MW01114619

THE NOBLE QUR'AN

a word for word interlinear translation

based on
The Qur'an Arabic Corpus
By Kais Dukes

AL SADIQIN PRESS

License

The Quranic Arabic Corpus is based on version 0.4 of the Quranic Arabic Corpus morphological data. A subset of that information is reproduced here in accordance with these terms and conditions of the GNU public license with terms of use.

The Quranic Arabic Corpus is Copyright © Kais Dukes, 2009-2011. E-mail: sckd@leeds.ac.uk as an open source project. The following information must be included in any derivative works:

Quranic Arabic Corpus (Version 0.4)
Copyright (C) 2011 Kais Dukes
License: GNU General Public License
#
The Quranic Arabic Corpus includes syntactic and morphological
annotation of the Quran, and builds on the verified Arabic text
distributed by the Tanzil project.
#
TERMS OF USE:
#
- Permission is granted to copy and distribute verbatim copies
of this file, but CHANGING IT IS NOT ALLOWED.
#
- This annotation can be used in any website or application,
provided its source (the Quranic Arabic Corpus) is clearly
indicated, and a link is made to http://corpus.quran.com to enable
users to keep track of changes.
#
- This copyright notice shall be included in all verbatim copies
of the text, and shall be reproduced appropriately in all works
derived from or containing substantial portion of this file.
#
Please check updates at: http://corpus.quran.com/download

All parts not covered by GPL License are Copyright © 2018 Al Sadiqin Press.
For reprint permission or other information write to:

ISBN 13: 978-1720554448
ISBN 10: 1720554447

Reprint Department
Al Sadiqin Press books@alsadiqin.org www.alsadiqin.org

Editor: Rebecca Abrahamson
Interior Designer: The Publishing Pro, LLC, Colorado Springs, Colorado

Table of Contents

Introduction by the director of al-Maehad al-Sadiqin (the Al-Sadiqin Institute).

In the name of Allah, the Most Beneficent, the Most Merciful.

Our research at Al Sadiqin necessitated a translation of the Holy Qur'an that allowed easy comparison between similar *ayat* (verses) and immediate reference to the original Arabic text for those not fluent in Arabic.

Kais Duke's website *corpus.quran.org* provides this, plus morphological data and a complete index to every usage of every word in the Holy Qur'an. It is an indispensably tool for the scholar and the standard translation used in all our research. The only thing lacking was a convenient way to include this translation in scholarly works.

Al Sadiqin contributes to Kais Duke's open source project by providing this publication. In the online form of this book, it makes for easy "copy and paste" of *ayat* for use in research papers. In the printed form, it allows the reader who may not be fluent in Arabic to become more acquainted with the nuances of the original Arabic text.

This book is published at cost. I offer *dua* that this work, and all the publications of Al Sadiqin press, may increase *iman* in the world.

Sincerely
Ben Abrahamson

Chapter (1) Sūrat l-Fātiḥah (The Opening)

1:1 In the name of Allah, the Most Gracious, the Most Merciful.
In the name (bis'mi) | of Allah (l-lahi), | the Most Gracious (l-raḥmāni), | the Most Merciful (l-raḥīmi).

1:2 All praises and thanks be to Allah, the Lord of the universe
All praises and thanks (al-ḥamdu) | be to Allah (lillahi), | the Lord (rabbi) | of the universe (l-ʿālamīna)

1:3 The Most Gracious, the Most Merciful.
The Most Gracious (al-raḥmāni), | the Most Merciful (l-raḥīmi).

1:4 The Master of the Day of the Judgment.
The Master (māliki) | of the Day (yawmi) | of the Judgment (l-dīni).

1:5 You Alone we worship, and You Alone we ask for help.
You Alone (iyyāka) | we worship (naʿbudu), | and You Alone (wa-iyyāka) | we ask for help (nastaʿīnu).

1:6 Guide us to the path, the straight.
Guide us (ih'dinā) | to the path (l-ṣirāṭa), | the straight (l-mus'taqīma).

1:7 The path of those You have bestowed Your Favors on them, not of those who earned Your wrath on themselves and not of those who go astray.
The path (ṣirāṭa) | of those (alladhīna) | You have bestowed Your Favors (anʿamta) | on them (ʿalayhim), | not of (ghayri) | those who earned Your wrath (l-maghḍūbi) | on themselves (ʿalayhim) | and not (walā) | of those who go astray (l-ḍālīna).

Chapter (2) Sūrat l-Baqarah (The Cow)

2:1 Alif Laam Meem
Alif Laam Meem (alif-lam-meem)

2:2 That is the book no doubt in it, a Guidance for the God-conscious.
That (dhālika) | is the book (l-kitābu) | no (lā) | doubt (rayba) | in it (fīhi), | a Guidance (hudan) | for the God-conscious (lil'muttaqīna).

2:3 Those who believe in the unseen, and establish the prayer, and out of what We have provided them they spend.
Those who (alladhīna) | believe (yu'minūna) | in the unseen (bil-ghaybi), | and establish (wayuqīmūna) | the prayer (l-ṣalata), | and out of what (wamimmā) | We have provided them (razaqnāhum) | they spend (yunfiqūna).

2:4 And those who believe in what is sent down to you and what was sent down from before you and in the Hereafter they firmly believe.

And those who (wa-alladhīna) | believe (yu'minūna) | in what (bimā) | is sent down (unzila) | to you (ilayka) | and what (wamā) | was sent down (unzila) | from (min) | before you (qablika) | and in the Hereafter (wabil-ākhirati) | they (hum) | firmly believe (yūqinūna).

2:5 Those are on Guidance from their Lord, and those - they are the successful ones.

Those (ulāika) | are on (ʿalā) | Guidance (hudan) | from (min) | their Lord (rabbihim), | and those (wa-ulāika)- | they (humu) | are the successful ones (l-muf'liḥūna).

2:6 Indeed, those who disbelieve[d], it is same to them whether you warn them or not you warn them, not they believe.

Indeed (inna), | those who (alladhīna) | disbelieve[d] (kafarū), | it is same (sawāon) | to them (ʿalayhim) | whether you warn them (a-andhartahum) | or (am) | not (lam) | you warn them (tundhir'hum), | not (lā) | they believe (yu'minūna).

2:7 Has set a seal Allah on their hearts and on their hearing, and on their vision is a veil. And for them is a punishment great.

Has set a seal (khatama) | Allah (l-lahu) | on (ʿalā) | their hearts (qulūbihim) | and on (waʿalā) | their hearing (samʿihim), | and on (waʿalā) | their vision (abṣārihim) | is a veil (ghishāwatun). | And for them (walahum) | is a punishment (ʿadhābun) | great (ʿaẓīmun).

2:8 And of the people are some who say, "We believed in Allah and in the Day [the] Last," but not they are believers (at all).

And of (wamina) | the people (l-nāsi) | are some who (man) | say (yaqūlu), | "We believed (āmannā) | in Allah (bil-lahi) | and in the Day (wabil-yawmi) | [the] Last, (l-ākhiri)" | but not (wamā) | they (hum) | are believers (at all) (bimu'minīna).

2:9 They seek to deceive Allah and those who believe[d], and not they deceive except themselves, and not they realize it.

They seek to deceive (yukhādiʿūna) | Allah (l-laha) | and those who (wa-alladhīna) | believe[d] (āmanū), | and not (wamā) | they deceive (yakhdaʿūna) | except (illā) | themselves (anfusahum), | and not (wamā) | they realize it (yashʿurūna).

2:10 In their hearts is a disease, so has increased them Allah in disease; and for them is a punishment painful because they used to [they] lie.

In (fī) | their hearts (qulūbihim) | is a disease (maraḍun), | so has increased them (fazādahumu) | Allah (l-lahu) | in disease (maraḍan); | and for them (walahum) | is a punishment (ʿadhābun) | painful (alīmun) | because (bimā) | they used to (kānū) | [they] lie (yakdhibūna).

2:11 And when it is said to them, "Do not spread corruption in the earth," they say, "Only we are reformers."

And when (wa-idhā) | it is said (qīla) | to them (lahum), | "Do not (lā) | spread corruption (tuf'sidū) | in (fī) | the earth, (l-arḍi)" | they say (qālū), | "Only (innamā) | we (naḥnu) | are reformers. (muṣ'liḥūna)"

2:12 Beware, indeed they themselves are the ones who spread corruption, [and] but not they realize it.

Beware (alā), | indeed they (innahum) | themselves (humu) | are the ones who spread corruption (l-muf'sidūna), | [and] but (walākin) | not (lā) | they realize it (yashʿurūna).

2:13 And when it is said to them, "Believe as believed the people," they say, "Should we believe as believed the fools?" Beware, certainly they themselves are the fools [and] but not they know.

And when (wa-idhā) | it is said (qīla) | to them (lahum), | "Believe (āminū) | as (kamā) | believed (āmana) | the people, (l-nāsu)" | they say (qālū), | "Should we believe (anu'minu) | as (kamā) | believed (āmana) | the fools? (l-sufahāu)" | Beware (alā), | certainly they (innahum) | themselves (humu) | are the fools (l-sufahāu) | [and] but (walākin) | not (lā) | they know (yaʿlamūna).

2:14 And when they meet those who believe[d], they say, "We believe[d]." But when they are alone with their evil ones, they say, "Indeed, we are with you, only we are mockers."

And when (wa-idhā) | they meet (laqū) | those who (alladhīna) | believe[d] (āmanū), | they say (qālū), | "We believe[d]. (āmannā)" | But when (wa-idhā) | they are alone (khalaw) | with (ilā) | their evil ones (shayāṭīnihim), | they say (qālū), | "Indeed, we (innā) | are with you (maʿakum), | only (innamā) | we (naḥnu) | are mockers. (mus'tahziūna)"

2:15 Allah mocks at them, and prolongs them in their transgression, they wander blindly.

Allah (al-lahu) | mocks (yastahzi-u) | at them (bihim), | and prolongs them (wayamudduhum) | in (fī) | their transgression (ṭugh'yānihim), | they wander blindly (yaʿmahūna).

2:16 Those are the ones who bought [the] astraying for [the] guidance. So not profited their commerce and not were they guided-ones.

Those (ulāika) | are the ones who (alladhīna) | bought (ish'tarawū) | [the] astraying (l-ḍalālata) | for [the] guidance (bil-hudā). | So not (famā) | profited (rabiḥat) | their commerce (tijāratuhum) | and not (wamā) | were they (kānū) | guided-ones (muh'tadīna).

2:17 Their example is like (the) example of the one who kindled a fire, then, when it illuminated what was around him took away Allah their light and left them in darkness[es], so not do they see.

Their example (mathaluhum) | is like (the) example (kamathali) | of the one who (alladhī) | kindled (is'tawqada) | a fire (nāran), | then, when (falammā) | it illuminated (aḍāat) | what (mā) | was around him (ḥawlahu) | took away (dhahaba) | Allah (l-lahu) | their light (binūrihim) | and left them (watarakahum) | in (fī) | darkness[es] (ẓulumātin), | so not (lā) | do they see (yub'ṣirūna).

2:18 Deaf, dumb, blind, so they not [they] will not return.

Deaf (ṣummun), | dumb (buk'mun), | blind (ʿum'yun), | so they (fahum) | not (lā) | [they] will not return (yarjiʿūna).

2:19 Or like a rainstorm from the sky in it are darkness[es], and thunder, and lightning. They put their fingers in their ears from the thunderclaps in fear (of) [the] death. And Allah is [the One Who] encompasses the disbelievers.

Or (aw) | like a rainstorm (kaṣayyibin) | from (mina) | the sky (l-samāi) | in it are (fīhi) | darkness[es] (ẓulumātun), | and thunder (waraʿdun), | and lightning (wabarqun). | They put (yajʿalūna) | their fingers (aṣābiʿahum) | in (fī) | their ears (ādhānihim) | from (mina) | the thunderclaps (l-ṣawāʿiqi) | in fear (of (ḥadhara)) | [the] death (l-mawti). | And Allah (wal-lahu) | is [the One Who] encompasses (muḥīṭun) | the disbelievers (bil-kāfirīna).

2:20 Almost the lightning snatches away their sight. Whenever it flashes for them they walk in it, and when it darkens on them they stand still. And if had willed Allah, He would certainly have taken away their hearing, and their sight. Indeed, Allah is on every thing All-Powerful.

Almost (yakādu) | the lightning (l-barqu) | snatches away (yakhṭafu) | their sight (abṣārahum). | Whenever (kullamā) | it flashes (aḍāa) | for them (lahum) | they walk (mashaw) | in it (fīhi), | and when (wa-idhā) | it darkens (aẓlama) | on them (ʿalayhim) | they stand still (qāmū). | And if (walaw) | had willed (shāa) | Allah (l-lahu), | He would certainly have taken away (ladhahaba) | their hearing (bisamʿihim), | and their sight (wa-abṣārihim). | Indeed (inna), | Allah (l-laha) | is on (ʿalā) | every (kulli) | thing (shayin) | All-Powerful (qadīrun).

2:21 O mankind! worship your Lord, the One Who created you and those from before you, so that you may become righteous.

O (yāayyuhā) | mankind (l-nāsu)! | worship (uʿbudū) | your Lord (rabbakumu), | the One Who (alladhī) | created you (khalaqakum) | and those (wa-alladhīna) | from (min) | before you (qablikum), | so that you may (laʿallakum) | become righteous (tattaqūna).

2:22 The One Who made for you the earth a resting place and the sky a canopy, and sent down from the sky water, then brought forth therewith [of] the fruits as provision for you. So do not set up to Allah rivals while you [you] know.

The One Who (alladhī) | made (jaʿala) | for you (lakumu) | the earth (l-arḍa) | a resting place (firāshan) | and the sky (wal-samāa) | a canopy (bināan), | and sent down (wa-anzala) | from (mina) | the sky (l-samāi) | water (māan), | then brought forth (fa-akhraja) | therewith (bihi) | [of] (mina) | the fruits (l-thamarāti) | as provision (riz'qan) | for you (lakum). | So do not (falā) | set up (tajʿalū) | to Allah (lillahi) | rivals (andādan) | while you (wa-antum) | [you] know (taʿlamūna).

2:23 And if you are in doubt about what We have revealed to Our slave, then produce a chapter [of] like it and call your witnesses from other than Allah if you are truthful.

And if (wa-in) | you are (kuntum) | in (fī) | doubt (raybin) | about what (mimmā) | We have revealed (nazzalnā) | to (ʿalā) | Our slave (ʿabdinā), | then produce (fatū) | a chapter (bisūratin) | [of] (min) | like it (mith'lihi) | and call (wa-idʿū) | your witnesses (shuhadāakum) | from (min) | other than (dūni) | Allah (l-lahi) | if (in) | you are (kuntum) | truthful (ṣādiqīna).

2:24 But if not you do, and never will you do, then fear the Fire whose [its] fuel is [the] men and [the] stones, prepared for the disbelievers.

But if (fa-in) | not (lam) | you do (tafʿalū), | and never (walan) | will you do (tafʿalū), | then fear (fa-ittaqū) | the Fire (l-nāra) | whose (allatī) | [its] fuel (waqūduhā) | is [the] men (l-nāsu) | and [the] stones (wal-ḥijāratu), | prepared (uʿiddat) | for the disbelievers (lil'kāfirīna).

2:25 And give good news to those who believe, and do [the] righteous deeds, that for them will be Gardens, flow [from] under them the rivers. Every time they are provided therefrom of fruit as provision, they will say, "This is the one which we were provided from before." And they will be given therefrom things in resemblance; And for them therein spouses purified, and they therein will abide forever.

And give good news (wabashiri) | to those who (alladhīna) | believe (āmanū), | and do (waʿamilū) | [the] righteous deeds (l-ṣāliḥāti), | that (anna) | for them (lahum) | will be Gardens (jannātin), | flow (tajrī) | [from] (min) | under them (taḥtihā) | the rivers (l-anhāru). | Every time (kullamā) | they are provided (ruziqū) | therefrom (min'hā) | of (min) | fruit (thamaratin) | as provision (riz'qan), | they will say (qālū), | "This is (hādhā) | the one which (alladhī) | we were provided (ruziq'nā) | from (min) | before. (qablu)" | And they will be given (wa-utū) | therefrom (bihi) | things in resemblance (mutashābihan); | And for them (walahum) | therein (fīhā) | spouses (azwājun) | purified (muṭahharatun), | and they (wahum) | therein (fīhā) | will abide forever (khālidūna).

2:26 Indeed, Allah is not ashamed to set forth an example like even of a mosquito and even something above it. Then as for those who believed, [thus] they will know that it is the truth from their Lord. And as for those who disbelieved [thus] they will say what did intend Allah by this example? He lets go astray by it many and He guides by it many. And not He lets go astray by it except the defiantly disobedient.

Indeed (inna), | Allah (l-laha) | is not (lā) | ashamed (yastaḥyī) | to (an) | set forth (yaḍriba) | an example (mathalan) | like even (mā) | of a mosquito (baʿūḍatan) | and even something (famā) | above it (fawqahā). | Then as for (fa-ammā) | those who (alladhīna) | believed (āmanū), | [thus]

they will know (faya'lamūna) | that it (annahu) | is the truth (l-ḥaqu) | from (min) | their Lord (rabbihim). | And as for (wa-ammā) | those who (alladhīna) | disbelieved (kafarū) | [thus] they will say (fayaqūlūna) | what (mādhā) | did intend (arāda) | Allah (l-lahu) | by this (bihādhā) | example (mathalan)? | He lets go astray (yuḍillu) | by it (bihi) | many (kathīran) | and He guides (wayahdī) | by it (bihi) | many (kathīran). | And not (wamā) | He lets go astray (yuḍillu) | by it (bihi) | except (illā) | the defiantly disobedient (l-fāsiqīna).

2:27 Those who break the Covenant of Allah from after its ratification, and [they] cut what has ordered Allah it to be joined and [they] spread corruption in the earth. Those, they are the losers.

Those who (alladhīna) | break (yanquḍūna) | the Covenant ('ahda) | of Allah (l-lahi) | from (min) | after (ba'di) | its ratification (mīthāqihi), | and [they] cut (wayaqṭa'ūna) | what (mā) | has ordered (amara) | Allah (l-lahu) | it (bihi) | to (an) | be joined (yūṣala) | and [they] spread corruption (wayuf'sidūna) | in (fī) | the earth (l-arḍi). | Those (ulāika), | they (humu) | are the losers (l-khāsirūna).

2:28 How can you disbelieve in Allah? While you were dead then He gave you life; then He will cause you to die, then He will give you life, then to Him you will be returned.

How (kayfa) | can you disbelieve (takfurūna) | in Allah (bil-lahi)? | While you were (wakuntum) | dead (amwātan) | then He gave you life (fa-aḥyākum); | then (thumma) | He will cause you to die (yumītukum), | then (thumma) | He will give you life (yuḥ'yīkum), | then (thumma) | to Him (ilayhi) | you will be returned (tur'ja'ūna).

2:29 He is the One Who created for you what is in the earth, all. Moreover He turned to the heaven and fashioned them seven heavens. And He of every thing is All-Knowing.

He (huwa) | is the One Who (alladhī) | created (khalaqa) | for you (lakum) | what (mā) | is in (fī) | the earth (l-arḍi), | all (jamī'an). | Moreover (thumma) | He turned (is'tawā) | to (ilā) | the heaven (l-samāi) | and fashioned them (fasawwāhunna) | seven (sab'a) | heavens (samāwātin). | And He (wahuwa) | of every (bikulli) | thing (shayin) | is All-Knowing ('alīmun).

2:30 And when said your Lord to the angels, "Indeed, I am going to place in the earth a vicegerent, they said, "Will You place in it one who will spread corruption in it and will shed [the] blood[s], while we, [we] glorify You with Your praises and we sanctify [to] You." He said, "Indeed, I [I] know what not you know."

And when (wa-idh) | said (qāla) | your Lord (rabbuka) | to the angels (lil'malāikati), | "Indeed, I am (innī) | going to place (jā'ilun) | in (fī) | the earth (l-arḍi) | a vicegerent (khalīfatan), | they said (qālū), | "Will You place (ataj'alu) | in it (fīhā) | one who (man) | will spread corruption (yuf'sidu) | in it (fīhā) | and will shed (wayasfiku) | [the] blood[s] (l-dimāa), | while we (wanaḥnu), | [we] glorify You (nusabbiḥu) | with Your praises (biḥamdika) | and we sanctify (wanuqaddisu) | [to] You. (laka)" | He said (qāla), | "Indeed, I (innī) | [I] know (a'lamu) | what (mā) | not (lā) | you know. (ta'lamūna)"

2:31 And He taught Adam the names - all of them. Then He displayed them to the angels, then He said, "Inform Me of the names of these, if you are truthful."

And He taught (wa'allama) | Adam (ādama) | the names (l-asmāa)- | all of them (kullahā). | Then (thumma) | He displayed them ('araḍahum) | to ('alā) | the angels (l-malāikati), | then He said (faqāla), | "Inform Me (anbiūnī) | of the names (bi-asmāi) | of these (hāulāi), | if (in) | you are (kuntum) | truthful. (ṣādiqīna)"

2:32 They said, "Glory be to You! No knowledge is for us except what You have taught us. Indeed You! You are the All-Knowing, the All-Wise.

They said (qālū), | "Glory be to You (sub'ḥānaka)! | No (lā) | knowledge ('il'ma) | is for us (lanā) | except (illā) | what (mā) | You have taught us ('allamtanā). | Indeed You (innaka)! | You (anta) | are the All-Knowing (l-ʿalīmu), | the All-Wise (l-ḥakīmu).

2:33 He said, "O Adam! Inform them of their names." And when he had informed them of their names, He said, "Did not I say to you, Indeed, I [I] know the unseen of the heavens and the earth, and I know what you reveal and what you [were] conceal."

He said (qāla), | "O Adam (yāādamu)! | Inform them (anbi'hum) | of their names. (bi-asmāihim)" | And when (falammā) | he had informed them (anba-ahum) | of their names (bi-asmāihim), | He said (qāla), | "Did not (alam) | I say (aqul) | to you (lakum), | Indeed, I (innī) | [I] know (aʿlamu) | the unseen (ghayba) | of the heavens (l-samāwāti) | and the earth (wal-arḍi), | and I know (wa-aʿlamu) | what (mā) | you reveal (tub'dūna) | and what (wamā) | you [were] (kuntum) | conceal. (taktumūna)"

2:34 And when We said to the angels, "Prostrate to Adam," [so] they prostrated except Iblis. He refused and was arrogant and became of the disbelievers.

And when (wa-idh) | We said (qul'nā) | to the angels (lil'malāikati), | "Prostrate (us'judū) | to Adam, (liādama)" | [so] they prostrated (fasajadū) | except (illā) | Iblis (ib'līsa). | He refused (abā) | and was arrogant (wa-is'takbara) | and became (wakāna) | of (mina) | the disbelievers (l-kāfirīna).

2:35 And We said, "O Adam! Dwell you and your spouse in Paradise, and [you both] eat from it freely from wherever you [both] wish. But do not [you two] approach this [the] tree, lest you [both] be of the wrongdoers."

And We said (waqul'nā), | "O Adam (yāādamu)! | Dwell (us'kun) | you (anta) | and your spouse (wazawjuka) | in Paradise (l-janata), | and [you both] eat (wakulā) | from it (min'hā) | freely (raghadan) | from wherever (ḥaythu) | you [both] wish (shi'tumā). | But do not (walā) | [you two] approach (taqrabā) | this (hādhihi) | [the] tree (l-shajarata), | lest you [both] be (fatakūnā) | of (mina) | the wrongdoers. (l-ẓālimīna)"

2:36 Then made [both of] them slip the Shaitaan from it, and he got [both of] them out from what they [both] were in [it]. And We said, "Go down all of you, some of you to others as enemy; and for you in the earth is a dwelling place and a provision for a period."

Then made [both of] them slip (fa-azallahumā) | the Shaitaan (l-shayṭānu) | from it (ʿanhā), | and he got [both of] them out (fa-akhrajahumā) | from what (mimmā) | they [both] were (kānā) | in [it] (fīhi). | And We said (waqul'nā), | "Go down all of you (ih'biṭū), | some of you (baʿḍukum) | to others (libaʿḍin) | as enemy (ʿaduwwun); | and for you (walakum) | in (fī) | the earth (l-arḍi) | is a dwelling place (mus'taqarrun) | and a provision (wamatāʿun) | for (ilā) | a period. (ḥīnin)"

2:37 Then received Adam from his Lord words, So his Lord turned towards him. Indeed He! He is the Oft-returning (to mercy), the Most Merciful.

Then received (fatalaqqā) | Adam (ādamu) | from (min) | his Lord (rabbihi) | words (kalimātin), | So his Lord turned (fatāba) | towards him (ʿalayhi). | Indeed He (innahu)! | He (huwa) | is the Oft-returning (to mercy) (l-tawābu), | the Most Merciful (l-raḥīmu).

2:38 We said, "Go down from it all of you, and when, comes to you from Me Guidance, then whoever follows My Guidance, [then] no fear will be on them and not they will grieve.

We said (qul'nā), | "Go down (ih'biṭū) | from it (min'hā) | all of you (jamīʿan), | and when (fa-immā), | comes to you (yatiyannakum) | from Me (minnī) | Guidance (hudan), | then whoever (faman) | follows (tabiʿa) | My Guidance (hudāya), | [then] no (falā) | fear (khawfun) | will be on them (ʿalayhim) | and not (walā) | they (hum) | will grieve (yaḥzanūna).

2:39 And those who disbelieve[d] and deny Our Signs, those are the companions of the Fire; they in it will abide forever."

And those (wa-alladhīna) | who disbelieve[d] (kafarū) | and deny (wakadhabū) | Our Signs (biāyātinā), | those (ulāika) | are the companions (aṣḥābu) | of the Fire (l-nāri); | they (hum) | in it (fīhā) | will abide forever. (khālidūna)"

2:40 O Children of Israel! Remember My Favor which I bestowed upon you and fulfill, My Covenant I will fulfill your covenant and Me Alone fear [Me].

O Children (yābanī) | of Israel (is'rāīla)! | Remember (udh'kurū) | My Favor (niʿʿmatiya) | which (allatī) | I bestowed (anʿamtu) | upon you (ʿalaykum) | and fulfill (wa-awfū), | My Covenant (biʿahdī) | I will fulfill (ūfi) | your covenant (biʿahdikum) | and Me Alone (wa-iyyāya) | fear [Me] (fa-ir'habūni).

2:41 And believe in what I have sent down confirming that which is with you, and do not be the first disbeliever of it. And do not exchange My Signs for a price small, and Me Alone fear [Me].

And believe (waāminū) | in what (bimā) | I have sent down (anzaltu) | confirming (muṣaddiqan) | that which (limā) | is with you (maʿakum), | and do not (walā) | be (takūnū) | the first (awwala) | disbeliever (kāfirin) | of it (bihi). | And do not (walā) | exchange (tashtarū) | My Signs for (biāyātī) | a price (thamanan) | small (qalīlan), | and Me Alone (wa-iyyāya) | fear [Me] (fa-ittaqūni).

2:42 And do not mix the Truth with [the] falsehood and conceal the Truth while you [you] know.

And do not (walā) | mix (talbisū) | the Truth (l-ḥaqa) | with [the] falsehood (bil-bāṭili) | and conceal (wataktumū) | the Truth (l-ḥaqa) | while you (wa-antum) | [you] know (taʿlamūna).

2:43 And establish the prayer and give zakah and bow down with those who bow down.

And establish (wa-aqīmū) | the prayer (l-ṣalata) | and give (waātū) | zakah (l-zakata) | and bow down (wa-ir'kaʿū) | with (maʿa) | those who bow down (l-rākiʿīna).

2:44 Do you order [the] people [the] righteousness and you forget yourselves, while you [you] recite the Book? Then, will not you use reason?

Do you order (atamurūna) | [the] people (l-nāsa) | [the] righteousness (bil-biri) | and you forget (watansawna) | yourselves (anfusakum), | while you (wa-antum) | [you] recite (tatlūna) | the Book (l-kitāba)? | Then, will not (afalā) | you use reason (taʿqilūna)?

2:45 And seek help through patience and the prayer; and indeed, it is surely difficult except on the humble ones,

And seek help (wa-is'taʿīnū) | through patience (bil-ṣabri) | and the prayer (wal-ṣalati); | and indeed, it (wa-innahā) | is surely difficult (lakabīratun) | except (illā) | on (ʿalā) | the humble ones (l-khāshiʿīna),

2:46 Those who believe that they will meet their Lord and that they to Him will return.

Those who (alladhīna) | believe (yaẓunnūna) | that they (annahum) | will meet (mulāqū) | their Lord (rabbihim) | and that they (wa-annahum) | to Him (ilayhi) | will return (rājiʿūna).

2:47 O Children of Israel! Remember My Favor which I bestowed upon you and that I [I] preferred you over the worlds.

O Children (yābanī) | of Israel (is'rāīla)! | Remember (udh'kurū) | My Favor (niʿʿmatiya) | which (allatī) | I bestowed (anʿamtu) | upon you (ʿalaykum) | and that I (wa-annī) | [I] preferred you (faḍḍaltukum) | over (ʿalā) | the worlds (l-ʿālamīna).

2:48 And fear a day, will not avail any soul for another soul anything, and not will be accepted from it any intercession, and not will be taken from it a compensation, and not they will be helped.

And fear (wa-ittaqū) | a day (yawman), | will not (lā) | avail (tajzī) | any soul (nafsun) | for (ʿan) | another soul (nafsin) | anything (shayan), | and not (walā) | will be accepted (yuq'balu) |

from it (min'hā) | any intercession (shafāʿatun), | and not (walā) | will be taken (yu'khadhu) | from it (min'hā) | a compensation (ʿadlun), | and not (walā) | they (hum) | will be helped (yunṣarūna).

2:49 And when We saved you from the people of Firaun who were afflicting you (with) horrible torment, slaughtering your sons and letting live your women. And in that was a trial from your Lord great.

And when (wa-idh) | We saved you (najjaynākum) | from (min) | the people (āli) | of Firaun (fir'ʿawna) | who were afflicting you (with (yasūmūnakum)) | horrible (sūa) | torment (l-ʿadhābi), | slaughtering (yudhabbiḥūna) | your sons (abnāakum) | and letting live (wayastaḥyūna) | your women (nisāakum). | And in (wafī) | that (dhālikum) | was a trial (balāon) | from (min) | your Lord (rabbikum) | great (ʿaẓīmun).

2:50 And when We parted for you the sea, then We saved you, and We drowned the people of Firaun while you were looking.

And when (wa-idh) | We parted (faraqnā) | for you (bikumu) | the sea (l-baḥra), | then We saved you (fa-anjaynākum), | and We drowned (wa-aghraqnā) | the people (āla) | of Firaun (fir'ʿawna) | while you (wa-antum) | were looking (tanẓurūna).

2:51 And when We appointed for Musa forty nights. Then you took the calf from after him and you were wrongdoers.

And when (wa-idh) | We appointed (wāʿadnā) | for Musa (mūsā) | forty (arbaʿīna) | nights (laylatan). | Then (thumma) | you took (ittakhadhtumu) | the calf (l-ʿij'la) | from (min) | after him (baʿdihi) | and you (wa-antum) | were wrongdoers (ẓālimūna).

2:52 Then We forgave you from after that, so that you may be grateful.

Then (thumma) | We forgave (ʿafawnā) | you (ʿankum) | from (min) | after (baʿdi) | that (dhālika), | so that you may (laʿallakum) | be grateful (tashkurūna).

2:53 And when We gave Musa the Book and the Criterion, perhaps you would be guided.

And when (wa-idh) | We gave (ātaynā) | Musa (mūsā) | the Book (l-kitāba) | and the Criterion (wal-fur'qāna), | perhaps you (laʿallakum) | would be guided (tahtadūna).

2:54 And when said Musa to his people, "O my people! Indeed, you [you] have wronged yourselves by your taking the calf. So turn in repentance to your Creator, and kill yourselves. That is better for you with your Creator." Then He turned towards you. Indeed He! He is the-returning, the Most Merciful.

And when (wa-idh) | said (qāla) | Musa (mūsā) | to his people (liqawmihi), | "O my people (yāqawmi)! | Indeed, you (innakum) | [you] have wronged (ẓalamtum) | yourselves (anfusakum) | by your taking (bi-ittikhādhikumu) | the calf (l-ʿij'la). | So turn in repentance (fatūbū) | to (ilā) | your Creator (bāri-ikum), | and kill (fa-uq'tulū) | yourselves (anfusakum). | That (dhālikum) | is better (khayrun) | for you (lakum) | with (ʿinda) | your Creator. (bāri-ikum)" | Then He turned (fatāba) | towards you (ʿalaykum). | Indeed He (innahu)! | He (huwa) | is the-returning (l-tawābu), | the Most Merciful (l-raḥīmu).

2:55 And when you said, "O Musa! Never will we believe in you until we see Allah manifestly." So seized you the thunderbolt while you were looking.

And when (wa-idh) | you said (qul'tum), | "O Musa (yāmūsā)! | Never (lan) | will we believe (nu'mina) | in you (laka) | until (ḥattā) | we see (narā) | Allah (l-laha) | manifestly. (jahratan)" | So seized you (fa-akhadhatkumu) | the thunderbolt (l-ṣāʿiqatu) | while you (wa-antum) | were looking (tanẓurūna).

2:56 Then We revived you from after your death, so that you may be grateful.

Then (thumma) | We revived you (baʿathnākum) | from (min) | after (baʿdi) | your death (mawtikum), | so that you may (laʿallakum) | be grateful (tashkurūna).

2:57 And We shaded [over] you with [the] clouds and We sent down to you [the] manna and [the] quails, "Eat from the good things that We have provided you." And not they wronged Us, but they were to themselves doing wrong.

And We shaded (waẓallalnā) | [over] you (ʿalaykumu) | with [the] clouds (l-ghamāma) | and We sent down (wa-anzalnā) | to you (ʿalaykumu) | [the] manna (l-mana) | and [the] quails (wal-salwā), | "Eat (kulū) | from (min) | the good things (ṭayyibāti) | that (mā) | We have provided you. (razaqnākum)" | And not (wamā) | they wronged Us (ẓalamūnā), | but (walākin) | they were (kānū) | to themselves (anfusahum) | doing wrong (yaẓlimūna).

2:58 And when We said, "Enter this town, then eat from wherever you wish[ed] abundantly, and enter the gate prostrating. And say, "Repentance." We will forgive for you your sins. And We will increase the good-doers in reward."

And when (wa-idh) | We said (qul'nā), | "Enter (ud'khulū) | this (hādhihi) | town (l-qaryata), | then eat (fakulū) | from (min'hā) | wherever (ḥaythu) | you wish[ed] (shi'tum) | abundantly (raghadan), | and enter (wa-ud'khulū) | the gate (l-bāba) | prostrating (sujjadan). | And say (waqūlū), | "Repentance. (ḥiṭṭatun)" | We will forgive (naghfir) | for you (lakum) | your sins (khaṭāyākum). | And We will increase (wasanazīdu) | the good-doers in reward. (l-muḥ'sinīna)"

2:59 But changed those who wronged the word other than that which was said to them; so We sent down upon those who wronged, a punishment from the sky because they were defiantly disobeying.

But changed (fabaddala) | those who (alladhīna) | wronged (ẓalamū) | the word (qawlan) | other than (ghayra) | that which (alladhī) | was said (qīla) | to them (lahum); | so We sent down (fa-anzalnā) | upon (ʿalā) | those who (alladhīna) | wronged (ẓalamū), | a punishment (rij'zan) | from (mina) | the sky (l-samāi) | because (bimā) | they were (kānū) | defiantly disobeying (yafsuqūna).

2:60 And when asked for water Musa for his people, [so] We said, "Strike with your staff the stone." Then gushed forth from it of twelve springs. Indeed knew all the people their drinking place. "Eat and drink from the provision (of) Allah, and do not act wickedly in the earth spreading corruption."

And when (wa-idhi) | asked for water (is'tasqā) | Musa (mūsā) | for his people (liqawmihi), | [so] We said (faqul'nā), | "Strike (iḍ'rib) | with your staff (biʿaṣāka) | the stone. (l-ḥajara)" | Then gushed forth (fa-infajarat) | from it (min'hu) | of (ith'natā) | twelve (ʿashrata) | springs (ʿaynan). | Indeed (qad) | knew (ʿalima) | all (kullu) | the people (unāsin) | their drinking place (mashrabahum). | "Eat (kulū) | and drink (wa-ish'rabū) | from (min) | the provision (of (riz'qi)) | Allah (l-lahi), | and do not (walā) | act wickedly (taʿthaw) | in (fī) | the earth (l-arḍi) | spreading corruption. (muf'sidīna)"

2:61 And when you said, "O Musa! Never will we endure [on] food of one (kind), so pray for us to your Lord to bring forth for us out of what grows the earth, of its herbs, [and] its cucumbers, [and] its garlic, [and] its lentils, and its onions." He said, "Would you exchange that which [it] is inferior for that which [it] is better? Go down to a city, so indeed for you is what you have asked for." And were struck on them the humiliation and the misery and they drew on themselves wrath of Allah That was because they used to disbelieve in the Signs of Allah and kill the Prophets without any [the] right. That was because they disobeyed and they were transgressing.

And when (wa-idh) | you said (qul'tum), | "O Musa (yāmūsā)! | Never will (lan) | we endure (naṣbira) | [on] (ʿalā) | food (ṭaʿāmin) | of one (kind) (wāḥidin), | so pray (fa-udʿʿu) | for us (lanā) | to your Lord (rabbaka) | to bring forth (yukh'rij) | for us (lanā) | out of what (mimmā) | grows (tunbitu) | the earth (l-arḍu), | of (min) | its herbs (baqlihā), | [and] its cucumbers (waqithāihā), | [and] its garlic (wafūmihā), | [and] its lentils (wa'adasihā), | and its onions. (wabaṣalihā)" | He said (qāla), | "Would you exchange (atastabdilūna) | that which (alladhī) | [it] (huwa) | is inferior (adnā) | for that which (bi-alladhī) | [it] (huwa) | is better (khayrun)? | Go down (ih'biṭū) | to a city (miṣ'ran), | so indeed (fa-inna) | for you (lakum) | is what (mā) | you have asked for. (sa-altum)" | And were struck (waḍuribat) | on them ('alayhimu) | the humiliation (l-dhilatu) | and the misery (wal-maskanatu) | and they drew on themselves (wabāū) | wrath (bighaḍabin) | of (mina) | Allah (l-lahi) | That was (dhālika) | because they (bi-annahum) | used to (kānū) | disbelieve (yakfurūna) | in the Signs (biāyāti) | of Allah (l-lahi) | and kill (wayaqtulūna) | the Prophets (l-nabiyīna) | without any (bighayri) | [the] right (l-ḥaqi). | That (dhālika) | was because (bimā) | they disobeyed ('aṣaw) | and they were (wakānū) | transgressing (ya'tadūna).

2:62 Indeed, those who believed and those who became Jews and the Christians and the Sabians - who believed in Allah and the Day [the] Last and did righteous deeds, so for them their reward is with their Lord and no fear on them and not they will grieve.

Indeed (inna), | those who (alladhīna) | believed (āmanū) | and those who (wa-alladhīna) | became Jews (hādū) | and the Christians (wal-naṣārā) | and the Sabians (wal-ṣābiīna)- | who (man) | believed (āmana) | in Allah (bil-lahi) | and the Day (wal-yawmi) | [the] Last (l-ākhiri) | and did (wa'amila) | righteous deeds (ṣāliḥan), | so for them (falahum) | their reward (ajruhum) | is with ('inda) | their Lord (rabbihim) | and no (walā) | fear (khawfun) | on them ('alayhim) | and not (walā) | they (hum) | will grieve (yaḥzanūna).

2:63 And when We took your covenant and We raised over you the mount, "Hold what We have given you with strength, and remember what is in it, perhaps you would become righteous."

And when (wa-idh) | We took (akhadhnā) | your covenant (mīthāqakum) | and We raised (warafa'nā) | over you (fawqakumu) | the mount (l-ṭūra), | "Hold (khudhū) | what (mā) | We have given you (ātaynākum) | with strength (biquwwatin), | and remember (wa-udh'kurū) | what (mā) | is in it (fīhi), | perhaps you (la'allakum) | would become righteous. (tattaqūna)"

2:64 Then you turned away from after that. So if not for the Grace of Allah upon you and His Mercy, surely you would have been of the losers.

Then (thumma) | you turned away (tawallaytum) | from (min) | after (ba'di) | that (dhālika). | So if not (falawlā) | for the Grace (faḍlu) | of Allah (l-lahi) | upon you ('alaykum) | and His Mercy (waraḥmatuhu), | surely you would have been (lakuntum) | of (mina) | the losers (l-khāsirīna).

2:65 And indeed, you knew those who transgressed among you in the matter of Sabbath. So We said to them, "Be apes, despised."

And indeed (walaqad), | you knew ('alim'tumu) | those who (alladhīna) | transgressed (i''tadaw) | among you (minkum) | in (fī) | the matter of Sabbath (l-sabti). | So We said (faqul'nā) | to them (lahum), | "Be (kūnū) | apes (qiradatan), | despised. (khāsiīna)"

2:66 So We made it a deterrent punishment for those in front of them and those after them and an admonition for those who fear Allah.

So We made it (faja'alnāhā) | a deterrent punishment (nakālan) | for those (limā) | in front (bayna) | of them (yadayhā) | and those (wamā) | after them (khalfahā) | and an admonition (wamaw'iẓatan) | for those who fear Allah (lil'muttaqīna).

2:67 And when said Musa to his people, "Indeed, Allah commands you that you slaughter a cow." They said, "Do you take us in ridicule." He said, "I seek refuge in Allah that I be among the ignorant."

And when (wa-idh) | said (qāla) | Musa (mūsā) | to his people (liqawmihi), | "Indeed (inna), | Allah (l-laha) | commands you (yamurukum) | that (an) | you slaughter (tadhbaḥū) | a cow. (baqaratan)" | They said (qālū), | "Do you take us (atattakhidhunā) | in ridicule. (huzuwan)" | He said (qāla), | "I seek refuge (aʿūdhu) | in Allah (bil-lahi) | that (an) | I be (akūna) | among (mina) | the ignorant. (l-jāhilīna)"

2:68 They said, "Pray for us to your Lord to make clear to us what it is." He said, "Indeed, He says, "[Indeed] it is a cow not old and not young, middle aged between that," so do what you are commanded."

They said (qālū), | "Pray (udʿu) | for us (lanā) | to your Lord (rabbaka) | to make clear (yubayyin) | to us (lanā) | what (mā) | it is. (hiya)" | He said (qāla), | "Indeed, He (innahu) | says (yaqūlu), | "[Indeed] it (innahā) | is a cow (baqaratun) | not (lā) | old (fāriḍun) | and not (walā) | young (bik'run), | middle aged (ʿawānun) | between (bayna) | that, (dhālika)" | so do (fa-ifʿalū) | what (mā) | you are commanded. (tu'marūna)"

2:69 They said, "Pray for us to your Lord to make clear to us what is its color." He said, "Indeed, He says, '[Indeed] it is a cow yellow, bright in its color, pleasing to those who see (it).'"

They said (qālū), | "Pray (udʿu) | for us (lanā) | to your Lord (rabbaka) | to make clear (yubayyin) | to us (lanā) | what (mā) | is its color. (lawnuhā)" | He said (qāla), | "Indeed, He (innahu) | says (yaqūlu), | '[Indeed] it is (innahā) | a cow (baqaratun) | yellow (ṣafrāu), | bright (fāqiʿun) | in its color (lawnuhā), | pleasing (tasurru) | to those who see (it).' (l-nāẓirīna)"

2:70 They said, "Pray for us to your Lord to make clear to us what it is. Indeed, [the] cows look alike to us. And indeed we, if wills Allah, will surely be those who are guided."

They said (qālū), | "Pray (udʿu) | for us (lanā) | to your Lord (rabbaka) | to make clear (yubayyin) | to us (lanā) | what (mā) | it is (hiya). | Indeed (inna), | [the] cows (l-baqara) | look alike (tashābaha) | to us (ʿalaynā). | And indeed we (wa-innā), | if (in) | wills (shāa) | Allah (l-lahu), | will surely be those who are guided. (lamuh'tadūna)"

2:71 He said, "Indeed, He says, "[Indeed] it is a cow not trained to plough the earth, and not water the field; sound, no blemish in it." They said, "Now you have come with the truth." So they slaughtered it, and not they were near to doing (it).

He said (qāla), | "Indeed, He (innahu) | says (yaqūlu), | "[Indeed] it (innahā) | is a cow (baqaratun) | not (lā) | trained (dhalūlun) | to plough (tuthīru) | the earth (l-arḍa), | and not (walā) | water (tasqī) | the field (l-ḥartha); | sound (musallamatun), | no (la) | blemish (shiyata) | in it. (fīhā)" | They said (qālū), | "Now (l-āna) | you have come (ji'ta) | with the truth. (bil-ḥaqi)" | So they slaughtered it (fadhabaḥūhā), | and not (wamā) | they were near (kādū) | to doing (it) (yafʿalūna).

2:72 And when you killed a man, then you disputed concerning it, but Allah is the One Who brought forth what you were concealing.

And when (wa-idh) | you killed (qataltum) | a man (nafsan), | then you disputed (fa-iddāratum) | concerning it (fīhā), | but Allah (wal-lahu) | is the One Who brought forth (mukh'rijun) | what (mā) | you were (kuntum) | concealing (taktumūna).

2:73 So We said, "Strike him with a part of it." Like this revives Allah the dead, and shows you His Signs, perhaps you may use your intellect.

So We said (faqul'nā), | "Strike him (iḍ'ribūhu) | with a part of it. (bibaʿḍihā)" | Like this (kadhālika) | revives (yuḥ'yī) | Allah (l-lahu) | the dead (l-mawtā), | and shows you (wayurīkum) | His Signs (āyātihi), | perhaps you may (laʿallakum) | use your intellect (taʿqilūna).

2:74 Then hardened your hearts from after that so they became like [the] stones or stronger in hardness. And indeed, from the stones certainly there are some which gush forth from it [the] rivers, and indeed, from them certainly there are some which split, so comes out from it [the] water, and indeed, from them certainly there are some which fall down from fear of Allah. And not is Allah unaware of what you do.

Then (thumma) | hardened (qasat) | your hearts (qulūbukum) | from (min) | after (baʿdi) | that (dhālika) | so they (fahiya) | became like [the] stones (kal-ḥijārati) | or (aw) | stronger (ashaddu) | in hardness (qaswatan). | And indeed (wa-inna), | from (mina) | the stones (l-ḥijārati) | certainly there are some which (lamā) | gush forth (yatafajjaru) | from it (min'hu) | [the] rivers (l-anhāru), | and indeed (wa-inna), | from them (min'hā) | certainly there are some which (lamā) | split (yashaqqaqu), | so comes out (fayakhruju) | from it (min'hu) | [the] water (l-māu), | and indeed (wa-inna), | from them (min'hā) | certainly there are some which (lamā) | fall down (yahbiṭu) | from (min) | fear (khashyati) | of Allah (l-lahi). | And not (wamā) | is Allah (l-lahu) | unaware (bighāfilin) | of what (ʿammā) | you do (taʿmalūna).

2:75 Do you hope that they will believe [for] you while indeed there has been a party of them, who used to hear the words of Allah, then they distort it from after [what] they understood it, while they know?

Do you hope (afataṭmaʿūna) | that (an) | they will believe (yu'minū) | [for] you (lakum) | while indeed (waqad) | there has been (kāna) | a party (farīqun) | of them (min'hum), | who used to hear (yasmaʿūna) | the words (kalāma) | of Allah (l-lahi), | then (thumma) | they distort it (yuḥarrifūnahu) | from (min) | after (baʿdi) | [what] (mā) | they understood it (ʿaqalūhu), | while they (wahum) | know (yaʿlamūna)?

2:76 And when they meet those who believe[d], they say, "We have believed." But when meet in private some of them with some others, they say, "Do you tell them what has Allah to you so that they argue with you therewith before your Lord? Then do you not understand?"

And when (wa-idhā) | they meet (laqū) | those who (alladhīna) | believe[d] (āmanū), | they say (qālū), | "We have believed. (āmannā)" | But when (wa-idhā) | meet in private (khalā) | some of them (baʿḍuhum) | with (ilā) | some others (baʿḍin), | they say (qālū), | "Do you tell them (atuḥaddithūnahum) | what (bimā) | has (fataḥa) | Allah (l-lahu) | to you (ʿalaykum) | so that they argue with you (liyuḥājjūkum) | therewith (bihi) | before (ʿinda) | your Lord (rabbikum)? | Then do you not (afalā) | understand? (taʿqilūna)"

2:77 Do not they know that Allah knows what they conceal and what they declare?

Do not (awalā) | they know (yaʿlamūna) | that (anna) | Allah (l-laha) | knows (yaʿlamu) | what (mā) | they conceal (yusirrūna) | and what (wamā) | they declare (yuʿlinūna)?

2:78 And among them are unlettered ones, who do not know the book except wishful thinking and not they do anything except guess.

And among them (wamin'hum) | are unlettered ones (ummiyyūna), | who do not (lā) | know (yaʿlamūna) | the book (l-kitāba) | except (illā) | wishful thinking (amāniyya) | and not (wa-in) | they (hum) | do anything except (illā) | guess (yaẓunnūna).

2:79 So woe to those who write the book with their own hands then, they say, "This is from Allah," to barter with it for a price little. So woe to them for what have written their hands and woe to them for what they earn.

So woe (fawaylun) | to those who (lilladhīna) | write (yaktubūna) | the book (l-kitāba) | with their own hands (bi-aydīhim) | then (thumma), | they say (yaqūlūna), | "This (hādhā) | is (min) | from (ʿindi) | Allah, (l-lahi)" | to barter (liyashtarū) | with it (bihi) | for a price (thamanan) | little (qalīlan). | So woe (fawaylun) | to them (lahum) | for what (mimmā) | have written (katabat) | their hands (aydīhim) | and woe (wawaylun) | to them (lahum) | for what (mimmā) | they earn (yaksibūna).

2:80 And they say, "Never will touch us the Fire except for days numbered." Say, "Have you taken from Allah a covenant, so never will break Allah His Covenant? Or do you say against Allah what not you know?"

And they say (waqālū), | "Never (lan) | will touch us (tamassanā) | the Fire (l-nāru) | except (illā) | for days (ayyāman) | numbered. (maʿdūdatan)" | Say (qul), | "Have you taken (attakhadhtum) | from (ʿinda) | Allah (l-lahi) | a covenant (ʿahdan), | so never (falan) | will break (yukh'lifa) | Allah (l-lahu) | His Covenant (ʿahdahu)? | Or (am) | do you say (taqūlūna) | against (ʿalā) | Allah (l-lahi) | what (mā) | not (lā) | you know? (taʿlamūna)"

2:81 Yes, whoever earned evil and surrounded him with his sins - [so] those are the companions of the Fire; they in it will abide forever.

Yes (balā), | whoever (man) | earned (kasaba) | evil (sayyi-atan) | and surrounded him (wa-aḥāṭat) | with (bihi) | his sins (khaṭīatuhu)- | [so] those (fa-ulāika) | are the companions (aṣḥābu) | of the Fire (l-nāri); | they (hum) | in it (fīhā) | will abide forever (khālidūna).

2:82 And those who believed and did righteous deeds, those are the companions of Paradise; they in it will abide forever.

And those who (wa-alladhīna) | believed (āmanū) | and did (waʿamilū) | righteous deeds (l-ṣāliḥāti), | those (ulāika) | are the companions (aṣḥābu) | of Paradise (l-janati); | they (hum) | in it (fīhā) | will abide forever (khālidūna).

2:83 And when We took the covenant from the Children of Israel, "Not you will worship except Allah, and with [the] parents be good and with relatives and [the] orphans and the needy, and speak to [the] people good, and establish the prayer and give the zakah." Then you turned away, except a few of you, and you were refusing.

And when (wa-idh) | We took (akhadhnā) | the covenant (mīthāqa) | from the Children (banī) | of Israel (is'rāīla), | "Not (lā) | you will worship (taʿbudūna) | except (illā) | Allah (l-laha), | and with [the] parents (wabil-wālidayni) | be good (iḥ'sānan) | and with (wadhī) | relatives (l-qur'bā) | and [the] orphans (wal-yatāmā) | and the needy (wal-masākīni), | and speak (waqūlū) | to [the] people (lilnnāsi) | good (ḥus'nan), | and establish (wa-aqīmū) | the prayer (l-ṣalata) | and give (waātū) | the zakah. (l-zakata)" | Then (thumma) | you turned away (tawallaytum), | except (illā) | a few (qalīlan) | of you (minkum), | and you were (wa-antum) | refusing (muʿ'riḍūna).

2:84 And when We took your covenant, "Not will you shed your blood and not will evict yourselves from your homes," then you ratified while you were witnessing.

And when (wa-idh) | We took (akhadhnā) | your covenant (mīthāqakum), | "Not (lā) | will you shed (tasfikūna) | your blood (dimāakum) | and not (walā) | will evict (tukh'rijūna) | yourselves (anfusakum) | from (min) | your homes, (diyārikum)" | then (thumma) | you ratified (aqrartum) | while you (wa-antum) | were witnessing (tashhadūna).

2:85 Then you are those who kill yourselves and evict a party of you from their homes, you support one another against them in sin and [the] transgression. And if they come to you as captives, you ransom them, while it was forbidden to you their eviction. So do you believe in part of the Book and disbelieve in part? Then what should be the recompense for the one who does that among you, except disgrace in the life of the world; and on the Day of [the] Resurrection they will be sent back to the most severe punishment? And not is Allah unaware of what you do.

Then (thumma) | you (antum) | are those (hāulāi) | who kill (taqtulūna) | yourselves (anfusakum) | and evict (watukh'rijūna) | a party (farīqan) | of you (minkum) | from (min) | their homes (diyārihim), | you support one another (taẓāharūna) | against them (ʿalayhim) | in sin (bil-ith'mi) | and [the] transgression (wal-ʿud'wāni). | And if (wa-in) | they come to you (yatūkum) | as captives (usārā), | you ransom them (tufādūhum), | while it (wahuwa) | was forbidden (muḥarramun) | to you (ʿalaykum) | their eviction (ikh'rājuhum). | So do you believe (afatu'minūna) | in part of (bibaʿḍi) | the Book (l-kitābi) | and disbelieve (watakfurūna) | in part (bibaʿḍin)? | Then what (famā) | should be the recompense (jazāu) | for the one who (man) | does (yafʿalu) | that (dhālika) | among you (minkum), | except (illā) | disgrace (khiz'yun) | in (fī) | the life (l-ḥayati) | of the world (l-dun'yā); | and on the Day (wayawma) | of [the] Resurrection (l-qiyāmati) | they will be sent back (yuraddūna) | to (ilā) | the most severe (ashaddi) | punishment (l-ʿadhābi)? | And not (wamā) | is Allah (l-lahu) | unaware (bighāfilin) | of what (ʿammā) | you do (taʿmalūna).

2:86 Those are the ones who bought the life of the world for the Hereafter; so not will be lightened for them the punishment and not they will be helped.

Those (ulāika) | are the ones who (alladhīna) | bought (ish'tarawū) | the life (l-ḥayata) | of the world (l-dun'yā) | for the Hereafter (bil-ākhirati); | so not (falā) | will be lightened (yukhaffafu) | for them (ʿanhumu) | the punishment (l-ʿadhābu) | and not (walā) | they (hum) | will be helped (yunṣarūna).

2:87 And indeed We gave Musa the Book and We followed up from after him with [the] Messengers. And We gave Isa, the son of Maryam, [the] clear signs and We supported him with the Holy Spirit. Is it not so (that) whenever came to you a Messenger with what does not desire yourselves, you acted arrogantly? So a party you denied, and a party you killed.

And indeed (walaqad) | We gave (ātaynā) | Musa (mūsā) | the Book (l-kitāba) | and We followed up (waqaffaynā) | from (min) | after him (baʿdihi) | with [the] Messengers (bil-rusuli). | And We gave (waātaynā) | Isa (ʿīsā), | the son (ib'na) | of Maryam (maryama), | [the] clear signs (l-bayināti) | and We supported him (wa-ayyadnāhu) | with (birūḥi) | the Holy Spirit (l-qudusi). | Is it not so (that) whenever (afakullamā) | came to you (jāakum) | a Messenger (rasūlun) | with what (bimā) | does not (lā) | desire (tahwā) | yourselves (anfusukumu), | you acted arrogantly (is'takbartum)? | So a party (fafarīqan) | you denied (kadhabtum), | and a party (wafarīqan) | you killed (taqtulūna).

2:88 And they said, "Our hearts are wrapped." Nay, has cursed them Allah for their disbelief; so little is what they believe.

And they said (waqālū), | "Our hearts (qulūbunā) | are wrapped. (ghul'fun)" | Nay (bal), | has cursed them (laʿanahumu) | Allah (l-lahu) | for their disbelief (bikuf'rihim); | so little (faqalīlan) | is what (mā) | they believe (yu'minūna).

2:89 And when came to them a Book of from Allah confirming what was with them, though they used to from before that, pray for victory over those who disbelieved - then when came to them what they recognized, they disbelieved in it. So the curse of Allah is on the disbelievers.

And when (walammā) | came to them (jāahum) | a Book (kitābun) | of (min) | from (ʿindi) | Allah (l-lahi) | confirming (muṣaddiqun) | what was (limā) | with them (maʿahum), | though they used to (wakānū) | from (min) | before (qablu) | that, pray for victory (yastaftiḥūna) | over (ʿalā) | those who (alladhīna) | disbelieved (kafarū)- | then when (falammā) | came to them (jāahum) | what (mā) | they recognized (ʿarafū), | they disbelieved (kafarū) | in it (bihi). | So the curse (falaʿnatu) | of Allah (l-lahi) | is on (ʿalā) | the disbelievers (l-kāfirīna).

2:90 Evil is that for which they have sold with themselves, that they disbelieve in what has revealed Allah, grudging that sends down Allah of His Grace on whom He wills from His servants. So they have drawn on themselves wrath upon wrath. And for the disbelievers is a punishment humiliating.

Evil is that (bi'samā) | for which they have sold (ish'taraw) | with (bihi) | themselves (anfusahum), | that (an) | they disbelieve (yakfurū) | in what (bimā) | has revealed (anzala) | Allah (l-lahu), | grudging (baghyan) | that (an) | sends down (yunazzila) | Allah (l-lahu) | of (min) | His Grace (faḍlihi) | on (ʿalā) | whom (man) | He wills (yashāu) | from (min) | His servants (ʿibādihi). | So they have drawn on themselves (fabāū) | wrath (bighaḍabin) | upon (ʿalā) | wrath (ghaḍabin). | And for the disbelievers (walil'kāfirīna) | is a punishment (ʿadhābun) | humiliating (muhīnun).

2:91 And when it is said to them, "Believe in what has revealed Allah," they say, "We believe in what was revealed to us." And they disbelieve in what is besides it, while it is the truth confirming what is with them. Say, "Then why did you kill the Prophets of Allah from before, if you were believers?"

And when (wa-idhā) | it is said (qīla) | to them (lahum), | "Believe (āminū) | in what (bimā) | has revealed (anzala) | Allah, (l-lahu)" | they say (qālū), | "We believe (nu'minu) | in what (bimā) | was revealed (unzila) | to us. (ʿalaynā)" | And they disbelieve (wayakfurūna) | in what (bimā) | is besides it (warāahu), | while it (wahuwa) | is the truth (l-ḥaqu) | confirming (muṣaddiqan) | what (limā) | is with them (maʿahum). | Say (qul), | "Then why (falima) | did you kill (taqtulūna) | the Prophets (anbiyāa) | of Allah (l-lahi) | from (min) | before (qablu), | if (in) | you were (kuntum) | believers? (mu'minīna)"

2:92 And indeed came to you Musa with [the] clear signs, then you took the calf from after him and you were wrongdoers.

And indeed (walaqad) | came to you (jāakum) | Musa (mūsā) | with [the] clear signs (bil-bayināti), | then (thumma) | you took (ittakhadhtumu) | the calf (l-ʿij'la) | from (min) | after him (baʿdihi) | and you (wa-antum) | were wrongdoers (ẓālimūna).

2:93 And when We took your covenant and We raised over you the mount, "Hold what We gave you, with firmness and listen." They said, "We heard and we disobeyed." And they were made to drink in their hearts love of the calf because of their disbelief. Say, "Evil is that orders you to do it with your faith, if you are believers."

And when (wa-idh) | We took (akhadhnā) | your covenant (mīthāqakum) | and We raised (warafaʿnā) | over you (fawqakumu) | the mount (l-ṭūra), | "Hold (khudhū) | what (mā) | We gave you (ātaynākum), | with firmness (biquwwatin) | and listen. (wa-is'maʿū)" | They said (qālū), | "We heard (samiʿ'nā) | and we disobeyed. (waʿaṣaynā)" | And they were made to drink (wa-ush'ribū) | in (fī) | their hearts (qulūbihimu) | love of the calf (l-ʿij'la) | because of their disbelief (bikuf'rihim). | Say (qul), | "Evil is that (bi'samā) | orders you to do it (yamurukum) | with (bihi) | your faith (īmānukum), | if (in) | you are (kuntum) | believers. (mu'minīna)"

2:94 Say, "If - is for you the home of the Hereafter with Allah exclusively, from excluding the mankind, then wish for [the] death, if you are truthful."

Say (qul), | "If (in)- | is (kānat) | for you (lakumu) | the home (l-dāru) | of the Hereafter (l-ākhiratu) | with (ʿinda) | Allah (l-lahi) | exclusively (khāliṣatan), | from (min) | excluding (dūni) | the mankind (l-nāsi), | then wish (fatamannawū) | for [the] death (l-mawta), | if (in) | you are (kuntum) | truthful. (ṣādiqīna)"

2:95 And never will they wish for it, ever, because of what sent ahead their hands. And Allah is All-Knower of the wrongdoers.

And never will (walan) | they wish for it (yatamannawhu), | ever (abadan), | because (bimā) | of what sent ahead (qaddamat) | their hands (aydīhim). | And Allah (wal-lahu) | is All-Knower (ʿalīmun) | of the wrongdoers (bil-ẓālimīna).

2:96 And surely you will find them the most greedy of [the] mankind for life, and greedier than those who associate[d] partners with Allah. Loves each one of them if he could be granted a life of a thousand years. But not it will remove him from the punishment that he should be granted life. And Allah is All-Seer of what they do.

And surely you will find them (walatajidannahum) | the most greedy (aḥraṣa) | of [the] mankind (l-nāsi) | for (ʿalā) | life (ḥayatin), | and greedier than (wamina) | those who (alladhīna) | associate[d] partners with Allah (ashrakū). | Loves (yawaddu) | each one of them (aḥaduhum) | if (law) | he could be granted a life (yuʿammaru) | of a thousand (alfa) | years (sanatin). | But not (wamā) | it (huwa) | will remove him (bimuzaḥziḥihi) | from (mina) | the punishment (l-ʿadhābi) | that (an) | he should be granted life (yuʿammara). | And Allah (wal-lahu) | is All-Seer (baṣīrun) | of what (bimā) | they do (yaʿmalūna).

2:97 Say, "Whoever is an enemy to Jibreel - then indeed he brought it down on your heart by the permission of Allah confirming what was before it and a guidance and glad tidings for the believers."

Say (qul), | "Whoever (man) | is (kāna) | an enemy (ʿaduwwan) | to Jibreel (lijib'rīla)- | then indeed he (fa-innahu) | brought it down (nazzalahu) | on (ʿalā) | your heart (qalbika) | by the permission (bi-idh'ni) | of Allah (l-lahi) | confirming (muṣaddiqan) | what (limā) | was (bayna) | before it (yadayhi) | and a guidance (wahudan) | and glad tidings (wabush'rā) | for the believers. (lil'mu'minīna)"

2:98 Whoever is an enemy to Allah and His Angels, and His Messengers, and Jibreel, and Meekael, then indeed Allah is an enemy to the disbelievers.

Whoever (man) | is (kāna) | an enemy (ʿaduwwan) | to Allah (lillahi) | and His Angels (wamalāikatihi), | and His Messengers (warusulihi), | and Jibreel (wajib'rīla), | and Meekael (wamīkāla), | then indeed (fa-inna) | Allah (l-laha) | is an enemy (ʿaduwwun) | to the disbelievers (lil'kāfirīna).

2:99 And indeed We revealed to you Verses clear, and not disbelieves in them except the defiantly disobedient.

And indeed (walaqad) | We revealed (anzalnā) | to you (ilayka) | Verses (āyātin) | clear (bayyinātin), | and not (wamā) | disbelieves (yakfuru) | in them (bihā) | except (illā) | the defiantly disobedient (l-fāsiqūna).

2:100 And is it not that whenever they took a covenant, threw it away a party of them? Nay, most of them do not believe.

And is it not that whenever (awakullamā) | they took (ʿāhadū) | a covenant (ʿahdan), | threw it away (nabadhahu) | a party (farīqun) | of them (min'hum)? | Nay (bal), | most of them (aktharuhum) | do not (lā) | believe (yu'minūna).

2:101 And when came to them a Messenger of from Allah confirming what was with them, threw away a party of those who were given the Book of Allah behind their backs as if they do not know.

And when (walammā) | came to them (jāahum) | a Messenger (rasūlun) | of (min) | from (ʿindi) | Allah (l-lahi) | confirming (muṣaddiqun) | what (limā) | was with them (maʿahum), | threw away (nabadha) | a party (farīqun) | of (mina) | those who (alladhīna) | were given (ūtū) | the Book (l-kitāba) | the Book (kitāba) | of Allah (l-lahi) | behind (warāa) | their backs (ẓuhūrihim) | as if they (ka-annahum) | do not (lā) | know (yaʿlamūna).

2:102 And they followed what recited the devils over the kingdom of Sulaiman. And not disbelieved Sulaiman [and] but the devils disbelieved, they teach the people [the] magic and what was sent down to the two angels in Babylon, Harut and Marut. And not they both teach any one unless they [both] say, "Only we are a trial, so do not disbelieve." But they learn from those two what [they] causes separation with it between the man and his spouse. And not they could at all [be those who] harm with it any one except by permission of Allah. And they learn what harms them and not profits them. And indeed they knew that whoever buys it, not for him in the Hereafter any share. And surely evil is what they sold with it themselves, if they were to know.

And they followed (wa-ittabaʿū) | what (mā) | recited (tatlū) | the devils (l-shayāṭīnu) | over (ʿalā) | the kingdom (mul'ki) | of Sulaiman (sulaymāna). | And not (wamā) | disbelieved (kafara) | Sulaiman (sulaymānu) | [and] but (walākinna) | the devils (l-shayāṭīna) | disbelieved (kafarū), | they teach (yuʿallimūna) | the people (l-nāsa) | [the] magic (l-siḥ'ra) | and what (wamā) | was sent down (unzila) | to (ʿalā) | the two angels (l-malakayni) | in Babylon (bibābila), | Harut (hārūta) | and Marut (wamārūta). | And not (wamā) | they both teach (yuʿallimāni) | any (min) | one (aḥadin) | unless (ḥattā) | they [both] say (yaqūlā), | "Only (innamā) | we (naḥnu) | are a trial (fit'natun), | so do not (falā) | disbelieve. (takfur)" | But they learn (fayataʿallamūna) | from those two (min'humā) | what (mā) | [they] causes separation (yufarriqūna) | with it (bihi) | between (bayna) | the man (l-mari) | and his spouse (wazawjihi). | And not (wamā) | they could (hum) | at all [be those who] harm (biḍārrīna) | with it (bihi) | any (min) | one (aḥadin) | except (illā) | by permission (bi-idh'ni) | of Allah (l-lahi). | And they learn (wayataʿallamūna) | what (mā) | harms them (yaḍurruhum) | and not (walā) | profits them (yanfaʿuhum). | And indeed (walaqad) | they knew (ʿalimū) | that whoever (lamani) | buys it (ish'tarāhu), | not (mā) | for him (lahu) | in (fī) | the Hereafter (l-ākhirati) | any (min) | share (khalāqin). | And surely evil (walabi'sa) | is what (mā) | they sold (sharaw) | with it (bihi) | themselves (anfusahum), | if (law) | they were (kānū) | to know (yaʿlamūna).

2:103 And if [that] they had believed and feared Allah, surely the reward of from Allah would have been better, if they were to know.

And if (walaw) | [that] they (annahum) | had believed (āmanū) | and feared Allah (wa-ittaqaw), | surely the reward (lamathūbatun) | of (min) | from (ʿindi) | Allah (l-lahi) | would have been better (khayrun), | if (law) | they were (kānū) | to know (yaʿlamūna).

2:104 O you who believe[d]! "Do not say "Raina" and say "Unzurna" and listen. And for the disbelievers is a punishment painful.

O you (yāayyuhā) | who (alladhīna) | believe[d] (āmanū)! | "Do not (lā) | say (taqūlū) | "Raina (rāʿinā)" | and say (waqūlū) | "Unzurna (unẓur'nā)" | and listen (wa-is'maʿū). | And for the disbelievers (walil'kāfirīna) | is a punishment (ʿadhābun) | painful (alīmun).

2:105 Do not like those who disbelieve from the People of the Book and not those who associate partners with Allah, that there should be sent down to you any good from your Lord. And Allah chooses for His Mercy whom He wills. And Allah is the Possessor of [the] Bounty [the] Great.

Do not (mā) | like (yawaddu) | those who (alladhīna) | disbelieve (kafarū) | from (min) | the People (ahli) | of the Book (l-kitābi) | and not (walā) | those who associate partners with Allah (l-mush'rikīna), | that (an) | there should be sent down (yunazzala) | to you (ʿalaykum) | any (min) | good (khayrin) | from (min) | your Lord (rabbikum). | And Allah (wal-lahu) | chooses (yakhtaṣṣu) | for His Mercy (biraḥmatihi) | whom (man) | He wills (yashāu). | And Allah (wal-lahu) | is the Possessor (dhū) | of [the] Bounty (l-faḍli) | [the] Great (l-ʿaẓīmi).

2:106 What We abrogate of a sign or [We] cause it to be forgotten, We bring better than it or similar to it. Do not you know that Allah over every thing is All-Powerful?

What (mā) | We abrogate (nansakh) | of (min) | a sign (āyatin) | or (aw) | [We] cause it to be forgotten (nunsihā), | We bring (nati) | better (bikhayrin) | than it (min'hā) | or (aw) | similar to it (mith'lihā). | Do not (alam) | you know (taʿlam) | that (anna) | Allah (l-laha) | over (ʿalā) | every (kulli) | thing (shayin) | is All-Powerful (qadīrun)?

2:107 Do not you know that, Allah for Him is the Kingdom of the heavens and the earth? And not is for you from besides Allah any protector and not any helper.

Do not (alam) | you know (taʿlam) | that (anna), | Allah (l-laha) | for Him (lahu) | is the Kingdom (mul'ku) | of the heavens (l-samāwāti) | and the earth (wal-arḍi)? | And not (wamā) | is for you (lakum) | from (min) | besides (dūni) | Allah (l-lahi) | any (min) | protector (waliyyin) | and not (walā) | any helper (naṣīrin).

2:108 Or do you wish that you ask your Messenger as was asked Musa from before? And whoever exchanges [the] disbelief with [the] faith, so certainly he went astray from the evenness of the way.

Or (am) | do you wish (turīdūna) | that (an) | you ask (tasalū) | your Messenger (rasūlakum) | as (kamā) | was asked (su-ila) | Musa (mūsā) | from (min) | before (qablu)? | And whoever (waman) | exchanges (yatabaddali) | [the] disbelief (l-kuf'ra) | with [the] faith (bil-īmāni), | so certainly (faqad) | he went astray from (ḍalla) | the evenness (sawāa) | of the way (l-sabīli).

2:109 Wish[ed] many from the People of the Book if they could turn you back from after your having faith to disbelievers, out of jealousy from of themselves, even from after [what] became clear to them, the truth. So forgive and overlook until brings Allah His Command. Indeed, Allah on every thing is All-Powerful.

Wish[ed] (wadda) | many (kathīrun) | from (min) | the People (ahli) | of the Book (l-kitābi) | if (law) | they could turn you back (yaruddūnakum) | from (min) | after (baʿdi) | your having faith (īmānikum) | to disbelievers (kuffāran), | out of jealousy (ḥasadan) | from (min) | of (ʿindi) | themselves (anfusihim), | even from (min) | after (baʿdi) | [what] (mā) | became clear (tabayyana) | to them (lahumu), | the truth (l-ḥaqu). | So forgive (fa-iʿfū) | and overlook (wa-iṣ'faḥū) | until (ḥattā) | brings (yatiya) | Allah (l-lahu) | His Command (bi-amrihi). | Indeed (inna), | Allah (l-laha) | on (ʿalā) | every (kulli) | thing (shayin) | is All-Powerful (qadīrun).

2:110 And establish the prayer and give [the] zakah. And whatever you send forth for yourselves of good deeds, you will find it with Allah. Indeed, Allah of what you do is All-Seer.

And establish (wa-aqīmū) | the prayer (l-ṣalata) | and give (waātū) | [the] zakah (l-zakata). | And whatever (wamā) | you send forth (tuqaddimū) | for yourselves (li-anfusikum) | of (min) | good deeds (khayrin), | you will find it (tajidūhu) | with (ʿinda) | Allah (l-lahi). | Indeed (inna), | Allah (l-laha) | of what (bimā) | you do (taʿmalūna) | is All-Seer (baṣīrun).

2:111 And they said, "Never will enter the Paradise except who is a Jew[s] or a Christian[s]." That is their wishful thinking. Say, "Bring your proof if you are [those who are] truthful."

And they said (waqālū), | "Never (lan) | will enter (yadkhula) | the Paradise (l-janata) | except (illā) | who (man) | is (kāna) | a Jew[s] (hūdan) | or (aw) | a Christian[s]. (naṣārā)" | That (til'ka) | is their wishful thinking (amāniyyuhum). | Say (qul), | "Bring (hātū) | your proof (bur'hānakum) | if (in) | you are (kuntum) | [those who are] truthful. (ṣādiqīna)"

2:112 Yes, whoever submits his face to Allah and he is a good-doer, so for him is his reward with his Lord. And no fear will be on them and not they will grieve.

Yes (balā), | whoever (man) | submits (aslama) | his face (wajhahu) | to Allah (lillahi) | and he (wahuwa) | is a good-doer (muḥ'sinun), | so for him (falahu) | is his reward (ajruhu) | with (ʿinda) | his Lord (rabbihi). | And no (walā) | fear (khawfun) | will be on them (ʿalayhim) | and not (walā) | they (hum) | will grieve (yaḥzanūna).

2:113 And said the Jews, "Not the Christians are on anything," and said the Christians, "Not the Jews are on anything," although they recite the Book. Like that said those who do not know, similar their saying. [So] Allah will judge between them on the Day of Resurrection in what they were [in it] differing.

And said (waqālati) | the Jews (l-yahūdu), | "Not (laysati) | the Christians (l-naṣārā) | are on (ʿalā) | anything, (shayin)" | and said (waqālati) | the Christians (l-naṣārā), | "Not (laysati) | the Jews (l-yahūdu) | are on (ʿalā) | anything, (shayin)" | although they (wahum) | recite (yatlūna) | the Book (l-kitāba). | Like that (kadhālika) | said (qāla) | those who (alladhīna) | do not (lā) | know (yaʿlamūna), | similar (mith'la) | their saying (qawlihim). | [So] Allah (fal-lahu) | will judge (yaḥkumu) | between them (baynahum) | on the Day (yawma) | of Resurrection (l-qiyāmati) | in what (fīmā) | they were (kānū) | [in it] (fīhi) | differing (yakhtalifūna).

2:114 And who is more unjust than one who prevents the masajid of Allah to be mentioned in them His name, and strives for their destruction? Those! Not it is for them that they enter them except like those in fear. For them in the world is disgrace and for them in the Hereafter is a punishment great.

And who (waman) | is more unjust (aẓlamu) | than one who (mimman) | prevents (manaʿa) | the masajid (masājida) | of Allah (l-lahi) | to (an) | be mentioned (yudh'kara) | in them (fīhā) | His name (us'muhu), | and strives (wasaʿā) | for (fī) | their destruction (kharābihā)? | Those (ulāika)! | Not (mā) | it is (kāna) | for them (lahum) | that (an) | they enter them (yadkhulūhā) | except (illā) |

like those in fear (khāifīna). | For them (lahum) | in (fī) | the world (l-dun'yā) | is disgrace (khiz'yun) | and for them (walahum) | in (fī) | the Hereafter (l-ākhirati) | is a punishment (ʿadhābun) | great (ʿaẓīmun).

2:115 And for Allah is the east and the west, so wherever you turn [so] there is the face of Allah. Indeed, Allah is All-Encompassing, All-Knowing.

And for Allah (walillahi) | is the east (l-mashriqu) | and the west (wal-maghribu), | so wherever (fa-aynamā) | you turn (tuwallū) | [so] there (fathamma) | is the face (wajhu) | of Allah (l-lahi). | Indeed (inna), | Allah (l-laha) | is All-Encompassing (wāsiʿun), | All-Knowing (ʿalīmun).

2:116 And they said, "has taken Allah a son." Glory be to Him! Nay, for Him is what is in the heavens and the earth. All to Him are humbly obedient.

And they said (waqālū), | "has taken (ittakhadha) | Allah (l-lahu) | a son. (waladan)" | Glory be to Him (sub'ḥānahu)! | Nay (bal), | for Him (lahu) | is what (mā) | is in (fī) | the heavens (l-samāwāti) | and the earth (wal-arḍi). | All (kullun) | to Him (lahu) | are humbly obedient (qānitūna).

2:117 The Originator of the heavens and the earth! And when He decrees a matter, [so] only He says to it "Be," and it becomes.

The Originator (badīʿu) | of the heavens (l-samāwāti) | and the earth (wal-arḍi)! | And when (wa-idhā) | He decrees (qaḍā) | a matter (amran), | [so] only (fa-innamā) | He says (yaqūlu) | to it (lahu) | "Be, (kun)" | and it becomes (fayakūnu).

2:118 And said those who do not know, "Why not speaks to us Allah or comes to us a sign?" Like that said those from before them similar their saying. Became alike their hearts. Indeed, We have made clear the signs for people who firmly believe.

And said (waqāla) | those who (alladhīna) | do not (lā) | know (yaʿlamūna), | "Why not (lawlā) | speaks to us (yukallimunā) | Allah (l-lahu) | or (aw) | comes to us (tatīnā) | a sign? (āyatun)" | Like that (kadhālika) | said (qāla) | those (alladhīna) | from (min) | before them (qablihim) | similar (mith'la) | their saying (qawlihim). | Became alike (tashābahat) | their hearts (qulūbuhum). | Indeed (qad), | We have made clear (bayyannā) | the signs (l-āyāti) | for people (liqawmin) | who firmly believe (yūqinūna).

2:119 Indeed We! [We] have sent you with the truth, as a bearer of good news and as a warner. And not you will be asked about the companions of the blazing Fire.

Indeed We (innā)! | [We] have sent you (arsalnāka) | with the truth (bil-ḥaqi), | as a bearer of good news (bashīran) | and as a warner (wanadhīran). | And not (walā) | you will be asked (tus'alu) | about (ʿan) | the companions (aṣḥābi) | of the blazing Fire (l-jaḥīmi).

2:120 And never will be pleased with you the Jews and [not] the Christians until you follow their religion. Say, "Indeed, the Guidance of Allah, it is the Guidance." And if you follow their desires after what has come to you of the knowledge, not for you from Allah any protector and not any helper.

And never (walan) | will be pleased (tarḍā) | with you (ʿanka) | the Jews (l-yahūdu) | and [not] (walā) | the Christians (l-naṣārā) | until (ḥattā) | you follow (tattabiʿa) | their religion (millatahum). | Say (qul), | "Indeed (inna), | the Guidance (hudā) | of Allah (l-lahi), | it (huwa) | is the Guidance. (l-hudā)" | And if (wala-ini) | you follow (ittabaʿta) | their desires (ahwāahum) | after (baʿda) | what (alladhī) | has come to you (jāaka) | of (mina) | the knowledge (l-ʿil'mi), | not (mā) | for you (laka) | from (mina) | Allah (l-lahi) | any (min) | protector (waliyyin) | and not (walā) | any helper (naṣīrin).

2:121 Those, We have given them the Book recite it as it has the right of its recitation. Those people believe in it. And whoever disbelieves in it, then those, they are the losers.

Those (alladhīna), | We have given them (ātaynāhumu) | the Book (l-kitāba) | recite it (yatlūnahu) | as it has the right (ḥaqqa) | of its recitation (tilāwatihi). | Those people (ulāika) | believe (yu'minūna) | in it (bihi). | And whoever (waman) | disbelieves (yakfur) | in it (bihi), | then those (fa-ulāika), | they (humu) | are the losers (l-khāsirūna).

2:122 O Children of Israel! Remember My Favor which I bestowed upon you and that I [I] preferred you over the worlds.

O Children (yābanī) | of Israel (is'rāīla)! | Remember (udh'kurū) | My Favor (ni''matiya) | which (allatī) | I bestowed (an'amtu) | upon you ('alaykum) | and that I (wa-annī) | [I] preferred you (faḍḍaltukum) | over ('alā) | the worlds (l-'ālamīna).

2:123 And fear a day not will avail a soul of another soul anything and not will be accepted from it any compensation, and not will benefit it any intercession, and not they will be helped.

And fear (wa-ittaqū) | a day (yawman) | not (lā) | will avail (tajzī) | a soul (nafsun) | of ('an) | another soul (nafsin) | anything (shayan) | and not (walā) | will be accepted (yuq'balu) | from it (min'hā) | any compensation ('adlun), | and not (walā) | will benefit it (tanfa'uhā) | any intercession (shafā'atun), | and not (walā) | they (hum) | will be helped (yunṣarūna).

2:124 And when tried Ibrahim his Lord with words and he fulfilled them, He said, "Indeed I am the One to make you for the mankind a leader." He said, "And from my offspring?" He said, "Does not reach My Covenant to the wrongdoers."

And when (wa-idhi) | tried (ib'talā) | Ibrahim (ib'rāhīma) | his Lord (rabbuhu) | with words (bikalimātin) | and he fulfilled them (fa-atammahunna), | He said (qāla), | "Indeed I (innī) | am the One to make you (jā'iluka) | for the mankind (lilnnāsi) | a leader. (imāman)" | He said (qāla), | "And from (wamin) | my offspring? (dhurriyyatī)" | He said (qāla), | "Does not (lā) | reach (yanālu) | My Covenant ('ahdī) | to the wrongdoers. (l-ẓālimīna)"

2:125 And when We made the House a place of return for mankind and a place of security and said, "Take [from] the standing place of Ibrahim, as a place of prayer." And We made a covenant with Ibrahim and Ishmael [that], "[You both] purify My House for those who circumambulate and those who seclude themselves for devotion and prayer and those who bow down and those who prostrate."

And when (wa-idh) | We made (ja'alnā) | the House (l-bayta) | a place of return (mathābatan) | for mankind (lilnnāsi) | and a place of security (wa-amnan) | and said, "Take (wa-ittakhidhū) | [from] (min) | the standing place (maqāmi) | of Ibrahim (ib'rāhīma), | as a place of prayer. (muṣallan)" | And We made a covenant (wa'ahid'nā) | with (ilā) | Ibrahim (ib'rāhīma) | and Ishmael (wa-is'mā'īla) | [that] (an), | "[You both] purify (ṭahhirā) | My House (baytiya) | for those who circumambulate (lilṭṭāifīna) | and those who seclude themselves for devotion and prayer (wal-'ākifīna) | and those who bow down (wal-ruka'i) | and those who prostrate. (l-sujūdi)"

2:126 And when said Ibrahim, "My Lord make this a city secure and provide its people with fruits, to whoever believed from them in Allah and the Day the Last," He said, "And whoever disbelieved, [then] I will grant him enjoyment a little; then I will force him to the punishment of the Fire, and evil is the destination.

And when (wa-idh) | said (qāla) | Ibrahim (ib'rāhīmu), | "My Lord (rabbi) | make (ij''al) | this (hādhā) | a city (baladan) | secure (āminan) | and provide (wa-ur'zuq) | its people (ahlahu) | with (mina) | fruits (l-thamarāti), | to whoever (man) | believed (āmana) | from them (min'hum) | in Allah (bil-lahi) | and the Day (wal-yawmi) | the Last, (l-ākhiri)" | He said (qāla), | "And whoever (waman) | disbelieved (kafara), | [then] I will grant him enjoyment (fa-umatti'uhu) | a little (qalīlan); | then (thumma) | I will force him (aḍṭarruhu) | to (ilā) | the punishment ('adhābi) | of the Fire (l-nāri), | and evil (wabi'sa) | is the destination (l-maṣīru).

2:127 And when was raising Ibrahim the foundations of the House and Ishmael, saying, "Our Lord! Accept from us. Indeed You! [You] are the All-Hearing, the All-Knowing.

And when (wa-idh) | was raising (yarfaʿu) | Ibrahim (ib'rāhīmu) | the foundations (l-qawāʿida) | of (mina) | the House (l-bayti) | and Ishmael (wa-is'māʿīlu), | saying, "Our Lord (rabbanā)! | Accept (taqabbal) | from us (minnā). | Indeed You (innaka)! | [You] are (anta) | the All-Hearing (l-samīʿu), | the All-Knowing (l-ʿalīmu).

2:128 Our Lord! [and] Make us both submissive to You. And from our offspring a community submissive to You. And show us our ways of worship and turn to us. Indeed You! [You] are the Oft-returning, the Most Merciful.

Our Lord (rabbanā)! | [and] Make us (wa-ij'ʿalnā) | both submissive (mus'limayni) | to You (laka). | And from (wamin) | our offspring (dhurriyyatinā) | a community (ummatan) | submissive (mus'limatan) | to You (laka). | And show us (wa-arinā) | our ways of worship (manāsikanā) | and turn (watub) | to us (ʿalaynā). | Indeed You (innaka)! | [You] are (anta) | the Oft-returning (l-tawābu), | the Most Merciful (l-raḥīmu).

2:129 Our Lord! [And] raise up in them a Messenger from them who will recite to them Your Verses and will teach them the Book and the wisdom and purify them. Indeed You! You are the All-Mighty the All-Wise."

Our Lord (rabbanā)! | [And] raise up (wa-ib'ʿath) | in them (fīhim) | a Messenger (rasūlan) | from them (min'hum) | who will recite (yatlū) | to them (ʿalayhim) | Your Verses (āyātika) | and will teach them (wayuʿallimuhumu) | the Book (l-kitāba) | and the wisdom (wal-ḥik'mata) | and purify them (wayuzakkīhim). | Indeed You (innaka)! | You are (anta) | the All-Mighty (l-ʿazīzu) | the All-Wise. (l-ḥakīmu)"

2:130 And who will turn away from the religion of Ibrahim except who fooled himself? And indeed We chose him in the world, and indeed he, in, the Hereafter surely will be among the righteous.

And who (waman) | will turn away (yarghabu) | from (ʿan) | the religion (millati) | of Ibrahim (ib'rāhīma) | except (illā) | who (man) | fooled (safiha) | himself (nafsahu)? | And indeed (walaqadi) | We chose him (iṣ'ṭafaynāhu) | in (fī) | the world (l-dun'yā), | and indeed he (wa-innahu), | in (fī), | the Hereafter (l-ākhirati) | surely will be among (lamina) | the righteous (l-ṣāliḥīna).

2:131 When said to him his Lord "Submit yourself," he said, "I have submitted (myself) to the Lord of the worlds."

When (idh) | said (qāla) | to him (lahu) | his Lord (rabbuhu) | "Submit yourself, (aslim)" | he said (qāla), | "I have submitted (myself (aslamtu)) | to the Lord (lirabbi) | of the worlds. (l-ʿālamīna)"

2:132 And enjoined [it] Ibrahim upon his sons and Yaqub, "O my sons! Indeed, Allah has chosen for you the religion, so not should you die except while you are submissive."

And enjoined (wawaṣṣā) | [it] (bihā) | Ibrahim (ib'rāhīmu) | upon his sons (banīhi) | and Yaqub (wayaʿqūbu), | "O my sons (yābaniyya)! | Indeed (inna), | Allah (l-laha) | has chosen (iṣ'ṭafā) | for you (lakumu) | the religion (l-dīna), | so not (falā) | should you die (tamūtunna) | except (illā) | while you (wa-antum) | are submissive. (mus'limūna)"

2:133 Or were you witnesses when came to Yaqub [the] death, when he said to his sons, "What will you worship from after me?" They said, "We will worship your God and the God of your forefathers, Ibrahim and Ishmael and Isaac - God One. And we to Him are submissive."

Or (am) | were you (kuntum) | witnesses (shuhadāa) | when (idh) | came to (ḥaḍara) | Yaqub (yaʿqūba) | [the] death (l-mawtu), | when (idh) | he said (qāla) | to his sons (libanīhi), | "What (mā) | will you worship (taʿbudūna) | from (min) | after me? (baʿdī)" | They said (qālū), |

"We will worship (naʿbudu) | your God (ilāhaka) | and the God (wa-ilāha) | of your forefathers (ābāika), | Ibrahim (ib'rāhīma) | and Ishmael (wa-is'māʿīla) | and Isaac (wa-is'ḥāqa)- | God (ilāhan) | One (wāḥidan). | And we (wanaḥnu) | to Him (lahu) | are submissive. (mus'limūna)"

2:134 This was a community which has passed away, for it what it earned and for you what you have earned. And not you will be asked about what they used to do.

This (til'ka) | was a community (ummatun) | which (qad) | has passed away (khalat), | for it (lahā) | what (mā) | it earned (kasabat) | and for you (walakum) | what (mā) | you have earned (kasabtum). | And not (walā) | you will be asked (tus'alūna) | about what (ʿammā) | they used to (kānū) | do (yaʿmalūna).

2:135 And they said, "Be Jews or Christians, then you will be guided." Say, "Nay, the religion of Ibrahim, the upright; and not he was of those who associated partners with Allah."

And they said (waqālū), | "Be (kūnū) | Jews (hūdan) | or (aw) | Christians (naṣārā), | then you will be guided. (tahtadū)" | Say (qul), | "Nay (bal), | the religion (millata) | of Ibrahim (ib'rāhīma), | the upright (ḥanīfan); | and not (wamā) | he was (kāna) | of (mina) | those who associated partners with Allah. (l-mush'rikīna)"

2:136 Say, "We have believed in Allah and what is revealed to us and what was revealed to Ibrahim and Ishmael and Isaac and Yaqub and the descendants, and what was given to Musa and Isa and what was given to the Prophets from their Lord. Not we make distinction between any of them. And we to Him are submissive."

Say (qūlū), | "We have believed (āmannā) | in Allah (bil-lahi) | and what (wamā) | is revealed (unzila) | to us (ilaynā) | and what (wamā) | was revealed (unzila) | to (ilā) | Ibrahim (ib'rāhīma) | and Ishmael (wa-is'māʿīla) | and Isaac (wa-is'ḥāqa) | and Yaqub (wayaʿqūba) | and the descendants (wal-asbāṭi), | and what (wamā) | was given (ūtiya) | to Musa (mūsā) | and Isa (waʿīsā) | and what (wamā) | was given (ūtiya) | to the Prophets (l-nabiyūna) | from (min) | their Lord (rabbihim). | Not (lā) | we make distinction (nufarriqu) | between (bayna) | any (aḥadin) | of them (min'hum). | And we (wanaḥnu) | to Him (lahu) | are submissive. (mus'limūna)"

2:137 So if they believe[d] in the like of what you have believed in [it], then indeed, they are rightly guided. But if they turn away, then only they are in dissension. So will suffice you against them Allah, and He is the All-Hearing, the All-Knowing.

So if (fa-in) | they believe[d] (āmanū) | in the like (bimith'li) | of what (mā) | you have believed (āmantum) | in [it] (bihi), | then indeed (faqadi), | they are rightly guided (ih'tadaw). | But if (wa-in) | they turn away (tawallaw), | then only (fa-innamā) | they (hum) | are in (fī) | dissension (shiqāqin). | So will suffice you against them (fasayakfīkahumu) | Allah (l-lahu), | and He (wahuwa) | is the All-Hearing (l-samīʿu), | the All-Knowing (l-ʿalīmu).

2:138 The color (religion) of Allah! And who is better than Allah at coloring? And we to Him are worshippers.

The color (religion (ṣib'ghata)) | of Allah (l-lahi)! | And who (waman) | is better (aḥsanu) | than (mina) | Allah (l-lahi) | at coloring (ṣib'ghatan)? | And we (wanaḥnu) | to Him (lahu) | are worshippers (ʿābidūna).

2:139 Say, "Do you argue with us about Allah while He is our Lord and your Lord? And for us are our deeds and for you are your deeds and we to Him are sincere.

Say (qul), | "Do you argue with us (atuḥājjūnanā) | about (fī) | Allah (l-lahi) | while He (wahuwa) | is our Lord (rabbunā) | and your Lord (warabbukum)? | And for us (walanā) | are our deeds (aʿmālunā) | and for you (walakum) | are your deeds (aʿmālukum) | and we (wanaḥnu) | to Him (lahu) | are sincere (mukh'liṣūna).

2:140 Or do you say that Ibrahim and Ishmael and Isaac and Yaqub and the descendants were Jews or Christians?" Say, "Are you better knowing or is Allah?" And who is more unjust than the one who concealed a testimony that he has from Allah? And not is Allah unaware of what you do.

Or (am) | do you say (taqūlūna) | that (inna) | Ibrahim (ib'rāhīma) | and Ishmael (wa-is'mā'īla) | and Isaac (wa-is'ḥāqa) | and Yaqub (waya'qūba) | and the descendants (wal-asbāṭa) | were (kānū) | Jews (hūdan) | or (aw) | Christians? (naṣārā)" | Say (qul), | "Are you (a-antum) | better knowing (a'lamu) | or (ami) | is Allah? (l-lahu)" | And who (waman) | is more unjust (aẓlamu) | than the one who (mimman) | concealed (katama) | a testimony (shahādatan) | that he has ('indahu) | from (mina) | Allah (l-lahi)? | And not (wamā) | is Allah (l-lahu) | unaware (bighāfilin) | of what ('ammā) | you do (ta'malūna).

2:141 This was a community which has passed away, for it what it earned and for you what you have earned. And not you will be asked about what they used to do.

This (til'ka) | was a community (ummatun) | which (qad) | has passed away (khalat), | for it (lahā) | what (mā) | it earned (kasabat) | and for you (walakum) | what (mā) | you have earned (kasabtum). | And not (walā) | you will be asked (tus'alūna) | about what ('ammā) | they used to (kānū) | do (ya'malūna).

2:142 Will say the foolish ones from the people, "What has turned them from their direction of prayer which they were used to [on it]." Say, "For Allah is the east and the west. He guides whom He wills to a path straight."

Will say (sayaqūlu) | the foolish ones (l-sufahāu) | from (mina) | the people (l-nāsi), | "What (mā) | has turned them (wallāhum) | from ('an) | their direction of prayer (qib'latihimu) | which (allatī) | they were used to (kānū) | [on it]. ('alayhā)" | Say (qul), | "For Allah (lillahi) | is the east (l-mashriqu) | and the west (wal-maghribu). | He guides (yahdī) | whom (man) | He wills (yashāu) | to (ilā) | a path (ṣirāṭin) | straight. (mus'taqīmin)"

2:143 And thus We made you a community of the middle way so that you will be witnesses over the mankind, and will be the Messenger on you a witness. And not We made the direction of prayer which you were used to [on it] except that We make evident he who follows the Messenger from he who turns back on his heels. And indeed, it was certainly a great test except for those whom guided by Allah. And not will Allah let go waste your faith. Indeed, Allah is to [the] mankind Full of Kindness, Most Merciful.

And thus (wakadhālika) | We made you (ja'alnākum) | a community (ummatan) | of the middle way (wasaṭan) | so that you will be (litakūnū) | witnesses (shuhadāa) | over ('alā) | the mankind (l-nāsi), | and will be (wayakūna) | the Messenger (l-rasūlu) | on you ('alaykum) | a witness (shahīdan). | And not (wamā) | We made (ja'alnā) | the direction of prayer (l-qib'lata) | which (allatī) | you were used to (kunta) | [on it] ('alayhā) | except (illā) | that We make evident (lina'lama) | he who (man) | follows (yattabi'u) | the Messenger (l-rasūla) | from he who (mimman) | turns back (yanqalibu) | on ('alā) | his heels ('aqibayhi). | And indeed (wa-in), | it was (kānat) | certainly a great test (lakabīratan) | except (illā) | for ('alā) | those whom (alladhīna) | guided (hadā) | by Allah (l-lahu). | And not (wamā) | will (kāna) | Allah (l-lahu) | let go waste (liyuḍī'a) | your faith (īmānakum). | Indeed (inna), | Allah (l-laha) | is to [the] mankind (bil-nāsi) | Full of Kindness (laraūfun), | Most Merciful (raḥīmun).

2:144 Indeed, We see the turning of your face towards the heaven. So We will surely turn you to the direction of prayer you will be pleased with. So turn your face towards the direction of Al-Masjid Al-Haraam and wherever that you are [so] turn your faces in its direction. And indeed, those who were given the Book surely know that it is the truth from their Lord. And not is Allah unaware of what they do.

Indeed (qad), | We see (narā) | the turning (taqalluba) | of your face (wajhika) | towards (fī) | the heaven (l-samāi). | So We will surely turn you (falanuwalliyannaka) | to the direction of prayer (qib'latan) | you will be pleased with (tarḍāhā). | So turn (fawalli) | your face (wajhaka) | towards the direction (shaṭra) | of Al-Masjid (l-masjidi) | Al-Haraam (l-ḥarāmi) | and wherever (waḥaythu) | that (mā) | you are (kuntum) | [so] turn (fawallū) | your faces (wujūhakum) | in its direction (shaṭrahu). | And indeed (wa-inna), | those who (alladhīna) | were given (ūtū) | the Book (l-kitāba) | surely know (laya'lamūna) | that it (annahu) | is the truth (l-ḥaqu) | from (min) | their Lord (rabbihim). | And not (wamā) | is Allah (l-lahu) | unaware (bighāfilin) | of what ('ammā) | they do (ya'malūna).

2:145 And even if you come to those who were given the Book with all the signs, not they would follow your direction of prayer, and not will you (be) a follower of their direction of prayer. And not some of them are followers of the direction of prayer of each other. And if you followed their desires from after [what] came to you of the knowledge, indeed, you would then be surely among the wrongdoers.

And even if (wala-in) | you come (atayta) | to those who (alladhīna) | were given (ūtū) | the Book (l-kitāba) | with all (bikulli) | the signs (āyatin), | not (mā) | they would follow (tabi'ū) | your direction of prayer (qib'lataka), | and not (wamā) | will you (be (anta)) | a follower (bitābi'in) | of their direction of prayer (qib'latahum). | And not (wamā) | some of them (ba'ḍuhum) | are followers (bitābi'in) | of the direction of prayer (qib'lata) | of each other (ba'ḍin). | And if (wala-ini) | you followed (ittaba'ta) | their desires (ahwāahum) | from (min) | after (ba'di) | [what] (mā) | came to you (jāaka) | of (mina) | the knowledge (l-'il'mi), | indeed, you (innaka) | would then (idhan) | be surely among (lamina) | the wrongdoers (l-ẓālimīna).

2:146 To those whom We gave [them] the Book, they recognize it like they recognize their sons. And indeed, a group of them surely they conceal the Truth while they know.

To those whom (alladhīna) | We gave [them] (ātaynāhumu) | the Book (l-kitāba), | they recognize it (ya'rifūnahu) | like (kamā) | they recognize (ya'rifūna) | their sons (abnāahum). | And indeed (wa-inna), | a group (farīqan) | of them (min'hum) | surely they conceal (layaktumūna) | the Truth (l-ḥaqa) | while they (wahum) | know (ya'lamūna).

2:147 The Truth is from your Lord, so do not be among the doubters.

The Truth (al-ḥaqu) | is from (min) | your Lord (rabbika), | so do not (falā) | be (takūnanna) | among (mina) | the doubters (l-mum'tarīna).

2:148 And for everyone is a direction - he turns towards it, so race to the good. Wherever that you will be will bring you by Allah together. Indeed, Allah is on every thing All-Powerful.

And for everyone (walikullin) | is a direction (wij'hatun)- | he (huwa) | turns towards it (muwallīhā), | so race (fa-is'tabiqū) | to the good (l-khayrāti). | Wherever (ayna) | that (mā) | you will be (takūnū) | will bring (yati) | you (bikumu) | by Allah (l-lahu) | together (jamī'an). | Indeed (inna), | Allah (l-laha) | is on ('alā) | every (kulli) | thing (shayin) | All-Powerful (qadīrun).

2:149 And from wherever you start forth, [so] turn your face in the direction of Al-Masjid Al-Haraam. And indeed, it is surely the truth from your Lord. And not is Allah unaware of what you do.

And from (wamin) | wherever (ḥaythu) | you start forth (kharajta), | [so] turn (fawalli) | your face (wajhaka) | in the direction (shaṭra) | of Al-Masjid (l-masjidi) | Al-Haraam (l-ḥarāmi). | And indeed, it (wa-innahu) | is surely the truth (lalḥaqqu) | from (min) | your Lord (rabbika). | And not (wamā) | is Allah (l-lahu) | unaware (bighāfilin) | of what ('ammā) | you do (ta'malūna).

2:150 And from wherever you start forth [so] turn your face in the direction of Al-Masjid Al-Haraam. And wherever that you all are [so] turn your faces in its direction, so that not will be for the people against you any argument except those who wronged among them; so do not fear them, but fear Me. And that I complete My favor upon you [and] so that you may be guided.

And from (wamin) | wherever (ḥaythu) | you start forth (kharajta) | [so] turn (fawalli) |

your face (wajhaka) | in the direction (shaṭra) | of Al-Masjid (l-masjidi) | Al-Haraam (l-ḥarāmi). | And wherever (waḥaythu) | that (mā) | you all are (kuntum) | [so] turn (fawallū) | your faces (wujūhakum) | in its direction (shaṭrahu), | so that not (li-allā) | will be (yakūna) | for the people (lilnnāsi) | against you (ʿalaykum) | any argument (ḥujjatun) | except (illā) | those who (alladhīna) | wronged (ẓalamū) | among them (min'hum); | so do not (falā) | fear them (takhshawhum), | but fear Me (wa-ikh'shawnī). | And that I complete (wali-utimma) | My favor (niʿ'matī) | upon you (ʿalaykum) | [and] so that you may (walaʿallakum) | be guided (tahtadūna).

2:151 As We sent among you a Messenger from you who recites to you Our verses and purifies you and teaches you the Book and the wisdom and teaches you what not you were knowing.

As (kamā) | We sent (arsalnā) | among you (fīkum) | a Messenger (rasūlan) | from you (minkum) | who recites (yatlū) | to you (ʿalaykum) | Our verses (āyātinā) | and purifies you (wayuzakkīkum) | and teaches you (wayuʿallimukumu) | the Book (l-kitāba) | and the wisdom (wal-ḥik'mata) | and teaches you (wayuʿallimukum) | what (mā) | not (lam) | you were (takūnū) | knowing (taʿlamūna).

2:152 So remember Me, I will remember you and be grateful to Me and do not be ungrateful to Me.

So remember Me (fa-udh'kurūnī), | I will remember you (adhkur'kum) | and be grateful (wa-ush'kurū) | to Me (lī) | and do not (walā) | be ungrateful to Me (takfurūni).

2:153 O you who believe[d]! Seek help through patience and the prayer. Indeed, Allah is with the patient ones.

O you (yāayyuhā) | who (alladhīna) | believe[d] (āmanū)! | Seek help (is'taʿīnū) | through patience (bil-ṣabri) | and the prayer (wal-ṣalati). | Indeed (inna), | Allah (l-laha) | is with (maʿa) | the patient ones (l-ṣābirīna).

2:154 And do not say for the ones who are slain in the way of Allah "They are dead." Nay, they are alive [and] but you do not perceive.

And do not (walā) | say (taqūlū) | for the ones who (liman) | are slain (yuq'talu) | in (fī) | the way (sabīli) | of Allah (l-lahi) | "They are dead. (amwātun)" | Nay (bal), | they are alive (aḥyāon) | [and] but (walākin) | you do not (lā) | perceive (tashʿurūna).

2:155 And surely We will test you with something of [the] fear and [the] hunger and loss of [the] wealth and [the] lives and [the] fruits, but give good news to the patient ones.

And surely We will test you (walanabluwannakum) | with something (bishayin) | of (mina) | [the] fear (l-khawfi) | and [the] hunger (wal-jūʿi) | and loss (wanaqṣin) | of (mina) | [the] wealth (l-amwāli) | and [the] lives (wal-anfusi) | and [the] fruits (wal-thamarāti), | but give good news (wabashiri) | to the patient ones (l-ṣābirīna).

2:156 Those who, when strikes them a misfortune, they say, "Indeed, we belong to Allah and indeed we towards Him will return."

Those who (alladhīna), | when (idhā) | strikes them (aṣābathum) | a misfortune (muṣībatun), | they say (qālū), | "Indeed, we (innā) | belong to Allah (lillahi) | and indeed we (wa-innā) | towards Him (ilayhi) | will return. (rājiʿūna)"

2:157 Those on them are blessings from their Lord and Mercy. And those [they] are the guided ones.

Those (ulāika) | on them (ʿalayhim) | are blessings (ṣalawātun) | from (min) | their Lord (rabbihim) | and Mercy (waraḥmatun). | And those (wa-ulāika) | [they] (humu) | are the guided ones (l-muh'tadūna).

2:158 Indeed, the Safa and the Marwah are from the symbols of Allah. So whoever performs Hajj of the House or performs Umrah, so no blame on him that he walks between [both of] them. And whoever voluntarily does good, then indeed, Allah is All-Appreciative, All-Knowing.

Indeed (inna), | the Safa (l-ṣafā) | and the Marwah (wal-marwata) | are from (min) | the symbols (shaʿāiri) | of Allah (l-lahi). | So whoever (faman) | performs Hajj (ḥajja) | of the House (l-bayta) | or (awi) | performs Umrah (iʿ'tamara), | so no (falā) | blame (junāḥa) | on him (ʿalayhi) | that (an) | he walks (yaṭṭawwafa) | between [both of] them (bihimā). | And whoever (waman) | voluntarily does (taṭawwaʿa) | good (khayran), | then indeed (fa-inna), | Allah (l-laha) | is All-Appreciative (shākirun), | All-Knowing (ʿalīmun).

2:159 Indeed, those who conceal what We revealed of the clear proofs, and the Guidance, from after [what] We made clear to the people in the Book - those, curses them Allah and curse them the ones who curse.

Indeed (inna), | those who (alladhīna) | conceal (yaktumūna) | what (mā) | We revealed (anzalnā) | of (mina) | the clear proofs (l-bayināti), | and the Guidance (wal-hudā), | from (min) | after (baʿdi) | [what] (mā) | We made clear (bayyannāhu) | to the people (lilnnāsi) | in (fī) | the Book (l-kitābi)- | those (ulāika), | curses them (yalʿanuhumu) | Allah (l-lahu) | and curse them (wayalʿanuhumu) | the ones who curse (l-lāʿinūna).

2:160 Except those who repent[ed] and reform[ed] and openly declar[ed]. Then those, I will accept repentance from them, and I am the Acceptor of Repentance, the Most Merciful.

Except (illā) | those (alladhīna) | who repent[ed] (tābū) | and reform[ed] (wa-aṣlaḥū) | and openly declar[ed] (wabayyanū). | Then those (fa-ulāika), | I will accept repentance (atūbu) | from them (ʿalayhim), | and I am (wa-anā) | the Acceptor of Repentance (l-tawābu), | the Most Merciful (l-raḥīmu).

2:161 Indeed, those who disbelieve[d] and die[d] while they were disbelievers, those, on them is the curse of Allah, and the Angels, and the mankind, all together.

Indeed (inna), | those who (alladhīna) | disbelieve[d] (kafarū) | and die[d] (wamātū) | while they (wahum) | were disbelievers (kuffārun), | those (ulāika), | on them (ʿalayhim) | is the curse (laʿnatu) | of Allah (l-lahi), | and the Angels (wal-malāikati), | and the mankind (wal-nāsi), | all together (ajmaʿīna).

2:162 Will abide forever in it. Not will be lightened for them the punishment and not they will be reprieved.

Will abide forever (khālidīna) | in it (fīhā). | Not (lā) | will be lightened (yukhaffafu) | for them (ʿanhumu) | the punishment (l-ʿadhābu) | and not (walā) | they (hum) | will be reprieved (yunẓarūna).

2:163 And your God is God one only; there is no god except Him, the Most Gracious, the Most Merciful.

And your God (wa-ilāhukum) | is God (ilāhun) | one only (wāḥidun); | there is no (lā) | god (ilāha) | except (illā) | Him (huwa), | the Most Gracious (l-raḥmānu), | the Most Merciful (l-raḥīmu).

2:164 Indeed, in the creation of the heavens and the earth, and alternation of the night and the day, and the ships which sail in the sea with what benefits [the] people, and what has sent down Allah from the sky [of] water, giving life thereby to the earth after its death, and dispersing therein [of] every moving creature, and directing of the winds and the clouds [the] controlled between the sky and the earth, surely are Signs for a people who use their intellect.

Indeed (inna), | in (fī) | the creation (khalqi) | of the heavens (l-samāwāti) | and the earth (wal-arḍi), | and alternation (wa-ikh'tilāfi) | of the night (al-layli) | and the day (wal-nahāri), | and the ships (wal-ful'ki) | which (allatī) | sail (tajrī) | in (fī) | the sea (l-baḥri) | with what (bimā) | benefits (yanfaʿu) | [the] people (l-nāsa), | and what (wamā) | has sent down (anzala) | Allah (l-lahu)

| from (mina) | the sky (l-samāi) | [of] (min) | water (māin), | giving life (fa-aḥyā) | thereby (bihi) | to the earth (l-arḍa) | after (baʿda) | its death (mawtihā), | and dispersing (wabatha) | therein (fīhā) | [of] (min) | every (kulli) | moving creature (dābbatin), | and directing (wataṣrīfi) | of the winds (l-riyāḥi) | and the clouds (wal-saḥābi) | [the] controlled (l-musakhari) | between (bayna) | the sky (l-samāi) | and the earth (wal-arḍi), | surely are Signs (laāyātin) | for a people (liqawmin) | who use their intellect (yaʿqilūna).

2:165 And among the mankind who takes from besides Allah equals. They love them as they should love Allah. And those who believe[d] are stronger in love for Allah. And if would see those who wronged, when they will see the punishment that the power belongs to Allah all and [that] Allah is severe in [the] punishment.

And among (wamina) | the mankind (l-nāsi) | who (man) | takes (yattakhidhu) | from (min) | besides (dūni) | Allah (l-lahi) | equals (andādan). | They love them (yuḥibbūnahum) | as they should love (kaḥubbi) | Allah (l-lahi). | And those who (wa-alladhīna) | believe[d] (āmanū) | are stronger (ashaddu) | in love (ḥubban) | for Allah (lillahi). | And if (walaw) | would see (yarā) | those who (alladhīna) | wronged (ẓalamū), | when (idh) | they will see (yarawna) | the punishment (l-ʿadhāba) | that (anna) | the power (l-quwata) | belongs to Allah (lillahi) | all (jamīʿan) | and [that] (wa-anna) | Allah (l-laha) | is severe (shadīdu) | in [the] punishment (l-ʿadhābi).

2:166 When will disown those who were followed [from] those who followed and they will see the punishment, [and] will be cut off for them the relations.

When (idh) | will disown (tabarra-a) | those who (alladhīna) | were followed (ittubiʿū) | [from] (mina) | those who (alladhīna) | followed (ittabaʿū) | and they will see (wara-awū) | the punishment (l-ʿadhāba), | [and] will be cut off (wataqaṭṭaʿat) | for them (bihimu) | the relations (l-asbābu).

2:167 And said those who followed, "Only if [that] for us a return, then we will disown [from] them as they disown [from] us." Thus will show them Allah their deeds as regrets for them. And not they will come out from the Fire.

And said (waqāla) | those who (alladhīna) | followed (ittabaʿū), | "Only if (law) | [that] (anna) | for us (lanā) | a return (karratan), | then we will disown (fanatabarra-a) | [from] them (min'hum) | as (kamā) | they disown (tabarraū) | [from] us. (minnā)" | Thus (kadhālika) | will show them (yurīhimu) | Allah (l-lahu) | their deeds (aʿmālahum) | as regrets (ḥasarātin) | for them (ʿalayhim). | And not (wamā) | they (hum) | will come out (bikhārijīna) | from (mina) | the Fire (l-nāri).

2:168 O mankind! Eat of what is in the earth lawful and good. And do not follow the footsteps (of) the Shaitaan. Indeed, he is to you an enemy clear.

O (yāayyuhā) | mankind (l-nāsu)! | Eat (kulū) | of what (mimmā) | is in (fī) | the earth (l-arḍi) | lawful (ḥalālan) | and good (ṭayyiban). | And do not (walā) | follow (tattabiʿū) | the footsteps (of (khuṭuwāti)) | the Shaitaan (l-shayṭāni). | Indeed, he (innahu) | is to you (lakum) | an enemy (ʿaduwwun) | clear (mubīnun).

2:169 Only he commands you to do the evil and the shameful and that you say about Allah what not you know.

Only (innamā) | he commands you (yamurukum) | to do the evil (bil-sūi) | and the shameful (wal-faḥshāi) | and that (wa-an) | you say (taqūlū) | about (ʿalā) | Allah (l-lahi) | what (mā) | not (lā) | you know (taʿlamūna).

2:170 And when it is said to them, "Follow what has revealed Allah," they said, "Nay we follow what we found [on it] our forefathers following". Even though [were] their forefathers did not understand anything and not were they guided?

And when (wa-idhā) | it is said (qīla) | to them (lahumu), | "Follow (ittabiʿū) | what (mā) | has revealed (anzala) | Allah, (l-lahu)" | they said (qālū), | "Nay (bal) | we follow (nattabiʿu) | what (mā) | we found (alfaynā) | [on it] (ʿalayhi) | our forefathers following" (ābāanā). | Even though (awalaw) | [were] (kāna) | their forefathers (ābāuhum) | did not (lā) | understand (yaʿqilūna) | anything (shayan) | and not (walā) | were they guided (yahtadūna)?

2:171 And the example of those who disbelieve[d] is like (the) example of the one who shouts at what not does hear except calls and cries - deaf dumb, and blind, [so] they do not understand.

And the example (wamathalu) | of those who (alladhīna) | disbelieve[d] (kafarū) | is like (the) example (kamathali) | of the one who (alladhī) | shouts (yanʿiqu) | at what (bimā) | not (lā) | does hear (yasmaʿu) | except (illā) | calls (duʿāan) | and cries (wanidāan)- | deaf (ṣummun) | dumb (buk'mun), | and blind (ʿum'yun), | [so] they (fahum) | do not (lā) | understand (yaʿqilūna).

2:172 O you who believe[d]! Eat from the good of what We have provided you and be grateful to Allah if you alone worship Him.

O you (yāayyuhā) | who (alladhīna) | believe[d] (āmanū)! | Eat (kulū) | from (min) | the good (ṭayyibāti) | of what (mā) | We have provided you (razaqnākum) | and be grateful (wa-ush'kurū) | to Allah (lillahi) | if (in) | you (kuntum) | alone (iyyāhu) | worship Him (taʿbudūna).

2:173 Only He has forbidden to you the dead animals, and [the] blood, and flesh, of swine, and what has been dedicated [with it] to other than Allah. So whoever is forced by necessity without being disobedient and not transgressor, then no sin on him. Indeed, Allah is Oft-Forgiving, Most Merciful.

Only (innamā) | He has forbidden (ḥarrama) | to you (ʿalaykumu) | the dead animals (l-maytata), | and [the] blood (wal-dama), | and flesh (walaḥma), | of swine (l-khinzīri), | and what (wamā) | has been dedicated (uhilla) | [with it] (bihi) | to other than (lighayri) | Allah (l-lahi). | So whoever (famani) | is forced by necessity (uḍ'ṭurra) | without (ghayra) | being disobedient (bāghin) | and not (walā) | transgressor (ʿādin), | then no (falā) | sin (ith'ma) | on him (ʿalayhi). | Indeed (inna), | Allah (l-laha) | is Oft-Forgiving (ghafūrun), | Most Merciful (raḥīmun).

2:174 Indeed, those who conceal what has revealed Allah has of the Book, and they purchase there with a gain little. Those, not they eat in their bellies except the Fire. And not will speak to them Allah on the Day of [the] Judgment and not will He purify them, and for them is a punishment painful.

Indeed (inna), | those who (alladhīna) | conceal (yaktumūna) | what (mā) | has revealed (anzala) | Allah has (l-lahu) | of (mina) | the Book (l-kitābi), | and they purchase (wayashtarūna) | there with (bihi) | a gain (thamanan) | little (qalīlan). | Those (ulāika), | not (mā) | they eat (yakulūna) | in (fī) | their bellies (buṭūnihim) | except (illā) | the Fire (l-nāra). | And not (walā) | will speak to them (yukallimuhumu) | Allah (l-lahu) | on the Day (yawma) | of [the] Judgment (l-qiyāmati) | and not (walā) | will He purify them (yuzakkīhim), | and for them (walahum) | is a punishment (ʿadhābun) | painful (alīmun).

2:175 Those are they who purchase[d] [the] astraying for [the] Guidance, and [the] punishment for [the] forgiveness. So what is their endurance on the Fire!

Those (ulāika) | are they who (alladhīna) | purchase[d] (ish'tarawū) | [the] astraying (l-ḍalālata) | for [the] Guidance (bil-hudā), | and [the] punishment (wal-ʿadhāba) | for [the] forgiveness (bil-maghfirati). | So what is (famā) | their endurance (aṣbarahum) | on (ʿalā) | the Fire (l-nāri)!

2:176 That is because Allah revealed the Book with [the] Truth. And indeed, those who differed in the Book are surely in schism far.

That (dhālika) | is because (bi-anna) | Allah (l-laha) | revealed (nazzala) | the Book (l-kitāba) | with [the] Truth (bil-ḥaqi). | And indeed (wa-inna), | those (alladhīna) | who differed (ikh'talafū) |

in (fī) | the Book (l-kitābi) | are surely in (lafī) | schism (shiqāqin) | far (baʿīdin).

2:177 It is not [the] righteousness that you turn your faces towards the east and the west, [and] but the righteous[ness] is he who believes in Allah and the Day [the] Last, and the Angels, and the Book, and the Prophets, and gives the wealth in spite of his love for it to those of the near relatives, and the orphans, and the needy, and of the wayfarer, and those who ask, and in freeing the necks slaves and who establish the prayer, and give the zakah, and those who fulfill their covenant when they make it; and those who are patient in [the] suffering and [the] hardship, and the time of [the] stress. Those are the ones who are true and those, [they] are the righteous.

It is not (laysa) | [the] righteousness (l-bira) | that (an) | you turn (tuwallū) | your faces (wujūhakum) | towards (qibala) | the east (l-mashriqi) | and the west (wal-maghribi), | [and] but (walākinna) | the righteous[ness] (l-bira) | is he who (man) | believes (āmana) | in Allah (bil-lahi) | and the Day (wal-yawmi) | [the] Last (l-ākhiri), | and the Angels (wal-malāikati), | and the Book (wal-kitābi), | and the Prophets (wal-nabiyīna), | and gives (waātā) | the wealth (l-māla) | in (ʿalā) | spite of his love for it (ḥubbihi) | to those (dhawī) | of the near relatives (l-qur'bā), | and the orphans (wal-yatāmā), | and the needy (wal-masākīna), | and of (wa-ib'na) | the wayfarer (l-sabīli), | and those who ask (wal-sāilīna), | and in (wafī) | freeing the necks slaves (l-riqābi) | and who establish (wa-aqāma) | the prayer (l-ṣalata), | and give (waātā) | the zakah (l-zakata), | and those who fulfill (wal-mūfūna) | their covenant (biʿahdihim) | when (idhā) | they make it (ʿāhadū); | and those who are patient (wal-ṣābirīna) | in (fī) | [the] suffering (l-basāi) | and [the] hardship (wal-ḍarāi), | and the time (waḥīna) | of [the] stress (l-basi). | Those (ulāika) | are the ones who (alladhīna) | are true (ṣadaqū) | and those (wa-ulāika), | [they] (humu) | are the righteous (l-mutaqūna).

2:178 O you who believe[d]! Prescribed for you is the legal retribution in the matter of the murdered, the freeman for the freeman, and the slave for the slave, and the female for the female. But whoever is pardoned [for it] from his brother anything, then follows up with suitable [and] payment to him with kindness. That is a concession from your Lord and mercy. Then whoever transgresses after that, then for him is a punishment painful.

O you (yāayyuhā) | who (alladhīna) | believe[d] (āmanū)! | Prescribed (kutiba) | for you (ʿalaykumu) | is the legal retribution (l-qiṣāṣu) | in (fī) | the matter of the murdered (l-qatlā), | the freeman (l-ḥuru) | for the freeman (bil-ḥuri), | and the slave (wal-ʿabdu) | for the slave (bil-ʿabdi), | and the female (wal-unthā) | for the female (bil-unthā). | But whoever (faman) | is pardoned (ʿufiya) | [for it] (lahu) | from (min) | his brother (akhīhi) | anything (shayon), | then follows up (fa-ittibāʿun) | with suitable (bil-maʿrūfi) | [and] payment (wa-adāon) | to him (ilayhi) | with kindness (bi-iḥ'sānin). | That is (dhālika) | a concession (takhfīfun) | from (min) | your Lord (rabbikum) | and mercy (waraḥmatun). | Then whoever (famani) | transgresses (iʿ'tadā) | after (baʿda) | that (dhālika), | then for him (falahu) | is a punishment (ʿadhābun) | painful (alīmun).

2:179 And for you in the legal retribution is life, O men of understanding! So that you may become righteous.

And for you (walakum) | in (fī) | the legal retribution (l-qiṣāṣi) | is life (ḥayatun), | O men (yāulī) | of understanding (l-albābi)! | So that you may (laʿallakum) | become righteous (tattaqūna).

2:180 Prescribed for you when approaches any of you [the] death, if he leaves good making the will for the parents and the near relatives with due fairness a duty on the righteous ones.

Prescribed (kutiba) | for you (ʿalaykum) | when (idhā) | approaches (ḥaḍara) | any of you (aḥadakumu) | [the] death (l-mawtu), | if (in) | he leaves (taraka) | good (khayran) | making the will (l-waṣiyatu) | for the parents (lil'wālidayni) | and the near relatives (wal-aqrabīna) | with due fairness (bil-maʿrūfi) | a duty (ḥaqqan) | on (ʿalā) | the righteous ones (l-mutaqīna).

2:181 Then whoever changes it after what he has heard [it], so only its sin would be on those who alter it. Indeed, Allah is All-Hearing, All-Knowing.

Then whoever (faman) | changes it (baddalahu) | after what (baʿdamā) | he has heard [it] (samiʿahu), | so only (fa-innamā) | its sin (ith'muhu) | would be on (ʿalā) | those who (alladhīna) | alter it (yubaddilūnahu). | Indeed (inna), | Allah (l-laha) | is All-Hearing (samīʿun), | All-Knowing (ʿalīmun).

2:182 But whoever fears from the testator any error or sin, then reconciles between them, then there is no sin on him. Indeed, Allah is Oft-Forgiving, All-Merciful.

But whoever (faman) | fears (khāfa) | from (min) | the testator (mūṣin) | any error (janafan) | or (aw) | sin (ith'man), | then reconciles (fa-aṣlaḥa) | between them (baynahum), | then there is no (falā) | sin (ith'ma) | on him (ʿalayhi). | Indeed (inna), | Allah (l-laha) | is Oft-Forgiving (ghafūrun), | All-Merciful (raḥīmun).

2:183 O you who believe[d]! Is prescribed for you [the] fasting as was prescribed to those from before you, so that you may become righteous.

O you (yāayyuhā) | who (alladhīna) | believe[d] (āmanū)! | Is prescribed (kutiba) | for you (ʿalaykumu) | [the] fasting (l-ṣiyāmu) | as (kamā) | was prescribed (kutiba) | to (ʿalā) | those (alladhīna) | from (min) | before you (qablikum), | so that you may (laʿallakum) | become righteous (tattaqūna).

2:184 Fasting for days numbered. So whoever is among you sick or on a journey, then a prescribed number of days other. And on those who can afford it, a ransom of feeding a poor. And whoever volunteers good then it is better for him. And to fast is better for you, if you know.

Fasting for days (ayyāman) | numbered (maʿdūdātin). | So whoever (faman) | is (kāna) | among you (minkum) | sick (marīḍan) | or (aw) | on (ʿalā) | a journey (safarin), | then a prescribed number (faʿiddatun) | of (min) | days (ayyāmin) | other (ukhara). | And on (waʿalā) | those who (alladhīna) | can afford it (yuṭīqūnahu), | a ransom (fid'yatun) | of feeding (ṭaʿāmu) | a poor (mis'kīnin). | And whoever (faman) | volunteers (taṭawwaʿa) | good (khayran) | then it (fahuwa) | is better (khayrun) | for him (lahu). | And to (wa-an) | fast (taṣūmū) | is better (khayrun) | for you (lakum), | if (in) | you (kuntum) | know (taʿlamūna).

2:185 Month of Ramadhaan is that was revealed therein the Quran, a Guidance for mankind and clear proofs of [the] Guidance and the Criterion. So whoever witnesses among you the month, then he should fast in it, and whoever is sick or on a journey then prescribed number should be made up from days other. Intends Allah for you [the] ease and not intends for you [the] hardship, so that you complete the prescribed period and that you magnify Allah for [what] He guided you so that you may be grateful.

Month (shahru) | of Ramadhaan (ramaḍāna) | is that (alladhī) | was revealed (unzila) | therein (fīhi) | the Quran (l-qur'ānu), | a Guidance (hudan) | for mankind (lilnnāsi) | and clear proofs (wabayyinātin) | of (mina) | [the] Guidance (l-hudā) | and the Criterion (wal-fur'qāni). | So whoever (faman) | witnesses (shahida) | among you (minkumu) | the month (l-shahra), | then he should fast in it (falyaṣum'hu), | and whoever (waman) | is (kāna) | sick (marīḍan) | or (aw) | on (ʿalā) | a journey (safarin) | then prescribed number should be made up (faʿiddatun) | from (min) | days (ayyāmin) | other (ukhara). | Intends (yurīdu) | Allah (l-lahu) | for you (bikumu) | [the] ease (l-yus'ra) | and not (walā) | intends (yurīdu) | for you (bikumu) | [the] hardship (l-ʿus'ra), | so that you complete (walituk'milū) | the prescribed period (l-ʿidata) | and that you magnify (walitukabbirū) | Allah (l-laha) | for (ʿalā) | [what] (mā) | He guided you (hadākum) | so that you may (walaʿallakum) | be grateful (tashkurūna).

2:186 And when ask you My servants about Me, then indeed I am near. I respond to the invocation of the supplicant when he calls Me. So let them respond to Me and let them believe in Me, so that they may be led aright.

And when (wa-idhā) | ask you (sa-alaka) | My servants (ʿibādī) | about Me (ʿannī), | then indeed I am (fa-innī) | near (qarībun). | I respond (ujību) | to the invocation (daʿwata) | of the supplicant (l-dāʿi) | when (idhā) | he calls Me (daʿāni). | So let them respond (falyastajībū) | to Me (lī) | and let them believe (walyu'minū) | in Me (bī), | so that they may (laʿallahum) | be led aright (yarshudūna).

2:187 Permitted for you in the nights of fasting is the approach to your wives. They are garments for you and you are garments for them. Knows Allah that you used to deceive yourselves, so He turned towards you and He forgave [on] you. So now have relations with them and seek what has ordained Allah for you. And eat and drink until becomes distinct to you the thread [the] white from the thread [the] black of [the] dawn. Then complete the fast till the night. And do not have relations with them while you are secluded in the masajid. These are the limits set by Allah, so do not approach them. Thus makes clear Allah His verses for [the] people so that they may become righteous.

Permitted (uḥilla) | for you (lakum) | in the nights (laylata) | of fasting (l-ṣiyāmi) | is the approach (l-rafathu) | to (ilā) | your wives (nisāikum). | They (hunna) | are garments (libāsun) | for you (lakum) | and you (wa-antum) | are garments (libāsun) | for them (lahunna). | Knows (ʿalima) | Allah (l-lahu) | that you (annakum) | used to (kuntum) | deceive (takhtānūna) | yourselves (anfusakum), | so He turned (fatāba) | towards you (ʿalaykum) | and He forgave (waʿafā) | [on] you (ʿankum). | So now (fal-āna) | have relations with them (bāshirūhunna) | and seek (wa-ib'taghū) | what (mā) | has ordained (kataba) | Allah (l-lahu) | for you (lakum). | And eat (wakulū) | and drink (wa-ish'rabū) | until (ḥattā) | becomes distinct (yatabayyana) | to you (lakumu) | the thread (l-khayṭu) | [the] white (l-abyaḍu) | from (mina) | the thread (l-khayṭi) | [the] black (l-aswadi) | of (mina) | [the] dawn (l-fajri). | Then (thumma) | complete (atimmū) | the fast (l-ṣiyāma) | till (ilā) | the night (al-layli). | And do not (walā) | have relations with them (tubāshirūhunna) | while you (wa-antum) | are secluded (ʿākifūna) | in (fī) | the masajid (l-masājidi). | These (til'ka) | are the limits (ḥudūdu) | set by Allah (l-lahi), | so do not (falā) | approach them (taqrabūhā). | Thus (kadhālika) | makes clear (yubayyinu) | Allah (l-lahu) | His verses (āyātihi) | for [the] people (lilnnāsi) | so that they may (laʿallahum) | become righteous (yattaqūna).

2:188 And do not eat your properties among yourselves wrongfully and present [with] it to the authorities so that you may eat a portion from the wealth of the people sinfully while you know.

And do not (walā) | eat (takulū) | your properties (amwālakum) | among yourselves (baynakum) | wrongfully (bil-bāṭili) | and present (watud'lū) | [with] it (bihā) | to (ilā) | the authorities (l-ḥukāmi) | so that you may eat (litakulū) | a portion (farīqan) | from (min) | the wealth (amwāli) | of the people (l-nāsi) | sinfully (bil-ith'mi) | while you (wa-antum) | know (taʿlamūna).

2:189 They ask you about the new moons. Say, "They are indicators of periods for the people, and for the Hajj." And it is not [the] righteousness that you come to the houses from their backs, [and] but [the] righteous is one who fears Allah. And come to the houses from their doors. And fear Allah so that you may be successful.

They ask you (yasalūnaka) | about (ʿani) | the new moons (l-ahilati). | Say (qul), | "They (hiya) | are indicators of periods (mawāqītu) | for the people (lilnnāsi), | and for the Hajj. (wal-ḥaji)" | And it is not (walaysa) | [the] righteousness (l-biru) | that (bi-an) | you come (tatū) | to the houses (l-buyūta) | from (min) | their backs (ẓuhūrihā), | [and] but (walākinna) | [the] righteous (l-bira) | is one who (mani) | fears Allah (ittaqā). | And come (watū) | to the houses (l-buyūta) | from (min) | their doors (abwābihā). | And fear (wa-ittaqū) | Allah (l-laha) | so that you may (laʿallakum) | be successful (tuf'liḥūna).

2:190 And fight in the way of Allah those who fight you and do not transgress. Indeed, Allah does not like the transgressors.

And fight (waqātilū) | in (fī) | the way (sabīli) | of Allah (l-lahi) | those who (alladhīna) |

fight you (yuqātilūnakum) | and do not (walā) | transgress (taʿtadū). | Indeed (inna), | Allah (l-laha) | does not (lā) | like (yuḥibbu) | the transgressors (l-muʿʿtadīna).

2:191 And kill them wherever you find them, and drive them out from wherever they drove you out, and [the] oppression is worse than [the] killing. And do not fight them near Al-Masjid Al-Haraam until they fight you in it. Then if they fight you, then kill them. Such is the reward of the disbelievers.

And kill them (wa-uq'tulūhum) | wherever (ḥaythu) | you find them (thaqif'tumūhum), | and drive them out (wa-akhrijūhum) | from (min) | wherever (ḥaythu) | they drove you out (akhrajūkum), | and [the] oppression (wal-fit'natu) | is worse (ashaddu) | than (mina) | [the] killing (l-qatli). | And do not (walā) | fight them (tuqātilūhum) | near (ʿinda) | Al-Masjid (l-masjidi) | Al-Haraam (l-ḥarāmi) | until (ḥattā) | they fight you (yuqātilūkum) | in it (fīhi). | Then if (fa-in) | they fight you (qātalūkum), | then kill them (fa-uq'tulūhum). | Such (kadhālika) | is the reward (jazāu) | of the disbelievers (l-kāfirīna).

2:192 Then if they cease, then indeed, Allah is Oft-Forgiving, Most Merciful.

Then if (fa-ini) | they cease (intahaw), | then indeed (fa-inna), | Allah (l-laha) | is Oft-Forgiving (ghafūrun), | Most Merciful (raḥīmun).

2:193 And fight against them until not there is oppression, and becomes the religion for Allah Then if they cease then let there be no hostility except against the oppressors.

And fight against them (waqātilūhum) | until (ḥattā) | not (lā) | there is (takūna) | oppression (fit'natun), | and becomes (wayakūna) | the religion (l-dīnu) | for Allah (lillahi) | Then if (fa-ini) | they cease (intahaw) | then let there be no (falā) | hostility (ʿud'wāna) | except (illā) | against (ʿalā) | the oppressors (l-ẓālimīna).

2:194 The month [the] sacred is for the month [the] sacred, and for all the violations is legal retribution. Then whoever transgressed upon you then you transgress on him in the same manner as he transgressed upon you. And fear Allah and know that Allah is with those who fear Him.

The month (al-shahru) | [the] sacred (l-ḥarāmu) | is for the month (bil-shahri) | [the] sacred (l-ḥarāmi), | and for all the violations (wal-ḥurumātu) | is legal retribution (qiṣāṣun). | Then whoever (famani) | transgressed (iʿʿtadā) | upon you (ʿalaykum) | then you transgress (fa-iʿʿtadū) | on him (ʿalayhi) | in the same manner (bimith'li) | as (mā) | he transgressed (iʿʿtadā) | upon you (ʿalaykum). | And fear (wa-ittaqū) | Allah (l-laha) | and know (wa-iʿʿlamū) | that (anna) | Allah (l-laha) | is with (maʿa) | those who fear Him (l-mutaqīna).

2:195 And spend in the way of Allah and do not throw yourselves [with your hands] into [the] destruction. And do good; indeed, Allah loves the good-doers.

And spend (wa-anfiqū) | in (fī) | the way (sabīli) | of Allah (l-lahi) | and do not (walā) | throw yourselves (tul'qū) | [with your hands] (bi-aydīkum) | into (ilā) | [the] destruction (l-tahlukati). | And do good (wa-aḥsinū); | indeed (inna), | Allah (l-laha) | loves (yuḥibbu) | the good-doers (l-muḥ'sinīna).

2:196 And complete the Hajj and the Umrah for Allah. And if you are held back then offer whatever can be obtained with ease of the sacrificial animal. And do not shave your heads until reaches the sacrificial animal to its destination. Then whoever is among you ill or he has an ailment of his head then a ransom of fasting or charity or sacrifice. Then when you are secure then whoever took advantage of the Umrah followed by the Hajj, then offer whatever can be obtained with ease of the sacrificial animal. But whoever can not find - then a fast of three days during the Hajj and seven days when you return. This is ten (days) in all. That is for (the one) whose, not is his family present near Al-Masjid Al-Haraam. And fear Allah and know that Allah is severe in retribution.

And complete (wa-atimmū) | the Hajj (l-ḥaja) | and the Umrah (wal-ʿum'rata) | for Allah (lillahi). | And if (fa-in) | you are held back (uḥ'ṣir'tum) | then offer whatever (famā) | can be obtained with ease (is'taysara) | of (mina) | the sacrificial animal (l-hadyi). | And do not (walā) | shave (taḥliqū) | your heads (ruūsakum) | until (ḥattā) | reaches (yablugha) | the sacrificial animal (l-hadyu) | to its destination (maḥillahu). | Then whoever (faman) | is (kāna) | among you (minkum) | ill (marīḍan) | or (aw) | he has (bihi) | an ailment (adhan) | of (min) | his head (rasihi) | then a ransom (fafid'yatun) | of (min) | fasting (ṣiyāmin) | or (aw) | charity (ṣadaqatin) | or (aw) | sacrifice (nusukin). | Then when (fa-idhā) | you are secure (amintum) | then whoever (faman) | took advantage (tamatta'a) | of the Umrah (bil-'um'rati) | followed (ilā) | by the Hajj (l-ḥaji), | then offer whatever (famā) | can be obtained with ease (is'taysara) | of (mina) | the sacrificial animal (l-hadyi). | But whoever (faman) | can not (lam) | find (yajid)- | then a fast (faṣiyāmu) | of three (thalāthati) | days (ayyāmin) | during (fī) | the Hajj (l-ḥaji) | and seven days (wasab'atin) | when (idhā) | you return (raja'tum). | This (til'ka) | is ten (days ('asharatun)) | in all (kāmilatun). | That (dhālika) | is for (the one) whose (liman), | not (lam) | is (yakun) | his family (ahluhu) | present (ḥāḍirī) | near Al-Masjid (l-masjidi) | Al-Haraam (l-ḥarāmi). | And fear (wa-ittaqū) | Allah (l-laha) | and know (wa-i''lamū) | that (anna) | Allah (l-laha) | is severe (shadīdu) | in retribution (l-'iqābi).

2:197 For the Hajj are months well known, then whoever undertakes therein the Hajj then no sexual relations and no wickedness and no quarrelling during the Hajj. And whatever you do of good knows it Allah. And take provision, but indeed, the best provision is righteousness. And fear Me, O men of understanding!

For the Hajj (al-ḥaju) | are months (ashhurun) | well known (ma'lūmātun), | then whoever (faman) | undertakes (faraḍa) | therein (fīhinna) | the Hajj (l-ḥaja) | then no (falā) | sexual relations (rafatha) | and no (walā) | wickedness (fusūqa) | and no (walā) | quarrelling (jidāla) | during (fī) | the Hajj (l-ḥaji). | And whatever (wamā) | you do (taf'alū) | of (min) | good (khayrin) | knows it (ya'lamhu) | Allah (l-lahu). | And take provision (watazawwadū), | but indeed (fa-inna), | the best (khayra) | provision (l-zādi) | is righteousness (l-taqwā). | And fear Me (wa-ittaqūni), | O men (yāulī) | of understanding (l-albābi)!

2:198 Not is on you any sin that you seek bounty from your Lord. And when you depart from Mount Arafat then remember Allah near the Monument [the] Sacred. And remember Him as He has guided you, [and] though you were [from] before [it], surely among those who went astray.

Not is (laysa) | on you ('alaykum) | any sin (junāḥun) | that (an) | you seek (tabtaghū) | bounty (faḍlan) | from (min) | your Lord (rabbikum). | And when (fa-idhā) | you depart (afaḍtum) | from (min) | Mount Arafat ('arafātin) | then remember (fa-udh'kurū) | Allah (l-laha) | near ('inda) | the Monument (l-mash'ari) | [the] Sacred (l-ḥarāmi). | And remember Him (wa-udh'kurūhu) | as (kamā) | He has guided you (hadākum), | [and] though (wa-in) | you were (kuntum) | [from] (min) | before [it] (qablihi), | surely among (lamina) | those who went astray (l-ḍālīna).

2:199 Then depart from wherever depart the people and ask forgiveness of Allah. Indeed, Allah is Oft-Forgiving, Most Merciful.

Then (thumma) | depart (afīḍū) | from (min) | wherever (ḥaythu) | depart (afāḍa) | the people (l-nāsu) | and ask forgiveness (wa-is'taghfirū) | of Allah (l-laha). | Indeed (inna), | Allah (l-laha) | is Oft-Forgiving (ghafūrun), | Most Merciful (raḥīmun).

2:200 Then when you complete[d] your acts of worship then remember Allah as you remember your forefathers or with greater remembrance. And from the people who say, "Our Lord! Grant us in the world." And not for him in the Hereafter [of] any share.

Then when (fa-idhā) | you complete[d] (qaḍaytum) | your acts of worship (manāsikakum) | then remember (fa-udh'kurū) | Allah (l-laha) | as you remember (kadhik'rikum) | your forefathers (ābāakum) | or (aw) | with greater (ashadda) | remembrance (dhik'ran). | And from (famina) | the people (l-nāsi) | who (man) | say (yaqūlu), | "Our Lord (rabbanā)! | Grant us (ātinā) | in (fī) | the world. (l-dun'yā)" | And not (wamā) | for him (lahu) | in (fī) | the Hereafter (l-ākhirati) | [of] (min) | any share (khalāqin).

2:201 And from those who say, "Our Lord! Grant us in the world good and in the Hereafter good, and save us from the punishment of the Fire."

And from those (wamin'hum) | who (man) | say (yaqūlu), | "Our Lord (rabbanā)! | Grant us (ātinā) | in (fī) | the world (l-dun'yā) | good (ḥasanatan) | and in (wafī) | the Hereafter (l-ākhirati) | good (ḥasanatan), | and save us (waqinā) | from the punishment (ʿadhāba) | of the Fire. (l-nāri)"

2:202 Those - for them is a share of what they earned, and Allah is swift in taking account.

Those (ulāika)- | for them (lahum) | is a share (naṣībun) | of what (mimmā) | they earned (kasabū), | and Allah (wal-lahu) | is swift (sarīʿu) | in taking account (l-ḥisābi).

2:203 And remember Allah during days numbered. Then he who hurries in two days then no sin upon him, and whoever delays then no sin upon him for the one who fears. And fear Allah and know that you unto Him will be gathered.

And remember (wa-udh'kurū) | Allah (l-laha) | during (fī) | days (ayyāmin) | numbered (maʿdūdātin). | Then he who (faman) | hurries (taʿajjala) | in (fī) | two days (yawmayni) | then no (falā) | sin (ith'ma) | upon him (ʿalayhi), | and whoever (waman) | delays (ta-akhara) | then no (falā) | sin (ith'ma) | upon him (ʿalayhi) | for the one who (limani) | fears (ittaqā). | And fear (wa-ittaqū) | Allah (l-laha) | and know (wa-iʿ'lamū) | that you (annakum) | unto Him (ilayhi) | will be gathered (tuḥ'sharūna).

2:204 And of the people is the one who pleases you with his speech in the life of the world, and he calls to witness Allah on what is in his heart, and he is the most quarrelsome of opponents.

And of (wamina) | the people (l-nāsi) | is the one who (man) | pleases you (yuʿ'jibuka) | with his speech (qawluhu) | in (fī) | the life (l-ḥayati) | of the world (l-dun'yā), | and he calls to witness (wayush'hidu) | Allah (l-laha) | on (ʿalā) | what (mā) | is in (fī) | his heart (qalbihi), | and he (wahuwa) | is the most quarrelsome (aladdu) | of opponents (l-khiṣāmi).

2:205 And when he turns away he strives in the earth to spread corruption [in it], and destroys the crops and progeny. And Allah does not love [the] corruption.

And when (wa-idhā) | he turns away (tawallā) | he strives (saʿā) | in (fī) | the earth (l-arḍi) | to spread corruption (liyuf'sida) | [in it] (fīhā), | and destroys (wayuh'lika) | the crops (l-ḥartha) | and progeny (wal-nasla). | And Allah (wal-lahu) | does not (lā) | love (yuḥibbu) | [the] corruption (l-fasāda).

2:206 And when it is said to him "Fear Allah," takes him his pride to [the] sins. Then enough for him is Hell - [and] surely an evil [the] resting-place.

And when (wa-idhā) | it is said (qīla) | to him (lahu) | "Fear (ittaqi) | Allah, (l-laha)" | takes him (akhadhathu) | his pride (l-ʿizatu) | to [the] sins (bil-ith'mi). | Then enough for him (faḥasbuhu) | is Hell (jahannamu)- | [and] surely an evil (walabi'sa) | [the] resting-place (l-mihādu).

2:207 And of the people is the one who sells his own self seeking pleasure of Allah. And Allah is full of Kindness to His servants.

And of (wamina) | the people (l-nāsi) | is the one who (man) | sells (yashrī) | his own self (nafsahu) | seeking (ib'tighāa) | pleasure (marḍāti) | of Allah (l-lahi). | And Allah (wal-lahu) | is full of Kindness (raūfun) | to His servants (bil-ʿibādi).

2:208 O you who believe[d]! Enter in Islam completely, and do not follow footsteps of the Shaitaan. Indeed, he is for you an enemy open.

O you (yāayyuhā) | who (alladhīna) | believe[d] (āmanū)! | Enter (ud'khulū) | in (fī) | Islam (l-sil'mi) | completely (kāffatan), | and do not (walā) | follow (tattabiʿū) | footsteps (khuṭuwāti) | of the Shaitaan (l-shayṭāni). | Indeed, he (innahu) | is for you (lakum) | an enemy (ʿaduwwun) | open (mubīnun).

2:209 Then if you slip from after [what] came to you from the clear proofs, then know that Allah is All-Mighty, All-Wise.

Then if (fa-in) | you slip (zalaltum) | from (min) | after (baʿdi) | [what] (mā) | came to you (jāatkumu) | from the clear proofs (l-bayinātu), | then know (fa-iʿ'lamū) | that (anna) | Allah (l-laha) | is All-Mighty (ʿazīzun), | All-Wise (ḥakīmun).

2:210 Are they waiting [except] that comes to them Allah in the shadows of [the] clouds, and the Angels, and is decreed the matter? And to Allah return all the matters.

Are (hal) | they waiting (yanẓurūna) | [except] (illā) | that (an) | comes to them (yatiyahumu) | Allah (l-lahu) | in (fī) | the shadows (ẓulalin) | of (mina) | [the] clouds (l-ghamāmi), | and the Angels (wal-malāikatu), | and is decreed (waquḍiya) | the matter (l-amru)? | And to (wa-ilā) | Allah (l-lahi) | return (tur'jaʿu) | all the matters (l-umūru).

2:211 Ask the Children of Israel, how many We gave them of the Sign(s) clear. And whoever changes Favor of Allah from after [what] it has come to him - then indeed, Allah is severe in [the] chastising.

Ask (sal) | the Children (banī) | of Israel (is'rāīla), | how many (kam) | We gave them (ātaynāhum) | of (min) | the Sign(s (āyatin)) | clear (bayyinatin). | And whoever (waman) | changes (yubaddil) | Favor (niʿ'mata) | of Allah (l-lahi) | from (min) | after (baʿdi) | [what] (mā) | it has come to him (jāathu)- | then indeed (fa-inna), | Allah (l-laha) | is severe (shadīdu) | in [the] chastising (l-ʿiqābi).

2:212 Beautified for those who disbelieve[d] is the life of the world, and they ridicule [of] those who believe[d]. And those who fear Allah, they will be above them on the Day of Resurrection. And Allah provides whom He wills without measure.

Beautified (zuyyina) | for those who (lilladhīna) | disbelieve[d] (kafarū) | is the life (l-ḥayatu) | of the world (l-dun'yā), | and they ridicule (wayaskharūna) | [of] (mina) | those who (alladhīna) | believe[d] (āmanū). | And those who (wa-alladhīna) | fear Allah (ittaqaw), | they will be above them (fawqahum) | on the Day (yawma) | of Resurrection (l-qiyāmati). | And Allah (wal-lahu) | provides (yarzuqu) | whom (man) | He wills (yashāu) | without (bighayri) | measure (ḥisābin).

2:213 Was mankind a community single, then raised up Allah [the] Prophets as bearers of glad tidings and as warners, and sent down with them the Book in [the] truth to judge between [the] people in what they differed [in it]. And did not differ[ed] in it except those who were given it from after [what] came to them the clear proofs, out of jealousy among themselves. And guided Allah those who believe[d] regarding what they differed [in it] of the Truth with His permission. And Allah guides whom He wills to a path straight.

Was (kāna) | mankind (l-nāsu) | a community (ummatan) | single (wāḥidatan), | then raised up (fabaʿatha) | Allah (l-lahu) | [the] Prophets (l-nabiyīna) | as bearers of glad tidings (mubashirīna) | and as warners (wamundhirīna), | and sent down (wa-anzala) | with them (maʿahumu) | the Book (l-kitāba) | in [the] truth (bil-ḥaqi) | to judge (liyaḥkuma) | between (bayna) | [the] people (l-nāsi) | in what (fīmā) | they differed (ikh'talafū) | [in it] (fīhi). | And did not (wamā) | differ[ed] (ikh'talafa) | in it (fīhi) | except (illā) | those who (alladhīna) | were given it (ūtūhu) | from (min) | after (baʿdi) | [what] (mā) | came to them (jāathumu) | the clear proofs (l-bayinātu), | out of jealousy (baghyan) | among themselves (baynahum). | And guided (fahadā) | Allah (l-lahu) | those who (alladhīna) | believe[d] (āmanū) | regarding what (limā) | they differed (ikh'talafū) | [in it] (fīhi) | of (mina) | the Truth (l-ḥaqi) | with His permission (bi-idh'nihi). | And Allah (wal-lahu) | guides (yahdī) | whom (man) | He wills (yashāu) | to (ilā) | a path (ṣirāṭin) | straight (mus'taqīmin).

2:214 Or do you think that you will enter Paradise while not has come to you like came to those who passed away from before you? Touched them [the] adversity and [the] hardship, and they were shaken until said the Messenger and those who believed with him, "When [will] the help of Allah (come) Unquestionably, [Indeed] help of Allah is near.

Or (am) | do you think (ḥasib'tum) | that (an) | you will enter (tadkhulū) | Paradise (l-janata) | while not (walammā) | has come to you (yatikum) | like came to (mathalu) | those who (alladhīna) | passed away (khalaw) | from (min) | before you (qablikum)? | Touched them (massathumu) | [the] adversity (l-basāu) | and [the] hardship (wal-ḍarāu), | and they were shaken (wazul'zilū) | until (ḥattā) | said (yaqūla) | the Messenger (l-rasūlu) | and those who (wa-alladhīna) | believed (āmanū) | with him (maʿahu), | "When (matā) | [will] the help (naṣru) | of Allah (come (l-lahi)) | Unquestionably (alā), | [Indeed] (inna) | help (naṣra) | of Allah (l-lahi) | is near (qarībun).

2:215 They ask you what they should spend. Say, "Whatever you spend of good, is for parents, and the relatives, and the orphans, and the needy, and of the wayfarer. And whatever you do of good. So indeed, Allah of it is All-Aware.

They ask you (yasalūnaka) | what (mādhā) | they should spend (yunfiqūna). | Say (qul), | "Whatever (mā) | you spend (anfaqtum) | of (min) | good (khayrin), | is for parents (falil'wālidayni), | and the relatives (wal-aqrabīna), | and the orphans (wal-yatāmā), | and the needy (wal-masākīni), | and of (wa-ib'ni) | the wayfarer (l-sabīli). | And whatever (wamā) | you do (tafʿalū) | of (min) | good (khayrin). | So indeed (fa-inna), | Allah (l-laha) | of it (bihi) | is All-Aware (ʿalīmun).

2:216 Is prescribed upon you [the] fighting while it is hateful to you. But perhaps [that] you dislike a thing and it is good for you; and perhaps [that] you love a thing and it is bad for you. And Allah knows while you do not know.

Is prescribed (kutiba) | upon you (ʿalaykumu) | [the] fighting (l-qitālu) | while it (wahuwa) | is hateful (kur'hun) | to you (lakum). | But perhaps (waʿasā) | [that] (an) | you dislike (takrahū) | a thing (shayan) | and it (wahuwa) | is good (khayrun) | for you (lakum); | and perhaps (waʿasā) | [that] (an) | you love (tuḥibbū) | a thing (shayan) | and it (wahuwa) | is bad (sharrun) | for you (lakum). | And Allah (wal-lahu) | knows (yaʿlamu) | while you (wa-antum) | do not (lā) | know (taʿlamūna).

2:217 They ask you about the month [the] sacred - concerning fighting in it. Say, "Fighting therein is a great (sin); but hindering people from the way of Allah, and disbelief in Him and preventing access to Al-Masjid Al-Haraam, and driving out its people from it, is greater (sin) near Allah. And [the] oppression is greater than [the] killing." And not they will cease to fight with you until they turn you away from your religion, if they are able. And whoever turns away among you from his religion, then dies while he is a disbeliever for those became worthless their deeds in the world and the Hereafter. And those are companions of the Fire, they in it will abide forever.

They ask you (yasalūnaka) | about (ʿani) | the month (l-shahri) | [the] sacred (l-ḥarāmi)- | concerning fighting (qitālin) | in it (fīhi). | Say (qul), | "Fighting (qitālun) | therein (fīhi) | is a great (sin) (kabīrun); | but hindering people (waṣaddun) | from (ʿan) | the way (sabīli) | of Allah (l-lahi), | and disbelief (wakuf'run) | in Him (bihi) | and preventing access to Al-Masjid (wal-masjidi) | Al-Haraam (l-ḥarāmi), | and driving out (wa-ikh'rāju) | its people (ahlihi) | from it (min'hu), | is greater (sin (akbaru)) | near (ʿinda) | Allah (l-lahi). | And [the] oppression (wal-fit'natu) | is greater (akbaru) | than (mina) | [the] killing. (l-qatli)" | And not (walā) | they will cease (yazālūna) | to fight with you (yuqātilūnakum) | until (ḥattā) | they turn you away (yaruddūkum) | from (ʿan) | your religion (dīnikum), | if (ini) | they are able (is'taṭāʿū). | And whoever (waman) | turns away (yartadid) | among you (minkum) | from (ʿan) | his religion (dīnihi), | then dies (fayamut) | while he (wahuwa) | is a disbeliever (kāfirun) | for those (fa-ulāika) | became worthless (ḥabiṭat) | their deeds (aʿmāluhum) | in (fī) | the world (l-dun'yā) | and the Hereafter (wal-ākhirati). | And those (wa-ulāika) | are companions (aṣḥābu) | of the Fire (l-nāri), | they (hum) | in it (fīhā) | will abide forever (khālidūna).

2:218 Indeed, those who believed and those who emigrated and strove in the way of Allah - those, they hope for Mercy of Allah. And Allah is Oft-Forgiving, Most Merciful.

Indeed (inna), | those who (alladhīna) | believed (āmanū) | and those who (wa-alladhīna) | emigrated (hājarū) | and strove (wajāhadū) | in (fī) | the way (sabīli) | of Allah (l-lahi)- | those (ulāika), | they hope (yarjūna) | for Mercy (raḥmata) | of Allah (l-lahi). | And Allah (wal-lahu) | is Oft-Forgiving (ghafūrun), | Most Merciful (raḥīmun).

2:219 They ask you about [the] intoxicants and [the] games of chance Say, "In both of them is a sin great, and some benefits for [the] people. But sin of both of them is greater than the benefit of (the) two." And they ask you what they should spend. Say, "The surplus." Thus makes clear Allah to you [the] Verses so that you may ponder,

They ask you (yasalūnaka) | about (ʿani) | [the] intoxicants (l-khamri) | and [the] games of chance (wal-maysiri) | Say (qul), | "In both of them (fīhimā) | is a sin (ith'mun) | great (kabīrun), | and some benefits (wamanāfiʿu) | for [the] people (lilnnāsi). | But sin of both of them (wa-ith'muhumā) | is greater (akbaru) | than (min) | the benefit of (the) two. (nafʿihimā)" | And they ask you (wayasalūnaka) | what (mādhā) | they should spend (yunfiqūna). | Say (quli), | "The surplus. (l-ʿafwa)" | Thus (kadhālika) | makes clear (yubayyinu) | Allah (l-lahu) | to you (lakumu) | [the] Verses (l-āyāti) | so that you may (laʿallakum) | ponder (tatafakkarūna),

2:220 Concerning the world and the Hereafter. They ask you about the orphans. Say, "Setting right their affairs for them is best. And if you associate with them then they are your brothers. And Allah knows the corrupter from the amender. And if had willed Allah surely He could have put you in difficulties. Indeed, Allah is All-Mighty, All-Wise."

Concerning (fī) | the world (l-dun'yā) | and the Hereafter (wal-ākhirati). | They ask you (wayasalūnaka) | about (ʿani) | the orphans (l-yatāmā). | Say (qul), | "Setting right their affairs (iṣ'lāḥun) | for them (lahum) | is best (khayrun). | And if (wa-in) | you associate with them (tukhāliṭūhum) | then they are your brothers (fa-ikh'wānukum). | And Allah (wal-lahu) | knows (yaʿlamu) | the corrupter (l-muf'sida) | from (mina) | the amender (l-muṣ'liḥi). | And if (walaw) | had willed (shāa) | Allah (l-lahu) | surely He could have put you in difficulties (la-aʿnatakum). | Indeed (inna), | Allah (l-laha) | is All-Mighty (ʿazīzun), | All-Wise. (ḥakīmun)"

2:221 And do not [you] marry [the] polytheistic women until they believe. And a bondwoman who is believing is better than a polytheistic woman [and] even if she pleases you. And do not give in marriage your women to [the] polytheistic men until they believe, and a bondman who is believing is better than a polytheistic man [and] even if he pleases you. [Those] they invite to the Fire, and Allah invites to Paradise and [the] forgiveness by His permission. And He makes clear His Verses for the people so that they may take heed.

And do not (walā) | [you] marry (tankiḥū) | [the] polytheistic women (l-mush'rikāti) | until (ḥattā) | they believe (yu'minna). | And a bondwoman (wala-amatun) | who is believing (mu'minatun) | is better (khayrun) | than (min) | a polytheistic woman (mush'rikatin) | [and] even if (walaw) | she pleases you (aʿjabatkum). | And do not (walā) | give in marriage your women (tunkiḥū) | to [the] polytheistic men (l-mush'rikīna) | until (ḥattā) | they believe (yu'minū), | and a bondman (walaʿabdun) | who is believing (mu'minun) | is better (khayrun) | than (min) | a polytheistic man (mush'rikin) | [and] even if (walaw) | he pleases you (aʿjabakum). | [Those] (ulāika) | they invite (yadʿūna) | to (ilā) | the Fire (l-nāri), | and Allah (wal-lahu) | invites (yadʿū) | to (ilā) | Paradise (l-janati) | and [the] forgiveness (wal-maghfirati) | by His permission (bi-idh'nihi). | And He makes clear (wayubayyinu) | His Verses (āyātihi) | for the people (lilnnāsi) | so that they may (laʿallahum) | take heed (yatadhakkarūna).

2:222 And they ask you about [the] menstruation. Say, "It is a hurt, so keep away from [the] women during their [the] menstruation. And do not approach them until they are cleansed. Then when they are purified, then come to them from where has ordered you Allah." Indeed, Allah loves those who turn in repentance and loves those who purify themselves.

And they ask you (wayasalūnaka) | about (ʿani) | [the] menstruation (l-maḥīḍi). | Say (qul), | "It (huwa) | is a hurt (adhan), | so keep away from (fa-iʿʿtazilū) | [the] women (l-nisāa) | during (fī) | their [the] menstruation (l-maḥīḍi). | And do not (walā) | approach them (taqrabūhunna) | until (ḥattā) | they are cleansed (yaṭhur'na). | Then when (fa-idhā) | they are purified (taṭahharna), | then come to them (fatūhunna) | from (min) | where (ḥaythu) | has ordered you (amarakumu) | Allah. (l-lahu)" | Indeed (inna), | Allah (l-laha) | loves (yuḥibbu) | those who turn in repentance (l-tawābīna) | and loves (wayuḥibbu) | those who purify themselves (l-mutaṭahirīna).

2:223 Your wives are a tilth for you, so come to your tilth when you wish, and send forth good deeds for yourselves. And be conscious of Allah and know that you will meet Him. And give glad tidings to the believers.

Your wives (nisāukum) | are a tilth (ḥarthun) | for you (lakum), | so come (fatū) | to your tilth (ḥarthakum) | when (annā) | you wish (shi'tum), | and send forth good deeds (waqaddimū) | for yourselves (li-anfusikum). | And be conscious (wa-ittaqū) | of Allah (l-laha) | and know (wa-iʿʿlamū) | that you (annakum) | will meet Him (mulāqūhu). | And give glad tidings (wabashiri) | to the believers (l-mu'minīna).

2:224 And do not make Allah's name an excuse in your oaths that you do good, and be righteous and make peace between [the] people. And Allah is All-Hearing, All-Knowing.

And do not (walā) | make (tajʿalū) | Allah's name (l-laha) | an excuse (ʿur'ḍatan) | in your oaths (li-aymānikum) | that (an) | you do good (tabarrū), | and be righteous (watattaqū) | and make peace (watuṣ'liḥū) | between (bayna) | [the] people (l-nāsi). | And Allah (wal-lahu) | is All-Hearing (samīʿun), | All-Knowing (ʿalīmun).

2:225 Not will take you to task Allah for what is unintentional in your oaths, [and] but He takes you to task for what have earned your hearts. And Allah is Oft-Forgiving, Most Forbearing.

Not (lā) | will take you to task (yuākhidhukumu) | Allah (l-lahu) | for what is unintentional (bil-laghwi) | in (fī) | your oaths (aymānikum), | [and] but (walākin) | He takes you to task (yuākhidhukum) | for what (bimā) | have earned (kasabat) | your hearts (qulūbukum). | And Allah (wal-lahu) | is Oft-Forgiving (ghafūrun), | Most Forbearing (ḥalīmun).

2:226 For those who swear off from their wives is a waiting (of) four months, then if they return - then indeed, Allah is Oft-Forgiving, Most Merciful.

For those who (lilladhīna) | swear off (yu'lūna) | from (min) | their wives (nisāihim) | is a waiting (of (tarabbuṣu)) | four (arbaʿati) | months (ashhurin), | then if (fa-in) | they return (fāū)- | then indeed (fa-inna), | Allah (l-laha) | is Oft-Forgiving (ghafūrun), | Most Merciful (raḥīmun).

2:227 And if they resolve on [the] divorce - then indeed, Allah is All-Hearing, All-Knowing.

And if (wa-in) | they resolve (ʿazamū) | on [the] divorce (l-ṭalāqa)- | then indeed (fa-inna), | Allah (l-laha) | is All-Hearing (samīʿun), | All-Knowing (ʿalīmun).

2:228 And the women who are divorced shall wait concerning themselves for three monthly periods. And it is not lawful for them that they conceal what has been created by Allah in their wombs, if they believe in Allah and the Day [the] Last. And their husbands have better right to take them back in that period if they wish for reconciliation. And for them is the like of that which is on them in a reasonable manner, and for the men over them is a degree. And Allah is All-Mighty, All-Wise.

And the women who are divorced (wal-muṭalaqātu) | shall wait (yatarabbaṣna) | concerning themselves (bi-anfusihinna) | for three (thalāthata) | monthly periods (qurūin). | And it is not (walā) | lawful (yaḥillu) | for them (lahunna) | that (an) | they conceal (yaktum'na) | what (mā) | has been created (khalaqa) | by Allah (l-lahu) | in (fī) | their wombs (arḥāmihinna), | if (in) | they (kunna) | believe (yu'minna) | in Allah (bil-lahi) | and the Day (wal-yawmi) | [the] Last (l-ākhiri).

| And their husbands (wabuʿūlatuhunna) | have better right (aḥaqqu) | to take them back (biraddihinna) | in (fī) | that period (dhālika) | if (in) | they wish (arādū) | for reconciliation (iṣ'lāḥan). | And for them (walahunna) | is the like (mith'lu) | of that which (alladhī) | is on them (ʿalayhinna) | in a reasonable manner (bil-maʿrūfi), | and for the men (walilrrijāli) | over them (ʿalayhinna) | is a degree (darajatun). | And Allah (wal-lahu) | is All-Mighty (ʿazīzun), | All-Wise (ḥakīmun).

2:229 The divorce is twice. Then to retain in a reasonable manner or to release her with kindness. And it is not lawful for you that you take back whatever you have given them anything, except if both fear that not they both can keep the limits of Allah. But if you fear that not they both can keep the limits of Allah then there is no sin on both of them in what she ransoms concerning it. These are the limits of Allah, so do not transgress them. And whoever transgresses the limits of Allah then those - they are the wrongdoers.

The divorce (al-ṭalāqu) | is twice (marratāni). | Then to retain (fa-im'sākun) | in a reasonable manner (bimaʿrūfin) | or (aw) | to release her (tasrīḥun) | with kindness (bi-iḥ'sānin). | And it is not (walā) | lawful (yaḥillu) | for you (lakum) | that (an) | you take back (takhudhū) | whatever (mimmā) | you have given them (ātaytumūhunna) | anything (shayan), | except (illā) | if (an) | both fear (yakhāfā) | that not (allā) | they both can keep (yuqīmā) | the limits (ḥudūda) | of Allah (l-lahi). | But if (fa-in) | you fear (khif'tum) | that not (allā) | they both can keep (yuqīmā) | the limits (ḥudūda) | of Allah (l-lahi) | then there is no (falā) | sin (junāḥa) | on both of them (ʿalayhimā) | in what (fīmā) | she ransoms (if'tadat) | concerning it (bihi). | These (til'ka) | are the limits (ḥudūdu) | of Allah (l-lahi), | so do not (falā) | transgress them (taʿtadūhā). | And whoever (waman) | transgresses (yataʿadda) | the limits (ḥudūda) | of Allah (l-lahi) | then those (fa-ulāika)- | they (humu) | are the wrongdoers (l-ẓālimūna).

2:230 Then if he divorces her, then she is not lawful for him from after that until she marries a spouse other than him. Then if he divorces her then no sin on them if they return to each other if they believe that they will be able to keep the limits. of Allah. And these are the limits. of Allah. He makes them clear to a people who know.

Then if (fa-in) | he divorces her (ṭallaqahā), | then she is not (falā) | lawful (taḥillu) | for him (lahu) | from (min) | after that (baʿdu) | until (ḥattā) | she marries (tankiḥa) | a spouse (zawjan) | other than him (ghayrahu). | Then if (fa-in) | he divorces her (ṭallaqahā) | then no (falā) | sin (junāḥa) | on them (ʿalayhimā) | if (an) | they return to each other (yatarājaʿā) | if (in) | they believe (ẓannā) | that (an) | they will be able to keep (yuqīmā) | the limits (ḥudūda). | of Allah (l-lahi). | And these (watil'ka) | are the limits (ḥudūdu). | of Allah (l-lahi). | He makes them clear (yubayyinuhā) | to a people (liqawmin) | who know (yaʿlamūna).

2:231 And when you divorce the women and they reach their waiting term, then retain them in a fair manner or release them in a fair manner. And do not retain them to hurt so that you transgress. And whoever does that, then indeed, he wronged himself. And do not take the Verses of Allah in jest, and remember the Favors of Allah upon you and what is revealed to you of the Book and [the] wisdom; He instructs you with it. And fear Allah and know that Allah is of every thing All-Knower.

And when (wa-idhā) | you divorce (ṭallaqtumu) | the women (l-nisāa) | and they reach (fabalaghna) | their waiting term (ajalahunna), | then retain them (fa-amsikūhunna) | in a fair manner (bimaʿrūfin) | or (aw) | release them (sarriḥūhunna) | in a fair manner (bimaʿrūfin). | And do not (walā) | retain them (tum'sikūhunna) | to hurt (ḍirāran) | so that you transgress (litaʿtadū). | And whoever (waman) | does (yafʿal) | that (dhālika), | then indeed (faqad), | he wronged (ẓalama) | himself (nafsahu). | And do not (walā) | take (tattakhidhū) | the Verses (āyāti) | of Allah (l-lahi) | in jest (huzuwan), | and remember (wa-udh'kurū) | the Favors (niʿ'mata) | of Allah (l-lahi) | upon you (ʿalaykum) | and what (wamā) | is revealed (anzala) | to you (ʿalaykum) | of (mina) | the Book (l-kitābi) | and [the] wisdom (wal-ḥik'mati); | He instructs you (yaʿiẓukum) | with it (bihi). | And fear (wa-ittaqū) | Allah (l-laha) | and know (wa-iʿ'lamū) | that (anna) | Allah is (l-laha) | of every (bikulli)

| thing (shayin) | All-Knower (ʿalīmun).

2:232 And when you divorce [the] women and they reached their waiting term, then do not hinder them [that] from marrying their husbands when they agree between themselves in a fair manner. That is admonished with it whoever [is] among you believes in Allah and the Day [the] Last; that is more virtuous for you and more purer. And Allah knows and you do not know.

And when (wa-idhā) | you divorce (ṭallaqtumu) | [the] women (l-nisāa) | and they reached (fabalaghna) | their waiting term (ajalahunna), | then do not (falā) | hinder them (taʿḍulūhunna) | [that] (an) | from marrying (yankiḥ'na) | their husbands (azwājahunna) | when (idhā) | they agree (tarāḍaw) | between themselves (baynahum) | in a fair manner (bil-maʿrūfi). | That (dhālika) | is admonished (yūʿaẓu) | with it (bihi) | whoever (man) | [is] (kāna) | among you (minkum) | believes (yu'minu) | in Allah (bil-lahi) | and the Day (wal-yawmi) | [the] Last (l-ākhiri); | that (dhālikum) | is more virtuous (azkā) | for you (lakum) | and more purer (wa-aṭharu). | And Allah (wal-lahu) | knows (yaʿlamu) | and you (wa-antum) | do not (lā) | know (taʿlamūna).

2:233 And the mothers shall suckle their children for two years complete, for whoever wishes to complete the suckling. And upon the father on him is their provision and their clothing in a fair manner. Not is burdened any soul except its capacity. Not made to suffer the mother because of her child and not the father be because of his child. And on the father's heir is a duty like that of the father. Then if they both desire weaning through mutual consent of both of them and consultation, then no blame on both of them. And if you want to ask another women to suckle your child then there is no blame on you, when you pay what you give in a fair manner. And fear Allah and know that Allah of what you do is All-Seer.

And the mothers (wal-wālidātu) | shall suckle (yur'ḍiʿ'na) | their children (awlādahunna) | for two years (ḥawlayni) | complete (kāmilayni), | for whoever (liman) | wishes (arāda) | to (an) | complete (yutimma) | the suckling (l-raḍāʿata). | And upon (waʿalā) | the father (l-mawlūdi) | on him (lahu) | is their provision (riz'quhunna) | and their clothing (wakis'watuhunna) | in a fair manner (bil-maʿrūfi). | Not (lā) | is burdened (tukallafu) | any soul (nafsun) | except (illā) | its capacity (wus'ʿahā). | Not (lā) | made to suffer (tuḍārra) | the mother (wālidatun) | because of her child (biwaladihā) | and not (walā) | the father (mawlūdun) | be (lahu) | because of his child (biwaladihi). | And on (waʿalā) | the father's heir (l-wārithi) | is a duty like (mith'lu) | that of the father (dhālika). | Then if (fa-in) | they both desire (arādā) | weaning (fiṣālan) | through (ʿan) | mutual consent (tarāḍin) | of both of them (min'humā) | and consultation (watashāwurin), | then no (falā) | blame (junāḥa) | on both of them (ʿalayhimā). | And if (wa-in) | you want (aradttum) | to (an) | ask another women to suckle (tastarḍiʿū) | your child (awlādakum) | then there is no (falā) | blame (junāḥa) | on you (ʿalaykum), | when (idhā) | you pay (sallamtum) | what (mā) | you give (ātaytum) | in a fair manner (bil-maʿrūfi). | And fear (wa-ittaqū) | Allah (l-laha) | and know (wa-iʿ'lamū) | that (anna) | Allah (l-laha) | of what (bimā) | you do (taʿmalūna) | is All-Seer (baṣīrun).

2:234 And those who pass away among you and leave behind wives, the widows should wait for themselves for four months and ten days. Then when they reach their specified term, then there is no blame upon you for what they do concerning themselves in a fair manner. And Allah of what you do is All-Aware.

And those who (wa-alladhīna) | pass away (yutawaffawna) | among you (minkum) | and leave behind (wayadharūna) | wives (azwājan), | the widows should wait (yatarabbaṣna) | for themselves (bi-anfusihinna) | for four (arbaʿata) | months (ashhurin) | and ten days (waʿashran). | Then when (fa-idhā) | they reach (balaghna) | their specified term (ajalahunna), | then there is no (falā) | blame (junāḥa) | upon you (ʿalaykum) | for what (fīmā) | they do (faʿalna) | concerning (fī) | themselves (anfusihinna) | in a fair manner (bil-maʿrūfi). | And Allah (wal-lahu) | of what (bimā) | you do (taʿmalūna) | is All-Aware (khabīrun).

2:235 And there is no blame upon you in what you hint [with it] of marriage proposal [to] the women or you conceal it in yourselves. Knows Allah that you will mention them, [and] but do not promise them widows secretly except that you say a saying honorable. And do not resolve on the knot of marriage until reaches the prescribed term its end. And know that Allah knows what is within yourselves so beware of Him. And know that Allah is Oft-Forgiving, Most Forbearing.

And there is no (walā) | blame (junāḥa) | upon you (ʿalaykum) | in what (fīmā) | you hint (ʿarraḍtum) | [with it] (bihi) | of (min) | marriage proposal (khiṭ'bati) | [to] the women (l-nisāi) | or (aw) | you conceal it (aknantum) | in (fī) | yourselves (anfusikum). | Knows (ʿalima) | Allah (l-lahu) | that you (annakum) | will mention them (satadhkurūnahunna), | [and] but (walākin) | do not (lā) | promise them widows (tuwāʿidūhunna) | secretly (sirran) | except (illā) | that (an) | you say (taqūlū) | a saying (qawlan) | honorable (maʿrūfan). | And do not (walā) | resolve on (taʿzimū) | the knot (ʿuq'data) | of marriage (l-nikāḥi) | until (ḥattā) | reaches (yablugha) | the prescribed term (l-kitābu) | its end (ajalahu). | And know (wa-iʿ'lamū) | that (anna) | Allah (l-laha) | knows (yaʿlamu) | what (mā) | is within (fī) | yourselves (anfusikum) | so beware of Him (fa-iḥ'dharūhu). | And know (wa-iʿ'lamū) | that (anna) | Allah (l-laha) | is Oft-Forgiving (ghafūrun), | Most Forbearing (ḥalīmun).

2:236 There is no blame upon you if you divorce [the] women whom not you have touched nor you specified for them an obligation dower. And make provision for them - upon the wealthy according to his means and upon the poor according to his means - a provision in a fair manner, a duty upon the good-doers.

There is no (lā) | blame (junāḥa) | upon you (ʿalaykum) | if (in) | you divorce (ṭallaqtumu) | [the] women (l-nisāa) | whom (mā) | not (lam) | you have touched (tamassūhunna) | nor (aw) | you specified (tafriḍū) | for them (lahunna) | an obligation dower (farīḍatan). | And make provision for them (wamattiʿūhunna)- | upon (ʿalā) | the wealthy (l-mūsiʿi) | according to his means (qadaruhu) | and upon (waʿalā) | the poor (l-muq'tiri) | according to his means (qadaruhu)- | a provision (matāʿan) | in a fair manner (bil-maʿrūfi), | a duty (ḥaqqan) | upon (ʿalā) | the good-doers (l-muḥ'sinīna).

2:237 And if you divorce them from before [that] you have touched them while already you have specified for them an obligation dower, then give half of what you have specified, unless [that] they women forgo (it) or forgoes the one in whose hands is the knot of the marriage. And that you forgo, is nearer to [the] righteousness. And do not forget the graciousness among you. Indeed, Allah of what you do is All-Seer.

And if (wa-in) | you divorce them (ṭallaqtumūhunna) | from (min) | before (qabli) | [that] (an) | you have touched them (tamassūhunna) | while already (waqad) | you have specified (faraḍtum) | for them (lahunna) | an obligation dower (farīḍatan), | then give half (faniṣ'fu) | of what (mā) | you have specified (faraḍtum), | unless (illā) | [that] (an) | they women forgo (it (yaʿfūna)) | or (aw) | forgoes (yaʿfuwā) | the one (alladhī) | in whose hands (biyadihi) | is the knot (ʿuq'datu) | of the marriage (l-nikāḥi). | And that (wa-an) | you forgo (taʿfū), | is nearer (aqrabu) | to [the] righteousness (lilttaqwā). | And do not (walā) | forget (tansawū) | the graciousness (l-faḍla) | among you (baynakum). | Indeed (inna), | Allah (l-laha) | of what (bimā) | you do (taʿmalūna) | is All-Seer (baṣīrun).

2:238 Guard strictly [on] the prayers, and the prayer - [the] middle, and stand up for Allah devoutly obedient.

Guard strictly (ḥāfiẓū) | [on] (ʿalā) | the prayers (l-ṣalawāti), | and the prayer (wal-ṣalati)- | [the] middle (l-wus'ṭā), | and stand up (waqūmū) | for Allah (lillahi) | devoutly obedient (qānitīna).

2:239 And if you fear then pray on foot or riding. Then when you are secure then remember Allah as He has taught you what not you were knowing.

And if (fa-in) | you fear (khif'tum) | then pray on foot (farijālan) | or (aw) | riding (ruk'bānan). | Then when (fa-idhā) | you are secure (amintum) | then remember (fa-udh'kurū) |

Allah (l-laha) | as (kamā) | He has taught you (ʿallamakum) | what (mā) | not (lam) | you were (takūnū) | knowing (taʿlamūna).

2:240 And those who die among you and leave behind their wives should make a will for their wives, provision for the year without driving them out. But if they leave then no blame upon you in what they do concerning themselves [of] honorably. And Allah is All-Mighty, All-Wise.

And those who (wa-alladhīna) | die (yutawaffawna) | among you (minkum) | and leave behind (wayadharūna) | their wives (azwājan) | should make a will (waṣiyyatan) | for their wives (li-azwājihim), | provision (matāʿan) | for (ilā) | the year (l-ḥawli) | without (ghayra) | driving them out (ikh'rājin). | But if (fa-in) | they leave (kharajna) | then no (falā) | blame (junāḥa) | upon you (ʿalaykum) | in (fī) | what (mā) | they do (faʿalna) | concerning (fī) | themselves (anfusihinna) | [of] (min) | honorably (maʿrūfin). | And Allah (wal-lahu) | is All-Mighty (ʿazīzun), | All-Wise (ḥakīmun).

2:241 And for the divorced women, is a provision in a fair manner - a duty upon the righteous.

And for the divorced women (walil'muṭallaqāti), | is a provision (matāʿun) | in a fair manner (bil-maʿrūfi)- | a duty (ḥaqqan) | upon (ʿalā) | the righteous (l-mutaqīna).

2:242 Thus makes clear Allah for you His Verses so that you may use your intellect.

Thus (kadhālika) | makes clear (yubayyinu) | Allah (l-lahu) | for you (lakum) | His Verses (āyātihi) | so that you may (laʿallakum) | use your intellect (taʿqilūna).

2:243 Did not you see [to] those who went out from their homes and they were in thousands in fear of [the] death? Then said to them Allah, "Die;" then He restored them to life. Indeed, Allah is surely Possessor of bounty for [the] mankind [and] but most of the people are not grateful.

Did not (alam) | you see (tara) | [to] (ilā) | those who (alladhīna) | went out (kharajū) | from (min) | their homes (diyārihim) | and they (wahum) | were in thousands (ulūfun) | in fear (ḥadhara) | of [the] death (l-mawti)? | Then said (faqāla) | to them (lahumu) | Allah (l-lahu), | "Die; (mūtū)" | then (thumma) | He restored them to life (aḥyāhum). | Indeed (inna), | Allah (l-laha) | is surely Possessor (ladhū) | of bounty (faḍlin) | for (ʿalā) | [the] mankind (l-nāsi) | [and] but (walākinna) | most (akthara) | of the people (l-nāsi) | are not (lā) | grateful (yashkurūna).

2:244 And fight in the way of Allah, and know that Allah is All-Hearing, All-Knowing.

And fight (waqātilū) | in (fī) | the way (sabīli) | of Allah (l-lahi), | and know (wa-iʿ'lamū) | that (anna) | Allah (l-laha) | is All-Hearing (samīʿun), | All-Knowing (ʿalīmun).

2:245 Who is the one who will lend to Allah - a loan good, so that He multiplies it for him - manifolds many And Allah withholds and grants abundance, and to Him you will be returned.

Who (man) | is the one (dhā) | who (alladhī) | will lend (yuq'riḍu) | to Allah (l-laha)- | a loan (qarḍan) | good (ḥasanan), | so that He multiplies it (fayuḍāʿifahu) | for him (lahu)- | manifolds (aḍʿāfan) | many (kathīratan) | And Allah (wal-lahu) | withholds (yaqbiḍu) | and grants abundance (wayabṣuṭu), | and to Him (wa-ilayhi) | you will be returned (tur'jaʿūna).

2:246 Did not you see [towards] the chiefs of the Children of Israel from after Musa, when they said to a Prophet of theirs, "Appoint for us a king, we may fight in the way of Allah?" He said, "Would you perhaps - if prescribed upon you [the] fighting, that not you fight?" They said, "And what for us that not we fight in the way of Allah while surely we have been driven from our homes and our children?" Yet, when was prescribed upon them the fighting they turned away, except a few among them. And Allah is All-Knowing of the wrongdoers.

Did not (alam) | you see (tara) | [towards] (ilā) | the chiefs (l-mala-i) | of (min) | the Children (banī) | of Israel (is'rāīla) | from (min) | after (baʿdi) | Musa (mūsā), | when (idh) | they said (qālū) | to a Prophet (linabiyyin) | of theirs (lahumu), | "Appoint (ib'ʿath) | for us (lanā) | a king (malikan), | we may fight (nuqātil) | in (fī) | the way (sabīli) | of Allah? (l-lahi)" | He said (qāla), |

"Would (hal) | you perhaps (ʿasaytum)- | if (in) | prescribed (kutiba) | upon you (ʿalaykumu) | [the] fighting (l-qitālu), | that not (allā) | you fight? (tuqātilū)" | They said (qālū), | "And what (wamā) | for us (lanā) | that not (allā) | we fight (nuqātila) | in (fī) | the way (sabīli) | of Allah (l-lahi) | while surely (waqad) | we have been driven (ukh'rij'nā) | from (min) | our homes (diyārinā) | and our children? (wa-abnāinā)" | Yet, when (falammā) | was prescribed (kutiba) | upon them (ʿalayhimu) | the fighting (l-qitālu) | they turned away (tawallaw), | except (illā) | a few (qalīlan) | among them (min'hum). | And Allah (wal-lahu) | is All-Knowing (ʿalīmun) | of the wrongdoers (bil-ẓālimīna).

2:247 And said to them their Prophet, "Indeed, Allah has surely raised for you Talut as a king." They said, How can be for him the kingship over us, while we are more entitled to kingship than him, and not he has been given abundance of [the] wealth?" He said, "Indeed, Allah has chosen him over you and increased him abundantly in [the] knowledge and [the] physique. And Allah gives His kingdom to whom He wills. And Allah is All-Encompassing, All-Knowing."

And said (waqāla) | to them (lahum) | their Prophet (nabiyyuhum), | "Indeed (inna), | Allah (l-laha) | has surely (qad) | raised (baʿatha) | for you (lakum) | Talut (ṭālūta) | as a king. (malikan)" | They said (qālū), | How (annā) | can be (yakūnu) | for him (lahu) | the kingship (l-mul'ku) | over us (ʿalaynā), | while we (wanaḥnu) | are more entitled (aḥaqqu) | to kingship (bil-mul'ki) | than him (min'hu), | and not (walam) | he has been given (yu'ta) | abundance (saʿatan) | of (mina) | [the] wealth? (l-māli)" | He said (qāla), | "Indeed (inna), | Allah (l-laha) | has chosen him (iṣ'ṭafāhu) | over you (ʿalaykum) | and increased him (wazādahu) | abundantly (basṭatan) | in (fī) | [the] knowledge (l-ʿil'mi) | and [the] physique (wal-jis'mi). | And Allah (wal-lahu) | gives (yu'tī) | His kingdom (mul'kahu) | to whom (man) | He wills (yashāu). | And Allah (wal-lahu) | is All-Encompassing (wāsiʿun), | All-Knowing. (ʿalīmun)"

2:248 And said to them their Prophet, "Indeed, a sign of his kingship is that will come to you the ark, in it is tranquility from your Lord, and a remnant of what was left by the family of Musa and family of Harun will carry it the Angels. Indeed, in that is surely a sign for you if you are believers."

And said (waqāla) | to them (lahum) | their Prophet (nabiyyuhum), | "Indeed (inna), | a sign (āyata) | of his kingship (mul'kihi) | is that (an) | will come to you (yatiyakumu) | the ark (l-tābūtu), | in it (fīhi) | is tranquility (sakīnatun) | from (min) | your Lord (rabbikum), | and a remnant (wabaqiyyatun) | of what (mimmā) | was left (taraka) | by the family (ālu) | of Musa (mūsā) | and family (waālu) | of Harun (hārūna) | will carry it (taḥmiluhu) | the Angels (l-malāikatu). | Indeed (inna), | in (fī) | that (dhālika) | is surely a sign (laāyatan) | for you (lakum) | if (in) | you are (kuntum) | believers. (mu'minīna)"

2:249 Then when set out Talut with the forces he said, "Indeed, Allah will test you with a river. So whoever drinks from it then he is not from me, and whoever does not taste it then indeed, he is from me except whoever takes in the hollow of his hand." Then they drank from it except a few of them. Then when he crossed it, he and those who believed with him, they said, "No strength for us today against Jalut and his troops." Said those who were certain that they would meet Allah, "How many of a company small overcame a company large by the permission of Allah. And Allah is with the patient ones."

Then when (falammā) | set out (faṣala) | Talut (ṭālūtu) | with the forces (bil-junūdi) | he said (qāla), | "Indeed (inna), | Allah (l-laha) | will test you (mub'talīkum) | with a river (binaharin). | So whoever (faman) | drinks (shariba) | from it (min'hu) | then he is not (falaysa) | from me (minnī), | and whoever (waman) | does not (lam) | taste it (yaṭʿamhu) | then indeed, he (fa-innahu) | is from me (minnī) | except (illā) | whoever (mani) | takes (igh'tarafa) | in the hollow (ghur'fatan) | of his hand. (biyadihi)" | Then they drank (fasharibū) | from it (min'hu) | except (illā) | a few (qalīlan) | of them (min'hum). | Then when (falammā) | he crossed it (jāwazahu), | he (huwa) | and those who (wa-alladhīna) | believed (āmanū) | with him (maʿahu), | they said (qālū), | "No (lā) | strength (ṭāqata) | for us (lanā) | today (l-yawma) | against Jalut (bijālūta) | and his troops. (wajunūdihi)" | Said (qāla) | those who (alladhīna) | were certain (yaẓunnūna) | that they (annahum) | would meet (mulāqū) | Allah (l-lahi), | "How many (kam) | of (min) | a company (fi-atin) | small (qalīlatin) | overcame (ghalabat) | a company (fi-atan) | large (kathīratan) | by the permission (bi-idh'ni) | of Allah (l-lahi). | And Allah (wal-lahu) | is with (maʿa) | the patient ones. (l-ṣābirīna)"

2:250 And when they went forth to face Jalut and his troops they said, "Our Lord! Pour on us patience and make firm our feet, and help us against the people who are disbelieving."

And when (walammā) | they went forth (barazū) | to face Jalut (lijālūta) | and his troops (wajunūdihi) | they said (qālū), | "Our Lord (rabbanā)! | Pour (afrigh) | on us (ʿalaynā) | patience (ṣabran) | and make firm (wathabbit) | our feet (aqdāmanā), | and help us (wa-unṣur'nā) | against (ʿalā) | the people (l-qawmi) | who are disbelieving. (l-kāfirīna)"

2:251 So they defeated them by the permission of Allah, and killed Dawood Jalut, and gave him Allah the kingdom and the wisdom and taught him that which He willed. And if not for the repelling by Allah, [the] people - some of them with others, certainly would have corrupted the Earth, [and] but Allah is Possessor of bounty to the worlds.

So they defeated them (fahazamūhum) | by the permission (bi-idh'ni) | of Allah (l-lahi), | and killed (waqatala) | Dawood (dāwūdu) | Jalut (jālūta), | and gave him (waātāhu) | Allah (l-lahu) | the kingdom (l-mul'ka) | and the wisdom (wal-ḥik'mata) | and taught him (waʿallamahu) | that which (mimmā) | He willed (yashāu). | And if not (walawlā) | for the repelling (dafʿu) | by Allah (l-lahi), | [the] people (l-nāsa)- | some of them (baʿḍahum) | with others (bibaʿḍin), | certainly would have corrupted (lafasadati) | the Earth (l-arḍu), | [and] but (walākinna) | Allah (l-laha) | is Possessor (dhū) | of bounty (faḍlin) | to (ʿalā) | the worlds (l-ʿālamīna).

2:252 These are the Verses of Allah, We recite them to you in [the] truth. And indeed, you are surely of the Messengers.

These (til'ka) | are the Verses (āyātu) | of Allah (l-lahi), | We recite them (natlūhā) | to you (ʿalayka) | in [the] truth (bil-ḥaqi). | And indeed, you (wa-innaka) | are surely of (lamina) | the Messengers (l-mur'salīna).

2:253 These are the Messengers We have preferred some of them over others. Among them were those with whom spoke Allah, and He raised some of them in degrees. And We gave Isa, son of Maryam, the clear proofs and We supported him with Spirit [the] Holy. And if had willed Allah not would have fought each other those who came from after them, from after [what] came to them the clear proofs. [And] but they differed, [so] of them are some who believed and of them are some who denied. And if had willed Allah not they would have fought each other, [and] but Allah does what He intends.

These (til'ka) | are the Messengers (l-rusulu) | We have preferred (faḍḍalnā) | some of them (baʿḍahum) | over (ʿalā) | others (baʿḍin). | Among them (min'hum) | were those with whom (man) | spoke (kallama) | Allah (l-lahu), | and He raised (warafaʿa) | some of them (baʿḍahum) | in degrees (darajātin). | And We gave (waātaynā) | Isa (ʿīsā), | son (ib'na) | of Maryam (maryama), | the clear proofs (l-bayināti) | and We supported him (wa-ayyadnāhu) | with Spirit (birūḥi) | [the] Holy (l-qudusi). | And if (walaw) | had willed (shāa) | Allah (l-lahu) | not (mā) | would have fought each other (iq'tatala) | those who (alladhīna) | came from (min) | after them (baʿdihim), | from (min) | after (baʿdi) | [what] (mā) | came to them (jāathumu) | the clear proofs (l-bayinātu). | [And] but (walākini) | they differed (ikh'talafū), | [so] of them (famin'hum) | are some who (man) | believed (āmana) | and of them (wamin'hum) | are some who (man) | denied (kafara). | And if (walaw) | had willed (shāa) | Allah (l-lahu) | not (mā) | they would have fought each other (iq'tatalū), | [and] but (walākinna) | Allah (l-laha) | does (yafʿalu) | what (mā) | He intends (yurīdu).

2:254 O you who believe[d]! Spend of what We have provided you, from before that comes a Day no bargaining in it and no friendship and no intercession. And the deniers - they are the wrongdoers.

O you (yāayyuhā) | who (alladhīna) | believe[d] (āmanū)! | Spend (anfiqū) | of what (mimmā) | We have provided you (razaqnākum), | from (min) | before (qabli) | that (an) | comes (yatiya) | a Day (yawmun) | no (lā) | bargaining (bay'un) | in it (fīhi) | and no (walā) | friendship (khullatun) | and no (walā) | intercession (shafā'atun). | And the deniers (wal-kāfirūna)- | they (humu) | are the wrongdoers (l-ẓālimūna).

2:255 Allah - there is no God except Him, the Ever-Living, the Sustainer of all that exists. Not overtakes Him slumber [and] not sleep. To Him belongs whatever is in the heavens and whatever is in the earth. Who is the one who can intercede with Him except by His permission. He knows what is before them and what is behind them. And not they encompass anything of His Knowledge except [of] what He willed. Extends His Throne to the heavens and the earth. And not tires Him the guarding of both of them. And He is the Most High, the Most Great.

Allah (al-lahu)- | there is no (lā) | God (ilāha) | except (illā) | Him (huwa), | the Ever-Living (l-ḥayu), | the Sustainer of all that exists (l-qayūmu). | Not (lā) | overtakes Him (takhudhuhu) | slumber (sinatun) | [and] not (walā) | sleep (nawmun). | To Him belongs (lahu) | whatever (mā) | is in (fī) | the heavens (l-samāwāti) | and whatever (wamā) | is in (fī) | the earth (l-arḍi). | Who (man) | is the one (dhā) | who (alladhī) | can intercede (yashfa'u) | with Him ('indahu) | except (illā) | by His permission (bi-idh'nihi). | He knows (ya'lamu) | what (mā) | is (bayna) | before them (aydīhim) | and what (wamā) | is behind them (khalfahum). | And not (walā) | they encompass (yuḥīṭūna) | anything (bishayin) | of (min) | His Knowledge ('il'mihi) | except (illā) | [of] what (bimā) | He willed (shāa). | Extends (wasi'a) | His Throne (kur'siyyuhu) | to the heavens (l-samāwāti) | and the earth (wal-arḍa). | And not (walā) | tires Him (yaūduhu) | the guarding of both of them (ḥif'ẓuhumā). | And He (wahuwa) | is the Most High (l-'aliyu), | the Most Great (l-'aẓīmu).

2:256 There is no compulsion in the religion. Surely has become distinct the right path from the wrong. Then whoever disbelieves in false deities and believes in Allah, then surely he grasped the handhold - [the] firm, which not will break [for it]. And Allah is All-Hearing, All-Knowing.

There is no (lā) | compulsion (ik'rāha) | in (fī) | the religion (l-dīni). | Surely (qad) | has become distinct (tabayyana) | the right path (l-rush'du) | from (mina) | the wrong (l-ghayi). | Then whoever (faman) | disbelieves (yakfur) | in false deities (bil-ṭāghūti) | and believes (wayu'min) | in Allah (bil-lahi), | then surely (faqadi) | he grasped (is'tamsaka) | the handhold (bil-'ur'wati)- | [the] firm (l-wuth'qā), | which not (lā) | will break (infiṣāma) | [for it] (lahā). | And Allah (wal-lahu) | is All-Hearing (samī'un), | All-Knowing ('alīmun).

2:257 Allah is the Protecting Guardian of those who believe[d]. He brings them out from [the] darkness towards [the] light. And those who disbelieved their guardians are the evil ones, they bring them out from the light towards [the] darkness. Those are the companions of the Fire, they in it will abide forever.

Allah (al-lahu) | is the Protecting Guardian (waliyyu) | of those who (alladhīna) | believe[d] (āmanū). | He brings them out (yukh'rijuhum) | from (mina) | [the] darkness (l-ẓulumāti) | towards (ilā) | [the] light (l-nūri). | And those who (wa-alladhīna) | disbelieved (kafarū) | their guardians (awliyāuhumu) | are the evil ones (l-ṭāghūtu), | they bring them out (yukh'rijūnahum) | from (mina) | the light (l-nūri) | towards (ilā) | [the] darkness (l-ẓulumāti). | Those (ulāika) | are the companions (aṣḥābu) | of the Fire (l-nāri), | they (hum) | in it (fīhā) | will abide forever (khālidūna).

2:258 Did not you see [towards] the one who argued with Ibrahim concerning his Lord, because gave him Allah the kingdom? When Said Ibrahim, "My Lord is the One Who grants life and causes death." He said, "I give life and cause death." Said Ibrahim, "[Then] indeed Allah brings up the sun from the east, so you bring it from the west." So became dumbfounded the one who disbelieved, and Allah does not guide the people who are [the] wrongdoers.

Did not (alam) | you see (tara) | [towards] (ilā) | the one who (alladhī) | argued (ḥājja) |

with Ibrahim (ib'rāhīma) | concerning (fī) | his Lord (rabbihi), | because (an) | gave him (ātāhu) | Allah (l-lahu) | the kingdom (l-mul'ka)? | When (idh) | Said (qāla) | Ibrahim (ib'rāhīmu), | "My Lord (rabbiya) | is the One Who (alladhī) | grants life (yuḥ'yī) | and causes death. (wayumītu)" | He said (qāla), | "I (anā) | give life (uḥ'yī) | and cause death. (wa-umītu)" | Said (qāla) | Ibrahim (ib'rāhīmu), | "[Then] indeed (fa-inna) | Allah (l-laha) | brings up (yatī) | the sun (bil-shamsi) | from (mina) | the east (l-mashriqi), | so you bring (fati) | it (bihā) | from (mina) | the west. (l-maghribi)" | So became dumbfounded (fabuhita) | the one who (alladhī) | disbelieved (kafara), | and Allah (wal-lahu) | does not (lā) | guide (yahdī) | the people (l-qawma) | who are [the] wrongdoers (l-ẓālimīna).

2:259 Or like the one who passed by a township, and it had overturned on its roofs. He said, "How will bring to life this town Allah after its death?" Then he was made to die by Allah for a hundred years, then He raised him. He said, "How long have you remained?" He said, "I remained for a day or a part of a day." He said, "Nay, you have remained one hundred years. Then look at your food and your drink, they did not change with time, and look at your donkey, and We will make you a sign for the people. And look at the bones how We raise them, then We cover them with flesh." Then when became clear to him, he said, "I know that Allah is on every thing All-Powerful."

Or (aw) | like the one who (ka-alladhī) | passed (marra) | by (ʿalā) | a township (qaryatin), | and it (wahiya) | had overturned (khāwiyatun) | on (ʿalā) | its roofs (ʿurūshihā). | He said (qāla), | "How (annā) | will bring to life (yuḥ'yī) | this town (hādhihi) | Allah (l-lahu) | after (baʿda) | its death? (mawtihā)" | Then he was made to die (fa-amātahu) | by Allah (l-lahu) | for a hundred (mi-ata) | years (ʿāmin), | then (thumma) | He raised him (baʿathahu). | He said (qāla), | "How long (kam) | have you remained? (labith'ta)" | He said (qāla), | "I remained (labith'tu) | for a day (yawman) | or (aw) | a part (baʿḍa) | of a day. (yawmin)" | He said (qāla), | "Nay (bal), | you have remained (labith'ta) | one hundred (mi-ata) | years (ʿāmin). | Then look (fa-unẓur) | at (ilā) | your food (ṭaʿāmika) | and your drink (washarābika), | they did not (lam) | change with time (yatasannah), | and look (wa-unẓur) | at (ilā) | your donkey (ḥimārika), | and We will make you (walinajʿalaka) | a sign (āyatan) | for the people (lilnnāsi). | And look (wa-unẓur) | at (ilā) | the bones (l-ʿiẓāmi) | how (kayfa) | We raise them (nunshizuhā), | then (thumma) | We cover them (naksūhā) | with flesh. (laḥman)" | Then when (falammā) | became clear (tabayyana) | to him (lahu), | he said (qāla), | "I know (aʿlamu) | that (anna) | Allah (l-laha) | is on (ʿalā) | every (kulli) | thing (shayin) | All-Powerful. (qadīrun)"

2:260 And when said Ibrahim, "My Lord show me how You give life to the dead." He said, "Have not you believed?" He said, "Yes [and] but to satisfy my heart." He said "Then take four of the birds and incline them towards you, then put on each hill of them a portion; then call them, they will come to you in haste. And know that Allah is All-Mighty, All-Wise.

And when (wa-idh) | said (qāla) | Ibrahim (ib'rāhīmu), | "My Lord (rabbi) | show me (arinī) | how (kayfa) | You give life (tuḥ'yī) | to the dead. (l-mawtā)" | He said (qāla), | "Have not (awalam) | you believed? (tu'min)" | He said (qāla), | "Yes (balā) | [and] but (walākin) | to satisfy (liyaṭma-inna) | my heart. (qalbī)" | He said (qāla) | "Then take (fakhudh) | four (arbaʿatan) | of (mina) | the birds (l-ṭayri) | and incline them (faṣur'hunna) | towards you (ilayka), | then (thumma) | put (ijʿal) | on (ʿalā) | each (kulli) | hill (jabalin) | of them (min'hunna) | a portion (juz'an); | then (thumma) | call them (udʿuhunna), | they will come to you (yatīnaka) | in haste (saʿyan). | And know (wa-iʿlam) | that (anna) | Allah (l-laha) | is All-Mighty (ʿazīzun), | All-Wise (ḥakīmun).

2:261 Example of those who spend their wealth in the way of Allah, is like a grain which grows seven ears, in each ear hundred grains. And Allah gives manifold to whom He wills. And Allah is All-Encompassing, All-Knowing.

Example (mathalu) | of those who (alladhīna) | spend (yunfiqūna) | their wealth (amwālahum) | in (fī) | the way (sabīli) | of Allah (l-lahi), | is like (kamathali) | a grain (ḥabbatin) | which grows (anbatat) | seven (sabʿa) | ears (sanābila), | in (fī) | each (kulli) | ear (sunbulatin) | hundred (mi-atu) | grains (ḥabbatin). | And Allah (wal-lahu) | gives manifold (yuḍāʿifu) | to whom (liman) | He wills (yashāu). | And Allah (wal-lahu) | is All-Encompassing (wāsiʿun), | All-Knowing (ʿalīmun).

2:262 Those who spend their wealth in the way of Allah then not they follow what they spend with reminders of generosity and not hurt - for them their reward is with their Lord, and there will be no fear on them and not they will grieve.

Those who (alladhīna) | spend (yunfiqūna) | their wealth (amwālahum) | in (fī) | the way (sabīli) | of Allah (l-lahi) | then (thumma) | not (lā) | they follow (yut'biʿūna) | what (mā) | they spend (anfaqū) | with reminders of generosity (mannan) | and not (walā) | hurt (adhan)- | for them (lahum) | their reward (ajruhum) | is with (ʿinda) | their Lord (rabbihim), | and there will be no (walā) | fear (khawfun) | on them (ʿalayhim) | and not (walā) | they (hum) | will grieve (yaḥzanūna).

2:263 A word kind and seeking forgiveness are better than a charity followed [it] by hurt. And Allah is All-Sufficient, All-Forbearing.

A word (qawlun) | kind (maʿrūfun) | and seeking forgiveness (wamaghfiratun) | are better (khayrun) | than (min) | a charity (ṣadaqatin) | followed [it] (yatbaʿuhā) | by hurt (adhan). | And Allah (wal-lahu) | is All-Sufficient (ghaniyyun), | All-Forbearing (ḥalīmun).

2:264 O you who believe[d]! Do not render in vain your charities with reminders of it or [the] hurt, like the one who spends his wealth to be seen by the people, and does not believe in Allah and the Day [the] Last. Then his example is like that of a smooth rock upon it is dust, then fell on it heavy rain, then left it bare. Not they have control on anything of what they have earned. And Allah does not guide the people [the] disbelieving.

O you (yāayyuhā) | who (alladhīna) | believe[d] (āmanū)! | Do not (lā) | render in vain (tub'ṭilū) | your charities (ṣadaqātikum) | with reminders of it (bil-mani) | or [the] hurt (wal-adhā), | like the one who (ka-alladhī) | spends (yunfiqu) | his wealth (mālahu) | to be seen (riāa) | by the people (l-nāsi), | and does not (walā) | believe (yu'minu) | in Allah (bil-lahi) | and the Day (wal-yawmi) | [the] Last (l-ākhiri). | Then his example (famathaluhu) | is like (kamathali) | that of a smooth rock (ṣafwānin) | upon it (ʿalayhi) | is dust (turābun), | then fell on it (fa-aṣābahu) | heavy rain (wābilun), | then left it (fatarakahu) | bare (ṣaldan). | Not (lā) | they have control (yaqdirūna) | on (ʿalā) | anything (shayin) | of what (mimmā) | they have earned (kasabū). | And Allah (wal-lahu) | does not (lā) | guide (yahdī) | the people (l-qawma) | [the] disbelieving (l-kāfirīna).

2:265 And the example of those who spend their wealth seeking the pleasure of Allah, and certainty from their inner souls, is like a garden on a height, fell on it heavy rain so it yielded its harvest double. Then if does not fall on it heavy rain, then a drizzle. And Allah of what you do is All-Seer.

And the example (wamathalu) | of those who (alladhīna) | spend (yunfiqūna) | their wealth (amwālahumu) | seeking (ib'tighāa) | the pleasure (marḍāti) | of Allah (l-lahi), | and certainty (watathbītan) | from (min) | their inner souls (anfusihim), | is like (kamathali) | a garden (jannatin) | on a height (birabwatin), | fell on it (aṣābahā) | heavy rain (wābilun) | so it yielded (faātat) | its harvest (ukulahā) | double (ḍiʿ'fayni). | Then if (fa-in) | does not (lam) | fall on it (yuṣib'hā) | heavy rain (wābilun), | then a drizzle (faṭallun). | And Allah (wal-lahu) | of what (bimā) | you do (taʿmalūna) | is All-Seer (baṣīrun).

2:266 Would like any of you that it be for him a garden, of date-palms and grapevines flowing [from] underneath it the rivers, for him in it of all kinds of [the] fruits, and strikes him [the] old age and [for] his children are weak then falls on it whirlwind, in it is fire then it is burnt. Thus makes clear Allah for you His Signs so that you may ponder.

Would like (ayawaddu) | any of you (aḥadukum) | that (an) | it be (takūna) | for him (lahu) | a garden (jannatun), | of (min) | date-palms (nakhīlin) | and grapevines (wa-aʿnābin) | flowing (tajrī) | [from] (min) | underneath it (taḥtihā) | the rivers (l-anhāru), | for him (lahu) | in it (fīhā) | of (min) | all kinds (kulli) | of [the] fruits (l-thamarāti), | and strikes him (wa-aṣābahu) | [the] old age (l-kibaru) | and [for] his (walahu) | children (dhurriyyatun) | are weak (ḍuʿafāu) | then falls on it (fa-aṣābahā) | whirlwind (iʿ'ṣārun), | in it (fīhi) | is fire (nārun) | then it is burnt (fa-iḥ'taraqat). | Thus (kadhālika) | makes clear (yubayyinu) | Allah (l-lahu) | for you (lakumu) | His Signs (l-āyāti) | so that you may (laʿallakum) | ponder (tatafakkarūna).

2:267 O you who believe[d]! Spend from the good things that you have earned and whatever We brought forth for you from the earth. And do not aim at the bad of it, you spend, while you would not take it except [that] with close(d) eyes [in it], and know that Allah is Self-Sufficient, Praiseworthy.

O you (yāayyuhā) | who (alladhīna) | believe[d] (āmanū)! | Spend (anfiqū) | from (min) | the good things (ṭayyibāti) | that (mā) | you have earned (kasabtum) | and whatever (wamimmā) | We brought forth (akhrajnā) | for you (lakum) | from (mina) | the earth (l-arḍi). | And do not (walā) | aim at (tayammamū) | the bad (l-khabītha) | of it (min'hu), | you spend (tunfiqūna), | while you would not (walastum) | take it (biākhidhīhi) | except (illā) | [that] (an) | with close(d) eyes (tugh'miḍū) | [in it] (fīhi), | and know (wa-iʿ'lamū) | that (anna) | Allah (l-laha) | is Self-Sufficient (ghaniyyun), | Praiseworthy (ḥamīdun).

2:268 The Shaitaan promises you [the] poverty and orders you to immorality, while Allah promises you forgiveness from Him and bounty. And Allah is All-Encompassing, All-Knowing.

The Shaitaan (al-shayṭānu) | promises you (yaʿidukumu) | [the] poverty (l-faqra) | and orders you (wayamurukum) | to immorality (bil-faḥshāi), | while Allah (wal-lahu) | promises you (yaʿidukum) | forgiveness (maghfiratan) | from Him (min'hu) | and bounty (wafaḍlan). | And Allah (wal-lahu) | is All-Encompassing (wāsiʿun), | All-Knowing (ʿalīmun).

2:269 He grants [the] wisdom to whom He wills, and whoever is granted [the] wisdom, then certainly he is granted good abundant. And none remembers except those of understanding.

He grants (yu'tī) | [the] wisdom (l-ḥik'mata) | to whom (man) | He wills (yashāu), | and whoever (waman) | is granted (yu'ta) | [the] wisdom (l-ḥik'mata), | then certainly (faqad) | he is granted (ūtiya) | good (khayran) | abundant (kathīran). | And none (wamā) | remembers (yadhakkaru) | except (illā) | those (ulū) | of understanding (l-albābi).

2:270 And whatever you spend out of your expenditures or you vow of vows, then indeed, Allah knows it, and not for the wrongdoers any helpers.

And whatever (wamā) | you spend (anfaqtum) | out of (min) | your expenditures (nafaqatin) | or (aw) | you vow (nadhartum) | of (min) | vows (nadhrin), | then indeed (fa-inna), | Allah (l-laha) | knows it (yaʿlamuhu), | and not (wamā) | for the wrongdoers (lilẓẓālimīna) | any (min) | helpers (anṣārin).

2:271 If you disclose the charities then good it is. But if you keep it secret and give it to the poor, then it is better for you. And He will remove from you [of] your evil deeds. And Allah with what you do is All-Aware.

If (in) | you disclose (tub'dū) | the charities (l-ṣadaqāti) | then good (faniʿimmā) | it is (hiya). | But if (wa-in) | you keep it secret (tukh'fūhā) | and give it (watu'tūhā) | to the poor (l-fuqarāa), | then it (fahuwa) | is better (khayrun) | for you (lakum). | And He will remove (wayukaffiru) | from you (ʿankum) | [of] (min) | your evil deeds (sayyiātikum). | And Allah (wal-lahu) | with what (bimā) | you do (taʿmalūna) | is All-Aware (khabīrun).

2:272 Not on you is their guidance [and] but Allah guides whom He wills. And whatever you spend of good then it is for yourself, and not you spend except seeking the face of Allah. And whatever you spend of good, will be repaid in full to you and you will not be wronged.

Not (laysa) | on you (ʿalayka) | is their guidance (hudāhum) | [and] but (walākinna) | Allah (l-laha) | guides (yahdī) | whom (man) | He wills (yashāu). | And whatever (wamā) | you spend (tunfiqū) | of (min) | good (khayrin) | then it is for yourself (fali-anfusikum), | and not (wamā) | you spend (tunfiqūna) | except (illā) | seeking (ib'tighāa) | the face (wajhi) | of Allah (l-lahi). | And whatever (wamā) | you spend (tunfiqū) | of (min) | good (khayrin), | will be repaid in full (yuwaffa) | to you (ilaykum) | and you (wa-antum) | will not (lā) | be wronged (tuẓ'lamūna).

2:273 For the poor, those who are wrapped up in the way of Allah, not they are able to move about in the earth. Think about them, the ignorant one, that they are self-sufficient because of their restraint, you recognize them by their mark. Not do they ask the people with importunity. And whatever you spend of good, then indeed, Allah of it is All-Knower.

For the poor (lil'fuqarāi), | those who (alladhīna) | are wrapped up (uḥ'ṣirū) | in (fī) | the way (sabīli) | of Allah (l-lahi), | not (lā) | they are able (yastaṭīʿūna) | to move about (ḍarban) | in (fī) | the earth (l-arḍi). | Think about them (yaḥsabuhumu), | the ignorant one (l-jāhilu), | that they are self-sufficient (aghniyāa) | because of (mina) | their restraint (l-taʿafufi), | you recognize them (taʿrifuhum) | by their mark (bisīmāhum). | Not (lā) | do they ask (yasalūna) | the people (l-nāsa) | with importunity (il'ḥāfan). | And whatever (wamā) | you spend (tunfiqū) | of (min) | good (khayrin), | then indeed (fa-inna), | Allah (l-laha) | of it (bihi) | is All-Knower (ʿalīmun).

2:274 Those who spend their wealth by night and day secretly and openly, then for them is their reward with their Lord, and no fear on them and not they will grieve.

Those who (alladhīna) | spend (yunfiqūna) | their wealth (amwālahum) | by night (bi-al-layli) | and day (wal-nahāri) | secretly (sirran) | and openly (waʿalāniyatan), | then for them (falahum) | is their reward (ajruhum) | with (ʿinda) | their Lord (rabbihim), | and no (walā) | fear (khawfun) | on them (ʿalayhim) | and not (walā) | they (hum) | will grieve (yaḥzanūna).

2:275 Those who consume [the] usury not they can stand except like stands the one who, confounds him the Shaitaan with his touch. That is because they say, "Only the trade is like [the] usury." While has permitted Allah [the] trade but has forbidden [the] usury. Then whoever - comes to him the admonition from His Lord and he refrained, then for him what has passed, and his case is with Allah, and whoever repeated then those are the companions of the Fire, they in it will abide forever.

Those who (alladhīna) | consume (yakulūna) | [the] usury (l-riba) | not (lā) | they can stand (yaqūmūna) | except (illā) | like (kamā) | stands (yaqūmu) | the one who (alladhī), | confounds him (yatakhabbaṭuhu) | the Shaitaan (l-shayṭānu) | with (mina) | his touch (l-masi). | That (dhālika) | is because they (bi-annahum) | say (qālū), | "Only (innamā) | the trade (l-bayʿu) | is like (mith'lu) | [the] usury. (l-riba)" | While has permitted (wa-aḥalla) | Allah (l-lahu) | [the] trade (l-bayʿa) | but has forbidden (waḥarrama) | [the] usury (l-riba). | Then whoever (faman)- | comes to him (jāahu) | the admonition (mawʿiẓatun) | from (min) | His Lord (rabbihi) | and he refrained (fa-intahā), | then for him (falahu) | what (mā) | has passed (salafa), | and his case (wa-amruhu) | is with (ilā) | Allah (l-lahi), | and whoever (waman) | repeated (ʿāda) | then those (fa-ulāika) | are the companions (aṣḥābu) | of the Fire (l-nāri), | they (hum) | in it (fīhā) | will abide forever (khālidūna).

2:276 Destroys Allah the usury and gives increase for the charities. And Allah does not love every ungrateful sinner.

Destroys (yamḥaqu) | Allah (l-lahu) | the usury (l-riba) | and gives increase (wayur'bī) | for the charities (l-ṣadaqāti). | And Allah (wal-lahu) | does not (lā) | love (yuḥibbu) | every (kulla) | ungrateful (kaffārin) | sinner (athīmin).

2:277 Indeed, those who believe[d] and did good deeds and established the prayer and gave the zakah for them - their reward is with their Lord, and no fear on them and not they will grieve.

Indeed (inna), | those who (alladhīna) | believe[d] (āmanū) | and did (waʿamilū) | good deeds (l-ṣāliḥāti) | and established (wa-aqāmū) | the prayer (l-ṣalata) | and gave (waātawū) | the zakah (l-zakata) | for them (lahum)- | their reward (ajruhum) | is with (ʿinda) | their Lord (rabbihim), | and no (walā) | fear (khawfun) | on them (ʿalayhim) | and not (walā) | they (hum) | will grieve (yaḥzanūna).

2:278 O you who believe[d]! Fear Allah and give up what remained of [the] usury, if you are believers.

O you (yāayyuhā) | who (alladhīna) | believe[d] (āmanū)! | Fear (ittaqū) | Allah (l-laha) | and give up (wadharū) | what (mā) | remained (baqiya) | of (mina) | [the] usury (l-riba), | if (in) | you are (kuntum) | believers (mu'minīna).

2:279 And if not you do, then be informed of a war from Allah and His Messenger. And if you repent then for you is your capital - do not wrong and not you will be wronged.

And if (fa-in) | not (lam) | you do (tafʿalū), | then be informed (fadhanū) | of a war (biḥarbin) | from (mina) | Allah (l-lahi) | and His Messenger (warasūlihi). | And if (wa-in) | you repent (tub'tum) | then for you (falakum) | is (ruūsu) | your capital (amwālikum)- | do not (lā) | wrong (taẓlimūna) | and not (walā) | you will be wronged (tuẓ'lamūna).

2:280 And if is the debtor in difficulty, then postponement until ease. And if you remit as charity it is better for you. If you know.

And if (wa-in) | is (kāna) | the debtor (dhū) | in difficulty (ʿus'ratin), | then postponement (fanaẓiratun) | until (ilā) | ease (maysaratin). | And if (wa-an) | you remit as charity (taṣaddaqū) | it is better (khayrun) | for you (lakum). | If (in) | you (kuntum) | know (taʿlamūna).

2:281 And fear a Day you will be brought back [in it] to Allah. Then will be repaid in full every soul what it earned and they not will be wronged.

And fear (wa-ittaqū) | a Day (yawman) | you will be brought back (tur'jaʿūna) | [in it] (fīhi) | to (ilā) | Allah (l-lahi). | Then (thumma) | will be repaid in full (tuwaffā) | every (kullu) | soul (nafsin) | what (mā) | it earned (kasabat) | and they (wahum) | not (lā) | will be wronged (yuẓ'lamūna).

2:282 O you who believe[d]! When you contract with one another any debt for a term fixed then write it. And let write between you a scribe in justice. And not should refuse a scribe that he writes as has taught him Allah. So let him write and let dictate the one on whom is the right and let him fear Allah, his Lord, and let him not diminish from it anything. Then if is the one on him is the right, of limited understanding, or weak, or not capable that can dictate he, then let dictate his guardian with justice. And call for evidence two witnesses among your men. And if not there are two men then one man and two women of whom you agree of [the] witnesses, so that (if) [she] errs, one of the two, then will remind one of the two the other. And not should refuse the witnesses when that they are called. And not be weary that you write it - small or large for its term. That is more just near Allah, and more upright for evidence and nearer that not you have doubt, except that be a transaction present, you carry out among you, then not on you any sin that not you write it. And take witness when you make commercial transaction. And not should be harmed the scribe and not the witness, and if you do, then indeed it is sinful conduct for you, and fear Allah. And teaches Allah. And Allah of every thing is All-Knower.

O you (yāayyuhā) | who (alladhīna) | believe[d] (āmanū)! | When (idhā) | you contract with one another (tadāyantum) | any debt (bidaynin) | for (ilā) | a term (ajalin) | fixed (musamman) | then write it (fa-uk'tubūhu). | And let write (walyaktub) | between you (baynakum) | a scribe (kātibun) | in justice (bil-ʿadli). | And not (walā) | should refuse (yaba) | a scribe (kātibun) | that (an) | he writes (yaktuba) | as (kamā) | has taught him (ʿallamahu) | Allah (l-lahu). | So let him write (falyaktub) | and let dictate (walyum'lili) | the one (alladhī) | on whom (ʿalayhi) | is the right (l-ḥaqu) | and let him fear (walyattaqi) | Allah (l-laha), | his Lord (rabbahu), | and let him not (walā) | diminish (yabkhas) | from it (min'hu) | anything (shayan). | Then if (fa-in) | is (kāna) | the one (alladhī) | on him (ʿalayhi) | is the right (l-ḥaqu), | of limited understanding (safīhan), | or (aw) | weak (ḍaʿīfan), | or (aw) | not (lā) | capable (yastaṭīʿu) | that (an) | can dictate (yumilla) | he (huwa), | then let dictate (falyum'lil) | his guardian (waliyyuhu) | with justice (bil-ʿadli). | And call for evidence (wa-is'tashhidū) | two witnesses (shahīdayni) | among (min) | your men (rijālikum). | And if (fa-in) | not (lam) | there are (yakūnā) | two men (rajulayni) | then one man (farajulun) | and two women (wa-im'ra-atāni) | of whom (mimman) | you agree (tarḍawna) | of (mina) | [the] witnesses (l-shuhadāi), | so that (if (an)) | [she] errs (taḍilla), | one of the two (iḥ'dāhumā), | then will remind (fatudhakkira) | one of the two (iḥ'dāhumā) | the other (l-ukh'rā). | And not (walā) | should refuse (yaba) | the witnesses (l-shuhadāu) | when (idhā) | that (mā) | they are called (duʿū). | And not (walā) | be weary (tasamū) | that (an) | you write it (taktubūhu)- | small (ṣaghīran) | or (aw) | large (kabīran) | for (ilā) | its term (ajalihi). | That (dhālikum) | is more just (aqsaṭu) | near (ʿinda) | Allah (l-lahi), | and more upright (wa-aqwamu) | for evidence (lilshahādati) | and nearer (wa-adnā) | that not (allā) | you have doubt (tartābū), | except (illā) | that (an) | be (takūna) | a transaction (tijāratan) | present (ḥāḍiratan), | you carry out (tudīrūnahā) | among you (baynakum), | then not (falaysa) | on you (ʿalaykum) | any sin (junāḥun) | that not (allā) | you write it (taktubūhā). | And take witness (wa-ashhidū) | when (idhā) | you make commercial transaction (tabāyaʿtum). | And not (walā) | should be harmed (yuḍārra) | the scribe (kātibun) | and not (walā) | the witness (shahīdun), | and if (wa-in) | you do (tafʿalū), | then indeed it (fa-innahu) | is sinful conduct (fusūqun) | for you (bikum), | and fear (wa-ittaqū) | Allah (l-laha). | And teaches (wayuʿallimukumu) | Allah (l-lahu). | And Allah (wal-lahu) | of every (bikulli) | thing (shayin) | is All-Knower (ʿalīmun).

2:283 And if you are on a journey and not you find a scribe, then pledge in hand. Then if entrusts one of you to another then let discharge the one who is entrusted his trust. And let him fear Allah, his Lord. And do not conceal the evidence. And whoever conceals it, then indeed he is sinful - his heart. And Allah of what you do is All-Knower.

And if (wa-in) | you are (kuntum) | on (ʿalā) | a journey (safarin) | and not (walam) | you find (tajidū) | a scribe (kātiban), | then pledge (farihānun) | in hand (maqbūḍatun). | Then if (fa-in) | entrusts (amina) | one of you (baʿḍukum) | to another (baʿḍan) | then let discharge (falyu-addi) | the one who (alladhī) | is entrusted (u'tumina) | his trust (amānatahu). | And let him fear (walyattaqi) | Allah (l-laha), | his Lord (rabbahu). | And do not (walā) | conceal (taktumū) | the evidence (l-shahādata). | And whoever (waman) | conceals it (yaktum'hā), | then indeed he (fa-innahu) | is sinful (āthimun)- | his heart (qalbuhu). | And Allah (wal-lahu) | of what (bimā) | you do (taʿmalūna) | is All-Knower (ʿalīmun).

2:284 To Allah belongs whatever is in the heavens and whatever is in the earth. And if you disclose what is in yourselves or you conceal it, will call you to account for it Allah. Then, He will forgive [to] whom He wills, and He will punish whom He wills. And Allah on every thing is All-Powerful.

To Allah belongs (lillahi) | whatever (mā) | is in (fī) | the heavens (l-samāwāti) | and whatever (wamā) | is in (fī) | the earth (l-arḍi). | And if (wa-in) | you disclose (tub'dū) | what (mā) | is in (fī) | yourselves (anfusikum) | or (aw) | you conceal it (tukh'fūhu), | will call you to account (yuḥāsib'kum) | for it (bihi) | Allah (l-lahu). | Then, He will forgive (fayaghfiru) | [to] whom (liman) | He wills (yashāu), | and He will punish (wayuʿadhibu) | whom (man) | He wills (yashāu). | And Allah (wal-lahu) | on (ʿalā) | every (kulli) | thing (shayin) | is All-Powerful (qadīrun).

2:285 Believed the Messenger in what was revealed to him from his Lord and the believers. All believed in Allah, and His Angels, and His Books, and His Messengers. "Not we make distinction between any of His messengers." And they said, "We heard and we obeyed. Grant us Your forgiveness our Lord, and to You is the return."

Believed (āmana) | the Messenger (l-rasūlu) | in what (bimā) | was revealed (unzila) | to him (ilayhi) | from (min) | his Lord (rabbihi) | and the believers (wal-mu'minūna). | All (kullun) | believed (āmana) | in Allah (bil-lahi), | and His Angels (wamalāikatihi), | and His Books (wakutubihi), | and His Messengers (warusulihi). | "Not (lā) | we make distinction (nufarriqu) | between (bayna) |

any (aḥadin) | of (min) | His messengers. (rusulihi)" | And they said (waqālū), | "We heard (samiʿnā) | and we obeyed (wa-aṭaʿnā). | Grant us Your forgiveness (ghuf'rānaka) | our Lord (rabbanā), | and to You (wa-ilayka) | is the return. (l-maṣīru)"

2:286 Does not burden Allah any soul except its capacity, for it what it earned, and against it what it earned. "Our Lord! Do not take us to task if we forget or we err. Our Lord! And do not lay upon us a burden like that which You laid [it] on those who were from before us. Our Lord! [And] do not lay on us what not the strength we have [of it] to bear. And pardon [from] us, and forgive [for] us and have mercy on us. You are our Protector, so help us against the people - [the] disbelievers.

Does not (lā) | burden (yukallifu) | Allah (l-lahu) | any soul (nafsan) | except (illā) | its capacity (wusʿahā), | for it (lahā) | what (mā) | it earned (kasabat), | and against it (waʿalayhā) | what (mā) | it earned (ik'tasabat). | "Our Lord (rabbanā)! | Do not (lā) | take us to task (tuākhidh'nā) | if (in) | we forget (nasīnā) | or (aw) | we err (akhṭanā). | Our Lord (rabbanā)! | And do not (walā) | lay (taḥmil) | upon us (ʿalaynā) | a burden (iṣ'ran) | like that (kamā) | which You laid [it] (ḥamaltahu) | on (ʿalā) | those who (alladhīna) | were from (min) | before us (qablinā). | Our Lord (rabbanā)! | [And] do not (walā) | lay on us (tuḥammil'nā) | what (mā) | not (lā) | the strength (ṭāqata) | we have (lanā) | [of it] to bear (bihi). | And pardon (wa-uʿfu) | [from] us (ʿannā), | and forgive (wa-igh'fir) | [for] us (lanā) | and have mercy on us (wa-ir'ḥamnā). | You are (anta) | our Protector (mawlānā), | so help us (fa-unṣur'nā) | against (ʿalā) | the people (l-qawmi)- | [the] disbelievers (l-kāfirīna).

Chapter (3) Sūrat āl ʿIm'rān (The Family of Imrān)

3:1 Alif Laam Meem

Alif Laam Meem (alif-lam-meem)

3:2 Allah - there is no God except Him, the Ever-Living the Sustainer of all that exists.

Allah (al-lahu)- | there is no (lā) | God (ilāha) | except (illā) | Him (huwa), | the Ever-Living (l-ḥayu) | the Sustainer of all that exists (l-qayūmu).

3:3 He revealed to you the Book in [the] truth confirming that which was before it, and He revealed the Taurat and the Injeel,

He revealed (nazzala) | to you (ʿalayka) | the Book (l-kitāba) | in [the] truth (bil-ḥaqi) | confirming (muṣaddiqan) | that which (limā) | was (bayna) | before it (yadayhi), | and He revealed (wa-anzala) | the Taurat (l-tawrāta) | and the Injeel (wal-injīla),

3:4 From before this, as guidance for the mankind. And He revealed the Criterion. Verily, those who disbelieve[d] in the Verses of Allah, for them is a punishment severe. And Allah is All-Mighty, All-Able of retribution.

From (min) | before this (qablu), | as guidance (hudan) | for the mankind (lilnnāsi). | And

He revealed (wa-anzala) | the Criterion (l-fur'qāna). | Verily (inna), | those who (alladhīna) | disbelieve[d] (kafarū) | in the Verses (biāyāti) | of Allah (l-lahi), | for them (lahum) | is a punishment (ʿadhābun) | severe (shadīdun). | And Allah (wal-lahu) | is All-Mighty (ʿazīzun), | All-Able (dhū) | of retribution (intiqāmin).

3:5 Indeed Allah - not is hidden from Him anything in the earth and not in the heaven.

Indeed (inna) | Allah (l-laha)- | not (lā) | is hidden (yakhfā) | from Him (ʿalayhi) | anything (shayon) | in (fī) | the earth (l-arḍi) | and not (walā) | in (fī) | the heaven (l-samāi).

3:6 He is the One Who shapes you in the wombs however He wills. There is no god except Him, the All-Mighty, the All-Wise.

He (huwa) | is the One Who (alladhī) | shapes you (yuṣawwirukum) | in (fī) | the wombs (l-arḥāmi) | however (kayfa) | He wills (yashāu). | There is no (lā) | god (ilāha) | except (illā) | Him (huwa), | the All-Mighty (l-ʿazīzu), | the All-Wise (l-ḥakīmu).

3:7 He is the One Who revealed to you the Book, of it are Verses absolutely clear - they are the foundation of the Book, and others are allegorical. Then as for those in their hearts is perversity - [so] they follow what is allegorical of it, seeking [the] discord and seeking its interpretation. And not knows its interpretation except Allah. And those firm in [the] knowledge, they say, "We believe in it. All is from our Lord." And not will take heed except men of understanding.

He (huwa) | is the One Who (alladhī) | revealed (anzala) | to you (ʿalayka) | the Book (l-kitāba), | of it (min'hu) | are Verses (āyātun) | absolutely clear (muḥ'kamātun)- | they are (hunna) | the foundation (ummu) | of the Book (l-kitābi), | and others (wa-ukharu) | are allegorical (mutashābihātun). | Then as for (fa-ammā) | those (alladhīna) | in (fī) | their hearts (qulūbihim) | is perversity (zayghun)- | [so] they follow (fayattabiʿūna) | what (mā) | is allegorical (tashābaha) | of it (min'hu), | seeking (ib'tighāa) | [the] discord (l-fit'nati) | and seeking (wa-ib'tighāa) | its interpretation (tawīlihi). | And not (wamā) | knows (yaʿlamu) | its interpretation (tawīlahu) | except (illā) | Allah (l-lahu). | And those firm (wal-rāsikhūna) | in (fī) | [the] knowledge (l-ʿil'mi), | they say (yaqūlūna), | "We believe (āmannā) | in it (bihi). | All (kullun) | is (min) | from (ʿindi) | our Lord. (rabbinā)" | And not (wamā) | will take heed (yadhakkaru) | except (illā) | men (ulū) | of understanding (l-albābi).

3:8 "Our Lord! Do not deviate our hearts after [when] You have guided us, and grant for us from Yourself mercy. Indeed You, You are the Bestower.

"Our Lord (rabbanā)! | Do not (lā) | deviate (tuzigh) | our hearts (qulūbanā) | after (baʿda) | [when] (idh) | You have guided us (hadaytanā), | and grant (wahab) | for us (lanā) | from (min) | Yourself (ladunka) | mercy (raḥmatan). | Indeed You (innaka), | You (anta) | are the Bestower (l-wahābu).

3:9 Our Lord! Indeed, You will gather [the] mankind on a Day, there is no doubt in it. Indeed, Allah does not break the Promise."

Our Lord (rabbanā)! | Indeed, You (innaka) | will gather (jāmiʿu) | [the] mankind (l-nāsi) | on a Day (liyawmin), | there is no (lā) | doubt (rayba) | in it (fīhi). | Indeed (inna), | Allah (l-laha) | does not (lā) | break (yukh'lifu) | the Promise. (l-mīʿāda)"

3:10 Indeed, those who disbelieve[d] never will avail [for] them their wealth and not their children against Allah anything, and those - they are the fuel for the Fire.

Indeed (inna), | those who (alladhīna) | disbelieve[d] (kafarū) | never (lan) | will avail (tugh'niya) | [for] them (ʿanhum) | their wealth (amwāluhum) | and not (walā) | their children (awlāduhum) | against (mina) | Allah (l-lahi) | anything (shayan), | and those (wa-ulāika)- | they are (hum) | the fuel (waqūdu) | for the Fire (l-nāri).

3:11 Like behavior of the people of Firaun and those who were from before them. They denied Our Signs, so seized them Allah for their sins. And Allah is severe in [the] punishment.

Like behavior (kadabi) | of the people (āli) | of Firaun (fir''awna) | and those who (wa-alladhīna) | were from (min) | before them (qablihim). | They denied (kadhabū) | Our Signs (biāyātinā), | so seized them (fa-akhadhahumu) | Allah (l-lahu) | for their sins (bidhunūbihim). | And Allah (wal-lahu) | is severe (shadīdu) | in [the] punishment (l-ʿiqābi).

3:12 Say to those who disbelieve[d], "You will be overcome and you will be gathered to Hell, [and] an evil [the] resting place.

Say (qul) | to those who (lilladhīna) | disbelieve[d] (kafarū), | "You will be overcome (satugh'labūna) | and you will be gathered (watuḥ'sharūna) | to (ilā) | Hell (jahannama), | [and] an evil (wabi'sa) | [the] resting place (l-mihādu).

3:13 Surely it was for you a sign in the two hosts which met - one group fighting in the way of Allah and another disbelievers. They were seeing them twice of them with the sight of their eyes. And Allah supports with His help whom He wills. Indeed, in that surely is a lesson for the owners of vision.

Surely (qad) | it was (kāna) | for you (lakum) | a sign (āyatun) | in (fī) | the two hosts (fi-atayni) | which met (l-taqatā)- | one group (fi-atun) | fighting (tuqātilu) | in (fī) | the way (sabīli) | of Allah (l-lahi) | and another (wa-ukh'rā) | disbelievers (kāfiratun). | They were seeing them (yarawnahum) | twice of them (mith'layhim) | with the sight (raya) | of their eyes (l-ʿayni). | And Allah (wal-lahu) | supports (yu-ayyidu) | with His help (binaṣrihi) | whom (man) | He wills (yashāu). | Indeed (inna), | in (fī) | that (dhālika) | surely is a lesson (laʿib'ratan) | for the owners (li-ulī) | of vision (l-abṣāri).

3:14 Beautified for mankind is love of the (things they) desire - of [the] women and [the] sons and [the] heaps [the] stored up of [the] gold and [the] silver, and [the] horses [the] branded, and [the] cattle and [the] tilled land. That is provision of life of the world but Allah - with Him is an excellent [the] abode to return.

Beautified (zuyyina) | for mankind (lilnnāsi) | is love (ḥubbu) | of the (things they) desire (l-shahawāti)- | of (mina) | [the] women (l-nisāi) | and [the] sons (wal-banīna) | and [the] heaps (wal-qanāṭīri) | [the] stored up (l-muqanṭarati) | of (mina) | [the] gold (l-dhahabi) | and [the] silver (wal-fiḍati), | and [the] horses (wal-khayli) | [the] branded (l-musawamati), | and [the] cattle (wal-anʿāmi) | and [the] tilled land (wal-ḥarthi). | That (dhālika) | is provision (matāʿu) | of life (l-ḥayati) | of the world (l-dun'yā) | but Allah (wal-lahu)- | with Him (ʿindahu) | is an excellent (ḥus'nu) | [the] abode to return (l-maābi).

3:15 Say, "Shall I inform you of better than that. For those who fear[ed], with their Lord, are Gardens flows from underneath them [the] rivers - abiding forever in it, and spouses pure and approval from Allah. And Allah is All-Seer of His slaves."

Say (qul), | "Shall I inform you (a-unabbi-ukum) | of better (bikhayrin) | than (min) | that (dhālikum). | For those who (lilladhīna) | fear[ed] (ittaqaw), | with (ʿinda) | their Lord (rabbihim), | are Gardens (jannātun) | flows (tajrī) | from (min) | underneath them (taḥtihā) | [the] rivers (l-anhāru)- | abiding forever (khālidīna) | in it (fīhā), | and spouses (wa-azwājun) | pure (muṭahharatun) | and approval (wariḍ'wānun) | from (mina) | Allah (l-lahi). | And Allah (wal-lahu) | is All-Seer (baṣīrun) | of His slaves. (bil-ʿibādi)"

3:16 Those who say, "Our Lord! Indeed, we have believed, so forgive for us our sins and save us from punishment of the Fire."

Those who (alladhīna) | say (yaqūlūna), | "Our Lord (rabbanā)! | Indeed, we (innanā) | have believed (āmannā), | so forgive (fa-igh'fir) | for us (lanā) | our sins (dhunūbanā) | and save us (waqinā) | from punishment (ʿadhāba) | of the Fire. (l-nāri)"

3:17 The patient and the truthful and the obedient and those who spend and those who seek forgiveness [in the] before dawn.

The patient (al-ṣābirīna) | and the truthful (wal-ṣādiqīna) | and the obedient (wal-qānitīna) | and those who spend (wal-munfiqīna) | and those who seek forgiveness (wal-mus'taghfirīna) | [in the] before dawn (bil-asḥāri).

3:18 Bears witness Allah that [He], there is no god except Him, and so do the Angels, and owners of [the] knowledge - standing in justice. There is no god except Him the All-Mighty, the All-Wise.

Bears witness (shahida) | Allah (l-lahu) | that [He] (annahu), | there is no (lā) | god (ilāha) | except (illā) | Him (huwa), | and so do the Angels (wal-malāikatu), | and owners (wa-ulū) | of [the] knowledge (l-ʿil'mi)- | standing (qāiman) | in justice (bil-qis'ṭi). | There is no (lā) | god (ilāha) | except (illā) | Him (huwa) | the All-Mighty (l-ʿazīzu), | the All-Wise (l-ḥakīmu).

3:19 Indeed, the religion near Allah is Islam. And not differed those who were given the Book except from after [what] came to them [the] knowledge out of envy among them. And whoever disbelieves in the Verses of Allah, then indeed, Allah is swift in taking account.

Indeed (inna), | the religion (l-dīna) | near (ʿinda) | Allah (l-lahi) | is Islam (l-is'lāmu). | And not (wamā) | differed (ikh'talafa) | those who (alladhīna) | were given (ūtū) | the Book (l-kitāba) | except (illā) | from (min) | after (baʿdi) | [what] (mā) | came to them (jāahumu) | [the] knowledge (l-ʿil'mu) | out of envy (baghyan) | among them (baynahum). | And whoever (waman) | disbelieves (yakfur) | in the Verses (biāyāti) | of Allah (l-lahi), | then indeed (fa-inna), | Allah (l-laha) | is swift (sarīʿu) | in taking account (l-ḥisābi).

3:20 Then if they argue with you, then say, "I have submitted myself to Allah and those who follow me." And say to those who were given the Book, and the unlettered people, "Have you submitted yourselves?" Then if they submit then surely they are guided. But if they turn back then only on you is to [the] convey. And Allah is All-Seer of [His] slaves.

Then if (fa-in) | they argue with you (ḥājjūka), | then say (faqul), | "I have submitted (aslamtu) | myself (wajhiya) | to Allah (lillahi) | and those who (wamani) | follow me. (ittabaʿani)" | And say (waqul) | to those who (lilladhīna) | were given (ūtū) | the Book (l-kitāba), | and the unlettered people (wal-umiyīna), | "Have you submitted yourselves? (a-aslamtum)" | Then if (fa-in) | they submit (aslamū) | then surely (faqadi) | they are guided (ih'tadaw). | But if (wa-in) | they turn back (tawallaw) | then only (fa-innamā) | on you (ʿalayka) | is to [the] convey (l-balāghu). | And Allah (wal-lahu) | is All-Seer (baṣīrun) | of [His] slaves (bil-ʿibādi).

3:21 Indeed, those who disbelieve in the Signs (of) Allah and they kill the Prophets without right and they kill those who order [with] justice among the people, then give them tidings of a punishment painful.

Indeed (inna), | those who (alladhīna) | disbelieve (yakfurūna) | in the Signs (of (biāyāti)) | Allah (l-lahi) | and they kill (wayaqtulūna) | the Prophets (l-nabiyīna) | without (bighayri) | right (ḥaqqin) | and they kill (wayaqtulūna) | those who (alladhīna) | order (yamurūna) | [with] justice (bil-qis'ṭi) | among (mina) | the people (l-nāsi), | then give them tidings (fabashir'hum) | of a punishment (biʿadhābin) | painful (alīmin).

3:22 Those are the ones who - became worthless their deeds in the world and in the Hereafter. And not will be for them any helpers.

Those (ulāika) | are the ones who (alladhīna)- | became worthless (ḥabiṭat) | their deeds (aʿmāluhum) | in (fī) | the world (l-dun'yā) | and in the Hereafter (wal-ākhirati). | And not (wamā) | will be for them (lahum) | any (min) | helpers (nāṣirīna).

3:23 Have not you seen [to] those who were given a portion of the Scripture? They are invited to the Book of Allah that it should arbitrate between them, then turns away a party of them and they are those who are averse.

Have not (alam) | you seen (tara) | [to] (ilā) | those who (alladhīna) | were given (ūtū) | a portion (naṣīban) | of (mina) | the Scripture (l-kitābi)? | They are invited (yud''awna) | to (ilā) | the Book (kitābi) | of Allah (l-lahi) | that it should arbitrate (liyaḥkuma) | between them (baynahum), | then (thumma) | turns away (yatawallā) | a party (farīqun) | of them (min'hum) | and they are (wahum) | those who are averse (mu''riḍūna).

3:24 That is because they say, "Never will touch us the Fire except for days numbered." And deceived them in their religion what they were inventing.

That (dhālika) | is because they (bi-annahum) | say (qālū), | "Never (lan) | will touch us (tamassanā) | the Fire (l-nāru) | except (illā) | for days (ayyāman) | numbered. (maʿdūdātin)" | And deceived them (wagharrahum) | in (fī) | their religion (dīnihim) | what (mā) | they were (kānū) | inventing (yaftarūna).

3:25 Then how will it be when We will gather them on a Day - no doubt in it. And will be paid in full every soul what it earned and they will not be wronged.

Then how will it be (fakayfa) | when (idhā) | We will gather them (jamaʿnāhum) | on a Day (liyawmin)- | no (lā) | doubt (rayba) | in it (fīhi). | And will be paid in full (wawuffiyat) | every (kullu) | soul (nafsin) | what (mā) | it earned (kasabat) | and they (wahum) | will not (lā) | be wronged (yuẓ'lamūna).

3:26 Say "O Allah! Owner of the Dominion, You give the dominion to whom You will and You take away the dominion from whom You will, and You honor whom You will, and You humiliate whom You will. In Your hand is all the good. Indeed, You are on every thing All-Powerful.

Say (quli) | "O Allah (l-lahuma)! | Owner (mālika) | of the Dominion (l-mul'ki), | You give (tu'tī) | the dominion (l-mul'ka) | to whom (man) | You will (tashāu) | and You take away (watanziʿu) | the dominion (l-mul'ka) | from whom (mimman) | You will (tashāu), | and You honor (watuʿizzu) | whom (man) | You will (tashāu), | and You humiliate (watudhillu) | whom (man) | You will (tashāu). | In Your hand (biyadika) | is all the good (l-khayru). | Indeed, You (innaka) | are on (ʿalā) | every (kulli) | thing (shayin) | All-Powerful (qadīrun).

3:27 You cause to enter the night in the day and You cause to enter the day in the night, and You bring forth the living from the dead, and You bring forth the dead from the living, and You give provision to whom You will without measure."

You cause to enter (tūliju) | the night (al-layla) | in (fī) | the day (l-nahāri) | and You cause to enter (watūliju) | the day (l-nahāra) | in (fī) | the night (al-layli), | and You bring forth (watukh'riju) | the living (l-ḥaya) | from (mina) | the dead (l-mayiti), | and You bring forth (watukh'riju) | the dead (l-mayita) | from (mina) | the living (l-ḥayi), | and You give provision (watarzuqu) | to whom (man) | You will (tashāu) | without (bighayri) | measure. (ḥisābin)"

3:28 Let not take the believers, the disbelievers as allies from instead of the believers. And whoever does that, then not he has from Allah in anything except that you fear from them, as a precaution. And warns you Allah of Himself, and to Allah is the final return.

Let not (lā) | take (yattakhidhi) | the believers (l-mu'minūna), | the disbelievers (l-kāfirīna) | as allies (awliyāa) | from (min) | instead of (dūni) | the believers (l-mu'minīna). | And whoever (waman) | does (yafʿal) | that (dhālika), | then not he has (falaysa) | from (mina) | Allah (l-lahi) | in (fī) | anything (shayin) | except (illā) | that (an) | you fear (tattaqū) | from them (min'hum), | as a precaution (tuqātan). | And warns you (wayuḥadhirukumu) | Allah (l-lahu) | of Himself (nafsahu), | and to (wa-ilā) | Allah (l-lahi) | is the final return (l-maṣīru).

3:29 Say, "Whether you conceal what is in your breasts or you disclose it - knows it Allah. And He knows what is in the heavens and what is in the earth. And Allah is on every thing All-Powerful."

Say (qul), | "Whether (in) | you conceal (tukh'fū) | what (mā) | is in (fī) | your breasts (ṣudūrikum) | or (aw) | you disclose it (tub'dūhu)- | knows it (yaʿlamhu) | Allah (l-lahu). | And He knows (wayaʿlamu) | what (mā) | is in (fī) | the heavens (l-samāwāti) | and what (wamā) | is in (fī) | the earth (l-arḍi). | And Allah (wal-lahu) | is on (ʿalā) | every (kulli) | thing (shayin) | All-Powerful. (qadīrun)"

3:30 On the day will find every soul what it did of good - presented, and what it did of evil, it will wish [if] that between itself and between it evil was a distance great. And warns you Allah against Himself, and Allah is Most Kind to His [the] slaves.

On the day (yawma) | will find (tajidu) | every (kullu) | soul (nafsin) | what (mā) | it did (ʿamilat) | of (min) | good (khayrin)- | presented (muḥ'ḍaran), | and what (wamā) | it did (ʿamilat) | of (min) | evil (sūin), | it will wish (tawaddu) | [if] (law) | that (anna) | between itself (baynahā) | and between it evil (wabaynahu) | was a distance (amadan) | great (baʿīdan). | And warns you (wayuḥadhirukumu) | Allah (l-lahu) | against Himself (nafsahu), | and Allah (wal-lahu) | is Most Kind (raūfun) | to His [the] slaves (bil-ʿibādi).

3:31 Say, "If you love Allah, then follow me, will love you Allah and He will forgive for you your sins. And Allah is Oft-Forgiving, Most Merciful.

Say (qul), | "If (in) | you (kuntum) | love (tuḥibbūna) | Allah (l-laha), | then follow me (fa-ittabiʿūnī), | will love you (yuḥ'bib'kumu) | Allah (l-lahu) | and He will forgive (wayaghfir) | for you (lakum) | your sins (dhunūbakum). | And Allah (wal-lahu) | is Oft-Forgiving (ghafūrun), | Most Merciful (raḥīmun).

3:32 Say, "Obey Allah and the Messenger." Then if they turn away - then indeed, Allah does not love the disbelievers.

Say (qul), | "Obey (aṭīʿū) | Allah (l-laha) | and the Messenger. (wal-rasūla)" | Then if (fa-in) | they turn away (tawallaw)- | then indeed (fa-inna), | Allah (l-laha) | does not (lā) | love (yuḥibbu) | the disbelievers (l-kāfirīna).

3:33 Indeed, Allah chose Adam and Nuh, and the family of Ibrahim and the family of Imran over the worlds.

Indeed (inna), | Allah (l-laha) | chose (iṣ'ṭafā) | Adam (ādama) | and Nuh (wanūḥan), | and the family (waāla) | of Ibrahim (ib'rāhīma) | and the family (waāla) | of Imran (ʿim'rāna) | over (ʿalā) | the worlds (l-ʿālamīna).

3:34 Descendents, some of them from others. And Allah is All-Hearing, All-Knowing.

Descendents (dhurriyyatan), | some of them (baʿḍuhā) | from (min) | others (baʿḍin). | And Allah (wal-lahu) | is All-Hearing (samīʿun), | All-Knowing (ʿalīmun).

3:35 When [she] said the wife of Imran, "My Lord! Indeed, I [I] vowed to You what is in my womb, dedicated, so accept from me. Indeed, You, You are the All-Hearing, the All-Knowing.

When (idh) | [she] said (qālati) | the wife (im'ra-atu) | of Imran (ʿim'rāna), | "My Lord (rabbi)! | Indeed, I (innī) | [I] vowed (nadhartu) | to You (laka) | what (mā) | is in (fī) | my womb (baṭnī), | dedicated (muḥarraran), | so accept (fataqabbal) | from me (minnī). | Indeed, You (innaka), | You (anta) | are the All-Hearing (l-samīʿu), | the All-Knowing (l-ʿalīmu).

3:36 Then when she delivered her, she said, "My Lord, indeed I [I] have delivered [her] a female." And Allah knows better [of] what she delivered, and is not the male like the female. "And that I [I] have named her Maryam and that I [I] seek refuge for her in You and her offspring from the Shaitaan the rejected."

Then when (falammā) | she delivered her (waḍaʿathā), | she said (qālat), | "My Lord (rabbi), | indeed I (innī) | [I] have delivered [her] (waḍaʿtuhā) | a female. (unthā)" | And Allah (wal-lahu) | knows better (aʿlamu) | [of] what (bimā) | she delivered (waḍaʿat), | and is not (walaysa) | the male (l-dhakaru) | like the female (kal-unthā). | "And that I (wa-innī) | [I] have named her (sammaytuhā) | Maryam (maryama) | and that I (wa-innī) | [I] seek refuge for her (uʿīdhuhā) | in You (bika) | and her offspring (wadhurriyyatahā) | from (mina) | the Shaitaan (l-shayṭāni) | the rejected. (l-rajīmi)"

3:37 So accepted her, her Lord with acceptance good, and reared her - a rearing good, and put her in the care of Zakariya. Whenever entered upon her Zakariya [the] prayer chamber he found with her provision. He said, "O Maryam! From where for you is this?" She said, "This is from Allah. Indeed, Allah gives provision to whom He wills without measure."

So accepted her (fataqabbalahā), | her Lord (rabbuhā) | with acceptance (biqabūlin) | good (ḥasanin), | and reared her (wa-anbatahā)- | a rearing (nabātan) | good (ḥasanan), | and put her in the care (wakaffalahā) | of Zakariya (zakariyyā). | Whenever (kullamā) | entered (dakhala) | upon her (ʿalayhā) | Zakariya (zakariyyā) | [the] prayer chamber (l-miḥ'rāba) | he found (wajada) | with her (ʿindahā) | provision (riz'qan). | He said (qāla), | "O Maryam (yāmaryamu)! | From where (annā) | for you (laki) | is this? (hādhā)" | She said (qālat), | "This (huwa) | is (min) | from (ʿindi) | Allah (l-lahi). | Indeed (inna), | Allah (l-laha) | gives provision (yarzuqu) | to whom (man) | He wills (yashāu) | without (bighayri) | measure. (ḥisābin)"

3:38 There only, invoked Zakariya his Lord, he said, "My Lord grant [for] me from Yourself offspring pure. Indeed, You are All-Hearer of the prayer

There only (hunālika), | invoked (daʿā) | Zakariya (zakariyyā) | his Lord (rabbahu), | he said (qāla), | "My Lord (rabbi) | grant (hab) | [for] me (lī) | from (min) | Yourself (ladunka) | offspring (dhurriyyatan) | pure (ṭayyibatan). | Indeed, You (innaka) | are All-Hearer (samīʿu) | of the prayer (l-duʿāi)

3:39 Then called him the Angels when he was standing - praying in the prayer chamber. "Indeed, Allah gives you glad tidings of Yahya, confirming [of] a Word from Allah and a noble and chaste and a Prophet among the righteous.

Then called him (fanādathu) | the Angels (l-malāikatu) | when he (wahuwa) | was standing (qāimun)- | praying (yuṣallī) | in (fī) | the prayer chamber (l-miḥ'rābi). | "Indeed (anna), | Allah (l-laha) | gives you glad tidings (yubashiruka) | of Yahya (biyaḥyā), | confirming (muṣaddiqan) | [of] a Word (bikalimatin) | from (mina) | Allah (l-lahi) | and a noble (wasayyidan) | and chaste (waḥaṣūran) | and a Prophet (wanabiyyan) | among (mina) | the righteous (l-ṣāliḥīna).

3:40 He said, "My Lord how can there be for me a son, and verily has reached me [the] old age and my wife is [a] barren?" He said, "Thus; Allah does what He wills."

He said (qāla), | "My Lord (rabbi) | how (annā) | can there be (yakūnu) | for me (lī) | a son (ghulāmun), | and verily (waqad) | has reached me (balaghaniya) | [the] old age (l-kibaru) | and my wife (wa-im'ra-atī) | is [a] barren? (ʿāqirun)" | He said (qāla), | "Thus (kadhālika); | Allah (l-lahu) | does (yafʿalu) | what (mā) | He wills. (yashāu)"

3:41 He said, "My Lord make for me a sign." He said, your sign is that not you will speak to the people for three days except with gestures. And remember your Lord much, and glorify Him in the evening and in the morning."

He said (qāla), | "My Lord (rabbi) | make (ij'ʿal) | for me (lī) | a sign. (āyatan)" | He said (qāla), | your sign (āyatuka) | is that not (allā) | you will speak (tukallima) | to the people (l-nāsa) | for three (thalāthata) | days (ayyāmin) | except (illā) | with gestures (ramzan). | And remember (wa-udh'kur) | your Lord (rabbaka) | much (kathīran), | and glorify Him (wasabbiḥ) | in the evening (bil-ʿashiyi) | and in the morning. (wal-ib'kāri)"

3:42 And when said the Angels, "O Maryam! Indeed, Allah has chosen you and purified you and chosen you over the women of the worlds."

And when (wa-idh) | said (qālati) | the Angels (l-malāikatu), | "O Maryam (yāmaryamu)! | Indeed (inna), | Allah (l-laha) | has chosen you (iṣ'ṭafāki) | and purified you (waṭahharaki) | and chosen you (wa-iṣ'ṭafāki) | over (ʿalā) | the women (nisāi) | of the worlds. (l-ʿālamīna)"

3:43 "O Maryam! Be obedient to your Lord and prostrate and bow down with those who bow down."

"O Maryam (yāmaryamu)! | Be obedient (uq'nutī) | to your Lord (lirabbiki) | and prostrate (wa-us'judī) | and bow down (wa-ir'kaʿī) | with (maʿa) | those who bow down. (l-rākiʿīna)"

3:44 That is from the news of the unseen - We reveal it to you. And not you were with them when they cast their pens as to which of them takes charge of Maryam; and not you were with them when they were disputing.

That (dhālika) | is from (min) | the news (anbāi) | of the unseen (l-ghaybi)- | We reveal it (nūḥīhi) | to you (ilayka). | And not (wamā) | you were (kunta) | with them (ladayhim) | when (idh) | they cast (yul'qūna) | their pens (aqlāmahum) | as to which of them (ayyuhum) | takes charge of (yakfulu) | Maryam (maryama); | and not (wamā) | you were (kunta) | with them (ladayhim) | when (idh) | they were disputing (yakhtaṣimūna).

3:45 When said the Angels, "O Maryam! Indeed, Allah gives you glad tidings of a word from Him, his name is the Messiah, Isa, son of Maryam, honored in the world and in the Hereafter, and of those brought near to Allah.

When (idh) | said (qālati) | the Angels (l-malāikatu), | "O Maryam (yāmaryamu)! | Indeed (inna), | Allah (l-laha) | gives you glad tidings (yubashiruki) | of a word (bikalimatin) | from Him (min'hu), | his name (us'muhu) | is the Messiah (l-masīḥu), | Isa (ʿīsā), | son (ub'nu) | of Maryam (maryama), | honored (wajīhan) | in (fī) | the world (l-dun'yā) | and in the Hereafter (wal-ākhirati), | and of (wamina) | those brought near to Allah (l-muqarabīna).

3:46 And he will speak to the people in the cradle and in maturity; and he will be of the righteous."

And he will speak (wayukallimu) | to the people (l-nāsa) | in (fī) | the cradle (l-mahdi) | and in maturity (wakahlan); | and he will be of (wamina) | the righteous. (l-ṣāliḥīna)"

3:47 She said, "My Lord how is [it] for me a boy, and has not touched me any man?" He said, "Thus Allah creates what He wills. When He decrees a matter then only He says to it, "Be," and it becomes.

She said (qālat), | "My Lord (rabbi) | how (annā) | is [it] (yakūnu) | for me (lī) | a boy (waladun), | and has not (walam) | touched me (yamsasnī) | any man? (basharun)" | He said (qāla), | "Thus (kadhāliki) | Allah (l-lahu) | creates (yakhluqu) | what (mā) | He wills (yashāu). | When (idhā) | He decrees (qaḍā) | a matter (amran) | then only (fa-innamā) | He says (yaqūlu) | to it (lahu), | "Be, (kun)" | and it becomes (fayakūnu).

3:48 And He will teach him the Book, and [the] wisdom, and the Taurat, and the Injeel.

And He will teach him (wayuʿallimuhu) | the Book (l-kitāba), | and [the] wisdom (wal-ḥik'mata), | and the Taurat (wal-tawrāta), | and the Injeel (wal-injīla).

3:49 And make him a Messenger to the Children of Israel, "Indeed, I [surely] [I] have come (to) you with a sign from your Lord that I [I] design for you from [the] clay like the form of the bird, then I breath into it and it becomes a bird by the permission of Allah. And I cure the blind, and the leper, and I give life to the dead by the permission of Allah. And I inform you of what you eat and what you store in your houses. Indeed, in that is surely a sign for you, if you are believers.

And make him a Messenger (warasūlan) | to (ilā) | the Children (banī) | of Israel (is'rāīla), |

"Indeed, I (annī) | [surely] (qad) | [I] have come (to) you (ji'tukum) | with a sign (biāyatin) | from (min) | your Lord (rabbikum) | that I (annī) | [I] design (akhluqu) | for you (lakum) | from (mina) | [the] clay (l-ṭīni) | like the form (kahayati) | of the bird (l-ṭayri), | then I breath (fa-anfukhu) | into it (fīhi) | and it becomes (fayakūnu) | a bird (ṭayran) | by the permission (bi-idh'ni) | of Allah (l-lahi). | And I cure (wa-ub'ri-u) | the blind (l-akmaha), | and the leper (wal-abraṣa), | and I give life (wa-uḥ'yī) | to the dead (l-mawtā) | by the permission (bi-idh'ni) | of Allah (l-lahi). | And I inform you (wa-unabbi-ukum) | of what (bimā) | you eat (takulūna) | and what (wamā) | you store (taddakhirūna) | in (fī) | your houses (buyūtikum). | Indeed (inna), | in (fī) | that (dhālika) | is surely a sign (laāyatan) | for you (lakum), | if (in) | you are (kuntum) | believers (mu'minīna).

3:50 And confirming that which was before me of the Taurat, and so that I make lawful for you some of that which was forbidden to you. And I have come to you with a sign from your Lord. So fear Allah and obey me.

And confirming (wamuṣaddiqan) | that which (limā) | was (bayna) | before me (yadayya) | of (mina) | the Taurat (l-tawrāti), | and so that I make lawful (wali-uḥilla) | for you (lakum) | some (baʿḍa) | of that which (alladhī) | was forbidden (ḥurrima) | to you (ʿalaykum). | And I have come to you (waji'tukum) | with a sign (biāyatin) | from (min) | your Lord (rabbikum). | So fear (fa-ittaqū) | Allah (l-laha) | and obey me (wa-aṭīʿūni).

3:51 Indeed, Allah is my Lord and your Lord, so worship Him. This is the path straight."

Indeed (inna), | Allah (l-laha) | is my Lord (rabbī) | and your Lord (warabbukum), | so worship Him (fa-uʿ'budūhu). | This (hādhā) | is the path (ṣirāṭun) | straight. (mus'taqīmun)"

3:52 Then when perceived Isa from them [the] disbelief he said, "Who will be my helpers to Allah." Said the disciples "We will be the helpers of Allah, we believe[d] in Allah and bear witness that we are Muslims.

Then when (falammā) | perceived (aḥassa) | Isa (ʿīsā) | from them (min'humu) | [the] disbelief (l-kuf'ra) | he said (qāla), | "Who (man) | will be my helpers (anṣārī) | to (ilā) | Allah. (l-lahi)" | Said (qāla) | the disciples (l-ḥawāriyūna) | "We (naḥnu) | will be the helpers (anṣāru) | of Allah (l-lahi), | we believe[d] (āmannā) | in Allah (bil-lahi) | and bear witness (wa-ish'had) | that we (bi-annā) | are Muslims (mus'limūna).

3:53 Our Lord, we believe[d] in what You revealed and we follow[ed] the Messenger, then write us among the witnesses."

Our Lord (rabbanā), | we believe[d] (āmannā) | in what (bimā) | You revealed (anzalta) | and we follow[ed] (wa-ittabaʿnā) | the Messenger (l-rasūla), | then write us (fa-uk'tub'nā) | among (maʿa) | the witnesses. (l-shāhidīna)"

3:54 And they schemed, and planned Allah. And Allah is the best of the planners.

And they schemed (wamakarū), | and planned (wamakara) | Allah (l-lahu). | And Allah (wal-lahu) | is the best (khayru) | of the planners (l-mākirīna).

3:55 When said Allah "O Isa! Indeed, I will take you and raise you to Myself and purify you from those who disbelieve[d], and I will make those who follow[ed] you superior to those who disbelieve[d] on the Day of [the] Resurrection. Then to Me is your return and I will judge between you about what you were [in it] differing.

When (idh) | said (qāla) | Allah (l-lahu) | "O Isa (yāʿīsā)! | Indeed, I (innī) | will take you (mutawaffīka) | and raise you (warāfiʿuka) | to Myself (ilayya) | and purify you (wamuṭahhiruka) | from (mina) | those who (alladhīna) | disbelieve[d] (kafarū), | and I will make (wajāʿilu) | those who (alladhīna) | follow[ed] you (ittabaʿūka) | superior (fawqa) | to those who (alladhīna) | disbelieve[d] (kafarū) | on (ilā) | the Day (yawmi) | of [the] Resurrection (l-qiyāmati). | Then (thumma) | to Me (ilayya) | is your return (marjiʿukum) | and I will judge (fa-aḥkumu) | between you (baynakum) |

about what (fīmā) | you were (kuntum) | [in it] (fīhi) | differing (takhtalifūna).

3:56 Then as for those who disbelieve[d], then I will punish them with a punishment severe in the world and in the Hereafter. And not for them any helpers.

Then as for (fa-ammā) | those who (alladhīna) | disbelieve[d] (kafarū), | then I will punish them (fa-uʿadhibuhum) | with a punishment (ʿadhāban) | severe (shadīdan) | in (fī) | the world (l-dun'yā) | and in the Hereafter (wal-ākhirati). | And not (wamā) | for them (lahum) | any (min) | helpers (nāṣirīna).

3:57 And as for those who believe[d] and did [the] righteous deeds then He will grant them in full their reward. And Allah does not love the wrongdoers.

And as for (wa-ammā) | those who (alladhīna) | believe[d] (āmanū) | and did (waʿamilū) | [the] righteous deeds (l-ṣāliḥāti) | then He will grant them in full (fayuwaffīhim) | their reward (ujūrahum). | And Allah (wal-lahu) | does not (lā) | love (yuḥibbu) | the wrongdoers (l-ẓālimīna).

3:58 That is what We recite [it] to you of the Verses and the Reminder - [the] Wise.

That (dhālika) | is what We recite [it] (natlūhu) | to you (ʿalayka) | of (mina) | the Verses (l-āyāti) | and the Reminder (wal-dhik'ri)- | [the] Wise (l-ḥakīmi).

3:59 Indeed, the likeness of Isa near Allah is like (the) likeness of Adam. He created him from dust then He said to him, "Be," and he was.

Indeed (inna), | the likeness (mathala) | of Isa (ʿīsā) | near (ʿinda) | Allah (l-lahi) | is like (the) likeness (kamathali) | of Adam (ādama). | He created him (khalaqahu) | from (min) | dust (turābin) | then (thumma) | He said (qāla) | to him (lahu), | "Be, (kun)" | and he was (fayakūnu).

3:60 The truth is from your Lord, so do not be among the doubters.

The truth (al-ḥaqu) | is from (min) | your Lord (rabbika), | so do not (falā) | be (takun) | among (mina) | the doubters (l-mum'tarīna).

3:61 Then whoever argues with you concerning it from after what came to you of the knowledge then say, "Come, let us call our sons and your sons, and our women and your women, and ourselves and yourselves, then let us pray humbly, and [we] invoke the curse of Allah on the liars.

Then whoever (faman) | argues with you (ḥājjaka) | concerning it (fīhi) | from (min) | after (baʿdi) | what (mā) | came to you (jāaka) | of (mina) | the knowledge (l-ʿil'mi) | then say (faqul), | "Come (taʿālaw), | let us call (nadʿu) | our sons (abnāanā) | and your sons (wa-abnāakum), | and our women (wanisāanā) | and your women (wanisāakum), | and ourselves (wa-anfusanā) | and yourselves (wa-anfusakum), | then (thumma) | let us pray humbly (nabtahil), | and [we] invoke (fanajʿal) | the curse (laʿnata) | of Allah (l-lahi) | on (ʿalā) | the liars (l-kādhibīna).

3:62 Indeed this, surely it is the narration - [the] true. And there is no of god except Allah. And indeed, Allah, surely He is the All-Mighty, the All-Wise.

Indeed (inna) | this (hādhā), | surely it is (lahuwa) | the narration (l-qaṣaṣu)- | [the] true (l-ḥaqu). | And there is no (wamā) | of (min) | god (ilāhin) | except (illā) | Allah (l-lahu). | And indeed (wa-inna), | Allah (l-laha), | surely He (lahuwa) | is the All-Mighty (l-ʿazīzu), | the All-Wise (l-ḥakīmu).

3:63 And if they turn back, then indeed, Allah is All-Knowing, of the corrupters.

And if (fa-in) | they turn back (tawallaw), | then indeed (fa-inna), | Allah (l-laha) | is All-Knowing (ʿalīmun), | of the corrupters (bil-muf'sidīna).

3:64 Say, "O People of the Book! Come to a word equitable between us and between you - that not we worship except Allah, and not we associate partners with Him - anything and not take some of us to others as lords from besides Allah." Then if they turn away, then say, "Bear witness that we are Muslims."

Say (qul), | "O People (yāahla) | of the Book (l-kitābi)! | Come (taʿālaw) | to (ilā) | a word (kalimatin) | equitable (sawāin) | between us (baynanā) | and between you (wabaynakum)- | that not (allā) | we worship (naʿbuda) | except (illā) | Allah (l-laha), | and not (walā) | we associate partners (nush'rika) | with Him (bihi)- | anything (shayan) | and not (walā) | take (yattakhidha) | some of us (baʿḍunā) | to others (baʿḍan) | as lords (arbāban) | from (min) | besides (dūni) | Allah. (l-lahi)" | Then if (fa-in) | they turn away (tawallaw), | then say (faqūlū), | "Bear witness (ish'hadū) | that we (bi-annā) | are Muslims. (mus'limūna)"

3:65 O People of the Book! Why do you argue concerning Ibrahim while not was revealed the Taurat and the Injeel except from after him? Then why don't you use your intellect?

O People (yāahla) | of the Book (l-kitābi)! | Why (lima) | do you argue (tuḥājjūna) | concerning (fī) | Ibrahim (ib'rāhīma) | while not (wamā) | was revealed (unzilati) | the Taurat (l-tawrātu) | and the Injeel (wal-injīlu) | except (illā) | from (min) | after him (baʿdihi)? | Then why don't (afalā) | you use your intellect (taʿqilūna)?

3:66 Here you are - those who argued about what [for] you of it have some knowledge. Then why do you argue about what not for you of it any knowledge. And Allah knows, while you do not know.

Here you are (hāantum)- | those who (hāulāi) | argued (ḥājajtum) | about what (fīmā) | [for] you (lakum) | of it (bihi) | have some knowledge (ʿil'mun). | Then why (falima) | do you argue (tuḥājjūna) | about what (fīmā) | not (laysa) | for you (lakum) | of it (bihi) | any knowledge (ʿil'mun). | And Allah (wal-lahu) | knows (yaʿlamu), | while you (wa-antum) | do not (lā) | know (taʿlamūna).

3:67 Not was Ibrahim a Jew and not a Christian [and] but he was a true Muslim, and not he was from the polytheists.

Not (mā) | was (kāna) | Ibrahim (ib'rāhīmu) | a Jew (yahūdiyyan) | and not (walā) | a Christian (naṣrāniyyan) | [and] but (walākin) | he was (kāna) | a true (ḥanīfan) | Muslim (mus'liman), | and not (wamā) | he was (kāna) | from (mina) | the polytheists (l-mush'rikīna).

3:68 Indeed, the best to claim relationship of people with Ibrahim are those who follow him and this [the] Prophet and those who believe[d]. And Allah is a Guardian of the believers.

Indeed (inna), | the best to claim relationship (awlā) | of people (l-nāsi) | with Ibrahim (bi-ib'rāhīma) | are those who (lalladhīna) | follow him (ittabaʿūhu) | and this (wahādhā) | [the] Prophet (l-nabiyu) | and those who (wa-alladhīna) | believe[d] (āmanū). | And Allah (wal-lahu) | is a Guardian (waliyyu) | of the believers (l-mu'minīna).

3:69 Wished a group from the People of the Book if they could lead you astray, and not they lead astray except themselves and not they perceive.

Wished (waddat) | a group (ṭāifatun) | from (min) | the People (ahli) | of the Book (l-kitābi) | if (law) | they could lead you astray (yuḍillūnakum), | and not (wamā) | they lead astray (yuḍillūna) | except (illā) | themselves (anfusahum) | and not (wamā) | they perceive (yashʿurūna).

3:70 O People of the Book! Why do you deny [in] the Signs of Allah while you bear witness?

O People (yāahla) | of the Book (l-kitābi)! | Why do (lima) | you deny (takfurūna) | [in] the Signs (biāyāti) | of Allah (l-lahi) | while you (wa-antum) | bear witness (tashhadūna)?

3:71 O People of the Book! Why do you mix the truth with the falsehood and conceal the truth while you know?

O People (yāahla) | of the Book (l-kitābi)! | Why (lima) | do you mix (talbisūna) | the truth (l-ḥaqa) | with the falsehood (bil-bāṭili) | and conceal (wataktumūna) | the truth (l-ḥaqa) | while you (wa-antum) | know (taʿlamūna)?

3:72 And said a group of the People of the Book, "Believe in what was revealed on those who believe[d] at the beginning of the day, and reject at its end, perhaps they may return.

And said (waqālat) | a group (ṭāifatun) | of (min) | the People (ahli) | of the Book (l-kitābi), | "Believe (āminū) | in what (bi-alladhī) | was revealed (unzila) | on (ʿalā) | those who (alladhīna) | believe[d] (āmanū) | at the beginning (wajha) | of the day (l-nahāri), | and reject (wa-uk'furū) | at its end (ākhirahu), | perhaps they may (laʿallahum) | return (yarjiʿūna).

3:73 And do not believe except the one who follows your religion." Say, "Indeed the true guidance is the Guidance of Allah - lest is given to one - the like of what was given to you or they may argue with you near your Lord." Say, "Indeed, the Bounty is in the Hand of Allah. He gives it to whom He wills, and Allah is All-Encompassing, All-Knowing."

And do not (walā) | believe (tu'minū) | except (illā) | the one who (liman) | follows (tabiʿa) | your religion. (dīnakum)" | Say (qul), | "Indeed (inna) | the true guidance (l-hudā) | is the Guidance (hudā) | of Allah (l-lahi)- | lest (an) | is given (yu'tā) | to one (aḥadun)- | the like (mith'la) | of what (mā) | was given to you (ūtītum) | or (aw) | they may argue with you (yuḥājjūkum) | near (ʿinda) | your Lord. (rabbikum)" | Say (qul), | "Indeed (inna), | the Bounty (l-faḍla) | is in the Hand (biyadi) | of Allah (l-lahi). | He gives it (yu'tīhi) | to whom (man) | He wills (yashāu), | and Allah (wal-lahu) | is All-Encompassing (wāsiʿun), | All-Knowing. (ʿalīmun)"

3:74 He chooses for His Mercy whom He wills. And Allah is the Possessor of Bounty - [the] great.

He chooses (yakhtaṣṣu) | for His Mercy (biraḥmatihi) | whom (man) | He wills (yashāu). | And Allah (wal-lahu) | is the Possessor (dhū) | of Bounty (l-faḍli)- | [the] great (l-ʿaẓīmi).

3:75 And from the People of the Book is he who, if you entrust him with a great amount of wealth he will return it to you. And from them is he who, if you entrust him with a single coin not he will return it to you except that you keep constantly over him standing. That is because they said, "Not on us concerning the unlettered people any [way] accountability." And they say about Allah the lie while they know.

And from (wamin) | the People (ahli) | of the Book (l-kitābi) | is he who (man), | if (in) | you entrust him (tamanhu) | with a great amount of wealth (biqinṭārin) | he will return it (yu-addihi) | to you (ilayka). | And from them (wamin'hum) | is he who (man), | if (in) | you entrust him (tamanhu) | with a single coin (bidīnārin) | not (lā) | he will return it (yu-addihi) | to you (ilayka) | except (illā) | that (mā) | you keep constantly (dum'ta) | over him (ʿalayhi) | standing (qāiman). | That (dhālika) | is because they (bi-annahum) | said (qālū), | "Not (laysa) | on us (ʿalaynā) | concerning (fī) | the unlettered people (l-umiyīna) | any [way] accountability. (sabīlun)" | And they say (wayaqūlūna) | about (ʿalā) | Allah (l-lahi) | the lie (l-kadhiba) | while they (wahum) | know (yaʿlamūna).

3:76 Nay, whoever fulfills his covenant and fears Allah, then indeed, Allah loves those who fear Him.

Nay (balā), | whoever (man) | fulfills (awfā) | his covenant (biʿahdihi) | and fears Allah (wa-ittaqā), | then indeed (fa-inna), | Allah (l-laha) | loves (yuḥibbu) | those who fear Him (l-mutaqīna).

3:77 Indeed, those who exchange the Covenant of Allah and their oaths for a price little, those - no share for them in the Hereafter and not will speak to them Allah, and not look at them on the Day of the Resurrection and not purify them, and for them is a punishment painful.

Indeed (inna), | those who (alladhīna) | exchange (yashtarūna) | the Covenant (biʿahdi) | of Allah (l-lahi) | and their oaths (wa-aymānihim) | for a price (thamanan) | little (qalīlan), | those (ulāika)- | no (lā) | share (khalāqa) | for them (lahum) | in (fī) | the Hereafter (l-ākhirati) | and not (walā) | will speak to them (yukallimuhumu) | Allah (l-lahu), | and not (walā) | look (yanẓuru) | at them (ilayhim) | on the Day (yawma) | of the Resurrection (l-qiyāmati) | and not (walā) | purify them (yuzakkīhim), | and for them (walahum) | is a punishment (ʿadhābun) | painful (alīmun).

3:78 And indeed, among them surely is a group - they distort their tongues in reciting the Book so that you may think it is from the Book and not it is from the Book. And they say, "It is from Allah." But not it is from Allah. And they say about Allah the lie while they know.

And indeed (wa-inna), | among them (min'hum) | surely is a group (lafarīqan)- | they distort (yalwūna) | their tongues (alsinatahum) | in reciting the Book (bil-kitābi) | so that you may think it (litaḥsabūhu) | is from (mina) | the Book (l-kitābi) | and not (wamā) | it (huwa) | is from (mina) | the Book (l-kitābi). | And they say (wayaqūlūna), | "It (huwa) | is (min) | from (ʿindi) | Allah. (l-lahi)" | But not (wamā) | it (huwa) | is (min) | from (ʿindi) | Allah (l-lahi). | And they say (wayaqūlūna) | about (ʿalā) | Allah (l-lahi) | the lie (l-kadhiba) | while they (wahum) | know (yaʿlamūna).

3:79 Not is for a human that gives him Allah the Book, and the wisdom, and the Prophethood, then he says to the people, "Be worshippers of me from besides Allah, but would say "Be worshippers of the Lord because you have been teaching the Book and because you have been studying it."

Not (mā) | is (kāna) | for a human (libasharin) | that (an) | gives him (yu'tiyahu) | Allah (l-lahu) | the Book (l-kitāba), | and the wisdom (wal-ḥuk'ma), | and the Prophethood (wal-nubuwata), | then (thumma) | he says (yaqūla) | to the people (lilnnāsi), | "Be (kūnū) | worshippers (ʿibādan) | of me (lī) | from (min) | besides (dūni) | Allah (l-lahi), | but would say (walākin) | "Be (kūnū) | worshippers of the Lord (rabbāniyyīna) | because (bimā) | you have been (kuntum) | teaching (tuʿallimūna) | the Book (l-kitāba) | and because (wabimā) | you have been (kuntum) | studying it. (tadrusūna)"

3:80 And not he will order you that you take the Angels, and the Prophets as lords. Would he order you to [the] disbelief after [when] you have become Muslims?

And not (walā) | he will order you (yamurakum) | that (an) | you take (tattakhidhū) | the Angels (l-malāikata), | and the Prophets (wal-nabiyīna) | as lords (arbāban). | Would he order you (ayamurukum) | to [the] disbelief (bil-kuf'ri) | after (baʿda) | [when] (idh) | you have become (antum) | Muslims (mus'limūna)?

3:81 And when took Allah covenant of the Prophets, "Certainly, whatever I have given you of the Book and wisdom then comes to you a Messenger confirming that which is with you, you must believe in him and you must help him." He said, "Do you affirm and take on that condition My Covenant?" They said, "We affirm." He said, "Then bear witness, and I am with you among the witnesses."

And when (wa-idh) | took (akhadha) | Allah (l-lahu) | covenant (mīthāqa) | of the Prophets (l-nabiyīna), | "Certainly, whatever (lamā) | I have given you (ātaytukum) | of (min) | the Book (kitābin) | and wisdom (waḥik'matin) | then (thumma) | comes to you (jāakum) | a Messenger (rasūlun) | confirming (muṣaddiqun) | that which (limā) | is with you (maʿakum), | you must believe (latu'minunna) | in him (bihi) | and you must help him. (walatanṣurunnahu)" | He said (qāla), | "Do you affirm (a-aqrartum) | and take (wa-akhadhtum) | on (ʿalā) | that condition (dhālikum) | My Covenant? (iṣ'rī)" | They said (qālū), | "We affirm. (aqrarnā)" | He said (qāla), | "Then bear witness (fa-ish'hadū), | and I am (wa-anā) | with you (maʿakum) | among (mina) | the witnesses. (l-shāhidīna)"

3:82 Then whoever turns away after that, then those they are the defiantly disobedient.

Then whoever (faman) | turns away (tawallā) | after (baʿda) | that (dhālika), | then those (fa-ulāika) | they (humu) | are the defiantly disobedient (l-fāsiqūna).

3:83 So is it other than the religion of Allah they seek? While to Him have submitted whatever is in the heavens and the earth, willingly or unwillingly, and towards Him they will be returned.

So is it other than (afaghayra) | the religion (dīni) | of Allah (l-lahi) | they seek (yabghūna)? | While to Him (walahu) | have submitted (aslama) | whatever (man) | is in (fī) | the heavens (l-samāwāti) | and the earth (wal-arḍi), | willingly (ṭawʿan) | or unwillingly (wakarhan), | and towards Him (wa-ilayhi) | they will be returned (yur'jaʿūna).

3:84 Say, "We believed in Allah and what is revealed on us and what was revealed on Ibrahim, and Ishmael, and Isaac, and Yaqub, and the descendents and what was given to Musa, and Isa, and the Prophets from their Lord. Not we make distinction between any of them and we to Him are submissive.

Say (qul), | "We believed (āmannā) | in Allah (bil-lahi) | and what (wamā) | is revealed (unzila) | on us (ʿalaynā) | and what (wamā) | was revealed (unzila) | on (ʿalā) | Ibrahim (ib'rāhīma), | and Ishmael (wa-is'māʿīla), | and Isaac (wa-is'ḥāqa), | and Yaqub (wayaʿqūba), | and the descendents (wal-asbāṭi) | and what (wamā) | was given (ūtiya) | to Musa (mūsā), | and Isa (waʿīsā), | and the Prophets (wal-nabiyūna) | from (min) | their Lord (rabbihim). | Not (lā) | we make distinction (nufarriqu) | between (bayna) | any (aḥadin) | of them (min'hum) | and we (wanaḥnu) | to Him (lahu) | are submissive (mus'limūna).

3:85 And whoever seeks other than [the] Islam as religion then never will be accepted from him, and he in the Hereafter, will be from the losers.

And whoever (waman) | seeks (yabtaghi) | other than (ghayra) | [the] Islam (l-is'lāmi) | as religion (dīnan) | then never (falan) | will be accepted (yuq'bala) | from him (min'hu), | and he (wahuwa) | in (fī) | the Hereafter (l-ākhirati), | will be from (mina) | the losers (l-khāsirīna).

3:86 How shall guide Allah a people who disbelieved after their belief and had witnessed that the Messenger is true, and came to them the clear proofs? And Allah does not guide the people [the] wrongdoers.

How (kayfa) | shall guide (yahdī) | Allah (l-lahu) | a people (qawman) | who disbelieved (kafarū) | after (baʿda) | their belief (īmānihim) | and had witnessed (washahidū) | that (anna) | the Messenger (l-rasūla) | is true (ḥaqqun), | and came to them (wajāahumu) | the clear proofs (l-bayinātu)? | And Allah (wal-lahu) | does not (lā) | guide (yahdī) | the people (l-qawma) | [the] wrongdoers (l-ẓālimīna).

3:87 Those - their recompense, that on them is the curse of Allah and the Angels and the people all together.

Those (ulāika)- | their recompense (jazāuhum), | that (anna) | on them (ʿalayhim) | is the curse (laʿnata) | of Allah (l-lahi) | and the Angels (wal-malāikati) | and the people (wal-nāsi) | all together (ajmaʿīna).

3:88 They will abide forever in it. Not will be lightened for them the punishment and not they will be reprieved.

They will abide forever (khālidīna) | in it (fīhā). | Not (lā) | will be lightened (yukhaffafu) | for them (ʿanhumu) | the punishment (l-ʿadhābu) | and not (walā) | they (hum) | will be reprieved (yunẓarūna).

3:89 Except those who repent from after that, and reform[ed] themselves. Then indeed, Allah is Oft-Forgiving, Most Merciful.

Except (illā) | those who (alladhīna) | repent (tābū) | from (min) | after (baʿdi) | that (dhālika), | and reform[ed] themselves (wa-aṣlaḥū). | Then indeed (fa-inna), | Allah (l-laha) | is Oft-Forgiving (ghafūrun), | Most Merciful (raḥīmun).

3:90 Indeed, those who disbelieved after their belief then they increased in disbelief never will be accepted their repentance, and those - they are those who have gone astray.

Indeed (inna), | those who (alladhīna) | disbelieved (kafarū) | after (baʿda) | their belief (īmānihim) | then (thumma) | they increased (iz'dādū) | in disbelief (kuf'ran) | never (lan) | will be accepted (tuq'bala) | their repentance (tawbatuhum), | and those (wa-ulāika)- | they (humu) | are those who have gone astray (l-ḍālūna).

3:91 Indeed, those who disbelieve[d] and died while they are disbelievers, then never will be accepted from any one of them full earth of gold [and] even if he offered as ransom it. Those - for them is a punishment painful and not will be for them any helpers.

Indeed (inna), | those who (alladhīna) | disbelieve[d] (kafarū) | and died (wamātū) | while they (wahum) | are disbelievers (kuffārun), | then never (falan) | will be accepted (yuq'bala) | from (min) | any one of them (aḥadihim) | full (mil'u) | earth (l-arḍi) | of gold (dhahaban) | [and] even if (walawi) | he offered as ransom (if'tadā) | it (bihi). | Those (ulāika)- | for them (lahum) | is a punishment (ʿadhābun) | painful (alīmun) | and not (wamā) | will be for them (lahum) | any (min) | helpers (nāṣirīna).

3:92 Never will you attain [the] righteousness until you spend from what you love. And whatever you spend of a thing then indeed, Allah of it is All-Knowing.

Never (lan) | will you attain (tanālū) | [the] righteousness (l-bira) | until (ḥattā) | you spend (tunfiqū) | from what (mimmā) | you love (tuḥibbūna). | And whatever (wamā) | you spend (tunfiqū) | of (min) | a thing (shayin) | then indeed (fa-inna), | Allah (l-laha) | of it (bihi) | is All-Knowing (ʿalīmun).

3:93 All [the] food was lawful for the Children of Israel except what made unlawful Israel upon himself from before [that] was revealed the Taurat. Say, "So bring the Taurat and recite it if you are truthful."

All (kullu) | [the] food (l-ṭaʿāmi) | was (kāna) | lawful (ḥillan) | for the Children (libanī) | of Israel (is'rāīla) | except (illā) | what (mā) | made unlawful (ḥarrama) | Israel (is'rāīlu) | upon (ʿalā) | himself (nafsihi) | from (min) | before (qabli) | [that] (an) | was revealed (tunazzala) | the Taurat (l-tawrātu). | Say (qul), | "So bring (fatū) | the Taurat (bil-tawrāti) | and recite it (fa-it'lūhā) | if (in) | you are (kuntum) | truthful. (ṣādiqīna)"

3:94 Then whoever fabricates about Allah [the] lie from after that, then those - they are the wrongdoers.

Then whoever (famani) | fabricates (if'tarā) | about (ʿalā) | Allah (l-lahi) | [the] lie (l-kadhiba) | from (min) | after (baʿdi) | that (dhālika), | then those (fa-ulāika)- | they (humu) | are the wrongdoers (l-ẓālimūna).

3:95 Say, has spoken the truth Allah, then follow the religion of Ibrahim the upright, and not he was of the polytheists.

Say (qul), | has spoken the truth (ṣadaqa) | Allah (l-lahu), | then follow (fa-ittabiʿū) | the religion (millata) | of Ibrahim (ib'rāhīma) | the upright (ḥanīfan), | and not (wamā) | he was (kāna) | of (mina) | the polytheists (l-mush'rikīna).

3:96 Indeed, the First House set up for the mankind is the one which is at Bakkah, blessed and a guidance for the worlds.

Indeed (inna), | the First (awwala) | House (baytin) | set up (wuḍiʿa) | for the mankind (lilnnāsi) | is the one which (lalladhī) | is at Bakkah (bibakkata), | blessed (mubārakan) | and a guidance (wahudan) | for the worlds (lil'ʿālamīna).

3:97 In it are signs clear, standing place of Ibrahim, and whoever enters it - is safe. And due to Allah upon the mankind is pilgrimage of the House for one who is able to [it] find a way. And whoever disbelieved then indeed, Allah is free from need of the universe.

In it (fīhi) | are signs (āyātun) | clear (bayyinātun), | standing place (maqāmu) | of Ibrahim (ib'rāhīma), | and whoever (waman) | enters it (dakhalahu)- | is (kāna) | safe (āminan). | And due to Allah (walillahi) | upon (ʿalā) | the mankind (l-nāsi) | is pilgrimage (ḥijju) | of the House (l-bayti) | for one who (mani) | is able (is'taṭāʿa) | to [it] (ilayhi) | find a way (sabīlan). | And whoever (waman) | disbelieved (kafara) | then indeed (fa-inna), | Allah (l-laha) | is free from need (ghaniyyun) | of (ʿani) | the universe (l-ʿālamīna).

3:98 Say, "O People of the Book! Why do you disbelieve in the Verses of Allah, while Allah is a Witness over what you do?"

Say (qul), | "O People (yāahla) | of the Book (l-kitābi)! | Why (lima) | do you disbelieve (takfurūna) | in the Verses (biāyāti) | of Allah (l-lahi), | while Allah (wal-lahu) | is a Witness (shahīdun) | over (ʿalā) | what (mā) | you do? (taʿmalūna)"

3:99 Say, "O People of the Book! Why do you hinder from the way of Allah those who believe[d], seeking to make it seem crooked while you are witnesses? And not Allah is unaware of what you do.

Say (qul), | "O People (yāahla) | of the Book (l-kitābi)! | Why (lima) | do you hinder (taṣuddūna) | from (ʿan) | the way (sabīli) | of Allah (l-lahi) | those who (man) | believe[d] (āmana), | seeking to make it (tabghūnahā) | seem crooked (ʿiwajan) | while you (wa-antum) | are witnesses (shuhadāu)? | And not (wamā) | Allah (l-lahu) | is unaware (bighāfilin) | of what (ʿammā) | you do (taʿmalūna).

3:100 O you who believe[d]! If you obey a group from those who were given the Book they will turn you back after your belief as disbelievers.

O you (yāayyuhā) | who (alladhīna) | believe[d] (āmanū)! | If (in) | you obey (tuṭīʿū) | a group (farīqan) | from (mina) | those who (alladhīna) | were given (ūtū) | the Book (l-kitāba) | they will turn you back (yaruddūkum) | after (baʿda) | your belief (īmānikum) | as disbelievers (kāfirīna).

3:101 And how could you disbelieve while [you] is recited upon you the Verses of Allah and among you is His Messenger? And whoever holds firmly to Allah, then surely he is guided to a path straight.

And how could (wakayfa) | you disbelieve (takfurūna) | while [you] (wa-antum) | is recited (tut'lā) | upon you (ʿalaykum) | the Verses (āyātu) | of Allah (l-lahi) | and among you (wafīkum) | is His Messenger (rasūluhu)? | And whoever (waman) | holds firmly (yaʿtaṣim) | to Allah (bil-lahi), | then surely (faqad) | he is guided (hudiya) | to (ilā) | a path (ṣirāṭin) | straight (mus'taqīmin).

3:102 O you who believe[d]! Fear Allah as is His right that He (should) be feared and do not die except [while you] as Muslims.

O you (yāayyuhā) | who (alladhīna) | believe[d] (āmanū)! | Fear (ittaqū) | Allah (l-laha) | as is His right (ḥaqqa) | that He (should) be feared (tuqātihi) | and do not (walā) | die (tamūtunna) | except (illā) | [while you] (wa-antum) | as Muslims (mus'limūna).

3:103 And hold firmly to the rope of Allah all together and do not be divided. And remember the Favor of Allah on you when you were enemies then He made friendship between your hearts then you became by His Favor brothers. And you were on the brink of pit of the Fire then He saved you from it. Thus makes clear Allah for you His Verses so that you may be guided.

And hold firmly (wa-iʿ'taṣimū) | to the rope (biḥabli) | of Allah (l-lahi) | all together (jamīʿan) | and do not (walā) | be divided (tafarraqū). | And remember (wa-udh'kurū) | the Favor (niʿ'mata) | of Allah (l-lahi) | on you (ʿalaykum) | when (idh) | you were (kuntum) | enemies (aʿdāan) | then He made friendship (fa-allafa) | between (bayna) | your hearts (qulūbikum) | then you became (fa-aṣbaḥtum) | by His Favor (biniʿ'matihi) | brothers (ikh'wānan). | And you were (wakuntum) | on (ʿalā) | the brink (shafā) | of pit (ḥuf'ratin) | of (mina) | the Fire (l-nāri) | then He saved you (fa-anqadhakum) | from it (min'hā). | Thus (kadhālika) | makes clear (yubayyinu) | Allah (l-lahu) | for you (lakum) | His Verses (āyātihi) | so that you may (laʿallakum) | be guided (tahtadūna).

3:104 And let there be among you [a] people inviting to the good [and] enjoining the right, and forbidding from the wrong, and those - they are the successful ones.

And let there be (waltakun) | among you (minkum) | [a] people (ummatun) | inviting (yadʿūna) | to (ilā) | the good (l-khayri) | [and] enjoining (wayamurūna) | the right (bil-maʿrūfi), | and forbidding (wayanhawna) | from (ʿani) | the wrong (l-munkari), | and those (wa-ulāika)- | they (humu) | are the successful ones (l-muf'liḥūna).

3:105 And do not be like those who became divided and differed from after what came to them - the clear proofs. And those for them is a punishment great.

And do not (walā) | be (takūnū) | like those who (ka-alladhīna) | became divided (tafarraqū) | and differed (wa-ikh'talafū) | from (min) | after (baʿdi) | what (mā) | came to them (jāahumu)- | the clear proofs (l-bayinātu). | And those (wa-ulāika) | for them (lahum) | is a punishment (ʿadhābun) | great (ʿaẓīmun).

3:106 On the Day would become white some faces and would become black some faces. As for those whose turn black [their] faces - "Did you disbelieve after your belief? Then taste the punishment for what you used to disbelieve."

On the Day (yawma) | would become white (tabyaḍḍu) | some faces (wujūhun) | and would become black (wataswaddu) | some faces (wujūhun). | As for (fa-ammā) | those whose (alladhīna) | turn black (is'waddat) | [their] faces (wujūhuhum)- | "Did you disbelieve (akafartum) | after (baʿda) | your belief (īmānikum)? | Then taste (fadhūqū) | the punishment (l-ʿadhāba) | for what (bimā) | you used to (kuntum) | disbelieve. (takfurūna)"

3:107 But as for those whose turn white [their] faces then they will be in the Mercy of Allah, they in it will abide forever.

But as for (wa-ammā) | those whose (alladhīna) | turn white (ib'yaḍḍat) | [their] faces (wujūhuhum) | then they will be in (fafī) | the Mercy (raḥmati) | of Allah (l-lahi), | they (hum) | in it (fīhā) | will abide forever (khālidūna).

3:108 These are the Verses of Allah. We recite them to you in truth. And not Allah wants injustice to the worlds.

These (til'ka) | are the Verses (āyātu) | of Allah (l-lahi). | We recite them (natlūhā) | to you (ʿalayka) | in truth (bil-ḥaqi). | And not (wamā) | Allah (l-lahu) | wants (yurīdu) | injustice (ẓul'man) | to the worlds (lil'ʿālamīna).

3:109 And to Allah belongs whatever is in the heavens and whatever is in the earth. And to Allah will be returned the matters.

And to Allah belongs (walillahi) | whatever (mā) | is in (fī) | the heavens (l-samāwāti) | and whatever (wamā) | is in (fī) | the earth (l-arḍi). | And to (wa-ilā) | Allah (l-lahi) | will be returned (tur'jaʿu) | the matters (l-umūru).

3:110 You are the best of people raised for the mankind - enjoining the right and forbidding [from] the wrong and believing in Allah. And if believed the People of the Book surely would have been good for them. Among them are [the] believers, but most of them are defiantly disobedient.

You are (kuntum) | the best (khayra) | of people (ummatin) | raised (ukh'rijat) | for the mankind (lilnnāsi)- | enjoining (tamurūna) | the right (bil-maʿrūfi) | and forbidding (watanhawna) | [from] (ʿani) | the wrong (l-munkari) | and believing (watu'minūna) | in Allah (bil-lahi). | And if (walaw) | believed (āmana) | the People (ahlu) | of the Book (l-kitābi) | surely would have been (lakāna) | good (khayran) | for them (lahum). | Among them (min'humu) | are [the] believers (l-mu'minūna), | but most of them (wa-aktharuhumu) | are defiantly disobedient (l-fāsiqūna).

3:111 Never will they harm you except a hurt. And if they fight you, they will turn towards you the backs, then not they will be helped.

Never (lan) | will they harm you (yaḍurrūkum) | except (illā) | a hurt (adhan). | And if (wa-in) | they fight you (yuqātilūkum), | they will turn towards you (yuwallūkumu) | the backs (l-adbāra), | then (thumma) | not (lā) | they will be helped (yunṣarūna).

3:112 Struck on them the humiliation wherever that they are found except with a rope from Allah and a rope from the people. And they incurred wrath from Allah and struck on them the poverty. That is because they used to disbelieve in the Verses of Allah and they killed the Prophets without right. That is because they disobeyed and they used to transgress.

Struck (ḍuribat) | on them (ʿalayhimu) | the humiliation (l-dhilatu) | wherever (ayna) | that (mā) | they are found (thuqifū) | except (illā) | with a rope (biḥablin) | from (mina) | Allah (l-lahi) | and a rope (waḥablin) | from (mina) | the people (l-nāsi). | And they incurred (wabāū) | wrath (bighaḍabin) | from (mina) | Allah (l-lahi) | and struck (waḍuribat) | on them (ʿalayhimu) | the poverty (l-maskanatu). | That (dhālika) | is because (bi-annahum) | they used to (kānū) | disbelieve (yakfurūna) | in the Verses (biāyāti) | of Allah (l-lahi) | and they killed (wayaqtulūna) | the Prophets (l-anbiyāa) | without (bighayri) | right (ḥaqqin). | That (dhālika) | is because (bimā) | they disobeyed (ʿaṣaw) | and they used to (wakānū) | transgress (yaʿtadūna).

3:113 They are not the same; among the People of the Book is a community standing and reciting the Verses of Allah in the hours of the night and they prostrate.

They are not (laysū) | the same (sawāan); | among (min) | the People (ahli) | of the Book (l-kitābi) | is a community (ummatun) | standing (qāimatun) | and reciting (yatlūna) | the Verses (āyāti) | of Allah (l-lahi) | in the hours (ānāa) | of the night (al-layli) | and they (wahum) | prostrate (yasjudūna).

3:114 They believe in Allah and the Day the Last and they enjoin [with] the right and forbid [from] the wrong and they hasten in the good deeds. And those are from the righteous.

They believe (yu'minūna) | in Allah (bil-lahi) | and the Day (wal-yawmi) | the Last (l-ākhiri) | and they enjoin (wayamurūna) | [with] the right (bil-maʿrūfi) | and forbid (wayanhawna) | [from] (ʿani) | the wrong (l-munkari) | and they hasten (wayusāriʿūna) | in (fī) | the good deeds (l-khayrāti). | And those (wa-ulāika) | are from (mina) | the righteous (l-ṣāliḥīna).

3:115 And whatever they do of a good, then never will they be denied it. And Allah is All-Knowing of the God-fearing.

And whatever (wamā) | they do (yafʿalū) | of (min) | a good (khayrin), | then never (falan) | will they be denied it (yuk'farūhu). | And Allah (wal-lahu) | is All-Knowing (ʿalīmun) | of the God-fearing (bil-mutaqīna).

3:116 Indeed, those who disbelieved, never will avail [for] them their wealth and not their children against Allah anything, and those are the companions of the Fire, they in it will abide forever.

Indeed (inna), | those who (alladhīna) | disbelieved (kafarū), | never (lan) | will avail (tugh'niya) | [for] them (ʿanhum) | their wealth (amwāluhum) | and not (walā) | their children (awlāduhum) | against (mina) | Allah (l-lahi) | anything (shayan), | and those (wa-ulāika) | are the companions (aṣḥābu) | of the Fire (l-nāri), | they (hum) | in it (fīhā) | will abide forever (khālidūna).

3:117 Example of what they spend in this [the] life of the world is like (the) example of a wind in it is frost, it struck the harvest of a people who wronged themselves, then destroyed it. And not has wronged them Allah [and] but themselves they wronged.

Example (mathalu) | of what (mā) | they spend (yunfiqūna) | in (fī) | this (hādhihi) | [the] life (l-ḥayati) | of the world (l-dun'yā) | is like (the) example (kamathali) | of a wind (rīḥin) | in it (fīhā) | is frost (ṣirrun), | it struck (aṣābat) | the harvest (ḥartha) | of a people (qawmin) | who wrongeḍ (ẓalamū) | themselves (anfusahum), | then destroyed it (fa-ahlakathu). | And not (wamā) | has wronged them (ẓalamahumu) | Allah (l-lahu) | [and] but (walākin) | themselves (anfusahum) | they wronged (yaẓlimūna).

3:118 O you who believe[d]! Do not take as intimates from other than yourselves, not they will spare you any ruin. They wish what distresses you. Indeed, has become apparent the hatred from their mouths, and what conceals their breasts is greater. Certainly We made clear for you the Verses, if you were to use reason.

O you (yāayyuhā) | who (alladhīna) | believe[d] (āmanū)! | Do not (lā) | take (tattakhidhū) | as intimates (biṭānatan) | from (min) | other than yourselves (dūnikum), | not (lā) | they will spare you (yalūnakum) | any ruin (khabālan). | They wish (waddū) | what (mā) | distresses you (ʿanittum). | Indeed (qad), | has become apparent (badati) | the hatred (l-baghḍāu) | from (min) | their mouths (afwāhihim), | and what (wamā) | conceals (tukh'fī) | their breasts (ṣudūruhum) | is greater (akbaru). | Certainly (qad) | We made clear (bayyannā) | for you (lakumu) | the Verses (l-āyāti), | if (in) | you were (kuntum) | to use reason (taʿqilūna).

3:119 Lo! You are those, you love them but not they love you and you believe in the Book - all of it. And when they meet you they say, "We believe." And when they are alone they bite at you the finger tips out of [the] rage. Say, "Die in your rage. Indeed. Allah is All-Knowing of what is in the breasts."

Lo! You are (hāantum) | those (ulāi), | you love them (tuḥibbūnahum) | but not (walā) | they love you (yuḥibbūnakum) | and you believe (watu'minūna) | in the Book (bil-kitābi)- | all of it (kullihi). | And when (wa-idhā) | they meet you (laqūkum) | they say (qālū), | "We believe. (āmannā)" | And when (wa-idhā) | they are alone (khalaw) | they bite (ʿaḍḍū) | at you (ʿalaykumu) | the finger tips (l-anāmila) | out of (mina) | [the] rage (l-ghayẓi). | Say (qul), | "Die (mūtū) | in your rage (bighayẓikum). | Indeed (inna). | Allah (l-laha) | is All-Knowing (ʿalīmun) | of what (bidhāti) | is in the breasts. (l-ṣudūri)"

3:120 If touches you a good, it grieves them and if strikes you misfortune, they rejoice at it. And if you are patient and fear Allah, not will harm you their plot in anything. Indeed, Allah, of what they do is All-Encompassing.

If (in) | touches you (tamsaskum) | a good (ḥasanatun), | it grieves them (tasu'hum) | and if (wa-in) | strikes you (tuṣib'kum) | misfortune (sayyi-atun), | they rejoice (yafraḥū) | at it (bihā). | And if (wa-in) | you are patient (taṣbirū) | and fear Allah (watattaqū), | not (lā) | will harm you (yaḍurrukum) | their plot (kayduhum) | in anything (shayan). | Indeed (inna), | Allah (l-laha), | of what (bimā) | they do (yaʿmalūna) | is All-Encompassing (muḥīṭun).

3:121 And when you left early morning from your household to post the believers to take positions for the battle. And Allah is All-Hearing, All-Knowing.

And when (wa-idh) | you left early morning (ghadawta) | from (min) | your household (ahlika) | to post (tubawwi-u) | the believers (l-mu'minīna) | to take positions (maqāʿida) | for the battle (lil'qitāli). | And Allah (wal-lahu) | is All-Hearing (samīʿun), | All-Knowing (ʿalīmun).

3:122 When inclined two parties among you that they lost heart, but Allah was their protector. And on Allah let put their trust the believers.

When (idh) | inclined (hammat) | two parties (ṭāifatāni) | among you (minkum) | that (an) | they lost heart (tafshalā), | but Allah (wal-lahu) | was their protector (waliyyuhumā). | And on (waʿalā) | Allah (l-lahi) | let put their trust (falyatawakkali) | the believers (l-mu'minūna).

3:123 And certainly helped you Allah in Badr while you were weak. So fear Allah so that you may be grateful.

And certainly (walaqad) | helped you (naṣarakumu) | Allah (l-lahu) | in Badr (bibadrin) |

while you were (wa-antum) | weak (adhillatun). | So fear (fa-ittaqū) | Allah (l-laha) | so that you may (laʿallakum) | be grateful (tashkurūna).

3:124 When you said to the believers, "Is it not enough for you that reinforces you your Lord with three thousand[s] [of] [the] Angels [the ones] sent down?

When (idh) | you said (taqūlu) | to the believers (lil'mu'minīna), | "Is it not (alan) | enough for you (yakfiyakum) | that (an) | reinforces you (yumiddakum) | your Lord (rabbukum) | with three (bithalāthati) | thousand[s] (ālāfin) | [of] (mina) | [the] Angels (l-malāikati) | [the ones] sent down (munzalīna)?

3:125 Yes, if you are patient and fear Allah and they come upon you [of] suddenly, [this] will reinforce you your Lord with five thousand[s] [of] [the] Angels [the ones] having marks.

Yes (balā), | if (in) | you are patient (taṣbirū) | and fear Allah (watattaqū) | and they come upon you (wayatūkum) | [of] (min) | suddenly (fawrihim), | [this] (hādhā) | will reinforce you (yum'did'kum) | your Lord (rabbukum) | with five (bikhamsati) | thousand[s] (ālāfin) | [of] (mina) | [the] Angels (l-malāikati) | [the ones] having marks (musawwimīna).

3:126 And not made it Allah except as good news for you and to reassure your hearts with it. And there is no [the] victory except from [near] Allah, the All-Mighty, the All-Wise.

And not (wamā) | made it (jaʿalahu) | Allah (l-lahu) | except (illā) | as good news (bush'rā) | for you (lakum) | and to reassure (walitaṭma-inna) | your hearts (qulūbukum) | with it (bihi). | And there is no (wamā) | [the] victory (l-naṣru) | except (illā) | from (min) | [near] (ʿindi) | Allah (l-lahi), | the All-Mighty (l-ʿazīzi), | the All-Wise (l-ḥakīmi).

3:127 That He may cut off a part of those who disbelieved or suppress them so that they turn back disappointed.

That He may cut off (liyaqṭaʿa) | a part (ṭarafan) | of (mina) | those who (alladhīna) | disbelieved (kafarū) | or (aw) | suppress them (yakbitahum) | so that they turn back (fayanqalibū) | disappointed (khāibīna).

3:128 Not for you of the decision of anything whether He turns to them or punishes them for indeed, they are wrongdoers.

Not (laysa) | for you (laka) | of (mina) | the decision (l-amri) | of anything (shayon) | whether (aw) | He turns (yatūba) | to them (ʿalayhim) | or (aw) | punishes them (yuʿadhibahum) | for indeed, they (fa-innahum) | are wrongdoers (ẓālimūna).

3:129 And to Allah belongs what is in the heavens and what is in the earth, He forgives [for] whom He wills and punishes whom He wills. And Allah is Oft-Forgiving, Most Merciful.

And to Allah belongs (walillahi) | what (mā) | is in (fī) | the heavens (l-samāwāti) | and what (wamā) | is in (fī) | the earth (l-arḍi), | He forgives (yaghfiru) | [for] whom (liman) | He wills (yashāu) | and punishes (wayuʿadhibu) | whom (man) | He wills (yashāu). | And Allah (wal-lahu) | is Oft-Forgiving (ghafūrun), | Most Merciful (raḥīmun).

3:130 O you who believe! Do not eat the usury doubled multiplied. And fear Allah so that you may be successful.

O you (yāayyuhā) | who (alladhīna) | believe (āmanū)! | Do not (lā) | eat (takulū) | the usury (l-riba) | doubled (aḍʿāfan) | multiplied (muḍāʿafatan). | And fear (wa-ittaqū) | Allah (l-laha) | so that you may (laʿallakum) | be successful (tuf'liḥūna).

3:131 And fear the Fire which is prepared for the disbelievers.

And fear (wa-ittaqū) | the Fire (l-nāra) | which (allatī) | is prepared (uʿiddat) | for the disbelievers (lil'kāfirīna).

3:132 And obey Allah and the Messenger so that you may receive mercy.

And obey (wa-aṭīʿū) | Allah (l-laha) | and the Messenger (wal-rasūla) | so that you may (laʿallakum) | receive mercy (tur'ḥamūna).

3:133 And hasten to forgiveness from your Lord and a Garden - its width is like that of the heavens and the earth prepared for the pious.

And hasten (wasāriʿū) | to (ilā) | forgiveness (maghfiratin) | from (min) | your Lord (rabbikum) | and a Garden (wajannatin)- | its width (ʿarḍuhā) | is like that of the heavens (l-samāwātu) | and the earth (wal-arḍu) | prepared (uʿiddat) | for the pious (lil'muttaqīna).

3:134 Those who spend in [the] ease and in the hardship and those who restrain the anger and those who pardon [from] the people - and Allah loves the good-doers.

Those who (alladhīna) | spend (yunfiqūna) | in (fī) | [the] ease (l-sarāi) | and in the hardship (wal-ḍarāi) | and those who restrain (wal-kāẓimīna) | the anger (l-ghayẓa) | and those who pardon (wal-ʿāfīna) | [from] (ʿani) | the people (l-nāsi)- | and Allah (wal-lahu) | loves (yuḥibbu) | the good-doers (l-muḥ'sinīna).

3:135 And those when they did immorality or wronged themselves - they remember Allah then ask forgiveness for their sins - and who can forgive the sins except Allah? And not they persist on what they did while they know.

And those (wa-alladhīna) | when (idhā) | they did (faʿalū) | immorality (fāḥishatan) | or (aw) | wronged (ẓalamū) | themselves (anfusahum)- | they remember (dhakarū) | Allah (l-laha) | then ask forgiveness (fa-is'taghfarū) | for their sins (lidhunūbihim)- | and who (waman) | can forgive (yaghfiru) | the sins (l-dhunūba) | except (illā) | Allah (l-lahu)? | And not (walam) | they persist (yuṣirrū) | on (ʿalā) | what (mā) | they did (faʿalū) | while they (wahum) | know (yaʿlamūna).

3:136 Those - their reward is forgiveness from their Lord and Gardens flows from underneath it the rivers, abiding forever in it. And an excellent reward for the (righteous) workers.

Those (ulāika)- | their reward (jazāuhum) | is forgiveness (maghfiratun) | from (min) | their Lord (rabbihim) | and Gardens (wajannātun) | flows (tajrī) | from (min) | underneath it (taḥtihā) | the rivers (l-anhāru), | abiding forever (khālidīna) | in it (fīhā). | And an excellent (waniʿʿma) | reward (ajru) | for the (righteous) workers (l-ʿāmilīna).

3:137 Verily passed from before you situations, then travel in the earth and see how was the end of the deniers.

Verily (qad) | passed (khalat) | from (min) | before you (qablikum) | situations (sunanun), | then travel (fasīrū) | in (fī) | the earth (l-arḍi) | and see (fa-unẓurū) | how (kayfa) | was (kāna) | the end (ʿāqibatu) | of the deniers (l-mukadhibīna).

3:138 This is a declaration for the people and guidance and admonition for the God-fearing.

This (hādhā) | is a declaration (bayānun) | for the people (lilnnāsi) | and guidance (wahudan) | and admonition (wamawʿiẓatun) | for the God-fearing (lil'muttaqīna).

3:139 And do not weaken and do not grieve and you will be [the] superior, if you are believers.

And do not (walā) | weaken (tahinū) | and do not (walā) | grieve (taḥzanū) | and you will be (wa-antumu) | [the] superior (l-aʿlawna), | if (in) | you are (kuntum) | believers (mu'minīna).

3:140 If touched you a wound, so certainly has touched the people wound like it. And this [the] days We alternate them among the people [and] so that makes evident Allah those who believe[d] and take from you martyrs. And Allah does not love the wrongdoers.

If (in) | touched you (yamsaskum) | a wound (qarḥun), | so certainly (faqad) | has touched (massa) | the people (l-qawma) | wound (qarḥun) | like it (mith'luhu). | And this (watil'ka) | [the] days (l-ayāmu) | We alternate them (nudāwiluhā) | among (bayna) | the people (l-nāsi) | [and] so that makes evident (waliyaʿlama) | Allah (l-lahu) | those who (alladhīna) | believe[d] (āmanū) | and take (wayattakhidha) | from you (minkum) | martyrs (shuhadāa). | And Allah (wal-lahu) | does not (lā) | love (yuḥibbu) | the wrongdoers (l-ẓālimīna).

3:141 And so that may purify Allah those who believe and destroy the disbelievers.

And so that may purify (waliyumaḥḥiṣa) | Allah (l-lahu) | those who (alladhīna) | believe (āmanū) | and destroy (wayamḥaqa) | the disbelievers (l-kāfirīna).

3:142 Or do you think that you will enter Paradise while has not yet made evident Allah those who strove hard among you and made evident the steadfast.

Or (am) | do you think (ḥasib'tum) | that (an) | you will enter (tadkhulū) | Paradise (l-janata) | while has not yet (walammā) | made evident (yaʿlami) | Allah (l-lahu) | those who (alladhīna) | strove hard (jāhadū) | among you (minkum) | and made evident (wayaʿlama) | the steadfast (l-ṣābirīna).

3:143 And certainly you used to wish for death from before [that] you met it, then indeed, you have seen it while you were looking on.

And certainly (walaqad) | you used to (kuntum) | wish (tamannawna) | for death (l-mawta) | from (min) | before (qabli) | [that] (an) | you met it (talqawhu), | then indeed (faqad), | you have seen it (ra-aytumūhu) | while you were (wa-antum) | looking on (tanẓurūna).

3:144 And not is Muhammad - except a Messenger, certainly passed away from before him [the] other Messengers. So if he died or is slain will you turn back on your heels? And whoever turns back on his heels then never will he harm Allah in anything. And will reward Allah the grateful ones.

And not (wamā) | is Muhammad (muḥammadun)- | except (illā) | a Messenger (rasūlun), | certainly (qad) | passed away (khalat) | from (min) | before him (qablihi) | [the] other Messengers (l-rusulu). | So if (afa-in) | he died (māta) | or (aw) | is slain (qutila) | will you turn back (inqalabtum) | on (ʿalā) | your heels (aʿqābikum)? | And whoever (waman) | turns back (yanqalib) | on (ʿalā) | his heels (ʿaqibayhi) | then never (falan) | will he harm (yaḍurra) | Allah (l-laha) | in anything (shayan). | And will reward (wasayajzī) | Allah (l-lahu) | the grateful ones (l-shākirīna).

3:145 And not is for a soul that he dies except by the permission of Allah, at a decree determined. And whoever desires reward of the world - We will give him thereof; and whoever desires reward of the Hereafter We will give him thereof. And We will reward the grateful ones.

And not (wamā) | is (kāna) | for a soul (linafsin) | that (an) | he dies (tamūta) | except (illā) | by the permission (bi-idh'ni) | of Allah (l-lahi), | at a decree (kitāban) | determined (mu-ajjalan). | And whoever (waman) | desires (yurid) | reward (thawāba) | of the world (l-dun'yā)- | We will give him (nu'tihi) | thereof (min'hā); | and whoever (waman) | desires (yurid) | reward (thawāba) | of the Hereafter (l-ākhirati) | We will give him (nu'tihi) | thereof (min'hā). | And We will reward (wasanajzī) | the grateful ones (l-shākirīna).

3:146 And how many from a Prophet fought; with him were religious scholars many. But not they lost heart for what befell them in the way of Allah and not they weakened and not they gave in. And Allah loves the patient ones.

And how many (waka-ayyin) | from (min) | a Prophet (nabiyyin) | fought (qātala); | with him (maʿahu) | were religious scholars (ribbiyyūna) | many (kathīrun). | But not (famā) | they lost heart (wahanū) | for what (limā) | befell them (aṣābahum) | in (fī) | the way (sabīli) | of Allah (l-lahi) | and not (wamā) | they weakened (ḍaʿufū) | and not (wamā) | they gave in (is'takānū). | And Allah (wal-lahu) | loves (yuḥibbu) | the patient ones (l-ṣābirīna).

3:147 And not were their words except that they said, "Our Lord forgive for us our sins and our excesses in our affairs and make firm our feet and give us victory over [the people] the disbelievers."

And not (wamā) | were (kāna) | their words (qawlahum) | except (illā) | that (an) | they said (qālū), | "Our Lord (rabbanā) | forgive (igh'fir) | for us (lanā) | our sins (dhunūbanā) | and our excesses (wa-is'rāfanā) | in (fī) | our affairs (amrinā) | and make firm (wathabbit) | our feet (aqdāmanā) | and give us victory (wa-unṣur'nā) | over (ʿalā) | [the people] (l-qawmi) | the disbelievers. (l-kāfirīna)"

3:148 So gave them Allah reward in the world and good reward in the Hereafter. And Allah loves the good-doers.

So gave them (faātāhumu) | Allah (l-lahu) | reward (thawāba) | in the world (l-dun'yā) | and good (waḥus'na) | reward (thawābi) | in the Hereafter (l-ākhirati). | And Allah (wal-lahu) | loves (yuḥibbu) | the good-doers (l-muḥ'sinīna).

3:149 O you who believe! If you obey those who disbelieve, they will turn you back on your heels, then you will turn back as losers.

O you (yāayyuhā) | who (alladhīna) | believe (āmanū)! | If (in) | you obey (tuṭīʿū) | those who (alladhīna) | disbelieve (kafarū), | they will turn you back (yaruddūkum) | on (ʿalā) | your heels (aʿqābikum), | then you will turn back (fatanqalibū) | as losers (khāsirīna).

3:150 Nay, Allah is your Protector and He is the best of the Helpers.

Nay (bali), | Allah (l-lahu) | is your Protector (mawlākum) | and He (wahuwa) | is the best (khayru) | of the Helpers (l-nāṣirīna).

3:151 We will cast in the hearts of those who disbelieve [the] terror because they associated partners with Allah, what not He sent down about it any authority, and their refuge will be the Fire and wretched is the abode [of] the wrongdoers.

We will cast (sanul'qī) | in (fī) | the hearts (qulūbi) | of those who (alladhīna) | disbelieve (kafarū) | [the] terror (l-ruʿ'ba) | because (bimā) | they associated partners (ashrakū) | with Allah (bil-lahi), | what (mā) | not (lam) | He sent down (yunazzil) | about it (bihi) | any authority (sul'ṭānan), | and their refuge (wamawāhumu) | will be the Fire (l-nāru) | and wretched (wabi'sa) | is the abode (mathwā) | [of] the wrongdoers (l-ẓālimīna).

3:152 And certainly fulfilled to you Allah His promise, when you were killing them by His permission, until when you lost courage and you fell into dispute concerning the order and you disobeyed from after [what] He had shown you what you love. Among you are some who desire the world and among you are some who desire the Hereafter. Then He diverted you from them so that He may test you. And surely He forgave you. And Allah is the Possessor of Bounty for the believers.

And certainly (walaqad) | fulfilled to you (ṣadaqakumu) | Allah (l-lahu) | His promise (waʿdahu), | when (idh) | you were killing them (taḥussūnahum) | by His permission (bi-idh'nihi), | until (ḥattā) | when (idhā) | you lost courage (fashil'tum) | and you fell into dispute (watanāzaʿtum) | concerning (fī) | the order (l-amri) | and you disobeyed (waʿaṣaytum) | from (min) | after (baʿdi) | [what] (mā) | He had shown you (arākum) | what (mā) | you love (tuḥibbūna). | Among you (minkum) | are some who (man) | desire (yurīdu) | the world (l-dun'yā) | and among you (waminkum) | are some who (man) | desire (yurīdu) | the Hereafter (l-ākhirata). | Then (thumma) | He diverted you (ṣarafakum) | from them (ʿanhum) | so that He may test you (liyabtaliyakum). | And surely (walaqad) | He forgave (ʿafā) | you (ʿankum). | And Allah (wal-lahu) | is the Possessor (dhū) | of Bounty (faḍlin) | for (ʿalā) | the believers (l-mu'minīna).

3:153 When you were running uphill and not casting a glance on anyone while the Messenger was calling you [in] from behind you. So He repaid you with distress on distress so that not you grieve over what escaped you and not what had befallen you. And Allah is All-Aware of what you do.

When (idh) | you were running uphill (tuṣʿidūna) | and not (walā) | casting a glance (talwūna) | on (ʿalā) | anyone (aḥadin) | while the Messenger (wal-rasūlu) | was calling you (yadʿūkum) | [in] (fī) | from behind you (ukh'rākum). | So He repaid you (fa-athābakum) | with distress (ghamman) | on distress (bighammin) | so that not (likaylā) | you grieve (taḥzanū) | over (ʿalā) | what (mā) | escaped you (fātakum) | and not (walā) | what (mā) | had befallen you (aṣābakum). | And Allah (wal-lahu) | is All-Aware (khabīrun) | of what (bimā) | you do (taʿmalūna).

3:154 Then He sent down upon you from after the distress security - slumber overcoming a group of you, while a group certainly worried [them] about themselves thinking about Allah other than the truth - the thought of [the] ignorance. saying, "Is there for us from the matter any thing?" Say, "Indeed the matter all of it is for Allah." They hide in themselves what not they reveal to you, They say, "If was for us from the matter anything not we would have been killed here." Say, "If you were in your houses, surely would have come out those who - was decreed upon them [the] death towards their places of death. And that might test Allah what is in your breasts and that He may purge what is in your hearts. And Allah is All-Aware of what is in the breasts.

Then (thumma) | He sent down (anzala) | upon you (ʿalaykum) | from (min) | after (baʿdi) | the distress (l-ghami) | security (amanatan)- | slumber (nuʿāsan) | overcoming (yaghshā) | a group (ṭāifatan) | of you (minkum), | while a group (waṭāifatun) | certainly (qad) | worried [them] (ahammathum) | about themselves (anfusuhum) | thinking (yaẓunnūna) | about Allah (bil-lahi) | other than (ghayra) | the truth (l-ḥaqi)- | the thought (ẓanna) | of [the] ignorance (l-jāhiliyati). | saying (yaqūlūna), | "Is there (hal) | for us (lanā) | from (mina) | the matter (l-amri) | any (min) | thing? (shayin)" | Say (qul), | "Indeed (inna) | the matter (l-amra) | all of it (kullahu) | is for Allah. (lillahi)" | They hide (yukh'fūna) | in (fī) | themselves (anfusihim) | what (mā) | not (lā) | they reveal (yub'dūna) | to you (laka), | They say (yaqūlūna), | "If (law) | was (kāna) | for us (lanā) | from (mina) | the matter (l-amri) | anything (shayon) | not (mā) | we would have been killed (qutil'nā) | here. (hāhunā)" | Say (qul), | "If (law) | you were (kuntum) | in (fī) | your houses (buyūtikum), | surely would have come out (labaraza) | those who (alladhīna)- | was decreed (kutiba) | upon them (ʿalayhimu) | [the] death (l-qatlu) | towards (ilā) | their places of death (maḍājiʿihim). | And that might test (waliyabtaliya) | Allah (l-lahu) | what (mā) | is in (fī) | your breasts (ṣudūrikum) | and that He may purge (waliyumaḥḥiṣa) | what (mā) | is in (fī) | your hearts (qulūbikum). | And Allah (wal-lahu) | is All-Aware (ʿalīmun) | of what (bidhāti) | is in the breasts (l-ṣudūri).

3:155 Indeed, those who turned back among you on the day met the two hosts - only made them slip the Shaitaan for some of what they had earned. And surely forgave Allah [on] them, indeed, Allah is Oft-Forgiving, All-Forbearing.

Indeed (inna), | those who (alladhīna) | turned back (tawallaw) | among you (minkum) | on the day (yawma) | met (l-taqā) | the two hosts (l-jamʿāni)- | only (innamā) | made them slip (is'tazallahumu) | the Shaitaan (l-shayṭānu) | for some (bibaʿḍi) | of what (mā) | they had earned (kasabū). | And surely (walaqad) | forgave (ʿafā) | Allah (l-lahu) | [on] them (ʿanhum), | indeed (inna), | Allah (l-laha) | is Oft-Forgiving (ghafūrun), | All-Forbearing (ḥalīmun).

3:156 O you who believe[d]! Do not be like those who disbelieved and they said about their brothers when they traveled in the earth or they were fighting, "If they had been with us, not they would have died and not they would have been killed." So makes Allah that a regret in their hearts. And Allah gives life and causes death, and Allah of what you do is All-Seer.

O you (yāayyuhā) | who (alladhīna) | believe[d] (āmanū)! | Do not (lā) | be (takūnū) | like those who (ka-alladhīna) | disbelieved (kafarū) | and they said (waqālū) | about their brothers (li-ikh'wānihim) | when (idhā) | they traveled (ḍarabū) | in (fī) | the earth (l-arḍi) | or (aw) | they were (kānū) | fighting (ghuzzan), | "If (law) | they had been (kānū) | with us (ʿindanā), | not (mā) | they would have died (mātū) | and not (wamā) | they would have been killed. (qutilū)" | So makes (liyajʿala) | Allah (l-lahu) | that (dhālika) | a regret (ḥasratan) | in (fī) | their hearts (qulūbihim). |

And Allah (wal-lahu) | gives life (yuḥ'yī) | and causes death (wayumītu), | and Allah (wal-lahu) | of what (bimā) | you do (taʿmalūna) | is All-Seer (baṣīrun).

3:157 And if you are killed in the way of Allah or die[d] - certainly forgiveness from Allah and Mercy are better than what they accumulate.

And if (wala-in) | you are killed (qutil'tum) | in (fī) | the way (sabīli) | of Allah (l-lahi) | or (aw) | die[d] (muttum)- | certainly forgiveness (lamaghfiratun) | from (mina) | Allah (l-lahi) | and Mercy (waraḥmatun) | are better (khayrun) | than what (mimmā) | they accumulate (yajmaʿūna).

3:158 And if you die or are killed, surely to Allah you will be gathered.

And if (wala-in) | you die (muttum) | or (aw) | are killed (qutil'tum), | surely to (la-ilā) | Allah (l-lahi) | you will be gathered (tuḥ'sharūna).

3:159 So because of Mercy from Allah you dealt gently with them. And if you had been rude and harsh at [the] heart, surely they would have dispersed from around you. Then pardon [from] them and ask forgiveness for them and consult them in the matter. Then when you have decided, then put trust on Allah. Indeed, Allah loves the ones who put trust in Him.

So because (fabimā) | of Mercy (raḥmatin) | from (mina) | Allah (l-lahi) | you dealt gently (linta) | with them (lahum). | And if (walaw) | you had been (kunta) | rude (faẓẓan) | and harsh (ghalīẓa) | at [the] heart (l-qalbi), | surely they would have dispersed (la-infaḍḍū) | from (min) | around you (ḥawlika). | Then pardon (fa-uʿ'fu) | [from] them (ʿanhum) | and ask forgiveness (wa-is'taghfir) | for them (lahum) | and consult them (washāwir'hum) | in (fī) | the matter (l-amri). | Then when (fa-idhā) | you have decided (ʿazamta), | then put trust (fatawakkal) | on (ʿalā) | Allah (l-lahi). | Indeed (inna), | Allah (l-laha) | loves (yuḥibbu) | the ones who put trust in Him (l-mutawakilīna).

3:160 If helps you Allah, then not can overcome [for] you, and if He forsakes you, then who is the one who can help you from after Him? And on Allah - let put their trust. the believers.

If (in) | helps you (yanṣur'kumu) | Allah (l-lahu), | then not (falā) | can overcome (ghāliba) | [for] you (lakum), | and if (wa-in) | He forsakes you (yakhdhul'kum), | then who (faman) | is (dhā) | the one who (alladhī) | can help you (yanṣurukum) | from (min) | after Him (baʿdihi)? | And on (waʿalā) | Allah (l-lahi)- | let put their trust (falyatawakkali). | the believers (l-mu'minūna).

3:161 And not is for a Prophet that he defrauds. And whoever defrauds will bring what he had defrauded on the Day of Resurrection. Then is repaid in full every soul what it earned and they will not be wronged.

And not (wamā) | is (kāna) | for a Prophet (linabiyyin) | that (an) | he defrauds (yaghulla). | And whoever (waman) | defrauds (yaghlul) | will bring (yati) | what (bimā) | he had defrauded (ghalla) | on the Day (yawma) | of Resurrection (l-qiyāmati). | Then (thumma) | is repaid in full (tuwaffā) | every (kullu) | soul (nafsin) | what (mā) | it earned (kasabat) | and they (wahum) | will not (lā) | be wronged (yuẓ'lamūna).

3:162 So is the one who pursues the pleasure of Allah like the one who draws on himself wrath of Allah and his abode is hell, and wretched is the destination?

So is the one who (afamani) | pursues (ittabaʿa) | the pleasure (riḍ'wāna) | of Allah (l-lahi) | like the one who (kaman) | draws (bāa) | on himself wrath (bisakhaṭin) | of (mina) | Allah (l-lahi) | and his abode (wamawāhu) | is hell (jahannamu), | and wretched (wabi'sa) | is the destination (l-maṣīru)?

3:163 They are in varying degrees near Allah, and Allah is All-Seer of what they do.

They (hum) | are in varying degrees (darajātun) | near (ʿinda) | Allah (l-lahi), | and Allah (wal-lahu) | is All-Seer (baṣīrun) | of what (bimā) | they do (yaʿmalūna).

3:164 Certainly bestowed a Favor Allah upon the believers as He raised among them a Messenger from themselves reciting to them His Verses and purifying them, and teaching them the Book and the wisdom, although they were from before that certainly in the error clear.

Certainly (laqad) | bestowed a Favor (manna) | Allah (l-lahu) | upon (ʿalā) | the believers (l-mu'minīna) | as (idh) | He raised (baʿatha) | among them (fīhim) | a Messenger (rasūlan) | from (min) | themselves (anfusihim) | reciting (yatlū) | to them (ʿalayhim) | His Verses (āyātihi) | and purifying them (wayuzakkīhim), | and teaching them (wayuʿallimuhumu) | the Book (l-kitāba) | and the wisdom (wal-ḥik'mata), | although (wa-in) | they were (kānū) | from (min) | before that (qablu) | certainly in (lafī) | the error (ḍalālin) | clear (mubīnin).

3:165 Or when struck you disaster, surely you had struck (them) twice of it, you said, "From where is this?" Say, "It is from yourselves." Indeed, Allah is on every thing All-Powerful.

Or when (awalammā) | struck you (aṣābatkum) | disaster (muṣībatun), | surely (qad) | you had struck (them (aṣabtum)) | twice of it (mith'layhā), | you said (qul'tum), | "From where (annā) | is this? (hādhā)" | Say (qul), | "It (huwa) | is (min) | from (ʿindi) | yourselves. (anfusikum)" | Indeed (inna), | Allah (l-laha) | is on (ʿalā) | every (kulli) | thing (shayin) | All-Powerful (qadīrun).

3:166 And what struck you on the day when met the two hosts was by (the) permission of Allah and that He might make evident the believers.

And what (wamā) | struck you (aṣābakum) | on the day (yawma) | when met (l-taqā) | the two hosts (l-jamʿāni) | was by (the) permission (fabi-idh'ni) | of Allah (l-lahi) | and that He might make evident (waliyaʿlama) | the believers (l-mu'minīna).

3:167 And that He might make evident those who are hypocrites. And it was said to them, "Come, fight in the way of Allah or defend." They said, "If we knew fighting certainly we would have followed you." They - to disbelief that day were nearer than [them] to the faith, saying with their mouths what was not in their hearts. And Allah is Most Knowing of what they conceal.

And that He might make evident (waliyaʿlama) | those who (alladhīna) | are hypocrites (nāfaqū). | And it was said (waqīla) | to them (lahum), | "Come (taʿālaw), | fight (qātilū) | in (fī) | the way (sabīli) | of Allah (l-lahi) | or (awi) | defend. (id'fa'ū)" | They said (qālū), | "If (law) | we knew (naʿlamu) | fighting (qitālan) | certainly we would have followed you. (la-ittabaʿnākum)" | They (hum)- | to disbelief (lil'kuf'ri) | that day (yawma-idhin) | were nearer (aqrabu) | than [them] (min'hum) | to the faith (lil'īmāni), | saying (yaqūlūna) | with their mouths (bi-afwāhihim) | what (mā) | was not (laysa) | in (fī) | their hearts (qulūbihim). | And Allah (wal-lahu) | is Most Knowing (aʿlamu) | of what (bimā) | they conceal (yaktumūna).

3:168 Those who said about their brothers while they sat, "If they had obeyed us not they would have been killed." Say, "Then avert from yourselves [the] death if you are truthful.

Those who (alladhīna) | said (qālū) | about their brothers (li-ikh'wānihim) | while they sat (waqaʿadū), | "If (law) | they had obeyed us (aṭāʿūnā) | not (mā) | they would have been killed. (qutilū)" | Say (qul), | "Then avert (fa-id'raū) | from (ʿan) | yourselves (anfusikumu) | [the] death (l-mawta) | if (in) | you are (kuntum) | truthful (ṣādiqīna).

3:169 And do not think of those who are killed in the way of Allah as dead. Nay! They are alive, near their Lord; they are given provision.

And do not (walā) | think (taḥsabanna) | of those who (alladhīna) | are killed (qutilū) | in (fī) | the way (sabīli) | of Allah (l-lahi) | as dead (amwātan). | Nay (bal)! | They are alive (aḥyāon), | near (ʿinda) | their Lord (rabbihim); | they are given provision (yur'zaqūna).

3:170 Rejoicing in what bestowed them Allah of His Bounty, and they receive good tidings about those who have not yet joined [with] them [from] but are left behind - that there will be no fear on them and not they will grieve.

Rejoicing (fariḥīna) | in what (bimā) | bestowed them (ātāhumu) | Allah (l-lahu) | of (min) | His Bounty (faḍlihi), | and they receive good tidings (wayastabshirūna) | about those who (bi-alladhīna) | have not (lam) | yet joined (yalḥaqū) | [with] them (bihim) | [from] (min) | but are left behind (khalfihim)- | that there will be no (allā) | fear (khawfun) | on them (ʿalayhim) | and not (walā) | they (hum) | will grieve (yaḥzanūna).

3:171 They receive good tidings of Favor from Allah and Bounty and that Allah does not let go waste the reward of the believers.

They receive good tidings (yastabshirūna) | of Favor (biniʿ'matin) | from (mina) | Allah (l-lahi) | and Bounty (wafaḍlin) | and that (wa-anna) | Allah (l-laha) | does not (lā) | let go waste (yuḍīʿu) | the reward (ajra) | of the believers (l-mu'minīna).

3:172 Those who responded to Allah and the Messenger from after what befell them - the injury - for those who did good among them and feared Allah, is a reward - great.

Those who (alladhīna) | responded (is'tajābū) | to Allah (lillahi) | and the Messenger (wal-rasūli) | from (min) | after (baʿdi) | what (mā) | befell them (aṣābahumu)- | the injury (l-qarḥu)- | for those who (lilladhīna) | did good (aḥsanū) | among them (min'hum) | and feared Allah (wa-ittaqaw), | is a reward (ajrun)- | great (ʿaẓīmun).

3:173 Those who said to them [the people], "Indeed the people have certainly gathered against you, so fear them." But it increased them in faith and they said, "Sufficient for us is Allah and He is the best [the] Disposer of affairs."

Those who (alladhīna) | said (qāla) | to them (lahumu) | [the people] (l-nāsu), | "Indeed (inna) | the people (l-nāsa) | have certainly (qad) | gathered (jamaʿū) | against you (lakum), | so fear them. (fa-ikh'shawhum)" | But it increased them (fazādahum) | in faith (īmānan) | and they said (waqālū), | "Sufficient for us (ḥasbunā) | is Allah (l-lahu) | and He is the best (waniʿ'ma) | [the] Disposer of affairs. (l-wakīlu)"

3:174 So they returned with the Favor of Allah and Bounty, not touched them any harm. And they followed the pleasure of Allah, and Allah is Possessor of Bounty great.

So they returned (fa-inqalabū) | with the Favor (biniʿ'matin) | of (mina) | Allah (l-lahi) | and Bounty (wafaḍlin), | not (lam) | touched them (yamsashum) | any harm (sūon). | And they followed (wa-ittabaʿū) | the pleasure (riḍ'wāna) | of Allah (l-lahi), | and Allah (wal-lahu) | is Possessor (dhū) | of Bounty (faḍlin) | great (ʿaẓīmin).

3:175 It is only that the Shaitaan frightens you of his allies. So do not fear them, but fear Me, if you are believers.

It is only (innamā) | that (dhālikumu) | the Shaitaan (l-shayṭānu) | frightens you (yukhawwifu) | of his allies (awliyāahu). | So do not (falā) | fear them (takhāfūhum), | but fear Me (wakhāfūni), | if (in) | you are (kuntum) | believers (mu'minīna).

3:176 And let not grieve you those who hasten into [the] disbelief. Indeed, they never will harm Allah in anything. intends Allah that not He will set for them any portion in the Hereafter. And for them is a punishment great.

And let not (walā) | grieve you (yaḥzunka) | those who (alladhīna) | hasten (yusāriʿūna) | into (fī) | [the] disbelief (l-kuf'ri). | Indeed, they (innahum) | never (lan) | will harm (yaḍurrū) | Allah (l-laha) | in anything (shayan). | intends (yurīdu) | Allah (l-lahu) | that not (allā) | He will set (yajʿala) | for them (lahum) | any portion (ḥaẓẓan) | in (fī) | the Hereafter (l-ākhirati). | And for them (walahum) | is a punishment (ʿadhābun) | great (ʿaẓīmun).

3:177 Indeed, those who have purchased [the] disbelief with the faith never will they harm Allah in anything, and for them is a punishment painful.

Indeed (inna), | those who (alladhīna) | have purchased (ish'tarawū) | [the] disbelief (l-kuf'ra) | with the faith (bil-īmāni) | never (lan) | will they harm (yaḍurrū) | Allah (l-laha) | in anything (shayan), | and for them (walahum) | is a punishment (ʿadhābun) | painful (alīmun).

3:178 And let not think those who disbelieved that We give respite to them is good for themselves. Only We give respite to them so that they may increase in sins, and for them is a punishment humiliating.

And let not (walā) | think (yaḥsabanna) | those who (alladhīna) | disbelieved (kafarū) | that (annamā) | We give respite (num'lī) | to them (lahum) | is good (khayrun) | for themselves (li-anfusihim). | Only (innamā) | We give respite (num'lī) | to them (lahum) | so that they may increase (liyazdādū) | in sins (ith'man), | and for them (walahum) | is a punishment (ʿadhābun) | humiliating (muhīnun).

3:179 Not is Allah to leave the believers on what you are in [it] until He separates the evil from the good. And not is Allah to inform you about the unseen, [and] but Allah chooses from His Messengers whom He wills, so believe in Allah and His Messengers, and if you believe and fear Allah then for you is a reward great.

Not (mā) | is (kāna) | Allah (l-lahu) | to leave (liyadhara) | the believers (l-mu'minīna) | on (ʿalā) | what (mā) | you are (antum) | in [it] (ʿalayhi) | until (ḥattā) | He separates (yamīza) | the evil (l-khabītha) | from (mina) | the good (l-ṭayibi). | And not (wamā) | is (kāna) | Allah (l-lahu) | to inform you (liyuṭ'liʿakum) | about (ʿalā) | the unseen (l-ghaybi), | [and] but (walākinna) | Allah (l-laha) | chooses (yajtabī) | from (min) | His Messengers (rusulihi) | whom (man) | He wills (yashāu), | so believe (faāminū) | in Allah (bil-lahi) | and His Messengers (warusulihi), | and if (wa-in) | you believe (tu'minū) | and fear Allah (watattaqū) | then for you (falakum) | is a reward (ajrun) | great (ʿaẓīmun).

3:180 And let not think those who withhold of what has given them Allah of His Bounty that it is good for them. Nay, it is bad for them. Their necks will be encircled with what they withheld [with it] on the Day of [the] Resurrection. And for Allah is the heritage of the heavens and the earth. And Allah, with what you do, is All-Aware.

And let not (walā) | think (yaḥsabanna) | those who (alladhīna) | withhold (yabkhalūna) | of what (bimā) | has given them (ātāhumu) | Allah (l-lahu) | of (min) | His Bounty (faḍlihi) | that it (huwa) | is good (khayran) | for them (lahum). | Nay (bal), | it (huwa) | is bad (sharrun) | for them (lahum). | Their necks will be encircled (sayuṭawwaqūna) | with what (mā) | they withheld (bakhilū) | [with it] (bihi) | on the Day (yawma) | of [the] Resurrection (l-qiyāmati). | And for Allah (walillahi) | is the heritage (mīrāthu) | of the heavens (l-samāwāti) | and the earth (wal-arḍi). | And Allah (wal-lahu), | with what (bimā) | you do (taʿmalūna), | is All-Aware (khabīrun).

3:181 Certainly, heard Allah the saying of those who said, "Indeed Allah is poor while we are rich." We will record what they said and their killing the Prophets without any right, and We will say, "Taste the punishment of the Burning Fire."

Certainly (laqad), | heard (samiʿa) | Allah (l-lahu) | the saying (qawla) | of those who (alladhīna) | said (qālū), | "Indeed (inna) | Allah (l-laha) | is poor (faqīrun) | while we (wanaḥnu) | are rich. (aghniyāu)" | We will record (sanaktubu) | what (mā) | they said (qālū) | and their killing (waqatlahumu) | the Prophets (l-anbiyāa) | without (bighayri) | any right (ḥaqqin), | and We will say (wanaqūlu), | "Taste (dhūqū) | the punishment (ʿadhāba) | of the Burning Fire. (l-ḥarīqi)"

3:182 That is because of what sent forth your hands and that Allah is not unjust to His slaves.

That (dhālika) | is because (bimā) | of what sent forth (qaddamat) | your hands (aydīkum) | and that (wa-anna) | Allah (l-laha) | is not (laysa) | unjust (biẓallāmin) | to His slaves (lilʿabīdi).

3:183 Those who said, "Indeed Allah has taken promise from us that not we should believe in a Messenger until he brings to us a sacrifice - consumes it the fire." Say, "Surely came to you Messengers from before me with the clear Signs and with what you speak. So why you killed them, if you are truthful.

Those who (alladhīna) | said (qālū), | "Indeed (inna) | Allah (l-laha) | has taken promise (ʿahida) | from us (ilaynā) | that not (allā) | we should believe (nu'mina) | in a Messenger (lirasūlin) | until (ḥattā) | he brings to us (yatiyanā) | a sacrifice (biqur'bānin)- | consumes it (takuluhu) | the fire. (l-nāru)" | Say (qul), | "Surely (qad) | came to you (jāakum) | Messengers (rusulun) | from (min) | before me (qablī) | with the clear Signs (bil-bayināti) | and with what (wabi-alladhī) | you speak (qul'tum). | So why (falima) | you killed them (qataltumūhum), | if (in) | you are (kuntum) | truthful (ṣādiqīna).

3:184 Then if they reject you, then certainly were rejected Messengers from before you who came with the clear Signs and the Scriptures and the Book - [the] Enlightening.

Then if (fa-in) | they reject you (kadhabūka), | then certainly (faqad) | were rejected (kudhiba) | Messengers (rusulun) | from (min) | before you (qablika) | who came (jāū) | with the clear Signs (bil-bayināti) | and the Scriptures (wal-zuburi) | and the Book (wal-kitābi)- | [the] Enlightening (l-munīri).

3:185 Every soul will taste [the] death, and only you will be paid in full your reward on the Day of [the] Resurrection. Then whoever is drawn away from the Fire and admitted to Paradise then surely he is successful. And not is the life of the world except enjoyment of delusion.

Every (kullu) | soul (nafsin) | will taste (dhāiqatu) | [the] death (l-mawti), | and only (wa-innamā) | you will be paid in full (tuwaffawna) | your reward (ujūrakum) | on the Day (yawma) | of [the] Resurrection (l-qiyāmati). | Then whoever (faman) | is drawn away (zuḥ'ziḥa) | from (ʿani) | the Fire (l-nāri) | and admitted (wa-ud'khila) | to Paradise (l-janata) | then surely (faqad) | he is successful (fāza). | And not (wamā) | is the life (l-ḥayatu) | of the world (l-dun'yā) | except (illā) | enjoyment (matāʿu) | of delusion (l-ghurūri).

3:186 You will certainly be tested in your wealth and yourselves. And you will certainly hear from those who were given the Book from before you and from those who associate partners with Allah - hurtful things many, and if you are patient and fear Allah then indeed, that is of the matters of determination.

You will certainly be tested (latub'lawunna) | in (fī) | your wealth (amwālikum) | and yourselves (wa-anfusikum). | And you will certainly hear (walatasmaʿunna) | from (mina) | those who (alladhīna) | were given (ūtū) | the Book (l-kitāba) | from (min) | before you (qablikum) | and from (wamina) | those who (alladhīna) | associate partners with Allah (ashrakū)- | hurtful things (adhan) | many (kathīran), | and if (wa-in) | you are patient (taṣbirū) | and fear Allah (watattaqū) | then indeed (fa-inna), | that (dhālika) | is of (min) | the matters (ʿazmi) | of determination (l-umūri).

3:187 And when took Allah a Covenant from those who were given the Book, "You certainly make it clear to the mankind and do not conceal it. Then they threw it behind their backs and they exchanged [with] it for a price little. And wretched is what they purchase.

And when (wa-idh) | took (akhadha) | Allah (l-lahu) | a Covenant (mīthāqa) | from those who (alladhīna) | were given (ūtū) | the Book (l-kitāba), | "You certainly make it clear (latubayyinunnahu) | to the mankind (lilnnāsi) | and do not (walā) | conceal it (taktumūnahu). | Then they threw it (fanabadhūhu) | behind (warāa) | their backs (ẓuhūrihim) | and they exchanged (wa-ish'taraw) | [with] it (bihi) | for a price (thamanan) | little (qalīlan). | And wretched (fabi'sa) | is what (mā) | they purchase (yashtarūna).

3:188 Do not think that those who rejoice in what they have brought and they love that they be praised for what not they do - so do not think that they will escape from the punishment; and for them is a punishment painful.

Do not (lā) | think (taḥsabanna) | that those who (alladhīna) | rejoice (yafraḥūna) | in what (bimā) | they have brought (ataw) | and they love (wayuḥibbūna) | that (an) | they be praised (yuḥ'madū) | for what (bimā) | not (lam) | they do (yafʿalū)- | so do not (falā) | think that they (taḥsabannahum) | will escape (bimafāzatin) | from (mina) | the punishment (l-ʿadhābi); | and for them (walahum) | is a punishment (ʿadhābun) | painful (alīmun).

3:189 And for Allah is the dominion of the heavens and the earth, and Allah is on every thing All-Powerful.

And for Allah (walillahi) | is the dominion (mul'ku) | of the heavens (l-samāwāti) | and the earth (wal-arḍi), | and Allah (wal-lahu) | is on (ʿalā) | every (kulli) | thing (shayin) | All-Powerful (qadīrun).

3:190 Indeed, in the creation of the heavens and the earth and in the alternation of the night and the day are surely Signs for men of understanding.

Indeed (inna), | in (fī) | the creation (khalqi) | of the heavens (l-samāwāti) | and the earth (wal-arḍi) | and in the alternation (wa-ikh'tilāfi) | of the night (al-layli) | and the day (wal-nahāri) | are surely Signs (laāyātin) | for men (li-ulī) | of understanding (l-albābi).

3:191 Those who remember Allah standing, and sitting and on their sides and they reflect on the creation of the heavens and the earth, "Our Lord, not You have created this in vain. Glory be to You, so save us from the punishment of the Fire.

Those who (alladhīna) | remember (yadhkurūna) | Allah (l-laha) | standing (qiyāman), | and sitting (waquʿūdan) | and on (waʿalā) | their sides (junūbihim) | and they reflect (wayatafakkarūna) | on (fī) | the creation (khalqi) | of the heavens (l-samāwāti) | and the earth (wal-arḍi), | "Our Lord (rabbanā), | not (mā) | You have created (khalaqta) | this (hādhā) | in vain (bāṭilan). | Glory be to You (sub'ḥānaka), | so save us (faqinā) | from the punishment (ʿadhāba) | of the Fire (l-nāri).

3:192 Our Lord, indeed [You] whom You admit to the Fire then surely You have disgraced him, and not for the wrongdoers are any helpers.

Our Lord (rabbanā), | indeed [You] (innaka) | whom (man) | You admit (tud'khili) | to the Fire (l-nāra) | then surely (faqad) | You have disgraced him (akhzaytahu), | and not (wamā) | for the wrongdoers (lilẓẓālimīna) | are any (min) | helpers (anṣārin).

3:193 Our Lord, indeed we [we] heard a caller calling to the faith that "Believe in your Lord," so we have believed. Our Lord so forgive for us our sins and remove from us our evil deeds, and cause us to die with the righteous.

Our Lord (rabbanā), | indeed we (innanā) | [we] heard (samiʿ'nā) | a caller (munādiyan) | calling (yunādī) | to the faith (lil'īmāni) | that (an) | "Believe (āminū) | in your Lord, (birabbikum)" | so we have believed (faāmannā). | Our Lord (rabbanā) | so forgive (fa-igh'fir) | for us (lanā) | our sins (dhunūbanā) | and remove (wakaffir) | from us (ʿannā) | our evil deeds (sayyiātinā), | and cause us to die (watawaffanā) | with (maʿa) | the righteous (l-abrāri).

3:194 Our Lord, grant us what You promised us through Your Messengers and do not disgrace us on the Day of [the] Resurrection. Indeed, You do not break the promise."

Our Lord (rabbanā), | grant us (waātinā) | what (mā) | You promised us (waʿadttanā) | through (ʿalā) | Your Messengers (rusulika) | and do not (walā) | disgrace us (tukh'zinā) | on the Day (yawma) | of [the] Resurrection (l-qiyāmati). | Indeed, You (innaka) | do not (lā) | break (tukh'lifu) | the promise. (l-mīʿāda)"

3:195 Then responded to them their Lord, "Indeed, I will not let go waste deeds of the doer among you [from] whether male or female each of you from the other. So those who emigrated and were driven out from their homes, and were harmed in My way and fought and were killed - surely I will remove from them their evil deeds and surely I will admit them to Gardens flowing from underneath them the rivers - a reward from [near] Allah. And Allah - with Him is the best reward."

Then responded (fa-is'tajāba) | to them (lahum) | their Lord (rabbuhum), | "Indeed, I (annī) | will not (lā) | let go waste (uḍīʿu) | deeds (ʿamala) | of the doer (ʿāmilin) | among you (minkum) | [from] (min) | whether male (dhakarin) | or (aw) | female (unthā) | each of you (baʿḍukum) | from (min) | the other (baʿḍin). | So those who (fa-alladhīna) | emigrated (hājarū) | and were driven out (wa-ukh'rijū) | from (min) | their homes (diyārihim), | and were harmed (waūdhū) | in (fī) | My way (sabīlī) | and fought (waqātalū) | and were killed (waqutilū)- | surely I will remove (la-ukaffiranna) | from them (ʿanhum) | their evil deeds (sayyiātihim) | and surely I will admit them (wala-ud'khilannahum) | to Gardens (jannātin) | flowing (tajrī) | from (min) | underneath them (taḥtihā) | the rivers (l-anhāru)- | a reward (thawāban) | from (min) | [near] (ʿindi) | Allah (l-lahi). | And Allah (wal-lahu)- | with Him (ʿindahu) | is the best (ḥus'nu) | reward. (l-thawābi)"

3:196 Let not deceive you the movement of those who disbelieved in the land.

Let not (lā) | deceive you (yaghurrannaka) | the movement (taqallubu) | of those who (alladhīna) | disbelieved (kafarū) | in (fī) | the land (l-bilādi).

3:197 An enjoyment little, then their abode is hell - [and] a wretched [the] resting place.

An enjoyment (matāʿun) | little (qalīlun), | then (thumma) | their abode (mawāhum) | is hell (jahannamu)- | [and] a wretched (wabi'sa) | [the] resting place (l-mihādu).

3:198 But those who fear their Lord, for them will be Gardens flows from underneath them the rivers, will abide forever in it - a hospitality from [near] Allah. And what is with Allah is best for the righteous.

But (lākini) | those who (alladhīna) | fear (ittaqaw) | their Lord (rabbahum), | for them (lahum) | will be Gardens (jannātun) | flows (tajrī) | from (min) | underneath them (taḥtihā) | the rivers (l-anhāru), | will abide forever (khālidīna) | in it (fīhā)- | a hospitality (nuzulan) | from (min) | [near] (ʿindi) | Allah (l-lahi). | And what (wamā) | is with (ʿinda) | Allah (l-lahi) | is best (khayrun) | for the righteous (lil'abrāri).

3:199 And indeed, among the People of the Book are those who believe in Allah and what was revealed to you and what was revealed to them - humbly submissive to Allah. Not do they exchange [with] the Verses of Allah for a price little. Those, for them, their reward is with their Lord. Indeed, Allah is swift in taking the account.

And indeed (wa-inna), | among (min) | the People (ahli) | of the Book (l-kitābi) | are those who (laman) | believe (yu'minu) | in Allah (bil-lahi) | and what (wamā) | was revealed (unzila) | to you (ilaykum) | and what (wamā) | was revealed (unzila) | to them (ilayhim)- | humbly submissive (khāshiʿīna) | to Allah (lillahi). | Not (lā) | do they exchange (yashtarūna) | [with] the Verses (biāyāti) | of Allah (l-lahi) | for a price (thamanan) | little (qalīlan). | Those (ulāika), | for them (lahum), | their reward (ajruhum) | is with (ʿinda) | their Lord (rabbihim). | Indeed (inna), | Allah (l-laha) | is swift (sarīʿu) | in taking the account (l-ḥisābi).

3:200 O you who believe[d]! Be steadfast and [be] patient and [be] constant and fear Allah so that you may be successful.

O you (yāayyuhā) | who (alladhīna) | believe[d] (āmanū)! | Be steadfast (iṣ'birū) | and [be] patient (waṣābirū) | and [be] constant (warābiṭū) | and fear (wa-ittaqū) | Allah (l-laha) | so that you may (laʿallakum) | be successful (tuf'liḥūna).

Chapter (4) Sūrat l-Nisāa (The Women)

4:1 O mankind! Fear your Lord the One Who created you from a soul single and created from it its mate and dispersed from both of them men many and women. And fear Allah through Whom you ask [with it] and the wombs. Indeed, Allah is over you Ever-Watchful.

O (yāayyuhā) | mankind (l-nāsu)! | Fear (ittaqū) | your Lord (rabbakumu) | the One Who (alladhī) | created you (khalaqakum) | from (min) | a soul (nafsin) | single (wāḥidatin) | and created (wakhalaqa) | from it (min'hā) | its mate (zawjahā) | and dispersed (wabatha) | from both of them (min'humā) | men (rijālan) | many (kathīran) | and women (wanisāan). | And fear (wa-ittaqū) | Allah (l-laha) | through Whom (alladhī) | you ask (tasāalūna) | [with it] (bihi) | and the wombs (wal-arḥāma). | Indeed (inna), | Allah (l-laha) | is (kāna) | over you (ʿalaykum) | Ever-Watchful (raqīban).

4:2 And give to the orphans their wealth, and do not exchange the bad with the good, and do not consume their wealth with your wealth. Indeed, it is a sin great.

And give (waātū) | to the orphans (l-yatāmā) | their wealth (amwālahum), | and do not (walā) | exchange (tatabaddalū) | the bad (l-khabītha) | with the good (bil-ṭayibi), | and do not (walā) | consume (takulū) | their wealth (amwālahum) | with (ilā) | your wealth (amwālikum). | Indeed, it (innahu) | is (kāna) | a sin (ḥūban) | great (kabīran).

4:3 And if you fear that not you will be able to do justice with the orphans, then marry what seems suitable to you from the women two, or three, or four. But if you fear that not you can do justice then marry one or what possesses your right hand. That is more appropriate that may not you oppress.

And if (wa-in) | you fear (khif'tum) | that not (allā) | you will be able to do justice (tuq'siṭū) | with (fī) | the orphans (l-yatāmā), | then marry (fa-inkiḥū) | what (mā) | seems suitable (ṭāba) | to you (lakum) | from (mina) | the women (l-nisāi) | two (mathnā), | or three (wathulātha), | or four (warubāʿa). | But if (fa-in) | you fear (khif'tum) | that not (allā) | you can do justice (taʿdilū) | then marry one (fawāḥidatan) | or (aw) | what (mā) | possesses (malakat) | your right hand (aymānukum). | That (dhālika) | is more appropriate (adnā) | that may not (allā) | you oppress (taʿūlū).

4:4 And give the women their dower graciously. But if they remit to you of anything of it on their own, then eat it in satisfaction and ease.

And give (waātū) | the women (l-nisāa) | their dower (ṣaduqātihinna) | graciously (niḥ'latan). | But if (fa-in) | they remit (ṭib'na) | to you (lakum) | of (ʿan) | anything (shayin) | of it (min'hu) | on their own (nafsan), | then eat it (fakulūhu) | in satisfaction (hanīan) | and ease (marīan).

4:5 And do not give the foolish your wealth which was made by Allah for you a means of support but provide (for) them with it and clothe them and speak to them words of kindness.

And do not (walā) | give (tu'tū) | the foolish (l-sufahāa) | your wealth (amwālakumu) | which (allatī) | was made (jaʿala) | by Allah (l-lahu) | for you (lakum) | a means of support (qiyāman) | but provide (for) them (wa-ur'zuqūhum) | with it (fīhā) | and clothe them (wa-ik'sūhum) | and speak (waqūlū) | to them (lahum) | words (qawlan) | of kindness (maʿrūfan).

4:6 And test the orphans until [when] they reach[ed] the age of marriage, then if you perceive in them sound judgement then deliver to them their wealth. And do not eat it extravagantly and hastily fearing that they will grow up. And whoever is rich then he should refrain, and whoever is poor then let him eat of it in a fair manner. Then when you deliver to them their wealth then take witnesses on them. And is sufficient Allah as a Reckoner.

And test (wa-ib'talū) | the orphans (l-yatāmā) | until (ḥattā) | [when] (idhā) | they reach[ed] (balaghū) | the age of marriage (l-nikāḥa), | then if (fa-in) | you perceive (ānastum) | in them (min'hum) | sound judgement (rush'dan) | then deliver (fa-id'fa'ū) | to them (ilayhim) | their wealth (amwālahum). | And do not (walā) | eat it (takulūhā) | extravagantly (is'rāfan) | and hastily (wabidāran) | fearing that (an) | they will grow up (yakbarū). | And whoever (waman) | is (kāna) | rich (ghaniyyan) | then he should refrain (falyastaʿfif), | and whoever (waman) | is (kāna) | poor (faqīran) | then let him eat of it (falyakul) | in a fair manner (bil-maʿrūfi). | Then when (fa-idhā) | you deliver (dafaʿtum) | to them (ilayhim) | their wealth (amwālahum) | then take witnesses (fa-ashhidū) | on them (ʿalayhim). | And is sufficient (wakafā) | Allah (bil-lahi) | as a Reckoner (ḥasīban).

4:7 For the men a portion of what is left by the parents, and the near relatives and for the women a portion of what is left by parents and the near relatives of what is little of it or much - a portion obligatory.

For the men (lilrrijāli) | a portion (naṣībun) | of what (mimmā) | is left (taraka) | by the parents (l-wālidāni), | and the near relatives (wal-aqrabūna) | and for the women (walilnnisāi) | a portion (naṣībun) | of what (mimmā) | is left (taraka) | by parents (l-wālidāni) | and the near relatives (wal-aqrabūna) | of what (mimmā) | is little (qalla) | of it (min'hu) | or (aw) | much (kathura)- | a portion (naṣīban) | obligatory (mafrūḍan).

4:8 And when present at the (time of) division of the relatives and the orphans and the poor, then provide them from it and speak to them words of kindness.

And when (wa-idhā) | present (ḥaḍara) | at the (time of) division (l-qis'mata) | of (ulū) | the relatives (l-qur'bā) | and the orphans (wal-yatāmā) | and the poor (wal-masākīnu), | then provide them (fa-ur'zuqūhum) | from it (min'hu) | and speak (waqūlū) | to them (lahum) | words (qawlan) | of kindness (maʿrūfan).

4:9 And let fear - those who, if they left from behind offspring weak and they would have feared about them. So let them fear Allah and let them speak words appropriate.

And let fear (walyakhsha)- | those who (alladhīna), | if (law) | they left (tarakū) | from (min) | behind (khalfihim) | offspring (dhurriyyatan) | weak (ḍiʿāfan) | and they would have feared (khāfū) | about them (ʿalayhim). | So let them fear (falyattaqū) | Allah (l-laha) | and let them speak (walyaqūlū) | words (qawlan) | appropriate (sadīdan).

4:10 Indeed, those who consume wealth of the orphans wrongfully, only they consume in their bellies fire, and they will be burned in a Blazing Fire.

Indeed (inna), | those who (alladhīna) | consume (yakulūna) | wealth (amwāla) | of the orphans (l-yatāmā) | wrongfully (ẓul'man), | only (innamā) | they consume (yakulūna) | in (fī) | their bellies (buṭūnihim) | fire (nāran), | and they will be burned (wasayaṣlawna) | in a Blazing Fire (saʿīran).

4:11 Instructs you Allah concerning your children - for the male like the portion of two females. But if there are only women more than two, then for them two thirds of what he left. And if there is only one, then for her is half. And for his parents, for each one of them a sixth of what is left, if is for him a child. But if not is for him any child and inherit[ed] him his parents, then for his mother is one third. And if are for him brothers and sisters, then for his mother is the sixth from after any will he has made [of which] or any debt. Your parents and your children - not you know which of them is nearer to you in benefit. An obligation from Allah. Indeed, Allah is All-Knowing, All-Wise.

Instructs you (yūṣīkumu) | Allah (l-lahu) | concerning (fī) | your children (awlādikum)- | for the male (lildhakari) | like (mith'lu) | the portion (ḥaẓẓi) | of two females (l-unthayayni). | But if (fa-in) | there are (kunna) | only women (nisāan) | more than (fawqa) | two (ith'natayni), | then for them (falahunna) | two thirds (thuluthā) | of what (mā) | he left (taraka). | And if (wa-in) | there is (kānat) | only one (wāḥidatan), | then for her (falahā) | is half (l-niṣ'fu). | And for his parents (wali-abawayhi), | for each (likulli) | one (wāḥidin) | of them (min'humā) | a sixth (l-sudusu) | of what (mimmā) | is left (taraka), | if (in) | is (kāna) | for him (lahu) | a child (waladun). | But if (fa-in) | not (lam) | is (yakun) | for him (lahu) | any child (waladun) | and inherit[ed] him (wawarithahu) | his parents (abawāhu), | then for his mother (fali-ummihi) | is one third (l-thuluthu). | And if (fa-in) | are (kāna) | for him (lahu) | brothers and sisters (ikh'watun), | then for his mother (fali-ummihi) | is the sixth (l-sudusu) | from (min) | after (baʿdi) | any will (waṣiyyatin) | he has made (yūṣī) | [of which] (bihā) | or (aw) | any debt (daynin). | Your parents (ābāukum) | and your children (wa-abnāukum)- | not (lā) | you know (tadrūna) | which of them (ayyuhum) | is nearer (aqrabu) | to you (lakum) | in benefit (nafʿan). | An obligation (farīḍatan) | from (mina) | Allah (l-lahi). | Indeed (inna), | Allah (l-laha) | is (kāna) | All-Knowing (ʿalīman), | All-Wise (ḥakīman).

4:12 And for you is half of what is left by your wives if not is for them a child. But if is for them a child, then for you is the fourth of what they left, from after any will they have made [for which] or any debt. And for them is the fourth of what you left, if not is for you a child. But if is for you a child, then for them is the eighth of what you left from after any will you have made [for which] or any debt. And if [is] a man whose wealth is to be inherited has no parent or child or a women and for him is a brother or a sister, then for each one of the two is the sixth. But if they are more than that, then they are partners in the third, from after any will was made [for which] or any debt without being harmful. An ordinance from Allah. And Allah is All-Knowing, All-Forbearing.

And for you (walakum) | is half (niṣ'fu) | of what (mā) | is left (taraka) | by your wives (azwājukum) | if (in) | not (lam) | is (yakun) | for them (lahunna) | a child (waladun). | But if (fa-in) | is (kāna) | for them (lahunna) | a child (waladun), | then for you (falakumu) | is the fourth (l-rubuʿu) | of what (mimmā) | they left (tarakna), | from (min) | after (baʿdi) | any will (waṣiyyatin) | they have made (yūṣīna) | [for which] (bihā) | or (aw) | any debt (daynin). | And for them (walahunna) | is the fourth (l-rubuʿu) | of what (mimmā) | you left (taraktum), | if (in) | not (lam) | is (yakun) | for you (lakum) | a child (waladun). | But if (fa-in) | is (kāna) | for you (lakum) | a child (waladun), | then for them (falahunna) | is the eighth (l-thumunu) | of what (mimmā) | you left (taraktum) | from (min) | after (baʿdi) | any will (waṣiyyatin) | you have made (tūṣūna) | [for which] (bihā) | or (aw) | any debt (daynin). | And if (wa-in) | [is] (kāna) | a man (rajulun) | whose wealth is to be inherited (yūrathu) | has no parent or child (kalālatan) | or (awi) | a women (im'ra-atun) | and for him (walahu) | is a brother (akhun) | or (aw) | a sister (ukh'tun), | then for each (falikulli) | one (wāḥidin) | of the two (min'humā) | is the sixth (l-sudusu). | But if (fa-in) | they are (kānū) | more (akthara) | than (min) | that (dhālika), | then they (fahum) | are partners (shurakāu) | in (fī) | the third (l-thuluthi), | from (min) | after (baʿdi) | any will (waṣiyyatin) | was made (yūṣā) | [for which] (bihā) | or (aw) | any debt (daynin) | without (ghayra) | being harmful (muḍārrin). | An ordinance (waṣiyyatan) | from (mina) | Allah (l-lahi). | And Allah (wal-lahu) | is All-Knowing (ʿalīmun), | All-Forbearing (ḥalīmun).

4:13 These are the limits of Allah, and whoever obeys Allah and His Messenger, He will admit him to Gardens flows from underneath them the rivers - will abide forever in it. And that is the success [the] great.

These (til'ka) | are the limits (ḥudūdu) | of Allah (l-lahi), | and whoever (waman) | obeys (yuṭiʿi) | Allah (l-laha) | and His Messenger (warasūlahu), | He will admit him (yud'khil'hu) | to Gardens (jannātin) | flows (tajrī) | from (min) | underneath them (taḥtihā) | the rivers (l-anhāru)- | will abide forever (khālidīna) | in it (fīhā). | And that (wadhālika) | is the success (l-fawzu) | [the] great (l-ʿaẓīmu).

4:14 And whoever disobeys Allah and His Messenger and transgresses His limits - He will admit him to Fire will abide forever in it. And for him is a punishment humiliating.

And whoever (waman) | disobeys (yaʿṣi) | Allah (l-laha) | and His Messenger (warasūlahu) | and transgresses (wayataʿadda) | His limits (ḥudūdahu)- | He will admit him (yud'khil'hu) | to

Fire (nāran) | will abide forever (khālidan) | in it (fīhā). | And for him (walahu) | is a punishment (ʿadhābun) | humiliating (muhīnun).

4:15 And those who commit [the] immorality from your women then call to witness against them four among you. And if they testify then confine them in their houses until comes to them [the] death or makes Allah for them a way.

And those who (wa-allātī) | commit (yatīna) | [the] immorality (l-fāḥishata) | from (min) | your women (nisāikum) | then call to witness (fa-is'tashhidū) | against them (ʿalayhinna) | four (arbaʿatan) | among you (minkum). | And if (fa-in) | they testify (shahidū) | then confine them (fa-amsikūhunna) | in (fī) | their houses (l-buyūti) | until (ḥattā) | comes to them (yatawaffāhunna) | [the] death (l-mawtu) | or (aw) | makes (yajʿala) | Allah (l-lahu) | for them (lahunna) | a way (sabīlan).

4:16 And the two who commit it among you, then punish both of them. But if they repent and correct themselves, then turn away from both of them. Indeed, Allah is Oft-Forgiving, Most-Merciful.

And the two who (wa-alladhāni) | commit it (yatiyānihā) | among you (minkum), | then punish both of them (faādhūhumā). | But if (fa-in) | they repent (tābā) | and correct themselves (wa-aṣlaḥā), | then turn away (fa-aʿriḍū) | from both of them (ʿanhumā). | Indeed (inna), | Allah (l-laha) | is (kāna) | Oft-Forgiving (tawwāban), | Most-Merciful (raḥīman).

4:17 Only the acceptance of repentance by Allah is for those who do the evil in ignorance, then they repent from soon after. Then those will have forgiveness from Allah upon them, and is Allah All-Knowing, All-Wise.

Only (innamā) | the acceptance of repentance (l-tawbatu) | by (ʿalā) | Allah (l-lahi) | is for those who (lilladhīna) | do (yaʿmalūna) | the evil (l-sūa) | in ignorance (bijahālatin), | then (thumma) | they repent (yatūbūna) | from (min) | soon after (qarībin). | Then those (fa-ulāika) | will have forgiveness (yatūbu) | from Allah (l-lahu) | upon them (ʿalayhim), | and is (wakāna) | Allah (l-lahu) | All-Knowing (ʿalīman), | All-Wise (ḥakīman).

4:18 And not is the acceptance of repentance for those who do the evil deeds until when approaches one of them [the] death, he says, "Indeed I repent now;" and not those who die while they are disbelievers. Those - We have prepared for them a punishment painful.

And not (walaysati) | is the acceptance of repentance (l-tawbatu) | for those who (lilladhīna) | do (yaʿmalūna) | the evil deeds (l-sayiāti) | until (ḥattā) | when (idhā) | approaches (ḥaḍara) | one of them (aḥadahumu) | [the] death (l-mawtu), | he says (qāla), | "Indeed I (innī) | repent (tub'tu) | now; (l-āna)" | and not (walā) | those who (alladhīna) | die (yamūtūna) | while they (wahum) | are disbelievers (kuffārun). | Those (ulāika)- | We have prepared (aʿtadnā) | for them (lahum) | a punishment (ʿadhāban) | painful (alīman).

4:19 O you who believe[d]! Not is lawful for you that you inherit the women by force. And not you constraint them so that you may take a part of what you have given them except that they commit immorality open. And live with them in kindness. But if you dislike them, then perhaps that you dislike a thing and has placed Allah in it good much.

O you (yāayyuhā) | who (alladhīna) | believe[d] (āmanū)! | Not (lā) | is lawful (yaḥillu) | for you (lakum) | that (an) | you inherit (tarithū) | the women (l-nisāa) | by force (karhan). | And not (walā) | you constraint them (taʿḍulūhunna) | so that you may take (litadhhabū) | a part (bibaʿḍi) | of what (mā) | you have given them (ātaytumūhunna) | except (illā) | that (an) | they commit (yatīna) | immorality (bifāḥishatin) | open (mubayyinatin). | And live with them (waʿāshirūhunna) | in kindness (bil-maʿrūfi). | But if (fa-in) | you dislike them (karih'tumūhunna), | then perhaps (faʿasā) | that (an) | you dislike (takrahū) | a thing (shayan) | and has placed (wayajʿala) | Allah (l-lahu) | in it (fīhi) | good (khayran) | much (kathīran).

4:20 And if you intend replacing a wife in place of a wife and you have given one of them heap of gold then do not take away from it anything. Would you take it by slander and a sin open?

And if (wa-in) | you intend (aradttumu) | replacing (is'tib'dāla) | a wife (zawjin) | in place (makāna) | of a wife (zawjin) | and you have given (waātaytum) | one of them (iḥ'dāhunna) | heap of gold (qinṭāran) | then do not (falā) | take away (takhudhū) | from it (min'hu) | anything (shayan). | Would you take it (atakhudhūnahu) | by slander (buh'tānan) | and a sin (wa-ith'man) | open (mubīnan)?

4:21 And how could you take it when surely has gone - one of you to another, and they have taken from you covenant strong?

And how (wakayfa) | could you take it (takhudhūnahu) | when surely (waqad) | has gone (afḍā)- | one of you (baʿḍukum) | to (ilā) | another (baʿḍin), | and they have taken (wa-akhadhna) | from you (minkum) | covenant (mīthāqan) | strong (ghalīẓan)?

4:22 And do not marry whom married your fathers of the women except what has passed before, indeed it was an immorality and hateful, and an evil way.

And do not (walā) | marry (tankiḥū) | whom (mā) | married (nakaḥa) | your fathers (ābāukum) | of (mina) | the women (l-nisāi) | except (illā) | what (mā) | has (qad) | passed before (salafa), | indeed it (innahu) | was (kāna) | an immorality (fāḥishatan) | and hateful (wamaqtan), | and an evil (wasāa) | way (sabīlan).

4:23 Forbidden to you are your mothers and your daughters and your sisters and your father's sisters and your mother's sisters and daughters of brothers, and daughters of sisters and the mothers who nursed you and your sisters from the nursing and mothers of your wives and your step daughters who are in your guardianship of your women whom you had relations with them, but if not you had relations with them, then there is no sin on you. And wives of your sons, those who are from your loins and that you gather together [between] two sisters except what has passed before. Indeed, Allah is Oft-Forgiving, Most-Merciful.

Forbidden (ḥurrimat) | to you (ʿalaykum) | are your mothers (ummahātukum) | and your daughters (wabanātukum) | and your sisters (wa-akhawātukum) | and your father's sisters (waʿammātukum) | and your mother's sisters (wakhālātukum) | and daughters (wabanātu) | of brothers (l-akhi), | and daughters (wabanātu) | of sisters (l-ukh'ti) | and the mothers (wa-ummahātukumu) | who (allātī) | nursed you (arḍaʿnakum) | and your sisters (wa-akhawātukum) | from (mina) | the nursing (l-raḍāʿati) | and mothers (wa-ummahātu) | of your wives (nisāikum) | and your step daughters (warabāibukumu) | who (allātī) | are in (fī) | your guardianship (ḥujūrikum) | of (min) | your women (nisāikumu) | whom (allātī) | you had relations (dakhaltum) | with them (bihinna), | but if (fa-in) | not (lam) | you had (takūnū) | relations (dakhaltum) | with them (bihinna), | then there is no (falā) | sin (junāḥa) | on you (ʿalaykum). | And wives (waḥalāilu) | of your sons (abnāikumu), | those who (alladhīna) | are from (min) | your loins (aṣlābikum) | and that (wa-an) | you gather together (tajmaʿū) | [between] (bayna) | two sisters (l-ukh'tayni) | except (illā) | what (mā) | has (qad) | passed before (salafa). | Indeed (inna), | Allah (l-laha) | is (kāna) | Oft-Forgiving (ghafūran), | Most-Merciful (raḥīman).

4:24 And prohibited are the ones who are married of the women except whom you possess rightfully. Decree of Allah upon you. And are lawful to you what is beyond that; that you seek with your wealth desiring to be chaste not to be lustful. So what you benefit[ed] of it from them, so you give them their bridal due as an obligation. And there is no sin on you concerning what you mutually agree of it from beyond the obligation. Indeed, Allah is All-Knowing, All-Wise.

And prohibited are the ones who are married (wal-muḥ'ṣanātu) | of (mina) | the women (l-nisāi) | except (illā) | whom (mā) | you possess (malakat) | rightfully (aymānukum). | Decree (kitāba) | of Allah (l-lahi) | upon you (ʿalaykum). | And are lawful (wa-uḥilla) | to you (lakum) | what (mā) | is beyond (warāa) | that (dhālikum); | that (an) | you seek (tabtaghū) | with your wealth (bi-amwālikum) | desiring to be chaste (muḥ'ṣinīna) | not (ghayra) | to be lustful (musāfiḥīna). | So what (famā) | you benefit[ed] (is'tamtaʿtum) | of it (bihi) | from them (min'hunna), | so you give them (faātūhunna) | their bridal due (ujūrahunna) | as an obligation (farīḍatan). | And there is no (walā) | sin (junāḥa) | on you (ʿalaykum) | concerning what (fīmā) | you mutually agree (tarāḍaytum) | of it (bihi) | from (min) | beyond (baʿdi) | the obligation (l-farīḍati). | Indeed (inna), | Allah (l-laha) | is (kāna) | All-Knowing (ʿalīman), | All-Wise (ḥakīman).

4:25 And whoever is not able to among you afford to marry the free chaste [the] believing women then marry from what possess[ed] your right hands of your slave girls - of the believers. And Allah knows best about your faith. You are from one another. So marry them with the permission of their family and give them their bridal due in a fair manner. They should be chaste not those who commit immorality and not those who take secret lovers. Then when they are married and if they commit adultery then for them is half of what is on the free chaste women of the punishment. That is for whoever fears committing sin among you and that you be patient is better for you. And Allah is Oft-Forgiving, Most Merciful.

And whoever (waman) | is not (lam) | able to (yastaṭiʿ) | among you (minkum) | afford (ṭawlan) | to (an) | marry (yankiḥa) | the free chaste (l-muḥ'ṣanāti) | [the] believing women (l-mu'mināti) | then marry from (famin) | what (mā) | possess[ed] (malakat) | your right hands (aymānukum) | of (min) | your slave girls (fatayātikumu)- | of the believers (l-mu'mināti). | And Allah (wal-lahu) | knows best (aʿlamu) | about your faith (biīmānikum). | You (baʿḍukum) | are from (min) | one another (baʿḍin). | So marry them (fa-inkiḥūhunna) | with the permission (bi-idh'ni) | of their family (ahlihinna) | and give them (waātūhunna) | their bridal due (ujūrahunna) | in a fair manner (bil-maʿrūfi). | They should be chaste (muḥ'ṣanātin) | not (ghayra) | those who commit immorality (musāfiḥātin) | and not (walā) | those who take (muttakhidhāti) | secret lovers (akhdānin). | Then when (fa-idhā) | they are married (uḥ'ṣinna) | and if (fa-in) | they commit (atayna) | adultery (bifāḥishatin) | then for them (faʿalayhinna) | is half (niṣ'fu) | of what (mā) | is on (ʿalā) | the free chaste women (l-muḥ'ṣanāti) | of (mina) | the punishment (l-ʿadhābi). | That (dhālika) | is for whoever (liman) | fears (khashiya) | committing sin (l-ʿanata) | among you (minkum) | and that (wa-an) | you be patient (taṣbirū) | is better (khayrun) | for you (lakum). | And Allah (wal-lahu) | is Oft-Forgiving (ghafūrun), | Most Merciful (raḥīmun).

4:26 Wishes Allah to make clear to you and to guide you to ways of those from before you and to accept repentance from you. And Allah is All-Knowing, All-Wise.

Wishes (yurīdu) | Allah (l-lahu) | to make clear (liyubayyina) | to you (lakum) | and to guide you (wayahdiyakum) | to ways (sunana) | of those (alladhīna) | from (min) | before you (qablikum) | and to accept repentance (wayatūba) | from you (ʿalaykum). | And Allah (wal-lahu) | is All-Knowing (ʿalīmun), | All-Wise (ḥakīmun).

4:27 And Allah wishes to accept repentance from you, but wish those who follow the passions that you deviate - into a deviation great.

And Allah (wal-lahu) | wishes (yurīdu) | to (an) | accept repentance (yatūba) | from you (ʿalaykum), | but wish (wayurīdu) | those who (alladhīna) | follow (yattabiʿūna) | the passions (l-shahawāti) | that (an) | you deviate (tamīlū)- | into a deviation (maylan) | great (ʿaẓīman).

4:28 Wishes Allah to lighten for you; and was created the mankind weak.

Wishes (yurīdu) | Allah (l-lahu) | to (an) | lighten (yukhaffifa) | for you (ʿankum); | and was created (wakhuliqa) | the mankind (l-insānu) | weak (ḍaʿīfan).

4:29 O you who believe[d]! Do not eat your wealth between yourselves unjustly. But that there be business on mutual consent among you. And do not kill yourselves. Indeed, Allah is to you Most Merciful.

O you (yāayyuhā) | who (alladhīna) | believe[d] (āmanū)! | Do not (lā) | eat (takulū) | your wealth (amwālakum) | between yourselves (baynakum) | unjustly (bil-bāṭili). | But (illā) | that (an) | there be (takūna) | business (tijāratan) | on (ʿan) | mutual consent (tarāḍin) | among you (minkum). | And do not (walā) | kill (taqtulū) | yourselves (anfusakum). | Indeed (inna), | Allah (l-laha) | is (kāna) | to you (bikum) | Most Merciful (raḥīman).

4:30 And whoever does that in aggression and injustice, then soon We will cast him into a Fire. And is that for Allah easy.

And whoever (waman) | does (yafʿal) | that (dhālika) | in aggression (ʿud'wānan) | and injustice (waẓul'man), | then soon (fasawfa) | We will cast him (nuṣ'līhi) | into a Fire (nāran). | And is (wakāna) | that (dhālika) | for (ʿalā) | Allah (l-lahi) | easy (yasīran).

4:31 If you avoid great sins of what you are forbidden from [it], We will remove from you your evil deeds and We will admit you to an entrance noble.

If (in) | you avoid (tajtanibū) | great sins (kabāira) | of what (mā) | you are forbidden (tun'hawna) | from [it] (ʿanhu), | We will remove (nukaffir) | from you (ʿankum) | your evil deeds (sayyiātikum) | and We will admit you (wanud'khil'kum) | to an entrance (mud'khalan) | noble (karīman).

4:32 And do not covet what has bestowed Allah [with it] some of you over others. For men is a share of what they earned, and for women is a share of what they earned. And ask Allah of His bounty. Indeed, Allah is of every thing All-Knower.

And do not (walā) | covet (tatamannaw) | what (mā) | has bestowed (faḍḍala) | Allah (l-lahu) | [with it] (bihi) | some of you (baʿḍakum) | over (ʿalā) | others (baʿḍin). | For men (lilrrijāli) | is a share (naṣībun) | of what (mimmā) | they earned (ik'tasabū), | and for women (walilnnisāi) | is a share (naṣībun) | of what (mimmā) | they earned (ik'tasabna). | And ask (wasalū) | Allah (l-laha) | of (min) | His bounty (faḍlihi). | Indeed (inna), | Allah (l-laha) | is (kāna) | of every (bikulli) | thing (shayin) | All-Knower (ʿalıman).

4:33 And for all We have made heirs of what is left by the parents and the relatives. And those whom pledged your right hands - then give them their share. Indeed, Allah is over every thing a Witness.

And for all (walikullin) | We have made (jaʿalnā) | heirs (mawāliya) | of what (mimmā) | is left (taraka) | by the parents (l-wālidāni) | and the relatives (wal-aqrabūna). | And those whom (wa-alladhīna) | pledged (ʿaqadat) | your right hands (aymānukum)- | then give them (faātūhum) | their share (naṣībahum). | Indeed (inna), | Allah (l-laha) | is (kāna) | over (ʿalā) | every (kulli) | thing (shayin) | a Witness (shahīdan).

4:34 [The] men are protectors of the women because has bestowed Allah some of them over others and because they spend from their wealth. So the righteous women are obedient, guarding in the unseen that which orders them to guard by Allah. And those from whom you fear their ill-conduct then advise them, and forsake them in the bed and [finally] strike them. Then if they obey you then do not seek against them a way. Indeed, Allah is Most High, Most Great.

[The] men (al-rijālu) | are protectors (qawwāmūna) | of (ʿalā) | the women (l-nisāi) | because (bimā) | has bestowed (faḍḍala) | Allah (l-lahu) | some of them (baʿḍahum) | over (ʿalā) | others (baʿḍin) | and because (wabimā) | they spend (anfaqū) | from (min) | their wealth (amwālihim). | So the righteous women (fal-ṣāliḥātu) | are obedient (qānitātun), | guarding (ḥāfiẓātun) | in the unseen (lil'ghaybi) | that which (bimā) | orders them to guard (ḥafiẓa) | by Allah (l-lahu). | And those from whom (wa-allātī) | you fear (takhāfūna) | their ill-conduct (nushūzahunna) | then advise them (faʿiẓūhunna), | and forsake them (wa-uh'jurūhunna) | in (fī) | the bed (l-maḍājiʿi) | and [finally] strike them (wa-iḍ'ribūhunna). | Then if (fa-in) | they obey you (aṭaʿnakum) | then do not (falā) | seek (tabghū) | against them (ʿalayhinna) | a way (sabīlan). | Indeed (inna), |

Allah (l-laha) | is (kāna) | Most High (ʿaliyyan), | Most Great (kabīran).

4:35 And if you fear a dissension between the two of them, then send an arbitrator from his family and an arbitrator from her family. If they both wish reconciliation, will cause reconciliation Allah between both of them. Indeed, Allah is All-Knower, All-Aware.

And if (wa-in) | you fear (khif'tum) | a dissension (shiqāqa) | between the two of them (baynihimā), | then send (fa-ib'ʿathū) | an arbitrator (ḥakaman) | from (min) | his family (ahlihi) | and an arbitrator (waḥakaman) | from (min) | her family (ahlihā). | If (in) | they both wish (yurīdā) | reconciliation (iṣ'lāḥan), | will cause reconciliation (yuwaffiqi) | Allah (l-lahu) | between both of them (baynahumā). | Indeed (inna), | Allah (l-laha) | is (kāna) | All-Knower (ʿalīman), | All-Aware (khabīran).

4:36 And worship Allah And do not associate with Him anything, and to the parents do good, and with the relatives, and the orphans, and the needy and the neighbor who is near, and the neighbor who is farther away, and the companion by your side and the traveler and what possess[ed] your right hands. Indeed, Allah does not love the one who is [a] proud and [a] boastful.

And worship (wa-uʿ'budū) | Allah (l-laha) | And do not (walā) | associate (tush'rikū) | with Him (bihi) | anything (shayan), | and to the parents (wabil-wālidayni) | do good (iḥ'sānan), | and with (wabidhī) | the relatives (l-qur'bā), | and the orphans (wal-yatāmā), | and the needy (wal-masākīni) | and the neighbor (wal-jāri) | who is (dhī) | near (l-qur'bā), | and the neighbor (wal-jāri) | who is farther away (l-junubi), | and the companion (wal-ṣāḥibi) | by your side (bil-janbi) | and the (wa-ib'ni) | traveler (l-sabīli) | and what (wamā) | possess[ed] (malakat) | your right hands (aymānukum). | Indeed (inna), | Allah (l-laha) | does not (lā) | love (yuḥibbu) | the one who (man) | is (kāna) | [a] proud (mukh'tālan) | and [a] boastful (fakhūran).

4:37 Those who are stingy and order the people [of] stinginess and hide what has given them Allah of His Bounty - and We have prepared for the disbelievers a punishment humiliating.

Those who (alladhīna) | are stingy (yabkhalūna) | and order (wayamurūna) | the people (l-nāsa) | [of] stinginess (bil-bukh'li) | and hide (wayaktumūna) | what (mā) | has given them (ātāhumu) | Allah (l-lahu) | of (min) | His Bounty (faḍlihi)- | and We have prepared (wa-aʿtadnā) | for the disbelievers (lil'kāfirīna) | a punishment (ʿadhāban) | humiliating (muhīnan).

4:38 And those who spend their wealth to be seen by the people and not they believe in Allah and not in the Day the Last, and whoever has the Shaitaan for him as companion - then evil is he as a companion.

And those who (wa-alladhīna) | spend (yunfiqūna) | their wealth (amwālahum) | to be seen (riāa) | by the people (l-nāsi) | and not (walā) | they believe (yu'minūna) | in Allah (bil-lahi) | and not (walā) | in the Day (bil-yawmi) | the Last (l-ākhiri), | and whoever (waman) | has (yakuni) | the Shaitaan (l-shayṭānu) | for him (lahu) | as companion (qarīnan)- | then evil (fasāa) | is he as a companion (qarīnan).

4:39 And what is against them if they believed in Allah and the Day the Last and spent from what has provided them Allah? And is Allah about them All-Knower.

And what (wamādhā) | is against them (ʿalayhim) | if (law) | they believed (āmanū) | in Allah (bil-lahi) | and the Day (wal-yawmi) | the Last (l-ākhiri) | and spent (wa-anfaqū) | from what (mimmā) | has provided them (razaqahumu) | Allah (l-lahu)? | And is (wakāna) | Allah (l-lahu) | about them (bihim) | All-Knower (ʿalīman).

4:40 Indeed, Allah does not wrong as much as weight of an atom. And if there is a good He doubles it and gives from near Him a reward great.

Indeed (inna), | Allah (l-laha) | does not (lā) | wrong (yaẓlimu) | as much as weight (mith'qāla) | of an atom (dharratin). | And if (wa-in) | there is (taku) | a good (ḥasanatan) | He doubles it (yuḍāʿif'hā) | and gives (wayu'ti) | from (min) | near Him (ladun'hu) | a reward (ajran) | great (ʿaẓīman).

4:41 So how will it be when We bring from every nation a witness and We bring you against these people as a witness.

So how will it be (fakayfa) | when (idhā) | We bring (ji'nā) | from (min) | every (kulli) | nation (ummatin) | a witness (bishahīdin) | and We bring (waji'nā) | you (bika) | against (ʿalā) | these people (hāulāi) | as a witness (shahīdan).

4:42 On that Day will wish those who disbelieved and disobeyed the Messenger if was leveled with them the earth and not they will be able to hide from Allah any statement.

On that Day (yawma-idhin) | will wish (yawaddu) | those who (alladhīna) | disbelieved (kafarū) | and disobeyed (waʿaṣawū) | the Messenger (l-rasūla) | if (law) | was leveled (tusawwā) | with them (bihimu) | the earth (l-arḍu) | and not (walā) | they will be able to hide (yaktumūna) | from Allah (l-laha) | any statement (ḥadīthan).

4:43 O you who believe[d]! Do not go near the prayer while you are intoxicated until you know what you are saying and not when you are impure except when passing through a way until you have bathed. And if you are ill or on a journey or came one of you from the toilet, or you have touched the women and not you find water, then do tayammum with earth clean and wipe with it your faces and your hands. Indeed, Allah is Oft-Pardoning, Oft-Forgiving.

O you (yāayyuhā) | who (alladhīna) | believe[d] (āmanū)! | Do not (lā) | go near (taqrabū) | the prayer (l-ṣalata) | while you (wa-antum) | are intoxicated (sukārā) | until (ḥattā) | you know (taʿlamū) | what (mā) | you are saying (taqūlūna) | and not (walā) | when you are impure (junuban) | except (illā) | when passing (ʿābirī) | through a way (sabīlin) | until (ḥattā) | you have bathed (taghtasilū). | And if (wa-in) | you are (kuntum) | ill (marḍā) | or (aw) | on (ʿalā) | a journey (safarin) | or (aw) | came (jāa) | one (aḥadun) | of you (minkum) | from (mina) | the toilet (l-ghāiṭi), | or (aw) | you have touched (lāmastumu) | the women (l-nisāa) | and not (falam) | you find (tajidū) | water (māan), | then do tayammum (fatayammamū) | with earth (ṣaʿīdan) | clean (ṭayyiban) | and wipe with it (fa-im'saḥū) | your faces (biwujūhikum) | and your hands (wa-aydīkum). | Indeed (inna), | Allah (l-laha) | is (kāna) | Oft-Pardoning (ʿafuwwan), | Oft-Forgiving (ghafūran).

4:44 Did not you see, [towards] those who were given a portion of the Book, purchasing [the] error and wishing that you stray from the way?

Did not (alam) | you see (tara), | [towards] (ilā) | those who (alladhīna) | were given (ūtū) | a portion (naṣīban) | of (mina) | the Book (l-kitābi), | purchasing (yashtarūna) | [the] error (l-ḍalālata) | and wishing (wayurīdūna) | that (an) | you stray (taḍillū) | from the way (l-sabīla)?

4:45 And Allah knows better about your enemies and is sufficient Allah as a Protector, and sufficient is Allah as a Helper.

And Allah (wal-lahu) | knows better (aʿlamu) | about your enemies (bi-aʿdāikum) | and is sufficient (wakafā) | Allah (bil-lahi) | as a Protector (waliyyan), | and sufficient (wakafā) | is Allah (bil-lahi) | as a Helper (naṣīran).

4:46 Of those who are Jews, they distort the words from their places and they say, "We hear[d] and we disobey[ed]" and "Hear not to be heard and "Raina" twisting [with] their tongues and defaming [in] the religion. And if [that] they had said, "We hear[d] and we obey[ed]" and "Hear and look at us," surely it would have been better for them and more suitable. [And] but cursed them Allah for their disbelief, so not they believe except a few.

Of (mina) | those who (alladhīna) | are Jews (hādū), | they distort (yuḥarrifūna) | the words (l-kalima) | from (ʿan) | their places (mawāḍiʿihi) | and they say (wayaqūlūna), | "We hear[d] (samiʿnā) | and we disobey[ed] (waʿaṣaynā)" | and "Hear (wa-is'maʿ) | not (ghayra) | to be heard (mus'maʿin) | and "Raina (warāʿinā)" | twisting (layyan) | [with] their tongues (bi-alsinatihim) | and defaming (waṭaʿnan) | [in] (fī) | the religion (l-dīni). | And if (walaw) | [that] they (annahum) | had said (qālū), | "We hear[d] (samiʿnā) | and we obey[ed] (wa-aṭaʿnā)" | and "Hear (wa-is'maʿ) | and look at us, (wa-unẓur'nā)" | surely it would have been (lakāna) | better (khayran) | for them (lahum) | and more suitable (wa-aqwama). | [And] but (walākin) | cursed them (laʿanahumu) | Allah (l-lahu) | for their disbelief (bikuf'rihim), | so not (falā) | they believe (yu'minūna) | except (illā) | a few (qalīlan).

4:47 O you who have been given the Book, believe in what We have revealed confirming what is with you, from before [that] We efface faces and turn them on their backs or We curse them as We cursed companions of the Sabbath. And is the command of Allah always executed.

O you (yāayyuhā) | who (alladhīna) | have been given (ūtū) | the Book (l-kitāba), | believe (āminū) | in what (bimā) | We have revealed (nazzalnā) | confirming (muṣaddiqan) | what is (limā) | with you (maʿakum), | from (min) | before (qabli) | [that] (an) | We efface (naṭmisa) | faces (wujūhan) | and turn them (fanaruddahā) | on (ʿalā) | their backs (adbārihā) | or (aw) | We curse them (nalʿanahum) | as (kamā) | We cursed (laʿannā) | companions (aṣḥāba) | of the Sabbath (l-sabti). | And is (wakāna) | the command (amru) | of Allah (l-lahi) | always executed (mafʿūlan).

4:48 Indeed, Allah does not forgive that partners be associated with Him, but He forgives from other than that for whom He wills. And whoever associates partners with Allah, then surely he has fabricated a sin - tremendous.

Indeed (inna), | Allah (l-laha) | does not (lā) | forgive (yaghfiru) | that (an) | partners be associated (yush'raka) | with Him (bihi), | but He forgives (wayaghfiru) | from (mā) | other than (dūna) | that (dhālika) | for whom (liman) | He wills (yashāu). | And whoever (waman) | associates partners (yush'rik) | with Allah (bil-lahi), | then surely (faqadi) | he has fabricated (if'tarā) | a sin (ith'man)- | tremendous (ʿaẓīman).

4:49 Do not you see [towards] those who claim purity for themselves? Nay, it is Allah, He purifies whom He wills and not they will be wronged even as much as a hair on a date-seed.

Do not (alam) | you see (tara) | [towards] (ilā) | those who (alladhīna) | claim purity (yuzakkūna) | for themselves (anfusahum)? | Nay (bali), | it is Allah (l-lahu), | He purifies (yuzakkī) | whom (man) | He wills (yashāu) | and not (walā) | they will be wronged (yuẓ'lamūna) | even as much as a hair on a date-seed (fatīlan).

4:50 See how they invent about Allah [the] lie, and sufficient is it - as a sin manifest.

See (unẓur) | how (kayfa) | they invent (yaftarūna) | about (ʿalā) | Allah (l-lahi) | [the] lie (l-kadhiba), | and sufficient (wakafā) | is it (bihi)- | as a sin (ith'man) | manifest (mubīnan).

4:51 Do not you see [towards] those who were given a portion of the Book? They believe in the superstition and the false deities, and they say for those who disbelieve[d] "These are better guided than those who believe[d] as to the way.

Do not (alam) | you see (tara) | [towards] (ilā) | those who (alladhīna) | were given (ūtū) | a portion (naṣīban) | of (mina) | the Book (l-kitābi)? | They believe (yu'minūna) | in the superstition (bil-jib'ti) | and the false deities (wal-ṭāghūti), | and they say (wayaqūlūna) | for those who (lilladhīna) | disbelieve[d] (kafarū) | "These (hāulāi) | are better guided (ahdā) | than (mina) | those who (alladhīna) | believe[d] (āmanū) | as to the way (sabīlan).

4:52 Those are the ones who have been cursed by Allah, and whoever is cursed by Allah then never will you find for him any helper.

Those (ulāika) | are the ones (alladhīna) | who have been cursed (laʿanahumu) | by Allah (l-lahu), | and whoever (waman) | is cursed (yalʿani) | by Allah (l-lahu) | then never (falan) | will you find (tajida) | for him (lahu) | any helper (naṣīran).

4:53 Or for them is a share of the Kingdom? Then not would they give the people even as much as the speck on a date seed.

Or (am) | for them (lahum) | is a share (naṣībun) | of (mina) | the Kingdom (l-mul'ki)? | Then (fa-idhan) | not would (lā) | they give (yu'tūna) | the people (l-nāsa) | even as much as the speck on a date seed (naqīran).

4:54 Or are they jealous of the people for what gave them Allah from His Bounty? But surely We gave the family of Ibrahim the Book and [the] wisdom and [We] gave them a kingdom great.

Or (am) | are they jealous (yaḥsudūna) | of the people (l-nāsa) | for (ʿalā) | what (mā) | gave them (ātāhumu) | Allah (l-lahu) | from (min) | His Bounty (faḍlihi)? | But surely (faqad) | We gave (ātaynā) | the family (āla) | of Ibrahim (ib'rāhīma) | the Book (l-kitāba) | and [the] wisdom (wal-ḥik'mata) | and [We] gave them (waātaynāhum) | a kingdom (mul'kan) | great (ʿaẓīman).

4:55 Then of them are some who believed in him and of them are some who turned away from him, and sufficient is Hell as a Blazing Fire.

Then of them (famin'hum) | are some who (man) | believed (āmana) | in him (bihi) | and of them (wamin'hum) | are some who (man) | turned away (ṣadda) | from him (ʿanhu), | and sufficient (wakafā) | is Hell (bijahannama) | as a Blazing Fire (saʿīran).

4:56 Indeed, those who disbelieved in Our Signs, soon We will burn them in a Fire. Every time are roasted their skins We will change their skins for other than that, so that they may taste the punishment. Indeed, Allah is All-Mighty, All-Wise.

Indeed (inna), | those who (alladhīna) | disbelieved (kafarū) | in Our Signs (biāyātinā), | soon (sawfa) | We will burn them (nuṣ'līhim) | in a Fire (nāran). | Every time (kullamā) | are roasted (naḍijat) | their skins (julūduhum) | We will change their (baddalnāhum) | skins (julūdan) | for other than that (ghayrahā), | so that they may taste (liyadhūqū) | the punishment (l-ʿadhāba). | Indeed (inna), | Allah (l-laha) | is (kāna) | All Mighty (ʿazīzan), | All-Wise (ḥakīman).

4:57 And those who believe[d] and did the good deeds We will admit them in Gardens flows from underneath it the rivers, will abide in it forever. For them in it are spouses pure, and We will admit them in the shade thick.

And those who (wa-alladhīna) | believe[d] (āmanū) | and did (waʿamilū) | the good deeds (l-ṣāliḥāti) | We will admit them (sanud'khiluhum) | in Gardens (jannātin) | flows (tajrī) | from (min) | underneath it (taḥtihā) | the rivers (l-anhāru), | will abide (khālidīna) | in it (fīhā) | forever (abadan). | For them (lahum) | in it (fīhā) | are spouses (azwājun) | pure (muṭahharatun), | and We will admit them (wanud'khiluhum) | in the shade (ẓillan) | thick (ẓalīlan).

4:58 Indeed, Allah orders you to render the trusts to their owners, and when you judge between the people to judge with justice. Indeed, Allah excellently advises you with it. Indeed, Allah is All-Hearing, All-Seeing.

Indeed (inna), | Allah (l-laha) | orders you (yamurukum) | to (an) | render (tu-addū) | the trusts (l-amānāti) | to (ilā) | their owners (ahlihā), | and when (wa-idhā) | you judge (ḥakamtum) | between (bayna) | the people (l-nāsi) | to (an) | judge (taḥkumū) | with justice (bil-ʿadli). | Indeed (inna), | Allah (l-laha) | excellently (niʿimmā) | advises you (yaʿiẓukum) | with it (bihi). | Indeed (inna), | Allah (l-laha) | is (kāna) | All-Hearing (samīʿan), | All-Seeing (baṣīran).

4:59 O you who believe[d]! Obey Allah and obey the Messenger and those having authority among you. Then if you disagree in anything, refer it to Allah and the Messenger, if you believe in Allah and the Day [the] Last. That is best and more suitable for final determination.

O you (yāayyuhā) | who (alladhīna) | believe[d] (āmanū)! | Obey (aṭīʿū) | Allah (l-laha) | and obey (wa-aṭīʿū) | the Messenger (l-rasūla) | and those (wa-ulī) | having authority (l-amri) |

among you (minkum). | Then if (fa-in) | you disagree (tanāzaʿtum) | in (fī) | anything (shayin), | refer it (faruddūhu) | to (ilā) | Allah (l-lahi) | and the Messenger (wal-rasūli), | if (in) | you (kuntum) | believe (tu'minūna) | in Allah (bil-lahi) | and the Day (wal-yawmi) | [the] Last (l-ākhiri). | That (dhālika) | is best (khayrun) | and more suitable (wa-aḥsanu) | for final determination (tawīlan).

4:60 Do not you see [towards] those who claim that they believe in what is revealed to you and what was revealed from before you? They wish to go for judgment to the false deities and surely they were ordered to reject [with] it. And wishes the Shaitaan to mislead them astray - far away.

Do not (alam) | you see (tara) | [towards] (ilā) | those who (alladhīna) | claim (yazʿumūna) | that they (annahum) | believe (āmanū) | in what (bimā) | is revealed (unzila) | to you (ilayka) | and what (wamā) | was revealed (unzila) | from (min) | before you (qablika)? | They wish (yurīdūna) | to (an) | go for judgment (yataḥākamū) | to (ilā) | the false deities (l-ṭāghūti) | and surely (waqad) | they were ordered (umirū) | to (an) | reject (yakfurū) | [with] it (bihi). | And wishes (wayurīdu) | the Shaitaan (l-shayṭānu) | to (an) | mislead them (yuḍillahum) | astray (ḍalālan)- | far away (baʿīdan).

4:61 And when it is said to them, "Come to what has revealed Allah and to the Messenger," you see the hypocrites turning away from you in aversion.

And when (wa-idhā) | it is said (qīla) | to them (lahum), | "Come (taʿālaw) | to (ilā) | what (mā) | has revealed (anzala) | Allah (l-lahu) | and to (wa-ilā) | the Messenger, (l-rasūli)" | you see (ra-ayta) | the hypocrites (l-munāfiqīna) | turning away (yaṣuddūna) | from you (ʿanka) | in aversion (ṣudūdan).

4:62 So how when befalls them disaster for what sent forth their hands then they come to you swearing by Allah, "Not we intended except good and reconciliation."

So how (fakayfa) | when (idhā) | befalls them (aṣābathum) | disaster (muṣībatun) | for what (bimā) | sent forth (qaddamat) | their hands (aydīhim) | then (thumma) | they come to you (jāūka) | swearing (yaḥlifūna) | by Allah (bil-lahi), | "Not (in) | we intended (aradnā) | except (illā) | good (iḥ'sānan) | and reconciliation. (watawfīqan)"

4:63 Those are the ones who - knows Allah what is in their hearts, so turn away from them and admonish them, and say to them concerning their souls a word penetrating.

Those (ulāika) | are the ones who (alladhīna)- | knows (yaʿlamu) | Allah (l-lahu) | what (mā) | is in (fī) | their hearts (qulūbihim), | so turn away (fa-aʿriḍ) | from them (ʿanhum) | and admonish them (waʿiẓ'hum), | and say (waqul) | to them (lahum) | concerning (fī) | their souls (anfusihim) | a word (qawlan) | penetrating (balīghan).

4:64 And not We sent any Messenger except to be obeyed by the permission of Allah. And if [that] they, when they wronged themselves, had come to you and asked forgiveness of Allah, and asked forgiveness for them the Messenger, surely they would have found Allah Oft-Forgiving, Most Merciful.

And not (wamā) | We sent (arsalnā) | any (min) | Messenger (rasūlin) | except (illā) | to be obeyed (liyuṭāʿa) | by the permission (bi-idh'ni) | of Allah (l-lahi). | And if (walaw) | [that] they (annahum), | when (idh) | they wronged (ẓalamū) | themselves (anfusahum), | had come to you (jāūka) | and asked forgiveness (fa-is'taghfarū) | of Allah (l-laha), | and asked forgiveness (wa-is'taghfara) | for them (lahumu) | the Messenger (l-rasūlu), | surely they would have found (lawajadū) | Allah (l-laha) | Oft-Forgiving (tawwāban), | Most Merciful (raḥīman).

4:65 But no, by your Lord, not will they believe until they make you judge about what arises between them, then not they find in themselves any discomfort about what you have decided and submit in full submission.

But no (falā), | by your Lord (warabbika), | not (lā) | will they believe (yu'minūna) | until (ḥattā) | they make you judge (yuḥakkimūka) | about what (fīmā) | arises (shajara) | between them (baynahum), | then (thumma) | not (lā) | they find (yajidū) | in (fī) | themselves (anfusihim) | any discomfort (ḥarajan) | about what (mimmā) | you have decided (qaḍayta) | and submit (wayusallimū) | in full submission (taslīman).

4:66 And if [that] We had decreed on them that, "Kill yourselves" or "Go forth from your homes," not they would have done it except a few of them. But if [that] they had done what they were advised with [it], surely it would have been better for them and stronger strengthening.

And if (walaw) | [that] We (annā) | had decreed (katabnā) | on them (ʿalayhim) | that (ani), | "Kill (uq'tulū) | yourselves (anfusakum)" | or (awi) | "Go forth (ukh'rujū) | from (min) | your homes, (diyārikum)" | not (mā) | they would have done it (faʿalūhu) | except (illā) | a few (qalīlun) | of them (min'hum). | But if (walaw) | [that] they (annahum) | had done (faʿalū) | what (mā) | they were advised (yūʿaẓūna) | with [it] (bihi), | surely it would have been (lakāna) | better (khayran) | for them (lahum) | and stronger (wa-ashadda) | strengthening (tathbītan).

4:67 And then We would have given them from Ourselves a reward, great.

And then (wa-idhan) | We would have given them (laātaynāhum) | from (min) | Ourselves (ladunnā) | a reward (ajran), | great (ʿaẓīman).

4:68 And We would have guided them to the way, the straight.

And We would have guided them (walahadaynāhum) | to the way (ṣirāṭan), | the straight (mus'taqīman).

4:69 And whoever obeys Allah and the Messenger then those will be with those whom has bestowed His Favor Allah upon them - of the Prophets, and the truthful, and the martyrs, and the righteous. And excellent are those companions.

And whoever (waman) | obeys (yuṭiʿi) | Allah (l-laha) | and the Messenger (wal-rasūla) | then those (fa-ulāika) | will be with (maʿa) | those whom (alladhīna) | has bestowed His Favor (anʿama) | Allah (l-lahu) | upon them (ʿalayhim)- | of (mina) | the Prophets (l-nabiyīna), | and the truthful (wal-ṣidīqīna), | and the martyrs (wal-shuhadāi), | and the righteous (wal-ṣāliḥīna). | And excellent (waḥasuna) | are those (ulāika) | companions (rafīqan).

4:70 That is the Bounty of Allah, and sufficient Allah, as All-Knower.

That (dhālika) | is the Bounty (l-faḍlu) | of (mina) | Allah (l-lahi), | and sufficient (wakafā) | Allah (bil-lahi), | as All-Knower (ʿalīman).

4:71 O you who believe[d]! Take your precautions and advance in groups or advance all together.

O you (yāayyuhā) | who (alladhīna) | believe[d] (āmanū)! | Take (khudhū) | your precautions (ḥidh'rakum) | and advance (fa-infirū) | in groups (thubātin) | or (awi) | advance (infirū) | all together (jamīʿan).

4:72 And indeed, among you is he who lags behind then if befalls you a disaster he said, "Verily has favored Allah [on] me [when] that not I was with them, present."

And indeed (wa-inna), | among you (minkum) | is he who (laman) | lags behind (layubaṭṭi-anna) | then if (fa-in) | befalls you (aṣābatkum) | a disaster (muṣībatun) | he said (qāla), | "Verily (qad) | has favored (anʿama) | Allah (l-lahu) | [on] me (ʿalayya) | [when] (idh) | that not (lam) | I was (akun) | with them (maʿahum), | present. (shahīdan)"

4:73 And if befalls you bounty from Allah he would surely say as if had not there been between you and between him any affection, "Oh! I wish I had been with them then I would have attained a success great."

And if (wala-in) | befalls you (aṣābakum) | bounty (faḍlun) | from (mina) | Allah (l-lahi) |

he would surely say (layaqūlanna) | as if (ka-an) | had not (lam) | there been (takun) | between you (baynakum) | and between him (wabaynahu) | any affection (mawaddatun), | "Oh! I wish (yālaytanī) | I had been (kuntu) | with them (maʿahum) | then I would have attained (fa-afūza) | a success (fawzan) | great. (ʿaẓīman)"

4:74 So let fight in the way of Allah those who sell the life of the world for the Hereafter. And whoever fights in the way of Allah, then he is killed or achieves victory then soon We will grant him a reward a great.

So let fight (falyuqātil) | in (fī) | the way (sabīli) | of Allah (l-lahi) | those who (alladhīna) | sell (yashrūna) | the life (l-ḥayata) | of the world (l-dun'yā) | for the Hereafter (bil-ākhirati). | And whoever (waman) | fights (yuqātil) | in (fī) | the way (sabīli) | of Allah (l-lahi), | then he is killed (fayuq'tal) | or (aw) | achieves victory (yaghlib) | then soon (fasawfa) | We will grant him (nu'tīhi) | a reward (ajran) | a great (ʿaẓīman).

4:75 And what for you that not you fight in the way of Allah, and for those who are weak among the men and the women and the children, those who say, "Our Lord take us out of this [the] town [the] oppressors are its people and appoint for us from Yourself a protector and appoint for us from Yourself a helper.

And what (wamā) | for you (lakum) | that not (lā) | you fight (tuqātilūna) | in (fī) | the way (sabīli) | of Allah (l-lahi), | and for those who are weak (wal-mus'taḍʿafīna) | among (mina) | the men (l-rijāli) | and the women (wal-nisāi) | and the children (wal-wil'dāni), | those who (alladhīna) | say (yaqūlūna), | "Our Lord (rabbanā) | take us out (akhrij'nā) | of (min) | this (hādhihi) | [the] town (l-qaryati) | [the] oppressors (l-ẓālimi) | are its people (ahluhā) | and appoint (wa-ij'ʿal) | for us (lanā) | from (min) | Yourself (ladunka) | a protector (waliyyan) | and appoint (wa-ij'ʿal) | for us (lanā) | from (min) | Yourself (ladunka) | a helper (naṣīran).

4:76 Those who believe, they fight in the way of Allah; and those who disbelieve, they fight in the way of the false deities. So fight against the friends of the Shaitaan. Indeed, the strategy of the Shaitaan is weak.

Those who (alladhīna) | believe (āmanū), | they fight (yuqātilūna) | in (fī) | the way (sabīli) | of Allah (l-lahi); | and those (wa-alladhīna) | who disbelieve (kafarū), | they fight (yuqātilūna) | in (fī) | the way (sabīli) | of the false deities (l-ṭāghūti). | So fight against (faqātilū) | the friends (awliyāa) | of the Shaitaan (l-shayṭāni). | Indeed (inna), | the strategy (kayda) | of the Shaitaan (l-shayṭāni) | is (kāna) | weak (ḍaʿīfan).

4:77 Have not you seen [towards] those who when it was said to them, "Restrain your hands and establish the prayer and give the zakah?" Then when was ordained on them the fighting, then a group of them [they] fear the people as they fear Allah or more intense fear, and they said, "Our Lord why have You ordained upon us [the] fighting? Why not You postpone it for us to a term, near." Say, "Enjoyment of the world is little and the Hereafter is better for whoever fears Allah and not you will be wronged even as much as a hair on a date-seed."

Have not (alam) | you seen (tara) | [towards] (ilā) | those who (alladhīna) | when it was said (qīla) | to them (lahum), | "Restrain (kuffū) | your hands (aydiyakum) | and establish (wa-aqīmū) | the prayer (l-ṣalata) | and give (waātū) | the zakah? (l-zakata)" | Then when (falammā) | was ordained (kutiba) | on them (ʿalayhimu) | the fighting (l-qitālu), | then (idhā) | a group (farīqun) | of them (min'hum) | [they] fear (yakhshawna) | the people (l-nāsa) | as they fear (kakhashyati) | Allah (l-lahi) | or (aw) | more intense (ashadda) | fear (khashyatan), | and they said (waqālū), | "Our Lord (rabbanā) | why (lima) | have You ordained (katabta) | upon us (ʿalaynā) | [the] fighting (l-qitāla)? | Why not (lawlā) | You postpone it for us (akhartanā) | to (ilā) | a term (ajalin), | near. (qarībin)" | Say (qul), | "Enjoyment (matāʿu) | of the world (l-dun'yā) | is little (qalīlun) | and the Hereafter (wal-ākhiratu) | is better (khayrun) | for whoever (limani) | fears Allah (ittaqā) | and not (walā) | you will be wronged (tuẓ'lamūna) | even as much as a hair on a date-seed.

(fatīlan)"

4:78 Wherever you be will overtake you [the] death even if you are in towers lofty. And if befalls them any good they say, "This is from Allah." And if befalls them any evil they say, "This is from you." Say, "All is from Allah." So what is wrong with these [the] people, not do they seem to understand any statement.

Wherever (aynamā) | you be (takūnū) | will overtake you (yud'rikkumu) | [the] death (l-mawtu) | even if (walaw) | you are (kuntum) | in (fī) | towers (burūjin) | lofty (mushayyadatin). | And if (wa-in) | befalls them (tuṣib'hum) | any good (ḥasanatun) | they say (yaqūlū), | "This (hādhihi) | is (min) | from (ʿindi) | Allah. (l-lahi)" | And if (wa-in) | befalls them (tuṣib'hum) | any evil (sayyi-atun) | they say (yaqūlū), | "This (hādhihi) | is (min) | from you. (ʿindika)" | Say (qul), | "All (kullun) | is (min) | from (ʿindi) | Allah. (l-lahi)" | So what is wrong (famāli) | with these (hāulāi) | [the] people (l-qawmi), | not (lā) | do they seem (yakādūna) | to understand (yafqahūna) | any statement (ḥadīthan).

4:79 Whatever befalls you of the good is from Allah, and whatever befalls you of the evil is from yourself. And We have sent you for the people as a Messenger, and is sufficient Allah as a Witness.

Whatever (mā) | befalls you (aṣābaka) | of (min) | the good (ḥasanatin) | is from (famina) | Allah (l-lahi), | and whatever (wamā) | befalls you (aṣābaka) | of (min) | the evil (sayyi-atin) | is from (famin) | yourself (nafsika). | And We have sent you (wa-arsalnāka) | for the people (lilnnāsi) | as a Messenger (rasūlan), | and is sufficient (wakafā) | Allah (bil-lahi) | as a Witness (shahīdan).

4:80 He who obeys the Messenger then surely he obeyed Allah, and whoever turns away - then not We have sent you over them as a guardian.

He who (man) | obeys (yuṭiʿi) | the Messenger (l-rasūla) | then surely (faqad) | he obeyed (aṭāʿa) | Allah (l-laha), | and whoever (waman) | turns away (tawallā)- | then not (famā) | We have sent you (arsalnāka) | over them (ʿalayhim) | as a guardian (ḥafīẓan).

4:81 And they say, "We pledge obedience." Then when they leave from you, plan by night a group of them other than that which you say. But Allah records what they plan by night. So turn away from them and put your trust in Allah. And sufficient is Allah as a Trustee.

And they say (wayaqūlūna), | "We pledge obedience. (ṭāʿatun)" | Then when (fa-idhā) | they leave (barazū) | from (min) | you (ʿindika), | plan by night (bayyata) | a group (ṭāifatun) | of them (min'hum) | other than (ghayra) | that which (alladhī) | you say (taqūlu). | But Allah (wal-lahu) | records (yaktubu) | what (mā) | they plan by night (yubayyitūna). | So turn away (fa-aʿriḍ) | from them (ʿanhum) | and put your trust (watawakkal) | in (ʿalā) | Allah (l-lahi). | And sufficient (wakafā) | is Allah (bil-lahi) | as a Trustee (wakīlan).

4:82 Then do not they ponder on the Quran? And if it had been of from other than Allah, surely they would have found in it contradiction, much.

Then do not (afalā) | they ponder (yatadabbarūna) | on the Quran (l-qur'āna)? | And if (walaw) | it had been (kāna) | of (min) | from (ʿindi) | other than (ghayri) | Allah (l-lahi), | surely they would have found (lawajadū) | in it (fīhi) | contradiction (ikh'tilāfan), | much (kathīran).

4:83 And when comes to them a matter of the security or [the] fear they spread [with] it. But if they had referred it to the Messenger and to those having authority among them, surely would have known it those who draw correct conclusion from it among them. And if not had been the bounty of Allah on you and His Mercy, surely you would have followed the Shaitaan except a few.

And when (wa-idhā) | comes to them (jāahum) | a matter (amrun) | of (mina) | the security (l-amni) | or (awi) | [the] fear (l-khawfi) | they spread (adhāʿū) | [with] it (bihi). | But if (walaw) | they had referred it (raddūhu) | to (ilā) | the Messenger (l-rasūli) | and to (wa-ilā) | those (ulī) | having authority (l-amri) | among them (min'hum), | surely would have known it (laʿalimahu)

| those who (alladhīna) | draw correct conclusion from it (yastanbiṭūnahu) | among them (min'hum). | And if not (walawlā) | had been the bounty (faḍlu) | of Allah (l-lahi) | on you (ʿalaykum) | and His Mercy (waraḥmatuhu), | surely you would have followed (la-ittabaʿtumu) | the Shaitaan (l-shayṭāna) | except (illā) | a few (qalīlan).

4:84 So fight in the way of Allah; not are you responsible except for yourself. And encourage the believers, perhaps Allah will restrain the might of those who disbelieved. And Allah is Stronger in Might and Stronger in punishment.

So fight (faqātil) | in (fī) | the way (sabīli) | of Allah (l-lahi); | not (lā) | are you responsible (tukallafu) | except (illā) | for yourself (nafsaka). | And encourage (waḥarriḍi) | the believers (l-mu'minīna), | perhaps (ʿasā) | Allah (l-lahu) | will (an) | restrain (yakuffa) | the might (basa) | of those who (alladhīna) | disbelieved (kafarū). | And Allah (wal-lahu) | is Stronger (ashaddu) | in Might (basan) | and Stronger (wa-ashaddu) | in punishment (tankīlan).

4:85 Whoever intercedes - an intercession good, will have for him a share of it; and whoever intercedes - an intercession evil, will have for him a portion of it. And is Allah on every thing a Keeper.

Whoever (man) | intercedes (yashfaʿ)- | an intercession (shafāʿatan) | good (ḥasanatan), | will have (yakun) | for him (lahu) | a share (naṣībun) | of it (min'hā); | and whoever (waman) | intercedes (yashfaʿ)- | an intercession (shafāʿatan) | evil (sayyi-atan), | will have (yakun) | for him (lahu) | a portion (kif'lun) | of it (min'hā). | And is (wakāna) | Allah (l-lahu) | on (ʿalā) | every (kulli) | thing (shayin) | a Keeper (muqītan).

4:86 And when you are greeted with a greeting, then greet with better than it or return it. Indeed, Allah is of every thing an Accountant.

And when (wa-idhā) | you are greeted (ḥuyyītum) | with a greeting (bitaḥiyyatin), | then greet (faḥayyū) | with better (bi-aḥsana) | than it (min'hā) | or (aw) | return it (ruddūhā). | Indeed (inna), | Allah (l-laha) | is (kāna) | of (ʿalā) | every (kulli) | thing (shayin) | an Accountant (ḥasīban).

4:87 Allah - there is no god except Him, surely He will gather you to the Day of Resurrection - no doubt about it. And who is more truthful than Allah in statement.

Allah (al-lahu)- | there is no (lā) | god (ilāha) | except (illā) | Him (huwa), | surely He will gather you (layajmaʿannakum) | to (ilā) | the Day (yawmi) | of Resurrection (l-qiyāmati)- | no (lā) | doubt (rayba) | about it (fīhi). | And who (waman) | is more truthful (aṣdaqu) | than (mina) | Allah (l-lahi) | in statement (ḥadīthan).

4:88 So what is the matter with you concerning the hypocrites that you have become two parties? While Allah cast them back for what they earned. Do you wish that you guide whom is let astray by Allah? And whoever is let astray by Allah, then never will you find for him a way.

So what (famā) | is the matter with you (lakum) | concerning (fī) | the hypocrites that (l-munāfiqīna) | you have become two parties (fi-atayni)? | While Allah (wal-lahu) | cast them back (arkasahum) | for what (bimā) | they earned (kasabū). | Do you wish (aturīdūna) | that (an) | you guide (tahdū) | whom (man) | is let astray (aḍalla) | by Allah (l-lahu)? | And whoever (waman) | is let astray (yuḍ'lili) | by Allah (l-lahu), | then never (falan) | will you find (tajida) | for him (lahu) | a way (sabīlan).

4:89 They wish if you disbelieve as they disbelieved and you would be alike. So do not take from them allies until they emigrate in the way of Allah. But if they turn back, seize them and kill them wherever you find them. And do not take from them any ally and not any helper,

They wish (waddū) | if (law) | you disbelieve (takfurūna) | as (kamā) | they disbelieved (kafarū) | and you would be (fatakūnūna) | alike (sawāan). | So do not (falā) | take (tattakhidhū) | from them (min'hum) | allies (awliyāa) | until (ḥattā) | they emigrate (yuhājirū) | in (fī) | the way (sabīli) | of Allah (l-lahi). | But if (fa-in) | they turn back (tawallaw), | seize them (fakhudhūhum) | and kill them (wa-uq'tulūhum) | wherever (ḥaythu) | you find them (wajadttumūhum). | And do not (walā) | take (tattakhidhū) | from them (min'hum) | any ally (waliyyan) | and not (walā) | any helper (naṣīran),

4:90 Except those who join [to] a group between you and between them is a treaty or those who come to you restraining their hearts that they fight you or they fight their people. And if had willed Allah, surely He would have given them power over you, and surely they would have fought you. So if they withdraw from you and do not fight against you and offer to you [the] peace then not has made Allah for you against them a way.

Except (illā) | those who (alladhīna) | join (yaṣilūna) | [to] (ilā) | a group (qawmin) | between you (baynakum) | and between them (wabaynahum) | is a treaty (mīthāqun) | or (aw) | those who come to you (jāūkum) | restraining (ḥaṣirat) | their hearts (ṣudūruhum) | that (an) | they fight you (yuqātilūkum) | or (aw) | they fight (yuqātilū) | their people (qawmahum). | And if (walaw) | had willed (shāa) | Allah (l-lahu), | surely He would have given them power (lasallaṭahum) | over you (ʿalaykum), | and surely they would have fought you (falaqātalūkum). | So if (fa-ini) | they withdraw from you (iʿ'tazalūkum) | and do not (falam) | fight against you (yuqātilūkum) | and offer (wa-alqaw) | to you (ilaykumu) | [the] peace (l-salama) | then not (famā) | has made (jaʿala) | Allah (l-lahu) | for you (lakum) | against them (ʿalayhim) | a way (sabīlan).

4:91 You will find others wishing that they be secure from you and they be secure from their people, Everytime that they are returned to the temptation, they are plunged into it. So if not they withdraw from you and offer to you [the] peace and they restrain their hands, then seize them and kill them wherever you find them. And those - We made for you against them an authority clear.

You will find (satajidūna) | others (ākharīna) | wishing (yurīdūna) | that (an) | they be secure from you (yamanūkum) | and they be secure from (wayamanū) | their people (qawmahum), | Everytime (kulla) | that (mā) | they are returned (ruddū) | to (ilā) | the temptation (l-fit'nati), | they are plunged (ur'kisū) | into it (fīhā). | So if (fa in) | not (lam) | they withdraw from you (yaʿtazilūkum) | and offer (wayul'qū) | to you (ilaykumu) | [the] peace (l-salama) | and they restrain (wayakuffū) | their hands (aydiyahum), | then seize them (fakhudhūhum) | and kill them (wa-uq'tulūhum) | wherever (ḥaythu) | you find them (thaqif'tumūhum). | And those (wa-ulāikum)- | We made (jaʿalnā) | for you (lakum) | against them (ʿalayhim) | an authority (sul'ṭānan) | clear (mubīnan).

4:92 And not is for a believer that he kills a believer except by mistake. And whoever killed a believer by mistake, then freeing of a slave - believing and blood money is to be paid to his family unless that they remit as charity. But if he was from a people hostile to you and he was a believer then freeing of a believing slave. - believing. And if he was from a people between you and between them, is a treaty, then blood money is to be paid to his family, and freeing of a slave - believing. And whoever does not find, then fasting for two months consecutively, seeking repentance from Allah, and is Allah All-Knowing, All-Wise.

And not (wamā) | is (kāna) | for a believer (limu'minin) | that (an) | he kills (yaqtula) | a believer (mu'minan) | except (illā) | by mistake (khaṭa-an). | And whoever (waman) | killed (qatala) | a believer (mu'minan) | by mistake (khaṭa-an), | then freeing (fataḥrīru) | of a slave (raqabatin) | - believing (mu'minatin) | and blood money (wadiyatun) | is to be paid (musallamatun) | to (ilā) | his family (ahlihi) | unless (illā) | that (an) | they remit as charity (yaṣṣaddaqū). | But if (fa-in) | he was (kāna) | from (min) | a people (qawmin) | hostile (ʿaduwwin) | to you (lakum) | and he was (wahuwa) | a believer (mu'minun) | then freeing (fataḥrīru) | of a believing slave (raqabatin). | - believing (mu'minatin). | And if (wa-in) | he was (kāna) | from (min) | a people (qawmin) | between you (baynakum) | and between them (wabaynahum), | is a treaty (mīthāqun), | then blood money (fadiyatun) | is to be paid (musallamatun) | to (ilā) | his family (ahlihi), | and freeing (wataḥrīru) | of a slave (raqabatin) | - believing (mu'minatin). | And whoever (faman) | does not (lam) | find (yajid),

| then fasting (faṣiyāmu) | for two months (shahrayni) | consecutively (mutatābiʿayni), | seeking repentance (tawbatan) | from (mina) | Allah (l-lahi), | and is (wakāna) | Allah (l-lahu) | All-Knowing (ʿalīman), | All-Wise (ḥakīman).

4:93 And whoever kills a believer intentionally then his recompense is Hell, abiding forever in it and will fall the wrath of Allah on him and He will curse him and He has prepared for him a punishment great.

And whoever (waman) | kills (yaqtul) | a believer (mu'minan) | intentionally (mutaʿammidan) | then his recompense (fajazāuhu) | is Hell (jahannamu), | abiding forever (khālidan) | in it (fīhā) | and will fall the wrath (waghaḍiba) | of Allah (l-lahu) | on him (ʿalayhi) | and He will curse him (walaʿanahu) | and He has prepared (wa-aʿadda) | for him (lahu) | a punishment (ʿadhāban) | great (ʿaẓīman).

4:94 O you who believe[d]! When you go forth in the way of Allah then investigate, and do not say to the one who offers to you a greeting of peace, "You are not a believer," seeking transitory gains of the life of the world, for with Allah are booties abundant. Like that you were from before, then conferred favor Allah upon you; so investigate. Indeed, Allah is of what you do All-Aware.

O you (yāayyuhā) | who (alladhīna) | believe[d] (āmanū)! | When (idhā) | you go forth (ḍarabtum) | in (fī) | the way (sabīli) | of Allah (l-lahi) | then investigate (fatabayyanū), | and do not (walā) | say (taqūlū) | to the one who (liman) | offers (alqā) | to you (ilaykumu) | a greeting of peace (l-salāma), | "You are not (lasta) | a believer, (mu'minan)" | seeking (tabtaghūna) | transitory gains (ʿaraḍa) | of the life (l-ḥayati) | of the world (l-dun'yā), | for with (faʿinda) | Allah (l-lahi) | are booties (maghānimu) | abundant (kathīratun). | Like that (kadhālika) | you were (kuntum) | from (min) | before (qablu), | then conferred favor (famanna) | Allah (l-lahu) | upon you (ʿalaykum); | so investigate (fatabayyanū). | Indeed (inna), | Allah (l-laha) | is (kāna) | of what (bimā) | you do (taʿmalūna) | All-Aware (khabīran).

4:95 Not are equal the ones who sit among the believers, other than the ones who are [the] disabled, and the ones who strive in the way of Allah with their wealth and their lives. Preferred has Allah the ones who strive with their wealth and their lives to the ones who sit in rank. And to all promised has Allah the best. preferred has Allah the ones who strive over the ones who sit with a reward great,

Not (lā) | are equal (yastawī) | the ones who sit (l-qāʿidūna) | among (mina) | the believers (l-mu'minīna), | other than (ghayru) | the ones who are (ulī) | [the] disabled (l-ḍarari), | and the ones who strive (wal-mujāhidūna) | in (fī) | the way (sabīli) | of Allah (l-lahi) | with their wealth (bi-amwālihim) | and their lives (wa-anfusihim). | Preferred (faḍḍala) | has Allah (l-lahu) | the ones who strive (l-mujāhidīna) | with their wealth (bi-amwālihim) | and their lives (wa-anfusihim) | to (ʿalā) | the ones who sit (l-qāʿidīna) | in rank (darajatan). | And to all (wakullan) | promised (waʿada) | has Allah (l-lahu) | the best (l-ḥus'nā). | preferred (wafaḍḍala) | has Allah (l-lahu) | the ones who strive (l-mujāhidīna) | over (ʿalā) | the ones who sit (l-qāʿidīna) | with a reward (ajran) | great (ʿaẓīman),

4:96 Ranks from Him and forgiveness, and mercy. And is Allah Oft-Forgiving, Most Merciful.

Ranks (darajātin) | from Him (min'hu) | and forgiveness (wamaghfiratan), | and mercy (waraḥmatan). | And is (wakāna) | Allah (l-lahu) | Oft-Forgiving (ghafūran), | Most Merciful (raḥīman).

4:97 Indeed, those whom - take them in death the Angels while they (were) wronging themselves they say, "In what condition were you?" They said, "We were oppressed in the earth." They said, "Not was the earth of Allah spacious enough so that you could emigrate in it?" Then those will have their abode in Hell - and it is an evil destination.

Indeed (inna), | those whom (alladhīna)- | take them in death (tawaffāhumu) | the

Angels (l-malāikatu) | while they (were) wronging (ẓālimī) | themselves (anfusihim) | they say (qālū), | "In what condition (fīma) | were you? (kuntum)" | They said (qālū), | "We were (kunnā) | oppressed (mus'taḍʿafīna) | in (fī) | the earth. (l-arḍi)" | They said (qālū), | "Not (alam) | was (takun) | the earth (arḍu) | of Allah (l-lahi) | spacious enough (wāsiʿatan) | so that you could emigrate (fatuhājirū) | in it? (fīhā)" | Then those (fa-ulāika) | will have their abode (mawāhum) | in Hell (jahannamu)- | and it is an evil (wasāat) | destination (maṣīran).

4:98 Except the oppressed among the men and the women and the children who not are able to plan and not they are directed to a way.

Except (illā) | the oppressed (l-mus'taḍʿafīna) | among (mina) | the men (l-rijāli) | and the women (wal-nisāi) | and the children (wal-wil'dāni) | who not (lā) | are able to (yastaṭīʿūna) | plan (ḥīlatan) | and not (walā) | they are directed (yahtadūna) | to a way (sabīlan).

4:99 Then those, may be, Allah will pardon [on] them, and is Allah Oft-Pardoning, Oft-Forgiving.

Then those (fa-ulāika), | may be (ʿasā), | Allah (l-lahu) | will (an) | pardon (yaʿfuwa) | [on] them (ʿanhum), | and is (wakāna) | Allah (l-lahu) | Oft-Pardoning (ʿafuwwan), | Oft-Forgiving (ghafūran).

4:100 And whoever emigrates in the way of Allah, will find in the earth places of refuge - many, and abundance. And whoever leaves from his home as an emigrant to Allah and His Messenger, then overtakes him [the] death, then certainly became incumbent his reward on Allah. And is Allah Oft-Forgiving, Most Merciful.

And whoever (waman) | emigrates (yuhājir) | in (fī) | the way (sabīli) | of Allah (l-lahi), | will find (yajid) | in (fī) | the earth (l-arḍi) | places of refuge (murāghaman)- | many (kathīran), | and abundance (wasaʿatan). | And whoever (waman) | leaves (yakhruj) | from (min) | his home (baytihi) | as an emigrant (muhājiran) | to (ilā) | Allah (l-lahi) | and His Messenger (warasūlihi), | then (thumma) | overtakes him (yud'rik'hu) | [the] death (l-mawtu), | then certainly (faqad) | became incumbent (waqaʿa) | his reward (ajruhu) | on (ʿalā) | Allah (l-lahi). | And is (wakāna) | Allah (l-lahu) | Oft-Forgiving (ghafūran), | Most Merciful (raḥīman).

4:101 And when you travel in the earth then not upon you is any blame that you shorten [of] the prayer if you fear that may harm you those who disbelieved. Indeed, the disbelievers are for you an enemy open.

And when (wa-idhā) | you travel (ḍarabtum) | in (fī) | the earth (l-arḍi) | then not (falaysa) | upon you (ʿalaykum) | is any blame (junāḥun) | that (an) | you shorten (taqṣurū) | [of] (mina) | the prayer (l-ṣalati) | if (in) | you fear (khif'tum) | that (an) | may harm you (yaftinakumu) | those who (alladhīna) | disbelieved (kafarū). | Indeed (inna), | the disbelievers (l-kāfirīna) | are (kānū) | for you (lakum) | an enemy (ʿaduwwan) | open (mubīnan).

4:102 And when you are among them and you lead for them the prayer, then let stand a group of them with you and let them take their arms. Then when they have prostrated, then let them be from behind you and let come forward a group - other, which has not prayed, and let them pray with you and let them take their precautions and their arms. Wished those who disbelieved if you neglect [about] your arms and your baggage, so that they (can) assault [upon] you in an attack, single. But there is no blame upon you if was with you any trouble because of rain or you are sick that you lay down your arms, but take your precautions. Indeed, Allah has prepared for the disbelievers a punishment humiliating.

And when (wa-idhā) | you are (kunta) | among them (fīhim) | and you lead (fa-aqamta) | for them (lahumu) | the prayer (l-ṣalata), | then let stand (faltaqum) | a group (ṭāifatun) | of them (min'hum) | with you (maʿaka) | and let them take (walyakhudhū) | their arms (asliḥatahum). | Then when (fa-idhā) | they have prostrated (sajadū), | then let them be (falyakūnū) | from (min) | behind you (warāikum) | and let come forward (waltati) | a group (ṭāifatun)- | other (ukh'rā), |

which has not (lam) | prayed (yuṣallū), | and let them pray (falyuṣallū) | with you (maʿaka) | and let them take (walyakhudhū) | their precautions (ḥidh'rahum) | and their arms (wa-asliḥatahum). | Wished (wadda) | those who (alladhīna) | disbelieved (kafarū) | if (law) | you neglect (taghfulūna) | [about] (ʿan) | your arms (asliḥatikum) | and your baggage (wa-amtiʿatikum), | so that they (can) assault (fayamīlūna) | [upon] you (ʿalaykum) | in an attack (maylatan), | single (wāḥidatan). | But there is no (walā) | blame (junāḥa) | upon you (ʿalaykum) | if (in) | was (kāna) | with you (bikum) | any trouble (adhan) | because of (min) | rain (maṭarin) | or (aw) | you are (kuntum) | sick (marḍā) | that (an) | you lay down (taḍaʿū) | your arms (asliḥatakum), | but take (wakhudhū) | your precautions (ḥidh'rakum). | Indeed (inna), | Allah (l-laha) | has prepared (aʿadda) | for the disbelievers (lil'kāfirīna) | a punishment (ʿadhāban) | humiliating (muhīnan).

4:103 Then when you have finished the prayer, then remember Allah standing and sitting and lying on your sides. But when you are secure then establish the regular prayer. Indeed, the prayer is on the believers prescribed at fixed times.

Then when (fa-idhā) | you have finished (qaḍaytumu) | the prayer (l-ṣalata), | then remember (fa-udh'kurū) | Allah (l-laha) | standing (qiyāman) | and sitting (waquʿūdan) | and lying on (waʿalā) | your sides (junūbikum). | But when (fa-idhā) | you are secure (iṭ'manantum) | then establish (fa-aqīmū) | the regular prayer (l-ṣalata). | Indeed (inna), | the prayer (l-ṣalata) | is (kānat) | on (ʿalā) | the believers (l-mu'minīna) | prescribed (kitāban) | at fixed times (mawqūtan).

4:104 And do not be weak in pursuit of the people. If you are suffering, then indeed, they are also suffering like what you are suffering, while you have hope from Allah what not they hope. And is Allah All-Knowing, All-Wise.

And do not (walā) | be weak (tahinū) | in (fī) | pursuit (ib'tighāi) | of the people (l-qawmi). | If (in) | you are (takūnū) | suffering (talamūna), | then indeed, they (fa-innahum) | are also suffering (yalamūna) | like what (kamā) | you are suffering (talamūna), | while you have hope (watarjūna) | from (mina) | Allah (l-lahi) | what (mā) | not (lā) | they hope (yarjūna). | And is (wakāna) | Allah (l-lahu) | All-Knowing (ʿalīman), | All-Wise (ḥakīman).

4:105 Indeed, We have sent down to you the Book with the truth so that you may judge between the people with what has shown you Allah. And do not be for the deceitful a pleader.

Indeed (innā), | We have sent down (anzalnā) | to you (ilayka) | the Book (l-kitāba) | with the truth (bil-ḥaqi) | so that you may judge (litaḥkuma) | between (bayna) | the people (l-nāsi) | with what (bimā) | has shown you (arāka) | Allah (l-lahu). | And do not (walā) | be (takun) | for the deceitful (lil'khāinīna) | a pleader (khaṣīman).

4:106 And seek forgiveness of Allah. Indeed, Allah is Oft-Forgiving, Most Merciful.

And seek forgiveness (wa-is'taghfiri) | of Allah (l-laha). | Indeed (inna), | Allah (l-laha) | is (kāna) | Oft-Forgiving (ghafūran), | Most Merciful (raḥīman).

4:107 And do not argue for those who deceive themselves. Indeed, Allah does not love the one who is treacherous and sinful.

And do not (walā) | argue (tujādil) | for (ʿani) | those who (alladhīna) | deceive (yakhtānūna) | themselves (anfusahum). | Indeed (inna), | Allah (l-laha) | does not (lā) | love (yuḥibbu) | the one who (man) | is (kāna) | treacherous (khawwānan) | and sinful (athīman).

4:108 They seek to hide from the people but not can they hide from Allah and He is with them when they plot by night what not does he approve of the word. And is Allah of what they do - All-Encompassing.

They seek to hide (yastakhfūna) | from (mina) | the people (l-nāsi) | but not (walā) | can they hide (yastakhfūna) | from (mina) | Allah (l-lahi) | and He (wahuwa) | is with them (maʿahum) | when (idh) | they plot by night (yubayyitūna) | what (mā) | not (lā) | does he approve (yarḍā) | of (mina) | the word (l-qawli). | And is (wakāna) | Allah (l-lahu) | of what (bimā) | they do (yaʿmalūna)- | All-Encompassing (muḥīṭan).

4:109 Here you are - those who [you] argue for them in the life of the world, but who will argue with Allah for them on the Day of [the] Resurrection or who will be [over them] their defender.

Here you are (hāantum)- | those who (hāulāi) | [you] argue (jādaltum) | for them (ʿanhum) | in (fī) | the life (l-ḥayati) | of the world (l-dun'yā), | but who (faman) | will argue (yujādilu) | with Allah (l-laha) | for them (ʿanhum) | on the Day (yawma) | of [the] Resurrection (l-qiyāmati) | or (am) | who (man) | will be (yakūnu) | [over them] (ʿalayhim) | their defender (wakīlan).

4:110 And whoever does evil or wrongs his soul then seeks forgiveness of Allah he will find Allah Oft-Forgiving, Most Merciful.

And whoever (waman) | does (yaʿmal) | evil (sūan) | or (aw) | wrongs (yaẓlim) | his soul (nafsahu) | then (thumma) | seeks forgiveness (yastaghfiri) | of Allah (l-laha) | he will find (yajidi) | Allah (l-laha) | Oft-Forgiving (ghafūran), | Most Merciful (raḥīman).

4:111 And whoever earns sin, then only he earns it against his soul. And is Allah All-Knowing, All-Wise.

And whoever (waman) | earns (yaksib) | sin (ith'man), | then only (fa-innamā) | he earns it (yaksibuhu) | against (ʿalā) | his soul (nafsihi). | And is (wakāna) | Allah (l-lahu) | All-Knowing (ʿalīman), | All-Wise (ḥakīman).

4:112 And whoever earns a fault or a sin then throws it on an innocent, then surely he has burdened (himself) with a slander and a sin manifest.

And whoever (waman) | earns (yaksib) | a fault (khaṭīatan) | or (aw) | a sin (ith'man) | then (thumma) | throws (yarmi) | it (bihi) | on an innocent (barīan), | then surely (faqadi) | he has burdened (himself (iḥ'tamala)) | with a slander (buh'tānan) | and a sin (wa-ith'man) | manifest (mubīnan).

4:113 And if not for the Grace of Allah upon you and His Mercy - surely had resolved a group of them to mislead you. But not they mislead except themselves, and not they will harm you in anything. And has sent down Allah to you the Book and [the] Wisdom and taught you what not you did know. And is the Grace of Allah upon you great.

And if not (walawlā) | for the Grace (faḍlu) | of Allah (l-lahi) | upon you (ʿalayka) | and His Mercy (waraḥmatuhu)- | surely had resolved (lahammat) | a group (ṭāifatun) | of them (min'hum) | to (an) | mislead you (yuḍillūka). | But not (wamā) | they mislead (yuḍillūna) | except (illā) | themselves (anfusahum), | and not (wamā) | they will harm you (yaḍurrūnaka) | in (min) | anything (shayin). | And has sent down (wa-anzala) | Allah (l-lahu) | to you (ʿalayka) | the Book (l-kitāba) | and [the] Wisdom (wal-ḥik'mata) | and taught you (waʿallamaka) | what (mā) | not (lam) | you did (takun) | know (taʿlamu). | And is (wakāna) | the Grace (faḍlu) | of Allah (l-lahi) | upon you (ʿalayka) | great (ʿaẓīman).

4:114 There is no good in much of their secret talk except he who orders charity or kindness or conciliation between the people. And who does that seeking pleasure of Allah then soon We will give him a reward great.

There is no (lā) | good (khayra) | in (fī) | much (kathīrin) | of (min) | their secret talk (najwāhum) | except (illā) | he who (man) | orders (amara) | charity (biṣadaqatin) | or (aw) | kindness (maʿrūfin) | or (aw) | conciliation (iṣ'lāḥin) | between (bayna) | the people (l-nāsi). | And who (waman) | does (yafʿal) | that (dhālika) | seeking (ib'tighāa) | pleasure (marḍāti) | of Allah (l-lahi) | then soon (fasawfa) | We will give him (nu'tīhi) | a reward (ajran) | great (ʿaẓīman).

4:115 And whoever opposes the Messenger from after what has become clear to him of the guidance, and he follows other than the way of the believers, We will turn him to what he has turned and We will burn him in Hell and evil it is as a destination.

And whoever (waman) | opposes (yushāqiqi) | the Messenger (l-rasūla) | from (min) | after (baʿdi) | what (mā) | has become clear (tabayyana) | to him (lahu) | of the guidance (l-hudā), | and he follows (wayattabiʿ) | other than (ghayra) | the way (sabīli) | of the believers (l-mu'minīna), | We will turn him (nuwallihi) | to what (mā) | he has turned (tawallā) | and We will burn him (wanuṣ'lihi) | in Hell (jahannama) | and evil it is (wasāat) | as a destination (maṣīran).

4:116 Indeed, Allah does not forgive that partners be associated with Him, but He forgives [what] other than that for whom He wills. And whoever associates partners with Allah then surely he lost the way, straying far away.

Indeed (inna), | Allah (l-laha) | does not (lā) | forgive (yaghfiru) | that (an) | partners be associated (yush'raka) | with Him (bihi), | but He forgives (wayaghfiru) | [what] (mā) | other than (dūna) | that (dhālika) | for whom (liman) | He wills (yashāu). | And whoever (waman) | associates partners (yush'rik) | with Allah (bil-lahi) | then surely (faqad) | he lost the way (ḍalla), | straying (ḍalālan) | far away (baʿīdan).

4:117 Not they invoke from besides Him but female deities and not they invoke except Shaitaan - rebellious.

Not (in) | they invoke (yadʿūna) | from (min) | besides Him (dūnihi) | but (illā) | female deities (ināthan) | and not (wa-in) | they invoke (yadʿūna) | except (illā) | Shaitaan (shayṭānan)- | rebellious (marīdan).

4:118 He was cursed by Allah and he said, "I will surely take from your slaves a portion appointed."

He was cursed (laʿanahu) | by Allah (l-lahu) | and he said (waqāla), | "I will surely take (la-attakhidhanna) | from (min) | your slaves (ʿibādika) | a portion (naṣīban) | appointed. (mafrūḍan)"

4:119 "And I will surely mislead them and surely arouse desires in them, and surely I will order them so they will surely cut off the ears of the cattle and surely I will order them so they will surely change the creation of Allah." And whoever takes the Shaitaan as a friend from besides Allah, then surely he has lost - a loss manifest.

"And I will surely mislead them (wala-uḍillannahum) | and surely arouse desires in them (wala-umanniyannahum), | and surely I will order them (walaāmurannahum) | so they will surely cut off (falayubattikunna) | the ears (ādhāna) | of the cattle (l-anʿāmi) | and surely I will order them (walaāmurannahum) | so they will surely change (falayughayyirunna) | the creation (khalqa) | of Allah. (l-lahi)" | And whoever (waman) | takes (yattakhidhi) | the Shaitaan (l-shayṭāna) | as a friend (waliyyan) | from (min) | besides (dūni) | Allah (l-lahi), | then surely (faqad) | he has lost (khasira)- | a loss (khus'rānan) | manifest (mubīnan).

4:120 He promises them and arouses desires in them and not promises them the Shaitaan - except deception.

He promises them (yaʿiduhum) | and arouses desires in them (wayumannīhim) | and not (wamā) | promises them (yaʿiduhumu) | the Shaitaan (l-shayṭānu)- | except (illā) | deception (ghurūran).

4:121 Those - their abode is Hell and not they will find from it any escape.

Those (ulāika)- | their abode (mawāhum) | is Hell (jahannamu) | and not (walā) | they will find (yajidūna) | from it (ʿanhā) | any escape (maḥīṣan).

4:122 And those who believe[d] and do [the] righteous deeds We will admit them in Gardens flow from underneath it the rivers, will abide in it forever. A Promise of Allah in truth, and who is truer than Allah in statement?

And those who (wa-alladhīna) | believe[d] (āmanū) | and do (waʿamilū) | [the] righteous deeds (l-ṣāliḥāti) | We will admit them (sanud'khiluhum) | in Gardens (jannātin) | flow (tajrī) | from (min) | underneath it (taḥtihā) | the rivers (l-anhāru), | will abide (khālidīna) | in it (fīhā) | forever (abadan). | A Promise (waʿda) | of Allah (l-lahi) | in truth (ḥaqqan), | and who (waman) | is truer (aṣdaqu) | than (mina) | Allah (l-lahi) | in statement (qīlan)?

4:123 Not by your desire and not by the desire of the People of the Book. Whoever does evil will be recompensed for it and not he will find for him from besides Allah any protector and not any helper.

Not (laysa) | by your desire (bi-amāniyyikum) | and not (walā) | by the desire (amāniyyi) | of the People (ahli) | of the Book (l-kitābi). | Whoever (man) | does (yaʿmal) | evil (sūan) | will be recompensed (yuj'za) | for it (bihi) | and not (walā) | he will find (yajid) | for him (lahu) | from (min) | besides (dūni) | Allah (l-lahi) | any protector (waliyyan) | and not (walā) | any helper (naṣīran).

4:124 And whoever does [of] [the] righteous deeds from the male or female, and he is a believer, then those will enter Paradise and not they will be wronged even as much as the speck on a date-seed.

And whoever (waman) | does (yaʿmal) | [of] (mina) | [the] righteous deeds (l-ṣāliḥāti) | from (min) | the male (dhakarin) | or (aw) | female (unthā), | and he (wahuwa) | is a believer (mu'minun), | then those (fa-ulāika) | will enter (yadkhulūna) | Paradise (l-janata) | and not (walā) | they will be wronged (yuẓ'lamūna) | even as much as the speck on a date-seed (naqīran).

4:125 And who is better in religion than one who submits his face to Allah and he is a good-doer and follows the religion of Ibrahim the upright? And was taken by Allah Ibrahim as a friend.

And who (waman) | is better (aḥsanu) | in religion (dīnan) | than one who (mimman) | submits (aslama) | his face (wajhahu) | to Allah (lillahi) | and he (wahuwa) | is a good-doer (muḥ'sinun) | and follows (wa-ittabaʿa) | the religion (millata) | of Ibrahim (ib'rāhīma) | the upright (ḥanīfan)? | And was taken (wa-ittakhadha) | by Allah (l-lahu) | Ibrahim (ib'rāhīma) | as a friend (khalīlan).

4:126 And for Allah is what is in the heavens and what is in the earth, and is Allah of every thing All-Encompassing.

And for Allah (walillahi) | is what (mā) | is in (fī) | the heavens (l-samāwāti) | and what (wamā) | is in (fī) | the earth (l-arḍi), | and is (wakāna) | Allah (l-lahu) | of every (bikulli) | thing (shayin) | All-Encompassing (muḥīṭan).

4:127 And they seek your ruling concerning the women. Say, "Allah gives you the ruling about them and what is recited to you in the Book concerning orphans of girls to whom not do you give them what is ordained for them and you desire to marry them, and the ones who are weak of the children and to stand for orphans with justice. And whatever you do of good then indeed, Allah is about it All-Knowing.

And they seek your ruling (wayastaftūnaka) | concerning (fī) | the women (l-nisāi). | Say (quli), | "Allah (l-lahu) | gives you the ruling (yuf'tīkum) | about them (fīhinna) | and what (wamā) | is recited (yut'lā) | to you (ʿalaykum) | in (fī) | the Book (l-kitābi) | concerning (fī) | orphans (yatāmā) | of girls (l-nisāi) | to whom (allātī) | not (lā) | do you give them (tu'tūnahunna) | what (mā) | is ordained (kutiba) | for them (lahunna) | and you desire (watarghabūna) | to (an) | marry them (tankiḥūhunna), | and the ones who are weak (wal-mus'taḍʿafīna) | of (mina) | the children (l-wil'dāni) | and to (wa-an) | stand (taqūmū) | for orphans (lil'yatāmā) | with justice (bil-qis'ṭi). | And whatever (wamā) | you do (tafʿalū) | of (min) | good (khayrin) | then indeed (fa-inna), | Allah (l-laha) | is (kāna) | about it (bihi) | All-Knowing (ʿalīman).

4:128 And if a woman fears from her husband ill-conduct or desertion then there is no sin on both of them that they make terms of peace between themselves - a reconciliation and [the] reconciliation is best. And are swayed the souls by greed. But if you do good and fear Allah, then indeed, Allah is of what you do All-Aware.

And if (wa-ini) | a woman (im'ra-atun) | fears (khāfat) | from (min) | her husband (baʿlihā) | ill-conduct (nushūzan) | or (aw) | desertion (iʿ'rāḍan) | then there is no (falā) | sin (junāḥa) | on both of them (ʿalayhimā) | that (an) | they make terms of peace (yuṣ'liḥā) | between themselves (baynahumā)- | a reconciliation (ṣul'ḥan) | and [the] reconciliation (wal-ṣul'ḥu) | is best (khayrun). | And are swayed (wa-uḥ'ḍirati) | the souls (l-anfusu) | by greed (l-shuḥa). | But if (wa-in) | you do good (tuḥ'sinū) | and fear Allah (watattaqū), | then indeed (fa-inna), | Allah (l-laha) | is (kāna) | of what (bimā) | you do (taʿmalūna) | All-Aware (khabīran).

4:129 And never will you be able to deal justly between [the] women even if you desired, but do not incline with all the inclination and leave her the other like the suspended one. And if you reconcile and fear Allah then indeed, Allah is Oft-Forgiving, Most Merciful.

And never (walan) | will you be able (tastaṭīʿū) | to (an) | deal justly (taʿdilū) | between (bayna) | [the] women (l-nisāi) | even if (walaw) | you desired (ḥaraṣtum), | but do not (falā) | incline (tamīlū) | with all (kulla) | the inclination (l-mayli) | and leave her the other (fatadharūhā) | like the suspended one (kal-muʿalaqati). | And if (wa-in) | you reconcile (tuṣ'liḥū) | and fear Allah (watattaqū) | then indeed (fa-inna), | Allah (l-laha) | is (kāna) | Oft-Forgiving (ghafūran), | Most Merciful (raḥīman).

4:130 And if they separate, will be enriched by Allah each of them from His abundance, and is Allah All-Encompassing, All-Wise.

And if (wa-in) | they separate (yatafarraqā), | will be enriched (yugh'ni) | by Allah (l-lahu) | each of them (kullan) | from (min) | His abundance (saʿatihi), | and is (wakāna) | Allah (l-lahu) | All-Encompassing (wāsiʿan), | All-Wise (ḥakīman).

4:131 And for Allah is whatever is in the heavens and whatever is in the earth. And surely We have instructed those who were given the Book from before you and yourselves that you fear Allah. But if you disbelieve - then indeed for Allah is whatever is in the heavens and whatever is in the earth. And is Allah Free of need, Praiseworthy.

And for Allah (walillahi) | is whatever (mā) | is in (fī) | the heavens (l-samāwāti) | and whatever (wamā) | is in (fī) | the earth (l-arḍi). | And surely (walaqad) | We have instructed (waṣṣaynā) | those who (alladhīna) | were given (ūtū) | the Book (l-kitāba) | from (min) | before you (qablikum) | and yourselves (wa-iyyākum) | that (ani) | you fear (ittaqū) | Allah (l-laha). | But if (wa-in) | you disbelieve (takfurū)- | then indeed (fa-inna) | for Allah (lillahi) | is whatever (mā) | is in (fī) | the heavens (l-samāwāti) | and whatever (wamā) | is in (fī) | the earth (l-arḍi). | And is (wakāna) | Allah (l-lahu) | Free of need (ghaniyyan), | Praiseworthy (ḥamīdan).

4:132 And for Allah is whatever is in the heavens and whatever is in the earth. And is sufficient Allah as a Disposer of affairs.

And for Allah (walillahi) | is whatever (mā) | is in (fī) | the heavens (l-samāwāti) | and whatever (wamā) | is in (fī) | the earth (l-arḍi). | And is sufficient (wakafā) | Allah (bil-lahi) | as a Disposer of affairs (wakīlan).

4:133 If He wills He can take you away O people, and bring others. And is Allah over that All-Powerful.

If (in) | He wills (yasha) | He can take you away (yudh'hib'kum) | O (ayyuhā) | people (l-nāsu), | and bring (wayati) | others (biākharīna). | And is (wakāna) | Allah (l-lahu) | over (ʿalā) | that (dhālika) | All-Powerful (qadīran).

4:134 Whoever [is] desires reward of the world - then with Allah is the reward of the world and the Hereafter. And is Allah All-Hearing, All-Seeing.

Whoever (man) | [is] (kāna) | desires (yurīdu) | reward (thawāba) | of the world (l-dun'yā)- | then with (faʿinda) | Allah (l-lahi) | is the reward (thawābu) | of the world (l-dun'yā) | and the Hereafter (wal-ākhirati). | And is (wakāna) | Allah (l-lahu) | All-Hearing (samīʿan), | All-Seeing (baṣīran).

4:135 O you who believe[d]! Be custodians of justice as witnesses to Allah, even if it is against yourselves or the parents and the relatives. if he be rich or poor, for Allah is nearer to both of them. So do not follow the desire lest you deviate. And if you distort or refrain, then indeed, Allah is of what you do All-Aware.

O you (yāayyuhā) | who (alladhīna) | believe[d] (āmanū)! | Be (kūnū) | custodians (qawwāmīna) | of justice (bil-qis'ṭi) | as witnesses (shuhadāa) | to Allah (lillahi), | even if (walaw) | it is against (ʿalā) | yourselves (anfusikum) | or (awi) | the parents (l-wālidayni) | and the relatives (wal-aqrabīna). | if (in) | he be (yakun) | rich (ghaniyyan) | or (aw) | poor (faqīran), | for Allah (fal-lahu) | is nearer (awlā) | to both of them (bihimā). | So do not (falā) | follow (tattabiʿū) | the desire (l-hawā) | lest (an) | you deviate (taʿdilū). | And if (wa-in) | you distort (talwū) | or (aw) | refrain (tuʿ'riḍū), | then indeed (fa-inna), | Allah (l-laha) | is (kāna) | of what (bimā) | you do (taʿmalūna) | All-Aware (khabīran).

4:136 O you who believe[d]! Believe in Allah and His Messenger, and the Book which He revealed upon His Messenger and the Book which He revealed from before. And whoever disbelieves in Allah and His Angels, and His Books, and His Messengers and the Day the Last, then surely he has lost (the) way, straying far away.

O you (yāayyuhā) | who (alladhīna) | believe[d] (āmanū)! | Believe (āminū) | in Allah (bil-lahi) | and His Messenger (warasūlihi), | and the Book (wal-kitābi) | which (alladhī) | He revealed (nazzala) | upon (ʿalā) | His Messenger (rasūlihi) | and the Book (wal-kitābi) | which (alladhī) | He revealed (anzala) | from (min) | before (qablu). | And whoever (waman) | disbelieves (yakfur) | in Allah (bil-lahi) | and His Angels (wamalāikatihi), | and His Books (wakutubihi), | and His Messengers (warusulihi) | and the Day (wal-yawmi) | the Last (l-ākhiri), | then surely (faqad) | he has lost (the) way (ḍalla), | straying (ḍalālan) | far away (baʿīdan).

4:137 Indeed, those who believed, then disbelieved, then again believed, then disbelieved, then increased in disbelief - not will Allah forgive [for] them and not will guide them to a (right) way.

Indeed (inna), | those who (alladhīna) | believed (āmanū), | then (thumma) | disbelieved (kafarū), | then (thumma) | again believed (āmanū), | then (thumma) | disbelieved (kafarū), | then (thumma) | increased (iz'dādū) | in disbelief (kuf'ran)- | not (lam) | will (yakuni) | Allah (l-lahu) | forgive (liyaghfira) | [for] them (lahum) | and not (walā) | will guide them (liyahdiyahum) | to a (right) way (sabīlan).

4:138 Give tidings to the hypocrites that for them is a punishment painful -

Give tidings (bashiri) | to the hypocrites (l-munāfiqīna) | that (bi-anna) | for them (lahum) | is a punishment (ʿadhāban) | painful (alīman)-

4:139 Those who take the disbelievers as allies from instead of the believers. Do they seek with them the honor? But indeed, the honor is for Allah, all.

Those who (alladhīna) | take (yattakhidhūna) | the disbelievers (l-kāfirīna) | as allies (awliyāa) | from (min) | instead of (dūni) | the believers (l-mu'minīna). | Do they seek (ayabtaghūna) | with them (ʿindahumu) | the honor (l-ʿizata)? | But indeed (fa-inna), | the honor (l-ʿizata) | is for Allah (lillahi), | all (jamīʿan).

4:140 And surely He has revealed to you in the Book that when you hear the Verses of Allah being rejected [it] and ridiculed at [it], then do not sit with them until they engage in a conversation other than that. Indeed, you then, would be like them. Indeed, Allah will gather the hypocrites and the disbelievers in Hell all together.

And surely (waqad) | He has revealed (nazzala) | to you (ʿalaykum) | in (fī) | the Book (l-kitābi) | that (an) | when (idhā) | you hear (samiʿtum) | the Verses (āyāti) | of Allah (l-lahi) | being rejected (yuk'faru) | [it] (bihā) | and ridiculed (wayus'tahza-u) | at [it] (bihā), | then do not (falā) | sit (taqʿudū) | with them (maʿahum) | until (ḥattā) | they engage (yakhūḍū) | in (fī) | a conversation (ḥadīthin) | other than that (ghayrihi). | Indeed, you (innakum) | then (idhan), | would be like them (mith'luhum). | Indeed (inna), | Allah (l-laha) | will gather (jāmiʿu) | the hypocrites (l-munāfiqīna) | and the disbelievers (wal-kāfirīna) | in (fī) | Hell (jahannama) | all together (jamīʿan).

4:141 Those who are waiting for you. Then if was for you a victory from Allah they say, "Were not we with you?" But if there was for the disbelievers a chance they said, "Did not we have advantage over you and we protected you from the believers?" And Allah will judge between you on the Day of the Resurrection, and never will make Allah for the disbelievers over the believers a way.

Those who (alladhīna) | are waiting (yatarabbaṣūna) | for you (bikum). | Then if (fa-in) | was (kāna) | for you (lakum) | a victory (fatḥun) | from (mina) | Allah (l-lahi) | they say (qālū), | "Were not (alam) | we (nakun) | with you? (maʿakum)" | But if (wa-in) | there was (kāna) | for the disbelievers (lil'kāfirīna) | a chance (naṣībun) | they said (qālū), | "Did not (alam) | we have advantage (nastaḥwidh) | over you (ʿalaykum) | and we protected you (wanamnaʿkum) | from (mina) | the believers? (l-mu'minīna)" | And Allah (fal-lahu) | will judge (yaḥkumu) | between you (baynakum) | on the Day (yawma) | of the Resurrection (l-qiyāmati), | and never (walan) | will make (yajʿala) | Allah (l-lahu) | for the disbelievers (lil'kāfirīna) | over (ʿalā) | the believers (l-mu'minīna) | a way (sabīlan).

4:142 Indeed, the hypocrites seek to deceive Allah and it is He who deceives them. And when they stand for the prayer, they stand lazily, showing off to the people and not they remember Allah except a little.

Indeed (inna), | the hypocrites (l-munāfiqīna) | seek to deceive (yukhādiʿūna) | Allah (l-laha) | and it is He (wahuwa) | who deceives them (khādiʿuhum). | And when (wa-idhā) | they stand (qāmū) | for (ilā) | the prayer (l-ṣalati), | they stand (qāmū) | lazily (kusālā), | showing off (yurāūna) | to the people (l-nāsa) | and not (walā) | they remember (yadhkurūna) | Allah (l-laha) | except (illā) | a little (qalīlan).

4:143 Wavering between that, not to these and not to those. And whoever has been lead astray by Allah - then never you will find for him a way.

Wavering (mudhabdhabīna) | between (bayna) | that (dhālika), | not (lā) | to (ilā) | these (hāulāi) | and not (walā) | to (ilā) | those (hāulāi). | And whoever (waman) | has been lead astray (yuḍ'lili) | by Allah (l-lahu)- | then never (falan) | you will find (tajida) | for him (lahu) | a way (sabīlan).

4:144 O you who believe[d]! Do not take the disbelievers as allies from instead of the believers. Do you wish that you make for Allah against you an evidence clear?

O you (yāayyuhā) | who (alladhīna) | believe[d] (āmanū)! | Do not (lā) | take (tattakhidhū) | the disbelievers (l-kāfirīna) | as allies (awliyāa) | from (min) | instead of (dūni) | the believers (l-mu'minīna). | Do you wish (aturīdūna) | that (an) | you make (tajʿalū) | for Allah (lillahi) | against you (ʿalaykum) | an evidence (sul'ṭānan) | clear (mubīnan)?

4:145 Indeed, the hypocrites will be in the depths, the lowest, of the Fire, and never you will find for them any helper

Indeed (inna), | the hypocrites (l-munāfiqīna) | will be in (fī) | the depths (l-darki), | the lowest (l-asfali), | of (mina) | the Fire (l-nāri), | and never (walan) | you will find (tajida) | for them (lahum) | any helper (naṣīran)

4:146 Except those who repent and correct themselves and hold fast to Allah and are sincere in their religion for Allah, then those will be with the believers. And soon will be given by Allah the believers a reward, great.

Except (illā) | those who (alladhīna) | repent (tābū) | and correct themselves (wa-aṣlaḥū) | and hold fast (wa-iʿtaṣamū) | to Allah (bil-lahi) | and are sincere (wa-akhlaṣū) | in their religion (dīnahum) | for Allah (lillahi), | then those will be (fa-ulāika) | with (maʿa) | the believers (l-mu'minīna). | And soon (wasawfa) | will be given (yu'ti) | by Allah (l-lahu) | the believers (l-mu'minīna) | a reward (ajran), | great (ʿaẓīman).

4:147 What would do Allah by punishing you if you are grateful and you believe? And is Allah All-Appreciative, All-Knowing.

What (mā) | would do (yafʿalu) | Allah (l-lahu) | by punishing you (biʿadhābikum) | if (in) | you are grateful (shakartum) | and you believe (waāmantum)? | And is (wakāna) | Allah (l-lahu) | All-Appreciative (shākiran), | All-Knowing (ʿalīman).

4:148 Does not love Allah the public mention of [the] evil [of] [the] words except by the one who has been wronged. And is Allah All-Hearing, All-Knowing.

Does not (lā) | love (yuḥibbu) | Allah (l-lahu) | the public mention (l-jahra) | of [the] evil (bil-sūi) | [of] (mina) | [the] words (l-qawli) | except (illā) | by the one who (man) | has been wronged (ẓulima). | And is (wakāna) | Allah (l-lahu) | All-Hearing (samīʿan), | All-Knowing (ʿalīman).

4:149 If you disclose a good or you conceal it or pardon [of] an evil, then indeed, Allah is Oft-Pardoning, All-Powerful.

If (in) | you disclose (tub'dū) | a good (khayran) | or (aw) | you conceal it (tukh'fūhu) | or (aw) | pardon (taʿfū) | [of] (ʿan) | an evil (sūin), | then indeed (fa-inna), | Allah (l-laha) | is (kāna) | Oft-Pardoning (ʿafuwwan), | All-Powerful (qadīran).

4:150 Indeed, those who disbelieve in Allah and His Messengers and they wish that they differentiate between Allah and His Messengers and they say, "We believe in some and we disbelieve in others." And they wish that they take between that a way.

Indeed (inna), | those who (alladhīna) | disbelieve (yakfurūna) | in Allah (bil-lahi) | and His Messengers (warusulihi) | and they wish (wayurīdūna) | that (an) | they differentiate (yufarriqū) | between (bayna) | Allah (l-lahi) | and His Messengers (warusulihi) | and they say (wayaqūlūna), | "We believe (nu'minu) | in some (bibaʿḍin) | and we disbelieve (wanakfuru) | in others. (bibaʿḍin)" | And they wish (wayurīdūna) | that (an) | they take (yattakhidhū) | between (bayna) | that (dhālika) | a way (sabīlan).

4:151 Those - they are the disbelievers truly. And We have prepared for the disbelievers a punishment humiliating.

Those (ulāika)- | they (humu) | are the disbelievers (l-kāfirūna) | truly (ḥaqqan). | And We have prepared (wa-aʿtadnā) | for the disbelievers (lil'kāfirīna) | a punishment (ʿadhāban) | humiliating (muhīnan).

4:152 And those who believe in Allah and His Messengers and not they differentiate between any one of them, those - soon He will give them their reward. And is Allah Oft-Forgiving, Most Merciful.

And those who (wa-alladhīna) | believe (āmanū) | in Allah (bil-lahi) | and His Messengers (warusulihi) | and not (walam) | they differentiate (yufarriqū) | between (bayna) | any one (aḥadin) | of them (min'hum), | those (ulāika)- | soon (sawfa) | He will give them (yu'tīhim) | their reward (ujūrahum). | And is (wakāna) | Allah (l-lahu) | Oft-Forgiving (ghafūran), | Most Merciful (raḥīman).

4:153 Ask you the People of the Book that you bring down to them a book from the heaven. Then indeed, they had asked Musa greater than that for they said, "Show us Allah manifestly," so struck them the thunderbolt for their wrongdoing. Then they took the calf for worship from after [what] came to them the clear proofs, then We forgave them for that. And We gave Musa an authority clear.

Ask you (yasaluka) | the People (ahlu) | of the Book (l-kitābi) | that (an) | you bring down (tunazzila) | to them (ʿalayhim) | a book (kitāban) | from (mina) | the heaven (l-samāi). | Then indeed (faqad), | they had asked (sa-alū) | Musa (mūsā) | greater (akbara) | than (min) | that (dhālika) | for they said (faqālū), | "Show us (arinā) | Allah (l-laha) | manifestly, (jahratan)" | so struck them (fa-akhadhathumu) | the thunderbolt (l-ṣāʿiqatu) | for their wrongdoing (biẓul'mihim). | Then (thumma) | they took (ittakhadhū) | the calf for worship (l-ʿij'la) | from (min) | after (baʿdi) | [what] (mā) | came to them (jāathumu) | the clear proofs (l-bayinātu), | then We forgave them (faʿafawnā) | for (ʿan) | that (dhālika). | And We gave (waātaynā) | Musa (mūsā) | an authority (sul'ṭānan) | clear (mubīnan).

4:154 And We raised over them the mount for their covenant, and We said to them, "Enter the gate, prostrating." And We said to them. "Do not transgress in the Sabbath." And We took from them a covenant solemn.

And We raised (warafaʿnā) | over them (fawqahumu) | the mount (l-ṭūra) | for their covenant (bimīthāqihim), | and We said (waqul'nā) | to them (lahumu), | "Enter (ud'khulū) | the gate (l-bāba), | prostrating. (sujjadan)" | And We said (waqul'nā) | to them (lahum). | "Do not (lā) | transgress (taʿdū) | in (fī) | the Sabbath. (l-sabti)" | And We took (wa-akhadhnā) | from them (min'hum) | a covenant (mīthāqan) | solemn (ghalīẓan).

4:155 Then because of their breaking of their covenant and their disbelief in the Signs of Allah and their killing of the Prophets without any right and their saying, "Our hearts are wrapped." Nay, has set a seal Allah on their hearts for their disbelief so not they believe except a few.

Then because of (fabimā) | their breaking (naqḍihim) | of their covenant (mīthāqahum) | and their disbelief (wakuf'rihim) | in the Signs (biāyāti) | of Allah (l-lahi) | and their killing (waqatlihimu) | of the Prophets (l-anbiyāa) | without (bighayri) | any right (ḥaqqin) | and their saying (waqawlihim), | "Our hearts (qulūbunā) | are wrapped. (ghul'fun)" | Nay (bal), | has set a seal (ṭabaʿa) | Allah (l-lahu) | on their hearts (ʿalayhā) | for their disbelief (bikuf'rihim) | so not (falā) | they believe (yu'minūna) | except (illā) | a few (qalīlan).

4:156 And for their disbelief and their saying against Maryam a slander great.

And for their disbelief (wabikuf'rihim) | and their saying (waqawlihim) | against (ʿalā) | Maryam (maryama) | a slander (buh'tānan) | great (ʿaẓīman).

4:157 And for their saying, "Indeed, we killed the Messiah, Isa, son of Maryam, the Messenger of Allah." And not they killed him and not they crucified him but it was made to appear so to them. And indeed, those who differ in it are surely in doubt about it. Not for them about it [of] any knowledge except the following of assumption. And not they killed him, certainly.

And for their saying (waqawlihim), | "Indeed, we (innā) | killed (qatalnā) | the Messiah (l-masīḥa), | Isa (ʿīsā), | son (ib'na) | of Maryam (maryama), | the Messenger (rasūla) | of Allah. (l-lahi)" | And not (wamā) | they killed him (qatalūhu) | and not (wamā) | they crucified him (ṣalabūhu) | but (walākin) | it was made to appear so (shubbiha) | to them (lahum). | And indeed (wa-inna), | those who (alladhīna) | differ (ikh'talafū) | in it (fīhi) | are surely in (lafī) | doubt (shakkin) | about it (min'hu). | Not (mā) | for them (lahum) | about it (bihi) | [of] (min) | any knowledge (ʿil'min) | except (illā) | the following (ittibāʿa) | of assumption (l-ẓani). | And not (wamā) | they killed him (qatalūhu), | certainly (yaqīnan).

4:158 Nay, he was raised by Allah towards Him. And is Allah All-Mighty, All-Wise.

Nay (bal), | he was raised (rafaʿahu) | by Allah (l-lahu) | towards Him (ilayhi). | And is (wakāna) | Allah (l-lahu) | All-Mighty (ʿazīzan), | All-Wise (ḥakīman).

4:159 And there is not from the People of the Book but surely he believes in him before his death. And on the Day of the Resurrection he will be against them a witness.

And there is not (wa-in) | from (min) | the People (ahli) | of the Book (l-kitābi) | but (illā) | surely he believes (layu'minanna) | in him (bihi) | before (qabla) | his death (mawtihi). | And on the Day (wayawma) | of the Resurrection (l-qiyāmati) | he will be (yakūnu) | against them (ʿalayhim) | a witness (shahīdan).

4:160 Then for the wrongdoing of those who were Jews, We made unlawful for them good things which had been lawful for them and for their hindering from the way of Allah - many.

Then for the wrongdoing (fabiẓul'min) | of (mina) | those who (alladhīna) | were Jews (hādū), | We made unlawful (ḥarramnā) | for them (ʿalayhim) | good things (ṭayyibātin) | which had been lawful (uḥillat) | for them (lahum) | and for their hindering (wabiṣaddihim) | from (ʿan) | the way (sabīli) | of Allah (l-lahi)- | many (kathīran).

4:161 And for their taking of [the] usury while certainly they were forbidden from it and for their consuming wealth of the people wrongfully. And We have prepared for the disbelievers among them a punishment painful.

And for their taking (wa-akhdhihimu) | of [the] usury (l-riba) | while certainly (waqad) | they were forbidden (nuhū) | from it (ʿanhu) | and for their consuming (wa-aklihim) | wealth (amwāla) | of the people (l-nāsi) | wrongfully (bil-bāṭili). | And We have prepared (wa-aʿtadnā) | for the disbelievers (lil'kāfirīna) | among them (min'hum) | a punishment (ʿadhāban) | painful (alīman).

4:162 But the ones who are firm in the knowledge among them and the believers believe in what is revealed to you and what was revealed from before you. And the ones who establish the prayer and the ones who give the zakah and the ones who believe in Allah and the Day the Last - those, We will give them a reward, great.

But (lākini) | the ones who are firm (l-rāsikhūna) | in (fī) | the knowledge (l-ʿil'mi) | among them (min'hum) | and the believers (wal-mu'minūna) | believe (yu'minūna) | in what (bimā) | is revealed (unzila) | to you (ilayka) | and what (wamā) | was revealed (unzila) | from (min) | before you (qablika). | And the ones who establish (wal-muqīmīna) | the prayer (l-ṣalata) | and the ones who give (wal-mu'tūna) | the zakah (l-zakata) | and the ones who believe (wal-mu'minūna) | in Allah (bil-lahi) | and the Day (wal-yawmi) | the Last (l-ākhiri)- | those (ulāika), | We will give them (sanu'tīhim) | a reward (ajran), | great (ʿaẓīman).

4:163 Indeed, We have revealed to you as We revealed to Nuh and the Prophets from after him, and We revealed to Ibrahim and Ishmael, and Isaac and Yaqub, and the tribes, and Isa and Ayyub, and Yunus, and Harun and Sulaiman and We gave to Dawood the Zaboor.

Indeed, We (innā) | have revealed (awḥaynā) | to you (ilayka) | as (kamā) | We revealed (awḥaynā) | to (ilā) | Nuh (nūḥin) | and the Prophets (wal-nabiyīna) | from (min) | after him (baʿdihi), | and We revealed (wa-awḥaynā) | to (ilā) | Ibrahim (ib'rāhīma) | and Ishmael (wa-is'māʿīla), | and Isaac (wa-is'ḥāqa) | and Yaqub (wayaʿqūba), | and the tribes (wal-asbāṭi), | and Isa (waʿīsā) | and Ayyub (wa-ayyūba), | and Yunus (wayūnusa), | and Harun (wahārūna) | and Sulaiman (wasulaymāna) | and We gave (waātaynā) | to Dawood (dāwūda) | the Zaboor (zabūran).

4:164 And Messengers surely We have mentioned them to you from before and Messengers not We have mentioned them to you. And spoke Allah to Musa in a conversation.

And Messengers (warusulan) | surely (qad) | We have mentioned them (qaṣaṣnāhum) | to you (ʿalayka) | from (min) | before (qablu) | and Messengers (warusulan) | not (lam) | We have mentioned them (naqṣuṣ'hum) | to you (ʿalayka). | And spoke (wakallama) | Allah (l-lahu) | to Musa (mūsā) | in a conversation (taklīman).

4:165 Messengers, bearers of glad tidings and warners, so that not there is for mankind against Allah any argument after the Messengers. And is Allah All-Mighty, All-Wise.

Messengers (rusulan), | bearers of glad tidings (mubashirīna) | and warners (wamundhirīna), | so that not (li-allā) | there is (yakūna) | for mankind (lilnnāsi) | against (ʿalā) | Allah (l-lahi) | any argument (ḥujjatun) | after (baʿda) | the Messengers (l-rusuli). | And is (wakāna) | Allah (l-lahu) | All-Mighty (ʿazīzan), | All-Wise (ḥakīman).

4:166 But Allah bears witness to what He has revealed to you. He has sent it down with His Knowledge and the Angels bear witness. And is sufficient Allah as a Witness.

But (lākini) | Allah (l-lahu) | bears witness (yashhadu) | to what (bimā) | He has revealed (anzala) | to you (ilayka). | He has sent it down (anzalahu) | with His Knowledge (biʿil'mihi) | and the Angels (wal-malāikatu) | bear witness (yashhadūna). | And is sufficient (wakafā) | Allah (bil-lahi) | as a Witness (shahīdan).

4:167 Indeed, those who disbelieve and hinder from the way of Allah, surely they have strayed, straying far away.

Indeed (inna), | those who (alladhīna) | disbelieve (kafarū) | and hinder (waṣaddū) | from (ʿan) | the way (sabīli) | of Allah (l-lahi), | surely (qad) | they have strayed (ḍallū), | straying (ḍalālan) | far away (baʿīdan).

4:168 Indeed, those who disbelieved and did wrong, not will Allah [to] forgive them and not He will guide them to a way,

Indeed (inna), | those who (alladhīna) | disbelieved (kafarū) | and did wrong (waẓalamū), | not (lam) | will (yakuni) | Allah (l-lahu) | [to] forgive (liyaghfira) | them (lahum) | and not (walā) | He will guide them (liyahdiyahum) | to a way (ṭarīqan),

4:169 Except the way to Hell, abiding in it forever. And is that for Allah easy.

Except (illā) | the way (ṭarīqa) | to Hell (jahannama), | abiding (khālidīna) | in it (fīhā) | forever (abadan). | And is (wakāna) | that (dhālika) | for (ʿalā) | Allah (l-lahi) | easy (yasīran).

4:170 O mankind! Surely has come to you the Messenger with the truth from your Lord so believe, it is better for you. But if you disbelieve, then indeed, to Allah belongs whatever is in the heavens and the earth. And is Allah All-Knowing, All-Wise.

O (yāayyuhā) | mankind (l-nāsu)! | Surely (qad) | has come to you (jāakumu) | the Messenger (l-rasūlu) | with the truth (bil-ḥaqi) | from (min) | your Lord (rabbikum) | so believe (faāminū), | it is better (khayran) | for you (lakum). | But if (wa-in) | you disbelieve (takfurū), | then indeed (fa-inna), | to Allah belongs (lillahi) | whatever (mā) | is in (fī) | the heavens (l-samāwāti) | and the earth (wal-arḍi). | And is (wakāna) | Allah (l-lahu) | All-Knowing (ʿalīman), | All-Wise (ḥakīman).

4:171 O People of the Book! Do not commit excess in your religion and do not say about Allah except the truth. Only the Messiah, Isa, son of Maryam, was a Messenger of Allah and His word which He conveyed to Maryam and a spirit from Him. So believe in Allah and His Messengers. And do not say, "Three;" desist it is better for you. Only Allah is God One. Glory be to Him! That He should have for Him a son. To Him belongs whatever is in the heavens and whatever is in the earth. And is sufficient Allah as a Disposer of affairs.

O People (yāahla) | of the Book (l-kitābi)! | Do not (lā) | commit excess (taghlū) | in (fī) | your religion (dīnikum) | and do not (walā) | say (taqūlū) | about (ʿalā) | Allah (l-lahi) | except (illā) | the truth (l-ḥaqa). | Only (innamā) | the Messiah (l-masīḥu), | Isa (ʿīsā), | son (ub'nu) | of Maryam (maryama), | was a Messenger (rasūlu) | of Allah (l-lahi) | and His word (wakalimatuhu) | which He conveyed (alqāhā) | to (ilā) | Maryam (maryama) | and a spirit (warūḥun) | from Him (min'hu). | So believe (faāminū) | in Allah (bil-lahi) | and His Messengers (warusulihi). | And do not (walā) | say (taqūlū), | "Three; (thalāthatun)" | desist (intahū) | it is better (khayran) | for you (lakum). | Only (innamā) | Allah (l-lahu) | is God (ilāhun) | One (wāḥidun). | Glory be to Him (sub'ḥānahu)! | That (an) | He should have (yakūna) | for Him (lahu) | a son (waladun). | To Him belongs (lahu) | whatever (mā) | is in (fī) | the heavens (l-samāwāti) | and whatever (wamā) | is in (fī) | the earth (l-arḍi). | And is sufficient (wakafā) | Allah (bil-lahi) | as a Disposer of affairs (wakīlan).

4:172 Never will disdain the Messiah to be a slave of Allah and not the Angels, the ones who are near to Allah. And whoever disdains from His worship and is arrogant then He will gather them towards Him all together.

Never (lan) | will disdain (yastankifa) | the Messiah (l-masīḥu) | to (an) | be (yakūna) | a slave (ʿabdan) | of Allah (lillahi) | and not (walā) | the Angels (l-malāikatu), | the ones who are near to Allah (l-muqarabūna). | And whoever (waman) | disdains (yastankif) | from (ʿan) | His worship (ʿibādatihi) | and is arrogant (wayastakbir) | then He will gather them (fasayaḥshuruhum) | towards Him (ilayhi) | all together (jamīʿan).

4:173 Then as for those who believed and did the righteous deeds then He will give them in full their reward and give them more from His Bounty. And as for those who disdained and were arrogant then He will punish them with a punishment painful, and not will they find for themselves from besides Allah any protector and not any helper.

Then as for (fa-ammā) | those who (alladhīna) | believed (āmanū) | and did (waʿamilū) | the righteous deeds (l-ṣāliḥāti) | then He will give them in full (fayuwaffīhim) | their reward (ujūrahum) | and give them more (wayazīduhum) | from (min) | His Bounty (faḍlihi). | And as for (wa-ammā) | those who (alladhīna) | disdained (is'tankafū) | and were arrogant (wa-is'takbarū) | then He will punish them (fayuʿadhibuhum) | with a punishment (ʿadhāban) | painful (alīman), | and not (walā) | will they find (yajidūna) | for themselves (lahum) | from (min) | besides (dūni) | Allah (l-lahi) | any protector (waliyyan) | and not (walā) | any helper (naṣīran).

4:174 O mankind! Surely has come to you a convincing proof from your Lord, and We have sent down to you a light, clear.

O (yāayyuhā) | mankind (l-nāsu)! | Surely (qad) | has come to you (jāakum) | a convincing proof (bur'hānun) | from (min) | your Lord (rabbikum), | and We have sent down (wa-anzalnā) | to you (ilaykum) | a light (nūran), | clear (mubīnan).

4:175 So as for those who believed in Allah and held fast to Him, then He will admit them in Mercy from Himself and Bounty and will guide them to Himself on a way, straight.

So as for (fa-ammā) | those who (alladhīna) | believed (āmanū) | in Allah (bil-lahi) | and held fast (wa-iʿ'taṣamū) | to Him (bihi), | then He will admit them (fasayud'khiluhum) | in (fī) | Mercy (raḥmatin) | from Himself (min'hu) | and Bounty (wafaḍlin) | and will guide them (wayahdīhim) | to Himself (ilayhi) | on a way (ṣirāṭan), | straight (mus'taqīman).

4:176 They seek your ruling. Say, "Allah gives you a ruling concerning the Kalala if a man died and not he has a child and he has a sister, then for her is a half of what he left. And he will inherit from her if not is for her a child. But if there were two females then for them two thirds of what he left. But if they were brothers and sisters men and women, then the male will have like share of the two females. makes clear Allah to you lest you go astray. And Allah of every thing is All-Knower.

They seek your ruling (yastaftūnaka). | Say (quli), | "Allah (l-lahu) | gives you a ruling (yuf'tīkum) | concerning (fī) | the Kalala (l-kalālati) | if (ini) | a man (im'ru-on) | died (halaka) | and not (laysa) | he has (lahu) | a child (waladun) | and he has (walahu) | a sister (ukh'tun), | then for her (falahā) | is a half (niṣ'fu) | of what (mā) | he left (taraka). | And he (wahuwa) | will inherit from her (yarithuhā) | if (in) | not (lam) | is (yakun) | for her (lahā) | a child (waladun). | But if (fa-in) | there were (kānatā) | two females (ith'natayni) | then for them (falahumā) | two thirds (l-thuluthāni) | of what (mimmā) | he left (taraka). | But if (wa-in) | they were (kānū) | brothers and sisters (ikh'watan) | men (rijālan) | and women (wanisāan), | then the male will have (falildhakari) | like (mith'lu) | share (ḥaẓẓi) | of the two females (l-unthayayni). | makes clear (yubayyinu) | Allah (l-lahu) | to you (lakum) | lest (an) | you go astray (taḍillū). | And Allah (wal-lahu) | of every (bikulli) | thing (shayin) | is All-Knower (ʿalīmun).

Chapter (5) Sūrat l-Māidah (The Table spread with Food)

5:1 O you who believe! Fulfil the contracts. Are made lawful for you the quadruped of the grazing livestock except what is recited on you, not being permitted to hunt while you are in Ihram. Indeed, Allah decrees what He wills.

O (yāayyuhā) | you who (alladhīna) | believe (āmanū)! | Fulfil (awfū) | the contracts (bil-ʿuqūdi). | Are made lawful (uḥillat) | for you (lakum) | the quadruped (bahīmatu) | of the grazing livestock (l-anʿāmi) | except (illā) | what (mā) | is recited (yut'lā) | on you (ʿalaykum), | not (ghayra) | being permitted (muḥillī) | to hunt (l-ṣaydi) | while you (wa-antum) | are in Ihram (ḥurumun). | Indeed (inna), | Allah (l-laha) | decrees (yaḥkumu) | what (mā) | He wills (yurīdu).

5:2 O you who believe! Do not violate the rites of Allah, and not the month, the sacred, and not the sacrificial animals and not the garlanded and not those coming to the House, the Sacred, seeking Bounty of their Lord and good pleasure. And when you come out of Ihram then you may hunt. And let not incite you the hatred for a people as they stopped you from Al-Masjid Al-Haraam that you commit transgression. And help one another in [the] righteousness and [the] piety, but do not help one another in [the] sin and [the] transgression. And fear Allah; indeed, Allah is severe in [the] punishment.

O (yāayyuhā) | you who (alladhīna) | believe (āmanū)! | Do not (lā) | violate (tuḥillū) | the rites (shaʿāira) | of Allah (l-lahi), | and not (walā) | the month (l-shahra), | the sacred (l-ḥarāma), | and not (walā) | the sacrificial animals (l-hadya) | and not (walā) | the garlanded (l-qalāida) | and not (walā) | those coming (āmmīna) | to the House (l-bayta), | the Sacred (l-ḥarāma), | seeking (yabtaghūna) | Bounty (faḍlan) | of (min) | their Lord (rabbihim) | and good pleasure (wariḍ'wānan). | And when (wa-idhā) | you come out of Ihram (ḥalaltum) | then you may hunt (fa-iṣ'ṭādū). | And let not (walā) | incite you (yajrimannakum) | the hatred (shanaānu) | for a people (qawmin) | as (an) | they stopped you (ṣaddūkum) | from (ʿani) | Al-Masjid (l-masjidi) | Al-Haraam (l-ḥarāmi) | that (an) | you commit transgression (taʿtadū). | And help one another (wataʿāwanū) | in (ʿalā) | [the] righteousness (l-biri) | and [the] piety (wal-taqwā), | but do not (walā) | help one another (taʿāwanū) | in (ʿalā) | [the] sin (l-ith'mi) | and [the] transgression (wal-ʿud'wāni). | And fear (wa-ittaqū) | Allah (l-laha); | indeed (inna), | Allah (l-laha) | is severe (shadīdu) | in [the] punishment (l-ʿiqābi).

5:3 Are made unlawful on you the dead animals, and the blood, and flesh of the swine, and what has been dedicated to other than Allah, [on it], and that which is strangled to death, and that which is hit fatally, and that which has a fatal fall, and that which is gored by horns, and that which ate it the wild animal except what you slaughtered, and what is sacrificed on the stone altars, and that you seek division by divining arrows - that is grave disobedience. This day have despaired those who disbelieved of your religion, so do not fear them, but fear Me. This day I have perfected for you your religion and I have completed upon you My Favor and I have approved for you [the] Islam as a religion. But whoever is forced by hunger and not inclining to sin, then indeed, Allah is Oft-Forgiving, Most Merciful.

Are made unlawful (ḥurrimat) | on you (ʿalaykumu) | the dead animals (l-maytatu), | and the blood (wal-damu), | and flesh (walaḥmu) | of the swine (l-khinzīri), | and what (wamā) | has been dedicated (uhilla) | to other than (lighayri) | Allah (l-lahi), | [on it] (bihi), | and that which is strangled to death (wal-mun'khaniqatu), | and that which is hit fatally (wal-mawqūdhatu), | and that which has a fatal fall (wal-mutaradiyatu), | and that which is gored by horns (wal-naṭīḥatu), | and that which (wamā) | ate it (akala) | the wild animal (l-sabuʿu) | except (illā) | what (mā) | you slaughtered (dhakkaytum), | and what (wamā) | is sacrificed (dhubiḥa) | on (ʿalā) | the stone altars (l-nuṣubi), | and that (wa-an) | you seek division (tastaqsimū) | by divining arrows (bil-azlāmi)- | that (dhālikum) | is grave disobedience (fis'qun). | This day (l-yawma) | have despaired (ya-isa) | those who (alladhīna) | disbelieved (kafarū) | of (min) | your religion (dīnikum), | so do not (falā) | fear them (takhshawhum), | but fear Me (wa-ikh'shawni). | This day (l-yawma) | I have perfected (akmaltu) | for you (lakum) | your religion (dīnakum) | and I have completed (wa-atmamtu) | upon you (ʿalaykum) | My Favor (niʿʾmatī) | and I have approved (waraḍītu) | for you (lakumu) | [the] Islam (l-is'lāma) | as a religion (dīnan). | But whoever (famani) | is forced (uḍ'ṭurra) | by (fī) | hunger (makhmaṣatin) | and not (ghayra) | inclining (mutajānifin) | to sin (li-ith'min), | then indeed (fa-inna), | Allah (l-laha) | is Oft-Forgiving (ghafūrun), | Most Merciful (raḥīmun).

5:4 They ask you what is made lawful for them. Say, "Are made lawful for you the good things and what you have taught of your hunting animals, ones who train animals to hunt, you teach them of what has taught you Allah. So eat of what they catch for you, but mention the name of Allah on it, and fear Allah. Indeed, Allah is swift in taking account.

They ask you (yasalūnaka) | what (mādhā) | is made lawful (uḥilla) | for them (lahum). | Say (qul), | "Are made lawful (uḥilla) | for you (lakumu) | the good things (l-ṭayibātu) | and what (wamā) | you have taught (ʿallamtum) | of (mina) | your hunting animals (l-jawāriḥi), | ones who train animals to hunt (mukallibīna), | you teach them (tuʿallimūnahunna) | of what (mimmā) | has taught you (ʿallamakumu) | Allah (l-lahu). | So eat (fakulū) | of what (mimmā) | they catch (amsakna) | for you (ʿalaykum), | but mention (wa-udh'kurū) | the name (is'ma) | of Allah (l-lahi) | on it (ʿalayhi), | and fear (wa-ittaqū) | Allah (l-laha). | Indeed (inna), | Allah (l-laha) | is swift (sarīʿu) | in taking account (l-ḥisābi).

5:5 This day are made lawful for you the good things; and the food of those who were given the Book is lawful for you, and your food is lawful for them. And the chaste women from the believers and the chaste women from those who were given the Book from before you, when you have given them their bridal due, being chaste not being lewd and not ones who are taking secret lovers. And whoever denies the faith - then surely are wasted his deeds and he, in the Hereafter, will be among the losers.

This day (al-yawma) | are made lawful (uḥilla) | for you (lakumu) | the good things (l-ṭayibātu); | and the food (waṭaʿāmu) | of those who (alladhīna) | were given (ūtū) | the Book (l-kitāba) | is lawful (ḥillun) | for you (lakum), | and your food (waṭaʿāmukum) | is lawful (ḥillun) | for them (lahum). | And the chaste women (wal-muḥ'ṣanātu) | from (mina) | the believers (l-mu'mināti) | and the chaste women (wal-muḥ'ṣanātu) | from (mina) | those who (alladhīna) | were given (ūtū) | the Book (l-kitāba) | from (min) | before you (qablikum), | when (idhā) | you have given them (ātaytumūhunna) | their bridal due (ujūrahunna), | being chaste (muḥ'ṣinīna) | not (ghayra) | being lewd (musāfiḥīna) | and not (walā) | ones who are taking (muttakhidhī) | secret lovers (akhdānin). | And whoever (waman) | denies (yakfur) | the faith (bil-īmāni)- | then surely (faqad) | are wasted (ḥabiṭa) | his deeds (ʿamaluhu) | and he (wahuwa), | in (fī) | the Hereafter (l-ākhirati), | will be among (mina) | the losers (l-khāsirīna).

5:6 O you who believe! When you stand up for the prayer, then wash your faces and your hands till the elbows and wipe your heads and your feet till the ankles. But if you are in a state of ceremonial impurity then purify yourselves. But if you are ill or on a journey or has come anyone of you from the toilet or has had contact with the women and not you find water, then do tayyammum with earth clean, then wipe your faces and your hands with it. Does not intend Allah to make for you any difficulty but He intends to purify you and to complete His Favor upon you so that you may be grateful.

O you (yāayyuhā) | who (alladhīna) | believe (āmanū)! | When (idhā) | you stand up (qum'tum) | for (ilā) | the prayer (l-ṣalati), | then wash (fa-igh'silū) | your faces (wujūhakum) | and your hands (wa-aydiyakum) | till (ilā) | the elbows (l-marāfiqi) | and wipe (wa-im'saḥū) | your heads (biruūsikum) | and your feet (wa-arjulakum) | till (ilā) | the ankles (l-kaʿbayni). | But if (wa-in) | you are (kuntum) | in a state of ceremonial impurity (junuban) | then purify yourselves (fa-iṭṭahharū). | But if (wa-in) | you are (kuntum) | ill (marḍā) | or (aw) | on (ʿalā) | a journey (safarin) | or (aw) | has come (jāa) | anyone (aḥadun) | of you (minkum) | from (mina) | the toilet (l-ghāiṭi) | or (aw) | has had contact (lāmastumu) | with the women (l-nisāa) | and not (falam) | you find (tajidū) | water (māan), | then do tayyammum (fatayammamū) | with earth (ṣaʿīdan) | clean (ṭayyiban), | then wipe (fa-im'saḥū) | your faces (biwujūhikum) | and your hands (wa-aydīkum) | with it (min'hu). | Does not (mā) | intend (yurīdu) | Allah (l-lahu) | to make (liyajʿala) | for you (ʿalaykum) | any (min) | difficulty (ḥarajin) | but (walākin) | He intends (yurīdu) | to purify you (liyuṭahhirakum) | and to complete (waliyutimma) | His Favor (niʿ'matahu) | upon you (ʿalaykum) | so that you may (laʿallakum) | be grateful (tashkurūna).

5:7 And remember the Favor of Allah upon you and His covenant which He bound you with [it] when you said, "We heard and we obeyed;" and fear Allah. Indeed, Allah is All-Knower of what is in the breasts.

And remember (wa-udh'kurū) | the Favor (niʿ'mata) | of Allah (l-lahi) | upon you (ʿalaykum) | and His covenant (wamīthāqahu) | which (alladhī) | He bound you (wāthaqakum) | with [it] (bihi) | when (idh) | you said (qul'tum), | "We heard (samiʿ'nā) | and we obeyed; (wa-aṭaʿnā)" | and fear (wa-ittaqū) | Allah (l-laha). | Indeed (inna), | Allah (l-laha) | is All-Knower (ʿalīmun) | of what (bidhāti) | is in the breasts (l-ṣudūri).

5:8 O you who believe! Be steadfast for Allah as witnesses in justice, and let not prevent you hatred of a people [upon] that not you do justice. Be just it is nearer to [the] piety. And fear Allah; indeed, Allah is All-Aware of what you do.

O you (yāayyuhā) | who (alladhīna) | believe (āmanū)! | Be (kūnū) | steadfast (qawwāmīna) | for Allah (lillahi) | as witnesses (shuhadāa) | in justice (bil-qis'ṭi), | and let not (walā) | prevent you (yajrimannakum) | hatred (shanaānu) | of a people (qawmin) | [upon] (ʿalā) | that not (allā) | you do justice (taʿdilū). | Be just (iʿ'dilū) | it (huwa) | is nearer (aqrabu) | to [the] piety (lilttaqwā). | And fear (wa-ittaqū) | Allah (l-laha); | indeed (inna), | Allah (l-laha) | is All-Aware (khabīrun) | of what (bimā) | you do (taʿmalūna).

5:9 Has promised Allah those who believe and do the righteous deeds - for them is forgiveness and a reward great.

Has promised (waʿada) | Allah (l-lahu) | those who (alladhīna) | believe (āmanū) | and do (waʿamilū) | the righteous deeds (l-ṣāliḥāti)- | for them (lahum) | is forgiveness (maghfiratun) | and a reward (wa-ajrun) | great (ʿaẓīmun).

5:10 And those who disbelieve and deny Our Signs - those are the companions of the Hellfire.

And those who (wa-alladhīna) | disbelieve (kafarū) | and deny (wakadhabū) | Our Signs (biāyātinā)- | those (ulāika) | are the companions (aṣḥābu) | of the Hellfire (l-jaḥīmi).

5:11 O you who believe! Remember the Favor of Allah upon you when determined a people that they stretch towards you their hands, but He restrained their hands from you. And fear Allah. And upon Allah so let put the trust the believers.

O you (yāayyuhā) | who (alladhīna) | believe (āmanū)! | Remember (udh'kurū) | the Favor (ni''mata) | of Allah (l-lahi) | upon you ('alaykum) | when (idh) | determined (hamma) | a people (qawmun) | that (an) | they stretch (yabsuṭū) | towards you (ilaykum) | their hands (aydiyahum), | but He restrained (fakaffa) | their hands (aydiyahum) | from you ('ankum). | And fear (wa-ittaqū) | Allah (l-laha). | And upon (wa'alā) | Allah (l-lahi) | so let put the trust (falyatawakkali) | the believers (l-mu'minūna).

5:12 And certainly took Allah a Covenant from the Children of Israel and We appointed among them two and ten leaders. And said Allah, "Indeed, I am with you, if you establish the prayer and give the zakah and you believe in My Messengers and you assist them and you loan to Allah a loan goodly surely I will remove from you your evil deeds and I will surely admit you to gardens flow from underneath them the rivers. But whoever disbelieved after that among you, then certainly he strayed from the way, the right.

And certainly (walaqad) | took (akhadha) | Allah (l-lahu) | a Covenant (mīthāqa) | from the Children (banī) | of Israel (is'rāīla) | and We appointed (waba'athnā) | among them (min'humu) | two (ith'nay) | and ten ('ashara) | leaders (naqīban). | And said (waqāla) | Allah (l-lahu), | "Indeed, I am (innī) | with you (ma'akum), | if (la-in) | you establish (aqamtumu) | the prayer (l-ṣalata) | and give (waātaytumu) | the zakah (l-zakata) | and you believe (waāmantum) | in My Messengers (birusulī) | and you assist them (wa'azzartumūhum) | and you loan (wa-aqraḍtumu) | to Allah (l-laha) | a loan (qarḍan) | goodly (ḥasanan) | surely I will remove (la-ukaffiranna) | from you ('ankum) | your evil deeds (sayyiātikum) | and I will surely admit you (wala-ud'khilannakum) | to gardens (jannātin) | flow (tajrī) | from (min) | underneath them (taḥtihā) | the rivers (l-anhāru). | But whoever (faman) | disbelieved (kafara) | after (ba'da) | that (dhālika) | among you (minkum), | then certainly (faqad) | he strayed (ḍalla) | from the way (sawāa), | the right (l-sabīli).

5:13 So for their breaking of their covenant We cursed them and We made their hearts hard. They distort the words from their places, and forgot a part of what they were reminded of [it]. And not will you cease to discover of treachery from them except a few of them. But forgive them and overlook. Indeed, Allah loves the good-doers.

So for (fabimā) | their breaking (naqḍihim) | of their covenant (mīthāqahum) | We cursed them (la'annāhum) | and We made (waja'alnā) | their hearts (qulūbahum) | hard (qāsiyatan). | They distort (yuḥarrifūna) | the words (l-kalima) | from ('an) | their places (mawāḍi'ihi), | and forgot (wanasū) | a part (ḥaẓẓan) | of what (mimmā) | they were reminded (dhukkirū) | of [it] (bihi). | And not (walā) | will you cease (tazālu) | to discover (taṭṭali'u) | of ('alā) | treachery (khāinatin) | from them (min'hum) | except (illā) | a few (qalīlan) | of them (min'hum). | But forgive (fa-u''fu) | them ('anhum) | and overlook (wa-iṣ'faḥ). | Indeed (inna), | Allah (l-laha) | loves (yuḥibbu) | the good-doers (l-muḥ'sinīna).

5:14 And from those who said, Indeed we are Christians," We took their covenant; but they forgot a part of what they were reminded of [it]. So We aroused between them [the] enmity and [the] hatred till the Day of the Resurrection. And soon will inform them Allah of what they used to do.

And from (wamina) | those who (alladhīna) | said (qālū), | Indeed we (innā) | are Christians, (naṣārā)" | We took (akhadhnā) | their covenant (mīthāqahum); | but they forgot (fanasū) | a part (ḥaẓẓan) | of what (mimmā) | they were reminded (dhukkirū) | of [it] (bihi). | So We aroused (fa-aghraynā) | between them (baynahumu) | [the] enmity (l-'adāwata) | and [the] hatred (wal-baghḍāa) | till (ilā) | the Day (yawmi) | of the Resurrection (l-qiyāmati). | And soon (wasawfa) | will inform them (yunabbi-uhumu) | Allah (l-lahu) | of what (bimā) | they used to (kānū) | do (yaṣna'ūna).

5:15 O People of the Book! Surely has come to you Our Messenger making clear to you much of what you used to conceal of the Scripture and overlooking of much. Surely has come to you from

Allah a light and a Book, clear.

O People (yāahla) | of the Book (l-kitābi)! | Surely (qad) | has come to you (jāakum) | Our Messenger (rasūlunā) | making clear (yubayyinu) | to you (lakum) | much (kathīran) | of what (mimmā) | you used to (kuntum) | conceal (tukh'fūna) | of (mina) | the Scripture (l-kitābi) | and overlooking (wayaʿfū) | of (ʿan) | much (kathīrin). | Surely (qad) | has come to you (jāakum) | from (mina) | Allah (l-lahi) | a light (nūrun) | and a Book (wakitābun), | clear (mubīnun).

5:16 Guides with it Allah those who seek His pleasure to the ways of the peace, and brings them out from the darknessess to the light by His permission, and guides them to the way, the straight.

Guides (yahdī) | with it (bihi) | Allah (l-lahu) | those who (mani) | seek (ittabaʿa) | His pleasure (riḍ'wānahu) | to the ways (subula) | of the peace (l-salāmi), | and brings them out (wayukh'rijuhum) | from (mina) | the darknessess (l-ẓulumāti) | to (ilā) | the light (l-nūri) | by His permission (bi-idh'nihi), | and guides them (wayahdīhim) | to (ilā) | the way (ṣirāṭin), | the straight (mus'taqīmin).

5:17 Certainly disbelieved - those who said, "Indeed, Allah, He is the Messiah, son of Maryam." Say, "Then who has power against Allah in anything if He intends to destroy the Messiah, son of Maryam, and his mother and whoever is in the earth all?" And for Allah is the dominion of the heavens and the earth and what is between both of them. He creates what He wills, and Allah is on every thing All-Powerful.

Certainly (laqad) | disbelieved (kafara)- | those who (alladhīna) | said (qālū), | "Indeed (inna), | Allah (l-laha), | He (huwa) | is the Messiah (l-masīḥu), | son (ub'nu) | of Maryam. (maryama)" | Say (qul), | "Then who (faman) | has power (yamliku) | against (mina) | Allah (l-lahi) | in anything (shayan) | if (in) | He intends (arāda) | to (an) | destroy (yuh'lika) | the Messiah (l-masīḥa), | son (ib'na) | of Maryam (maryama), | and his mother (wa-ummahu) | and whoever (waman) | is in (fī) | the earth (l-arḍi) | all? (jamīʿan)" | And for Allah (walillahi) | is the dominion (mul'ku) | of the heavens (l-samāwāti) | and the earth (wal-arḍi) | and what (wamā) | is between both of them (baynahumā). | He creates (yakhluqu) | what (mā) | He wills (yashāu), | and Allah (wal-lahu) | is on (ʿalā) | every (kulli) | thing (shayin) | All-Powerful (qadīrun).

5:18 And said, the Jews and the Christians "We are the children of Allah and His beloved." Say, "Then why does He punish you for your sins?" Nay, you are human beings from among those He created. He forgives [for] whom He wills and punishes whom He wills. And for Allah is the dominion of the heavens and the earth and whatever is between them, and to Him is the final return.

And said (waqālati), | the Jews (l-yahūdu) | and the Christians (wal-naṣārā) | "We are (naḥnu) | the children (abnāu) | of Allah (l-lahi) | and His beloved. (wa-aḥibbāuhu)" | Say (qul), | "Then why (falima) | does He punish you (yuʿadhibukum) | for your sins? (bidhunūbikum)" | Nay (bal), | you are (antum) | human beings (basharun) | from among those (mimman) | He created (khalaqa). | He forgives (yaghfiru) | [for] whom (liman) | He wills (yashāu) | and punishes (wayuʿadhibu) | whom (man) | He wills (yashāu). | And for Allah (walillahi) | is the dominion (mul'ku) | of the heavens (l-samāwāti) | and the earth (wal-arḍi) | and whatever (wamā) | is between them (baynahumā), | and to Him (wa-ilayhi) | is the final return (l-maṣīru).

5:19 O People of the Book! Surely has come to you Our Messenger, he makes clear to you [on] after an interval (of cessation) of the Messengers, lest you say "Not has come to us any bearer of glad tidings and not a warner." But surely has come to you a bearer of glad tidings and a warner. And Allah is on every thing All-Powerful.

O People (yāahla) | of the Book (l-kitābi)! | Surely (qad) | has come to you (jāakum) | Our Messenger (rasūlunā), | he makes clear (yubayyinu) | to you (lakum) | [on] (ʿalā) | after an interval (of cessation (fatratin)) | of (mina) | the Messengers (l-rusuli), | lest (an) | you say (taqūlū) | "Not (mā) | has come to us (jāanā) | any (min) | bearer of glad tidings (bashīrin) | and not (walā) | a warner. (nadhīrin)" | But surely (faqad) | has come to you (jāakum) | a bearer of glad tidings (bashīrun) | and a warner (wanadhīrun). | And Allah (wal-lahu) | is on (ʿalā) | every (kulli) | thing (shayin) | All-Powerful (qadīrun).

5:20 And when said Musa to his people, "O my people, remember the Favor of Allah upon you when He placed among you Prophets and made you kings and He gave you what not He had given to anyone from the worlds.

And when (wa-idh) | said (qāla) | Musa (mūsā) | to his people (liqawmihi), | "O my people (yāqawmi), | remember (udh'kurū) | the Favor (niʿ'mata) | of Allah (l-lahi) | upon you (ʿalaykum) | when (idh) | He placed (jaʿala) | among you (fīkum) | Prophets (anbiyāa) | and made you (wajaʿalakum) | kings (mulūkan) | and He gave you (waātākum) | what (mā) | not (lam) | He had given (yu'ti) | to anyone (aḥadan) | from (mina) | the worlds (l-ʿālamīna).

5:21 "O my people! Enter the land, the Holy, which has been ordained by Allah for you and do not turn on your backs, then you will turn back as losers."

"O my people (yāqawmi)! | Enter (ud'khulū) | the land (l-arḍa), | the Holy (l-muqadasata), | which (allatī) | has been ordained (kataba) | by Allah (l-lahu) | for you (lakum) | and do not (walā) | turn (tartaddū) | on (ʿalā) | your backs (adbārikum), | then you will turn back (fatanqalibū) | as losers. (khāsirīna)"

5:22 They said, "O Musa! Indeed, in it are people of tyrannical strength and indeed, we never will enter it until they leave from it, and if they leave [from] it then certainly we will enter it."

They said (qālū), | "O Musa (yāmūsā)! | Indeed (inna), | in it (fīhā) | are people (qawman) | of tyrannical strength (jabbārīna) | and indeed, we (wa-innā) | never (lan) | will enter it (nadkhulahā) | until (ḥattā) | they leave (yakhrujū) | from it (min'hā), | and if (fa-in) | they leave (yakhrujū) | [from] it (min'hā) | then certainly we will (fa-innā) | enter it. (dākhilūna)"

5:23 Said two men from those who feared Allah, had favored Allah [on] both of them, "Enter upon them through the gate then when you have entered it then indeed, you will be victorious. And upon Allah then put your trust if you are believers.

Said (qāla) | two men (rajulāni) | from (mina) | those who (alladhīna) | feared Allah (yakhāfūna), | had favored (anʿama) | Allah (l-lahu) | [on] both of them (ʿalayhimā), | "Enter (ud'khulū) | upon them (ʿalayhimu) | through the gate (l-bāba) | then when (fa-idhā) | you have entered it (dakhaltumūhu) | then indeed, you will be (fa-innakum) | victorious (ghālibūna). | And upon (waʿalā) | Allah (l-lahi) | then put your trust (fatawakkalū) | if (in) | you are (kuntum) | believers (mu'minīna).

5:24 They said, O Musa! Indeed, we never will enter it, ever, for as long as they are in it. So go you and your Lord and you both fight. Indeed, we are [here] sitting."

They said (qālū), | O Musa (yāmūsā)! | Indeed, we (innā) | never (lan) | will enter it (nadkhulahā), | ever (abadan), | for (mā) | as long as they are (dāmū) | in it (fīhā). | So go (fa-idh'hab) | you (anta) | and your Lord (warabbuka) | and you both fight (faqātilā). | Indeed, we (innā) | are [here] (hāhunā) | sitting. (qāʿidūna)"

5:25 He said "O my Lord! Indeed, I do not have power except over myself and my brother, so make a separation between us and between the people, the defiantly disobedient."

He said (qāla) | "O my Lord (rabbi)! | Indeed, I (innī) | do not (lā) | have power (amliku) | except (illā) | over myself (nafsī) | and my brother (wa-akhī), | so make a separation (fa-uf'ruq) | between us (baynanā) | and between (wabayna) | the people (l-qawmi), | the defiantly disobedient. (l-fāsiqīna)"

5:26 Allah said, "Then indeed it will be forbidden to them for forty years, they will wander in the earth. So do not grieve over the people, the defiantly disobedient."

Allah said (qāla), | "Then indeed it (fa-innahā) | will be forbidden (muḥarramatun) | to them (ʿalayhim) | for forty (arbaʿīna) | years (sanatan), | they will wander (yatīhūna) | in (fī) | the earth (l-arḍi). | So do not (falā) | grieve (tasa) | over (ʿalā) | the people (l-qawmi), | the defiantly disobedient. (l-fāsiqīna)"

5:27 And recite to them the story of two sons of Adam, in truth, when both offered a sacrifice, and it was accepted from one of them and not was accepted from the other. Said the latter, "Surely I will kill you." Said the former, "Only accepts does Allah from the God fearing.

And recite (wa-ut'lu) | to them (ʿalayhim) | the story (naba-a) | of two sons (ib'nay) | of Adam (ādama), | in truth (bil-ḥaqi), | when (idh) | both offered (qarrabā) | a sacrifice (qur'bānan), | and it was accepted (fatuqubbila) | from (min) | one of them (aḥadihimā) | and not (walam) | was accepted (yutaqabbal) | from (mina) | the other (l-ākhari). | Said the latter (qāla), | "Surely I will kill you. (la-aqtulannaka)" | Said the former (qāla), | "Only (innamā) | accepts (yataqabbalu) | does Allah (l-lahu) | from (mina) | the God fearing (l-mutaqīna).

5:28 If you stretch towards me your hand to kill me, not will I stretch my hand towards you to kill you, indeed I fear Allah the Lord of the worlds."

If (la-in) | you stretch (basaṭta) | towards me (ilayya) | your hand (yadaka) | to kill me (litaqtulanī), | not (mā) | will I (anā) | stretch (bibāsiṭin) | my hand (yadiya) | towards you (ilayka) | to kill you (li-aqtulaka), | indeed I (innī) | fear (akhāfu) | Allah (l-laha) | the Lord (rabba) | of the worlds. (l-ʿālamīna)"

5:29 "Indeed, I wish that you be laden with my sin and your sin so you will be among the companions of the Fire, and that is the recompense of the wrong-doers."

"Indeed, I (innī) | wish (urīdu) | that (an) | you be laden (tabūa) | with my sin (bi-ith'mī) | and your sin (wa-ith'mika) | so you will be (fatakūna) | among (min) | the companions (aṣḥābi) | of the Fire (l-nāri), | and that (wadhālika) | is the recompense (jazāu) | of the wrong-doers. (l-ẓālimīna)"

5:30 Then prompted to him his soul to kill his brother, so he killed him and became of the losers.

Then prompted (faṭawwaʿat) | to him (lahu) | his soul (nafsuhu) | to kill (qatla) | his brother (akhīhi), | so he killed him (faqatalahu) | and became (fa-aṣbaḥa) | of (mina) | the losers (l-khāsirīna).

5:31 Then was sent by Allah a crow, it was scratching in the earth to show him how to hide the dead body of his brother. He said, "Woe to me! Am I unable that I can be like this [the] crow and hide the dead body of my brother?" Then he became of the regretful.

Then was sent (fabaʿatha) | by Allah (l-lahu) | a crow (ghurāban), | it was scratching (yabḥathu) | in (fī) | the earth (l-arḍi) | to show him (liyuriyahu) | how (kayfa) | to hide (yuwārī) | the dead body (sawata) | of his brother (akhīhi). | He said (qāla), | "Woe to me (yāwaylatā)! | Am I unable (aʿajaztu) | that (an) | I can be (akūna) | like (mith'la) | this (hādhā) | [the] crow (l-ghurābi) | and hide (fa-uwāriya) | the dead body (sawata) | of my brother? (akhī)" | Then he became (fa-aṣbaḥa) | of (mina) | the regretful (l-nādimīna).

5:32 From time that, We ordained on the Children of Israel that he who kills a soul other than for a soul or for spreading corruption in the earth then it is as if he has killed mankind, all, and whoever saves it then it is as if he has saved mankind. all. And surely came to them Our Messengers with clear Signs yet, indeed, many of them after that in the earth are surely those who commit excesses.

From (min) | time (ajli) | that (dhālika), | We ordained (katabnā) | on (ʿalā) | the Children (banī) | of Israel (is'rāīla) | that he (annahu) | who (man) | kills (qatala) | a soul (nafsan) | other than (bighayri) | for a soul (nafsin) | or (aw) | for spreading corruption (fasādin) | in (fī) | the earth (l-arḍi) | then it is as if (faka-annamā) | he has killed (qatala) | mankind (l-nāsa), | all (jamīʿan), |

and whoever (waman) | saves it (aḥyāhā) | then it is as if (faka-annamā) | he has saved (aḥyā) | mankind (l-nāsa). | all (jamīʿan). | And surely (walaqad) | came to them (jāathum) | Our Messengers (rusulunā) | with clear Signs (bil-bayināti) | yet (thumma), | indeed (inna), | many (kathīran) | of them (min'hum) | after (baʿda) | that (dhālika) | in (fī) | the earth (l-arḍi) | are surely those who commit excesses (lamus'rifūna).

5:33 Only the recompense for those who wage war against Allah and His Messenger and strive in the earth spreading corruption is that they be killed or they be crucified or be cut off their hands and their feet of opposite sides or they be exiled from the land. That is for them disgrace in the world and for them in the Hereafter is a punishment great.

Only (innamā) | the recompense (jazāu) | for those who (alladhīna) | wage war (yuḥāribūna) | against Allah (l-laha) | and His Messenger (warasūlahu) | and strive (wayasʿawna) | in (fī) | the earth (l-arḍi) | spreading corruption (fasādan) | is that (an) | they be killed (yuqattalū) | or (aw) | they be crucified (yuṣallabū) | or (aw) | be cut off (tuqaṭṭaʿa) | their hands (aydīhim) | and their feet (wa-arjuluhum) | of (min) | opposite sides (khilāfin) | or (aw) | they be exiled (yunfaw) | from (mina) | the land (l-arḍi). | That (dhālika) | is for them (lahum) | disgrace (khiz'yun) | in (fī) | the world (l-dun'yā) | and for them (walahum) | in (fī) | the Hereafter (l-ākhirati) | is a punishment (ʿadhābun) | great (ʿaẓīmun).

5:34 Except those who repent from before that you overpower [over] them, then know that Allah is Oft-Forgiving, Most Merciful.

Except (illā) | those who (alladhīna) | repent (tābū) | from (min) | before (qabli) | that (an) | you overpower (taqdirū) | [over] them (ʿalayhim), | then know (fa-iʿ'lamū) | that (anna) | Allah (l-laha) | is Oft-Forgiving (ghafūrun), | Most Merciful (raḥīmun).

5:35 O you who believe! Fear Allah and seek towards Him the means and strive hard in His way, so that you may succeed.

O you (yāayyuhā) | who (alladhīna) | believe (āmanū)! | Fear (ittaqū) | Allah (l-laha) | and seek (wa-ib'taghū) | towards Him (ilayhi) | the means (l-wasīlata) | and strive hard (wajāhidū) | in (fī) | His way (sabīlihi), | so that you may (laʿallakum) | succeed (tuf'liḥūna).

5:36 Indeed, those who disbelieve, if that for them is what is in the earth all and the like of it with it, to ransom themselves with it, from the punishment of the Day of the Resurrection, not will be accepted from them, and for them is a punishment painful.

Indeed (inna), | those who (alladhīna) | disbelieve (kafarū), | if (law) | that (anna) | for them (lahum) | is what (mā) | is in (fī) | the earth (l-arḍi) | all (jamīʿan) | and the like of it (wamith'lahu) | with it (maʿahu), | to ransom themselves (liyaftadū) | with it (bihi), | from (min) | the punishment (ʿadhābi) | of the Day (yawmi) | of the Resurrection (l-qiyāmati), | not (mā) | will be accepted (tuqubbila) | from them (min'hum), | and for them (walahum) | is a punishment (ʿadhābun) | painful (alīmun).

5:37 They will wish that they come out of the Fire but not they will come out of it. And for them is a punishment lasting.

They will wish (yurīdūna) | that (an) | they come out (yakhrujū) | of (mina) | the Fire (l-nāri) | but not (wamā) | they (hum) | will come out (bikhārijīna) | of it (min'hā). | And for them (walahum) | is a punishment (ʿadhābun) | lasting (muqīmun).

5:38 And for the male thief and the female thief - [then] cut off their hands as a recompense for what they earned as an exemplary (punishment) from Allah. And Allah is All-Mighty, All-Wise.

And for the male thief (wal-sāriqu) | and the female thief (wal-sāriqatu)- | [then] cut off (fa-iq'ṭaʿū) | their hands (aydiyahumā) | as a recompense (jazāan) | for what (bimā) | they earned (kasabā) | as an exemplary (punishment (nakālan)) | from (mina) | Allah (l-lahi). | And Allah (wal-lahu) | is All-Mighty (ʿazīzun), | All-Wise (ḥakīmun).

5:39 But whoever repented from after his wrongdoing and reforms, then indeed, Allah will turn in forgiveness to him. Indeed, Allah is Oft-Forgiving, Most Merciful.

But whoever (faman) | repented (tāba) | from (min) | after (baʿdi) | his wrongdoing (ẓul'mihi) | and reforms (wa-aṣlaḥa), | then indeed (fa-inna), | Allah (l-laha) | will turn in forgiveness (yatūbu) | to him (ʿalayhi). | Indeed (inna), | Allah (l-laha) | is Oft-Forgiving (ghafūrun), | Most Merciful (raḥīmun).

5:40 Do not you know that Allah, to Him belongs the dominion of the heavens and the earth? He punishes whom He wills and He forgives [to] whom He wills. And Allah is on every thing All-Powerful.

Do not (alam) | you know (taʿlam) | that (anna) | Allah (l-laha), | to Him belongs (lahu) | the dominion (mul'ku) | of the heavens (l-samāwāti) | and the earth (wal-arḍi)? | He punishes (yuʿadhibu) | whom (man) | He wills (yashāu) | and He forgives (wayaghfiru) | [to] whom (liman) | He wills (yashāu). | And Allah (wal-lahu) | is on (ʿalā) | every (kulli) | thing (shayin) | All-Powerful (qadīrun).

5:41 O Messenger! Let not grieve you those who hasten in to [the] disbelief - of those who said, "We believe" with their mouths and not believe their hearts, and from those who are Jews. They are listeners to falsehood, and listeners for people, other, who have not come to you. They distort the words from after their context, saying, "If you are given this [so] take it but if not you are given it then beware." And for whom intends Allah his trial, then never will you have power for him against Allah anything. Those are the ones never will intend Allah that He purifies their hearts. For them in the world is disgrace and for them in the Hereafter is a punishment great.

O (yāayyuhā) | Messenger (l-rasūlu)! | Let not (lā) | grieve you (yaḥzunka) | those who (alladhīna) | hasten (yusāriʿūna) | in to (fī) | [the] disbelief (l-kuf'ri)- | of (mina) | those who (alladhīna) | said (qālū), | "We believe (āmannā)" | with their mouths (bi-afwāhihim) | and not (walam) | believe (tu'min) | their hearts (qulūbuhum), | and from (wamina) | those who (alladhīna) | are Jews (hādū). | They are listeners (sammāʿūna) | to falsehood (lil'kadhibi), | and listeners (sammāʿūna) | for people (liqawmin), | other (ākharīna), | who have not (lam) | come to you (yatūka). | They distort (yuḥarrifūna) | the words (l-kalima) | from (min) | after (baʿdi) | their context (mawāḍiʿihi), | saying (yaqūlūna), | "If (in) | you are given (ūtītum) | this (hādhā) | [so] take it (fakhudhūhu) | but if (wa-in) | not (lam) | you are given it (tu'tawhu) | then beware. (fa-iḥ'dharū)" | And for whom (waman) | intends (yuridi) | Allah (l-lahu) | his trial (fit'natahu), | then never (falan) | will you have power (tamlika) | for him (lahu) | against (mina) | Allah (l-lahi) | anything (shayan). | Those (ulāika) | are the ones (alladhīna) | never (lam) | will intend (yuridi) | Allah (l-lahu) | that (an) | He purifies (yuṭahhira) | their hearts (qulūbahum). | For them (lahum) | in (fī) | the world (l-dun'yā) | is disgrace (khiz'yun) | and for them (walahum) | in (fī) | the Hereafter (l-ākhirati) | is a punishment (ʿadhābun) | great (ʿaẓīmun).

5:42 Listeners to [the] falsehood, devourers of the forbidden. So if they come to you then judge between them or turn away from them. And if you turn away from them, then never will they harm you in anything. And if you judge, then judge between them with [the] justice. Indeed, Allah loves the ones who are just.

Listeners (sammāʿūna) | to [the] falsehood (lil'kadhibi), | devourers (akkālūna) | of the forbidden (lilssuḥ'ti). | So if (fa-in) | they come to you (jāūka) | then judge (fa-uḥ'kum) | between them (baynahum) | or (aw) | turn away (aʿriḍ) | from them (ʿanhum). | And if (wa-in) | you turn away (tuʿ'riḍ) | from them (ʿanhum), | then never (falan) | will they harm you (yaḍurrūka) | in anything (shayan). | And if (wa-in) | you judge (ḥakamta), | then judge (fa-uḥ'kum) | between them (baynahum) | with [the] justice (bil-qis'ṭi). | Indeed (inna), | Allah (l-laha) | loves (yuḥibbu) | the ones who are just (l-muq'siṭīna).

5:43 But how can they appoint you a judge while they have with them the Taurat, in it is the Command of Allah? Then they turn away from after that, and not those are the believers.

But how can (wakayfa) | they appoint you a judge (yuḥakkimūnaka) | while they have with them (waʿindahumu) | the Taurat (l-tawrātu), | in it (fīhā) | is the Command (ḥuk'mu) | of Allah (l-lahi)? | Then (thumma) | they turn away (yatawallawna) | from (min) | after (baʿdi) | that (dhālika), | and not (wamā) | those (ulāika) | are the believers (bil-mu'minīna).

5:44 Indeed, We revealed the Taurat in it was Guidance and light; judged by it the Prophets, those who had submitted to Allah for those who were Jews, and the Rabbis, and the scholars, with what they were entrusted of the Book of Allah and they were to it witnesses. So do not fear the people but fear Me, and do not sell My Verses for a price, little. And whoever does not judge by what has revealed Allah, then those [they] are the disbelievers.

Indeed (innā), | We revealed (anzalnā) | the Taurat (l-tawrāta) | in it (fīhā) | was Guidance (hudan) | and light (wanūrun); | judged (yaḥkumu) | by it (bihā) | the Prophets (l-nabiyūna), | those who (alladhīna) | had submitted to Allah (aslamū) | for those who (lilladhīna) | were Jews (hādū), | and the Rabbis (wal-rabāniyūna), | and the scholars (wal-aḥbāru), | with what (bimā) | they were entrusted (us'tuḥ'fiẓū) | of (min) | the Book (kitābi) | of Allah (l-lahi) | and they were (wakānū) | to it (ʿalayhi) | witnesses (shuhadāa). | So do not (falā) | fear (takhshawū) | the people (l-nāsa) | but fear Me (wa-ikh'shawni), | and do not (walā) | sell (tashtarū) | My Verses (biāyātī) | for a price (thamanan), | little (qalīlan). | And whoever (waman) | does not (lam) | judge (yaḥkum) | by what (bimā) | has revealed (anzala) | Allah (l-lahu), | then those (fa-ulāika) | [they] (humu) | are the disbelievers (l-kāfirūna).

5:45 And We ordained for them in it that - the life for the life, and the eye for the eye, and the nose for the nose, and the ear for the ear, and the tooth for the tooth, and for wounds is retribution. But whoever gives charity with it, then it is an expiation for him. And whoever does not judge by what has revealed Allah, then those [they] are the wrongdoers.

And We ordained (wakatabnā) | for them (ʿalayhim) | in it (fīhā) | that (anna)- | the life (l-nafsa) | for the life (bil-nafsi), | and the eye (wal-ʿayna) | for the eye (bil-ʿayni), | and the nose (wal-anfa) | for the nose (bil-anfi), | and the ear (wal-udhuna) | for the ear (bil-udhuni), | and the tooth (wal-sina) | for the tooth (bil-sini), | and for wounds (wal-jurūḥa) | is retribution (qiṣāṣun). | But whoever (faman) | gives charity (taṣaddaqa) | with it (bihi), | then it is (fahuwa) | an expiation (kaffāratun) | for him (lahu). | And whoever (waman) | does not (lam) | judge (yaḥkum) | by what (bimā) | has revealed (anzala) | Allah (l-lahu), | then those (fa-ulāika) | [they] (humu) | are the wrongdoers (l-ẓālimūna).

5:46 And We sent on their footsteps Isa, son of Maryam, confirming what was between his hands of the Taurat, and We gave him the Injeel, in it was Guidance and light and confirming what was between his hands of the Taurat and a Guidance and an admonition for the God conscious.

And We sent (waqaffaynā) | on (ʿalā) | their footsteps (āthārihim) | Isa (biʿīsā), | son (ib'ni) | of Maryam (maryama), | confirming (muṣaddiqan) | what (limā) | was between (bayna) | his hands (yadayhi) | of (mina) | the Taurat (l-tawrāti), | and We gave him (waātaynāhu) | the Injeel (l-injīla), | in it (fīhi) | was Guidance (hudan) | and light (wanūrun) | and confirming (wamuṣaddiqan) | what (limā) | was between (bayna) | his hands (yadayhi) | of (mina) | the Taurat (l-tawrāti) | and a Guidance (wahudan) | and an admonition (wamawʿiẓatan) | for the God conscious (lil'muttaqīna).

5:47 And let judge the People of the Injeel by what has revealed Allah in it. And whoever does not judge by what has revealed Allah then those [they] are the defiantly disobedient.

And let judge (walyaḥkum) | the People (ahlu) | of the Injeel (l-injīli) | by what (bimā) | has revealed (anzala) | Allah (l-lahu) | in it (fīhi). | And whoever (waman) | does not (lam) | judge (yaḥkum) | by what (bimā) | has revealed (anzala) | Allah (l-lahu) | then those (fa-ulāika) | [they]

are (humu) | the defiantly disobedient (l-fāsiqūna).

5:48 And We revealed to you the Book in [the] truth, confirming what was before his hands of the Book and a guardian over it. So judge between them by what has revealed Allah and do not follow their vain desires when has come to you of the truth. For each We have made for you a law and a clear way. And if had willed Allah He would have made you a community, one, [and] but to test you in what He has given you, so race to the good. To Allah you will return, all, then He will inform you of what you were concerning it differing.

And We revealed (wa-anzalnā) | to you (ilayka) | the Book (l-kitāba) | in [the] truth (bil-ḥaqi), | confirming (muṣaddiqan) | what (limā) | was before (bayna) | his hands (yadayhi) | of (mina) | the Book (l-kitābi) | and a guardian (wamuhayminan) | over it (ʿalayhi). | So judge (fa-uḥ'kum) | between them (baynahum) | by what (bimā) | has revealed (anzala) | Allah (l-lahu) | and do not (walā) | follow (tattabiʿ) | their vain desires (ahwāahum) | when (ʿammā) | has come to you (jāaka) | of (mina) | the truth (l-ḥaqi). | For each (likullin) | We have made (jaʿalnā) | for you (minkum) | a law (shir'ʿatan) | and a clear way (wamin'hājan). | And if (walaw) | had willed (shāa) | Allah (l-lahu) | He would have made you (lajaʿalakum) | a community (ummatan), | one (wāḥidatan), | [and] but (walākin) | to test you (liyabluwakum) | in (fī) | what (mā) | He has given you (ātākum), | so race (fa-is'tabiqū) | to the good (l-khayrāti). | To (ilā) | Allah (l-lahi) | you will return (marjiʿukum), | all (jamīʿan), | then He will inform you (fayunabbi-ukum) | of what (bimā) | you were (kuntum) | concerning it (fīhi) | differing (takhtalifūna).

5:49 And that you judge between them by what has revealed Allah and do not follow their vain desires and beware of them lest they tempt you away from some of what has revealed Allah to you. And if they turn away then know that only intends Allah to afflict them for some of their sins. And indeed, many of the people are defiantly disobedient.

And that (wa-ani) | you judge (uḥ'kum) | between them (baynahum) | by what (bimā) | has revealed (anzala) | Allah (l-lahu) | and do not (walā) | follow (tattabiʿ) | their vain desires (ahwāahum) | and beware of them (wa-iḥ'dharhum) | lest (an) | they tempt you away (yaftinūka) | from (ʿan) | some (baʿḍi) | of what (mā) | has revealed (anzala) | Allah (l-lahu) | to you (ilayka). | And if (fa-in) | they turn away (tawallaw) | then know that (fa-iʿ'lam) | only (annamā) | intends (yurīdu) | Allah (l-lahu) | to (an) | afflict them (yuṣībahum) | for some (bibaʿḍi) | of their sins (dhunūbihim). | And indeed (wa-inna), | many (kathīran) | of (mina) | the people (l-nāsi) | are defiantly disobedient (lafāsiqūna).

5:50 Is it then the judgment of the time of ignorance they seek? And who is better than Allah in judgment for a people who firmly believe.

Is it then the judgment (afaḥuk'ma) | of the time of ignorance (l-jāhiliyati) | they seek (yabghūna)? | And who is (waman) | better (aḥsanu) | than (mina) | Allah (l-lahi) | in judgment (ḥuk'man) | for a people (liqawmin) | who firmly believe (yūqinūna).

5:51 O you who believe! Do not take the Jews and the Christians as allies. Some of them are allies to others. And whoever takes them as allies among you, then indeed, he is of them. Indeed, Allah does not guide the people, the wrongdoing.

O you (yāayyuhā) | who (alladhīna) | believe (āmanū)! | Do not (lā) | take (tattakhidhū) | the Jews (l-yahūda) | and the Christians (wal-naṣārā) | as allies (awliyāa). | Some of them (baʿḍuhum) | are allies (awliyāu) | to others (baʿḍin). | And whoever (waman) | takes them as allies (yatawallahum) | among you (minkum), | then indeed, he (fa-innahu) | is of them (min'hum). | Indeed (inna), | Allah (l-laha) | does not (lā) | guide (yahdī) | the people (l-qawma), | the wrongdoing (l-ẓālimīna).

5:52 And you see those - in their hearts is a disease they hasten to them saying, "We fear that may strike us a misfortune." But perhaps Allah [that] will bring the victory or a decision from of Him.

Then they will become for what they had concealed within themselves, regretful.

And you see (fatarā) | those (alladhīna)- | in (fī) | their hearts (qulūbihim) | is a disease (maraḍun) | they hasten (yusāriʿūna) | to them (fīhim) | saying (yaqūlūna), | "We fear (nakhshā) | that (an) | may strike us (tuṣībanā) | a misfortune. (dāiratun)" | But perhaps (faʿasā) | Allah (l-lahu) | [that] (an) | will bring (yatiya) | the victory (bil-fatḥi) | or (aw) | a decision (amrin) | from (min) | of Him (ʿindihi). | Then they will become (fayuṣ'biḥū) | for (ʿalā) | what (mā) | they had concealed (asarrū) | within (fī) | themselves (anfusihim), | regretful (nādimīna).

5:53 And will say those who believe, "Are these those who swore by Allah strongest, of their oaths, indeed, they were with you?" Became worthless their deeds, and they became the losers.

And will say (wayaqūlu) | those who (alladhīna) | believe (āmanū), | "Are these (ahāulāi) | those who (alladhīna) | swore (aqsamū) | by Allah (bil-lahi) | strongest (jahda), | of their oaths (aymānihim), | indeed, they (innahum) | were with you? (lamaʿakum)" | Became worthless (ḥabiṭat) | their deeds (aʿmāluhum), | and they became (fa-aṣbaḥū) | the losers (khāsirīna).

5:54 O you who believe! Whoever turns back among you from his religion, then soon will be brought by Allah a people whom He loves and they love Him, humble towards the believers and stern towards the disbelievers; striving in the way of Allah and not fearing the blame of a critic. That is the Grace of Allah, He grants whom He wills. And Allah is All-Encompassing, All-Knowing.

O you (yāayyuhā) | who (alladhīna) | believe (āmanū)! | Whoever (man) | turns back (yartadda) | among you (minkum) | from (ʿan) | his religion (dīnihi), | then soon (fasawfa) | will be brought (yatī) | by Allah (l-lahu) | a people (biqawmin) | whom He loves (yuḥibbuhum) | and they love Him (wayuḥibbūnahu), | humble (adhillatin) | towards (ʿalā) | the believers (l-mu'minīna) | and stern (aʿizzatin) | towards (ʿalā) | the disbelievers (l-kāfirīna); | striving (yujāhidūna) | in (fī) | the way (sabīli) | of Allah (l-lahi) | and not (walā) | fearing (yakhāfūna) | the blame (lawmata) | of a critic (lāimin). | That (dhālika) | is the Grace (faḍlu) | of Allah (l-lahi), | He grants (yu'tīhi) | whom (man) | He wills (yashāu). | And Allah (wal-lahu) | is All-Encompassing (wāsiʿun), | All-Knowing (ʿalīmun).

5:55 Only your ally is Allah and His Messenger, and those who believe, and those who establish the prayer and give zakah and they are those who bow down.

Only (innamā) | your ally (waliyyukumu) | is Allah (l-lahu) | and His Messenger (warasūluhu), | and those who (wa-alladhīna) | believe (āmanū), | and those who (alladhīna) | establish (yuqīmūna) | the prayer (l-ṣalata) | and give (wayu'tūna) | zakah (l-zakata) | and they (wahum) | are those who bow down (rākiʿūna).

5:56 And whoever takes as an ally Allah and His Messenger and those who believe, then indeed. the party of Allah - they are the victorious.

And whoever (waman) | takes as an ally (yatawalla) | Allah (l-laha) | and His Messenger (warasūlahu) | and those who (wa-alladhīna) | believe (āmanū), | then indeed (fa-inna). | the party (ḥiz'ba) | of Allah (l-lahi)- | they (humu) | are the victorious (l-ghālibūna).

5:57 O you who believe! Do not take those who take your religion in ridicule and fun from those who are given the Book from before you and the disbelievers as allies. And fear Allah, if you are believers.

O you (yāayyuhā) | who (alladhīna) | believe (āmanū)! | Do not (lā) | take (tattakhidhū) | those who (alladhīna) | take (ittakhadhū) | your religion (dīnakum) | in ridicule (huzuwan) | and fun (walaʿiban) | from (mina) | those who (alladhīna) | are given (ūtū) | the Book (l-kitāba) | from (min) | before you (qablikum) | and the disbelievers (wal-kufāra) | as allies (awliyāa). | And fear (wa-ittaqū) | Allah (l-laha), | if (in) | you are (kuntum) | believers (mu'minīna).

5:58 And when you make a call for the prayer, they take it in ridicule and fun. That is because they are a people who do not understand.

And when (wa-idhā) | you make a call (nādaytum) | for (ilā) | the prayer (l-ṣalati), | they take it (ittakhadhūhā) | in ridicule (huzuwan) | and fun (walaʿiban). | That (dhālika) | is because they (bi-annahum) | are a people (qawmun) | who do not (lā) | understand (yaʿqilūna).

5:59 Say, "O People of the Book! Do you resent [of] us except that we believe in Allah and what has been revealed to us and what was revealed from before, and that most of you are defiantly disobedient."

Say (qul), | "O People (yāahla) | of the Book (l-kitābi)! | Do (hal) | you resent (tanqimūna) | [of] us (minnā) | except (illā) | that (an) | we believe (āmannā) | in Allah (bil-lahi) | and what (wamā) | has been revealed (unzila) | to us (ilaynā) | and what (wamā) | was revealed (unzila) | from (min) | before (qablu), | and that (wa-anna) | most of you (aktharakum) | are defiantly disobedient. (fāsiqūna)"

5:60 Say, "Shall I inform you of worse than that as recompense from Allah? Whom has been cursed by Allah and He became angry with him and made of them [the] apes and [the] swines, and who worshipped the false deities. Those are worse in position and farthest astray from the even way."

Say (qul), | "Shall (hal) | I inform you (unabbi-ukum) | of worse (bisharrin) | than (min) | that (dhālika) | as recompense (mathūbatan) | from (ʿinda) | Allah (l-lahi)? | Whom (man) | has been cursed (laʿanahu) | by Allah (l-lahu) | and He became angry (waghaḍiba) | with him (ʿalayhi) | and made (wajaʿala) | of them (min'humu) | [the] apes (l-qiradata) | and [the] swines (wal-khanāzīra), | and who worshipped (waʿabada) | the false deities (l-ṭāghūta). | Those (ulāika) | are worse (sharrun) | in position (makānan) | and farthest astray (wa-aḍallu) | from (ʿan) | the even (sawāi) | way. (l-sabīli)"

5:61 And when they come to you they say, "We believe." But certainly they entered with disbelief and they certainly went out with it. And Allah knows best [of] what they were hiding.

And when (wa-idhā) | they come to you (jāūkum) | they say (qālū), | "We believe. (āmannā)" | But certainly (waqad) | they entered (dakhalū) | with disbelief (bil-kuf'ri) | and they (wahum) | certainly (qad) | went out (kharajū) | with it (bihi). | And Allah (wal-lahu) | knows best (aʿlamu) | [of] what (bimā) | they were (kānū) | hiding (yaktumūna).

5:62 And you see many of them hastening into [the] sin and [the] transgression and eating the forbidden. Surely evil is what they were doing.

And you see (watarā) | many (kathīran) | of them (min'hum) | hastening (yusāriʿūna) | into (fī) | [the] sin (l-ith'mi) | and [the] transgression (wal-ʿud'wāni) | and eating (wa-aklihimu) | the forbidden (l-suḥ'ta). | Surely evil (labi'sa) | is what (mā) | they were (kānū) | doing (yaʿmalūna).

5:63 Why do not forbid them, the Rabbis and the religious scholars from their saying the sinful and their eating of the forbidden? Surely, evil is what they used to do.

Why do not (lawlā) | forbid them (yanhāhumu), | the Rabbis (l-rabāniyūna) | and the religious scholars (wal-aḥbāru) | from (ʿan) | their saying (qawlihimu) | the sinful (l-ith'ma) | and their eating (wa-aklihimu) | of the forbidden (l-suḥ'ta)? | Surely, evil (labi'sa) | is what (mā) | they used to (kānū) | do (yaṣnaʿūna).

5:64 And said the Jews, "The Hand of Allah is chained." Are chained their hands, and they have been cursed for what they said. Nay, His Hands are stretched out He spends how He wills. And surely increase many of them, what has been revealed to you from your Lord, in rebellion and disbelief. And We have cast among them [the] enmity and [the] hatred till the Day of the Resurrection. Every time they kindled the fire of [the] war, it was extinguished by Allah. And they strive in the earth spreading corruption. And Allah does not love the corrupters.

And said (waqālati) | the Jews (l-yahūdu), | "The Hand (yadu) | of Allah (l-lahi) | is chained.

(maghlūlatun)" | Are chained (ghullat) | their hands (aydīhim), | and they have been cursed (waluʿinū) | for what (bimā) | they said (qālū). | Nay (bal), | His Hands (yadāhu) | are stretched out (mabsūṭatāni) | He spends (yunfiqu) | how (kayfa) | He wills (yashāu). | And surely increase (walayazīdanna) | many (kathīran) | of them (min'hum), | what (mā) | has been revealed (unzila) | to you (ilayka) | from (min) | your Lord (rabbika), | in rebellion (ṭugh'yānan) | and disbelief (wakuf'ran). | And We have cast (wa-alqaynā) | among them (baynahumu) | [the] enmity (l-ʿadāwata) | and [the] hatred (wal-baghḍāa) | till (ilā) | the Day (yawmi) | of the Resurrection (l-qiyāmati). | Every time (kullamā) | they kindled (awqadū) | the fire (nāran) | of [the] war (lil'ḥarbi), | it was extinguished (aṭfa-ahā) | by Allah (l-lahu). | And they strive (wayasʿawna) | in (fī) | the earth (l-arḍi) | spreading corruption (fasādan). | And Allah (wal-lahu) | does not (lā) | love (yuḥibbu) | the corrupters (l-muf'sidīna).

5:65 And if that the People of the Book had believed and feared Allah, surely We would have removed from them their evil deeds and surely We would have admitted them to Gardens of Bliss.

And if (walaw) | that (anna) | the People (ahla) | of the Book (l-kitābi) | had believed (āmanū) | and feared Allah (wa-ittaqaw), | surely We would have removed (lakaffarnā) | from them (ʿanhum) | their evil deeds (sayyiātihim) | and surely We would have admitted them (wala-adkhalnāhum) | to Gardens (jannāti) | of Bliss (l-naʿīmi).

5:66 And if that they had stood firmly by the Taurat and the Injeel and what was revealed to them from their Lord, surely they would have eaten from above them and from beneath their feet. Among them is a community moderate, but many of them - evil is what they do.

And if (walaw) | that they (annahum) | had stood firmly (aqāmū) | by the Taurat (l-tawrāta) | and the Injeel (wal-injīla) | and what (wamā) | was revealed (unzila) | to them (ilayhim) | from (min) | their Lord (rabbihim), | surely they would have eaten (la-akalū) | from (min) | above them (fawqihim) | and from (wamin) | beneath (taḥti) | their feet (arjulihim). | Among them (min'hum) | is a community (ummatun) | moderate (muq'taṣidatun), | but many (wakathīrun) | of them (min'hum)- | evil (sāa) | is what (mā) | they do (yaʿmalūna).

5:67 O Messenger! Convey what has been revealed to you from your Lord, and if not you do then not you have conveyed His Message. And Allah will protect you from the people. Indeed, Allah does not guide the people, the disbelieving.

O (yāayyuhā) | Messenger (l-rasūlu)! | Convey (balligh) | what (mā) | has been revealed (unzila) | to you (ilayka) | from (min) | your Lord (rabbika), | and if (wa-in) | not (lam) | you do (tafʿal) | then not (famā) | you have conveyed (ballaghta) | His Message (risālatahu). | And Allah (wal-lahu) | will protect you (yaʿṣimuka) | from (mina) | the people (l-nāsi). | Indeed (inna), | Allah (l-laha) | does not (lā) | guide (yahdī) | the people (l-qawma), | the disbelieving (l-kāfirīna).

5:68 Say, "O People of the Book! You are not on anything until you stand firmly by the Taurat and the Injeel and what has been revealed to you from your Lord. And surely increase many of them, what has been revealed to you from your Lord, in rebellion and disbelief. So do not grieve over the people, the disbelieving.

Say (qul), | "O People (yāahla) | of the Book (l-kitābi)! | You are not (lastum) | on (ʿalā) | anything (shayin) | until (ḥattā) | you stand firmly (tuqīmū) | by the Taurat (l-tawrāta) | and the Injeel (wal-injīla) | and what (wamā) | has been revealed (unzila) | to you (ilaykum) | from (min) | your Lord (rabbikum). | And surely increase (walayazīdanna) | many (kathīran) | of them (min'hum), | what (mā) | has been revealed (unzila) | to you (ilayka) | from (min) | your Lord (rabbika), | in rebellion (ṭugh'yānan) | and disbelief (wakuf'ran). | So do not (falā) | grieve (tasa) | over (ʿalā) | the people (l-qawmi), | the disbelieving (l-kāfirīna).

5:69 Indeed, those who believed and those who became Jews and the Sabians and the Christians, whoever believed in Allah and the Day, the Last and did good deeds, then no fear on them and not they will grieve.

Indeed (inna), | those who (alladhīna) | believed (āmanū) | and those who (wa-alladhīna) | became Jews (hādū) | and the Sabians (wal-ṣābiūna) | and the Christians (wal-naṣārā), | whoever (man) | believed (āmana) | in Allah (bil-lahi) | and the Day (wal-yawmi), | the Last (l-ākhiri) | and did (waʿamila) | good deeds (ṣāliḥan), | then no (falā) | fear (khawfun) | on them (ʿalayhim) | and not (walā) | they (hum) | will grieve (yaḥzanūna).

5:70 Certainly We took a Covenant from the Children of Israel and We sent to them Messengers. Whenever came to them any Messenger with what not desired their souls, a group they denied and a group they kill.

Certainly (laqad) | We took (akhadhnā) | a Covenant (mīthāqa) | from the Children (banī) | of Israel (is'rāīla) | and We sent (wa-arsalnā) | to them (ilayhim) | Messengers (rusulan). | Whenever (kullamā) | came to them (jāahum) | any Messenger (rasūlun) | with what (bimā) | not (lā) | desired (tahwā) | their souls (anfusuhum), | a group (farīqan) | they denied (kadhabū) | and a group (wafarīqan) | they kill (yaqtulūna).

5:71 And they thought that not will be for them a trial, so they became blind and they became deaf. Then turned Allah to them, then again they became blind and they became deaf, many of them. And Allah is All-Seer of what they do.

And they thought (waḥasibū) | that not (allā) | will be for them (takūna) | a trial (fit'natun), | so they became blind (faʿamū) | and they became deaf (waṣammū). | Then (thumma) | turned (tāba) | Allah (l-lahu) | to them (ʿalayhim), | then again (thumma) | they became blind (ʿamū) | and they became deaf (waṣammū), | many (kathīrun) | of them (min'hum). | And Allah (wal-lahu) | is All-Seer (baṣīrun) | of what (bimā) | they do (yaʿmalūna).

5:72 Certainly disbelieved those who say, "Indeed Allah - He is the Messiah, son of Maryam." While said the Messiah, "O Children of Israel! Worship Allah, my Lord and your Lord." Indeed, he who associates partners with Allah, then surely has forbidden Allah for him Paradise and his abode will be the Fire. And not for the wrongdoers any helpers.

Certainly (laqad) | disbelieved (kafara) | those who (alladhīna) | say (qālū), | "Indeed (inna) | Allah (l-laha)- | He (huwa) | is the Messiah (l-masīḥu), | son (ub'nu) | of Maryam. (maryama)" | While said (waqāla) | the Messiah (l-masīḥu), | "O Children (yābanī) | of Israel (is'rāīla)! | Worship (uʿ'budū) | Allah (l-laha), | my Lord (rabbī) | and your Lord. (warabbakum)" | Indeed, he (innahu) | who (man) | associates partners (yush'rik) | with Allah (bil-lahi), | then surely (faqad) | has forbidden (ḥarrama) | Allah (l-lahu) | for him (ʿalayhi) | Paradise (l-janata) | and his abode (wamawāhu) | will be the Fire (l-nāru). | And not (wamā) | for the wrongdoers (lilẓẓālimīna) | any (min) | helpers (anṣārin).

5:73 Certainly disbelieved those who say, "Indeed Allah is the third of three." And there is no [of] god except the God, the One. And if not they desist from what they are saying surely will afflict those who disbelieved among them, a punishment painful.

Certainly (laqad) | disbelieved (kafara) | those who (alladhīna) | say (qālū), | "Indeed (inna) | Allah (l-laha) | is the third (thālithu) | of three. (thalāthatin)" | And there is no (wamā) | [of] (min) | god (ilāhin) | except (illā) | the God (ilāhun), | the One (wāḥidun). | And if (wa-in) | not (lam) | they desist (yantahū) | from what (ʿammā) | they are saying (yaqūlūna) | surely will afflict (layamassanna) | those who (alladhīna) | disbelieved (kafarū) | among them (min'hum), | a punishment (ʿadhābun) | painful (alīmun).

5:74 So will not they turn in repentance to Allah and seek His forgiveness? And Allah is Oft-Forgiving, Most Merciful.

So will not (afalā) | they turn in repentance (yatūbūna) | to (ilā) | Allah (l-lahi) | and seek His forgiveness (wayastaghfirūnahu)? | And Allah (wal-lahu) | is Oft-Forgiving (ghafūrun), | Most

Merciful (raḥīmun).

5:75 Not is the Messiah, son of Maryam but a Messenger, certainly had passed from before him the Messengers. And his mother was truthful. They both used to eat [the] food. See how We make clear to them the Signs, then see how they are deluded.

Not (mā) | is the Messiah (l-masīḥu), | son (ub'nu) | of Maryam (maryama) | but (illā) | a Messenger (rasūlun), | certainly (qad) | had passed (khalat) | from (min) | before him (qablihi) | the Messengers (l-rusulu). | And his mother (wa-ummuhu) | was truthful (ṣiddīqatun). | They both used to (kānā) | eat (yakulāni) | [the] food (l-ṭaʿāma). | See (unẓur) | how (kayfa) | We make clear (nubayyinu) | to them (lahumu) | the Signs (l-āyāti), | then (thumma) | see (unẓur) | how (annā) | they are deluded (yu'fakūna).

5:76 Say, "Do you worship from besides Allah what not has power to cause you any harm and not any benefit, while Allah, He is the All-Hearing, the All-Knowing?

Say (qul), | "Do you worship (ataʿbudūna) | from (min) | besides (dūni) | Allah (l-lahi) | what (mā) | not (lā) | has power (yamliku) | to cause you (lakum) | any harm (ḍarran) | and not (walā) | any benefit (nafʿan), | while Allah (wal-lahu), | He (huwa) | is the All-Hearing (l-samīʿu), | the All-Knowing (l-ʿalīmu)?

5:77 Say, "O People of the Book! Do not exceed in your religion other than the truth, and do not follow vain desires of a people certainly who went astray from before, and they misled many, and they have strayed from the right [the] way.

Say (qul), | "O People (yāahla) | of the Book (l-kitābi)! | Do not (lā) | exceed (taghlū) | in (fī) | your religion (dīnikum) | other than (ghayra) | the truth (l-ḥaqi), | and do not (walā) | follow (tattabiʿū) | vain desires (ahwāa) | of a people (qawmin) | certainly (qad) | who went astray (ḍallū) | from (min) | before (qablu), | and they misled (wa-aḍallū) | many (kathīran), | and they have strayed (waḍallū) | from (ʿan) | the right (sawāi) | [the] way (l-sabīli).

5:78 Were cursed those who disbelieved from the Children of Israel by the tongue of Dawood and Isa, son of Maryam, that was because they disobeyed and they were transgressing.

Were cursed (luʿina) | those who (alladhīna) | disbelieved (kafarū) | from (min) | the Children (banī) | of Israel (is'rāīla) | by (ʿalā) | the tongue (lisāni) | of Dawood (dāwūda) | and Isa (waʿīsā), | son (ib'ni) | of Maryam (maryama), | that was (dhālika) | because (bimā) | they disobeyed (ʿaṣaw) | and they were (wakānū) | transgressing (yaʿtadūna).

5:79 They had been not forbidding each other from wrongdoing they did [it]. Surely, evil was what they were doing.

They had been (kānū) | not (lā) | forbidding each other (yatanāhawna) | from (ʿan) | wrongdoing (munkarin) | they did [it] (faʿalūhu). | Surely, evil (labi'sa) | was what (mā) | they were (kānū) | doing (yafʿalūna).

5:80 You see many of them taking as allies those who disbelieved. Surely evil is what sent forth for them their souls, that became angry Allah with them and in the punishment they will abide forever.

You see (tarā) | many (kathīran) | of them (min'hum) | taking as allies (yatawallawna) | those who (alladhīna) | disbelieved (kafarū). | Surely evil (labi'sa) | is what (mā) | sent forth (qaddamat) | for them (lahum) | their souls (anfusuhum), | that (an) | became angry (sakhiṭa) | Allah (l-lahu) | with them (ʿalayhim) | and in (wafī) | the punishment (l-ʿadhābi) | they (hum) | will abide forever (khālidūna).

5:81 And if they had believed in Allah and the Prophet and what has been revealed to him, not they would have taken them as allies; [and] but many of them are defiantly disobedient.

And if (walaw) | they had (kānū) | believed (yu'minūna) | in Allah (bil-lahi) | and the

Prophet (wal-nabiyi) | and what (wamā) | has been revealed (unzila) | to him (ilayhi), | not (mā) | they would have taken them (ittakhadhūhum) | as allies (awliyāa); | [and] but (walākinna) | many (kathīran) | of them (min'hum) | are defiantly disobedient (fāsiqūna).

5:82 Surely you will find strongest of the people in enmity to those who believe, the Jews and those who are polytheists; and surely you will find nearest of them in affection to those who believe, those who say, "We are Christians." That is because among them are priests and monks, and that they are not arrogant.

Surely you will find (latajidanna) | strongest (ashadda) | of the people (l-nāsi) | in enmity (ʿadāwatan) | to those who (lilladhīna) | believe (āmanū), | the Jews (l-yahūda) | and those who (wa-alladhīna) | are polytheists (ashrakū); | and surely you will find (walatajidanna) | nearest of them (aqrabahum) | in affection (mawaddatan) | to those who (lilladhīna) | believe (āmanū), | those who (alladhīna) | say (qālū), | "We (innā) | are Christians. (naṣārā)" | That is (dhālika) | because (bi-anna) | among them (min'hum) | are priests (qissīsīna) | and monks (waruh'bānan), | and that they (wa-annahum) | are not (lā) | arrogant (yastakbirūna).

5:83 And when they listen to what has been revealed to the Messenger, you see their eyes overflowing with the tears, for what they recognized of the truth. They say, "Our Lord, we have believed so write us with the witnesses.

And when (wa-idhā) | they listen (samiʿū) | to what (mā) | has been revealed (unzila) | to (ilā) | the Messenger (l-rasūli), | you see (tarā) | their eyes (aʿyunahum) | overflowing (tafīḍu) | with (mina) | the tears (l-damʿi), | for what (mimmā) | they recognized (ʿarafū) | of (mina) | the truth (l-ḥaqi). | They say (yaqūlūna), | "Our Lord (rabbanā), | we have believed (āmannā) | so write us (fa-uk'tub'nā) | with (maʿa) | the witnesses (l-shāhidīna).

5:84 And what for us that not we believe in Allah and what came to us from the truth? And we hope that will admit us our Lord with the people, the righteous."

And what (wamā) | for us that (lanā) | not (lā) | we believe (nu'minu) | in Allah (bil-lahi) | and what (wamā) | came to us (jāanā) | from (mina) | the truth (l-ḥaqi)? | And we hope (wanaṭmaʿu) | that (an) | will admit us (yud'khilanā) | our Lord (rabbunā) | with (maʿa) | the people (l-qawmi), | the righteous. (l-ṣāliḥīna)"

5:85 So rewarded them Allah for what they said with Gardens flows from underneath them the rivers, will abide forever in it. And that is the reward of the good-doers.

So rewarded them (fa-athābahumu) | Allah (l-lahu) | for what (bimā) | they said (qālū) | with Gardens (jannātin) | flows (tajrī) | from (min) | underneath them (taḥtihā) | the rivers (l-anhāru), | will abide forever (khālidīna) | in it (fīhā). | And that (wadhālika) | is the reward (jazāu) | of the good-doers (l-muḥ'sinīna).

5:86 And those who disbelieved and denied Our Signs, those are the companions of the Hellfire.

And those who (wa-alladhīna) | disbelieved (kafarū) | and denied (wakadhabū) | Our Signs (biāyātinā), | those (ulāika) | are the companions (aṣḥābu) | of the Hellfire (l-jaḥīmi).

5:87 O you who believe! Do not make unlawful the good things of what has been made lawful by Allah for you, and do not transgress. Indeed, Allah does not love the transgressors.

O you (yāayyuhā) | who (alladhīna) | believe (āmanū)! | Do not (lā) | make unlawful (tuḥarrimū) | the good things (ṭayyibāti) | of what (mā) | has been made lawful (aḥalla) | by Allah (l-lahu) | for you (lakum), | and do not (walā) | transgress (taʿtadū). | Indeed (inna), | Allah (l-laha) | does not (lā) | love (yuḥibbu) | the transgressors (l-muʿ'tadīna).

5:88 And eat of what has provided you Allah - lawful good. And fear Allah, the One you are in Him believers.

And eat (wakulū) | of what (mimmā) | has provided you (razaqakumu) | Allah (l-lahu)- | lawful (ḥalālan) | good (ṭayyiban). | And fear (wa-ittaqū) | Allah (l-laha), | the One (alladhī) | you are (antum) | in Him (bihi) | believers (mu'minūna).

5:89 Not will call you to account Allah for the thoughtless utterances in your oaths but He will call you to account for what you contracted of the oath. So its expiation is feeding of ten needy people of average of what you feed your families or clothing them or freeing a slave. But whoever does not find that, then fasting for three days. That is the expiation of your oaths when you have sworn. And guard your oaths. Thus makes clear Allah to you His Verses so that you may be grateful.

Not (lā) | will call you to account (yuākhidhukumu) | Allah (l-lahu) | for the thoughtless utterances (bil-laghwi) | in (fī) | your oaths (aymānikum) | but (walākin) | He will call you to account (yuākhidhukum) | for what (bimā) | you contracted (ʿaqqadttumu) | of the oath (l-aymāna). | So its expiation (fakaffāratuhu) | is feeding (iṭ'ʿāmu) | of ten (ʿasharati) | needy people (masākīna) | of (min) | average (awsaṭi) | of what (mā) | you feed (tuṭ'ʿimūna) | your families (ahlīkum) | or (aw) | clothing them (kis'watuhum) | or (aw) | freeing (taḥrīru) | a slave (raqabatin). | But whoever (faman) | does not (lam) | find (yajid) | that, then fasting (faṣiyāmu) | for three (thalāthati) | days (ayyāmin). | That (dhālika) | is the expiation (kaffāratu) | of your oaths (aymānikum) | when (idhā) | you have sworn (ḥalaftum). | And guard (wa-iḥ'faẓū) | your oaths (aymānakum). | Thus (kadhālika) | makes clear (yubayyinu) | Allah (l-lahu) | to you (lakum) | His Verses (āyātihi) | so that you may (laʿallakum) | be grateful (tashkurūna).

5:90 O you who believe! Verily the intoxicants and [the] games of chance and sacrifices at altars and divining arrows are an abomination from the work of the Shaitaan, so avoid it so that you may be successful.

O you (yāayyuhā) | who (alladhīna) | believe (āmanū)! | Verily (innamā) | the intoxicants (l-khamru) | and [the] games of chance (wal-maysiru) | and sacrifices at altars (wal-anṣābu) | and divining arrows (wal-azlāmu) | are an abomination (rij'sun) | from (min) | the work (ʿamali) | of the Shaitaan (l-shayṭāni), | so avoid it (fa-ij'tanibūhu) | so that you may (laʿallakum) | be successful (tuf'liḥūna).

5:91 Only intends the Shaitaan to cause between you [the] enmity and [the] hatred through intoxicants and gambling, and hinders you from the remembrance of Allah and from the prayer. So will you be the ones who abstain?

Only (innamā) | intends (yurīdu) | the Shaitaan (l-shayṭānu) | to (an) | cause (yūqiʿa) | between you (baynakumu) | [the] enmity (l-ʿadāwata) | and [the] hatred (wal-baghḍāa) | through (fī) | intoxicants (l-khamri) | and gambling (wal-maysiri), | and hinders you (wayaṣuddakum) | from (ʿan) | the remembrance (dhik'ri) | of Allah (l-lahi) | and from (waʿani) | the prayer (l-ṣalati). | So will (fahal) | you (antum) | be the ones who abstain (muntahūna)?

5:92 And obey Allah and obey the Messenger and beware. And if you turn away, then know only upon Our Messenger is to convey (the Message) clearly.

And obey (wa-aṭīʿū) | Allah (l-laha) | and obey (wa-aṭīʿū) | the Messenger (l-rasūla) | and beware (wa-iḥ'dharū). | And if (fa-in) | you turn away (tawallaytum), | then know (fa-iʿlamū) | only (annamā) | upon (ʿalā) | Our Messenger (rasūlinā) | is to convey (the Message (l-balāghu)) | clearly (l-mubīnu).

5:93 Not on those who believe and do the good deeds any sin for what they ate when that they fear Allah and they believe and they do [the] good deeds then they fear Allah and believe, then they fear Allah and do good, and Allah loves the good-doers.

Not (laysa) | on (ʿalā) | those who (alladhīna) | believe (āmanū) | and do (waʿamilū) | the good deeds (l-ṣāliḥāti) | any sin (junāḥun) | for what (fīmā) | they ate (ṭaʿimū) | when (idhā) | that (mā) | they fear Allah (ittaqaw) | and they believe (waāmanū) | and they do (waʿamilū) | [the] good deeds (l-ṣāliḥāti) | then (thumma) | they fear Allah (ittaqaw) | and believe (waāmanū), | then (thumma) | they fear Allah (ittaqaw) | and do good (wa-aḥsanū), | and Allah (wal-lahu) | loves (yuḥibbu) | the good-doers (l-muḥ'sinīna).

5:94 O you who believe! Surely will test you Allah through something of the game - can reach it your hands and your spears that may make evident Allah who fears Him in the unseen. And whoever transgressed after that, then for him is a punishment painful.

O you (yāayyuhā) | who (alladhīna) | believe (āmanū)! | Surely will test you (layabluwannakumu) | Allah (l-lahu) | through something (bishayin) | of (mina) | the game (l-ṣaydi)- | can reach it (tanāluhu) | your hands (aydīkum) | and your spears (warimāḥukum) | that may make evident (liyaʿlama) | Allah (l-lahu) | who (man) | fears Him (yakhāfuhu) | in the unseen (bil-ghaybi). | And whoever (famani) | transgressed (iʿtadā) | after (baʿda) | that (dhālika), | then for him (falahu) | is a punishment (ʿadhābun) | painful (alīmun).

5:95 O you who believe! Do not kill the game while you are in Ihram. And whoever killed it among you intentionally, then penalty is similar to what he killed of the cattle, judging it two men, just, among you as an offering reaching the Kabah or an expiation - feeding needy people or equivalent of that in fasting, that he may taste the consequence of his deed. Pardoned by Allah what has passed, but whoever returned, then will take retribution Allah from him. And Allah is All-Mighty, Owner of Retribution.

O you (yāayyuhā) | who (alladhīna) | believe (āmanū)! | Do not (lā) | kill (taqtulū) | the game (l-ṣayda) | while you (wa-antum) | are in Ihram (ḥurumun). | And whoever (waman) | killed it (qatalahu) | among you (minkum) | intentionally (mutaʿammidan), | then penalty (fajazāon) | is similar (mith'lu) | to what (mā) | he killed (qatala) | of (mina) | the cattle (l-naʿami), | judging (yaḥkumu) | it (bihi) | two men (dhawā), | just (ʿadlin), | among you (minkum) | as an offering (hadyan) | reaching (bāligha) | the Kabah (l-kaʿbati) | or (aw) | an expiation (kaffāratun)- | feeding (ṭaʿāmu) | needy people (masākīna) | or (aw) | equivalent (ʿadlu) | of that (dhālika) | in fasting (ṣiyāman), | that he may taste (liyadhūqa) | the consequence (wabāla) | of his deed (amrihi). | Pardoned (ʿafā) | by Allah (l-lahu) | what (ʿammā) | has passed (salafa), | but whoever (waman) | returned (ʿāda), | then will take retribution (fayantaqimu) | Allah (l-lahu) | from him (min'hu). | And Allah (wal-lahu) | is All-Mighty (ʿazīzun), | Owner (dhū) | of Retribution (intiqāmin).

5:96 Is made lawful for you game of the sea and its food as provision for you and for the travelers, and is made unlawful on you game of the land as long as you are in Ihram, And be conscious of Allah the One to Him you will be gathered.

Is made lawful (uḥilla) | for you (lakum) | game (ṣaydu) | of the sea (l-baḥri) | and its food (waṭaʿāmuhu) | as provision (matāʿan) | for you (lakum) | and for the travelers (walilssayyārati), | and is made unlawful (waḥurrima) | on you (ʿalaykum) | game (ṣaydu) | of the land (l-bari) | as (mā) | long as you (dum'tum) | are in Ihram (ḥuruman), | And be conscious (wa-ittaqū) | of Allah (l-laha) | the One (alladhī) | to Him (ilayhi) | you will be gathered (tuḥ'sharūna).

5:97 Has been made by Allah the Kabah, the House, the Sacred, an establishment for mankind and the months [the] sacred and the animals for offering and the garlands. That is so that you may know that Allah knows what is in the heavens and what is in the earth, and that Allah of every thing is All-Knowing.

Has been made (jaʿala) | by Allah (l-lahu) | the Kabah (l-kaʿbata), | the House (l-bayta), | the Sacred (l-ḥarāma), | an establishment (qiyāman) | for mankind (lilnnāsi) | and the months (wal-shahra) | [the] sacred (l-ḥarāma) | and the animals for offering (wal-hadya) | and the garlands (wal-qalāida). | That is (dhālika) | so that you may know (litaʿlamū) | that (anna) | Allah (l-laha) | knows (yaʿlamu) | what (mā) | is in (fī) | the heavens (l-samāwāti) | and what (wamā) | is in (fī) | the earth (l-arḍi), | and that (wa-anna) | Allah (l-laha) | of every (bikulli) | thing (shayin) | is All-Knowing (ʿalīmun).

5:98 Know that Allah is severe in punishment and that Allah is Oft-Forgiving, Most Merciful.
Know (i'lamū) | that (anna) | Allah (l-laha) | is severe (shadīdu) | in punishment (l-ʿiqābi) | and that (wa-anna) | Allah (l-laha) | is Oft-Forgiving (ghafūrun), | Most Merciful (raḥīmun).

5:99 Not on the Messenger except the conveyance. And Allah knows what you reveal and what you conceal.
Not (mā) | on (ʿalā) | the Messenger (l-rasūli) | except (illā) | the conveyance (l-balāghu). | And Allah (wal-lahu) | knows (yaʿlamu) | what (mā) | you reveal (tub'dūna) | and what (wamā) | you conceal (taktumūna).

5:100 Say, "Not are equal the evil and the good even if impresses you abundance of the evil. So fear Allah, O men of understanding, so that you may be successful."
Say (qul), | "Not (lā) | are equal (yastawī) | the evil (l-khabīthu) | and the good (wal-ṭayibu) | even if (walaw) | impresses you (aʿjabaka) | abundance (kathratu) | of the evil (l-khabīthi). | So fear (fa-ittaqū) | Allah (l-laha), | O men (yāulī) | of understanding (l-albābi), | so that you may (laʿallakum) | be successful. (tuf'liḥūna)"

5:101 O you who believe! Do not ask about things if made clear to you, it may distress you and if you ask about it when is being revealed the Quran it would be made clear to you. has been pardoned by Allah [about] it, and Allah is Oft-Forgiving, All-Forbearing.
O you (yāayyuhā) | who (alladhīna) | believe (āmanū)! | Do not (lā) | ask (tasalū) | about (ʿan) | things (ashyāa) | if (in) | made clear (tub'da) | to you (lakum), | it may distress you (tasu'kum) | and if (wa-in) | you ask (tasalū) | about it (ʿanhā) | when (ḥīna) | is being revealed (yunazzalu) | the Quran (l-qur'ānu) | it would be made clear (tub'da) | to you (lakum). | has been pardoned (ʿafā) | by Allah (l-lahu) | [about] it (ʿanhā), | and Allah (wal-lahu) | is Oft-Forgiving (ghafūrun), | All-Forbearing (ḥalīmun).

5:102 Indeed, asked them a people from before you, then they became thereby disbelievers.
Indeed (qad), | asked them (sa-alahā) | a people (qawmun) | from (min) | before you (qablikum), | then (thumma) | they became (aṣbaḥū) | thereby (bihā) | disbelievers (kāfirīna).

5:103 Not has been made by Allah of a Bahirah and not a Saibah and not a Wasilah and not a Hami. [And] but those who disbelieved they invent against Allah the lie, and most of them do not use reason.
Not (mā) | has been made (jaʿala) | by Allah (l-lahu) | of (min) | a Bahirah (baḥīratin) | and not (walā) | a Saibah (sāibatin) | and not (walā) | a Wasilah (waṣīlatin) | and not (walā) | a Hami (ḥāmin). | [And] but (walākinna) | those who (alladhīna) | disbelieved (kafarū) | they invent (yaftarūna) | against (ʿalā) | Allah (l-lahi) | the lie (l-kadhiba), | and most of them (wa-aktharuhum) | do not (lā) | use reason (yaʿqilūna).

5:104 And when it is said to them, "Come to what has been revealed by Allah and to the Messenger," they said, "Sufficient for us is what we found upon it our forefathers." Even though that their forefathers were not knowing anything and not they were guided?
And when (wa-idhā) | it is said (qīla) | to them (lahum), | "Come (taʿālaw) | to (ilā) | what (mā) | has been revealed (anzala) | by Allah (l-lahu) | and to (wa-ilā) | the Messenger, (l-rasūli)" | they said (qālū), | "Sufficient for us (ḥasbunā) | is what (mā) | we found (wajadnā) | upon it (ʿalayhi) | our forefathers. (ābāanā)" | Even though (awalaw) | that (kāna) | their forefathers (ābāuhum) | were not (lā) | knowing (yaʿlamūna) | anything (shayan) | and not (walā) | they were guided (yahtadūna)?

5:105 O you who believe! Upon you is to guard yourselves. Not will harm you those who have gone astray when you have been guided. To Allah is your return - all; then He will inform you of what you used to do.

O you (yāayyuhā) | who (alladhīna) | believe (āmanū)! | Upon you (ʿalaykum) | is to guard yourselves (anfusakum). | Not (lā) | will harm you (yaḍurrukum) | those who (man) | have gone astray (ḍalla) | when (idhā) | you have been guided (ih'tadaytum). | To (ilā) | Allah (l-lahi) | is your return (marjiʿukum)- | all (jamīʿan); | then He will inform you (fayunabbi-ukum) | of what (bimā) | you used to (kuntum) | do (taʿmalūna).

5:106 O you who believe! Take testimony among you when approaches one of you [the] death, at the time (of making) [the] a will two men, just, among you, or two others from other than you if you are travel(ing) in the earth then befalls you calamity of [the] death. Detain both of them from after the prayer and let them both swear by Allah if you doubt, "Not we will exchange it for a price even if he is of a near relative, and not we will conceal testimony of Allah. Indeed, we then will surely (be) of the sinners."

O you (yāayyuhā) | who (alladhīna) | believe (āmanū)! | Take testimony (shahādatu) | among you (baynikum) | when (idhā) | approaches (ḥaḍara) | one of you (aḥadakumu) | [the] death (l-mawtu), | at the time (of making (ḥīna)) | [the] a will (l-waṣiyati) | two (ith'nāni) | men (dhawā), | just (ʿadlin), | among you (minkum), | or (aw) | two others (ākharāni) | from (min) | other than you (ghayrikum) | if (in) | you (antum) | are travel(ing (ḍarabtum)) | in (fī) | the earth (l-arḍi) | then befalls you (fa-aṣābatkum) | calamity (muṣībatu) | of [the] death (l-mawti). | Detain both of them (taḥbisūnahumā) | from (min) | after (baʿdi) | the prayer (l-ṣalati) | and let them both swear (fayuq'simāni) | by Allah (bil-lahi) | if (ini) | you doubt (ir'tabtum), | "Not (lā) | we will exchange (nashtarī) | it for (bihi) | a price (thamanan) | even if (walaw) | he is (kāna) | of (dhā) | a near relative (qur'bā), | and not (walā) | we will conceal (naktumu) | testimony (shahādata) | of Allah (l-lahi). | Indeed, we (innā) | then (idhan) | will surely (be) of (lamina) | the sinners. (l-āthimīna)"

5:107 Then if it is discovered on that the two were guilty of sin, then let two others stand in their place from those who have a lawful right over them - the former two - and let them both swear by Allah "Surely our testimony is truer than testimony of the other two and not we have transgressed. Indeed, we then will be of the wrongdoers."

Then if (fa-in) | it is discovered (ʿuthira) | on (ʿalā) | that the two (annahumā) | were guilty (is'taḥaqqā) | of sin (ith'man), | then let two others (faākharāni) | stand (yaqūmāni) | in their place (maqāmahumā) | from (mina) | those who (alladhīna) | have a lawful right (is'taḥaqqa) | over them (ʿalayhimu)- | the former two (l-awlayāni)- | and let them both swear (fayuq'simāni) | by Allah (bil-lahi) | "Surely our testimony (lashahādatunā) | is truer (aḥaqqu) | than (min) | testimony of the other two (shahādatihimā) | and not (wamā) | we have transgressed (iʿ'tadaynā). | Indeed, we (innā) | then (idhan) | will be of (lamina) | the wrongdoers. (l-ẓālimīna)"

5:108 That is closer that they will give the testimony in its true form or they would fear that will be refuted their oaths after their others oaths. And fear Allah and listen; and Allah does not guide the people. the defiantly disobedient.

That (dhālika) | is closer (adnā) | that (an) | they will give (yatū) | the testimony (bil-shahādati) | in (ʿalā) | its true form (wajhihā) | or (aw) | they would fear (yakhāfū) | that (an) | will be refuted (turadda) | their oaths (aymānun) | after (baʿda) | their others oaths (aymānihim). | And fear (wa-ittaqū) | Allah (l-laha) | and listen (wa-is'maʿū); | and Allah (wal-lahu) | does not (lā) | guide (yahdī) | the people (l-qawma). | the defiantly disobedient (l-fāsiqīna).

5:109 The day will be gathered by Allah the Messengers and He will say, "What was the response you received?" They said, "There is no knowledge for us. Indeed You, You are the Knower of the unseen."

The day (yawma) | will be gathered (yajmaʿu) | by Allah (l-lahu) | the Messengers (l-rusula)

| and He will say (fayaqūlu), | "What (mādhā) | was the response you received? (ujib'tum)" | They said (qālū), | "There is no (lā) | knowledge (ʿil'ma) | for us (lanā). | Indeed You (innaka), | You (anta) | are the Knower (ʿallāmu) | of the unseen. (l-ghuyūbi)"

5:110 When said Allah, "O Isa, son of Maryam! Remember My Favor upon you and upon your mother when I strengthened you with the Spirit, the Holy, you spoke to the people in the cradle and in maturity. And when I taught you the Book and the wisdom and the Taurat and the Injeel; and when you make from the clay like the shape of the bird by My permission then you breath into it and it becomes a bird by My permission, and you heal the born blind and the leper by My permission, and when you bring forth the dead by My permission. And when I restrained the Children of Israel from you when you came to them with the clear proofs then said those who disbelieved among them "Not is this but magic, clear."

When (idh) | said (qāla) | Allah (l-lahu), | "O Isa (yāʿīsā), | son (ib'na) | of Maryam (maryama)! | Remember (udh'kur) | My Favor (niʿ'matī) | upon you (ʿalayka) | and upon (waʿalā) | your mother (wālidatika) | when (idh) | I strengthened you (ayyadttuka) | with the Spirit (birūḥi), | the Holy (l-qudusi), | you spoke (tukallimu) | to the people (l-nāsa) | in (fī) | the cradle (l-mahdi) | and in maturity (wakahlan). | And when (wa-idh) | I taught you (ʿallamtuka) | the Book (l-kitāba) | and the wisdom (wal-ḥik'mata) | and the Taurat (wal-tawrāta) | and the Injeel (wal-injīla); | and when (wa-idh) | you make (takhluqu) | from (mina) | the clay (l-ṭīni) | like the shape (kahayati) | of the bird (l-ṭayri) | by My permission (bi-idh'nī) | then you breath (fatanfukhu) | into it (fīhā) | and it becomes (fatakūnu) | a bird (ṭayran) | by My permission (bi-idh'nī), | and you heal (watub'ri-u) | the born blind (l-akmaha) | and the leper (wal-abraṣa) | by My permission (bi-idh'nī), | and when (wa-idh) | you bring forth (tukh'riju) | the dead (l-mawtā) | by My permission (bi-idh'nī). | And when (wa-idh) | I restrained (kafaftu) | the Children (banī) | of Israel (is'rāīla) | from you (ʿanka) | when (idh) | you came to them (ji'tahum) | with the clear proofs (bil-bayināti) | then said (faqāla) | those who (alladhīna) | disbelieved (kafarū) | among them (min'hum) | "Not (in) | is this (hādhā) | but (illā) | magic (siḥ'run), | clear. (mubīnun)"

5:111 And when I inspired to the disciples to believe in Me and in My Messenger they said, "We believe and bear witness that indeed we are Muslims.

And when (wa-idh) | I inspired (awḥaytu) | to (ilā) | the disciples (l-ḥawāriyīna) | to (an) | believe (āminū) | in Me (bī) | and in My Messenger (wabirasūlī) | they said (qālū), | "We believe (āmannā) | and bear witness (wa-ish'had) | that indeed we (bi-annanā) | are Muslims (mus'limūna).

5:112 When said the disciples, "O Isa, son of Maryam! Is able your Lord to send down to us a table spread from the heaven?" He said, "Fear Allah, if you are believers."

When (idh) | said (qāla) | the disciples (l-ḥawāriyūna), | "O Isa (yāʿīsā), | son (ib'na) | of Maryam (maryama)! | Is (hal) | able (yastaṭīʿu) | your Lord (rabbuka) | to (an) | send down (yunazzila) | to us (ʿalaynā) | a table spread (māidatan) | from (mina) | the heaven? (l-samāi)" | He said (qāla), | "Fear (ittaqū) | Allah (l-laha), | if (in) | you are (kuntum) | believers. (mu'minīna)"

5:113 They said, "We wish that we eat from it and satisfy our hearts and we know that certainly you have spoken the truth to us and we be over it among the witnesses.

They said (qālū), | "We wish (nurīdu) | that (an) | we eat (nakula) | from it (min'hā) | and satisfy (wataṭma-inna) | our hearts (qulūbunā) | and we know (wanaʿlama) | that (an) | certainly (qad) | you have spoken the truth to us (ṣadaqtanā) | and we be (wanakūna) | over it (ʿalayhā) | among (mina) | the witnesses (l-shāhidīna).

5:114 Said Isa, son of Maryam, "O Allah, our Lord, send down to us a table spread from the heaven to be for us a festival for first of us and last of us and a sign from You. And provide us, and You are best of the providers.

Said (qāla) | Isa (ʿīsā), | son (ub'nu) | of Maryam (maryama), | "O Allah (l-lahuma), | our

Lord (rabbanā), | send down (anzil) | to us (ʿalaynā) | a table spread (māidatan) | from (mina) | the heaven (l-samāi) | to be (takūnu) | for us (lanā) | a festival (ʿīdan) | for first of us (li-awwalinā) | and last of us (waākhirinā) | and a sign (waāyatan) | from You (minka). | And provide us (wa-ur'zuq'nā), | and You (wa-anta) | are best (khayru) | of the providers (l-rāziqīna).

5:115 Said Allah, "Indeed I will send it down to you, then whoever disbelieves after that among you, then indeed I [I] will punish him with a punishment not I have punished anyone among the worlds."

Said (qāla) | Allah (l-lahu), | "Indeed I (innī) | will send it down (munazziluhā) | to you (ʿalaykum), | then whoever (faman) | disbelieves (yakfur) | after that (baʿdu) | among you (minkum), | then indeed I (fa-innī) | [I] will punish him (uʿadhibuhu) | with a punishment (ʿadhāban) | not (lā) | I have punished (uʿadhibuhu) | anyone (aḥadan) | among (mina) | the worlds. (l-ʿālamīna)"

5:116 And when said Allah, "O Isa, son of Maryam! Did you say to the people, "Take me and my mother as two gods from besides Allah?" He said, "Glory be to You! Not was for me that I say what not I had right. If I had said it, then surely You would have known it. You know what is in myself, and not I know what is in Yourself. Indeed, You, You are All-Knower of the unseen.

And when (wa-idh) | said (qāla) | Allah (l-lahu), | "O Isa (yāʿīsā), | son (ib'na) | of Maryam (maryama)! | Did you (a-anta) | say (qul'ta) | to the people (lilnnāsi), | "Take me (ittakhidhūnī) | and my mother (wa-ummiya) | as two gods (ilāhayni) | from (min) | besides (dūni) | Allah? (l-lahi)" | He said (qāla), | "Glory be to You (sub'ḥānaka)! | Not (mā) | was (yakūnu) | for me (lī) | that (an) | I say (aqūla) | what (mā) | not (laysa) | I (lī) | had right (biḥaqqin). | If (in) | I had (kuntu) | said it (qul'tuhu), | then surely (faqad) | You would have known it (ʿalim'tahu). | You know (taʿlamu) | what (mā) | is in (fī) | myself (nafsī), | and not (walā) | I know (aʿlamu) | what (mā) | is in (fī) | Yourself (nafsika). | Indeed, You (innaka), | You (anta) | are All-Knower (ʿallāmu) | of the unseen (l-ghuyūbi).

5:117 Not I said to them except what You commanded me [with it] that "You worship Allah, my Lord and your Lord." And I was over them a witness that as long as I was among them, then when You raised me You were [You] the Watcher over them, and You are on every thing a Witness.

Not (mā) | I said (qul'tu) | to them (lahum) | except (illā) | what (mā) | You commanded me (amartanī) | [with it] (bihi) | that (ani) | "You worship (uʿ'budū) | Allah (l-laha), | my Lord (rabbī) | and your Lord. (warabbakum)" | And I was (wakuntu) | over them (ʿalayhim) | a witness (shahīdan) | that (mā) | as long as I (dum'tu) | was among them (fīhim), | then when (falammā) | You raised me (tawaffaytanī) | You were (kunta) | [You] (anta) | the Watcher (l-raqība) | over them (ʿalayhim), | and You (wa-anta) | are on (ʿalā) | every (kulli) | thing (shayin) | a Witness (shahīdun).

5:118 If You punish them, then indeed they are Your slaves, and if You forgive [for] them then indeed You, You are the All-Mighty, the All-Wise."

If (in) | You punish them (tuʿadhib'hum), | then indeed they (fa-innahum) | are Your slaves (ʿibāduka), | and if (wa-in) | You forgive (taghfir) | [for] them (lahum) | then indeed You (fa-innaka), | You (anta) | are the All-Mighty (l-ʿazīzu), | the All-Wise. (l-ḥakīmu)"

5:119 Will say Allah, "This Day will profit the truthful their truthfulness." For them are Gardens flows from underneath it the rivers will abide in it forever." is pleased Allah with them and they are pleased with Him. That is the success, the great.

Will say (qāla) | Allah (l-lahu), | "This (hādhā) | Day (yawmu) | will profit (yanfaʿu) | the truthful (l-ṣādiqīna) | their truthfulness. (ṣid'quhum)" | For them (lahum) | are Gardens (jannātun) | flows (tajrī) | from (min) | underneath it (taḥtihā) | the rivers (l-anhāru) | will abide (khālidīna) | in it (fīhā) | forever. (abadan)" | is pleased (raḍiya) | Allah (l-lahu) | with them (ʿanhum) | and they are pleased (waraḍū) | with Him (ʿanhu). | That (dhālika) | is the success (l-fawzu), | the great (l-ʿaẓīmu).

5:120 To Allah belongs the dominion of the heavens and the earth and what is in them. And He is on every thing All-Powerful.

To Allah belongs (lillahi) | the dominion (mul'ku) | of the heavens (l-samāwāti) | and the earth (wal-arḍi) | and what (wamā) | is in them (fīhinna). | And He (wahuwa) | is on (ʿalā) | every (kulli) | thing (shayin) | All-Powerful (qadīrun).

Chapter (6) Sūrat l-Anʿām (The Cattle)

6:1 All the praises and thanks be to Allah, the One Who created the heavens and the earth and made the darkness[es] and the light. Then those who disbelieved in their Lord equate others with Him.

All the praises and thanks (al-ḥamdu) | be to Allah (lillahi), | the One Who (alladhī) | created (khalaqa) | the heavens (l-samāwāti) | and the earth (wal-arḍa) | and made (wajaʿala) | the darkness[es] (l-ẓulumāti) | and the light (wal-nūra). | Then (thumma) | those who (alladhīna) | disbelieved (kafarū) | in their Lord (birabbihim) | equate others with Him (yaʿdilūna).

6:2 He is the One Who created you from clay then He decreed a term - and a term specified with Him, yet you doubt.

He (huwa) | is the One Who (alladhī) | created you (khalaqakum) | from (min) | clay (ṭīnin) | then (thumma) | He decreed (qaḍā) | a term (ajalan)- | and a term (wa-ajalun) | specified (musamman) | with Him (ʿindahu), | yet (thumma) | you (antum) | doubt (tamtarūna).

6:3 And He is Allah in the heavens and in the earth. He knows your secret and what you make public and He knows what you earn.

And He (wahuwa) | is Allah (l-lahu) | in (fī) | the heavens (l-samāwāti) | and in (wafī) | the earth (l-arḍi). | He knows (yaʿlamu) | your secret (sirrakum) | and what you make public (wajahrakum) | and He knows (wayaʿlamu) | what (mā) | you earn (taksibūna).

6:4 And not comes to them [of] any sign from the Signs of their Lord but they are from it turning away.

And not (wamā) | comes to them (tatīhim) | [of] (min) | any sign (āyatin) | from (min) | the Signs (āyāti) | of their Lord (rabbihim) | but (illā) | they are (kānū) | from it (ʿanhā) | turning away (muʿ'riḍīna).

6:5 Then indeed, they denied the truth when it came to them, but soon will come to them news of what they used to [at it] mock.

Then indeed (faqad), | they denied (kadhabū) | the truth (bil-ḥaqi) | when (lammā) | it came to them (jāahum), | but soon (fasawfa) | will come to them (yatīhim) | news (anbāu) | of what (mā) | they used to (kānū) | [at it] (bihi) | mock (yastahziūna).

6:6 Did not they see how many We destroyed from before them of generations We had established them in the earth what not We have established for you? And We sent rain from the sky upon them showering abundantly and We made the rivers flow from underneath them. Then We destroyed them for their sins and We raised from after them generations, other.

Did not (alam) | they see (yaraw) | how many (kam) | We destroyed (ahlaknā) | from (min) | before them (qablihim) | of (min) | generations (qarnin) | We had established them (makkannāhum) | in (fī) | the earth (l-arḍi) | what (mā) | not (lam) | We have established (numakkin) | for you (lakum)? | And We sent (wa-arsalnā) | rain from the sky (l-samāa) | upon them (ʿalayhim) | showering abundantly (mid'rāran) | and We made (wajaʿalnā) | the rivers (l-anhāra) | flow (tajrī) | from (min) | underneath them (taḥtihim). | Then We destroyed them (fa-ahlaknāhum) | for their sins (bidhunūbihim) | and We raised (wa-anshanā) | from (min) | after them (baʿdihim) | generations (qarnan), | other (ākharīna).

6:7 And even if We had sent down to you a written Scripture in a parchment and they touched it with their hands, surely would have said those who disbelieved, "Not is this but magic, clear."

And even if (walaw) | We had sent down (nazzalnā) | to you (ʿalayka) | a written Scripture (kitāban) | in (fī) | a parchment (qir'ṭāsin) | and they touched it (falamasūhu) | with their hands (bi-aydīhim), | surely would have said (laqāla) | those who (alladhīna) | disbelieved (kafarū), | "Not (in) | is this (hādhā) | but (illā) | magic (siḥ'run), | clear. (mubīnun)"

6:8 And they said, "Why has not been sent down to him an Angel?" And if We had sent down an Angel, surely would have been decided the matter then no respite would have been granted to them.

And they said (waqālū), | "Why has not been (lawlā) | sent down (unzila) | to him (ʿalayhi) | an Angel? (malakun)" | And if (walaw) | We had sent down (anzalnā) | an Angel (malakan), | surely would have been decided (laquḍiya) | the matter (l-amru) | then (thumma) | no (lā) | respite would have been granted to them (yunẓarūna).

6:9 And if We had made him an Angel, certainly We would have made him a man, and certainly We would have obscured to them what they are obscuring.

And if (walaw) | We had made him (jaʿalnāhu) | an Angel (malakan), | certainly We would have made him (lajaʿalnāhu) | a man (rajulan), | and certainly We would have obscured (walalabasnā) | to them (ʿalayhim) | what (mā) | they are obscuring (yalbisūna).

6:10 And indeed were mocked Messengers from before you but surrounded those who scoffed of them what they used to [at it] mock.

And indeed (walaqadi) | were mocked (us'tuh'zi-a) | Messengers (birusulin) | from (min) | before you (qablika) | but surrounded (faḥāqa) | those who (bi-alladhīna) | scoffed (sakhirū) | of them (min'hum) | what (mā) | they used to (kānū) | [at it] (bihi) | mock (yastahziūna).

6:11 Say, "Travel in the earth and see how was the end of the rejecters."

Say (qul), | "Travel (sīrū) | in (fī) | the earth (l-arḍi) | and (thumma) | see (unẓurū) | how (kayfa) | was (kāna) | the end (ʿāqibatu) | of the rejecters. (l-mukadhibīna)"

6:12 Say, "To whom belongs what is in the heavens and the earth?" Say, "To Allah." He has decreed upon Himself the Mercy. Surely He will assemble you on the Day of the Resurrection, there is no doubt about it. Those who have lost themselves, then they do not believe.

Say (qul), | "To whom belongs (liman) | what (mā) | is in (fī) | the heavens (l-samāwāti) | and the earth? (wal-arḍi)" | Say (qul), | "To Allah. (lillahi)" | He has decreed (kataba) | upon (ʿalā) | Himself (nafsihi) | the Mercy (l-raḥmata). | Surely He will assemble you (layajmaʿannakum) | on (ilā) | the Day (yawmi) | of the Resurrection (l-qiyāmati), | there is no (lā) | doubt (rayba) | about it (fīhi). | Those who (alladhīna) | have lost (khasirū) | themselves (anfusahum), | then they (fahum) | do not (lā) | believe (yu'minūna).

6:13 And for Him is whatever dwells in the night and the day, and He is All-Hearing, All-Knowing.

And for Him (walahu) | is whatever (mā) | dwells (sakana) | in (fī) | the night (al-layli) | and the day (wal-nahāri), | and He (wahuwa) | is All-Hearing (l-samīʿu), | All-Knowing (l-ʿalīmu).

6:14 Say, "Is it other than Allah I should take as a protector, Creator, of the heavens and the earth, while it is He Who feeds and not He is fed?" Say, "Indeed I [I] am commanded that I be the first who submits to Allah and not be of the polytheists."

Say (qul), | "Is it other than (aghayra) | Allah (l-lahi) | I should take (attakhidhu) | as a protector (waliyyan), | Creator (fāṭiri), | of the heavens (l-samāwāti) | and the earth (wal-arḍi), | while it is He (wahuwa) | Who feeds (yuṭ'ʿimu) | and not (walā) | He is fed? (yuṭ'ʿamu)" | Say (qul), | "Indeed I (innī) | [I] am commanded (umir'tu) | that (an) | I be (akūna) | the first (awwala) | who (man) | submits to Allah (aslama) | and not (walā) | be (takūnanna) | of (mina) | the polytheists. (l-mush'rikīna)"

6:15 Say, "Indeed, I [I] fear if I disobeyed my Lord, punishment of a Day, Mighty."

Say (qul), | "Indeed, I (innī) | [I] fear (akhāfu) | if (in) | I disobeyed (ʿaṣaytu) | my Lord (rabbī), | punishment (ʿadhāba) | of a Day (yawmin), | Mighty. (ʿaẓīmin)"

6:16 Whoever is averted from it that Day then surely He had Mercy on him. And that is the success the clear.

Whoever (man) | is averted (yuṣ'raf) | from it (ʿanhu) | that Day (yawma-idhin) | then surely (faqad) | He had Mercy on him (raḥimahu). | And that (wadhālika) | is the success (l-fawzu) | the clear (l-mubīnu).

6:17 And if touches you Allah with affliction then no remover of it except Him. And if He touches you with good, then He is on every thing All-Powerful.

And if (wa-in) | touches you (yamsaska) | Allah (l-lahu) | with affliction (biḍurrin) | then no (falā) | remover (kāshifa) | of it (lahu) | except (illā) | Him (huwa). | And if (wa-in) | He touches you (yamsaska) | with good (bikhayrin), | then He (fahuwa) | is on (ʿalā) | every (kulli) | thing (shayin) | All-Powerful (qadīrun).

6:18 And He is the Subjugator over His slaves. And He is the All-Wise, the All-Aware.

And He (wahuwa) | is the Subjugator (l-qāhiru) | over (fawqa) | His slaves (ʿibādihi). | And He (wahuwa) | is the All-Wise (l-ḥakīmu), | the All-Aware (l-khabīru).

6:19 Say, "What thing is greatest as a testimony?" Say, "Allah is Witness between me and between you, and has been revealed to me this [the] Quran that I may warn you with it and whoever it reaches. Do you truly testify that with Allah there are gods other?" Say, Not do I testify. Say, "Only He is God, One. and indeed, I am free of what you associate with Him.

Say (qul), | "What (ayyu) | thing (shayin) | is greatest (akbaru) | as a testimony? (shahādatan)" | Say (quli), | "Allah (l-lahu) | is Witness (shahīdun) | between me (baynī) | and between you (wabaynakum), | and has been revealed (waūḥiya) | to me (ilayya) | this (hādhā) | [the] Quran (l-qur'ānu) | that I may warn you (li-undhirakum) | with it (bihi) | and whoever (waman) | it reaches (balagha). | Do you truly (a-innakum) | testify (latashhadūna) | that (anna) | with (maʿa) | Allah (l-lahi) | there are gods (ālihatan) | other? (ukh'rā)" | Say (qul), | Not (lā) | do I testify (ashhadu). | Say (qul), | "Only (innamā) | He (huwa) | is God (ilāhun), | One (wāḥidun). | and indeed, I am (wa-innanī) | free (barīon) | of what (mimmā) | you associate with Him (tush'rikūna).

6:20 Those to whom We have given them the Book they recognize him as they recognize their sons. Those who lost themselves then they do not believe.

Those to whom (alladhīna) | We have given them (ātaynāhumu) | the Book (l-kitāba) | they recognize him (yaʿrifūnahu) | as (kamā) | they recognize (yaʿrifūna) | their sons (abnāahumu).

| Those who (alladhīna) | lost (khasirū) | themselves (anfusahum) | then they (fahum) | do not (lā) | believe (yu'minūna).

6:21 And who is more unjust than he who invents against Allah a lie or rejects His Signs? Indeed, not will be successful the wrongdoers.

And who (waman) | is more unjust (aẓlamu) | than he who (mimmani) | invents (if'tarā) | against (ʿalā) | Allah (l-lahi) | a lie (kadhiban) | or (aw) | rejects (kadhaba) | His Signs (biāyātihi)? | Indeed (innahu), | not (lā) | will be successful (yuf'liḥu) | the wrongdoers (l-ẓālimūna).

6:22 And the Day We will gather them all, then We will say to those who associated others with Allah, "Where are your partners, those whom you used to claim?"

And the Day (wayawma) | We will gather them (naḥshuruhum) | all (jamīʿan), | then (thumma) | We will say (naqūlu) | to those who (lilladhīna) | associated others with Allah (ashrakū), | "Where are (ayna) | your partners (shurakāukumu), | those whom (alladhīna) | you used to (kuntum) | claim? (tazʿumūna)"

6:23 Then not will be for them a plea except that they say, "By Allah, our Lord, not we were those who associated others with Allah."

Then (thumma) | not (lam) | will be (takun) | for them a plea (fit'natuhum) | except (illā) | that (an) | they say (qālū), | "By Allah (wal-lahi), | our Lord (rabbinā), | not (mā) | we were (kunnā) | those who associated others with Allah. (mush'rikīna)"

6:24 Look how they lied against themselves. And lost from them what they used to invent.

Look (unẓur) | how (kayfa) | they lied (kadhabū) | against (ʿalā) | themselves (anfusihim). | And lost (waḍalla) | from them (ʿanhum) | what (mā) | they used to (kānū) | invent (yaftarūna).

6:25 And among them are those who listen to you, but We have placed over their hearts coverings lest they understand it, and in their ears deafness. And if they see every sign not will they believe in it. Until, when they come to you and argue with you say those who disbelieved, "Not is this but the tales of the former (people)."

And among them (wamin'hum) | are those who (man) | listen (yastamiʿu) | to you (ilayka), | but We have placed (wajaʿalnā) | over (ʿalā) | their hearts (qulūbihim) | coverings (akinnatan) | lest (an) | they understand it (yafqahūhu), | and in (wafī) | their ears (ādhānihim) | deafness (waqran). | And if (wa-in) | they see (yaraw) | every (kulla) | sign (āyatin) | not (lā) | will they believe (yu'minū) | in it (bihā). | Until (ḥattā), | when (idhā) | they come to you (jāūka) | and argue with you (yujādilūnaka) | say (yaqūlu) | those who (alladhīna) | disbelieved (kafarū), | "Not (in) | is this (hādhā) | but (illā) | the tales (asāṭīru) | of the former (people). (l-awalīna)"

6:26 And they forbid others from it and they keep away from it. And not they destroy except themselves and not they perceive.

And they (wahum) | forbid others (yanhawna) | from it (ʿanhu) | and they keep away (wayanawna) | from it (ʿanhu). | And not (wa-in) | they destroy (yuh'likūna) | except (illā) | themselves (anfusahum) | and not (wamā) | they perceive (yashʿurūna).

6:27 And if you could see when they are made to stand by the Fire then they will say, "Oh! Would that we were sent back and not we would deny the Signs of our Lord and we would be among the believers."

And if (walaw) | you could see (tarā) | when (idh) | they are made to stand (wuqifū) | by (ʿalā) | the Fire (l-nāri) | then they will say (faqālū), | "Oh! Would that we (yālaytanā) | were sent back (nuraddu) | and not (walā) | we would deny (nukadhiba) | the Signs (biāyāti) | of our Lord (rabbinā) | and we would be (wanakūna) | among (mina) | the believers. (l-mu'minīna)"

6:28 Nay, became manifest for them what they used to conceal from before. And if they were sent back certainly they would return to what they were forbidden from it, and indeed they certainly are liars.

Nay (bal), | became manifest (badā) | for them (lahum) | what (mā) | they used to (kānū) | conceal (yukh'fūna) | from (min) | before (qablu). | And if (walaw) | they were sent back (ruddū) | certainly they would return (laʿādū) | to what (limā) | they were forbidden (nuhū) | from it (ʿanhu), | and indeed they (wa-innahum) | certainly are liars (lakādhibūna).

6:29 And they said, "Not it is except our life of the world and not we will be resurrected."

And they said (waqālū), | "Not (in) | it is (hiya) | except (illā) | our life (ḥayātunā) | of the world (l-dun'yā) | and not (wamā) | we (naḥnu) | will be resurrected. (bimabʿūthīna)"

6:30 And if you could see when they will be made to stand before their Lord. He will say, "Is not this the truth?" They will say, "Yes, by our Lord." He will say, "So taste the punishment because you used to disbelieve."

And if (walaw) | you could see (tarā) | when (idh) | they will be made to stand (wuqifū) | before (ʿalā) | their Lord (rabbihim). | He will say (qāla), | "Is not (alaysa) | this (hādhā) | the truth? (bil-ḥaqi)" | They will say (qālū), | "Yes (balā), | by our Lord. (warabbinā)" | He will say (qāla), | "So taste (fadhūqū) | the punishment (l-ʿadhāba) | because (bimā) | you used to (kuntum) | disbelieve. (takfurūna)"

6:31 Indeed, incurred loss those who denied in the meeting with Allah, until when came to them the Hour suddenly they said, "Oh! Our regret over what we neglected concerning it," while they will bear their burdens on their backs. Unquestionably! Evil is what they bear.

Indeed (qad), | incurred loss (khasira) | those who (alladhīna) | denied (kadhabū) | in the meeting (biliqāi) | with Allah (l-lahi), | until (ḥattā) | when (idhā) | came to them (jāathumu) | the Hour (l-sāʿatu) | suddenly (baghtatan) | they said (qālū), | "Oh! Our regret (yāḥasratanā) | over (ʿalā) | what (mā) | we neglected (farraṭnā) | concerning it, (fīhā)" | while they (wahum) | will bear (yaḥmilūna) | their burdens (awzārahum) | on (ʿalā) | their backs (ẓuhūrihim). | Unquestionably (alā)! | Evil (sāa) | is what (mā) | they bear (yazirūna).

6:32 And not is the life of the world except a play and amusement; but the home of the Hereafter is best for those who are God conscious. Then not will you reason?

And not (wamā) | is the life (l-ḥayatu) | of the world (l-dun'yā) | except (illā) | a play (laʿibun) | and amusement (walahwun); | but the home (walalddāru) | of the Hereafter (l-ākhiratu) | is best (khayrun) | for those who (lilladhīna) | are God conscious (yattaqūna). | Then not (afalā) | will you reason (taʿqilūna)?

6:33 Indeed, We know that it grieves you what they say. And indeed, they do not deny you but the wrongdoers - the Verses of Allah they reject.

Indeed (qad), | We know (naʿlamu) | that it (innahu) | grieves you (layaḥzunuka) | what (alladhī) | they say (yaqūlūna). | And indeed, they (fa-innahum) | do not (lā) | deny you (yukadhibūnaka) | but (walākinna) | the wrongdoers (l-ẓālimīna)- | the Verses (biāyāti) | of Allah (l-lahi) | they reject (yajḥadūna).

6:34 And surely were rejected Messengers from before you, but they were patient over what they were rejected and they were harmed until came to them Our help. And no one can alter the words of Allah, and surely has come to you of the news of the Messengers.

And surely (walaqad) | were rejected (kudhibat) | Messengers (rusulun) | from (min) | before you (qablika), | but they were patient (faṣabarū) | over (ʿalā) | what (mā) | they were rejected (kudhibū) | and they were harmed (waūdhū) | until (ḥattā) | came to them (atāhum) | Our help (naṣrunā). | And no (walā) | one can alter (mubaddila) | the words (likalimāti) | of Allah (l-lahi),

| and surely (walaqad) | has come to you (jāaka) | of (min) | the news (naba-i) | of the Messengers (l-mur'salīna).

6:35 And if is difficult for you their aversion then if you are able to seek a tunnel in the earth or a ladder into the sky so that you bring to them a Sign. But if had willed Allah surely He would have gathered them on the guidance. So do not be of the ignorant.

And if (wa-in) | is (kāna) | difficult (kabura) | for you (ʿalayka) | their aversion (iʿ'rāḍuhum) | then if (fa-ini) | you are able (is'taṭaʿta) | to (an) | seek (tabtaghiya) | a tunnel (nafaqan) | in (fī) | the earth (l-arḍi) | or (aw) | a ladder (sullaman) | into (fī) | the sky (l-samāi) | so that you bring to them (fatatiyahum) | a Sign (biāyatin). | But if (walaw) | had willed (shāa) | Allah (l-lahu) | surely He would have gathered them (lajamaʿahum) | on (ʿalā) | the guidance (l-hudā). | So do not (falā) | be (takūnanna) | of (mina) | the ignorant (l-jāhilīna).

6:36 Only respond those who listen. But the dead - will resurrect them Allah then to Him they will be returned.

Only (innamā) | respond (yastajību) | those who (alladhīna) | listen (yasmaʿūna). | But the dead (wal-mawtā)- | will resurrect them (yabʿathuhumu) | Allah (l-lahu) | then (thumma) | to Him (ilayhi) | they will be returned (yur'jaʿūna).

6:37 And they said, "Why is not sent down to him a Sign from his Lord?" Say, "Indeed Allah is Able [on] to send down a Sign, but most of them do not know."

And they said (waqālū), | "Why is not (lawlā) | sent down (nuzzila) | to him (ʿalayhi) | a Sign (āyatun) | from (min) | his Lord? (rabbihi)" | Say (qul), | "Indeed (inna) | Allah (l-laha) | is Able (qādirun) | [on] (ʿalā) | to (an) | send down (yunazzila) | a Sign (āyatan), | but (walākinna) | most of them (aktharahum) | do not (lā) | know. (yaʿlamūna)"

6:38 And not [of] any animal in the earth and not a bird that flies with its wings - but are communities like you. Not We have neglected in the Book [of] anything, then to their Lord they will be gathered.

And not (wamā) | [of] (min) | any animal (dābbatin) | in (fī) | the earth (l-arḍi) | and not (walā) | a bird (ṭāirin) | that flies (yaṭīru) | with its wings (bijanāḥayhi)- | but (illā) | are communities (umamun) | like you (amthālukum). | Not (mā) | We have neglected (farraṭnā) | in (fī) | the Book (l-kitābi) | [of] (min) | anything (shayin), | then (thumma) | to (ilā) | their Lord (rabbihim) | they will be gathered (yuḥ'sharūna).

6:39 And those who rejected Our Verses are deaf and dumb in the darkness[es]. Whoever wills Allah - He lets him go astray and whoever He wills - He places him on the way, the straight.

And those who (wa-alladhīna) | rejected (kadhabū) | Our Verses (biāyātinā) | are deaf (ṣummun) | and dumb (wabuk'mun) | in (fī) | the darkness[es] (l-ẓulumāti). | Whoever (man) | wills (yasha-i) | Allah (l-lahu)- | He lets him go astray (yuḍ'lil'hu) | and whoever (waman) | He wills (yasha)- | He places him (yajʿalhu) | on (ʿalā) | the way (ṣirāṭin), | the straight (mus'taqīmin).

6:40 Say, "Have you seen if there came to you punishment of Allah or there came to you the Hour - is it other than Allah you call, if you are truthful?"

Say (qul), | "Have you seen (ara-aytakum) | if (in) | there came to you (atākum) | punishment (ʿadhābu) | of Allah (l-lahi) | or (aw) | there came to you (atatkumu) | the Hour (l-sāʿatu)- | is it other (aghayra) | than Allah (l-lahi) | you call (tadʿūna), | if (in) | you are (kuntum) | truthful? (ṣādiqīna)"

6:41 "Nay, Him Alone you call and He would remove what you call upon Him if He wills, and you will forget what you associate with Him."

"Nay (bal), | Him Alone (iyyāhu) | you call (tadʿūna) | and He would remove (fayakshifu) |

what (mā) | you call (tad'ūna) | upon Him (ilayhi) | if (in) | He wills (shāa), | and you will forget (watansawna) | what (mā) | you associate with Him. (tush'rikūna)"

6:42 And certainly We sent Messengers to nations from before you, then We seized them with adversity and hardship so that they may humble themselves.

And certainly (walaqad) | We sent Messengers (arsalnā) | to (ilā) | nations (umamin) | from (min) | before you (qablika), | then We seized them (fa-akhadhnāhum) | with adversity (bil-basāi) | and hardship (wal-ḍarāi) | so that they may (la'allahum) | humble themselves (yataḍarra'ūna).

6:43 Then why not when came to them Our punishment, they humbled themselves? But became hardened their hearts and made fair-seeming to them the Shaitaan what they used to do.

Then why not (falawlā) | when (idh) | came to them (jāahum) | Our punishment (basunā), | they humbled themselves (taḍarra'ū)? | But (walākin) | became hardened (qasat) | their hearts (qulūbuhum) | and made fair-seeming (wazayyana) | to them (lahumu) | the Shaitaan (l-shayṭānu) | what (mā) | they used to (kānū) | do (ya'malūna).

6:44 So when they forgot what they were reminded of [it], We opened on them gates of every thing, until when they rejoiced in what they were given, We seized them suddenly and then they were dumbfounded.

So when (falammā) | they forgot (nasū) | what (mā) | they were reminded (dhukkirū) | of [it] (bihi), | We opened (fataḥnā) | on them ('alayhim) | gates (abwāba) | of every (kulli) | thing (shayin), | until (ḥattā) | when (idhā) | they rejoiced (fariḥū) | in what (bimā) | they were given (ūtū), | We seized them (akhadhnāhum) | suddenly (baghtatan) | and then (fa-idhā) | they (hum) | were dumbfounded (mub'lisūna).

6:45 So was cut off the remnant of the people [those] who did wrong. And all praises and thanks be to Allah Lord of the worlds.

So was cut off (faquṭi'a) | the remnant (dābiru) | of the people (l-qawmi) | [those] who (alladhīna) | did wrong (ẓalamū). | And all praises and thanks (wal-ḥamdu) | be to Allah (lillahi) | Lord (rabbi) | of the worlds (l-'ālamīna).

6:46 Say, "Have you seen if took away Allah your hearing and your sight and sealed [on] your hearts, who is the god other than Allah to bring [back] to you with it? See how We explain the Signs; yet they turn away."

Say (qul), | "Have you seen (ara-aytum) | if (in) | took away (akhadha) | Allah (l-lahu) | your hearing (sam'akum) | and your sight (wa-abṣārakum) | and sealed (wakhatama) | [on] ('alā) | your hearts (qulūbikum), | who (man) | is the god (ilāhun) | other than (ghayru) | Allah (l-lahi) | to bring [back] to you (yatīkum) | with it (bihi)? | See (unẓur) | how (kayfa) | We explain (nuṣarrifu) | the Signs (l-āyāti); | yet (thumma) | they (hum) | turn away. (yaṣdifūna)"

6:47 Say, "Have you seen if comes to you punishment of Allah suddenly or openly, will any be destroyed except the people - the wrongdoers?

Say (qul), | "Have you seen (ara-aytakum) | if (in) | comes to you (atākum) | punishment ('adhābu) | of Allah (l-lahi) | suddenly (baghtatan) | or (aw) | openly (jahratan), | will (hal) | any be destroyed (yuh'laku) | except (illā) | the people (l-qawmu)- | the wrongdoers (l-ẓālimūna)?

6:48 And not We send the Messengers except as bearer of glad tidings and as warners. So whoever believed and reformed, then no fear upon them and not they will grieve.

And not (wamā) | We send (nur'silu) | the Messengers (l-mur'salīna) | except (illā) | as bearer of glad tidings (mubashirīna) | and as warners (wamundhirīna). | So whoever (faman) | believed (āmana) | and reformed (wa-aṣlaḥa), | then no (falā) | fear (khawfun) | upon them

(ʿalayhim) | and not (walā) | they (hum) | will grieve (yaḥzanūna).

6:49 And those who denied [in] Our Verses will touch them the punishment for what they used to defiantly disobey.

And those who (wa-alladhīna) | denied (kadhabū) | [in] Our Verses (biāyātinā) | will touch them (yamassuhumu) | the punishment (l-ʿadhābu) | for what (bimā) | they used to (kānū) | defiantly disobey (yafsuqūna).

6:50 Say, "Not do I say to you that with me are the treasures of Allah and not that I know the unseen and not I say to you that I am an Angel. Not do I follow except what is revealed to me." Say, "Can be equal the blind and the seeing one?" Then will not you give thought?

Say (qul), | "Not (lā) | do I say (aqūlu) | to you (lakum) | that with me (ʿindī) | are the treasures (khazāinu) | of Allah (l-lahi) | and not (walā) | that I know (aʿlamu) | the unseen (l-ghayba) | and not (walā) | I say (aqūlu) | to you (lakum) | that I am (innī) | an Angel (malakun). | Not (in) | do I follow (attabiʿu) | except (illā) | what (mā) | is revealed (yūḥā) | to me. (ilayya)" | Say (qul), | "Can (hal) | be equal (yastawī) | the blind (l-aʿmā) | and the seeing one? (wal-baṣīru)" | Then will not (afalā) | you give thought (tatafakkarūna)?

6:51 And warn with it those who fear that they will be gathered to their Lord, not for them of other than Him any protector and not any intercessor, so that they may become righteous.

And warn (wa-andhir) | with it (bihi) | those who (alladhīna) | fear (yakhāfūna) | that (an) | they will be gathered (yuḥ'sharū) | to (ilā) | their Lord (rabbihim), | not (laysa) | for them (lahum) | of (min) | other than Him (dūnihi) | any protector (waliyyun) | and not (walā) | any intercessor (shafīʿun), | so that they may (laʿallahum) | become righteous (yattaqūna).

6:52 And do not send away those who call their Lord in the morning and the evening desiring His Countenance. Not is on you of their account [of] anything, and not from your account on them [of] anything. So were you to send them away, then you would be of the wrongdoers.

And do not (walā) | send away (taṭrudi) | those who (alladhīna) | call (yadʿūna) | their Lord (rabbahum) | in the morning (bil-ghadati) | and the evening (wal-ʿashiyi) | desiring (yurīdūna) | His Countenance (wajhahu). | Not (mā) | is on you (ʿalayka) | of (min) | their account (ḥisābihim) | [of] (min) | anything (shayin), | and not (wamā) | from (min) | your account (ḥisābika) | on them (ʿalayhim) | [of] (min) | anything (shayin). | So were you to send them away (fataṭrudahum), | then you would be (fatakūna) | of (mina) | the wrongdoers (l-ẓālimīna).

6:53 And thus We try some of them with others that they say, "Are these whom has been favored by Allah [upon them] from among us?" is not Allah most knowing of those who are grateful?

And thus (wakadhālika) | We try (fatannā) | some of them (baʿḍahum) | with others (bibaʿḍin) | that they say (liyaqūlū), | "Are these (ahāulāi) | whom has been favored (manna) | by Allah (l-lahu) | [upon them] (ʿalayhim) | from (min) | among us? (bayninā)" | is not (alaysa) | Allah (l-lahu) | most knowing (bi-aʿlama) | of those who are grateful (bil-shākirīna)?

6:54 And when come to you those who believe in Our Verses then say, "Peace be upon you. Has Prescribed your Lord upon Himself the Mercy, that he who does among you evil in ignorance then repents from after it and reforms, then, indeed He is Oft-Forgiving, Most Merciful."

And when (wa-idhā) | come to you (jāaka) | those who (alladhīna) | believe (yu'minūna) | in Our Verses (biāyātinā) | then say (faqul), | "Peace (salāmun) | be upon you (ʿalaykum). | Has Prescribed (kataba) | your Lord (rabbukum) | upon (ʿalā) | Himself (nafsihi) | the Mercy (l-raḥmata), | that he (annahu) | who (man) | does (ʿamila) | among you (minkum) | evil (sūan) | in ignorance (bijahālatin) | then (thumma) | repents (tāba) | from (min) | after it (baʿdihi) | and reforms (wa-aṣlaḥa), | then, indeed He (fa-annahu) | is Oft-Forgiving (ghafūrun), | Most Merciful. (raḥīmun)"

6:55 And thus We explain the Verses, so that becomes manifest the way of the criminals.

And thus (wakadhālika) | We explain (nufaṣṣilu) | the Verses (l-āyāti), | so that becomes manifest (walitastabīna) | the way (sabīlu) | of the criminals (l-muj'rimīna).

6:56 Say, "Indeed I [I] am forbidden that I worship those whom you call from besides Allah." Say, "Not I follow your vain desires, certainly I would go astray then, and not I would be from the guided-ones."

Say (qul), | "Indeed I (innī) | [I] am forbidden (nuhītu) | that (an) | I worship (aʿbuda) | those whom (alladhīna) | you call (tadʿūna) | from (min) | besides (dūni) | Allah. (l-lahi)" | Say (qul), | "Not (lā) | I follow (attabiʿu) | your vain desires (ahwāakum), | certainly (qad) | I would go astray (ḍalaltu) | then (idhan), | and not (wamā) | I would be (anā) | from (mina) | the guided-ones. (l-muh'tadīna)"

6:57 Say, "Indeed, I am on clear proof from my Lord, while you deny [with] it. Not I have what you seek to hasten of it. Not is the decision except for Allah. He relates the truth, and He is the best of the Deciders."

Say (qul), | "Indeed, I am (innī) | on (ʿalā) | clear proof (bayyinatin) | from (min) | my Lord (rabbī), | while you deny (wakadhabtum) | [with] it (bihi). | Not (mā) | I have (ʿindī) | what (mā) | you seek to hasten (tastaʿjilūna) | of it (bihi). | Not (ini) | is the decision (l-ḥuk'mu) | except (illā) | for Allah (lillahi). | He relates (yaquṣṣu) | the truth (l-ḥaqa), | and He (wahuwa) | is the best (khayru) | of the Deciders. (l-fāṣilīna)"

6:58 Say, "If that were with me what you seek to hasten of it, surely would have been decided the matter between me and between you. And Allah is most knowing of the wrongdoers.

Say (qul), | "If (law) | that (anna) | were with me (ʿindī) | what (mā) | you seek to hasten (tastaʿjilūna) | of it (bihi), | surely would have been decided (laquḍiya) | the matter (l-amru) | between me (baynī) | and between you (wabaynakum). | And Allah (wal-lahu) | is most knowing (aʿlamu) | of the wrongdoers (bil-ẓālimīna).

6:59 And with Him are the keys of the unseen, no one knows them except Him. And He knows what is in the land and in the sea. And not falls of any leaf but He knows it. And not a grain in the darkness[es] of the earth and not moist and not dry but is in a Record Clear.

And with Him (waʿindahu) | are the keys (mafātiḥu) | of the unseen (l-ghaybi), | no one (lā) | knows them (yaʿlamuhā) | except (illā) | Him (huwa). | And He knows (wayaʿlamu) | what (mā) | is in (fī) | the land (l-bari) | and in the sea (wal-baḥri). | And not (wamā) | falls (tasquṭu) | of (min) | any leaf (waraqatin) | but (illā) | He knows it (yaʿlamuhā). | And not (walā) | a grain (ḥabbatin) | in (fī) | the darkness[es] (ẓulumāti) | of the earth (l-arḍi) | and not (walā) | moist (raṭbin) | and not (walā) | dry (yābisin) | but (illā) | is in (fī) | a Record (kitābin) | Clear (mubīnin).

6:60 And He is the One Who takes your soul by the night and He knows what you committed by the day. Then He raises you up therein, so that is fulfilled the term specified. Then to Him will be your return then He will inform you about what you used to do.

And He (wahuwa) | is the One Who (alladhī) | takes your soul (yatawaffākum) | by the night (bi-al-layli) | and He knows (wayaʿlamu) | what (mā) | you committed (jaraḥtum) | by the day (bil-nahāri). | Then (thumma) | He raises you up (yabʿathukum) | therein (fīhi), | so that is fulfilled (liyuq'ḍā) | the term (ajalun) | specified (musamman). | Then (thumma) | to Him (ilayhi) | will be your return (marjiʿukum) | then (thumma) | He will inform you (yunabbi-ukum) | about what (bimā) | you used to (kuntum) | do (taʿmalūna).

6:61 And He is the Subjugator over His slaves, and He sends over you guardians until when comes to anyone of you the death take him Our messengers, and they do not fail.

And He (wahuwa) | is the Subjugator (l-qāhiru) | over (fawqa) | His slaves (ʿibādihi), | and He sends (wayur'silu) | over you (ʿalaykum) | guardians (ḥafaẓatan) | until (ḥattā) | when (idhā) | comes (jāa) | to anyone of you (aḥadakumu) | the death (l-mawtu) | take him (tawaffathu) | Our messengers (rusulunā), | and they (wahum) | do not (lā) | fail (yufarriṭūna).

6:62 Then they are returned to Allah their Protector - [the] True, Unquestionably, for Him is the judgment? And He is swiftest of the Reckoners.

Then (thumma) | they are returned (ruddū) | to (ilā) | Allah (l-lahi) | their Protector (mawlāhumu)- | [the] True (l-ḥaqi), | Unquestionably (alā), | for Him (lahu) | is the judgment (l-ḥuk'mu)? | And He (wahuwa) | is swiftest (asraʿu) | of the Reckoners (l-ḥāsibīna).

6:63 Say, "Who saves you from darkness[es] of the land and the sea, you call Him humbly and secretly, "If He saves us from this, surely we will be from the grateful ones."

Say (qul), | "Who (man) | saves you (yunajjīkum) | from (min) | darkness[es] (ẓulumāti) | of the land (l-bari) | and the sea (wal-baḥri), | you call Him (tadʿūnahu) | humbly (taḍarruʿan) | and secretly (wakhuf'yatan), | "If (la-in) | He saves us (anjānā) | from (min) | this (hādhihi), | surely we will be (lanakūnanna) | from (mina) | the grateful ones. (l-shākirīna)"

6:64 Say, "Allah saves you from it and from every distress, yet you associate partners with Allah."

Say (quli), | "Allah (l-lahu) | saves you (yunajjīkum) | from it (min'hā) | and from (wamin) | every (kulli) | distress (karbin), | yet (thumma) | you (antum) | associate partners with Allah. (tush'rikūna)"

6:65 Say, "He is All-Capable [on] to send upon you punishment from above you or from beneath your feet or to confuse you into sects and make you taste - some of you violence of others." See how We explain the Signs so that they may understand.

Say (qul), | "He (huwa) | is All-Capable (l-qādiru) | [on] (ʿalā) | to (an) | send (yabʿatha) | upon you (ʿalaykum) | punishment (ʿadhāban) | from (min) | above you (fawqikum) | or (aw) | from (min) | beneath (taḥti) | your feet (arjulikum) | or (aw) | to confuse you (yalbisakum) | into sects (shiyaʿan) | and make you taste (wayudhīqa)- | some of you (baʿḍakum) | violence (basa) | of others. (baʿḍin)" | See (unẓur) | how (kayfa) | We explain (nuṣarrifu) | the Signs (l-āyāti) | so that they may (laʿallahum) | understand (yafqahūna).

6:66 But denied it - your people while it is the truth. Say, "I am not over you a manager."

But denied (wakadhaba) | it (bihi)- | your people (qawmuka) | while it (wahuwa) | is the truth (l-ḥaqu). | Say (qul), | "I am not (lastu) | over you (ʿalaykum) | a manager. (biwakīlin)"

6:67 For every news is a fixed time, and soon you will know.

For every (likulli) | news (naba-in) | is a fixed time (mus'taqarrun), | and soon (wasawfa) | you will know (taʿlamūna).

6:68 And when you see those who engage in vain talks about Our Verses, then turn away from them until they engage in a talk other than it. And if causes you to forget the Shaitaan, then do not sit after the reminder with the people - the wrongdoers.

And when (wa-idhā) | you see (ra-ayta) | those who (alladhīna) | engage in vain talks (yakhūḍūna) | about (fī) | Our Verses (āyātinā), | then turn away (fa-aʿriḍ) | from them (ʿanhum) | until (ḥattā) | they engage (yakhūḍū) | in (fī) | a talk (ḥadīthin) | other than it (ghayrihi). | And if (wa-immā) | causes you to forget (yunsiyannaka) | the Shaitaan (l-shayṭānu), | then do not (falā) | sit (taqʿud) | after (baʿda) | the reminder (l-dhik'rā) | with (maʿa) | the people (l-qawmi)- | the wrongdoers (l-ẓālimīna).

6:69 And not is on those who fear Allah of their account [of] anything; but for reminder, so that they may fear Allah.

And not (wamā) | is on (ʿalā) | those who (alladhīna) | fear Allah (yattaqūna) | of (min) | their account (ḥisābihim) | [of] (min) | anything (shayin); | but (walākin) | for reminder (dhik'rā), | so that they may (laʿallahum) | fear Allah (yattaqūna).

6:70 And leave those who take their religion as a play and amusement and deluded them the life of the world. But remind with it, lest is given up to destruction a soul for what it has earned, not is for it from besides Allah any protector and not any intercessor. And if it offers ransom - every ransom, not will it be taken from it. Those are ones who are given to destruction for what they earned. For them will be a drink of boiling water and a punishment painful because they used to disbelieve.

And leave (wadhari) | those who (alladhīna) | take (ittakhadhū) | their religion (dīnahum) | as a play (laʿiban) | and amusement (walahwan) | and deluded them (wagharrathumu) | the life (l-ḥayatu) | of the world (l-dun'yā). | But remind (wadhakkir) | with it (bihi), | lest (an) | is given up to destruction (tub'sala) | a soul (nafsun) | for what (bimā) | it has earned (kasabat), | not (laysa) | is for it (lahā) | from (min) | besides (dūni) | Allah (l-lahi) | any protector (waliyyun) | and not (walā) | any intercessor (shafīʿun). | And if (wa-in) | it offers ransom (taʿdil)- | every (kulla) | ransom (ʿadlin), | not (lā) | will it be taken (yu'khadh) | from it (min'hā). | Those (ulāika) | are ones who (alladhīna) | are given to destruction (ub'silū) | for what (bimā) | they earned (kasabū). | For them (lahum) | will be a drink (sharābun) | of (min) | boiling water (ḥamīmin) | and a punishment (waʿadhābun) | painful (alīmun) | because (bimā) | they used to (kānū) | disbelieve (yakfurūna).

6:71 Say, "Shall we call from besides Allah what not benefits us and not harms us, and we turn back on our heels after [when] has guided us Allah? Like the one whom has been enticed by the Shaitaan in the earth, confused, he has companions who call him towards the guidance, 'Come to us.'" Say, "Indeed, the Guidance of Allah, it is the Guidance, and we have been commanded that we submit to the Lord of the worlds

Say (qul), | "Shall we call (anadʿū) | from (min) | besides (dūni) | Allah (l-lahi) | what (mā) | not (lā) | benefits us (yanfaʿunā) | and not (walā) | harms us (yaḍurrunā), | and we turn back (wanuraddu) | on (ʿalā) | our heels (aʿqābinā) | after (baʿda) | [when] (idh) | has guided us (hadānā) | Allah (l-lahu)? | Like the one (ka-alladhī) | whom has been enticed (is'tahwathu) | by the Shaitaan (l-shayāṭīnu) | in (fī) | the earth (l-arḍi), | confused (ḥayrāna), | he has (lahu) | companions (aṣḥābun) | who call him (yadʿūnahu) | towards (ilā) | the guidance (l-hudā), | 'Come to us.' (i'tinā)" | Say (qul), | "Indeed (inna), | the Guidance (hudā) | of Allah (l-lahi), | it (huwa) | is the Guidance (l-hudā), | and we have been commanded (wa-umir'nā) | that we submit (linus'lima) | to the Lord (lirabbi) | of the worlds (l-ʿālamīna)

6:72 And to establish the prayer and fear Him. And He is the One to Him you will be gathered."

And to (wa-an) | establish (aqīmū) | the prayer (l-ṣalata) | and fear Him (wa-ittaqūhu). | And He (wahuwa) | is the One (alladhī) | to Him (ilayhi) | you will be gathered. (tuḥ'sharūna)"

6:73 And it is He Who created the heavens and the earth in truth. And the Day He says, "Be" and it is, His word is the truth. And for Him is the Dominion on the Day will be blown in the trumpet. He is All-Knower of the unseen and the seen. And He is the All-Wise, the All-Aware.

And it is He (wahuwa) | Who (alladhī) | created (khalaqa) | the heavens (l-samāwāti) | and the earth (wal-arḍa) | in truth (bil-ḥaqi). | And the Day (wayawma) | He says (yaqūlu), | "Be (kun)" | and it is (fayakūnu), | His word (qawluhu) | is the truth (l-ḥaqu). | And for Him (walahu) | is the Dominion (l-mul'ku) | on the Day (yawma) | will be blown (yunfakhu) | in (fī) | the trumpet (l-ṣūri). | He is All-Knower (ʿālimu) | of the unseen (l-ghaybi) | and the seen (wal-shahādati). | And He (wahuwa) | is the All-Wise (l-ḥakīmu), | the All-Aware (l-khabīru).

6:74 And when said Ibrahim to his father Azar, "Do you take idols as gods? Indeed, I [I] see you and your people in error manifest."

And when (wa-idh) | said (qāla) | Ibrahim (ib'rāhīmu) | to his father (li-abīhi) | Azar (āzara), | "Do you take (atattakhidhu) | idols (aṣnāman) | as gods (ālihatan)? | Indeed, I (innī) | [I] see you (arāka) | and your people (waqawmaka) | in (fī) | error (ḍalālin) | manifest. (mubīnin)"

6:75 And thus We showed Ibrahim the kingdom of the heavens and the earth, so that he would be among the ones who are certain.

And thus (wakadhālika) | We showed (nurī) | Ibrahim (ib'rāhīma) | the kingdom (malakūta) | of the heavens (l-samāwāti) | and the earth (wal-arḍi), | so that he would be (waliyakūna) | among (mina) | the ones who are certain (l-mūqinīna).

6:76 So when covered over him the night, he saw a star. He said, "This is my Lord." But when it set, he said "Not do I like the ones that set."

So when (falammā) | covered (janna) | over him (ʿalayhi) | the night (al-laylu), | he saw (raā) | a star (kawkaban). | He said (qāla), | "This (hādhā) | is my Lord. (rabbī)" | But when (falammā) | it set (afala), | he said (qāla) | "Not (lā) | do I like (uḥibbu) | the ones that set. (l-āfilīna)"

6:77 When he saw the moon rising he said, "This is my Lord." But when it set he said, "If does not guide me my Lord, I will surely be among the people who went astray."

When (falammā) | he saw (raā) | the moon (l-qamara) | rising (bāzighan) | he said (qāla), | "This (hādhā) | is my Lord. (rabbī)" | But when (falammā) | it set (afala) | he said (qāla), | "If (la-in) | does not (lam) | guide me (yahdinī) | my Lord (rabbī), | I will surely be (la-akūnanna) | among (mina) | the people (l-qawmi) | who went astray. (l-ḍālīna)"

6:78 When he saw the sun rising he said, "This is my Lord, this is greater." But when it set, he said, "O my people! Indeed, I am free of what you associate with Allah."

When (falammā) | he saw (raā) | the sun (l-shamsa) | rising (bāzighatan) | he said (qāla), | "This is (hādhā) | my Lord (rabbī), | this is (hādhā) | greater. (akbaru)" | But when (falammā) | it set (afalat), | he said (qāla), | "O my people (yāqawmi)! | Indeed, I am (innī) | free (barīon) | of what (mimmā) | you associate with Allah. (tush'rikūna)"

6:79 Indeed, I [I] have turned my face to the One Who created the heavens and the earth as a true monotheist, and not I am of the polytheists.

Indeed, I (innī) | [I] have turned (wajjahtu) | my face (wajhiya) | to the One Who (lilladhī) | created (faṭara) | the heavens (l-samāwāti) | and the earth (wal-arḍa) | as a true monotheist (ḥanīfan), | and not (wamā) | I am (anā) | of (mina) | the polytheists (l-mush'rikīna).

6:80 And argued with him his people. He said, "Do you argue with me concerning Allah while certainly He has guided me? And not do I fear what you associate with Him, unless [that] wills my Lord anything. Encompasses my Lord every thing in knowledge. Then will not you take heed?

And argued with him (waḥājjahu) | his people (qawmuhu). | He said (qāla), | "Do you argue with me (atuḥājjūnnī) | concerning (fī) | Allah (l-lahi) | while certainly (waqad) | He has guided me (hadāni)? | And not (walā) | do I fear (akhāfu) | what (mā) | you associate (tush'rikūna) | with Him (bihi), | unless (illā) | [that] (an) | wills (yashāa) | my Lord (rabbī) | anything (shayan). | Encompasses (wasiʿa) | my Lord (rabbī) | every (kulla) | thing (shayin) | in knowledge (ʿil'man). | Then will not (afalā) | you take heed (tatadhakkarūna)?

6:81 And how could I fear what you associate with Allah while not you fear that you have associated with Allah what not did He send down for it to you any authority. So which of the two parties has more right to security if you know?"

And how (wakayfa) | could I fear (akhāfu) | what (mā) | you associate with Allah (ashraktum) | while not (walā) | you fear (takhāfūna) | that you (annakum) | have associated (ashraktum) | with Allah (bil-lahi) | what (mā) | not (lam) | did He send down (yunazzil) | for it (bihi) | to you (ʿalaykum) | any authority (sul'ṭānan). | So which (fa-ayyu) | of the two parties (l-farīqayni) | has more right (aḥaqqu) | to security (bil-amni) | if (in) | you (kuntum) | know? (taʿlamūna)"

6:82 Those who believed and did not mix their belief with wrong, those, for them, is the security and they are rightly guided.

Those who (alladhīna) | believed (āmanū) | and did not (walam) | mix (yalbisū) | their belief (īmānahum) | with wrong (biẓul'min), | those (ulāika), | for them (lahumu), | is the security (l-amnu) | and they (wahum) | are rightly guided (muh'tadūna).

6:83 And this is Our argument, We gave it to Ibrahim against his people. We raise by degrees whom We will. Indeed, your Lord is All-Wise, All-Knowing.

And this (watil'ka) | is Our argument (ḥujjatunā), | We gave it (ātaynāhā) | to Ibrahim (ib'rāhīma) | against (ʿalā) | his people (qawmihi). | We raise (narfaʿu) | by degrees (darajātin) | whom (man) | We will (nashāu). | Indeed (inna), | your Lord (rabbaka) | is All-Wise (ḥakīmun), | All-Knowing (ʿalīmun).

6:84 And We bestowed to him Isaac and Yaqub, all We guided. And Nuh, We guided from before; and of his descendents, Dawood and Sulaiman and Ayyub and Yusuf and Musa and Harun. And thus We reward the good-doers.

And We bestowed (wawahabnā) | to him (lahu) | Isaac (is'ḥāqa) | and Yaqub (wayaʿqūba), | all (kullan) | We guided (hadaynā). | And Nuh (wanūḥan), | We guided (hadaynā) | from (min) | before (qablu); | and of (wamin) | his descendents (dhurriyyatihi), | Dawood (dāwūda) | and Sulaiman (wasulaymāna) | and Ayyub (wa-ayyūba) | and Yusuf (wayūsufa) | and Musa (wamūsā) | and Harun (wahārūna). | And thus (wakadhālika) | We reward (najzī) | the good-doers (l-muḥ'sinīna).

6:85 And Zakariya and Yahya and Isa and Elijah - all were of the righteous.

And Zakariya (wazakariyyā) | and Yahya (wayaḥyā) | and Isa (waʿīsā) | and Elijah (wa-il'yāsa)- | all were (kullun) | of (mina) | the righteous (l-ṣāliḥīna).

6:86 And Ishmael and Elisha and Yunus and Lut, and all We preferred over the worlds.

And Ishmael (wa-is'māʿīla) | and Elisha (wal-yasaʿa) | and Yunus (wayūnusa) | and Lut (walūṭan), | and all (wakullan) | We preferred (faḍḍalnā) | over (ʿalā) | the worlds (l-ʿālamīna).

6:87 And from their fathers and their descendents and their brothers - and We chose them and We guided them to a path, straight.

And from (wamin) | their fathers (ābāihim) | and their descendents (wadhurriyyātihim) | and their brothers (wa-ikh'wānihim)- | and We chose them (wa-ij'tabaynāhum) | and We guided them (wahadaynāhum) | to (ilā) | a path (ṣirāṭin), | straight (mus'taqīmin).

6:88 That is the Guidance of Allah, He guides with it whom He wills of His slaves. But if they had associated partners (with Allah), surely would be worthless for them what they used to do.

That (dhālika) | is the Guidance (hudā) | of Allah (l-lahi), | He guides (yahdī) | with it (bihi) | whom (man) | He wills (yashāu) | of (min) | His slaves (ʿibādihi). | But if (walaw) | they had associated partners (with Allah) (ashrakū), | surely would be worthless (laḥabiṭa) | for them (ʿanhum) | what (mā) | they used to (kānū) | do (yaʿmalūna).

6:89 Those - are ones whom We gave them the Book and the judgment and the Prophethood. But if disbelieve in it these, then indeed, We have entrusted it to a people who are not therein disbelievers.

Those (ulāika)- | are ones whom (alladhīna) | We gave them (ātaynāhumu) | the Book (l-kitāba) | and the judgment (wal-ḥuk'ma) | and the Prophethood (wal-nubuwata). | But if (fa-in) | disbelieve (yakfur) | in it (bihā) | these (hāulāi), | then indeed (faqad), | We have entrusted (wakkalnā) | it (bihā) | to a people (qawman) | who are not (laysū) | therein (bihā) | disbelievers (bikāfirīna).

6:90 Those are ones whom have been guided by Allah so of their guidance you follow. Say, "Not I ask you for it any reward. Not is it but a reminder for the worlds."

Those (ulāika) | are ones whom (alladhīna) | have been guided (hadā) | by Allah (l-lahu) | so of their guidance (fabihudāhumu) | you follow (iq'tadih). | Say (qul), | "Not (lā) | I ask you (asalukum) | for it (ʿalayhi) | any reward (ajran). | Not (in) | is it (huwa) | but (illā) | a reminder (dhik'rā) | for the worlds. (lil'ʿālamīna)"

6:91 And not they appraised Allah with true [of his] appraisal when they said, "Not revealed by Allah on a human being [of] anything." Say, "Who revealed the Book which brought [it] Musa as a light and guidance for the people? You make it into parchments, you disclose some of it and you conceal much of it. And you were taught what not knew you and not your forefathers." Say, "Allah revealed it." Then leave them in their discourse - playing.

And not (wamā) | they appraised (qadarū) | Allah (l-laha) | with true (ḥaqqa) | [of his] appraisal (qadrihi) | when (idh) | they said (qālū), | "Not (mā) | revealed (anzala) | by Allah (l-lahu) | on (ʿalā) | a human being (basharin) | [of] (min) | anything. (shayin)" | Say (qul), | "Who (man) | revealed (anzala) | the Book (l-kitāba) | which (alladhī) | brought (jāa) | [it] (bihi) | Musa (mūsā) | as a light (nūran) | and guidance (wahudan) | for the people (lilnnāsi)? | You make it (tajʿalūnahu) | into parchments (qarāṭīsa), | you disclose some of it (tub'dūnahā) | and you conceal (watukh'fūna) | much of it (kathīran). | And you were taught (waʿullim'tum) | what (mā) | not (lam) | knew (taʿlamū) | you (antum) | and not (walā) | your forefathers. (ābāukum)" | Say (quli), | "Allah revealed it. (l-lahu)" | Then (thumma) | leave them (dharhum) | in (fī) | their discourse (khawḍihim)- | playing (yalʿabūna).

6:92 And this is a Book, We have revealed it, blessed, confirming which came before its hands, so that you may warn the mother of the cities and who are around it. And those who believe in the Hereafter, they believe in it, and they, over their prayers are guarding.

And this (wahādhā) | is a Book (kitābun), | We have revealed it (anzalnāhu), | blessed (mubārakun), | confirming (muṣaddiqu) | which (alladhī) | came before (bayna) | its hands (yadayhi), | so that you may warn (walitundhira) | the mother (umma) | of the cities (l-qurā) | and who (waman) | are around it (ḥawlahā). | And those who (wa-alladhīna) | believe (yu'minūna) | in the Hereafter (bil-ākhirati), | they believe (yu'minūna) | in it (bihi), | and they (wahum), | over (ʿalā) | their prayers (ṣalātihim) | are guarding (yuḥāfiẓūna).

6:93 And who is more unjust than one who invents about Allah a lie or said, "It has been inspired to me" while not it was inspired to him anything, and one who said, "I will reveal like what has been revealed by Allah." And if you could see when the wrongdoers are in agonies of [the] death while the Angels are stretching out their hands saying, "Discharge your souls! Today you will be recompensed with punishment, humiliating, because you used to say against Allah other than the truth and you were towards His Verses being arrogant."

And who (waman) | is more unjust (aẓlamu) | than one who (mimmani) | invents (if'tarā) | about (ʿalā) | Allah (l-lahi) | a lie (kadhiban) | or (aw) | said (qāla), | "It has been inspired (ūḥiya) | to me (ilayya)" | while not (walam) | it was inspired (yūḥa) | to him (ilayhi) | anything (shayon), | and one who (waman) | said (qāla), | "I will reveal (sa-unzilu) | like (mith'la) | what (mā) | has been revealed (anzala) | by Allah. (l-lahu)" | And if (walaw) | you could see (tarā) | when (idhi) | the wrongdoers (l-ẓālimūna) | are in (fī) | agonies (ghamarāti) | of [the] death (l-mawti) | while the Angels (wal-malāikatu) | are stretching out (bāsiṭū) | their hands saying (aydīhim), | "Discharge (akhrijū) | your souls (anfusakumu)! | Today (l-yawma) | you will be recompensed (tuj'zawna) |

with punishment (ʿadhāba), | humiliating (l-hūni), | because (bimā) | you used to (kuntum) | say (taqūlūna) | against (ʿalā) | Allah (l-lahi) | other than (ghayra) | the truth (l-ḥaqi) | and you were (wakuntum) | towards (ʿan) | His Verses (āyātihi) | being arrogant. (tastakbirūna)"

6:94 And certainly you have come to Us alone as We created you the first time, and you have left whatever We bestowed on you behind your backs. And not We see with you your intercessors those whom you claimed that they were in your matters partners with Allah. Indeed, have been severed bonds between you and is lost from you what you used to claim."

And certainly (walaqad) | you have come to Us (ji'tumūnā) | alone (furādā) | as (kamā) | We created you (khalaqnākum) | the first (awwala) | time (marratin), | and you have left (wataraktum) | whatever (mā) | We bestowed on you (khawwalnākum) | behind (warāa) | your backs (ẓuhūrikum). | And not (wamā) | We see (narā) | with you (maʿakum) | your intercessors (shufaʿāakumu) | those whom (alladhīna) | you claimed (zaʿamtum) | that they were (annahum) | in your matters (fīkum) | partners with Allah (shurakāu). | Indeed (laqad), | have been severed bonds (taqaṭṭaʿa) | between you (baynakum) | and is lost (waḍalla) | from you (ʿankum) | what (mā) | you used to (kuntum) | claim. (tazʿumūna)"

6:95 Indeed, Allah is the Cleaver of the grain and the date-seed. He brings forth the living from the dead and brings forth the dead from the living. That is Allah, so how are you deluded?

Indeed (inna), | Allah (l-laha) | is the Cleaver (fāliqu) | of the grain (l-ḥabi) | and the date-seed (wal-nawā). | He brings forth (yukh'riju) | the living (l-ḥaya) | from (mina) | the dead (l-mayiti) | and brings forth (wamukh'riju) | the dead (l-mayiti) | from (mina) | the living (l-ḥayi). | That (dhālikumu) | is Allah (l-lahu), | so how (fa-annā) | are you deluded (tu'fakūna)?

6:96 He is the Cleaver of the daybreak and He has made the night for rest and the sun and the moon for reckoning. That is the ordaining of the All-Mighty, the All-Knowing.

He is the Cleaver (fāliqu) | of the daybreak (l-iṣ'bāḥi) | and He has made (wajaʿala) | the night (al-layla) | for rest (sakanan) | and the sun (wal-shamsa) | and the moon (wal-qamara) | for reckoning (ḥus'bānan). | That (dhālika) | is the ordaining (taqdīru) | of the All-Mighty (l-ʿazīzi), | the All-Knowing (l-ʿalīmi).

6:97 And He is the One Who made for you the stars that you may guide yourselves with them in the darkness[es] of the land and the sea. Certainly, We have made clear the Signs for a people who know.

And He (wahuwa) | is the One Who (alladhī) | made (jaʿala) | for you (lakumu) | the stars (l-nujūma) | that you may guide yourselves (litahtadū) | with them (bihā) | in (fī) | the darkness[es] (ẓulumāti) | of the land (l-bari) | and the sea (wal-baḥri). | Certainly (qad), | We have made clear (faṣṣalnā) | the Signs (l-āyāti) | for a people (liqawmin) | who know (yaʿlamūna).

6:98 And He is the One Who has produced you from a soul, single, so there is a place of dwelling and a resting place. Certainly, We have made clear the Signs for a people who understand.

And He (wahuwa) | is the One Who (alladhī) | has produced you (ansha-akum) | from (min) | a soul (nafsin), | single (wāḥidatin), | so there is a place of dwelling (famus'taqarrun) | and a resting place (wamus'tawdaʿun). | Certainly (qad), | We have made clear (faṣṣalnā) | the Signs (l-āyāti) | for a people (liqawmin) | who understand (yafqahūna).

6:99 And He is the One Who sends down from the sky water, then We bring forth with it vegetation of every thing. Then We bring forth from it green plant, We bring forth from it grain - thick clustered. And from the date-palm, from its spathe clusters of dates hanging low. And gardens of grapes and the olives and the pomegranates resembling and not resembling. Look at its fruit when it bears fruit and its ripening. Indeed, in that are signs for a people who believe.

And He (wahuwa) | is the One Who (alladhī) | sends down (anzala) | from (mina) | the sky (l-samāi) | water (māan), | then We bring forth (fa-akhrajnā) | with it (bihi) | vegetation (nabāta) | of every (kulli) | thing (shayin). | Then We bring forth (fa-akhrajnā) | from it (min'hu) | green plant (khaḍiran), | We bring forth (nukh'riju) | from it (min'hu) | grain (ḥabban)- | thick clustered (mutarākiban). | And from (wamina) | the date-palm (l-nakhli), | from (min) | its spathe (ṭalʿihā) | clusters of dates (qin'wānun) | hanging low (dāniyatun). | And gardens (wajannātin) | of (min) | grapes (aʿnābin) | and the olives (wal-zaytūna) | and the pomegranates (wal-rumāna) | resembling (mush'tabihan) | and not (waghayra) | resembling (mutashābihin). | Look (unẓurū) | at (ilā) | its fruit (thamarihi) | when (idhā) | it bears fruit (athmara) | and its ripening (wayanʿihi). | Indeed (inna), | in (fī) | that (dhālikum) | are signs (laāyātin) | for a people (liqawmin) | who believe (yu'minūna).

6:100 And they make with Allah partners - jinn though He has created them, and they falsely attribute to Him sons and daughters without knowledge. Glorified is He and Exalted above what they attribute.

And they make (wajaʿalū) | with Allah (lillahi) | partners (shurakāa)- | jinn (l-jina) | though He has created them (wakhalaqahum), | and they falsely attribute (wakharaqū) | to Him (lahu) | sons (banīna) | and daughters (wabanātin) | without (bighayri) | knowledge (ʿil'min). | Glorified is He (sub'ḥānahu) | and Exalted (wataʿālā) | above what (ʿammā) | they attribute (yaṣifūna).

6:101 Originator of the heavens and the earth. How can be for Him a son while not there is for Him a companion, and He created every thing? And He is of every thing All-Knower.

Originator (badīʿu) | of the heavens (l-samāwāti) | and the earth (wal-arḍi). | How (annā) | can be (yakūnu) | for Him (lahu) | a son (waladun) | while not (walam) | there is (takun) | for Him (lahu) | a companion (ṣāḥibatun), | and He created (wakhalaqa) | every (kulla) | thing (shayin)? | And He (wahuwa) | is of every (bikulli) | thing (shayin) | All-Knower (ʿalīmun).

6:102 That is Allah your Lord, there is no god except Him, the Creator of every thing, so worship Him. And He is on every thing a Guardian.

That (dhālikumu) | is Allah (l-lahu) | your Lord (rabbukum), | there is no (lā) | god (ilāha) | except (illā) | Him (huwa), | the Creator (khāliqu) | of every (kulli) | thing (shayin), | so worship Him (fa-uʿ'budūhu). | And He (wahuwa) | is on (ʿalā) | every (kulli) | thing (shayin) | a Guardian (wakīlun).

6:103 Not can grasp Him the visions but He can grasp all the vision, and He is the All-Subtle, the All-Aware.

Not can (lā) | grasp Him (tud'rikuhu) | the visions (l-abṣāru) | but He (wahuwa) | can grasp (yud'riku) | all the vision (l-abṣāra), | and He is (wahuwa) | the All-Subtle (l-laṭīfu), | the All-Aware (l-khabīru).

6:104 Verily, has come to you enlightenment from your Lord. Then whoever sees, then it is for his soul, and whoever is blind then it is against himself. And not am I over you a guardian.

Verily (qad), | has come to you (jāakum) | enlightenment (baṣāiru) | from (min) | your Lord (rabbikum). | Then whoever (faman) | sees (abṣara), | then it is for his soul (falinafsihi), | and whoever (waman) | is blind (ʿamiya) | then it is against himself (faʿalayhā). | And not (wamā) | am I (anā) | over you (ʿalaykum) | a guardian (biḥafīẓin).

6:105 And thus We explain the Signs that they may say, "You have studied," and that We may make it clear for a people who know.

And thus (wakadhālika) | We explain (nuṣarrifu) | the Signs (l-āyāti) | that they may say (waliyaqūlū), | "You have studied, (darasta)" | and that We may make it clear (walinubayyinahu) | for a people (liqawmin) | who know (yaʿlamūna).

6:106 Follow, what has been inspired to you from your Lord, there is no god except Him, and turn away from the polytheists.

Follow (ittabiʿ), | what (mā) | has been inspired (ūḥiya) | to you (ilayka) | from (min) | your Lord (rabbika), | there is no (lā) | god (ilāha) | except (illā) | Him (huwa), | and turn away (wa-aʿriḍ) | from (ʿani) | the polytheists (l-mush'rikīna).

6:107 And if had willed Allah, not they would have associated partners with Him. And not We have made you over them a guardian, and not you are over them a manager.

And if (walaw) | had willed (shāa) | Allah (l-lahu), | not they would have (mā) | associated partners with Him (ashrakū). | And not (wamā) | We have made you (jaʿalnāka) | over them (ʿalayhim) | a guardian (ḥafīẓan), | and not (wamā) | you (anta) | are over them (ʿalayhim) | a manager (biwakīlin).

6:108 And do not insult those whom they invoke from other than Allah, lest they insult Allah in enmity without knowledge. Thus We have made fair-seeming to every community their deed. Then to their Lord is their return, then He will inform them about what they used to do.

And do not (walā) | insult (tasubbū) | those whom (alladhīna) | they invoke (yadʿūna) | from (min) | other than (dūni) | Allah (l-lahi), | lest they insult (fayasubbū) | Allah (l-laha) | in enmity (ʿadwan) | without (bighayri) | knowledge (ʿil'min). | Thus (kadhālika) | We have made fair-seeming (zayyannā) | to every (likulli) | community (ummatin) | their deed (ʿamalahum). | Then (thumma) | to (ilā) | their Lord (rabbihim) | is their return (marjiʿuhum), | then He will inform them (fayunabbi-uhum) | about what (bimā) | they used to (kānū) | do (yaʿmalūna).

6:109 And they swear by Allah strongest of their oaths that if came to them a sign, they would surely believe in it. Say, "Only the signs are with Allah." And what will make you perceive that [it] when it comes not they will believe.

And they swear (wa-aqsamū) | by Allah (bil-lahi) | strongest (jahda) | of their oaths (aymānihim) | that if (la-in) | came to them (jāathum) | a sign (āyatun), | they would surely believe (layu'minunna) | in it (bihā). | Say (qul), | "Only (innamā) | the signs (l-āyātu) | are with (ʿinda) | Allah. (l-lahi)" | And what (wamā) | will make you perceive (yush'ʿirukum) | that [it] (annahā) | when (idhā) | it comes (jāat) | not (lā) | they will believe (yu'minūna).

6:110 And We will turn their hearts and their sights just as not they believe in it the first time. And We will leave them in their transgression wandering blindly.

And We will turn (wanuqallibu) | their hearts (afidatahum) | and their sights (wa-abṣārahum) | just as (kamā) | not (lam) | they believe (yu'minū) | in it (bihi) | the first (awwala) | time (marratin). | And We will leave them (wanadharuhum) | in (fī) | their transgression (ṭugh'yānihim) | wandering blindly (yaʿmahūna).

6:111 And even if [that] We had [We] sent down to them the Angels and spoken to them the dead and We gathered before them every thing face to face, not they were to believe unless [that] wills Allah. But most of them are ignorant.

And even if (walaw) | [that] We had (annanā) | [We] sent down (nazzalnā) | to them (ilayhimu) | the Angels (l-malāikata) | and spoken to them (wakallamahumu) | the dead (l-mawtā) | and We gathered (waḥasharnā) | before them (ʿalayhim) | every (kulla) | thing (shayin) | face to face (qubulan), | not (mā) | they were (kānū) | to believe (liyu'minū) | unless (illā) | [that] (an) | wills (yashāa) | Allah (l-lahu). | But (walākinna) | most of them (aktharahum) | are ignorant (yajhalūna).

6:112 And thus We made for every Prophet an enemy - devils from the mankind and the jinn, inspiring some of them to others with decorative [the] speech in deception. But if had willed your

Lord not they would have done it, so leave them and what they invent.

And thus (wakadhālika) | We made (jaʿalnā) | for every (likulli) | Prophet (nabiyyin) | an enemy (ʿaduwwan)- | devils (shayāṭīna) | from the mankind (l-insi) | and the jinn (wal-jini), | inspiring (yūḥī) | some of them (baʿḍuhum) | to (ilā) | others (baʿḍin) | with decorative (zukh'rufa) | [the] speech (l-qawli) | in deception (ghurūran). | But if (walaw) | had willed (shāa) | your Lord (rabbuka) | not (mā) | they would have done it (faʿalūhu), | so leave them (fadharhum) | and what (wamā) | they invent (yaftarūna).

6:113 And so that incline to it hearts of those who do not believe in the Hereafter, and so that they may be pleased with it and so that they may commit what they are committing.

And so that incline (walitaṣghā) | to it (ilayhi) | hearts (afidatu) | of those who (alladhīna) | do not (lā) | believe (yu'minūna) | in the Hereafter (bil-ākhirati), | and so that they may be pleased with it (waliyarḍawhu) | and so that they may commit (waliyaqtarifū) | what (mā) | they (hum) | are committing (muq'tarifūna).

6:114 "Then is it other than Allah I seek as judge, while He is the One Who has revealed to you the Book explained in detail?" And those to whom We gave them the Book, they know that it is sent down from your Lord in truth, so do not be among the ones who doubt.

"Then is it other than (afaghayra) | Allah (l-lahi) | I seek (abtaghī) | as judge (ḥakaman), | while He (wahuwa) | is the One Who (alladhī) | has revealed (anzala) | to you (ilaykumu) | the Book (l-kitāba) | explained in detail? (mufaṣṣalan)" | And those to whom (wa-alladhīna) | We gave them (ātaynāhumu) | the Book (l-kitāba), | they know (yaʿlamūna) | that it (annahu) | is sent down (munazzalun) | from (min) | your Lord (rabbika) | in truth (bil-ḥaqi), | so do not (falā) | be (takūnanna) | among (mina) | the ones who doubt (l-mum'tarīna).

6:115 And has been fulfilled the word of your Lord in truth and justice. No one can change His words, and He is the All-Hearer, the All-Knower.

And has been fulfilled (watammat) | the word (kalimatu) | of your Lord (rabbika) | in truth (ṣid'qan) | and justice (waʿadlan). | No (lā) | one can change (mubaddila) | His words (likalimātihi), | and He (wahuwa) | is the All-Hearer (l-samīʿu), | the All-Knower (l-ʿalīmu).

6:116 And if you obey most of those in the earth they will mislead you from the way of Allah. Not they follow except [the] assumption, and not they do except guess.

And if (wa-in) | you obey (tuṭiʿ) | most (akthara) | of (man) | those in (fī) | the earth (l-arḍi) | they will mislead you (yuḍillūka) | from (ʿan) | the way (sabīli) | of Allah (l-lahi). | Not (in) | they follow (yattabiʿūna) | except (illā) | [the] assumption (l-ẓana), | and not (wa-in) | they do (hum) | except (illā) | guess (yakhruṣūna).

6:117 Indeed, your Lord, He knows best who strays from His way, and He is most knowing of the guided-ones.

Indeed (inna), | your Lord (rabbaka), | He (huwa) | knows best (aʿlamu) | who (man) | strays (yaḍillu) | from (ʿan) | His way (sabīlihi), | and He (wahuwa) | is most knowing (aʿlamu) | of the guided-ones (bil-muh'tadīna).

6:118 So eat of what is mentioned the name of Allah on it, if you are in His Verses - believers.

So eat (fakulū) | of what (mimmā) | is mentioned (dhukira) | the name (us'mu) | of Allah (l-lahi) | on it (ʿalayhi), | if (in) | you are (kuntum) | in His Verses (biāyātihi)- | believers (mu'minīna).

6:119 And what for you that not you eat of what has been mentioned the name of Allah on it, when indeed, He has explained in detail to you what He has forbidden to you except what you are compelled to it. And indeed, many surely lead astray by their vain desires without knowledge.

Indeed, your Lord, He is most knowing of the transgressors.

And what (wamā) | for you (lakum) | that not (allā) | you eat (takulū) | of what (mimmā) | has been mentioned (dhukira) | the name (us'mu) | of Allah (l-lahi) | on it (ʿalayhi), | when indeed (waqad), | He has explained in detail (faṣṣala) | to you (lakum) | what (mā) | He has forbidden (ḥarrama) | to you (ʿalaykum) | except (illā) | what (mā) | you are compelled (uḍ'ṭurir'tum) | to it (ilayhi). | And indeed (wa-inna), | many (kathīran) | surely lead astray (layuḍillūna) | by their vain desires (bi-ahwāihim) | without (bighayri) | knowledge (ʿil'min). | Indeed (inna), | your Lord (rabbaka), | He (huwa) | is most knowing (aʿlamu) | of the transgressors (bil-muʿ'tadīna).

6:120 Forsake open [the] sins and the secret. Indeed, those who earn [the] sin they will be recompensed for what they used to commit.

Forsake (wadharū) | open (ẓāhira) | [the] sins (l-ith'mi) | and the secret (wabāṭinahu). | Indeed (inna), | those who (alladhīna) | earn (yaksibūna) | [the] sin (l-ith'ma) | they will be recompensed (sayuj'zawna) | for what (bimā) | they used to (kānū) | commit (yaqtarifūna).

6:121 And do not eat of that, not has been mentioned the name of Allah on it, and indeed, it is grave disobedience. And indeed, the devils inspire to their friends so that they dispute with you, and if you obey them, indeed, you would be the polytheists.

And do not (walā) | eat (takulū) | of that (mimmā), | not (lam) | has been mentioned (yudh'kari) | the name (us'mu) | of Allah (l-lahi) | on it (ʿalayhi), | and indeed, it is (wa-innahu) | grave disobedience (lafis'qun). | And indeed (wa-inna), | the devils (l-shayāṭīna) | inspire (layūḥūna) | to (ilā) | their friends (awliyāihim) | so that they dispute with you (liyujādilūkum), | and if (wa-in) | you obey them (aṭaʿtumūhum), | indeed, you (innakum) | would be the polytheists (lamush'rikūna).

6:122 Is one who was dead and We gave him life and We made for him light, he walks whereby among the people, like one who [similar to him] is in the darknesses, not he comes out of it? Thus is made fair-seeming to the disbelievers what they were doing.

Is one who (awaman) | was (kāna) | dead (maytan) | and We gave him life (fa-aḥyaynāhu) | and We made (wajaʿalnā) | for him (lahu) | light (nūran), | he walks (yamshī) | whereby (bihi) | among (fī) | the people (l-nāsi), | like one who (kaman) | [similar to him] (mathaluhu) | is in (fī) | the darknesses (l-ẓulumāti), | not (laysa) | he comes out (bikhārijin) | of it (min'hā)? | Thus (kadhālika) | is made fair-seeming (zuyyina) | to the disbelievers (lil'kāfirīna) | what (mā) | they were (kānū) | doing (yaʿmalūna).

6:123 And thus We placed in every city greatest of its criminals, so that they plot therein. And not they plot except against themselves and not they perceive.

And thus (wakadhālika) | We placed (jaʿalnā) | in (fī) | every (kulli) | city (qaryatin) | greatest (akābira) | of its criminals (muj'rimīhā), | so that they plot (liyamkurū) | therein (fīhā). | And not (wamā) | they plot (yamkurūna) | except (illā) | against themselves (bi-anfusihim) | and not (wamā) | they perceive (yashʿurūna).

6:124 And when comes to them a Sign they say, "Never we will believe until we are given like what was given to the Messengers of Allah." Allah knows best where He places His Message. Will afflict those who committed crimes a humiliation from Allah and a punishment severe for what they used to plot.

And when (wa-idhā) | comes to them (jāathum) | a Sign (āyatun) | they say (qālū), | "Never (lan) | we will believe (nu'mina) | until (ḥattā) | we are given (nu'tā) | like (mith'la) | what (mā) | was given (ūtiya) | to the Messengers (rusulu) | of Allah. (l-lahi)" | Allah (l-lahu) | knows best (aʿlamu) | where (ḥaythu) | He places (yajʿalu) | His Message (risālatahu). | Will afflict (sayuṣību) | those who (alladhīna) | committed crimes (ajramū) | a humiliation (ṣaghārun) | from (ʿinda) | Allah (l-lahi) | and a punishment (waʿadhābun) | severe (shadīdun) | for what (bimā) | they used to (kānū) | plot (yamkurūna).

6:125 So whoever wants Allah that He guides him - He expands his breast to Islam; and whoever He wants that He lets him go astray He makes his breast tight and constricted as though he were climbing into the sky. Thus places Allah the filth on those who do not believe.

So whoever (faman) | wants (yuridi) | Allah (l-lahu) | that (an) | He guides him (yahdiyahu)- | He expands (yashraḥ) | his breast (ṣadrahu) | to Islam (lil'is'lāmi); | and whoever (waman) | He wants (yurid) | that (an) | He lets him go astray (yuḍillahu) | He makes (yajʿal) | his breast (ṣadrahu) | tight (ḍayyiqan) | and constricted (ḥarajan) | as though (ka-annamā) | he were climbing (yaṣṣaʿʿadu) | into (fī) | the sky (l-samāi). | Thus (kadhālika) | places (yajʿalu) | Allah (l-lahu) | the filth (l-rij'sa) | on (ʿalā) | those who (alladhīna) | do not (lā) | believe (yu'minūna).

6:126 And this is the way of your Lord - straight. Certainly We have detailed the Verses for a people who take heed.

And this (wahādhā) | is the way (ṣirāṭu) | of your Lord (rabbika)- | straight (mus'taqīman). | Certainly (qad) | We have detailed (faṣṣalnā) | the Verses (l-āyāti) | for a people (liqawmin) | who take heed (yadhakkarūna).

6:127 For them will be home of [the] peace with their Lord. And He will be their protecting friend because of what they used to do.

For them (lahum) | will be home (dāru) | of [the] peace (l-salāmi) | with (ʿinda) | their Lord (rabbihim). | And He (wahuwa) | will be their protecting friend (waliyyuhum) | because (bimā) | of what they used to (kānū) | do (yaʿmalūna).

6:128 And the Day He will gather them all, and will say, "O assembly of [the] jinn! Certainly, you have misled many of the mankind." And will say their friends among the men, "Our Lord profited some of us by others, and we have reached our term which You appointed for us." He will say, "The Fire is your abode, will abide forever in it, except for what wills Allah Indeed, your Lord is All-Wise, All-Knowing.

And the Day (wayawma) | He will gather them (yaḥshuruhum) | all (jamīʿan), | and will say, "O assembly (yāmaʿshara) | of [the] jinn (l-jini)! | Certainly (qadi), | you have misled many (is'takthartum) | of (mina) | the mankind. (l-insi)" | And will say (waqāla) | their friends (awliyāuhum) | among (mina) | the men (l-insi), | "Our Lord (rabbanā) | profited (is'tamtaʿa) | some of us (baʿḍunā) | by others (bibaʿḍin), | and we have reached (wabalaghnā) | our term (ajalanā) | which (alladhī) | You appointed (ajjalta) | for us. (lanā)" | He will say (qāla), | "The Fire (l-nāru) | is your abode (mathwākum), | will abide forever (khālidīna) | in it (fīhā), | except (illā) | for what (mā) | wills (shāa) | Allah (l-lahu) | Indeed (inna), | your Lord (rabbaka) | is All-Wise (ḥakīmun), | All-Knowing (ʿalīmun).

6:129 And thus We make friends, some of the wrongdoers to others for what they used to earn.

And thus (wakadhālika) | We make friends (nuwallī), | some of (baʿḍa) | the wrongdoers (l-ẓālimīna) | to others (baʿḍan) | for what (bimā) | they used to (kānū) | earn (yaksibūna).

6:130 O assembly of [the] jinn and [the] men! Did there not come to you Messengers from among you, relating to you My Verses and warning you of the meeting of your day, this?" They will say, "We bear witness against ourselves." And deluded them the life of the world, and they will bear witness against themselves that they were disbelievers.

O assembly (yāmaʿshara) | of [the] jinn (l-jini) | and [the] men (wal-insi)! | Did there not (alam) | come to you (yatikum) | Messengers (rusulun) | from among you (minkum), | relating (yaquṣṣūna) | to you (ʿalaykum) | My Verses (āyātī) | and warning you (wayundhirūnakum) | of the meeting (liqāa) | of your day (yawmikum), | this? (hādhā)" | They will say (qālū), | "We bear witness (shahid'nā) | against (ʿalā) | ourselves. (anfusinā)" | And deluded them (wagharrathumu) | the life (l-ḥayatu) | of the world (l-dun'yā), | and they will bear witness (washahidū) | against (ʿalā) |

themselves (anfusihim) | that they (annahum) | were (kānū) | disbelievers (kāfirīna).

6:131 That is because [that] not is your Lord one who destroys the cities for their wrongdoing while their people are unaware.

That is because (dhālika) | [that] (an) | not (lam) | is (yakun) | your Lord (rabbuka) | one who destroys (muh'lika) | the cities (l-qurā) | for their wrongdoing (biẓul'min) | while their people (wa-ahluhā) | are unaware (ghāfilūna).

6:132 And for all will be degrees for what they did. And not is your Lord unaware about what they do.

And for all (walikullin) | will be degrees (darajātun) | for what (mimmā) | they did (ʿamilū). | And not (wamā) | is your Lord (rabbuka) | unaware (bighāfilin) | about what (ʿammā) | they do (yaʿmalūna).

6:133 And your Lord is the Self-Sufficient, the Possessor of mercy. If He wills He can take you away and grant succession from after you to whom He wills. as He raised you from the descendants of people, other.

And your Lord (warabbuka) | is the Self-Sufficient (l-ghaniyu), | the Possessor (dhū) | of mercy (l-raḥmati). | If (in) | He wills (yasha) | He can take you away (yudh'hib'kum) | and grant succession (wayastakhlif) | from (min) | after you (baʿdikum) | to whom (mā) | He wills (yashāu). | as (kamā) | He raised you (ansha-akum) | from (min) | the descendants (dhurriyyati) | of people (qawmin), | other (ākharīna).

6:134 Indeed, what you are promised is sure to come. And not can you escape it.

Indeed (inna), | what (mā) | you are promised (tūʿadūna) | is sure to come (laātin). | And not (wamā) | can you (antum) | escape it (bimuʿʿjizīna).

6:135 Say, "O my people! Work on your position. Indeed, I am a worker. And soon you will know who will have for himself in the end, a good home. Indeed [he], will not succeed the wrongdoers."

Say (qul), | "O my people (yāqawmi)! | Work (iʿʿmalū) | on (ʿalā) | your position (makānatikum). | Indeed, I am (innī) | a worker (ʿāmilun). | And soon (fasawfa) | you will know (taʿlamūna) | who (man) | will have (takūnu) | for himself (lahu) | in the end (ʿāqibatu), | a good home (l-dāri). | Indeed [he] (innahu), | will not (lā) | succeed (yuf'liḥu) | the wrongdoers. (l-ẓālimūna)"

6:136 And they assign to Allah out of what He produced of the crops and the cattle a share and they say, "This is for Allah," by their claim, "And this is for our partners." But what is for their partners does not reach [to] Allah, while what is for Allah then it reaches [to] their partners. Evil is what they judge.

And they assign (wajaʿalū) | to Allah (lillahi) | out of what (mimmā) | He produced (dhara-a) | of (mina) | the crops (l-ḥarthi) | and the cattle (wal-anʿāmi) | a share (naṣīban) | and they say (faqālū), | "This (hādhā) | is for Allah, (lillahi)" | by their claim (bizaʿmihim), | "And this (wahādhā) | is for our partners. (lishurakāinā)" | But what (famā) | is (kāna) | for their partners (lishurakāihim) | does not (falā) | reach (yaṣilu) | [to] (ilā) | Allah (l-lahi), | while what (wamā) | is (kāna) | for Allah (lillahi) | then it (fahuwa) | reaches (yaṣilu) | [to] (ilā) | their partners (shurakāihim). | Evil (sāa) | is what (mā) | they judge (yaḥkumūna).

6:137 And likewise made pleasing to many of the polytheists - the killing of their children - their partners - so that they may ruin them and that they make confusing to them their religion. And if had willed Allah not would they have done so. So leave them and what they invent.

And likewise (wakadhālika) | made pleasing (zayyana) | to many (likathīrin) | of (mina) | the polytheists (l-mush'rikīna)- | the killing (qatla) | of their children (awlādihim)- | their partners (shurakāuhum)- | so that they may ruin them (liyur'dūhum) | and that they make confusing (waliyalbisū) | to them (ʿalayhim) | their religion (dīnahum). | And if (walaw) | had willed (shāa) | Allah (l-lahu) | not (mā) | would they have done so (faʿalūhu). | So leave them (fadharhum) | and what (wamā) | they invent (yaftarūna).

6:138 And they say, "These are cattle and crops, forbidden, no one can eat them except whom we will," by their claim. And cattle, forbidden are their backs and cattle not they mention the name of Allah on it as an invention against Him. He will recompense them for what they used to invent.

And they say (waqālū), | "These (hādhihi) | are cattle (anʿāmun) | and crops (waḥarthun), | forbidden (ḥij'run), | no one (lā) | can eat them (yaṭʿamuhā) | except (illā) | whom (man) | we will, (nashāu)" | by their claim (bizaʿmihim). | And cattle (wa-anʿāmun), | forbidden (ḥurrimat) | are their backs (ẓuhūruhā) | and cattle (wa-anʿāmun) | not (lā) | they mention (yadhkurūna) | the name (is'ma) | of Allah (l-lahi) | on it (ʿalayhā) | as an invention (if'tirāan) | against Him (ʿalayhi). | He will recompense them (sayajzīhim) | for what (bimā) | they used to (kānū) | invent (yaftarūna).

6:139 And they say, "What is in the wombs of these cattle is exclusively for our males and forbidden on our spouses. But if is born dead, then they all in it are partners." He will recompense them for their attribution. Indeed, He is All-Wise, All-Knowing.

And they say (waqālū), | "What (mā) | is in (fī) | the wombs (buṭūni) | of these (hādhihi) | cattle (l-anʿāmi) | is exclusively (khāliṣatun) | for our males (lidhukūrinā) | and forbidden (wamuḥarramun) | on (ʿalā) | our spouses (azwājinā). | But if (wa-in) | is (yakun) | born dead (maytatan), | then they all (fahum) | in it (fīhi) | are partners. (shurakāu)" | He will recompense them (sayajzīhim) | for their attribution (waṣfahum). | Indeed, He (innahu) | is All-Wise (ḥakīmun), | All-Knowing (ʿalīmun).

6:140 Certainly, are lost those who killed their children in foolishness without knowledge and forbid what bas been provided (to) them by Allah - inventing lies against Allah. Certainly, they have gone astray and not they are guided-ones.

Certainly (qad), | are lost (khasira) | those who (alladhīna) | killed (qatalū) | their children (awlādahum) | in foolishness (safahan) | without (bighayri) | knowledge (ʿil'min) | and forbid (waḥarramū) | what (mā) | bas been provided (to) them (razaqahumu) | by Allah (l-lahu)- | inventing lies (if'tirāan) | against (ʿalā) | Allah (l-lahi). | Certainly (qad), | they have gone astray (ḍallū) | and not (wamā) | they are (kānū) | guided-ones (muh'tadīna).

6:141 And He is the One Who produced gardens trellised and other than trellised and the date-palm and the crops, diverse are its taste, and the olives and the pomegranates similar and other than similar. Eat of its fruit when it bears fruit, and give its due on the day of its harvest. And do not be extravagant. Indeed, He does not love the ones who are extravagant.

And He (wahuwa) | is the One Who (alladhī) | produced (ansha-a) | gardens (jannātin) | trellised (maʿrūshātin) | and other than (waghayra) | trellised (maʿrūshātin) | and the date-palm (wal-nakhla) | and the crops (wal-zarʿa), | diverse (mukh'talifan) | are its taste (ukuluhu), | and the olives (wal-zaytūna) | and the pomegranates (wal-rumāna) | similar (mutashābihan) | and other than (waghayra) | similar (mutashābihin). | Eat (kulū) | of (min) | its fruit (thamarihi) | when (idhā) | it bears fruit (athmara), | and give (waātū) | its due (ḥaqqahu) | on the day (yawma) | of its harvest (ḥaṣādihi). | And do not (walā) | be extravagant (tus'rifū). | Indeed, He (innahu) | does not (lā) | love (yuḥibbu) | the ones who are extravagant (l-mus'rifīna).

6:142 And of the cattle are some for burden and some for meat. Eat of what has been provided (to) you by Allah, and do not follow the footsteps of Shaitaan. Indeed, he is to you an enemy open.

And of (wamina) | the cattle (l-anʿāmi) | are some for burden (ḥamūlatan) | and some for meat (wafarshan). | Eat (kulū) | of what (mimmā) | has been provided (to) you (razaqakumu) | by Allah (l-lahu), | and do not (walā) | follow (tattabiʿū) | the footsteps (khuṭuwāti) | of Shaitaan (l-shayṭāni). | Indeed, he (innahu) | is to you (lakum) | an enemy (ʿaduwwun) | open (mubīnun).

6:143 Eight pairs - of the sheep, two and of the goats two. Say, "Are the two males He has forbidden or the two females or what contains [in it] the wombs of the two females? Inform me with knowledge, if you are truthful."

Eight (thamāniyata) | pairs (azwājin)- | of (mina) | the sheep (l-ḍani), | two (ith'nayni) | and of (wamina) | the goats (l-maʿzi) | two (ith'nayni). | Say (qul), | "Are the two males (āldhakarayni) | He has forbidden (ḥarrama) | or (ami) | the two females (l-unthayayni) | or what (ammā) | contains (ish'tamalat) | [in it] (ʿalayhi) | the wombs (arḥāmu) | of the two females (l-unthayayni)? | Inform me (nabbiūnī) | with knowledge (biʿil'min), | if (in) | you are (kuntum) | truthful. (ṣādiqīna)"

6:144 And of the camels two and of the cows two. Say, "Is it the two males He has forbidden or the two females or what contains [in it] the wombs of the two females? Or were you witnesses when enjoined you Allah with this? Then who is more unjust than one who invents against Allah a lie to mislead the people without knowledge? Indeed, Allah does not guide the people, the wrongdoing."

And of (wamina) | the camels (l-ibili) | two (ith'nayni) | and of (wamina) | the cows (l-baqari) | two (ith'nayni). | Say (qul), | "Is it the two males (āldhakarayni) | He has forbidden (ḥarrama) | or (ami) | the two females (l-unthayayni) | or what (ammā) | contains (ish'tamalat) | [in it] (ʿalayhi) | the wombs (arḥāmu) | of the two females (l-unthayayni)? | Or (am) | were you (kuntum) | witnesses (shuhadāa) | when (idh) | enjoined you (waṣṣākumu) | Allah (l-lahu) | with this (bihādhā)? | Then who (faman) | is more unjust (aẓlamu) | than one who (mimmani) | invents (if'tarā) | against (ʿalā) | Allah (l-lahi) | a lie (kadhiban) | to mislead (liyuḍilla) | the people (l-nāsa) | without (bighayri) | knowledge (ʿil'min)? | Indeed (inna), | Allah (l-laha) | does not (lā) | guide (yahdī) | the people (l-qawma), | the wrongdoing. (l-ẓālimīna)"

6:145 Say, "Not do I find in what has been revealed to me anything forbidden to an eater who eats it except that it be dead or blood poured forth or the flesh of swine - for indeed, it is filth - or it be disobedience, [is] dedicated to other than Allah [on it]. But whoever is compelled not desiring and not transgressing, then indeed, your Lord is Oft-Forgiving, Most Merciful."

Say (qul), | "Not (lā) | do I find (ajidu) | in (fī) | what (mā) | has been revealed (ūḥiya) | to me (ilayya) | anything forbidden (muḥarraman) | to (ʿalā) | an eater (ṭāʿimin) | who eats it (yaṭʿamuhu) | except (illā) | that (an) | it be (yakūna) | dead (maytatan) | or (aw) | blood (daman) | poured forth (masfūḥan) | or (aw) | the flesh (laḥma) | of swine (khinzīrin)- | for indeed, it (fa-innahu) | is filth (rij'sun)- | or (aw) | it be disobedience (fis'qan), | [is] dedicated (uhilla) | to other than (lighayri) | Allah (l-lahi) | [on it] (bihi). | But whoever (famani) | is compelled (uḍ'ṭurra) | not (ghayra) | desiring (bāghin) | and not (walā) | transgressing (ʿādin), | then indeed (fa-inna), | your Lord (rabbaka) | is Oft-Forgiving (ghafūrun), | Most Merciful. (raḥīmun)"

6:146 And to those who are Jews We forbade every animal with claws, and of the cows and the sheep We forbade to them their fat except what carried their backs or the entrails or what is joined with the bone. That is their recompense for their rebellion. And indeed, We [surely] are truthful.

And to (waʿalā) | those who (alladhīna) | are Jews (hādū) | We forbade (ḥarramnā) | every (kulla) | animal with (dhī) | claws (ẓufurin), | and of (wamina) | the cows (l-baqari) | and the sheep (wal-ghanami) | We forbade (ḥarramnā) | to them (ʿalayhim) | their fat (shuḥūmahumā) | except (illā) | what (mā) | carried (ḥamalat) | their backs (ẓuhūruhumā) | or (awi) | the entrails (l-ḥawāyā) | or (aw) | what (mā) | is joined (ikh'talaṭa) | with the bone (biʿaẓmin). | That (dhālika) | is their recompense (jazaynāhum) | for their rebellion (bibaghyihim). | And indeed, We (wa-innā) | [surely] are truthful (laṣādiqūna).

6:147 But if they deny you then say, "Your Lord is the Possessor of Mercy Vast, but not will be turned back His wrath from the people who are criminals."

But if (fa-in) | they deny you (kadhabūka) | then say (faqul), | "Your Lord (rabbukum) | is the Possessor (dhū) | of Mercy (raḥmatin) | Vast (wāsiʿatin), | but not (walā) | will be turned back (yuraddu) | His wrath (basuhu) | from (ʿani) | the people (l-qawmi) | who are criminals. (l-muj'rimīna)"

6:148 Will say those who associate partners with Allah, "If Had willed Allah, not we would have associated partners (with Allah) and not our forefathers and not we would have forbidden [of] anything." Likewise denied those who were from before them until they tasted Our wrath. Say, "Is with you [of] any knowledge then produce it for us? Not you follow except the assumption, and not you do but guess."

Will say (sayaqūlu) | those who (alladhīna) | associate partners with Allah (ashrakū), | "If (law) | Had willed (shāa) | Allah (l-lahu), | not (mā) | we would have associated partners (with Allah (ashraknā)) | and not (walā) | our forefathers (ābāunā) | and not (walā) | we would have forbidden (ḥarramnā) | [of] (min) | anything. (shayin)" | Likewise (kadhālika) | denied (kadhaba) | those who (alladhīna) | were from (min) | before them (qablihim) | until (ḥattā) | they tasted (dhāqū) | Our wrath (basanā). | Say (qul), | "Is (hal) | with you (ʿindakum) | [of] (min) | any knowledge (ʿil'min) | then produce it (fatukh'rijūhu) | for us (lanā)? | Not (in) | you follow (tattabiʿūna) | except (illā) | the assumption (l-ẓana), | and not (wa-in) | you do (antum) | but (illā) | guess. (takhruṣūna)"

6:149 Say, "With Allah is the argument - the conclusive. And if He had willed, surely He would have guided you all."

Say (qul), | "With Allah (falillahi) | is the argument (l-ḥujatu)- | the conclusive (l-bālighatu). | And if (falaw) | He had willed (shāa), | surely He would have guided you (lahadākum) | all. (ajmaʿīna)"

6:150 Say, "Bring forward your witnesses, those who testify that Allah prohibited this." Then if they testify then do not testify with them. And do not follow the desires of those who denied Our Signs and those who do not believe in the Hereafter, while they with their Lord set up equals.

Say (qul), | "Bring forward (halumma) | your witnesses (shuhadāakumu), | those who (alladhīna) | testify (yashhadūna) | that (anna) | Allah (l-laha) | prohibited (ḥarrama) | this. (hādhā)" | Then if (fa-in) | they testify (shahidū) | then do not (falā) | testify (tashhad) | with them (maʿahum). | And do not (walā) | follow (tattabiʿ) | the desires (ahwāa) | of those who (alladhīna) | denied (kadhabū) | Our Signs (biāyātinā) | and those who (wa-alladhīna) | do not (lā) | believe (yu'minūna) | in the Hereafter (bil-ākhirati), | while they (wahum) | with their Lord (birabbihim) | set up equals (yaʿdilūna).

6:151 Say, "Come, I will recite what has prohibited your Lord to you. That do not associate with Him anything, and with the parents be good, and do not kill your children out of poverty, We provide for you and for them. And do not go near [the] immoralities what is apparent of them and what is concealed. And do not kill the soul which has been forbidden by Allah except by legal right. That He has enjoined on you with it, so that you may use reason."

Say (qul), | "Come (taʿālaw), | I will recite (atlu) | what (mā) | has prohibited (ḥarrama) | your Lord (rabbukum) | to you (ʿalaykum). | That do not (allā) | associate (tush'rikū) | with Him (bihi) | anything (shayan), | and with the parents (wabil-wālidayni) | be good (iḥ'sānan), | and do not (walā) | kill (taqtulū) | your children (awlādakum) | out of (min) | poverty (im'lāqin), | We (naḥnu) | provide for you (narzuqukum) | and for them (wa-iyyāhum). | And do not (walā) | go near (taqrabū) | [the] immoralities (l-fawāḥisha) | what (mā) | is apparent (ẓahara) | of them (min'hā) | and what (wamā) | is concealed (baṭana). | And do not (walā) | kill (taqtulū) | the soul (l-nafsa) | which (allatī) | has been forbidden (ḥarrama) | by Allah (l-lahu) | except (illā) | by legal right (bil-ḥaqi). | That (dhālikum) | He has enjoined on you (waṣṣākum) | with it (bihi), | so that you may (laʿallakum) | use reason. (taʿqilūna)"

6:152 And do not go near wealth of the orphans except with that which is best until he reaches his maturity. And give full [the] measure and the weight with justice. Not We burden any soul except to its capacity. And when you speak then be just even if he is one of. a near relative. And the Covenant of Allah fulfil. That He has enjoined on you with it so that you may remember.

And do not (walā) | go near (taqrabū) | wealth (māla) | of the orphans (l-yatīmi) | except (illā) | with that (bi-allatī) | which (hiya) | is best (aḥsanu) | until (ḥattā) | he reaches (yablugha) | his maturity (ashuddahu). | And give full (wa-awfū) | [the] measure (l-kayla) | and the weight (wal-mīzāna) | with justice (bil-qis'ṭi). | Not (lā) | We burden (nukallifu) | any soul (nafsan) | except (illā) | to its capacity (wus''ahā). | And when (wa-idhā) | you speak (qul'tum) | then be just (fa-i''dilū) | even if (walaw) | he is (kāna) | one of (dhā). | a near relative (qur'bā). | And the Covenant (wabi'ahdi) | of Allah (l-lahi) | fulfil (awfū). | That (dhālikum) | He has enjoined on you (waṣṣākum) | with it (bihi) | so that you may (la'allakum) | remember (tadhakkarūna).

6:153 And that, this is My path, straight, so follow it. And do not follow the other paths, then they will separate you from His path. That He has enjoined on you [with it] so that you may become righteous.

And that (wa-anna), | this (hādhā) | is My path (ṣirāṭī), | straight (mus'taqīman), | so follow it (fa-ittabi'ūhu). | And do not (walā) | follow (tattabi'ū) | the other paths (l-subula), | then they will separate (fatafarraqa) | you (bikum) | from ('an) | His path (sabīlihi). | That (dhālikum) | He has enjoined on you (waṣṣākum) | [with it] (bihi) | so that you may (la'allakum) | become righteous (tattaqūna).

6:154 Moreover We gave Musa the Book, completing Our Favor on the one who did good and an explanation of every thing, and a guidance and mercy, so that they may in the meeting with their Lord believe.

Moreover (thumma) | We gave (ātaynā) | Musa (mūsā) | the Book (l-kitāba), | completing Our Favor (tamāman) | on ('alā) | the one who (alladhī) | did good (aḥsana) | and an explanation (watafṣīlan) | of every (likulli) | thing (shayin), | and a guidance (wahudan) | and mercy (waraḥmatan), | so that they may (la'allahum) | in the meeting (biliqāi) | with their Lord (rabbihim) | believe (yu'minūna).

6:155 And this is a Book We have revealed it - blessed, so follow it and fear Allah so that you may receive mercy.

And this (wahādhā) | is a Book (kitābun) | We have revealed it (anzalnāhu)- | blessed (mubārakun), | so follow it (fa-ittabi'ūhu) | and fear Allah (wa-ittaqū) | so that you may (la'allakum) | receive mercy (tur'ḥamūna).

6:156 Lest you say, "Only was revealed the Book on the two groups from before us, and indeed we were about their study certainly unaware."

Lest (an) | you say (taqūlū), | "Only (innamā) | was revealed (unzila) | the Book (l-kitābu) | on ('alā) | the two groups (ṭāifatayni) | from (min) | before us (qablinā), | and indeed (wa-in) | we were (kunnā) | about ('an) | their study (dirāsatihim) | certainly unaware. (laghāfilīna)"

6:157 Or you say, "If [that] was revealed to us the Book surely we would have been better guided than them. So verily has come to you clear proofs from your Lord and a Guidance and a Mercy. Then who is more unjust than he who denies [with] the Verses of Allah, and turns away from them? We will recompense those who turn away from Our Signs with an evil punishment because they used to turn away.

Or (aw) | you say (taqūlū), | "If (law) | [that] (annā) | was revealed (unzila) | to us ('alaynā) | the Book (l-kitābu) | surely we would have been (lakunnā) | better guided (ahdā) | than them (min'hum). | So verily (faqad) | has come to you (jāakum) | clear proofs (bayyinatun) | from (min) | your Lord (rabbikum) | and a Guidance (wahudan) | and a Mercy (waraḥmatun). | Then who (faman)

| is more unjust (aẓlamu) | than he who (mimman) | denies (kadhaba) | [with] the Verses (biāyāti) | of Allah (l-lahi), | and turns away (waṣadafa) | from them (ʿanhā)? | We will recompense (sanajzī) | those who (alladhīna) | turn away (yaṣdifūna) | from (ʿan) | Our Signs (āyātinā) | with an evil (sūa) | punishment (l-ʿadhābi) | because (bimā) | they used to (kānū) | turn away (yaṣdifūna).

6:158 Are they waiting except that comes to them the Angels or comes your Lord or comes some of the Signs of your Lord? The Day when comes some of the Signs of your Lord, not will benefit a soul its faith, not if it had believed from before or earned through its faith any good. Say, "Wait. Indeed, we are those who wait."

Are (hal) | they waiting (yanẓurūna) | except (illā) | that (an) | comes to them (tatiyahumu) | the Angels (l-malāikatu) | or (aw) | comes (yatiya) | your Lord (rabbuka) | or (aw) | comes (yatiya) | some of (baʿḍu) | the Signs (āyāti) | of your Lord (rabbika)? | The Day (yawma) | when comes (yatī) | some of (baʿḍu) | the Signs (āyāti) | of your Lord (rabbika), | not (lā) | will benefit (yanfaʿu) | a soul (nafsan) | its faith (īmānuhā), | not (lam) | if it had (takun) | believed (āmanat) | from (min) | before (qablu) | or (aw) | earned (kasabat) | through (fī) | its faith (īmānihā) | any good (khayran). | Say (quli), | "Wait (intaẓirū). | Indeed, we (innā) | are those who wait. (muntaẓirūna)"

6:159 Indeed, those who divide their religion and become sects, you are not with them in anything. Only their affair is with Allah, then He will inform them of what they used to do.

Indeed (inna), | those who (alladhīna) | divide (farraqū) | their religion (dīnahum) | and become (wakānū) | sects (shiyaʿan), | you are not (lasta) | with them (min'hum) | in (fī) | anything (shayin). | Only (innamā) | their affair (amruhum) | is with (ilā) | Allah (l-lahi), | then (thumma) | He will inform them (yunabbi-uhum) | of what (bimā) | they used to (kānū) | do (yafʿalūna).

6:160 Whoever came with a good deed, then for him is ten (times) the like of it. And whoever came with an evil deed then not he will be recompensed except the like of it, and they will not be wronged.

Whoever (man) | came (jāa) | with a good deed (bil-ḥasanati), | then for him (falahu) | is ten (times) (ʿashru)) | the like of it (amthālihā). | And whoever (waman) | came (jāa) | with an evil deed (bil-sayi-ati) | then not (falā) | he will be recompensed (yuj'zā) | except (illā) | the like of it (mith'lahā), | and they (wahum) | will not (lā) | be wronged (yuẓ'lamūna).

6:161 Say, "Indeed as for me, has guided me my Lord to a path, straight - a religion right, religion of Ibrahim - a true monotheist. And not he was from the polytheists.

Say (qul), | "Indeed as for me (innanī), | has guided me (hadānī) | my Lord (rabbī) | to (ilā) | a path (ṣirāṭin), | straight (mus'taqīmin)- | a religion (dīnan) | right (qiyaman), | religion (millata) | of Ibrahim (ib'rāhīma)- | a true monotheist (ḥanīfan). | And not (wamā) | he was (kāna) | from (mina) | the polytheists (l-mush'rikīna).

6:162 Say, "Indeed, my prayer, and my rites of sacrifice, and my living, and my dying are for Allah, Lord of the worlds.

Say (qul), | "Indeed (inna), | my prayer (ṣalātī), | and my rites of sacrifice (wanusukī), | and my living (wamaḥyāya), | and my dying (wamamātī) | are for Allah (lillahi), | Lord (rabbi) | of the worlds (l-ʿālamīna).

6:163 No partners for Him; and with that I have been commanded. And I am the first of the ones who surrender (to Him).

No (lā) | partners (sharīka) | for Him (lahu); | and with that (wabidhālika) | I have been commanded (umir'tu). | And I am (wa-anā) | the first (awwalu) | of the ones who surrender (to Him) (l-mus'limīna).

6:164 Say, "Is it other than Allah I should seek as a Lord, while He is the Lord of every thing?" And not earns every soul except against itself, and not bears any bearer of burden, burden of another. Then to your Lord is your return then He will inform you about what you were concerning it differing.

Say (qul), | "Is it other than (aghayra) | Allah (l-lahi) | I should seek (abghī) | as a Lord (rabban), | while He (wahuwa) | is the Lord (rabbu) | of every (kulli) | thing? (shayin)" | And not (walā) | earns (taksibu) | every (kullu) | soul (nafsin) | except (illā) | against itself (ʿalayhā), | and not (walā) | bears (taziru) | any bearer of burden (wāziratun), | burden (wiz'ra) | of another (ukh'rā). | Then (thumma) | to (ilā) | your Lord (rabbikum) | is your return (marjiʿukum) | then He will inform you (fayunabbi-ukum) | about what (bimā) | you were (kuntum) | concerning it (fīhi) | differing (takhtalifūna).

6:165 And He is the One Who has made you successors of the earth and raised some of you above others in ranks, so that He may test you in what He has given you. Indeed, your Lord is swift in the punishment, and indeed, He is [certainly], Oft-Forgiving, Most Merciful.

And He (wahuwa) | is the One Who (alladhī) | has made you (jaʿalakum) | successors (khalāifa) | of the earth (l-arḍi) | and raised (warafaʿa) | some of you (baʿḍakum) | above (fawqa) | others (baʿḍin) | in ranks (darajātin), | so that He may test you (liyabluwakum) | in (fī) | what (mā) | He has given you (ātākum). | Indeed (inna), | your Lord (rabbaka) | is swift (sarīʿu) | in the punishment (l-ʿiqābi), | and indeed, He is (wa-innahu) | [certainly], Oft-Forgiving (laghafūrun), | Most Merciful (raḥīmun).

Chapter (7) Sūrat l-Aʿrāf (The Heights)

7:1 Alif Laam Meem Saad.

Alif Laam Meem Saad (alif-lam-meem-sad).

7:2 This is a Book revealed to you so let not be in your breast any uneasiness from it that you warn with it, and a reminder for the believers.

This is a Book (kitābun) | revealed (unzila) | to you (ilayka) | so let not (falā) | be (yakun) | in (fī) | your breast (ṣadrika) | any uneasiness (ḥarajun) | from it (min'hu) | that you warn (litundhira) | with it (bihi), | and a reminder (wadhik'rā) | for the believers (lil'mu'minīna).

7:3 Follow what has been revealed to you from your Lord, and do not follow from beside Him any allies. Little is what you remember.

Follow (ittabiʿū) | what (mā) | has been revealed (unzila) | to you (ilaykum) | from (min) | your Lord (rabbikum), | and do not (walā) | follow (tattabiʿū) | from (min) | beside Him (dūnihi) | any allies (awliyāa). | Little (qalīlan) | is what (mā) | you remember (tadhakkarūna).

7:4 And how many of a city We destroyed it, and came to it Our punishment at night or while they were sleeping at noon.

And how many (wakam) | of (min) | a city (qaryatin) | We destroyed it (ahlaknāhā), | and came to it (fajāahā) | Our punishment (basunā) | at night (bayātan) | or (aw) | while they (hum) | were sleeping at noon (qāilūna).

7:5 Then not was their plea when came to them Our punishment except that they said, "Indeed, we were wrongdoers."

Then not (famā) | was (kāna) | their plea (daʿwāhum) | when (idh) | came to them (jāahum) | Our punishment (basunā) | except (illā) | that (an) | they said (qālū), | "Indeed, we (innā) | were (kunnā) | wrongdoers. (ẓālimīna)"

7:6 Then surely We will question those to whom were sent to them Messengers, and surely We will question the Messengers.

Then surely We will question (falanasalanna) | those to whom (alladhīna) | were sent (ur'sila) | to them Messengers (ilayhim), | and surely We will question (walanasalanna) | the Messengers (l-mur'salīna).

7:7 Then surely We will narrate to them with knowledge, and not were We absent.

Then surely We will narrate (falanaquṣṣanna) | to them (ʿalayhim) | with knowledge (biʿil'min), | and not (wamā) | were We (kunnā) | absent (ghāibīna).

7:8 And the weighing that day will be the truth. So whose - will be heavy his scales, then those [they] will be the successful ones.

And the weighing (wal-waznu) | that day (yawma-idhin) | will be the truth (l-ḥaqu). | So whose (faman)- | will be heavy (thaqulat) | his scales (mawāzīnuhu), | then those (fa-ulāika) | [they] (humu) | will be the successful ones (l-muf'liḥūna).

7:9 And for those will be light his scales, so those will be the ones who lost, themselves because they were to Our Verses doing injustice.

And for those (waman) | will be light (khaffat) | his scales (mawāzīnuhu), | so those (fa-ulāika) | will be the ones who (alladhīna) | lost (khasirū), | themselves (anfusahum) | because (bimā) | they were (kānū) | to Our Verses (biāyātinā) | doing injustice (yaẓlimūna).

7:10 And certainly We established you in the earth and We made for you in it livelihood. Little is what you are grateful.

And certainly (walaqad) | We established you (makkannākum) | in (fī) | the earth (l-arḍi) | and We made (wajaʿalnā) | for you (lakum) | in it (fīhā) | livelihood (maʿāyisha). | Little (qalīlan) | is what (mā) | you are grateful (tashkurūna).

7:11 And certainly We created you then We fashioned you. Then We said to the Angels, "Prostrate to Adam," So they prostrated, except Iblis. Not he was of those who prostrated.

And certainly (walaqad) | We created you (khalaqnākum) | then (thumma) | We fashioned you (ṣawwarnākum). | Then (thumma) | We said (qul'nā) | to the Angels (lil'malāikati), | "Prostrate (us'judū) | to Adam, (liādama)" | So they prostrated (fasajadū), | except (illā) | Iblis (ib'līsa). | Not (lam) | he was (yakun) | of (mina) | those who prostrated (l-sājidīna).

7:12 Allah said, "What prevented you that not you prostrate when I commanded you?" Shaitaan said, "I am better than him. You created me from fire and You created him from clay."

Allah said (qāla), | "What (mā) | prevented you (manaʿaka) | that not (allā) | you prostrate (tasjuda) | when (idh) | I commanded you? (amartuka)" | Shaitaan said (qāla), | "I am (anā) | better (khayrun) | than him (min'hu). | You created me (khalaqtanī) | from (min) | fire (nārin) | and You created him (wakhalaqtahu) | from (min) | clay. (ṭīnin)"

7:13 Allah said, "Then go down from it, for not it is for you that you be arrogant in it. So get out; indeed, you are of the disgraced ones."

Allah said (qāla), | "Then go down (fa-ih'biṭ) | from it (min'hā), | for not (famā) | it is (yakūnu) | for you (laka) | that (an) | you be arrogant (tatakabbara) | in it (fīhā). | So get out (fa-ukh'ruj); | indeed, you (innaka) | are of (mina) | the disgraced ones. (l-ṣāghirīna)"

7:14 Shaitaan said, "Give me respite till the Day they are raised up."

Shaitaan said (qāla), | "Give me respite (anẓir'nī) | till (ilā) | the Day (yawmi) | they are raised up. (yub'ʿathūna)"

7:15 Allah said, "Indeed, you are of the ones given respite."

Allah said (qāla), | "Indeed, you (innaka) | are of (mina) | the ones given respite. (l-munẓarīna)"

7:16 Shaitaan said, "Because You have sent me astray, surely I will sit for them on Your path, the straight.

Shaitaan said (qāla), | "Because (fabimā) | You have sent me astray (aghwaytanī), | surely I will sit (la-aqʿudanna) | for them (lahum) | on Your path (ṣirāṭaka), | the straight (l-mus'taqīma).

7:17 Then surely, I will come to them from before them and from behind them and from their right and from their left, and not You will find most of them grateful."

Then (thumma) | surely, I will come to them (laātiyannahum) | from (min) | before (bayni) | them (aydīhim) | and from (wamin) | behind them (khalfihim) | and from (waʿan) | their right (aymānihim) | and from (waʿan) | their left (shamāilihim), | and not (walā) | You will find (tajidu) | most of them (aktharahum) | grateful. (shākirīna)"

7:18 Allah said, "Get out of it disgraced and expelled. Certainly, whoever follows you among them, surely, I will fill Hell with you all.

Allah said (qāla), | "Get out (ukh'ruj) | of it (min'hā) | disgraced (madhūman) | and expelled (madḥūran). | Certainly, whoever (laman) | follows you (tabiʿaka) | among them (min'hum), | surely, I will fill (la-amla-anna) | Hell (jahannama) | with you (minkum) | all (ajmaʿīna).

7:19 And O Adam! Dwell, you and your wife, in the Garden, and you both eat from wherever you both wish, but do not approach [both of you] this [the] tree lest you both be among the wrongdoers."

And O Adam (wayāādamu)! | Dwell (us'kun), | you (anta) | and your wife (wazawjuka), | in the Garden (l-janata), | and you both eat (fakulā) | from (min) | wherever (ḥaythu) | you both wish (shi'tumā), | but do not (walā) | approach [both of you] (taqrabā) | this (hādhihi) | [the] tree (l-shajarata) | lest you both be (fatakūnā) | among (mina) | the wrongdoers. (l-ẓālimīna)"

7:20 Then whispered to both of them the Shaitaan to make apparent to both of them what was concealed from both of them of their shame. And he said, "Did not forbid you both your Lord from this [the] tree except that you two become Angels or you two become of the immortals."

Then whispered (fawaswasa) | to both of them (lahumā) | the Shaitaan (l-shayṭānu) | to make apparent (liyub'diya) | to both of them (lahumā) | what (mā) | was concealed (wūriya) | from both of them (ʿanhumā) | of (min) | their shame (sawātihimā). | And he said (waqāla), | "Did not (mā) | forbid you both (nahākumā) | your Lord (rabbukumā) | from (ʿan) | this (hādhihi) | [the] tree (l-shajarati) | except (illā) | that (an) | you two become (takūnā) | Angels (malakayni) | or (aw) | you two become (takūnā) | of (mina) | the immortals. (l-khālidīna)"

7:21 And he swore to both of them, "Indeed, I am to both of you among the sincere advisors."

And he swore to both of them (waqāsamahumā), | "Indeed, I am (innī) | to both of you (lakumā) | among (lamina) | the sincere advisors. (l-nāṣiḥīna)"

7:22 So he made both of them fall by deception. Then when they both tasted the tree, became apparent to both of them their shame, and they began to fasten over themselves from the leaves of the Garden. And called them both their Lord, "Did not I forbid you both from this [the] tree and [I] say to both of you, that [the] Shaitaan to both of you is an enemy, open?"

So he made both of them fall (fadallāhumā) | by deception (bighurūrin). | Then when (falammā) | they both tasted (dhāqā) | the tree (l-shajarata), | became apparent (badat) | to both of them (lahumā) | their shame (sawātuhumā), | and they began (waṭafiqā) | to fasten (yakhṣifāni) | over themselves (ʿalayhimā) | from (min) | the leaves (waraqi) | of the Garden (l-janati). | And called them both (wanādāhumā) | their Lord (rabbuhumā), | "Did not (alam) | I forbid you both (anhakumā) | from (ʿan) | this (til'kumā) | [the] tree (l-shajarati) | and [I] say (wa-aqul) | to both of you (lakumā), | that (inna) | [the] Shaitaan (l-shayṭāna) | to both of you (lakumā) | is an enemy (ʿaduwwun), | open? (mubīnun)"

7:23 Both of them said, "Our Lord we have wronged ourselves, and if not You forgive [for] us and have mercy on us, surely, we will be among the losers."

Both of them said (qālā), | "Our Lord (rabbanā) | we have wronged (ẓalamnā) | ourselves (anfusanā), | and if (wa-in) | not (lam) | You forgive (taghfir) | [for] us (lanā) | and have mercy on us (watarḥamnā), | surely, we will be (lanakūnanna) | among (mina) | the losers. (l-khāsirīna)"

7:24 Allah said, "Get down some of you to some others as enemy. And for you in the earth is a dwelling place and livelihood for a time."

Allah said (qāla), | "Get down (ih'biṭū) | some of you (baʿḍukum) | to some others (libaʿḍin) | as enemy (ʿaduwwun). | And for you (walakum) | in (fī) | the earth (l-arḍi) | is a dwelling place (mus'taqarrun) | and livelihood (wamatāʿun) | for (ilā) | a time. (ḥīnin)"

7:25 He said, "In it you will live and in it you will die and from it you will be brought forth."

He said (qāla), | "In it (fīhā) | you will live (taḥyawna) | and in it (wafīhā) | you will die (tamūtūna) | and from it (wamin'hā) | you will be brought forth. (tukh'rajūna)"

7:26 O Children of Adam! Verily We have sent down to you clothing, it covers your shame and as an adornment. But the clothing of [the] righteousness - that is best. That is from the Signs of Allah so that they may remember.

O Children (yābanī) | of Adam (ādama)! | Verily (qad) | We have sent down (anzalnā) | to you (ʿalaykum) | clothing (libāsan), | it covers (yuwārī) | your shame (sawātikum) | and as an adornment (warīshan). | But the clothing (walibāsu) | of [the] righteousness (l-taqwā)- | that (dhālika) | is best (khayrun). | That (dhālika) | is from (min) | the Signs (āyāti) | of Allah (l-lahi) | so that they may (laʿallahum) | remember (yadhakkarūna).

7:27 O Children of Adam! Let not tempt you [the] Shaitaan as he drove out your parents from Paradise, stripping from both of them their clothing to show both of them their shame. Indeed, he sees you - he and his tribe from where not you see them. Indeed, We have made the devils friends of those who do not believe.

O Children (yābanī) | of Adam (ādama)! | Let not (lā) | tempt you (yaftinannakumu) | [the] Shaitaan (l-shayṭānu) | as (kamā) | he drove out (akhraja) | your parents (abawaykum) | from (mina) | Paradise (l-janati), | stripping (yanziʿu) | from both of them (ʿanhumā) | their clothing (libāsahumā) | to show both of them (liyuriyahumā) | their shame (sawātihimā). | Indeed, he (innahu) | sees you (yarākum)- | he (huwa) | and his tribe (waqabīluhu) | from (min) | where (ḥaythu) | not (lā) | you see them (tarawnahum). | Indeed (innā), | We have made (jaʿalnā) | the devils (l-shayāṭīna) | friends (awliyāa) | of those who (lilladhīna) | do not (lā) | believe (yu'minūna).

7:28 And when they do immorality they say, "We found on it our forefathers and Allah has ordered us of it." Say, "Indeed, Allah does not order immorality. Do you say about Allah what not you know?"

And when (wa-idhā) | they do (faʿalū) | immorality (fāḥishatan) | they say (qālū), | "We found (wajadnā) | on it (ʿalayhā) | our forefathers (ābāanā) | and Allah (wal-lahu) | has ordered us (amaranā) | of it. (bihā)" | Say (qul), | "Indeed (inna), | Allah (l-laha) | does not (lā) | order (yamuru) | immorality (bil-faḥshāi). | Do you say (ataqūlūna) | about (ʿalā) | Allah (l-lahi) | what (mā) | not (lā) | you know? (taʿlamūna)"

7:29 Say, "Has been ordered by my Lord, justice and set your faces at every masjid and invoke Him being sincere to Him in the religion. As He originated you so will you return."

Say (qul), | "Has been ordered (amara) | by my Lord (rabbī), | justice (bil-qis'ṭi) | and set (wa-aqīmū) | your faces (wujūhakum) | at (ʿinda) | every (kulli) | masjid (masjidin) | and invoke Him (wa-id'ʿūhu) | being sincere (mukh'liṣīna) | to Him (lahu) | in the religion (l-dīna). | As (kamā) | He originated you (bada-akum) | so will you return. (taʿūdūna)"

7:30 A group He guided and a group deserved - [on] they the astraying. Indeed, they take the devils as allies from besides Allah while they think that they are the guided-ones.

A group (farīqan) | He guided (hadā) | and a group (wafarīqan) | deserved (ḥaqqa)- | [on] they (ʿalayhimu) | the astraying (l-ḍalālatu). | Indeed, they (innahumu) | take (ittakhadhū) | the devils (l-shayāṭīna) | as allies (awliyāa) | from (min) | besides (dūni) | Allah (l-lahi) | while they think (wayaḥsabūna) | that they (annahum) | are the guided-ones (muh'tadūna).

7:31 O Children of Adam! Take your adornment at every masjid, and eat and drink but do not be extravagant. Indeed, He does not love the extravagant ones.

O Children (yābanī) | of Adam (ādama)! | Take (khudhū) | your adornment (zīnatakum) | at (ʿinda) | every (kulli) | masjid (masjidin), | and eat (wakulū) | and drink (wa-ish'rabū) | but do not (walā) | be extravagant (tus'rifū). | Indeed, He (innahu) | does not (lā) | love (yuḥibbu) | the extravagant ones (l-mus'rifīna).

7:32 Say, "Who has forbidden the adornment from Allah which He has brought forth for His slaves, and the pure things of sustenance?" Say, "They are for those who believe during the life of the world, exclusively for them on the Day of Resurrection. Thus We explain the Signs for the people who know."

Say (qul), | "Who (man) | has forbidden (ḥarrama) | the adornment (zīnata) | from Allah (l-lahi) | which (allatī) | He has brought forth (akhraja) | for His slaves (liʿibādihi), | and the pure things (wal-ṭayibāti) | of (mina) | sustenance? (l-riz'qi)" | Say (qul), | "They (hiya) | are for those who (lilladhīna) | believe (āmanū) | during (fī) | the life (l-ḥayati) | of the world (l-dun'yā), | exclusively for them (khāliṣatan) | on the Day (yawma) | of Resurrection (l-qiyāmati). | Thus (kadhālika) | We explain (nufaṣṣilu) | the Signs (l-āyāti) | for the people (liqawmin) | who know. (yaʿlamūna)"

7:33 Say, "Only had forbidden my Lord the shameful deeds what is apparent of it and what is concealed, and the sin, and the oppression without [the] right, and that you associate others with Allah what not He has sent down of it any authority, and that you say about Allah what not you know."

Say (qul), | "Only (innamā) | had forbidden (ḥarrama) | my Lord (rabbiya) | the shameful deeds (l-fawāḥisha) | what (mā) | is apparent (ẓahara) | of it (min'hā) | and what (wamā) | is concealed (baṭana), | and the sin (wal-ith'ma), | and the oppression (wal-baghya) | without (bighayri) | [the] right (l-ḥaqi), | and that (wa-an) | you associate others (tush'rikū) | with Allah (bil-lahi) | what (mā) | not (lam) | He has sent down (yunazzil) | of it (bihi) | any authority (sul'ṭānan), | and that (wa-an) | you say (taqūlū) | about (ʿalā) | Allah (l-lahi) | what (mā) | not (lā) | you know. (taʿlamūna)"

7:34 And for every nation is a fixed term. So when comes their term, they can not seek to delay an hour, and not seek to advance it.

And for every (walikulli) | nation (ummatin) | is a fixed term (ajalun). | So when (fa-idhā) |

comes (jāa) | their term (ajaluhum), | they can not (lā) | seek to delay (yastakhirūna) | an hour (sāʿatan), | and not (walā) | seek to advance it (yastaqdimūna).

7:35 O Children of Adam! If come to you Messengers from you relating to you My Verses, then whoever fears Allah, and reforms, then no fear on them and not they will grieve.

O Children (yābanī) | of Adam (ādama)! | If (immā) | come to you (yatiyannakum) | Messengers (rusulun) | from you (minkum) | relating (yaquṣṣūna) | to you (ʿalaykum) | My Verses (āyātī), | then whoever (famani) | fears Allah (ittaqā), | and reforms (wa-aṣlaḥa), | then no (falā) | fear (khawfun) | on them (ʿalayhim) | and not (walā) | they (hum) | will grieve (yaḥzanūna).

7:36 But those who deny Our Verses and are arrogant towards them those are the companions of the Fire, they in it will abide forever.

But those who (wa-alladhīna) | deny (kadhabū) | Our Verses (biāyātinā) | and are arrogant (wa-is'takbarū) | towards them (ʿanhā) | those (ulāika) | are the companions (aṣḥābu) | of the Fire (l-nāri), | they (hum) | in it (fīhā) | will abide forever (khālidūna).

7:37 Then who is more unjust than one who invented against Allah a lie or denies His Verses? Those - will reach them their portion from the Book, until when comes to them Our messengers Angels to take them in death they say, "Where are those whom you used to invoke from besides Allah?" They say, "They strayed from us," and they will testify against themselves that they were disbelievers.

Then who (faman) | is more unjust (aẓlamu) | than one who (mimmani) | invented (if'tarā) | against (ʿalā) | Allah (l-lahi) | a lie (kadhiban) | or (aw) | denies (kadhaba) | His Verses (biāyātihi)? | Those (ulāika)- | will reach them (yanāluhum) | their portion (naṣībuhum) | from (mina) | the Book (l-kitābi), | until (ḥattā) | when (idhā) | comes to them (jāathum) | Our messengers Angels (rusulunā) | to take them in death (yatawaffawnahum) | they say (qālū), | "Where are (ayna) | those whom (mā) | you used to (kuntum) | invoke (tadʿūna) | from (min) | besides (dūni) | Allah? (l-lahi)" | They say (qālū), | "They strayed (ḍallū) | from us, (ʿannā)" | and they will testify (washahidū) | against (ʿalā) | themselves (anfusihim) | that they (annahum) | were (kānū) | disbelievers (kāfirīna).

7:38 He will say, "Enter among the nations who passed away from before you of the jinn and the men in the Fire." Every time entered a nation it cursed its sister nation until when they had overtaken one another in it all, will say the last of them about the first of them, "Our Lord, these misled us so give them punishment, double, of the Fire." He will say, "For each is a double [and] but not you know."

He will say (qāla), | "Enter (ud'khulū) | among (fī) | the nations (umamin) | who (qad) | passed away (khalat) | from (min) | before you (qablikum) | of (mina) | the jinn (l-jini) | and the men (wal-insi) | in (fī) | the Fire. (l-nāri)" | Every time (kullamā) | entered (dakhalat) | a nation (ummatun) | it cursed (laʿanat) | its sister nation (ukh'tahā) | until (ḥattā) | when (idhā) | they had overtaken one another (iddārakū) | in it (fīhā) | all (jamīʿan), | will say (qālat) | the last of them (ukh'rāhum) | about the first of them (liūlāhum), | "Our Lord (rabbanā), | these (hāulāi) | misled us (aḍallūnā) | so give them (faātihim) | punishment (ʿadhāban), | double (ḍiʿ'fan), | of (mina) | the Fire. (l-nāri)" | He will say (qāla), | "For each (likullin) | is a double (ḍiʿ'fun) | [and] but (walākin) | not (lā) | you know. (taʿlamūna)"

7:39 And will say the first of them to the last of them, "Then not is for you upon us any superiority, so taste the punishment for what you used to earn."

And will say (waqālat) | the first of them (ūlāhum) | to the last of them (li-ukh'rāhum), | "Then not (famā) | is (kāna) | for you (lakum) | upon us (ʿalaynā) | any (min) | superiority (faḍlin), | so taste (fadhūqū) | the punishment (l-ʿadhāba) | for what (bimā) | you used to (kuntum) | earn. (taksibūna)"

7:40 Indeed, those who denied Our Verses and were arrogant towards them, will not be opened for them the doors of the heaven, and not they will enter Paradise until passes the camel through the eye of the needle. And thus We recompense the criminals.

Indeed (inna), | those who (alladhīna) | denied (kadhabū) | Our Verses (biāyātinā) | and were arrogant (wa-is'takbarū) | towards them (ʿanhā), | will not (lā) | be opened (tufattaḥu) | for them (lahum) | the doors (abwābu) | of the heaven (l-samāi), | and not (walā) | they will enter (yadkhulūna) | Paradise (l-janata) | until (ḥattā) | passes (yalija) | the camel (l-jamalu) | through (fī) | the eye (sammi) | of the needle (l-khiyāṭi). | And thus (wakadhālika) | We recompense (najzī) | the criminals (l-muj'rimīna).

7:41 For them of the Hell is a bed and from over them coverings. And thus We recompense the wrongdoers.

For them (lahum) | of (min) | the Hell (jahannama) | is a bed (mihādun) | and from (wamin) | over them (fawqihim) | coverings (ghawāshin). | And thus (wakadhālika) | We recompense (najzī) | the wrongdoers (l-ẓālimīna).

7:42 But those who believe and do [the] righteous deeds not We burden any soul except to its capacity. Those are the companions of Paradise, they in it will abide forever.

But those who (wa-alladhīna) | believe (āmanū) | and do (waʿamilū) | [the] righteous deeds (l-ṣāliḥāti) | not (lā) | We burden (nukallifu) | any soul (nafsan) | except (illā) | to its capacity (wus'ʿahā). | Those (ulāika) | are the companions (aṣḥābu) | of Paradise (l-janati), | they (hum) | in it (fīhā) | will abide forever (khālidūna).

7:43 And We will remove whatever is in their breasts of malice. Flows from underneath them the rivers. And they will say, "All the praise is for Allah, the One Who guided us to this, and not we were to receive guidance if not [that] had guided us Allah. Certainly, came Messengers of our Lord with the truth." And they will be addressed, [that] "This is Paradise, you have been made to inherit it for what you used to do."

And We will remove (wanazaʿnā) | whatever (mā) | is in (fī) | their breasts (ṣudūrihim) | of (min) | malice (ghillin). | Flows (tajrī) | from (min) | underneath them (taḥtihimu) | the rivers (l-anhāru). | And they will say (waqālū), | "All the praise (l-ḥamdu) | is for Allah (lillahi), | the One Who (alladhī) | guided us (hadānā) | to this (lihādhā), | and not (wamā) | we were (kunnā) | to receive guidance (linahtadiya) | if not (lawlā) | [that] (an) | had guided us (hadānā) | Allah (l-lahu). | Certainly (laqad), | came (jāat) | Messengers (rusulu) | of our Lord (rabbinā) | with the truth. (bil-ḥaqi)" | And they will be addressed (wanūdū), | [that] (an) | "This (til'kumu) | is Paradise (l-janatu), | you have been made to inherit it (ūrith'tumūhā) | for what (bimā) | you used to (kuntum) | do. (taʿmalūna)"

7:44 And will call out the companions of Paradise to the companions of the Fire that, "Indeed, we found what had promised us our Lord true. So have you found what was promised by your Lord to be true?" They will say, "Yes." Then will announce an announcer among them, [that] "The curse of Allah is on the wrongdoers,

And will call out (wanādā) | the companions (aṣḥābu) | of Paradise (l-janati) | to the companions (aṣḥāba) | of the Fire (l-nāri) | that (an), | "Indeed (qad), | we found (wajadnā) | what (mā) | had promised us (waʿadanā) | our Lord (rabbunā) | true (ḥaqqan). | So have (fahal) | you found (wajadttum) | what (mā) | was promised (waʿada) | by your Lord (rabbukum) | to be true? (ḥaqqan)" | They will say (qālū), | "Yes. (naʿam)" | Then will announce (fa-adhana) | an announcer (mu-adhinun) | among them (baynahum), | [that] (an) | "The curse (laʿnatu) | of Allah (l-lahi) | is on (ʿalā) | the wrongdoers (l-ẓālimīna),

7:45 Those who hinder from the way of Allah and seek in it crookedness while they are concerning the Hereafter, disbelievers."

Those who (alladhīna) | hinder (yaṣuddūna) | from (ʿan) | the way (sabīli) | of Allah (l-lahi) | and seek in it (wayabghūnahā) | crookedness (ʿiwajan) | while they are (wahum) | concerning the Hereafter (bil-ākhirati), | disbelievers. (kāfirūna)"

7:46 And between them will be a partition, and on the heights will be men recognizing all by their marks. And they will call out to the companions of Paradise that "Peace be upon you." Not they have entered it but they hope.

And between them (wabaynahumā) | will be a partition (ḥijābun), | and on (waʿalā) | the heights (l-aʿrāfi) | will be men (rijālun) | recognizing (yaʿrifūna) | all (kullan) | by their marks (bisīmāhum). | And they will call out (wanādaw) | to the companions (aṣḥāba) | of Paradise (l-janati) | that (an) | "Peace (salāmun) | be upon you. (ʿalaykum)" | Not (lam) | they have entered it (yadkhulūhā) | but they (wahum) | hope (yaṭmaʿūna).

7:47 And when are turned their eyes towards the companions of the Fire, they will say, "Our Lord! Do not place us with the people - the wrongdoers."

And when (wa-idhā) | are turned (ṣurifat) | their eyes (abṣāruhum) | towards (til'qāa) | the companions (aṣḥābi) | of the Fire (l-nāri), | they will say (qālū), | "Our Lord (rabbanā)! | Do not (lā) | place us (tajʿalnā) | with (maʿa) | the people (l-qawmi)- | the wrongdoers. (l-ẓālimīna)"

7:48 And will call out the companions of the heights to men whom they recognize by their marks saying, "Not has availed [to] you your gathering and what you were arrogant about."

And will call out (wanādā) | the companions (aṣḥābu) | of the heights (l-aʿrāfi) | to men (rijālan) | whom they recognize (yaʿrifūnahum) | by their marks (bisīmāhum) | saying (qālū), | "Not (mā) | has availed (aghnā) | [to] you (ʿankum) | your gathering (jamʿukum) | and what (wamā) | you were (kuntum) | arrogant about. (tastakbirūna)"

7:49 Are these the ones whom you had sworn that not will grant them Allah Mercy? "Enter Paradise. There will be no fear upon you and not you will grieve."

Are these (ahāulāi) | the ones whom (alladhīna) | you had sworn (aqsamtum) | that not (lā) | will grant them (yanāluhumu) | Allah (l-lahu) | Mercy (biraḥmatin)? | "Enter (ud'khulū) | Paradise (l-janata). | There will be no (lā) | fear (khawfun) | upon you (ʿalaykum) | and not (walā) | you (antum) | will grieve. (taḥzanūna)"

7:50 And will call out the companions of the Fire to the companions of Paradise [that], "Pour upon us [of] some water or of what has been provided (to) you by Allah." They will say, "Indeed, Allah has forbidden both to the disbelievers,

And will call out (wanādā) | the companions (aṣḥābu) | of the Fire (l-nāri) | to the companions (aṣḥāba) | of Paradise (l-janati) | [that] (an), | "Pour (afīḍū) | upon us (ʿalaynā) | [of] (mina) | some water (l-māi) | or (aw) | of what (mimmā) | has been provided (to) you (razaqakumu) | by Allah. (l-lahu)" | They will say (qālū), | "Indeed (inna), | Allah (l-laha) | has forbidden both (ḥarramahumā) | to (ʿalā) | the disbelievers (l-kāfirīna),

7:51 Those who took their religion as an amusement and play and deluded them the life of the world." So today We forget them as they forgot the meeting of their day, this, and [what] as they used to with Our Verses they reject.

Those who (alladhīna) | took (ittakhadhū) | their religion (dīnahum) | as an amusement (lahwan) | and play (walaʿiban) | and deluded them (wagharrathumu) | the life (l-ḥayatu) | of the world. (l-dun'yā)" | So today (fal-yawma) | We forget them (nansāhum) | as (kamā) | they forgot (nasū) | the meeting (liqāa) | of their day (yawmihim), | this (hādhā), | and [what] (wamā) | as they used to (kānū) | with Our Verses (biāyātinā) | they reject (yajḥadūna).

7:52 And certainly We had brought them a Book which We have explained with knowledge - as guidance and mercy for a people who believe.

And certainly (walaqad) | We had brought them (ji'nāhum) | a Book (bikitābin) | which We have explained (faṣṣalnāhu) | with (ʿalā) | knowledge ('il'min)- | as guidance (hudan) | and mercy (waraḥmatan) | for a people (liqawmin) | who believe (yu'minūna).

7:53 Do they wait except for its fulfillment The Day will come its fulfillment, will say those who had forgotten it from before, "Verily had come the Messengers of our Lord with the truth, so are there for us any intercessors so that they intercede for us or we are sent back so that we do (deeds) other than that which we used to do." Verily, they lost themselves, and strayed from them what they used to invent.

Do (hal) | they wait (yanẓurūna) | except (illā) | for its fulfillment (tawīlahu) | The Day (yawma) | will come (yatī) | its fulfillment (tawīluhu), | will say (yaqūlu) | those who (alladhīna) | had forgotten it (nasūhu) | from (min) | before (qablu), | "Verily (qad) | had come (jāat) | the Messengers (rusulu) | of our Lord (rabbinā) | with the truth (bil-ḥaqi), | so are there (fahal) | for us (lanā) | any (min) | intercessors (shufaʿāa) | so that they intercede (fayashfaʿū) | for us (lanā) | or (aw) | we are sent back (nuraddu) | so that we do (deeds (fanaʿmala)) | other than (ghayra) | that which (alladhī) | we used to (kunnā) | do. (naʿmalu)" | Verily (qad), | they lost (khasirū) | themselves (anfusahum), | and strayed (waḍalla) | from them (ʿanhum) | what (mā) | they used to (kānū) | invent (yaftarūna).

7:54 Indeed, your Lord is Allah the One Who created the heavens and the earth in six epochs, then He ascended on the Throne. He covers the night with the day seeking it rapidly and the sun and the moon and the stars - subjected by His command. Unquestionably for Him is the creation and the command, blessed is Allah, Lord of the worlds.

Indeed (inna), | your Lord (rabbakumu) | is Allah (l-lahu) | the One Who (alladhī) | created (khalaqa) | the heavens (l-samāwāti) | and the earth (wal-arḍa) | in (fī) | six (sittati) | epochs (ayyāmin), | then (thumma) | He ascended (is'tawā) | on (ʿalā) | the Throne (l-ʿarshi). | He covers (yugh'shī) | the night (al-layla) | with the day (l nahāra) | seeking it (yaṭlubuhu) | rapidly (ḥathīthan) | and the sun (wal-shamsa) | and the moon (wal-qamara) | and the stars (wal-nujūma)- | subjected (musakharātin) | by His command (bi-amrihi). | Unquestionably (alā) | for Him (lahu) | is the creation (l-khalqu) | and the command (wal-amru), | blessed (tabāraka) | is Allah (l-lahu), | Lord (rabbu) | of the worlds (l-ʿālamīna).

7:55 Call upon your Lord humbly and privately. Indeed, He does not love the transgressors.

Call upon (id'ʿū) | your Lord (rabbakum) | humbly (taḍarruʿan) | and privately (wakhuf'yatan). | Indeed, He (innahu) | does not (lā) | love (yuḥibbu) | the transgressors (l-muʿ'tadīna).

7:56 And do not cause corruption in the earth after its reformation. And call Him in fear and hope. Indeed, the Mercy of Allah is near for the good-doers.

And do not (walā) | cause corruption (tuf'sidū) | in (fī) | the earth (l-arḍi) | after (baʿda) | its reformation (iṣ'lāḥihā). | And call Him (wa-id'ʿūhu) | in fear (khawfan) | and hope (waṭamaʿan). | Indeed (inna), | the Mercy (raḥmata) | of Allah (l-lahi) | is near (qarībun) | for (mina) | the good-doers (l-muḥ'sinīna).

7:57 And He is the One Who sends the winds as glad tidings from before His Mercy, until, when they have carried clouds - heavy, We drive them to a land, dead, then We send down from it the water then We bring forth from it of all kinds of fruits. Thus We will bring forth the dead so that you may take heed.

And He (wahuwa) | is the One Who (alladhī) | sends (yur'silu) | the winds (l-riyāḥa) | as glad tidings (bush'ran) | from (bayna) | before (yaday) | His Mercy (raḥmatihi), | until (ḥattā), | when (idhā) | they have carried (aqallat) | clouds (saḥāban)- | heavy (thiqālan), | We drive them (suq'nāhu) | to a land (libaladin), | dead (mayyitin), | then We send down (fa-anzalnā) | from it (bihi) | the water (l-māa) | then We bring forth (fa-akhrajnā) | from it (bihi) | of (min) | all kinds (kulli) | of fruits (l-thamarāti). | Thus (kadhālika) | We will bring forth (nukh'riju) | the dead (l-mawtā) | so that you may (laʿallakum) | take heed (tadhakkarūna).

7:58 And the land - [the] pure, comes forth its vegetation by the permission of its Lord, but which is bad - does not come forth except with difficulty. Thus We explain the Signs for a people who are grateful.

And the land (wal-baladu)- | [the] pure (l-ṭayibu), | comes forth (yakhruju) | its vegetation (nabātuhu) | by the permission (bi-idh'ni) | of its Lord (rabbihi), | but which (wa-alladhī) | is bad (khabutha)- | does not (lā) | come forth (yakhruju) | except (illā) | with difficulty (nakidan). | Thus (kadhālika) | We explain (nuṣarrifu) | the Signs (l-āyāti) | for a people (liqawmin) | who are grateful (yashkurūna).

7:59 Certainly, We sent Nuh to his people and he said, "O my people! Worship Allah, not for you any god other than Him. Indeed, I [I] fear for you punishment of the Day Great."

Certainly (laqad), | We sent (arsalnā) | Nuh (nūḥan) | to (ilā) | his people (qawmihi) | and he said (faqāla), | "O my people (yāqawmi)! | Worship (uʿ'budū) | Allah (l-laha), | not (mā) | for you (lakum) | any (min) | god (ilāhin) | other than Him (ghayruhu). | Indeed, I (innī) | [I] fear (akhāfu) | for you (ʿalaykum) | punishment (ʿadhāba) | of the Day (yawmin) | Great. (ʿaẓīmin)"

7:60 Said the chiefs of his people, "Indeed, we surely see you in error, clear."

Said (qāla) | the chiefs (l-mala-u) | of (min) | his people (qawmihi), | "Indeed, we (innā) | surely see you (lanarāka) | in (fī) | error (ḍalālin), | clear. (mubīnin)"

7:61 He said, "O my people! There is not in me error, but I am a Messenger from the Lord of the worlds.

He said (qāla), | "O my people (yāqawmi)! | There is not (laysa) | in me (bī) | error (ḍalālatun), | but I am (walākinnī) | a Messenger (rasūlun) | from (min) | the Lord (rabbi) | of the worlds (l-ʿālamīna).

7:62 I convey to you the Messages of my Lord and [I] advise [to] you, and I know from Allah what not you know.

I convey to you (uballighukum) | the Messages (risālāti) | of my Lord (rabbī) | and [I] advise (wa-anṣaḥu) | [to] you (lakum), | and I know (wa-aʿlamu) | from (mina) | Allah (l-lahi) | what (mā) | not (lā) | you know (taʿlamūna).

7:63 Do you wonder that has come to you a reminder from your Lord on a man among you, that he may warn you and that you may fear, and so that you may receive mercy."

Do you wonder (awaʿajib'tum) | that (an) | has come to you (jāakum) | a reminder (dhik'run) | from (min) | your Lord (rabbikum) | on (ʿalā) | a man (rajulin) | among you (minkum), | that he may warn you (liyundhirakum) | and that you may fear (walitattaqū), | and so that you may (walaʿallakum) | receive mercy. (tur'ḥamūna)"

7:64 But they denied him, so We saved him and those who were with him in the ship. And We drowned those who denied Our Verses. Indeed, they were a people blind.

But they denied him (fakadhabūhu), | so We saved him (fa-anjaynāhu) | and those who (wa-alladhīna) | were with him (maʿahu) | in (fī) | the ship (l-ful'ki). | And We drowned (wa-aghraqnā) | those who (alladhīna) | denied (kadhabū) | Our Verses (biāyātinā). | Indeed, they (innahum) | were (kānū) | a people (qawman) | blind (ʿamīna).

7:65 And to Aad We sent their brother Hud. He said, "O my people! Worship Allah, not for you any god other than Him. Then will not you fear Allah?"

And to (wa-ilā) | Aad (ʿādin) | We sent their brother (akhāhum) | Hud (hūdan). | He said (qāla), | "O my people (yāqawmi)! | Worship (uʿ'budū) | Allah (l-laha), | not (mā) | for you (lakum) | any (min) | god (ilāhin) | other than Him (ghayruhu). | Then will not (afalā) | you fear Allah? (tattaqūna)"

7:66 Said the chiefs of those who disbelieved from his people, "Indeed, we surely, see you in foolishness and indeed, we [we] think you are of the liars."

Said (qāla) | the chiefs (l-mala-u) | of those who (alladhīna) | disbelieved (kafarū) | from (min) | his people (qawmihi), | "Indeed, we (innā) | surely, see you (lanarāka) | in (fī) | foolishness (safāhatin) | and indeed, we (wa-innā) | [we] think you (lanaẓunnuka) | are of (mina) | the liars. (l-kādhibīna)"

7:67 He said, "O my people! There is not in me foolishness, but I am a Messenger from the Lord of the worlds.

He said (qāla), | "O my people (yāqawmi)! | There is not (laysa) | in me (bī) | foolishness (safāhatun), | but I am (walākinnī) | a Messenger (rasūlun) | from (min) | the Lord (rabbi) | of the worlds (l-ʿālamīna).

7:68 I convey to you Messages of my Lord and I am to you an adviser - trustworthy.

I convey to you (uballighukum) | Messages (risālāti) | of my Lord (rabbī) | and I am (wa-anā) | to you (lakum) | an adviser (nāṣiḥun)- | trustworthy (amīnun).

7:69 Do you wonder that has come to you a reminder from your Lord on a man among you that he may warn you? And remember when He made you successors from after the people of Nuh, and increased you in the stature extensively. So remember the Bounties of Allah so that you may succeed."

Do you wonder (awaʿajib'tum) | that (an) | has come to you (jāakum) | a reminder (dhik'run) | from (min) | your Lord (rabbikum) | on (ʿalā) | a man (rajulin) | among you (minkum) | that he may warn you (liyundhirakum)? | And remember (wa-udh'kurū) | when (idh) | He made you (jaʿalakum) | successors (khulafāa) | from (min) | after (baʿdi) | the people (qawmi) | of Nuh (nūḥin), | and increased you (wazādakum) | in (fī) | the stature (l-khalqi) | extensively (baṣ'ṭatan). | So remember (fa-udh'kurū) | the Bounties (ālāa) | of Allah (l-lahi) | so that you may (laʿallakum) | succeed. (tuf'liḥūna)"

7:70 They said, "Have you come to us that we should worship Allah Alone and we forsake what used to worship our forefathers? Then bring us of what you promise us, if you are of the truthful."

They said (qālū), | "Have you come to us (aji'tanā) | that we should worship (linaʿbuda) | Allah (l-laha) | Alone (waḥdahu) | and we forsake (wanadhara) | what (mā) | used to (kāna) | worship (yaʿbudu) | our forefathers (ābāunā)? | Then bring us (fatinā) | of what (bimā) | you promise us (taʿidunā), | if (in) | you are (kunta) | of (mina) | the truthful. (l-ṣādiqīna)"

7:71 He said, "Verily has fallen upon you from your Lord punishment and anger. Do you dispute with me concerning names you have named them - you and your forefathers Not has been sent down by Allah for it any authority? Then wait, indeed, I am with you of the ones who wait.

He said (qāla), | "Verily (qad) | has fallen (waqaʿa) | upon you (ʿalaykum) | from (min) | your Lord (rabbikum) | punishment (rij'sun) | and anger (waghaḍabun). | Do you dispute with me (atujādilūnanī) | concerning (fī) | names (asmāin) | you have named them (sammaytumūhā)- | you (antum) | and your forefathers (waābāukum) | Not (mā) | has been sent down (nazzala) | by Allah (l-lahu) | for it (bihā) | any (min) | authority (sul'ṭānin)? | Then wait (fa-intaẓirū), | indeed, I am (innī) | with you (maʿakum) | of (mina) | the ones who wait (l-muntaẓirīna).

7:72 So We saved him and those with him by Mercy from Us. And We cut off the roots of those who denied Our Signs, and not they were believers.

So We saved him (fa-anjaynāhu) | and those (wa-alladhīna) | with him (maʿahu) | by Mercy (biraḥmatin) | from Us (minnā). | And We cut off (waqaṭaʿnā) | the roots (dābira) | of those who (alladhīna) | denied (kadhabū) | Our Signs (biāyātinā), | and not (wamā) | they were (kānū) | believers (mu'minīna).

7:73 And to Thamud We sent their brother Salih. He said, "O my people! Worship Allah, not for you any god other than Him. Verily has come to you a clear proof from your Lord, This is a she-camel of Allah it is for you a Sign. So you leave her to eat on the earth of Allah, and do not touch her with harm, lest seizes you a punishment painful."

And to (wa-ilā) | Thamud (thamūda) | We sent their brother (akhāhum) | Salih (ṣāliḥan). | He said (qāla), | "O my people (yāqawmi)! | Worship (uʿ'budū) | Allah (l-laha), | not (mā) | for you (lakum) | any (min) | god (ilāhin) | other than Him (ghayruhu). | Verily (qad) | has come to you (jāatkum) | a clear proof (bayyinatun) | from (min) | your Lord (rabbikum), | This (hādhihi) | is a she-camel (nāqatu) | of Allah (l-lahi) | it is for you (lakum) | a Sign (āyatan). | So you leave her (fadharūhā) | to eat (takul) | on (fī) | the earth (arḍi) | of Allah (l-lahi), | and do not (walā) | touch her (tamassūhā) | with harm (bisūin), | lest seizes you (fayakhudhakum) | a punishment (ʿadhābun) | painful. (alīmun)"

7:74 And remember when He made you successors from after Aad, and settled you in the earth. You take from its plains palaces and you carve out the mountains as homes. So remember the Bounties of Allah and do not act wickedly in the earth spreading corruption.

And remember (wa-udh'kurū) | when (idh) | He made you (jaʿalakum) | successors (khulafāa) | from (min) | after (baʿdi) | Aad (ʿādin), | and settled you (wabawwa-akum) | in (fī) | the earth (l-arḍi). | You take (tattakhidhūna) | from (min) | its plains (suhūlihā) | palaces (quṣūran) | and you carve out (watanḥitūna) | the mountains (l-jibāla) | as homes (buyūtan). | So remember (fa-udh'kurū) | the Bounties (ālāa) | of Allah (l-lahi) | and do not (walā) | act wickedly (taʿthaw) | in (fī) | the earth (l-arḍi) | spreading corruption (muf'sidīna).

7:75 Said the chiefs - those who were arrogant among his people, to those who were oppressed - [to] those who believed among them, "Do you know that Salih is the one sent from his Lord?" They said, "Indeed, we in what he has been sent with [it] are believers."

Said (qāla) | the chiefs (l-mala-u) | - those (alladhīna) | who were arrogant (is'takbarū) | among (min) | his people (qawmihi), | to those who (lilladhīna) | were oppressed (us'tuḍʿifū)- | [to] those who (liman) | believed (āmana) | among them (min'hum), | "Do you know (ataʿlamūna) | that (anna) | Salih (ṣāliḥan) | is the one sent (mur'salun) | from (min) | his Lord? (rabbihi)" | They said (qālū), | "Indeed, we (innā) | in what (bimā) | he has been sent (ur'sila) | with [it] (bihi) | are believers. (mu'minūna)"

7:76 Said those who were arrogant, "Indeed we, in that which you believe in it are disbelievers."

Said (qāla) | those who (alladhīna) | were arrogant (is'takbarū), | "Indeed we (innā), | in that which (bi-alladhī) | you believe (āmantum) | in it (bihi) | are disbelievers. (kāfirūna)"

7:77 Then they hamstrung the she-camel and were insolent towards the command of their Lord and they said, "O Salih! Bring us what you promise us if you are of the Messengers."

Then they hamstrung (faʿaqarū) | the she-camel (l-nāqata) | and were insolent (waʿataw) | towards (ʿan) | the command (amri) | of their Lord (rabbihim) | and they said (waqālū), | "O Salih (yāṣāliḥu)! | Bring us (i'tinā) | what (bimā) | you promise us (taʿidunā) | if (in) | you are (kunta) | of (mina) | the Messengers. (l-mur'salīna)"

7:78 So seized them the earthquake, then they became in their homes fallen prone.

So seized them (fa-akhadhathumu) | the earthquake (l-rajfatu), | then they became (fa-aṣbaḥū) | in (fī) | their homes (dārihim) | fallen prone (jāthimīna).

7:79 So he turned away from them and he said, "O my people! Verily, I have conveyed to you the Message of my Lord and [I] advised [to] you but not you like the advisers."

So he turned away (fatawallā) | from them (ʿanhum) | and he said (waqāla), | "O my people (yāqawmi)! | Verily (laqad), | I have conveyed to you (ablaghtukum) | the Message (risālata) | of my Lord (rabbī) | and [I] advised (wanaṣaḥtu) | [to] you (lakum) | but (walākin) | not (lā) | you like (tuḥibbūna) | the advisers. (l-nāṣiḥīna)"

7:80 And Lut, when he said to his people, "Do you commit such immorality not has preceded you therein any one of the worlds?

And Lut (walūṭan), | when (idh) | he said (qāla) | to his people (liqawmihi), | "Do you commit (atatūna) | such immorality (l-fāḥishata) | not (mā) | has preceded you (sabaqakum) | therein (bihā) | any (min) | one (aḥadin) | of (mina) | the worlds (l-ʿālamīna)?

7:81 Indeed, you you approach the men lustfully from instead of the women. Nay, you are a people who commit excesses."

Indeed, you (innakum) | you approach (latatūna) | the men (l-rijāla) | lustfully (shahwatan) | from (min) | instead of (dūni) | the women (l-nisāi). | Nay (bal), | you (antum) | are a people (qawmun) | who commit excesses. (mus'rifūna)"

7:82 And not was the answer of his people except that they said, "Drive them out of your town. Indeed, they are people who keep themselves pure."

And not (wamā) | was (kāna) | the answer (jawāba) | of his people (qawmihi) | except (illā) | that (an) | they said (qālū), | "Drive them out (akhrijūhum) | of (min) | your town (qaryatikum). | Indeed, they (innahum) | are people (unāsun) | who keep themselves pure. (yataṭahharūna)"

7:83 So We saved him and his family except his wife, she was of those who stayed behind.

So We saved him (fa-anjaynāhu) | and his family (wa-ahlahu) | except (illā) | his wife (im'ra-atahu), | she was (kānat) | of (mina) | those who stayed behind (l-ghābirīna).

7:84 And We showered upon them a rain. So see how was the end of the criminals.

And We showered (wa-amṭarnā) | upon them (ʿalayhim) | a rain (maṭaran). | So see (fa-unẓur) | how (kayfa) | was (kāna) | the end (ʿāqibatu) | of the criminals (l-muj'rimīna).

7:85 And to Madyan, his brother Shuaib. He said, "O my people! Worship Allah, not for you any god other than Him. Verily, has came to you a clear proof from your Lord. So give full [the] measure and the weight and do not deprive [the] people in their things and do not cause corruption in the earth after its reformation. That is better for you if you are believers.

And to (wa-ilā) | Madyan (madyana), | his brother (akhāhum) | Shuaib (shuʿayban). | He said (qāla), | "O my people (yāqawmi)! | Worship (uʿbudū) | Allah (l-laha), | not (mā) | for you (lakum) | any (min) | god (ilāhin) | other than Him (ghayruhu). | Verily (qad), | has came to you (jāatkum) | a clear proof (bayyinatun) | from (min) | your Lord (rabbikum). | So give full (fa-awfū) | [the] measure (l-kayla) | and the weight (wal-mīzāna) | and do not (walā) | deprive (tabkhasū) | [the] people (l-nāsa) | in their things (ashyāahum) | and do not (walā) | cause corruption (tuf'sidū) | in (fī) | the earth (l-arḍi) | after (baʿda) | its reformation (iṣ'lāḥihā). | That (dhālikum) | is better (khayrun) | for you (lakum) | if (in) | you are (kuntum) | believers (mu'minīna).

7:86 And do not sit on every path threatening and hindering from the way of Allah those who believe in Him, and seeking to make it crooked. And remember when you were few and He increased you. And see how was the end of the corrupters.

And do not (walā) | sit (taqʿudū) | on every (bikulli) | path (ṣirāṭin) | threatening (tūʿidūna) | and hindering (wataṣuddūna) | from (ʿan) | the way (sabīli) | of Allah (l-lahi) | those who (man) | believe (āmana) | in Him (bihi), | and seeking to make it (watabghūnahā) | crooked (ʿiwajan). | And remember (wa-udh'kurū) | when (idh) | you were (kuntum) | few (qalīlan) | and He increased you (fakatharakum). | And see (wa-unẓurū) | how (kayfa) | was (kāna) | the end (ʿāqibatu) | of the corrupters (l-muf'sidīna).

7:87 And if there is a group among you who has believed in that which I have been sent with [it], and a group not they believe, then be patient until judges Allah between us. And He is the Best of [the] Judges."

And if (wa-in) | there is (kāna) | a group (ṭāifatun) | among you (minkum) | who has believed (āmanū) | in that which (bi-alladhī) | I have been sent (ur'sil'tu) | with [it] (bihi), | and a group (waṭāifatun) | not (lam) | they believe (yu'minū), | then be patient (fa-iṣ'birū) | until (ḥattā) | judges (yaḥkuma) | Allah (l-lahu) | between us (baynanā). | And He (wahuwa) | is the Best (khayru) | of [the] Judges. (l-ḥākimīna)"

7:88 Said the chiefs of those who were arrogant among his people, "We will surely drive you out O Shuaib! And those who have believed with you from our city, or you must return to our religion." He said, "Even if we are the ones who hate (it)?

Said (qāla) | the chiefs (l-mala-u) | of those who (alladhīna) | were arrogant (is'takbarū) | among (min) | his people (qawmihi), | "We will surely drive you out (lanukh'rijannaka) | O Shuaib (yāshuʿaybu)! | And those who (wa-alladhīna) | have believed (āmanū) | with you (maʿaka) | from (min) | our city (qaryatinā), | or (aw) | you must return (lataʿūdunna) | to (fī) | our religion. (millatinā)" | He said (qāla), | "Even if (awalaw) | we are (kunnā) | the ones who hate (it) (kārihīna)?

7:89 Verily, we would have fabricated against Allah a lie if we returned in your religion after [when] saved us Allah from it. And not it is for us that we return in it except that wills Allah - our Lord. Encompasses by Our Lord every thing in knowledge. Upon Allah we put our trust. Our Lord! Decide between us and between our people in truth and You are the Best of those who Decide."

Verily (qadi), | we would have fabricated (if'taraynā) | against (ʿalā) | Allah (l-lahi) | a lie (kadhiban) | if (in) | we returned (ʿud'nā) | in (fī) | your religion (millatikum) | after (baʿda) | [when] (idh) | saved us (najjānā) | Allah (l-lahu) | from it (min'hā). | And not (wamā) | it is (yakūnu) | for us (lanā) | that (an) | we return (naʿūda) | in it (fīhā) | except (illā) | that (an) | wills (yashāa) | Allah (l-lahu)- | our Lord (rabbunā). | Encompasses (wasiʿa) | by Our Lord (rabbunā) | every (kulla) | thing (shayin) | in knowledge (ʿil'man). | Upon (ʿalā) | Allah (l-lahi) | we put our trust (tawakkalnā). | Our Lord (rabbanā)! | Decide (if'taḥ) | between us (baynanā) | and between (wabayna) | our people (qawminā) | in truth (bil-ḥaqi) | and You (wa-anta) | are the Best (khayru) | of those who Decide. (l-fātiḥīna)"

7:90 And said the chiefs of those who disbelieved among his people, "If you follow Shuaib, indeed, you then will be certainly losers."

And said (waqāla) | the chiefs (l-mala-u) | of those who (alladhīna) | disbelieved (kafarū) | among (min) | his people (qawmihi), | "If (la-ini) | you follow (ittabaʿtum) | Shuaib (shuʿayban), | indeed, you (innakum) | then (idhan) | will be certainly losers. (lakhāsirūna)"

7:91 Then seized them the earthquake, then they became in their homes fallen prone.

Then seized them (fa-akhadhathumu) | the earthquake (l-rajfatu), | then they became (fa-aṣbaḥū) | in (fī) | their homes (dārihim) | fallen prone (jāthimīna).

7:92 Those who denied Shuaib became as if not they had lived therein. Those who denied Shuaib, they were them the losers.

Those who (alladhīna) | denied (kadhabū) | Shuaib (shuʿayban) | became as if (ka-an) | not (lam) | they had lived (yaghnaw) | therein (fīhā). | Those who (alladhīna) | denied (kadhabū) | Shuaib (shuʿayban), | they were (kānū) | them (humu) | the losers (l-khāsirīna).

7:93 So he turned away from them and said, "O my people! Verily, I have conveyed to you the Messages of my Lord and advised [to] you. So how could I grieve for a people who are disbelievers?"

So he turned away (fatawallā) | from them (ʿanhum) | and said (waqāla), | "O my people (yāqawmi)! | Verily (laqad), | I have conveyed to you (ablaghtukum) | the Messages (risālāti) | of my Lord (rabbī) | and advised (wanaṣaḥtu) | [to] you (lakum). | So how could (fakayfa) | I grieve (āsā) | for (ʿalā) | a people (qawmin) | who are disbelievers? (kāfirīna)"

7:94 And not We sent in a city any Prophet except We seized its people with adversity and hardship, so that they may become humble.

And not (wamā) | We sent (arsalnā) | in (fī) | a city (qaryatin) | any (min) | Prophet (nabiyyin) | except (illā) | We seized (akhadhnā) | its people (ahlahā) | with adversity (bil-basāi) | and hardship (wal-ḍarāi), | so that they may (laʿallahum) | become humble (yaḍḍarraʿūna).

7:95 Then We changed in place of the bad the good, until they increased and said, "Verily, had touched our forefathers the adversity and the ease." So We seized them suddenly, while they did not perceive.

Then (thumma) | We changed (baddalnā) | in place (makāna) | of the bad (l-sayi-ati) | the good (l-ḥasanata), | until (ḥattā) | they increased (ʿafaw) | and said (waqālū), | "Verily (qad), | had touched (massa) | our forefathers (ābāanā) | the adversity (l-ḍarāu) | and the ease. (wal-sarāu)" | So We seized them (fa-akhadhnāhum) | suddenly (baghtatan), | while they (wahum) | did not (lā) | perceive (yashʿurūna).

7:96 And if [that] people of the cities had believed and feared Allah surely We would have opened upon them blessings from the heaven and the earth but they denied. So We seized them for what they used to earn.

And if (walaw) | [that] (anna) | people (ahla) | of the cities (l-qurā) | had believed (āmanū) | and feared Allah (wa-ittaqaw) | surely We would have opened (lafataḥnā) | upon them (ʿalayhim) | blessings (barakātin) | from (mina) | the heaven (l-samāi) | and the earth (wal-arḍi) | but (walākin) | they denied (kadhabū). | So We seized them (fa-akhadhnāhum) | for what (bimā) | they used to (kānū) | earn (yaksibūna).

7:97 Then did feel secure the people of the cities that comes to them Our punishment at night while they were asleep?

Then did feel secure (afa-amina) | the people (ahlu) | of the cities (l-qurā) | that (an) | comes to them (yatiyahum) | Our punishment (basunā) | at night (bayātan) | while they (wahum) | were asleep (nāimūna)?

7:98 Or felt secure the people of the cities that comes to them Our punishment in daylight while they were playing?

Or felt secure (awa-amina) | the people (ahlu) | of the cities (l-qurā) | that (an) | comes to them (yatiyahum) | Our punishment (basunā) | in daylight (ḍuḥan) | while they (wahum) | were playing (yalʿabūna)?

7:99 Then did they feel secure from the plan of Allah? But not feel secure from the plan of Allah except the people who are the losers.

Then did they feel secure (afa-aminū) | from the plan (makra) | of Allah (l-lahi)? | But not (falā) | feel secure (yamanu) | from the plan (makra) | of Allah (l-lahi) | except (illā) | the people (l-qawmu) | who are the losers (l-khāsirūna).

7:100 Would it not guide [for] those who inherit the land from after its people that if We willed, We could afflict them for their sins and We put a seal over their hearts so they do not hear?

Would it not (awalam) | guide (yahdi) | [for] those who (lilladhīna) | inherit (yarithūna) | the land (l-arḍa) | from (min) | after (baʿdi) | its people (ahlihā) | that (an) | if (law) | We willed (nashāu), | We could afflict them (aṣabnāhum) | for their sins (bidhunūbihim) | and We put a seal (wanaṭbaʿu) | over (ʿalā) | their hearts (qulūbihim) | so they (fahum) | do not (lā) | hear (yasmaʿūna)?

7:101 These were the cities - We relate to you of their news. And certainly came to them their Messengers with clear proofs, but not they were to believe in what they had denied from before. Thus has been put a seal by Allah on the hearts of the disbelievers.

These (til'ka) | were the cities (l-qurā)- | We relate (naquṣṣu) | to you (ʿalayka) | of (min) | their news (anbāihā). | And certainly (walaqad) | came to them (jāathum) | their Messengers (rusuluhum) | with clear proofs (bil-bayināti), | but not (famā) | they were (kānū) | to believe (liyu'minū) | in what (bimā) | they had denied (kadhabū) | from (min) | before (qablu). | Thus (kadhālika) | has been put a seal (yaṭbaʿu) | by Allah (l-lahu) | on (ʿalā) | the hearts (qulūbi) | of the disbelievers (l-kāfirīna).

7:102 And not We found for most of them any covenant. But We found most of them certainly, defiantly disobedient.

And not (wamā) | We found (wajadnā) | for most of them (li-aktharihim) | any (min) | covenant (ʿahdin). | But (wa-in) | We found (wajadnā) | most of them (aktharahum) | certainly, defiantly disobedient (lafāsiqīna).

7:103 Then We sent from after them Musa with Our Signs to Firaun and his chiefs, But they were unjust to them. So see how was the end of the corrupters.

Then (thumma) | We sent (baʿathnā) | from (min) | after them (baʿdihim) | Musa (mūsā) | with Our Signs (biāyātinā) | to (ilā) | Firaun (firʿawna) | and his chiefs (wamala-ihi), | But they were unjust (faẓalamū) | to them (bihā). | So see (fa-unẓur) | how (kayfa) | was (kāna) | the end (ʿāqibatu) | of the corrupters (l-muf'sidīna).

7:104 And said Musa, "O Firaun! Indeed, I am a Messenger from the Lord of the worlds

And said (waqāla) | Musa (mūsā), | "O Firaun (yāfirʿawnu)! | Indeed, I am (innī) | a Messenger (rasūlun) | from (min) | the Lord (rabbi) | of the worlds (l-ʿālamīna)

7:105 Obligated on that not I say about Allah except the truth. Verily, I have come to you with a clear Sign from your Lord, so send with me the Children of Israel."

Obligated (ḥaqīqun) | on (ʿalā) | that (an) | not (lā) | I say (aqūla) | about (ʿalā) | Allah (l-lahi) | except (illā) | the truth (l-ḥaqa). | Verily (qad), | I have come to you (ji'tukum) | with a clear Sign (bibayyinatin) | from (min) | your Lord (rabbikum), | so send (fa-arsil) | with me (maʿiya) | the Children (banī) | of Israel. (is'rāīla)"

7:106 He said, "If you have come with a Sign, then bring it if you are of the truthful."

He said (qāla), | "If (in) | you have (kunta) | come (ji'ta) | with a Sign (biāyatin), | then bring (fati) | it (bihā) | if (in) | you are (kunta) | of (mina) | the truthful. (l-ṣādiqīna)"

7:107 So he threw his staff, and suddenly it was a serpent, manifest.

So he threw (fa-alqā) | his staff (ʿaṣāhu), | and suddenly (fa-idhā) | it (hiya) | was a serpent (thuʿbānun), | manifest (mubīnun).

7:108 And he drew out his hand and suddenly it was white for the observers.

And he drew out (wanazaʿa) | his hand (yadahu) | and suddenly (fa-idhā) | it (hiya) | was white (bayḍāu) | for the observers (lilnnāẓirīna).

7:109 Said the chiefs of the people of Firaun, "Indeed, this is surely a magician - learned.
Said (qāla) | the chiefs (l-mala-u) | of (min) | the people (qawmi) | of Firaun (firʿawna), | "Indeed (inna), | this (hādhā) | is surely a magician (lasāḥirun)- | learned (ʿalīmun).

7:110 He wants to drive you out from your land, so what do you instruct?"
He wants (yurīdu) | to (an) | drive you out (yukh'rijakum) | from (min) | your land (arḍikum), | so what (famādhā) | do you instruct? (tamurūna)"

7:111 They said, "Postpone him and his brother, and send in the cities gatherers.
They said (qālū), | "Postpone him (arjih) | and his brother (wa-akhāhu), | and send (wa-arsil) | in (fī) | the cities (l-madāini) | gatherers (ḥāshirīna).

7:112 They will bring to you [with] every magician, learned."
They will bring to you (yatūka) | [with] every (bikulli) | magician (sāḥirin), | learned. (ʿalīmin)"

7:113 So came the magicians to Firaun. They said, "Indeed, for us surely will be a reward if we are [we] the victors."
So came (wajāa) | the magicians (l-saḥaratu) | to Firaun (firʿawna). | They said (qālū), | "Indeed (inna), | for us (lanā) | surely will be a reward (la-ajran) | if (in) | we are (kunnā) | [we] (naḥnu) | the victors. (l-ghālibīna)"

7:114 He said, "Yes, and indeed you surely will be of the ones who are near."
He said (qāla), | "Yes (naʿam), | and indeed you (wa-innakum) | surely will be of (lamina) | the ones who are near. (l-muqarabīna)"

7:115 They said, "O Musa! Whether [that] you throw or Whether [that] we will be [we] the ones to throw?"
They said (qālū), | "O Musa (yāmūsā)! | Whether (immā) | [that] (an) | you throw (tul'qiya) | or Whether (wa-immā) | [that] (an) | we will be (nakūna) | [we] (naḥnu) | the ones to throw? (l-mul'qīna)"

7:116 He said, "Throw." Then when they threw, they bewitched the eyes of the people, and terrified them and came up with a magic great.
He said (qāla), | "Throw. (alqū)" | Then when (falammā) | they threw (alqaw), | they bewitched (saḥarū) | the eyes (aʿyuna) | of the people (l-nāsi), | and terrified them (wa-is'tarhabūhum) | and came up (wajāū) | with a magic (bisiḥ'rin) | great (ʿaẓīmin).

7:117 And We inspired to Musa that, "Throw your staff," and suddenly it swallowed what they were falsifying.
And We inspired (wa-awḥaynā) | to (ilā) | Musa (mūsā) | that (an), | "Throw (alqi) | your staff, (ʿaṣāka)" | and suddenly (fa-idhā) | it (hiya) | swallowed (talqafu) | what (mā) | they were falsifying (yafikūna).

7:118 So was established the truth, and became futile what they used to do.
So was established (fawaqaʿa) | the truth (l-ḥaqu), | and became futile (wabaṭala) | what (mā) | they used to (kānū) | do (yaʿmalūna).

7:119 So they were defeated there and returned humiliated.

So they were defeated (faghulibū) | there (hunālika) | and returned (wa-inqalabū) | humiliated (ṣāghirīna).

7:120 And fell down the magicians prostrate.
And fell down (wa-ul'qiya) | the magicians (l-saḥaratu) | prostrate (sājidīna).

7:121 They said, "We believe in the Lord of the worlds
They said (qālū), | "We believe (āmannā) | in the Lord (birabbi) | of the worlds (l-ʿālamīna)

7:122 Lord of Musa and Harun."
Lord (rabbi) | of Musa (mūsā) | and Harun. (wahārūna)"

7:123 Said Firaun, "You believed in him before [that] I give permission to you. Indeed, this is surely a plot you have plotted it in the city so that you may drive out from it its people. But soon you will know.
Said (qāla) | Firaun (fir'ʿawnu), | "You believed (āmantum) | in him (bihi) | before (qabla) | [that] (an) | I give permission (ādhana) | to you (lakum). | Indeed (inna), | this (hādhā) | is surely a plot (lamakrun) | you have plotted it (makartumūhu) | in (fī) | the city (l-madīnati) | so that you may drive out (litukh'rijū) | from it (min'hā) | its people (ahlahā). | But soon (fasawfa) | you will know (taʿlamūna).

7:124 I will surely cut off your hands and your feet of opposite sides. Then I will surely crucify you all."
I will surely cut off (la-uqaṭṭiʿanna) | your hands (aydiyakum) | and your feet (wa-arjulakum) | of (min) | opposite sides (khilāfin). | Then (thumma) | I will surely crucify you (la-uṣallibannakum) | all. (ajmaʿīna)"

7:125 They said, "Indeed, we to our Lord will return.
They said (qālū), | "Indeed, we (innā) | to (ilā) | our Lord (rabbinā) | will return (munqalibūna).

7:126 And not you take revenge from us except that we believed in the Signs of our Lord when they came to us. Our Lord! Pour upon us patience and cause us to die as Muslims."
And not (wamā) | you take revenge (tanqimu) | from us (minnā) | except (illā) | that (an) | we believed (āmannā) | in the Signs (biāyāti) | of our Lord (rabbinā) | when (lammā) | they came to us (jāatnā). | Our Lord (rabbanā)! | Pour (afrigh) | upon us (ʿalaynā) | patience (ṣabran) | and cause us to die (watawaffanā) | as Muslims. (mus'limīna)"

7:127 And said the chiefs of the people of Firaun, "Will you leave Musa and his people so that they cause corruption in the earth and forsake you and your gods?" He said, "We will kill their sons and we will let live their women, and indeed, we over them are subjugators."
And said (waqāla) | the chiefs (l-mala-u) | of (min) | the people (qawmi) | of Firaun (fir'ʿawna), | "Will you leave (atadharu) | Musa (mūsā) | and his people (waqawmahu) | so that they cause corruption (liyuf'sidū) | in (fī) | the earth (l-arḍi) | and forsake you (wayadharaka) | and your gods? (waālihataka)" | He said (qāla), | "We will kill (sanuqattilu) | their sons (abnāahum) | and we will let live (wanastaḥyī) | their women (nisāahum), | and indeed, we (wa-innā) | over them (fawqahum) | are subjugators. (qāhirūna)"

7:128 Said Musa to his people, "Seek help from Allah and be patient. Indeed, the earth belongs to Allah. He causes to inherit it whom He wills of His servants. And the end is for the righteous."
Said (qāla) | Musa (mūsā) | to his people (liqawmihi), | "Seek help (is'taʿīnū) | from Allah (bil-lahi) | and be patient (wa-iṣ'birū). | Indeed (inna), | the earth (l-arḍa) | belongs to Allah (lillahi).

| He causes to inherit it (yūrithuhā) | whom (man) | He wills (yashāu) | of (min) | His servants (ʿibādihi). | And the end (wal-ʿāqibatu) | is for the righteous. (lil'muttaqīna)"

7:129 They said, "We have been harmed from before [that] you came to us from and after [what] you have come to us." He said, "Perhaps your Lord [that] will destroy your enemy and make you successors in the earth, then see how you will do."

They said (qālū), | "We have been harmed (ūdhīnā) | from (min) | before (qabli) | [that] (an) | you came to us (tatiyanā) | from (wamin) | and after (baʿdi) | [what] (mā) | you have come to us. (ji'tanā)" | He said (qāla), | "Perhaps (ʿasā) | your Lord (rabbukum) | [that] (an) | will destroy (yuh'lika) | your enemy (ʿaduwwakum) | and make you successors (wayastakhlifakum) | in (fī) | the earth (l-arḍi), | then see (fayanẓura) | how (kayfa) | you will do. (taʿmalūna)"

7:130 And certainly, We seized the people of Firaun with years of famine and a deficit of [the] fruits, so that they may receive admonition.

And certainly (walaqad), | We seized (akhadhnā) | the people (āla) | of Firaun (fir'ʿawna) | with years of famine (bil-sinīna) | and a deficit (wanaqṣin) | of (mina) | [the] fruits (l-thamarāti), | so that they may (laʿallahum) | receive admonition (yadhakkarūna).

7:131 But when came to them the good they said, "For us is this." And if afflicts them bad, they ascribe evil omens to Musa and who were with him. Behold! Only their evil omens are with Allah but most of them do not know.

But when (fa-idhā) | came to them (jāathumu) | the good (l-ḥasanatu) | they said (qālū), | "For us (lanā) | is this. (hādhihi)" | And if (wa-in) | afflicts them (tuṣib'hum) | bad (sayyi-atun), | they ascribe evil omens (yaṭṭayyarū) | to Musa (bimūsā) | and who (waman) | were with him (maʿahu). | Behold (alā)! | Only (innamā) | their evil omens (ṭāiruhum) | are with (ʿinda) | Allah (l-lahi) | but (walākinna) | most of them (aktharahum) | do not (lā) | know (yaʿlamūna).

7:132 And they said, "Whatever you bring us therewith of the sign so that you bewitch us with it, then not we will be in you believers."

And they said (waqālū), | "Whatever (mahmā) | you bring us (tatinā) | therewith (bihi) | of (min) | the sign (āyatin) | so that you bewitch us (litasḥaranā) | with it (bihā), | then not (famā) | we (naḥnu) | will be in you (laka) | believers. (bimu'minīna)"

7:133 So We sent on them the flood and the locusts and the lice and the frogs and the blood as signs manifest, but they showed arrogance and they were a people, criminal.

So We sent (fa-arsalnā) | on them (ʿalayhimu) | the flood (l-ṭūfāna) | and the locusts (wal-jarāda) | and the lice (wal-qumala) | and the frogs (wal-ḍafādiʿa) | and the blood (wal-dama) | as signs (āyātin) | manifest (mufaṣṣalātin), | but they showed arrogance (fa-is'takbarū) | and they were (wakānū) | a people (qawman), | criminal (muj'rimīna).

7:134 And when fell on them the punishment, they said, "O Musa! Invoke for us your Lord by what He has promised to you. If you remove from us the punishment surely, we will believe [for] you and surely, we will send with you the Children of Israel."

And when (walammā) | fell (waqaʿa) | on them (ʿalayhimu) | the punishment (l-rij'zu), | they said (qālū), | "O Musa (yāmūsā)! | Invoke (ud'ʿu) | for us (lanā) | your Lord (rabbaka) | by what (bimā) | He has promised (ʿahida) | to you (ʿindaka). | If (la-in) | you remove (kashafta) | from us (ʿannā) | the punishment (l-rij'za) | surely, we will believe (lanu'minanna) | [for] you (laka) | and surely, we will send (walanur'silanna) | with you (maʿaka) | the Children (banī) | of Israel. (is'rāīla)"

7:135 But when We removed from them the punishment till a fixed term which they were to reach [it], then, they broke the word.

But when (falammā) | We removed (kashafnā) | from them (ʿanhumu) | the punishment (l-rij'za) | till (ilā) | a fixed term (ajalin) | which they (hum) | were to reach [it] (bālighūhu), | then (idhā), | they (hum) | broke the word (yankuthūna).

7:136 So We took retribution from them and We drowned them in the sea because they denied Our Signs, and they were to them heedless.

So We took retribution (fa-intaqamnā) | from them (min'hum) | and We drowned them (fa-aghraqnāhum) | in (fī) | the sea (l-yami) | because they (bi-annahum) | denied (kadhabū) | Our Signs (biāyātinā), | and they were (wakānū) | to them (ʿanhā) | heedless (ghāfilīna).

7:137 And We made inheritors the people those who were considered weak - the eastern (parts) of the land and the western parts of it, which We blessed [in it]. And was fulfilled the word of your Lord - the best for the Children of Israel because they were patient. And We destroyed what used to make Firaun and his people, and what they used to erect.

And We made inheritors (wa-awrathnā) | the people (l-qawma) | those who (alladhīna) | were (kānū) | considered weak (yus'taḍʿafūna)- | the eastern (parts (mashāriqa)) | of the land (l-arḍi) | and the western parts of it (wamaghāribahā), | which (allatī) | We blessed (bāraknā) | [in it] (fīhā). | And was fulfilled (watammat) | the word (kalimatu) | of your Lord (rabbika)- | the best (l-ḥus'nā) | for (ʿalā) | the Children (banī) | of Israel (is'rāīla) | because (bimā) | they were patient (ṣabarū). | And We destroyed (wadammarnā) | what (mā) | used to (kāna) | make (yaṣnaʿu) | Firaun (fir'ʿawnu) | and his people (waqawmuhu), | and what (wamā) | they used to (kānū) | erect (yaʿrishūna).

7:138 And We led across the Children of Israel the sea. Then they came upon a people devoted to idols of theirs. They said, "O Musa! Make for us a god like what they have gods. He said, "Indeed, you are a people ignorant.

And We led across (wajāwaznā) | the Children (bibanī) | of Israel (is'rāīla) | the sea (l-baḥra). | Then they came (fa-ataw) | upon (ʿalā) | a people (qawmin) | devoted (yaʿkufūna) | to (ʿalā) | idols (aṣnāmin) | of theirs (lahum). | They said (qālū), | "O Musa (yāmūsā)! | Make (ij'ʿal) | for us (lanā) | a god (ilāhan) | like what (kamā) | they have (lahum) | gods (ālihatun). | He said (qāla), | "Indeed, you (innakum) | are a people (qawmun) | ignorant (tajhalūna).

7:139 Indeed these, destroyed is what they are in it and vain is what they used to do."

Indeed (inna) | these (hāulāi), | destroyed (mutabbarun) | is what (mā) | they (hum) | are in it (fīhi) | and vain (wabāṭilun) | is what (mā) | they used to (kānū) | do. (yaʿmalūna)"

7:140 He said, "Should other than Allah I seek for you a god, while He has preferred you over the worlds?"

He said (qāla), | "Should other than (aghayra) | Allah (l-lahi) | I seek for you (abghīkum) | a god (ilāhan), | while He (wahuwa) | has preferred you (faḍḍalakum) | over (ʿalā) | the worlds? (l-ʿālamīna)"

7:141 And when We saved you from the people of Firaun who were afflicting you with worst of torment, they were killing your sons and letting live your women. And in that was a trial from your Lord great.

And when (wa-idh) | We saved you (anjaynākum) | from (min) | the people (āli) | of Firaun (fir'ʿawna) | who were afflicting you (yasūmūnakum) | with worst (sūa) | of torment (l-ʿadhābi), | they were killing (yuqattilūna) | your sons (abnāakum) | and letting live (wayastaḥyūna) | your women (nisāakum). | And in (wafī) | that (dhālikum) | was a trial (balāon) | from (min) | your Lord (rabbikum) | great (ʿaẓīmun).

7:142 And We appointed for Musa thirty nights and We completed them with ten more, so was completed the set term of his Lord of forty nights. And said Musa to his brother Harun, "Take my place in my people, and do right and do not follow the way of the corrupters."

And We appointed (wawāʿadnā) | for Musa (mūsā) | thirty (thalāthīna) | nights (laylatan) | and We completed them (wa-atmamnāhā) | with ten more (biʿashrin), | so was completed (fatamma) | the set term (mīqātu) | of his Lord (rabbihi) | of forty (arbaʿīna) | nights (laylatan). | And said (waqāla) | Musa (mūsā) | to his brother (li-akhīhi) | Harun (hārūna), | "Take my place (ukh'luf'nī) | in (fī) | my people (qawmī), | and do right (wa-aṣliḥ) | and do not (walā) | follow (tattabiʿ) | the way (sabīla) | of the corrupters. (l-muf'sidīna)"

7:143 And when came Musa to Our appointed place and spoke to him his Lord, he said, "O my Lord! Show me that I may look at You." He said, "Never you can see Me, but look at the mountain [then] if it remains in its place then you will see Me." But when revealed His Glory his Lord to the mountain, He made it crumbled to dust and fell down Musa unconscious. And when he recovered he said, "Glory be to You! I turn in repentance to you, and I am the first of the believers."

And when (walammā) | came (jāa) | Musa (mūsā) | to Our appointed place (limīqātinā) | and spoke to him (wakallamahu) | his Lord (rabbuhu), | he said (qāla), | "O my Lord (rabbi)! | Show me (arinī) | that I may look (anẓur) | at You. (ilayka)" | He said (qāla), | "Never (lan) | you can see Me (tarānī), | but (walākini) | look (unẓur) | at (ilā) | the mountain (l-jabali) | [then] if (fa-ini) | it remains (is'taqarra) | in its place (makānahu) | then (fasawfa) | you will see Me. (tarānī)" | But when (falammā) | revealed His Glory (tajallā) | his Lord (rabbuhu) | to the mountain (lil'jabali), | He made it (jaʿalahu) | crumbled to dust (dakkan) | and fell down (wakharra) | Musa (mūsā) | unconscious (ṣaʿiqan). | And when (falammā) | he recovered (afāqa) | he said (qāla), | "Glory be to You (sub'ḥānaka)! | I turn in repentance (tub'tu) | to you (ilayka), | and I am (wa-anā) | the first (awwalu) | of the believers. (l-mu'minīna)"

7:144 He said, "O Musa! Indeed, I have chosen you over the people with My Messages and with My words. So take what I have given you and be among the grateful."

He said (qāla), | "O Musa (yāmūsā)! | Indeed, I (innī) | have chosen you (iṣ'ṭafaytuka) | over (ʿalā) | the people (l-nāsi) | with My Messages (birisālātī) | and with My words (wabikalāmī). | So take (fakhudh) | what (mā) | I have given you (ātaytuka) | and be (wakun) | among (mina) | the grateful. (l-shākirīna)"

7:145 And We ordained laws for him in the tablets - of every thing, an instruction and explanation for every thing, "So take them with firmness and order your people to take the best of it. I will show you the home of the defiantly disobedient."

And We ordained laws (wakatabnā) | for him (lahu) | in (fī) | the tablets (l-alwāḥi)- | of (min) | every (kulli) | thing (shayin), | an instruction (mawʿiẓatan) | and explanation (watafṣīlan) | for every (likulli) | thing (shayin), | "So take them (fakhudh'hā) | with firmness (biquwwatin) | and order (wamur) | your people (qawmaka) | to take (yakhudhū) | the best of it (bi-aḥsanihā). | I will show you (sa-urīkum) | the home (dāra) | of the defiantly disobedient. (l-fāsiqīna)"

7:146 I will turn away from My Signs those who are arrogant in the earth without [the] right; and if they see every sign, not will they believe in it. And if they see the way of the righteousness, not will they take it as a way, but if they see the way of [the] error, they will take it as a way. That is because they denied Our Signs and they were of them heedless.

I will turn away (sa-aṣrifu) | from (ʿan) | My Signs (āyātiya) | those who (alladhīna) | are arrogant (yatakabbarūna) | in (fī) | the earth (l-arḍi) | without (bighayri) | [the] right (l-ḥaqi); | and if (wa-in) | they see (yaraw) | every (kulla) | sign (āyatin), | not (lā) | will they believe (yu'minū) | in it (bihā). | And if (wa-in) | they see (yaraw) | the way (sabīla) | of the righteousness (l-rush'di), | not (lā) | will they take it (yattakhidhūhu) | as a way (sabīlan), | but if (wa-in) | they see (yaraw) | the way (sabīla) | of [the] error (l-ghayi), | they will take it (yattakhidhūhu) | as a way (sabīlan). | That (dhālika) | is because they (bi-annahum) | denied (kadhabū) | Our Signs (biāyātinā) | and they were (wakānū) | of them (ʿanhā) | heedless (ghāfilīna).

7:147 And those who denied Our Signs and the meeting of the Hereafter - worthless are their deeds. Will they be recompensed except for what they used to do?

And those who (wa-alladhīna) | denied (kadhabū) | Our Signs (biāyātinā) | and the meeting (waliqāi) | of the Hereafter (l-ākhirati)- | worthless (ḥabiṭat) | are their deeds (aʿmāluhum). | Will (hal) | they be recompensed (yuj'zawna) | except (illā) | for what (mā) | they used to (kānū) | do (yaʿmalūna)?

7:148 And took the people of Musa, from after him from their ornaments a calf - an image [for] it had a lowing sound. Did not they see that it could not speak to them and not guide them to a way? They took it for worship and they were wrongdoers.

And took (wa-ittakhadha) | the people (qawmu) | of Musa (mūsā), | from (min) | after him (baʿdihi) | from (min) | their ornaments (ḥuliyyihim) | a calf (ʿij'lan)- | an image (jasadan) | [for] it (lahu) | had a lowing sound (khuwārun). | Did not (alam) | they see (yaraw) | that it (annahu) | could not (lā) | speak to them (yukallimuhum) | and not (walā) | guide them (yahdīhim) | to a way (sabīlan)? | They took it for worship (ittakhadhūhu) | and they were (wakānū) | wrongdoers (ẓālimīna).

7:149 And when it was made to fall into their hands and they saw that they had indeed gone astray, they said, "If not has Mercy on us, Our Lord, and forgive [for] us, we will surely be among the losers."

And when (walammā) | it was made to fall (suqiṭa) | into (fī) | their hands (aydīhim) | and they saw (wara-aw) | that they (annahum) | had indeed (qad) | gone astray (ḍallū), | they said (qālū), | "If (la-in) | not (lam) | has Mercy on us (yarḥamnā), | Our Lord (rabbunā), | and forgive (wayaghfir) | [for] us (lanā), | we will surely be (lanakūnanna) | among (mina) | the losers. (l-khāsirīna)"

7:150 And when returned Musa to his people - angry, and grieved, he said, "Evil is what you have done in my place from after me. Were you impatient over the matter of your Lord?" And he cast down the tablets and seized by head, his brother dragging him to himself. He said, "O son of my mother! Indeed, the people considered me weak and were about to kill me. So let not rejoice over me the enemies, and do not place me with the people who are wrongdoing.

And when (walammā) | returned (rajaʿa) | Musa (mūsā) | to (ilā) | his people (qawmihi)- | angry (ghaḍbāna), | and grieved (asifan), | he said (qāla), | "Evil is what (bi'samā) | you have done in my place (khalaftumūnī) | from (min) | after me (baʿdī). | Were you impatient (aʿajil'tum) | over the matter (amra) | of your Lord? (rabbikum)" | And he cast down (wa-alqā) | the tablets (l-alwāḥa) | and seized (wa-akhadha) | by head (birasi), | his brother (akhīhi) | dragging him (yajurruhu) | to himself (ilayhi). | He said (qāla), | "O son (ib'na) | of my mother (umma)! | Indeed (inna), | the people (l-qawma) | considered me weak (is'taḍʿafūnī) | and were about to (wakādū) | kill me (yaqtulūnanī). | So let not (falā) | rejoice (tush'mit) | over me (biya) | the enemies (l-aʿdāa), | and do not (walā) | place me (tajʿalnī) | with (maʿa) | the people (l-qawmi) | who are wrongdoing (l-ẓālimīna).

7:151 He said, "O my Lord! Forgive me and my brother and admit us into Your Mercy, for You are the Most Merciful of the merciful."

He said (qāla), | "O my Lord (rabbi)! | Forgive (igh'fir) | me (lī) | and my brother (wali-akhī) | and admit us (wa-adkhil'nā) | into (fī) | Your Mercy (raḥmatika), | for You (wa-anta) | are the Most Merciful (arḥamu) | of the merciful. (l-rāḥimīna)"

7:152 Indeed, those who took the calf, will reach them wrath from their Lord, and humiliation in the life of the world. And thus We recompense the ones who invent falsehood.

Indeed (inna), | those who (alladhīna) | took (ittakhadhū) | the calf (l-ʿij'la), | will reach them (sayanāluhum) | wrath (ghaḍabun) | from (min) | their Lord (rabbihim), | and humiliation (wadhillatun) | in (fī) | the life (l-ḥayati) | of the world (l-dun'yā). | And thus (wakadhālika) | We recompense (najzī) | the ones who invent falsehood (l-muf'tarīna).

7:153 And those who do the evil deeds then repented from after that and believed, indeed, your Lord from after that is surely Oft-Forgiving, Most Merciful.

And those who (wa-alladhīna) | do (ʿamilū) | the evil deeds (l-sayiāti) | then (thumma) | repented (tābū) | from (min) | after that (baʿdihā) | and believed (waāmanū), | indeed (inna), | your Lord (rabbaka) | from (min) | after that (baʿdihā) | is surely Oft-Forgiving (laghafūrun), | Most Merciful (raḥīmun).

7:154 And when was calmed from Musa the anger, he took up the tablets and in their inscription was guidance and mercy for those who [they] of their Lord are fearful.

And when (walammā) | was calmed (sakata) | from (ʿan) | Musa (mūsā) | the anger (l-ghaḍabu), | he took up (akhadha) | the tablets (l-alwāḥa) | and in (wafī) | their inscription (nus'khatihā) | was guidance (hudan) | and mercy (waraḥmatun) | for those who (lilladhīna) | [they] (hum) | of their Lord (lirabbihim) | are fearful (yarhabūna).

7:155 And chose Musa from his people seventy men for Our appointment. Then when seized them the earthquake he said, "O my Lord! If you had willed, You could have destroyed them from before and me. Would You destroy us for what did the foolish among us? Not it was but Your trial, You let go astray by it whom You will and You guide whom You will. You are our Protector, so forgive us and have mercy upon us, and You are Best of Forgivers.

And chose (wa-ikh'tāra) | Musa (mūsā) | from his people (qawmahu) | seventy (sabʿīna) | men (rajulan) | for Our appointment (limīqātinā). | Then when (falammā) | seized them (akhadhathumu) | the earthquake (l-rajfatu) | he said (qāla), | "O my Lord (rabbi)! | If (law) | you had willed (shi'ta), | You could have destroyed them (ahlaktahum) | from (min) | before (qablu) | and me (wa-iyyāya). | Would You destroy us (atuh'likunā) | for what (bimā) | did (faʿala) | the foolish (l-sufahāu) | among us (minnā)? | Not (in) | it was (hiya) | but (illā) | Your trial (fit'natuka), | You let go astray (tuḍillu) | by it (bihā) | whom (man) | You will (tashāu) | and You guide (watahdī) | whom (man) | You will (tashāu). | You (anta) | are our Protector (waliyyunā), | so forgive (fa-igh'fir) | us (lanā) | and have mercy upon us (wa-ir'ḥamnā), | and You (wa-anta) | are Best (khayru) | of Forgivers (l-ghāfirīna).

7:156 And ordain for us in this [the] world, good and in the Hereafter. Indeed, we we have turned to You." He said, "My punishment - I afflict with it whom I will, but My Mercy encompasses every thing. So I will ordain it for those who are righteous and give zakah and those who [they] in Our Verses, they believe.

And ordain (wa-uk'tub) | for us (lanā) | in (fī) | this (hādhihi) | [the] world (l-dun'yā), | good (ḥasanatan) | and in (wafī) | the Hereafter (l-ākhirati). | Indeed, we (innā) | we have turned (hud'nā) | to You. (ilayka)" | He said (qāla), | "My punishment (ʿadhābī)- | I afflict (uṣību) | with it (bihi) | whom (man) | I will (ashāu), | but My Mercy (waraḥmatī) | encompasses (wasiʿat) | every (kulla) | thing (shayin). | So I will ordain it (fasa-aktubuhā) | for those who (lilladhīna) | are righteous (yattaqūna) | and give (wayu'tūna) | zakah (l-zakata) | and those who (wa-alladhīna) | [they] (hum) | in Our Verses (biāyātinā), | they believe (yu'minūna).

7:157 Those who follow the Messenger, the Prophet, the unlettered, whom they find him written with them in the Taurat and the Injeel. He commands them to the right and forbids them from the wrong, and he makes lawful for them the pure things and makes unlawful for them the impure things and he relieves from them their burden and the fetters which were upon them. So those who believe in him and honor him, and help him and follow the light which has been sent down with him - Those are [they] the successful ones."

Those who (alladhīna) | follow (yattabiʿūna) | the Messenger (l-rasūla), | the Prophet (l-nabiya), | the unlettered (l-umiya), | whom (alladhī) | they find him (yajidūnahu) | written (maktūban) | with them (ʿindahum) | in (fī) | the Taurat (l-tawrāti) | and the Injeel (wal-injīli). | He commands them (yamuruhum) | to the right (bil-maʿrūfi) | and forbids them (wayanhāhum) | from (ʿani) | the wrong (l-munkari), | and he makes lawful (wayuḥillu) | for them (lahumu) | the pure things (l-ṭayibāti) | and makes unlawful (wayuḥarrimu) | for them (ʿalayhimu) | the impure things (l-khabāitha) | and he relieves (wayaḍaʿu) | from them (ʿanhum) | their burden (iṣ'rahum) | and the fetters (wal-aghlāla) | which (allatī) | were (kānat) | upon them (ʿalayhim). | So those who (fa-alladhīna) | believe (āmanū) | in him (bihi) | and honor him (waʿazzarūhu), | and help him (wanaṣarūhu) | and follow (wa-ittabaʿū) | the light (l-nūra) | which (alladhī) | has been sent down (unzila) | with him (maʿahu)- | Those are (ulāika) | [they] (humu) | the successful ones. (l-muf'liḥūna)"

7:158 Say, "O mankind! Indeed I am the Messenger of Allah to you all, the One for Whom is the dominion of the heavens and the earth. There is no god except Him, He gives life and causes death. So believe in Allah and His Messenger, the Prophet, the unlettered the one who believes in Allah and His Words, and follow him so that you may be guided."

Say (qul), | "O (yāayyuhā) | mankind (l-nāsu)! | Indeed I am (innī) | the Messenger (rasūlu) | of Allah (l-lahi) | to you (ilaykum) | all (jamīʿan), | the One (alladhī) | for Whom (lahu) | is the dominion (mul'ku) | of the heavens (l-samāwāti) | and the earth (wal-arḍi). | There is no (lā) | god (ilāha) | except (illā) | Him (huwa), | He gives life (yuḥ'yī) | and causes death (wayumītu). | So believe (faāminū) | in Allah (bil-lahi) | and His Messenger (warasūlihi), | the Prophet (l-nabiyi), | the unlettered (l-umiyi) | the one who (alladhī) | believes (yu'minu) | in Allah (bil-lahi) | and His Words (wakalimātihi), | and follow him (wa-ittabiʿūhu) | so that you may (laʿallakum) | be guided. (tahtadūna)"

7:159 And among the people of Musa is a community which guides with truth and by it establishes justice.

And among (wamin) | the people (qawmi) | of Musa (mūsā) | is a community (ummatun) | which guides (yahdūna) | with truth (bil-ḥaqi) | and by it (wabihi) | establishes justice (yaʿdilūna).

7:160 And We divided them into two and ten [i.e. twelve] tribes as communities. And We inspired to Musa, when asked him for water his people, [that] "Strike with your staff the stone." Then gushed forth from it two and ten [i.e. twelve] springs. Certainly, knew each people their drinking place. And We shaded [on] them with the clouds and We sent down upon them, the manna and the quails. "Eat from the good things which We have provided you." And not they wronged Us but they were to themselves doing wrong.

And We divided them (waqaṭṭaʿnāhumu) | into two (ith'natay) | and ten [i.e. twelve] (ʿashrata) | tribes (asbāṭan) | as communities (umaman). | And We inspired (wa-awḥaynā) | to (ilā) | Musa (mūsā), | when (idhi) | asked him for water (is'tasqāhu) | his people (qawmuhu), | [that] (ani) | "Strike (iḍ'rib) | with your staff (biʿaṣāka) | the stone. (l-ḥajara)" | Then gushed forth (fa-inbajasat) | from it (min'hu) | two (ith'natā) | and ten [i.e. twelve] (ʿashrata) | springs (ʿaynan). | Certainly (qad), | knew (ʿalima) | each (kullu) | people (unāsin) | their drinking place (mashrabahum). | And We shaded (waẓallalnā) | [on] them (ʿalayhimu) | with the clouds (l-ghamāma) | and We sent down (wa-anzalnā) | upon them (ʿalayhimu), | the manna (l-mana) | and the quails (wal-salwā). | "Eat (kulū) | from (min) | the good things (ṭayyibāti) | which (mā) | We have provided you. (razaqnākum)" | And not (wamā) | they wronged Us (ẓalamūnā) | but (walākin) | they were (kānū) | to themselves (anfusahum) | doing wrong (yaẓlimūna).

7:161 And when it was said to them, "Live in this city and eat from it wherever you wish and say, "Repentance," and enter the gate prostrating, We will forgive for you your sins. We will increase reward of the good-doers."

And when (wa-idh) | it was said (qīla) | to them (lahumu), | "Live (us'kunū) | in this (hādhihi) | city (l-qaryata) | and eat (wakulū) | from it (min'hā) | wherever (ḥaythu) | you wish (shi'tum) | and say (waqūlū), | "Repentance, (ḥiṭṭatun)" | and enter (wa-ud'khulū) | the gate (l-bāba) | prostrating (sujjadan), | We will forgive (naghfir) | for you (lakum) | your sins (khaṭīātikum). | We will increase reward (sanazīdu) | of the good-doers. (l-muḥ'sinīna)"

7:162 But changed those who wronged among them word other than that which was said to them. So We sent upon them torment from the sky because they were doing wrong.

But changed (fabaddala) | those who (alladhīna) | wronged (ẓalamū) | among them (min'hum) | word (qawlan) | other than (ghayra) | that which (alladhī) | was said (qīla) | to them (lahum). | So We sent (fa-arsalnā) | upon them (ʿalayhim) | torment (rij'zan) | from (mina) | the sky (l-samāi) | because (bimā) | they were (kānū) | doing wrong (yaẓlimūna).

7:163 And ask them about the town which was situated by the sea, when they transgressed in the matter of Sabbath, when came to them their fish on the day of their Sabbath visibly and on the day not they had Sabbath they did not come to them. Thus We test them because they were defiantly disobeying.

And ask them (wasalhum) | about (ʿani) | the town (l-qaryati) | which (allatī) | was (kānat) | situated (ḥāḍirata) | by the sea (l-baḥri), | when (idh) | they transgressed (yaʿdūna) | in (fī) | the matter of Sabbath (l-sabti), | when (idh) | came to them (tatīhim) | their fish (ḥītānuhum) | on the day (yawma) | of their Sabbath (sabtihim) | visibly (shurraʿan) | and on the day (wayawma) | not (lā) | they had Sabbath (yasbitūna) | they did not (lā) | come to them (tatīhim). | Thus (kadhālika) | We test them (nablūhum) | because (bimā) | they were (kānū) | defiantly disobeying (yafsuqūna).

7:164 And when said a community among them, "Why do you preach a people, whom Allah is going to destroy them or punish them with a punishment severe?" They said, "To be absolved before your Lord and that they may become righteous."

And when (wa-idh) | said (qālat) | a community (ummatun) | among them (min'hum), | "Why (lima) | do you preach (taʿiẓūna) | a people (qawman), | whom Allah (l-lahu) | is going to destroy them (muh'likuhum) | or (aw) | punish them (muʿadhibuhum) | with a punishment (ʿadhāban) | severe? (shadīdan)" | They said (qālū), | "To be absolved (maʿdhiratan) | before (ilā) | your Lord (rabbikum) | and that they may (walaʿallahum) | become righteous. (yattaqūna)"

7:165 So when they forgot what they had been reminded with [it], We saved those who forbade [from] the evil, and We seized those who wronged with a punishment wretched, because they were defiantly disobeying.

So when (falammā) | they forgot (nasū) | what (mā) | they had been reminded (dhukkirū) | with [it] (bihi), | We saved (anjaynā) | those who (alladhīna) | forbade (yanhawna) | [from] (ʿani) | the evil (l-sūi), | and We seized (wa-akhadhnā) | those who (alladhīna) | wronged (ẓalamū) | with a punishment (biʿadhābin) | wretched (baīsin), | because (bimā) | they were (kānū) | defiantly disobeying (yafsuqūna).

7:166 So when they exceeded all bounds about what they were forbidden from it, We said to them, "Be apes, despised."

So when (falammā) | they exceeded all bounds (ʿataw) | about (ʿan) | what (mā) | they were forbidden (nuhū) | from it (ʿanhu), | We said (qul'nā) | to them (lahum), | "Be (kūnū) | apes (qiradatan), | despised. (khāsiīna)"

7:167 And when declared your Lord that He would surely send upon them till the Day of the Resurrection those who would afflict them with a grievous [the] punishment. Indeed, your Lord is surely swift in the retribution, but indeed, He is surely Oft-Forgiving, Most Merciful.

And when (wa-idh) | declared (ta-adhana) | your Lord (rabbuka) | that He would surely send (layabʿathanna) | upon them (ʿalayhim) | till (ilā) | the Day (yawmi) | of the Resurrection (l-qiyāmati) | those who (man) | would afflict them (yasūmuhum) | with a grievous (sūa) | [the] punishment (l-ʿadhābi). | Indeed (inna), | your Lord (rabbaka) | is surely swift (lasarīʿu) | in the retribution (l-ʿiqābi), | but indeed, He (wa-innahu) | is surely Oft-Forgiving (laghafūrun), | Most Merciful (raḥīmun).

7:168 And We divided them in the earth as nations. Among them are the righteous and among them are other than that. And We tested them with the good and the bad, so that they may return.

And We divided them (waqaṭṭaʿnāhum) | in (fī) | the earth (l-arḍi) | as nations (umaman). | Among them (min'humu) | are the righteous (l-ṣāliḥūna) | and among them (wamin'hum) | are other than (dūna) | that (dhālika). | And We tested them (wabalawnāhum) | with the good (bil-ḥasanāti) | and the bad (wal-sayiāti), | so that they may (laʿallahum) | return (yarjiʿūna).

7:169 Then succeeded from after them successors who inherited the Book taking goods of this the lower life and they say, "It will be forgiven for us." And if comes to them goods similar to it they will take it. Was not taken on them Covenant of the Book that not they will say about Allah except the truth while they studied what is in it? And the home of the Hereafter is better for those who fear Allah. So will not you use intellect?

Then succeeded (fakhalafa) | from (min) | after them (baʿdihim) | successors (khalfun) | who inherited (warithū) | the Book (l-kitāba) | taking (yakhudhūna) | goods (ʿaraḍa) | of this (hādhā) | the lower life (l-adnā) | and they say (wayaqūlūna), | "It will be forgiven (sayugh'faru) | for us. (lanā)" | And if (wa-in) | comes to them (yatihim) | goods (ʿaraḍun) | similar to it (mith'luhu) | they will take it (yakhudhūhu). | Was not (alam) | taken (yu'khadh) | on them (ʿalayhim) | Covenant (mīthāqu) | of the Book (l-kitābi) | that (an) | not (lā) | they will say (yaqūlū) | about (ʿalā) | Allah (l-lahi) | except (illā) | the truth (l-ḥaqa) | while they studied (wadarasū) | what (mā) | is in it (fīhi)? | And the home (wal-dāru) | of the Hereafter (l-ākhiratu) | is better (khayrun) | for those who (lilladhīna) | fear Allah (yattaqūna). | So will not (afalā) | you use intellect (taʿqilūna)?

7:170 And those who hold fast to the Book, and establish the prayer, indeed, We will not [We] let go waste the reward of the reformers.

And those who (wa-alladhīna) | hold fast (yumassikūna) | to the Book (bil-kitābi), | and establish (wa-aqāmū) | the prayer (l-ṣalata), | indeed, We (innā) | will not (lā) | [We] let go waste (nuḍīʿu) | the reward (ajra) | of the reformers (l-muṣ'liḥīna).

7:171 And when We raised the mountain above them as if it was a canopy and they thought that it would fall upon them, We said, "Take what We have given you with strength and remember what is in it so that you may fear Allah."

And when (wa-idh) | We raised (nataqnā) | the mountain (l-jabala) | above them (fawqahum) | as if it was (ka-annahu) | a canopy (ẓullatun) | and they thought (waẓannū) | that it (annahu) | would fall (wāqiʿun) | upon them (bihim), | We said, "Take (khudhū) | what (mā) | We have given you (ātaynākum) | with strength (biquwwatin) | and remember (wa-udh'kurū) | what (mā) | is in it (fīhi) | so that you may (laʿallakum) | fear Allah. (tattaqūna)"

7:172 And when was taken by your Lord from the Children of Adam - from their loins - their descendants and made them testify over themselves, "Am I not your Lord?" They said, "Yes we have testified." Lest you say on the Day of the Resurrection, "Indeed, we were about this unaware."

And when (wa-idh) | was taken (akhadha) | by your Lord (rabbuka) | from (min) | the Children (banī) | of Adam (ādama)- | from (min) | their loins (ẓuhūrihim)- | their descendants (dhurriyyatahum) | and made them testify (wa-ashhadahum) | over (ʿalā) | themselves (anfusihim), | "Am I not (alastu) | your Lord? (birabbikum)" | They said (qālū), | "Yes (balā) | we have testified. (shahid'nā)" | Lest (an) | you say (taqūlū) | on the Day (yawma) | of the Resurrection (l-qiyāmati), | "Indeed (innā), | we were (kunnā) | about (ʿan) | this (hādhā) | unaware. (ghāfilīna)"

7:173 Or you say, "Only partners were associated (with Allah) by our forefathers from before us and we are descendants from after them. So will You destroy us for what did the falsifiers?"

Or (aw) | you say (taqūlū), | "Only (innamā) | partners were associated (with Allah (ashraka)) | by our forefathers (ābāunā) | from (min) | before us (qablu) | and we are (wakunnā) | descendants (dhurriyyatan) | from (min) | after them (baʿdihim). | So will You destroy us (afatuh'likunā) | for what (bimā) | did (faʿala) | the falsifiers? (l-mub'ṭilūna)"

7:174 And thus We explain the Verses so that they may return.

And thus (wakadhālika) | We explain (nufaṣṣilu) | the Verses (l-āyāti) | so that they may (walaʿallahum) | return (yarjiʿūna).

7:175 And recite to them the story of the one whom We gave [him] Our Verses, but he detached [from] them, so followed him the Shaitaan and he became of those gone astray.

And recite (wa-ut'lu) | to them (ʿalayhim) | the story (naba-a) | of the one whom (alladhī) | We gave [him] (ātaynāhu) | Our Verses (āyātinā), | but he detached (fa-insalakha) | [from] them (min'hā), | so followed him (fa-atbaʿahu) | the Shaitaan (l-shayṭānu) | and he became (fakāna) | of (mina) | those gone astray (l-ghāwīna).

7:176 And if We willed surely, We could have raised him with these [and] but he adhered to the earth and followed his vain desires. So his example is like (the) example of the dog, if you attack [on] him, he lolls out his tongue or if you leave him, he lolls out his tongue. That is the example of the people who denied [in] Our Signs. So relate the story so that they may reflect.

And if (walaw) | We willed (shi'nā) | surely, We could have raised him (larafaʿnāhu) | with these (bihā) | [and] but he (walākinnahu) | adhered (akhlada) | to (ilā) | the earth (l-arḍi) | and followed (wa-ittabaʿa) | his vain desires (hawāhu). | So his example (famathaluhu) | is like (the) example (kamathali) | of the dog (l-kalbi), | if (in) | you attack (taḥmil) | [on] him (ʿalayhi), | he lolls out his tongue (yalhath) | or (aw) | if you leave him (tatruk'hu), | he lolls out his tongue (yalhath). | That (dhālika) | is the example (mathalu) | of the people (l-qawmi) | who (alladhīna) | denied (kadhabū) | [in] Our Signs (biāyātinā). | So relate (fa-uq'ṣuṣi) | the story (l-qaṣaṣa) | so that they may (laʿallahum) | reflect (yatafakkarūna).

7:177 Evil as an example are the people those who denied Our Signs and themselves they used to wrong.

Evil (sāa) | as an example (mathalan) | are the people (l-qawmu) | those who (alladhīna) | denied (kadhabū) | Our Signs (biāyātinā) | and themselves (wa-anfusahum) | they used to (kānū) | wrong (yaẓlimūna).

7:178 Whoever is guided by Allah then he is the guided one while whoever He lets go astray then those [they] are the losers.

Whoever (man) | is guided (yahdi) | by Allah (l-lahu) | then he (fahuwa) | is the guided one (l-muh'tadī) | while whoever (waman) | He lets go astray (yuḍ'lil) | then those (fa-ulāika) | [they] (humu) | are the losers (l-khāsirūna).

7:179 And certainly We have created for Hell many of the jinn and men. For them are hearts but not they understand with them, and for them are eyes but not they see with them, and for them are ears but not they hear with them. Those are like cattle, nay they are more astray. Those - they are the heedless.

And certainly (walaqad) | We have created (dharanā) | for Hell (lijahannama) | many (kathīran) | of (mina) | the jinn (l-jini) | and men (wal-insi). | For them (lahum) | are hearts (qulūbun) | but not (lā) | they understand (yafqahūna) | with them (bihā), | and for them (walahum) | are eyes (aʿyunun) | but not (lā) | they see (yub'ṣirūna) | with them (bihā), | and for them (walahum) | are ears (ādhānun) | but not (lā) | they hear (yasmaʿūna) | with them (bihā). | Those (ulāika) | are like cattle (kal-anʿāmi), | nay (bal) | they (hum) | are more astray (aḍallu). | Those (ulāika)- | they (humu) | are the heedless (l-ghāfilūna).

7:180 And for Allah are the names - the most beautiful, so invoke Him by them. And leave those who deviate concerning His names. They will be recompensed for what they used to do.

And for Allah (walillahi) | are the names (l-asmāu)- | the most beautiful (l-ḥus'nā), | so invoke Him (fa-id''ūhu) | by them (bihā). | And leave (wadharū) | those who (alladhīna) | deviate (yul'ḥidūna) | concerning (fī) | His names (asmāihi). | They will be recompensed (sayuj'zawna) | for what (mā) | they used to (kānū) | do (yaʿmalūna).

7:181 And of those whom We have created is a nation, who guides with the truth and thereby they establish justice.

And of those whom (wamimman) | We have created (khalaqnā) | is a nation (ummatun), | who guides (yahdūna) | with the truth (bil-ḥaqi) | and thereby (wabihi) | they establish justice (yaʿdilūna).

7:182 But those who denied Our Signs, We will gradually lead them from where not they know.

But those who (wa-alladhīna) | denied (kadhabū) | Our Signs (biāyātinā), | We will gradually lead them (sanastadrijuhum) | from (min) | where (ḥaythu) | not (lā) | they know (yaʿlamūna).

7:183 And I will give respite to them. Indeed, My plan is firm.

And I will give respite (wa-um'lī) | to them (lahum). | Indeed (inna), | My plan (kaydī) | is firm (matīnun).

7:184 Do not they reflect? Not in their companion [of] is any madness. Not he is but a warner, clear.

Do not (awalam) | they reflect (yatafakkarū)? | Not (mā) | in their companion (biṣāḥibihim) | [of] (min) | is any madness (jinnatin). | Not (in) | he (huwa) | is but (illā) | a warner (nadhīrun), | clear (mubīnun).

7:185 Do not they look in the dominion of the heavens and the earth and what has been created by Allah of everything and that perhaps [that] has verily come near - their term? So in what statement after this will they believe?

Do not (awalam) | they look (yanẓurū) | in (fī) | the dominion (malakūti) | of the heavens (l-samāwāti) | and the earth (wal-arḍi) | and what (wamā) | has been created (khalaqa) | by Allah (l-lahu) | of (min) | everything (shayin) | and that (wa-an) | perhaps (ʿasā) | [that] (an) | has (yakūna) | verily (qadi) | come near (iq'taraba)- | their term (ajaluhum)? | So in what (fabi-ayyi) | statement (ḥadīthin) | after this (baʿdahu) | will they believe (yu'minūna)?

7:186 Whoever is let go astray by Allah then there is no guide for him. And He leaves them in their transgression wandering blindly.

Whoever (man) | is let go astray (yuḍ'lili) | by Allah (l-lahu) | then there is no (falā) | guide (hādiya) | for him (lahu). | And He leaves them (wayadharuhum) | in (fī) | their transgression (ṭugh'yānihim) | wandering blindly (yaʿmahūna).

7:187 They ask you about the Hour, when will be its appointed time? Say, "Only its knowledge is with my Lord, no one can reveal [it] its time except Him. It lays heavily in the heavens and the earth. Not will it come to you but suddenly." They ask you as if you were well informed about it. Say, "Only its knowledge is with Allah, but most of the people do not know."

They ask you (yasalūnaka) | about (ʿani) | the Hour (l-sāʿati), | when will be (ayyāna) | its appointed time (mur'sāhā)? | Say (qul), | "Only (innamā) | its knowledge (ʿil'muhā) | is with (ʿinda) |

my Lord (rabbī), | no one (lā) | can reveal [it] (yujallīhā) | its time (liwaqtihā) | except (illā) | Him (huwa). | It lays heavily (thaqulat) | in (fī) | the heavens (l-samāwāti) | and the earth (wal-arḍi). | Not (lā) | will it come to you (tatīkum) | but (illā) | suddenly. (baghtatan)" | They ask you (yasalūnaka) | as if you (ka-annaka) | were well informed (ḥafiyyun) | about it (ʿanhā). | Say (qul), | "Only (innamā) | its knowledge (ʿil'muhā) | is with (ʿinda) | Allah (l-lahi), | but (walākinna) | most (akthara) | of the people (l-nāsi) | do not (lā) | know. (yaʿlamūna)"

7:188 Say, "Not I have power for myself to benefit and no power to harm, except what wills Allah. And if I would know of the unseen surely I could have multiplied of the good and not could have touched me the evil. Not am I except a warner and a bearer of good tidings to a people who believe."

Say (qul), | "Not (lā) | I have power (amliku) | for myself (linafsī) | to benefit (nafʿan) | and no (walā) | power to harm (ḍarran), | except (illā) | what (mā) | wills (shāa) | Allah (l-lahu). | And if (walaw) | I would (kuntu) | know (aʿlamu) | of the unseen (l-ghayba) | surely I could have multiplied (la-is'takthartu) | of (mina) | the good (l-khayri) | and not (wamā) | could have touched me (massaniya) | the evil (l-sūu). | Not (in) | am I (anā) | except (illā) | a warner (nadhīrun) | and a bearer of good tidings (wabashīrun) | to a people (liqawmin) | who believe. (yu'minūna)"

7:189 He is the One Who created you from a soul, single and made from it its mate that he might live with her. And when he covers her, she carries a burden light and continues with it. But when she grows heavy, they both invoke Allah, their Lord, "If You give us a righteous child, surely we will be among the thankful."

He (huwa) | is the One Who (alladhī) | created you (khalaqakum) | from (min) | a soul (nafsin), | single (wāḥidatin) | and made (wajaʿala) | from it (min'hā) | its mate (zawjahā) | that he might live (liyaskuna) | with her (ilayhā). | And when (falammā) | he covers her (taghashāhā), | she carries (ḥamalat) | a burden (ḥamlan) | light (khafīfan) | and continues (famarrat) | with it (bihi). | But when (falammā) | she grows heavy (athqalat), | they both invoke (daʿawā) | Allah (l-laha), | their Lord (rabbahumā), | "If (la-in) | You give us (ātaytanā) | a righteous child (ṣāliḥan), | surely we will be (lanakūnanna) | among (mina) | the thankful. (l-shākirīna)"

7:190 But when He gives them a good, child they make for Him partners in what He has given them. But exalted is Allah above what they associate with Him.

But when (falammā) | He gives them (ātāhumā) | a good, child (ṣāliḥan) | they make (jaʿalā) | for Him (lahu) | partners (shurakāa) | in what (fīmā) | He has given them (ātāhumā). | But exalted (fataʿālā) | is Allah (l-lahu) | above what (ʿammā) | they associate with Him (yush'rikūna).

7:191 Do they associate what can not create anything and they are created?

Do they associate (ayush'rikūna) | what (mā) | can not (lā) | create (yakhluqu) | anything (shayan) | and they (wahum) | are created (yukh'laqūna)?

7:192 And not they are able to give them any help and not themselves can they help.

And not (walā) | they are able (yastaṭīʿūna) | to give them (lahum) | any help (naṣran) | and not (walā) | themselves (anfusahum) | can they help (yanṣurūna).

7:193 And if you call them to the guidance, not will they follow you. It is same for you whether you call them or you remain silent.

And if (wa-in) | you call them (tadʿūhum) | to (ilā) | the guidance (l-hudā), | not (lā) | will they follow you (yattabiʿūkum). | It is same (sawāon) | for you (ʿalaykum) | whether you call them (adaʿawtumūhum) | or (am) | you (antum) | remain silent (ṣāmitūna).

7:194 Indeed, those whom you call from besides Allah are slaves like you. So invoke them and let them respond to you, if you are truthful.

Indeed (inna), | those whom (alladhīna) | you call (tadʿūna) | from (min) | besides (dūni) | Allah (l-lahi) | are slaves (ʿibādun) | like you (amthālukum). | So invoke them (fa-idʿʿūhum) | and let them respond (falyastajībū) | to you (lakum), | if (in) | you are (kuntum) | truthful (ṣādiqīna).

7:195 Are for them feet to walk with [it], or for them hands to hold with [it], or for them eyes to see with [it], or for them ears to hear with [it]? Say, "Call your partners, then scheme against me and do not give me respite."

Are for them (alahum) | feet (arjulun) | to walk (yamshūna) | with [it] (bihā), | or (am) | for them (lahum) | hands (aydin) | to hold (yabṭishūna) | with [it] (bihā), | or (am) | for them (lahum) | eyes (aʿyunun) | to see (yub'ṣirūna) | with [it] (bihā), | or (am) | for them (lahum) | ears (ādhānun) | to hear (yasmaʿūna) | with [it] (bihā)? | Say (quli), | "Call (idʿʿū) | your partners (shurakāakum), | then (thumma) | scheme against me (kīdūni) | and do not (falā) | give me respite. (tunẓirūni)"

7:196 Indeed, my protector is Allah the One Who revealed the Book. And He protects the righteous.

Indeed (inna), | my protector (waliyyiya) | is Allah (l-lahu) | the One Who (alladhī) | revealed (nazzala) | the Book (l-kitāba). | And He (wahuwa) | protects (yatawallā) | the righteous (l-ṣāliḥīna).

7:197 And those whom you invoke from besides Him, not they are able to help you and not themselves can they help.

And those whom (wa-alladhīna) | you invoke (tadʿūna) | from (min) | besides Him (dūnihi), | not (lā) | they are able (yastaṭīʿūna) | to help you (naṣrakum) | and not (walā) | themselves (anfusahum) | can they help (yanṣurūna).

7:198 And if you call them to the guidance not do they not. And you see them looking at you but they - not do they see.

And if (wa-in) | you call them (tadʿūhum) | to (ilā) | the guidance (l-hudā) | not (lā) | do they not (yasmaʿū). | And you see them (watarāhum) | looking (yanẓurūna) | at you (ilayka) | but they (wahum)- | not (lā) | do they see (yub'ṣirūna).

7:199 Hold to forgiveness and enjoin the good, and turn away from the ignorant.

Hold (khudhi) | to forgiveness (l-ʿafwa) | and enjoin (wamur) | the good (bil-ʿur'fi), | and turn away (wa-aʿriḍ) | from (ʿani) | the ignorant (l-jāhilīna).

7:200 And if an evil suggestion comes to you from [the] Shaitaan [an evil suggestion], then seek refuge in Allah. Indeed, He is All-Hearing, All-Knowing.

And if (wa-immā) | an evil suggestion comes to you (yanzaghannaka) | from (mina) | [the] Shaitaan (l-shayṭāni) | [an evil suggestion] (nazghun), | then seek refuge (fa-is'taʿidh) | in Allah (bil-lahi). | Indeed, He (innahu) | is All-Hearing (samīʿun), | All-Knowing (ʿalīmun).

7:201 Indeed, those who fear Allah when touches them an evil thought from the Shaitaan, they remember Allah and then they are those who see (aright).

Indeed (inna), | those who (alladhīna) | fear Allah (ittaqaw) | when (idhā) | touches them (massahum) | an evil thought (ṭāifun) | from (mina) | the Shaitaan (l-shayṭāni), | they remember Allah (tadhakkarū) | and then (fa-idhā) | they (hum) | are those who see (aright) (mub'ṣirūna).

7:202 But their brothers they plunge them in the error, then not they cease.

But their brothers (wa-ikh'wānuhum) | they plunge them (yamuddūnahum) | in (fī) | the error (l-ghayi), | then (thumma) | not (lā) | they cease (yuq'ṣirūna).

7:203 And when not you bring them a Sign they say, "Why have not you devised it?" Say, "Only I follow what is revealed to me from my Lord. This is enlightenment from your Lord and guidance and mercy for a people who believe."

And when (wa-idhā) | not (lam) | you bring them (tatihim) | a Sign (biāyatin) | they say (qālū), | "Why have not (lawlā) | you devised it? (ij'tabaytahā)" | Say (qul), | "Only (innamā) | I follow (attabiʿu) | what (mā) | is revealed (yūḥā) | to me (ilayya) | from (min) | my Lord (rabbī). | This is (hādhā) | enlightenment (baṣāiru) | from (min) | your Lord (rabbikum) | and guidance (wahudan) | and mercy (waraḥmatun) | for a people (liqawmin) | who believe. (yu'minūna)"

7:204 And when is recited the Quran, then listen to it and pay attention so that you may receive mercy.

And when (wa-idhā) | is recited (quri-a) | the Quran (l-qur'ānu), | then listen (fa-is'tamiʿū) | to it (lahu) | and pay attention (wa-anṣitū) | so that you may (laʿallakum) | receive mercy (tur'ḥamūna).

7:205 And remember your Lord in yourself humbly and in fear and without the loudness of [the] words, in the mornings and in the evenings. And do not be among the heedless.

And remember (wa-udh'kur) | your Lord (rabbaka) | in (fī) | yourself (nafsika) | humbly (taḍarruʿan) | and in fear (wakhīfatan) | and without (wadūna) | the loudness (l-jahri) | of (mina) | [the] words (l-qawli), | in the mornings (bil-ghuduwi) | and in the evenings (wal-āṣāli). | And do not (walā) | be (takun) | among (mina) | the heedless (l-ghāfilīna).

7:206 Indeed, those who are near your Lord, not do they turn away in pride from His worship. And they glorify Him and to Him they prostrate.

Indeed (inna), | those who (alladhīna) | are near (ʿinda) | your Lord (rabbika), | not (lā) | do they turn away in pride (yastakbirūna) | from (ʿan) | His worship (ʿibādatihi). | And they glorify Him (wayusabbiḥūnahu) | and to Him (walahu) | they prostrate (yasjudūna).

Chapter (8) Sūrat l-Anfāl (The Spoils of War)

8:1 They ask you about the spoils of war. Say, "The spoils of war are for Allah and the Messenger. So fear Allah and set right that which is between you and obey Allah and His Messenger, if you are believers."

They ask you (yasalūnaka) | about (ʿani) | the spoils of war (l-anfāli). | Say (quli), | "The spoils of war (l-anfālu) | are for Allah (lillahi) | and the Messenger (wal-rasūli). | So fear (fa-ittaqū) | Allah (l-laha) | and set right (wa-aṣliḥū) | that (dhāta) | which is between you (baynikum) | and obey (wa-aṭīʿū) | Allah (l-laha) | and His Messenger (warasūlahu), | if (in) | you are (kuntum) | believers. (mu'minīna)"

8:2 Only the believers are those who when is mentioned Allah feel fear their hearts, and when are recited to them His Verses, they increase them in faith, and upon their Lord they put their trust.

Only (innamā) | the believers (l-mu'minūna) | are those who (alladhīna) | when (idhā) | is mentioned (dhukira) | Allah (l-lahu) | feel fear (wajilat) | their hearts (qulūbuhum), | and when (wa-idhā) | are recited (tuliyat) | to them (ʿalayhim) | His Verses (āyātuhu), | they increase them (zādathum) | in faith (īmānan), | and upon (waʿalā) | their Lord (rabbihim) | they put their trust (yatawakkalūna).

8:3 Those who establish the prayer and out of what We have provided them they spend.

Those who (alladhīna) | establish (yuqīmūna) | the prayer (l-ṣalata) | and out of what (wamimmā) | We have provided them (razaqnāhum) | they spend (yunfiqūna).

8:4 Those - they are the believers in truth. For them are ranks with their Lord and forgiveness and a provision noble.

Those (ulāika)- | they are (humu) | the believers (l-mu'minūna) | in truth (ḥaqqan). | For them (lahum) | are ranks (darajātun) | with (ʿinda) | their Lord (rabbihim) | and forgiveness (wamaghfiratun) | and a provision (wariz'qun) | noble (karīmun).

8:5 As brought you out your Lord from your home in truth, while indeed, a party among the believers certainly disliked.

As (kamā) | brought you out (akhrajaka) | your Lord (rabbuka) | from (min) | your home (baytika) | in truth (bil-ḥaqi), | while indeed (wa-inna), | a party (farīqan) | among (mina) | the believers (l-mu'minīna) | certainly disliked (lakārihūna).

8:6 They dispute with you concerning the truth after what was made clear, as if they were driven to [the] death while they were looking.

They dispute with you (yujādilūnaka) | concerning (fī) | the truth (l-ḥaqi) | after what (baʿdamā) | was made clear (tabayyana), | as if (ka-annamā) | they were driven (yusāqūna) | to (ilā) | [the] death (l-mawti) | while they (wahum) | were looking (yanẓurūna).

8:7 And when promised you Allah one of the two groups - that it would be for you - and you wished that one other than that of the armed would be for you. But intended Allah to justify the truth by His words, and cut off the roots of the disbelievers

And when (wa-idh) | promised you (yaʿidukumu) | Allah (l-lahu) | one (iḥ'dā) | of the two groups (l-ṭāifatayni)- | that it would be (annahā) | for you (lakum)- | and you wished (watawaddūna) | that (anna) | one other than (ghayra) | that (dhāti) | of the armed (l-shawkati) | would be (takūnu) | for you (lakum). | But intended (wayurīdu) | Allah (l-lahu) | to (an) | justify (yuḥiqqa) | the truth (l-ḥaqa) | by His words (bikalimātihi), | and cut off (wayaqṭaʿa) | the roots (dābira) | of the disbelievers (l-kāfirīna)

8:8 That He might justify the truth and prove false the falsehood, even if disliked it the criminals.

That He might justify (liyuḥiqqa) | the truth (l-ḥaqa) | and prove false (wayub'ṭila) | the falsehood (l-bāṭila), | even if (walaw) | disliked it (kariha) | the criminals (l-muj'rimūna).

8:9 When you were seeking help of your Lord and He answered [to] you, "Indeed, I am going to reinforce you with a thousand of the Angels one after another."

When (idh) | you were seeking help (tastaghīthūna) | of your Lord (rabbakum) | and He answered (fa-is'tajāba) | [to] you (lakum), | "Indeed, I am (annī) | going to reinforce you (mumiddukum) | with a thousand (bi-alfin) | of (mina) | the Angels (l-malāikati) | one after another. (mur'difīna)"

8:10 And not it was made by Allah but good tidings and so that might be at rest with it your hearts. And there is no [the] victory except from [of] Allah. Indeed, Allah is All-Mighty, All-Wise.

And not (wamā) | it was made (jaʿalahu) | by Allah (l-lahu) | but (illā) | good tidings (bush'rā) | and so that might be at rest (walitaṭma-inna) | with it (bihi) | your hearts (qulūbukum). | And there is no (wamā) | [the] victory (l-naṣru) | except (illā) | from (min) | [of] (ʿindi) | Allah (l-lahi). | Indeed (inna), | Allah (l-laha) | is All-Mighty (ʿazīzun), | All-Wise (ḥakīmun).

8:11 When He covered you with [the] slumber, a security from Him, and sent down upon you from the sky water, so that He may purify you with it, and take away from you evil suggestions of the Shaitaan. And to strengthen [on] your hearts and make firm with it your feet.

When (idh) | He covered you (yughashīkumu) | with [the] slumber (l-nuʿāsa), | a security (amanatan) | from Him (min'hu), | and sent down (wayunazzilu) | upon you (ʿalaykum) | from (mina) | the sky (l-samāi) | water (māan), | so that He may purify you (liyuṭahhirakum) | with it (bihi), | and take away (wayudh'hiba) | from you (ʿankum) | evil suggestions (rij'za) | of the Shaitaan (l-shayṭāni). | And to strengthen (waliyarbiṭa) | [on] (ʿalā) | your hearts (qulūbikum) | and make firm (wayuthabbita) | with it (bihi) | your feet (l-aqdāma).

8:12 When inspired your Lord to the Angels, "I am with you, so strengthen those who believed. I will cast in the hearts of those who disbelieved - the terror, so strike above the necks and strike from them every fingertip[s]."

When (idh) | inspired (yūḥī) | your Lord (rabbuka) | to (ilā) | the Angels (l-malāikati), | "I am (annī) | with you (maʿakum), | so strengthen (fathabbitū) | those who (alladhīna) | believed (āmanū). | I will cast (sa-ul'qī) | in (fī) | the hearts (qulūbi) | of those who (alladhīna) | disbelieved (kafarū)- | the terror (l-ruʿ'ba), | so strike (fa-iḍ'ribū) | above (fawqa) | the necks (l-aʿnāqi) | and strike (wa-iḍ'ribū) | from them (min'hum) | every (kulla) | fingertip[s]. (banānin)"

8:13 That is because they opposed Allah and His Messenger. And whoever opposes Allah and His Messenger, then indeed, Allah is severe in [the] penalty.

That (dhālika) | is because they (bi-annahum) | opposed (shāqqū) | Allah (l-laha) | and His Messenger (warasūlahu). | And whoever (waman) | opposes (yushāqiqi) | Allah (l-laha) | and His Messenger (warasūlahu), | then indeed (fa-inna), | Allah (l-laha) | is severe (shadīdu) | in [the] penalty (l-ʿiqābi).

8:14 That - "So taste it." And that, for the disbelievers is the punishment of the Fire.

That (dhālikum)- | "So taste it. (fadhūqūhu)" | And that (wa-anna), | for the disbelievers (lil'kāfirīna) | is the punishment (ʿadhāba) | of the Fire (l-nāri).

8:15 O you who believe! When you meet those who disbelieve advancing, then do not turn to them the backs.

O you (yāayyuhā) | who (alladhīna) | believe (āmanū)! | When (idhā) | you meet (laqītumu) | those who (alladhīna) | disbelieve (kafarū) | advancing (zaḥfan), | then do not (falā) | turn to them (tuwallūhumu) | the backs (l-adbāra).

8:16 And whoever turns to them that day his back except as a strategy of war or to join to a group, certainly he has incurred wrath of Allah and his abode is Hell, a wretched destination.

And whoever (waman) | turns to them (yuwallihim) | that day (yawma-idhin) | his back (duburahu) | except (illā) | as a strategy (mutaḥarrifan) | of war (liqitālin) | or (aw) | to join (mutaḥayyizan) | to (ilā) | a group (fi-atin), | certainly (faqad) | he has incurred (bāa) | wrath (bighaḍabin) | of (mina) | Allah (l-lahi) | and his abode (wamawāhu) | is Hell (jahannamu), | a wretched (wabi'sa) | destination (l-maṣīru).

8:17 And not you kill them, but Allah killed them. And not you threw when you threw, but Allah threw and that He may test the believers from Him with a trial good. Indeed, Allah is All-Hearing, All-Knowing.

And not (falam) | you kill them (taqtulūhum), | but (walākinna) | Allah (l-laha) | killed them (qatalahum). | And not (wamā) | you threw (ramayta) | when (idh) | you threw (ramayta), | but (walākinna) | Allah (l-laha) | threw (ramā) | and that He may test (waliyub'liya) | the believers (l-mu'minīna) | from Him (min'hu) | with a trial (balāan) | good (ḥasanan). | Indeed (inna), | Allah (l-laha) | is All-Hearing (samīʿun), | All-Knowing (ʿalīmun).

8:18 That is the case and that, Allah is one who makes weak the plan of the disbelievers.

That is the case (dhālikum) | and that (wa-anna), | Allah is (l-laha) | one who makes weak (mūhinu) | the plan (kaydi) | of the disbelievers (l-kāfirīna).

8:19 If you ask for victory then certainly has come to you the victory. And if you desist, then it is good for you, but if you return, We will return too. And never will avail you your forces anything, even if they are numerous. And that Allah is with the believers.

If (in) | you ask for victory (tastaftiḥū) | then certainly (faqad) | has come to you (jāakumu) | the victory (l-fatḥu). | And if (wa-in) | you desist (tantahū), | then it is (fahuwa) | good (khayrun) | for you (lakum), | but if (wa-in) | you return (taʿūdū), | We will return too (naʿud). | And never (walan) | will avail (tugh'niya) | you (ʿankum) | your forces (fi-atukum) | anything (shayan), | even if (walaw) | they are numerous (kathurat). | And that (wa-anna) | Allah (l-laha) | is with (maʿa) | the believers (l-mu'minīna).

8:20 O you who believe! Obey Allah and His Messenger. And do not turn away from him while you hear.

O you (yāayyuhā) | who (alladhīna) | believe (āmanū)! | Obey (aṭīʿū) | Allah (l-laha) | and His Messenger (warasūlahu). | And do not (walā) | turn away (tawallaw) | from him (ʿanhu) | while you (wa-antum) | hear (tasmaʿūna).

8:21 And do not be like those who say, "We heard," while they do not hear.

And do not (walā) | be (takūnū) | like those who (ka-alladhīna) | say (qālū), | "We heard, (samiʿ'nā)" | while they (wahum) | do not (lā) | hear (yasmaʿūna).

8:22 Indeed, worst of the living creatures near Allah are the deaf, the dumb - those who do not use their intellect.

Indeed (inna), | worst (sharra) | of the living creatures (l-dawābi) | near (ʿinda) | Allah (l-lahi) | are the deaf (l-ṣumu), | the dumb (l-buk'mu)- | those who (alladhīna) | do not (lā) | use their intellect (yaʿqilūna).

8:23 And if had known Allah in them any good, surely, He would have made them hear. And if He had made them hear, surely they would have turned away, while they were averse.

And if (walaw) | had known (ʿalima) | Allah (l-lahu) | in them (fīhim) | any good (khayran), | surely, He would have made them hear (la-asmaʿahum). | And if (walaw) | He had made them hear (asmaʿahum), | surely they would have turned away (latawallaw), | while they (wahum) | were averse (muʿ'riḍūna).

8:24 O you who believe! Respond to Allah and His Messenger when he calls you to what gives you life. And know that Allah comes in between a man and his heart, and that to Him you will be gathered.

O you (yāayyuhā) | who (alladhīna) | believe (āmanū)! | Respond (is'tajībū) | to Allah (lillahi) | and His Messenger (walilrrasūli) | when (idhā) | he calls you (daʿākum) | to what (limā) | gives you life (yuḥ'yīkum). | And know (wa-iʿ'lamū) | that (anna) | Allah (l-laha) | comes (yaḥūlu) | in between (bayna) | a man (l-mari) | and his heart (waqalbihi), | and that (wa-annahu) | to Him (ilayhi) | you will be gathered (tuḥ'sharūna).

8:25 And fear a trial not which will afflict those who do wrong among you exclusively. And know that Allah is severe in the penalty.

And fear (wa-ittaqū) | a trial (fit'natan) | not (lā) | which will afflict (tuṣībanna) | those who (alladhīna) | do wrong (ẓalamū) | among you (minkum) | exclusively (khāṣṣatan). | And know (wa-i''lamū) | that (anna) | Allah (l-laha) | is severe (shadīdu) | in the penalty (l-ʿiqābi).

8:26 And remember when you were few and deemed weak in the earth fearing that might do away with you the men, then He sheltered you, and strengthened you with His help, and provided you of the good things so that you may be thankful.

And remember (wa-udh'kurū) | when (idh) | you (antum) | were few (qalīlun) | and deemed weak (mus'taḍʿafūna) | in (fī) | the earth (l-arḍi) | fearing (takhāfūna) | that (an) | might do away with you (yatakhaṭṭafakumu) | the men (l-nāsu), | then He sheltered you (faāwākum), | and strengthened you (wa-ayyadakum) | with His help (binaṣrihi), | and provided you (warazaqakum) | of (mina) | the good things (l-ṭayibāti) | so that you may (laʿallakum) | be thankful (tashkurūna).

8:27 O you who believe! Do not betray Allah and the Messenger, or betray your trusts while you know.

O you (yāayyuhā) | who (alladhīna) | believe (āmanū)! | Do not (lā) | betray (takhūnū) | Allah (l-laha) | and the Messenger (wal-rasūla), | or betray (watakhūnū) | your trusts (amānātikum) | while you (wa-antum) | know (taʿlamūna).

8:28 And know that your wealth and your children are a trial. And that Allah - with Him is a reward great.

And know (wa-i''lamū) | that (annamā) | your wealth (amwālukum) | and your children (wa-awlādukum) | are a trial (fit'natun). | And that (wa-anna) | Allah (l-laha)- | with Him (ʿindahu) | is a reward (ajrun) | great (ʿaẓīmun).

8:29 O you who believe! If you fear Allah, He will grant you a criterion and will remove from you your evil deeds and forgive you. And Allah is the Possessor of Bounty, the Great.

O you (yāayyuhā) | who (alladhīna) | believe (āmanū)! | If (in) | you fear (tattaqū) | Allah (l-laha), | He will grant (yajʿal) | you (lakum) | a criterion (fur'qānan) | and will remove (wayukaffir) | from you (ʿankum) | your evil deeds (sayyiātikum) | and forgive (wayaghfir) | you (lakum). | And Allah (wal-lahu) | is the Possessor (dhū) | of Bounty (l-faḍli), | the Great (l-ʿaẓīmi).

8:30 And when plotted against you those who disbelieved that they restrain you or kill you or drive you out. And they were planning and also was planning Allah. And Allah is the Best of the Planners.

And when (wa-idh) | plotted (yamkuru) | against you (bika) | those who (alladhīna) | disbelieved (kafarū) | that they restrain you (liyuth'bitūka) | or (aw) | kill you (yaqtulūka) | or (aw) | drive you out (yukh'rijūka). | And they were planning (wayamkurūna) | and also was planning (wayamkuru) | Allah (l-lahu). | And Allah (wal-lahu) | is the Best (khayru) | of the Planners (l-mākirīna).

8:31 And when are recited to them Our Verses they say, "Verily we have heard. if we wish surely, we could say like this. Not is this but tales of the former (people)."

And when (wa-idhā) | are recited (tut'lā) | to them (ʿalayhim) | Our Verses (āyātunā) | they say (qālū), | "Verily (qad) | we have heard (sami''nā). | if (law) | we wish (nashāu) | surely, we could say (laqul'nā) | like (mith'la) | this (hādhā). | Not (in) | is this (hādhā) | but (illā) | tales (asāṭīru) | of the former (people). (l-awalīna)"

8:32 And when they said, "O Allah! If was this [it] the truth [of] from You then send rain upon us of stones from the sky or bring upon us a punishment painful."

And when (wa-idh) | they said (qālū), | "O Allah (l-lahuma)! | If (in) | was (kāna) | this (hādhā) | [it] (huwa) | the truth (l-ḥaqa) | [of] (min) | from You (ʿindika) | then send rain (fa-amṭir) | upon us (ʿalaynā) | of stones (ḥijāratan) | from (mina) | the sky (l-samāi) | or (awi) | bring upon us (i'tinā) | a punishment (biʿadhābin) | painful. (alīmin)"

8:33 But not is for Allah that He punishes them while you are among them, and not is Allah the One Who punishes them while they seek forgiveness.

But not (wamā) | is (kāna) | for Allah (l-lahu) | that He punishes them (liyuʿadhibahum) | while you (wa-anta) | are among them (fīhim), | and not (wamā) | is (kāna) | Allah (l-lahu) | the One Who punishes them (muʿadhibahum) | while they (wahum) | seek forgiveness (yastaghfirūna).

8:34 But what is for them that not should punish them Allah while they hinder people from Al-Masjid Al-Haraam, while not they are its guardians? Not can be its guardians except the ones who fear Allah, but most of them do not know.

But what (wamā) | is for them (lahum) | that not (allā) | should punish them (yuʿadhibahumu) | Allah (l-lahu) | while they (wahum) | hinder people (yaṣuddūna) | from (ʿani) | Al-Masjid (l-masjidi) | Al-Haraam (l-ḥarāmi), | while not (wamā) | they are (kānū) | its guardians (awliyāahu)? | Not can be (in) | its guardians (awliyāuhu) | except (illā) | the ones who fear Allah (l-mutaqūna), | but (walākinna) | most of them (aktharahum) | do not (lā) | know (yaʿlamūna).

8:35 And not was their prayer at the House except whistling and clapping. So taste the punishment because you used to disbelieve.

And not (wamā) | was (kāna) | their prayer (ṣalātuhum) | at (ʿinda) | the House (l-bayti) | except (illā) | whistling (mukāan) | and clapping (wataṣdiyatan). | So taste (fadhūqū) | the punishment (l-ʿadhāba) | because (bimā) | you used to (kuntum) | disbelieve (takfurūna).

8:36 Indeed, those who disbelieve, they spend their wealth to hinder people from the way of Allah. So they will spend it, then it will be for them a regret, then they will be overcome. And those who disbelieve, to Hell they will be gathered.

Indeed (inna), | those who (alladhīna) | disbelieve (kafarū), | they spend (yunfiqūna) | their wealth (amwālahum) | to hinder people (liyaṣuddū) | from (ʿan) | the way (sabīli) | of Allah (l-lahi). | So they will spend it (fasayunfiqūnahā), | then (thumma) | it will be (takūnu) | for them (ʿalayhim) | a regret (ḥasratan), | then (thumma) | they will be overcome (yugh'labūna). | And those who (wa-alladhīna) | disbelieve (kafarū), | to (ilā) | Hell (jahannama) | they will be gathered (yuḥ'sharūna).

8:37 That may distinguish Allah the wicked from the good, and place the wicked some of them on others and heap them all together, and put them in Hell. Those - they are the losers.

That may distinguish (liyamīza) | Allah (l-lahu) | the wicked (l-khabītha) | from (mina) | the good (l-ṭayibi), | and place (wayajʿala) | the wicked (l-khabītha) | some of them (baʿḍahu) | on (ʿalā) | others (baʿḍin) | and heap them (fayarkumahu) | all together (jamīʿan), | and put them (fayajʿalahu) | in (fī) | Hell (jahannama). | Those (ulāika)- | they (humu) | are the losers (l-khāsirūna).

8:38 Say to those who disbelieve if they cease will be forgiven for them what [verily] is past. But if they return then verily preceded the practice of the former (people).

Say (qul) | to those who (lilladhīna) | disbelieve (kafarū) | if (in) | they cease (yantahū) | will be forgiven (yugh'far) | for them (lahum) | what (mā) | [verily] (qad) | is past (salafa). | But if (wa-in) | they return (yaʿūdū) | then verily (faqad) | preceded (maḍat) | the practice (sunnatu) | of the former (people) (l-awalīna).

8:39 And fight them until not there is oppression and is the religion all of it for Allah. But if they cease, then indeed, Allah of what they do is All-Seer.

And fight them (waqātilūhum) | until (ḥattā) | not (lā) | there is (takūna) | oppression (fit'natun) | and is (wayakūna) | the religion (l-dīnu) | all of it (kulluhu) | for Allah (lillahi). | But if (fa-ini) | they cease (intahaw), | then indeed (fa-inna), | Allah (l-laha) | of what (bimā) | they do (yaʿmalūna) | is All-Seer (baṣīrun).

8:40 And if they turn away then know that Allah is your Protector, Excellent is the Protector, and Excellent is the Helper.

And if (wa-in) | they turn away (tawallaw) | then know (fa-iʿ'lamū) | that (anna) | Allah (l-laha) | is your Protector (mawlākum), | Excellent (niʿ'ma) | is the Protector (l-mawlā), | and Excellent (waniʿ'ma) | is the Helper (l-naṣīru).

8:41 And know that what you obtain as spoils of war of anything, then that, for Allah is one fifth of it and for the Messenger and for the near relatives, and the orphans and the needy and the wayfarer, if you believe in Allah, and in what We sent down to Our slave on the day of the criterion, the day when met the two forces. And Allah is on every thing All-Powerful.

And know (wa-iʿ'lamū) | that what (annamā) | you obtain as spoils of war (ghanim'tum) | of (min) | anything (shayin), | then that (fa-anna), | for Allah (lillahi) | is one fifth of it (khumusahu) | and for the Messenger (walilrrasūli) | and for the (walidhī) | near relatives (l-qur'bā), | and the orphans (wal-yatāmā) | and the needy (wal-masākīni) | and the (wa-ib'ni) | wayfarer (l-sabīli), | if (in) | you (kuntum) | believe (āmantum) | in Allah (bil-lahi), | and in what (wamā) | We sent down (anzalnā) | to (ʿalā) | Our slave (ʿabdinā) | on the day (yawma) | of the criterion (l-fur'qāni), | the day (yawma) | when met (l-taqā) | the two forces (l-jamʿāni). | And Allah (wal-lahu) | is on (ʿalā) | every (kulli) | thing (shayin) | All-Powerful (qadīrun).

8:42 When you were on side of the valley, the nearer and they were on the side, the farther and the caravan was lower than you. And if you had made an appointment certainly you would have failed in the appointment. But that might accomplish Allah a matter that was destined, that might be destroyed those who were to be destroyed on a clear evidence and might live those who were to live on a clear evidence. And indeed, Allah is All-Hearing, All-Knowing.

When (idh) | you were (antum) | on side of the valley (bil-ʿud'wati), | the nearer (l-dun'yā) | and they (wahum) | were on the side (bil-ʿud'wati), | the farther (l-quṣ'wā) | and the caravan (wal-rakbu) | was lower (asfala) | than you (minkum). | And if (walaw) | you had made an appointment (tawāʿadttum) | certainly you would have failed (la-ikh'talaftum) | in (fī) | the appointment (l-mīʿādi). | But (walākin) | that might accomplish (liyaqḍiya) | Allah (l-lahu) | a matter (amran) | that was (kāna) | destined (mafʿūlan), | that might be destroyed (liyahlika) | those who (man) | were to be destroyed (halaka) | on (ʿan) | a clear evidence (bayyinatin) | and might live (wayaḥyā) | those who (man) | were to live (ḥayya) | on (ʿan) | a clear evidence (bayyinatin). | And indeed (wa-inna), | Allah (l-laha) | is All-Hearing (lasamīʿun), | All-Knowing (ʿalīmun).

8:43 When you where shown them by Allah in your dream as few, and if He had shown them to you as many surely you would have lost courage and surely you would have disputed in the matter, but Allah saved you. Indeed, He is All-Knower of what is in the breasts.

When (idh) | you where shown them (yurīkahumu) | by Allah (l-lahu) | in (fī) | your dream (manāmika) | as few (qalīlan), | and if (walaw) | He had shown them to you (arākahum) | as many (kathīran) | surely you would have lost courage (lafashil'tum) | and surely you would have disputed (walatanāzaʿtum) | in (fī) | the matter (l-amri), | but (walākinna) | Allah (l-laha) | saved you (sallama). | Indeed, He (innahu) | is All-Knower (ʿalīmun) | of what is in (bidhāti) | the breasts (l-ṣudūri).

8:44 And when He showed them to you, when you met - in your eyes as few and He made you appear as few in their eyes that might accomplish Allah might accomplish a matter that was already destined. And to Allah return all the matters.

And when (wa-idh) | He showed them to you (yurīkumūhum), | when (idhi) | you met (l-taqaytum)- | in (fī) | your eyes (aʿyunikum) | as few (qalīlan) | and He made you appear as few (wayuqallilukum) | in (fī) | their eyes (aʿyunihim) | that might accomplish (liyaqḍiya) | Allah might accomplish (l-lahu) | a matter (amran) | that was (kāna) | already destined (mafʿūlan). | And to (wa-ilā) | Allah (l-lahi) | return (tur'ja'u) | all the matters (l-umūru).

8:45 O you who believe! When you meet a force, then be firm and remember Allah much, so that you may be successful.

O you (yāayyuhā) | who (alladhīna) | believe (āmanū)! | When (idhā) | you meet (laqītum) | a force (fi-atan), | then be firm (fa-uth'butū) | and remember (wa-udh'kurū) | Allah (l-laha) | much (kathīran), | so that you may (la'allakum) | be successful (tuf'liḥūna).

8:46 And obey Allah and His Messenger, and do not dispute lest you lose courage and would depart your strength, and be patient. Indeed, Allah is with the patient ones.

And obey (wa-aṭī'ū) | Allah (l-laha) | and His Messenger (warasūlahu), | and do not (walā) | dispute (tanāza'ū) | lest you lose courage (fatafshalū) | and would depart (watadhhaba) | your strength (rīḥukum), | and be patient (wa-iṣ'birū). | Indeed (inna), | Allah (l-laha) | is with (ma'a) | the patient ones (l-ṣābirīna).

8:47 And do not be like those who came forth from their homes boastfully and showing off to the people, and hinder them from the way of Allah. And Allah of what they do is All-Encompassing.

And do not (walā) | be (takūnū) | like those who (ka-alladhīna) | came forth (kharajū) | from (min) | their homes (diyārihim) | boastfully (baṭaran) | and showing off (wariāa) | to the people (l-nāsi), | and hinder them (wayaṣuddūna) | from ('an) | the way (sabīli) | of Allah (l-lahi). | And Allah (wal-lahu) | of what (bimā) | they do (ya'malūna) | is All-Encompassing (muḥīṭun).

8:48 And when made fair-seeming to them the Shaitaan their deeds and he said, "No one can overcome [to] you today from the people and indeed, I am a neighbor for you." But when came in sight the two forces he turned away on his heels and said, "Indeed, I am free of you. Indeed, I see what not you see, indeed, I [I] fear Allah. And Allah is severe in the penalty."

And when (wa-idh) | made fair-seeming (zayyana) | to them (lahumu) | the Shaitaan (l-shayṭānu) | their deeds (a'mālahum) | and he said (waqāla), | "No one (lā) | can overcome (ghāliba) | [to] you (lakumu) | today (l-yawma) | from (mina) | the people (l-nāsi) | and indeed, I am (wa-innī) | a neighbor (jārun) | for you. (lakum)" | But when (falammā) | came in sight (tarāati) | the two forces (l-fi-atāni) | he turned away (nakaṣa) | on ('alā) | his heels ('aqibayhi) | and said (waqāla), | "Indeed, I am (innī) | free (barīon) | of you (minkum). | Indeed, I (innī) | see (arā) | what (mā) | not (lā) | you see (tarawna), | indeed, I (innī) | [I] fear (akhāfu) | Allah (l-laha). | And Allah (wal-lahu) | is severe (shadīdu) | in the penalty. (l-'iqābi)"

8:49 When said the hypocrites and those who - in their hearts was a disease, "Had deluded these people their religion." But whoever puts his trust in Allah then indeed, Allah is All-Mighty, All-Wise."

When (idh) | said (yaqūlu) | the hypocrites (l-munāfiqūna) | and those who (wa-alladhīna)- | in (fī) | their hearts (qulūbihim) | was a disease (maraḍun), | "Had deluded (gharra) | these people (hāulāi) | their religion. (dīnuhum)" | But whoever (waman) | puts his trust (yatawakkal) | in ('alā) | Allah (l-lahi) | then indeed (fa-inna), | Allah (l-laha) | is All-Mighty ('azīzun), | All-Wise. (ḥakīmun)"

8:50 And if you could see when take away souls of those who disbelieve the Angels, striking their faces and their backs "Taste the punishment of the Blazing Fire."

And if (walaw) | you could see (tarā) | when (idh) | take away souls (yatawaffā) | of those who (alladhīna) | disbelieve (kafarū) | the Angels (l-malāikatu), | striking (yaḍribūna) | their faces (wujūhahum) | and their backs (wa-adbārahum) | "Taste (wadhūqū) | the punishment ('adhāba) | of the Blazing Fire. (l-ḥarīqi)"

8:51 That is for what sent forth your hands. And indeed, Allah is not unjust to His slaves.

That (dhālika) | is for what (bimā) | sent forth (qaddamat) | your hands (aydīkum). | And indeed (wa-anna), | Allah (l-laha) | is not (laysa) | unjust (biẓallāmin) | to His slaves (lil''abīdi).

8:52 Like the way of people of Firaun and those who were from before them. They disbelieved in the Signs of Allah, so seized them Allah for their sins. Indeed, Allah is All-Strong and severe in the penalty.

Like the way (kadabi) | of people (āli) | of Firaun (fir''awna) | and those who (wa-alladhīna) | were from (min) | before them (qablihim). | They disbelieved (kafarū) | in the Signs (biāyāti) | of Allah (l-lahi), | so seized them (fa-akhadhahumu) | Allah (l-lahu) | for their sins (bidhunūbihim). | Indeed (inna), | Allah (l-laha) | is All-Strong (qawiyyun) | and severe (shadīdu) | in the penalty (l-'iqābi).

8:53 That is because Allah not is One Who changes a favor which He had bestowed on a people until they change what is in themselves. And indeed, Allah is All-Hearing, All-Knowing.

That (dhālika) | is because (bi-anna) | Allah (l-laha) | not (lam) | is (yaku) | One Who changes (mughayyiran) | a favor (ni''matan) | which He had bestowed (an'amahā) | on ('alā) | a people (qawmin) | until (ḥattā) | they change (yughayyirū) | what (mā) | is in themselves (bi-anfusihim). | And indeed (wa-anna), | Allah (l-laha) | is All-Hearing (samī'un), | All-Knowing ('alīmun).

8:54 Like the way of people of Firaun and those who were from before them. They denied the Signs of their Lord, so We destroyed them for their sins and We drowned the people of Firaun and they all were wrongdoers.

Like the way (kadabi) | of people (āli) | of Firaun (fir''awna) | and those who (wa-alladhīna) | were from (min) | before them (qablihim). | They denied (kadhabū) | the Signs (biāyāti) | of their Lord (rabbihim), | so We destroyed them (fa-ahlaknāhum) | for their sins (bidhunūbihim) | and We drowned (wa-aghraqnā) | the people (āla) | of Firaun (fir''awna) | and they all (wakullun) | were (kānū) | wrongdoers (ẓālimīna).

8:55 Indeed, the worst of the living creatures near Allah are those who disbelieve, and they will not believe.

Indeed (inna), | the worst (sharra) | of the living creatures (l-dawābi) | near ('inda) | Allah (l-lahi) | are those who (alladhīna) | disbelieve (kafarū), | and they (fahum) | will not (lā) | believe (yu'minūna).

8:56 Those who - you made a covenant with them then they break their covenant [in] every time, and they do not fear Allah.

Those who (alladhīna)- | you made a covenant ('āhadtta) | with them (min'hum) | then (thumma) | they break (yanquḍūna) | their covenant ('ahdahum) | [in] (fī) | every (kulli) | time (marratin), | and they (wahum) | do not (lā) | fear Allah (yattaqūna).

8:57 So if you gain dominance over them in the war, disperse by them those who are behind them, so that they may take heed.

So if (fa-immā) | you gain dominance over them (tathqafannahum) | in (fī) | the war (l-ḥarbi), | disperse (fasharrid) | by them (bihim) | those who (man) | are behind them (khalfahum), | so that they may (la'allahum) | take heed (yadhakkarūna).

8:58 And if you fear from a people betrayal throw back to them on equal terms. Indeed, Allah does not love the traitors.

And if (wa-immā) | you fear (takhāfanna) | from (min) | a people (qawmin) | betrayal (khiyānatan) | throw back (fa-inbidh) | to them (ilayhim) | on ('alā) | equal terms (sawāin). | Indeed (inna), | Allah (l-laha) | does not (lā) | love (yuḥibbu) | the traitors (l-khāinīna).

8:59 And let not think those who disbelieve they can outstrip. Indeed, they can not escape.

And let not (walā) | think (yaḥsabanna) | those who (alladhīna) | disbelieve (kafarū) | they can outstrip (sabaqū). | Indeed, they (innahum) | can not (lā) | escape (yuʿʿjizūna).

8:60 And prepare for them whatever you able to of force and of tethered horses to terrify therewith the enemy the enemy, and your enemy and others from besides them, not do you know them but Allah knows them. And whatever you spend from any thing in the way of Allah it will be fully repaid to you, and you will not be wronged.

And prepare (wa-aʿiddū) | for them (lahum) | whatever (mā) | you able to (is'taṭaʿtum) | of (min) | force (quwwatin) | and of (wamin) | tethered (ribāṭi) | horses (l-khayli) | to terrify (tur'hibūna) | therewith (bihi) | the enemy (ʿaduwwa) | the enemy (l-lahi), | and your enemy (waʿaduwwakum) | and others (waākharīna) | from (min) | besides them (dūnihim), | not (lā) | do you know them (taʿlamūnahumu) | but Allah (l-lahu) | knows them (yaʿlamuhum). | And whatever (wamā) | you spend (tunfiqū) | from (min) | any thing (shayin) | in (fī) | the way (sabīli) | of Allah (l-lahi) | it will be fully repaid (yuwaffa) | to you (ilaykum), | and you (wa-antum) | will not (lā) | be wronged (tuẓ'lamūna).

8:61 And if they incline to peace, then you also incline to it, and put your trust in Allah. Indeed, He is All-Hearer, All-Knower.

And if (wa-in) | they incline (janaḥū) | to peace (lilssalmi), | then you also incline (fa-ij'naḥ) | to it (lahā), | and put your trust (watawakkal) | in (ʿalā) | Allah (l-lahi). | Indeed (innahu), | He (huwa) | is All-Hearer (l-samīʿu), | All-Knower (l-ʿalīmu).

8:62 But if they intend to deceive you, then indeed, is sufficient for you, Allah. He is the One Who supported you with His help and with the believers

But if (wa-in) | they intend (yurīdū) | to (an) | deceive you (yakhdaʿūka), | then indeed (fa-inna), | is sufficient for you (ḥasbaka), | Allah (l-lahu). | He (huwa) | is the One Who (alladhī) | supported you (ayyadaka) | with His help (binaṣrihi) | and with the believers (wabil-mu'minīna)

8:63 And He has put affection between their hearts. If you had spent whatever is in the earth all not could you (have) put affection between their hearts, but Allah has put affection between them. Indeed, He is All-Mighty, All-Wise.

And He has put affection (wa-allafa) | between (bayna) | their hearts (qulūbihim). | If (law) | you had spent (anfaqta) | whatever (mā) | is in (fī) | the earth (l-arḍi) | all (jamīʿan) | not (mā) | could you (have) put affection (allafta) | between (bayna) | their hearts (qulūbihim), | but (walākinna) | Allah (l-laha) | has put affection (allafa) | between them (baynahum). | Indeed, He (innahu) | is All-Mighty (ʿazīzun), | All-Wise (ḥakīmun).

8:64 O Prophet! Sufficient for you is Allah and whoever follows you of the believers.

O (yāayyuhā) | Prophet (l-nabiyu)! | Sufficient for you (ḥasbuka) | is Allah (l-lahu) | and whoever (wamani) | follows you (ittabaʿaka) | of (mina) | the believers (l-mu'minīna).

8:65 O Prophet! Urge the believers to [the] fight. If there are among you twenty steadfast they will overcome two hundred. And if there are among you a hundred, they will overcome a thousand of those who disbelieve, because they are a people who do not understand.

O (yāayyuhā) | Prophet (l-nabiyu)! | Urge (ḥarriḍi) | the believers (l-mu'minīna) | to (ʿalā) | [the] fight (l-qitāli). | If (in) | there are (yakun) | among you (minkum) | twenty (ʿish'rūna) | steadfast (ṣābirūna) | they will overcome (yaghlibū) | two hundred (mi-atayni). | And if (wa-in) | there are (yakun) | among you (minkum) | a hundred (mi-atun), | they will overcome (yaghlibū) | a thousand (alfan) | of (mina) | those who (alladhīna) | disbelieve (kafarū), | because they (bi-annahum) | are a people (qawmun) | who do not (lā) | understand (yafqahūna).

8:66 Now has been lightened by Allah for you, and He knows that in you there is weakness. So if there are among you a hundred steadfast, they will overcome two hundred. And if there are among you a thousand, they will overcome two thousand with the permission of Allah. And Allah is with the steadfast.

Now (al-āna) | has been lightened (khaffafa) | by Allah (l-lahu) | for you (ʿankum), | and He knows (waʿalima) | that (anna) | in you (fīkum) | there is weakness (ḍaʿfan). | So if (fa-in) | there are (yakun) | among you (minkum) | a hundred (mi-atun) | steadfast (ṣābiratun), | they will overcome (yaghlibū) | two hundred (mi-atayni). | And if (wa-in) | there are (yakun) | among you (minkum) | a thousand (alfun), | they will overcome (yaghlibū) | two thousand (alfayni) | with the permission (bi-idh'ni) | of Allah (l-lahi). | And Allah (wal-lahu) | is with (maʿa) | the steadfast (l-ṣābirīna).

8:67 Not is for a Prophet that there should be for him prisoners of war until he has battled strenuously in the land. You desire the commodities of the world, but Allah desires for you the Hereafter. And Allah is All-Mighty, All-Wise.

Not (mā) | is (kāna) | for a Prophet (linabiyyin) | that (an) | there should be (yakūna) | for him (lahu) | prisoners of war (asrā) | until (ḥattā) | he has battled strenuously (yuth'khina) | in (fī) | the land (l-arḍi). | You desire (turīdūna) | the commodities (ʿaraḍa) | of the world (l-dun'yā), | but Allah (wal-lahu) | desires (yurīdu) | for you the Hereafter (l-ākhirata). | And Allah (wal-lahu) | is All-Mighty (ʿazīzun), | All-Wise (ḥakīmun).

8:68 Had not an ordainment from Allah preceded, surely would have touched you for what you took - a punishment great.

Had not (lawlā) | an ordainment (kitābun) | from (mina) | Allah (l-lahi) | preceded (sabaqa), | surely would have touched you (lamassakum) | for what (fīmā) | you took (akhadhtum)- | a punishment (ʿadhābun) | great (ʿaẓīmun).

8:69 So eat from what you got as war booty - lawful and good, and fear Allah. Indeed, Allah is Oft-Forgiving, Most Merciful.

So eat (fakulū) | from what (mimmā) | you got as war booty (ghanim'tum)- | lawful (ḥalālan) | and good (ṭayyiban), | and fear (wa-ittaqū) | Allah (l-laha). | Indeed (inna), | Allah (l-laha) | is Oft-Forgiving (ghafūrun), | Most Merciful (raḥīmun).

8:70 O Prophet! Say to whoever is in your hands of the captives, "If knows Allah in your hearts any good, He will give you better than what was taken from you, and He will forgive you. And Allah is Oft-Forgiving, Most Merciful."

O (yāayyuhā) | Prophet (l-nabiyu)! | Say (qul) | to whoever (liman) | is in (fī) | your hands (aydīkum) | of (mina) | the captives (l-asrā), | "If (in) | knows (yaʿlami) | Allah (l-lahu) | in (fī) | your hearts (qulūbikum) | any good (khayran), | He will give you (yu'tikum) | better (khayran) | than what (mimmā) | was taken (ukhidha) | from you (minkum), | and He will forgive (wayaghfir) | you (lakum). | And Allah (wal-lahu) | is Oft-Forgiving (ghafūrun), | Most Merciful. (raḥīmun)"

8:71 But if they intend to betray you certainly they have betrayed Allah from before. So He gave you power over them. And Allah is All-Knower, All-Wise.

But if (wa-in) | they intend (yurīdū) | to betray you (khiyānataka) | certainly (faqad) | they have betrayed (khānū) | Allah (l-laha) | from (min) | before (qablu). | So He gave you power (fa-amkana) | over them (min'hum). | And Allah (wal-lahu) | is All-Knower (ʿalīmun), | All-Wise (ḥakīmun).

8:72 Indeed, those who believed and emigrated and strove hard with their wealth and their lives in the way of Allah and those who gave shelter and helped those - some of them are allies of another. But those who believed and did not emigrate, it is not for you of their protection in in anything, until they emigrate. And if they seek your help in the religion, then upon you is to help them except against a people between you and between them is a treaty. And Allah of what you do is All-Seer.

Indeed (inna), | those who (alladhīna) | believed (āmanū) | and emigrated (wahājarū) | and strove hard (wajāhadū) | with their wealth (bi-amwālihim) | and their lives (wa-anfusihim) | in (fī) | the way (sabīli) | of Allah (l-lahi) | and those who (wa-alladhīna) | gave shelter (āwaw) | and helped (wanaṣarū) | those (ulāika)- | some of them (baʿḍuhum) | are allies (awliyāu) | of another (baʿḍin). | But those who (wa-alladhīna) | believed (āmanū) | and did not (walam) | emigrate (yuhājirū), | it is not (mā) | for you (lakum) | of (min) | their protection (walāyatihim) | in (min) | in anything (shayin), | until (ḥattā) | they emigrate (yuhājirū). | And if (wa-ini) | they seek your help (is'tanṣarūkum) | in (fī) | the religion (l-dīni), | then upon you (faʿalaykumu) | is to help them (l-naṣru) | except (illā) | against (ʿalā) | a people (qawmin) | between you (baynakum) | and between them (wabaynahum) | is a treaty (mīthāqun). | And Allah (wal-lahu) | of what (bimā) | you do (taʿmalūna) | is All-Seer (baṣīrun).

8:73 And those who disbelieve, some of them are allies to another. If not you do it, there will be oppression in the earth and corruption great.

And those who (wa-alladhīna) | disbelieve (kafarū), | some of them (baʿḍuhum) | are allies (awliyāu) | to another (baʿḍin). | If not (illā) | you do it (tafʿalūhu), | there will be (takun) | oppression (fit'natun) | in (fī) | the earth (l-arḍi) | and corruption (wafasādun) | great (kabīrun).

8:74 And those who believed and emigrated and strove hard in the way of Allah and those who gave shelter and helped, those - they are the believers in truth. For them is forgiveness and a provision noble.

And those who (wa-alladhīna) | believed (āmanū) | and emigrated (wahājarū) | and strove hard (wajāhadū) | in (fī) | the way (sabīli) | of Allah (l-lahi) | and those who (wa-alladhīna) | gave shelter (āwaw) | and helped (wanaṣarū), | those (ulāika)- | they are (humu) | the believers (l-mu'minūna) | in truth (ḥaqqan). | For them (lahum) | is forgiveness (maghfiratun) | and a provision (wariz'qun) | noble (karīmun).

8:75 And those who believed from afterwards, and emigrated and strove hard with you, then those are of you. But those of blood relationship, some of them are nearer to another in the Book of Allah. Indeed, Allah of every thing is All-Knower.

And those who (wa-alladhīna) | believed (āmanū) | from (min) | afterwards (baʿdu), | and emigrated (wahājarū) | and strove hard (wajāhadū) | with you (maʿakum), | then those (fa-ulāika) | are of you (minkum). | But those (wa-ulū) | of blood relationship (l-arḥāmi), | some of them (baʿḍuhum) | are nearer (awlā) | to another (bibaʿḍin) | in (fī) | the Book (kitābi) | of Allah (l-lahi). | Indeed (inna), | Allah (l-laha) | of every (bikulli) | thing (shayin) | is All-Knower (ʿalīmun).

Chapter (9) Sūrat l-Tawbah (The Repentance)

9:1 Freedom from obligations from Allah and His Messenger to those with whom you made a covenant from the polytheists.

Freedom from obligations (barāatun) | from (mina) | Allah (l-lahi) | and His Messenger (warasūlihi) | to (ilā) | those with whom (alladhīna) | you made a covenant (ʿāhadttum) | from (mina) | the polytheists (l-mush'rikīna).

9:2 So move about in the land during four months but know that you can not escape Allah and that Allah is the One Who (will) disgrace the disbelievers.

So move about (fasīḥū) | in (fī) | the land (l-arḍi) | during four (arbaʿata) | months (ashhurin) | but know (wa-iʿ'lamū) | that you (annakum) | can not (ghayru) | escape (muʿ'jizī) | Allah (l-lahi) | and that (wa-anna) | Allah (l-laha) | is the One Who (will) disgrace (mukh'zī) | the disbelievers (l-kāfirīna).

9:3 And an announcement from Allah and His Messenger to the people on the day of the greater Pilgrimage that Allah is free from obligations [of] to the polytheists, and so is His Messenger. So if you repent, then, it is best for you. But if you turn away then know that you can not escape Allah. And give glad tidings to those who disbelieve of a punishment painful.

And an announcement (wa-adhānun) | from Allah (mina) | from Allah (l-lahi) | and His Messenger (warasūlihi) | to (ilā) | the people (l-nāsi) | on the day (yawma) | of the greater Pilgrimage (l-ḥaji) | of the greater Pilgrimage (l-akbari) | that (anna) | Allah (l-laha) | is free from obligations (barīon) | [of] (mina) | to the polytheists (l-mush'rikīna), | and so is His Messenger (warasūluhu). | So if (fa-in) | you repent (tub'tum), | then, it is (fahuwa) | best (khayrun) | for you (lakum). | But if (wa-in) | you turn away (tawallaytum) | then know (fa-iʿ'lamū) | that you (annakum) | can not (ghayru) | escape (muʿ'jizī) | Allah (l-lahi). | And give glad tidings (wabashiri) | to those who (alladhīna) | disbelieve (kafarū) | of a punishment (biʿadhābin) | painful (alīmin).

9:4 Except those with whom you have a covenant among the polytheists, then not they have failed you in any thing and not they have supported against you anyone, so fulfil to them their treaty till their term. Indeed, Allah loves the righteous.

Except (illā) | those with whom (alladhīna) | you have a covenant (ʿāhadttum) | among (mina) | the polytheists (l-mush'rikīna), | then (thumma) | not (lam) | they have failed you (yanquṣūkum) | in any thing (shayan) | and not (walam) | they have supported (yuẓāhirū) | against you (ʿalaykum) | anyone (aḥadan), | so fulfil (fa-atimmū) | to them (ilayhim) | their treaty (ʿahdahum) | till (ilā) | their term (muddatihim). | Indeed (inna), | Allah (l-laha) | loves (yuḥibbu) | the righteous (l-mutaqīna).

9:5 Then when have passed the sacred months, then kill the polytheists wherever you find them and seize them and besiege them and sit in wait for them at every place of ambush. But if they repent and establish the prayer and give the zakah then leave their way. Indeed, Allah is Oft-Forgiving, Most Merciful.

Then when (fa-idhā) | have passed (insalakha) | the sacred months (l-ashhuru), | the sacred months (l-ḥurumu), | then kill (fa-uq'tulū) | the polytheists (l-mush'rikīna) | wherever (ḥaythu) | you find them (wajadttumūhum) | and seize them (wakhudhūhum) | and besiege them (wa-uḥ'ṣurūhum) | and sit in wait (wa-uq'ʿudū) | for them (lahum) | at every (kulla) | place of ambush (marṣadin). | But if (fa-in) | they repent (tābū) | and establish (wa-aqāmū) | the prayer (l-ṣalata) | and give (waātawū) | the zakah (l-zakata) | then leave (fakhallū) | their way (sabīlahum). | Indeed (inna), | Allah (l-laha) | is Oft-Forgiving (ghafūrun), | Most Merciful (raḥīmun).

9:6 And if anyone of the polytheists seek your protection then grant him protection until he hears the Words of Allah. Then escort him to his place of safety. That is because they are a people who do not know.

And if (wa-in) | anyone (aḥadun) | of (mina) | the polytheists (l-mush'rikīna) | seek your protection (is'tajāraka) | then grant him protection (fa-ajir'hu) | until (ḥattā) | he hears (yasmaʿa) | the Words of Allah (kalāma). | the Words of Allah (l-lahi). | Then (thumma) | escort him (abligh'hu) | to his place of safety (mamanahu). | That (dhālika) | is because they (bi-annahum) | are a people (qawmun) | who do not know (lā). | who do not know (yaʿlamūna).

9:7 How can there be for the polytheists a covenant with Allah and with His Messenger, except those with whom you made a covenant near Al-Masjid Al-Haraam? So long as they are upright to you then you be upright to them. Indeed, Allah loves the righteous.

How (kayfa) | can there be (yakūnu) | for the polytheists (lil'mush'rikīna) | a covenant (ʿahdun) | with (ʿinda) | Allah (l-lahi) | and with (waʿinda) | His Messenger (rasūlihi), | except (illā) | those with whom (alladhīna) | you made a covenant (ʿāhadttum) | near (ʿinda) | Al-Masjid (l-masjidi) | Al-Haraam (l-ḥarāmi)? | So long as (famā) | they are upright (is'taqāmū) | to you (lakum) | then you be upright (fa-is'taqīmū) | to them (lahum). | Indeed (inna), | Allah (l-laha) | loves (yuḥibbu) | the righteous (l-mutaqīna).

9:8 How while, if they gain dominance over you they do not regard the ties with you of kinship and not covenant of protection? They satisfy you with their mouths but refuse, their hearts and most of them are defiantly disobedient.

How (kayfa) | while, if (wa-in) | they gain dominance (yaẓharū) | over you (ʿalaykum) | they do not regard the ties (lā) | they do not regard the ties (yarqubū) | with you (fīkum) | of kinship (illan) | and not (walā) | covenant of protection (dhimmatan)? | They satisfy you (yur'ḍūnakum) | with their mouths (bi-afwāhihim) | but refuse (watabā), | their hearts (qulūbuhum) | and most of them (wa-aktharuhum) | are defiantly disobedient (fāsiqūna).

9:9 They exchange [with] the Verses of Allah for a little price, and they hinder people from His way. Indeed, evil is what they used to do.

They exchange (ish'taraw) | [with] the Verses of Allah (biāyāti) | [with] the Verses of Allah (l-lahi) | for a little price (thamanan), | for a little price (qalīlan), | and they hinder people (faṣaddū) | from (ʿan) | His way (sabīlihi). | Indeed (innahum), | evil (sāa) | is what (mā) | they used to (kānū) | do (yaʿmalūna).

9:10 Not they respect the ties towards a believer of kinship and not covenant of protection. And those [they] are the transgressors.

Not (lā) | they respect the ties (yarqubūna) | towards (fī) | a believer (mu'minin) | of kinship (illan) | and not (walā) | covenant of protection (dhimmatan). | And those (wa-ulāika) | [they] (humu) | are the transgressors (l-muʿ'tadūna).

9:11 But if they repent and establish the prayer and give the zakah, then they are your brothers in [the] religion. And We explain in detail the Verses for a people who know.

But if (fa-in) | they repent (tābū) | and establish (wa-aqāmū) | the prayer (l-ṣalata) | and give (waātawū) | the zakah (l-zakata), | then they are your brothers (fa-ikh'wānukum) | in (fī) | [the] religion (l-dīni). | And We explain in detail (wanufaṣṣilu) | the Verses (l-āyāti) | for a people (liqawmin) | who know (yaʿlamūna).

9:12 And if they break their oaths after their treaty and defame [in] your religion, then fight the leaders of [the] disbelief, indeed, they - no oaths for them, so that they may cease.

And if (wa-in) | they break (nakathū) | their oaths (aymānahum) | after (min) | after (baʿdi) | their treaty (ʿahdihim) | and defame (waṭaʿanū) | [in] (fī) | your religion (dīnikum), | then fight (faqātilū) | the leaders (a-immata) | of [the] disbelief (l-kuf'ri), | indeed, they (innahum)- | no (lā) | oaths (aymāna) | for them (lahum), | so that they may (laʿallahum) | cease (yantahūna).

9:13 Will not you fight a people who broke their oaths and determined to drive out the Messenger and they began to attack you first time? Do you fear them? But Allah has more right that you should fear Him, if you are believers.

Will not (alā) | you fight (tuqātilūna) | a people (qawman) | who broke (nakathū) | their oaths (aymānahum) | and determined (wahammū) | to drive out (bi-ikh'rāji) | the Messenger (l-rasūli) | and they (wahum) | began to attack you (badaūkum) | first (awwala) | time (marratin)? | Do you fear them (atakhshawnahum)? | But Allah (fal-lahu) | has more right (aḥaqqu) | that (an) | you should fear Him (takhshawhu), | if (in) | you are (kuntum) | believers (mu'minīna).

9:14 Fight them - Allah will punish them by your hands and disgrace them and give you victory over them, and will heal the breasts of a people who are believers.

Fight them (qātilūhum)- | Allah will punish them (yuʿadhib'humu) | Allah will punish them (l-lahu) | by your hands (bi-aydīkum) | and disgrace them (wayukh'zihim) | and give you victory (wayanṣur'kum) | over them (ʿalayhim), | and will heal (wayashfi) | the breasts (ṣudūra) | of a people (qawmin) | who are believers (mu'minīna).

9:15 And remove the anger of their hearts. And Allah accepts repentance of whom He wills. And Allah is All-Knower, All-Wise.

And remove (wayudh'hib) | the anger (ghayẓa) | of their hearts (qulūbihim). | And Allah accepts repentance (wayatūbu) | And Allah accepts repentance (l-lahu) | of (ʿalā) | whom (man) | He wills (yashāu). | And Allah (wal-lahu) | is All-Knower (ʿalīmun), | All-Wise (ḥakīmun).

9:16 Or do you think that you would be left while not Allah made evident those who strive among you, and not take besides Allah and not His Messenger and not the believers as intimates? And Allah is All-Aware of what you do.

Or (am) | do you think (ḥasib'tum) | that (an) | you would be left (tut'rakū) | while not (walammā) | Allah made evident (yaʿlami) | Allah made evident (l-lahu) | those who (alladhīna) | strive (jāhadū) | among you (minkum), | and not (walam) | take (yattakhidhū) | besides Allah (min) | besides Allah (dūni) | besides Allah (l-lahi) | and not (walā) | His Messenger (rasūlihi) | and not (walā) | the believers (l-mu'minīna) | as intimates (walījatan)? | And Allah (wal-lahu) | is All-Aware (khabīrun) | of what (bimā) | you do (taʿmalūna).

9:17 It is not for the polytheists that they maintain the masajid of Allah while witnessing against themselves [with] disbelief. For those, worthless are their deeds, and in the Fire they will abide forever.

It is not (mā) | It is not (kāna) | for the polytheists (lil'mush'rikīna) | that (an) | they maintain (yaʿmurū) | the masajid of Allah (masājida) | the masajid of Allah (l-lahi) | while witnessing (shāhidīna) | against (ʿalā) | themselves (anfusihim) | [with] disbelief (bil-kuf'ri). | For those (ulāika), | worthless (ḥabiṭat) | are their deeds (aʿmāluhum), | and in (wafī) | the Fire (l-nāri) | they (hum) | will abide forever (khālidūna).

9:18 Only will maintain the masajid of Allah the one who believes in Allah and the Day the Last, and establishes the prayer and gives the zakah and not fear except Allah. Then perhaps those, [that] they are of the guided ones.

Only (innamā) | will maintain (yaʿmuru) | the masajid of Allah (masājida) | the masajid of Allah (l-lahi) | the one who (man) | believes (āmana) | in Allah (bil-lahi) | and the Day (wal-yawmi) | the Last (l-ākhiri), | and establishes (wa-aqāma) | the prayer (l-ṣalata) | and gives (waātā) | the zakah (l-zakata) | and not (walam) | fear (yakhsha) | except (illā) | Allah (l-laha). | Then perhaps (faʿasā) | those (ulāika), | [that] (an) | they are (yakūnū) | of (mina) | the guided ones (l-muh'tadīna).

9:19 Do you make the providing of water to the pilgrims and the maintenance of Al-Masjid Al-Haraam like the one who believes in Allah and the Day the Last, and strives in the way of Allah? They are not equal near Allah. And Allah does not guide the people - the wrongdoers.

Do you make (ajaʿaltum) | the providing of water (siqāyata) | to the pilgrims (l-ḥāji) | and the maintenance (waʿimārata) | of Al-Masjid Al-Haraam (l-masjidi) | of Al-Masjid Al-Haraam (l-ḥarāmi) | like the one who (kaman) | believes (āmana) | in Allah (bil-lahi) | and the Day (wal-yawmi) | the Last (l-ākhiri), | and strives (wajāhada) | in (fī) | the way (sabīli) | of Allah (l-lahi)? | They are not equal (lā) | They are not equal (yastawūna) | near (ʿinda) | Allah (l-lahi). | And Allah (wal-lahu) | does not (lā) | guide (yahdī) | the people (l-qawma)- | the wrongdoers (l-ẓālimīna).

9:20 Those who believed and emigrated and strove in the way of Allah with their wealth and their lives are greater in rank near Allah. And those - they are the successful.

Those who (alladhīna) | believed (āmanū) | and emigrated (wahājarū) | and strove (wajāhadū) | in (fī) | the way (sabīli) | of Allah (l-lahi) | with their wealth (bi-amwālihim) | and their lives (wa-anfusihim) | are greater (aʿẓamu) | in rank (darajatan) | near (ʿinda) | Allah (l-lahi). | And those (wa-ulāika)- | they (humu) | are the successful (l-fāizūna).

9:21 Their Lord gives them glad tidings of Mercy from Him and Pleasure, and Gardens for them - in it is bliss enduring.

Their Lord gives them glad tidings (yubashiruhum) | Their Lord gives them glad tidings (rabbuhum) | of Mercy (biraḥmatin) | from Him (min'hu) | and Pleasure (wariḍ'wānin), | and Gardens (wajannātin) | for them (lahum)- | in it (fīhā) | is bliss (naʿīmun) | enduring (muqīmun).

9:22 They will abide in it forever. Indeed, Allah - with Him is a reward great.

They will abide (khālidīna) | in it (fīhā) | forever (abadan). | Indeed (inna), | Allah (l-laha)- | with Him (ʿindahu) | is a reward (ajrun) | great (ʿaẓīmun).

9:23 O you who believe! Do not take your fathers and your brothers as allies if they prefer [the] disbelief over [the] belief. And whoever takes them as allies among you, then those [they] are the wrongdoers.

O you (yāayyuhā) | who (alladhīna) | believe (āmanū)! | Do not (lā) | take (tattakhidhū) | your fathers (ābāakum) | and your brothers (wa-ikh'wānakum) | as allies (awliyāa) | if (ini) | they prefer (is'taḥabbū) | [the] disbelief (l-kuf'ra) | over (ʿalā) | [the] belief (l-īmāni). | And whoever (waman) | takes them as allies (yatawallahum) | among you (minkum), | then those (fa-ulāika) | [they] (humu) | are the wrongdoers (l-ẓālimūna).

9:24 Say, "If are your fathers, and your sons, and your brothers, and your spouses, and your relatives, and wealth that you have acquired and the commerce, you fear a decline in it and the dwellings you delight in it are more beloved to you than Allah, and His Messenger and striving in His way, then wait until Allah brings His Command. And Allah does not guide the people - the defiantly disobedient."

Say (qul), | "If (in) | are (kāna) | your fathers (ābāukum), | and your sons (wa-abnāukum), | and your brothers (wa-ikh'wānukum), | and your spouses (wa-azwājukum), | and your relatives (waʿashīratukum), | and wealth (wa-amwālun) | that you have acquired (iq'taraftumūhā) | and the commerce (watijāratun), | you fear (takhshawna) | a decline in it (kasādahā) | and the dwellings (wamasākinu) | you delight in it (tarḍawnahā) | are more beloved (aḥabba) | to you (ilaykum) | than (mina) | Allah (l-lahi), | and His Messenger (warasūlihi) | and striving (wajihādin) | in (fī) | His way (sabīlihi), | then wait (fatarabbaṣū) | until (ḥattā) | Allah brings (yatiya) | Allah brings (l-lahu) | His Command (bi-amrihi). | And Allah (wal-lahu) | does not (lā) | guide (yahdī) | the people (l-qawma)- | the defiantly disobedient. (l-fāsiqīna)"

9:25 Verily, Allah helped you in regions many, and on the day of Hunain, when pleased you your multitude, but not availed you anything and was straitened for you the earth in spite of its vastness, then you turned back, fleeing.

Verily (laqad), | Allah helped you (naṣarakumu) | Allah helped you (l-lahu) | in (fī) | regions (mawāṭina) | many (kathīratin), | and on the day (wayawma) | of Hunain (ḥunaynin), | when (idh) | pleased you (aʿjabatkum) | your multitude (kathratukum), | but not (falam) | availed (tugh'ni) | you (ʿankum) | anything (shayan) | and was straitened (waḍāqat) | for you (ʿalaykumu) | the earth (l-arḍu) | in spite of its vastness (bimā), | in spite of its vastness (raḥubat), | then (thumma) | you turned back (wallaytum), | fleeing (mud'birīna).

9:26 Then Allah sent down His tranquility on His Messenger, and on the believers and sent down forces, which you did not see and He punished those who disbelieved. And that is the recompense of the disbelievers.

Then (thumma) | Allah sent down (anzala) | Allah sent down (l-lahu) | His tranquility (sakīnatahu) | on (ʿalā) | His Messenger (rasūlihi), | and on (waʿalā) | the believers (l-mu'minīna) | and sent down (wa-anzala) | forces (junūdan), | which you did not see (lam) | which you did not see (tarawhā) | and He punished (waʿadhaba) | those who (alladhīna) | disbelieved (kafarū). | And that (wadhālika) | is the recompense (jazāu) | of the disbelievers (l-kāfirīna).

9:27 Then Allah accepts repentance after that for whom He wills. And Allah is Oft-Forgiving, Most Merciful.

Then (thumma) | Allah accepts repentance (yatūbu) | Allah accepts repentance (l-lahu) | after (min) | after (baʿdi) | that (dhālika) | for (ʿalā) | whom (man) | He wills (yashāu). | And Allah (wal-lahu) | is Oft-Forgiving (ghafūrun), | Most Merciful (raḥīmun).

9:28 O you who believe! Indeed, the polytheists are unclean, so let them not come near Al-Masjid Al-Haraam after this, their final year. And if you fear poverty, then soon Allah will enrich you from His Bounty, if He wills. Indeed, Allah is All-Knower, All-Wise.

O you who believe (yāayyuhā)! | O you who believe (alladhīna)! | O you who believe (āmanū)! | Indeed (innamā), | the polytheists (l-mush'rikūna) | are unclean (najasun), | so let them not come near (falā) | so let them not come near (yaqrabū) | Al-Masjid Al-Haraam (l-masjida) | Al-Masjid Al-Haraam (l-ḥarāma) | after (baʿda) | this, their final year (ʿāmihim). | this, their final year (hādhā). | And if (wa-in) | you fear (khif'tum) | poverty (ʿaylatan), | then soon (fasawfa) | Allah will enrich you (yugh'nīkumu) | Allah will enrich you (l-lahu) | from (min) | His Bounty (faḍlihi), | if (in) | He wills (shāa). | Indeed (inna), | Allah (l-laha) | is All-Knower (ʿalīmun), | All-Wise (ḥakīmun).

9:29 Fight those who do not believe in Allah and not in the Day the Last, and not they make unlawful what Allah has made unlawful and His Messenger, and not they acknowledge the religion of the truth, from those who were given the Scripture, until they pay the jizyah willingly, while they are subdued.

Fight (qātilū) | those who (alladhīna) | do not (lā) | believe (yu'minūna) | in Allah (bil-lahi) | and not (walā) | in the Day (bil-yawmi) | the Last (l-ākhiri), | and not (walā) | they make unlawful (yuḥarrimūna) | what (mā) | Allah has made unlawful (ḥarrama) | Allah has made unlawful (l-lahu) | and His Messenger (warasūluhu), | and not (walā) | they acknowledge (yadīnūna) | the religion (dīna) | of the truth (l-ḥaqi), | from (mina) | those who (alladhīna) | were given (ūtū) | the Scripture (l-kitāba), | until (ḥattā) | they pay (yuʿ'ṭū) | the jizyah (l-jiz'yata) | willingly (ʿan), | willingly (yadin), | while they (wahum) | are subdued (ṣāghirūna).

9:30 And said the Jews, "Uzair is son of Allah." And said the Christians, "Messiah is son of Allah." That is their saying with their mouths, they imitate the saying of those who disbelieved before. May Allah destroy them. How deluded are they!

And said (waqālati) | the Jews (l-yahūdu), | "Uzair (ʿuzayrun) | is son (ub'nu) | of Allah. (l-lahi)" | And said (waqālati) | the Christians (l-naṣārā), | "Messiah (l-masīḥu) | is son (ub'nu) | of Allah. (l-lahi)" | That (dhālika) | is their saying (qawluhum) | with their mouths (bi-afwāhihim), | they imitate (yuḍāhiūna) | the saying (qawla) | of those who (alladhīna) | disbelieved (kafarū) | before (min). | before (qablu). | May Allah destroy them (qātalahumu). | May Allah destroy them (l-lahu). | How (annā) | deluded are they (yu'fakūna)!

9:31 They have taken their rabbis and their monks as Lords besides Allah and the Messiah, son of

Maryam. And not they were commanded except that they worship One God. There is no god except Him. Glory be to Him from what they associate with Him.

They have taken (ittakhadhū) | their rabbis (aḥbārahum) | and their monks (waruh'bānahum) | as Lords (arbāban) | besides (min) | besides (dūni) | Allah (l-lahi) | and the Messiah (wal-masīḥa), | son (ib'na) | of Maryam (maryama). | And not (wamā) | they were commanded (umirū) | except (illā) | that they worship (liyaʿbudū) | One God (ilāhan). | One God (wāḥidan). | There is no (lā) | god (ilāha) | except (illā) | Him (huwa). | Glory be to Him (sub'ḥānahu) | from what (ʿammā) | they associate with Him (yush'rikūna).

9:32 They want to extinguish Allah's light with their mouths, but Allah refuses except to perfect His Light even if the disbelievers dislike it.

They want (yurīdūna) | to (an) | extinguish (yuṭ'fiū) | Allah's light (nūra) | Allah's light (l-lahi) | with their mouths (bi-afwāhihim), | but Allah refuses (wayabā) | but Allah refuses (l-lahu) | except (illā) | to (an) | perfect (yutimma) | His Light (nūrahu) | even if (walaw) | the disbelievers dislike it (kariha). | the disbelievers dislike it (l-kāfirūna).

9:33 He is the One Who has sent His Messenger with the guidance and the religion of [the] truth, to manifest it over all religions. Even if dislike it the polytheists.

He (huwa) | is the One Who (alladhī) | has sent (arsala) | His Messenger (rasūlahu) | with the guidance (bil-hudā) | and the religion (wadīni) | of [the] truth (l-ḥaqi), | to manifest it (liyuẓ'hirahu) | over (ʿalā) | all religions (l-dīni). | all religions (kullihi). | Even if (walaw) | dislike it (kariha) | the polytheists (l-mush'rikūna).

9:34 O you who believe! Indeed, many of the rabbis and the monks surely eat the wealth of the people in falsehood, and hinder from the way of Allah. And those who hoard the gold and the silver, and do not spend it in the way of Allah, [so] give them tidings of a punishment painful.

O you who believe (yāayyuhā)! | O you who believe (alladhīna)! | O you who believe (āmanū)! | Indeed (inna), | many (kathīran) | of (mina) | the rabbis (l-aḥbāri) | and the monks (wal-ruh'bāni) | surely eat (layakulūna) | the wealth (amwāla) | of the people (l-nāsi) | in falsehood (bil-bāṭili), | and hinder (wayaṣuddūna) | from (ʿan) | the way (sabīli) | of Allah (l-lahi). | And those who (wa-alladhīna) | hoard (yaknizūna) | the gold (l-dhahaba) | and the silver (wal-fiḍata), | and do not (walā) | spend it (yunfiqūnahā) | in (fī) | the way (sabīli) | of Allah (l-lahi), | [so] give them tidings (fabashir'hum) | of a punishment (biʿadhābin) | painful (alīmin).

9:35 The Day it will be heated [on it] in the Fire of Hell, and will be branded with it their foreheads and their flanks and their backs, "This is what you hoarded for yourselves, so taste what you used to hoard."

The Day (yawma) | it will be heated [on it] (yuḥ'mā) | it will be heated [on it] (ʿalayhā) | in (fī) | the Fire (nāri) | of Hell (jahannama), | and will be branded (fatuk'wā) | with it (bihā) | their foreheads (jibāhuhum) | and their flanks (wajunūbuhum) | and their backs (waẓuhūruhum), | "This (hādhā) | is what (mā) | you hoarded (kanaztum) | for yourselves (li-anfusikum), | so taste (fadhūqū) | what (mā) | you used to (kuntum) | hoard. (taknizūna)"

9:36 Indeed, the number of the months with Allah is twelve months in the ordinance of Allah from the Day He created the heavens and the earth; of them, four are sacred. That is the religion the upright, so do not wrong therein yourselves. And fight the polytheists all together, as they fight you all together. And know that Allah is with the righteous.

Indeed (inna), | the number (ʿiddata) | of the months (l-shuhūri) | with (ʿinda) | Allah (l-lahi) | is twelve (ith'nā) | is twelve (ʿashara) | months (shahran) | in (fī) | the ordinance (kitābi) | of Allah (l-lahi) | from the Day (yawma) | He created (khalaqa) | the heavens (l-samāwāti) | and the earth (wal-arḍa); | of them (min'hā), | four (arbaʿatun) | are sacred (ḥurumun). | That (dhālika) | is the religion (l-dīnu) | the upright (l-qayimu), | so do not (falā) | wrong (taẓlimū) | therein (fīhinna) |

yourselves (anfusakum). | And fight (waqātilū) | the polytheists (l-mush'rikīna) | all together (kāffatan), | as (kamā) | they fight you (yuqātilūnakum) | all together (kāffatan). | And know (wa-i''lamū) | that (anna) | Allah (l-laha) | is with (maʿa) | the righteous (l-mutaqīna).

9:37 Indeed, the postponing is an increase in the disbelief, are led astray by it those who disbelieve. They make it lawful one year and make it unlawful another year, to adjust the number which Allah has made unlawful and making lawful what Allah has made unlawful. Is made fair-seeming to them the evil of their deeds. And Allah does not guide the people - the disbelievers.

Indeed (innamā), | the postponing (l-nasīu) | is an increase (ziyādatun) | in (fī) | the disbelief (l-kuf'ri), | are led astray (yuḍallu) | by it (bihi) | those who (alladhīna) | disbelieve (kafarū). | They make it lawful (yuḥillūnahu) | one year (ʿāman) | and make it unlawful (wayuḥarrimūnahu) | another year (ʿāman), | to adjust (liyuwāṭiū) | the number (ʿiddata) | which (mā) | Allah has made unlawful (ḥarrama) | Allah has made unlawful (l-lahu) | and making lawful (fayuḥillū) | what (mā) | Allah has made unlawful (ḥarrama). | Allah has made unlawful (l-lahu). | Is made fair-seeming (zuyyina) | to them (lahum) | the evil (sūu) | of their deeds (aʿmālihim). | And Allah (wal-lahu) | does not (lā) | guide (yahdī) | the people (l-qawma)- | the disbelievers (l-kāfirīna).

9:38 O you who believe! What is the matter with you when it is said to you go forth in the way of Allah, you cling heavily to the earth? Are you pleased with the life of the world rather than the Hereafter? But what is the enjoyment of the life of the world in comparison to the hereafter except a little.

O you who believe (yāayyuhā)! | O you who believe (alladhīna)! | O you who believe (āmanū)! | What (mā) | is the matter with you (lakum) | when (idhā) | it is said (qīla) | to you (lakumu) | go forth (infirū) | in (fī) | the way (sabīli) | of Allah (l-lahi), | you cling heavily (ithāqaltum) | to (ilā) | the earth (l-arḍi)? | Are you pleased (araḍītum) | with the life (bil-ḥayati) | of the world (l-dun'yā) | rather than (mina) | the Hereafter (l-ākhirati)? | But what (famā) | is the enjoyment (matāʿu) | of the life (l-ḥayati) | of the world (l-dun'yā) | in comparison to (fī) | the hereafter (l-ākhirati) | except (illā) | a little (qalīlun).

9:39 If not you go forth, He will punish you with a painful punishment, and will replace you with a people other than you, and not you can harm Him in anything. And Allah is on every thing All-Powerful.

If not (illā) | you go forth (tanfirū), | He will punish you (yuʿadhib'kum) | with a painful punishment (ʿadhāban), | with a painful punishment (alīman), | and will replace you (wayastabdil) | with a people (qawman) | other than you (ghayrakum), | and not (walā) | you can harm Him (taḍurrūhu) | in anything (shayan). | And Allah (wal-lahu) | is on (ʿalā) | every (kulli) | thing (shayin) | All-Powerful (qadīrun).

9:40 If not you help him, certainly, Allah helped him, when drove him out those who disbelieved, the second of the two, when they both were in the cave, when he said to his companion, "Do not grieve, indeed, Allah is with us." Then Allah sent down His tranquility upon him, and supported him with forces which you did not see, and made the word of those who disbelieved the lowest, while the Word of Allah it is the highest. And Allah is All-Mighty, All-Wise.

If not (illā) | you help him (tanṣurūhu), | certainly (faqad), | Allah helped him (naṣarahu), | Allah helped him (l-lahu), | when (idh) | drove him out (akhrajahu) | those who (alladhīna) | disbelieved (kafarū), | the second (thāniya) | of the two (ith'nayni), | when (idh) | they both (humā) | were in (fī) | the cave (l-ghāri), | when (idh) | he said (yaqūlu) | to his companion (liṣāḥibihi), | "Do not (lā) | grieve (taḥzan), | indeed (inna), | Allah (l-laha) | is with us. (maʿanā)" | Then Allah sent down (fa-anzala) | Then Allah sent down (l-lahu) | His tranquility (sakīnatahu) | upon him (ʿalayhi), | and supported him (wa-ayyadahu) | with forces (bijunūdin) | which you did not see (lam), | which you did not see (tarawhā), | and made (wajaʿala) | the word (kalimata) | of those who (alladhīna) | disbelieved (kafarū) | the lowest (l-suf'lā), | while the Word (wakalimatu) | of Allah (l-lahi) | it is (hiya) | the highest (l-ʿul'yā). | And Allah (wal-lahu) | is All-Mighty (ʿazīzun), | All-Wise (ḥakīmun).

9:41 Go forth, light or heavy and strive with your wealth and your lives in the way of Allah. That is better for you, if you know.

Go forth (infirū), | light (khifāfan) | or heavy (wathiqālan) | and strive (wajāhidū) | with your wealth (bi-amwālikum) | and your lives (wa-anfusikum) | in (fī) | the way (sabīli) | of Allah (l-lahi). | That (dhālikum) | is better (khayrun) | for you (lakum), | if (in) | you (kuntum) | know (taʿlamūna).

9:42 If it had been a gain near and a journey easy, surely they would have followed you but was long for them the distance. And they will swear by Allah, "If we were able, certainly we would have come forth with you." They destroy their own selves and Allah knows that indeed, they are surely liars.

If (law) | it had been (kāna) | a gain (ʿaraḍan) | near (qarīban) | and a journey (wasafaran) | easy (qāṣidan), | surely they would have followed you (la-ittabaʿūka) | but (walākin) | was long (baʿudat) | for them (ʿalayhimu) | the distance (l-shuqatu). | And they will swear (wasayaḥlifūna) | by Allah (bil-lahi), | "If (lawi) | we were able (is'taṭaʿnā), | certainly we would have come forth (lakharajnā) | with you. (maʿakum)" | They destroy (yuh'likūna) | their own selves (anfusahum) | and Allah (wal-lahu) | knows (yaʿlamu) | that indeed, they (innahum) | are surely liars (lakādhibūna).

9:43 May Allah forgive you! Why did you grant leave to them until became evident to you those who were truthful, and you knew the liars?

May Allah forgive (ʿafā) | May Allah forgive (l-lahu) | you (ʿanka)! | Why did (lima) | you grant leave (adhinta) | to them (lahum) | until (ḥattā) | became evident (yatabayyana) | to you (laka) | those who (alladhīna) | were truthful (ṣadaqū), | and you knew (wataʿlama) | the liars (l-kādhibīna)?

9:44 Would not ask your permission those who believe in Allah and the Day the Last that they strive with their wealth and their lives. And Allah is All-Knower of the righteous.

Would not ask your permission (lā) | Would not ask your permission (yastadhinuka) | those who (alladhīna) | believe (yu'minūna) | in Allah (bil-lahi) | and the Day (wal-yawmi) | the Last (l-ākhiri) | that (an) | they strive (yujāhidū) | with their wealth (bi-amwālihim) | and their lives (wa-anfusihim). | And Allah (wal-lahu) | is All-Knower (ʿalīmun) | of the righteous (bil-mutaqīna).

9:45 Only ask your leave those who do not believe in Allah and the Day the Last, and are in doubts their hearts, so they in their doubts they waver.

Only (innamā) | ask your leave (yastadhinuka) | those who (alladhīna) | do not (lā) | believe (yu'minūna) | in Allah (bil-lahi) | and the Day (wal-yawmi) | the Last (l-ākhiri), | and are in doubts (wa-ir'tābat) | their hearts (qulūbuhum), | so they (fahum) | in (fī) | their doubts (raybihim) | they waver (yataraddadūna).

9:46 And if they had wished to go forth, surely they would have prepared for it some preparation. But Allah disliked their being sent, so He made them lag behind and it was said, "Sit with those who sit."

And if (walaw) | they had wished (arādū) | to go forth (l-khurūja), | surely they would have prepared (la-aʿaddū) | for it (lahu) | some preparation (ʿuddatan). | But (walākin) | Allah disliked (kariha) | Allah disliked (l-lahu) | their being sent (inbiʿāthahum), | so He made them lag behind (fathabbaṭahum) | and it was said (waqīla), | "Sit (uq''udū) | with (maʿa) | those who sit. (l-qāʿidīna)"

9:47 If they had gone forth with you, not they would have increased you except in confusion and would have been active in your midst seeking for you dissension. And among you are some who would have listened to them. And Allah is All-Knower, of the wrongdoers.

If (law) | they had gone forth (kharajū) | with you (fīkum), | not (mā) | they would have increased you (zādūkum) | except (illā) | in confusion (khabālan) | and would have been active (wala-awḍaʿū) | in your midst (khilālakum) | seeking for you (yabghūnakumu) | dissension (l-fit'nata). | And among you are some (wafīkum) | who would have listened (sammāʿūna) | to them (lahum). | And Allah (wal-lahu) | is All-Knower (ʿalīmun), | of the wrongdoers (bil-ẓālimīna).

9:48 Verily, they had sought dissension before and had upset for you the matters until came the truth and became manifest the Order of Allah, while they disliked it.

Verily (laqadi), | they had sought (ib'taghawū) | dissension (l-fit'nata) | before (min) | before (qablu) | and had upset (waqallabū) | for you (laka) | the matters (l-umūra) | until (ḥattā) | came (jāa) | the truth (l-ḥaqu) | and became manifest (waẓahara) | the Order of Allah (amru), | the Order of Allah (l-lahi), | while they (wahum) | disliked it (kārihūna).

9:49 And among them is he who says, "Grant me leave and do not put me to trial." Surely, in the trial they have fallen. And indeed, Hell will surely surround the disbelievers.

And among them (wamin'hum) | is he who (man) | says (yaqūlu), | "Grant me leave (i'dhan) | "Grant me leave (lī) | and do not (walā) | put me to trial. (taftinnī)" | Surely (alā), | in (fī) | the trial (l-fit'nati) | they have fallen (saqaṭū). | And indeed (wa-inna), | Hell (jahannama) | will surely surround (lamuḥīṭatun) | the disbelievers (bil-kāfirīna).

9:50 If befalls you good, it distresses them, but if befalls you a calamity they say, "Verily, we took our matter before." And they turn away while they are rejoicing.

If (in) | befalls you (tuṣib'ka) | good (ḥasanatun), | it distresses them (tasu'hum), | but if (wa-in) | befalls you (tuṣib'ka) | a calamity (muṣībatun) | they say (yaqūlū), | "Verily (qad), | we took (akhadhnā) | our matter (amranā) | before. (min)" | before. (qablu)" | And they turn away (wayatawallaw) | while they (wahum) | are rejoicing (fariḥūna).

9:51 Say, "Never will befall us except what Allah has decreed for us, He is our Protector." And on Allah [so] let the believers put their trust.

Say (qul), | "Never (lan) | will befall us (yuṣībanā) | except (illā) | what (mā) | Allah has decreed (kataba) | Allah has decreed (l-lahu) | for us (lanā), | He (huwa) | is our Protector. (mawlānā)" | And on (waʿalā) | Allah (l-lahi) | [so] let the believers put their trust (falyatawakkali). | [so] let the believers put their trust (l-mu'minūna).

9:52 Say, "Do you await for us except one of the two best (things) while we [we] await for you that Allah will afflict you with a punishment from [near] Him, or by our hands? So wait, indeed, we with you are waiting."

Say (qul), | "Do (hal) | you await (tarabbaṣūna) | for us (binā) | except (illā) | one (iḥ'dā) | of the two best (things (l-ḥus'nayayni)) | while we (wanaḥnu) | [we] await (natarabbaṣu) | for you (bikum) | that (an) | Allah will afflict you (yuṣībakumu) | Allah will afflict you (l-lahu) | with a punishment (biʿadhābin) | from (min) | [near] Him (ʿindihi), | or (aw) | by our hands (bi-aydīnā)? | So wait (fatarabbaṣū), | indeed, we (innā) | with you (maʿakum) | are waiting. (mutarabbiṣūna)"

9:53 Say, "Spend willingly or unwillingly; never will be accepted from you. Indeed, you [you] are a people defiantly disobedient."

Say (qul), | "Spend (anfiqū) | willingly (ṭawʿan) | or (aw) | unwillingly (karhan); | never (lan) | will be accepted (yutaqabbala) | from you (minkum). | Indeed, you (innakum) | [you] are (kuntum) | a people (qawman) | defiantly disobedient. (fāsiqīna)"

9:54 And not prevents them that is accepted from them their contributions except that they disbelieve in Allah and in His Messenger, and not they come to the prayer except while they are lazy, and not they spend except while they are unwilling.

And not (wamā) | prevents them (manaʿahum) | that (an) | is accepted (tuq'bala) | from them (min'hum) | their contributions (nafaqātuhum) | except (illā) | that they (annahum) | disbelieve (kafarū) | in Allah (bil-lahi) | and in His Messenger (wabirasūlihi), | and not (walā) | they come (yatūna) | to the prayer (l-ṣalata) | except (illā) | while they (wahum) | are lazy (kusālā), | and not (walā) | they spend (yunfiqūna) | except (illā) | while they (wahum) | are unwilling (kārihūna).

9:55 So let not impress you their wealth and not their children. Only Allah intends to punish them with it in the life of the world, and should depart their souls while they are disbelievers.

So let not (falā) | impress you (tuʿ'jib'ka) | their wealth (amwāluhum) | and not (walā) | their children (awlāduhum). | Only (innamā) | Allah intends (yurīdu) | Allah intends (l-lahu) | to punish them (liyuʿadhibahum) | with it (bihā) | in (fī) | the life (l-ḥayati) | of the world (l-dun'yā), | and should depart (watazhaqa) | their souls (anfusuhum) | while they (wahum) | are disbelievers (kāfirūna).

9:56 And they swear by Allah indeed, they surely are of you, while not they are of you, but they are a people who are afraid.

And they swear (wayaḥlifūna) | by Allah (bil-lahi) | indeed, they (innahum) | surely are of you (laminkum), | while not (wamā) | they (hum) | are of you (minkum), | but they (walākinnahum) | are a people (qawmun) | who are afraid (yafraqūna).

9:57 If they could find a refuge or caves or a place to enter, surely, they would turn to it, and they run wild.

If (law) | they could find (yajidūna) | a refuge (malja-an) | or (aw) | caves (maghārātin) | or (aw) | a place to enter (muddakhalan), | surely, they would turn (lawallaw) | to it (ilayhi), | and they (wahum) | run wild (yajmaḥūna).

9:58 And among them is he who criticizes you concerning the charities. Then if they are given from it, they are pleased; but if not they are given from it, then they are enraged.

And among them (wamin'hum) | is he who (man) | criticizes you (yalmizuka) | concerning (fī) | the charities (l-ṣadaqāti). | Then if (fa-in) | they are given (uʿ'ṭū) | from it (min'hā), | they are pleased (raḍū); | but if (wa-in) | not (lam) | they are given (yuʿ'ṭaw) | from it (min'hā), | then (idhā) | they (hum) | are enraged (yaskhaṭūna).

9:59 And if [that] they were satisfied with what Allah gave them and His Messenger, and said, "Sufficient for us is Allah, Allah will give us of His Bounty and His Messenger. Indeed, we to Allah turn our hopes."

And if (walaw) | [that] they (annahum) | were satisfied (raḍū) | with what (mā) | Allah gave them (ātāhumu) | Allah gave them (l-lahu) | and His Messenger (warasūluhu), | and said (waqālū), | "Sufficient for us (ḥasbunā) | is Allah (l-lahu), | Allah will give us (sayu'tīnā) | Allah will give us (l-lahu) | of (min) | His Bounty (faḍlihi) | and His Messenger (warasūluhu). | Indeed, we (innā) | to (ilā) | Allah (l-lahi) | turn our hopes. (rāghibūna)"

9:60 Only the charities are for the poor, and the needy and those who collect them, and the ones inclined their hearts, and in the freeing of the necks, and for those in debt and in the way of Allah, and the wayfarer - an obligation from Allah. And Allah is All-Knowing, All-Wise.

Only (innamā) | the charities (l-ṣadaqātu) | are for the poor (lil'fuqarāi), | and the needy (wal-masākīni) | and those who collect (wal-ʿāmilīna) | them (ʿalayhā), | and the ones inclined (wal-mu-alafati) | their hearts (qulūbuhum), | and in (wafī) | the freeing of the necks (l-riqābi), | and for those in debt (wal-ghārimīna) | and in (wafī) | the way (sabīli) | of Allah (l-lahi), | and the wayfarer (wa-ib'ni)- | and the wayfarer (l-sabīli)- | an obligation (farīḍatan) | from (mina) | Allah (l-lahi). | And Allah (wal-lahu) | is All-Knowing (ʿalīmun), | All-Wise (ḥakīmun).

9:61 And among them are those who hurt the Prophet and they say, "He is all ear." Say, "An ear of goodness for you, he believes in Allah, and believes the believers, and is a mercy to those who believe among you." And those who hurt the Messenger of Allah, for them is a punishment painful.

And among them (wamin'humu) | are those who (alladhīna) | hurt (yu'dhūna) | the Prophet (l-nabiya) | and they say (wayaqūlūna), | "He is (huwa) | all ear. (udhunun)" | Say (qul), | "An ear (udhunu) | of goodness (khayrin) | for you (lakum), | he believes (yu'minu) | in Allah (bil-lahi), | and believes (wayu'minu) | the believers (lil'mu'minīna), | and is a mercy (waraḥmatun) | to those who (lilladhīna) | believe (āmanū) | among you. (minkum)" | And those who (wa-alladhīna) | hurt (yu'dhūna) | the Messenger (rasūla) | of Allah (l-lahi), | for them (lahum) | is a punishment (ʿadhābun) | painful (alīmun).

9:62 They swear by Allah to you to please you. And Allah and His Messenger have more right that they should please Him, if they are believers.

They swear (yaḥlifūna) | by Allah (bil-lahi) | to you (lakum) | to please you (liyur'ḍūkum). | And Allah (wal-lahu) | and His Messenger (warasūluhu) | have more right (aḥaqqu) | that (an) | they should please Him (yur'ḍūhu), | if (in) | they are (kānū) | believers (mu'minīna).

9:63 Do not they know that he who opposes Allah and His Messenger, [then] that, for him is the Fire of Hell, will abide forever in it? That is the disgrace the great.

Do not (alam) | they know (yaʿlamū) | that he (annahu) | who (man) | opposes (yuḥādidi) | Allah (l-laha) | and His Messenger (warasūlahu), | [then] that (fa-anna), | for him (lahu) | is the Fire (nāra) | of Hell (jahannama), | will abide forever (khālidan) | in it (fīhā)? | That (dhālika) | is the disgrace (l-khiz'yu) | the great (l-ʿaẓīmu).

9:64 Fear the hypocrites lest be revealed about them a Surah, informing them of what is in their hearts. Say, "Mock, indeed, Allah will bring forth what you fear."

Fear (yaḥdharu) | the hypocrites (l-munāfiqūna) | lest (an) | be revealed (tunazzala) | about them (ʿalayhim) | a Surah (sūratun), | informing them (tunabbi-uhum) | of what (bimā) | is in (fī) | their hearts (qulūbihim). | Say (quli), | "Mock (is'tahziū), | indeed (inna), | Allah (l-laha) | will bring forth (mukh'rijun) | what (mā) | you fear. (taḥdharūna)"

9:65 And if you ask them, surely they will say, "Only we were conversing and playing." Say, "Is it Allah and His Verses and His Messenger that you were mocking?"

And if (wala-in) | you ask them (sa-altahum), | surely they will say (layaqūlunna), | "Only (innamā) | we were (kunnā) | conversing (nakhūḍu) | and playing. (wanalʿabu)" | Say (qul), | "Is it Allah (abil-lahi) | and His Verses (waāyātihi) | and His Messenger (warasūlihi) | that you were (kuntum) | mocking? (tastahziūna)"

9:66 Do not make excuse; verily, you have disbelieved after your belief. If We pardon [on] a party of you We will punish a party, because they were criminals.

Do not (lā) | make excuse (taʿtadhirū); | verily (qad), | you have disbelieved (kafartum) | after (baʿda) | your belief (īmānikum). | If (in) | We pardon (naʿfu) | [on] (ʿan) | a party (ṭāifatin) | of you (minkum) | We will punish (nuʿadhib) | a party (ṭāifatan), | because they (bi-annahum) | were (kānū) | criminals (muj'rimīna).

9:67 The hypocrite men and the hypocrite women, some of them are of others. They enjoin the wrong and forbid what is the right, and they close their hands. They forget Allah, so He has forgotten them. Indeed, the hypocrites, they are the defiantly disobedient.

The hypocrite men (al-munāfiqūna) | and the hypocrite women (wal-munāfiqātu), | some of them (baʿḍuhum) | are of (min) | others (baʿḍin). | They enjoin (yamurūna) | the wrong (bil-munkari) | and forbid (wayanhawna) | what (ʿani) | is the right (l-maʿrūfi), | and they close (wayaqbiḍūna) | their hands (aydiyahum). | They forget (nasū) | Allah (l-laha), | so He has forgotten them (fanasiyahum). | Indeed (inna), | the hypocrites (l-munāfiqīna), | they are (humu) | the defiantly disobedient (l-fāsiqūna).

9:68 Allah has promised the hypocrite men, and the hypocrite women and the disbelievers, Fire of Hell, they will abide forever in it. It is sufficient for them. And Allah has cursed them, and for them is a punishment enduring.

Allah has promised (waʿada) | Allah has promised (l-lahu) | the hypocrite men (l-munāfiqīna), | and the hypocrite women (wal-munāfiqāti) | and the disbelievers (wal-kufāra), | Fire (nāra) | of Hell (jahannama), | they will abide forever (khālidīna) | in it (fīhā). | It is (hiya) | sufficient for them (ḥasbuhum). | And Allah has cursed them (walaʿanahumu), | And Allah has cursed them (l-lahu), | and for them (walahum) | is a punishment (ʿadhābun) | enduring (muqīmun).

9:69 Like those before you they were mightier than you in strength, and more abundant in wealth and children. So they enjoyed their portion, and you have enjoyed your portion like enjoyed those before you their portion, and you indulge like the one who indulges in idle talk. Those, worthless, are their deeds in the world and in the Hereafter. And those, they are the losers.

Like those (ka-alladhīna) | before you (min) | before you (qablikum) | they were (kānū) | mightier (ashadda) | than you (minkum) | in strength (quwwatan), | and more abundant (wa-akthara) | in wealth (amwālan) | and children (wa-awlādan). | So they enjoyed (fa-is'tamtaʿū) | their portion (bikhalāqihim), | and you have enjoyed (fa-is'tamtaʿtum) | your portion (bikhalāqikum) | like (kamā) | enjoyed (is'tamtaʿa) | those (alladhīna) | before you (min) | before you (qablikum) | their portion (bikhalāqihim), | and you indulge (wakhuḍ'tum) | like the one who (ka-alladhī) | indulges in idle talk (khāḍū). | Those (ulāika), | worthless (ḥabiṭat), | are their deeds (aʿmāluhum) | in (fī) | the world (l-dun'yā) | and in the Hereafter (wal-ākhirati). | And those (wa-ulāika), | they (humu) | are the losers (l-khāsirūna).

9:70 Has not come to them the news of those who were before them, the people of Nuh, and Aad, and Thamud, and the people of Ibrahim and the companions of Madyan, and the towns overturned? Came to them their Messengers with clear proofs. And not was Allah to wrong them but they were to themselves doing wrong.

Has not (alam) | come to them (yatihim) | the news (naba-u) | of those who (alladhīna) | were before them (min), | were before them (qablihim), | the people (qawmi) | of Nuh (nūḥin), | and Aad (waʿādin), | and Thamud (wathamūda), | and the people (waqawmi) | of Ibrahim (ib'rāhīma) | and the companions (wa-aṣḥābi) | of Madyan (madyana), | and the towns overturned (wal-mu'tafikāti)? | Came to them (atathum) | their Messengers (rusuluhum) | with clear proofs (bil-bayināti). | And not (famā) | was (kāna) | Allah (l-lahu) | to wrong them (liyaẓlimahum) | but (walākin) | they were to (kānū) | themselves (anfusahum) | doing wrong (yaẓlimūna).

9:71 And the believing men and the believing women, some of them are allies of others. They enjoin the right, and forbid from the wrong, and they establish the prayer and give the zakah, and they obey Allah and His Messenger. Those, Allah will have mercy on them. Indeed, Allah is All-Mighty, All-Wise.

And the believing men (wal-mu'minūna) | and the believing women (wal-mu'minātu), | some of them (baʿḍuhum) | are allies (awliyāu) | of others (baʿḍin). | They enjoin (yamurūna) | the right (bil-maʿrūfi), | and forbid (wayanhawna) | from (ʿani) | the wrong (l-munkari), | and they establish (wayuqīmūna) | the prayer (l-ṣalata) | and give (wayu'tūna) | the zakah (l-zakata), | and they obey (wayuṭīʿūna) | Allah (l-laha) | and His Messenger (warasūlahu). | Those (ulāika), | Allah will have mercy on them (sayarḥamuhumu). | Allah will have mercy on them (l-lahu). | Indeed (inna), | Allah (l-laha) | is All-Mighty (ʿazīzun), | All-Wise (ḥakīmun).

9:72 Has been promised by Allah to the believing men and the believing women Gardens, flow from underneath it the rivers will abide forever in it and dwellings blessed in Gardens of everlasting bliss. But the pleasure of Allah is greater. That, it is the success great.

Has been promised (waʿada) | by Allah (l-lahu) | to the believing men (l-mu'minīna) | and the believing women (wal-mu'mināti) | Gardens (jannātin), | flow (tajrī) | from (min) | underneath it (taḥtihā) | the rivers (l-anhāru) | will abide forever (khālidīna) | in it (fīhā) | and dwellings (wamasākina) | blessed (ṭayyibatan) | in (fī) | Gardens (jannāti) | of everlasting bliss (ʿadnin). | But the pleasure (wariḍ'wānun) | of (mina) | Allah (l-lahi) | is greater (akbaru). | That (dhālika), | it (huwa) | is the success (l-fawzu) | great (l-ʿaẓīmu).

9:73 O Prophet! Strive against the disbelievers and the hypocrites and be stern with them. And their abode is Hell, and wretched is the destination.

O Prophet (yāayyuhā)! | O Prophet (l-nabiyu)! | Strive against (jāhidi) | the disbelievers (l-kufāra) | and the hypocrites (wal-munāfiqīna) | and be stern (wa-ugh'luẓ) | with them (ʿalayhim). | And their abode (wamawāhum) | is Hell (jahannamu), | and wretched (wabi'sa) | is the destination (l-maṣīru).

9:74 They swear by Allah that they said nothing, while certainly they said the word of the disbelief and disbelieved after their pretense of Islam, and planned [of] what not they could attain. And not they were resentful except that Allah had enriched them and His Messenger of His Bounty. So if they repent, it is better for them, and if they turn away, Allah will punish them with a punishment painful, in the world and in the Hereafter. And not for them in the earth any protector and not a helper.

They swear (yaḥlifūna) | by Allah (bil-lahi) | that they said nothing (mā), | that they said nothing (qālū), | while certainly (walaqad) | they said (qālū) | the word (kalimata) | of the disbelief (l-kuf'ri) | and disbelieved (wakafarū) | after (baʿda) | their pretense of Islam (is'lāmihim), | and planned (wahammū) | [of] what (bimā) | not (lam) | they could attain (yanālū). | And not (wamā) | they were resentful (naqamū) | except (illā) | that (an) | Allah had enriched them (aghnāhumu) | Allah had enriched them (l-lahu) | and His Messenger (warasūluhu) | of (min) | His Bounty (faḍlihi). | So if (fa-in) | they repent (yatūbū), | it is (yaku) | better (khayran) | for them (lahum), | and if (wa-in) | they turn away (yatawallaw), | Allah will punish them (yuʿadhib'humu) | Allah will punish them (l-lahu) | with a punishment (ʿadhāban) | painful (alīman), | in (fī) | the world (l-dun'yā) | and in the Hereafter (wal-ākhirati). | And not (wamā) | for them (lahum) | in (fī) | the earth (l-arḍi) | any (min) | protector (waliyyin) | and not (walā) | a helper (naṣīrin).

9:75 And among them is he who made a covenant with Allah, "If He gives us of His bounty, surely we will give charity and surely we will be among the righteous."

And among them (wamin'hum) | is he who (man) | made a covenant (ʿāhada) | with Allah (l-laha), | "If (la-in) | He gives us (ātānā) | of (min) | His bounty (faḍlihi), | surely we will give charity (lanaṣṣaddaqanna) | and surely we will be (walanakūnanna) | among (mina) | the righteous. (l-ṣāliḥīna)"

9:76 But when He gave them of His Bounty, they became stingy with it and turned away while they were averse.

But when (falammā) | He gave them (ātāhum) | of (min) | His Bounty (faḍlihi), | they became stingy (bakhilū) | with it (bihi) | and turned away (watawallaw) | while they (wahum) | were averse (muʿ'riḍūna).

9:77 So He penalized them with hypocrisy in their hearts until the day when they will meet Him, because they broke the covenant with Allah what they had promised Him, and because they used to lie.

So He penalized them (fa-aʿqabahum) | with hypocrisy (nifāqan) | in (fī) | their hearts (qulūbihim) | until (ilā) | the day (yawmi) | when they will meet Him (yalqawnahu), | because (bimā) | they broke (akhlafū) | the covenant with Allah (l-laha) | what (mā) | they had promised Him (waʿadūhu), | and because (wabimā) | they used to (kānū) | lie (yakdhibūna).

9:78 Do not they know that Allah knows their secret and their secret conversation, and that Allah is All-Knower of the unseen?

Do not (alam) | they know (yaʿlamū) | that (anna) | Allah (l-laha) | knows (yaʿlamu) | their secret (sirrahum) | and their secret conversation (wanajwāhum), | and that (wa-anna) | Allah (l-laha) | is All-Knower (ʿallāmu) | of the unseen (l-ghuyūbi)?

9:79 Those who criticize the ones who give willingly of the believers concerning the charities, and those who not find except their effort, so they ridicule them, Allah will ridicule them, and for them is a punishment painful.

Those who (alladhīna) | criticize (yalmizūna) | the ones who give willingly (l-muṭawiʿīna) | of (mina) | the believers (l-mu'minīna) | concerning (fī) | the charities (l-ṣadaqāti), | and those who (wa-alladhīna) | not (lā) | find (yajidūna) | except (illā) | their effort (juh'dahum), | so they ridicule (fayaskharūna) | them (min'hum), | Allah will ridicule (sakhira) | Allah will ridicule (l-lahu) | them (min'hum), | and for them (walahum) | is a punishment (ʿadhābun) | painful (alīmun).

9:80 Ask forgiveness for them or do not ask forgiveness for them. If you ask forgiveness for them seventy times, never will Allah forgive [for] them. That is because they disbelieved in Allah and His Messenger, and Allah does not guide the people, the defiantly disobedient.

Ask forgiveness (is'taghfir) | for them (lahum) | or (aw) | do not (lā) | ask forgiveness (tastaghfir) | for them (lahum). | If (in) | you ask forgiveness (tastaghfir) | for them (lahum) | seventy (sabʿīna) | times (marratan), | never (falan) | will Allah forgive (yaghfira) | will Allah forgive (l-lahu) | [for] them (lahum). | That (dhālika) | is because they (bi-annahum) | disbelieved (kafarū) | in Allah (bil-lahi) | and His Messenger (warasūlihi), | and Allah (wal-lahu) | does not (lā) | guide (yahdī) | the people (l-qawma), | the defiantly disobedient (l-fāsiqīna).

9:81 Rejoice those who remained behind in their staying behind the Messenger of Allah, and they disliked to strive with their wealth and their lives in the way of Allah and they said, "Do not go forth in the heat." Say, "The Fire of Hell is more intense in heat." If only they could understand.

Rejoice (fariḥa) | those who remained behind (l-mukhalafūna) | in their staying (bimaqʿadihim) | behind (khilāfa) | the Messenger (rasūli) | of Allah (l-lahi), | and they disliked (wakarihū) | to (an) | strive (yujāhidū) | with their wealth (bi-amwālihim) | and their lives (wa-anfusihim) | in (fī) | the way (sabīli) | of Allah (l-lahi) | and they said (waqālū), | "Do not (lā) | go forth (tanfirū) | in (fī) | the heat. (l-ḥari)" | Say (qul), | "The Fire (nāru) | of Hell (jahannama) | is more intense (ashaddu) | in heat. (ḥarran)" | If only (law) | they could (kānū) | understand (yafqahūna).

9:82 So let them laugh a little, and let them weep much as a recompense for what they used to earn.

So let them laugh (falyaḍḥakū) | a little (qalīlan), | and let them weep (walyabkū) | much (kathīran) | as a recompense (jazāan) | for what (bimā) | they used to (kānū) | earn (yaksibūna).

9:83 Then if Allah returns you to a group of them, and they ask you permission to go out, then say, "Never will you come out with me ever and never will you fight with me any enemy. Indeed, you were satisfied with sitting the first time, so sit with those who stay behind."

Then if (fa-in) | Allah returns you (rajaʿaka) | Allah returns you (l-lahu) | to (ilā) | a group (ṭāifatin) | of them (min'hum), | and they ask you permission (fa-is'tadhanūka) | to go out (lil'khurūji), | then say (faqul), | "Never (lan) | will you come out (takhrujū) | with me (maʿiya) | ever (abadan) | and never (walan) | will you fight (tuqātilū) | with me (maʿiya) | any enemy (ʿaduwwan). | Indeed, you (innakum) | were satisfied (raḍītum) | with sitting (bil-quʿūdi) | the first (awwala) | time (marratin), | so sit (fa-uqʿʿudū) | with (maʿa) | those who stay behind. (l-khālifīna)"

9:84 And not you pray for any of them who dies, ever, and not you stand by his grave. Indeed, they disbelieved in Allah and His Messenger, and died while they were defiantly disobedient.

And not (walā) | you pray (tuṣalli) | for (ʿalā) | any (aḥadin) | of them (min'hum) | who dies (māta), | ever (abadan), | and not (walā) | you stand (taqum) | by (ʿalā) | his grave (qabrihi). | Indeed, they (innahum) | disbelieved (kafarū) | in Allah (bil-lahi) | and His Messenger (warasūlihi), | and died (wamātū) | while they were (wahum) | defiantly disobedient (fāsiqūna).

9:85 And let not impress you their wealth and their children. Only Allah intends to punish them with it in the world, and will depart their souls while they are disbelievers.

And let not (walā) | impress you (tuʿʿjib'ka) | their wealth (amwāluhum) | and their children (wa-awlāduhum). | Only (innamā) | Allah intends (yurīdu) | Allah intends (l-lahu) | to (an) | punish them (yuʿadhibahum) | with it (bihā) | in (fī) | the world (l-dun'yā), | and will depart (watazhaqa) | their souls (anfusuhum) | while they (wahum) | are disbelievers (kāfirūna).

9:86 And when was revealed a Surah that; believe in Allah and strive with His Messenger, ask your permission the men of wealth among them and said, "Leave us, to be with those who sit."

And when (wa-idhā) | was revealed (unzilat) | a Surah (sūratun) | that (an); | believe (āminū) | in Allah (bil-lahi) | and strive (wajāhidū) | with (maʿa) | His Messenger (rasūlihi), | ask your permission (is'tadhanaka) | the men (ulū) | of wealth (l-ṭawli) | among them (min'hum) | and said (waqālū), | "Leave us (dharnā), | to be (nakun) | with (maʿa) | those who sit. (l-qāʿidīna)"

9:87 They were satisfied to be with those who stay behind, and were sealed [on] their hearts, so they do not understand.

They were satisfied (raḍū) | to (bi-an) | be (yakūnū) | with (maʿa) | those who stay behind (l-khawālifi), | and were sealed (waṭubiʿa) | [on] (ʿalā) | their hearts (qulūbihim), | so they (fahum) | do not (lā) | understand (yafqahūna).

9:88 But the Messenger and those who believed with him strove with their wealth and their lives. And those, for them are the good things, and those - they are the successful ones.

But (lākini) | the Messenger (l-rasūlu) | and those who (wa-alladhīna) | believed (āmanū) | with him (maʿahu) | strove (jāhadū) | with their wealth (bi-amwālihim) | and their lives (wa-anfusihim). | And those (wa-ulāika), | for them (lahumu) | are the good things (l-khayrātu), | and those (wa-ulāika)- | they (humu) | are the successful ones (l-muf'liḥūna).

9:89 Allah has prepared for them Gardens flows from underneath it the rivers, will abide forever in it. That is the success the great.

Allah has prepared (aʿadda) | Allah has prepared (l-lahu) | for them (lahum) | Gardens (jannātin) | flows (tajrī) | from (min) | underneath it (taḥtihā) | the rivers (l-anhāru), | will abide forever (khālidīna) | in it (fīhā). | That (dhālika) | is the success (l-fawzu) | the great (l-ʿaẓīmu).

9:90 And came the ones who make excuses of the bedouins, that permission be granted to them, and sat, those who lied to Allah and His Messenger. Will strike those who disbelieved among them a punishment painful.

And came (wajāa) | the ones who make excuses (l-muʿadhirūna) | of (mina) | the bedouins (l-aʿrābi), | that permission be granted (liyu'dhana) | to them (lahum), | and sat (waqaʿada), | those who (alladhīna) | lied (kadhabū) | to Allah (l-laha) | and His Messenger (warasūlahu). | Will strike (sayuṣību) | those who (alladhīna) | disbelieved (kafarū) | among them (min'hum) | a punishment

(ʿadhābun) | painful (alīmun).

9:91 Not on the weak and not on the sick and not on those who not they find what they can spend any blame if they are sincere to Allah and His Messenger. Not is on the good-doers any way for blame. And Allah is Oft-Forgiving, Most Merciful.

Not (laysa) | on (ʿalā) | the weak (l-ḍuʿafāi) | and not (walā) | on (ʿalā) | the sick (l-marḍā) | and not (walā) | on (ʿalā) | those who (alladhīna) | not (lā) | they find (yajidūna) | what (mā) | they can spend (yunfiqūna) | any blame (ḥarajun) | if (idhā) | they are sincere (naṣaḥū) | to Allah (lillahi) | and His Messenger (warasūlihi). | Not (mā) | is on (ʿalā) | the good-doers (l-muḥ'sinīna) | any (min) | way for blame (sabīlin). | And Allah (wal-lahu) | is Oft-Forgiving (ghafūrun), | Most Merciful (raḥīmun).

9:92 And not on those who, when they came to you that you provide them with mounts, you said, "Not I find what to mount you on [it]. They turned back with their eyes flowing [of] with the tears, of sorrow that not they find what they could spend.

And not (walā) | on (ʿalā) | those who (alladhīna), | when (idhā) | when (mā) | they came to you (atawka) | that you provide them with mounts (litaḥmilahum), | you said (qul'ta), | "Not (lā) | I find (ajidu) | what (mā) | to mount you (aḥmilukum) | on [it] (ʿalayhi). | They turned back (tawallaw) | with their eyes (wa-aʿyunuhum) | flowing (tafīḍu) | [of] (mina) | with the tears (l-damʿi), | of sorrow (ḥazanan) | that not (allā) | they find (yajidū) | what (mā) | they could spend (yunfiqūna).

9:93 Only the way blame is on those who ask your permission while they are rich. They are satisfied to be with those who stay behind, and Allah sealed [on] their hearts, so they do not know.

Only (innamā) | the way blame (l-sabīlu) | is on (ʿalā) | those who (alladhīna) | ask your permission (yastadhinūnaka) | while they (wahum) | are rich (aghniyāu). | They are satisfied (raḍū) | to (bi-an) | be (yakūnū) | with (maʿa) | those who stay behind (l-khawālifi), | and Allah sealed (waṭabaʿa) | and Allah sealed (l-lahu) | [on] (ʿalā) | their hearts (qulūbihim), | so they (fahum) | do not (lā) | know (yaʿlamūna).

9:94 They will make excuses to you when you have returned to them. Say, "Do not make excuse, never we will believe you. Verily, Allah has informed us of your news, and Allah will see your deeds, and His Messenger. Then you will be brought back to, the Knower of the unseen and the seen, then He will inform you of what you used to do."

They will make excuses (yaʿtadhirūna) | to you (ilaykum) | when (idhā) | you have returned (rajaʿtum) | to them (ilayhim). | Say (qul), | "Do not (lā) | make excuse (taʿtadhirū), | never (lan) | we will believe (nu'mina) | you (lakum). | Verily (qad), | Allah has informed us (nabba-anā) | Allah has informed us (l-lahu) | of (min) | your news (akhbārikum), | and Allah will see (wasayarā) | and Allah will see (l-lahu) | your deeds (ʿamalakum), | and His Messenger (warasūluhu). | Then (thumma) | you will be brought back (turaddūna) | to (ilā), | the Knower (ʿālimi) | of the unseen (l-ghaybi) | and the seen (wal-shahādati), | then He will inform you (fayunabbi-ukum) | of what (bimā) | you used to (kuntum) | do. (taʿmalūna)"

9:95 They will swear by Allah to you when you returned to them, that you may turn away from them. So turn away from them, indeed, they are impure and their abode is Hell, a recompense for what they used to earn.

They will swear (sayaḥlifūna) | by Allah (bil-lahi) | to you (lakum) | when (idhā) | you returned (inqalabtum) | to them (ilayhim), | that you may turn away (lituʿ'riḍū) | from them (ʿanhum). | So turn away (fa-aʿriḍū) | from them (ʿanhum), | indeed, they (innahum) | are impure (rij'sun) | and their abode (wamawāhum) | is Hell (jahannamu), | a recompense (jazāan) | for what (bimā) | they used to (kānū) | earn (yaksibūna).

9:96 They swear to you that you may be pleased with them. But if you are pleased with them, then indeed, Allah is not pleased with the people who are defiantly disobedient.

They swear (yaḥlifūna) | to you (lakum) | that you may be pleased (litarḍaw) | with them (ʿanhum). | But if (fa-in) | you are pleased (tarḍaw) | with them (ʿanhum), | then indeed (fa-inna), | Allah (l-laha) | is not pleased (lā) | is not pleased (yarḍā) | with (ʿani) | the people (l-qawmi) | who are defiantly disobedient (l-fāsiqīna).

9:97 The bedouins are stronger in disbelief and hypocrisy, and more likely that not they know the limits of what Allah has revealed to His Messenger. And Allah is All-Knower, All-Wise.

The bedouins (al-aʿrābu) | are stronger (ashaddu) | in disbelief (kuf'ran) | and hypocrisy (wanifāqan), | and more likely (wa-ajdaru) | that not (allā) | they know (yaʿlamū) | the limits (ḥudūda) | of what (mā) | Allah has revealed (anzala) | Allah has revealed (l-lahu) | to (ʿalā) | His Messenger (rasūlihi). | And Allah (wal-lahu) | is All-Knower (ʿalīmun), | All-Wise (ḥakīmun).

9:98 And among the bedouins is he who takes what he spends as a loss, and he awaits for you the turns of misfortune. Upon them will be the turn of the evil. And Allah is All-Hearer, All-Knower.

And among (wamina) | the bedouins (l-aʿrābi) | is he who (man) | takes (yattakhidhu) | what (mā) | he spends (yunfiqu) | as a loss (maghraman), | and he awaits (wayatarabbaṣu) | for you (bikumu) | the turns of misfortune (l-dawāira). | Upon them (ʿalayhim) | will be the turn (dāiratu) | of the evil (l-sawi). | And Allah (wal-lahu) | is All-Hearer (samīʿun), | All-Knower (ʿalīmun).

9:99 But among the bedouins is he who, believes in Allah and the Day the Last, and takes what he spends as means of nearness with Allah and blessings of the Messenger. Behold! Indeed, it is a means of nearness for them. Allah will admit them to His Mercy. Indeed, Allah is Oft-Forgiving, Most Merciful.

But among (wamina) | the bedouins (l-aʿrābi) | is he who (man), | believes (yu'minu) | in Allah (bil-lahi) | and the Day (wal-yawmi) | the Last (l-ākhiri), | and takes (wayattakhidhu) | what (mā) | he spends (yunfiqu) | as means of nearness (qurubātin) | with (ʿinda) | Allah (l-lahi) | and blessings (waṣalawāti) | of the Messenger (l-rasūli). | Behold (alā)! | Indeed, it (innahā) | is a means of nearness (qur'batun) | for them (lahum). | Allah will admit them (sayud'khiluhumu) | Allah will admit them (l-lahu) | to (fī) | His Mercy (raḥmatihi). | Indeed (inna), | Allah (l-laha) | is Oft-Forgiving (ghafūrun), | Most Merciful (raḥīmun).

9:100 And the forerunners, the first among the emigrants and the helpers and those who followed them in righteousness, Allah is pleased with them, and they are pleased with Him. And He has prepared for them Gardens flows underneath it the rivers, will abide in it forever. That is the success the great.

And the forerunners (wal-sābiqūna), | the first (l-awalūna) | among (mina) | the emigrants (l-muhājirīna) | and the helpers (wal-anṣāri) | and those who (wa-alladhīna) | followed them (ittabaʿūhum) | in righteousness (bi-iḥ'sānin), | Allah is pleased (raḍiya) | Allah is pleased (l-lahu) | with them (ʿanhum), | and they are pleased (waraḍū) | with Him (ʿanhu). | And He has prepared (wa-aʿadda) | for them (lahum) | Gardens (jannātin) | flows (tajrī) | underneath it (taḥtahā) | the rivers (l-anhāru), | will abide (khālidīna) | in it (fīhā) | forever (abadan). | That (dhālika) | is the success (l-fawzu) | the great (l-ʿaẓīmu).

9:101 And among those around you of the bedouins are hypocrites and also from people of the Madinah. They persist in the hypocrisy, not you know them, We [We] know them. We will punish them twice then they will be returned to a punishment great.

And among those (wamimman) | around you (ḥawlakum) | of (mina) | the bedouins (l-aʿrābi) | are hypocrites (munāfiqūna) | and also from (wamin) | people (ahli) | of the Madinah (l-madīnati). | They persist (maradū) | in (ʿalā) | the hypocrisy (l-nifāqi), | not (lā) | you know them (taʿlamuhum), | We (naḥnu) | [We] know them (naʿlamuhum). | We will punish them (sanuʿadhibuhum) | twice (marratayni) | then (thumma) | they will be returned (yuraddūna) | to (ilā) | a punishment (ʿadhābin) | great (ʿaẓīmin).

9:102 And others who have acknowledged their sins. They had mixed a deed righteous with other that was evil. Perhaps Allah [that] will turn in mercy to them. Indeed, Allah is Oft-Forgiving, Most Merciful.

And others (waākharūna) | who have acknowledged (iʿ'tarafū) | their sins (bidhunūbihim). | They had mixed (khalaṭū) | a deed (ʿamalan) | righteous (ṣāliḥan) | with other (waākhara) | that was evil (sayyi-an). | Perhaps (ʿasā) | Allah (l-lahu) | [that] (an) | will turn in mercy (yatūba) | to them (ʿalayhim). | Indeed (inna), | Allah (l-laha) | is Oft-Forgiving (ghafūrun), | Most Merciful (raḥīmun).

9:103 Take from their wealth a charity, purifying them and cause them increase by it, and bless [upon] them. Indeed, your blessings are a reassurance for them. And Allah is All-Hearer, All-Knower.

Take (khudh) | from (min) | their wealth (amwālihim) | a charity (ṣadaqatan), | purifying them (tuṭahhiruhum) | and cause them increase (watuzakkīhim) | by it (bihā), | and bless (waṣalli) | [upon] them (ʿalayhim). | Indeed (inna), | your blessings (ṣalataka) | are a reassurance (sakanun) | for them (lahum). | And Allah (wal-lahu) | is All-Hearer (samīʿun), | All-Knower (ʿalīmun).

9:104 Do not they know that Allah is He Who accepts the repentance from His slaves and takes the charities, and that Allah, He is the Acceptor of repentance, the Most Merciful.

Do not (alam) | they know (yaʿlamū) | that (anna) | Allah (l-laha) | is He (huwa) | Who accepts (yaqbalu) | the repentance (l-tawbata) | from (ʿan) | His slaves (ʿibādihi) | and takes (wayakhudhu) | the charities (l-ṣadaqāti), | and that (wa-anna) | Allah (l-laha), | He (huwa) | is the Acceptor of repentance (l-tawābu), | the Most Merciful (l-raḥīmu).

9:105 And say, "Do, then Allah will see your deed and His Messenger, and the believers. And you will be brought back to the Knower of the unseen and the seen, then He will inform you of what you used to do."

And say (waquli), | "Do (iʿ'malū), | then Allah will see (fasayarā) | then Allah will see (l-lahu) | your deed (ʿamalakum) | and His Messenger (warasūluhu), | and the believers (wal-mu'minūna). | And you will be brought back (wasaturaddūna) | to (ilā) | the Knower (ʿālimi) | of the unseen (l-ghaybi) | and the seen (wal-shahādati), | then He will inform you (fayunabbi-ukum) | of what (bimā) | you used to (kuntum) | do. (taʿmalūna)"

9:106 And others deferred for the Command of Allah - whether He will punish them or He will turn in mercy to them. And Allah is All-Knower, All-Wise.

And others (waākharūna) | deferred (mur'jawna) | for the Command of Allah (li-amri)- | for the Command of Allah (l-lahi)- | whether (immā) | He will punish them (yuʿadhibuhum) | or (wa-immā) | He will turn in mercy (yatūbu) | to them (ʿalayhim). | And Allah (wal-lahu) | is All-Knower (ʿalīmun), | All-Wise (ḥakīmun).

9:107 And those who take a masjid for causing harm and for disbelief, and for division among the believers, and as a station for whoever warred against Allah and His Messenger before. And surely they will swear, "Not we wish except the good." But Allah bears witness indeed, they are surely liars.

And those who (wa-alladhīna) | take (ittakhadhū) | a masjid (masjidan) | for causing harm (ḍirāran) | and for disbelief (wakuf'ran), | and for division (watafrīqan) | among (bayna) | the believers (l-mu'minīna), | and as a station (wa-ir'ṣādan) | for whoever (liman) | warred (ḥāraba) | against Allah (l-laha) | and His Messenger (warasūlahu) | before (min). | before (qablu). | And surely they will swear (walayaḥlifunna), | "Not (in) | we wish (aradnā) | except (illā) | the good. (l-ḥus'nā)" | But Allah (wal-lahu) | bears witness (yashhadu) | indeed, they (innahum) | are surely liars (lakādhibūna).

9:108 Do not stand in it ever. A masjid founded on the righteousness from the first day is more worthy that you stand in it. Within it are men who love to purify themselves, and Allah loves the ones who purify themselves.

Do not (lā) | stand (taqum) | in it (fīhi) | ever (abadan). | A masjid (lamasjidun) | founded (ussisa) | on (ʿalā) | the righteousness (l-taqwā) | from (min) | the first (awwali) | day (yawmin) | is more worthy (aḥaqqu) | that (an) | you stand (taqūma) | in it (fīhi). | Within it (fīhi) | are men (rijālun) | who love (yuḥibbūna) | to (an) | purify themselves (yataṭahharū), | and Allah (wal-lahu) | loves (yuḥibbu) | the ones who purify themselves (l-muṭahirīna).

9:109 Then is one who founded his building on righteousness from Allah and His pleasure better or one who founded his building on edge of a cliff about to collapse, so it collapsed with him in the Fire of Hell. And Allah does not guide the wrongdoing people.

Then is one who (afaman) | founded (assasa) | his building (bun'yānahu) | on (ʿalā) | righteousness (taqwā) | from (mina) | Allah (l-lahi) | and His pleasure (wariḍ'wānin) | better (khayrun) | or (am) | one who (man) | founded (assasa) | his building (bun'yānahu) | on (ʿalā) | edge (shafā) | of a cliff (jurufin) | about to collapse (hārin), | so it collapsed (fa-in'hāra) | with him (bihi) | in (fī) | the Fire (nāri) | of Hell (jahannama). | And Allah (wal-lahu) | does not (lā) | guide (yahdī) | the wrongdoing people (l-qawma). | the wrongdoing people (l-ẓālimīna).

9:110 Not will cease their building which they built a cause of doubt in their hearts except that are cut into pieces their hearts. And Allah is All-Knower, All-Wise.

Not (lā) | will cease (yazālu) | their building (bun'yānuhumu) | which (alladhī) | they built (banaw) | a cause of doubt (rībatan) | in (fī) | their hearts (qulūbihim) | except (illā) | that (an) | are cut into pieces (taqaṭṭaʿa) | their hearts (qulūbuhum). | And Allah (wal-lahu) | is All-Knower (ʿalīmun), | All-Wise (ḥakīmun).

9:111 Indeed, Allah has purchased from the believers their lives and their wealth, because for them is Paradise. They fight in the way of Allah, they slay and they are slain. A promise upon Him true, in the Taurat and the Injeel and the Quran. And who is more faithful to his promise than Allah? So rejoice in your transaction which you have contracted [with it]. And that it is the success the great.

Indeed (inna), | Allah (l-laha) | has purchased (ish'tarā) | from (mina) | the believers (l-mu'minīna) | their lives (anfusahum) | and their wealth (wa-amwālahum), | because (bi-anna) | for them (lahumu) | is Paradise (l-janata). | They fight (yuqātilūna) | in (fī) | the way (sabīli) | of Allah (l-lahi), | they slay (fayaqtulūna) | and they are slain (wayuq'talūna). | A promise (waʿdan) | upon Him (ʿalayhi) | true (ḥaqqan), | in (fī) | the Taurat (l-tawrāti) | and the Injeel (wal-injīli) | and the Quran (wal-qur'āni). | And who (waman) | is more faithful (awfā) | to his promise (biʿahdihi) | than (mina) | Allah (l-lahi)? | So rejoice (fa-is'tabshirū) | in your transaction (bibayʿikumu) | which (alladhī) | you have contracted (bāyaʿtum) | [with it] (bihi). | And that (wadhālika) | it (huwa) | is the success (l-fawzu) | the great (l-ʿaẓīmu).

9:112 Those who turn in repentance, those who worship, those who praise, those who go out, those who bow down, those who prostrate, those who enjoin the right and those who forbid [on] the wrong, and those who observe the limits of Allah. And give glad tidings to the believers.

Those who turn in repentance (al-tāibūna), | those who worship (l-ʿābidūna), | those who praise (l-ḥāmidūna), | those who go out (l-sāiḥūna), | those who bow down (l-rākiʿūna), | those who prostrate (l-sājidūna), | those who enjoin (l-āmirūna) | the right (bil-maʿrūfi) | and those who forbid (wal-nāhūna) | [on] (ʿani) | the wrong (l-munkari), | and those who observe (wal-ḥāfiẓūna) | the limits (liḥudūdi) | of Allah (l-lahi). | And give glad tidings (wabashiri) | to the believers (l-mu'minīna).

9:113 Not it is for the Prophet and those who believe that they ask forgiveness for the polytheists, even though they be near of kin, after [what] has become clear to them, that they are the companions of the Hellfire.

Not (mā) | it is (kāna) | for the Prophet (lilnnabiyyi) | and those who (wa-alladhīna) | believe (āmanū) | that (an) | they ask forgiveness (yastaghfirū) | for the polytheists (lil'mush'rikīna), | even though (walaw) | they be (kānū) | near of kin (ulī), | near of kin (qur'bā), | after (min) | after (baʿdi) | [what] (mā) | has become clear (tabayyana) | to them (lahum), | that they (annahum) | are the companions (aṣḥābu) | of the Hellfire (l-jaḥīmi).

9:114 And not was the asking of forgiveness by Ibrahim for his father except because of a promise he had promised it to him. But when it became clear to him that he was an enemy to Allah, he disassociated from him. Indeed, Ibrahim was compassionate, forbearing.

And not (wamā) | was (kāna) | the asking of forgiveness (is'tigh'fāru) | by Ibrahim (ib'rāhīma) | for his father (li-abīhi) | except (illā) | because (ʿan) | of a promise (mawʿidatin) | he had promised it (waʿadahā) | to him (iyyāhu). | But when (falammā) | it became clear (tabayyana) | to him (lahu) | that he (annahu) | was an enemy (ʿaduwwun) | to Allah (lillahi), | he disassociated (tabarra-a) | from him (min'hu). | Indeed (inna), | Ibrahim (ib'rāhīma) | was compassionate (la-awwāhun), | forbearing (ḥalīmun).

9:115 And not is for Allah that He lets go astray a people after [when] He has guided them until He makes clear to them what they should fear. Indeed, Allah of every thing is All-Knower.

And not (wamā) | is (kāna) | for Allah (l-lahu) | that He lets go astray (liyuḍilla) | a people (qawman) | after (baʿda) | [when] (idh) | He has guided them (hadāhum) | until (ḥattā) | He makes clear (yubayyina) | to them (lahum) | what (mā) | they should fear (yattaqūna). | Indeed (inna), | Allah (l-laha) | of every (bikulli) | thing (shayin) | is All-Knower (ʿalīmun).

9:116 Indeed, Allah to Him belongs the dominion of the heavens and the earth, He gives life, and He causes death. And not for you besides Allah any protector and not any helper.

Indeed (inna), | Allah (l-laha) | to Him belongs (lahu) | the dominion (mul'ku) | of the heavens (l-samāwāti) | and the earth (wal-arḍi), | He gives life (yuḥ'yī), | and He causes death (wayumītu). | And not (wamā) | for you (lakum) | besides Allah (min) | besides Allah (dūni) | besides Allah (l-lahi) | any (min) | protector (waliyyin) | and not (walā) | any helper (naṣīrin).

9:117 Verily, Allah turned in mercy to the Prophet, and the emigrants, and the helpers [those] who followed him, in the hour of difficulty after [what] had nearly deviated the hearts of a party of them, then He turned in mercy to them. Indeed, He to them is Most Kind, Most Merciful.

Verily (laqad), | Allah turned in mercy (tāba) | Allah turned in mercy (l-lahu) | to (ʿalā) | the Prophet (l-nabiyi), | and the emigrants (wal-muhājirīna), | and the helpers (wal-anṣāri) | [those] who (alladhīna) | followed him (ittabaʿūhu), | in (fī) | the hour (sāʿati) | of difficulty (l-ʿus'rati) | after (min) | after (baʿdi) | [what] (mā) | had nearly (kāda) | deviated (yazīghu) | the hearts (qulūbu) | of a party (farīqin) | of them (min'hum), | then (thumma) | He turned in mercy (tāba) | to them (ʿalayhim). | Indeed, He (innahu) | to them (bihim) | is Most Kind (raūfun), | Most Merciful (raḥīmun).

9:118 And on the three of those who were left behind, until when was straitened for them the earth, though it was vast. And was straitened for them their own souls and they were certain that there is no refuge from Allah except to Him. Then He turned in mercy to them that they may repent. Indeed, Allah, He is the Acceptor of repentance, the Most Merciful.

And on (waʿalā) | the three (l-thalāthati) | of those who (alladhīna) | were left behind (khullifū), | until (ḥattā) | when (idhā) | was straitened (ḍāqat) | for them (ʿalayhimu) | the earth (l-arḍu), | though (bimā) | it was vast (raḥubat). | And was straitened (waḍāqat) | for them (ʿalayhim) | their own souls (anfusuhum) | and they were certain (waẓannū) | that (an) | there is no (lā) | refuge (malja-a) | from (mina) | Allah (l-lahi) | except (illā) | to Him (ilayhi). | Then (thumma) |

He turned in mercy (tāba) | to them (ʿalayhim) | that they may repent (liyatūbū). | Indeed (inna), | Allah (l-laha), | He (huwa) | is the Acceptor of repentance (l-tawābu), | the Most Merciful (l-raḥīmu).

9:119 O you who believe! Fear Allah and be with those who are truthful.

O you who believe (yāayyuhā)! | O you who believe (alladhīna)! | O you who believe (āmanū)! | Fear (ittaqū) | Allah (l-laha) | and be (wakūnū) | with (maʿa) | those who are truthful (l-ṣādiqīna).

9:120 Not it was for the people of the Madinah and who were around them of the bedouins, that they remain behind after the Messenger of Allah, and not they prefer their lives to his life. That is because [they] does not afflict them thirst and not fatigue and not hunger in the way of Allah, and not they step any step that angers the disbelievers and not they inflict on an enemy an infliction except is recorded for them in it as a deed righteous. Indeed, Allah does not allow to be lost the reward of the good-doers.

Not (mā) | it was (kāna) | for the people (li-ahli) | of the Madinah (l-madīnati) | and who (waman) | were around them (ḥawlahum) | of (mina) | the bedouins (l-aʿrābi), | that (an) | they remain behind (yatakhallafū) | after (ʿan) | the Messenger (rasūli) | of Allah (l-lahi), | and not (walā) | they prefer (yarghabū) | their lives (bi-anfusihim) | to (ʿan) | his life (nafsihi). | That is (dhālika) | because [they] (bi-annahum) | does not (lā) | afflict them (yuṣībuhum) | thirst (ẓama-on) | and not (walā) | fatigue (naṣabun) | and not (walā) | hunger (makhmaṣatun) | in (fī) | the way (sabīli) | of Allah (l-lahi), | and not (walā) | they step (yaṭaūna) | any step (mawṭi-an) | that angers (yaghīẓu) | the disbelievers (l-kufāra) | and not (walā) | they inflict (yanālūna) | on (min) | an enemy (ʿaduwwin) | an infliction (naylan) | except (illā) | is recorded (kutiba) | for them (lahum) | in it (bihi) | as a deed (ʿamalun) | righteous (ṣāliḥun). | Indeed (inna), | Allah (l-laha) | does not (lā) | allow to be lost (yuḍīʿu) | the reward (ajra) | of the good-doers (l-muḥ'sinīna).

9:121 And not they spend any spending small and not big, and not they cross a valley but is recorded for them, that Allah may reward them the best of what they used to do.

And not (walā) | they spend (yunfiqūna) | any spending (nafaqatan) | small (ṣaghīratan) | and not (walā) | big (kabīratan), | and not (walā) | they cross (yaqṭaʿūna) | a valley (wādiyan) | but (illā) | is recorded (kutiba) | for them (lahum), | that Allah may reward them (liyajziyahumu) | that Allah may reward them (l-lahu) | the best (aḥsana) | of what (mā) | they used to (kānū) | do (yaʿmalūna).

9:122 And not is for the believers that they go forth all together. So if not go forth from every group among them a party that they may obtain understanding in the religion, and that they may warn their people when they return to them, so that they may beware.

And not (wamā) | is (kāna) | for the believers (l-mu'minūna) | that they go forth (liyanfirū) | all together (kāffatan). | So if not (falawlā) | go forth (nafara) | from (min) | every (kulli) | group (fir'qatin) | among them (min'hum) | a party (ṭāifatun) | that they may obtain understanding (liyatafaqqahū) | in (fī) | the religion (l-dīni), | and that they may warn (waliyundhirū) | their people (qawmahum) | when (idhā) | they return (rajaʿū) | to them (ilayhim), | so that they may (laʿallahum) | beware (yaḥdharūna).

9:123 O you who believe! Fight those who are close to you of the disbelievers, and let them find in you harshness. And know that Allah is with those who fear Him.

O you who believe (yāayyuhā)! | O you who believe (alladhīna)! | O you who believe (āmanū)! | Fight (qātilū) | those who (alladhīna) | are close to you (yalūnakum) | of (mina) | the disbelievers (l-kufāri), | and let them find (walyajidū) | in you (fīkum) | harshness (ghil'ẓatan). | And know (wa-iʿ'lamū) | that (anna) | Allah (l-laha) | is with (maʿa) | those who fear Him (l-mutaqīna).

9:124 And whenever is revealed a Surah, among them are some who say, "Which of you has increased [it] by this in faith?" As for those who believe then it has increased them in faith and they rejoice.

And whenever (wa-idhā) | And whenever (mā) | is revealed (unzilat) | a Surah (sūratun), | among them (famin'hum) | are some who (man) | say (yaqūlu), | "Which of you (ayyukum) | has increased [it] (zādathu) | by this (hādhihi) | in faith? (īmānan)" | As for (fa-ammā) | those who (alladhīna) | believe (āmanū) | then it has increased them (fazādathum) | in faith (īmānan) | and they (wahum) | rejoice (yastabshirūna).

9:125 But as for those, in their hearts is a disease, it increases them in evil to their evil. And they die while they are disbelievers.

But as for (wa-ammā) | those (alladhīna), | in (fī) | their hearts (qulūbihim) | is a disease (maraḍun), | it increases them (fazādathum) | in evil (rij'san) | to (ilā) | their evil (rij'sihim). | And they die (wamātū) | while they (wahum) | are disbelievers (kāfirūna).

9:126 Do not they see that they are tried [in] every year once or twice? Yet not they turn in repentance, and not they pay heed.

Do not (awalā) | they see (yarawna) | that they (annahum) | are tried (yuf'tanūna) | [in] (fī) | every (kulli) | year (ʿāmin) | once (marratan) | or (aw) | twice (marratayni)? | Yet (thumma) | not (lā) | they turn in repentance (yatūbūna), | and not (walā) | they (hum) | pay heed (yadhakkarūna).

9:127 And whenever is revealed a Surah, look some of them to others, "Does see you any one?" Then they turn away. Allah has turned away their hearts because they are a people not they understand.

And whenever (wa-idhā) | And whenever (mā) | is revealed (unzilat) | a Surah (sūratun), | look (naẓara) | some of them (baʿḍuhum) | to (ilā) | others (baʿḍin), | "Does (hal) | see you (yarākum) | any (min) | one? (aḥadin)" | Then (thumma) | they turn away (inṣarafū). | Allah has turned away (ṣarafa) | Allah has turned away (l-lahu) | their hearts (qulūbahum) | because they (bi-annahum) | are a people (qawmun) | not (lā) | they understand (yafqahūna).

9:128 Certainly, has come to you a Messenger from yourselves. Grievous to him is what you suffer, he is concerned over you, to the believers he is kind and merciful.

Certainly (laqad), | has come to you (jāakum) | a Messenger (rasūlun) | from (min) | yourselves (anfusikum). | Grievous (ʿazīzun) | to him (ʿalayhi) | is what (mā) | you suffer (ʿanittum), | he is concerned (ḥarīṣun) | over you (ʿalaykum), | to the believers (bil-mu'minīna) | he is kind (raūfun) | and merciful (raḥīmun).

9:129 But if they turn away, then say, "Sufficient for me is Allah. There is no god except Him. On Him I put my trust. And He is the Lord of the Throne, the Great."

But if (fa-in) | they turn away (tawallaw), | then say (faqul), | "Sufficient for me (ḥasbiya) | is Allah (l-lahu). | There is no (lā) | god (ilāha) | except (illā) | Him (huwa). | On Him (ʿalayhi) | I put my trust (tawakkaltu). | And He (wahuwa) | is the Lord (rabbu) | of the Throne (l-ʿarshi), | the Great. (l-ʿaẓīmi)"

Chapter (10) Sūrat Yūnus (Jonah)

10:1 Alif Lam Ra. These are the verses of the Book the wise.

Alif Lam Ra (alif-lam-ra). | These (til'ka) | are the verses (āyātu) | of the Book (l-kitābi) | the wise (l-ḥakīmi).

10:2 Is it for the mankind a wonder that We revealed to a man from among them that, "Warn the mankind and give glad tidings to those who believe that for them will be a respectable position near their Lord?" Said the disbelievers, "Indeed, this is surely a magician obvious."

Is it (akāna) | for the mankind (lilnnāsi) | a wonder (ʿajaban) | that (an) | We revealed (awḥaynā) | to (ilā) | a man (rajulin) | from among them (min'hum) | that (an), | "Warn (andhiri) | the mankind (l-nāsa) | and give glad tidings (wabashiri) | to those who (alladhīna) | believe (āmanū) | that (anna) | for them (lahum) | will be a respectable position (qadama) | will be a respectable position (ṣid'qin) | near (ʿinda) | their Lord? (rabbihim)" | Said (qāla) | the disbelievers (l-kāfirūna), | "Indeed (inna), | this (hādhā) | is surely a magician (lasāḥirun) | obvious. (mubīnun)"

10:3 Indeed, your Lord is Allah the One Who created the heavens and the earth in six periods, then He established on the Throne, disposing the affairs. Not is any intercessor except after His permission. That is Allah, your Lord, so worship Him. Then will not you remember?

Indeed (inna), | your Lord (rabbakumu) | is Allah (l-lahu) | the One Who (alladhī) | created (khalaqa) | the heavens (l-samāwāti) | and the earth (wal-arḍa) | in (fī) | six (sittati) | periods (ayyāmin), | then (thumma) | He established (is'tawā) | on (ʿalā) | the Throne (l-ʿarshi), | disposing (yudabbiru) | the affairs (l-amra). | Not (mā) | is any intercessor (min) | is any intercessor (shafīʿin) | except (illā) | after (min) | after (baʿdi) | His permission (idh'nihi). | That (dhālikumu) | is Allah (l-lahu), | your Lord (rabbukum), | so worship Him (fa-uʿ'budūhu). | Then will not (afalā) | you remember (tadhakkarūna)?

10:4 To Him, will be your return [all]. Promise of Allah is true. Indeed, He originates the creation, then He repeats it, that He may reward those who believed and did the good deeds, in justice. But those who disbelieved, for them will be a drink of boiling fluids and a punishment painful, because they used to disbelieve.

To Him (ilayhi), | will be your return (marjiʿukum) | [all] (jamīʿan). | Promise (waʿda) | of Allah (l-lahi) | is true (ḥaqqan). | Indeed, He (innahu) | originates (yabda-u) | the creation (l-khalqa), | then (thumma) | He repeats it (yuʿīduhu), | that He may reward (liyajziya) | those who (alladhīna) | believed (āmanū) | and did (waʿamilū) | the good deeds (l-ṣāliḥāti), | in justice (bil-qis'ṭi). | But those who (wa-alladhīna) | disbelieved (kafarū), | for them (lahum) | will be a drink (sharābun) | of (min) | boiling fluids (ḥamīmin) | and a punishment (waʿadhābun) | painful (alīmun), | because (bimā) | they used to (kānū) | disbelieve (yakfurūna).

10:5 He is the One Who made the sun a shining light, and the moon a reflected light and determined for it phases, that you may know the number of the years and the count of time. Not created Allah that except in truth. He explains the Signs for a people who know.

He (huwa) | is the One Who (alladhī) | made (jaʿala) | the sun (l-shamsa) | a shining light (ḍiyāan), | and the moon (wal-qamara) | a reflected light (nūran) | and determined for it (waqaddarahu) | phases (manāzila), | that you may know (litaʿlamū) | the number (ʿadada) | of the years (l-sinīna) | and the count of time (wal-ḥisāba). | Not (mā) | created (khalaqa) | Allah (l-lahu) | that (dhālika) | except (illā) | in truth (bil-ḥaqi). | He explains (yufaṣṣilu) | the Signs (l-āyāti) | for a people (liqawmin) | who know (yaʿlamūna).

10:6 Indeed, in the alternation of the night and the day and what has been created by Allah in the heavens, and the earth are Signs for a people who are God conscious.

Indeed (inna), | in (fī) | the alternation (ikh'tilāfi) | of the night (al-layli) | and the day (wal-nahāri) | and what (wamā) | has been created (khalaqa) | by Allah (l-lahu) | in (fī) | the heavens (l-samāwāti), | and the earth (wal-arḍi) | are Signs (laāyātin) | for a people (liqawmin) | who are God conscious (yattaqūna).

10:7 Indeed, those who do not expect the meeting with Us and are pleased with the life of the world, and feel satisfied with it and those - they are of Our Signs, heedless.

Indeed (inna), | those who (alladhīna) | do not (lā) | expect (yarjūna) | the meeting with Us (liqāanā) | and are pleased (waraḍū) | with the life (bil-ḥayati) | of the world (l-dun'yā), | and feel satisfied (wa-iṭ'ma-annū) | with it (bihā) | and those (wa-alladhīna)- | they (hum) | are of (ʿan) | Our Signs (āyātinā), | heedless (ghāfilūna).

10:8 Those - their abode will be the Fire, for what they used to earn.

Those (ulāika)- | their abode (mawāhumu) | will be the Fire (l-nāru), | for what (bimā) | they used to (kānū) | earn (yaksibūna).

10:9 Indeed, those who believed and did good deeds, will guide them their Lord, by their faith. Will flow from underneath them the rivers, in Gardens of Delight.

Indeed (inna), | those who (alladhīna) | believed (āmanū) | and did (waʿamilū) | good deeds (l-ṣāliḥāti), | will guide them (yahdīhim) | their Lord (rabbuhum), | by their faith (biīmānihim). | Will flow (tajrī) | from (min) | underneath them (taḥtihimu) | the rivers (l-anhāru), | in (fī) | Gardens (jannāti) | of Delight (l-naʿīmi).

10:10 Their prayer therein will be, "Glory be to You, O Allah!" And their greeting therein will be, "Peace." And the last of their call will be [that] "All the Praise be to Allah, Lord of the worlds."

Their prayer (daʿwāhum) | therein (fīhā) | will be, "Glory be to You (sub'ḥānaka), | O Allah! (l-lahuma)" | And their greeting (wataḥiyyatuhum) | therein will be (fīhā), | "Peace. (salāmun)" | And the last (waākhiru) | of their call (daʿwāhum) | will be [that] (ani) | "All the Praise be (l-ḥamdu) | to Allah (lillahi), | Lord (rabbi) | of the worlds. (l-ʿālamīna)"

10:11 And if hastens by Allah for the mankind the evil, as He hastens for them the good, surely, would have been decreed for them their term. But We leave those who do not expect the meeting with Us, in their transgression, wandering blindly.

And if (walaw) | hastens (yuʿajjilu) | by Allah (l-lahu) | for the mankind (lilnnāsi) | the evil (l-shara), | as He hastens for them (is'tiʿ'jālahum) | the good (bil-khayri), | surely, would have been decreed (laquḍiya) | for them (ilayhim) | their term (ajaluhum). | But We leave (fanadharu) | those who (alladhīna) | do not (lā) | expect (yarjūna) | the meeting with Us (liqāanā), | in (fī) | their transgression (ṭugh'yānihim), | wandering blindly (yaʿmahūna).

10:12 And when touches the man the affliction he calls Us, lying on his side or sitting or standing. But when We remove from him his affliction he passes on as if he had not called Us for the affliction that touched him. Thus it is made fair seeming to the extravagant what they used to do.

And when (wa-idhā) | touches (massa) | the man (l-insāna) | the affliction (l-ḍuru) | he calls Us (daʿānā), | lying on his side (lijanbihi) | or (aw) | sitting (qāʿidan) | or (aw) | standing (qāiman). | But when (falammā) | We remove (kashafnā) | from him (ʿanhu) | his affliction (ḍurrahu) | he passes on (marra) | as if he (ka-an) | had not (lam) | called Us (yadʿunā) | for (ilā) | the affliction (ḍurrin) | that touched him (massahu). | Thus (kadhālika) | it is made fair seeming (zuyyina) | to the extravagant (lil'mus'rifīna) | what (mā) | they used to (kānū) | do (yaʿmalūna).

10:13 And verily We destroyed the generations before you when they wronged, and came to them their Messengers with clear proofs, but not they were to believe. Thus We recompense the people who are criminals.

And verily (walaqad) | We destroyed (ahlaknā) | the generations (l-qurūna) | before you (min) | before you (qablikum) | when (lammā) | they wronged (ẓalamū), | and came to them (wajāathum) | their Messengers (rusuluhum) | with clear proofs (bil-bayināti), | but not (wamā) | they were (kānū) | to believe (liyu'minū). | Thus (kadhālika) | We recompense (najzī) | the people (l-qawma) | who are criminals (l-muj'rimīna).

10:14 Then We made you successors in the earth after them so that We may see how you do.

Then (thumma) | We made you (jaʿalnākum) | successors (khalāifa) | in (fī) | the earth (l-arḍi) | after them (min) | after them (baʿdihim) | so that We may see (linanẓura) | how (kayfa) | you do (taʿmalūna).

10:15 And when are recited to them Our Verses as clear proofs said those who do not hope for the meeting (with) Us, "Bring us a Quran other than this or change it." Say, "Not it is for me that I change it of my own accord. Not I follow except what is revealed to me. Indeed, I [I] fear if I were to disobey my Lord, the punishment of a Day, Great."

And when (wa-idhā) | are recited (tut'lā) | to them (ʿalayhim) | Our Verses (āyātunā) | as clear proofs (bayyinātin) | said (qāla) | those who (alladhīna) | do not (lā) | hope (yarjūna) | for the meeting (with) Us (liqāanā), | "Bring us (i'ti) | a Quran (biqur'ānin) | other than (ghayri) | this (hādhā) | or (aw) | change it. (baddil'hu)" | Say (qul), | "Not (mā) | it is (yakūnu) | for me (lī) | that (an) | I change it (ubaddilahu) | of (min) | my own accord (til'qāi). | my own accord (nafsī). | Not (in) | I follow (attabiʿu) | except (illā) | what (mā) | is revealed (yūḥā) | to me (ilayya). | Indeed, I (innī) | [I] fear (akhāfu) | if (in) | I were to disobey (ʿaṣaytu) | my Lord (rabbī), | the punishment (ʿadhāba) | of a Day (yawmin), | Great. (ʿaẓīmin)"

10:16 Say, "If had willed Allah, not I would have recited it to you, and not He would have made it known to you. Verily, I have stayed among you a lifetime before it. Then will not you use reason?"

Say (qul), | "If (law) | had willed (shāa) | Allah (l-lahu), | not (mā) | I would have recited it (talawtuhu) | to you (ʿalaykum), | and not (walā) | He would have made it known to you (adrākum). | He would have made it known to you (bihi). | Verily (faqad), | I have stayed (labith'tu) | among you (fīkum) | a lifetime (ʿumuran) | before it (min). | before it (qablihi). | Then will not (afalā) | you use reason? (taʿqilūna)"

10:17 So who is more wrong than he who invents against Allah a lie or denies His Signs? Indeed, not will succeed the criminals.

So who (faman) | is more wrong (aẓlamu) | than he who (mimmani) | invents (if'tarā) | against (ʿalā) | Allah (l-lahi) | a lie (kadhiban) | or (aw) | denies (kadhaba) | His Signs (biāyātihi)? | Indeed (innahu), | not (lā) | will succeed (yuf'liḥu) | the criminals (l-muj'rimūna).

10:18 And they worship from other than Allah that which does not harm them and not benefit them, and they say, "These are our intercessors with Allah." Say, "Do you inform Allah of what not he knows in the heavens and not in the earth?" Glorified is He and Exalted above what they associate with Him.

And they worship (wayaʿbudūna) | from (min) | other than (dūni) | Allah (l-lahi) | that which (mā) | does not (lā) | harm them (yaḍurruhum) | and not (walā) | benefit them (yanfaʿuhum), | and they say (wayaqūlūna), | "These (hāulāi) | are our intercessors (shufaʿāunā) | with (ʿinda) | Allah. (l-lahi)" | Say (qul), | "Do you inform (atunabbiūna) | Allah (l-laha) | of what (bimā) | not (lā) | he knows (yaʿlamu) | in (fī) | the heavens (l-samāwāti) | and not (walā) | in (fī) | the earth? (l-arḍi)" | Glorified is He (sub'ḥānahu) | and Exalted (wataʿālā) | above what (ʿammā) | they associate with Him (yush'rikūna).

10:19 And not was the mankind but a community, one, then they differed. And had it not been a word that preceded from your Lord, surely, it would have been judged between them concerning what [therein] they differ.

And not (wamā) | was (kāna) | the mankind (l-nāsu) | but (illā) | a community (ummatan), | one (wāḥidatan), | then they differed (fa-ikh'talafū). | And had it not been (walawlā) | a word (kalimatun) | that preceded (sabaqat) | from (min) | your Lord (rabbika), | surely, it would have been judged (laquḍiya) | between them (baynahum) | concerning what (fīmā) | [therein] (fīhi) | they differ (yakhtalifūna).

10:20 And they say, "Why not is sent down to him a Sign from his Lord?" So say, "Only the unseen is for Allah, so wait; indeed, I am with you among the ones who wait."

And they say (wayaqūlūna), | "Why not (lawlā) | is sent down (unzila) | to him (ʿalayhi) | a Sign (āyatun) | from (min) | his Lord? (rabbihi)" | So say (faqul), | "Only (innamā) | the unseen (l-ghaybu) | is for Allah (lillahi), | so wait (fa-intaẓirū); | indeed, I am (innī) | with you (maʿakum) | among (mina) | the ones who wait. (l-muntaẓirīna)"

10:21 And when We let [the] mankind taste mercy after adversity has touched them, behold! They have a plot against Our Verses. Say, "Allah is more swift in planning." Indeed, Our Messengers write down what you plot.

And when (wa-idhā) | We let [the] mankind taste (adhaqnā) | We let [the] mankind taste (l-nāsa) | mercy (raḥmatan) | after (min) | after (baʿdi) | adversity (ḍarrāa) | has touched them (massathum), | behold (idhā)! | They have (lahum) | a plot (makrun) | against (fī) | Our Verses (āyātinā). | Say (quli), | "Allah (l-lahu) | is more swift (asraʿu) | in planning. (makran)" | Indeed (inna), | Our Messengers (rusulanā) | write down (yaktubūna) | what (mā) | you plot (tamkurūna).

10:22 He is the One Who enables you to travel in the land and the sea, until, when you are in the ships and they sail with them with a wind good, and they rejoice therein comes to it a wind stormy, and comes to them the waves from every place, and they assume that they are surrounded with them. They call Allah sincerely to Him in the religion, saying, "If You save us from this, surely we will be among the thankful."

He (huwa) | is the One Who (alladhī) | enables you to travel (yusayyirukum) | in (fī) | the land (l-bari) | and the sea (wal-baḥri), | until (ḥattā), | when (idhā) | you are (kuntum) | in (fī) | the ships (l-ful'ki) | and they sail (wajarayna) | with them (bihim) | with a wind (birīḥin) | good (ṭayyibatin), | and they rejoice (wafariḥū) | therein (bihā) | comes to it (jāathā) | a wind (rīḥun) | stormy (ʿāṣifun), | and comes to them (wajāahumu) | the waves (l-mawju) | from (min) | every (kulli) | place (makānin), | and they assume (waẓannū) | that they (annahum) | are surrounded (uḥīṭa) | with them (bihim). | They call (daʿawū) | Allah (l-laha) | sincerely (mukh'liṣīna) | to Him (lahu) | in the religion (l-dīna), | saying, "If (la-in) | You save us (anjaytanā) | from (min) | this (hādhihi), | surely we will be (lanakūnanna) | among (mina) | the thankful. (l-shākirīna)"

10:23 But when He saved them, behold! They rebel in the earth without [the] right. O mankind! Only your rebellion is against yourselves, the enjoyment of the life of the world. Then to Us is your return and We will inform you of what you used to do.

But when (falammā) | He saved them (anjāhum), | behold (idhā)! | They (hum) | rebel (yabghūna) | in (fī) | the earth (l-arḍi) | without (bighayri) | [the] right (l-ḥaqi). | O mankind (yāayyuhā)! | O mankind (l-nāsu)! | Only (innamā) | your rebellion (baghyukum) | is against (ʿalā) | yourselves (anfusikum), | the enjoyment (matāʿa) | of the life (l-ḥayati) | of the world (l-dun'yā). | Then (thumma) | to Us (ilaynā) | is your return (marjiʿukum) | and We will inform you (fanunabbi-ukum) | of what (bimā) | you used to (kuntum) | do (taʿmalūna).

10:24 Only the example of the life of the world is like (the) water which We sent down from the sky, so absorbs [with] it, the plants of the earth from which eat the men and the cattle, until when takes the earth its adornment and is beautified and think its people that they have the power over it, comes to it Our command by night or by day, and We make it a harvest clean-mown, as if not it had flourished yesterday. Thus We explain the Signs for a people who reflect.

Only (innamā) | the example (mathalu) | of the life (l-ḥayati) | of the world (l-dun'yā) | is like (the) water (kamāin) | which We sent down (anzalnāhu) | from (mina) | the sky (l-samāi), | so absorbs (fa-ikh'talaṭa) | [with] it (bihi), | the plants (nabātu) | of the earth (l-arḍi) | from which (mimmā) | eat (yakulu) | the men (l-nāsu) | and the cattle (wal-anʿāmu), | until (ḥattā) | when (idhā) | takes (akhadhati) | the earth (l-arḍu) | its adornment (zukh'rufahā) | and is beautified (wa-izzayyanat) | and think (waẓanna) | its people (ahluhā) | that they (annahum) | have the power (qādirūna) | over it (ʿalayhā), | comes to it (atāhā) | Our command (amrunā) | by night (laylan) | or (aw) | by day (nahāran), | and We make it (fajaʿalnāhā) | a harvest clean-mown (ḥaṣīdan), | as if (ka-an) | not (lam) | it had flourished (taghna) | yesterday (bil-amsi). | Thus (kadhālika) | We explain (nufaṣṣilu) | the Signs (l-āyāti) | for a people (liqawmin) | who reflect (yatafakkarūna).

10:25 And Allah calls to the Home of the Peace, and guides whom He wills to the straight path.

And Allah (wal-lahu) | calls (yadʿū) | to (ilā) | the Home (dāri) | of the Peace (l-salāmi), | and guides (wayahdī) | whom (man) | He wills (yashāu) | to (ilā) | the straight path (ṣirāṭin). | the straight path (mus'taqīmin).

10:26 For those who do good is the best and more. And not will cover their faces dust and not humiliation. Those are the companions of Paradise, they in it will abide forever.

For those who (lilladhīna) | do good (aḥsanū) | is the best (l-ḥus'nā) | and more (waziyādatun). | And not (walā) | will cover (yarhaqu) | their faces (wujūhahum) | dust (qatarun) | and not (walā) | humiliation (dhillatun). | Those (ulāika) | are the companions (aṣḥābu) | of Paradise (l-janati), | they (hum) | in it (fīhā) | will abide forever (khālidūna).

10:27 And those who earned the evil deeds, the recompense of an evil deed is like it, and will cover them humiliation. They will not have from Allah any defender. As if had been covered their faces with pieces from the darkness of night. Those are the companions of the Fire, they in it will abide forever.

And those who (wa-alladhīna) | earned (kasabū) | the evil deeds (l-sayiāti), | the recompense (jazāu) | of an evil deed (sayyi-atin) | is like it (bimith'lihā), | and will cover them (watarhaquhum) | humiliation (dhillatun). | They will not have (mā) | They will not have (lahum) | from (mina) | Allah (l-lahi) | any (min) | defender (ʿāṣimin). | As if (ka-annamā) | had been covered (ugh'shiyat) | their faces (wujūhuhum) | with pieces (qiṭaʿan) | from (mina) | the darkness of night (al-layli). | the darkness of night (muẓ'liman). | Those (ulāika) | are the companions (aṣḥābu) | of the Fire (l-nāri), | they (hum) | in it (fīhā) | will abide forever (khālidūna).

10:28 And the Day We will gather them all together, then We will say to those who associate partners with Allah, "Remain in your place you and your partners." Then We will separate [between] them, and will say their partners, "Not you used to worship us."

And the Day (wayawma) | We will gather them (naḥshuruhum) | all together (jamīʿan), | then (thumma) | We will say (naqūlu) | to those who (lilladhīna) | associate partners with Allah (ashrakū), | "Remain in your place (makānakum) | you (antum) | and your partners. (washurakāukum)" | Then We will separate (fazayyalnā) | [between] them (baynahum), | and will say (waqāla) | their partners (shurakāuhum), | "Not (mā) | you used to (kuntum) | worship us. (iyyānā)" | worship us. (taʿbudūna)"

10:29 So sufficient is Allah as a witness between us and between you that we were of your worship certainly unaware.

So sufficient (fakafā) | is Allah (bil-lahi) | as a witness (shahīdan) | between us (baynanā) | and between you (wabaynakum) | that (in) | we were (kunnā) | of (ʿan) | your worship (ʿibādatikum) | certainly unaware (laghāfilīna).

10:30 There will be put to trial every soul for what it did previously, and they will be returned to Allah their Lord the true, and will be lost from them what they used to invent.

There (hunālika) | will be put to trial (tablū) | every (kullu) | soul (nafsin) | for what (mā) | it did previously (aslafat), | and they will be returned (waruddū) | to (ilā) | Allah (l-lahi) | their Lord (mawlāhumu) | the true (l-ḥaqi), | and will be lost (waḍalla) | from them (ʿanhum) | what (mā) | they used to (kānū) | invent (yaftarūna).

10:31 Say, "Who provides for you from the sky and the earth? Or who controls the hearing and the sight? And who brings out the living from the dead, and brings forth the dead from the living? And who disposes the affairs?" Then they will say, "Allah." Then say, "Then will not you fear Him?"

Say (qul), | "Who (man) | provides for you (yarzuqukum) | from (mina) | the sky (l-samāi) | and the earth (wal-arḍi)? | Or who (amman) | controls (yamliku) | the hearing (l-samʿa) | and the sight (wal-abṣāra)? | And who (waman) | brings out (yukh'riju) | the living (l-ḥaya) | from (mina) | the dead (l-mayiti), | and brings forth (wayukh'riju) | the dead (l-mayita) | from (mina) | the living (l-ḥayi)? | And who (waman) | disposes (yudabbiru) | the affairs? (l-amra)" | Then they will say (fasayaqūlūna), | "Allah. (l-lahu)" | Then say (faqul), | "Then will not (afalā) | you fear Him? (tattaqūna)"

10:32 For that is Allah, your Lord, the true. So what can be after the truth except the error? So how are you turned away.

For that (fadhālikumu) | is Allah (l-lahu), | your Lord (rabbukumu), | the true (l-ḥaqu). | So what can be (famādhā) | after (baʿda) | the truth (l-ḥaqi) | except (illā) | the error (l-ḍalālu)? | So how (fa-annā) | are you turned away (tuṣ'rafūna).

10:33 Thus is proved true the Word of your Lord upon those who defiantly disobeyed, that they will not believe.

Thus (kadhālika) | is proved true (ḥaqqat) | the Word (kalimatu) | of your Lord (rabbika) | upon (ʿalā) | those who (alladhīna) | defiantly disobeyed (fasaqū), | that they (annahum) | will not (lā) | believe (yu'minūna).

10:34 Say, "Is there of your partners any who originates the creation then repeats it?" Say, "Allah originates the creation then repeats it. So how you are deluded?"

Say (qul), | "Is there (hal) | of (min) | your partners (shurakāikum) | any who (man) | originates (yabda-u) | the creation (l-khalqa) | then (thumma) | repeats it? (yuʿīduhu)" | Say (quli), | "Allah (l-lahu) | originates (yabda-u) | the creation (l-khalqa) | then (thumma) | repeats it (yuʿīduhu). | So how (fa-annā) | you are deluded? (tu'fakūna)"

10:35 Say, "Is there of your partners any who guides to the truth?" Say, "Allah guides to the truth. Is then he who guides to the truth more worthy that he should be followed or he who does not guide unless [that] he is guided? Then what is for you, how you judge?"

Say (qul), | "Is there (hal) | of (min) | your partners (shurakāikum) | any who (man) | guides (yahdī) | to (ilā) | the truth? (l-ḥaqi)" | Say (quli), | "Allah (l-lahu) | guides (yahdī) | to the truth (lil'ḥaqqi). | Is then he who (afaman) | guides (yahdī) | to (ilā) | the truth (l-ḥaqi) | more worthy (aḥaqqu) | that (an) | he should be followed (yuttabaʿa) | or he who (amman) | does not (lā) | guide (yahiddī) | unless (illā) | [that] (an) | he is guided (yuh'dā)? | Then what (famā) | is for you (lakum), | how (kayfa) | you judge? (taḥkumūna)"

10:36 And not follow most of them except assumption. Indeed, the assumption does not avail against the truth anything. Indeed, Allah is All-Knower of what they do.

And not (wamā) | follow (yattabiʿu) | most of them (aktharuhum) | except (illā) | assumption (ẓannan). | Indeed (inna), | the assumption (l-ẓana) | does not (lā) | avail (yugh'nī) | against (mina) | the truth (l-ḥaqi) | anything (shayan). | Indeed (inna), | Allah (l-laha) | is All-Knower

(ʿalīmun) | of what (bimā) | they do (yafʿalūna).

10:37 And not is this the Quran, that it could be produced by other than Allah, but it is a confirmation of that which was before it and a detailed explanation of the Book, there is no doubt in it, from the Lord of the worlds.

And not (wamā) | is (kāna) | this (hādhā) | the Quran (l-qur'ānu), | that (an) | it could be produced (yuf'tarā) | by (min) | other than Allah (dūni), | other than Allah (l-lahi), | but (walākin) | it is a confirmation (taṣdīqa) | of that which (alladhī) | was before it (bayna) | was before it (yadayhi) | and a detailed explanation (watafṣīla) | of the Book (l-kitābi), | there is no (lā) | doubt (rayba) | in it (fīhi), | from (min) | the Lord (rabbi) | of the worlds (l-ʿālamīna).

10:38 Or do they say, "He has invented it?" Say, "Then bring a Surah like it and call whoever you can besides Allah, if you are truthful."

Or (am) | do they say (yaqūlūna), | "He has invented it? (if'tarāhu)" | Say (qul), | "Then bring (fatū) | a Surah (bisūratin) | like it (mith'lihi) | and call (wa-id'ʿū) | whoever (mani) | you can (is'taṭaʿtum) | besides Allah (min), | besides Allah (dūni), | besides Allah (l-lahi), | if (in) | you are (kuntum) | truthful. (ṣādiqīna)"

10:39 Nay, they denied what not they could encompass of its knowledge and not has come to them its interpretation. Thus denied those before them, then see how was the end of the wrongdoers.

Nay (bal), | they denied (kadhabū) | what (bimā) | not (lam) | they could encompass (yuḥīṭū) | of its knowledge (biʿil'mihi) | and not (walammā) | has come to them (yatihim) | its interpretation (tawīluhu). | Thus (kadhālika) | denied (kadhaba) | those (alladhīna) | before them (min), | before them (qablihim), | then see (fa-unẓur) | how (kayfa) | was (kāna) | the end (ʿāqibatu) | of the wrongdoers (l-ẓālimīna).

10:40 And of them is one who believes in it, and of them is one who does not believe in it. And your Lord is All-Knower of the corrupters.

And of them (wamin'hum) | is one who (man) | believes (yu'minu) | in it (bihi), | and of them (wamin'hum) | is one who (man) | does not (lā) | believe (yu'minu) | in it (bihi). | And your Lord (warabbuka) | is All-Knower (aʿlamu) | of the corrupters (bil-muf'sidīna).

10:41 And if they deny you then say, "For me are my deeds, and for you are your deeds. You are disassociated from what I do, and I am disassociated from what you do."

And if (wa-in) | they deny you (kadhabūka) | then say (faqul), | "For me (lī) | are my deeds (ʿamalī), | and for you (walakum) | are your deeds (ʿamalukum). | You (antum) | are disassociated (barīūna) | from what (mimmā) | I do (aʿmalu), | and I am (wa-anā) | disassociated (barīon) | from what (mimmā) | you do. (taʿmalūna)"

10:42 And among them are some who listen to you. But can you cause the deaf to hear even though they [were] do not use reason?

And among them (wamin'hum) | are some who (man) | listen (yastamiʿūna) | to you (ilayka). | But can you (afa-anta) | cause the deaf to hear (tus'miʿu) | cause the deaf to hear (l-ṣuma) | even though (walaw) | they [were] (kānū) | do not (lā) | use reason (yaʿqilūna)?

10:43 And among them are some who look at you. But can you guide the blind even though they [were] do not see?

And among them (wamin'hum) | are some who (man) | look (yanẓuru) | at you (ilayka). | But can you (afa-anta) | guide (tahdī) | the blind (l-ʿum'ya) | even though (walaw) | they [were] (kānū) | do not (lā) | see (yub'ṣirūna)?

10:44 Indeed, Allah does not wrong the people in anything, but the people wrong themselves.

Indeed (inna), | Allah (l-laha) | does not (lā) | wrong (yaẓlimu) | the people (l-nāsa) | in anything (shayan), | but (walākinna) | the people (l-nāsa) | wrong themselves (anfusahum). | wrong themselves (yaẓlimūna).

10:45 And the Day He will gather them, as if they had not remained except an hour of the day, they will recognize each other between them. Certainly, will have lost those who denied the meeting with Allah, and not they were the guided ones.

And the Day (wayawma) | He will gather them (yaḥshuruhum), | as if (ka-an) | they had not remained (lam) | they had not remained (yalbathū) | except (illā) | an hour (sāʿatan) | of (mina) | the day (l-nahāri), | they will recognize each other (yataʿārafūna) | between them (baynahum). | Certainly (qad), | will have lost (khasira) | those who (alladhīna) | denied (kadhabū) | the meeting (biliqāi) | with Allah (l-lahi), | and not (wamā) | they were (kānū) | the guided ones (muh'tadīna).

10:46 And whether We show you some of that which We promised them or We cause you to die, then to Us is their return, then Allah is a Witness over what they do.

And whether (wa-immā) | We show you (nuriyannaka) | some (baʿḍa) | of that which (alladhī) | We promised them (naʿiduhum) | or (aw) | We cause you to die (natawaffayannaka), | then to Us (fa-ilaynā) | is their return (marjiʿuhum), | then (thumma) | Allah (l-lahu) | is a Witness (shahīdun) | over (ʿalā) | what (mā) | they do (yafʿalūna).

10:47 And for every nation is a Messenger. So when comes their Messenger, it will be judged between them in justice, and they will not be wronged.

And for every (walikulli) | nation (ummatin) | is a Messenger (rasūlun). | So when (fa-idhā) | comes (jāa) | their Messenger (rasūluhum), | it will be judged (quḍiya) | between them (baynahum) | in justice (bil-qis'ṭi), | and they (wahum) | will not (lā) | be wronged (yuẓ'lamūna).

10:48 And they say, "When will this, the promise be fulfilled, if you are truthful?"

And they say (wayaqūlūna), | "When (matā) | will this (hādhā), | the promise be fulfilled (l-waʿdu), | if (in) | you are (kuntum) | truthful? (ṣādiqīna)"

10:49 Say, "Not I have power for myself for any harm and not for any profit except what Allah wills. For every nation is a term. When comes their term, then not they remain behind an hour, and not they can precede it."

Say (qul), | "Not (lā) | I have power (amliku) | for myself (linafsī) | for any harm (ḍarran) | and not (walā) | for any profit (nafʿan) | except (illā) | what (mā) | Allah wills (shāa). | Allah wills (l-lahu). | For every (likulli) | nation (ummatin) | is a term (ajalun). | When (idhā) | comes (jāa) | their term (ajaluhum), | then not (falā) | they remain behind (yastakhirūna) | an hour (sāʿatan), | and not (walā) | they can precede it. (yastaqdimūna)"

10:50 Say, "Do you see, if comes to you His punishment by night or by day, what portion of it would wish to hasten the criminals?"

Say (qul), | "Do you see (ara-aytum), | if (in) | comes to you (atākum) | His punishment (ʿadhābuhu) | by night (bayātan) | or (aw) | by day (nahāran), | what portion (mādhā) | of it would wish to hasten (yastaʿjilu) | of it would wish to hasten (min'hu) | the criminals? (l-muj'rimūna)"

10:51 Is it then when it had occurred you will believe in it? Now? And certainly you were seeking to hasten it.

Is it then (athumma) | when (idhā) | when (mā) | it had occurred (waqaʿa) | you will believe (āmantum) | in it (bihi)? | Now (āl'āna)? | And certainly (waqad) | you were (kuntum) | seeking to hasten it (bihi). | seeking to hasten it (tastaʿjilūna).

10:52 Then it will be said to those who wronged, "Taste punishment the everlasting. Are you being recompensed except for what you used to earn?"

Then (thumma) | it will be said (qīla) | to those who (lilladhīna) | wronged (ẓalamū), | "Taste (dhūqū) | punishment (ʿadhāba) | the everlasting (l-khul'di). | Are you being recompensed (hal) | Are you being recompensed (tuj'zawna) | except (illā) | for what (bimā) | you used to (kuntum) | earn? (taksibūna)"

10:53 And they ask you to inform "Is it true?" Say, "Yes, by my Lord! Indeed, it is surely the truth, and not you can escape (it)."

And they ask you to inform (wayastanbiūnaka) | "Is it true? (aḥaqqun)" | "Is it true? (huwa)" | Say (qul), | "Yes (ī), | by my Lord (warabbī)! | Indeed, it (innahu) | is surely the truth (laḥaqqun), | and not (wamā) | you (antum) | can escape (it). (bimuʿjizīna)"

10:54 And if that for every soul that wronged, whatever is in the earth, it would seek to ransom with it, and they will confide the regret when they see the punishment. But will be judged between them in justice, and they will not be wronged.

And if (walaw) | that (anna) | for every (likulli) | soul (nafsin) | that wronged (ẓalamat), | whatever (mā) | is in (fī) | the earth (l-arḍi), | it would seek to ransom (la-if'tadat) | with it (bihi), | and they will confide (wa-asarrū) | the regret (l-nadāmata) | when (lammā) | they see (ra-awū) | the punishment (l-ʿadhāba). | But will be judged (waquḍiya) | between them (baynahum) | in justice (bil-qis'ṭi), | and they (wahum) | will not (lā) | be wronged (yuẓ'lamūna).

10:55 No doubt, indeed, for Allah is whatever is in the heavens and the earth. No doubt indeed, the Promise of Allah is true. But most of them do not know.

No doubt (alā), | indeed (inna), | for Allah (lillahi) | is whatever (mā) | is in (fī) | the heavens (l-samāwāti) | and the earth (wal-arḍi). | No doubt (alā) | indeed (inna), | the Promise of Allah (waʿda) | the Promise of Allah (l-lahi) | is true (ḥaqqun). | But (walākinna) | most of them (aktharahum) | do not (lā) | know (yaʿlamūna).

10:56 He gives life and causes death, and to Him you will be returned.

He (huwa) | gives life (yuḥ'yī) | and causes death (wayumītu), | and to Him (wa-ilayhi) | you will be returned (tur'jaʿūna).

10:57 O mankind! Verily has come to you an instruction from your Lord, and a healing for what is in your breasts, and guidance and mercy for the believers.

O mankind (yāayyuhā)! | O mankind (l-nāsu)! | Verily (qad) | has come to you (jāatkum) | an instruction (mawʿiẓatun) | from (min) | your Lord (rabbikum), | and a healing (washifāon) | for what (limā) | is in (fī) | your breasts (l-ṣudūri), | and guidance (wahudan) | and mercy (waraḥmatun) | for the believers (lil'mu'minīna).

10:58 Say, "In the Bounty of Allah and in His Mercy so in that let them rejoice." It is better than what they accumulate.

Say (qul), | "In the Bounty (bifaḍli) | of Allah (l-lahi) | and in His Mercy (wabiraḥmatihi) | so in that (fabidhālika) | let them rejoice. (falyafraḥū)" | It (huwa) | is better (khayrun) | than what (mimmā) | they accumulate (yajmaʿūna).

10:59 Say, "Have you seen what has been sent down by Allah for you of the provision, and you have made of it unlawful and lawful?" Say, "Has Allah permitted [to] you, or about Allah you invent lies?"

Say (qul), | "Have you seen (ara-aytum) | what (mā) | has been sent down (anzala) | by Allah (l-lahu) | for you (lakum) | of (min) | the provision (riz'qin), | and you have made (fajaʿaltum) | of it (min'hu) | unlawful (ḥarāman) | and lawful? (waḥalālan)" | Say (qul), | "Has Allah (āllahu) | permitted (adhina) | [to] you (lakum), | or (am) | about (ʿalā) | Allah (l-lahi) | you invent lies? (taftarūna)"

10:60 And what will be the assumption of those who invent against Allah the lie on the Day of the Judgment? Indeed, Allah is surely Full (of) Bounty to the mankind, but most of them are not grateful.

And what (wamā) | will be the assumption (ẓannu) | of those who (alladhīna) | invent (yaftarūna) | against (ʿalā) | Allah (l-lahi) | the lie (l-kadhiba) | on the Day (yawma) | of the Judgment (l-qiyāmati)? | Indeed (inna), | Allah (l-laha) | is surely Full (of) Bounty (ladhū) | is surely Full (of) Bounty (faḍlin) | to (ʿalā) | the mankind (l-nāsi), | but (walākinna) | most of them (aktharahum) | are not (lā) | grateful (yashkurūna).

10:61 And not you are [in] any situation, and not you recite of it from the Quran and not you do any deed except We are over you witnesses when you are engaged in it. And not escapes from your Lord of the weight of an atom in the earth, and not in the heavens and not smaller than that and not greater but is in a Record clear.

And not (wamā) | you are (takūnu) | [in] (fī) | any situation (shanin), | and not (wamā) | you recite (tatlū) | of it (min'hu) | from (min) | the Quran (qur'ānin) | and not (walā) | you do (taʿmalūna) | any (min) | deed (ʿamalin) | except (illā) | We are (kunnā) | over you (ʿalaykum) | witnesses (shuhūdan) | when (idh) | you are engaged (tufīḍūna) | in it (fīhi). | And not (wamā) | escapes (yaʿzubu) | from (ʿan) | your Lord (rabbika) | of (min) | the weight (mith'qāli) | of an atom (dharratin) | in (fī) | the earth (l-arḍi), | and not (walā) | in (fī) | the heavens (l-samāi) | and not (walā) | smaller (aṣghara) | than (min) | that (dhālika) | and not (walā) | greater (akbara) | but (illā) | is in (fī) | a Record (kitābin) | clear (mubīnin).

10:62 No doubt! Indeed, the friends of Allah there will be no fear upon then and not they will grieve.

No doubt (alā)! | Indeed (inna), | the friends (awliyāa) | of Allah (l-lahi) | there will be no (lā) | fear (khawfun) | upon then (ʿalayhim) | and not (walā) | they (hum) | will grieve (yaḥzanūna).

10:63 Those who believe and are conscious of Allah,

Those who (alladhīna) | believe (āmanū) | and are (wakānū) | conscious of Allah (yattaqūna),

10:64 For them are the glad tidings in the life of the world and in the Hereafter. No change is there in the Words of Allah. That is the success the great.

For them (lahumu) | are the glad tidings (l-bush'rā) | in (fī) | the life (l-ḥayati) | of the world (l-dun'yā) | and in (wafī) | the Hereafter (l-ākhirati). | No (lā) | change (tabdīla) | is there in the Words (likalimāti) | of Allah (l-lahi). | That (dhālika) | is (huwa) | the success (l-fawzu) | the great (l-ʿaẓīmu).

10:65 And let not grieve you their speech. Indeed, the honor belongs to Allah all. He is the All-Hearer, the All-Knower.

And let not (walā) | grieve you (yaḥzunka) | their speech (qawluhum). | Indeed (inna), | the honor (l-ʿizata) | belongs to Allah (lillahi) | all (jamīʿan). | He (huwa) | is the All-Hearer (l-samīʿu), | the All-Knower (l-ʿalīmu).

10:66 No doubt! Indeed, to Allah belongs whoever is in the heavens and whoever is in the earth. And not follow those who invoke other than Allah partners. Not they follow but the assumption and not they but guess.

No doubt (alā)! | Indeed (inna), | to Allah belongs (lillahi) | whoever (man) | is in (fī) | the heavens (l-samāwāti) | and whoever (waman) | is in (fī) | the earth (l-arḍi). | And not (wamā) | follow (yattabiʿu) | those who (alladhīna) | invoke (yadʿūna) | other than Allah (min) | other than Allah (dūni) | other than Allah (l-lahi) | partners (shurakāa). | Not (in) | they follow (yattabiʿūna) |

but (illā) | the assumption (l-ẓana) | and not (wa-in) | they (hum) | but (illā) | guess (yakhruṣūna).

10:67 He is the One Who made for you the night that you may rest in it and the day giving visibility. Indeed, in that surely are Signs for a people who listen.

He (huwa) | is the One Who (alladhī) | made (jaʿala) | for you (lakumu) | the night (al-layla) | that you may rest (litaskunū) | in it (fīhi) | and the day (wal-nahāra) | giving visibility (mub'ṣiran). | Indeed (inna), | in (fī) | that (dhālika) | surely are Signs (laāyātin) | for a people (liqawmin) | who listen (yasmaʿūna).

10:68 They say, "Allah has taken a son." Glory be to Him! He is the Self-sufficient. To Him belongs whatever is in the heavens and whatever is in the earth. Not you have any authority for this. Do you say about Allah what not you know?

They say (qālū), | "Allah has taken (ittakhadha) | "Allah has taken (l-lahu) | a son. (waladan)" | Glory be to Him (sub'ḥānahu)! | He (huwa) | is the Self-sufficient (l-ghaniyu). | To Him belongs (lahu) | whatever (mā) | is in (fī) | the heavens (l-samāwāti) | and whatever (wamā) | is in (fī) | the earth (l-arḍi). | Not (in) | you have (ʿindakum) | any (min) | authority (sul'ṭānin) | for this (bihādhā). | Do you say (ataqūlūna) | about (ʿalā) | Allah (l-lahi) | what (mā) | not (lā) | you know (taʿlamūna)?

10:69 Say, "Indeed those who invent against Allah the lie, they will not succeed."

Say (qul), | "Indeed (inna) | those who (alladhīna) | invent (yaftarūna) | against (ʿalā) | Allah (l-lahi) | the lie (l-kadhiba), | they will not succeed. (lā)" | they will not succeed. (yuf'liḥūna)"

10:70 An enjoyment in the world, then to Us is their return, then We will make them taste the punishment the severe because they used to disbelieve.

An enjoyment (matāʿun) | in (fī) | the world (l-dun'yā), | then (thumma) | to Us (ilaynā) | is their return (marjiʿuhum), | then (thumma) | We will make them taste (nudhīquhumu) | the punishment (l-ʿadhāba) | the severe (l-shadīda) | because (bimā) | they used to (kānū) | disbelieve (yakfurūna).

10:71 And recite to them the news of Nuh when he said to his people, "O my people! If is hard on you my stay and my reminding the Signs of Allah, then on Allah I put my trust. So you all resolve your plan and your partners. Then let not be in your plan for you any doubt. Then carry it out upon me and do not give me respite.

And recite (wa-ut'lu) | to them (ʿalayhim) | the news (naba-a) | of Nuh (nūḥin) | when (idh) | he said (qāla) | to his people (liqawmihi), | "O my people (yāqawmi)! | If (in) | is (kāna) | hard (kabura) | on you (ʿalaykum) | my stay (maqāmī) | and my reminding (watadhkīrī) | the Signs of Allah (biāyāti), | the Signs of Allah (l-lahi), | then on (faʿalā) | Allah (l-lahi) | I put my trust (tawakkaltu). | So you all resolve (fa-ajmiʿū) | your plan (amrakum) | and your partners (washurakāakum). | Then (thumma) | let not be (lā) | let not be (yakun) | in your plan (amrukum) | for you (ʿalaykum) | any doubt (ghummatan). | Then (thumma) | carry it out (iq'ḍū) | upon me (ilayya) | and do not (walā) | give me respite (tunẓirūni).

10:72 But if you turn away then not I have asked you any reward. Not is my reward but on Allah, and I have been commanded that I be of the Muslims."

But if (fa-in) | you turn away (tawallaytum) | then not (famā) | I have asked you (sa-altukum) | any (min) | reward (ajrin). | Not (in) | is my reward (ajriya) | but (illā) | on (ʿalā) | Allah (l-lahi), | and I have been commanded (wa-umir'tu) | that (an) | I be (akūna) | of (mina) | the Muslims. (l-mus'limīna)"

10:73 But they denied him, so We saved him and those who were with him in the ship, and We made them successors, and We drowned those who denied Our Signs. Then see how was the end of those who were warned.

But they denied him (fakadhabūhu), | so We saved him (fanajjaynāhu) | and those who (waman) | were with him (maʿahu) | in (fī) | the ship (l-ful'ki), | and We made them (wajaʿalnāhum) | successors (khalāifa), | and We drowned (wa-aghraqnā) | those who (alladhīna) | denied (kadhabū) | Our Signs (biāyātinā). | Then see (fa-unẓur) | how (kayfa) | was (kāna) | the end (ʿāqibatu) | of those who were warned (l-mundharīna).

10:74 Then We sent after him Messengers to their people, and they came to them with clear proofs. But not they were to believe what they had denied [it] before. Thus We seal [on] the hearts of the transgressors.

Then (thumma) | We sent (baʿathnā) | after him (min) | after him (baʿdihi) | Messengers (rusulan) | to (ilā) | their people (qawmihim), | and they came to them (fajāūhum) | with clear proofs (bil-bayināti). | But not (famā) | they were (kānū) | to believe (liyu'minū) | what (bimā) | they had denied (kadhabū) | [it] (bihi) | before (min). | before (qablu). | Thus (kadhālika) | We seal (naṭbaʿu) | [on] (ʿalā) | the hearts (qulūbi) | of the transgressors (l-muʿ'tadīna).

10:75 Then We sent after them Musa and Harun to Firaun and his chiefs with Our Signs, but they were arrogant and were a people criminal.

Then (thumma) | We sent (baʿathnā) | after them (min) | after them (baʿdihim) | Musa (mūsā) | and Harun (wahārūna) | to (ilā) | Firaun (fir'ʿawna) | and his chiefs (wamala-ihi) | with Our Signs (biāyātinā), | but they were arrogant (fa-is'takbarū) | and were (wakānū) | a people (qawman) | criminal (muj'rimīna).

10:76 So when came to them the truth from Us, they said, "Indeed this is surely, a magic clear."

So when (falammā) | came to them (jāahumu) | the truth (l-ḥaqu) | from Us (min), | from Us (ʿindinā), | they said (qālū), | "Indeed (inna) | this (hādhā) | is surely, a magic (lasiḥ'run) | clear. (mubīnun)"

10:77 Musa said, "Do you say about the truth when it has come to you? Is this magic? But will not succeed the magicians."

Musa said (qāla), | Musa said (mūsā), | "Do you say (ataqūlūna) | about the truth (lil'ḥaqqi) | when (lammā) | it has come to you (jāakum)? | Is this magic (asiḥ'run)? | Is this magic (hādhā)? | But will not (walā) | succeed (yuf'liḥu) | the magicians. (l-sāḥirūna)"

10:78 They said, "Have you come to us to turn us away from that we found on it our forefathers, and you two may have the greatness in the land? And we are not in you two believers."

They said (qālū), | "Have you come to us (aji'tanā) | to turn us away (litalfitanā) | from that (ʿammā) | we found (wajadnā) | on it (ʿalayhi) | our forefathers (ābāanā), | and you two may have (watakūna) | and you two may have (lakumā) | the greatness (l-kib'riyāu) | in (fī) | the land (l-arḍi)? | And we are not (wamā) | And we are not (naḥnu) | in you two (lakumā) | believers. (bimu'minīna)"

10:79 And Firaun said, "Bring to me every magician learned."

And Firaun said (waqāla), | And Firaun said (fir'ʿawnu), | "Bring to me (i'tūnī) | every (bikulli) | magician (sāḥirin) | learned. (ʿalīmin)"

10:80 So when came the magicians, said to them Musa, "Throw whatever you wish to throw."

So when (falammā) | came (jāa) | the magicians (l-saḥaratu), | said (qāla) | to them (lahum) | Musa (mūsā), | "Throw (alqū) | whatever (mā) | you (antum) | wish to throw. (mul'qūna)"

10:81 Then when they had thrown, Musa said, "What you have brought [it] is the magic. Indeed, Allah will nullify it. Indeed, Allah does not amend the work of the corrupters.

Then when (falammā) | they had thrown (alqaw), | Musa said (qāla), | Musa said (mūsā), | "What (mā) | you have brought (ji'tum) | [it] (bihi) | is the magic (l-siḥ'ru). | Indeed (inna), | Allah (l-laha) | will nullify it (sayub'ṭiluhu). | Indeed (inna), | Allah (l-laha) | does not (lā) | amend (yuṣ'liḥu) | the work (ʿamala) | of the corrupters (l-muf'sidīna).

10:82 And Allah will establish the truth by His words, even if dislike it the criminals."

And Allah will establish (wayuḥiqqu) | And Allah will establish (l-lahu) | the truth (l-ḥaqa) | by His words (bikalimātihi), | even if (walaw) | dislike it (kariha) | the criminals. (l-muj'rimūna)"

10:83 But none believed Musa except the offspring among his people for fear of Firaun and their chiefs, lest they persecute them. And indeed, Firaun was a tyrant in the earth, and indeed, he was of the ones who commit excesses.

But none (famā) | believed (āmana) | Musa (limūsā) | except (illā) | the offspring (dhurriyyatun) | among (min) | his people (qawmihi) | for (ʿalā) | fear (khawfin) | of (min) | Firaun (fir'ʿawna) | and their chiefs (wamala-ihim), | lest (an) | they persecute them (yaftinahum). | And indeed (wa-inna), | Firaun (fir'ʿawna) | was a tyrant (laʿālin) | in (fī) | the earth (l-arḍi), | and indeed, he (wa-innahu) | was of (lamina) | the ones who commit excesses (l-mus'rifīna).

10:84 And Musa said, "O my people! If you have believed in Allah, then on Him put your trust, if you are Muslims."

And Musa said (waqāla), | And Musa said (mūsā), | "O my people (yāqawmi)! | If (in) | you have (kuntum) | believed (āmantum) | in Allah (bil-lahi), | then on Him (faʿalayhi) | put your trust (tawakkalū), | if (in) | you are (kuntum) | Muslims. (mus'limīna)"

10:85 Then they said, "Upon Allah we put our trust. Our Lord! Do not make us a trial for the people - the wrongdoers.

Then they said (faqālū), | "Upon (ʿalā) | Allah (l-lahi) | we put our trust (tawakkalnā). | Our Lord (rabbanā)! | Do not (lā) | make us (tajʿalnā) | a trial (fit'natan) | for the people (lil'qawmi)- | the wrongdoers (l-ẓālimīna).

10:86 And save us by Your Mercy from the people - the disbelievers."

And save us (wanajjinā) | by Your Mercy (biraḥmatika) | from (mina) | the people (l-qawmi)- | the disbelievers. (l-kāfirīna)"

10:87 And We inspired to Musa and his brother that, "Settle your people in Egypt in houses, and make your houses as places of worship, and establish the prayer. And give glad tidings to the believers."

And We inspired (wa-awḥaynā) | to (ilā) | Musa (mūsā) | and his brother (wa-akhīhi) | that (an), | "Settle (tabawwaā) | your people (liqawmikumā) | in Egypt (bimiṣ'ra) | in houses (buyūtan), | and make (wa-ij'ʿalū) | your houses (buyūtakum) | as places of worship (qib'latan), | and establish (wa-aqīmū) | the prayer (l-ṣalata). | And give glad tidings (wabashiri) | to the believers. (l-mu'minīna)"

10:88 And Musa said, "Our Lord! Indeed, You have given Firaun and his chiefs splendor and wealth in the life of the world. Our Lord! That they may lead astray from Your way. Our Lord! Destroy [on] their wealth and harden [on] their hearts, so that not they believe until they see the punishment - the painful."

And Musa said (waqāla), | And Musa said (mūsā), | "Our Lord (rabbanā)! | Indeed, You (innaka) | have given (ātayta) | Firaun (fir'ʿawna) | and his chiefs (wamala-ahu) | splendor (zīnatan) | and wealth (wa-amwālan) | in (fī) | the life (l-ḥayati) | of the world (l-dun'yā). | Our Lord (rabbanā)! | That they may lead astray (liyuḍillū) | from (ʿan) | Your way (sabīlika). | Our Lord (rabbanā)! | Destroy (iṭ'mis) | [on] (ʿalā) | their wealth (amwālihim) | and harden (wa-ush'dud) |

[on] (ʿalā) | their hearts (qulūbihim), | so that not (falā) | they believe (yu'minū) | until (ḥattā) | they see (yarawū) | the punishment (l-ʿadhāba)- | the painful. (l-alīma)"

10:89 He said, "Verily, has been answered the invocation of both of you. So you two keep to the straight way. And do not follow the way of those who do not know."

He said (qāla), | "Verily (qad), | has been answered (ujībat) | the invocation of both of you (daʿwatukumā). | So you two keep to the straight way (fa-is'taqīmā). | And do not (walā) | follow (tattabiʿānni) | the way (sabīla) | of those who (alladhīna) | do not (lā) | know. (yaʿlamūna)"

10:90 And We took across the Children of Israel - the sea, and followed them Firaun and his hosts in rebellion and enmity, until when overtook him the drowning, he said, "I believe that there is no god except the One, in Whom believe the Children of Israel, and I am of the Muslims."

And We took across (wajāwaznā) | the Children (bibanī) | of Israel (is'rāīla)- | the sea (l-baḥra), | and followed them (fa-atbaʿahum) | Firaun (fir'ʿawnu) | and his hosts (wajunūduhu) | in rebellion (baghyan) | and enmity (waʿadwan), | until (ḥattā) | when (idhā) | overtook him (adrakahu) | the drowning (l-gharaqu), | he said (qāla), | "I believe (āmantu) | that (annahu) | there is no (lā) | god (ilāha) | except (illā) | the One (alladhī), | in Whom believe (āmanat) | in Whom believe (bihi) | the Children of Israel (banū), | the Children of Israel (is'rāīla), | and I am (wa-anā) | of (mina) | the Muslims. (l-mus'limīna)"

10:91 "Now? And verily, you had disobeyed before and you were of the corrupters?"

"Now (āl'āna)? | And verily (waqad), | you had disobeyed (ʿaṣayta) | before (qablu) | and you were (wakunta) | of (mina) | the corrupters? (l-muf'sidīna)"

10:92 So today We will save you in your body, that you may be for those who succeed you a sign. And indeed, many among the mankind of Our Signs are surely heedless."

So today (fal-yawma) | We will save you (nunajjīka) | in your body (bibadanika), | that you may be (litakūna) | for those who (liman) | succeed you (khalfaka) | a sign (āyatan). | And indeed (wa-inna), | many (kathīran) | among (mina) | the mankind (l-nāsi) | of (ʿan) | Our Signs (āyātinā) | are surely heedless. (laghāfilūna)"

10:93 And verily, We settled the Children of Israel in a settlement honorable, and We provided them with the good things, and not they differ until came to them the knowledge. Indeed, your Lord will judge between them on the Day of the Resurrection, concerning what they used to [in it] differ.

And verily (walaqad), | We settled (bawwanā) | the Children (banī) | of Israel (is'rāīla) | in a settlement (mubawwa-a) | honorable (ṣid'qin), | and We provided them (warazaqnāhum) | with (mina) | the good things (l-ṭayibāti), | and not (famā) | they differ (ikh'talafū) | until (ḥattā) | came to them (jāahumu) | the knowledge (l-ʿil'mu). | Indeed (inna), | your Lord (rabbaka) | will judge (yaqḍī) | between them (baynahum) | on the Day (yawma) | of the Resurrection (l-qiyāmati), | concerning what (fīmā) | they used to (kānū) | [in it] (fīhi) | differ (yakhtalifūna).

10:94 So if you are in doubt of what We have revealed to you, then ask those who have been reading the Book before you. Verily, has come to you the truth from your Lord, so do not be among the doubters.

So if (fa-in) | you are (kunta) | in (fī) | doubt (shakkin) | of what (mimmā) | We have revealed (anzalnā) | to you (ilayka), | then ask (fasali) | those who (alladhīna) | have been reading (yaqraūna) | the Book (l-kitāba) | before you (min). | before you (qablika). | Verily (laqad), | has come to you (jāaka) | the truth (l-ḥaqu) | from (min) | your Lord (rabbika), | so do not (falā) | be (takūnanna) | among (mina) | the doubters (l-mum'tarīna).

10:95 And do not be of those who deny the Signs of Allah, then you will be among the losers.

And do not (walā) | be (takūnanna) | of (mina) | those who (alladhīna) | deny (kadhabū) |

the Signs of Allah (biāyāti), | the Signs of Allah (l-lahi), | then you will be (fatakūna) | among (mina) | the losers (l-khāsirīna).

10:96 Indeed, those [whom], has become due on them the Word of your Lord will not believe.

Indeed (inna), | those [whom] (alladhīna), | has become due (ḥaqqat) | on them (ʿalayhim) | the Word (kalimatu) | of your Lord (rabbika) | will not (lā) | believe (yu'minūna).

10:97 Even if comes to them every Sign until they see the punishment - the painful.

Even if (walaw) | comes to them (jāathum) | every (kullu) | Sign (āyatin) | until (ḥattā) | they see (yarawū) | the punishment (l-ʿadhāba)- | the painful (l-alīma).

10:98 So why not was any town that believed, and benefited it its faith, except the people of Yunus? When they believed, We removed from them the punishment of the disgrace in the life of the world and We granted them enjoyment for a time.

So why not (falawlā) | was (kānat) | any town (qaryatun) | that believed (āmanat), | and benefited it (fanafaʿahā) | its faith (īmānuhā), | except (illā) | the people (qawma) | of Yunus (yūnusa)? | When (lammā) | they believed (āmanū), | We removed (kashafnā) | from them (ʿanhum) | the punishment (ʿadhāba) | of the disgrace (l-khiz'yi) | in (fī) | the life (l-ḥayati) | of the world (l-dun'yā) | and We granted them enjoyment (wamattaʿnāhum) | for (ilā) | a time (ḥīnin).

10:99 And if had willed your Lord surely, would have believed who are in the earth all of them together. Then, will you compel the mankind until they become believers?

And if (walaw) | had willed (shāa) | your Lord (rabbuka) | surely, would have believed (laāmana) | who (man) | are in (fī) | the earth (l-arḍi) | all of them (kulluhum) | together (jamīʿan). | Then, will you (afa-anta) | compel (tuk'rihu) | the mankind (l-nāsa) | until (ḥattā) | they become (yakūnū) | believers (mu'minīna)?

10:100 And not is for a soul to believe except by the permission of Allah. And He will place the wrath on those who do not use reason.

And not (wamā) | is (kāna) | for a soul (linafsin) | to (an) | believe (tu'mina) | except (illā) | by the permission (bi-idh'ni) | of Allah (l-lahi). | And He will place (wayajʿalu) | the wrath (l-rij'sa) | on (ʿalā) | those who (alladhīna) | do not (lā) | use reason (yaʿqilūna).

10:101 Say, "See, what is in the heavens and the earth." But not will avail the Signs and the warners to a people who do not believe.

Say (quli), | "See (unẓurū), | what (mādhā) | is in (fī) | the heavens (l-samāwāti) | and the earth. (wal-arḍi)" | But not (wamā) | will avail (tugh'nī) | the Signs (l-āyātu) | and the warners (wal-nudhuru) | to (ʿan) | a people (qawmin) | who do not (lā) | believe (yu'minūna).

10:102 Then do they wait except like the days of those who passed away before them? Say, "Then wait indeed, I am with you among the ones who wait."

Then do (fahal) | they wait (yantaẓirūna) | except (illā) | like (mith'la) | the days (ayyāmi) | of those who (alladhīna) | passed away (khalaw) | before them (min)? | before them (qablihim)? | Say (qul), | "Then wait (fa-intaẓirū) | indeed, I am (innī) | with you (maʿakum) | among (mina) | the ones who wait. (l-muntaẓirīna)"

10:103 Then We will save Our Messengers and those who believe. Thus, it is an obligation upon Us that We save the believers.

Then (thumma) | We will save (nunajjī) | Our Messengers (rusulanā) | and those who (wa-alladhīna) | believe (āmanū). | Thus (kadhālika), | it is an obligation (ḥaqqan) | upon Us (ʿalaynā) | that We save (nunji) | the believers (l-mu'minīna).

10:104 Say, "O mankind! If you are in doubt of my religion, then not I worship those whom you worship besides Allah, but I worship Allah, the One Who causes you to die. And I am commanded that I be of the believers."

Say (qul), | "O mankind (yāayyuhā)! | "O mankind (l-nāsu)! | If (in) | you are (kuntum) | in (fī) | doubt (shakkin) | of (min) | my religion (dīnī), | then not (falā) | I worship (aʿbudu) | those whom (alladhīna) | you worship (taʿbudūna) | besides Allah (min), | besides Allah (dūni), | besides Allah (l-lahi), | but (walākin) | I worship (aʿbudu) | Allah (l-laha), | the One Who (alladhī) | causes you to die (yatawaffākum). | And I am commanded (wa-umir'tu) | that (an) | I be (akūna) | of (mina) | the believers. (l-mu'minīna)"

10:105 And that, "Direct your face to the religion upright, and do not be of the polytheists.

And that (wa-an), | "Direct (aqim) | your face (wajhaka) | to the religion (lilddīni) | upright (ḥanīfan), | and do not (walā) | be (takūnanna) | of (mina) | the polytheists (l-mush'rikīna).

10:106 And do not invoke besides Allah what will not benefit you and not harm you. But if you did so indeed, you then will be of the wrongdoers."

And do not (walā) | invoke (tadʿu) | besides Allah (min) | besides Allah (dūni) | besides Allah (l-lahi) | what (mā) | will not (lā) | benefit you (yanfaʿuka) | and not (walā) | harm you (yaḍurruka). | But if (fa-in) | you did so (faʿalta) | indeed, you (fa-innaka) | then will be (idhan) | of (mina) | the wrongdoers. (l-ẓālimīna)"

10:107 And if Allah touches you with adversity there is no remover of it except Him, and if He intends for you any good then there is no repeller of His Bounty. He causes it to reach whom He wills of His slaves. And He is the Oft-Forgiving, the Most Merciful.

And if (wa-in) | Allah touches you (yamsaska) | Allah touches you (l-lahu) | with adversity (biḍurrin) | there is no (falā) | remover (kāshifa) | of it (lahu) | except (illā) | Him (huwa), | and if (wa-in) | He intends for you (yurid'ka) | any good (bikhayrin) | then there is no (falā) | repeller (rādda) | of His Bounty (lifaḍlihi). | He causes it to reach (yuṣību) | He causes it to reach (bihi) | whom (man) | He wills (yashāu) | of (min) | His slaves (ʿibādihi). | And He (wahuwa) | is the Oft-Forgiving (l-ghafūru), | the Most Merciful (l-raḥīmu).

10:108 Say, "O mankind! Verily has come to you the truth from your Lord. So whoever is guided then only he is guided for his soul, and whoever goes astray then only he strays against it. And I am not over you a guardian."

Say (qul), | "O mankind (yāayyuhā)! | "O mankind (l-nāsu)! | Verily (qad) | has come to you (jāakumu) | the truth (l-ḥaqu) | from (min) | your Lord (rabbikum). | So whoever (famani) | is guided (ih'tadā) | then only (fa-innamā) | he is guided (yahtadī) | for his soul (linafsihi), | and whoever (waman) | goes astray (ḍalla) | then only (fa-innamā) | he strays (yaḍillu) | against it (ʿalayhā). | And I am not (wamā) | And I am not (anā) | over you (ʿalaykum) | a guardian. (biwakīlin)"

10:109 And follow what is revealed to you and be patient until Allah gives judgment. And He is the Best of the Judges.

And follow (wa-ittabiʿ) | what (mā) | is revealed (yūḥā) | to you (ilayka) | and be patient (wa-iṣ'bir) | until (ḥattā) | Allah gives judgment (yaḥkuma). | Allah gives judgment (l-lahu). | And He (wahuwa) | is the Best (khayru) | of the Judges (l-ḥākimīna).

Chapter (11) Sūrat Hūd (Hud)

11:1 Alif Lam Ra. This is a Book are perfected its Verses moreover, explained in detail from he One Who is All-Wise, All-Aware.

Alif Lam Ra (alif-lam-ra). | This is a Book (kitābun) | are perfected (uḥ'kimat) | its Verses (āyātuhu) | moreover (thumma), | explained in detail (fuṣṣilat) | from he One Who (min) | from he One Who (ladun) | is All-Wise (ḥakīmin), | All-Aware (khabīrin).

11:2 That "Not you worship but Allah. Indeed, I am to you from Him a warner and a bearer of glad tidings."

That "Not (allā) | you worship (taʿbudū) | but (illā) | Allah (l-laha). | Indeed, I am (innanī) | to you (lakum) | from Him (min'hu) | a warner (nadhīrun) | and a bearer of glad tidings. (wabashīrun)"

11:3 And that "Seek forgiveness of your Lord and turn in repentance to Him, He will let you enjoy a good for a term appointed. And give to every owner of grace His Grace. But if you turn away then indeed, I fear for you the punishment of a Great Day.

And that (wa-ani) | "Seek forgiveness (is'taghfirū) | of your Lord (rabbakum) | and (thumma) | turn in repentance (tūbū) | to Him (ilayhi), | He will let you (yumattiʿ'kum) | enjoy (matāʿan) | a good (ḥasanan) | for (ilā) | a term (ajalin) | appointed (musamman). | And give (wayu'ti) | to every (kulla) | owner (dhī) | of grace (faḍlin) | His Grace (faḍlahu). | But if (wa-in) | you turn away (tawallaw) | then indeed, I (fa-innī) | fear (akhāfu) | for you (ʿalaykum) | the punishment (ʿadhāba) | of a Great Day (yawmin). | of a Great Day (kabīrin).

11:4 To Allah is your return, and He is on every thing All-Powerful."

To (ilā) | Allah (l-lahi) | is your return (marjiʿukum), | and He (wahuwa) | is on (ʿalā) | every (kulli) | thing (shayin) | All-Powerful. (qadīrun)"

11:5 No doubt! They fold up their breasts that they may hide from Him. Surely, when they cover themselves with their garments, He knows what they conceal and what they reveal. Indeed, He is All-Knower of what is in the breasts.

No doubt (alā)! | They (innahum) | fold up (yathnūna) | their breasts (ṣudūrahum) | that they may hide (liyastakhfū) | from Him (min'hu). | Surely (alā), | when (ḥīna) | they cover themselves (yastaghshūna) | with their garments (thiyābahum), | He knows (yaʿlamu) | what (mā) | they conceal (yusirrūna) | and what (wamā) | they reveal (yuʿ'linūna). | Indeed, He (innahu) | is All-Knower (ʿalīmun) | of what (bidhāti) | is in the breasts (l-ṣudūri).

11:6 And not any moving creature in the earth but on Allah is its provision. And He knows its dwelling place and its place of storage. All is in a Record clear.

And not (wamā) | any (min) | moving creature (dābbatin) | in (fī) | the earth (l-arḍi) | but (illā) | on (ʿalā) | Allah (l-lahi) | is its provision (riz'quhā). | And He knows (wayaʿlamu) | its dwelling place (mus'taqarrahā) | and its place of storage (wamus'tawdaʿahā). | All (kullun) | is in (fī) | a Record (kitābin) | clear (mubīnin).

11:7 And He is the One Who created the heavens and the earth in six epochs, and His throne was on the water that He might test [you] which of you is best in deed. But if you say, "Indeed, you will be resurrected after [the] death," surely would say those who disbelieved, "This is not but a magic clear."

And He (wahuwa) | is the One Who (alladhī) | created (khalaqa) | the heavens (l-samāwāti) | and the earth (wal-arḍa) | in (fī) | six (sittati) | epochs (ayyāmin), | and His throne was (wakāna) | and His throne was (ʿarshuhu) | on (ʿalā) | the water (l-māi) | that He might test [you] (liyabluwakum) | which of you (ayyukum) | is best (aḥsanu) | in deed (ʿamalan). | But if (wala-in) | you say (qul'ta), | "Indeed, you (innakum) | will be resurrected (mabʿūthūna) | after (min) | after (baʿdi) | [the] death, (l-mawti)" | surely would say (layaqūlanna) | those who (alladhīna) | disbelieved (kafarū), | "This is not (in) | "This is not (hādhā) | but (illā) | a magic (siḥ'run) | clear. (mubīnun)"

11:8 And if We delay from them the punishment for a time determined, they will surely say, "What detains it?" No doubt! On the Day it comes to them not will be averted from them and will surround them what they used to mock at [it].

And if (wala-in) | We delay (akharnā) | from them (ʿanhumu) | the punishment (l-ʿadhāba) | for (ilā) | a time (ummatin) | determined (maʿdūdatin), | they will surely say (layaqūlunna), | "What (mā) | detains it? (yaḥbisuhu)" | No doubt (alā)! | On the Day (yawma) | it comes to them (yatīhim) | not (laysa) | will be averted (maṣrūfan) | from them (ʿanhum) | and will surround (waḥāqa) | them (bihim) | what (mā) | they used to (kānū) | mock at [it] (bihi). | mock at [it] (yastahziūna).

11:9 And if We give man a taste of Mercy from Us, then We withdraw it from him, indeed, he is despairing and ungrateful.

And if (wala-in) | We give man a taste (adhaqnā) | We give man a taste (l-insāna) | of Mercy from Us (minnā), | of Mercy from Us (raḥmatan), | then (thumma) | We withdraw it (nazaʿnāhā) | from him (min'hu), | indeed, he (innahu) | is despairing (layaūsun) | and ungrateful (kafūrun).

11:10 But if We give him a taste of favor after hardship has touched him, surely, he will say, "Have gone the evils from me." Indeed, he is exultant and boastful.

But if (wala-in) | We give him a taste (adhaqnāhu) | of favor (naʿmāa) | after (baʿda) | hardship (ḍarrāa) | has touched him (massathu), | surely, he will say (layaqūlanna), | "Have gone (dhahaba) | the evils (l-sayiātu) | from me. (ʿannī)" | Indeed, he (innahu) | is exultant (lafariḥun) | and boastful (fakhūrun).

11:11 Except those who are patient and do the good deeds, those for them will be forgiveness and a reward great.

Except (illā) | those who (alladhīna) | are patient (ṣabarū) | and do (waʿamilū) | the good deeds (l-ṣāliḥāti), | those (ulāika) | for them (lahum) | will be forgiveness (maghfiratun) | and a reward (wa-ajrun) | great (kabīrun).

11:12 Then possibly you may give up a part of what is revealed to you and straitened by it your breast because they say, "Why not is sent down for him a treasure or has come with him an Angel?" Only you are a warner. And Allah is on every thing a Guardian.

Then possibly you (falaʿallaka) | may give up (tārikun) | a part (baʿḍa) | of what (mā) | is revealed (yūḥā) | to you (ilayka) | and straitened (waḍāiqun) | by it (bihi) | your breast (ṣadruka) | because (an) | they say (yaqūlū), | "Why not (lawlā) | is sent down (unzila) | for him (ʿalayhi) | a treasure (kanzun) | or (aw) | has come (jāa) | with him (maʿahu) | an Angel? (malakun)" | Only (innamā) | you (anta) | are a warner (nadhīrun). | And Allah (wal-lahu) | is on (ʿalā) | every (kulli) | thing (shayin) | a Guardian (wakīlun).

11:13 Or they say, "He has fabricated it." Say, "Then bring ten Surahs like it fabricated, and call whoever you can besides Allah if you are truthful."

Or (am) | they say (yaqūlūna), | "He has fabricated it. (if'tarāhu)" | Say (qul), | "Then bring (fatū) | ten (biʿashri) | Surahs (suwarin) | like it (mith'lihi) | fabricated (muf'tarayātin), | and call (wa-id'ʿū) | whoever (mani) | you can (is'taṭaʿtum) | besides Allah (min) | besides Allah (dūni) | besides Allah (l-lahi) | if (in) | you are (kuntum) | truthful. (ṣādiqīna)"

11:14 Then if not they respond to you then know that it was sent down with the knowledge of Allah, and that there is no god except Him. Then, would you be Muslims?

Then if not (fa-illam) | they respond (yastajībū) | to you (lakum) | then know (fa-iʿlamū) | that (annamā) | it was sent down (unzila) | with the knowledge of Allah (biʿil'mi), | with the knowledge of Allah (l-lahi), | and that (wa-an) | there is no (lā) | god (ilāha) | except (illā) | Him (huwa). | Then, would (fahal) | you (antum) | be Muslims (mus'limūna)?

11:15 Whoever [is] desires the life of the world and its adornments, We will repay in full to them for their deeds therein, and they in it will not be lessened.

Whoever [is] (man) | Whoever [is] (kāna) | desires (yurīdu) | the life (l-ḥayata) | of the world (l-dun'yā) | and its adornments (wazīnatahā), | We will repay in full (nuwaffi) | to them (ilayhim) | for their deeds (aʿmālahum) | therein (fīhā), | and they (wahum) | in it (fīhā) | will not be lessened (lā). | will not be lessened (yub'khasūna).

11:16 Those are the ones who - is not for them in the Hereafter except the Fire. And has gone in vain what they did therein, and is worthless what they used to do.

Those (ulāika) | are the ones who (alladhīna)- | is not (laysa) | for them (lahum) | in (fī) | the Hereafter (l-ākhirati) | except (illā) | the Fire (l-nāru). | And has gone in vain (waḥabiṭa) | what (mā) | they did (ṣanaʿū) | therein (fīhā), | and is worthless (wabāṭilun) | what (mā) | they used to (kānū) | do (yaʿmalūna).

11:17 Then is he who is on a clear proof from his Lord, and recites it, a witness from Him, and before it was a Book of Musa as a guide and as mercy? Those believe in it. But whoever disbelieves in it among the sects, then the Fire will be his promised (meeting) place. So do not be in doubt about it. Indeed, it is the truth from your Lord, but most of the people do not believe.

Then is he who (afaman) | is (kāna) | on (ʿalā) | a clear proof (bayyinatin) | from (min) | his Lord (rabbihi), | and recites it (wayatlūhu), | a witness (shāhidun) | from Him (min'hu), | and before it (wamin) | and before it (qablihi) | was a Book (kitābu) | of Musa (mūsā) | as a guide (imāman) | and as mercy (waraḥmatan)? | Those (ulāika) | believe (yu'minūna) | in it (bihi). | But whoever (waman) | disbelieves (yakfur) | in it (bihi) | among (mina) | the sects (l-aḥzābi), | then the Fire (fal-nāru) | will be his promised (meeting) place (mawʿiduhu). | So do not (falā) | be (taku) | in (fī) | doubt (mir'yatin) | about it (min'hu). | Indeed, it (innahu) | is the truth (l-ḥaqu) | from (min) | your Lord (rabbika), | but (walākinna) | most (akthara) | of the people (l-nāsi) | do not (lā) | believe (yu'minūna).

11:18 And who is more unjust than he who invents against Allah a lie? Those will be presented before their Lord, and will say the witnesses, "These are those who lied against their Lord." No doubt! The curse of Allah is on the wrongdoers.

And who (waman) | is more unjust (aẓlamu) | than he who (mimmani) | invents (if'tarā) | against (ʿalā) | Allah (l-lahi) | a lie (kadhiban)? | Those (ulāika) | will be presented (yuʿraḍūna) | before (ʿalā) | their Lord (rabbihim), | and will say (wayaqūlu) | the witnesses (l-ashhādu), | "These are (hāulāi) | those who (alladhīna) | lied (kadhabū) | against (ʿalā) | their Lord. (rabbihim)" | No doubt (alā)! | The curse of Allah (laʿnatu) | The curse of Allah (l-lahi) | is on (ʿalā) | the wrongdoers (l-ẓālimīna).

11:19 Those who hinder from the way of Allah and seek in it crookedness, while they in the Hereafter [they] are disbelievers.

Those who (alladhīna) | hinder (yaṣuddūna) | from (ʿan) | the way (sabīli) | of Allah (l-lahi) | and seek in it (wayabghūnahā) | crookedness (ʿiwajan), | while they (wahum) | in the Hereafter (bil-ākhirati) | [they] (hum) | are disbelievers (kāfirūna).

11:20 Those not will be able to escape in the earth and not is for them besides Allah any protectors. And will be doubled for them the punishment. Not they were able to hear and not they used to see.

Those (ulāika) | not (lam) | will be (yakūnū) | able to escape (muʿjizīna) | in (fī) | the earth (l-arḍi) | and not (wamā) | is (kāna) | for them (lahum) | besides (min) | besides (dūni) | Allah (l-lahi) | any (min) | protectors (awliyāa). | And will be doubled (yuḍāʿafu) | for them (lahumu) | the punishment (l-ʿadhābu). | Not (mā) | they were (kānū) | able (yastaṭīʿūna) | to hear (l-samʿa) | and not (wamā) | they used to (kānū) | see (yub'ṣirūna).

11:21 Those are the ones who have lost their souls, and lost from them is what they used to invent.

Those (ulāika) | are the ones who (alladhīna) | have lost (khasirū) | their souls (anfusahum), | and lost (waḍalla) | from them (ʿanhum) | is what (mā) | they used (kānū) | to invent (yaftarūna).

11:22 No doubt that they in the Hereafter [they] will be the greatest losers.

No (lā) | doubt (jarama) | that they (annahum) | in (fī) | the Hereafter (l-ākhirati) | [they] (humu) | will be the greatest losers (l-akhsarūna).

11:23 Indeed, those who believe and do good deeds and humble themselves before their Lord, those are the companions of Paradise, they in it will abide forever.

Indeed (inna), | those who (alladhīna) | believe (āmanū) | and do (waʿamilū) | good deeds (l-ṣāliḥāti) | and humble themselves (wa-akhbatū) | before (ilā) | their Lord (rabbihim), | those (ulāika) | are the companions (aṣḥābu) | of Paradise (l-janati), | they (hum) | in it (fīhā) | will abide forever (khālidūna).

11:24 The example of the two parties is like the blind and the deaf, and the seer and the hearer. Are they equal in comparison? Then, will not you take heed?

The example (mathalu) | of the two parties (l-farīqayni) | is like the blind (kal-aʿmā) | and the deaf (wal-aṣami), | and the seer (wal-baṣīri) | and the hearer (wal-samīʿi). | Are (hal) | they equal (yastawiyāni) | in comparison (mathalan)? | Then, will not (afalā) | you take heed (tadhakkarūna)?

11:25 And verily We sent Nuh to his people, "Indeed, I am to you a warner clear.

And verily (walaqad) | We sent (arsalnā) | Nuh (nūḥan) | to (ilā) | his people (qawmihi), | "Indeed, I am (innī) | to you (lakum) | a warner (nadhīrun) | clear (mubīnun).

11:26 That do not worship except Allah. Indeed, I [I] fear for you the punishment of a Day painful."

That (an) | do not (lā) | worship (taʿbudū) | except (illā) | Allah (l-laha). | Indeed, I (innī) | [I] fear (akhāfu) | for you (ʿalaykum) | the punishment (ʿadhāba) | of a Day (yawmin) | painful. (alīmin)"

11:27 So said the chiefs of those who disbelieved from his people, "Not we see you but a man like us, and not we see you followed [you] except those who [they] are the lowest of us immature in opinion. And not we see in you over us any merit; nay, we think you are liars."

So said (faqāla) | the chiefs (l-mala-u) | of those who (alladhīna) | disbelieved (kafarū) | from (min) | his people (qawmihi), | "Not (mā) | we see you (narāka) | but (illā) | a man (basharan) | like us (mith'lanā), | and not (wamā) | we see you (narāka) | followed [you] (ittabaʿaka) | except (illā) | those who (alladhīna) | [they] (hum) | are the lowest of us (arādhilunā) | immature in opinion (bādiya). | immature in opinion (l-rayi). | And not (wamā) | we see (narā) | in you (lakum) | over us (ʿalaynā) | any (min) | merit (faḍlin); | nay (bal), | we think you (naẓunnukum) | are liars. (kādhibīna)"

11:28 He said, "O my people! Do you see if I was on the clear proof from my Lord, while He has given me mercy from Himself but it has been obscured from you, should We compel you to accept it while you are averse to it?

He said (qāla), | "O my people (yāqawmi)! | Do you see (ara-aytum) | if (in) | I was (kuntu) | on (ʿalā) | the clear proof (bayyinatin) | from (min) | my Lord (rabbī), | while He has given me (waātānī) | mercy (raḥmatan) | from (min) | Himself (ʿindihi) | but it has been obscured (faʿummiyat) | from you (ʿalaykum), | should We compel you to accept it (anul'zimukumūhā) | while you are (wa-antum) | averse to it (lahā)? | averse to it (kārihūna)?

11:29 And O my people! not I ask of you for it any wealth. Not is my reward except from Allah. And not I am going to drive away those who believed. Indeed, they will be meeting their Lord, but I see you are a people ignorant.

And O my people (wayāqawmi)! | not (lā) | I ask of you (asalukum) | for it (ʿalayhi) | any wealth (mālan). | Not (in) | is my reward (ajriya) | except (illā) | from (ʿalā) | Allah (l-lahi). | And not (wamā) | I am (anā) | going to drive away (biṭāridi) | those who (alladhīna) | believed (āmanū). | Indeed, they (innahum) | will be meeting (mulāqū) | their Lord (rabbihim), | but I (walākinnī) | see you (arākum) | are a people (qawman) | ignorant (tajhalūna).

11:30 And O my people! Who would help me against Allah if I drove them away? Then, will not you take heed?

And O my people (wayāqawmi)! | Who (man) | would help me (yanṣurunī) | against (mina) | Allah (l-lahi) | if (in) | I drove them away (ṭaradttuhum)? | Then, will not (afalā) | you take heed (tadhakkarūna)?

11:31 And not I say to you that with me are the treasures of Allah, and not I know the unseen, and not I say that I am an Angel, and not I say for those whom look down upon your eyes, never will Allah give them any good. Allah knows best what is in their souls. Indeed, I then will be surely of the wrongdoers."

And not (walā) | I say (aqūlu) | to you (lakum) | that with me (ʿindī) | are the treasures (khazāinu) | of Allah (l-lahi), | and not (walā) | I know (aʿlamu) | the unseen (l-ghayba), | and not (walā) | I say (aqūlu) | that I am (innī) | an Angel (malakun), | and not (walā) | I say (aqūlu) | for those whom (lilladhīna) | look down upon (tazdarī) | your eyes (aʿyunukum), | never (lan) | will Allah give them (yu'tiyahumu) | will Allah give them (l-lahu) | any good (khayran). | Allah (l-lahu) | knows best (aʿlamu) | what (bimā) | is in (fī) | their souls (anfusihim). | Indeed, I (innī) | then (idhan) | will be surely of (lamina) | the wrongdoers. (l-ẓālimīna)"

11:32 They said, "O Nuh! Indeed, you disputed with us and you have been frequent in dispute with us. So bring us what you threaten us with, if you are of the truthful."

They said (qālū), | "O Nuh (yānūḥu)! | Indeed (qad), | you disputed with us (jādaltanā) | and you have been frequent (fa-aktharta) | in dispute with us (jidālanā). | So bring us (fatinā) | what (bimā) | you threaten us with (taʿidunā), | if (in) | you are (kunta) | of (mina) | the truthful. (l-ṣādiqīna)"

11:33 He said, "Only will bring it on you Allah, if He wills, and not you are one who can escape (it).

He said (qāla), | "Only (innamā) | will bring it on you (yatīkum) | will bring it on you (bihi) | Allah (l-lahu), | if (in) | He wills (shāa), | and not (wamā) | you are (antum) | one who can escape (it) (bimuʿʿjizīna).

11:34 And will not benefit you my advice even if I wish to [I] advise [to] you, if it was Allah's will to let you go astray. He is your Lord, and to Him you will be returned."

And will not (walā) | benefit you (yanfaʿukum) | my advice (nuṣ'ḥī) | even if (in) | I wish (aradttu) | to (an) | [I] advise (anṣaḥa) | [to] you (lakum), | if (in) | it was Allah's (kāna) | it was Allah's (l-lahu) | will (yurīdu) | to (an) | let you go astray (yugh'wiyakum). | He is (huwa) | your Lord (rabbukum), | and to Him (wa-ilayhi) | you will be returned. (tur'jaʿūna)"

11:35 Or do they say, "He has invented it?" Say, "If I have invented it, then on me is my crime, but I am innocent of what crimes you commit."

Or (am) | do they say (yaqūlūna), | "He has invented it? (if'tarāhu)" | Say (qul), | "If (ini) | I have invented it (if'taraytuhu), | then on me (faʿalayya) | is my crime (ij'rāmī), | but I am (wa-anā) | innocent (barīon) | of what (mimmā) | crimes you commit. (tuj'rimūna)"

11:36 And it was revealed to Nuh, "That will never believe from your people except those who have already believed. So do not be distressed by what they have been doing.

And it was revealed (waūḥiya) | to (ilā) | Nuh (nūḥin), | "That (annahu) | will never (lan) | believe (yu'mina) | from (min) | your people (qawmika) | except (illā) | those who (man) | have already (qad) | believed (āmana). | So do not (falā) | be distressed (tabta-is) | by what (bimā) | they have been (kānū) | doing (yafʿalūna).

11:37 And construct the ship under Our Eyes, and Our inspiration and do not address Me concerning those who wronged; indeed, they are the ones to be drowned."

And construct (wa-iṣ'naʿi) | the ship (l-ful'ka) | under Our Eyes (bi-aʿyuninā), | and Our inspiration (wawaḥyinā) | and do not (walā) | address Me (tukhāṭib'nī) | concerning (fī) | those who (alladhīna) | wronged (ẓalamū); | indeed, they are (innahum) | the ones to be drowned. (mugh'raqūna)"

11:38 And he was constructing the ship, and every time passed by him the chiefs of his people, they ridiculed [of] him. He said, "If you ridicule us, then we can ridicule you as you ridicule.

And he was constructing (wayaṣnaʿu) | the ship (l-ful'ka), | and every time (wakullamā) | passed (marra) | by him (ʿalayhi) | the chiefs (mala-on) | of (min) | his people (qawmihi), | they ridiculed (sakhirū) | [of] him (min'hu). | He said (qāla), | "If (in) | you ridicule (taskharū) | us (minnā), | then we (fa-innā) | can ridicule (naskharu) | you (minkum) | as (kamā) | you ridicule (taskharūna).

11:39 And soon you will know on whom will come a punishment that will disgrace him, and will descend on him a punishment lasting."

And soon (fasawfa) | you will know (taʿlamūna) | on whom (man) | will come (yatīhi) | a punishment (ʿadhābun) | that will disgrace him (yukh'zīhi), | and will descend (wayaḥillu) | on him (ʿalayhi) | a punishment (ʿadhābun) | lasting. (muqīmun)"

11:40 Till when came Our command, and overflowed the oven, We said, "Load in it of every kind a pair two, and your family except who has preceded against him the word, and whoever believed." And not believed with him except a few.

Till (ḥattā) | when (idhā) | came (jāa) | Our command (amrunā), | and overflowed (wafāra) | the oven (l-tanūru), | We said (qul'nā), | "Load (iḥ'mil) | in it (fīhā) | of (min) | every kind (kullin) | a pair (zawjayni) | two (ith'nayni), | and your family (wa-ahlaka) | except (illā) | who (man) | has preceded (sabaqa) | against him (ʿalayhi) | the word (l-qawlu), | and whoever (waman) | believed. (āmana)" | And not (wamā) | believed (āmana) | with him (maʿahu) | except (illā) | a few (qalīlun).

11:41 And he said, "Embark in it, in the name of Allah is its course and its anchorage. Indeed, my Lord is certainly Oft-Forgiving, Most Merciful."

And he said (waqāla), | "Embark (ir'kabū) | in it (fīhā), | in the name (bis'mi) | of Allah (l-lahi) | is its course (majrahā) | and its anchorage (wamur'sāhā). | Indeed (inna), | my Lord (rabbī) | is certainly Oft-Forgiving (laghafūrun), | Most Merciful. (raḥīmun)"

11:42 And it sailed with them on the waves like mountains, and Nuh called out to his son, and he was [in] apart, "O my son! Embark with us and do not be with the disbelievers."

And it (wahiya) | sailed (tajrī) | with them (bihim) | on (fī) | the waves (mawjin) | like mountains (kal-jibāli), | and Nuh called out (wanādā) | and Nuh called out (nūḥun) | to his son (ib'nahu), | and he was (wakāna) | [in] (fī) | apart (maʿzilin), | "O my son (yābunayya)! | Embark (ir'kab) | with us (maʿanā) | and do not (walā) | be (takun) | with (maʿa) | the disbelievers. (l-kāfirīna)"

11:43 He said, "I will betake myself to a mountain, that will save me from the water." He said, "There is no protector today from the Command of Allah except, on whom He has mercy." And came in between them the waves, so he was among the drowned.

He said (qāla), | "I will betake myself (saāwī) | to (ilā) | a mountain (jabalin), | that will save me (yaʿṣimunī) | from (mina) | the water. (l-māi)" | He said (qāla), | "There is no (lā) | protector (ʿāṣima) | today (l-yawma) | from (min) | the Command of Allah (amri) | the Command of Allah (l-lahi) | except (illā), | on whom (man) | He has mercy. (raḥima)" | And came (waḥāla) | in between them (baynahumā) | the waves (l-mawju), | so he was (fakāna) | among (mina) | the drowned (l-mugh'raqīna).

11:44 And it was said, "O earth! Swallow your water, and O sky! Withhold." And subsided the water, and was fulfilled the Command. And it rested on the Judi. And it was said, "Away with the people the wrongdoers."

And it was said (waqīla), | "O earth (yāarḍu)! | Swallow (ib'laʿī) | your water (māaki), | and O sky (wayāsamāu)! | Withhold. (aqliʿī)" | And subsided (waghīḍa) | the water (l-māu), | and was fulfilled (waquḍiya) | the Command (l-amru). | And it rested (wa-is'tawat) | on (ʿalā) | the Judi (l-jūdiyi). | And it was said (waqīla), | "Away (buʿ'dan) | with the people (lil'qawmi) | the wrongdoers. (l-ẓālimīna)"

11:45 And Nuh called to his Lord and said, "O my Lord! Indeed, my son is of my family, and indeed, Your promise is true, and You are the Most Just of the judges."

And Nuh called (wanādā) | And Nuh called (nūḥun) | to his Lord (rabbahu) | and said (faqāla), | "O my Lord (rabbi)! | Indeed (inna), | my son (ib'nī) | is of (min) | my family (ahlī), | and indeed (wa-inna), | Your promise (waʿdaka) | is true (l-ḥaqu), | and You (wa-anta) | are the Most Just (aḥkamu) | of the judges. (l-ḥākimīna)"

11:46 He said, "O Nuh! Indeed, he is not of your family; indeed, [he] his deed is other than righteous, so do not ask Me about what not you have of it any knowledge. Indeed, I admonish you lest you be among the ignorant."

He said (qāla), | "O Nuh (yānūḥu)! | Indeed, he (innahu) | is not (laysa) | of (min) | your family (ahlika); | indeed, [he] (innahu) | his deed (ʿamalun) | is other than (ghayru) | righteous (ṣāliḥin), | so do not (falā) | ask Me (tasalni) | about what (mā) | not (laysa) | you have (laka) | of it (bihi) | any knowledge (ʿil'mun). | Indeed, I (innī) | admonish you (aʿiẓuka) | lest (an) | you be (takūna) | among (mina) | the ignorant. (l-jāhilīna)"

11:47 He said, "O my Lord! Indeed, I seek refuge in You, that I should ask You what not I have of it knowledge. And unless You forgive me and You have mercy on me, I will be among the losers."

He said (qāla), | "O my Lord (rabbi)! | Indeed, I (innī) | seek refuge (aʿūdhu) | in You (bika), | that (an) | I should ask You (asalaka) | what (mā) | not (laysa) | I have (lī) | of it (bihi) | knowledge (ʿil'mun). | And unless (wa-illā) | You forgive (taghfir) | me (lī) | and You have mercy on me (watarḥamnī), | I will be (akun) | among (mina) | the losers. (l-khāsirīna)"

11:48 It was said, "O Nuh! Go down with peace from Us and blessings on you and on the nations from those with you. But to other nations We will grant enjoyment; then will touch them from Us a punishment painful."

It was said (qīla), | "O Nuh (yānūḥu)! | Go down (ih'biṭ) | with peace (bisalāmin) | from Us (minnā) | and blessings (wabarakātin) | on you (ʿalayka) | and on (waʿalā) | the nations (umamin) |

from those (mimman) | with you (ma'aka). | But to other nations (wa-umamun) | We will grant enjoyment (sanumatti'uhum); | then (thumma) | will touch them (yamassuhum) | from Us (minnā) | a punishment ('adhābun) | painful. (alīmun)"

11:49 This is from the news of the unseen, which We reveal to you. Not you were knowing it, you and not your people from before this. So be patient; indeed, the end is for the God fearing."

This (til'ka) | is from (min) | the news (anbāi) | of the unseen (l-ghaybi), | which We reveal (nūḥīhā) | to you (ilayka). | Not (mā) | you were (kunta) | knowing it (ta'lamuhā), | you (anta) | and not (walā) | your people (qawmuka) | from (min) | before (qabli) | this (hādhā). | So be patient (fa-iṣ'bir); | indeed (inna), | the end (l-'āqibata) | is for the God fearing. (lil'muttaqīna)"

11:50 And to Aad We sent their brother Hud. He said, "O my people! Worship Allah, not is for you any god, other than Him. Not you are but inventors.

And to (wa-ilā) | Aad ('ādin) | We sent their brother (akhāhum) | Hud (hūdan). | He said (qāla), | "O my people (yāqawmi)! | Worship (u''budū) | Allah (l-laha), | not (mā) | is for you (lakum) | any (min) | god (ilāhin), | other than Him (ghayruhu). | Not (in) | you (antum) | are but (illā) | inventors (muf'tarūna).

11:51 O my people! Not I ask you for it any reward. Not is my reward except from the One Who created me. Then will not you use reason?

O my people (yāqawmi)! | Not (lā) | I ask you (asalukum) | for it ('alayhi) | any reward (ajran). | Not (in) | is my reward (ajriya) | except (illā) | from ('alā) | the One Who (alladhī) | created me (faṭaranī). | Then will not (afalā) | you use reason (ta'qilūna)?

11:52 And O my people! Ask forgiveness of your Lord, then turn in repentance to Him. He will send from the sky (rain) upon you in abundance and increase you in strength added to your strength. And do not turn away as criminals."

And O my people (wayāqawmi)! | Ask forgiveness (is'taghfirū) | of your Lord (rabbakum), | then (thumma) | turn in repentance (tūbū) | to Him (ilayhi). | He will send (yur'sili) | from the sky (rain (l-samāa)) | upon you ('alaykum) | in abundance (mid'rāran) | and increase you (wayazid'kum) | in strength (quwwatan) | added to (ilā) | your strength (quwwatikum). | And do not (walā) | turn away (tatawallaw) | as criminals. (muj'rimīna)"

11:53 They said, "O Hud! You have not brought us clear proofs, and not we will leave our gods on your saying, and not we are in you believers.

They said (qālū), | "O Hud (yāhūdu)! | You have not brought us (mā) | You have not brought us (ji'tanā) | clear proofs (bibayyinatin), | and not (wamā) | we (naḥnu) | will leave (bitārikī) | our gods (ālihatinā) | on ('an) | your saying (qawlika), | and not (wamā) | we are (naḥnu) | in you (laka) | believers (bimu'minīna).

11:54 Not we say, except that, have seized you some of our gods with evil." He said, "Indeed, I [I] call Allah to witness and you bear witness that I am innocent of what you associate,

Not (in) | we say (naqūlu), | except that (illā), | have seized you (i''tarāka) | some (ba'ḍu) | of our gods (ālihatinā) | with evil. (bisūin)" | He said (qāla), | "Indeed, I (innī) | [I] call Allah to witness (ush'hidu) | [I] call Allah to witness (l-laha) | and you bear witness (wa-ish'hadū) | that I am (annī) | innocent (barīon) | of what (mimmā) | you associate (tush'rikūna),

11:55 Other than Him. So plot against me all together, then do not give me respite.

Other than Him (min). | Other than Him (dūnihi). | So plot against me (fakīdūnī) | all together (jamī'an), | then (thumma) | do not (lā) | give me respite (tunẓirūni).

11:56 Indeed, I [I] put my trust upon Allah my Lord, and your Lord. There is not of a moving creature but He has grasp of its forelock. Indeed, my Lord is on a path straight.

Indeed, I (innī) | [I] put my trust (tawakkaltu) | upon (ʿalā) | Allah (l-lahi) | my Lord (rabbī), | and your Lord (warabbikum). | There is not (mā) | of a moving creature (min) | of a moving creature (dābbatin) | but (illā) | He (huwa) | has grasp (ākhidhun) | of its forelock (bināṣiyatihā). | Indeed (inna), | my Lord (rabbī) | is on (ʿalā) | a path (ṣirāṭin) | straight (mus'taqīmin).

11:57 So if you turn away, then verily I have conveyed to you what I was sent with [it] to you. And my Lord will give succession to a people other than you, and not you will harm Him in anything. Indeed, my Lord is on all things a Guardian."

So if (fa-in) | you turn away (tawallaw), | then verily (faqad) | I have conveyed to you (ablaghtukum) | what (mā) | I was sent (ur'sil'tu) | with [it] (bihi) | to you (ilaykum). | And my Lord will give succession (wayastakhlifu) | And my Lord will give succession (rabbī) | to a people (qawman) | other than you (ghayrakum), | and not (walā) | you will harm Him (taḍurrūnahu) | in anything (shayan). | Indeed (inna), | my Lord (rabbī) | is on (ʿalā) | all (kulli) | things (shayin) | a Guardian. (ḥafīẓun)"

11:58 And when came Our command, We saved Hud and those who believed with him, by a Mercy from Us and We saved them from a punishment severe.

And when (walammā) | came (jāa) | Our command (amrunā), | We saved (najjaynā) | Hud (hūdan) | and those who (wa-alladhīna) | believed (āmanū) | with him (maʿahu), | by a Mercy (biraḥmatin) | from Us (minnā) | and We saved them (wanajjaynāhum) | from (min) | a punishment (ʿadhābin) | severe (ghalīẓin).

11:59 And this was Aad, they rejected the Signs of their Lord and disobeyed His Messengers and followed the command of every tyrant obstinate.

And this (watil'ka) | was Aad (ʿādun), | they rejected (jaḥadū) | the Signs (biāyāti) | of their Lord (rabbihim) | and disobeyed (waʿaṣaw) | His Messengers (rusulahu) | and followed (wa-ittabaʿū) | the command (amra) | of every (kulli) | tyrant (jabbārin) | obstinate (ʿanīdin).

11:60 And they were followed in this world with a curse and on the Day of the Resurrection. No doubt! Indeed, Aad disbelieved their Lord, So away with Aad, the people of Hud.

And they were followed (wa-ut'biʿū) | in (fī) | this (hādhihi) | world (l-dun'yā) | with a curse (laʿnatan) | and on the Day (wayawma) | of the Resurrection (l-qiyāmati). | No doubt (alā)! | Indeed (inna), | Aad (ʿādan) | disbelieved (kafarū) | their Lord (rabbahum), | So (alā) | away (buʿʿdan) | with Aad (liʿādin), | the people (qawmi) | of Hud (hūdin).

11:61 And to Thamud We sent their brother Salih. He said, "O my people! Worship Allah, not you have any god other than Him. He produced you from the earth and settled you in it. So ask forgiveness of Him, then turn in repentance to Him. Indeed, my Lord is near, All-Responsive."

And to (wa-ilā) | Thamud (thamūda) | We sent their brother (akhāhum) | Salih (ṣāliḥan). | He said (qāla), | "O my people (yāqawmi)! | Worship (uʿʿbudū) | Allah (l-laha), | not (mā) | you have (lakum) | any (min) | god (ilāhin) | other than Him (ghayruhu). | He (huwa) | produced you (ansha-akum) | from (mina) | the earth (l-arḍi) | and settled you (wa-is'taʿmarakum) | in it (fīhā). | So ask forgiveness of Him (fa-is'taghfirūhu), | then (thumma) | turn in repentance (tūbū) | to Him (ilayhi). | Indeed (inna), | my Lord (rabbī) | is near (qarībun), | All-Responsive. (mujībun)"

11:62 They said, O Salih! Verily you were among us the one in whom hope was placed before this. Do you forbid us that we worship what our forefathers worshipped? And indeed we surely are in doubt about what you call us to it, suspicious."

They said (qālū), | O Salih (yāṣāliḥu)! | Verily (qad) | you were (kunta) | among us (fīnā) | the one in whom hope was placed (marjuwwan) | before (qabla) | this (hādhā). | Do you forbid us (atanhānā) | that (an) | we worship (naʿbuda) | what (mā) | our forefathers worshipped (yaʿbudu)?

| our forefathers worshipped (ābāunā)? | And indeed we (wa-innanā) | surely are in (lafī) | doubt (shakkin) | about what (mimmā) | you call us (tadʿūnā) | to it (ilayhi), | suspicious. (murībin)"

11:63 He said, "O my people! Do you see, if I am on a clear proof from my Lord, and He has given me from Him, a Mercy then who can help me against Allah, if I were to disobey Him? So not you would increase me but in loss.

He said (qāla), | "O my people (yāqawmi)! | Do you see (ara-aytum), | if (in) | I am (kuntu) | on (ʿalā) | a clear proof (bayyinatin) | from (min) | my Lord (rabbī), | and He has given me (waātānī) | from Him (min'hu), | a Mercy (raḥmatan) | then who (faman) | can help me (yanṣurunī) | against (mina) | Allah (l-lahi), | if (in) | I were to disobey Him (ʿaṣaytuhu)? | So not (famā) | you would increase me (tazīdūnanī) | but (ghayra) | in loss (takhsīrin).

11:64 And O my people! This she-camel of Allah is for you a Sign, so leave her to eat in the earth of Allah, and do not touch her with harm, lest will seize you a punishment impending."

And O my people (wayāqawmi)! | This (hādhihi) | she-camel (nāqatu) | of Allah (l-lahi) | is for you (lakum) | a Sign (āyatan), | so leave her (fadharūhā) | to eat (takul) | in (fī) | the earth (arḍi) | of Allah (l-lahi), | and do not (walā) | touch her (tamassūhā) | with harm (bisūin), | lest will seize you (fayakhudhakum) | a punishment (ʿadhābun) | impending. (qarībun)"

11:65 But they hamstrung her. So he said, "Enjoy yourselves in your homes for three days. That is a promise not to be belied."

But they hamstrung her (faʿaqarūhā). | So he said (faqāla), | "Enjoy yourselves (tamattaʿū) | in (fī) | your homes (dārikum) | for three (thalāthata) | days (ayyāmin). | That (dhālika) | is a promise (waʿdun) | not (ghayru) | to be belied. (makdhūbin)"

11:66 So when came Our command We saved Salih, and those who believed with him, by a Mercy from Us, and from the disgrace of that Day. Indeed, your Lord, He is All-Strong, All-Mighty.

So when (falammā) | came (jāa) | Our command (amrunā) | We saved (najjaynā) | Salih (ṣāliḥan), | and those who (wa-alladhīna) | believed (āmanū) | with him (maʿahu), | by a Mercy (biraḥmatin) | from Us (minnā), | and from (wamin) | the disgrace (khiz'yi) | of that Day (yawmi-idhin). | Indeed (inna), | your Lord (rabbaka), | He (huwa) | is All-Strong (l-qawiyu), | All-Mighty (l-ʿazīzu).

11:67 And seized those who wronged, the thunderous blast then they became in their homes fallen prone.

And seized (wa-akhadha) | those who (alladhīna) | wronged (ẓalamū), | the thunderous blast (l-ṣayḥatu) | then they became (fa-aṣbaḥū) | in (fī) | their homes (diyārihim) | fallen prone (jāthimīna).

11:68 As if not they had prospered therein. No doubt, indeed, Thamud disbelieved in their Lord, so away with Thamud.

As if (ka-an) | not (lam) | they had prospered (yaghnaw) | therein (fīhā). | No doubt (alā), | indeed (inna), | Thamud (thamūdā) | disbelieved (kafarū) | in their Lord (rabbahum), | so (alā) | away (buʿ'dan) | with Thamud (lithamūda).

11:69 And certainly came Our messengers to Ibrahim with glad tidings, they said, "Peace." He said, "Peace," and not he delayed to bring a calf roasted.

And certainly (walaqad) | came (jāat) | Our messengers (rusulunā) | to Ibrahim (ib'rāhīma) | with glad tidings (bil-bush'rā), | they said (qālū), | "Peace. (salāman)" | He said (qāla), | "Peace, (salāmun)" | and not he delayed (famā) | and not he delayed (labitha) | to (an) | bring (jāa) | a calf (biʿij'lin) | roasted (ḥanīdhin).

11:70 But when he saw their hands not reaching to it, he felt unfamiliar of them and felt apprehension from them [a fear]. They said, "Do not fear. Indeed, we [we] have been sent to the people of Lut."

But when (falammā) | he saw (raā) | their hands (aydiyahum) | not (lā) | reaching (taṣilu) | to it (ilayhi), | he felt unfamiliar of them (nakirahum) | and felt apprehension (wa-awjasa) | from them (min'hum) | [a fear] (khīfatan). | They said (qālū), | "Do not (lā) | fear (takhaf). | Indeed, we (innā) | [we] have been sent (ur'sil'nā) | to (ilā) | the people (qawmi) | of Lut. (lūṭin)"

11:71 And his wife was standing and she laughed. Then We gave her glad tidings of Isaac, and after Isaac of Yaqub.

And his wife (wa-im'ra-atuhu) | was standing (qāimatun) | and she laughed (faḍaḥikat). | Then We gave her glad tidings (fabasharnāhā) | of Isaac (bi-is'ḥāqa), | and after (wamin) | and after (warāi) | Isaac (is'ḥāqa) | of Yaqub (yaʿqūba).

11:72 She said, "Woe to me! Shall I bear a child while I am an old woman and this, my husband, is an old man? Indeed, this is surely a thing amazing."

She said (qālat), | "Woe to me (yāwaylatā)! | Shall I bear a child (a-alidu) | while I am (wa-anā) | an old woman (ʿajūzun) | and this (wahādhā), | my husband (baʿlī), | is an old man (shaykhan)? | Indeed (inna), | this (hādhā) | is surely a thing (lashayon) | amazing. (ʿajībun)"

11:73 They said, "Are you amazed at the decree of Allah? The Mercy of Allah and His blessings be upon you, people of the house. Indeed, He is All-Praiseworthy, All-Glorious."

They said (qālū), | "Are you amazed (ataʿjabīna) | at (min) | the decree of Allah (amri)? | the decree of Allah (l-lahi)? | The Mercy of Allah (raḥmatu) | The Mercy of Allah (l-lahi) | and His blessings (wabarakātuhu) | be upon you (ʿalaykum), | people (ahla) | of the house (l-bayti). | Indeed, He (innahu) | is All-Praiseworthy (ḥamīdun), | All-Glorious. (majīdun)"

11:74 And when had gone away from Ibrahim the fright, and had reached him the glad tidings, he argued with Us, concerning the people of Lut.

And when (falammā) | had gone away (dhahaba) | from (ʿan) | Ibrahim (ib'rāhīma) | the fright (l-rawʿu), | and had reached him (wajāathu) | the glad tidings (l-bush'rā), | he argued with Us (yujādilunā), | concerning (fī) | the people (qawmi) | of Lut (lūṭin).

11:75 Indeed, Ibrahim was certainly forbearing, imploring, and oft-returning.

Indeed (inna), | Ibrahim (ib'rāhīma) | was certainly forbearing (laḥalīmun), | imploring (awwāhun), | and oft-returning (munībun).

11:76 O Ibrahim! Turn away from this. Indeed, it certainly has come, the Command of your Lord and indeed, [they] will come (for) them a punishment which cannot be repelled.

O Ibrahim (yāib'rāhīmu)! | Turn away (aʿriḍ) | from (ʿan) | this (hādhā). | Indeed, it (innahu) | certainly (qad) | has come (jāa), | the Command (amru) | of your Lord (rabbika) | and indeed, [they] (wa-innahum) | will come (for) them (ātīhim) | a punishment (ʿadhābun) | which cannot (ghayru) | be repelled (mardūdin).

11:77 And when came Our messengers to Lut, he was distressed for them and felt straitened for them and uneasy, and said, "This is a day distressful."

And when (walammā) | came (jāat) | Our messengers (rusulunā) | to Lut (lūṭan), | he was distressed (sīa) | for them (bihim) | and felt straitened (waḍāqa) | for them (bihim) | and uneasy (dharʿan), | and said (waqāla), | "This (hādhā) | is a day (yawmun) | distressful. (ʿaṣībun)"

11:78 And came to him his people rushing, to him, and before they had been doing the evil deeds. He said, "O my people! These are my daughters, they are purer for you. So fear Allah and do not disgrace me concerning my guests. Is there not among you a man right-minded?"

And came to him (wajāahu) | his people (qawmuhu) | rushing (yuh'ra'ūna), | to him (ilayhi), | and before (wamin) | and before (qablu) | they had been (kānū) | doing (ya'malūna) | the evil deeds (l-sayiāti). | He said (qāla), | "O my people (yāqawmi)! | These (hāulāi) | are my daughters (banātī), | they (hunna) | are purer (aṭharu) | for you (lakum). | So fear (fa-ittaqū) | Allah (l-laha) | and do not (walā) | disgrace me (tukh'zūni) | concerning (fī) | my guests (ḍayfī). | Is there not (alaysa) | among you (minkum) | a man (rajulun) | right-minded? (rashīdun)"

11:79 They said, "Verily you know that not we have concerning your daughters any right. And indeed, you surely know what we want."

They said (qālū), | "Verily (laqad) | you know ('alim'ta) | that not (mā) | we have (lanā) | concerning (fī) | your daughters (banātika) | any (min) | right (ḥaqqin). | And indeed, you (wa-innaka) | surely know (lata'lamu) | what (mā) | we want. (nurīdu)"

11:80 He said, "If that I had over you power or I could take refuge in a support strong."

He said (qāla), | "If (law) | that (anna) | I had (lī) | over you (bikum) | power (quwwatan) | or (aw) | I could take refuge (āwī) | in (ilā) | a support (ruk'nin) | strong. (shadīdin)"

11:81 They said, "O Lut! Indeed, we are messengers of your Lord, never they will reach you. So travel with your family in a part of the night and let not look back anyone of you, except your wife. Indeed, it will strike her what will strike them. Indeed, their appointed time is morning. Is not the morning near?"

They said (qālū), | "O Lut (yālūṭu)! | Indeed, we (innā) | are messengers (rusulu) | of your Lord (rabbika), | never (lan) | they will reach (yaṣilū) | you (ilayka). | So travel (fa-asri) | with your family (bi-ahlika) | in a part (biqiṭ''in) | of (mina) | the night (al-layli) | and let not (walā) | look back (yaltafit) | anyone of you (minkum), | anyone of you (aḥadun), | except (illā) | your wife (im'ra-ataka). | Indeed, it (innahu) | will strike her (muṣībuhā) | what (mā) | will strike them (aṣābahum). | Indeed (inna), | their appointed time (maw'idahumu) | is morning (l-ṣub'ḥu). | Is not (alaysa) | the morning (l-ṣub'ḥu) | near? (biqarībin)"

11:82 So when came Our Command, We made its upside, its downside, and We rained upon them stones of baked clay in layers.

So when (falammā) | came (jāa) | Our Command (amrunā), | We made (ja'alnā) | its upside ('āliyahā), | its downside (sāfilahā), | and We rained (wa-amṭarnā) | upon them ('alayhā) | stones (ḥijāratan) | of (min) | baked clay (sijjīlin) | in layers (manḍūdin).

11:83 Marked from your Lord. And not it is from the wrongdoers far.

Marked (musawwamatan) | from ('inda) | your Lord (rabbika). | And not (wamā) | it (hiya) | is from (mina) | the wrongdoers (l-ẓālimīna) | far (biba'īdin).

11:84 And to Madyan, their brother Shuaib. He said, "O my people! Worship Allah not is for you any god other than Him. And do not decrease from the measure and the scale. Indeed, I see you in prosperity, but indeed, I fear for you punishment of a Day all-encompassing.

And to (wa-ilā) | Madyan (madyana), | their brother (akhāhum) | Shuaib (shu'ayban). | He said (qāla), | "O my people (yāqawmi)! | Worship (u''budū) | Allah (l-laha) | not (mā) | is for you (lakum) | any (min) | god (ilāhin) | other than Him (ghayruhu). | And do not (walā) | decrease (tanquṣū) | from the measure (l-mik'yāla) | and the scale (wal-mīzāna). | Indeed, I (innī) | see you (arākum) | in prosperity (bikhayrin), | but indeed, I (wa-innī) | fear (akhāfu) | for you ('alaykum) | punishment ('adhāba) | of a Day (yawmin) | all-encompassing (muḥīṭin).

11:85 And O my people! Give full measure, and weight in justice and do not deprive the people of their things, and do not act wickedly in the earth spreading corruption.

And O my people (wayāqawmi)! | Give full (awfū) | measure (l-mik'yāla), | and weight (wal-mīzāna) | in justice (bil-qis'ṭi) | and do not (walā) | deprive (tabkhasū) | the people (l-nāsa) | of their things (ashyāahum), | and do not (walā) | act wickedly (taʿthaw) | in (fī) | the earth (l-arḍi) | spreading corruption (muf'sidīna).

11:86 What remains from Allah is best for you, if you are believers. And not I am over you a guardian."

What remains (baqiyyatu) | from Allah (l-lahi) | is best (khayrun) | for you (lakum), | if (in) | you are (kuntum) | believers (mu'minīna). | And not (wamā) | I am (anā) | over you (ʿalaykum) | a guardian. (biḥafīẓin)"

11:87 They said, "O Shuaib! Does your prayer command you that we leave what worship our forefathers, or that we do concerning our wealth what we will? Indeed you, surely you are the forbearing, the right-minded."

They said (qālū), | "O Shuaib (yāshuʿaybu)! | Does your prayer (aṣalatuka) | command you (tamuruka) | that (an) | we leave (natruka) | what (mā) | worship (yaʿbudu) | our forefathers (ābāunā), | or (aw) | that (an) | we do (nafʿala) | concerning (fī) | our wealth (amwālinā) | what (mā) | we will (nashāu)? | Indeed you (innaka), | surely you (la-anta) | are the forbearing (l-ḥalīmu), | the right-minded. (l-rashīdu)"

11:88 He said, "O my people! Do you see if I am on a clear evidence from my Lord, and He has provided me from Himself a good provision? And not I intend that I differ from you in what I forbid you from it. Not I intend except the reform as much as I am able. And not is my success except with Allah. Upon Him I trust and to Him I turn.

He said (qāla), | "O my people (yāqawmi)! | Do you see (ara-aytum) | if (in) | I am (kuntu) | on (ʿalā) | a clear evidence (bayyinatin) | from (min) | my Lord (rabbī), | and He has provided me (warazaqanī) | from Himself (min'hu) | a good provision (riz'qan)? | a good provision (ḥasanan)? | And not (wamā) | I intend (urīdu) | that (an) | I differ from you (ukhālifakum) | in (ilā) | what (mā) | I forbid you (anhākum) | from it (ʿanhu). | Not (in) | I intend (urīdu) | except (illā) | the reform (l-iṣ'lāḥa) | as much as I am able (mā). | as much as I am able (is'taṭaʿtu). | And not (wamā) | is my success (tawfīqī) | except (illā) | with Allah (bil-lahi). | Upon Him (ʿalayhi) | I trust (tawakkaltu) | and to Him (wa-ilayhi) | I turn (unību).

11:89 And O my people! Let not cause you to sin my dissension lest befalls you similar to what befell the people of Nuh or the people of Hud or people of Salih. And not are the people of Lut from you far off.

And O my people (wayāqawmi)! | Let not cause you to sin (lā) | Let not cause you to sin (yajrimannakum) | my dissension (shiqāqī) | lest (an) | befalls you (yuṣībakum) | similar (mith'lu) | to what (mā) | befell (aṣāba) | the people of Nuh (qawma) | the people of Nuh (nūḥin) | or (aw) | the people of Hud (qawma) | the people of Hud (hūdin) | or (aw) | people of Salih (qawma). | people of Salih (ṣāliḥin). | And not (wamā) | are the people of Lut (qawmu) | are the people of Lut (lūṭin) | from you (minkum) | far off (bibaʿīdin).

11:90 And ask forgiveness of your Lord, then turn in repentance to Him. Indeed, my Lord is Most Merciful, Most Loving."

And ask forgiveness (wa-is'taghfirū) | of your Lord (rabbakum), | then (thumma) | turn in repentance (tūbū) | to Him (ilayhi). | Indeed (inna), | my Lord (rabbī) | is Most Merciful (raḥīmun), | Most Loving. (wadūdun)"

11:91 They said, "O Shuaib! Not we understand much of what you say, and indeed, we surely [we] see you among us weak. And if not for your family surely we would have stoned you, and you are not against us mighty."

They said (qālū), | "O Shuaib (yāshuʿaybu)! | Not (mā) | we understand (nafqahu) | much (kathīran) | of what (mimmā) | you say (taqūlu), | and indeed, we (wa-innā) | surely [we] see you (lanarāka) | among us (fīnā) | weak (ḍaʿīfan). | And if not (walawlā) | for your family (rahṭuka) | surely we would have stoned you (larajamnāka), | and you are not (wamā) | and you are not (anta) | against us (ʿalaynā) | mighty. (biʿazīzin)"

11:92 He said, "O my people! Is my family mightier on you than Allah? And you have taken Him, behind your backs. Indeed, my Lord of what you do is All-Encompassing.

He said (qāla), | "O my people (yāqawmi)! | Is my family (arahṭī) | mightier (aʿazzu) | on you (ʿalaykum) | than (mina) | Allah (l-lahi)? | And you have taken Him (wa-ittakhadhtumūhu), | behind your (warāakum) | backs (ẓih'riyyan). | Indeed (inna), | my Lord (rabbī) | of what (bimā) | you do (taʿmalūna) | is All-Encompassing (muḥīṭun).

11:93 And O my people! Work according to your position, indeed, I am working. Soon you will know on whom will come a punishment that will disgrace him, and who [he] is a liar. And watch, indeed, I am with you a watcher."

And O my people (wayāqawmi)! | Work (iʿ'malū) | according to (ʿalā) | your position (makānatikum), | indeed, I am (innī) | working (ʿāmilun). | Soon (sawfa) | you will know (taʿlamūna) | on whom (man) | will come (yatīhi) | a punishment (ʿadhābun) | that will disgrace him (yukh'zīhi), | and who (waman) | [he] (huwa) | is a liar (kādhibun). | And watch (wa-ir'taqibū), | indeed, I am (innī) | with you (maʿakum) | a watcher. (raqībun)"

11:94 And when came Our Command, We saved Shuaib and those who believed with him by a Mercy from Us. And seized those who wronged, the thunderous blast then they became in their homes fallen prone.

And when (walammā) | came (jāa) | Our Command (amrunā), | We saved (najjaynā) | Shuaib (shuʿayban) | and those who (wa-alladhīna) | believed (āmanū) | with him (maʿahu) | by a Mercy (biraḥmatin) | from Us (minnā). | And seized (wa-akhadhati) | those who (alladhīna) | wronged (ẓalamū), | the thunderous blast (l-ṣayḥatu) | then they became (fa-aṣbaḥū) | in (fī) | their homes (diyārihim) | fallen prone (jāthimīna).

11:95 As if not they had prospered therein. So, away with Madyan as was taken away the Thamud.

As if (ka-an) | not (lam) | they had prospered (yaghnaw) | therein (fīhā). | So (alā), | away (buʿ'dan) | with Madyan (limadyana) | as (kamā) | was taken away (baʿidat) | the Thamud (thamūdu).

11:96 And certainly We sent Musa with Our Signs and an authority clear,

And certainly (walaqad) | We sent (arsalnā) | Musa (mūsā) | with Our Signs (biāyātinā) | and an authority (wasul'ṭānin) | clear (mubīnin),

11:97 To Firaun and his chiefs, but they followed the command of Firaun, and not the command of Firaun was right.

To (ilā) | Firaun (firʿ'awna) | and his chiefs (wamala-ihi), | but they followed (fa-ittabaʿū) | the command of Firaun (amra), | the command of Firaun (firʿ'awna), | and not (wamā) | the command of Firaun (amru) | the command of Firaun (firʿ'awna) | was right (birashīdin).

11:98 He will precede his people on the Day of the Resurrection and lead them into the Fire. And wretched is the place to which they are led.

He will precede (yaqdumu) | his people (qawmahu) | on the Day (yawma) | of the Resurrection (l-qiyāmati) | and lead them (fa-awradahumu) | into the Fire (l-nāra). | And wretched (wabi'sa) | is the place (l-wir'du) | to which they are led (l-mawrūdu).

11:99 And they were followed in this by a curse and on the Day of the Resurrection. Wretched is the gift which will be given.

And they were followed (wa-ut'biʿū) | in (fī) | this (hādhihi) | by a curse (laʿnatan) | and on the Day (wayawma) | of the Resurrection (l-qiyāmati). | Wretched (bi'sa) | is the gift (l-rif'du) | which will be given (l-marfūdu).

11:100 That is from the news of the cities which We relate to you; of them, some are standing and some mown.

That (dhālika) | is from (min) | the news (anbāi) | of the cities (l-qurā) | which We relate (naquṣṣuhu) | to you (ʿalayka); | of them (min'hā), | some are standing (qāimun) | and some mown (waḥaṣīdun).

11:101 And not We wronged them but they wronged themselves. So not availed them their gods which they invoked other than Allah, any thing, when came the command (of) your Lord. And not they increased them other than ruin.

And not (wamā) | We wronged them (ẓalamnāhum) | but (walākin) | they wronged (ẓalamū) | themselves (anfusahum). | So not (famā) | availed (aghnat) | them (ʿanhum) | their gods (ālihatuhumu) | which (allatī) | they invoked (yadʿūna) | other than Allah (min), | other than Allah (dūni), | other than Allah (l-lahi), | any (min) | thing (shayin), | when (lammā) | came (jāa) | the command (of) your Lord (amru). | the command (of) your Lord (rabbika). | And not (wamā) | they increased them (zādūhum) | other than (ghayra) | ruin (tatbībin).

11:102 And thus is the seizure (of) your Lord when He seizes the cities while they are doing wrong. Indeed, His seizure is painful, and severe.

And thus (wakadhālika) | is the seizure (of) your Lord (akhdhu) | is the seizure (of) your Lord (rabbika) | when (idhā) | He seizes (akhadha) | the cities (l-qurā) | while they (wahiya) | are doing wrong (ẓālimatun). | Indeed (inna), | His seizure (akhdhahu) | is painful (alīmun), | and severe (shadīdun).

11:103 Indeed, in that is surely a Sign for those who fear the punishment of the Hereafter. That is a Day will be gathered on it the mankind, and that is a Day witnessed.

Indeed (inna), | in (fī) | that (dhālika) | is surely a Sign (laāyatan) | for those who (liman) | fear (khāfa) | the punishment (ʿadhāba) | of the Hereafter (l-ākhirati). | That (dhālika) | is a Day (yawmun) | will be gathered (majmūʿun) | on it (lahu) | the mankind (l-nāsu), | and that (wadhālika) | is a Day (yawmun) | witnessed (mashhūdun).

11:104 And not We delay it except for a term limited.

And not (wamā) | We delay it (nu-akhiruhu) | except (illā) | for a term (li-ajalin) | limited (maʿdūdin).

11:105 The Day it comes not will speak a soul except by His leave. Then among them will be the wretched, and the glad.

The Day (yawma) | it comes (yati) | not (lā) | will speak (takallamu) | a soul (nafsun) | except (illā) | by His leave (bi-idh'nihi). | Then among them (famin'hum) | will be the wretched (shaqiyyun), | and the glad (wasaʿīdun).

11:106 As for those who were wretched then they will be in the Fire. For them therein is sighing, and wailing.

As for (fa-ammā) | those who (alladhīna) | were wretched (shaqū) | then they will be in (fafī) | the Fire (l-nāri). | For them (lahum) | therein (fīhā) | is sighing (zafīrun), | and wailing (washahīqun).

11:107 Will be abiding therein as long as remain the heavens and the earth, except what your Lord wills. Indeed, your Lord is All-Accomplisher of what He intends.

Will be abiding (khālidīna) | therein (fīhā) | as long as remain (mā) | as long as remain (dāmati) | the heavens (l-samāwātu) | and the earth (wal-arḍu), | except (illā) | what your Lord wills (mā). | what your Lord wills (shāa). | what your Lord wills (rabbuka). | Indeed (inna), | your Lord (rabbaka) | is All-Accomplisher (faʿʿālun) | of what (limā) | He intends (yurīdu).

11:108 And as for those who were glad then they will be in Paradise, will be abiding therein as long as remains the heavens and the earth, except what your Lord wills - a bestowal not interrupted.

And as for (wa-ammā) | those who (alladhīna) | were glad (suʿidū) | then they will be in (fafī) | Paradise (l-janati), | will be abiding (khālidīna) | therein (fīhā) | as long as remains (mā) | as long as remains (dāmati) | the heavens (l-samāwātu) | and the earth (wal-arḍu), | except (illā) | what your Lord wills (mā)- | what your Lord wills (shāa)- | what your Lord wills (rabbuka)- | a bestowal (ʿaṭāan) | not (ghayra) | interrupted (majdhūdhin).

11:109 So do not be in doubt as to what worship these polytheists. Not they worship except as what worshipped their forefathers before. And indeed, We will surely pay them in full their share without being diminished.

So do not (falā) | be (taku) | in (fī) | doubt (mir'yatin) | as to what (mimmā) | worship (yaʿbudu) | these polytheists (hāulāi). | Not (mā) | they worship (yaʿbudūna) | except (illā) | as what (kamā) | worshipped (yaʿbudu) | their forefathers (ābāuhum) | before (min). | before (qablu). | And indeed, We (wa-innā) | will surely pay them in full (lamuwaffūhum) | their share (naṣībahum) | without (ghayra) | being diminished (manqūṣin).

11:110 And verily We gave Musa the Book, but differences arose therein. And if not for a Word that preceded from your Lord, surely would have been judged between them. And indeed, they surely are in doubt concerning it suspicious.

And verily (walaqad) | We gave (ātaynā) | Musa (mūsā) | the Book (l-kitāba), | but differences arose (fa-ukh'tulifa) | therein (fīhi). | And if not (walawlā) | for a Word (kalimatun) | that preceded (sabaqat) | from (min) | your Lord (rabbika), | surely would have been judged (laquḍiya) | between them (baynahum). | And indeed, they (wa-innahum) | surely are in (lafī) | doubt (shakkin) | concerning it (min'hu) | suspicious (murībin).

11:111 And indeed, to each [when] surely will pay them in full your Lord their deeds. Indeed, He of what they do is All-Aware.

And indeed (wa-inna), | to each [when] (kullan) | to each [when] (lammā) | surely will pay them in full (layuwaffiyannahum) | your Lord (rabbuka) | their deeds (aʿmālahum). | Indeed, He (innahu) | of what (bimā) | they do (yaʿmalūna) | is All-Aware (khabīrun).

11:112 So stand firm as you are commanded and those who turn in repentance with you, and do not transgress. Indeed, He of what you do is All-Seer.

So stand firm (fa-is'taqim) | as (kamā) | you are commanded (umir'ta) | and those who (waman) | turn in repentance (tāba) | with you (maʿaka), | and do not (walā) | transgress (taṭghaw). | Indeed, He (innahu) | of what (bimā) | you do (taʿmalūna) | is All-Seer (baṣīrun).

11:113 And do not incline to those who do wrong lest touches you the Fire, and not is for you besides Allah any protectors; then not you will be helped.

And do not (walā) | incline (tarkanū) | to (ilā) | those who (alladhīna) | do wrong (ẓalamū) | lest touches you (fatamassakumu) | the Fire (l-nāru), | and not (wamā) | is for you (lakum) | besides Allah (min) | besides Allah (dūni) | besides Allah (l-lahi) | any (min) | protectors (awliyāa); | then (thumma) | not (lā) | you will be helped (tunṣarūna).

11:114 And establish the prayer at the two ends of the day and at the approach of the night. Indeed, the good deeds remove the evil deeds. That is a reminder for those who remember.

And establish (wa-aqimi) | the prayer (l-ṣalata) | at the two ends (ṭarafayi) | of the day (l-nahāri) | and at the approach (wazulafan) | of (mina) | the night (al-layli). | Indeed (inna), | the good deeds (l-ḥasanāti) | remove (yudh'hib'na) | the evil deeds (l-sayiāti). | That (dhālika) | is a reminder (dhik'rā) | for those who remember (lildhākirīna).

11:115 And be patient, for indeed, Allah does not let go waste the reward of the good-doers.

And be patient (wa-iṣ'bir), | for indeed (fa-inna), | Allah (l-laha) | does not (lā) | let go waste (yuḍīʿu) | the reward (ajra) | of the good-doers (l-muḥ'sinīna).

11:116 So why not had been of the generations before you those possessing a remnant, forbidding from the corruption in the earth except a few of those We saved among them? But followed those who did wrong what luxury they were given therein, and they were criminals.

So why not (falawlā) | had been (kāna) | of (mina) | the generations (l-qurūni) | before you (min) | before you (qablikum) | those possessing a remnant (ulū), | those possessing a remnant (baqiyyatin), | forbidding (yanhawna) | from (ʿani) | the corruption (l-fasādi) | in (fī) | the earth (l-arḍi) | except (illā) | a few (qalīlan) | of those (mimman) | We saved (anjaynā) | among them (min'hum)? | But followed (wa-ittabaʿa) | those who (alladhīna) | did wrong (ẓalamū) | what (mā) | luxury they were given (ut'rifū) | therein (fīhi), | and they were (wakānū) | criminals (muj'rimīna).

11:117 And not would your Lord, destroy the cities unjustly while its people were reformers.

And not (wamā) | would (kāna) | your Lord (rabbuka), | destroy (liyuh'lika) | the cities (l-qurā) | unjustly (biẓul'min) | while its people (wa-ahluhā) | were reformers (muṣ'liḥūna).

11:118 And if your Lord had willed surely He could have made the mankind one community, but not they will cease to differ.

And if (walaw) | your Lord had willed (shāa) | your Lord had willed (rabbuka) | surely He could have made (lajaʿala) | the mankind (l-nāsa) | one community (ummatan), | one community (wāḥidatan), | but not (walā) | they will cease (yazālūna) | to differ (mukh'talifīna).

11:119 Except on whom your Lord has bestowed Mercy, and for that He created them. And will be fulfilled the Word of your Lord, "Surely I will fill Hell with the Jinn and the men all together."

Except (illā) | on whom (man) | your Lord has bestowed Mercy (raḥima), | your Lord has bestowed Mercy (rabbuka), | and for that (walidhālika) | He created them (khalaqahum). | And will be fulfilled (watammat) | the Word of your Lord (kalimatu), | the Word of your Lord (rabbika), | "Surely I will fill (la-amla-anna) | Hell (jahannama) | with (mina) | the Jinn (l-jinati) | and the men (wal-nāsi) | all together. (ajmaʿīna)"

11:120 And each, We relate to you of the news of the Messengers for that We may make firm with it your heart. And has come to you in this the truth and an admonition and a reminder for the believers.

And each (wakullan), | We relate (naquṣṣu) | to you (ʿalayka) | of (min) | the news (anbāi) | of the Messengers (l-rusuli) | for that (mā) | We may make firm (nuthabbitu) | with it (bihi) | your heart (fuādaka). | And has come to you (wajāaka) | in (fī) | this (hādhihi) | the truth (l-ḥaqu) | and an admonition (wamawʿiẓatun) | and a reminder (wadhik'rā) | for the believers (lil'mu'minīna).

11:121 And say to those who do not believe, "Work according to your position; indeed, we are also working.

And say (waqul) | to those who (lilladhīna) | do not (lā) | believe (yu'minūna), | "Work (iʿ'malū) | according to (ʿalā) | your position (makānatikum); | indeed, we (innā) | are also working (ʿāmilūna).

11:122 And wait; indeed, we are ones who wait."

And wait (wa-intaẓirū); | indeed, we (innā) | are ones who wait. (muntaẓirūna)"

11:123 And for Allah is the unseen of the heavens and the earth, and to Him will be returned the matter, all of it, so worship Him, and put your trust upon Him. And your Lord is not unaware of what you do.

And for Allah (walillahi) | is the unseen (ghaybu) | of the heavens (l-samāwāti) | and the earth (wal-arḍi), | and to Him (wa-ilayhi) | will be returned (yur'jaʿu) | the matter (l-amru), | all of it (kulluhu), | so worship Him (fa-uʿ'bud'hu), | and put your trust (watawakkal) | upon Him (ʿalayhi). | And your Lord is not (wamā) | And your Lord is not (rabbuka) | unaware (bighāfilin) | of what (ʿammā) | you do (taʿmalūna).

Chapter (12) Sūrat Yūsuf (Joseph)

12:1 Alif Laam Ra. These are the Verses of the Book [the] clear.

Alif Laam Ra (alif-lam-ra). | These (til'ka) | are the Verses (āyātu) | of the Book (l-kitābi) | [the] clear (l-mubīni).

12:2 Indeed, We, We have sent it down, as a Quran in Arabic so that you may understand.

Indeed, We (innā), | We have sent it down (anzalnāhu), | as a Quran in Arabic (qur'ānan) | as a Quran in Arabic (ʿarabiyyan) | so that you may (laʿallakum) | understand (taʿqilūna).

12:3 We relate to you the best of the narrations in what We have revealed to you of this the Quran, although you were, before it, surely among the unaware.

We (naḥnu) | relate (naquṣṣu) | to you (ʿalayka) | the best (aḥsana) | of the narrations (l-qaṣaṣi) | in what (bimā) | We have revealed (awḥaynā) | to you (ilayka) | of this (hādhā) | the Quran (l-qur'āna), | although (wa-in) | you were (kunta), | before it (min), | before it (qablihi), | surely among (lamina) | the unaware (l-ghāfilīna).

12:4 When said Yusuf to his father, "O my father! Indeed, I I saw eleven stars and the sun and the moon; I saw them to me prostrating."

When (idh) | said (qāla) | Yusuf (yūsufu) | to his father (li-abīhi), | "O my father (yāabati)! | Indeed, I (innī) | I saw (ra-aytu) | eleven (aḥada) | eleven (ʿashara) | stars (kawkaban) | and the sun (wal-shamsa) | and the moon (wal-qamara); | I saw them (ra-aytuhum) | to me (lī) | prostrating. (sājidīna)"

12:5 He said, "O my son! Do not relate your vision to your brothers lest they plan against you a plot. Indeed, the Shaitaan is to man an enemy open.

He said (qāla), | "O my son (yābunayya)! | Do not (lā) | relate (taqṣuṣ) | your vision (ru'yāka) | to (ʿalā) | your brothers (ikh'watika) | lest they plan (fayakīdū) | against you (laka) | a plot (kaydan). | Indeed (inna), | the Shaitaan (l-shayṭāna) | is to man (lil'insāni) | an enemy (ʿaduwwun) | open (mubīnun).

12:6 And thus will choose you your Lord and will teach you of the interpretation of the narratives and complete His Favor on you and on the family of Yaqub as He completed it on your two forefathers before - Ibrahim and Isaac. Indeed, your Lord is All-Knower, All-Wise."

And thus (wakadhālika) | will choose you (yajtabīka) | your Lord (rabbuka) | and will teach you (wayuʿallimuka) | of (min) | the interpretation (tawīli) | of the narratives (l-aḥādīthi) | and complete (wayutimmu) | His Favor (niʿʹmatahu) | on you (ʿalayka) | and on (waʿalā) | the family (āli) | of Yaqub (yaʿqūba) | as (kamā) | He completed it (atammahā) | on (ʿalā) | your two forefathers (abawayka) | before (min)- | before (qablu)- | Ibrahim (ib'rāhīma) | and Isaac (wa-is'ḥāqa). | Indeed (inna), | your Lord (rabbaka) | is All-Knower (ʿalīmun), | All-Wise. (ḥakīmun)"

12:7 Certainly were in Yusuf and his brothers signs for those who ask.

Certainly (laqad) | were (kāna) | in (fī) | Yusuf (yūsufa) | and his brothers (wa-ikh'watihi) | signs (āyātun) | for those who ask (lilssāilīna).

12:8 When they said, "Surely Yusuf and his brother are more beloved to our father than we, while we are a group. Indeed, our father is surely in an error clear.

When (idh) | they said (qālū), | "Surely Yusuf (layūsufu) | and his brother (wa-akhūhu) | are more beloved (aḥabbu) | to (ilā) | our father (abīnā) | than we (minnā), | while we (wanaḥnu) | are a group (ʿuṣ'batun). | Indeed (inna), | our father (abānā) | is surely in (lafī) | an error (ḍalālin) | clear (mubīnin).

12:9 Kill Yusuf or cast him to a land so will be free for you the face of your father, and you will be after that a people righteous."

Kill (uq'tulū) | Yusuf (yūsufa) | or (awi) | cast him (iṭ'raḥūhu) | to a land (arḍan) | so will be free (yakhlu) | for you (lakum) | the face (wajhu) | of your father (abīkum), | and you will be (watakūnū) | after that (min) | after that (baʿdihi) | a people (qawman) | righteous. (ṣāliḥīna)"

12:10 Said a speaker among them, "Do not kill Yusuf but throw him in the bottom of the well, will pick him some [the] caravan if you are doing."

Said (qāla) | a speaker (qāilun) | among them (min'hum), | "Do not (lā) | kill (taqtulū) | Yusuf (yūsufa) | but throw him (wa-alqūhu) | in (fī) | the bottom (ghayābati) | of the well (l-jubi), | will pick him (yaltaqiṭ'hu) | some (baʿḍu) | [the] caravan (l-sayārati) | if (in) | you are (kuntum) | doing. (fāʿilīna)"

12:11 They said, "O our father! Why do you not trust us with Yusuf, while indeed, we are for him surely well-wishers?

They said (qālū), | "O our father (yāabānā)! | Why (mā) | do you (laka) | not (lā) | trust us (tamannā) | with (ʿalā) | Yusuf (yūsufa), | while indeed, we (wa-innā) | are for him (lahu) | surely well-wishers (lanāṣiḥūna)?

12:12 Send him with us tomorrow, to enjoy and play. And indeed, we for him will surely (be) guardians."

Send him (arsil'hu) | with us (maʿanā) | tomorrow (ghadan), | to enjoy (yartaʿ) | and play (wayalʿab). | And indeed, we (wa-innā) | for him (lahu) | will surely (be) guardians. (laḥāfiẓūna)"

12:13 He said, "Indeed, [I] it surely saddens me that you should take him and I fear that would eat him a wolf while you of him are unaware."

He said (qāla), | "Indeed, [I] (innī) | it surely saddens me (layaḥzununī) | that (an) | you should take him (tadhhabū) | you should take him (bihi) | and I fear (wa-akhāfu) | that (an) | would eat him (yakulahu) | a wolf (l-dhi'bu) | while you (wa-antum) | of him (ʿanhu) | are unaware. (ghāfilūna)"

12:14 They said, "If eats him the wolf while we are a group, indeed, we then surely would be losers."

They said (qālū), | "If (la-in) | eats him (akalahu) | the wolf (l-dhi'bu) | while we (wanaḥnu) | are a group (ʿuṣ'batun), | indeed, we (innā) | then (idhan) | surely would be losers. (lakhāsirūna)"

12:15 So when they took him and agreed that they put him in the bottom of the well. But We inspired to him, "Surely, you will inform them about this affair, while they do not perceive."

So when (falammā) | they took him (dhahabū) | they took him (bihi) | and agreed (wa-ajmaʿū) | that (an) | they put him (yajʿalūhu) | in (fī) | the bottom (ghayābati) | of the well (l-jubi). | But We inspired (wa-awḥaynā) | to him (ilayhi), | "Surely, you will inform them (latunabbi-annahum) | about this affair (bi-amrihim), | about this affair (hādhā), | while they (wahum) | do not (lā) | perceive. (yashʿurūna)"

12:16 And they came to their father early at night weeping.

And they came (wajāū) | to their father (abāhum) | early at night (ʿishāan) | weeping (yabkūna).

12:17 They said, "O our father! Indeed, we [we] went racing each other and we left Yusuf with our possessions, and ate him the wolf. But not you will believe us, even if we are truthful."

They said (qālū), | "O our father (yāabānā)! | Indeed, we (innā) | [we] went (dhahabnā) | racing each other (nastabiqu) | and we left (wataraknā) | Yusuf (yūsufa) | with (ʿinda) | our possessions (matāʿinā), | and ate him (fa-akalahu) | the wolf (l-dhi'bu). | But not (wamā) | you (anta) | will believe (bimu'minin) | us (lanā), | even if (walaw) | we are (kunnā) | truthful. (ṣādiqīna)"

12:18 And they brought upon his shirt with false blood. He said, "Nay, has enticed you your souls to a matter, so patience is beautiful. And Allah is the One sought for help against what you describe."

And they brought (wajāū) | upon (ʿalā) | his shirt (qamīṣihi) | with false blood (bidamin). | with false blood (kadhibin). | He said (qāla), | "Nay (bal), | has enticed you (sawwalat) | has enticed you (lakum) | your souls (anfusukum) | to a matter (amran), | so patience (faṣabrun) | is beautiful (jamīlun). | And Allah (wal-lahu) | is the One sought for help (l-mus'taʿānu) | against (ʿalā) | what (mā) | you describe. (taṣifūna)"

12:19 And there came a caravan and they sent their water drawer then he let down his bucket. He said, "O good news! This is a boy." And they hid him as a merchandise. And Allah is All-Knower of what they do.

And there came (wajāat) | a caravan (sayyāratun) | and they sent (fa-arsalū) | their water drawer (wāridahum) | then he let down (fa-adlā) | his bucket (dalwahu). | He said (qāla), | "O good news (yābush'rā)! | This (hādhā) | is a boy. (ghulāmun)" | And they hid him (wa-asarrūhu) | as a merchandise (biḍāʿatan). | And Allah (wal-lahu) | is All-Knower (ʿalīmun) | of what (bimā) | they do (yaʿmalūna).

12:20 And they sold him for a price very low, dirhams few, and they were about him of those keen to give up.

And they sold him (washarawhu) | for a price (bithamanin) | very low (bakhsin), | dirhams (darāhima) | few (maʿdūdatin), | and they were (wakānū) | about him (fīhi) | of (mina) | those keen to give up (l-zāhidīna).

12:21 And said the one who bought him of Egypt to his wife, "Make comfortable his stay. Perhaps that he will benefit us or we will take him as a son." And thus We established Yusuf in the land that We might teach him the interpretation of the events. And Allah is Predominant over His affairs, but most of the people do not know.

And said (waqāla) | the one who (alladhī) | bought him (ish'tarāhu) | of (min) | Egypt (miṣ'ra) | to his wife (li-im'ra-atihi), | "Make comfortable (akrimī) | his stay (mathwāhu). | Perhaps (ʿasā) | that (an) | he will benefit us (yanfaʿanā) | or (aw) | we will take him (nattakhidhahu) | as a son. (waladan)" | And thus (wakadhālika) | We established (makkannā) | Yusuf (liyūsufa) | in (fī) | the land (l-arḍi) | that We might teach him (walinuʿallimahu) | the interpretation of (min) | the interpretation of (tawīli) | the events (l-aḥādīthi). | And Allah (wal-lahu) | is Predominant (ghālibun) | over (ʿalā) | His affairs (amrihi), | but (walākinna) | most (akthara) | of the people (l-nāsi) | do not (lā) | know (yaʿlamūna).

12:22 And when he reached his maturity, We gave him wisdom and knowledge. And thus We reward the good-doers.

And when (walammā) | he reached (balagha) | his maturity (ashuddahu), | We gave him (ātaynāhu) | wisdom (ḥuk'man) | and knowledge (waʿil'man). | And thus (wakadhālika) | We reward (najzī) | the good-doers (l-muḥ'sinīna).

12:23 And sought to seduce him she who, he was in her house from his self. And she closed the doors and she said, "Come on you." He said, "I seek refuge in Allah. Indeed, he is my lord who has made good my stay. Indeed, not will succeed the wrongdoers."

And sought to seduce him (warāwadathu) | she who (allatī), | he was (huwa) | in (fī) | her house (baytihā) | from (ʿan) | his self (nafsihi). | And she closed (waghallaqati) | the doors (l-abwāba) | and she said (waqālat), | "Come on (hayta) | you. (laka)" | He said (qāla), | "I seek refuge in Allah (maʿādha). | "I seek refuge in Allah (l-lahi). | Indeed, he (innahu) | is my lord (rabbī) | who has made good (aḥsana) | my stay (mathwāya). | Indeed (innahu), | not (lā) | will succeed (yuf'liḥu) | the wrongdoers. (l-ẓālimūna)"

12:24 And certainly she did desire him, and he would have desired her, if not that he saw the proof of his Lord. Thus, that We might avert from him the evil and the immorality. Indeed, he was of Our slaves the sincere.

And certainly (walaqad) | she did desire (hammat) | him (bihi), | and he would have desired (wahamma) | her (bihā), | if not (lawlā) | that (an) | he saw (raā) | the proof (bur'hāna) | of his Lord (rabbihi). | Thus (kadhālika), | that We might avert (linaṣrifa) | from him (ʿanhu) | the evil (l-sūa) | and the immorality (wal-faḥshāa). | Indeed, he (innahu) | was of (min) | Our slaves (ʿibādinā) | the sincere (l-mukh'laṣīna).

12:25 And they both raced to the door and she tore his shirt from the back, and they both found her husband at the door. She said, "What is the recompense of one who intended for your wife evil except that he be imprisoned or a punishment painful?"

And they both raced (wa-is'tabaqā) | to the door (l-bāba) | and she tore (waqaddat) | his shirt (qamīṣahu) | from (min) | the back (duburin), | and they both found (wa-alfayā) | her husband (sayyidahā) | at (ladā) | the door (l-bābi). | She said (qālat), | "What (mā) | is the recompense (jazāu) | of one who (man) | intended (arāda) | for your wife (bi-ahlika) | evil (sūan) | except (illā) | that (an) | he be imprisoned (yus'jana) | or (aw) | a punishment (ʿadhābun) | painful? (alīmun)"

12:26 He said, "She sought to seduce me about myself." And testified a witness of her family "If [is] his shirt is torn from the front then she has spoken the truth, and he is of the liars.

He said (qāla), | "She (hiya) | sought to seduce me (rāwadatnī) | about (ʿan) | myself. (nafsī)" | And testified (washahida) | a witness (shāhidun) | of (min) | her family (ahlihā) | "If (in) | [is] (kāna) | his shirt (qamīṣuhu) | is torn (qudda) | from (min) | the front (qubulin) | then she has spoken the truth (faṣadaqat), | and he (wahuwa) | is of (mina) | the liars (l-kādhibīna).

12:27 But if [is] his shirt is torn from the back then she has lied and he is of the truthful."

But if (wa-in) | [is] (kāna) | his shirt (qamīṣuhu) | is torn (qudda) | from (min) | the back (duburin) | then she has lied (fakadhabat) | and he (wahuwa) | is of (mina) | the truthful. (l-ṣādiqīna)"

12:28 So when he saw his shirt torn from the back he said, "Indeed, it is of your plot. Indeed, your plot is great.

So when (falammā) | he saw (raā) | his shirt (qamīṣahu) | torn (qudda) | from (min) | the back (duburin) | he said (qāla), | "Indeed, it (innahu) | is of (min) | your plot (kaydikunna). | Indeed (inna), | your plot (kaydakunna) | is great (ʿaẓīmun).

12:29 Yusuf, turn away from this. And ask forgiveness for your sin. Indeed, you are of the sinful."

Yusuf (yūsufu), | turn away (aʿriḍ) | from (ʿan) | this (hādhā). | And ask forgiveness (wa-is'taghfirī) | for your sin (lidhanbiki). | Indeed, you (innaki) | are (kunti) | of (mina) | the sinful. (l-khāṭiīna)"

12:30 And said women in the city, "The wife of Aziz is seeking to seduce her slave boy about himself; indeed, he has impassioned her with love. Indeed, we [we] surely see her in an error clear."

And said (waqāla) | women (nis'watun) | in (fī) | the city (l-madīnati), | "The wife of (im'ra-atu) | Aziz (l-ʿazīzi) | is seeking to seduce (turāwidu) | her slave boy (fatāhā) | about (ʿan) | himself (nafsihi); | indeed (qad), | he has impassioned her (shaghafahā) | with love (ḥubban). | Indeed, we (innā) | [we] surely see her (lanarāhā) | in (fī) | an error (ḍalālin) | clear. (mubīnin)"

12:31 So when she heard of their scheming, she sent for them and she prepared for them a banquet and she gave each one of them a knife and she said, "Come out before them." Then when they saw him they greatly admired him, and cut their hands, they said, "Forbid Allah, not is this a man not is this but an angel noble."

So when (falammā) | she heard (samiʿat) | of their scheming (bimakrihinna), | she sent (arsalat) | for them (ilayhinna) | and she prepared (wa-aʿtadat) | for them (lahunna) | a banquet (muttaka-an) | and she gave (waātat) | each (kulla) | one (wāḥidatin) | of them (min'hunna) | a knife (sikkīnan) | and she said (waqālati), | "Come out (ukh'ruj) | before them. (ʿalayhinna)" | Then when (falammā) | they saw him (ra-aynahu) | they greatly admired him (akbarnahu), | and cut (waqaṭṭaʿna) | their hands (aydiyahunna), | they said (waqul'na), | "Forbid (ḥāsha) | Allah (lillahi), | not (mā) | is this (hādhā) | a man (basharan) | not (in) | is this (hādhā) | but (illā) | an angel (malakun) | noble. (karīmun)"

12:32 She said, "That is the one, you blamed me about him. And certainly I sought to seduce him, [from] [himself] but he saved himself, and if not he does what I order him, surely, he will be imprisoned and certainly will be of those who are disgraced."

She said (qālat), | "That (fadhālikunna) | is the one (alladhī), | you blamed me (lum'tunnanī) | about him (fīhi). | And certainly (walaqad) | I sought to seduce him (rāwadttuhu), | [from] (ʿan) | [himself] (nafsihi) | but he saved himself (fa-is'taʿṣama), | and if (wala-in) | not (lam) | he does (yafʿal) | what (mā) | I order him (āmuruhu), | surely, he will be imprisoned (layus'janannа) | and certainly will be (walayakūnan) | of (mina) | those who are disgraced. (l-ṣāghirīna)"

12:33 He said, "My Lord, the prison is dearer to me than what they invite me to it. And unless You turn away from me their plot I might incline towards them and [I] be of the ignorant."

He said (qāla), | "My Lord (rabbi), | the prison (l-sij'nu) | is dearer (aḥabbu) | to me (ilayya) | than what (mimmā) | they invite me (yadʿūnanī) | to it (ilayhi). | And unless (wa-illā) | You turn away (taṣrif) | from me (ʿannī) | their plot (kaydahunna) | I might incline (aṣbu) | towards them (ilayhinna) | and [I] be (wa-akun) | of (mina) | the ignorant. (l-jāhilīna)"

12:34 So responded to him his Lord, and turned away from him their plot. Indeed, [He] He is All-Hearer, All-Knower.

So responded (fa-is'tajāba) | to him (lahu) | his Lord (rabbuhu), | and turned away (faṣarafa) | from him (ʿanhu) | their plot (kaydahunna). | Indeed, [He] (innahu) | He (huwa) | is All-Hearer (l-samīʿu), | All-Knower (l-ʿalīmu).

12:35 Then it appeared to them after [what] they had seen the signs, surely they should imprison him until a time.

Then (thumma) | it appeared (badā) | to them (lahum) | after (min) | after (baʿdi) | [what] (mā) | they had seen (ra-awū) | the signs (l-āyāti), | surely they should imprison him (layasjununnahu) | until (ḥattā) | a time (ḥīnin).

12:36 And entered with him in the prison two young men. Said one of them, "Indeed, I [I] see myself pressing wine." And said the other, "Indeed, I [I] see myself [I am] carrying over my head bread, were eating the birds from it. Inform us of its interpretation; indeed, we [we] see you of the good-doers."

And entered (wadakhala) | with him (maʿahu) | in the prison (l-sij'na) | two young men (fatayāni). | Said (qāla) | one of them (aḥaduhumā), | "Indeed, I (innī) | [I] see myself (arānī) | pressing (aʿṣiru) | wine. (khamran)" | And said (waqāla) | the other (l-ākharu), | "Indeed, I (innī) | [I] see myself (arānī) | [I am] carrying (aḥmilu) | over (fawqa) | my head (rasī) | bread (khub'zan), | were eating (takulu) | the birds (l-ṭayru) | from it (min'hu). | Inform us (nabbi'nā) | of its interpretation (bitawīlihi); | indeed, we (innā) | [we] see you (narāka) | of (mina) | the good-doers. (l-muḥ'sinīna)"

12:37 He said, "Not will come to both of you food you are provided with but I will inform both of you of its interpretation, before [that] [it] comes to both of you. That is of what has taught me my Lord. Indeed, I [I] abandon the religion of a people, not they believe in Allah, and they in the Hereafter [they] are disbelievers.

He said (qāla), | "Not (lā) | will come to both of you (yatīkumā) | food (ṭaʿāmun) | you are provided with (tur'zaqānihi) | but (illā) | I will inform both of you (nabbatukumā) | of its interpretation (bitawīlihi), | before (qabla) | [that] (an) | [it] comes to both of you (yatiyakumā). | That (dhālikumā) | is of what (mimmā) | has taught me (ʿallamanī) | my Lord (rabbī). | Indeed, I (innī) | [I] abandon (taraktu) | the religion (millata) | of a people (qawmin), | not (lā) | they believe (yu'minūna) | in Allah (bil-lahi), | and they (wahum) | in the Hereafter (bil-ākhirati) | [they] (hum) | are disbelievers (kāfirūna).

12:38 And I follow the religion of my forefathers, Ibrahim, and Isaac and Yaqub. Not was for us that we associate with Allah any thing. That is from the Grace of Allah upon us, and upon the mankind but most of the men are not grateful.

And I follow (wa-ittabaʿtu) | the religion (millata) | of my forefathers (ābāī), | Ibrahim (ib'rāhīma), | and Isaac (wa-is'ḥāqa) | and Yaqub (wayaʿqūba). | Not (mā) | was (kāna) | for us (lanā) | that (an) | we associate (nush'rika) | with Allah (bil-lahi) | any (min) | thing (shayin). | That (dhālika) | is from (min) | the Grace (faḍli) | of Allah (l-lahi) | upon us (ʿalaynā), | and upon (waʿalā) | the mankind (l-nāsi) | but (walākinna) | most (akthara) | of the men (l-nāsi) | are not (lā) | grateful (yashkurūna).

12:39 O my two companions of the prison! Are lords separate better or Allah, the One the Irresistible?

O my two companions (yāṣāḥibayi) | of the prison (l-sij'ni)! | Are lords (a-arbābun) | separate (mutafarriqūna) | better (khayrun) | or (ami) | Allah (l-lahu), | the One (l-wāḥidu) | the Irresistible (l-qahāru)?

12:40 Not you worship besides Him but names which you have named them, you and your forefathers, not has sent down Allah for it any authority. Not is the command but for Allah. He has commanded that not you worship but Him Alone. That is the religion the right, but most [the] men do not know.

Not (mā) | you worship (taʿbudūna) | besides Him (min) | besides Him (dūnihi) | but (illā) | names (asmāan) | which you have named them (sammaytumūhā), | you (antum) | and your forefathers (waābāukum), | not (mā) | has sent down (anzala) | Allah (l-lahu) | for it (bihā) | any (min) | authority (sul'ṭānin). | Not (ini) | is the command (l-ḥuk'mu) | but (illā) | for Allah (lillahi). | He has commanded (amara) | that not (allā) | you worship (taʿbudū) | but (illā) | Him Alone (iyyāhu). | That (dhālika) | is the religion (l-dīnu) | the right (l-qayimu), | but (walākinna) | most (akthara) | [the] men (l-nāsi) | do not (lā) | know (yaʿlamūna).

12:41 O my two companions of the prison! As for one of you he will give drink to his master wine; and as for the other he will be crucified, and will eat the birds from his head. Has been decreed the matter about which you both inquire."

O my two companions (yāṣāḥibayi) | of the prison (l-sij'ni)! | As for (ammā) | one of you (aḥadukumā) | he will give drink (fayasqī) | to his master (rabbahu) | wine (khamran); | and as for (wa-ammā) | the other (l-ākharu) | he will be crucified (fayuṣ'labu), | and will eat (fatakulu) | the birds (l-ṭayru) | from (min) | his head (rasihi). | Has been decreed (quḍiya) | the matter (l-amru) | about which (alladhī) | about which (fīhi) | you both inquire. (tastaftiyāni)"

12:42 And he said to the one whom he thought that he would be saved of both of them, "Mention me to your master." But made him forget the Shaitaan the mention to his master, so he remained in the prison several years.

And he said (waqāla) | to the one whom (lilladhī) | he thought (ẓanna) | that he (annahu) | would be saved (nājin) | of both of them (min'humā), | "Mention me (udh'kur'nī) | to (ʿinda) | your master. (rabbika)" | But made him forget (fa-ansāhu) | the Shaitaan (l-shayṭānu) | the mention (dhik'ra) | to his master (rabbihi), | so he remained (falabitha) | in (fī) | the prison (l-sij'ni) | several (biḍ''a) | years (sinīna).

12:43 And said the king, "Indeed, I [I] have seen seven cows fat, eating them seven lean ones, and seven ears of corn green, and others dry. O chiefs! Explain to me about my vision if you can of visions interpret."

And said (waqāla) | the king (l-maliku), | "Indeed, I (innī) | [I] have seen (arā) | seven (sabʿa) | cows (baqarātin) | fat (simānin), | eating them (yakuluhunna) | seven (sabʿun) | lean ones (ʿijāfun), | and seven (wasabʿa) | ears of corn (sunbulātin) | green (khuḍ'rin), | and others (wa-ukhara) | dry (yābisātin). | O (yāayyuhā) | chiefs (l-mala-u)! | Explain to me (aftūnī) | about (fī) | my vision (ru'yāya) | if (in) | you can (kuntum) | of visions (lilrru'yā) | interpret. (taʿburūna)"

12:44 They said, "Confused dreams, and not we are in the interpretation of the dreams learned."

They said (qālū), | "Confused (aḍghāthu) | dreams (aḥlāmin), | and not (wamā) | we (naḥnu) | are in the interpretation (bitawīli) | of the dreams (l-aḥlāmi) | learned. (biʿālimīna)"

12:45 But said the one who was saved of the two and remembered after a period, "I [I] will inform you of its interpretation so send me forth.

But said (waqāla) | the one who (alladhī) | was saved (najā) | of the two (min'humā) | and remembered (wa-iddakara) | after (baʿda) | a period (ummatin), | "I (anā) | [I] will inform you (unabbi-ukum) | of its interpretation (bitawīlihi) | so send me forth (fa-arsilūni).

12:46 Yusuf, O the truthful one! Explain to us about the seven cows fat eating them seven lean ones, and seven ears of corn green and other dry, that I may return to the people so that they may know."

Yusuf (yūsufu), | O (ayyuhā) | the truthful one (l-ṣidīqu)! | Explain to us (aftinā) | about (fī) | the seven (sabʿi) | cows (baqarātin) | fat (simānin) | eating them (yakuluhunna) | seven (sabʿun) | lean ones (ʿijāfun), | and seven (wasabʿi) | ears of corn (sunbulātin) | green (khuḍ'rin) | and other (wa-ukhara) | dry (yābisātin), | that I may (laʿallī) | return (arjiʿu) | to (ilā) | the people (l-nāsi) | so that they may (laʿallahum) | know. (yaʿlamūna)"

12:47 He said, "You will sow for seven years, as usual, and that which you reap so leave it in its ears except a little from which you will eat.

He said (qāla), | "You will sow (tazraʿūna) | for seven (sabʿa) | years (sinīna), | as usual (da-aban), | and that which (famā) | you reap (ḥaṣadttum) | so leave it (fadharūhu) | in (fī) | its ears (sunbulihi) | except (illā) | a little (qalīlan) | from which (mimmā) | you will eat (takulūna).

12:48 Then will come after that seven hard years which will consume what you advanced for them, except a little of what you will store.

Then (thumma) | will come (yatī) | after (min) | after (baʿdi) | that (dhālika) | seven (sabʿun) | hard years (shidādun) | which will consume (yakul'na) | what (mā) | you advanced (qaddamtum) | for them (lahunna), | except (illā) | a little (qalīlan) | of what (mimmā) | you will store (tuḥ'ṣinūna).

12:49 Then will come after that a year in it will be given abundant rain the people and in it they will press."

Then (thumma) | will come (yatī) | after (min) | after (baʿdi) | that (dhālika) | a year (ʿāmun) | in it (fīhi) | will be given abundant rain (yughāthu) | the people (l-nāsu) | and in it (wafīhi) | they will press. (yaʿṣirūna)"

12:50 And said the king, "Bring him to me." But when came to him the messenger, he said, "Return to your lord, and ask him what is the case of the women who cut their hands. Indeed, my Lord of their plot is All-Knower."

And said (waqāla) | the king (l-maliku), | "Bring him to me. (i'tūnī)" | "Bring him to me. (bihi)" | But when (falammā) | came to him (jāahu) | the messenger (l-rasūlu), | he said (qāla), | "Return (ir'jiʿ) | to (ilā) | your lord (rabbika), | and ask him (fasalhu) | what (mā) | is the case (bālu) | of the women (l-nis'wati) | who (allātī) | cut (qaṭṭaʿna) | their hands (aydiyahunna). | Indeed (inna), | my Lord (rabbī) | of their plot (bikaydihinna) | is All-Knower. (ʿalīmun)"

12:51 He said, "What was your affair when you sought to seduce Yusuf from himself?" They said, "Allah forbid! Not we know about him any evil." Said the wife of Aziz, "Now is manifest the truth. I sought to seduce him from himself, and indeed, he is surely of the truthful.

He said (qāla), | "What (mā) | was your affair (khaṭbukunna) | when (idh) | you sought to seduce (rāwadttunna) | Yusuf (yūsufa) | from (ʿan) | himself? (nafsihi)" | They said (qul'na), | "Allah forbid (ḥāsha)! | "Allah forbid (lillahi)! | Not (mā) | we know (ʿalim'nā) | about him (ʿalayhi) | any (min) | evil. (sūin)" | Said (qālati) | the wife (im'ra-atu) | of Aziz (l-ʿazīzi), | "Now (l-āna) | is manifest (ḥaṣḥaṣa) | the truth (l-ḥaqu). | I (anā) | sought to seduce him (rāwadttuhu) | from (ʿan) | himself (nafsihi), | and indeed, he (wa-innahu) | is surely of (lamina) | the truthful (l-ṣādiqīna).

12:52 That he may know that I not [I] betray him in secret, and that Allah does not guide the plan of the betrayers."

That (dhālika) | he may know (liyaʿlama) | that I (annī) | not (lam) | [I] betray him (akhun'hu) | in secret (bil-ghaybi), | and that (wa-anna) | Allah (l-laha) | does not (lā) | guide (yahdī) | the plan (kayda) | of the betrayers. (l-khāinīna)"

12:53 "And not I absolve myself. Indeed, the soul is a certain enjoiner of evil, unless [that] bestows Mercy my Lord. Indeed, my Lord is Oft-Forgiving, Most Merciful."

"And not (wamā) | I absolve (ubarri-u) | myself (nafsī). | Indeed (inna), | the soul (l-nafsa) | is a certain enjoiner (la-ammāratun) | of evil (bil-sūi), | unless (illā) | [that] (mā) | bestows Mercy (raḥima) | my Lord (rabbī). | Indeed (inna), | my Lord (rabbī) | is Oft-Forgiving (ghafūrun), | Most

Merciful. (raḥīmun)"

12:54 And said the king, "Bring him to me; I will select him for myself." Then when he spoke to him, he said, "Indeed, you are today with us firmly established and trusted."

And said (waqāla) | the king (l-maliku), | "Bring him to me (i'tūnī); | "Bring him to me (bihi); | I will select him (astakhliṣ'hu) | for myself. (linafsī)" | Then when (falammā) | he spoke to him (kallamahu), | he said (qāla), | "Indeed, you (innaka) | are today (l-yawma) | with us (ladaynā) | firmly established (makīnun) | and trusted. (amīnun)"

12:55 He said, "Appoint me over the treasuries of the land. Indeed, I will be a guardian knowing."

He said (qāla), | "Appoint me (ij'ʿalnī) | over (ʿalā) | the treasuries (khazāini) | of the land (l-arḍi). | Indeed, I (innī) | will be a guardian (ḥafīẓun) | knowing. (ʿalīmun)"

12:56 And thus We established [to] Yusuf in the land to settle therein where ever he willed. We bestow Our Mercy on whom We will. And not We let go waste the reward of the good-doers.

And thus (wakadhālika) | We established (makkannā) | [to] Yusuf (liyūsufa) | in (fī) | the land (l-arḍi) | to settle (yatabawwa-u) | therein (min'hā) | where ever (ḥaythu) | he willed (yashāu). | We bestow (nuṣību) | Our Mercy (biraḥmatinā) | on whom (man) | We will (nashāu). | And not (walā) | We let go waste (nuḍīʿu) | the reward (ajra) | of the good-doers (l-muḥ'sinīna).

12:57 And surely the reward of the Hereafter is better for those who believe and are God conscious.

And surely the reward (wala-ajru) | of the Hereafter (l-ākhirati) | is better (khayrun) | for those who (lilladhīna) | believe (āmanū) | and are (wakānū) | God conscious (yattaqūna).

12:58 And came the brothers of Yusuf and they entered upon him; and he recognized them, but they knew him not.

And came (wajāa) | the brothers (ikh'watu) | of Yusuf (yūsufa) | and they entered (fadakhalū) | upon him (ʿalayhi); | and he recognized them (faʿarafahum), | but they (wahum) | knew him not (lahu). | knew him not (munkirūna).

12:59 And when he had furnished them with their supplies, he said, "Bring to me a brother of yours, from your father. Do not you see that I [I] give full [the] measure, and that I am the best of the hosts?

And when (walammā) | he had furnished them (jahhazahum) | with their supplies (bijahāzihim), | he said (qāla), | "Bring to me (i'tūnī) | a brother (bi-akhin) | of yours (lakum), | from (min) | your father (abīkum). | Do not (alā) | you see (tarawna) | that I (annī) | [I] give full (ūfī) | [the] measure (l-kayla), | and that I am (wa-anā) | the best (khayru) | of the hosts (l-munzilīna)?

12:60 But if not you bring him to me then there will be no measure for you from me, and not you will come near me."

But if (fa-in) | not (lam) | you bring him to me (tatūnī) | you bring him to me (bihi) | then there will be no (falā) | measure (kayla) | for you (lakum) | from me (ʿindī), | and not (walā) | you will come near me. (taqrabūni)"

12:61 They said, "We will try to get permission for him from his father, and indeed we, surely will do."

They said (qālū), | "We will try to get permission (sanurāwidu) | for him (ʿanhu) | from his father (abāhu), | and indeed we (wa-innā), | surely will do. (lafāʿilūna)"

12:62 And he said to his servants, "Put their merchandise in their saddlebags so that they may recognize it when they go back to their people so that they may return."

And he said (waqāla) | to his servants (lifit'yānihi), | "Put (ij'ʿalū) | their merchandise (biḍāʿatahum) | in (fī) | their saddlebags (riḥālihim) | so that they (laʿallahum) | may recognize it (yaʿrifūnahā) | when (idhā) | they go back (inqalabū) | to (ilā) | their people (ahlihim) | so that they may (laʿallahum) | return. (yarjiʿūna)"

12:63 So when they returned to their father, they said, "O our father! Has been denied to us the measure, so send with us our brother that we will get measure. And indeed, we for him will surely (be) guardians."

So when (falammā) | they returned (rajaʿū) | to (ilā) | their father (abīhim), | they said (qālū), | "O our father (yāabānā)! | Has been denied (muniʿa) | to us (minnā) | the measure (l-kaylu), | so send (fa-arsil) | with us (maʿanā) | our brother (akhānā) | that we will get measure (naktal). | And indeed, we (wa-innā) | for him (lahu) | will surely (be) guardians. (laḥāfiẓūna)"

12:64 He said, "Should I entrust you with him except as I entrusted you with his brother before? But Allah is the best Guardian and He is the Most Merciful of the merciful."

He said (qāla), | "Should (hal) | I entrust you (āmanukum) | with him (ʿalayhi) | except (illā) | as (kamā) | I entrusted you (amintukum) | with (ʿalā) | his brother (akhīhi) | before (min)? | before (qablu)? | But Allah (fal-lahu) | is the best (khayrun) | Guardian (ḥāfiẓan) | and He (wahuwa) | is the Most Merciful (arḥamu) | of the merciful. (l-rāḥimīna)"

12:65 And when they opened their baggage, they found their merchandise returned to them. They said, "O our father! What could we desire? This is our merchandise returned to us. And we will get provision for our family, and we will protect our brother and get an increase measure of a camel's (load). That is a measurement easy."

And when (walammā) | they opened (fataḥū) | their baggage (matāʿahum), | they found (wajadū) | their merchandise (biḍāʿatahum) | returned (ruddat) | to them (ilayhim). | They said (qālū), | "O our father (yāabānā)! | What (mā) | could we desire (nabghī)? | This (hādhihi) | is our merchandise (biḍāʿatunā) | returned (ruddat) | to us (ilaynā). | And we will get provision (wanamīru) | for our family (ahlanā), | and we will protect (wanaḥfaẓu) | our brother (akhānā) | and get an increase (wanazdādu) | measure (kayla) | of a camel's (load) (baʿīrin). | That (dhālika) | is a measurement (kaylun) | easy. (yasīrun)"

12:66 He said, "Never will I send him with you until you give to me a promise by Allah that surely you will bring him to me unless that you are surrounded." And when they had given him their promise, he said, "Allah over what we say is a Guardian."

He said (qāla), | "Never (lan) | will I send him (ur'silahu) | with you (maʿakum) | until (ḥattā) | you give to me (tu'tūni) | a promise (mawthiqan) | by (mina) | Allah (l-lahi) | that surely you will bring him to me (latatunnanī) | that surely you will bring him to me (bihi) | unless (illā) | that (an) | you are surrounded. (yuḥāṭa)" | you are surrounded. (bikum)" | And when (falammā) | they had given him (ātawhu) | their promise (mawthiqahum), | he said (qāla), | "Allah (l-lahu) | over (ʿalā) | what (mā) | we say (naqūlu) | is a Guardian. (wakīlun)"

12:67 And he said, "O my sons! Do not enter from one gate, but enter from gates different. And not I can avail you against Allah any thing. Not is the decision except with Allah, upon Him I put my trust and upon Him, let put their trust the ones who put trust."

And he said (waqāla), | "O my sons (yābaniyya)! | Do not (lā) | enter (tadkhulū) | from (min) | one gate (bābin), | one gate (wāḥidin), | but enter (wa-ud'khulū) | from (min) | gates (abwābin) | different (mutafarriqatin). | And not (wamā) | I can avail (ugh'nī) | you (ʿankum) | against (mina) | Allah (l-lahi) | any (min) | thing (shayin). | Not (ini) | is the decision (l-ḥuk'mu) | except (illā) | with Allah (lillahi), | upon Him (ʿalayhi) | I put my trust (tawakkaltu) | and upon Him (waʿalayhi), | let put their trust (falyatawakkali) | the ones who put trust. (l-mutawakilūna)"

12:68 And when they entered from where ordered them their father, not it availed them against

Allah any thing but it was a need of Yaqub's soul, which he carried out. And indeed, he was a possessor of knowledge because We had taught him, but most of the people do not know.

And when (walammā) | they entered (dakhalū) | from (min) | where (ḥaythu) | ordered them (amarahum) | their father (abūhum), | not (mā) | it (kāna) | availed (yugh'nī) | them (ʿanhum) | against (mina) | Allah (l-lahi) | any (min) | thing (shayin) | but (illā) | it was a need (ḥājatan) | of (fī) | Yaqub's soul (nafsi), | Yaqub's soul (yaʿqūba), | which he carried out (qaḍāhā). | And indeed, he (wa-innahu) | was a possessor (ladhū) | of knowledge (ʿil'min) | because (limā) | We had taught him (ʿallamnāhu), | but (walākinna) | most (akthara) | of the people (l-nāsi) | do not (lā) | know (yaʿlamūna).

12:69 And when they entered upon Yusuf, he took to himself his brother. He said, "Indeed, I [I] am your brother so do not grieve for what they used to do."

And when (walammā) | they entered (dakhalū) | upon (ʿalā) | Yusuf (yūsufa), | he took (āwā) | to himself (ilayhi) | his brother (akhāhu). | He said (qāla), | "Indeed, I (innī) | [I] am (anā) | your brother (akhūka) | so do not (falā) | grieve (tabta-is) | for what (bimā) | they used to (kānū) | do. (yaʿmalūna)"

12:70 So when he had furnished them with their supplies, he put the drinking cup in the bag of his brother. Then called out an announcer "O you in the caravan! Indeed, you surely are thieves."

So when (falammā) | he had furnished them (jahhazahum) | with their supplies (bijahāzihim), | he put (jaʿala) | the drinking cup (l-siqāyata) | in (fī) | the bag (raḥli) | of his brother (akhīhi). | Then (thumma) | called out (adhana) | an announcer (mu-adhinun) | "O you (ayyatuhā) | in the caravan (l-ʿīru)! | Indeed, you (innakum) | surely are thieves. (lasāriqūna)"

12:71 They said turning towards them, "What is it you miss?"

They said (qālū) | turning towards (wa-aqbalū) | them (ʿalayhim), | "What is it (mādhā) | you miss? (tafqidūna)"

12:72 They said, "We are missing the cup of the king. And for one who brings it, is a load of a camel, and I for it is responsible."

They said (qālū), | "We are missing (nafqidu) | the cup (ṣuwāʿa) | of the king (l-maliki). | And for one who (waliman) | brings (jāa) | it (bihi), | is a load (ḥim'lu) | of a camel (baʿīrin), | and I (wa-anā) | for it (bihi) | is responsible. (zaʿīmun)"

12:73 They said, "By Allah certainly you know, not we came that we cause corruption in the land, and not we are thieves."

They said (qālū), | "By Allah (tal-lahi) | certainly (laqad) | you know (ʿalim'tum), | not (mā) | we came (ji'nā) | that we cause corruption (linuf'sida) | in (fī) | the land (l-arḍi), | and not (wamā) | we are (kunnā) | thieves. (sāriqīna)"

12:74 They said, "Then what will be the recompense (of) it if you are liars."

They said (qālū), | "Then what (famā) | will be the recompense (of) it (jazāuhu) | if (in) | you are (kuntum) | liars. (kādhibīna)"

12:75 They said, "Its recompense is that one who, it is found in his bag, then he will be his recompense. Thus do we recompense the wrongdoers."

They said (qālū), | "Its recompense (jazāuhu) | is that one who (man), | it is found (wujida) | in (fī) | his bag (raḥlihi), | then he (fahuwa) | will be his recompense (jazāuhu). | Thus (kadhālika) | do we recompense (najzī) | the wrongdoers. (l-ẓālimīna)"

12:76 So he began with their bags before the bag of his brother; then he brought it out from the bag of his brother. Thus did We plan for Yusuf. He could not take his brother by the law of the king, except that Allah willed. We raise in degrees whom We will, but over every possessor of knowledge is the All-Knower.

So he began (fabada-a) | with their bags (bi-awʿiyatihim) | before (qabla) | the bag (wiʿāi) | of his brother (akhīhi); | then (thumma) | he brought it out (is'takhrajahā) | from (min) | the bag (wiʿāi) | of his brother (akhīhi). | Thus (kadhālika) | did We plan (kid'nā) | for Yusuf (liyūsufa). | He could not (mā) | He could not (kāna) | take (liyakhudha) | his brother (akhāhu) | by (fī) | the law (dīni) | of the king (l-maliki), | except (illā) | that (an) | Allah willed (yashāa). | Allah willed (l-lahu). | We raise (narfaʿu) | in degrees (darajātin) | whom (man) | We will (nashāu), | but over (wafawqa) | every (kulli) | possessor (dhī) | of knowledge (ʿil'min) | is the All-Knower (ʿalīmun).

12:77 They said, "If he steals - then verily stole a brother of his before." But Yusuf kept it secret within himself, and did not reveal it to them. He said, "You are the worse in position, and Allah knows best of what you describe."

They said (qālū), | "If (in) | he steals (yasriq)- | then verily (faqad) | stole (saraqa) | a brother (akhun) | of his (lahu) | before. (min)" | before. (qablu)" | But Yusuf kept it secret (fa-asarrahā) | But Yusuf kept it secret (yūsufu) | within (fī) | himself (nafsihi), | and did not (walam) | reveal it (yub'dihā) | to them (lahum). | He said (qāla), | "You (antum) | are the worse (sharrun) | in position (makānan), | and Allah (wal-lahu) | knows best (aʿlamu) | of what (bimā) | you describe. (taṣifūna)"

12:78 They said, "O Aziz! Indeed, he has a father old [great], so take one of us in his place. Indeed, we [we] see you of the good-doers."

They said (qālū), | "O (yāayyuhā) | Aziz (l-ʿazīzu)! | Indeed (inna), | he has (lahu) | a father (aban) | old (shaykhan) | [great] (kabīran), | so take (fakhudh) | one of us (aḥadanā) | in his place (makānahu). | Indeed, we (innā) | [we] see you (narāka) | of (mina) | the good-doers. (l-muḥ'sinīna)"

12:79 He said, "Allah forbid that we take except one who, we found our possession with him. Indeed, we then surely would be wrongdoers."

He said (qāla), | "Allah forbid (maʿādha) | "Allah forbid (l-lahi) | that (an) | we take (nakhudha) | except (illā) | one who (man), | we found (wajadnā) | our possession (matāʿanā) | with him (ʿindahu). | Indeed, we (innā) | then (idhan) | surely would be wrongdoers. (laẓālimūna)"

12:80 So when they despaired of him, they secluded themselves in private consultation. Said the eldest among them, "Do not you know that your father, has taken upon you a promise by Allah, and before that you failed concerning Yusuf? So never will I leave the land until permits me my father or Allah decides for me, and He is the Best of the judges.

So when (falammā) | they despaired (is'tayasū) | of him (min'hu), | they secluded themselves (khalaṣū) | in private consultation (najiyyan). | Said (qāla) | the eldest among them (kabīruhum), | "Do not (alam) | you know (taʿlamū) | that (anna) | your father (abākum), | has taken (qad) | has taken (akhadha) | upon you (ʿalaykum) | a promise (mawthiqan) | by (mina) | Allah (l-lahi), | and before (wamin) | and before (qablu) | that (mā) | you failed (farraṭtum) | concerning (fī) | Yusuf (yūsufa)? | So never (falan) | will I leave (abraḥa) | the land (l-arḍa) | until (ḥattā) | permits (yadhana) | me (lī) | my father (abī) | or (aw) | Allah decides (yaḥkuma) | Allah decides (l-lahu) | for me (lī), | and He (wahuwa) | is the Best (khayru) | of the judges (l-ḥākimīna).

12:81 Return to your father and say, 'O our father! Indeed, your son has stolen, and not we testify except of what we knew. And not we were of the unseen guardians.

Return (ir'jiʿū) | to (ilā) | your father (abīkum) | and say (faqūlū), | 'O our father (yāabānā)! | Indeed (inna), | your son (ib'naka) | has stolen (saraqa), | and not (wamā) | we testify (shahid'nā) | except (illā) | of what (bimā) | we knew (ʿalim'nā). | And not (wamā) | we were (kunnā) | of the unseen (lil'ghaybi) | guardians (ḥāfiẓīna).

12:82 And ask the town where we were [in it], and the caravan which we returned [in it]. And indeed, we surely are truthful.'"

And ask (wasali) | the town (l-qaryata) | where (allatī) | we were (kunnā) | [in it] (fīhā), | and the caravan (wal-ʿīra) | which (allatī) | we returned (aqbalnā) | [in it] (fīhā). | And indeed, we (wa-innā) | surely are truthful.' (laṣādiqūna)"

12:83 He said, "Nay, have enticed you your souls something, so patience is beautiful. Perhaps Allah, will bring them to me all. Indeed, He He is the All-Knower, All-Wise."

He said (qāla), | "Nay (bal), | have enticed (sawwalat) | you (lakum) | your souls (anfusukum) | something (amran), | so patience (faṣabrun) | is beautiful (jamīlun). | Perhaps (ʿasā) | Allah (l-lahu), | will bring them to me (an) | will bring them to me (yatiyanī) | will bring them to me (bihim) | all (jamīʿan). | Indeed, He (innahu) | He (huwa) | is the All-Knower (l-ʿalīmu), | All-Wise. (l-ḥakīmu)"

12:84 And he turned away from them and said, "Alas, my grief over Yusuf!" And became white his eyes from the grief, and he was a suppressor.

And he turned away (watawallā) | from them (ʿanhum) | and said (waqāla), | "Alas, my grief (yāasafā) | over (ʿalā) | Yusuf! (yūsufa)" | And became white (wa-ib'yaḍḍat) | his eyes (ʿaynāhu) | from (mina) | the grief (l-ḥuz'ni), | and he was (fahuwa) | a suppressor (kaẓīmun).

12:85 They said, "By Allah, you will not cease remembering Yusuf until you become fatally ill or become of those who perish."

They said (qālū), | "By Allah (tal-lahi), | you will not cease (tafta-u) | remembering (tadhkuru) | Yusuf (yūsufa) | until (ḥattā) | you become (takūna) | fatally ill (ḥaraḍan) | or (aw) | become (takūna) | of (mina) | those who perish. (l-hālikīna)"

12:86 He said, "Only I complain of my suffering and my grief to Allah, and I know from Allah what not you know.

He said (qāla), | "Only (innamā) | I complain (ashkū) | of my suffering (bathī) | and my grief (waḥuz'nī) | to (ilā) | Allah (l-lahi), | and I know (wa-aʿlamu) | from (mina) | Allah (l-lahi) | what (mā) | not (lā) | you know (taʿlamūna).

12:87 O my sons! Go and inquire about Yusuf and his brother, and not despair of the Mercy of Allah. Indeed, none despairs of the Mercy of Allah except the people the disbelievers."

O my sons (yābaniyya)! | Go (idh'habū) | and inquire (fataḥassasū) | about (min) | Yusuf (yūsufa) | and his brother (wa-akhīhi), | and not (walā) | despair (tāy'asū) | of (min) | the Mercy of Allah (rawḥi). | the Mercy of Allah (l-lahi). | Indeed (innahu), | none (lā) | despairs (yāy'asu) | of (min) | the Mercy of Allah (rawḥi) | the Mercy of Allah (l-lahi) | except (illā) | the people (l-qawmu) | the disbelievers. (l-kāfirūna)"

12:88 So when they entered upon him they said, "O Aziz! Has touched us and our family the adversity, and we have come with goods of little value, but pay in full to us the measure and be charitable to us. Indeed, Allah rewards the charitable."

So when (falammā) | they entered (dakhalū) | upon him (ʿalayhi) | they said (qālū), | "O Aziz (yāayyuhā)! | "O Aziz (l-ʿazīzu)! | Has touched us (massanā) | and our family (wa-ahlanā) | the adversity (l-ḍuru), | and we have come (waji'nā) | with goods (bibiḍāʿatin) | of little value (muz'jātin), | but pay in full (fa-awfi) | to us (lanā) | the measure (l-kayla) | and be charitable (wataṣaddaq) | to us (ʿalaynā). | Indeed (inna), | Allah (l-laha) | rewards (yajzī) | the charitable. (l-mutaṣadiqīna)"

12:89 He said, "Do you know what you did with Yusuf and his brother, when you were ignorant?"

He said (qāla), | "Do (hal) | you know (ʿalim'tum) | what (mā) | you did (faʿaltum) | with Yusuf (biyūsufa) | and his brother (wa-akhīhi), | when (idh) | you were (antum) | ignorant? (jāhilūna)"

12:90 They said, "Are you indeed, surely you, Yusuf?" He said, "I am Yusuf and this is my brother. Indeed, Allah has been gracious to us. Indeed, he who fears Allah and is patient, then indeed, Allah does not let go waste the reward of the good-doers."

They said (qālū), | "Are you indeed (a-innaka), | surely you (la-anta), | Yusuf? (yūsufu)" | He said (qāla), | "I am (anā) | Yusuf (yūsufu) | and this (wahādhā) | is my brother (akhī). | Indeed (qad), | Allah has been gracious (manna) | Allah has been gracious (l-lahu) | to us (ʿalaynā). | Indeed, he (innahu) | who (man) | fears Allah (yattaqi) | and is patient (wayaṣbir), | then indeed (fa-inna), | Allah (l-laha) | does not (lā) | let go waste (yuḍīʿu) | the reward (ajra) | of the good-doers. (l-muḥ'sinīna)"

12:91 They said, "By Allah, certainly Allah has preferred you over us and indeed, we have been sinners."

They said (qālū), | "By Allah (tal-lahi), | certainly (laqad) | Allah has preferred you (ātharaka) | Allah has preferred you (l-lahu) | over us (ʿalaynā) | and indeed (wa-in), | we have been (kunnā) | sinners. (lakhāṭiīna)"

12:92 He said, "No blame upon you today. Allah will forgive you, and He is the Most Merciful of those who show mercy.

He said (qāla), | "No (lā) | blame (tathrība) | upon you (ʿalaykumu) | today (l-yawma). | Allah will forgive (yaghfiru) | Allah will forgive (l-lahu) | you (lakum), | and He (wahuwa) | is the Most Merciful (arḥamu) | of those who show mercy (l-rāḥimīna).

12:93 Go with this shirt of mine and cast it over the face of my father, he will regain sight. And bring to me your family all together."

Go (idh'habū) | with this shirt of mine (biqamīṣī) | with this shirt of mine (hādhā) | and cast it (fa-alqūhu) | over (ʿalā) | the face (wajhi) | of my father (abī), | he will regain sight (yati). | he will regain sight (baṣīran). | And bring to me (watūnī) | your family (bi-ahlikum) | all together. (ajmaʿīna)"

12:94 And when departed the caravan, their father said, "Indeed, I [I] find the smell of Yusuf, if not that you think me weakened in mind."

And when (walammā) | departed (faṣalati) | the caravan (l-ʿīru), | their father said (qāla), | their father said (abūhum), | "Indeed, I (innī) | [I] find (la-ajidu) | the smell (rīḥa) | of Yusuf (yūsufa), | if not (lawlā) | that (an) | you think me weakened in mind. (tufannidūni)"

12:95 They said, "By Allah indeed, you surely are in your error old."

They said (qālū), | "By Allah (tal-lahi) | indeed, you (innaka) | surely are in (lafī) | your error (ḍalālika) | old. (l-qadīmi)"

12:96 Then when [that] arrived the bearer of glad tidings, he cast it over his face, then returned his sight. He said, "Did not I say to you, indeed, I [I] know from Allah what not you know?"

Then when (falammā) | [that] (an) | arrived (jāa) | the bearer of glad tidings (l-bashīru), | he cast it (alqāhu) | over (ʿalā) | his face (wajhihi), | then returned his sight (fa-ir'tadda). | then returned his sight (baṣīran). | He said (qāla), | "Did not (alam) | I say (aqul) | to you (lakum), | indeed, I (innī) | [I] know (aʿlamu) | from (mina) | Allah (l-lahi) | what (mā) | not (lā) | you know? (taʿlamūna)"

12:97 They said, "O our father! Ask forgiveness for us of our sins. Indeed, we have been sinners."

They said (qālū), | "O our father (yāabānā)! | Ask forgiveness (is'taghfir) | for us (lanā) | of our sins (dhunūbanā). | Indeed, we (innā) | have been (kunnā) | sinners. (khāṭiīna)"

12:98 He said, "Soon I will ask forgiveness for you from my Lord. Indeed, He, He is the Oft-Forgiving, the Most Merciful."

He said (qāla), | "Soon (sawfa) | I will ask forgiveness (astaghfiru) | for you (lakum) | from my Lord (rabbī). | Indeed, He (innahu), | He (huwa) | is the Oft-Forgiving (l-ghafūru), | the Most Merciful. (l-raḥīmu)"

12:99 Then when they entered upon Yusuf, he took to himself his parents and said, "Enter Egypt if Allah wills, safe."

Then when (falammā) | they entered (dakhalū) | upon (ʿalā) | Yusuf (yūsufa), | he took (āwā) | to himself (ilayhi) | his parents (abawayhi) | and said (waqāla), | "Enter (ud'khulū) | Egypt (miṣ'ra) | if (in) | Allah wills (shāa), | Allah wills (l-lahu), | safe. (āminīna)"

12:100 And he raised his parents upon the throne and they fell down to him prostrate. And he said, "O my father! This is the interpretation of my dream, of before. Verily, has made it my Lord true. And indeed, He was good to me when He took me out of the prison, and brought you from the bedouin life after [that] had caused discord the Shaitaan between me and between my brothers. Indeed, my Lord is Most Subtle to what He wills. Indeed, He, He is the All-Knower, the All-Wise.

And he raised (warafaʿa) | his parents (abawayhi) | upon (ʿalā) | the throne (l-ʿarshi) | and they fell down (wakharrū) | to him (lahu) | prostrate (sujjadan). | And he said (waqāla), | "O my father (yāabati)! | This (hādhā) | is the interpretation (tawīlu) | of my dream (ru'yāya), | of before (min). | of before (qablu). | Verily (qad), | has made it (jaʿalahā) | my Lord (rabbī) | true (ḥaqqan). | And indeed (waqad), | He was good (aḥsana) | to me (bī) | when (idh) | He took me out (akhrajanī) | of (mina) | the prison (l-sij'ni), | and brought (wajāa) | you (bikum) | from (mina) | the bedouin life (l-badwi) | after (min) | after (baʿdi) | [that] (an) | had caused discord (nazagha) | the Shaitaan (l-shayṭānu) | between me (baynī) | and between (wabayna) | my brothers (ikh'watī). | Indeed (inna), | my Lord (rabbī) | is Most Subtle (laṭīfun) | to what (limā) | He wills (yashāu). | Indeed, He (innahu), | He (huwa) | is the All-Knower (l-ʿalīmu), | the All-Wise (l-ḥakīmu).

12:101 My Lord, indeed, you have given me of the sovereignty and taught me of the interpretation of the events. Creator of the heavens and the earth, You are my Protector, in the world and the Hereafter. Cause me to die as a Muslim, and join me with the righteous."

My Lord (rabbi), | indeed (qad), | you have given me (ātaytanī) | of (mina) | the sovereignty (l-mul'ki) | and taught me (waʿallamtanī) | of (min) | the interpretation (tawīli) | of the events (l-aḥādīthi). | Creator (fāṭira) | of the heavens (l-samāwāti) | and the earth (wal-arḍi), | You (anta) | are my Protector (waliyyī), | in (fī) | the world (l-dun'yā) | and the Hereafter (wal-ākhirati). | Cause me to die (tawaffanī) | as a Muslim (mus'liman), | and join me (wa-alḥiq'nī) | with the righteous. (bil-ṣāliḥīna)"

12:102 That is from the news of the unseen which We reveal to you. And not you were with them when they put together their plan while they were plotting.

That (dhālika) | is from (min) | the news (anbāi) | of the unseen (l-ghaybi) | which We reveal (nūḥīhi) | to you (ilayka). | And not (wamā) | you were (kunta) | with them (ladayhim) | when (idh) | they put together (ajmaʿū) | their plan (amrahum) | while they (wahum) | were plotting (yamkurūna).

12:103 And not most of the mankind, even though you desire, will be believers.

And not (wamā) | most (aktharu) | of the mankind (l-nāsi), | even though (walaw) | you desire (ḥaraṣta), | will be believers (bimu'minīna).

12:104 And not you ask them for it any reward. Not is it but a reminder to the worlds.

And not (wamā) | you ask them (tasaluhum) | for it (ʿalayhi) | any (min) | reward (ajrin). | Not (in) | is it (huwa) | but (illā) | a reminder (dhik'run) | to the worlds (lil'ʿālamīna).

12:105 And how many of a Sign in the heavens and the earth they pass over it, while they are from them the ones who turn away.

And how many (waka-ayyin) | of (min) | a Sign (āyatin) | in (fī) | the heavens (l-samāwāti) | and the earth (wal-arḍi) | they pass (yamurrūna) | over it (ʿalayhā), | while they (wahum) | are from them (ʿanhā) | the ones who turn away (muʿriḍūna).

12:106 And not believe most of them in Allah except while they associate partners with Him.

And not (wamā) | believe (yu'minu) | most of them (aktharuhum) | in Allah (bil-lahi) | except (illā) | while they (wahum) | associate partners with Him (mush'rikūna).

12:107 Do they then feel secure against that comes to them an overwhelming [of] punishment of Allah, or comes to them the Hour suddenly while they do not perceive?

Do they then feel secure (afa-aminū) | against that (an) | comes to them (tatiyahum) | an overwhelming (ghāshiyatun) | [of] (min) | punishment (ʿadhābi) | of Allah (l-lahi), | or (aw) | comes to them (tatiyahumu) | the Hour (l-sāʿatu) | suddenly (baghtatan) | while they (wahum) | do not (lā) | perceive (yashʿurūna)?

12:108 Say, "This is my way; I invite to Allah, with insight, I and whoever follows me. And Glory be to Allah and not I am of the polytheists."

Say (qul), | "This (hādhihi) | is my way (sabīlī); | I invite (adʿū) | to (ilā) | Allah (l-lahi), | with (ʿalā) | insight (baṣīratin), | I (anā) | and whoever (wamani) | follows me (ittabaʿanī). | And Glory be (wasub'ḥāna) | to Allah (l-lahi) | and not (wamā) | I am (anā) | of (mina) | the polytheists. (l-mush'rikīna)"

12:109 And not We sent before you, but men We revealed to them from among the people of the townships. So have not they traveled in the earth and seen how was the end of those who were before them? And surely the home of the Hereafter is best for those who fear Allah. Then will not you use reason?

And not (wamā) | We sent (arsalnā) | before you (min), | before you (qablika), | but (illā) | men (rijālan) | We revealed (nūḥī) | to them (ilayhim) | from among (min) | the people (ahli) | of the townships (l-qurā). | So have not (afalam) | they traveled (yasīrū) | in (fī) | the earth (l-arḍi) | and seen (fayanẓurū) | how (kayfa) | was (kāna) | the end (ʿāqibatu) | of those who (alladhīna) | were before them (min)? | were before them (qablihim)? | And surely the home (waladāru) | of the Hereafter (l-ākhirati) | is best (khayrun) | for those who (lilladhīna) | fear Allah (ittaqaw). | Then will not (afalā) | you use reason (taʿqilūna)?

12:110 Until when gave up hope the Messengers, and thought that they certainly were denied, then came to them Our help, and was saved whom We willed. And not can be repelled Our punishment from the people who are criminals.

Until (ḥattā) | when (idhā) | gave up hope (is'tayasa) | the Messengers (l-rusulu), | and thought (waẓannū) | that they (annahum) | certainly (qad) | were denied (kudhibū), | then came to them (jāahum) | Our help (naṣrunā), | and was saved (fanujjiya) | whom (man) | We willed (nashāu). | And not (walā) | can be repelled (yuraddu) | Our punishment (basunā) | from (ʿani) | the people (l-qawmi) | who are criminals (l-muj'rimīna).

12:111 Verily, there is in their stories a lesson for men of understanding. Not it is a narration invented, but a confirmation of that which was before it and a detailed explanation of all things, and a guidance and mercy for a people who believe.

Verily (laqad), | there is (kāna) | in (fī) | their stories (qaṣaṣihim) | a lesson (ʿib'ratun) | for men (li-ulī) | of understanding (l-albābi). | Not (mā) | it is (kāna) | a narration (ḥadīthan) | invented (yuf'tarā), | but (walākin) | a confirmation (taṣdīqa) | of that which (alladhī) | was before it (bayna) | was before it (yadayhi) | and a detailed explanation (watafṣīla) | of all (kulli) | things (shayin), | and a guidance (wahudan) | and mercy (waraḥmatan) | for a people (liqawmin) | who believe (yu'minūna).

Chapter (13) Sūrat l-Raʿd (The Thunder)

13:1 Alif Laam Mim Ra. These are the Verses of the Book. And that which has been revealed to you from your Lord is the truth, but most of the mankind do not believe.

Alif Laam Mim Ra (alif-lam-meem-ra). | These (til'ka) | are the Verses (āyātu) | of the Book (l-kitābi). | And that which (wa-alladhī) | has been revealed (unzila) | to you (ilayka) | from (min) | your Lord (rabbika) | is the truth (l-ḥaqu), | but (walākinna) | most (akthara) | of the mankind (l-nāsi) | do not (lā) | believe (yu'minūna).

13:2 Allah is the One Who raised the heavens without pillars that you see, then He established on the Throne and subjected the sun and the moon each running for a term appointed, He arranges the matter; He details the Signs so that you may in the meeting with your Lord believe with certainty.

Allah (al-lahu) | is the One Who (alladhī) | raised (rafaʿa) | the heavens (l-samāwāti) | without (bighayri) | pillars (ʿamadin) | that you see (tarawnahā), | then (thumma) | He established (is'tawā) | on (ʿalā) | the Throne (l-ʿarshi) | and subjected (wasakhara) | the sun (l-shamsa) | and the moon (wal-qamara) | each (kullun) | running (yajrī) | for a term (li-ajalin) | appointed (musamman), | He arranges (yudabbiru) | the matter (l-amra); | He details (yufaṣṣilu) | the Signs (l-āyāti) | so that you may (laʿallakum) | in the meeting (biliqāi) | with your Lord (rabbikum) | believe with certainty (tūqinūna).

13:3 And He is the One Who spread the earth, and placed in it firm mountains and rivers, and from all of the fruits He made in it pairs two. He covers the night with the day. Indeed, in that surely are Signs for a people who ponder.

And He (wahuwa) | is the One Who (alladhī) | spread (madda) | the earth (l-arḍa), | and placed (wajaʿala) | in it (fīhā) | firm mountains (rawāsiya) | and rivers (wa-anhāran), | and from (wamin) | all (kulli) | of the fruits (l-thamarāti) | He made (jaʿala) | in it (fīhā) | pairs (zawjayni) | two (ith'nayni). | He covers (yugh'shī) | the night (al-layla) | with the day (l-nahāra). | Indeed (inna), | in (fī) | that (dhālika) | surely are Signs (laāyātin) | for a people (liqawmin) | who ponder (yatafakkarūna).

13:4 And in the earth are tracks neighboring, and gardens of grapevines and crops and date-palms trees growing from a single root and not trees growing from a single root. watered with water, one; but We cause to exceed some of them over others in the fruit. Indeed, in that surely are Signs for a people who use reason.

And in (wafī) | the earth (l-arḍi) | are tracks (qiṭaʿun) | neighboring (mutajāwirātun), | and gardens (wajannātun) | of (min) | grapevines (aʿnābin) | and crops (wazarʿun) | and date-palms (wanakhīlun) | trees growing from a single root (ṣin'wānun) | and not (waghayru) | trees growing from a single root (ṣin'wānin). | watered (yus'qā) | with water (bimāin), | one (wāḥidin); | but We cause to exceed (wanufaḍḍilu) | some of them (baʿḍahā) | over (ʿalā) | others (baʿḍin) | in (fī) | the fruit (l-ukuli). | Indeed (inna), | in (fī) | that (dhālika) | surely are Signs (laāyātin) | for a people (liqawmin) | who use reason (yaʿqilūna).

13:5 And if you are astonished, then astonishing is their saying, "When we are dust, will we be indeed, in a creation new?" Those are the ones who disbelieved in their Lord, and those the iron chains will be in their necks, those are the companions of the Fire, they in it will abide forever.

And if (wa-in) | you are astonished (taʿjab), | then astonishing (faʿajabun) | is their saying (qawluhum), | "When (a-idhā) | we are (kunnā) | dust (turāban), | will we (a-innā) | be indeed, in (lafī) | a creation (khalqin) | new? (jadīdin)" | Those (ulāika) | are the ones who (alladhīna) | disbelieved (kafarū) | in their Lord (birabbihim), | and those (wa-ulāika) | the iron chains (l-aghlālu) | will be in (fī) | their necks (aʿnāqihim), | those (wa-ulāika) | are the companions (aṣḥābu) | of the Fire (l-nāri), | they (hum) | in it (fīhā) | will abide forever (khālidūna).

13:6 And they ask you to hasten the evil before the good and verily has occurred from before them [the] similar punishments. And indeed, your Lord is full of forgiveness for mankind for their wrongdoing, and indeed, your Lord is severe in the penalty.

And they ask you to hasten (wayastaʿjilūnaka) | the evil (bil-sayi-ati) | before (qabla) | the good (l-ḥasanati) | and verily (waqad) | has occurred (khalat) | from (min) | before them (qablihimu) | [the] similar punishments (l-mathulātu). | And indeed (wa-inna), | your Lord (rabbaka) | is full (ladhū) | of forgiveness (maghfiratin) | for mankind (lilnnāsi) | for (ʿalā) | their wrongdoing (ẓul'mihim), | and indeed (wa-inna), | your Lord (rabbaka) | is severe (lashadīdu) | in the penalty (l-ʿiqābi).

13:7 And say those who disbelieved, "Why not has been sent down to him a sign from his Lord?" Only you are a warner, and for every people is a guide.

And say (wayaqūlu) | those who (alladhīna) | disbelieved (kafarū), | "Why not (lawlā) | has been sent down (unzila) | to him (ʿalayhi) | a sign (āyatun) | from (min) | his Lord? (rabbihi)" | Only (innamā) | you (anta) | are a warner (mundhirun), | and for every (walikulli) | people (qawmin) | is a guide (hādin).

13:8 Allah knows what carries every female, and what fall short the womb, and what they exceed. And every thing with Him is in due proportion.

Allah (al-lahu) | knows (yaʿlamu) | what (mā) | carries (taḥmilu) | every (kullu) | female (unthā), | and what (wamā) | fall short (taghīḍu) | the womb (l-arḥāmu), | and what (wamā) | they exceed (tazdādu). | And every (wakullu) | thing (shayin) | with Him (ʿindahu) | is in due proportion (bimiq'dārin).

13:9 Knower of the unseen and the witnessed, the Most Great, the Most High.

Knower (ʿālimu) | of the unseen (l-ghaybi) | and the witnessed (wal-shahādati), | the Most Great (l-kabīru), | the Most High (l-mutaʿāli).

13:10 It is same (to Him) [of you] one who conceals the speech or one who publicizes it and one who [he] is hidden by night or goes freely by day.

It is same (to Him (sawāon)) | [of you] (minkum) | one who (man) | conceals (asarra) | the speech (l-qawla) | or one who (waman) | publicizes (jahara) | it (bihi) | and one who (waman) | [he] (huwa) | is hidden (mus'takhfin) | by night (bi-al-layli) | or goes freely (wasāribun) | by day (bil-nahāri).

13:11 For him are successive (Angels) from before him and from and behind him, who guard him by the command of Allah. Indeed, Allah does not change the condition of a people, until they change what is in themselves. And when wills Allah for a people misfortune, then there is no turning away of it, and not for them from besides Him any protector.

For him (lahu) | are successive (Angels (muʿaqqibātun)) | from (min) | before (bayni) | him (yadayhi) | and from (wamin) | and behind him (khalfihi), | who guard him (yaḥfaẓūnahu) | by (min) | the command (amri) | of Allah (l-lahi). | Indeed (inna), | Allah (l-laha) | does not (lā) | change (yughayyiru) | the condition (mā) | of a people (biqawmin), | until (ḥattā) | they change (yughayyirū) | what (mā) | is in themselves (bi-anfusihim). | And when (wa-idhā) | wills (arāda) | Allah (l-lahu) | for a people (biqawmin) | misfortune (sūan), | then there is no (falā) | turning away (maradda) | of it (lahu), | and not (wamā) | for them (lahum) | from (min) | besides Him (dūnihi) | any (min) | protector (wālin).

13:12 He is the One Who shows you the lightning, a fear and a hope and brings up the clouds, the heavy.

He (huwa) | is the One Who (alladhī) | shows you (yurīkumu) | the lightning (l-barqa), | a fear (khawfan) | and a hope (waṭamaʿan) | and brings up (wayunshi-u) | the clouds (l-saḥāba), | the heavy (l-thiqāla).

13:13 And glorifies the thunder with his praise - and the Angels for fear of Him. And He sends the thunderbolts and strikes with it whom He wills, yet they dispute about Allah. And He is Mighty in Strength.

And glorifies (wayusabbiḥu) | the thunder (l-raʿdu) | with his praise (biḥamdihi)- | and the Angels (wal-malāikatu) | for (min) | fear of Him (khīfatihi). | And He sends (wayur'silu) | the thunderbolts (l-ṣawāʿiqa) | and strikes (fayuṣību) | with it (bihā) | whom (man) | He wills (yashāu), | yet they (wahum) | dispute (yujādilūna) | about (fī) | Allah (l-lahi). | And He (wahuwa) | is Mighty (shadīdu) | in Strength (l-miḥāli).

13:14 To Him is supplication of the truth. And those whom they invoke besides Him not they respond to them with a thing except like one who stretches his hands towards water to reach his mouth, but not it reaches it. And not is the supplication of the disbelievers but in error.

To Him (lahu) | is supplication (daʿwatu) | of the truth (l-ḥaqi). | And those whom (wa-alladhīna) | they invoke (yadʿūna) | besides Him (min) | besides Him (dūnihi) | not (lā) | they respond (yastajībūna) | to them (lahum) | with a thing (bishayin) | except (illā) | like one who stretches (kabāsiṭi) | his hands (kaffayhi) | towards (ilā) | water (l-māi) | to reach (liyablugha) | his mouth (fāhu), | but not (wamā) | it (huwa) | reaches it (bibālighihi). | And not (wamā) | is the supplication (duʿāu) | of the disbelievers (l-kāfirīna) | but (illā) | in (fī) | error (ḍalālin).

13:15 And to Allah prostrates whoever is in the heavens and the earth, willingly or unwillingly, and so do their shadows in the mornings and in the afternoons.

And to Allah (walillahi) | prostrates (yasjudu) | whoever (man) | is in (fī) | the heavens (l-samāwāti) | and the earth (wal-arḍi), | willingly (ṭawʿan) | or unwillingly (wakarhan), | and so do their shadows (waẓilāluhum) | in the mornings (bil-ghuduwi) | and in the afternoons (wal-āṣāli).

13:16 Say, "Who is the Lord of the heavens and the earth?" Say, "Allah." Say, "Have you then taken from besides Him, protectors, not they have power for themselves to benefit and not to harm?" Say, "Is equal the blind and the seeing? Or is equal the darkness[es] and the light? Or they attribute to Allah partners who created like His creation, so that seemed alike the creation to them?" Say, "Allah is the Creator of all things, and He is the One the Irresistible."

Say (qul), | "Who (man) | is the Lord (rabbu) | of the heavens (l-samāwāti) | and the earth? (wal-arḍi)" | Say (quli), | "Allah. (l-lahu)" | Say (qul), | "Have you then taken (afa-ittakhadhtum) | from (min) | besides Him (dūnihi), | protectors (awliyāa), | not (lā) | they have power (yamlikūna) | for themselves (li-anfusihim) | to benefit (nafʿan) | and not (walā) | to harm? (ḍarran)" | Say (qul), |

"Is (hal) | equal (yastawī) | the blind (l-aʿmā) | and the seeing (wal-baṣīru)? | Or (am) | is (hal) | equal (tastawī) | the darkness[es] (l-ẓulumātu) | and the light (wal-nūru)? | Or (am) | they attribute (jaʿalū) | to Allah (lillahi) | partners (shurakāa) | who created (khalaqū) | like His creation (kakhalqihi), | so that seemed alike (fatashābaha) | the creation (l-khalqu) | to them? (ʿalayhim)" | Say (quli), | "Allah (l-lahu) | is the Creator (khāliqu) | of all (kulli) | things (shayin), | and He (wahuwa) | is the One (l-wāḥidu) | the Irresistible. (l-qahāru)"

13:17 He sends down from the sky water and flows the valleys according to their measure, and carries the torrent a foam rising. And from what they heat [on] it in the fire in order to make ornaments or utensils, a foam like it. Thus sets forth Allah the truth and the falsehood. Then as for the foam it passes away as scum, and as for what benefits the mankind, remains in the earth. Thus Allah sets forth the examples.

He sends down (anzala) | from (mina) | the sky (l-samāi) | water (māan) | and flows (fasālat) | the valleys (awdiyatun) | according to their measure (biqadarihā), | and carries (fa-iḥ'tamala) | the torrent (l-saylu) | a foam (zabadan) | rising (rābiyan). | And from what (wamimmā) | they heat (yūqidūna) | [on] it (ʿalayhi) | in (fī) | the fire (l-nāri) | in order to make (ib'tighāa) | ornaments (ḥil'yatin) | or (aw) | utensils (matāʿin), | a foam (zabadun) | like it (mith'luhu). | Thus (kadhālika) | sets forth (yaḍribu) | Allah (l-lahu) | the truth (l-ḥaqa) | and the falsehood (wal-bāṭila). | Then as for (fa-ammā) | the foam (l-zabadu) | it passes away (fayadhhabu) | as scum (jufāan), | and as for (wa-ammā) | what (mā) | benefits (yanfaʿu) | the mankind (l-nāsa), | remains (fayamkuthu) | in (fī) | the earth (l-arḍi). | Thus (kadhālika) | Allah sets forth (yaḍribu) | Allah sets forth (l-lahu) | the examples (l-amthāla).

13:18 For those who responded to their Lord is the bliss. And for those who did not respond to Him, if that they had whatever is in the earth all and like of it with it, surely they would offer ransom with it. Those for them is a terrible reckoning, and their abode is Hell, and wretched is the resting place.

For those who (lilladhīna) | responded (is'tajābū) | to their Lord (lirabbihimu) | is the bliss (l-ḥus'na). | And for those who (wa-alladhīna) | did not (lam) | respond (yastajībū) | to Him (lahu), | if (law) | that (anna) | they had (lahum) | whatever (mā) | is in (fī) | the earth (l-arḍi) | all (jamīʿan) | and like of it (wamith'lahu) | with it (maʿahu), | surely they would offer ransom (la-if'tadaw) | with it (bihi). | Those (ulāika) | for them (lahum) | is a terrible (sūu) | reckoning (l-ḥisābi), | and their abode (wamawāhum) | is Hell (jahannamu), | and wretched (wabi'sa) | is the resting place (l-mihādu).

13:19 Then is he who knows that which has been revealed to you from your Lord is the truth like one who [he] is blind? Only pay heed men of understanding.

Then is he who (afaman) | knows (yaʿlamu) | that which (annamā) | has been revealed (unzila) | to you (ilayka) | from (min) | your Lord (rabbika) | is the truth (l-ḥaqu) | like one who (kaman) | [he] (huwa) | is blind (aʿmā)? | Only (innamā) | pay heed (yatadhakkaru) | men (ulū) | of understanding (l-albābi).

13:20 Those who fulfill the covenant of Allah and not they break the contract,

Those who (alladhīna) | fulfill (yūfūna) | the covenant (biʿahdi) | of Allah (l-lahi) | and not (walā) | they break (yanquḍūna) | the contract (l-mīthāqa),

13:21 And those who join what has been commanded by Allah [for it] to be joined, and fear their Lord and are afraid of the evil the account,

And those who (wa-alladhīna) | join (yaṣilūna) | what (mā) | has been commanded (amara) | by Allah (l-lahu) | [for it] (bihi) | to (an) | be joined (yūṣala), | and fear (wayakhshawna) | their Lord (rabbahum) | and are afraid (wayakhāfūna) | of the evil (sūa) | the account (l-ḥisābi),

13:22 And those who are patient, seeking the Face of their Lord and establish the prayer and spend from what We have provided them, secretly and publicly and they repel with the good the evil - those for them is the final attainment of the Home -

And those who (wa-alladhīna) | are patient (ṣabarū), | seeking (ib'tighāa) | the Face (wajhi) | of their Lord (rabbihim) | and establish (wa-aqāmū) | the prayer (l-ṣalata) | and spend (wa-anfaqū) | from what (mimmā) | We have provided them (razaqnāhum), | secretly (sirran) | and publicly (waʿalāniyatan) | and they repel (wayadraūna) | with the good (bil-ḥasanati) | the evil (l-sayi-ata)- | those (ulāika) | for them (lahum) | is the final attainment (ʿuq'bā) | of the Home (l-dāri)-

13:23 Gardens of Eden, they will enter them and whoever were righteous among their fathers and their spouses, and their offsprings. And the Angels will enter upon them from every gate,

Gardens (jannātu) | of Eden (ʿadnin), | they will enter them (yadkhulūnahā) | and whoever (waman) | were righteous (ṣalaḥa) | among (min) | their fathers (ābāihim) | and their spouses (wa-azwājihim), | and their offsprings (wadhurriyyātihim). | And the Angels (wal-malāikatu) | will enter (yadkhulūna) | upon them (ʿalayhim) | from (min) | every (kulli) | gate (bābin),

13:24 Saying, "Peace be upon you for what you patiently endured. And excellent is the final attainment of the Home."

Saying, "Peace (salāmun) | be upon you (ʿalaykum) | for what (bimā) | you patiently endured (ṣabartum). | And excellent (faniʿʿma) | is the final attainment (ʿuq'bā) | of the Home. (l-dāri)"

13:25 And those who break the covenant of Allah from after contracting it, and sever what has been commanded by Allah for it to be joined and spread corruption in the earth. Those - for them is the curse, and for them is an evil home.

And those who (wa-alladhīna) | break (yanquḍūna) | the covenant (ʿahda) | of Allah (l-lahi) | from (min) | after (baʿdi) | contracting it (mīthāqihi), | and sever (wayaqṭaʿūna) | what (mā) | has been commanded (amara) | by Allah (l-lahu) | for it (bihi) | to (an) | be joined (yūṣala) | and spread corruption (wayuf'sidūna) | in (fī) | the earth (l-arḍi). | Those (ulāika)- | for them (lahumu) | is the curse (l-laʿnatu), | and for them (walahum) | is an evil (sūu) | home (l-dāri).

13:26 Allah extends the provision for whom He wills and restricts. And they rejoice in the life of the world and nothing is the life of the world in comparison to the Hereafter, except an enjoyment.

Allah (al-lahu) | extends (yabsuṭu) | the provision (l-riz'qa) | for whom (liman) | He wills (yashāu) | and restricts (wayaqdiru). | And they rejoice (wafariḥū) | in the life (bil-ḥayati) | of the world (l-dun'yā) | and nothing (wamā) | is the life (l-ḥayatu) | of the world (l-dun'yā) | in comparison to (fī) | the Hereafter (l-ākhirati), | except (illā) | an enjoyment (matāʿun).

13:27 And say those who disbelieved, "Why has not been sent down upon him a Sign from his Lord?" Say, "Indeed, Allah lets go astray whom He wills and guides to Himself whoever turns back,

And say (wayaqūlu) | those who (alladhīna) | disbelieved (kafarū), | "Why has not (lawlā) | been sent down (unzila) | upon him (ʿalayhi) | a Sign (āyatun) | from (min) | his Lord? (rabbihi)" | Say (qul), | "Indeed (inna), | Allah (l-laha) | lets go astray (yuḍillu) | whom (man) | He wills (yashāu) | and guides (wayahdī) | to Himself (ilayhi) | whoever (man) | turns back (anāba),

13:28 Those who believed and find satisfaction their hearts in the remembrance of Allah. No doubt, in the remembrance of Allah find satisfaction the hearts."

Those who (alladhīna) | believed (āmanū) | and find satisfaction (wataṭma-innu) | their hearts (qulūbuhum) | in the remembrance (bidhik'ri) | of Allah (l-lahi). | No doubt (alā), | in the remembrance (bidhik'ri) | of Allah (l-lahi) | find satisfaction (taṭma-innu) | the hearts. (l-qulūbu)"

13:29 Those who believed and did righteous deeds, blessedness is for them and a beautiful place of return.

Those who (alladhīna) | believed (āmanū) | and did (waʿamilū) | righteous deeds (l-ṣāliḥāti), | blessedness (ṭūbā) | is for them (lahum) | and a beautiful (waḥus'nu) | place of return (maābin).

13:30 Thus We have sent you to a nation verily have passed away from before it nations, so that you might recite to them what We revealed to you, while they disbelieve in the Most Gracious. Say, "He is my Lord, there is no god except Him. Upon Him I put my trust and to Him is my return."

Thus (kadhālika) | We have sent you (arsalnāka) | to (fī) | a nation (ummatin) | verily (qad) | have passed away (khalat) | from (min) | before it (qablihā) | nations (umamun), | so that you might recite (litatluwā) | to them (ʿalayhimu) | what (alladhī) | We revealed (awḥaynā) | to you (ilayka), | while they (wahum) | disbelieve (yakfurūna) | in the Most Gracious (bil-raḥmāni). | Say (qul), | "He (huwa) | is my Lord (rabbī), | there is no (lā) | god (ilāha) | except (illā) | Him (huwa). | Upon Him (ʿalayhi) | I put my trust (tawakkaltu) | and to Him (wa-ilayhi) | is my return. (matābi)"

13:31 And if that was any Quran, could be moved by it the mountains, or could be cloven asunder by it the earth, or could be made to speak by it the dead. Nay, with Allah is the command all. Then do not know those who believe that if had willed Allah, surely, He would have guided all? all of the mankind? And not will cease those who disbelieve to strike them for what they did a disaster, or it settles close from their homes until comes the promise of Allah. Indeed, Allah will not fail in the Promise.

And if (walaw) | that was (anna) | any Quran (qur'ānan), | could be moved (suyyirat) | by it (bihi) | the mountains (l-jibālu), | or (aw) | could be cloven asunder (quṭṭiʿat) | by it (bihi) | the earth (l-arḍu), | or (aw) | could be made to speak (kullima) | by it (bihi) | the dead (l-mawtā). | Nay (bal), | with Allah (lillahi) | is the command (l-amru) | all (jamīʿan). | Then do not (afalam) | know (yāy'asi) | those who (alladhīna) | believe (āmanū) | that (an) | if (law) | had willed (yashāu) | Allah (l-lahu), | surely, He would have guided (lahadā) | all (l-nāsa)? | all of the mankind (jamīʿan)? | And not (walā) | will cease (yazālu) | those who (alladhīna) | disbelieve (kafarū) | to strike them (tuṣībuhum) | for what (bimā) | they did (ṣanaʿū) | a disaster (qāriʿatun), | or (aw) | it settles (taḥullu) | close (qarīban) | from (min) | their homes (dārihim) | until (ḥattā) | comes (yatiya) | the promise (waʿdu) | of Allah (l-lahi). | Indeed (inna), | Allah (l-laha) | will not (lā) | fail (yukh'lifu) | in the Promise (l-mīʿāda).

13:32 And certainly, were mocked Messengers from before you, but I granted respite to those who disbelieved; then I seized them, and how was My penalty.

And certainly (walaqadi), | were mocked (us'tuh'zi-a) | Messengers (birusulin) | from (min) | before you (qablika), | but I granted respite (fa-amlaytu) | to those who (lilladhīna) | disbelieved (kafarū); | then (thumma) | I seized them (akhadhtuhum), | and how (fakayfa) | was (kāna) | My penalty (ʿiqābi).

13:33 Is then He Who He is a Maintainer of every soul for what it has earned? Yet they ascribe to Allah partners. Say, "Name them. Or do you inform Him of what not He knows in the earth or of the apparent of the words?" Nay, is made fair-seeming to those who disbelieve their plotting, and they are hindered from the Path. And whoever by Allah Allah lets go astray then not for him any guide.

Is then He Who (afaman) | He (huwa) | is a Maintainer (qāimun) | of (ʿalā) | every (kulli) | soul (nafsin) | for what (bimā) | it has earned (kasabat)? | Yet they ascribe (wajaʿalū) | to Allah (lillahi) | partners (shurakāa). | Say (qul), | "Name them (sammūhum). | Or (am) | do you inform Him (tunabbiūnahu) | of what (bimā) | not (lā) | He knows (yaʿlamu) | in (fī) | the earth (l-arḍi) | or (am) | of the apparent (biẓāhirin) | of (mina) | the words? (l-qawli)" | Nay (bal), | is made fair-seeming (zuyyina) | to those who (lilladhīna) | disbelieve (kafarū) | their plotting (makruhum), | and they are hindered (waṣuddū) | from (ʿani) | the Path (l-sabīli). | And whoever (waman) | by Allah (yuḍ'lili) | Allah lets go astray (l-lahu) | then not (famā) | for him (lahu) | any (min) | guide (hādin).

13:34 For them is a punishment in the life of the world and surely the punishment of the Hereafter is harder. And not for them against Allah any defender.

For them (lahum) | is a punishment (ʿadhābun) | in (fī) | the life (l-ḥayati) | of the world (l-dun'yā) | and surely the punishment (walaʿadhābu) | of the Hereafter (l-ākhirati) | is harder (ashaqqu). | And not (wamā) | for them (lahum) | against (mina) | Allah (l-lahi) | any (min) | defender (wāqin).

13:35 The example of Paradise which is promised to the righteous, flows from underneath it the rivers. Its food is everlasting, and its shade. This is the end of those who are righteous, and the end of the disbelievers is the Fire.

The example (mathalu) | of Paradise (l-janati) | which (allatī) | is promised (wuʿida) | to the righteous (l-mutaqūna), | flows (tajrī) | from (min) | underneath it (taḥtihā) | the rivers (l-anhāru). | Its food (ukuluhā) | is everlasting (dāimun), | and its shade (waẓilluhā). | This (til'ka) | is the end (ʿuq'bā) | of those who (alladhīna) | are righteous (ittaqaw), | and the end (waʿuq'bā) | of the disbelievers (l-kāfirīna) | is the Fire (l-nāru).

13:36 And those to whom We have given them the Book, rejoice at what has been revealed to you, but among the groups those who deny a part of it. Say, "Only I have been commanded that I worship Allah, and not I associate partners with Him. To Him I call and to Him is my return."

And those to whom (wa-alladhīna) | We have given them (ātaynāhumu) | the Book (l-kitāba), | rejoice (yafraḥūna) | at what (bimā) | has been revealed (unzila) | to you (ilayka), | but among (wamina) | the groups (l-aḥzābi) | those who (man) | deny (yunkiru) | a part of it (baʿḍahu). | Say (qul), | "Only (innamā) | I have been commanded (umir'tu) | that (an) | I worship (aʿbuda) | Allah (l-laha), | and not (walā) | I associate partners (ush'rika) | with Him (bihi). | To Him (ilayhi) | I call (adʿū) | and to Him (wa-ilayhi) | is my return. (maābi)"

13:37 And thus We have revealed it to be a judgment of authority in Arabic. And if you follow their desires after what came to you of the knowledge, not for you against Allah any protector and not defender.

And thus (wakadhālika) | We have revealed it (anzalnāhu) | to be a judgment of authority (ḥuk'man) | in Arabic (ʿarabiyyan). | And if (wala-ini) | you follow (ittabaʿta) | their desires (ahwāahum) | after what (baʿdamā) | came to you (jāaka) | of (mina) | the knowledge (l-ʿil'mi), | not (mā) | for you (laka) | against (mina) | Allah (l-lahi) | any (min) | protector (waliyyin) | and not (walā) | defender (wāqin).

13:38 And certainly, We sent Messengers from before you and We made for them wives and offspring. And not was for a Messenger that he comes with a sign except by the leave of Allah. For everything is a time prescribed.

And certainly (walaqad), | We sent (arsalnā) | Messengers (rusulan) | from (min) | before you (qablika) | and We made (wajaʿalnā) | for them (lahum) | wives (azwājan) | and offspring (wadhurriyyatan). | And not (wamā) | was (kāna) | for a Messenger (lirasūlin) | that (an) | he comes (yatiya) | with a sign (biāyatin) | except (illā) | by the leave (bi-idh'ni) | of Allah (l-lahi). | For everything (likulli) | is a time (ajalin) | prescribed (kitābun).

13:39 Is eliminated by Allah what He wills, and confirms, and with Him is the Mother (of) the Book.

Is eliminated (yamḥū) | by Allah (l-lahu) | what (mā) | He wills (yashāu), | and confirms (wayuth'bitu), | and with Him (waʿindahu) | is the Mother (of) the Book (ummu). | is the Mother (of) the Book (l-kitābi).

13:40 And whether what We show you a part of what We have promised them or We cause you to die, so only on you is the conveyance, and on Us is the reckoning.

And whether (wa-in) | what (mā) | We show you (nuriyannaka) | a part (baʿḍa) | of what (alladhī) | We have promised them (naʿiduhum) | or (aw) | We cause you to die (natawaffayannaka), | so only (fa-innamā) | on you (ʿalayka) | is the conveyance (l-balāghu), | and on Us (waʿalaynā) | is the reckoning (l-ḥisābu).

13:41 Did not they see that We come to the land, reducing it from its borders? And Allah judges; there is no adjuster of His Judgment. And He is Swift in the reckoning.

Did not (awalam) | they see (yaraw) | that We (annā) | come (natī) | to the land (l-arḍa), | reducing it (nanquṣuhā) | from (min) | its borders (aṭrāfihā)? | And Allah (wal-lahu) | judges (yaḥkumu); | there is no (lā) | adjuster (muʿaqqiba) | of His Judgment (liḥuk'mihi). | And He (wahuwa) | is Swift (sarīʿu) | in the reckoning (l-ḥisābi).

13:42 And certainly plotted those who were from before them, but for Allah is the plot all. He knows what earns every soul, and will know the disbelievers for whom is the final the home.

And certainly (waqad) | plotted (makara) | those who (alladhīna) | were from (min) | before them (qablihim), | but for Allah (falillahi) | is the plot (l-makru) | all (jamīʿan). | He knows (yaʿlamu) | what (mā) | earns (taksibu) | every (kullu) | soul (nafsin), | and will know (wasayaʿlamu) | the disbelievers (l-kufāru) | for whom (liman) | is the final (ʿuq'bā) | the home (l-dāri).

13:43 And say those who disbelieve, "You are not a Messenger." Say, "Sufficient is Allah as a Witness between me and between you, and whoever [he] has knowledge of the Book."

And say (wayaqūlu) | those who (alladhīna) | disbelieve (kafarū), | "You are not (lasta) | a Messenger. (mur'salan)" | Say (qul), | "Sufficient (kafā) | is Allah (bil-lahi) | as a Witness (shahīdan) | between me (baynī) | and between you (wabaynakum), | and whoever (waman) | [he] has (ʿindahu) | knowledge (ʿil'mu) | of the Book. (l-kitābi)"

Chapter (14) Sūrat Ib'rāhīm (Abraham)

14:1 Alif Laam Ra. A Book which We have revealed to you, so that you may bring out the mankind from the darkness[es] to the light by the permission of their Lord, to the Path of the All-Mighty, the Praiseworthy.

Alif Laam Ra (alif-lam-ra). | A Book (kitābun) | which We have revealed (anzalnāhu) | to you (ilayka), | so that you may bring out (litukh'rija) | the mankind (l-nāsa) | from (mina) | the darkness[es] (l-ẓulumāti) | to (ilā) | the light (l-nūri) | by the permission (bi-idh'ni) | of their Lord (rabbihim), | to (ilā) | the Path (ṣirāṭi) | of the All-Mighty (l-ʿazīzi), | the Praiseworthy (l-ḥamīdi).

14:2 Allah is the One to Him belongs whatever is in the heavens and whatever is in the earth. And woe to the disbelievers from the punishment severe.

Allah (al-lahi) | is the One (alladhī) | to Him belongs (lahu) | whatever (mā) | is in (fī) | the heavens (l-samāwāti) | and whatever (wamā) | is in (fī) | the earth (l-arḍi). | And woe (wawaylun) | to the disbelievers (lil'kāfirīna) | from (min) | the punishment (ʿadhābin) | severe (shadīdin).

14:3 Those who love more the life of the world than the Hereafter, and hinder from the Path of Allah, and seek in it crookedness, those [in] are far astray.

Those who (alladhīna) | love more (yastaḥibbūna) | the life (l-ḥayata) | of the world (l-dun'yā) | than (ʿalā) | the Hereafter (l-ākhirati), | and hinder (wayaṣuddūna) | from (ʿan) | the Path (sabīli) | of Allah (l-lahi), | and seek in it (wayabghūnahā) | crookedness (ʿiwajan), | those (ulāika) | [in] (fī) | are far astray (ḍalālin). | are far astray (baʿīdin).

14:4 And not We sent any Messenger except with the language of his people so that he might make clear for them. Then Allah lets go astray whom He wills and guides whom He wills. And He is the All-Mighty, the All-Wise.

And not (wamā) | We sent (arsalnā) | any (min) | Messenger (rasūlin) | except (illā) | with the language (bilisāni) | of his people (qawmihi) | so that he might make clear (liyubayyina) | for them (lahum). | Then Allah lets go astray (fayuḍillu) | Then Allah lets go astray (l-lahu) | whom (man) | He wills (yashāu) | and guides (wayahdī) | whom (man) | He wills (yashāu). | And He (wahuwa) | is the All-Mighty (l-ʿazīzu), | the All-Wise (l-ḥakīmu).

14:5 And verily We sent Musa with Our Signs, that "Bring out your people from the darkness[es] to the light. And remind them of the days of Allah." Indeed, in that surely are the signs for everyone patient and thankful.

And verily (walaqad) | We sent (arsalnā) | Musa (mūsā) | with Our Signs (biāyātinā), | that (an) | "Bring out (akhrij) | your people (qawmaka) | from (mina) | the darkness[es] (l-ẓulumāti) | to (ilā) | the light (l-nūri). | And remind them (wadhakkir'hum) | of the days (bi-ayyāmi) | of Allah. (l-lahi)" | Indeed (inna), | in (fī) | that (dhālika) | surely are the signs (laāyātin) | for everyone (likulli) | patient (ṣabbārin) | and thankful (shakūrin).

14:6 And when said Musa to his people, "Remember the Favor of Allah upon you, when He saved you from the people of Firaun, they were afflicting you with evil torment and were slaughtering your sons and letting live your women. And in that was a trial from your Lord great."

And when (wa-idh) | said (qāla) | Musa (mūsā) | to his people (liqawmihi), | "Remember (udh'kurū) | the Favor of Allah (niʿ'mata) | the Favor of Allah (l-lahi) | upon you (ʿalaykum), | when (idh) | He saved you (anjākum) | from (min) | the people (āli) | of Firaun (firʿ'awna), | they were afflicting you (yasūmūnakum) | with evil (sūa) | torment (l-ʿadhābi) | and were slaughtering (wayudhabbiḥūna) | your sons (abnāakum) | and letting live (wayastaḥyūna) | your women (nisāakum). | And in (wafī) | that (dhālikum) | was a trial (balāon) | from (min) | your Lord (rabbikum) | great. (ʿaẓīmun)"

14:7 And when proclaimed your Lord, "If you are thankful, surely I will increase you; but if you are ungrateful indeed, My punishment is surely severe."

And when (wa-idh) | proclaimed (ta-adhana) | your Lord (rabbukum), | "If (la-in) | you are thankful (shakartum), | surely I will increase you (la-azīdannakum); | but if (wala-in) | you are ungrateful (kafartum) | indeed (inna), | My punishment (ʿadhābī) | is surely severe. (lashadīdun)"

14:8 And said Musa, "If you disbelieve, you and whoever is in the earth all, then indeed, Allah certainly is Free of need, Praiseworthy."

And said (waqāla) | Musa (mūsā), | "If (in) | you disbelieve (takfurū), | you (antum) | and whoever (waman) | is in (fī) | the earth (l-arḍi) | all (jamīʿan), | then indeed (fa-inna), | Allah (l-laha) | certainly is Free of need (laghaniyyun), | Praiseworthy. (ḥamīdun)"

14:9 Has not come to you the news of those who were before you, the people of Nuh, and Aad and Thamud and those who were after them? None knows them except Allah. Came to them their Messengers with clear proofs but they returned their hands in their mouths and they said, "Indeed we [we] disbelieve in what you have been sent with [it], and indeed, we are surely in doubt about what you invite us to it suspicious."

Has not (alam) | come to you (yatikum) | the news (naba-u) | of those who (alladhīna) |

were before you (min), | were before you (qablikum), | the people (qawmi) | of Nuh (nūḥin), | and Aad (waʿādin) | and Thamud (wathamūda) | and those who (wa-alladhīna) | were after them (min)? | were after them (baʿdihim)? | None (lā) | knows them (yaʿlamuhum) | except (illā) | Allah (l-lahu). | Came to them (jāathum) | their Messengers (rusuluhum) | with clear proofs (bil-bayināti) | but they returned (faraddū) | their hands (aydiyahum) | in (fī) | their mouths (afwāhihim) | and they said (waqālū), | "Indeed we (innā) | [we] disbelieve (kafarnā) | in what (bimā) | you have been sent (ur'sil'tum) | with [it] (bihi), | and indeed, we (wa-innā) | are surely in (lafī) | doubt (shakkin) | about what (mimmā) | you invite us (tadʿūnanā) | to it (ilayhi) | suspicious. (murībin)"

14:10 Said their Messengers, "Can there be about Allah any doubt, the Creator of the heavens and the earth? He invites you, so that He may forgive for you [of] your sins, and give you respite for a term appointed." They said, "Not you are but a human like us, you wish to hinder us from what used to worship our forefathers. So bring us an authority clear."

Said (qālat) | their Messengers (rusuluhum), | "Can there be about (afī) | Allah (l-lahi) | any doubt (shakkun), | the Creator (fāṭiri) | of the heavens (l-samāwāti) | and the earth (wal-arḍi)? | He invites you (yadʿūkum), | so that He may forgive (liyaghfira) | for you (lakum) | [of] (min) | your sins (dhunūbikum), | and give you respite (wayu-akhirakum) | for (ilā) | a term (ajalin) | appointed. (musamman)" | They said (qālū), | "Not (in) | you (antum) | are but (illā) | a human (basharun) | like us (mith'lunā), | you wish (turīdūna) | to (an) | hinder us (taṣuddūnā) | from what (ʿammā) | used to (kāna) | worship (yaʿbudu) | our forefathers (ābāunā). | So bring us (fatūnā) | an authority (bisul'ṭānin) | clear. (mubīnin)"

14:11 Said to them their Messengers, "Not we are but a human like you, but Allah bestows His Grace on whom He wills of His slaves. And not is for us that we bring you an authority except by the permission of Allah. And upon Allah so let put their trust the believers.

Said (qālat) | to them (lahum) | their Messengers (rusuluhum), | "Not (in) | we are (naḥnu) | but (illā) | a human (basharun) | like you (mith'lukum), | but (walākinna) | Allah (l-laha) | bestows His Grace (yamunnu) | on (ʿalā) | whom (man) | He wills (yashāu) | of (min) | His slaves (ʿibādihi). | And not (wamā) | is (kāna) | for us (lanā) | that (an) | we bring you (natiyakum) | an authority (bisul'ṭānin) | except (illā) | by the permission of Allah (bi-idh'ni). | by the permission of Allah (l-lahi). | And upon (waʿalā) | Allah (l-lahi) | so let put their trust (falyatawakkali) | the believers (l-mu'minūna).

14:12 And what is for us that not we put our trust upon Allah, while certainly He has guided us to our ways? And surely we will bear with patience on what harm you may cause us. And upon Allah so let put their trust the ones who put their trust."

And what (wamā) | is for us (lanā) | that not (allā) | we put our trust (natawakkala) | upon (ʿalā) | Allah (l-lahi), | while certainly (waqad) | He has guided us (hadānā) | to our ways (subulanā)? | And surely we will bear with patience (walanaṣbiranna) | on (ʿalā) | what (mā) | harm you may cause us (ādhaytumūnā). | And upon (waʿalā) | Allah (l-lahi) | so let put their trust (falyatawakkali) | the ones who put their trust. (l-mutawakilūna)"

14:13 And said those who disbelieved to their Messengers, "Surely we will drive you out of our land or surely you should return to our religion." So inspired to them their Lord, "We will surely destroy the wrongdoers.

And said (waqāla) | those who (alladhīna) | disbelieved (kafarū) | to their Messengers (lirusulihim), | "Surely we will drive you out (lanukh'rijannakum) | of (min) | our land (arḍinā) | or (aw) | surely you should return (lataʿūdunna) | to (fī) | our religion. (millatinā)" | So inspired (fa-awḥā) | to them (ilayhim) | their Lord (rabbuhum), | "We will surely destroy (lanuh'likanna) | the wrongdoers (l-ẓālimīna).

14:14 And surely We will make you dwell in the land after them. That is for whoever fears standing before Me and fears My Threat."

And surely We will make you dwell (walanus'kinannakumu) | in the land (l-arḍa) | after them (min). | after them (baʿdihim). | That (dhālika) | is for whoever (liman) | fears (khāfa) | standing before Me (maqāmī) | and fears (wakhāfa) | My Threat. (waʿīdi)"

14:15 And they sought victory and disappointed every tyrant obstinate.

And they sought victory (wa-is'taftaḥū) | and disappointed (wakhāba) | every (kullu) | tyrant (jabbārin) | obstinate (ʿanīdin).

14:16 Ahead of him is Hell, and he will be made to drink of water purulent.

Ahead of him (min) | Ahead of him (warāihi) | is Hell (jahannamu), | and he will be made to drink (wayus'qā) | of (min) | water (māin) | purulent (ṣadīdin).

14:17 He will sip it but not he will be near to swallowing it. And will come to him the death from every side, but not he will die. And ahead of him is a punishment harsh.

He will sip it (yatajarraʿuhu) | but not (walā) | he will be near (yakādu) | to swallowing it (yusīghuhu). | And will come to him (wayatīhi) | the death (l-mawtu) | from (min) | every (kulli) | side (makānin), | but not (wamā) | he (huwa) | will die (bimayyitin). | And ahead of him (wamin) | And ahead of him (warāihi) | is a punishment (ʿadhābun) | harsh (ghalīẓun).

14:18 The example of those who disbelieve in their Lord, their deeds are like ashes blows furiously on it the wind in a day stormy. No control they have of what they have earned on anything. That, [it] is the straying far.

The example (mathalu) | of those who (alladhīna) | disbelieve (kafarū) | in their Lord (birabbihim), | their deeds (aʿmāluhum) | are like ashes (karamādin) | blows furiously (ish'taddat) | on it (bihi) | the wind (l-rīḥu) | in (fī) | a day (yawmin) | stormy (ʿāṣifin). | No (lā) | control they have (yaqdirūna) | of what (mimmā) | they have earned (kasabū) | on (ʿalā) | anything (shayin). | That (dhālika), | [it] (huwa) | is the straying (l-ḍalālu) | far (l-baʿīdu).

14:19 Do not you see, that Allah created the heavens and the earth in truth? If He wills, He can remove you and bring a creation new.

Do not (alam) | you see (tara), | that (anna) | Allah (l-laha) | created (khalaqa) | the heavens (l-samāwāti) | and the earth (wal-arḍa) | in truth (bil-ḥaqi)? | If (in) | He wills (yasha), | He can remove you (yudh'hib'kum) | and bring (wayati) | a creation (bikhalqin) | new (jadīdin).

14:20 And not is that on Allah great.

And not (wamā) | is that (dhālika) | on (ʿalā) | Allah (l-lahi) | great (biʿazīzin).

14:21 And they will come forth before Allah all together, then will say the weak to those who were arrogant, "Indeed we, we were your followers, so can you be the one who avails us from the punishment of Allah anything?" They will say, "If Allah had guided us surely we would have guided you. It is same for us whether we show intolerance or we are patient, not is for us any place of escape."

And they will come forth (wabarazū) | before Allah (lillahi) | all together (jamīʿan), | then will say (faqāla) | the weak (l-ḍuʿafāu) | to those who (lilladhīna) | were arrogant (is'takbarū), | "Indeed we (innā), | we were (kunnā) | your (lakum) | followers (tabaʿan), | so can (fahal) | you be (antum) | the one who avails (mugh'nūna) | us (ʿannā) | from (min) | the punishment (ʿadhābi) | of Allah (l-lahi) | anything? (min)" | anything? (shayin)" | They will say (qālū), | "If (law) | Allah had guided us (hadānā) | Allah had guided us (l-lahu) | surely we would have guided you (lahadaynākum). | It is same (sawāon) | for us (ʿalaynā) | whether we show intolerance (ajaziʿ'nā) | or (am) | we are patient (ṣabarnā), | not (mā) | is for us (lanā) | any (min) | place of escape. (maḥīṣin)"

14:22 And will say the Shaitaan, when has been decided the matter, "Indeed, Allah promised you a promise of truth. And I promised you, but I betrayed you. But not I had over you any authority except that I invited you, and you responded to me. So do not blame me, but blame yourselves. Not can I be your helper and not you can be my helper. Indeed, I deny [of what] your association of me with Allah before. Indeed, the wrongdoers, for them is a punishment painful."

And will say (waqāla) | the Shaitaan (l-shayṭānu), | when (lammā) | has been decided (quḍiya) | the matter (l-amru), | "Indeed (inna), | Allah (l-laha) | promised you (waʿadakum) | a promise (waʿda) | of truth (l-ḥaqi). | And I promised you (wawaʿadttukum), | but I betrayed you (fa-akhlaftukum). | But not (wamā) | I had (kāna) | I had (liya) | over you (ʿalaykum) | any (min) | authority (sul'ṭānin) | except (illā) | that (an) | I invited you (daʿawtukum), | and you responded (fa-is'tajabtum) | to me (lī). | So do not (falā) | blame me (talūmūnī), | but blame (walūmū) | yourselves (anfusakum). | Not (mā) | can I (anā) | be your helper (bimuṣ'rikhikum) | and not (wamā) | you can (antum) | be my helper (bimuṣ'rikhiyya). | Indeed, I (innī) | deny (kafartu) | [of what] (bimā) | your association of me with Allah (ashraktumūni) | before (min). | before (qablu). | Indeed (inna), | the wrongdoers (l-ẓālimīna), | for them (lahum) | is a punishment (ʿadhābun) | painful. (alīmun)"

14:23 And will be admitted, those who believed and did righteous deeds to Gardens flows from underneath it the rivers will abide forever in it by the permission of their Lord; their greetings therein will be peace.

And will be admitted (wa-ud'khila), | those who (alladhīna) | believed (āmanū) | and did (waʿamilū) | righteous deeds (l-ṣāliḥāti) | to Gardens (jannātin) | flows (tajrī) | from (min) | underneath it (taḥtihā) | the rivers (l-anhāru) | will abide forever (khālidīna) | in it (fīhā) | by the permission (bi-idh'ni) | of their Lord (rabbihim); | their greetings (taḥiyyatuhum) | therein (fīhā) | will be peace (salāmun).

14:24 Do not you see how Allah sets forth the example, a word good is like a tree good, its root is firm and its branches are in the sky?

Do not (alam) | you see (tara) | how (kayfa) | Allah sets forth (ḍaraba) | Allah sets forth (l-lahu) | the example (mathalan), | a word (kalimatan) | good (ṭayyibatan) | is like a tree (kashajaratin) | good (ṭayyibatin), | its root (aṣluhā) | is firm (thābitun) | and its branches (wafarʿuhā) | are in (fī) | the sky (l-samāi)?

14:25 Giving its fruit all time by the permission of its Lord. And Allah sets forth the examples for mankind so that they may remember.

Giving (tu'tī) | its fruit (ukulahā) | all (kulla) | time (ḥīnin) | by the permission (bi-idh'ni) | of its Lord (rabbihā). | And Allah sets forth (wayaḍribu) | And Allah sets forth (l-lahu) | the examples (l-amthāla) | for mankind (lilnnāsi) | so that they may (laʿallahum) | remember (yatadhakkarūna).

14:26 And the example of a word evil is like a tree evil, uprooted from the surface of the earth, not for it is any stability.

And the example (wamathalu) | of a word (kalimatin) | evil (khabīthatin) | is like a tree (kashajaratin) | evil (khabīthatin), | uprooted (uj'tuthat) | from (min) | the surface (fawqi) | of the earth (l-arḍi), | not (mā) | for it (lahā) | is any (min) | stability (qarārin).

14:27 Allah keeps firm those who believe with the firm word in the life of the world and in the Hereafter. And Allah lets go astray the wrongdoers. And Allah does what He wills.

Allah keeps firm (yuthabbitu) | Allah keeps firm (l-lahu) | those who (alladhīna) | believe (āmanū) | with the firm word (bil-qawli) | with the firm word (l-thābiti) | in (fī) | the life (l-ḥayati) | of the world (l-dun'yā) | and in (wafī) | the Hereafter (l-ākhirati). | And Allah lets go astray (wayuḍillu) | And Allah lets go astray (l-lahu) | the wrongdoers (l-ẓālimīna). | And Allah does (wayafʿalu) | And Allah does (l-lahu) | what (mā) | He wills (yashāu).

14:28 Have not you seen [to] those who have changed the Favor of Allah for disbelief and they led their people to the house of destruction?

Have not (alam) | you seen (tara) | [to] (ilā) | those who (alladhīna) | have changed (baddalū) | the Favor (niʿmata) | of Allah (l-lahi) | for disbelief (kuf'ran) | and they led (wa-aḥallū) | their people (qawmahum) | to the house (dāra) | of destruction (l-bawāri)?

14:29 Hell, in it they will burn and a wretched place to settle.

Hell (jahannama), | in it they will burn (yaṣlawnahā) | and a wretched (wabi'sa) | place to settle (l-qarāru).

14:30 And they set up to Allah equals so that they mislead from His Path. Say, "Enjoy, but indeed, your destination is to the Fire."

And they set up (wajaʿalū) | to Allah (lillahi) | equals (andādan) | so that they mislead (liyuḍillū) | from (ʿan) | His Path (sabīlihi). | Say (qul), | "Enjoy (tamattaʿū), | but indeed (fa-inna), | your destination (maṣīrakum) | is to (ilā) | the Fire. (l-nāri)"

14:31 Say to My slaves those who believe to establish the prayers, and to spend from what We have provided them, secretly and publicly, before [that] comes a Day not any trade in it and not any friendship.

Say (qul) | to My slaves (liʿibādiya) | those who (alladhīna) | believe (āmanū) | to establish (yuqīmū) | the prayers (l-ṣalata), | and to spend (wayunfiqū) | from what (mimmā) | We have provided them (razaqnāhum), | secretly (sirran) | and publicly (waʿalāniyatan), | before (min) | before (qabli) | [that] (an) | comes (yatiya) | a Day (yawmun) | not (lā) | any trade (bayʿun) | in it (fīhi) | and not (walā) | any friendship (khilālun).

14:32 Allah is the One Who created the heavens and the earth, and sent down from the sky water, then brought forth from it of the fruits as a provision for you, and subjected for you the ships, so that they may sail in the sea by His command, and subjected for you the rivers.

Allah (al-lahu) | is the One Who (alladhī) | created (khalaqa) | the heavens (l-samāwāti) | and the earth (wal-arḍa), | and sent down (wa-anzala) | from (mina) | the sky (l-samāi) | water (māan), | then brought forth (fa-akhraja) | from it (bihi) | of (mina) | the fruits (l-thamarāti) | as a provision (riz'qan) | for you (lakum), | and subjected (wasakhara) | for you (lakumu) | the ships (l-ful'ka), | so that they may sail (litajriya) | in (fī) | the sea (l-baḥri) | by His command (bi-amrihi), | and subjected (wasakhara) | for you (lakumu) | the rivers (l-anhāra).

14:33 And He subjected for you the sun and the moon, both constantly pursuing their courses, and subjected for you the night and the day.

And He subjected (wasakhara) | for you (lakumu) | the sun (l-shamsa) | and the moon (wal-qamara), | both constantly pursuing their courses (dāibayni), | and subjected (wasakhara) | for you (lakumu) | the night (al-layla) | and the day (wal-nahāra).

14:34 And He gave you of all what you asked of Him. And if you count the Favor of Allah not you will be able to count them. Indeed, the mankind is surely unjust and ungrateful.

And He gave you (waātākum) | of (min) | all (kulli) | what (mā) | you asked of Him (sa-altumūhu). | And if (wa-in) | you count (taʿuddū) | the Favor of Allah (niʿmata) | the Favor of Allah (l-lahi) | not (lā) | you will be able to count them (tuḥ'ṣūhā). | Indeed (inna), | the mankind (l-insāna) | is surely unjust (laẓalūmun) | and ungrateful (kaffārun).

14:35 And when said Ibrahim, "My Lord! Make this city safe, and keep me away and my sons that we worship the idols.

And when (wa-idh) | said (qāla) | Ibrahim (ib'rāhīmu), | "My Lord (rabbi)! | Make (ij''al) | this (hādhā) | city (l-balada) | safe (āminan), | and keep me away (wa-uj'nub'nī) | and my sons (wabaniyya) | that (an) | we worship (na'buda) | the idols (l-aṣnāma).

14:36 My Lord! Indeed, they have led astray many among the mankind. So whoever follows me then indeed, he is of me, and whoever disobeys me, then indeed, You are Oft-Forgiving, Most Merciful.

My Lord (rabbi)! | Indeed, they (innahunna) | have led astray (aḍlalna) | many (kathīran) | among (mina) | the mankind (l-nāsi). | So whoever (faman) | follows me (tabi'anī) | then indeed, he (fa-innahu) | is of me (minnī), | and whoever (waman) | disobeys me ('aṣānī), | then indeed, You (fa-innaka) | are Oft-Forgiving (ghafūrun), | Most Merciful (raḥīmun).

14:37 Our Lord! Indeed, I [I] have settled some of my offsprings in a valley not with cultivation near Your Sacred House, our Lord! That they may establish the prayers. So make hearts of the men incline towards them, and provide them with the fruits so that they may be grateful.

Our Lord (rabbanā)! | Indeed, I (innī) | [I] have settled (askantu) | some of (min) | my offsprings (dhurriyyatī) | in a valley (biwādin) | not (ghayri) | with (dhī) | cultivation (zar'in) | near ('inda) | Your Sacred House (baytika), | Your Sacred House (l-muḥarami), | our Lord (rabbanā)! | That they may establish (liyuqīmū) | the prayers (l-ṣalata). | So make (fa-ij''al) | hearts (afidatan) | of (mina) | the men (l-nāsi) | incline (tahwī) | towards them (ilayhim), | and provide them (wa-ur'zuq'hum) | with (mina) | the fruits (l-thamarāti) | so that they may (la'allahum) | be grateful (yashkurūna).

14:38 Our Lord! Indeed, You You know what we conceal and what we proclaim. And not is hidden from Allah any thing in the earth and not in the heaven.

Our Lord (rabbanā)! | Indeed, You (innaka) | You know (ta'lamu) | what (mā) | we conceal (nukh'fī) | and what (wamā) | we proclaim (nu''linu). | And not (wamā) | is hidden (yakhfā) | from ('alā) | Allah (l-lahi) | any (min) | thing (shayin) | in (fī) | the earth (l-arḍi) | and not (walā) | in (fī) | the heaven (l-samāi).

14:39 All the Praise is for Allah the One Who has granted me in the old age Ishmael and Isaac. Indeed, my Lord is All-Hearer of the prayer.

All the Praise (al-ḥamdu) | is for Allah (lillahi) | the One Who (alladhī) | has granted (wahaba) | me (lī) | in ('alā) | the old age (l-kibari) | Ishmael (is'mā'īla) | and Isaac (wa-is'ḥāqa). | Indeed (inna), | my Lord (rabbī) | is All-Hearer (lasamī'u) | of the prayer (l-du'āi).

14:40 My Lord! Make me an establisher of the prayer, and from my offsprings. Our Lord! and accept my prayer.

My Lord (rabbi)! | Make me (ij''alnī) | an establisher (muqīma) | of the prayer (l-ṣalati), | and from (wamin) | my offsprings (dhurriyyatī). | Our Lord (rabbanā)! | and accept (wataqabbal) | my prayer (du'āi).

14:41 Our Lord! Forgive me and my parents and the believers on the Day will be established the account."

Our Lord (rabbanā)! | Forgive (igh'fir) | me (lī) | and my parents (waliwālidayya) | and the believers (walil'mu'minīna) | on the Day (yawma) | will be established (yaqūmu) | the account. (l-ḥisābu)"

14:42 And do not think that Allah is unaware of what do the wrongdoers. Only He gives them respite to a Day will stare in it the eyes.

And do not (walā) | think (taḥsabanna) | that Allah (l-laha) | is unaware (ghāfilan) | of what ('ammā) | do (ya'malu) | the wrongdoers (l-ẓālimūna). | Only (innamā) | He gives them respite (yu-akhiruhum) | to a Day (liyawmin) | will stare (tashkhaṣu) | in it (fīhi) | the eyes (l-abṣāru).

14:43 Racing ahead, raised up their heads, not returning towards them their gaze, and their hearts are empty.

Racing ahead (muh'ṭiʿīna), | raised up (muq'niʿī) | their heads (ruūsihim), | not (lā) | returning (yartaddu) | towards them (ilayhim) | their gaze (ṭarfuhum), | and their hearts (wa-afidatuhum) | are empty (hawāon).

14:44 And warn the mankind of a Day when will come to them the punishment, then will say those who did wrong, "Our Lord! Respite us for a term short; we will answer Your call and we will follow the Messengers." "Had not you sworn before not for you any end?

And warn (wa-andhiri) | the mankind (l-nāsa) | of a Day (yawma) | when will come to them (yatīhimu) | the punishment (l-ʿadhābu), | then will say (fayaqūlu) | those who (alladhīna) | did wrong (ẓalamū), | "Our Lord (rabbanā)! | Respite us (akhir'nā) | for (ilā) | a term (ajalin) | short (qarībin); | we will answer (nujib) | Your call (daʿwataka) | and we will follow (wanattabiʿi) | the Messengers. (l-rusula)" | "Had not (awalam) | you (takūnū) | sworn (aqsamtum) | before (min) | before (qablu) | not (mā) | for you (lakum) | any (min) | end (zawālin)?

14:45 And you dwelt in the dwellings of those who wronged themselves, and it had become clear to you how We dealt with them, and We put forth for you the examples."

And you dwelt (wasakantum) | in (fī) | the dwellings (masākini) | of those who (alladhīna) | wronged (ẓalamū) | themselves (anfusahum), | and it had become clear (watabayyana) | to you (lakum) | how (kayfa) | We dealt (faʿalnā) | with them (bihim), | and We put forth (waḍarabnā) | for you (lakumu) | the examples. (l-amthāla)"

14:46 And indeed they planned their plan, but with Allah was their plan, even if was their plan that should be moved by it the mountains.

And indeed (waqad) | they planned (makarū) | their plan (makrahum), | but with (waʿinda) | Allah (l-lahi) | was their plan (makruhum), | even if (wa-in) | was (kāna) | their plan (makruhum) | that should be moved (litazūla) | by it (min'hu) | the mountains (l-jibālu).

14:47 So do not think that Allah will fail to keep His Promise to His Messengers. Indeed, Allah is All-Mighty, Owner of Retribution.

So do not (falā) | think (taḥsabanna) | that Allah (l-laha) | will fail (mukh'lifa) | to keep His Promise (waʿdihi) | to His Messengers (rusulahu). | Indeed (inna), | Allah (l-laha) | is All-Mighty (ʿazīzun), | Owner of Retribution (dhū). | Owner of Retribution (intiqāmin).

14:48 On the Day will be changed the earth to other (than) the earth, and the heavens, and they will come forth before Allah, the One, the Irresistible.

On the Day (yawma) | will be changed (tubaddalu) | the earth (l-arḍu) | to other (than (ghayra)) | the earth (l-arḍi), | and the heavens (wal-samāwātu), | and they will come forth (wabarazū) | before Allah (lillahi), | the One (l-wāḥidi), | the Irresistible (l-qahāri).

14:49 And you will see the criminals, on that Day bound together in the chains,

And you will see (watarā) | the criminals (l-muj'rimīna), | on that Day (yawma-idhin) | bound together (muqarranīna) | in (fī) | the chains (l-aṣfādi),

14:50 Their garments of tar, and will cover their faces the Fire.

Their garments (sarābīluhum) | of (min) | tar (qaṭirānin), | and will cover (wataghshā) | their faces (wujūhahumu) | the Fire (l-nāru).

14:51 So that Allah may recompense each soul for what it earned. Indeed, Allah is Swift in the reckoning.

So that Allah may recompense (liyajziya) | So that Allah may recompense (l-lahu) | each (kulla) | soul (nafsin) | for what (mā) | it earned (kasabat). | Indeed (inna), | Allah (l-laha) | is Swift (sarīʿu) | in the reckoning (l-ḥisābi).

14:52 This is a Message for the mankind, that they may be warned with it, and that they may know that only He is One God, and that may take heed men of understanding.

This (hādhā) | is a Message (balāghun) | for the mankind (lilnnāsi), | that they may be warned (waliyundharū) | with it (bihi), | and that they may know (waliyaʿlamū) | that only (annamā) | He (huwa) | is One God (ilāhun), | is One God (wāḥidun), | and that may take heed (waliyadhakkara) | men (ulū) | of understanding (l-albābi).

Chapter (15) Sūrat l-Ḥij'r (The Rocky Tract)

15:1 Alif Laam Ra. These are the Verses of the Book and Quran clear.

Alif Laam Ra (alif-lam-ra). | These (til'ka) | are the Verses (āyātu) | of the Book (l-kitābi) | and Quran (waqur'ānin) | clear (mubīnin).

15:2 Perhaps will wish those who disbelieved, if they had been Muslims.

Perhaps (rubamā) | will wish (yawaddu) | those who (alladhīna) | disbelieved (kafarū), | if (law) | they had been (kānū) | Muslims (mus'limīna).

15:3 Leave them to eat and enjoy and diverted them the hope, then soon they will come to know.

Leave them (dharhum) | to eat (yakulū) | and enjoy (wayatamattaʿū) | and diverted them (wayul'hihimu) | the hope (l-amalu), | then soon (fasawfa) | they will come to know (yaʿlamūna).

15:4 And not We destroyed any town but there was for it a decree known.

And not (wamā) | We destroyed (ahlaknā) | any (min) | town (qaryatin) | but (illā) | there was for it (walahā) | a decree (kitābun) | known (maʿlūmun).

15:5 Not can advance any nation its term and not can delay it.

Not (mā) | can advance (tasbiqu) | any (min) | nation (ummatin) | its term (ajalahā) | and not (wamā) | can delay it (yastakhirūna).

15:6 And they say, "O you to whom has been sent down [on him] the Reminder, indeed, you are surely mad.

And they say (waqālū), | "O you (yāayyuhā) | to whom (alladhī) | has been sent down (nuzzila) | [on him] (ʿalayhi) | the Reminder (l-dhik'ru), | indeed, you (innaka) | are surely mad (lamajnūnun).

15:7 Why not you bring to us the Angels, if you are of the truthful?"

Why (law) | not (mā) | you bring to us (tatīnā) | the Angels (bil-malāikati), | if (in) | you are (kunta) | of (mina) | the truthful? (l-ṣādiqīna)"

15:8 Not We send down the Angels except with the truth; and not they would be then given respite.
Not (mā) | We send down (nunazzilu) | the Angels (l-malāikata) | except (illā) | with the truth (bil-ḥaqi); | and not (wamā) | they would be (kānū) | then (idhan) | given respite (munẓarīna).

15:9 Indeed, We We have sent down the Reminder, and indeed, We of it are surely Guardians.
Indeed, We (innā) | We (naḥnu) | have sent down (nazzalnā) | the Reminder (l-dhik'ra), | and indeed, We (wa-innā) | of it (lahu) | are surely Guardians (laḥāfiẓūna).

15:10 And certainly We had sent before you in the sects of the former (people).
And certainly (walaqad) | We had sent (arsalnā) | before you (min) | before you (qablika) | in (fī) | the sects (shiyaʿi) | of the former (people) (l-awalīna).

15:11 And not came to them any Messenger but they did at him mock.
And not (wamā) | came to them (yatīhim) | any (min) | Messenger (rasūlin) | but (illā) | they did (kānū) | at him (bihi) | mock (yastahziūna).

15:12 Thus We let it enter in the hearts of the criminals.
Thus (kadhālika) | We let it enter (naslukuhu) | in (fī) | the hearts (qulūbi) | of the criminals (l-muj'rimīna).

15:13 Not they believe in it, and verily have passed the ways of the former (people).
Not (lā) | they believe (yu'minūna) | in it (bihi), | and verily (waqad) | have passed (khalat) | the ways (sunnatu) | of the former (people) (l-awalīna).

15:14 And even if We opened to them a gate from the heaven, and they were to continue therein to ascend,
And even if (walaw) | We opened (fataḥnā) | to them (ʿalayhim) | a gate (bāban) | from (mina) | the heaven (l-samāi), | and they were to continue (faẓallū) | therein (fīhi) | to ascend (yaʿrujūna),

15:15 They would surely say "Only have been dazzled our eyes. Nay, we are a people bewitched."
They would surely say (laqālū) | "Only (innamā) | have been dazzled (sukkirat) | our eyes (abṣārunā). | Nay (bal), | we (naḥnu) | are a people (qawmun) | bewitched. (masḥūrūna)"

15:16 And verily We have placed in the heavens constellations and We have beautified it for the observers.
And verily (walaqad) | We have placed (jaʿalnā) | in (fī) | the heavens (l-samāi) | constellations (burūjan) | and We have beautified it (wazayyannāhā) | for the observers (lilnnāẓirīna).

15:17 And We have protected it from every devil accursed.
And We have protected it (waḥafiẓ'nāhā) | from (min) | every (kulli) | devil (shayṭānin) | accursed (rajīmin).

15:18 Except one who steals the hearing, then follows him a burning flame clear.
Except (illā) | one who (mani) | steals (is'taraqa) | the hearing (l-samʿa), | then follows him (fa-atbaʿahu) | a burning flame (shihābun) | clear (mubīnun).

15:19 And the earth, We have spread it and [We] cast therein firm mountains and [We] caused to grow therein of every thing well-balanced.
And the earth (wal-arḍa), | We have spread it (madadnāhā) | and [We] cast (wa-alqaynā) | therein (fīhā) | firm mountains (rawāsiya) | and [We] caused to grow (wa-anbatnā) | therein (fīhā) |

of (min) | every (kulli) | thing (shayin) | well-balanced (mawzūnin).

15:20 And We have made for you therein means of living and whom you are not for him providers.
And We have made (wajaʿalnā) | for you (lakum) | therein (fīhā) | means of living (maʿāyisha) | and whom (waman) | you are not (lastum) | for him (lahu) | providers (birāziqīna).

15:21 And not is any thing but with Us are its treasures, and not We send it down except in a measure known.
And not (wa-in) | is any (min) | thing (shayin) | but (illā) | with Us (ʿindanā) | are its treasures (khazāinuhu), | and not (wamā) | We send it down (nunazziluhu) | except (illā) | in a measure (biqadarin) | known (maʿlūmin).

15:22 And We have sent the winds fertilizing, and We sent down from the sky water, and We gave it to you to drink. And not you of it are retainers.
And We have sent (wa-arsalnā) | the winds (l-riyāḥa) | fertilizing (lawāqiḥa), | and We sent down (fa-anzalnā) | from (mina) | the sky (l-samāi) | water (māan), | and We gave it to you to drink (fa-asqaynākumūhu). | And not (wamā) | you (antum) | of it (lahu) | are retainers (bikhāzinīna).

15:23 And indeed, We, surely [We] We give life and We cause death, and We are the Inheritors.
And indeed, We (wa-innā), | surely [We] (lanaḥnu) | We give life (nuḥ'yī) | and We cause death (wanumītu), | and We (wanaḥnu) | are the Inheritors (l-wārithūna).

15:24 And verily We know the preceding ones among you and verily, We know the later ones.
And verily (walaqad) | We know (ʿalim'nā) | the preceding ones (l-mus'taqdimīna) | among you (minkum) | and verily (walaqad), | We know (ʿalim'nā) | the later ones (l-mus'takhirīna).

15:25 And indeed, your Lord, He will gather them. Indeed, He is All-Wise, All-Knowing.
And indeed (wa-inna), | your Lord (rabbaka), | He (huwa) | will gather them (yaḥshuruhum). | Indeed, He (innahu) | is All-Wise (ḥakīmun), | All-Knowing (ʿalīmun).

15:26 And verily, We created humankind out of sounding clay from black mud altered.
And verily (walaqad), | We created (khalaqnā) | humankind (l-insāna) | out of (min) | sounding clay (ṣalṣālin) | from (min) | black mud (ḥama-in) | altered (masnūnin).

15:27 And the jinn We created it before from fire scorching.
And the jinn (wal-jāna) | We created it (khalaqnāhu) | before (min) | before (qablu) | from (min) | fire (nāri) | scorching (l-samūmi).

15:28 And when your Lord said to the Angels, "Indeed, I will create a human being out of clay from black mud altered.
And when (wa-idh) | your Lord said (qāla) | your Lord said (rabbuka) | to the Angels (lil'malāikati), | "Indeed, I (innī) | will create (khāliqun) | a human being (basharan) | out of (min) | clay (ṣalṣālin) | from (min) | black mud (ḥama-in) | altered (masnūnin).

15:29 So, when I have fashioned him and [I] breathed into him of My spirit, then fall down to him prostrating."
So, when (fa-idhā) | I have fashioned him (sawwaytuhu) | and [I] breathed (wanafakhtu) | into him (fīhi) | of (min) | My spirit (rūḥī), | then fall down (faqaʿū) | to him (lahu) | prostrating. (sājidīna)"

15:30 So prostrated the Angels all of them together,
So prostrated (fasajada) | the Angels (l-malāikatu) | all of them (kulluhum) | together

(ajmaʿūna),

15:31 Except Iblis. He refused to be with those who prostrated.
Except (illā) | Iblis (ib'līsa). | He refused (abā) | to (an) | be (yakūna) | with (maʿa) | those who prostrated (l-sājidīna).

15:32 He said, "O Iblis! What is for you that not you are with those who prostrated?"
He said (qāla), | "O Iblis (yāib'līsu)! | What (mā) | is for you (laka) | that not (allā) | you are (takūna) | with (maʿa) | those who prostrated? (l-sājidīna)"

15:33 He said, "I am not one to prostrate to a human whom You created, out of clay from black mud altered."
He said (qāla), | "I am not (lam) | "I am not (akun) | one to prostrate (li-asjuda) | to a human (libasharin) | whom You created (khalaqtahu), | out of (min) | clay (ṣalṣālin) | from (min) | black mud (ḥama-in) | altered. (masnūnin)"

15:34 He said, "Then get out of it, for indeed, you are expelled.
He said (qāla), | "Then get out (fa-ukh'ruj) | of it (min'hā), | for indeed, you (fa-innaka) | are expelled (rajīmun).

15:35 And indeed, upon you will be the curse till the Day of [the] Judgment."
And indeed (wa-inna), | upon you (ʿalayka) | will be the curse (l-laʿnata) | till (ilā) | the Day (yawmi) | of [the] Judgment. (l-dīni)"

15:36 He said, "O my Lord! Then give me respite till the Day they are raised."
He said (qāla), | "O my Lord (rabbi)! | Then give me respite (fa-anẓir'nī) | till (ilā) | the Day (yawmi) | they are raised. (yub'ʿathūna)"

15:37 He said, "Then indeed you, are of the ones given respite.
He said (qāla), | "Then indeed you (fa-innaka), | are of (mina) | the ones given respite (l-munẓarīna).

15:38 Till the Day of the time well-known."
Till (ilā) | the Day (yawmi) | of the time (l-waqti) | well-known. (l-maʿlūmi)"

15:39 He said, "My Lord! Because You misled me, surely, I will make evil fair-seeming to them in the earth and I will mislead them all
He said (qāla), | "My Lord (rabbi)! | Because (bimā) | You misled me (aghwaytanī), | surely, I will make evil fair-seeming (la-uzayyinanna) | to them (lahum) | in (fī) | the earth (l-arḍi) | and I will mislead them (wala-ugh'wiyannahum) | all (ajmaʿīna)

15:40 Except, Your slaves among them the ones who are sincere."
Except (illā), | Your slaves (ʿibādaka) | among them (min'humu) | the ones who are sincere. (l-mukh'laṣīna)"

15:41 He said, "This is the way to Me straight.
He said (qāla), | "This (hādhā) | is the way (ṣirāṭun) | to Me (ʿalayya) | straight (mus'taqīmun).

15:42 Indeed, My slaves, not you have over them any authority, except those who follow you, of the ones who go astray."
Indeed (inna), | My slaves (ʿibādī), | not (laysa) | you have (laka) | over them (ʿalayhim) |

any authority (sul'ṭānun), | except (illā) | those who (mani) | follow you (ittabaʿaka), | of (mina) | the ones who go astray. (l-ghāwīna)"

15:43 And indeed, Hell is surely the promised place for them all.
And indeed (wa-inna), | Hell (jahannama) | is surely the promised place for them (lamawʿiduhum) | all (ajmaʿīna).

15:44 For it are seven gates, for each gate among them is a portion assigned.
For it (lahā) | are seven (sabʿatu) | gates (abwābin), | for each (likulli) | gate (bābin) | among them (min'hum) | is a portion (juz'on) | assigned (maqsūmun).

15:45 Indeed, the righteous will be in Gardens and water springs.
Indeed (inna), | the righteous (l-mutaqīna) | will be in (fī) | Gardens (jannātin) | and water springs (waʿuyūnin).

15:46 "Enter it in peace, secure."
"Enter it (ud'khulūhā) | in peace (bisalāmin), | secure. (āminīna)"

15:47 And We will remove what is in their breasts of rancor they will be brothers on thrones facing each other.
And We will remove (wanazaʿnā) | what (mā) | is in (fī) | their breasts (ṣudūrihim) | of (min) | rancor (ghillin) | they will be brothers (ikh'wānan) | on (ʿalā) | thrones (sururin) | facing each other (mutaqābilīna).

15:48 Not will touch them therein fatigue, and not they from it will be removed.
Not (lā) | will touch them (yamassuhum) | therein (fīhā) | fatigue (naṣabun), | and not (wamā) | they (hum) | from it (min'hā) | will be removed (bimukh'rajīna).

15:49 Inform My slaves that I, I am the Oft-Forgiving, the Most Merciful.
Inform (nabbi) | My slaves (ʿibādī) | that I (annī), | I am (anā) | the Oft-Forgiving (l-ghafūru), | the Most Merciful (l-raḥīmu).

15:50 And that My punishment, it is the punishment the most painful.
And that (wa-anna) | My punishment (ʿadhābī), | it (huwa) | is the punishment (l-ʿadhābu) | the most painful (l-alīmu).

15:51 And inform them about the guests of Ibrahim,
And inform them (wanabbi'hum) | about (ʿan) | the guests (ḍayfi) | of Ibrahim (ib'rāhīma),

15:52 When they entered upon him and said, "Peace." He said, "Indeed, we are of you afraid."
When (idh) | they entered (dakhalū) | upon him (ʿalayhi) | and said (faqālū), | "Peace. (salāman)" | He said (qāla), | "Indeed, we (innā) | are of you (minkum) | afraid. (wajilūna)"

15:53 They said, "Do not be afraid, indeed, we [we] bring glad tidings to you of a boy learned."
They said (qālū), | "Do not (lā) | be afraid (tawjal), | indeed, we (innā) | [we] bring glad tidings to you (nubashiruka) | of a boy (bighulāmin) | learned. (ʿalīmin)"

15:54 He said, "Do you give me glad tidings although has overtaken me old age? Then about what you give glad tidings?"
He said (qāla), | "Do you give me glad tidings (abashartumūnī) | "Do you give me glad tidings (ʿalā) | although (an) | has overtaken me (massaniya) | old age (l-kibaru)? | Then about what (fabima) | you give glad tidings? (tubashirūna)"

15:55 They said, "We give you glad tidings in truth, so do not be of the despairing."
They said (qālū), | "We give you glad tidings (basharnāka) | in truth (bil-ḥaqi), | so do not (falā) | be (takun) | of (mina) | the despairing. (l-qāniṭīna)"

15:56 He said, "And who despairs of the Mercy of his Lord except those who are astray."
He said (qāla), | "And who (waman) | despairs (yaqnaṭu) | of (min) | the Mercy (raḥmati) | of his Lord (rabbihi) | except (illā) | those who are astray. (l-ḍālūna)"

15:57 He said, "Then what is your business, O messengers?"
He said (qāla), | "Then what (famā) | is your business (khaṭbukum), | O messengers? (ayyuhā)" | O messengers? (l-mur'salūna)"

15:58 They said, "Indeed, we [we] have been sent to a people - criminals,
They said (qālū), | "Indeed, we (innā) | [we] have been sent (ur'sil'nā) | to (ilā) | a people (qawmin)- | criminals (muj'rimīna),

15:59 Except the family of Lut; indeed, we surely will save them all
Except (illā) | the family (āla) | of Lut (lūṭin); | indeed, we (innā) | surely will save them (lamunajjūhum) | all (ajmaʿīna)

15:60 Except his wife." We have decreed that she is surely of those who remain behind.
Except (illā) | his wife. (im'ra-atahu)" | We have decreed (qaddarnā) | that she (innahā) | is surely of (lamina) | those who remain behind (l-ghābirīna).

15:61 And when came to the family of Lut the messengers,
And when (falammā) | came (jāa) | to the family (āla) | of Lut (lūṭin) | the messengers (l-mur'salūna),

15:62 He said, "Indeed, you are a people unknown."
He said (qāla), | "Indeed, you (innakum) | are a people (qawmun) | unknown. (munkarūna)"

15:63 They said, "Nay, we have come to you with what they were in it disputing,
They said (qālū), | "Nay (bal), | we have come to you (ji'nāka) | with what (bimā) | they were (kānū) | in it (fīhi) | disputing (yamtarūna),

15:64 And we have come to you with the truth, and indeed, we surely are truthful.
And we have come to you (wa-ataynāka) | with the truth (bil-ḥaqi), | and indeed, we (wa-innā) | surely are truthful (laṣādiqūna).

15:65 So travel with your family in a portion of the night and follow their backs, and not let look back among you anyone, and go on where you are ordered."
So travel (fa-asri) | with your family (bi-ahlika) | in a portion (biqiṭ'ʿin) | of (mina) | the night (al-layli) | and follow (wa-ittabiʿ) | their backs (adbārahum), | and not (walā) | let look back (yaltafit) | among you (minkum) | anyone (aḥadun), | and go on (wa-im'ḍū) | where (ḥaythu) | you are ordered. (tu'marūna)"

15:66 And We conveyed to him [that] the matter that the root of these would be cut off by early morning.
And We conveyed (waqaḍaynā) | to him (ilayhi) | [that] (dhālika) | the matter (l-amra) | that (anna) | the root (dābira) | of these (hāulāi) | would be cut off (maqṭūʿun) | by early morning

(muṣ'biḥīna).

15:67 And came the people of the city, rejoicing.
And came (wajāa) | the people (ahlu) | of the city (l-madīnati), | rejoicing (yastabshirūna).

15:68 He said, "Indeed, these are my guests, so do not shame me.
He said (qāla), | "Indeed (inna), | these (hāulāi) | are my guests (ḍayfī), | so do not (falā) | shame me (tafḍaḥūni).

15:69 And fear Allah, and do not disgrace me."
And fear (wa-ittaqū) | Allah (l-laha), | and do not (walā) | disgrace me. (tukh'zūni)"

15:70 They said, "Did not we forbid you from the world?"
They said (qālū), | "Did not (awalam) | we forbid you (nanhaka) | from (ʿani) | the world? (l-ʿālamīna)"

15:71 He said, "These are my daughters if you would be doers."
He said (qāla), | "These (hāulāi) | are my daughters (banātī) | if (in) | you would be (kuntum) | doers. (fāʿilīna)"

15:72 By your life indeed, they were in their intoxication, wandering blindly.
By your life (laʿamruka) | indeed, they (innahum) | were in (lafī) | their intoxication (sakratihim), | wandering blindly (yaʿmahūna).

15:73 So, seized them the awful cry at sunrise.
So, seized them (fa-akhadhathumu) | the awful cry (l-ṣayḥatu) | at sunrise (mush'riqīna).

15:74 And We made its highest part its lowest, and We rained upon them stones of baked clay.
And We made (fajaʿalnā) | its highest part (ʿāliyahā) | its lowest (sāfilahā), | and We rained (wa-amṭarnā) | upon them (ʿalayhim) | stones (ḥijāratan) | of (min) | baked clay (sijjīlin).

15:75 Indeed, in that are the Signs for those who discern.
Indeed (inna), | in (fī) | that (dhālika) | are the Signs (laāyātin) | for those who discern (lil'mutawassimīna).

15:76 And indeed, it is on a road established.
And indeed, it (wa-innahā) | is on a road (labisabīlin) | established (muqīmin).

15:77 Indeed, in that surely is a Sign for the believers.
Indeed (inna), | in (fī) | that (dhālika) | surely is a Sign (laāyatan) | for the believers (lil'mu'minīna).

15:78 And were the companions of the wood surely wrongdoers.
And were (wa-in) | And were (kāna) | the companions (aṣḥābu) | of the wood (l-aykati) | surely wrongdoers (laẓālimīna).

15:79 So We took retribution from them, and indeed, they both were on a highway clear.
So We took retribution (fa-intaqamnā) | from them (min'hum), | and indeed, they both (wa-innahumā) | were on a highway (labi-imāmin) | clear (mubīnin).

15:80 And certainly denied the companions of the Rocky Tract, the Messengers.
And certainly (walaqad) | denied (kadhaba) | the companions (aṣḥābu) | of the Rocky

Tract (l-ḥij'ri), | the Messengers (l-mur'salīna).

15:81 And We gave them Our Signs, but they were from them turning away.
And We gave them (waātaynāhum) | Our Signs (āyātinā), | but they were (fakānū) | from them (ʿanhā) | turning away (muʿʿriḍīna).

15:82 And they used to carve from the mountains, houses, secure.
And they used to (wakānū) | carve (yanḥitūna) | from (mina) | the mountains (l-jibāli), | houses (buyūtan), | secure (āminīna).

15:83 But seized them the awful cry at early morning,
But seized them (fa-akhadhathumu) | the awful cry (l-ṣayḥatu) | at early morning (muṣ'biḥīna),

15:84 And not availed them what they used to earn.
And not (famā) | availed (aghnā) | them (ʿanhum) | what (mā) | they used to (kānū) | earn (yaksibūna).

15:85 And not We created the heavens and the earth and whatever is between them except in truth. And indeed, the Hour is surely coming. So overlook with forgiveness gracious.
And not (wamā) | We created (khalaqnā) | the heavens (l-samāwāti) | and the earth (wal-arḍa) | and whatever (wamā) | is between them (baynahumā) | except (illā) | in truth (bil-ḥaqi). | And indeed (wa-inna), | the Hour (l-sāʿata) | is surely coming (laātiyatun). | So overlook (fa-iṣ'faḥi) | with forgiveness (l-ṣafḥa) | gracious (l-jamīla).

15:86 Indeed, your Lord, He is the Creator the All-Knower.
Indeed (inna), | your Lord (rabbaka), | He (huwa) | is the Creator (l-khalāqu) | the All-Knower (l-ʿalīmu).

15:87 And certainly, We have given you seven of the oft-repeated and the Quran Great.
And certainly (walaqad), | We have given you (ātaynāka) | seven (sabʿan) | of (mina) | the oft-repeated (l-mathānī) | and the Quran (wal-qur'āna) | Great (l-ʿaẓīma).

15:88 Do not extend your eyes towards what We have bestowed with it to categories of them and do not grieve over them. And lower your wing to the believers.
Do not (lā) | extend (tamuddanna) | your eyes (ʿaynayka) | towards (ilā) | what (mā) | We have bestowed (mattaʿnā) | with it (bihi) | to categories (azwājan) | of them (min'hum) | and do not (walā) | grieve (taḥzan) | over them (ʿalayhim). | And lower (wa-ikh'fiḍ) | your wing (janāḥaka) | to the believers (lil'mu'minīna).

15:89 And say, "Indeed, I [I] am a warner clear."
And say (waqul), | "Indeed, I (innī) | [I] am (anā) | a warner (l-nadhīru) | clear. (l-mubīnu)"

15:90 As We sent down on those who divided.
As (kamā) | We sent down (anzalnā) | on (ʿalā) | those who divided (l-muq'tasimīna).

15:91 Those who have made the Quran in parts.
Those who (alladhīna) | have made (jaʿalū) | the Quran (l-qur'āna) | in parts (ʿiḍīna).

15:92 So by your Lord, surely We will question them all
So by your Lord (fawarabbika), | surely We will question them (lanasalannahum) | all (ajmaʿīna)

15:93 About what they used to do.
About what (ʿammā) | they used to (kānū) | do (yaʿmalūna).

15:94 So proclaim of what you are ordered and turn away from the polytheists.
So proclaim (fa-iṣ'daʿ) | of what (bimā) | you are ordered (tu'maru) | and turn away (wa-aʿriḍ) | from (ʿani) | the polytheists (l-mush'rikīna).

15:95 Indeed, We [We] are sufficient for you against the mockers
Indeed, We (innā) | [We] are sufficient for you (kafaynāka) | against the mockers (l-mus'tahziīna)

15:96 Those who set up with Allah god another. But soon they will come to know.
Those who (alladhīna) | set up (yajʿalūna) | with (maʿa) | Allah (l-lahi) | god (ilāhan) | another (ākhara). | But soon (fasawfa) | they will come to know (yaʿlamūna).

15:97 And verily, We know that [you] is straitened your breast by what they say.
And verily (walaqad), | We know (naʿlamu) | that [you] (annaka) | is straitened (yaḍīqu) | your breast (ṣadruka) | by what (bimā) | they say (yaqūlūna).

15:98 So glorify with the praise of your Lord and be of those who prostrate.
So glorify (fasabbiḥ) | with the praise (biḥamdi) | of your Lord (rabbika) | and be (wakun) | of (mina) | those who prostrate (l-sājidīna).

15:99 And worship your Lord until comes to you the certainty.
And worship (wa-uʿ'bud) | your Lord (rabbaka) | until (ḥattā) | comes to you (yatiyaka) | the certainty (l-yaqīnu).

Chapter (16) Sūrat l-Naḥl (The Bees)

16:1 Will come the command of Allah so do not be impatient for it. Glorified is He and Exalted is He above what they associate.
Will come (atā) | the command of Allah (amru) | the command of Allah (l-lahi) | so do not (falā) | be impatient for it (tastaʿjilūhu). | Glorified is He (sub'ḥānahu) | and Exalted is He (wataʿālā) | above what (ʿammā) | they associate (yush'rikūna).

16:2 He sends down the Angels with the inspiration of His Command, upon whom He wills of His slaves, that "Warn that [He] there is no god except Me, so fear Me."
He sends down (yunazzilu) | the Angels (l-malāikata) | with the inspiration (bil-rūḥi) | of (min) | His Command (amrihi), | upon (ʿalā) | whom (man) | He wills (yashāu) | of (min) | His slaves (ʿibādihi), | that (an) | "Warn (andhirū) | that [He] (annahu) | there is no (lā) | god (ilāha) | except (illā) | Me (anā), | so fear Me. (fa-ittaqūni)"

16:3 He created the heavens and the earth, in truth. Exalted is He above what they associate.
He created (khalaqa) | the heavens (l-samāwāti) | and the earth (wal-arḍa), | in truth

(bil-ḥaqi). | Exalted is He (taʿālā) | above what (ʿammā) | they associate (yush'rikūna).

16:4 He created the human kind from a minute quantity of semen then behold, he is an opponent clear.

He created (khalaqa) | the human kind (l-insāna) | from (min) | a minute quantity of semen (nuṭ'fatin) | then behold (fa-idhā), | he (huwa) | is an opponent (khaṣīmun) | clear (mubīnun).

16:5 And the cattle, He created them for you, in them is warmth and benefits and from them you eat.

And the cattle (wal-anʿāma), | He created them (khalaqahā) | for you (lakum), | in them (fīhā) | is warmth (dif'on) | and benefits (wamanāfiʿu) | and from them (wamin'hā) | you eat (takulūna).

16:6 And for you in them is beauty when you bring them in and when you take them out.

And for you (walakum) | in them (fīhā) | is beauty (jamālun) | when (ḥīna) | you bring them in (turīḥūna) | and when (waḥīna) | you take them out (tasraḥūna).

16:7 And they carry your loads to a land not you could reach it except with great trouble to yourselves. Indeed, your Lord surely is Most Kind, Most Merciful.

And they carry (wataḥmilu) | your loads (athqālakum) | to (ilā) | a land (baladin) | not (lam) | you could (takūnū) | reach it (bālighīhi) | except (illā) | with great trouble (bishiqqi) | to yourselves (l-anfusi). | Indeed (inna), | your Lord (rabbakum) | surely is Most Kind (laraūfun), | Most Merciful (raḥīmun).

16:8 And horses and mules and donkeys for you to ride them and as adornment. And He creates what not you know.

And horses (wal-khayla) | and mules (wal-bighāla) | and donkeys (wal-ḥamīra) | for you to ride them (litarkabūhā) | and as adornment (wazīnatan). | And He creates (wayakhluqu) | what (mā) | not (lā) | you know (taʿlamūna).

16:9 And upon Allah is the direction of the way, and among them are crooked. And if He willed, surely He would have guided you all.

And upon (waʿalā) | Allah (l-lahi) | is the direction (qaṣdu) | of the way (l-sabīli), | and among them (wamin'hā) | are crooked (jāirun). | And if (walaw) | He willed (shāa), | surely He would have guided you (lahadākum) | all (ajmaʿīna).

16:10 He is the One Who sends down from the sky water for you of it is drink, and from it grows vegetation in which you pasture your cattle.

He (huwa) | is the One Who (alladhī) | sends down (anzala) | from (mina) | the sky (l-samāi) | water (māan) | for you (lakum) | of it (min'hu) | is drink (sharābun), | and from it (wamin'hu) | grows vegetation (shajarun) | in which (fīhi) | you pasture your cattle (tusīmūna).

16:11 He causes to grow for you with it, the crops and the olives and the date-palms and the grapes and of every kind of fruits. Indeed, in that surely is a sign for a people who reflect.

He causes to grow (yunbitu) | for you (lakum) | with it (bihi), | the crops (l-zarʿa) | and the olives (wal-zaytūna) | and the date-palms (wal-nakhīla) | and the grapes (wal-aʿnāba) | and of (wamin) | every kind (kulli) | of fruits (l-thamarāti). | Indeed (inna), | in (fī) | that (dhālika) | surely is a sign (laāyatan) | for a people (liqawmin) | who reflect (yatafakkarūna).

16:12 And He has subjected for you the night and the day, and the sun and the moon, and the stars are subjected by His command. Indeed, in that surely are signs for a people who use reason.

And He has subjected (wasakhara) | for you (lakumu) | the night (al-layla) | and the day (wal-nahāra), | and the sun (wal-shamsa) | and the moon (wal-qamara), | and the stars (wal-nujūmu) | are subjected (musakharātun) | by His command (bi-amrihi). | Indeed (inna), | in (fī) | that (dhālika) | surely are signs (laāyātin) | for a people (liqawmin) | who use reason (yaʿqilūna).

16:13 And whatever He multiplied for you in the earth of varying colors. Indeed, in that surely is a sign for a people who remember.

And whatever (wamā) | He multiplied (dhara-a) | for you (lakum) | in (fī) | the earth (l-arḍi) | of varying (mukh'talifan) | colors (alwānuhu). | Indeed (inna), | in (fī) | that (dhālika) | surely is a sign (laāyatan) | for a people (liqawmin) | who remember (yadhakkarūna).

16:14 And He is the One Who subjected the sea for you to eat from it meat fresh and that you bring forth from it, ornaments that you wear them. And you see the ships ploughing through it, and that you may seek of His Bounty, and that you may be grateful.

And He (wahuwa) | is the One Who (alladhī) | subjected (sakhara) | the sea (l-baḥra) | for you to eat (litakulū) | from it (min'hu) | meat (laḥman) | fresh (ṭariyyan) | and that you bring forth (watastakhrijū) | from it (min'hu), | ornaments (ḥil'yatan) | that you wear them (talbasūnahā). | And you see (watarā) | the ships (l-ful'ka) | ploughing (mawākhira) | through it (fīhi), | and that you may seek (walitabtaghū) | of (min) | His Bounty (faḍlihi), | and that you may (walaʿallakum) | be grateful (tashkurūna).

16:15 And He has cast in the earth firm mountains, lest it should shake with you, and rivers and roads so that you may be guided,

And He has cast (wa-alqā) | in (fī) | the earth (l-arḍi) | firm mountains (rawāsiya), | lest (an) | it should shake (tamīda) | with you (bikum), | and rivers (wa-anhāran) | and roads (wasubulan) | so that you may (laʿallakum) | be guided (tahtadūna),

16:16 And landmarks. And by the stars they guide themselves.

And landmarks (waʿalāmātin). | And by the stars (wabil-najmi) | they (hum) | guide themselves (yahtadūna).

16:17 Then is He Who creates like one who does not create? Then will you not remember?

Then is He Who (afaman) | creates (yakhluqu) | like one who (kaman) | does not (lā) | create (yakhluqu)? | Then will you not (afalā) | remember (tadhakkarūna)?

16:18 And if you should count the Favors of Allah, not you could enumerate them. Indeed, Allah is Oft-Forgiving, Most Merciful.

And if (wa-in) | you should count (taʿuddū) | the Favors of Allah (niʿ'mata), | the Favors of Allah (l-lahi), | not (lā) | you could enumerate them (tuḥ'ṣūhā). | Indeed (inna), | Allah (l-laha) | is Oft-Forgiving (laghafūrun), | Most Merciful (raḥīmun).

16:19 And Allah knows what you conceal and what you reveal.

And Allah (wal-lahu) | knows (yaʿlamu) | what (mā) | you conceal (tusirrūna) | and what (wamā) | you reveal (tuʿ'linūna).

16:20 And those whom they invoke besides Allah not they create anything, but are themselves created.

And those whom (wa-alladhīna) | they invoke (yadʿūna) | besides (min) | besides (dūni) | Allah (l-lahi) | not (lā) | they create (yakhluqūna) | anything (shayan), | but are themselves (wahum) | created (yukh'laqūna).

16:21 They are dead not alive. And not they perceive when they will be resurrected.

They are dead (amwātun) | not alive (ghayru). | not alive (aḥyāin). | And not (wamā) | they perceive (yashʿurūna) | when (ayyāna) | they will be resurrected (yubʿʿathūna).

16:22 Your god is God One. But those who do not believe in the Hereafter, their hearts refuse, and they are arrogant.

Your god (ilāhukum) | is God (ilāhun) | One (wāḥidun). | But those who (fa-alladhīna) | do not (lā) | believe (yu'minūna) | in the Hereafter (bil-ākhirati), | their hearts (qulūbuhum) | refuse (munkiratun), | and they (wahum) | are arrogant (mus'takbirūna).

16:23 No doubt that Allah knows what they conceal and what they reveal. Indeed, He does not love the arrogant ones.

No doubt (lā) | No doubt (jarama) | that (anna) | Allah (l-laha) | knows (yaʿlamu) | what (mā) | they conceal (yusirrūna) | and what (wamā) | they reveal (yuʿʿlinūna). | Indeed, He (innahu) | does not (lā) | love (yuḥibbu) | the arrogant ones (l-mus'takbirīna).

16:24 And when it is said to them, "What has your Lord sent down? They say, "Tales of the ancient."

And when (wa-idhā) | it is said (qīla) | to them (lahum), | "What (mādhā) | has your Lord sent down (anzala)? | has your Lord sent down (rabbukum)? | They say (qālū), | "Tales (asāṭīru) | of the ancient. (l-awalīna)"

16:25 That they may bear their own burdens in full on the Day of the Resurrection, and of the burdens of those whom they misled [them] without knowledge. Unquestionably, evil is what they will bear.

That they may bear (liyaḥmilū) | their own burdens (awzārahum) | in full (kāmilatan) | on the Day (yawma) | of the Resurrection (l-qiyāmati), | and of (wamin) | the burdens (awzāri) | of those whom (alladhīna) | they misled [them] (yuḍillūnahum) | without (bighayri) | knowledge (ʿil'min). | Unquestionably (alā), | evil (sāa) | is what (mā) | they will bear (yazirūna).

16:26 Verily, plotted those who were before them, but Allah came at their building from the foundations, so fell upon them the roof from above them, and came to them the punishment from where they did not perceive.

Verily (qad), | plotted (makara) | those who (alladhīna) | were before them (min), | were before them (qablihim), | but Allah came (fa-atā) | but Allah came (l-lahu) | at their building (bun'yānahum) | from (mina) | the foundations (l-qawāʿidi), | so fell (fakharra) | upon them (ʿalayhimu) | the roof (l-saqfu) | from (min) | above them (fawqihim), | and came to them (wa-atāhumu) | the punishment (l-ʿadhābu) | from (min) | where (ḥaythu) | they did not perceive (lā). | they did not perceive (yashʿurūna).

16:27 Then on the Day of the Resurrection, He will disgrace them and say, "Where are My partners those for whom you used to oppose [in them]?" Will say those who were given the knowledge, "Indeed, the disgrace, this Day and evil are upon the disbelievers"

Then (thumma) | on the Day (yawma) | of the Resurrection (l-qiyāmati), | He will disgrace them (yukh'zīhim) | and say (wayaqūlu), | "Where (ayna) | are My partners (shurakāiya) | those for whom (alladhīna) | you used to (kuntum) | oppose (tushāqqūna) | [in them]? (fīhim)" | Will say (qāla) | those who (alladhīna) | were given (ūtū) | the knowledge (l-ʿil'ma), | "Indeed (inna), | the disgrace (l-khiz'ya), | this Day (l-yawma) | and evil (wal-sūa) | are upon (ʿalā) | the disbelievers (l-kāfirīna)"

16:28 Those whom - take them in death the Angels while wronging themselves, then they would offer the submission, "Not we were doing any evil." Nay, indeed, Allah is All-Knower of what you used to do.

Those whom (alladhīna)- | take them in death (tatawaffāhumu) | the Angels (l-malāikatu)

| while wronging (ẓālimī) | themselves (anfusihim), | then they would offer (fa-alqawū) | the submission (l-salama), | "Not (mā) | we were (kunnā) | doing (naʿmalu) | any (min) | evil. (sūin)" | Nay (balā), | indeed (inna), | Allah (l-laha) | is All-Knower (ʿalīmun) | of what (bimā) | you used to (kuntum) | do (taʿmalūna).

16:29 So enter the gates of Hell to abide forever in it. Surely, wretched is the abode of the arrogant.

So enter (fa-ud'khulū) | the gates (abwāba) | of Hell (jahannama) | to abide forever (khālidīna) | in it (fīhā). | Surely, wretched (falabi'sa) | is the abode (mathwā) | of the arrogant (l-mutakabirīna).

16:30 And it will be said to those who fear Allah, "What has your Lord sent down?" They will say, "Good." For those who do good in this world is a good, and the home of the Hereafter is better. And surely excellent is the home of the righteous.

And it will be said (waqīla) | to those who (lilladhīna) | fear Allah (ittaqaw), | "What (mādhā) | has your Lord sent down? (anzala)" | has your Lord sent down? (rabbukum)" | They will say (qālū), | "Good. (khayran)" | For those who (lilladhīna) | do good (aḥsanū) | in (fī) | this (hādhihi) | world (l-dun'yā) | is a good (ḥasanatun), | and the home (waladāru) | of the Hereafter (l-ākhirati) | is better (khayrun). | And surely excellent (walaniʿʿma) | is the home (dāru) | of the righteous (l-mutaqīna).

16:31 Gardens of Eden - which they will enter, flows from underneath them the rivers. For them therein will be whatever they wish. Thus Allah rewards the righteous,

Gardens (jannātu) | of Eden (ʿadnin)- | which they will enter (yadkhulūnahā), | flows (tajrī) | from (min) | underneath them (taḥtihā) | the rivers (l-anhāru). | For them (lahum) | therein (fīhā) | will be whatever (mā) | they wish (yashāūna). | Thus (kadhālika) | Allah rewards (yajzī) | Allah rewards (l-lahu) | the righteous (l-mutaqīna),

16:32 Those whom take them in death the Angels when they are pure saying, "Peace be upon you. Enter Paradise for what you used to do."

Those whom (alladhīna) | take them in death (tatawaffāhumu) | the Angels (l-malāikatu) | when they are pure (ṭayyibīna) | saying (yaqūlūna), | "Peace (salāmun) | be upon you (ʿalaykumu). | Enter (ud'khulū) | Paradise (l-janata) | for what (bimā) | you used to (kuntum) | do. (taʿmalūna)"

16:33 Do they wait except that should come to them the Angels or should come the Command of your Lord? Thus did those who were before them. And not wronged them Allah but they were themselves wronging.

Do (hal) | they wait (yanẓurūna) | except (illā) | that (an) | should come to them (tatiyahumu) | the Angels (l-malāikatu) | or (aw) | should come (yatiya) | the Command (amru) | of your Lord (rabbika)? | Thus (kadhālika) | did (faʿala) | those who (alladhīna) | were before them (min). | were before them (qablihim). | And not (wamā) | wronged them (ẓalamahumu) | Allah (l-lahu) | but (walākin) | they were (kānū) | themselves (anfusahum) | wronging (yaẓlimūna).

16:34 Then struck them the evil (results) of what they did, and surrounded them what they used to [of it] mock.

Then struck them (fa-aṣābahum) | the evil (results (sayyiātu)) | of what (mā) | they did (ʿamilū), | and surrounded (waḥāqa) | them (bihim) | what (mā) | they used to (kānū) | [of it] (bihi) | mock (yastahziūna).

16:35 And said those who associate partners with Allah, "If Allah had willed not we would have worshipped other than Him any thing, we and not our forefathers and not we would have forbidden other than Him anything." Thus did those who were before them. Then is there on the messengers except the conveyance clear?

And said (waqāla) | those who (alladhīna) | associate partners with Allah (ashrakū), | "If (law) | Allah had willed (shāa) | Allah had willed (l-lahu) | not (mā) | we would have worshipped (ʿabadnā) | other than Him (min) | other than Him (dūnihi) | any (min) | thing (shayin), | we (naḥnu) | and not (walā) | our forefathers (ābāunā) | and not (walā) | we would have forbidden (ḥarramnā) | other than Him (min) | other than Him (dūnihi) | anything. (min)" | anything. (shayin)" | Thus (kadhālika) | did (faʿala) | those who (alladhīna) | were before them (min). | were before them (qablihim). | Then is there (fahal) | on (ʿalā) | the messengers (l-rusuli) | except (illā) | the conveyance (l-balāghu) | clear (l-mubīnu)?

16:36 And certainly, We sent into every nation a Messenger, that, "Worship Allah, and avoid the false deities." Then among them were some whom Allah guided, and among them were some was justified on them the straying. So travel in the earth and see how was the end of the deniers.

And certainly (walaqad), | We sent (baʿathnā) | into (fī) | every (kulli) | nation (ummatin) | a Messenger (rasūlan), | that (ani), | "Worship (uʿ'budū) | Allah (l-laha), | and avoid (wa-ij'tanibū) | the false deities. (l-ṭāghūta)" | Then among them (famin'hum) | were some whom (man) | Allah guided (hadā), | Allah guided (l-lahu), | and among them (wamin'hum) | were some (man) | was justified (ḥaqqat) | on them (ʿalayhi) | the straying (l-ḍalālatu). | So travel (fasīrū) | in (fī) | the earth (l-arḍi) | and see (fa-unẓurū) | how (kayfa) | was (kāna) | the end (ʿāqibatu) | of the deniers (l-mukadhibīna).

16:37 If you desire [for] their guidance, then indeed, Allah will not guide whom He lets go astray, and not are for them any helpers.

If (in) | you desire (taḥriṣ) | [for] (ʿalā) | their guidance (hudāhum), | then indeed (fa-inna), | Allah (l-laha) | will not (lā) | guide (yahdī) | whom (man) | He lets go astray (yuḍillu), | and not are (wamā) | for them (lahum) | any (min) | helpers (nāṣirīna).

16:38 And they swear by Allah strongest of their oaths, Allah will not resurrect one who dies. Nay, it is a promise upon Him in truth, but most of the mankind do not know.

And they swear (wa-aqsamū) | by Allah (bil-lahi) | strongest (jahda) | of their oaths (aymānihim), | Allah will not resurrect (lā) | Allah will not resurrect (yabʿathu) | Allah will not resurrect (l-lahu) | one who (man) | dies (yamūtu). | Nay (balā), | it is a promise (waʿdan) | upon Him (ʿalayhi) | in truth (ḥaqqan), | but (walākinna) | most (akthara) | of the mankind (l-nāsi) | do not (lā) | know (yaʿlamūna).

16:39 That He will make clear to them that they differ wherein, and that may know those who disbelieved that they were liars.

That He will make clear (liyubayyina) | to them (lahumu) | that (alladhī) | they differ (yakhtalifūna) | wherein (fīhi), | and that may know (waliyaʿlama) | those who (alladhīna) | disbelieved (kafarū) | that they (annahum) | were (kānū) | liars (kādhibīna).

16:40 Only Our Word to a thing when We intend it is that We say to it, "Be" and it is.

Only (innamā) | Our Word (qawlunā) | to a thing (lishayin) | when (idhā) | We intend it (aradnāhu) | is that (an) | We say (naqūla) | to it (lahu), | "Be (kun)" | and it is (fayakūnu).

16:41 And those who emigrated in the way of Allah after [what] they were wronged, surely We will give them position in the world good, but surely the reward of the Hereafter is greater, if they know.

And those who (wa-alladhīna) | emigrated (hājarū) | in the way (fī) | of Allah (l-lahi) | after (min) | after (baʿdi) | [what] (mā) | they were wronged (ẓulimū), | surely We will give them position (lanubawwi-annahum) | in (fī) | the world (l-dun'yā) | good (ḥasanatan), | but surely the reward (wala-ajru) | of the Hereafter (l-ākhirati) | is greater (akbaru), | if (law) | they (kānū) | know (yaʿlamūna).

16:42 Those who are patient and on their Lord they put their trust.

Those who (alladhīna) | are patient (ṣabarū) | and on (waʿalā) | their Lord (rabbihim) | they put their trust (yatawakkalūna).

16:43 And not We sent before you except men, We revealed to them, so ask the people of the Reminder if you do not know.

And not (wamā) | We sent (arsalnā) | before you (min) | before you (qablika) | except (illā) | men (rijālan), | We revealed (nūḥī) | to them (ilayhim), | so ask (fasalū) | the people (ahla) | of the Reminder (l-dhik'ri) | if (in) | you (kuntum) | do not (lā) | know (taʿlamūna).

16:44 With the clear proofs and the Books. And We sent down to you the Remembrance, that you may make clear to the mankind, what has been sent down to them and that they may reflect.

With the clear proofs (bil-bayināti) | and the Books (wal-zuburi). | And We sent down (wa-anzalnā) | to you (ilayka) | the Remembrance (l-dhik'ra), | that you may make clear (litubayyina) | to the mankind (lilnnāsi), | what (mā) | has been sent down (nuzzila) | to them (ilayhim) | and that they may (walaʿallahum) | reflect (yatafakkarūna).

16:45 Do then feel secure those who plotted the evil deeds that Allah will cave with them the earth or will come to them the punishment from where not they perceive?

Do then feel secure (afa-amina) | those who (alladhīna) | plotted (makarū) | the evil deeds (l-sayiāti) | that (an) | Allah will cave (yakhsifa) | Allah will cave (l-lahu) | with them (bihimu) | the earth (l-arḍa) | or (aw) | will come to them (yatiyahumu) | the punishment (l-ʿadhābu) | from (min) | where (ḥaythu) | not (lā) | they perceive (yashʿurūna)?

16:46 Or that He may seize them in their going to and fro then not they will be able to escape?

Or (aw) | that He may seize them (yakhudhahum) | in (fī) | their going to and fro (taqallubihim) | then not (famā) | they (hum) | will be able to escape (bimuʿ'jizīna)?

16:47 Or that He may seize them with a gradual wasting But indeed, your Lord is surely Full of Kindness, Most Merciful.

Or (aw) | that He may seize them (yakhudhahum) | with (ʿalā) | a gradual wasting (takhawwufin) | But indeed (fa-inna), | your Lord (rabbakum) | is surely Full of Kindness (laraūfun), | Most Merciful (raḥīmun).

16:48 Have not they seen [towards] what Allah has created from a thing? Incline their shadows to the right and to the left, prostrating to Allah while they are humble?

Have not (awalam) | they seen (yaraw) | [towards] (ilā) | what (mā) | Allah has created (khalaqa) | Allah has created (l-lahu) | from (min) | a thing (shayin)? | Incline (yatafayya-u) | their shadows (ẓilāluhu) | to (ʿani) | the right (l-yamīni) | and to the left (wal-shamāili), | prostrating (sujjadan) | to Allah (lillahi) | while they (wahum) | are humble (dākhirūna)?

16:49 And to Allah prostrate whatever is in the heavens and whatever is in the earth of moving creatures and the Angels, and they are not arrogant.

And to Allah (walillahi) | prostrate (yasjudu) | whatever (mā) | is in (fī) | the heavens (l-samāwāti) | and whatever (wamā) | is in (fī) | the earth (l-arḍi) | of (min) | moving creatures (dābbatin) | and the Angels (wal-malāikatu), | and they (wahum) | are not (lā) | arrogant (yastakbirūna).

16:50 They fear their Lord above them, and they do what they are commanded.

They fear (yakhāfūna) | their Lord (rabbahum) | above them (min), | above them (fawqihim), | and they do (wayafʿalūna) | what (mā) | they are commanded (yu'marūna).

16:51 And Allah has said, "Do not take [two] gods two, only He is God One, so Me Alone you fear [Me]."

And Allah has said (waqāla), | And Allah has said (l-lahu), | "Do not (lā) | take (tattakhidhū) | [two] gods (ilāhayni) | two (ith'nayni), | only (innamā) | He (huwa) | is God (ilāhun) | One (wāḥidun), | so Me Alone (fa-iyyāya) | you fear [Me]. (fa-ir'habūni)"

16:52 And to Him belongs whatever is in the heavens and the earth and to Him is due the worship constantly. Then is it other than Allah you fear?

And to Him belongs (walahu) | whatever (mā) | is in (fī) | the heavens (l-samāwāti) | and the earth (wal-arḍi) | and to Him (walahu) | is due the worship (l-dīnu) | constantly (wāṣiban). | Then is it other than (afaghayra) | Allah (l-lahi) | you fear (tattaqūna)?

16:53 And whatever you have of favor is from Allah. Then when touches you the adversity then to Him you cry for help.

And whatever (wamā) | you have (bikum) | of (min) | favor (niʿ'matin) | is from (famina) | Allah (l-lahi). | Then (thumma) | when (idhā) | touches you (massakumu) | the adversity (l-ḍuru) | then to Him (fa-ilayhi) | you cry for help (tajarūna).

16:54 Then when He removes the adversity from you, behold! A group of you with their Lord associate others,

Then (thumma) | when (idhā) | He removes (kashafa) | the adversity (l-ḍura) | from you (ʿankum), | behold (idhā)! | A group (farīqun) | of you (minkum) | with their Lord (birabbihim) | associate others (yush'rikūna),

16:55 So as to deny that which We have given them. Then enjoy yourselves, soon you will know.

So as to deny (liyakfurū) | that which (bimā) | We have given them (ātaynāhum). | Then enjoy yourselves (fatamattaʿū), | soon (fasawfa) | you will know (taʿlamūna).

16:56 And they assign to what not they know - a portion, of what We have provided them. By Allah surely you will be asked about what you used to invent.

And they assign (wayajʿalūna) | to what (limā) | not (lā) | they know (yaʿlamūna)- | a portion (naṣīban), | of what (mimmā) | We have provided them (razaqnāhum). | By Allah (tal-lahi) | surely you will be asked (latus'alunna) | about what (ʿammā) | you used to (kuntum) | invent (taftarūna).

16:57 And they assign to Allah daughters. Glory be to Him! And for them is what they desire.

And they assign (wayajʿalūna) | to Allah (lillahi) | daughters (l-banāti). | Glory be to Him (sub'ḥānahu)! | And for them (walahum) | is what (mā) | they desire (yashtahūna).

16:58 And when is given good news to one of them of a female, turns his face dark and he suppresses grief.

And when (wa-idhā) | is given good news (bushira) | to one of them (aḥaduhum) | of a female (bil-unthā), | turns (ẓalla) | his face (wajhuhu) | dark (mus'waddan) | and he (wahuwa) | suppresses grief (kaẓīmun).

16:59 He hides himself from the people because of the evil of what he has been given good news about. Should he keep it in humiliation or bury it in the dust? Unquestionably, evil is what they decide.

He hides himself (yatawārā) | from (mina) | the people (l-qawmi) | because of (min) | the evil (sūi) | of what (mā) | he has been given good news (bushira) | about (bihi). | Should he keep it (ayum'sikuhu) | in (ʿalā) | humiliation (hūnin) | or (am) | bury it (yadussuhu) | in (fī) | the dust (l-turābi)? | Unquestionably (alā), | evil (sāa) | is what (mā) | they decide (yaḥkumūna).

16:60 For those who do not believe in the Hereafter, is a similitude of the evil, and for Allah is the similitude the Highest. And He is the All-Mighty, All-Wise.

For those who (lilladhīna) | do not (lā) | believe (yu'minūna) | in the Hereafter (bil-ākhirati), | is a similitude (mathalu) | of the evil (l-sawi), | and for Allah (walillahi) | is the similitude (l-mathalu) | the Highest (l-aʿlā). | And He (wahuwa) | is the All-Mighty (l-ʿazīzu), | All-Wise (l-ḥakīmu).

16:61 And if Allah were to seize the mankind for their wrongdoing not He would have left upon it any moving creature, but He defers them for a term appointed. Then when comes their terms not they will remain behind an hour and not they can advance it.

And if (walaw) | Allah were to seize (yuākhidhu) | Allah were to seize (l-lahu) | the mankind (l-nāsa) | for their wrongdoing (biẓul'mihim) | not (mā) | He would have left (taraka) | upon it (ʿalayhā) | any (min) | moving creature (dābbatin), | but (walākin) | He defers them (yu-akhiruhum) | for (ilā) | a term (ajalin) | appointed (musamman). | Then when (fa-idhā) | comes (jāa) | their terms (ajaluhum) | not (lā) | they will remain behind (yastakhirūna) | an hour (sāʿatan) | and not (walā) | they can advance it (yastaqdimūna).

16:62 And they assign to Allah what they dislike and assert their tongues the lie that for them is the best. No doubt that for them is the Fire and that they will be abandoned.

And they assign (wayajʿalūna) | to Allah (lillahi) | what (mā) | they dislike (yakrahūna) | and assert (wataṣifu) | their tongues (alsinatuhumu) | the lie (l-kadhiba) | that (anna) | for them (lahumu) | is the best (l-ḥus'nā). | No (lā) | doubt (jarama) | that (anna) | for them (lahumu) | is the Fire (l-nāra) | and that they (wa-annahum) | will be abandoned (muf'raṭūna).

16:63 By Allah, certainly We have sent to nations before you but made fair-seeming to them the Shaitaan their deeds. So he is their ally today, and for them is a punishment painful.

By Allah (tal-lahi), | certainly (laqad) | We have sent (arsalnā) | to (ilā) | nations (umamin) | before you (min) | before you (qablika) | but made fair-seeming (fazayyana) | to them (lahumu) | the Shaitaan (l-shayṭānu) | their deeds (aʿmālahum). | So he (fahuwa) | is their ally (waliyyuhumu) | today (l-yawma), | and for them (walahum) | is a punishment (ʿadhābun) | painful (alīmun).

16:64 And not We revealed to you the Book except that you make clear to them that which they differed in it, and as a guidance and mercy for a people who believe.

And not (wamā) | We revealed (anzalnā) | to you (ʿalayka) | the Book (l-kitāba) | except (illā) | that you make clear (litubayyina) | to them (lahumu) | that which (alladhī) | they differed (ikh'talafū) | in it (fīhi), | and as a guidance (wahudan) | and mercy (waraḥmatan) | for a people (liqawmin) | who believe (yu'minūna).

16:65 And Allah has sent down from the sky water, then gives life by it to the earth after its death. Indeed, in that is surely a Sign for a people who listen.

And Allah (wal-lahu) | has sent down (anzala) | from (mina) | the sky (l-samāi) | water (māan), | then gives life (fa-aḥyā) | by it (bihi) | to the earth (l-arḍa) | after (baʿda) | its death (mawtihā). | Indeed (inna), | in (fī) | that (dhālika) | is surely a Sign (laāyatan) | for a people (liqawmin) | who listen (yasmaʿūna).

16:66 And indeed, for you in the cattle is a lesson. We give you to drink from what is in their bellies, from between bowels and blood, milk pure, palatable to the drinkers.

And indeed (wa-inna), | for you (lakum) | in (fī) | the cattle (l-anʿāmi) | is a lesson (laʿib'ratan). | We give you to drink (nus'qīkum) | from what (mimmā) | is in (fī) | their bellies (buṭūnihi), | from (min) | between (bayni) | bowels (farthin) | and blood (wadamin), | milk (labanan)

| pure (khāliṣan), | palatable (sāighan) | to the drinkers (lilshāribīna).

16:67 And from fruits the date-palm, and the grapes, you take from it intoxicant and a provision good. Indeed, in that is surely a Sign for a people who use reason.

And from (wamin) | fruits (thamarāti) | the date-palm (l-nakhīli), | and the grapes (wal-aʿnābi), | you take (tattakhidhūna) | from it (min'hu) | intoxicant (sakaran) | and a provision (wariz'qan) | good (ḥasanan). | Indeed (inna), | in (fī) | that (dhālika) | is surely a Sign (laāyatan) | for a people (liqawmin) | who use reason (yaʿqilūna).

16:68 And inspired your Lord to the bee, [that] "Take among the mountains, houses and among the trees, and in what they construct.

And inspired (wa-awḥā) | your Lord (rabbuka) | to (ilā) | the bee (l-naḥli), | [that] (ani) | "Take (ittakhidhī) | among (mina) | the mountains (l-jibāli), | houses (buyūtan) | and among (wamina) | the trees (l-shajari), | and in what (wamimmā) | they construct (yaʿrishūna).

16:69 Then eat from all the fruits and follow the ways of your Lord made smooth." Comes forth from their bellies a drink of varying colors, in it is a healing for the mankind. Indeed, in that is surely a Sign for a people who reflect.

Then (thumma) | eat (kulī) | from (min) | all (kulli) | the fruits (l-thamarāti) | and follow (fa-us'lukī) | the ways (subula) | of your Lord (rabbiki) | made smooth. (dhululan)" | Comes forth (yakhruju) | from (min) | their bellies (buṭūnihā) | a drink (sharābun) | of varying (mukh'talifun) | colors (alwānuhu), | in it (fīhi) | is a healing (shifāon) | for the mankind (lilnnāsi). | Indeed (inna), | in (fī) | that (dhālika) | is surely a Sign (laāyatan) | for a people (liqawmin) | who reflect (yatafakkarūna).

16:70 And Allah created you, then will cause you to die. And among you is one who is sent back to the worst of the age, so that not he will know after knowledge a thing. Indeed, Allah is All-Knowing, All-Powerful.

And Allah (wal-lahu) | created you (khalaqakum), | then (thumma) | will cause you to die (yatawaffākum). | And among you (waminkum) | is one who (man) | is sent back (yuraddu) | to (ilā) | the worst (ardhali) | of the age (l-ʿumuri), | so that (likay) | not (lā) | he will know (yaʿlama) | after (baʿda) | knowledge (ʿil'min) | a thing (shayan). | Indeed (inna), | Allah (l-laha) | is All-Knowing (ʿalīmun), | All-Powerful (qadīrun).

16:71 And Allah has favored some of you over others in [the] provision. But not those who were favored would hand over their provision to whom possess their right hands, so that they are in it equal. Then is it the Favor of Allah they reject?

And Allah (wal-lahu) | has favored (faḍḍala) | some of you (baʿḍakum) | over (ʿalā) | others (baʿḍin) | in (fī) | [the] provision (l-riz'qi). | But not (famā) | those who (alladhīna) | were favored (fuḍḍilū) | would hand over (birāddī) | their provision (riz'qihim) | to (ʿalā) | whom (mā) | possess (malakat) | their right hands (aymānuhum), | so that they (fahum) | are in it (fīhi) | equal (sawāon). | Then is it the Favor (afabiniʿ'mati) | of Allah (l-lahi) | they reject (yajḥadūna)?

16:72 And Allah has made for you from yourselves spouses, and has made for you from your spouses sons and grandsons and has provided for you from the good things. Then in falsehood do they believe, and the Favor of Allah they disbelieve?

And Allah (wal-lahu) | has made (jaʿala) | for you (lakum) | from (min) | yourselves (anfusikum) | spouses (azwājan), | and has made (wajaʿala) | for you (lakum) | from (min) | your spouses (azwājikum) | sons (banīna) | and grandsons (waḥafadatan) | and has provided for you (warazaqakum) | from (mina) | the good things (l-ṭayibāti). | Then in falsehood do (afabil-bāṭili) | they believe (yu'minūna), | and the Favor (wabiniʿ'mati) | of Allah (l-lahi) | they (hum) | disbelieve (yakfurūna)?

16:73 And they worship other than Allah which not possesses for them any provision from the heavens and the earth [anything], and not they are able.

And they worship (wayaʿbudūna) | other than (min) | other than (dūni) | Allah (l-lahi) | which (mā) | not (lā) | possesses (yamliku) | for them (lahum) | any provision (riz'qan) | from (mina) | the heavens (l-samāwāti) | and the earth (wal-arḍi) | [anything] (shayan), | and not (walā) | they are able (yastaṭīʿūna).

16:74 So do not put forth for Allah the similitude. Indeed, Allah knows and you do not know.

So do not (falā) | put forth (taḍribū) | for Allah (lillahi) | the similitude (l-amthāla). | Indeed (inna), | Allah (l-laha) | knows (yaʿlamu) | and you (wa-antum) | do not (lā) | know (taʿlamūna).

16:75 Allah sets forth the example of a slave who is owned, not he has power on anything and one whom We provided him from Us a provision good, so he spends from it, secretly and publicly. Can they be equal? All praise is for Allah! Nay, but most of them do not know.

Allah sets forth (ḍaraba) | Allah sets forth (l-lahu) | the example (mathalan) | of a slave (ʿabdan) | who is owned (mamlūkan), | not (lā) | he has power (yaqdiru) | on (ʿalā) | anything (shayin) | and one whom (waman) | We provided him (razaqnāhu) | from Us (minnā) | a provision (riz'qan) | good (ḥasanan), | so he (fahuwa) | spends (yunfiqu) | from it (min'hu), | secretly (sirran) | and publicly (wajahran). | Can (hal) | they be equal (yastawūna)? | All praise (l-ḥamdu) | is for Allah (lillahi)! | Nay (bal), | but most of them (aktharuhum) | do not (lā) | know (yaʿlamūna).

16:76 And Allah sets forth an example of two men, one of them is dumb, not he has power on anything, while he is a burden on his master. Wherever he directs him not he comes with any good. Is equal he and the one who commands [of] justice, and he is on a path straight?

And Allah sets forth (waḍaraba) | And Allah sets forth (l-lahu) | an example (mathalan) | of two men (rajulayni), | one of them (aḥaduhumā) | is dumb (abkamu), | not (lā) | he has power (yaqdiru) | on (ʿalā) | anything (shayin), | while he (wahuwa) | is a burden (kallun) | on (ʿalā) | his master (mawlāhu). | Wherever (aynamā) | he directs him (yuwajjihhu) | not (lā) | he comes (yati) | with any good (bikhayrin). | Is (hal) | equal (yastawī) | he (huwa) | and the one who (waman) | commands (yamuru) | [of] justice (bil-ʿadli), | and he (wahuwa) | is on (ʿalā) | a path (ṣirāṭin) | straight (mus'taqīmin)?

16:77 And to Allah belongs the unseen of the heavens and the earth. And not is the matter of the Hour but as a twinkling of the eye or it is nearer. Indeed, Allah on every thing is All-Powerful.

And to Allah belongs (walillahi) | the unseen (ghaybu) | of the heavens (l-samāwāti) | and the earth (wal-arḍi). | And not (wamā) | is the matter (amru) | of the Hour (l-sāʿati) | but (illā) | as a twinkling (kalamḥi) | of the eye (l-baṣari) | or (aw) | it (huwa) | is nearer (aqrabu). | Indeed (inna), | Allah (l-laha) | on (ʿalā) | every (kulli) | thing (shayin) | is All-Powerful (qadīrun).

16:78 And Allah brought you forth from the wombs of your mothers, not knowing anything, and made for you the hearing and the sight and the hearts so that you may give thanks.

And Allah (wal-lahu) | brought you forth (akhrajakum) | from (min) | the wombs (buṭūni) | of your mothers (ummahātikum), | not (lā) | knowing (taʿlamūna) | anything (shayan), | and made (wajaʿala) | for you (lakumu) | the hearing (l-samʿa) | and the sight (wal-abṣāra) | and the hearts (wal-afidata) | so that you may (laʿallakum) | give thanks (tashkurūna).

16:79 Do not they see towards the birds controlled in the midst of the sky? None holds them up except Allah. Indeed, in that are Signs for a people who believe.

Do not (alam) | they see (yaraw) | towards (ilā) | the birds (l-ṭayri) | controlled (musakharātin) | in (fī) | the midst (jawwi) | of the sky (l-samāi)? | None (mā) | holds them up (yum'sikuhunna) | except (illā) | Allah (l-lahu). | Indeed (inna), | in (fī) | that (dhālika) | are Signs (laāyātin) | for a people (liqawmin) | who believe (yu'minūna).

16:80 And Allah has made for you [from] your homes a resting place, and made for you from the hides of the cattle tents, which you find light on the day of your travel and the day of your encampment; and from their wool and their fur and their hair is furnishing and a provision for a time.

And Allah (wal-lahu) | has made (jaʿala) | for you (lakum) | [from] (min) | your homes (buyūtikum) | a resting place (sakanan), | and made (wajaʿala) | for you (lakum) | from (min) | the hides (julūdi) | of the cattle (l-anʿāmi) | tents (buyūtan), | which you find light (tastakhiffūnahā) | on the day (yawma) | of your travel (ẓaʿnikum) | and the day (wayawma) | of your encampment (iqāmatikum); | and from (wamin) | their wool (aṣwāfihā) | and their fur (wa-awbārihā) | and their hair (wa-ashʿārihā) | is furnishing (athāthan) | and a provision (wamatāʿan) | for (ilā) | a time (ḥīnin).

16:81 And Allah has made for you from what He created, shades and has made for you from the mountains, shelters and has made for you garments to protect you from the heat and garments to protect you from your mutual violence. Thus He completes His Favor upon you so that you may submit.

And Allah (wal-lahu) | has made (jaʿala) | for you (lakum) | from what (mimmā) | He created (khalaqa), | shades (ẓilālan) | and has made (wajaʿala) | for you (lakum) | from (mina) | the mountains (l-jibāli), | shelters (aknānan) | and has made (wajaʿala) | for you (lakum) | garments (sarābīla) | to protect you (taqīkumu) | from the heat (l-ḥara) | and garments (wasarābīla) | to protect you (taqīkum) | from your mutual violence (basakum). | Thus (kadhālika) | He completes (yutimmu) | His Favor (niʿʿmatahu) | upon you (ʿalaykum) | so that you may (laʿallakum) | submit (tus'limūna).

16:82 Then, if they turn away then only upon you is the conveyance the clear.

Then, if (fa-in) | they turn away (tawallaw) | then only (fa-innamā) | upon you (ʿalayka) | is the conveyance (l-balāghu) | the clear (l-mubīnu).

16:83 They recognize the Favor of Allah; then they deny it. And most of them are the disbelievers.

They recognize (yaʿrifūna) | the Favor (niʿʿmata) | of Allah (l-lahi); | then (thumma) | they deny it (yunkirūnahā). | And most of them (wa-aktharuhumu) | are the disbelievers (l-kāfirūna).

16:84 And the Day We will resurrect from every nation a witness, then not will be permitted to those who disbelieved and not they will be asked to make amends.

And the Day (wayawma) | We will resurrect (nabʿathu) | from (min) | every (kulli) | nation (ummatin) | a witness (shahīdan), | then (thumma) | not (lā) | will be permitted (yu'dhanu) | to those who (lilladhīna) | disbelieved (kafarū) | and not (walā) | they (hum) | will be asked to make amends (yus'taʿtabūna).

16:85 And when will see those who wronged the punishment, then not it will be lightened for them and not they will be given respite.

And when (wa-idhā) | will see (raā) | those who (alladhīna) | wronged (ẓalamū) | the punishment (l-ʿadhāba), | then not (falā) | it will be lightened (yukhaffafu) | for them (ʿanhum) | and not (walā) | they (hum) | will be given respite (yunẓarūna).

16:86 And when will see those who associated partners with Allah their partners. They will say, "Our Lord, these are our partners those whom we used to invoke besides You." But they will throw back at them their word, "Indeed, you are surely liars."

And when (wa-idhā) | will see (raā) | those who (alladhīna) | associated partners with

Allah (ashrakū) | their partners (shurakāahum). | They will say (qālū), | "Our Lord (rabbanā), | these (hāulāi) | are our partners (shurakāunā) | those whom (alladhīna) | we used to (kunnā) | invoke (nadʿū) | besides You. (min)" | besides You. (dūnika)" | But they will throw back (fa-alqaw) | at them (ilayhimu) | their word (l-qawla), | "Indeed, you (innakum) | are surely liars. (lakādhibūna)"

16:87 And they will offer to Allah on that Day the submission, and is lost from them what they used to invent.

And they will offer (wa-alqaw) | to (ilā) | Allah (l-lahi) | on that Day (yawma-idhin) | the submission (l-salama), | and is lost (waḍalla) | from them (ʿanhum) | what (mā) | they used to (kānū) | invent (yaftarūna).

16:88 And those who disbelieved and hindered from the way of Allah, We will increase them in punishment over punishment because they used to spread corruption.

And those who (alladhīna) | disbelieved (kafarū) | and hindered (waṣaddū) | from (ʿan) | the way (sabīli) | of Allah (l-lahi), | We will increase them (zid'nāhum) | in punishment (ʿadhāban) | over (fawqa) | punishment (l-ʿadhābi) | because (bimā) | they used to (kānū) | spread corruption (yuf'sidūna).

16:89 And the Day We will resurrect among every nation a witness over them from themselves. And We will bring you as a witness over these. And We sent down to you the Book as a clarification of every thing and a guidance and mercy and glad tidings for the Muslims.

And the Day (wayawma) | We will resurrect (nabʿathu) | among (fī) | every (kulli) | nation (ummatin) | a witness (shahīdan) | over them (ʿalayhim) | from (min) | themselves (anfusihim). | And We will bring (waji'nā) | you (bika) | as a witness (shahīdan) | over (ʿalā) | these (hāulāi). | And We sent down (wanazzalnā) | to you (ʿalayka) | the Book (l-kitāba) | as a clarification (tib'yānan) | of every (likulli) | thing (shayin) | and a guidance (wahudan) | and mercy (waraḥmatan) | and glad tidings (wabush'rā) | for the Muslims (lil'mus'limīna).

16:90 Indeed, Allah commands justice and the good, and giving to relatives, and forbids [from] the immorality and the bad and the oppression. He admonishes you so that you may take heed.

Indeed (inna), | Allah (l-laha) | commands (yamuru) | justice (bil-ʿadli) | and the good (wal-iḥ'sāni), | and giving (waītāi) | to relatives (dhī), | to relatives (l-qur'bā), | and forbids (wayanhā) | [from] (ʿani) | the immorality (l-faḥshāi) | and the bad (wal-munkari) | and the oppression (wal-baghyi). | He admonishes you (yaʿiẓukum) | so that you may (laʿallakum) | take heed (tadhakkarūna).

16:91 And fulfil the covenant of Allah when you have taken a covenant, and do not break oaths after their confirmation while verily you have made Allah over you a surety. Indeed, Allah knows what you do.

And fulfil (wa-awfū) | the covenant (biʿahdi) | of Allah (l-lahi) | when (idhā) | you have taken a covenant (ʿāhadttum), | and do not (walā) | break (tanquḍū) | oaths (l-aymāna) | after (baʿda) | their confirmation (tawkīdihā) | while verily (waqad) | you have made (jaʿaltumu) | Allah (l-laha) | over you (ʿalaykum) | a surety (kafīlan). | Indeed (inna), | Allah (l-laha) | knows (yaʿlamu) | what (mā) | you do (tafʿalūna).

16:92 And do not be like her who untwists her spun yarn after strength into untwisted strands; you take your oaths as a deception between you, because is a community [it] more numerous than another community. Only, Allah tests you by it. And He will make clear to you on the Day of the Resurrection, what you used to in it differ.

And do not (walā) | be (takūnū) | like her who (ka-allatī) | untwists (naqaḍat) | her spun yarn (ghazlahā) | after (min) | after (baʿdi) | strength (quwwatin) | into untwisted strands (ankāthan); | you take (tattakhidhūna) | your oaths (aymānakum) | as a deception (dakhalan) |

between you (baynakum), | because (an) | is (takūna) | a community (ummatun) | [it] (hiya) | more numerous (arbā) | than (min) | another community (ummatin). | Only (innamā), | Allah tests you (yablūkumu) | Allah tests you (l-lahu) | by it (bihi). | And He will make clear (walayubayyinanna) | to you (lakum) | on the Day (yawma) | of the Resurrection (l-qiyāmati), | what (mā) | you used to (kuntum) | in it (fīhi) | differ (takhtalifūna).

16:93 And if Allah had willed surely He could have made you a nation one, but He lets go astray whom He wills and guides whom He wills. And surely you will be questioned about what you used to do.

And if (walaw) | Allah had willed (shāa) | Allah had willed (l-lahu) | surely He could have made you (laja'alakum) | a nation (ummatan) | one (wāḥidatan), | but (walākin) | He lets go astray (yuḍillu) | whom (man) | He wills (yashāu) | and guides (wayahdī) | whom (man) | He wills (yashāu). | And surely you will be questioned (walatus'alunna) | about what ('ammā) | you used to (kuntum) | do (ta'malūna).

16:94 And do not take your oaths as a deception between you, lest, should slip a foot after it is firmly planted, and you would taste the evil for what you hindered from the way of Allah and for you is a punishment great.

And do not (walā) | take (tattakhidhū) | your oaths (aymānakum) | as a deception (dakhalan) | between you (baynakum), | lest, should slip (fatazilla) | a foot (qadamun) | after (ba'da) | it is firmly planted (thubūtihā), | and you would taste (watadhūqū) | the evil (l-sūa) | for what (bimā) | you hindered (ṣadadttum) | from ('an) | the way (sabīli) | of Allah (l-lahi) | and for you (walakum) | is a punishment ('adhābun) | great ('aẓīmun).

16:95 And do not exchange the covenant of Allah, for a price little. Indeed, what is with Allah, it is better for you if you were to know.

And do not (walā) | exchange (tashtarū) | the covenant (bi'ahdi) | of Allah (l-lahi), | for a price (thamanan) | little (qalīlan). | Indeed, what (innamā) | is with ('inda) | Allah (l-lahi), | it (huwa) | is better (khayrun) | for you (lakum) | if (in) | you were to (kuntum) | know (ta'lamūna).

16:96 Whatever is with you will be exhausted, and whatever is with Allah will be remaining. And surely We will pay those who are patient their reward to the best of what they used to do.

Whatever (mā) | is with you ('indakum) | will be exhausted (yanfadu), | and whatever (wamā) | is with ('inda) | Allah (l-lahi) | will be remaining (bāqin). | And surely We will pay (walanajziyanna) | those who (alladhīna) | are patient (ṣabarū) | their reward (ajrahum) | to the best (bi-aḥsani) | of what (mā) | they used to (kānū) | do (ya'malūna).

16:97 Whoever does righteous deeds whether male or female while he is a believer, then surely We will give him life, a life good, and We will pay them their reward to the best of what they used to do.

Whoever (man) | does ('amila) | righteous deeds (ṣāliḥan) | whether (min) | male (dhakarin) | or (aw) | female (unthā) | while he (wahuwa) | is a believer (mu'minun), | then surely We will give him life (falanuḥ'yiyannahu), | a life (ḥayatan) | good (ṭayyibatan), | and We will pay them (walanajziyannahum) | their reward (ajrahum) | to the best (bi-aḥsani) | of what (mā) | they used to (kānū) | do (ya'malūna).

16:98 So when you recite the Quran, seek refuge in Allah from the Shaitaan, the accursed.

So when (fa-idhā) | you recite (qarata) | the Quran (l-qur'āna), | seek refuge (fa-is'ta'idh) | in Allah (bil-lahi) | from (mina) | the Shaitaan (l-shayṭāni), | the accursed (l-rajīmi).

16:99 Indeed he, not for him is any authority on those who believe and upon their Lord they put their trust.

Indeed he (innahu), | not (laysa) | for him (lahu) | is any authority (sul'ṭānun) | on ('alā) |

those who (alladhīna) | believe (āmanū) | and upon (waʿalā) | their Lord (rabbihim) | they put their trust (yatawakkalūna).

16:100 Only his authority is over those who take him as an ally and those who [they] with Him associate partners.

Only (innamā) | his authority (sul'ṭānuhu) | is over (ʿalā) | those who (alladhīna) | take him as an ally (yatawallawnahu) | and those who (wa-alladhīna) | [they] (hum) | with Him (bihi) | associate partners (mush'rikūna).

16:101 And when We substitute a Verse in place of a Verse, and Allah - is most knowing of what He sends down they say, "Only you are an inventor." Nay, most of them do not know.

And when (wa-idhā) | We substitute (baddalnā) | a Verse (āyatan) | in place (makāna) | of a Verse (āyatin), | and Allah (wal-lahu)- | is most knowing (aʿlamu) | of what (bimā) | He sends down (yunazzilu) | they say (qālū), | "Only (innamā) | you (anta) | are an inventor. (muf'tarin)" | Nay (bal), | most of them (aktharuhum) | do not (lā) | know (yaʿlamūna).

16:102 Say, "Has brought it down the Holy Spirit from your Lord in truth, to make firm those who believe and as a guidance and glad tidings to the Muslims."

Say (qul), | "Has brought it down (nazzalahu) | the Holy Spirit (rūḥu) | the Holy Spirit (l-qudusi) | from (min) | your Lord (rabbika) | in truth (bil-ḥaqi), | to make firm (liyuthabbita) | those who (alladhīna) | believe (āmanū) | and as a guidance (wahudan) | and glad tidings (wabush'rā) | to the Muslims. (lil'mus'limīna)"

16:103 And certainly We know that they say, "Only teaches him a human being." The tongue of the one they refer to him is foreign while this is a language Arabic clear.

And certainly (walaqad) | We know (naʿlamu) | that they (annahum) | say (yaqūlūna), | "Only (innamā) | teaches him (yuʿallimuhu) | a human being. (basharun)" | The tongue (lisānu) | of the one (alladhī) | they refer (yul'ḥidūna) | to him (ilayhi) | is foreign (aʿjamiyyun) | while this (wahādhā) | is a language (lisānun) | Arabic (ʿarabiyyun) | clear (mubīnun).

16:104 Indeed, those who do not believe in the Verses of Allah, not Allah will guide them and for them is a punishment painful.

Indeed (inna), | those who (alladhīna) | do not (lā) | believe (yu'minūna) | in the Verses (biāyāti) | of Allah (l-lahi), | not (lā) | Allah will guide them (yahdīhimu) | Allah will guide them (l-lahu) | and for them (walahum) | is a punishment (ʿadhābun) | painful (alīmun).

16:105 Only they invent the falsehood those who do not believe in the Verses of Allah, and those - they are the liars.

Only (innamā) | they invent (yaftarī) | the falsehood (l-kadhiba) | those who (alladhīna) | do not (lā) | believe (yu'minūna) | in the Verses (biāyāti) | of Allah (l-lahi), | and those (wa-ulāika)- | they (humu) | are the liars (l-kādhibūna).

16:106 Whoever disbelieves in Allah after his belief, except one who is forced while his heart is content with the faith. But one who opens to disbelief his breast, then upon them is a wrath of Allah and for them is a punishment great.

Whoever (man) | disbelieves (kafara) | in Allah (bil-lahi) | after (min) | after (baʿdi) | his belief (īmānihi), | except (illā) | one who (man) | is forced (uk'riha) | while his heart (waqalbuhu) | is content (muṭ'ma-innun) | with the faith (bil-īmāni). | But (walākin) | one who (man) | opens (sharaḥa) | to disbelief (bil-kuf'ri) | his breast (ṣadran), | then upon them (faʿalayhim) | is a wrath (ghaḍabun) | of (mina) | Allah (l-lahi) | and for them (walahum) | is a punishment (ʿadhābun) | great (ʿaẓīmun).

16:107 That is because they preferred the life of the world over the Hereafter and that Allah does not guide the people the disbelievers.

That is (dhālika) | because (bi-annahumu) | they preferred (is'taḥabbū) | the life (l-ḥayata) | of the world (l-dun'yā) | over (ʿalā) | the Hereafter (l-ākhirati) | and that (wa-anna) | Allah (l-laha) | does not (lā) | guide (yahdī) | the people (l-qawma) | the disbelievers (l-kāfirīna).

16:108 Those are the ones - Allah has set a seal over their hearts and their hearing and their sight. And those - they are the heedless.

Those (ulāika) | are the ones (alladhīna)- | Allah has set a seal (ṭabaʿa) | Allah has set a seal (l-lahu) | over (ʿalā) | their hearts (qulūbihim) | and their hearing (wasamʿihim) | and their sight (wa-abṣārihim). | And those (wa-ulāika)- | they are (humu) | the heedless (l-ghāfilūna).

16:109 No doubt that they in the Hereafter [they] are the losers.

No (lā) | doubt (jarama) | that they (annahum) | in (fī) | the Hereafter (l-ākhirati) | [they] (humu) | are the losers (l-khāsirūna).

16:110 Then indeed, your Lord, to those who emigrated after what they had been put to trials then strove hard and were patient. Indeed, your Lord, after it, surely is Oft-Forgiving, Most Merciful.

Then (thumma) | indeed (inna), | your Lord (rabbaka), | to those who (lilladhīna) | emigrated (hājarū) | after (min) | after (baʿdi) | what (mā) | they had been put to trials (futinū) | then (thumma) | strove hard (jāhadū) | and were patient (waṣabarū). | Indeed (inna), | your Lord (rabbaka), | after it (min), | after it (baʿdihā), | surely is Oft-Forgiving (laghafūrun), | Most Merciful (raḥīmun).

16:111 On the Day when will come every soul pleading for itself, and will be paid in full every soul what it did and they will not be wronged.

On the Day (yawma) | when will come (tatī) | every (kullu) | soul (nafsin) | pleading (tujādilu) | for (ʿan) | itself (nafsihā), | and will be paid in full (watuwaffā) | every (kullu) | soul (nafsin) | what (mā) | it did (ʿamilat) | and they (wahum) | will not (lā) | be wronged (yuẓ'lamūna).

16:112 And Allah sets forth a similitude of a town that was secure and content, coming to it its provision in abundance from every place, but it denied the Favors of Allah, so Allah made it taste the garb of the hunger and the fear for what they used to do.

And Allah sets forth (waḍaraba) | And Allah sets forth (l-lahu) | a similitude (mathalan) | of a town (qaryatan) | that was (kānat) | secure (āminatan) | and content (muṭ'ma-innatan), | coming to it (yatīhā) | its provision (riz'quhā) | in abundance (raghadan) | from (min) | every (kulli) | place (makānin), | but it denied (fakafarat) | the Favors of Allah (bi-anʿumi), | the Favors of Allah (l-lahi), | so Allah made it taste (fa-adhāqahā) | so Allah made it taste (l-lahu) | the garb (libāsa) | of the hunger (l-jūʿi) | and the fear (wal-khawfi) | for what (bimā) | they used to (kānū) | do (yaṣnaʿūna).

16:113 And certainly came to them a Messenger from among them but they denied him; so seized them the punishment while they were wrongdoers.

And certainly (walaqad) | came to them (jāahum) | a Messenger (rasūlun) | from among them (min'hum) | but they denied him (fakadhabūhu); | so seized them (fa-akhadhahumu) | the punishment (l-ʿadhābu) | while they (wahum) | were wrongdoers (ẓālimūna).

16:114 So eat of what Allah has provided you - lawful and good. And be grateful for the Favor of Allah, if [you] Him Alone you worship.

So eat (fakulū) | of what (mimmā) | Allah has provided you (razaqakumu)- | Allah has provided you (l-lahu)- | lawful (ḥalālan) | and good (ṭayyiban). | And be grateful (wa-ush'kurū) | for the Favor (niʿ'mata) | of Allah (l-lahi), | if (in) | [you] (kuntum) | Him Alone (iyyāhu) | you worship (taʿbudūna).

16:115 Only He has forbidden to you the dead animal and the blood and the flesh of the swine, and what has been dedicated to other than Allah [with it]. But if one is forced - without being disobedient, and not a transgressor - then indeed, Allah is Oft-Forgiving, Most Merciful.

Only (innamā) | He has forbidden (ḥarrama) | to you (ʿalaykumu) | the dead animal (l-maytata) | and the blood (wal-dama) | and the flesh (walaḥma) | of the swine (l-khinzīri), | and what (wamā) | has been dedicated (uhilla) | to other than (lighayri) | Allah (l-lahi) | [with it] (bihi). | But if one (famani) | is forced (uḍ'ṭurra)- | without being (ghayra) | disobedient (bāghin), | and not (walā) | a transgressor (ʿādin)- | then indeed (fa-inna), | Allah (l-laha) | is Oft-Forgiving (ghafūrun), | Most Merciful (raḥīmun).

16:116 And do not say for that which assert your tongues, the lie, "This is lawful and this is forbidden," so that you invent about Allah the lie. Indeed, those who invent about Allah the lie, they will not succeed.

And do not (walā) | say (taqūlū) | for that which (limā) | assert (taṣifu) | your tongues (alsinatukumu), | the lie (l-kadhiba), | "This (hādhā) | is lawful (ḥalālun) | and this (wahādhā) | is forbidden, (ḥarāmun)" | so that you invent (litaftarū) | about (ʿalā) | Allah (l-lahi) | the lie (l-kadhiba). | Indeed (inna), | those who (alladhīna) | invent (yaftarūna) | about (ʿalā) | Allah (l-lahi) | the lie (l-kadhiba), | they will not succeed (lā). | they will not succeed (yuf'liḥūna).

16:117 An enjoyment little and for them is a punishment painful.

An enjoyment (matāʿun) | little (qalīlun) | and for them (walahum) | is a punishment (ʿadhābun) | painful (alīmun).

16:118 And to those who are Jews We have forbidden what We related to you before. And not We wronged them but they used to themselves wrong.

And to (waʿalā) | those who (alladhīna) | are Jews (hādū) | We have forbidden (ḥarramnā) | what (mā) | We related (qaṣaṣnā) | to you (ʿalayka) | before (min). | before (qablu). | And not (wamā) | We wronged them (ẓalamnāhum) | but (walākin) | they used to (kānū) | themselves (anfusahum) | wrong (yaẓlimūna).

16:119 Then indeed, your Lord, to those who did evil in ignorance, then repented after that, and corrected themselves - indeed, your Lord, after that is surely Oft-Forgiving, Most Merciful.

Then (thumma) | indeed (inna), | your Lord (rabbaka), | to those who (lilladhīna) | did (ʿamilū) | evil (l-sūa) | in ignorance (bijahālatin), | then (thumma) | repented (tābū) | after (min) | after (baʿdi) | that (dhālika), | and corrected themselves (wa-aṣlaḥū)- | indeed (inna), | your Lord (rabbaka), | after that (min) | after that (baʿdihā) | is surely Oft-Forgiving (laghafūrun), | Most Merciful (raḥīmun).

16:120 Indeed, Ibrahim was a nation obedient to Allah upright, and not he was of the polytheists.

Indeed (inna), | Ibrahim (ib'rāhīma) | was (kāna) | a nation (ummatan) | obedient (qānitan) | to Allah (lillahi) | upright (ḥanīfan), | and not (walam) | he was (yaku) | of (mina) | the polytheists (l-mush'rikīna).

16:121 Thankful for His favors. He chose him and guided him to the way straight.

Thankful (shākiran) | for His favors (li-anʿumihi). | He chose him (ij'tabāhu) | and guided him (wahadāhu) | to (ilā) | the way (ṣirāṭin) | straight (mus'taqīmin).

16:122 And We gave him in the world good, and indeed, he in the Hereafter he will surely (be) among the righteous.

And We gave him (waātaynāhu) | in (fī) | the world (l-dun'yā) | good (ḥasanatan), | and indeed, he (wa-innahu) | in (fī) | the Hereafter (l-ākhirati) | he will surely (be) among (lamina) | the righteous (l-ṣāliḥīna).

16:123 Then We revealed to you, that, "You follow the religion of Ibrahim upright; and not he was of the polytheists."

Then (thumma) | We revealed (awḥaynā) | to you (ilayka), | that (ani), | "You follow (ittabiʿ) | the religion (millata) | of Ibrahim (ib'rāhīma) | upright (ḥanīfan); | and not (wamā) | he was (kāna) | of (mina) | the polytheists. (l-mush'rikīna)"

16:124 Only was appointed the Sabbath for those who differed in it. And indeed, your Lord will surely judge between them on the Day of the Resurrection in what they used to [in it] differ.

Only (innamā) | was appointed (juʿila) | the Sabbath (l-sabtu) | for (ʿalā) | those who (alladhīna) | differed (ikh'talafū) | in it (fīhi). | And indeed (wa-inna), | your Lord (rabbaka) | will surely judge (layaḥkumu) | between them (baynahum) | on the Day (yawma) | of the Resurrection (l-qiyāmati) | in what (fīmā) | they used to (kānū) | [in it] (fīhi) | differ (yakhtalifūna).

16:125 Call to the way of your Lord with the wisdom and the instruction the good, and discuss with them in that which is best. Indeed, your Lord, He is most knowing of who has strayed from His way, And He is most knowing of the guided ones.

Call (ud'ʿu) | to (ilā) | the way (sabīli) | of your Lord (rabbika) | with the wisdom (bil-ḥik'mati) | and the instruction (wal-mawʿiẓati) | the good (l-ḥasanati), | and discuss with them (wajādil'hum) | in that (bi-allatī) | which (hiya) | is best (aḥsanu). | Indeed (inna), | your Lord (rabbaka), | He (huwa) | is most knowing (aʿlamu) | of who (biman) | has strayed (ḍalla) | from (ʿan) | His way (sabīlihi), | And He (wahuwa) | is most knowing (aʿlamu) | of the guided ones (bil-muh'tadīna).

16:126 And if you retaliate, then retaliate with the like of what you were afflicted with [it]. But if you are patient, surely it is better for those who are patient.

And if (wa-in) | you retaliate (ʿāqabtum), | then retaliate (faʿāqibū) | with the like (bimith'li) | of what (mā) | you were afflicted (ʿūqib'tum) | with [it] (bihi). | But if (wala-in) | you are patient (ṣabartum), | surely it is (lahuwa) | better (khayrun) | for those who are patient (lilṣṣābirīna).

16:127 And be patient and not is your patience but from Allah. And do not grieve over them and do not be in distress for what they plot.

And be patient (wa-iṣ'bir) | and not (wamā) | is your patience (ṣabruka) | but (illā) | from Allah (bil-lahi). | And do not (walā) | grieve (taḥzan) | over them (ʿalayhim) | and do not (walā) | be (taku) | in (fī) | distress (ḍayqin) | for what (mimmā) | they plot (yamkurūna).

16:128 Indeed, Allah is with those who fear Him and those who [they] are good-doers.

Indeed (inna), | Allah (l-laha) | is with (maʿa) | those who (alladhīna) | fear Him (ittaqaw) | and those who (wa-alladhīna) | [they] (hum) | are good-doers (muḥ'sinūna).

Chapter (17) Sūrat l-Isrā (The Night Journey)

17:1 Exalted is the One Who took His servant by night from Al-Masjid Al-Haraam, to Al-Masjid Al-Aqsa which We blessed its surroundings, that We may show him of Our Signs. Indeed He, He is the All-Hearer, the All-Seer.

Exalted (sub'ḥāna) | is the One Who (alladhī) | took (asrā) | His servant (biʿabdihi) | by night (laylan) | from (mina) | Al-Masjid Al-Haraam (l-masjidi), | Al-Masjid Al-Haraam (l-ḥarāmi), | to (ilā) | Al-Masjid Al-Aqsa (l-masjidi) | Al-Masjid Al-Aqsa (l-aqṣā) | which (alladhī) | We blessed (bāraknā) | its surroundings (ḥawlahu), | that We may show him (linuriyahu) | of (min) | Our Signs (āyātinā). | Indeed He (innahu), | He (huwa) | is the All-Hearer (l-samīʿu), | the All-Seer (l-baṣīru).

17:2 And We gave Musa the Book, and made it a guidance for the Children of Israel, "That not you take other than Me as a Disposer of affairs."

And We gave (waātaynā) | Musa (mūsā) | the Book (l-kitāba), | and made it (wajaʿalnāhu) | a guidance (hudan) | for the Children (libanī) | of Israel (is'rāīla), | "That not (allā) | you take (tattakhidhū) | other than Me (min) | other than Me (dūnī) | as a Disposer of affairs. (wakīlan)"

17:3 Offsprings of one who We carried with Nuh. Indeed, he was a servant grateful.

Offsprings (dhurriyyata) | of one who (man) | We carried (ḥamalnā) | with (maʿa) | Nuh (nūḥin). | Indeed, he (innahu) | was (kāna) | a servant (ʿabdan) | grateful (shakūran).

17:4 And We decreed for the Children of Israel in the Book, "Surely you will cause corruption in the earth twice, and surely you will reach, haughtiness great."

And We decreed (waqaḍaynā) | for (ilā) | the Children (banī) | of Israel (is'rāīla) | in (fī) | the Book (l-kitābi), | "Surely you will cause corruption (latuf'sidunna) | in (fī) | the earth (l-arḍi) | twice (marratayni), | and surely you will reach (walataʿlunna), | haughtiness (ʿuluwwan) | great. (kabīran)"

17:5 So when came the promise for the first of the two, We raised against you servants of Ours those of great military might and they entered the inner most part of the homes, and it was a promise fulfilled.

So when (fa-idhā) | came (jāa) | the promise (waʿdu) | for the first of the two (ūlāhumā), | We raised (baʿathnā) | against you (ʿalaykum) | servants (ʿibādan) | of Ours (lanā) | those of great military might (ulī) | those of great military might (basin) | those of great military might (shadīdin) | and they entered (fajāsū) | the inner most part (khilāla) | of the homes (l-diyāri), | and it was (wakāna) | a promise (waʿdan) | fulfilled (mafʿūlan).

17:6 Then We gave back to you the return victory over them. And We reinforced you with the wealth and sons and made you more numerous.

Then (thumma) | We gave back (radadnā) | to you (lakumu) | the return victory (l-karata) | over them (ʿalayhim). | And We reinforced you (wa-amdadnākum) | with the wealth (bi-amwālin) | and sons (wabanīna) | and made you (wajaʿalnākum) | more (akthara) | numerous (nafīran).

17:7 If you do good, you do good for yourselves; and if you do evil, then it is for it. So when came promise the last, to sadden your faces and to enter the Masjid just as they had entered it first time, and to destroy what they had conquered with destruction.

If (in) | you do good (aḥsantum), | you do good (aḥsantum) | for yourselves (li-anfusikum); | and if (wa-in) | you do evil (asatum), | then it is for it (falahā). | So when (fa-idhā) | came (jāa) | promise (waʿdu) | the last (l-ākhirati), | to sadden (liyasūū) | your faces (wujūhakum) | and to enter (waliyadkhulū) | the Masjid (l-masjida) | just as (kamā) | they had entered it (dakhalūhu) | first (awwala) | time (marratin), | and to destroy (waliyutabbirū) | what (mā) | they had conquered (ʿalaw) | with destruction (tatbīran).

17:8 "It may be that your Lord may have mercy upon you. But if you return, We will return. And We have made Hell, for the disbelievers, a prison-bed."

"It may be (ʿasā) | that your Lord (rabbukum) | that your Lord (an) | may have mercy upon you (yarḥamakum). | But if (wa-in) | you return (ʿudttum), | We will return (ʿud'nā). | And We have made (wajaʿalnā) | Hell (jahannama), | for the disbelievers (lil'kāfirīna), | a prison-bed. (ḥaṣīran)"

17:9 Indeed, this, the Quran, guides to that which is most straight and gives glad tidings to the believers - those who do the righteous deeds, that for them is a reward great,

Indeed (inna), | this (hādhā), | the Quran (l-qur'āna), | guides (yahdī) | to that (lillatī) | which (hiya) | is most straight (aqwamu) | and gives glad tidings (wayubashiru) | to the believers (l-mu'minīna)- | those who (alladhīna) | do (yaʿmalūna) | the righteous deeds (l-ṣāliḥāti), | that (anna) | for them (lahum) | is a reward (ajran) | great (kabīran),

17:10 And that those who do not believe in the Hereafter, We have prepared for them a punishment painful.

And that (wa-anna) | those who (alladhīna) | do not (lā) | believe (yu'minūna) | in the Hereafter (bil-ākhirati), | We have prepared (aʿtadnā) | for them (lahum) | a punishment (ʿadhāban) | painful (alīman).

17:11 And prays the man for evil as he prays for the good. And is the man ever hasty.

And prays (wayadʿu) | the man (l-insānu) | for evil (bil-shari) | as he prays (duʿāahu) | for the good (bil-khayri). | And is (wakāna) | the man (l-insānu) | ever hasty (ʿajūlan).

17:12 And We have made the night and the day as two signs. Then We erased the sign of the night, and We made the sign of the day visible, that you may seek bounty from your Lord, and that you may know the number of the years, and the account. And every thing - We have explained it in detail.

And We have made (wajaʿalnā) | the night (al-layla) | and the day (wal-nahāra) | as two signs (āyatayni). | Then We erased (famaḥawnā) | the sign (āyata) | of the night (al-layli), | and We made (wajaʿalnā) | the sign (āyata) | of the day (l-nahāri) | visible (mub'ṣiratan), | that you may seek (litabtaghū) | bounty (faḍlan) | from (min) | your Lord (rabbikum), | and that you may know (walitaʿlamū) | the number (ʿadada) | of the years (l-sinīna), | and the account (wal-ḥisāba). | And every (wakulla) | thing (shayin)- | We have explained it (faṣṣalnāhu) | in detail (tafṣīlan).

17:13 And for every man We have fastened to him his fate in his neck, and We will bring forth for him on the Day of the Resurrection a record which he will find wide open.

And for every (wakulla) | man (insānin) | We have fastened to him (alzamnāhu) | his fate (ṭāirahu) | in (fī) | his neck (ʿunuqihi), | and We will bring forth (wanukh'riju) | for him (lahu) | on the Day (yawma) | of the Resurrection (l-qiyāmati) | a record (kitāban) | which he will find (yalqāhu) | wide open (manshūran).

17:14 "Read your record. Sufficient is yourself today, against you as accountant."

"Read (iq'ra) | your record (kitābaka). | Sufficient (kafā) | is yourself (binafsika) | today (l-yawma), | against you (ʿalayka) | as accountant. (ḥasīban)"

17:15 Whoever is guided then only he is guided for his soul. And whoever goes astray then only he goes astray against it And not will bear a bearer of burden, burden of another. And not We are to punish until, We have sent a Messenger.

Whoever (mani) | is guided (ih'tadā) | then only (fa-innamā) | he is guided (yahtadī) | for his soul (linafsihi). | And whoever (waman) | goes astray (ḍalla) | then only (fa-innamā) | he goes astray (yaḍillu) | against it (ʿalayhā) | And not (walā) | will bear (taziru) | a bearer of burden (wāziratun), | burden (wiz'ra) | of another (ukh'rā). | And not (wamā) | We (kunnā) | are to punish (muʿadhibīna) | until (ḥattā), | We have sent (nabʿatha) | a Messenger (rasūlan).

17:16 And when We intend that We destroy a town, We order its wealthy people but they defiantly disobey therein; so is proved true against it the word, and We destroy it with destruction.

And when (wa-idhā) | We intend (aradnā) | that (an) | We destroy (nuh'lika) | a town (qaryatan), | We order (amarnā) | its wealthy people (mut'rafīhā) | but they defiantly disobey (fafasaqū) | therein (fīhā); | so is proved true (faḥaqqa) | against it (ʿalayhā) | the word (l-qawlu), | and We destroy it (fadammarnāhā) | with destruction (tadmīran).

17:17 And how many We destroyed from the generations after Nuh! And sufficient is your Lord concerning the sins of His servants All-Aware, All-Seer.

And how many (wakam) | We destroyed (ahlaknā) | from (mina) | the generations (l-qurūni) | after (min) | after (baʿdi) | Nuh (nūḥin)! | And sufficient (wakafā) | is your Lord (birabbika) | concerning the sins (bidhunūbi) | of His servants (ʿibādihi) | All-Aware (khabīran), | All-Seer (baṣīran).

17:18 Whoever should desire the immediate We hasten for him in it what We will to whom We intend. Then We have made for him Hell, he will burn disgraced rejected.

Whoever (man) | should (kāna) | desire (yurīdu) | the immediate (l-ʿājilata) | We hasten (ʿajjalnā) | for him (lahu) | in it (fīhā) | what (mā) | We will (nashāu) | to whom (liman) | We intend (nurīdu). | Then (thumma) | We have made (jaʿalnā) | for him (lahu) | Hell (jahannama), | he will burn (yaṣlāhā) | disgraced (madhmūman) | rejected (madḥūran).

17:19 And whoever desires the Hereafter and exerts for it the effort, while he is a believer, then those [are] their effort, is appreciated.

And whoever (waman) | desires (arāda) | the Hereafter (l-ākhirata) | and exerts (wasaʿā) | for it (lahā) | the effort (saʿyahā), | while he (wahuwa) | is a believer (mu'minun), | then those (fa-ulāika) | [are] (kāna) | their effort (saʿyuhum), | is appreciated (mashkūran).

17:20 To each We extend to these and to these, from the gift of your Lord. And not is the gift of your Lord restricted.

To each (kullan) | We extend (numiddu) | to these (hāulāi) | and to these (wahāulāi), | from (min) | the gift (ʿaṭāi) | of your Lord (rabbika). | And not (wamā) | is (kāna) | the gift (ʿaṭāu) | of your Lord (rabbika) | restricted (maḥẓūran).

17:21 See how We preferred some of them over others. And surely the Hereafter is greater in degrees and greater in excellence.

See (unẓur) | how (kayfa) | We preferred (faḍḍalnā) | some of them (baʿḍahum) | over (ʿalā) | others (baʿḍin). | And surely the Hereafter (walalākhiratu) | is greater (akbaru) | in degrees (darajātin) | and greater (wa-akbaru) | in excellence (tafḍīlan).

17:22 Do not make with Allah god another, lest you will sit disgraced, forsaken.

Do not (lā) | make (tajʿal) | with (maʿa) | Allah (l-lahi) | god (ilāhan) | another (ākhara), | lest you will sit (fataqʿuda) | disgraced (madhmūman), | forsaken (makhdhūlan).

17:23 And has decreed your Lord, that do not worship except Him Alone and to the parents be good. Whether reach with you the old age one of them, or both of them, then do not say to both of them a word of disrespect and do not repel them, but speak to them a word noble.

And has decreed (waqaḍā) | your Lord (rabbuka), | that do not (allā) | worship (taʿbudū) | except (illā) | Him Alone (iyyāhu) | and to the parents (wabil-wālidayni) | be good (iḥ'sānan). | Whether (immā) | reach (yablughanna) | with you (ʿindaka) | the old age (l-kibara) | one of them (aḥaduhumā), | or (aw) | both of them (kilāhumā), | then do not (falā) | say (taqul) | to both of them (lahumā) | a word of disrespect (uffin) | and do not (walā) | repel them (tanharhumā), | but speak (waqul) | to them (lahumā) | a word (qawlan) | noble (karīman).

17:24 And lower to them the wing of humility out of [the] mercy and say, "My Lord! Have mercy on both of them as they brought me up when I was small."

And lower (wa-ikh'fiḍ) | to them (lahumā) | the wing (janāḥa) | of humility (l-dhuli) | out of (mina) | [the] mercy (l-raḥmati) | and say (waqul), | "My Lord (rabbi)! | Have mercy on both of them (ir'ḥamhumā) | as (kamā) | they brought me up (rabbayānī) | when I was small. (ṣaghīran)"

17:25 Your Lord is most knowing of what is in yourselves. If you are righteous, then indeed, He is to those who often turn to Him Most Forgiving.

Your Lord (rabbukum) | is most knowing (aʿlamu) | of what (bimā) | is in (fī) | yourselves (nufūsikum). | If (in) | you are (takūnū) | righteous (ṣāliḥīna), | then indeed, He (fa-innahu) | is (kāna) | to those who often turn to Him (lil'awwābīna) | Most Forgiving (ghafūran).

17:26 And give the relatives his right, and the needy, and the wayfarer, and do not spend wastefully.

And give (waāti) | the relatives (dhā) | the relatives (l-qur'bā) | his right (ḥaqqahu), | and the needy (wal-mis'kīna), | and the wayfarer (wa-ib'na), | and the wayfarer (l-sabīli), | and do not (walā) | spend (tubadhir) | wastefully (tabdhīran).

17:27 Indeed, the spendthrifts are brothers of the devils. And is the Shaitaan to his Lord ungrateful.

Indeed (inna), | the spendthrifts (l-mubadhirīna) | are (kānū) | brothers (ikh'wāna) | of the devils (l-shayāṭīni). | And is (wakāna) | the Shaitaan (l-shayṭānu) | to his Lord (lirabbihi) | ungrateful (kafūran).

17:28 And if you turn away from them seeking mercy from your Lord, which you expect then say to them a word gentle.

And if (wa-immā) | you turn away (tuʿ'riḍanna) | from them (ʿanhumu) | seeking (ib'tighāa) | mercy (raḥmatin) | from (min) | your Lord (rabbika), | which you expect (tarjūhā) | then say (faqul) | to them (lahum) | a word (qawlan) | gentle (maysūran).

17:29 And do not make your hand chained to your neck, and not extend it to its utmost reach, so that you sit blameworthy, insolvent.

And do not (walā) | make (tajʿal) | your hand (yadaka) | chained (maghlūlatan) | to (ilā) | your neck (ʿunuqika), | and not (walā) | extend it (tabsuṭ'hā) | to its utmost (kulla) | reach (l-basṭi), | so that you sit (fataqʿuda) | blameworthy (malūman), | insolvent (maḥsūran).

17:30 Indeed, your Lord extends the provision for whom He wills, and straitens. Indeed, He is of His slaves All-Aware, All-Seer.

Indeed (inna), | your Lord (rabbaka) | extends (yabsuṭu) | the provision (l-riz'qa) | for whom (liman) | He wills (yashāu), | and straitens (wayaqdiru). | Indeed, He (innahu) | is (kāna) | of His slaves (biʿibādihi) | All-Aware (khabīran), | All-Seer (baṣīran).

17:31 And do not kill your children for fear of poverty. We We provide for them and for you. Indeed, their killing is a sin great.

And do not (walā) | kill (taqtulū) | your children (awlādakum) | for fear (khashyata) | of poverty (im'lāqin). | We (naḥnu) | We provide for them (narzuquhum) | and for you (wa-iyyākum). | Indeed (inna), | their killing (qatlahum) | is (kāna) | a sin (khiṭ'an) | great (kabīran).

17:32 And do not go near adultery. Indeed, it is an immorality and an evil way.

And do not (walā) | go near (taqrabū) | adultery (l-zinā). | Indeed, it (innahu) | is (kāna) | an immorality (fāḥishatan) | and an evil (wasāa) | way (sabīlan).

17:33 And do not kill the soul which Allah has forbidden, except by right. And whoever is killed wrongfully, verily We have made for his heir an authority, but not he should exceed in the killing. Indeed, he is helped.

And do not (walā) | kill (taqtulū) | the soul (l-nafsa) | which (allatī) | Allah has forbidden (ḥarrama), | Allah has forbidden (l-lahu), | except (illā) | by right (bil-ḥaqi). | And whoever (waman) | is killed (qutila) | wrongfully (maẓlūman), | verily (faqad) | We have made (ja'alnā) | for his heir (liwaliyyihi) | an authority (sul'ṭānan), | but not (falā) | he should exceed (yus'rif) | in (fī) | the killing (l-qatli). | Indeed, he (innahu) | is (kāna) | helped (manṣūran).

17:34 And do not come near the wealth of the orphan, except with what [it] is best until he reaches his maturity. And fulfil the covenant. Indeed, the covenant will be questioned.

And do not (walā) | come near (taqrabū) | the wealth (māla) | of the orphan (l-yatīmi), | except (illā) | with what (bi-allatī) | [it] is (hiya) | best (aḥsanu) | until (ḥattā) | he reaches (yablugha) | his maturity (ashuddahu). | And fulfil (wa-awfū) | the covenant (bil-'ahdi). | Indeed (inna), | the covenant (l-'ahda) | will be (kāna) | questioned (masūlan).

17:35 And give full [the] measure when you measure, and weigh with the balance the straight. That is good and best in result.

And give full (wa-awfū) | [the] measure (l-kayla) | when (idhā) | you measure (kil'tum), | and weigh (wazinū) | with the balance (bil-qis'ṭāsi) | the straight (l-mus'taqīmi). | That (dhālika) | is good (khayrun) | and best (wa-aḥsanu) | in result (tawīlan).

17:36 And do not pursue what not you have of it any knowledge. Indeed, the hearing, and the sight, and the heart all those will be [about it] questioned.

And do not (walā) | pursue (taqfu) | what (mā) | not (laysa) | you have (laka) | of it (bihi) | any knowledge ('il'mun). | Indeed (inna), | the hearing (l-sam'a), | and the sight (wal-baṣara), | and the heart (wal-fuāda) | all (kullu) | those (ulāika) | will be (kāna) | [about it] ('anhu) | questioned (masūlan).

17:37 And do not walk in the earth with insolence. Indeed, you will never tear the earth and will never reach the mountains in height.

And do not (walā) | walk (tamshi) | in (fī) | the earth (l-arḍi) | with insolence (maraḥan). | Indeed, you (innaka) | will never (lan) | tear (takhriqa) | the earth (l-arḍa) | and will never (walan) | reach (tablugha) | the mountains (l-jibāla) | in height (ṭūlan).

17:38 All that is [its] evil near your Lord, hateful.

All (kullu) | that (dhālika) | is (kāna) | [its] evil (sayyi-uhu) | near ('inda) | your Lord (rabbika), | hateful (makrūhan).

17:39 That is from what was revealed to you from your Lord of the wisdom. And do not make with Allah god other lest you should be thrown in Hell, blameworthy, abandoned.

That (dhālika) | is from what (mimmā) | was revealed (awḥā) | to you (ilayka) | from your Lord (rabbuka) | of (mina) | the wisdom (l-ḥik'mati). | And do not (walā) | make (taj'al) | with (ma'a) | Allah (l-lahi) | god (ilāhan) | other (ākhara) | lest you should be thrown (fatul'qā) | in (fī) | Hell (jahannama), | blameworthy (malūman), | abandoned (madḥūran).

17:40 Then has your Lord chosen for you sons and He has taken from the Angels daughters? Indeed, you surely say a word grave.

Then has your Lord chosen for you (afa-aṣfākum) | Then has your Lord chosen for you (rabbukum) | sons (bil-banīna) | and He has taken (wa-ittakhadha) | from (mina) | the Angels (l-malāikati) | daughters (ināthan)? | Indeed, you (innakum) | surely say (lataqūlūna) | a word (qawlan) | grave ('aẓīman).

17:41 And verily, We have explained in this the Quran, that they may take heed, but not it increases them except in aversion.

And verily (walaqad), | We have explained (ṣarrafnā) | in (fī) | this (hādhā) | the Quran (l-qur'āni), | that they may take heed (liyadhakkarū), | but not (wamā) | it increases them (yazīduhum) | except (illā) | in aversion (nufūran).

17:42 Say, "If there were with Him gods as they say, then surely they would have sought to the Owner of the Throne a way."

Say (qul), | "If (law) | there were (kāna) | with Him (maʿahu) | gods (ālihatun) | as (kamā) | they say (yaqūlūna), | then (idhan) | surely they would have sought (la-ib'taghaw) | to (ilā) | the Owner (dhī) | of the Throne (l-ʿarshi) | a way. (sabīlan)"

17:43 Glorified is He and Exalted is He above what they say by height great.

Glorified is He (sub'ḥānahu) | and Exalted is He (wataʿālā) | above what (ʿammā) | they say (yaqūlūna) | by height (ʿuluwwan) | great (kabīran).

17:44 Glorify [to] Him the seven heavens and the earth and whatever is in them. And there is not any thing except glorifies His Praise, but not you understand their glorification. Indeed, He is Ever-Forbearing, Oft-Forgiving."

Glorify (tusabbiḥu) | [to] Him (lahu) | the seven heavens (l-samāwātu) | the seven heavens (l-sabʿu) | and the earth (wal-arḍu) | and whatever (waman) | is in them (fīhinna). | And there is not (wa-in) | any (min) | thing (shayin) | except (illā) | glorifies (yusabbiḥu) | His Praise (biḥamdihi), | but (walākin) | not (lā) | you understand (tafqahūna) | their glorification (tasbīḥahum). | Indeed, He (innahu) | is (kāna) | Ever-Forbearing (ḥalīman), | Oft-Forgiving. (ghafūran)"

17:45 And when you recite the Quran, We place between you and between those who do not believe in the Hereafter a barrier hidden.

And when (wa-idhā) | you recite (qarata) | the Quran (l-qur'āna), | We place (jaʿalnā) | between you (baynaka) | and between (wabayna) | those who (alladhīna) | do not (lā) | believe (yu'minūna) | in the Hereafter (bil-ākhirati) | a barrier (ḥijāban) | hidden (mastūran).

17:46 And We have placed over their hearts coverings, lest they understand it, and in their ears deafness. And when you mention your Lord in the Quran Alone, they turn on their backs in aversion.

And We have placed (wajaʿalnā) | over (ʿalā) | their hearts (qulūbihim) | coverings (akinnatan), | lest (an) | they understand it (yafqahūhu), | and in (wafī) | their ears (ādhānihim) | deafness (waqran). | And when (wa-idhā) | you mention (dhakarta) | your Lord (rabbaka) | in (fī) | the Quran (l-qur'āni) | Alone (waḥdahu), | they turn (wallaw) | on (ʿalā) | their backs (adbārihim) | in aversion (nufūran).

17:47 We know best [of] what they listen to [it] when they listen to you, and when they are in private conversation, when say the wrongdoers, "Not you follow but a man bewitched."

We (naḥnu) | know best (aʿlamu) | [of] what (bimā) | they listen (yastamiʿūna) | to [it] (bihi) | when (idh) | they listen (yastamiʿūna) | to you (ilayka), | and when (wa-idh) | they (hum) | are in private conversation (najwā), | when (idh) | say (yaqūlu) | the wrongdoers (l-ẓālimūna), | "Not (in) | you follow (tattabiʿūna) | but (illā) | a man (rajulan) | bewitched. (masḥūran)"

17:48 See how they put forth for you the examples; but they have gone astray so not they can find a way.

See (unẓur) | how (kayfa) | they put forth (ḍarabū) | for you (laka) | the examples (l-amthāla); | but they have gone astray (faḍallū) | so not (falā) | they can (yastaṭīʿūna) | find a way (sabīlan).

17:49 And they say, "Is it when we are bones and crumbled particles, will we surely be resurrected as a creation new."

And they say (waqālū), | "Is it when (a-idhā) | we are (kunnā) | bones (ʿiẓāman) | and crumbled particles (warufātan), | will we (a-innā) | surely be resurrected (lamabʿūthūna) | as a creation (khalqan) | new. (jadīdan)"

17:50 Say, "Be stones or iron.

Say (qul), | "Be (kūnū) | stones (ḥijāratan) | or (aw) | iron (ḥadīdan).

17:51 Or a creation of what is great in your breasts." Then they will say, "Who will restore us?" Say, "He Who created you the first time." Then they will shake at you their heads and they say, "When will it be?" Say, "Perhaps that it will be soon."

Or (aw) | a creation (khalqan) | of what (mimmā) | is great (yakburu) | in (fī) | your breasts. (ṣudūrikum)" | Then they will say (fasayaqūlūna), | "Who (man) | will restore us? (yuʿīdunā)" | Say (quli), | "He Who (alladhī) | created you (faṭarakum) | the first (awwala) | time. (marratin)" | Then they will shake (fasayun'ghiḍūna) | at you (ilayka) | their heads (ruūsahum) | and they say (wayaqūlūna), | "When will (matā) | it be? (huwa)" | Say (qul), | "Perhaps (ʿasā) | that (an) | it will be (yakūna) | soon. (qarīban)"

17:52 On the Day He will call you and you will respond with His Praise, and you will think, not you had remained except a little while.

On the Day (yawma) | He will call you (yadʿūkum) | and you will respond (fatastajībūna) | with His Praise (biḥamdihi), | and you will think (wataẓunnūna), | not (in) | you had remained (labith'tum) | except (illā) | a little while (qalīlan).

17:53 And say to My slaves to say that which is best. Indeed, the Shaitaan sows discord between them. Indeed, the Shaitaan is to the man an enemy clear.

And say (waqul) | to My slaves (liʿibādī) | to say (yaqūlū) | that (allatī) | which (hiya) | is best (aḥsanu). | Indeed (inna), | the Shaitaan (l-shayṭāna) | sows discord (yanzaghu) | between them (baynahum). | Indeed (inna), | the Shaitaan (l-shayṭāna) | is (kāna) | to the man (lil'insāni) | an enemy (ʿaduwwan) | clear (mubīnan).

17:54 Your Lord is most knowing of you. If He wills, He will have mercy on you; or if He wills He will punish you. And not We have sent you over them as a guardian.

Your Lord (rabbukum) | is most knowing (aʿlamu) | of you (bikum). | If (in) | He wills (yasha), | He will have mercy on you (yarḥamkum); | or (aw) | if (in) | He wills (yasha) | He will punish you (yuʿadhib'kum). | And not (wamā) | We have sent you (arsalnāka) | over them (ʿalayhim) | as a guardian (wakīlan).

17:55 And your Lord is most knowing of whoever is in the heavens and the earth. And verily We have preferred some of the Prophets to others. And We gave Dawood Zaboor.

And your Lord (warabbuka) | is most knowing (aʿlamu) | of whoever (biman) | is in (fī) | the heavens (l-samāwāti) | and the earth (wal-arḍi). | And verily (walaqad) | We have preferred (faḍḍalnā) | some (baʿḍa) | of the Prophets (l-nabiyīna) | to (ʿalā) | others (baʿḍin). | And We gave (waātaynā) | Dawood (dāwūda) | Zaboor (zabūran).

17:56 Say, "Call those whom you claimed besides Him, [then] not they have power to remove the misfortunes from you and not to transfer (it)."

Say (quli), | "Call (id'ʿū) | those whom (alladhīna) | you claimed (zaʿamtum) | besides Him (min), | besides Him (dūnihi), | [then] not (falā) | they have power (yamlikūna) | to remove (kashfa) | the misfortunes (l-ḍuri) | from you (ʿankum) | and not (walā) | to transfer (it). (taḥwīlan)"

17:57 Those whom they call, seek to their Lord the means of access, which of them is nearest, and they hope for His mercy and fear His punishment. Indeed, the punishment of your Lord is ever feared.

Those (ulāika) | whom (alladhīna) | they call (yadʿūna), | seek (yabtaghūna) | to (ilā) | their Lord (rabbihimu) | the means of access (l-wasīlata), | which of them (ayyuhum) | is nearest (aqrabu), | and they hope (wayarjūna) | for His mercy (raḥmatahu) | and fear (wayakhāfūna) | His punishment (ʿadhābahu). | Indeed (inna), | the punishment (ʿadhāba) | of your Lord (rabbika) | is (kāna) | ever feared (maḥdhūran).

17:58 And not is any town but We will destroy it before the Day of the Resurrection or punish it with a punishment severe. That is in the Book written.

And not (wa-in) | is any (min) | town (qaryatin) | but (illā) | We (naḥnu) | will destroy it (muh'likūhā) | before (qabla) | the Day (yawmi) | of the Resurrection (l-qiyāmati) | or (aw) | punish it (muʿadhibūhā) | with a punishment (ʿadhāban) | severe (shadīdan). | That is (kāna) | That is (dhālika) | in (fī) | the Book (l-kitābi) | written (masṭūran).

17:59 And not stopped Us that We send the Signs except that denied them the former people And We gave Thamud the she-camel as a visible sign, but they wronged her. And not We send the Signs except as a warning.

And not (wamā) | stopped Us (manaʿanā) | that (an) | We send (nur'sila) | the Signs (bil-āyāti) | except (illā) | that (an) | denied (kadhaba) | them (bihā) | the former people (l-awalūna) | And We gave (waātaynā) | Thamud (thamūda) | the she-camel (l-nāqata) | as a visible sign (mub'ṣiratan), | but they wronged (faẓalamū) | her (bihā). | And not (wamā) | We send (nur'silu) | the Signs (bil-āyāti) | except (illā) | as a warning (takhwīfan).

17:60 And when We said to you, "Indeed, your Lord has encompassed the mankind." And not We made the vision which We showed you except as a trial for mankind, and the tree the accursed in the Quran. And We threaten them but not it increases them except in transgression great.

And when (wa-idh) | We said (qul'nā) | to you (laka), | "Indeed (inna), | your Lord (rabbaka) | has encompassed (aḥāṭa) | the mankind. (bil-nāsi)" | And not (wamā) | We made (jaʿalnā) | the vision (l-ru'yā) | which (allatī) | We showed you (araynāka) | except (illā) | as a trial (fit'natan) | for mankind (lilnnāsi), | and the tree (wal-shajarata) | the accursed (l-malʿūnata) | in (fī) | the Quran (l-qur'āni). | And We threaten them (wanukhawwifuhum) | but not (famā) | it increases them (yazīduhum) | except (illā) | in transgression (ṭugh'yānan) | great (kabīran).

17:61 And when We said to the Angels, "Prostrate to Adam." So they prostrated except Iblis. He said, "Shall I prostrate to one whom You created from clay?"

And when (wa-idh) | We said (qul'nā) | to the Angels (lil'malāikati), | "Prostrate (us'judū) | to Adam. (liādama)" | So they prostrated (fasajadū) | except (illā) | Iblis (ib'līsa). | He said (qāla), | "Shall I prostrate (a-asjudu) | to one whom (liman) | You created (khalaqta) | from clay? (ṭīnan)"

17:62 He said, "Do You see this whom You have honored, above me? If You give me respite till the Day of the Resurrection, I will surely destroy his offspring except a few."

He said (qāla), | "Do You see (ara-aytaka) | this (hādhā) | whom (alladhī) | You have honored (karramta), | above me (ʿalayya)? | If (la-in) | You give me respite (akhartani) | till (ilā) | the Day (yawmi) | of the Resurrection (l-qiyāmati), | I will surely destroy (la-aḥtanikanna) | his offspring (dhurriyyatahu) | except (illā) | a few. (qalīlan)"

17:63 He said, "Go, and whoever follows you among them then indeed, Hell is your recompense - a recompense ample.

He said (qāla), | "Go (idh'hab), | and whoever (faman) | follows you (tabiʿaka) | among them (min'hum) | then indeed (fa-inna), | Hell (jahannama) | is your recompense (jazāukum)- | a recompense (jazāan) | ample (mawfūran).

17:64 And incite whoever you can among them with your voice, and assault [on] them with your cavalry and infantry and be a partner in the wealth and the children, and promise them." And not promises them the Shaitaan except delusion.

And incite (wa-is'tafziz) | whoever (mani) | you can (is'taṭaʿta) | among them (min'hum) | with your voice (biṣawtika), | and assault (wa-ajlib) | [on] them (ʿalayhim) | with your cavalry (bikhaylika) | and infantry (warajilika) | and be a partner (washārik'hum) | in (fī) | the wealth (l-amwāli) | and the children (wal-awlādi), | and promise them. (waʿid'hum)" | And not (wamā) | promises them (yaʿiduhumu) | the Shaitaan (l-shayṭānu) | except (illā) | delusion (ghurūran).

17:65 "Indeed, My slaves not for you over them any authority. And sufficient is your Lord as a Guardian."

"Indeed (inna), | My slaves (ʿibādī) | not (laysa) | for you (laka) | over them (ʿalayhim) | any authority (sul'ṭānun). | And sufficient (wakafā) | is your Lord (birabbika) | as a Guardian. (wakīlan)"

17:66 Your Lord is the One Who drives for you the ship in the sea, that you may seek of His Bounty. Indeed, He is to you Ever Merciful.

Your Lord (rabbukumu) | is the One Who (alladhī) | drives (yuz'jī) | for you (lakumu) | the ship (l-ful'ka) | in (fī) | the sea (l-baḥri), | that you may seek (litabtaghū) | of (min) | His Bounty (faḍlihi). | Indeed, He (innahu) | is (kāna) | to you (bikum) | Ever Merciful (raḥīman).

17:67 And when touches you the hardship in the sea, lost are who you call except Him Alone. But when He delivers you to the land you turn away. And is man ungrateful.

And when (wa-idhā) | touches you (massakumu) | the hardship (l-ḍuru) | in (fī) | the sea (l-baḥri), | lost (ḍalla) | are who (man) | you call (tadʿūna) | except (illā) | Him Alone (iyyāhu). | But when (falammā) | He delivers you (najjākum) | to (ilā) | the land (l-bari) | you turn away (aʿraḍtum). | And is (wakāna) | man (l-insānu) | ungrateful (kafūran).

17:68 Do you then feel secure that not He will cause to swallow you, side of the land or send against you a storm of stones? Then not you will find for you a guardian?

Do you then feel secure (afa-amintum) | that not (an) | He will cause to swallow (yakhsifa) | you (bikum), | side (jāniba) | of the land (l-bari) | or (aw) | send (yur'sila) | against you (ʿalaykum) | a storm of stones (ḥāṣiban)? | Then (thumma) | not (lā) | you will find (tajidū) | for you (lakum) | a guardian (wakīlan)?

17:69 Or do you feel secure that not He will send you back into it another time, and send upon you a hurricane of the wind, and drown you because you disbelieved? Then not you will find for you against Us therein an avenger?

Or (am) | do you feel secure (amintum) | that not (an) | He will send you back (yuʿīdakum) | into it (fīhi) | another time (tāratan), | another time (ukh'rā), | and send (fayur'sila) | upon you (ʿalaykum) | a hurricane (qāṣifan) | of (mina) | the wind (l-rīḥi), | and drown you (fayugh'riqakum) | because (bimā) | you disbelieved (kafartum)? | Then (thumma) | not (lā) | you will find (tajidū) | for you (lakum) | against Us (ʿalaynā) | therein (bihi) | an avenger (tabīʿan)?

17:70 And certainly, We have honored the children of Adam and We carried them on the land and the sea, and We have provided them of the good things and We preferred them over many of those whom We have created with preference.

And certainly (walaqad), | We have honored (karramnā) | the children of Adam (banī) | the children of Adam (ādama) | and We carried them (waḥamalnāhum) | on (fī) | the land (l-bari) |

and the sea (wal-baḥri), | and We have provided them (warazaqnāhum) | of (mina) | the good things (l-ṭayibāti) | and We preferred them (wafaḍḍalnāhum) | over (ʿalā) | many (kathīrin) | of those whom (mimman) | We have created (khalaqnā) | with preference (tafḍīlan).

17:71 The Day We will call all human beings with their record, then whoever is given his record in his right hand, then those will read their records, and not they will be wronged even as much as a hair on a date seed.

The Day (yawma) | We will call (nadʿū) | all (kulla) | human beings (unāsin) | with their record (bi-imāmihim), | then whoever (faman) | is given (ūtiya) | his record (kitābahu) | in his right hand (biyamīnihi), | then those (fa-ulāika) | will read (yaqraūna) | their records (kitābahum), | and not (walā) | they will be wronged (yuẓ'lamūna) | even as much as a hair on a date seed (fatīlan).

17:72 And whoever is in this world blind, then he in the Hereafter will be blind, and more astray from the path.

And whoever (waman) | is (kāna) | in (fī) | this world (hādhihi) | blind (aʿmā), | then he (fahuwa) | in (fī) | the Hereafter (l-ākhirati) | will be blind (aʿmā), | and more astray (wa-aḍallu) | from the path (sabīlan).

17:73 And indeed, they were about to tempt you away from that which We revealed, to you that you invent about Us other than it. And then surely they would take you as a friend.

And indeed (wa-in), | they were about to (kādū) | tempt you away (layaftinūnaka) | from (ʿani) | that which (alladhī) | We revealed (awḥaynā), | to you (ilayka) | that you invent (litaftariya) | about Us (ʿalaynā) | other than it (ghayrahu). | And then (wa-idhan) | surely they would take you (la-ittakhadhūka) | as a friend (khalīlan).

17:74 And if not [that] We had strengthened you, certainly, you almost would have inclined to them in something a little.

And if not (walawlā) | [that] (an) | We had strengthened you (thabbatnāka), | certainly (laqad), | you almost (kidtta) | would have inclined (tarkanu) | to them (ilayhim) | in something (shayan) | a little (qalīlan).

17:75 Then We would have made you taste double in the life, and double after the death. Then not you would have found for you against Us any helper.

Then (idhan) | We would have made you taste (la-adhaqnāka) | double (ḍiʿfa) | in the life (l-ḥayati), | and double (waḍiʿfa) | after the death (l-mamāti). | Then (thumma) | not (lā) | you would have found (tajidu) | for you (laka) | against Us (ʿalaynā) | any helper (naṣīran).

17:76 And indeed, they were about to scare you from the land, that they evict you from it. But then not they would have stayed after you except a little.

And indeed (wa-in), | they were about (kādū) | to scare you (layastafizzūnaka) | from (mina) | the land (l-arḍi), | that they evict you (liyukh'rijūka) | from it (min'hā). | But then (wa-idhan) | not (lā) | they would have stayed (yalbathūna) | after you (khilāfaka) | except (illā) | a little (qalīlan).

17:77 Such is Our Way for whom [verily] We sent before you of Our Messengers. And not you will find in Our way any alteration.

Such is Our Way (sunnata) | for whom (man) | [verily] (qad) | We sent (arsalnā) | before you (qablaka) | of (min) | Our Messengers (rusulinā). | And not (walā) | you will find (tajidu) | in Our way (lisunnatinā) | any alteration (taḥwīlan).

17:78 Establish the prayer, at the decline of the sun till the darkness of the night and Quran at dawn, indeed, the Quran at the dawn is ever witnessed.

Establish (aqimi) | the prayer (l-ṣalata), | at the decline (lidulūki) | of the sun (l-shamsi) | till (ilā) | the darkness (ghasaqi) | of the night (al-layli) | and Quran (waqur'āna) | at dawn (l-fajri), | indeed (inna), | the Quran (qur'āna) | at the dawn (l-fajri) | is (kāna) | ever witnessed (mashhūdan).

17:79 And from the night arise from sleep for prayer with it as additional for you; it may be that will raise you your Lord to a station praiseworthy.

And from (wamina) | the night (al-layli) | arise from sleep for prayer (fatahajjad) | with it (bihi) | as additional (nāfilatan) | for you (laka); | it may be (ʿasā) | that (an) | will raise you (yabʿathaka) | your Lord (rabbuka) | to a station (maqāman) | praiseworthy (maḥmūdan).

17:80 And say, "My Lord! Cause me to enter an entrance sound, and cause me to exit an exit sound and make for me from near You an authority helping."

And say (waqul), | "My Lord (rabbi)! | Cause me to enter (adkhil'nī) | an entrance (mud'khala) | sound (ṣid'qin), | and cause me to exit (wa-akhrij'nī) | an exit (mukh'raja) | sound (ṣid'qin) | and make (wa-ij'ʿal) | for me (lī) | from (min) | near You (ladunka) | an authority (sul'ṭānan) | helping. (naṣīran)"

17:81 And say, "Has come the truth and perished the falsehood. Indeed, the falsehood is bound to perish."

And say (waqul), | "Has come (jāa) | the truth (l-ḥaqu) | and perished (wazahaqa) | the falsehood (l-bāṭilu). | Indeed (inna), | the falsehood (l-bāṭila) | is (kāna) | bound to perish. (zahūqan)"

17:82 And We reveal from the Quran that it is a healing and a mercy for the believers, but not it increases the wrongdoers except in loss.

And We reveal (wanunazzilu) | from (mina) | the Quran (l-qur'āni) | that (mā) | it (huwa) | is a healing (shifāon) | and a mercy (waraḥmatun) | for the believers (lil'mu'minīna), | but not (walā) | it increases (yazīdu) | the wrongdoers (l-ẓālimīna) | except (illā) | in loss (khasāran).

17:83 And when We bestow favor on man he turns away and becomes remote on his side. And when touches him the evil he is in despair.

And when (wa-idhā) | We bestow favor (anʿamnā) | on (ʿalā) | man (l-insāni) | he turns away (aʿraḍa) | and becomes remote (wanaā) | on his side (bijānibihi). | And when (wa-idhā) | touches him (massahu) | the evil (l-sharu) | he is (kāna) | in despair (yaūsan).

17:84 Say, "Each works on his manner, but your Lord is most knowing of who [he] is best guided in way."

Say (qul), | "Each (kullun) | works (yaʿmalu) | on (ʿalā) | his manner (shākilatihi), | but your Lord (farabbukum) | is most knowing (aʿlamu) | of who (biman) | [he] (huwa) | is best guided (ahdā) | in way. (sabīlan)"

17:85 And they ask you concerning the soul. Say, "The soul is of the affair of my Lord. And not you have been given of the knowledge except a little."

And they ask you (wayasalūnaka) | concerning (ʿani) | the soul (l-rūḥi). | Say (quli), | "The soul (l-rūḥu) | is of (min) | the affair (amri) | of my Lord (rabbī). | And not (wamā) | you have been given (ūtītum) | of (mina) | the knowledge (l-ʿil'mi) | except (illā) | a little. (qalīlan)"

17:86 And if We willed, We would have surely taken away that which We have revealed to you. Then not you would find for you concerning it against Us any advocate,

And if (wala-in) | We willed (shi'nā), | We would have surely taken away (lanadhhabanna) | that which (bi-alladhī) | We have revealed (awḥaynā) | to you (ilayka). | Then (thumma) | not (lā) | you would find (tajidu) | for you (laka) | concerning it (bihi) | against Us (ʿalaynā) | any advocate (wakīlan),

17:87 Except a mercy from your Lord. Indeed, His Bounty is upon you great.

Except (illā) | a mercy (raḥmatan) | from (min) | your Lord (rabbika). | Indeed (inna), | His Bounty (faḍlahu) | is (kāna) | upon you (ʿalayka) | great (kabīran).

17:88 Say, "If gathered the mankind and the jinn to [that] bring the like of this Quran, not they could bring the like of it, even if were some of them to some others assistants."

Say (qul), | "If (la-ini) | gathered (ij'tamaʿati) | the mankind (l-insu) | and the jinn (wal-jinu) | to (ʿalā) | [that] (an) | bring (yatū) | the like (bimith'li) | of this (hādhā) | Quran (l-qur'āni), | not (lā) | they could bring (yatūna) | the like of it (bimith'lihi), | even if (walaw) | were (kāna) | some of them (baʿḍuhum) | to some others (libaʿḍin) | assistants. (ẓahīran)"

17:89 And verily We have explained to mankind in this Quran from every example, but refused most of the mankind except disbelief.

And verily (walaqad) | We have explained (ṣarrafnā) | to mankind (lilnnāsi) | in (fī) | this (hādhā) | Quran (l-qur'āni) | from (min) | every (kulli) | example (mathalin), | but refused (fa-abā) | most (aktharu) | of the mankind (l-nāsi) | except (illā) | disbelief (kufūran).

17:90 And they say, "Never we will believe in you until you cause to gush forth for us from the earth a spring.

And they say (waqālū), | "Never (lan) | we will believe (nu'mina) | in you (laka) | until (ḥattā) | you cause to gush forth (tafjura) | for us (lanā) | from (mina) | the earth (l-arḍi) | a spring (yanbūʿan).

17:91 Or you have for you a garden of date-palms and grapes, and cause to gush forth the rivers within them abundantly.

Or (aw) | you have (takūna) | for you (laka) | a garden (jannatun) | of (min) | date-palms (nakhīlin) | and grapes (waʿinabin), | and cause to gush forth (fatufajjira) | the rivers (l-anhāra) | within them (khilālahā) | abundantly (tafjīran).

17:92 Or you cause to fall the sky, as you have claimed, upon us in pieces or you bring Allah and the Angels before us.

Or (aw) | you cause to fall (tus'qiṭa) | the sky (l-samāa), | as (kamā) | you have claimed (zaʿamta), | upon us (ʿalaynā) | in pieces (kisafan) | or (aw) | you bring (tatiya) | Allah (bil-lahi) | and the Angels (wal-malāikati) | before us (qabīlan).

17:93 Or is for you a house of ornament or you ascend into the sky. And never we will believe in your ascension until you bring down to us a book we could read it." Say, "Glorified is my Lord! "What am I but a human, a Messenger."

Or (aw) | is (yakūna) | for you (laka) | a house (baytun) | of (min) | ornament (zukh'rufin) | or (aw) | you ascend (tarqā) | into (fī) | the sky (l-samāi). | And never (walan) | we will believe (nu'mina) | in your ascension (liruqiyyika) | until (ḥattā) | you bring down (tunazzila) | to us (ʿalaynā) | a book (kitāban) | we could read it. (naqra-uhu)" | Say (qul), | "Glorified is (sub'ḥāna) | my Lord (rabbī)! | "What (hal) | am I (kuntu) | but (illā) | a human (basharan), | a Messenger. (rasūlan)"

17:94 And what prevented the people that they believe when came to them the guidance except that they said, "Has Allah sent a human Messenger?"

And what (wamā) | prevented (manaʿa) | the people (l-nāsa) | that (an) | they believe (yu'minū) | when (idh) | came to them (jāahumu) | the guidance (l-hudā) | except (illā) | that (an) | they said (qālū), | "Has Allah sent (abaʿatha) | "Has Allah sent (l-lahu) | a human (basharan) | Messenger? (rasūlan)"

17:95 Say, "If there were in the earth Angels walking securely, surely We would have sent down to them from the heaven an Angel as a Messenger."

Say (qul), | "If (law) | there were (kāna) | in (fī) | the earth (l-arḍi) | Angels (malāikatun) | walking (yamshūna) | securely (muṭ'ma-innīna), | surely We would have sent down (lanazzalnā) | to them (ʿalayhim) | from (mina) | the heaven (l-samāi) | an Angel (malakan) | as a Messenger. (rasūlan)"

17:96 Say, "Sufficient is Allah as a witness between me and between you. Indeed, He is of His slaves All-Aware, All-Seer."

Say (qul), | "Sufficient is (kafā) | Allah (bil-lahi) | as a witness (shahīdan) | between me (baynī) | and between you (wabaynakum). | Indeed, He (innahu) | is (kāna) | of His slaves (biʿibādihi) | All-Aware (khabīran), | All-Seer. (baṣīran)"

17:97 And whoever Allah guides then he is the guided one; and whoever He lets go astray - then never you will find for them protectors besides Him. And We will gather them on the Day of the Resurrection on their faces - blind and dumb and deaf. Their abode is Hell; every time it subsides, We will increase (for) them the blazing fire.

And whoever (waman) | Allah guides (yahdi) | Allah guides (l-lahu) | then he is (fahuwa) | the guided one (l-muh'tadi); | and whoever (waman) | He lets go astray (yuḍ'lil)- | then never (falan) | you will find (tajida) | for them (lahum) | protectors (awliyāa) | besides Him (min). | besides Him (dūnihi). | And We will gather them (wanaḥshuruhum) | on the Day (yawma) | of the Resurrection (l-qiyāmati) | on (ʿalā) | their faces (wujūhihim)- | blind (ʿum'yan) | and dumb (wabuk'man) | and deaf (waṣumman). | Their abode (mawāhum) | is Hell (jahannamu); | every time (kullamā) | it subsides (khabat), | We will increase (for) them (zid'nāhum) | the blazing fire (saʿīran).

17:98 That is their recompense because they disbelieved in Our Verses and said, "When we are bones and crumbled particles, will we surely be resurrected as a creation new."

That (dhālika) | is their recompense (jazāuhum) | because they (bi-annahum) | disbelieved (kafarū) | in Our Verses (biāyātinā) | and said (waqālū), | "When (a-idhā) | we are (kunnā) | bones (ʿiẓāman) | and crumbled particles (warufātan), | will we (a-innā) | surely be resurrected (lamabʿūthūna) | as a creation (khalqan) | new. (jadīdan)"

17:99 Do not they see that Allah, the One Who, created the heavens and the earth is Able [on] to create the like of them? And He has made for them a term, no doubt in it. But refused the wrongdoers except disbelief.

Do not (awalam) | they see (yaraw) | that (anna) | Allah (l-laha), | the One Who (alladhī), | created (khalaqa) | the heavens (l-samāwāti) | and the earth (wal-arḍa) | is Able (qādirun) | [on] (ʿalā) | to (an) | create (yakhluqa) | the like of them (mith'lahum)? | And He has made (wajaʿala) | for them (lahum) | a term (ajalan), | no (lā) | doubt (rayba) | in it (fīhi). | But refused (fa-abā) | the wrongdoers (l-ẓālimūna) | except (illā) | disbelief (kufūran).

17:100 Say, "If you possess the treasures of the Mercy of my Lord, then surely you would withhold out of fear of spending." And is man stingy.

Say (qul), | "If (law) | you (antum) | possess (tamlikūna) | the treasures (khazāina) | of the Mercy (raḥmati) | of my Lord (rabbī), | then (idhan) | surely you would withhold (la-amsaktum) | out of fear (khashyata) | of spending. (l-infāqi)" | And is (wakāna) | man (l-insānu) | stingy (qatūran).

17:101 And certainly We had given Musa nine Signs clear, so ask the Children of Israel when he came to them, then said to him Firaun, "Indeed, I [I] think you - O Musa! you are bewitched."

And certainly (walaqad) | We had given (ātaynā) | Musa (mūsā) | nine (tis''a) | Signs (āyātin) | clear (bayyinātin), | so ask (fasal) | the Children of Israel (banī) | the Children of Israel (is'rāīla) | when (idh) | he came to them (jāahum), | then said (faqāla) | to him (lahu) | Firaun (fir''awnu), | "Indeed, I (innī) | [I] think you (la-aẓunnuka)- | O Musa (yāmūsā)! | you are bewitched. (masḥūran)"

17:102 He said, "Verily, you have known none has sent down these except the Lord of the heavens and the earth as evidence, and indeed, I [I] surely think you O Firaun! you are destroyed."

He said (qāla), | "Verily (laqad), | you have known (ʿalim'ta) | none (mā) | has sent down (anzala) | these (hāulāi) | except (illā) | the Lord (rabbu) | of the heavens (l-samāwāti) | and the earth (wal-arḍi) | as evidence (baṣāira), | and indeed, I (wa-innī) | [I] surely think you (la-aẓunnuka) | O Firaun (yāfir''awnu)! | you are destroyed. (mathbūran)"

17:103 So he intended to drive them out from the land, but We drowned him and who were with him all.

So he intended (fa-arāda) | to (an) | drive them out (yastafizzahum) | from (mina) | the land (l-arḍi), | but We drowned him (fa-aghraqnāhu) | and who (waman) | were with him (maʿahu) | all (jamīʿan).

17:104 And We said after him to the Children of Israel, "Dwell in the land, then when comes the promise of the Hereafter, We will bring you as a mixed crowd."

And We said (waqul'nā) | after him (min) | after him (baʿdihi) | to the Children of Israel (libanī), | to the Children of Israel (is'rāīla), | "Dwell (us'kunū) | in the land (l-arḍa), | then when (fa-idhā) | comes (jāa) | the promise (waʿdu) | of the Hereafter (l-ākhirati), | We will bring (ji'nā) | you (bikum) | as a mixed crowd. (lafīfan)"

17:105 And with the truth We sent it down, and with the truth it descended. And not We sent you except as a bearer of glad tidings and a warner.

And with the truth (wabil-ḥaqi) | We sent it down (anzalnāhu), | and with the truth (wabil-ḥaqi) | it descended (nazala). | And not (wamā) | We sent you (arsalnāka) | except (illā) | as a bearer of glad tidings (mubashiran) | and a warner (wanadhīran).

17:106 And the Quran We have divided, that you might recite it to the people at intervals. And We have revealed it in stages.

And the Quran (waqur'ānan) | We have divided (faraqnāhu), | that you might recite it (litaqra-ahu) | to (ʿalā) | the people (l-nāsi) | at (ʿalā) | intervals (muk'thin). | And We have revealed it (wanazzalnāhu) | in stages (tanzīlan).

17:107 Say, "Believe in it or do not believe. Indeed, those who were given the knowledge before it, when it is recited to them, they fall on their faces in prostration."

Say (qul), | "Believe (āminū) | in it (bihi) | or (aw) | do not (lā) | believe (tu'minū). | Indeed (inna), | those who (alladhīna) | were given (ūtū) | the knowledge (l-ʿil'ma) | before it (min), | before it (qablihi), | when (idhā) | it is recited (yut'lā) | to them (ʿalayhim), | they fall (yakhirrūna) | on their faces (lil'adhqāni) | in prostration. (sujjadan)"

17:108 And they say, "Glory be to our Lord! Indeed, is the promise of our Lord surely fulfilled."

And they say (wayaqūlūna), | "Glory be to (sub'ḥāna) | our Lord (rabbinā)! | Indeed (in), | is (kāna) | the promise (waʿdu) | of our Lord (rabbinā) | surely fulfilled. (lamafʿūlan)"

17:109 And they fall on their faces weeping, and it increases them in humility.

And they fall (wayakhirrūna) | on their faces (lil'adhqāni) | weeping (yabkūna), | and it increases them (wayazīduhum) | in humility (khushūʿan).

17:110 Say, "Invoke Allah or invoke the Most Gracious. By whatever name you invoke, to Him belongs the Most Beautiful Names. And do not be loud in your prayers and not be silent therein, but seek between that a way."

Say (quli), | "Invoke (id''ū) | Allah (l-laha) | or (awi) | invoke (id''ū) | the Most Gracious (l-raḥmāna). | By whatever name (ayyan) | By whatever name (mā) | you invoke (tad'ū), | to Him belongs (falahu) | the Most Beautiful Names (l-asmāu). | the Most Beautiful Names (l-ḥus'nā). | And do not (walā) | be loud (tajhar) | in your prayers (biṣalātika) | and not (walā) | be silent (tukhāfit) | therein (bihā), | but seek (wa-ib'taghi) | between (bayna) | that (dhālika) | a way. (sabīlan)"

17:111 And say, "All Praise is for Allah the One Who has not taken a son and not is for Him a partner in the dominion, and not is for Him any protector out of weakness. And magnify Him with all magnificence."

And say (waquli), | "All Praise (l-ḥamdu) | is for Allah (lillahi) | the One Who (alladhī) | has not taken (lam) | has not taken (yattakhidh) | a son (waladan) | and not (walam) | is (yakun) | for Him (lahu) | a partner (sharīkun) | in (fī) | the dominion (l-mul'ki), | and not (walam) | is (yakun) | for Him (lahu) | any protector (waliyyun) | out of (mina) | weakness (l-dhuli). | And magnify Him (wakabbir'hu) | with all magnificence. (takbīran)"

Chapter (18) Sūrat l-Kahf (The Cave)

18:1 All Praise is for Allah the One Who has revealed to His slave the Book, and not has made in it any crookedness.

All Praise (al-ḥamdu) | is for Allah (lillahi) | the One Who (alladhī) | has revealed (anzala) | to ('alā) | His slave ('abdihi) | the Book (l-kitāba), | and not (walam) | has made (yaj'al) | in it (lahu) | any crookedness ('iwajā).

18:2 Straight, to warn of a punishment severe, from near Him, and give glad tidings to the believers, those who do righteous deeds, that for them is a good reward.

Straight (qayyiman), | to warn (liyundhira) | of a punishment (basan) | severe (shadīdan), | from (min) | near Him (ladun'hu), | and give glad tidings (wayubashira) | to the believers (l-mu'minīna), | those who (alladhīna) | do (ya'malūna) | righteous deeds (l-ṣāliḥāti), | that (anna) | for them (lahum) | is a good reward (ajran). | is a good reward (ḥasanan).

18:3 They will abide in it forever.

They will abide (mākithīna) | in it (fīhi) | forever (abadan).

18:4 And to warn those who say, "Allah has taken a son."

And to warn (wayundhira) | those who (alladhīna) | say (qālū), | "Allah has taken (ittakhadha) | "Allah has taken (l-lahu) | a son. (waladan)"

18:5 Not they have about it any knowledge and not their forefathers. Grave is the word that comes out of their mouths. Not they say except a lie.

Not (mā) | they have (lahum) | about it (bihi) | any (min) | knowledge ('il'min) | and not (walā) | their forefathers (liābāihim). | Grave is (kaburat) | the word (kalimatan) | that comes out (takhruju) | of (min) | their mouths (afwāhihim). | Not (in) | they say (yaqūlūna) | except (illā) | a lie (kadhiban).

18:6 Then perhaps you would be the one who kills yourself over their footsteps, if not they believe in this [the] narration, in grief.

Then perhaps you would be (fala'allaka) | the one who kills (bākhi'un) | yourself (nafsaka) | over ('alā) | their footsteps (āthārihim), | if (in) | not (lam) | they believe (yu'minū) | in this (bihādhā) | [the] narration (l-ḥadīthi), | in grief (asafan).

18:7 Indeed, We We have made what is on the earth adornment for it, that We may test [them] which of them is best in deed.

Indeed, We (innā) | We have made (ja'alnā) | what (mā) | is on ('alā) | the earth (l-arḍi) | adornment (zīnatan) | for it (lahā), | that We may test [them] (linabluwahum) | which of them (ayyuhum) | is best (aḥsanu) | in deed ('amalan).

18:8 And indeed, We will surely make what is on it soil barren.

And indeed, We (wa-innā) | will surely make (lajā'ilūna) | what (mā) | is on it ('alayhā) | soil (ṣa'īdan) | barren (juruzan).

18:9 Or have you thought that the companions of the cave and the inscription were, among Our Signs, a wonder?

Or (am) | have you thought (ḥasib'ta) | that (anna) | the companions (aṣḥāba) | of the cave (l-kahfi) | and the inscription (wal-raqīmi) | were (kānū), | among (min) | Our Signs (āyātinā), | a wonder ('ajaban)?

18:10 When retreated the youths to the cave, and they said, "Our Lord! Grant us from Yourself Mercy, and facilitate for us [from] our affair in the right way."

When (idh) | retreated (awā) | the youths (l-fit'yatu) | to (ilā) | the cave (l-kahfi), | and they said (faqālū), | "Our Lord (rabbanā)! | Grant us (ātinā) | from (min) | Yourself (ladunka) | Mercy (raḥmatan), | and facilitate (wahayyi) | for us (lanā) | [from] (min) | our affair (amrinā) | in the right way. (rashadan)"

18:11 So We cast over their ears in the cave years - a number.

So We cast (faḍarabnā) | over ('alā) | their ears (ādhānihim) | in (fī) | the cave (l-kahfi) | years (sinīna)- | a number ('adadan).

18:12 Then We raised them up that We make evident which of the two parties best calculated for what they had remained in time.

Then (thumma) | We raised them up (ba'athnāhum) | that We make evident (lina'lama) | which (ayyu) | of the two parties (l-ḥiz'bayni) | best calculated (aḥṣā) | for what (limā) | they had remained (labithū) | in time (amadan).

18:13 We narrate to you their story in truth. Indeed, they were youths who believed in their Lord, and We increased them in guidance.

We (naḥnu) | narrate (naquṣṣu) | to you ('alayka) | their story (naba-ahum) | in truth (bil-ḥaqi). | Indeed, they were (innahum) | youths (fit'yatun) | who believed (āmanū) | in their Lord (birabbihim), | and We increased them (wazid'nāhum) | in guidance (hudan).

18:14 And We made firm [on] their hearts when they stood up and said, "Our Lord is the Lord of the heavens and the earth. Never we will invoke besides Him any god. Certainly, we would have said, then, an enormity.

And We made firm (warabaṭnā) | [on] (ʿalā) | their hearts (qulūbihim) | when (idh) | they stood up (qāmū) | and said (faqālū), | "Our Lord (rabbunā) | is the Lord (rabbu) | of the heavens (l-samāwāti) | and the earth (wal-arḍi). | Never (lan) | we will invoke (nadʿuwā) | besides Him (min) | besides Him (dūnihi) | any god (ilāhan). | Certainly (laqad), | we would have said (qul'nā), | then (idhan), | an enormity (shaṭaṭan).

18:15 These, our people, have taken besides Him gods. Why not they come to them with an authority clear? And who is more wrong than one who invents against Allah a lie?

These (hāulāi), | our people (qawmunā), | have taken (ittakhadhū) | besides Him (min) | besides Him (dūnihi) | gods (ālihatan). | Why not (lawlā) | they come (yatūna) | to them (ʿalayhim) | with an authority (bisul'ṭānin) | clear (bayyinin)? | And who (faman) | is more wrong (aẓlamu) | than one who (mimmani) | invents (if'tarā) | against (ʿalā) | Allah (l-lahi) | a lie (kadhiban)?

18:16 And when you withdraw from them and what they worship except Allah, then retreat to the cave. Will spread for you your Lord of His Mercy and will facilitate for you [from] your affair in ease."

And when (wa-idhi) | you withdraw from them (iʿ'tazaltumūhum) | and what (wamā) | they worship (yaʿbudūna) | except (illā) | Allah (l-laha), | then retreat (fawū) | to (ilā) | the cave (l-kahfi). | Will spread (yanshur) | for you (lakum) | your Lord (rabbukum) | of (min) | His Mercy (raḥmatihi) | and will facilitate (wayuhayyi) | for you (lakum) | [from] (min) | your affair (amrikum) | in ease. (mir'faqan)"

18:17 And you might have seen the sun, when it rose, inclining away from their cave to the right, and when it set, passing away from them to the left while they lay in the open space thereof. That was from the Signs of Allah. Whoever Allah guides and he is the guided one, and whoever He lets go astray then never you will find for him a protector, a guide.

And you might have seen (watarā) | the sun (l-shamsa), | when (idhā) | it rose (ṭalaʿat), | inclining away (tazāwaru) | from (ʿan) | their cave (kahfihim) | to (dhāta) | the right (l-yamīni), | and when (wa-idhā) | it set (gharabat), | passing away from them (taqriḍuhum) | to (dhāta) | the left (l-shimāli) | while they (wahum) | lay in (fī) | the open space (fajwatin) | thereof (min'hu). | That (dhālika) | was from (min) | the Signs (āyāti) | of Allah (l-lahi). | Whoever (man) | Allah guides (yahdi) | Allah guides (l-lahu) | and he (fahuwa) | is the guided one (l-muh'tadi), | and whoever (waman) | He lets go astray (yuḍ'lil) | then never (falan) | you will find (tajida) | for him (lahu) | a protector (waliyyan), | a guide (mur'shidan).

18:18 And you would think them awake while they were asleep. And We turned them to the right and to the left, while their dog stretched his two forelegs at the entrance. If you had looked at them, you would have surely turned back from them in flight and surely you would have been filled by them with terror.

And you would think them (wataḥsabuhum) | awake (ayqāẓan) | while they (wahum) | were asleep (ruqūdun). | And We turned them (wanuqallibuhum) | to (dhāta) | the right (l-yamīni) | and to (wadhāta) | the left (l-shimāli), | while their dog (wakalbuhum) | stretched (bāsiṭun) | his two forelegs (dhirāʿayhi) | at the entrance (bil-waṣīdi). | If (lawi) | you had looked (iṭṭalaʿta) | at them (ʿalayhim), | you would have surely turned back (lawallayta) | from them (min'hum) | in flight (firāran) | and surely you would have been filled (walamuli'ta) | by them (min'hum) | with terror (ruʿ'ban).

18:19 And similarly, We raised them that they might question among them. Said a speaker among them, "How long have you remained?" They said, "We have remained a day or a part of a day." They said, "Your Lord knows best how long you have remained. So send one of you with this silver coin of yours to the city, and let him see which is the purest food, and let him bring to you provision from it, and let him be cautious. And let not be aware about you anyone."

And similarly (wakadhālika), | We raised them (baʿathnāhum) | that they might question (liyatasāalū) | among them (baynahum). | Said (qāla) | a speaker (qāilun) | among them (min'hum), | "How long (kam) | have you remained? (labith'tum)" | They said (qālū), | "We have remained (labith'nā) | a day (yawman) | or (aw) | a part (baʿḍa) | of a day. (yawmin)" | They said (qālū), | "Your Lord (rabbukum) | knows best (aʿlamu) | how long (bimā) | you have remained (labith'tum). | So send (fa-ib'ʿathū) | one of you (aḥadakum) | with this silver coin of yours (biwariqikum) | with this silver coin of yours (hādhihi) | to (ilā) | the city (l-madīnati), | and let him see (falyanẓur) | which is (ayyuhā) | the purest (azkā) | food (ṭaʿāman), | and let him bring to you (falyatikum) | provision (biriz'qin) | from it (min'hu), | and let him be cautious (walyatalaṭṭaf). | And let not be aware (walā) | And let not be aware (yush'ʿiranna) | about you (bikum) | anyone. (aḥadan)"

18:20 "Indeed, [they] if they come to know about you, they will stone you or return you to their religion. And never will you succeed then - ever."

"Indeed, [they] (innahum) | if (in) | they come to know (yaẓharū) | about you (ʿalaykum), | they will stone you (yarjumūkum) | or (aw) | return you (yuʿīdūkum) | to (fī) | their religion (millatihim). | And never (walan) | will you succeed (tuf'liḥū) | then (idhan)- | ever. (abadan)"

18:21 And similarly, We made known about them that they might know that the Promise of Allah is true, and that about the Hour there is no doubt in it. When they disputed among themselves about their affair and they said, "Construct over them a structure. Their Lord knows best about them." Said those who prevailed in their matter, "Surely we will take over them a place of worship."

And similarly (wakadhālika), | We made known (aʿtharnā) | about them (ʿalayhim) | that they might know (liyaʿlamū) | that (anna) | the Promise (waʿda) | of Allah (l-lahi) | is true (ḥaqqun), | and that (wa-anna) | about the Hour (l-sāʿata) | there is no (lā) | doubt (rayba) | in it (fīhā). | When (idh) | they disputed (yatanāzaʿūna) | among themselves (baynahum) | about their affair (amrahum) | and they said (faqālū), | "Construct (ib'nū) | over them (ʿalayhim) | a structure (bun'yānan). | Their Lord (rabbuhum) | knows best (aʿlamu) | about them. (bihim)" | Said (qāla) | those who (alladhīna) | prevailed (ghalabū) | in (ʿalā) | their matter (amrihim), | "Surely we will take (lanattakhidhanna) | over them (ʿalayhim) | a place of worship. (masjidan)"

18:22 They say, they were three, the forth of them their dog; and they say they were five the sixth of them their dog - guessing about the unseen; and they say, they were seven and the eight of them their dog. Say, "My Lord, knows best their number. None knows them except a few. So do not argue about them except with an argument obvious, and do not inquire about them among them from anyone."

They say (sayaqūlūna), | they were three (thalāthatun), | the forth of them (rābiʿuhum) | their dog (kalbuhum); | and they say (wayaqūlūna) | they were five (khamsatun) | the sixth of them (sādisuhum) | their dog (kalbuhum)- | guessing (rajman) | about the unseen (bil-ghaybi); | and they say (wayaqūlūna), | they were seven (sabʿatun) | and the eight of them (wathāminuhum) | their dog (kalbuhum). | Say (qul), | "My Lord (rabbī), | knows best (aʿlamu) | their number (biʿiddatihim). | None (mā) | knows them (yaʿlamuhum) | except (illā) | a few (qalīlun). | So do not (falā) | argue (tumāri) | about them (fīhim) | except (illā) | with an argument (mirāan) | obvious (ẓāhiran), | and do not (walā) | inquire (tastafti) | about them (fīhim) | among them (min'hum) | from anyone. (aḥadan)"

18:23 And do not say of anything, "Indeed, I will do that tomorrow."

And do not (walā) | say (taqūlanna) | of anything (lishāy'in), | "Indeed, I (innī) | will do (fāʿilun) | that (dhālika) | tomorrow. (ghadan)"

18:24 Except, "If Allah wills." And remember your Lord when you forget and say, "Perhaps [that] will guide me my Lord to a nearer way than this right way."

Except (illā), | "If (an) | Allah wills. (yashāa)" | Allah wills. (l-lahu)" | And remember (wa-udh'kur) | your Lord (rabbaka) | when (idhā) | you forget (nasīta) | and say (waqul), | "Perhaps (ʿasā) | [that] (an) | will guide me (yahdiyani) | my Lord (rabbī) | to a nearer way (li-aqraba) | than (min) | this (hādhā) | right way. (rashadan)"

18:25 And they remained in their cave for three hundred years and add nine.

And they remained (walabithū) | in (fī) | their cave (kahfihim) | for three (thalātha) | hundred (mi-atin) | years (sinīna) | and add (wa-iz'dādū) | nine (tis'ʿan).

18:26 Say, "Allah knows best about what period they remained. For Him is the unseen of the heavens and the earth. How clearly He sees! [of it] And how clearly He hears! Not for them besides Him any protector, and not He shares [in] His Commands with anyone."

Say (quli), | "Allah (l-lahu) | knows best (aʿlamu) | about what period (bimā) | they remained (labithū). | For Him (lahu) | is the unseen (ghaybu) | of the heavens (l-samāwāti) | and the earth (wal-arḍi). | How clearly He sees (abṣir)! | [of it] (bihi) | And how clearly He hears (wa-asmiʿ)! | Not (mā) | for them (lahum) | besides Him (min) | besides Him (dūnihi) | any (min) | protector (waliyyin), | and not (walā) | He shares (yush'riku) | [in] (fī) | His Commands (ḥuk'mihi) | with anyone. (aḥadan)"

18:27 And recite what has been revealed to you of the Book of your Lord. None can change His Words and never you will find besides Him a refuge.

And recite (wa-ut'lu) | what (mā) | has been revealed (ūḥiya) | to you (ilayka) | of (min) | the Book (kitābi) | of your Lord (rabbika). | None (lā) | can change (mubaddila) | His Words (likalimātihi) | and never (walan) | you will find (tajida) | besides Him (min) | besides Him (dūnihi) | a refuge (mul'taḥadan).

18:28 And be patient, yourself, with those who call their Lord in the morning and the evening desiring His Face. And let not pass beyond your eyes over them, desiring adornment of the life of the world, and do not obey whom We have made heedless his heart of Our remembrance, and follows his desires and is his affair in excess.

And be patient (wa-iṣ'bir), | yourself (nafsaka), | with (maʿa) | those who (alladhīna) | call (yadʿūna) | their Lord (rabbahum) | in the morning (bil-ghadati) | and the evening (wal-ʿashiyi) | desiring (yurīdūna) | His Face (wajhahu). | And let not (walā) | pass beyond (taʿdu) | your eyes (ʿaynāka) | over them (ʿanhum), | desiring (turīdu) | adornment (zīnata) | of the life (l-ḥayati) | of the world (l-dun'yā), | and do not (walā) | obey (tuṭiʿ) | whom (man) | We have made heedless (aghfalnā) | his heart (qalbahu) | of (ʿan) | Our remembrance (dhik'rinā), | and follows (wa-ittabaʿa) | his desires (hawāhu) | and is (wakāna) | his affair (amruhu) | in excess (furuṭan).

18:29 And say, "The truth is from your Lord, so whoever wills - let him believe and whoever wills - let him disbelieve." Indeed, We have prepared for the wrongdoers a Fire, will surround them its walls. And if they call for relief, they will be relieved with water like molten brass, which scalds the faces. Wretched is the drink, and evil is the resting place.

And say (waquli), | "The truth (l-ḥaqu) | is from (min) | your Lord (rabbikum), | so whoever (faman) | wills (shāa)- | let him believe (falyu'min) | and whoever (waman) | wills (shāa)- | let him disbelieve. (falyakfur)" | Indeed, We (innā) | have prepared (aʿtadnā) | for the wrongdoers (lilẓẓālimīna) | a Fire (nāran), | will surround (aḥāṭa) | them (bihim) | its walls (surādiquhā). | And if (wa-in) | they call for relief (yastaghīthū), | they will be relieved (yughāthū) | with water (bimāin) | like molten brass (kal-muh'li), | which scalds (yashwī) | the faces (l-wujūha). | Wretched (bi'sa) | is the drink (l-sharābu), | and evil (wasāat) | is the resting place (mur'tafaqan).

18:30 Indeed, those who believed and did the good deeds, indeed, We will not let go waste the reward of one who does good deeds.

Indeed (inna), | those who (alladhīna) | believed (āmanū) | and did (waʿamilū) | the good deeds (l-ṣāliḥāti), | indeed, We (innā) | will not let go waste (lā) | will not let go waste (nuḍīʿu) | the reward (ajra) | of one who (man) | does good (aḥsana) | deeds (ʿamalan).

18:31 Those, for them are Gardens of Eden, flows from underneath them the rivers. They will be adorned therein [of] with bracelets of gold and will wear garments, green, of fine silk and heavy brocade, reclining therein on adorned couches. Excellent is the reward, and good is the resting place.

Those (ulāika), | for them (lahum) | are Gardens (jannātu) | of Eden (ʿadnin), | flows (tajrī) | from (min) | underneath them (taḥtihimu) | the rivers (l-anhāru). | They will be adorned (yuḥallawna) | therein (fīhā) | [of] with (min) | bracelets (asāwira) | of (min) | gold (dhahabin) | and will wear (wayalbasūna) | garments (thiyāban), | green (khuḍ'ran), | of (min) | fine silk (sundusin) | and heavy brocade (wa-is'tabraqin), | reclining (muttakiīna) | therein (fīhā) | on (ʿalā) | adorned couches (l-arāiki). | Excellent (niʿʿma) | is the reward (l-thawābu), | and good (waḥasunat) | is the resting place (mur'tafaqan).

18:32 And set forth to them the example of two men: We provided for one of them two gardens of grapes, and We bordered them with date-palms, and We placed between both of them crops.

And set forth (wa-iḍ'rib) | to them (lahum) | the example (mathalan) | of two men (rajulayni): | We provided (jaʿalnā) | for one of them (li-aḥadihimā) | two gardens (jannatayni) | of (min) | grapes (aʿnābin), | and We bordered them (waḥafafnāhumā) | with date-palms (binakhlin), | and We placed (wajaʿalnā) | between both of them (baynahumā) | crops (zarʿan).

18:33 Each of the two gardens brought forth its produce and not did wrong of it anything. And We caused to gush forth within them a river.

Each (kil'tā) | of the two gardens (l-janatayni) | brought forth (ātat) | its produce (ukulahā) | and not (walam) | did wrong (taẓlim) | of it (min'hu) | anything (shayan). | And We caused to gush forth (wafajjarnā) | within them (khilālahumā) | a river (naharan).

18:34 And was for him fruit, so he said to his companion while he was talking with him, "I am greater than you in wealth and stronger in men."

And was (wakāna) | for him (lahu) | fruit (thamarun), | so he said (faqāla) | to his companion (liṣāḥibihi) | while he (wahuwa) | was talking with him (yuḥāwiruhu), | "I am (anā) | greater (aktharu) | than you (minka) | in wealth (mālan) | and stronger (wa-aʿazzu) | in men. (nafaran)"

18:35 And he entered his garden while he was unjust to himself. He said, "Not I think that will perish this ever.

And he entered (wadakhala) | his garden (jannatahu) | while he (wahuwa) | was unjust (ẓālimun) | to himself (linafsihi). | He said (qāla), | "Not (mā) | I think (aẓunnu) | that (an) | will perish (tabīda) | this (hādhihi) | ever (abadan).

18:36 And not I think the Hour will occur. And if I am brought back to my Lord, I will surely find better than this as a return."

And not (wamā) | I think (aẓunnu) | the Hour (l-sāʿata) | will occur (qāimatan). | And if (wala-in) | I am brought back (rudidttu) | to (ilā) | my Lord (rabbī), | I will surely find (la-ajidanna) | better (khayran) | than this (min'hā) | as a return. (munqalaban)"

18:37 Said to him his companion while he was talking to him, "Do you disbelieve in One Who created you from dust then from a minute quantity of semen. then fashioned you into a man?

Said (qāla) | to him (lahu) | his companion (ṣāḥibuhu) | while he (wahuwa) | was talking to him (yuḥāwiruhu), | "Do you disbelieve (akafarta) | in One Who (bi-alladhī) | created you (khalaqaka) | from (min) | dust (turābin) | then (thumma) | from (min) | a minute quantity of semen (nuṭ'fatin). | then (thumma) | fashioned you (sawwāka) | into a man (rajulan)?

18:38 But as for me, He is Allah, my Lord, and not I associate with my Lord anyone.
But as for me (lākinnā), | He (huwa) | is Allah (l-lahu), | my Lord (rabbī), | and not (walā) | I associate (ush'riku) | with my Lord (birabbī) | anyone (aḥadan).

18:39 And why did you not, when you entered your garden say, "What wills Allah; there is no power except with Allah." If you see me me lesser than you in wealth and children,
And why did you not (walawlā), | when (idh) | you entered (dakhalta) | your garden (jannataka) | say (qul'ta), | "What (mā) | wills (shāa) | Allah (l-lahu); | there is no (lā) | power (quwwata) | except (illā) | with Allah. (bil-lahi)" | If (in) | you see me (tarani) | me (anā) | lesser (aqalla) | than you (minka) | in wealth (mālan) | and children (wawaladan),

18:40 It may be that my Lord will give me better than your garden and will send upon it a calamity from the sky, then it will become ground slippery,
It may be (faʿasā) | that my Lord (rabbī) | that my Lord (an) | will give me (yu'tiyani) | better (khayran) | than (min) | your garden (jannatika) | and will send (wayur'sila) | upon it (ʿalayhā) | a calamity (ḥus'bānan) | from (mina) | the sky (l-samāi), | then it will become (fatuṣ'biḥa) | ground (ṣaʿīdan) | slippery (zalaqan),

18:41 Or will become, its water, sunken, so never you will be able to find it."
Or (aw) | will become (yuṣ'biḥa), | its water (māuhā), | sunken (ghawran), | so never (falan) | you will be able (tastaṭīʿa) | to find it. (lahu)" | to find it. (ṭalaban)"

18:42 And were surrounded his fruits, so he began twisting his hands over what he had spent on it, while it had collapsed on its trellises, and he said, "Oh! I wish I had not associated with my Lord anyone."
And were surrounded (wa-uḥīṭa) | his fruits (bithamarihi), | so he began (fa-aṣbaḥa) | twisting (yuqallibu) | his hands (kaffayhi) | over (ʿalā) | what (mā) | he had spent (anfaqa) | on it (fīhā), | while it had (wahiya) | collapsed (khāwiyatun) | on (ʿalā) | its trellises (ʿurūshihā), | and he said (wayaqūlu), | "Oh! I wish (yālaytanī) | I had not associated (lam) | I had not associated (ush'rik) | with my Lord (birabbī) | anyone. (aḥadan)"

18:43 And not was for him a group to help him other than Allah, and not was he supported.
And not (walam) | was (takun) | for him (lahu) | a group (fi-atun) | to help him (yanṣurūnahu) | other than (min) | other than (dūni) | Allah (l-lahi), | and not (wamā) | was (kāna) | he supported (muntaṣiran).

18:44 There, the protection is from Allah the True. He is the best to reward and the best for the final end.
There (hunālika), | the protection (l-walāyatu) | is from Allah (lillahi) | the True (l-ḥaqi). | He (huwa) | is the best (khayrun) | to reward (thawāban) | and the best (wakhayrun) | for the final end (ʿuq'ban).

18:45 And present to them the example of the life of the world, like water which We send down from the sky, then mingles with it the vegetation of the earth then becomes dry stalks, it is scattered by the winds. And Allah over every thing is All Able.
And present (wa-iḍ'rib) | to them (lahum) | the example (mathala) | of the life (l-ḥayati) | of the world (l-dun'yā), | like water (kamāin) | which We send down (anzalnāhu) | from (mina) | the sky (l-samāi), | then mingles (fa-ikh'talaṭa) | with it (bihi) | the vegetation (nabātu) | of the earth (l-arḍi) | then becomes (fa-aṣbaḥa) | dry stalks (hashīman), | it is scattered (tadhrūhu) | by the winds (l-riyāḥu). | And Allah (wakāna) | And Allah (l-lahu) | over (ʿalā) | every (kulli) | thing (shayin)

| is All Able (muq'tadiran).

18:46 The wealth and children are adornment of the life of the world. But the enduring good deeds are better near your Lord for reward and better for hope.

The wealth (al-mālu) | and children (wal-banūna) | are adornment (zīnatu) | of the life (l-ḥayati) | of the world (l-dun'yā). | But the enduring (wal-bāqiyātu) | good deeds (l-ṣāliḥātu) | are better (khayrun) | near (ʿinda) | your Lord (rabbika) | for reward (thawāban) | and better (wakhayrun) | for hope (amalan).

18:47 And the Day We will cause to move the mountains and you will see the earth as a leveled plain and We will gather them and not We will leave behind from them anyone.

And the Day (wayawma) | We will cause to move (nusayyiru) | the mountains (l-jibāla) | and you will see (watarā) | the earth (l-arḍa) | as a leveled plain (bārizatan) | and We will gather them (waḥasharnāhum) | and not (falam) | We will leave behind (nughādir) | from them (min'hum) | anyone (aḥadan).

18:48 And they will be presented before your Lord in rows, "Certainly, you have come to Us as We created you the first time. Nay, you claimed that not We made for you an appointment."

And they will be presented (waʿuriḍū) | before (ʿalā) | your Lord (rabbika) | in rows (ṣaffan), | "Certainly (laqad), | you have come to Us (ji'tumūnā) | as (kamā) | We created you (khalaqnākum) | the first (awwala) | time (marratin). | Nay (bal), | you claimed (zaʿamtum) | that not (allan) | We made (najʿala) | for you (lakum) | an appointment. (mawʿidan)"

18:49 And will be placed the Book and you will see the criminals fearful of what is in it, and they will say, "Oh, woe to us! What is for this [the] Book, not leaves a small and not a great except has enumerated it?" And they will find what they did presented. And not deals unjustly your Lord with anyone.

And will be placed (wawuḍiʿa) | the Book (l-kitābu) | and you will see (fatarā) | the criminals (l-muj'rimīna) | fearful (mush'fiqīna) | of what (mimmā) | is in it (fīhi), | and they will say (wayaqūlūna), | "Oh, woe to us (yāwaylatanā)! | What is for (māli) | this (hādhā) | [the] Book (l-kitābi), | not (lā) | leaves (yughādiru) | a small (ṣaghīratan) | and not (walā) | a great (kabīratan) | except (illā) | has enumerated it? (aḥṣāhā)" | And they will find (wawajadū) | what (mā) | they did (ʿamilū) | presented (ḥāḍiran). | And not (walā) | deals unjustly (yaẓlimu) | your Lord (rabbuka) | with anyone (aḥadan).

18:50 And when We said to the Angels, "Prostrate to Adam," so they prostrated except Iblis. He was of the jinn, and he rebelled against the Command of his Lord. Will you then take him and his offspring as protectors other than Me, while they are to you enemies? Wretched for the wrongdoers is the exchange.

And when (wa-idh) | We said (qul'nā) | to the Angels (lil'malāikati), | "Prostrate (us'judū) | to Adam, (liādama)" | so they prostrated (fasajadū) | except (illā) | Iblis (ib'līsa). | He was (kāna) | of (mina) | the jinn (l-jini), | and he rebelled (fafasaqa) | against (ʿan) | the Command (amri) | of his Lord (rabbihi). | Will you then take him (afatattakhidhūnahu) | and his offspring (wadhurriyyatahu) | as protectors (awliyāa) | other than Me (min), | other than Me (dūnī), | while they (wahum) | are to you (lakum) | enemies (ʿaduwwun)? | Wretched (bi'sa) | for the wrongdoers (lilẓẓālimīna) | is the exchange (badalan).

18:51 Not I made them witness the creation of the heavens and the earth and not the creation of themselves and not I Am the One to take the misleaders as helper(s).

Not (mā) | I made them witness (ashhadttuhum) | the creation (khalqa) | of the heavens (l-samāwāti) | and the earth (wal-arḍi) | and not (walā) | the creation (khalqa) | of themselves (anfusihim) | and not (wamā) | I Am (kuntu) | the One to take (muttakhidha) | the misleaders (l-muḍilīna) | as helper(s) (ʿaḍudan).

18:52 And the Day He will say, "Call My partners, those who you claimed," then they will call them but not they will respond to them. And We will make between them a barrier.

And the Day (wayawma) | He will say (yaqūlu), | "Call (nādū) | My partners (shurakāiya), | those who (alladhīna) | you claimed, (zaʿamtum)" | then they will call them (fadaʿawhum) | but not (falam) | they will respond (yastajībū) | to them (lahum). | And We will make (wajaʿalnā) | between them (baynahum) | a barrier (mawbiqan).

18:53 And will see the criminals the Fire, and they will be certain that they are to fall in it. And not they will find from it a way of escape.

And will see (waraā) | the criminals (l-muj'rimūna) | the Fire (l-nāra), | and they will be certain (faẓannū) | that they (annahum) | are to fall in it (muwāqiʿūhā). | And not (walam) | they will find (yajidū) | from it (ʿanhā) | a way of escape (maṣrifan).

18:54 And certainly, We have explained in this the Quran for mankind of every example. But is the man in most things quarrelsome.

And certainly (walaqad), | We have explained (ṣarrafnā) | in (fī) | this (hādhā) | the Quran (l-qur'āni) | for mankind (lilnnāsi) | of (min) | every (kulli) | example (mathalin). | But is (wakāna) | the man (l-insānu) | in most (akthara) | things (shayin) | quarrelsome (jadalan).

18:55 And nothing prevents men that they believe when has come to them the guidance and they ask forgiveness of their Lord, except that comes to them the way of the former (people) or comes to them the punishment before them?

And nothing (wamā) | prevents (manaʿa) | men (l-nāsa) | that (an) | they believe (yu'minū) | when (idh) | has come to them (jāahumu) | the guidance (l-hudā) | and they ask forgiveness (wayastaghfirū) | of their Lord (rabbahum), | except (illā) | that (an) | comes to them (tatiyahum) | the way (sunnatu) | of the former (people (l-awalīna)) | or (aw) | comes to them (yatiyahumu) | the punishment (l-ʿadhābu) | before them (qubulan)?

18:56 And not We send the Messengers except as bearers of glad tidings and as warners. And dispute those who disbelieve with falsehood, to refute thereby the truth. And they take My Verses and what they are warned in ridicule.

And not (wamā) | We send (nur'silu) | the Messengers (l-mur'salīna) | except (illā) | as bearers of glad tidings (mubashirīna) | and as warners (wamundhirīna). | And dispute (wayujādilu) | those who (alladhīna) | disbelieve (kafarū) | with falsehood (bil-bāṭili), | to refute (liyud'ḥiḍū) | thereby (bihi) | the truth (l-ḥaqa). | And they take (wa-ittakhadhū) | My Verses (āyātī) | and what (wamā) | they are warned (undhirū) | in ridicule (huzuwan).

18:57 And who is more wrong than he who is reminded of the Verses of his Lord, but turns away from them, and forgets what have sent forth his hands? Indeed, We [We] have placed over their hearts coverings, lest they understand it and in their ears is deafness. And if you call them to the guidance, then never they will be guided then ever.

And who (waman) | is more wrong (aẓlamu) | than he who (mimman) | is reminded (dhukkira) | of the Verses (biāyāti) | of his Lord (rabbihi), | but turns away (fa-aʿraḍa) | from them (ʿanhā), | and forgets (wanasiya) | what (mā) | have sent forth (qaddamat) | his hands (yadāhu)? | Indeed, We (innā) | [We] have placed (jaʿalnā) | over (ʿalā) | their hearts (qulūbihim) | coverings (akinnatan), | lest (an) | they understand it (yafqahūhu) | and in (wafī) | their ears (ādhānihim) | is deafness (waqran). | And if (wa-in) | you call them (tadʿuhum) | to (ilā) | the guidance (l-hudā), | then never (falan) | they will be guided (yahtadū) | then (idhan) | ever (abadan).

18:58 And your Lord is the Most Forgiving, Owner of the Mercy. If He were to seize them for what they have earned, surely, He would have hastened for them the punishment. But for them is an appointment, never they will find other than it an escape.

And your Lord (warabbuka) | is the Most Forgiving (l-ghafūru), | Owner (dhū) | of the Mercy (l-raḥmati). | If (law) | He were to seize them (yuākhidhuhum) | for what (bimā) | they have earned (kasabū), | surely, He would have hastened (laʿajjala) | for them (lahumu) | the punishment (l-ʿadhāba). | But (bal) | for them (lahum) | is an appointment (mawʿidun), | never (lan) | they will find (yajidū) | other than it (min) | other than it (dūnihi) | an escape (mawilan).

18:59 And these [the] towns, We destroyed them when they wronged, and We made for their destruction an appointed time.

And these (watil'ka) | [the] towns (l-qurā), | We destroyed them (ahlaknāhum) | when (lammā) | they wronged (ẓalamū), | and We made (wajaʿalnā) | for their destruction (limahlikihim) | an appointed time (mawʿidan).

18:60 And when said Musa to his boy, "Not I will cease until I reach the junction of the two seas or I continue for a long period."

And when (wa-idh) | said (qāla) | Musa (mūsā) | to his boy (lifatāhu), | "Not (lā) | I will cease (abraḥu) | until (ḥattā) | I reach (ablugha) | the junction (majmaʿa) | of the two seas (l-baḥrayni) | or (aw) | I continue (amḍiya) | for a long period. (ḥuquban)"

18:61 But when they reached the junction between them, they forgot their fish, and it took its way into the sea, slipping away.

But when (falammā) | they reached (balaghā) | the junction (majmaʿa) | between them (baynihimā), | they forgot (nasiyā) | their fish (ḥūtahumā), | and it took (fa-ittakhadha) | its way (sabīlahu) | into (fī) | the sea (l-baḥri), | slipping away (saraban).

18:62 Then when they had passed beyond he said to his boy, "Bring us our morning meal. Certainly we have suffered in our journey this, fatigue."

Then when (falammā) | they had passed beyond (jāwazā) | he said (qāla) | to his boy (lifatāhu), | "Bring us (ātinā) | our morning meal (ghadāanā). | Certainly (laqad) | we have suffered (laqīnā) | in (min) | our journey (safarinā) | this (hādhā), | fatigue. (naṣaban)"

18:63 He said, "Did you see, when we retired to the rock? Then indeed, I [I] forgot the fish. And not made me forget it except the Shaitaan that I mention it. And it took its way into the sea amazingly."

He said (qāla), | "Did you see (ara-ayta), | when (idh) | we retired (awaynā) | to (ilā) | the rock (l-ṣakhrati)? | Then indeed, I (fa-innī) | [I] forgot (nasītu) | the fish (l-ḥūta). | And not (wamā) | made me forget it (ansānīhu) | except (illā) | the Shaitaan (l-shayṭānu) | that (an) | I mention it (adhkurahu). | And it took (wa-ittakhadha) | its way (sabīlahu) | into (fī) | the sea (l-baḥri) | amazingly. (ʿajaban)"

18:64 He said, "That is what we were seeking." So they returned on their footprints, retracing.

He said (qāla), | "That (dhālika) | is what (mā) | we were (kunnā) | seeking. (nabghi)" | So they returned (fa-ir'taddā) | on (ʿalā) | their footprints (āthārihimā), | retracing (qaṣaṣan).

18:65 Then they found a servant from Our servants, whom We had given mercy from Us, and We had taught him from Us a knowledge.

Then they found (fawajadā) | a servant (ʿabdan) | from (min) | Our servants (ʿibādinā), | whom We had given (ātaynāhu) | mercy (raḥmatan) | from (min) | Us (ʿindinā), | and We had taught him (waʿallamnāhu) | from (min) | Us (ladunnā) | a knowledge (ʿil'man).

18:66 Said to him Musa, "May, I follow you on that you teach me of what you have been taught of right guidance?"

Said (qāla) | to him (lahu) | Musa (mūsā), | "May (hal), | I follow you (attabiʿuka) | on (ʿalā) | that (an) | you teach me (tuʿallimani) | of what (mimmā) | you have been taught (ʿullim'ta) | of right guidance? (rush'dan)"

18:67 He said, "Indeed, you never will be able, with me, to have patience.

He said (qāla), | "Indeed, you (innaka) | never (lan) | will be able (tastaṭīʿa), | with me (maʿiya), | to have patience (ṣabran).

18:68 And how can you have patience for what not you encompass of it any knowledge."

And how can (wakayfa) | you have patience (taṣbiru) | for (ʿalā) | what (mā) | not (lam) | you encompass (tuḥiṭ) | of it (bihi) | any knowledge. (khub'ran)"

18:69 He said, "You will find me, if Allah wills, patient, and not I will disobey your order."

He said (qāla), | "You will find me (satajidunī), | if (in) | Allah wills (shāa), | Allah wills (l-lahu), | patient (ṣābiran), | and not (walā) | I will disobey (aʿṣī) | your (laka) | order. (amran)"

18:70 He said, "Then if you follow me, do not ask me about anything until I present to you of it a mention."

He said (qāla), | "Then if (fa-ini) | you follow me (ittabaʿtanī), | do not (falā) | ask me (tasalnī) | about (ʿan) | anything (shayin) | until (ḥattā) | I present (uḥ'ditha) | to you (laka) | of it (min'hu) | a mention. (dhik'ran)"

18:71 So they both set out until when they had embarked on the ship he made a hole in it. He said, "Have you made a hole in it, to drown its people? Certainly, you have done a thing grave."

So they both set out (fa-inṭalaqā) | until (ḥattā) | when (idhā) | they had embarked (rakibā) | on (fī) | the ship (l-safīnati) | he made a hole in it (kharaqahā). | He said (qāla), | "Have you made a hole in it (akharaqtahā), | to drown (litugh'riqa) | its people (ahlahā)? | Certainly (laqad), | you have done (ji'ta) | a thing (shayan) | grave. (im'ran)"

18:72 He said, "Did not I say, indeed, you never will be able with me to have patience?"

He said (qāla), | "Did not (alam) | I say (aqul), | indeed, you (innaka) | never (lan) | will be able (tastaṭīʿa) | with me (maʿiya) | to have patience? (ṣabran)"

18:73 He said, "Do not, blame me for what I forgot and do not be hard upon me in my affair raising difficulty."

He said (qāla), | "Do not (lā), | blame me (tuākhidh'nī) | for what (bimā) | I forgot (nasītu) | and do not (walā) | be hard upon me (tur'hiq'nī) | in (min) | my affair (amrī) | raising difficulty. (ʿus'ran)"

18:74 Then they both set out until when they met a boy, then he killed him. He said, "Have you killed a soul, pure, for other than a soul? Certainly, you have done a thing evil."

Then they both set out (fa-inṭalaqā) | until (ḥattā) | when (idhā) | they met (laqiyā) | a boy (ghulāman), | then he killed him (faqatalahu). | He said (qāla), | "Have you killed (aqatalta) | a soul (nafsan), | pure (zakiyyatan), | for other than (bighayri) | a soul (nafsin)? | Certainly (laqad), | you have done (ji'ta) | a thing (shayan) | evil. (nuk'ran)"

18:75 He said, "Did not I say to you that you, never will be able with me to have patience?"

He said (qāla), | "Did not (alam) | I say (aqul) | to you (laka) | that you (innaka), | never (lan) | will be able (tastaṭīʿa) | with me (maʿiya) | to have patience? (ṣabran)"

18:76 He said, "If I ask you about anything after it, then do not keep me as a companion. Verily, you have reached from me an excuse."

He said (qāla), | "If (in) | I ask you (sa-altuka) | about (ʿan) | anything (shayin) | after it (baʿdahā), | then do not (falā) | keep me as a companion (tuṣāḥib'nī). | Verily (qad), | you have reached (balaghta) | from me (min) | from me (ladunnī) | an excuse. (ʿudh'ran)"

18:77 So they set out until when they came to the people of a town, they asked for food from its people, but they refused to offer them hospitality. Then they found in it a wall that want(ed) to collapse, so he set it straight. He said, "If you wished surely you could have taken for it a payment."

So they set out (fa-inṭalaqā) | until (ḥattā) | when (idhā) | they came (atayā) | to the people (ahla) | of a town (qaryatin), | they asked for food (is'taṭʿamā) | from its people (ahlahā), | but they refused (fa-abaw) | to (an) | offer them hospitality (yuḍayyifūhumā). | Then they found (fawajadā) | in it (fīhā) | a wall (jidāran) | that want(ed (yurīdu)) | to (an) | collapse (yanqaḍḍa), | so he set it straight (fa-aqāmahu). | He said (qāla), | "If (law) | you wished (shi'ta) | surely you could have taken (lattakhadhta) | for it (ʿalayhi) | a payment. (ajran)"

18:78 He said, "This is parting between me and between you. I will inform you of the interpretation of what not you were able on it to have patience.

He said (qāla), | "This (hādhā) | is parting (firāqu) | between me (baynī) | and between you (wabaynika). | I will inform you (sa-unabbi-uka) | of the interpretation (bitawīli) | of what (mā) | not (lam) | you were able (tastaṭiʿ) | on it (ʿalayhi) | to have patience (ṣabran).

18:79 As for the ship, it was of the poor people working in the sea. So I intended that I cause defect in it as there was after them a king who seized every ship by force.

As for (ammā) | the ship (l-safīnatu), | it was (fakānat) | of the poor people (limasākīna) | working (yaʿmalūna) | in (fī) | the sea (l-baḥri). | So I intended (fa-aradttu) | that (an) | I cause defect in it (aʿībahā) | as there was (wakāna) | after them (warāahum) | a king (malikun) | who seized (yakhudhu) | every (kulla) | ship (safīnatin) | by force (ghaṣban).

18:80 And as for the boy his parents were believers, and we feared that he would overburden them by transgression and disbelief.

And as for (wa-ammā) | the boy (l-ghulāmu) | his parents were (fakāna) | his parents were (abawāhu) | believers (mu'minayni), | and we feared (fakhashīnā) | that (an) | he would overburden them (yur'hiqahumā) | by transgression (ṭugh'yānan) | and disbelief (wakuf'ran).

18:81 So we intended that would change for them their Lord, a better than him in purity and nearer in affection.

So we intended (fa-aradnā) | that (an) | would change for them (yub'dilahumā) | their Lord (rabbuhumā), | a better (khayran) | than him (min'hu) | in purity (zakatan) | and nearer (wa-aqraba) | in affection (ruḥ'man).

18:82 And as for the wall, it was for two orphan boys, in the town, and was underneath it a treasure for them and was their father righteous. So intended your Lord that they reach their maturity, and bring forth their treasure as a mercy from your Lord. And not I did it on my own accord. That is the interpretation of what not you were able on it to have patience."

And as for (wa-ammā) | the wall (l-jidāru), | it was (fakāna) | for two orphan boys (lighulāmayni), | for two orphan boys (yatīmayni), | in (fī) | the town (l-madīnati), | and was (wakāna) | underneath it (taḥtahu) | a treasure (kanzun) | for them (lahumā) | and was (wakāna) | their father (abūhumā) | righteous (ṣāliḥan). | So intended (fa-arāda) | your Lord (rabbuka) | that (an) | they reach (yablughā) | their maturity (ashuddahumā), | and bring forth (wayastakhrijā) | their treasure (kanzahumā) | as a mercy (raḥmatan) | from (min) | your Lord (rabbika). | And not (wamā) | I did it (faʿaltuhu) | on (ʿan) | my own accord (amrī). | That (dhālika) | is the interpretation (tawīlu) | of what (mā) | not (lam) | you were able (tasṭiʿ) | on it (ʿalayhi) | to have patience. (ṣabran)"

18:83 And they ask you about Dhul-qarnain. Say, "I will recite to you about him a remembrance."

And they ask you (wayasalūnaka) | about (ʿan) | Dhul-qarnain (dhī). | Dhul-qarnain (l-qarnayni). | Say (qul), | "I will recite (sa-atlū) | to you (ʿalaykum) | about him (min'hu) | a remembrance. (dhik'ran)"

18:84 Indeed, We [We] established [for] him in the earth, and We gave him of every thing a means.

Indeed, We (innā) | [We] established (makkannā) | [for] him (lahu) | in (fī) | the earth (l-arḍi), | and We gave him (waātaynāhu) | of (min) | every (kulli) | thing (shayin) | a means (sababan).

18:85 So he followed a course

So he followed (fa-atbaʿa) | a course (sababan)

18:86 Until, when he reached the setting place of the sun, he found it setting in a spring of dark mud, and he found near it a community. We said, "O Dhul-qarnain! Either [that] you punish or [that] you take [in] them with goodness."

Until (ḥattā), | when (idhā) | he reached (balagha) | the setting place (maghriba) | of the sun (l-shamsi), | he found it (wajadahā) | setting (taghrubu) | in (fī) | a spring (ʿaynin) | of dark mud (ḥami-atin), | and he found (wawajada) | near it (ʿindahā) | a community (qawman). | We said (qul'nā), | "O Dhul-qarnain (yādhā)! | "O Dhul-qarnain (l-qarnayni)! | Either (immā) | [that] (an) | you punish (tuʿadhiba) | or (wa-immā) | [that] (an) | you take (tattakhidha) | [in] them (fīhim) | with goodness. (ḥus'nan)"

18:87 He said, "As for one who wrongs, then soon we will punish him. Then he will be returned to his Lord, and He will punish him with a punishment terrible.

He said (qāla), | "As for (ammā) | one who (man) | wrongs (ẓalama), | then soon (fasawfa) | we will punish him (nuʿadhibuhu). | Then (thumma) | he will be returned (yuraddu) | to (ilā) | his Lord (rabbihi), | and He will punish him (fayuʿadhibuhu) | with a punishment (ʿadhāban) | terrible (nuk'ran).

18:88 But as for one who believes and does righteous deeds, then for him is a reward good. And we will speak to him from our command with ease."

But as for (wa-ammā) | one who (man) | believes (āmana) | and does (waʿamila) | righteous deeds (ṣāliḥan), | then for him (falahu) | is a reward (jazāan) | good (l-ḥus'nā). | And we will speak (wasanaqūlu) | to him (lahu) | from (min) | our command (amrinā) | with ease. (yus'ran)"

18:89 Then he followed a course

Then (thumma) | he followed (atbaʿa) | a course (sababan)

18:90 Until, when he reached the rising place of the sun, and he found it rising on a community not We made for them against it any shelter.

Until (ḥattā), | when (idhā) | he reached (balagha) | the rising place (maṭliʿa) | of the sun (l-shamsi), | and he found it (wajadahā) | rising (taṭluʿu) | on (ʿalā) | a community (qawmin) | not (lam) | We made (najʿal) | for them (lahum) | against it (min) | against it (dūnihā) | any shelter (sit'ran).

18:91 Thus. And verily, We encompassed of what was with him of the information.

Thus (kadhālika). | And verily (waqad), | We encompassed (aḥaṭnā) | of what (bimā) | was with him (ladayhi) | of the information (khub'ran).

18:92 Then he followed a course

Then (thumma) | he followed (atbaʿa) | a course (sababan)

18:93 Until, when he reached between the two mountains, he found besides them a community, not who would almost understand his speech.

Until (ḥattā), | when (idhā) | he reached (balagha) | between (bayna) | the two mountains (l-sadayni), | he found (wajada) | besides them (min) | besides them (dūnihimā) | a community (qawman), | not (lā) | who would almost (yakādūna) | understand (yafqahūna) | his speech (qawlan).

18:94 They said, "O Dhul-qarnain! Indeed, Yajuj and Majuj are corrupters in the land. So may we make for you an expenditure [on] that you make between us and between them a barrier?"

They said (qālū), | "O Dhul-qarnain (yādhā)! | "O Dhul-qarnain (l-qarnayni)! | Indeed (inna), | Yajuj (yajūja) | and Majuj (wamajūja) | are corrupters (muf'sidūna) | in (fī) | the land (l-arḍi). | So may (fahal) | we make (najʿalu) | for you (laka) | an expenditure (kharjan) | [on] (ʿalā) | that (an) | you make (tajʿala) | between us (baynanā) | and between them (wabaynahum) | a barrier? (saddan)"

18:95 He said, "What has established me [in it] my Lord is better, but assist me with strength, I will make between you and between them a barrier.

He said (qāla), | "What (mā) | has established me (makkannī) | [in it] (fīhi) | my Lord (rabbī) | is better (khayrun), | but assist me (fa-aʿīnūnī) | with strength (biquwwatin), | I will make (ajʿal) | between you (baynakum) | and between them (wabaynahum) | a barrier (radman).

18:96 Bring me sheets of iron" until, when he had leveled between the two cliffs, he said, "Blow," until when he made it fire, he said, "Bring me, I pour over it molten copper."

Bring me (ātūnī) | sheets (zubara) | of iron (l-ḥadīdi)" | until (ḥattā), | when (idhā) | he had leveled (sāwā) | between (bayna) | the two cliffs (l-ṣadafayni), | he said (qāla), | "Blow, (unfukhū)" | until (ḥattā) | when (idhā) | he made it (jaʿalahu) | fire (nāran), | he said (qāla), | "Bring me (ātūnī), | I pour (uf'righ) | over it (ʿalayhi) | molten copper. (qiṭ'ran)"

18:97 So not they were able to scale it and not they were able in it to do any penetration.

So not (famā) | they were able (is'ṭāʿū) | to (an) | scale it (yaẓharūhu) | and not (wamā) | they were able (is'taṭāʿū) | in it (lahu) | to do any penetration (naqban).

18:98 He said, "This is a mercy from my Lord. But when comes the Promise of my Lord, He will make it level. And is the Promise of my Lord true."

He said (qāla), | "This (hādhā) | is a mercy (raḥmatun) | from (min) | my Lord (rabbī). | But when (fa-idhā) | comes (jāa) | the Promise (waʿdu) | of my Lord (rabbī), | He will make it (jaʿalahu) | level (dakkāa). | And is (wakāna) | the Promise (waʿdu) | of my Lord (rabbī) | true. (ḥaqqan)"

18:99 And We will leave some of them on that Day to surge over others, and will be blown in the trumpet, then We will gather them all together.

And We will leave (wataraknā) | some of them (baʿḍahum) | on that Day (yawma-idhin) | to surge (yamūju) | over (fī) | others (baʿḍin), | and will be blown (wanufikha) | in (fī) | the trumpet (l-ṣūri), | then We will gather them (fajamaʿnāhum) | all together (jamʿan).

18:100 And We will present Hell on that Day to the disbelievers, on display

And We will present (waʿaraḍnā) | Hell (jahannama) | on that Day (yawma-idhin) | to the disbelievers (lil'kāfirīna), | on display (ʿarḍan)

18:101 Those had been their eyes within a cover from My remembrance, and were not able to hear.

Those (alladhīna) | had been (kānat) | their eyes (aʿyunuhum) | within (fī) | a cover (ghiṭāin) | from (ʿan) | My remembrance (dhik'rī), | and were (wakānū) | not (lā) | able (yastaṭīʿūna) | to hear (samʿan).

18:102 Do then think those who disbelieve that they can take My servants besides Me as protectors? Indeed, We - We have prepared Hell for the disbelievers as a lodging.

Do then think (afaḥasiba) | those who (alladhīna) | disbelieve (kafarū) | that (an) | they can take (yattakhidhū) | My servants (ʿibādī) | besides Me (min) | besides Me (dūnī) | as protectors (awliyāa)? | Indeed, We (innā)- | We have prepared (aʿtadnā) | Hell (jahannama) | for the disbelievers (lil'kāfirīna) | as a lodging (nuzulan).

18:103 Say, "Shall We inform you of the greatest losers as to their deeds?

Say (qul), | "Shall (hal) | We inform you (nunabbi-ukum) | of the greatest losers (bil-akhsarīna) | as to their deeds (aʿmālan)?

18:104 Those - is lost their effort in the life of the world, while they think that they were acquiring good in work."

Those (alladhīna)- | is lost (ḍalla) | their effort (saʿyuhum) | in (fī) | the life (l-ḥayati) | of the world (l-dun'yā), | while they (wahum) | think (yaḥsabūna) | that they (annahum) | were acquiring good (yuḥ'sinūna) | in work. (ṣun'ʿan)"

18:105 Those are the ones who disbelieve in the Verses of their Lord, and the meeting with Him. So are vain their deeds, so not We will assign for them on the Day of the Resurrection any weight.

Those (ulāika) | are the ones who (alladhīna) | disbelieve (kafarū) | in the Verses (biāyāti) | of their Lord (rabbihim), | and the meeting with Him (waliqāihi). | So are vain (faḥabiṭat) | their deeds (aʿmāluhum), | so not (falā) | We will assign (nuqīmu) | for them (lahum) | on the Day (yawma) | of the Resurrection (l-qiyāmati) | any weight (waznan).

18:106 That is their recompense - Hell - because they disbelieved, and took My Verses and My Messengers in ridicule.

That (dhālika) | is their recompense (jazāuhum)- | Hell (jahannamu)- | because (bimā) | they disbelieved (kafarū), | and took (wa-ittakhadhū) | My Verses (āyātī) | and My Messengers (warusulī) | in ridicule (huzuwan).

18:107 Indeed, those who believed and did righteous deeds, for them will be Gardens of the Paradise as a lodging,

Indeed (inna), | those who (alladhīna) | believed (āmanū) | and did (waʿamilū) | righteous deeds (l-ṣāliḥāti), | for them will be (kānat) | for them will be (lahum) | Gardens (jannātu) | of the Paradise (l-fir'dawsi) | as a lodging (nuzulan),

18:108 Abiding forever in it. Not they will desire from it any transfer.

Abiding forever (khālidīna) | in it (fīhā). | Not (lā) | they will desire (yabghūna) | from it (ʿanhā) | any transfer (ḥiwalan).

18:109 Say, "If were the sea ink, for the Words of my Lord, surely would be exhausted the sea before [that] were exhausted the Words of my Lord, even if We brought the like (of) it as a supplement."

Say (qul), | "If (law) | were (kāna) | the sea (l-baḥru) | ink (midādan), | for the Words (likalimāti) | of my Lord (rabbī), | surely would be exhausted (lanafida) | the sea (l-baḥru) | before (qabla) | [that] (an) | were exhausted (tanfada) | the Words (kalimātu) | of my Lord (rabbī), | even if (walaw) | We brought (ji'nā) | the like (of) it (bimith'lihi) | as a supplement. (madadan)"

18:110 Say, "Only I am a man like you. Has been revealed to me that your God is God One. So whoever is hoping for the meeting with his Lord, let him do deeds righteous and not associate in the worship of his Lord anyone."

Say (qul), | "Only (innamā) | I (anā) | am a man (basharun) | like you (mith'lukum). | Has been revealed (yūḥā) | to me (ilayya) | that (annamā) | your God (ilāhukum) | is God (ilāhun) | One (wāḥidun). | So whoever (faman) | is (kāna) | hoping (yarjū) | for the meeting (liqāa) | with his Lord (rabbihi), | let him do (falyaʿmal) | deeds (ʿamalan) | righteous (ṣāliḥan) | and not (walā) | associate (yush'rik) | in the worship (biʿibādati) | of his Lord (rabbihi) | anyone. (aḥadan)"

Chapter (19) Sūrat Maryam (Mary)

19:1 Kaaf Ha Ya Ain Sad.

Kaaf Ha Ya Ain Sad (kaf-ha-ya-ain-sad).

19:2 A mention of the Mercy of your Lord to His servant Zakariya

A mention (dhik'ru) | of the Mercy (raḥmati) | of your Lord (rabbika) | to His servant (ʿabdahu) | Zakariya (zakariyyā)

19:3 When he called to his Lord a call - secret.

When (idh) | he called (nādā) | to his Lord (rabbahu) | a call (nidāan)- | secret (khafiyyan).

19:4 He said, "My Lord! Indeed, [I] have weakened my bones, and flared my head with white, and not I have been in my supplication (to) You my Lord unblessed.

He said (qāla), | "My Lord (rabbi)! | Indeed, [I] (innī) | have weakened (wahana) | my bones (l-ʿaẓmu), | my bones (minnī), | and flared (wa-ish'taʿala) | my head (l-rasu) | with white (shayban), | and not (walam) | I have been (akun) | in my supplication (to) You (biduʿāika) | my Lord (rabbi) | unblessed (shaqiyyan).

19:5 And indeed, I [I] fear the successors after me, and is my wife barren. So give [to] me from Yourself an heir

And indeed, I (wa-innī) | [I] fear (khif'tu) | the successors (l-mawāliya) | after me (min), | after me (warāī), | and is (wakānati) | my wife (im'ra-atī) | barren (ʿāqiran). | So give (fahab) | [to] me (lī) | from (min) | Yourself (ladunka) | an heir (waliyyan)

19:6 Who will inherit me and inherit from the family of Yaqub. And make him my Lord, pleasing."

Who will inherit me (yarithunī) | and inherit (wayarithu) | from (min) | the family (āli) | of Yaqub (yaʿqūba). | And make him (wa-ij'ʿalhu) | my Lord (rabbi), | pleasing. (raḍiyyan)"

19:7 "O Zakariya! Indeed, We [We] give you glad tidings of a boy his name will be Yahya, not We have assigned [for] it before this name."

"O Zakariya (yāzakariyyā)! | Indeed, We (innā) | [We] give you glad tidings (nubashiruka) | of a boy (bighulāmin) | his name (us'muhu) | will be Yahya (yaḥyā), | not (lam) | We have assigned (najʿal) | [for] it (lahu) | before (min) | before (qablu) | this name. (samiyyan)"

19:8 He said, "My Lord! How can I have a boy, while is my wife barren, and indeed, I have reached of the old age extreme?"

He said (qāla), | "My Lord (rabbi)! | How (annā) | can (yakūnu) | I have (lī) | a boy (ghulāmun), | while is (wakānati) | my wife (im'ra-atī) | barren (ʿāqiran), | and indeed (waqad), | I have reached (balaghtu) | of (mina) | the old age (l-kibari) | extreme? (ʿitiyyan)"

19:9 He said, "Thus, said your Lord, 'It is easy for Me and certainly I have created you before, while not you were anything.'"

He said (qāla), | "Thus (kadhālika), | said (qāla) | your Lord (rabbuka), | 'It (huwa) | is easy for Me (ʿalayya) | is easy for Me (hayyinun) | and certainly (waqad) | I have created you (khalaqtuka) | before (min), | before (qablu), | while not (walam) | you were (taku) | anything.' (shayan)"

19:10 He said, "My Lord! Make for me a sign." He said, "Your sign is that not you will speak to the people, for three nights sound."

He said (qāla), | "My Lord (rabbi)! | Make (ijʿal) | for me (lī) | a sign. (āyatan)" | He said (qāla), | "Your sign (āyatuka) | is that not (allā) | you will speak (tukallima) | to the people (l-nāsa), | for three (thalātha) | nights (layālin) | sound. (sawiyyan)"

19:11 Then he came out to his people from the prayer chamber, and he signaled to them to glorify Allah in the morning and in the evening.

Then he came out (fakharaja) | to (ʿalā) | his people (qawmihi) | from (mina) | the prayer chamber (l-miḥ'rābi), | and he signaled (fa-awḥā) | to them (ilayhim) | to (an) | glorify Allah (sabbiḥū) | in the morning (buk'ratan) | and in the evening (waʿashiyyan).

19:12 "O Yahya! Hold the Scripture with strength." And We gave him [the] wisdom when he was a child

"O Yahya (yāyaḥyā)! | Hold (khudhi) | the Scripture (l-kitāba) | with strength. (biquwwatin)" | And We gave him (waātaynāhu) | [the] wisdom (l-ḥuk'ma) | when he was a child (ṣabiyyan)

19:13 And affection from Us and purity and he was righteous

And affection (waḥanānan) | from (min) | Us (ladunnā) | and purity (wazakatan) | and he was (wakāna) | righteous (taqiyyan)

19:14 And dutiful to his parents, and not he was a tyrant disobedient.

And dutiful (wabarran) | to his parents (biwālidayhi), | and not (walam) | he was (yakun) | a tyrant (jabbāran) | disobedient (ʿaṣiyyan).

19:15 And peace be upon him the day he was born and the day he dies and the day he will be raised alive.

And peace be (wasalāmun) | upon him (ʿalayhi) | the day (yawma) | he was born (wulida) | and the day (wayawma) | he dies (yamūtu) | and the day (wayawma) | he will be raised (yubʿathu) | alive (ḥayyan).

19:16 And mention in the Book Maryam, when she withdrew from her family to a place eastern.

And mention (wa-udh'kur) | in (fī) | the Book (l-kitābi) | Maryam (maryama), | when (idhi) | she withdrew (intabadhat) | from (min) | her family (ahlihā) | to a place (makānan) | eastern (sharqiyyan).

19:17 Then she took from them a screen. Then We sent to her Our Spirit then he assumed for her the likeness of a man well-proportioned.

Then she took (fa-ittakhadhat) | from them (min) | from them (dūnihim) | a screen (ḥijāban). | Then We sent (fa-arsalnā) | to her (ilayhā) | Our Spirit (rūḥanā) | then he assumed for her the likeness (fatamathala) | then he assumed for her the likeness (lahā) | of a man (basharan) |

well-proportioned (sawiyyan).

19:18 She said, "Indeed, I [I] seek refuge with the Most Gracious from you if you are God fearing."
She said (qālat), | "Indeed, I (innī) | [I] seek refuge (aʿūdhu) | with the Most Gracious (bil-raḥmāni) | from you (minka) | if (in) | you are (kunta) | God fearing. (taqiyyan)"

19:19 He said, "Only I am a Messenger from your Lord, that I may bestow on you a son pure."
He said (qāla), | "Only (innamā) | I am (anā) | a Messenger (rasūlu) | from your Lord (rabbiki), | that I may bestow (li-ahaba) | on you (laki) | a son (ghulāman) | pure. (zakiyyan)"

19:20 She said, "How can be for me a son, when not has touched me a man, and not I am unchaste?"
She said (qālat), | "How (annā) | can be (yakūnu) | for me (lī) | a son (ghulāmun), | when not (walam) | has touched me (yamsasnī) | a man (basharun), | and not (walam) | I am (aku) | unchaste? (baghiyyan)"

19:21 He said, "Thus; said your Lord, 'It is for Me easy, and so that We will make him a sign for the mankind and a Mercy from Us. And it is a matter decreed.'"
He said (qāla), | "Thus (kadhāliki); | said (qāla) | your Lord (rabbuki), | 'It (huwa) | is for Me (ʿalayya) | easy (hayyinun), | and so that We will make him (walinajʿalahu) | a sign (āyatan) | for the mankind (lilnnāsi) | and a Mercy (waraḥmatan) | from Us (minnā). | And it is (wakāna) | a matter (amran) | decreed.' (maqḍiyyan)"

19:22 So she conceived him, and she withdrew with him to a place remote.
So she conceived him (faḥamalathu), | and she withdrew (fa-intabadhat) | with him (bihi) | to a place (makānan) | remote (qaṣiyyan).

19:23 Then drove her the pains of childbirth to the trunk of the date-palm. She said, "O! I wish I had died before this and I was in oblivion, forgotten."
Then drove her (fa-ajāahā) | the pains of childbirth (l-makhāḍu) | to (ilā) | the trunk (jidhʿi) | of the date-palm (l-nakhlati). | She said (qālat), | "O! I wish (yālaytanī) | I had died (mittu) | before (qabla) | this (hādhā) | and I was (wakuntu) | in oblivion (nasyan), | forgotten. (mansiyyan)"

19:24 So cried to her from beneath her, "That do not grieve verily, has placed your Lord beneath you, a stream.
So cried to her (fanādāhā) | from (min) | beneath her (taḥtihā), | "That do not (allā) | grieve (taḥzanī) | verily (qad), | has placed (jaʿala) | your Lord (rabbuki) | beneath you (taḥtaki), | a stream (sariyyan).

19:25 And shake towards you the trunk of the date-palm, it will drop upon you fresh dates ripe.
And shake (wahuzzī) | towards you (ilayki) | the trunk (bijidhʿi) | of the date-palm (l-nakhlati), | it will drop (tusāqiṭ) | upon you (ʿalayki) | fresh dates (ruṭaban) | ripe (janiyyan).

19:26 So eat and drink and cool your eyes. And if you see from human being anyone then say, "Indeed, I [I] have vowed to the Most Gracious a fast, so not I will speak today to any human being."
So eat (fakulī) | and drink (wa-ish'rabī) | and cool (waqarrī) | your eyes (ʿaynan). | And if (fa-immā) | you see (tarayinna) | from (mina) | human being (l-bashari) | anyone (aḥadan) | then say (faqūlī), | "Indeed, I (innī) | [I] have vowed (nadhartu) | to the Most Gracious (lilrraḥmāni) | a fast (ṣawman), | so not (falan) | I will speak (ukallima) | today (l-yawma) | to any human being. (insiyyan)"

19:27 Then she came with him to her people, carrying him. They said, "O Maryam! Certainly, you have brought an amazing thing.

Then she came (fa-atat) | with him (bihi) | to her people (qawmahā), | carrying him (taḥmiluhu). | They said (qālū), | "O Maryam (yāmaryamu)! | Certainly (laqad), | you have brought (ji'ti) | an amazing thing (shayan). | an amazing thing (fariyyan).

19:28 O sister of Harun! Not was your father an evil man, and not was your mother unchaste."

O sister (yāukh'ta) | of Harun (hārūna)! | Not (mā) | was (kāna) | your father (abūki) | an evil man (im'ra-a), | an evil man (sawin), | and not (wamā) | was (kānat) | your mother (ummuki) | unchaste. (baghiyyan)"

19:29 Then she pointed to him. They said, "How can we speak to one who is in the cradle, a child?"

Then she pointed (fa-ashārat) | to him (ilayhi). | They said (qālū), | "How (kayfa) | can we speak (nukallimu) | to one who (man) | is (kāna) | in (fī) | the cradle (l-mahdi), | a child? (ṣabiyyan)"

19:30 He said, "Indeed, I am a slave of Allah. He gave me the Scripture and made me a Prophet.

He said (qāla), | "Indeed, I am (innī) | a slave (ʿabdu) | of Allah (l-lahi). | He gave me (ātāniya) | the Scripture (l-kitāba) | and made me (wajaʿalanī) | a Prophet (nabiyyan).

19:31 And He has made me blessed wherever I am and has enjoined on me [of] the prayer and zakah, as long as I am alive

And He has made me (wajaʿalanī) | blessed (mubārakan) | wherever (ayna) | wherever (mā) | I am (kuntu) | and has enjoined on me (wa-awṣānī) | [of] the prayer (bil-ṣalati) | and zakah (wal-zakati), | as long as I am (mā) | as long as I am (dum'tu) | alive (ḥayyan)

19:32 And dutiful to my mother, and not He has made me insolent, unblessed.

And dutiful (wabarran) | to my mother (biwālidatī), | and not (walam) | He has made me (yajʿalnī) | insolent (jabbāran), | unblessed (shaqiyyan).

19:33 And peace be on me the day I was born and the day I will die and the Day I will be raised alive."

And peace be (wal-salāmu) | on me (ʿalayya) | the day (yawma) | I was born (wulidttu) | and the day (wayawma) | I will die (amūtu) | and the Day (wayawma) | I will be raised (ub'ʿathu) | alive. (ḥayyan)"

19:34 That was Isa, the son of Maryam, a statement of truth that which about it they dispute.

That (dhālika) | was Isa (ʿīsā), | the son (ub'nu) | of Maryam (maryama), | a statement (qawla) | of truth (l-ḥaqi) | that which (alladhī) | about it (fīhi) | they dispute (yamtarūna).

19:35 Not it is for Allah that He should take any son. Glory be to Him! When He decrees a matter, then only He says to it, "Be" and it is.

Not (mā) | it is (kāna) | for Allah (lillahi) | that (an) | He should take (yattakhidha) | any son (min). | any son (waladin). | Glory be to Him (sub'ḥānahu)! | When (idhā) | He decrees (qaḍā) | a matter (amran), | then only (fa-innamā) | He says (yaqūlu) | to it (lahu), | "Be (kun)" | and it is (fayakūnu).

19:36 "And indeed, Allah is my Lord and your Lord, so worship Him. This is a path straight."

"And indeed (wa-inna), | Allah (l-laha) | is my Lord (rabbī) | and your Lord (warabbukum), | so worship Him (fa-uʿ'budūhu). | This (hādhā) | is a path (ṣirāṭun) | straight. (mus'taqīmun)"

19:37 But differed the sects from among them, so woe to those who disbelieve from the witnessing of a Day great.

But differed (fa-ikh'talafa) | the sects (l-aḥzābu) | from among them (min), | from among them (baynihim), | so woe (fawaylun) | to those who (lilladhīna) | disbelieve (kafarū) | from (min) | the witnessing (mashhadi) | of a Day (yawmin) | great (ʿaẓīmin).

19:38 How they will hear! and how they will see! the Day they will come to Us, but the wrongdoers today are in error clear.

How they will hear (asmiʿ)! | How they will hear (bihim)! | and how they will see (wa-abṣir)! | the Day (yawma) | they will come to Us (yatūnanā), | but (lākini) | the wrongdoers (l-ẓālimūna) | today (l-yawma) | are in (fī) | error (ḍalālin) | clear (mubīnin).

19:39 And warn them of the Day of the Regret, when has been decided the matter. And they are in heedlessness, and they do not believe.

And warn them (wa-andhir'hum) | of the Day (yawma) | of the Regret (l-ḥasrati), | when (idh) | has been decided (quḍiya) | the matter (l-amru). | And they (wahum) | are in (fī) | heedlessness (ghaflatin), | and they (wahum) | do not (lā) | believe (yu'minūna).

19:40 Indeed, We [We] [We] will inherit the earth and whoever is on it, and to Us they will be returned.

Indeed, We (innā) | [We] (naḥnu) | [We] will inherit (narithu) | the earth (l-arḍa) | and whoever (waman) | is on it (ʿalayhā), | and to Us (wa-ilaynā) | they will be returned (yur'jaʿūna).

19:41 And mention in the Book Ibrahim. Indeed, he was a man of truth, a Prophet.

And mention (wa-udh'kur) | in (fī) | the Book (l-kitābi) | Ibrahim (ib'rāhīma). | Indeed, he (innahu) | was (kāna) | a man of truth (ṣiddīqan), | a Prophet (nabiyyan).

19:42 When he said to his father, "O my father! Why do you worship that which not hears and not sees and not benefits [to] you in anything?

When (idh) | he said (qāla) | to his father (li-abīhi), | "O my father (yāabati)! | Why (lima) | do you worship (taʿbudu) | that which (mā) | not (lā) | hears (yasmaʿu) | and not (walā) | sees (yub'ṣiru) | and not (walā) | benefits (yugh'nī) | [to] you (ʿanka) | in anything (shayan)?

19:43 O my father! Indeed, [I] verily has come to me of the knowledge what not came to you, so follow me; I will guide you to the path even.

O my father (yāabati)! | Indeed, [I] (innī) | verily (qad) | has come to me (jāanī) | of (mina) | the knowledge (l-ʿil'mi) | what (mā) | not (lam) | came to you (yatika), | so follow me (fa-ittabiʿ'nī); | I will guide you (ahdika) | to the path (ṣirāṭan) | even (sawiyyan).

19:44 O my father! Do not worship the Shaitaan. Indeed, the Shaitaan is to the Most Gracious disobedient.

O my father (yāabati)! | Do not (lā) | worship (taʿbudi) | the Shaitaan (l-shayṭāna). | Indeed (inna), | the Shaitaan (l-shayṭāna) | is (kāna) | to the Most Gracious (lilrraḥmāni) | disobedient (ʿaṣiyyan).

19:45 O my father! Indeed, I [I] fear that will touch you a punishment from the Most Gracious, so you would be to the Shaitaan a friend."

O my father (yāabati)! | Indeed, I (innī) | [I] fear (akhāfu) | that (an) | will touch you (yamassaka) | a punishment (ʿadhābun) | from (mina) | the Most Gracious (l-raḥmāni), | so you would be (fatakūna) | to the Shaitaan (lilshayṭāni) | a friend. (waliyyan)"

19:46 He said, "Do you hate from my gods, O Ibrahim? Surely, if not you desist surely, I will stone you, so leave me for a prolonged time."

He said (qāla), | "Do you hate (arāghibun) | "Do you hate (anta) | from (ʿan) | my gods (ālihatī), | O Ibrahim (yāib'rāhīmu)? | Surely, if (la-in) | not (lam) | you desist (tantahi) | surely, I will stone you (la-arjumannaka), | so leave me (wa-uh'jur'nī) | for a prolonged time. (maliyyan)"

19:47 He said, "Peace be on you. I will ask forgiveness for you from my Lord. Indeed, He is to me Ever Gracious.

He said (qāla), | "Peace be (salāmun) | on you (ʿalayka). | I will ask forgiveness (sa-astaghfiru) | for you (laka) | from my Lord (rabbī). | Indeed, He (innahu) | is (kāna) | to me (bī) | Ever Gracious (ḥafiyyan).

19:48 And I will leave you and what you invoke besides Allah and I will invoke my Lord. May be that not I will be in invocation to my Lord unblessed."

And I will leave you (wa-aʿtazilukum) | and what (wamā) | you invoke (tadʿūna) | besides (min) | besides (dūni) | Allah (l-lahi) | and I will invoke (wa-adʿū) | my Lord (rabbī). | May be (ʿasā) | that not (allā) | I will be (akūna) | in invocation (biduʿāi) | to my Lord (rabbī) | unblessed. (shaqiyyan)"

19:49 So when he left them and what they worshipped besides Allah, [and] We bestowed [to] him Isaac and Yaqub, and each of them We made a Prophet.

So when (falammā) | he left them (iʿ'tazalahum) | and what (wamā) | they worshipped (yaʿbudūna) | besides Allah (min), | besides Allah (dūni), | besides Allah (l-lahi), | [and] We bestowed (wahabnā) | [to] him (lahu) | Isaac (is'ḥāqa) | and Yaqub (wayaʿqūba), | and each of them (wakullan) | We made (jaʿalnā) | a Prophet (nabiyyan).

19:50 And We bestowed to them of Our Mercy, and We made for them a truthful mention, high.

And We bestowed (wawahabnā) | to them (lahum) | of (min) | Our Mercy (raḥmatinā), | and We made (wajaʿalnā) | for them (lahum) | a truthful mention (lisāna), | a truthful mention (ṣid'qin), | high (ʿaliyyan).

19:51 And mention in the Book, Musa. Indeed, he was chosen and was a Messenger, a Prophet.

And mention (wa-udh'kur) | in (fī) | the Book (l-kitābi), | Musa (mūsā). | Indeed, he (innahu) | was (kāna) | chosen (mukh'laṣan) | and was (wakāna) | a Messenger (rasūlan), | a Prophet (nabiyyan).

19:52 And We called him from the side of the Mount the right, and brought him near for conversation.

And We called him (wanādaynāhu) | from (min) | the side (jānibi) | of the Mount (l-ṭūri) | the right (l-aymani), | and brought him near (waqarrabnāhu) | for conversation (najiyyan).

19:53 And We bestowed [to] him from Our Mercy his brother Harun, a Prophet.

And We bestowed (wawahabnā) | [to] him (lahu) | from (min) | Our Mercy (raḥmatinā) | his brother (akhāhu) | Harun (hārūna), | a Prophet (nabiyyan).

19:54 And mention in the Book, Ishmael. Indeed, he was true to his promise and was a Messenger - a Prophet.

And mention (wa-udh'kur) | in (fī) | the Book (l-kitābi), | Ishmael (is'māʿīla). | Indeed, he (innahu) | was (kāna) | true (ṣādiqa) | to his promise (l-waʿdi) | and was (wakāna) | a Messenger (rasūlan)- | a Prophet (nabiyyan).

19:55 And he used to enjoin on his people the prayer and zakah and was near his Lord pleasing.

And he used (wakāna) | to enjoin (yamuru) | on his people (ahlahu) | the prayer (bil-ṣalati) | and zakah (wal-zakati) | and was (wakāna) | near (ʿinda) | his Lord (rabbihi) | pleasing (marḍiyyan).

19:56 And mention in the Book, Idris. Indeed, he was truthful, a Prophet.

And mention (wa-udh'kur) | in (fī) | the Book (l-kitābi), | Idris (id'rīsa). | Indeed, he (innahu) | was (kāna) | truthful (ṣiddīqan), | a Prophet (nabiyyan).

19:57 And We raised him to a position high.

And We raised him (warafaʿnāhu) | to a position (makānan) | high (ʿaliyyan).

19:58 Those were the ones whom Allah bestowed favor upon them from among the Prophets, of the offspring of Adam, and of those We carried with Nuh and of the offspring of Ibrahim and Israel and of those whom We guided and We chose. When were recited to them the Verses of the Most Gracious, they fell prostrating and weeping.

Those (ulāika) | were the ones whom (alladhīna) | Allah bestowed favor (anʿama) | Allah bestowed favor (l-lahu) | upon them (ʿalayhim) | from among (mina) | the Prophets (l-nabiyīna), | of (min) | the offspring (dhurriyyati) | of Adam (ādama), | and of those (wamimman) | We carried (ḥamalnā) | with (maʿa) | Nuh (nūḥin) | and of (wamin) | the offspring (dhurriyyati) | of Ibrahim (ib'rāhīma) | and Israel (wa-is'rāīla) | and of those whom (wamimman) | We guided (hadaynā) | and We chose (wa-ij'tabaynā). | When (idhā) | were recited (tut'lā) | to them (ʿalayhim) | the Verses (āyātu) | of the Most Gracious (l-raḥmāni), | they fell (kharrū) | prostrating (sujjadan) | and weeping (wabukiyyan).

19:59 Then succeeded after them successors, who neglected the prayer and they followed the lusts so soon, they will meet evil

Then succeeded (fakhalafa) | after them (min) | after them (baʿdihim) | successors (khalfun), | who neglected (aḍāʿū) | the prayer (l-ṣalata) | and they followed (wa-ittabaʿū) | the lusts (l-shahawāti) | so soon (fasawfa), | they will meet (yalqawna) | evil (ghayyan)

19:60 Except one who repented and believed and did good deeds. Then those will enter Paradise and not they will be wronged in anything.

Except (illā) | one who (man) | repented (tāba) | and believed (waāmana) | and did (waʿamila) | good deeds (ṣāliḥan). | Then those (fa-ulāika) | will enter (yadkhulūna) | Paradise (l-janata) | and not (walā) | they will be wronged (yuẓ'lamūna) | in anything (shayan).

19:61 Gardens of Eden, which promised the Most Gracious to His slaves in the unseen. Indeed, [it] is His promise sure to come.

Gardens (jannāti) | of Eden (ʿadnin), | which (allatī) | promised (waʿada) | the Most Gracious (l-raḥmānu) | to His slaves (ʿibādahu) | in the unseen (bil-ghaybi). | Indeed, [it] (innahu) | is (kāna) | His promise (waʿduhu) | sure to come (matiyyan).

19:62 Not they will hear therein vain talk but peace. And for them is their provision therein, morning and evening.

Not (lā) | they will hear (yasmaʿūna) | therein (fīhā) | vain talk (laghwan) | but (illā) | peace (salāman). | And for them (walahum) | is their provision (riz'quhum) | therein (fīhā), | morning (buk'ratan) | and evening (waʿashiyyan).

19:63 This is Paradise, which We give as inheritance [of] to Our slaves the one who is righteous.

This (til'ka) | is Paradise (l-janatu), | which (allatī) | We give as inheritance (nūrithu) | [of] to (min) | Our slaves (ʿibādinā) | the one who (man) | is (kāna) | righteous (taqiyyan).

19:64 And not we descend except by the Command of your Lord. To Him belongs what is before us and what is behind us, and what is between that. And not is your Lord forgetful

And not (wamā) | we descend (natanazzalu) | except (illā) | by the Command (bi-amri) | of your Lord (rabbika). | To Him belongs (lahu) | what (mā) | is before us (bayna) | is before us (aydīnā)

| and what (wamā) | is behind us (khalfanā), | and what (wamā) | is between (bayna) | that (dhālika). | And not (wamā) | is (kāna) | your Lord (rabbuka) | forgetful (nasiyyan)

19:65 Lord of the heavens and the earth and whatever is between both of them, so worship Him and be constant in His worship. Do you know for Him any similarity?

Lord (rabbu) | of the heavens (l-samāwāti) | and the earth (wal-arḍi) | and whatever (wamā) | is between both of them (baynahumā), | so worship Him (fa-uʿ'bud'hu) | and be constant (wa-iṣ'ṭabir) | in His worship (liʿibādatihi). | Do (hal) | you know (taʿlamu) | for Him (lahu) | any similarity (samiyyan)?

19:66 And says [the] man, "What! When I am dead, surely will I be brought forth alive?"

And says (wayaqūlu) | [the] man (l-insānu), | "What! When (a-idhā) | "What! When (mā) | I am dead (mittu), | surely will (lasawfa) | I be brought forth (ukh'raju) | alive? (ḥayyan)"

19:67 Does not remember [the] man that We, We created him before, while not he was anything?

Does not (awalā) | remember (yadhkuru) | [the] man (l-insānu) | that We (annā), | We created him (khalaqnāhu) | before (min), | before (qablu), | while not (walam) | he was (yaku) | anything (shayan)?

19:68 So by your Lord, surely, We will gather them and the devils, then surely, We will bring them around Hell bent on knees.

So by your Lord (fawarabbika), | surely, We will gather them (lanaḥshurannahum) | and the devils (wal-shayāṭīna), | then (thumma) | surely, We will bring them (lanuḥ'ḍirannahum) | around (ḥawla) | Hell (jahannama) | bent on knees (jithiyyan).

19:69 Then surely, We will drag out from every sect, those of them who were worst against the Most Gracious in rebellion.

Then (thumma) | surely, We will drag out (lananziʿanna) | from (min) | every (kulli) | sect (shīʿatin), | those of them (ayyuhum) | who were worst (ashaddu) | against (ʿalā) | the Most Gracious (l-raḥmāni) | in rebellion (ʿitiyyan).

19:70 Then surely, We know best [of] those who [they] are most worthy therein of being burnt.

Then (thumma) | surely, We (lanaḥnu) | know best (aʿlamu) | [of] those who (bi-alladhīna) | [they] (hum) | are most worthy (awlā) | therein (bihā) | of being burnt (ṣiliyyan).

19:71 And there is not any of you but will be passing over it. This is upon your Lord an inevitability decreed.

And there is not (wa-in) | any of you (minkum) | but (illā) | will be passing over it (wāriduhā). | This is (kāna) | upon (ʿalā) | your Lord (rabbika) | an inevitability (ḥatman) | decreed (maqḍiyyan).

19:72 Then We will deliver those who feared Allah, and We will leave the wrongdoers therein bent on knees.

Then (thumma) | We will deliver (nunajjī) | those who (alladhīna) | feared Allah (ittaqaw), | and We will leave (wanadharu) | the wrongdoers (l-ẓālimīna) | therein (fīhā) | bent on knees (jithiyyan).

19:73 And when are recited to them Our Verses clear, say those who disbelieved to those who believed, "Which of the two groups is better in position. and best in assembly?"

And when (wa-idhā) | are recited (tut'lā) | to them (ʿalayhim) | Our Verses (āyātunā) | clear (bayyinātin), | say (qāla) | those who (alladhīna) | disbelieved (kafarū) | to those who (lilladhīna) | believed (āmanū), | "Which (ayyu) | of the two groups (l-farīqayni) | is better (khayrun)

| in position (maqāman). | and best (wa-aḥsanu) | in assembly? (nadiyyan)"

19:74 And how many We destroyed before them of a generation - they were better in possessions and appearance?

And how many (wakam) | We destroyed (ahlaknā) | before them (qablahum) | of (min) | a generation (qarnin)- | they (hum) | were better (aḥsanu) | in possessions (athāthan) | and appearance (wari'yan)?

19:75 Say, "Whoever is in [the] error, then surely will extend for him the Most Gracious an extension, until when they see what they were promised, either the punishment or the Hour, then they will know who [he] is worst in position and weaker in forces."

Say (qul), | "Whoever (man) | is (kāna) | in (fī) | [the] error (l-ḍalālati), | then surely will extend (falyamdud) | for him (lahu) | the Most Gracious (l-raḥmānu) | an extension (maddan), | until (ḥattā) | when (idhā) | they see (ra-aw) | what (mā) | they were promised (yūʿadūna), | either (immā) | the punishment (l-ʿadhāba) | or (wa-immā) | the Hour (l-sāʿata), | then they will know (fasayaʿlamūna) | who (man) | [he] (huwa) | is worst (sharrun) | in position (makānan) | and weaker (wa-aḍʿafu) | in forces. (jundan)"

19:76 And Allah increases those who accept guidance, in guidance. And the everlasting good deeds are better near your Lord for reward and better for return.

And Allah increases (wayazīdu) | And Allah increases (l-lahu) | those who (alladhīna) | accept guidance (ih'tadaw), | in guidance (hudan). | And the everlasting (wal-bāqiyātu) | good deeds (l-ṣāliḥātu) | are better (khayrun) | near (ʿinda) | your Lord (rabbika) | for reward (thawāban) | and better (wakhayrun) | for return (maraddan).

19:77 Then, have you seen he who disbelieved in Our Verses, and said, "Surely, I will be given wealth and children?"

Then, have you seen (afara-ayta) | he who (alladhī) | disbelieved (kafara) | in Our Verses (biāyātinā), | and said (waqāla), | "Surely, I will be given (laūtayanna) | wealth (mālan) | and children? (wawaladan)"

19:78 Has he looked into the unseen, or has he taken from the Most Gracious a promise?

Has he looked (aṭṭalaʿa) | into the unseen (l-ghayba), | or (ami) | has he taken (ittakhadha) | from (ʿinda) | the Most Gracious (l-raḥmāni) | a promise (ʿahdan)?

19:79 Nay, We will record what he says, and We will extend for him from the punishment extensively.

Nay (kallā), | We will record (sanaktubu) | what (mā) | he says (yaqūlu), | and We will extend (wanamuddu) | for him (lahu) | from (mina) | the punishment (l-ʿadhābi) | extensively (maddan).

19:80 And We will inherit from him what he says, and he will come to Us alone.

And We will inherit from him (wanarithuhu) | what (mā) | he says (yaqūlu), | and he will come to Us (wayatīnā) | alone (fardan).

19:81 And they have taken besides Allah, gods, that they may be for them an honor.

And they have taken (wa-ittakhadhū) | besides Allah (min), | besides Allah (dūni), | besides Allah (l-lahi), | gods (ālihatan), | that they may be (liyakūnū) | for them (lahum) | an honor (ʿizzan).

19:82 Nay, they will deny their worship of them and they will be against them opponents.

Nay (kallā), | they will deny (sayakfurūna) | their worship of them (biʿibādatihim) | and they will be (wayakūnūna) | against them (ʿalayhim) | opponents (ḍiddan).

19:83 Do not you see, that We [We] have sent the devils upon the disbelievers, inciting them with incitement.

Do not (alam) | you see (tara), | that We (annā) | [We] have sent (arsalnā) | the devils (l-shayāṭīna) | upon (ʿalā) | the disbelievers (l-kāfirīna), | inciting them (ta-uzzuhum) | with incitement (azzan).

19:84 So do not make haste against them. Only We count for them a number.

So do not (falā) | make haste (taʿjal) | against them (ʿalayhim). | Only (innamā) | We count (naʿuddu) | for them (lahum) | a number (ʿaddan).

19:85 The Day We will gather the righteous to the Most Gracious as a delegation

The Day (yawma) | We will gather (naḥshuru) | the righteous (l-mutaqīna) | to (ilā) | the Most Gracious (l-raḥmāni) | as a delegation (wafdan)

19:86 And We will drive the criminals to Hell thirsty.

And We will drive (wanasūqu) | the criminals (l-muj'rimīna) | to (ilā) | Hell (jahannama) | thirsty (wir'dan).

19:87 Not they will have the power of the intercession except he who has taken from the Most Gracious a covenant.

Not (lā) | they will have the power (yamlikūna) | of the intercession (l-shafāʿata) | except (illā) | he who (mani) | has taken (ittakhadha) | from (ʿinda) | the Most Gracious (l-raḥmāni) | a covenant (ʿahdan).

19:88 And they say, "Has taken the Most Gracious a son."

And they say (waqālū), | "Has taken (ittakhadha) | the Most Gracious (l-raḥmānu) | a son. (waladan)"

19:89 Verily, you have put forth a thing atrocious.

Verily (laqad), | you have put forth (ji'tum) | a thing (shayan) | atrocious (iddan).

19:90 Almost the heavens get torn therefrom, and splits asunder the earth and collapse the mountain in devastation

Almost (takādu) | the heavens (l-samāwātu) | get torn (yatafaṭṭarna) | therefrom (min'hu), | and splits asunder (watanshaqqu) | the earth (l-arḍu) | and collapse (watakhirru) | the mountain (l-jibālu) | in devastation (haddan)

19:91 That they invoke to the Most Gracious a son.

That (an) | they invoke (daʿaw) | to the Most Gracious (lilrraḥmāni) | a son (waladan).

19:92 And not is appropriate for the Most Gracious that He should take a son.

And not (wamā) | is appropriate (yanbaghī) | for the Most Gracious (lilrraḥmāni) | that (an) | He should take (yattakhidha) | a son (waladan).

19:93 Not all who are in the heavens and the earth but will come to the Most Gracious as a slave.

Not (in) | all (kullu) | who (man) | are in (fī) | the heavens (l-samāwāti) | and the earth (wal-arḍi) | but (illā) | will come (ātī) | to the Most Gracious (l-raḥmāni) | as a slave (ʿabdan).

19:94 Verily, He has enumerated them and counted them, a counting.

Verily (laqad), | He has enumerated them (aḥṣāhum) | and counted them (waʿaddahum), | a counting (ʿaddan).

19:95 And all of them will come (to) Him on the Day of the Resurrection alone.
And all of them (wakulluhum) | will come (to) Him (ātīhi) | on the Day (yawma) | of the Resurrection (l-qiyāmati) | alone (fardan).

19:96 Indeed, those who believed and did good deeds, will bestow for them the Most Gracious affection.
Indeed (inna), | those who (alladhīna) | believed (āmanū) | and did (waʿamilū) | good deeds (l-ṣāliḥāti), | will bestow (sayajʿalu) | for them (lahumu) | the Most Gracious (l-raḥmānu) | affection (wuddan).

19:97 So, only We have made it easy in your tongue, that you may give glad tidings with it to the righteous and warn with it a people hostile.
So, only (fa-innamā) | We have made it easy (yassarnāhu) | in your tongue (bilisānika), | that you may give glad tidings (litubashira) | with it (bihi) | to the righteous (l-mutaqīna) | and warn (watundhira) | with it (bihi) | a people (qawman) | hostile (luddan).

19:98 And how many We have destroyed before them of a generation? Can you perceive of them any one or hear from them a sound?
And how many (wakam) | We have destroyed (ahlaknā) | before them (qablahum) | of (min) | a generation (qarnin)? | Can (hal) | you perceive (tuḥissu) | of them (min'hum) | any (min) | one (aḥadin) | or (aw) | hear (tasmaʿu) | from them (lahum) | a sound (rik'zan)?

Chapter (20) Sūrat Ṭā Hā

20:1 Ta Ha.
Ta Ha (tta-ha).

20:2 Not We have sent down to you the Quran that you be distressed
Not (mā) | We have sent down (anzalnā) | to you (ʿalayka) | the Quran (l-qur'āna) | that you be distressed (litashqā)

20:3 But as a reminder for those who fear
But (illā) | as a reminder (tadhkiratan) | for those who (liman) | fear (yakhshā)

20:4 A revelation from He Who created the earth and the heavens [the] high,
A revelation (tanzīlan) | from He Who (mimman) | created (khalaqa) | the earth (l-arḍa) | and the heavens (wal-samāwāti) | [the] high (l-ʿulā),

20:5 The Most Gracious over the Throne is established.
The Most Gracious (al-raḥmānu) | over (ʿalā) | the Throne (l-ʿarshi) | is established

(is'tawā).

20:6 To Him belongs whatever is in the heavens and whatever is in the earth, and whatever is between them and whatever is under the soil.

To Him belongs (lahu) | whatever (mā) | is in (fī) | the heavens (l-samāwāti) | and whatever (wamā) | is in (fī) | the earth (l-arḍi), | and whatever (wamā) | is between them (baynahumā) | and whatever (wamā) | is under (taḥta) | the soil (l-tharā).

20:7 And if you speak aloud the word, then indeed, He knows the secret and the more hidden.

And if (wa-in) | you speak aloud (tajhar) | the word (bil-qawli), | then indeed, He (fa-innahu) | knows (yaʿlamu) | the secret (l-sira) | and the more hidden (wa-akhfā).

20:8 Allah - there is no god except Him. To Him belong the Names, the Most Beautiful.

Allah (al-lahu)- | there is no (lā) | god (ilāha) | except (illā) | Him (huwa). | To Him belong (lahu) | the Names (l-asmāu), | the Most Beautiful (l-ḥus'nā).

20:9 And has come to you the narration of Musa?

And has (wahal) | come to you (atāka) | the narration (ḥadīthu) | of Musa (mūsā)?

20:10 When he saw a fire, then he said to his family, "Stay here; indeed, I [I] perceived a fire; perhaps I can bring you therefrom a burning brand, or I find at the fire guidance."

When (idh) | he saw (raā) | a fire (nāran), | then he said (faqāla) | to his family (li-ahlihi), | "Stay here (um'kuthū); | indeed, I (innī) | [I] perceived (ānastu) | a fire (nāran); | perhaps I can (laʿallī) | bring you (ātīkum) | therefrom (min'hā) | a burning brand (biqabasin), | or (aw) | I find (ajidu) | at (ʿalā) | the fire (l-nāri) | guidance. (hudan)"

20:11 Then when he came to it, he was called, "O Musa,

Then when (falammā) | he came to it (atāhā), | he was called (nūdiya), | "O Musa (yāmūsā),

20:12 Indeed, [I] I Am your Lord, so remove your shoes. Indeed, you are in the valley the sacred of Tuwa.

Indeed, [I] (innī) | I Am (anā) | your Lord (rabbuka), | so remove (fa-ikh'laʿ) | your shoes (naʿlayka). | Indeed, you (innaka) | are in the valley (bil-wādi) | the sacred (l-muqadasi) | of Tuwa (ṭuwan).

20:13 And I have chosen you, so listen to what is revealed.

And I (wa-anā) | have chosen you (ikh'tartuka), | so listen (fa-is'tamiʿ) | to what (limā) | is revealed (yūḥā).

20:14 Indeed, [I] I Am Allah. There is no god but I, so worship Me and establish the prayer for My remembrance.

Indeed, [I] (innanī) | I Am (anā) | Allah (l-lahu). | There is no (lā) | god (ilāha) | but (illā) | I (anā), | so worship Me (fa-uʿ'bud'nī) | and establish (wa-aqimi) | the prayer (l-ṣalata) | for My remembrance (lidhik'rī).

20:15 Indeed, the Hour will be coming. I almost [I] hide it that may be recompensed every soul for what it strives.

Indeed (inna), | the Hour (l-sāʿata) | will be coming (ātiyatun). | I almost (akādu) | [I] hide it (ukh'fīhā) | that may be recompensed (lituj'zā) | every (kullu) | soul (nafsin) | for what (bimā) | it strives (tasʿā).

20:16 So do not let avert you from it one who does not believe in it and follows his desires, lest you perish.

So do not (falā) | let avert you (yaṣuddannaka) | from it (ʿanhā) | one who (man) | does not (lā) | believe (yu'minu) | in it (bihā) | and follows (wa-ittabaʿa) | his desires (hawāhu), | lest you perish (fatardā).

20:17 And what is that in your right hand, O Musa?"

And what (wamā) | is that (til'ka) | in your right hand (biyamīnika), | O Musa? (yāmūsā)"

20:18 He said, "It is my staff; I lean upon it, and I bring down leaves with it for my sheep, and for me in it are uses other."

He said (qāla), | "It (hiya) | is my staff (ʿaṣāya); | I lean (atawakka-u) | upon it (ʿalayhā), | and I bring down leaves (wa-ahushu) | with it (bihā) | for (ʿalā) | my sheep (ghanamī), | and for me (waliya) | in it (fīhā) | are uses (maāribu) | other. (ukh'rā)"

20:19 He said, "Throw it down, O Musa!"

He said (qāla), | "Throw it down (alqihā), | O Musa! (yāmūsā)"

20:20 So he threw it down, and behold! It was a snake, moving swiftly.

So he threw it down (fa-alqāhā), | and behold (fa-idhā)! | It (hiya) | was a snake (ḥayyatun), | moving swiftly (tasʿā).

20:21 He said, "Seize it and do not fear. We will return it to its state the former.

He said (qāla), | "Seize it (khudh'hā) | and do not (walā) | fear (takhaf). | We will return it (sanuʿīduhā) | to its state (sīratahā) | the former (l-ūlā).

20:22 And draw near your hand to your side; it will come out white, without any disease as a sign another.

And draw near (wa-uḍ'mum) | your hand (yadaka) | to (ilā) | your side (janāḥika); | it will come out (takhruj) | white (bayḍāa), | without any (min) | without any (ghayri) | disease (sūin) | as a sign (āyatan) | another (ukh'rā).

20:23 That We may show you of Our Signs the Greatest.

That We may show you (linuriyaka) | of (min) | Our Signs (āyātinā) | the Greatest (l-kub'rā).

20:24 Go to Firaun. Indeed, he has transgressed."

Go (idh'hab) | to (ilā) | Firaun (fir'ʿawna). | Indeed, he (innahu) | has transgressed. (ṭaghā)"

20:25 He said, "My Lord! Expand for me my breast

He said (qāla), | "My Lord (rabbi)! | Expand (ish'raḥ) | for me (lī) | my breast (ṣadrī)

20:26 And ease for me my task

And ease (wayassir) | for me (lī) | my task (amrī)

20:27 And untie the knot from my tongue

And untie (wa-uḥ'lul) | the knot (ʿuq'datan) | from (min) | my tongue (lisānī)

20:28 That they may understand my speech.

That they may understand (yafqahū) | my speech (qawlī).

20:29 And appoint for me a minister from my family.

And appoint (wa-ij''al) | for me (lī) | a minister (wazīran) | from (min) | my family (ahlī).

20:30 Harun, my brother.
Harun (hārūna), | my brother (akhī).

20:31 Reinforce through him my strength.
Reinforce (ush'dud) | through him (bihi) | my strength (azrī).

20:32 And make him share [in] my task
And make him share (wa-ashrik'hu) | [in] (fī) | my task (amrī)

20:33 That we may glorify You much
That (kay) | we may glorify You (nusabbiḥaka) | much (kathīran)

20:34 And [we] remember You much.
And [we] remember You (wanadhkuraka) | much (kathīran).

20:35 Indeed, [You] You are of us All-Seer."
Indeed, [You] (innaka) | You are (kunta) | of us (binā) | All-Seer. (baṣīran)"

20:36 He said, "Verily, you are granted your request, O Musa!
He said (qāla), | "Verily (qad), | you are granted (ūtīta) | your request (su'laka), | O Musa (yāmūsā)!

20:37 And indeed, We conferred a favor on you another time,
And indeed (walaqad), | We conferred a favor (manannā) | on you (ʿalayka) | another time (marratan), | another time (ukh'rā),

20:38 When We inspired to your mother what is inspired,
When (idh) | We inspired (awḥaynā) | to (ilā) | your mother (ummika) | what (mā) | is inspired (yūḥā),

20:39 "That cast him in the chest then cast it in the river, then let cast it the river on the bank; will take him an enemy to Me, and an enemy to him." And I cast over you love from Me, and that you may be brought up under My eye.
"That (ani) | cast him (iq'dhifīhi) | in (fī) | the chest (l-tābūti) | then cast it (fa-iq'dhifīhi) | in (fī) | the river (l-yami), | then let cast it (falyul'qihi) | the river (l-yamu) | on the bank (bil-sāḥili); | will take him (yakhudh'hu) | an enemy (ʿaduwwun) | to Me (lī), | and an enemy (waʿaduwwun) | to him. (lahu)" | And I cast (wa-alqaytu) | over you (ʿalayka) | love (maḥabbatan) | from Me (minnī), | and that you may be brought up (walituṣ'naʿa) | under (ʿalā) | My eye (ʿaynī).

20:40 When was going your sister and she said, "Shall, I show you [to] one who will nurse and rear him?" So We returned you to your mother that may be cooled her eyes and not she grieves. And you killed a man, but We saved you from the distress, and We tried you with a trial. Then you remained some years with the people of Madyan. Then you came at the decreed time O Musa!
When (idh) | was going (tamshī) | your sister (ukh'tuka) | and she said (fataqūlu), | "Shall (hal), | I show you (adullukum) | [to] (ʿalā) | one who (man) | will nurse and rear him? (yakfuluhu)" | So We returned you (farajaʿnāka) | to (ilā) | your mother (ummika) | that (kay) | may be cooled (taqarra) | her eyes (ʿaynuhā) | and not (walā) | she grieves (taḥzana). | And you killed (waqatalta) | a man (nafsan), | but We saved you (fanajjaynāka) | from (mina) | the distress (l-ghami), | and We tried you (wafatannāka) | with a trial (futūnan). | Then you remained (falabith'ta) | some years (sinīna) | with (fī) | the people (ahli) | of Madyan (madyana). | Then (thumma) | you came (ji'ta) |

at (ʿalā) | the decreed time (qadarin) | O Musa (yāmūsā)!

20:41 And I have chosen you for Myself.
And I have chosen you (wa-iṣ'ṭanaʿtuka) | for Myself (linafsī).

20:42 Go, you and your brother with My Signs, and do not slacken in My remembrance.
Go (idh'hab), | you (anta) | and your brother (wa-akhūka) | with My Signs (biāyātī), | and do not (walā) | slacken (taniyā) | in (fī) | My remembrance (dhik'rī).

20:43 Go, both of you, to Firaun. Indeed, he has transgressed.
Go, both of you (idh'habā), | to (ilā) | Firaun (fir'ʿawna). | Indeed, he (innahu) | has transgressed (ṭaghā).

20:44 And speak to him a word gentle, perhaps he may take heed or fear."
And speak (faqūlā) | to him (lahu) | a word (qawlan) | gentle (layyinan), | perhaps he (laʿallahu) | may take heed (yatadhakkaru) | or (aw) | fear. (yakhshā)"

20:45 They said, "Our Lord! Indeed, we fear that he will hasten against us or that he will transgress."
They said (qālā), | "Our Lord (rabbanā)! | Indeed, we (innanā) | fear (nakhāfu) | that (an) | he will hasten (yafruṭa) | against us (ʿalaynā) | or (aw) | that (an) | he will transgress. (yaṭghā)"

20:46 He said, "Do not fear. Indeed, I Am with you both; I hear and I see.
He said (qāla), | "Do not (lā) | fear (takhāfā). | Indeed, I Am (innanī) | with you both (maʿakumā); | I hear (asmaʿu) | and I see (wa-arā).

20:47 So go to him and say, "Indeed, we both are Messengers of your Lord, so send with us the Children of Israel, and do not torment them. Verily, we came to you with a Sign from your Lord. And peace on one who follows the Guidance.
So go to him (fatiyāhu) | and say (faqūlā), | "Indeed, we (innā) | both are Messengers (rasūlā) | of your Lord (rabbika), | so send (fa-arsil) | with us (maʿanā) | the Children of Israel (banī), | the Children of Israel (is'rāīla), | and do not (walā) | torment them (tuʿadhib'hum). | Verily (qad), | we came to you (ji'nāka) | with a Sign (biāyatin) | from (min) | your Lord (rabbika). | And peace (wal-salāmu) | on (ʿalā) | one who (mani) | follows (ittabaʿa) | the Guidance (l-hudā).

20:48 Indeed, we verily, it has been revealed to us that the punishment will be on one who denies and turns away."
Indeed, we (innā) | verily (qad), | it has been revealed (ūḥiya) | to us (ilaynā) | that (anna) | the punishment (l-ʿadhāba) | will be on (ʿalā) | one who (man) | denies (kadhaba) | and turns away. (watawallā)"

20:49 He said, "Then who is your Lord, O Musa?"
He said (qāla), | "Then who (faman) | is your Lord (rabbukumā), | O Musa? (yāmūsā)"

20:50 He said, "Our Lord is the One Who gave to every thing its form, then He guided it."
He said (qāla), | "Our Lord (rabbunā) | is the One Who (alladhī) | gave (aʿṭā) | to every (kulla) | thing (shayin) | its form (khalqahu), | then (thumma) | He guided it. (hadā)"

20:51 He said, "Then what is the case of the generations of the former."
He said (qāla), | "Then what (famā) | is the case (bālu) | of the generations (l-qurūni) | of the former. (l-ūlā)"

20:52 He said, "Its knowledge is with my Lord, in a Record. Not errs my Lord and not forgets."

He said (qāla), | "Its knowledge (ʿil'muhā) | is with (ʿinda) | my Lord (rabbī), | in (fī) | a Record (kitābin). | Not (lā) | errs (yaḍillu) | my Lord (rabbī) | and not (walā) | forgets. (yansā)"

20:53 The One Who made for you the earth as a bed and inserted for you therein ways, and sent down from the sky water, then We have brought forth with it, pairs of plants diverse.

The One Who (alladhī) | made (jaʿala) | for you (lakumu) | the earth (l-arḍa) | as a bed (mahdan) | and inserted (wasalaka) | for you (lakum) | therein (fīhā) | ways (subulan), | and sent down (wa-anzala) | from (mina) | the sky (l-samāi) | water (māan), | then We have brought forth (fa-akhrajnā) | with it (bihi), | pairs (azwājan) | of (min) | plants (nabātin) | diverse (shattā).

20:54 Eat and pasture your cattle. Indeed, in that, surely are Signs for possessors of intelligence.

Eat (kulū) | and pasture (wa-ir''aw) | your cattle (anʿāmakum). | Indeed (inna), | in (fī) | that (dhālika), | surely are Signs (laāyātin) | for possessors (li-ulī) | of intelligence (l-nuhā).

20:55 From it We created you, and in it We will return you, and from it We will bring you out, time another.

From it (min'hā) | We created you (khalaqnākum), | and in it (wafīhā) | We will return you (nuʿīdukum), | and from it (wamin'hā) | We will bring you out (nukh'rijukum), | time (tāratan) | another (ukh'rā).

20:56 And verily, We showed him Our Signs, all of them, but he denied and refused.

And verily (walaqad), | We showed him (araynāhu) | Our Signs (āyātinā), | all of them (kullahā), | but he denied (fakadhaba) | and refused (wa-abā).

20:57 He said, "Have you come to us to drive us out of our land with your magic, O Musa?

He said (qāla), | "Have you come to us (aji'tanā) | to drive us out (litukh'rijanā) | of (min) | our land (arḍinā) | with your magic (bisiḥ'rika), | O Musa (yāmūsā)?

20:58 Then we will surely produce for you magic like it. So make between us and between you an appointment, not we will fail it [we] and not you, in a place even."

Then we will surely produce for you (falanatiyannaka) | magic (bisiḥ'rin) | like it (mith'lihi). | So make (fa-ij''al) | between us (baynanā) | and between you (wabaynaka) | an appointment (mawʿidan), | not (lā) | we will fail it (nukh'lifuhu) | [we] (naḥnu) | and not (walā) | you (anta), | in a place (makānan) | even. (suwan)"

20:59 He said, "Your appointment is on the day of the festival, and that will be assembled the people at forenoon."

He said (qāla), | "Your appointment (mawʿidukum) | is on the day (yawmu) | of the festival (l-zīnati), | and that (wa-an) | will be assembled (yuḥ'shara) | the people (l-nāsu) | at forenoon. (ḍuḥan)"

20:60 Then went away Firaun and put together his plan, then came.

Then went away (fatawallā) | Firaun (fir''awnu) | and put together (fajamaʿa) | his plan (kaydahu), | then (thumma) | came (atā).

20:61 Said to them Musa, "Woe to you! Do not invent against Allah a lie, lest He will destroy you with a punishment. And verily, he failed who invented."

Said (qāla) | to them (lahum) | Musa (mūsā), | "Woe to you (waylakum)! | Do not (lā) | invent (taftarū) | against (ʿalā) | Allah (l-lahi) | a lie (kadhiban), | lest He will destroy you (fayus'ḥitakum) | with a punishment (biʿadhābin). | And verily (waqad), | he failed (khāba) | who (mani) | invented. (if'tarā)"

20:62 Then they disputed in their affair among them, and they kept secret the private conversation.
Then they disputed (fatanāzaʿū) | in their affair (amrahum) | among them (baynahum), | and they kept secret (wa-asarrū) | the private conversation (l-najwā).

20:63 They said, "Indeed, these two [two] magicians they intend that they drive you out of your land with their magic and do away with your way the exemplary.
They said (qālū), | "Indeed (in), | these two (hādhāni) | [two] magicians (lasāḥirāni) | they intend (yurīdāni) | that (an) | they drive you out (yukh'rijākum) | of (min) | your land (arḍikum) | with their magic (bisiḥ'rihimā) | and do away (wayadhhabā) | with your way (biṭarīqatikumu) | the exemplary (l-muth'lā).

20:64 So put together your plan then come in a line. And verily, will be successful today who overcomes."
So put together (fa-ajmiʿū) | your plan (kaydakum) | then (thumma) | come (i'tū) | in a line (ṣaffan). | And verily (waqad), | will be successful (aflaḥa) | today (l-yawma) | who (mani) | overcomes. (is'taʿlā)"

20:65 They said, "O Musa! Either [that] you throw or [that] we will be the first who throws?"
They said (qālū), | "O Musa (yāmūsā)! | Either (immā) | [that] (an) | you throw (tul'qiya) | or (wa-immā) | [that] (an) | we will be (nakūna) | the first (awwala) | who (man) | throws? (alqā)"

20:66 He said, "Nay, you throw." Then behold! Their ropes and their staffs seemed to him by their magic that they were moving.
He said (qāla), | "Nay (bal), | you throw. (alqū)" | Then behold (fa-idhā)! | Their ropes (ḥibāluhum) | and their staffs (waʿiṣiyyuhum) | seemed (yukhayyalu) | to him (ilayhi) | by (min) | their magic (siḥ'rihim) | that they (annahā) | were moving (tasʿā).

20:67 So sensed in himself a fear, Musa.
So sensed (fa-awjasa) | in (fī) | himself (nafsihi) | a fear (khīfatan), | Musa (mūsā).

20:68 We said, "Do not fear. Indeed, you you will be superior.
We said (qul'nā), | "Do not (lā) | fear (takhaf). | Indeed, you (innaka) | you (anta) | will be superior (l-aʿlā).

20:69 And throw what is in your right hand; it will swallow up what they have made. Only they have made a trick of a magician and not will be successful the magician wherever he comes."
And throw (wa-alqi) | what (mā) | is in (fī) | your right hand (yamīnika); | it will swallow up (talqaf) | what (mā) | they have made (ṣanaʿū). | Only (innamā) | they have made (ṣanaʿū) | a trick (kaydu) | of a magician (sāḥirin) | and not (walā) | will be successful (yuf'liḥu) | the magician (l-sāḥiru) | wherever (ḥaythu) | he comes. (atā)"

20:70 So were thrown down the magicians prostrating. They said, "We believe in the Lord of Harun and Musa."
So were thrown down (fa-ul'qiya) | the magicians (l-saḥaratu) | prostrating (sujjadan). | They said (qālū), | "We believe (āmannā) | in the Lord (birabbi) | of Harun (hārūna) | and Musa. (wamūsā)"

20:71 He said, "You believe [to] him before [that] I gave permission to you. Indeed, he is your chief, the one who taught you the magic. So surely I will cut off your hands and your feet of opposite sides, and surely I will crucify you on the trunks of date-palms and surely you will know which of us is more severe in punishment and more lasting."
He said (qāla), | "You believe (āmantum) | [to] him (lahu) | before (qabla) | [that] (an) | I

gave permission (ādhana) | to you (lakum). | Indeed, he (innahu) | is your chief (lakabīrukumu), | the one who (alladhī) | taught you (ʿallamakumu) | the magic (l-siḥ'ra). | So surely I will cut off (fala-uqaṭṭiʿanna) | your hands (aydiyakum) | and your feet (wa-arjulakum) | of (min) | opposite sides (khilāfin), | and surely I will crucify you (wala-uṣallibannakum) | on (fī) | the trunks (judhūʿi) | of date-palms (l-nakhli) | and surely you will know (walataʿlamunna) | which of us (ayyunā) | is more severe (ashaddu) | in punishment (ʿadhāban) | and more lasting. (wa-abqā)"

20:72 They said, "Never we will prefer you over what has come to us of the clear proofs, and the One Who created us. So decree whatever you are decreeing. Only you can decree for this life of the world.

They said (qālū), | "Never (lan) | we will prefer you (nu'thiraka) | over (ʿalā) | what (mā) | has come to us (jāanā) | of (mina) | the clear proofs (l-bayināti), | and the One Who (wa-alladhī) | created us (faṭaranā). | So decree (fa-iq'ḍi) | whatever (mā) | you (anta) | are decreeing (qāḍin). | Only (innamā) | you can decree (taqḍī) | for this (hādhihi) | life (l-ḥayata) | of the world (l-dun'yā).

20:73 Indeed, [we] we believe in our Lord that He may forgive for us our sins and what you compelled us on it of the magic. And Allah is Best and Ever Lasting."

Indeed, [we] (innā) | we believe (āmannā) | in our Lord (birabbinā) | that He may forgive (liyaghfira) | for us (lanā) | our sins (khaṭāyānā) | and what (wamā) | you compelled us (akrahtanā) | on it (ʿalayhi) | of (mina) | the magic (l-siḥ'ri). | And Allah (wal-lahu) | is Best (khayrun) | and Ever Lasting. (wa-abqā)"

20:74 Indeed, he who comes to his Lord as a criminal then indeed, for him is Hell. Not he will die in it and not live.

Indeed, he (innahu) | who (man) | comes (yati) | to his Lord (rabbahu) | as a criminal (muj'riman) | then indeed (fa-inna), | for him (lahu) | is Hell (jahannama). | Not (lā) | he will die (yamūtu) | in it (fīhā) | and not (walā) | live (yaḥyā).

20:75 But whoever comes to Him as a believer verily, he has done the righteous deeds, then those for them will be the ranks, [the] high.

But whoever (waman) | comes to Him (yatihi) | as a believer (mu'minan) | verily (qad), | he has done (ʿamila) | the righteous deeds (l-ṣāliḥāti), | then those (fa-ulāika) | for them (lahumu) | will be the ranks (l-darajātu), | [the] high (l-ʿulā).

20:76 Gardens of Eden flows from underneath them the rivers, abiding forever in it. And that is the reward for him who purifies himself.

Gardens (jannātu) | of Eden (ʿadnin) | flows (tajrī) | from (min) | underneath them (taḥtihā) | the rivers (l-anhāru), | abiding forever (khālidīna) | in it (fīhā). | And that (wadhālika) | is the reward (jazāu) | for him who (man) | purifies himself (tazakkā).

20:77 And verily, We inspired to Musa that, "Travel by night with My slaves and strike for them a path in the sea dry; not fearing to be overtaken and not being afraid."

And verily (walaqad), | We inspired (awḥaynā) | to (ilā) | Musa (mūsā) | that (an), | "Travel by night (asri) | with My slaves (biʿibādī) | and strike (fa-iḍ'rib) | for them (lahum) | a path (ṭarīqan) | in (fī) | the sea (l-baḥri) | dry (yabasan); | not (lā) | fearing (takhāfu) | to be overtaken (darakan) | and not (walā) | being afraid. (takhshā)"

20:78 Then followed them Firaun with his forces, but covered them from the sea what covered them

Then followed them (fa-atbaʿahum) | Firaun (fir'ʿawnu) | with his forces (bijunūdihi), | but covered them (faghashiyahum) | from (mina) | the sea (l-yami) | what (mā) | covered them (ghashiyahum)

20:79 And led astray Firaun his people and did not guide them.

And led astray (wa-aḍalla) | Firaun (fir''awnu) | his people (qawmahu) | and did not (wamā) | guide them (hadā).

20:80 O Children of Israel! Verily, We delivered you from your enemy, and We made a covenant with you on the side of the Mount the right, and We sent down to you the Manna and the quails.

O Children of Israel (yābanī)! | O Children of Israel (is'rāīla)! | Verily (qad), | We delivered you (anjaynākum) | from (min) | your enemy (ʿaduwwikum), | and We made a covenant with you (wawāʿadnākum) | on the side (jāniba) | of the Mount (l-ṭūri) | the right (l-aymana), | and We sent down (wanazzalnā) | to you (ʿalaykumu) | the Manna (l-mana) | and the quails (wal-salwā).

20:81 Eat of the good things which We have provided you and do not transgress therein, lest should descend upon you My Anger. And whoever on whom descends My Anger, indeed, he has perished.

Eat (kulū) | of (min) | the good things (ṭayyibāti) | which (mā) | We have provided you (razaqnākum) | and do not (walā) | transgress (taṭghaw) | therein (fīhi), | lest should descend (fayaḥilla) | upon you (ʿalaykum) | My Anger (ghaḍabī). | And whoever (waman) | on whom descends (yaḥlil) | on whom descends (ʿalayhi) | My Anger (ghaḍabī), | indeed (faqad), | he has perished (hawā).

20:82 But indeed, I Am the Perpetual Forgiver of whoever repents and believes and does righteous deeds then remains guided.

But indeed, I Am (wa-innī) | the Perpetual Forgiver (laghaffārun) | of whoever (liman) | repents (tāba) | and believes (waāmana) | and does (waʿamila) | righteous deeds (ṣāliḥan) | then (thumma) | remains guided (ih'tadā).

20:83 "And what made you hasten from your people, O Musa?"

"And what (wamā) | made you hasten (aʿjalaka) | from (ʿan) | your people (qawmika), | O Musa? (yāmūsā)"

20:84 He said, "They are close upon my tracks, and I hastened to you my Lord, that You be pleased."

He said (qāla), | "They (hum) | are close (ulāi) | upon (ʿalā) | my tracks (atharī), | and I hastened (waʿajil'tu) | to you (ilayka) | my Lord (rabbi), | that You be pleased. (litarḍā)"

20:85 He said, "But indeed, We [verily] We have tried your people after you and has led them astray the Samiri."

He said (qāla), | "But indeed, We (fa-innā) | [verily] (qad) | We have tried (fatannā) | your people (qawmaka) | after you (min) | after you (baʿdika) | and has led them astray (wa-aḍallahumu) | the Samiri. (l-sāmiriyu)"

20:86 Then Musa returned to his people angry and sorrowful. He said, "O my people! Did not promise you your Lord a promise good? Then, did seem long to you the promise, or did you desire that descend upon you the Anger of your Lord, so you broke the promise to me?"

Then Musa returned (farajaʿa) | Then Musa returned (mūsā) | to (ilā) | his people (qawmihi) | angry (ghaḍbāna) | and sorrowful (asifan). | He said (qāla), | "O my people (yāqawmi)! | Did not (alam) | promise you (yaʿid'kum) | your Lord (rabbukum) | a promise (waʿdan) | good (ḥasanan)? | Then, did seem long (afaṭāla) | to you (ʿalaykumu) | the promise (l-ʿahdu), | or (am) | did you desire (aradttum) | that (an) | descend (yaḥilla) | upon you (ʿalaykum) | the Anger (ghaḍabun) | of (min) | your Lord (rabbikum), | so you broke (fa-akhlaftum) | the promise to me? (mawʿidī)"

20:87 They said, "Not we broke promise to you by our will, but we [we] were made to carry burdens from ornaments of the people, so we threw them and thus threw the Samiri."

They said (qālū), | "Not (mā) | we broke (akhlafnā) | promise to you (mawʿidaka) | by our will (bimalkinā), | but we (walākinnā) | [we] were made to carry (ḥummil'nā) | burdens (awzāran) | from (min) | ornaments (zīnati) | of the people (l-qawmi), | so we threw them (faqadhafnāhā) | and thus (fakadhālika) | threw (alqā) | the Samiri. (l-sāmiriyu)"

20:88 Then he brought forth for them a calf's body it had a lowing sound, and they said, "This is your god and the god of Musa, but he forgot."

Then he brought forth (fa-akhraja) | for them (lahum) | a calf's (ʿij'lan) | body (jasadan) | it had (lahu) | a lowing sound (khuwārun), | and they said (faqālū), | "This (hādhā) | is your god (ilāhukum) | and the god (wa-ilāhu) | of Musa (mūsā), | but he forgot. (fanasiya)"

20:89 Then, did not they see that not it could return to them a word and not possess for them any harm and not any benefit?

Then, did not (afalā) | they see (yarawna) | that not (allā) | it could return (yarjiʿu) | to them (ilayhim) | a word (qawlan) | and not (walā) | possess (yamliku) | for them (lahum) | any harm (ḍarran) | and not (walā) | any benefit (nafʿan)?

20:90 And verily had said to them Harun before, "O my people! Only you are being tested by it, and indeed, your Lord is the Most Gracious, so follow me and obey my order."

And verily (walaqad) | had said (qāla) | to them (lahum) | Harun (hārūnu) | before (min), | before (qablu), | "O my people (yāqawmi)! | Only (innamā) | you are being tested (futintum) | by it (bihi), | and indeed (wa-inna), | your Lord (rabbakumu) | is the Most Gracious (l-raḥmānu), | so follow me (fa-ittabiʿūnī) | and obey (wa-aṭīʿū) | my order. (amrī)"

20:91 They said, "Never we will cease being devoted to it until returns to us Musa."

They said (qālū), | "Never (lan) | we will cease (nabraḥa) | being devoted to it (ʿalayhi) | being devoted to it (ʿākifīna) | until (ḥattā) | returns (yarjiʿa) | to us (ilaynā) | Musa. (mūsā)"

20:92 He said, "O Harun! What prevented you, when you saw them going astray,

He said (qāla), | "O Harun (yāhārūnu)! | What (mā) | prevented you (manaʿaka), | when (idh) | you saw them (ra-aytahum) | going astray (ḍallū),

20:93 That not you follow me? Then, have you disobeyed my order?"

That not (allā) | you follow me (tattabiʿani)? | Then, have you disobeyed (afaʿaṣayta) | my order? (amrī)"

20:94 He said, "O son of my mother! Do not seize me by my beard and not by my head. Indeed, I [I] feared that you would say, "You caused division between the Children of Israel and not you respect my word."

He said (qāla), | "O son of my mother (yabna-umma)! | Do not (lā) | seize me (takhudh) | by my beard (biliḥ'yatī) | and not (walā) | by my head (birasī). | Indeed, I (innī) | [I] feared (khashītu) | that (an) | you would say (taqūla), | "You caused division (farraqta) | between (bayna) | the Children of Israel (banī) | the Children of Israel (is'rāīla) | and not (walam) | you respect (tarqub) | my word. (qawlī)"

20:95 He said, "Then what is your case, O Samiri?"

He said (qāla), | "Then what (famā) | is your case (khaṭbuka), | O Samiri? (yāsāmiriyyu)"

20:96 He said, "I perceived what not they perceive, in it, so I took a handful from the track of the Messenger then threw it, and thus suggested to me my soul."

He said (qāla), | "I perceived (baṣur'tu) | what (bimā) | not (lam) | they perceive (yabṣurū),

| in it (bihi), | so I took (faqabaḍtu) | a handful (qabḍatan) | from (min) | the track (athari) | of the Messenger (l-rasūli) | then threw it (fanabadhtuhā), | and thus (wakadhālika) | suggested (sawwalat) | to me (lī) | my soul. (nafsī)"

20:97 He said, "Then go. And indeed, for you in the life that you will say, "Do not touch." And indeed, for you is an appointment never you will fail to keep it. And look at your god that which you have remained to it devoted. Surely we will burn it then certainly we will scatter it in the sea in particles."

He said (qāla), | "Then go (fa-idh'hab). | And indeed (fa-inna), | for you (laka) | in (fī) | the life (l-ḥayati) | that (an) | you will say (taqūla), | "Do not (lā) | touch. (misāsa)" | And indeed (wa-inna), | for you (laka) | is an appointment (mawʿidan) | never (lan) | you will fail to keep it (tukh'lafahu). | And look (wa-unẓur) | at (ilā) | your god (ilāhika) | that which (alladhī) | you have remained (ẓalta) | to it (ʿalayhi) | devoted (ʿākifan). | Surely we will burn it (lanuḥarriqannahu) | then (thumma) | certainly we will scatter it (lanansifannahu) | in (fī) | the sea (l-yami) | in particles. (nasfan)"

20:98 Only your God is Allah the One, there is no god but He. He has encompassed all things in knowledge.

Only (innamā) | your God (ilāhukumu) | is Allah (l-lahu) | the One (alladhī), | there is no (lā) | god (ilāha) | but (illā) | He (huwa). | He has encompassed (wasiʿa) | all (kulla) | things (shayin) | in knowledge (ʿil'man).

20:99 Thus We relate to you from the news of what has preceded. And certainly We have given you from Us a Reminder.

Thus (kadhālika) | We relate (naquṣṣu) | to you (ʿalayka) | from (min) | the news (anbāi) | of what (mā) | has preceded (qad). | has preceded (sabaqa). | And certainly (waqad) | We have given you (ātaynāka) | from (min) | Us (ladunnā) | a Reminder (dhik'ran).

20:100 Whoever turns away from it, then indeed, he will bear on the Day of Resurrection a burden.

Whoever (man) | turns away (aʿraḍa) | from it (ʿanhu), | then indeed, he (fa-innahu) | will bear (yaḥmilu) | on the Day (yawma) | of Resurrection (l-qiyāmati) | a burden (wiz'ran).

20:101 Abiding forever in it, and evil for them on the Day of the Resurrection as a load

Abiding forever (khālidīna) | in it (fīhi), | and evil (wasāa) | for them (lahum) | on the Day (yawma) | of the Resurrection (l-qiyāmati) | as a load (ḥim'lan)

20:102 The Day will be blown in the Trumpet, and We will gather the criminals, that Day, blue-eyed.

The Day (yawma) | will be blown (yunfakhu) | in (fī) | the Trumpet (l-ṣūri), | and We will gather (wanaḥshuru) | the criminals (l-muj'rimīna), | that Day (yawma-idhin), | blue-eyed (zur'qan).

20:103 They are murmuring among themselves, "Not you remained except for ten."

They are murmuring (yatakhāfatūna) | among themselves (baynahum), | "Not (in) | you remained (labith'tum) | except for (illā) | ten. (ʿashran)"

20:104 We know best what they will say when will say, the best of them in conduct, "Not you remained except for a day."

We (naḥnu) | know best (aʿlamu) | what (bimā) | they will say (yaqūlūna) | when (idh) | will say (yaqūlu), | the best of them (amthaluhum) | in conduct (ṭarīqatan), | "Not (in) | you remained (labith'tum) | except for (illā) | a day. (yawman)"

20:105 And they ask you about the mountains, so say, "Will blast them my Lord into particles.

And they ask you (wayasalūnaka) | about (ʿani) | the mountains (l-jibāli), | so say (faqul), | "Will blast them (yansifuhā) | my Lord (rabbī) | into particles (nasfan).

20:106 Then He will leave it, a level plain.
Then He will leave it (fayadharuhā), | a level (qāʿan) | plain (ṣafṣafan).

20:107 Not you will see in it any crookedness and not any curve."
Not (lā) | you will see (tarā) | in it (fīhā) | any crookedness (ʿiwajan) | and not (walā) | any curve. (amtan)"

20:108 On that Day they will follow the caller, no deviation from it. And will be humbled the voices for the Most Gracious, so not you will hear except a faint sound.
On that Day (yawma-idhin) | they will follow (yattabiʿūna) | the caller (l-dāʿiya), | no (lā) | deviation (ʿiwaja) | from it (lahu). | And will be humbled (wakhashaʿati) | the voices (l-aṣwātu) | for the Most Gracious (lilrraḥmāni), | so not (falā) | you will hear (tasmaʿu) | except (illā) | a faint sound (hamsan).

20:109 On that Day not will benefit the intercession except to whom has given permission [to him] the Most Gracious, and He has accepted for him a word.
On that Day (yawma-idhin) | not (lā) | will benefit (tanfaʿu) | the intercession (l-shafāʿatu) | except (illā) | to whom (man) | has given permission (adhina) | [to him] (lahu) | the Most Gracious (l-raḥmānu), | and He has accepted (waraḍiya) | for him (lahu) | a word (qawlan).

20:110 He knows what is before them and what is behind them, while not they encompass it in knowledge.
He knows (yaʿlamu) | what (mā) | is before them (bayna) | is before them (aydīhim) | and what (wamā) | is behind them (khalfahum), | while not (walā) | they encompass (yuḥīṭūna) | it (bihi) | in knowledge (ʿil'man).

20:111 And will be humbled the faces before the Ever-Living, the Self-Subsisting. And verily will have failed he who carried wrongdoing.
And will be humbled (waʿanati) | the faces (l-wujūhu) | before the Ever-Living (lil'ḥayyi), | the Self-Subsisting (l-qayūmi). | And verily (waqad) | will have failed (khāba) | he who (man) | carried (ḥamala) | wrongdoing (ẓul'man).

20:112 But he who does of the righteous deeds while he is a believer, then not he will fear injustice and not deprivation.
But he who (waman) | does (yaʿmal) | of (mina) | the righteous deeds (l-ṣāliḥāti) | while he (wahuwa) | is a believer (mu'minun), | then not (falā) | he will fear (yakhāfu) | injustice (ẓul'man) | and not (walā) | deprivation (haḍman).

20:113 And thus We have sent it down, the Quran in Arabic and We have explained in it of the warnings that they may fear or it may cause [for] them remembrance.
And thus (wakadhālika) | We have sent it down (anzalnāhu), | the Quran (qur'ānan) | in Arabic (ʿarabiyyan) | and We have explained (waṣarrafnā) | in it (fīhi) | of (mina) | the warnings (l-waʿīdi) | that they may (laʿallahum) | fear (yattaqūna) | or (aw) | it may cause (yuḥ'dithu) | [for] them (lahum) | remembrance (dhik'ran).

20:114 So high above all is Allah the King, the True. And do not hasten with the Quran before [that] is completed to you its revelation, and say, "My Lord! Increase me in knowledge."
So high above all (fataʿālā) | is Allah (l-lahu) | the King (l-maliku), | the True (l-ḥaqu). | And do not (walā) | hasten (taʿjal) | with the Quran (bil-qur'āni) | before (min) | before (qabli) | [that] (an) | is completed (yuq'ḍā) | to you (ilayka) | its revelation (waḥyuhu), | and say (waqul), | "My Lord (rabbi)! | Increase me (zid'nī) | in knowledge. (ʿil'man)"

20:115 And verily We made a covenant with Adam before, but he forgot; and not We found in him determination.

And verily (walaqad) | We made a covenant (ʿahid'nā) | with (ilā) | Adam (ādama) | before (min), | before (qablu), | but he forgot (fanasiya); | and not (walam) | We found (najid) | in him (lahu) | determination (ʿazman).

20:116 And when We said to the Angels, "Prostrate to Adam," then they prostrated, except Iblis; he refused.

And when (wa-idh) | We said (qul'nā) | to the Angels (lil'malāikati), | "Prostrate (us'judū) | to Adam, (liādama)" | then they prostrated (fasajadū), | except (illā) | Iblis (ib'līsa); | he refused (abā).

20:117 Then We said, "O Adam! Indeed, this is an enemy to you and to your wife. So not let him drive you both from Paradise so that you would suffer.

Then We said (faqul'nā), | "O Adam (yāādamu)! | Indeed (inna), | this (hādhā) | is an enemy (ʿaduwwun) | to you (laka) | and to your wife (walizawjika). | So not (falā) | let him drive you both (yukh'rijannakumā) | from (mina) | Paradise (l-janati) | so that you would suffer (fatashqā).

20:118 Indeed, for you that not you will be hungry therein and not you will be unclothed.

Indeed (inna), | for you (laka) | that not (allā) | you will be hungry (tajūʿa) | therein (fīhā) | and not (walā) | you will be unclothed (taʿrā).

20:119 And that you not will suffer from thirst therein and not exposed to the sun's heat."

And that you (wa-annaka) | not (lā) | will suffer from thirst (taẓma-u) | therein (fīhā) | and not (walā) | exposed to the sun's heat. (taḍḥā)"

20:120 Then whispered to him Shaitaan, he said, "O Adam! Shall I direct you to the tree of the Eternity and a kingdom not that will deteriorate?"

Then whispered (fawaswasa) | to him (ilayhi) | Shaitaan (l-shayṭānu), | he said (qāla), | "O Adam (yāādamu)! | Shall (hal) | I direct you (adulluka) | to (ʿalā) | the tree (shajarati) | of the Eternity (l-khul'di) | and a kingdom (wamul'kin) | not (lā) | that will deteriorate? (yablā)"

20:121 Then they both ate from it, so became apparent to them their shame and they began, to fasten on themselves from the leaves of Paradise. And Adam disobeyed his Lord, and erred.

Then they both ate (fa-akalā) | from it (min'hā), | so became apparent (fabadat) | to them (lahumā) | their shame (sawātuhumā) | and they began (waṭafiqā), | to fasten (yakhṣifāni) | on themselves (ʿalayhimā) | from (min) | the leaves (waraqi) | of Paradise (l-janati). | And Adam disobeyed (waʿaṣā) | And Adam disobeyed (ādamu) | his Lord (rabbahu), | and erred (faghawā).

20:122 Then chose him his Lord, and turned to him and guided him.

Then (thumma) | chose him (ij'tabāhu) | his Lord (rabbuhu), | and turned (fatāba) | to him (ʿalayhi) | and guided him (wahadā).

20:123 He said, "Go down from it all, some of you to others as enemy. Then if comes to you from Me guidance then whoever, follows My guidance, then not he will go astray and not suffer.

He said (qāla), | "Go down (ih'biṭā) | from it (min'hā) | all (jamīʿan), | some of you (baʿḍukum) | to others (libaʿḍin) | as enemy (ʿaduwwun). | Then if (fa-immā) | comes to you (yatiyannakum) | from Me (minnī) | guidance (hudan) | then whoever (famani), | follows (ittabaʿa) | My guidance (hudāya), | then not (falā) | he will go astray (yaḍillu) | and not (walā) | suffer (yashqā).

20:124 And whoever turns away from My remembrance, then indeed, for him is a life straitened and We will gather him on the Day of the Resurrection blind."

And whoever (waman) | turns away (aʿraḍa) | from (ʿan) | My remembrance (dhik'rī), | then indeed (fa-inna), | for him (lahu) | is a life (maʿīshatan) | straitened (ḍankan) | and We will gather him (wanaḥshuruhu) | on the Day (yawma) | of the Resurrection (l-qiyāmati) | blind. (aʿmā)"

20:125 He will say, "My Lord! Why You raised me blind while [verily] I had sight."

He will say (qāla), | "My Lord (rabbi)! | Why (lima) | You raised me (ḥashartanī) | blind (aʿmā) | while [verily] (waqad) | I had (kuntu) | sight. (baṣīran)"

20:126 He will say, "Thus came to you Our Signs, but you forgot them, and thus today you will be forgotten."

He will say (qāla), | "Thus (kadhālika) | came to you (atatka) | Our Signs (āyātunā), | but you forgot them (fanasītahā), | and thus (wakadhālika) | today (l-yawma) | you will be forgotten. (tunsā)"

20:127 And thus We recompense he who transgresses, and not believes in the Signs of his Lord. And surely the punishment of the Hereafter is more severe and more lasting.

And thus (wakadhālika) | We recompense (najzī) | he who (man) | transgresses (asrafa), | and not (walam) | believes (yu'min) | in the Signs (biāyāti) | of his Lord (rabbihi). | And surely the punishment (walaʿadhābu) | of the Hereafter (l-ākhirati) | is more severe (ashaddu) | and more lasting (wa-abqā).

20:128 Then has not it guided [for] them how many We have destroyed before them, of the generations, as they walk in their dwellings? Indeed, in that surely are Signs for possessors of intelligence.

Then has not (afalam) | it guided (yahdi) | [for] them (lahum) | how many (kam) | We have destroyed (ahlakna) | before them (qablahum), | of (mina) | the generations (l-qurūni), | as they walk (yamshūna) | in (fī) | their dwellings (masākinihim)? | Indeed (inna), | in (fī) | that (dhālika) | surely are Signs (laāyātin) | for possessors (li-ulī) | of intelligence (l-nuhā).

20:129 And if not for a Word that preceded from your Lord, surely would have been an obligation and a term determined.

And if not (walawlā) | for a Word (kalimatun) | that preceded (sabaqat) | from (min) | your Lord (rabbika), | surely would have been (lakāna) | an obligation (lizāman) | and a term (wa-ajalun) | determined (musamman).

20:130 So be patient over what they say and glorify with praise of your Lord before the rising of the sun and before its setting; and from the hours of the night, and glorify at the ends of the day so that you may be satisfied.

So be patient (fa-iṣ'bir) | over (ʿalā) | what (mā) | they say (yaqūlūna) | and glorify (wasabbiḥ) | with praise (biḥamdi) | of your Lord (rabbika) | before (qabla) | the rising (ṭulūʿi) | of the sun (l-shamsi) | and before (waqabla) | its setting (ghurūbihā); | and from (wamin) | the hours (ānāi) | of the night (al-layli), | and glorify (fasabbiḥ) | at the ends (wa-aṭrāfa) | of the day (l-nahāri) | so that you may (laʿallaka) | be satisfied (tarḍā).

20:131 And do not extend your eyes towards what We have given for enjoyment [with it], pairs of them the splendor of the life of the world, that We may test them in it. And the provision of your Lord is better and more lasting.

And do not (walā) | extend (tamuddanna) | your eyes (ʿaynayka) | towards (ilā) | what (mā) | We have given for enjoyment (mattaʿnā) | [with it] (bihi), | pairs (azwājan) | of them (min'hum) | the splendor (zahrata) | of the life (l-ḥayati) | of the world (l-dun'yā), | that We may test them (linaftinahum) | in it (fīhi). | And the provision (wariz'qu) | of your Lord (rabbika) | is better (khayrun) | and more lasting (wa-abqā).

20:132 And enjoin on your family the prayer and be steadfast therein. Not We ask you for provision; We provide for you, and the outcome is for the righteous[ness].

And enjoin (wamur) | on your family (ahlaka) | the prayer (bil-ṣalati) | and be steadfast (wa-iṣ'ṭabir) | therein (ʿalayhā). | Not (lā) | We ask you (nasaluka) | for provision (riz'qan); | We (naḥnu) | provide for you (narzuquka), | and the outcome (wal-ʿāqibatu) | is for the righteous[ness] (lilttaqwā).

20:133 And they say, "Why not he brings us a sign from his Lord?" Has not come to them evidence of what was in the Scriptures the former?

And they say (waqālū), | "Why not (lawlā) | he brings us (yatīnā) | a sign (biāyatin) | from (min) | his Lord? (rabbihi)" | Has not (awalam) | come to them (tatihim) | evidence (bayyinatu) | of what (mā) | was in (fī) | the Scriptures (l-ṣuḥufi) | the former (l-ūlā)?

20:134 And if We had destroyed them with a punishment before him, surely they would have said, "Our Lord, why not You sent to us a Messenger, so we could have followed Your signs before [that] we were humiliated and disgraced."

And if (walaw) | We (annā) | had destroyed them (ahlaknāhum) | with a punishment (biʿadhābin) | before him (min), | before him (qablihi), | surely they would have said (laqālū), | "Our Lord (rabbanā), | why not (lawlā) | You sent (arsalta) | to us (ilaynā) | a Messenger (rasūlan), | so we could have followed (fanattabiʿa) | Your signs (āyātika) | before (min) | before (qabli) | [that] (an) | we were humiliated (nadhilla) | and disgraced. (wanakhzā)"

20:135 Say, "Each is waiting; so await. Then you will know who are the companions of the way [the] even, and who is guided."

Say (qul), | "Each (kullun) | is waiting (mutarabbiṣun); | so await (fatarabbaṣū). | Then you will know (fasataʿlamūna) | who (man) | are the companions (aṣḥābu) | of the way (l-ṣirāṭi) | [the] even (l-sawiyi), | and who (wamani) | is guided. (ih'tadā)"

Chapter (21) Sūrat l-Anbiyāa (The Prophets)

21:1 Has approached for [the] mankind their account, while they are in heedlessness turning away.

Has approached (iq'taraba) | for [the] mankind (lilnnāsi) | their account (ḥisābuhum), | while they (wahum) | are in (fī) | heedlessness (ghaflatin) | turning away (muʿ'riḍūna).

21:2 Not comes to them of a Reminder from their Lord, anew except they listen to it while they are at play

Not (mā) | comes to them (yatīhim) | of (min) | a Reminder (dhik'rin) | from (min) | their Lord (rabbihim), | anew (muḥ'dathin) | except (illā) | they listen to it (is'tamaʿūhu) | while they (wahum) | are at play (yalʿabūna)

21:3 Distracted their hearts. And they conceal the private conversation, those who [they] wronged, "Is this except a human being like you? So would you approach the magic while you see it?"

Distracted (lāhiyatan) | their hearts (qulūbuhum). | And they conceal (wa-asarrū) | the private conversation (l-najwā), | those who (alladhīna) | [they] wronged (ẓalamū), | "Is (hal) | this (hādhā) | except (illā) | a human being (basharun) | like you (mith'lukum)? | So would you approach (afatatūna) | the magic (l-siḥ'ra) | while you (wa-antum) | see it? (tub'ṣirūna)"

21:4 He said, "My Lord knows the word in the heavens and the earth. And He is the All-Hearer, the All-Knower."

He said (qāla), | "My Lord (rabbī) | knows (yaʿlamu) | the word (l-qawla) | in (fī) | the heavens (l-samāi) | and the earth (wal-arḍi). | And He (wahuwa) | is the All-Hearer (l-samīʿu), | the All-Knower. (l-ʿalīmu)"

21:5 Nay, they say, "Muddled dreams; nay, he has invented it; nay, he is a poet. So let him bring us a sign like what was sent to the former."

Nay (bal), | they say (qālū), | "Muddled (aḍghāthu) | dreams (aḥlāmin); | nay (bali), | he has invented it (if'tarāhu); | nay (bal), | he (huwa) | is a poet (shāʿirun). | So let him bring us (falyatinā) | a sign (biāyatin) | like what (kamā) | was sent (ur'sila) | to the former. (l-awalūna)"

21:6 Not believed before them any town which We destroyed, so will they believe?

Not (mā) | believed (āmanat) | before them (qablahum) | any (min) | town (qaryatin) | which We destroyed (ahlaknāhā), | so will they (afahum) | believe (yu'minūna)?

21:7 And not We sent before you except men, We revealed to them. So ask the people of the Reminder, if you do not know.

And not (wamā) | We sent (arsalnā) | before you (qablaka) | except (illā) | men (rijālan), | We revealed (nūḥī) | to them (ilayhim). | So ask (fasalū) | the people (ahla) | of the Reminder (l-dhik'ri), | if (in) | you (kuntum) | do not (lā) | know (taʿlamūna).

21:8 And not We made them bodies not eating the food, and not they were immortals.

And not (wamā) | We made them (jaʿalnāhum) | bodies (jasadan) | not (lā) | eating (yakulūna) | the food (l-ṭaʿāma), | and not (wamā) | they were (kānū) | immortals (khālidīna).

21:9 Then We fulfilled for them the promise, and We saved them and whom We willed, and We destroyed the transgressors.

Then (thumma) | We fulfilled for them (ṣadaqnāhumu) | the promise (l-waʿda), | and We saved them (fa-anjaynāhum) | and whom (waman) | We willed (nashāu), | and We destroyed (wa-ahlaknā) | the transgressors (l-mus'rifīna).

21:10 Indeed, We have sent down to you a Book in it is your mention. Then will not you use reason?

Indeed (laqad), | We have sent down (anzalnā) | to you (ilaykum) | a Book (kitāban) | in it (fīhi) | is your mention (dhik'rukum). | Then will not (afalā) | you use reason (taʿqilūna)?

21:11 And how many We have shattered of a town that was unjust, and We produced after them another people.

And how many (wakam) | We have shattered (qaṣamnā) | of (min) | a town (qaryatin) | that was (kānat) | unjust (ẓālimatan), | and We produced (wa-anshanā) | after them (baʿdahā) | another people (qawman). | another people (ākharīna).

21:12 Then when they perceived Our torment, behold, they from it were fleeing.

Then when (falammā) | they perceived (aḥassū) | Our torment (basanā), | behold (idhā), | they (hum) | from it (min'hā) | were fleeing (yarkuḍūna).

21:13 Flee not, but return to what you were given luxury in it and to your homes, so that you may be questioned.

Flee not (lā), | Flee not (tarkuḍū), | but return (wa-ir'jiʿū) | to (ilā) | what (mā) | you were given luxury (ut'rif'tum) | in it (fīhi) | and to your homes (wamasākinikum), | so that you may (laʿallakum) | be questioned (tus'alūna).

21:14 They said, "O woe to us! Indeed, [we] we were wrongdoers."

They said (qālū), | "O woe to us (yāwaylanā)! | Indeed, [we] (innā) | we were (kunnā) | wrongdoers. (ẓālimīna)"

21:15 Then not ceased [this] their cry until We made them reaped extinct.

Then not (famā) | ceased (zālat) | [this] (til'ka) | their cry (daʿwāhum) | until (ḥattā) | We made them (jaʿalnāhum) | reaped (ḥaṣīdan) | extinct (khāmidīna).

21:16 And not We created the heavens and the earth and what is between them for playing.

And not (wamā) | We created (khalaqnā) | the heavens (l-samāa) | and the earth (wal-arḍa) | and what (wamā) | is between them (baynahumā) | for playing (lāʿibīna).

21:17 If We intended that We take a pastime, surely We could have taken it from Us, if We were doers.

If (law) | We intended (aradnā) | that (an) | We take (nattakhidha) | a pastime (lahwan), | surely We could have taken it (la-ittakhadhnāhu) | from (min) | Us (ladunnā), | if (in) | We were (kunnā) | doers (fāʿilīna).

21:18 Nay, We hurl the truth against [the] falsehood, and it breaks its head, behold, it is vanishing. And for you is destruction for what you ascribe.

Nay (bal), | We hurl (naqdhifu) | the truth (bil-ḥaqi) | against (ʿalā) | [the] falsehood (l-bāṭili), | and it breaks its head (fayadmaghuhu), | behold (fa-idhā), | it is (huwa) | vanishing (zāhiqun). | And for you (walakumu) | is destruction (l-waylu) | for what (mimmā) | you ascribe (taṣifūna).

21:19 And to Him belongs whoever is in the heavens and the earth. And those who are near Him not they are arrogant to worship Him and not they tire.

And to Him belongs (walahu) | whoever (man) | is in (fī) | the heavens (l-samāwāti) | and the earth (wal-arḍi). | And those who (waman) | are near Him (ʿindahu) | not (lā) | they are arrogant (yastakbirūna) | to (ʿan) | worship Him (ʿibādatihi) | and not (walā) | they tire (yastaḥsirūna).

21:20 They glorify Him [the] night and [the] day, not they slacken.

They glorify Him (yusabbiḥūna) | [the] night (al-layla) | and [the] day (wal-nahāra), | not (lā) | they slacken (yafturūna).

21:21 Or have they taken gods from the earth, they raise the dead?

Or (ami) | have they taken (ittakhadhū) | gods (ālihatan) | from (mina) | the earth (l-arḍi), | they (hum) | raise the dead (yunshirūna)?

21:22 If there were in both of them gods besides Allah, surely they would have been ruined. So glorified is Allah, Lord of the Throne above what they attribute.

If (law) | there were (kāna) | in both of them (fīhimā) | gods (ālihatun) | besides (illā) | Allah (l-lahu), | surely they would have been ruined (lafasadatā). | So glorified (fasub'ḥāna) | is Allah (l-lahi), | Lord (rabbi) | of the Throne (l-ʿarshi) | above what (ʿammā) | they attribute (yaṣifūna).

21:23 Not He can be questioned about what He does, but they will be questioned.

Not (lā) | He can be questioned (yus'alu) | about what (ʿammā) | He does (yafʿalu), | but they (wahum) | will be questioned (yus'alūna).

21:24 Or have they taken besides Him gods? Say, "Bring your proof. This is a Reminder for those who are with me, and a Reminder for those who were before me." But most of them do not know the truth so they are averse.

Or (ami) | have they taken (ittakhadhū) | besides Him (min) | besides Him (dūnihi) | gods (ālihatan)? | Say (qul), | "Bring (hātū) | your proof (bur'hānakum). | This (hādhā) | is a Reminder (dhik'ru) | for those who (man) | are with me (maʿiya), | and a Reminder (wadhik'ru) | for those who (man) | were before me. (qablī)" | But (bal) | most of them (aktharuhum) | do not (lā) | know (yaʿlamūna) | the truth (l-ḥaqa) | so they (fahum) | are averse (muʿ'riḍūna).

21:25 And not We sent before you any Messenger but We revealed to him that [He], "There is no god except Me so worship Me."

And not (wamā) | We sent (arsalnā) | before you (min) | before you (qablika) | any (min) | Messenger (rasūlin) | but (illā) | We revealed (nūḥī) | to him (ilayhi) | that [He] (annahu), | "There is no (lā) | god (ilāha) | except (illā) | Me (anā) | so worship Me. (fa-uʿ'budūni)"

21:26 And they say, "Has taken the Most Gracious a son." Glorified is He! Nay, they are slaves honored.

And they say (waqālū), | "Has taken (ittakhadha) | the Most Gracious (l-raḥmānu) | a son. (waladan)" | Glorified is He (sub'ḥānahu)! | Nay (bal), | they are slaves (ʿibādun) | honored (muk'ramūna).

21:27 Not they can precede Him in word, and they by His command act.

Not (lā) | they can precede Him (yasbiqūnahu) | in word (bil-qawli), | and they (wahum) | by His command (bi-amrihi) | act (yaʿmalūna).

21:28 He knows what is before them, and what is behind them, and not they can intercede except for whom He approves. And they, from fear of Him, stand in awe.

He knows (yaʿlamu) | what (mā) | is before them (bayna), | is before them (aydīhim), | and what (wamā) | is behind them (khalfahum), | and not (walā) | they can intercede (yashfaʿūna) | except (illā) | for whom (limani) | He approves (ir'taḍā). | And they (wahum), | from (min) | fear of Him (khashyatihi), | stand in awe (mush'fiqūna).

21:29 And whoever says of them, "Indeed, I am a god besides Him." Then that We will recompense with Hell. Thus We recompense the wrongdoers.

And whoever (waman) | says (yaqul) | of them (min'hum), | "Indeed, I am (innī) | a god (ilāhun) | besides Him. (min)" | besides Him. (dūnihi)" | Then that (fadhālika) | We will recompense (najzīhi) | with Hell (jahannama). | Thus (kadhālika) | We recompense (najzī) | the wrongdoers (l-ẓālimīna).

21:30 Do not see those who disbelieved that the heavens and the earth were a joined entity, then We parted them and We made from [the] water every living thing? Then will not they believe?

Do not (awalam) | see (yara) | those who (alladhīna) | disbelieved (kafarū) | that (anna) | the heavens (l-samāwāti) | and the earth (wal-arḍa) | were (kānatā) | a joined entity (ratqan), | then We parted them (fafataqnāhumā) | and We made (wajaʿalnā) | from (mina) | [the] water (l-māi) | every (kulla) | living thing (shayin)? | living thing (ḥayyin)? | Then will not (afalā) | they believe (yu'minūna)?

21:31 And We have placed in the earth firmly set mountains, lest it should shake with them, and We made therein broad passes as ways, so that they may be guided.

And We have placed (wajaʿalnā) | in (fī) | the earth (l-arḍi) | firmly set mountains (rawāsiya), | lest (an) | it should shake (tamīda) | with them (bihim), | and We made (wajaʿalnā) | therein (fīhā) | broad passes (fijājan) | as ways (subulan), | so that they may (laʿallahum) | be guided (yahtadūna).

21:32 And We made the sky a roof protected. But they, from its Signs, turn away.

And We made (wajaʿalnā) | the sky (l-samāa) | a roof (saqfan) | protected (maḥfūẓan). | But they (wahum), | from (ʿan) | its Signs (āyātihā), | turn away (muʿʿriḍūna).

21:33 And He is the One Who created the night and the day, and the sun and the moon; each in an orbit floating.

And He (wahuwa) | is the One Who (alladhī) | created (khalaqa) | the night (al-layla) | and the day (wal-nahāra), | and the sun (wal-shamsa) | and the moon (wal-qamara); | each (kullun) | in (fī) | an orbit (falakin) | floating (yasbaḥūna).

21:34 And not We made for any man before you [the] immortality; so if you die, then would they live forever?

And not (wamā) | We made (jaʿalnā) | for any man (libasharin) | before you (min) | before you (qablika) | [the] immortality (l-khul'da); | so if (afa-in) | you die (mitta), | then would they (fahumu) | live forever (l-khālidūna)?

21:35 Every soul will taste [the] death. And We test you with [the] bad and [the] good as a trial; and to Us you will be returned.

Every (kullu) | soul (nafsin) | will taste (dhāiqatu) | [the] death (l-mawti). | And We test you (wanablūkum) | with [the] bad (bil-shari) | and [the] good (wal-khayri) | as a trial (fit'natan); | and to Us (wa-ilaynā) | you will be returned (tur'jaʿūna).

21:36 And when they see you, those who disbelieve not they take you except in ridicule, "Is this the one who mentions your gods?" And they at the mention of the Most Gracious [they] are disbelievers.

And when (wa-idhā) | they see you (raāka), | those who (alladhīna) | disbelieve (kafarū) | not (in) | they take you (yattakhidhūnaka) | except (illā) | in ridicule (huzuwan), | "Is this (ahādhā) | the one who (alladhī) | mentions (yadhkuru) | your gods? (ālihatakum)" | And they (wahum) | at the mention (bidhik'ri) | of the Most Gracious (l-raḥmāni) | [they] (hum) | are disbelievers (kāfirūna).

21:37 Is created the man of haste. I will show you My Signs so do not ask Me to hasten.

Is created (khuliqa) | the man (l-insānu) | of (min) | haste (ʿajalin). | I will show you (sa-urīkum) | My Signs (āyātī) | so do not (falā) | ask Me to hasten (tastaʿjilūni).

21:38 And they say, "When will be fulfilled this promise, if you are truthful?"

And they say (wayaqūlūna), | "When will be fulfilled (matā) | this (hādhā) | promise (l-waʿdu), | if (in) | you are (kuntum) | truthful? (ṣādiqīna)"

21:39 If knew those who disbelieved the time when not they will avert from their faces the Fire and not from their backs and not they will be helped!

If (law) | knew (yaʿlamu) | those who (alladhīna) | disbelieved (kafarū) | the time (ḥīna) | when not (lā) | they will avert (yakuffūna) | from (ʿan) | their faces (wujūhihimu) | the Fire (l-nāra) | and not (walā) | from (ʿan) | their backs (ẓuhūrihim) | and not (walā) | they (hum) | will be helped (yunṣarūna)!

21:40 Nay, it will come to them unexpectedly and bewilder them, then not they will be able to repel it, and not they will be given respite.

Nay (bal), | it will come to them (tatīhim) | unexpectedly (baghtatan) | and bewilder them (fatabhatuhum), | then not (falā) | they will be able (yastaṭīʿūna) | to repel it (raddahā), | and not (walā) | they (hum) | will be given respite (yunẓarūna).

21:41 And verily, were mocked Messengers before you then surrounded those who mocked from them what they used at it to mock.

And verily (walaqadi), | were mocked (us'tuh'zi-a) | Messengers (birusulin) | before you (min) | before you (qablika) | then surrounded (faḥāqa) | those who (bi-alladhīna) | mocked (sakhirū) | from them (min'hum) | what (mā) | they used (kānū) | at it (bihi) | to mock (yastahziūna).

21:42 Say, "Who can protect you in the night and the day from the Most Gracious?" Yet, they from the remembrance of their Lord turn away.

Say (qul), | "Who (man) | can protect you (yakla-ukum) | in the night (bi-al-layli) | and the day (wal-nahāri) | from (mina) | the Most Gracious? (l-raḥmāni)" | Yet (bal), | they (hum) | from (ʿan) | the remembrance (dhik'ri) | of their Lord (rabbihim) | turn away (muʿ'riḍūna).

21:43 Or have they gods to defend them from Us? Not they are able to help themselves and not they from Us can be protected.

Or (am) | have they (lahum) | gods (ālihatun) | to defend them (tamnaʿuhum) | from (min) | Us (dūninā)? | Not (lā) | they are able (yastaṭīʿūna) | to help (naṣra) | themselves (anfusihim) | and not (walā) | they (hum) | from Us (minnā) | can be protected (yuṣ'ḥabūna).

21:44 Nay, We gave provision to these and their fathers until grew long for them, the life. Then do not they see that We We come to the land, We reduce it from its borders? So is it they who will be overcoming?

Nay (bal), | We gave provision (mattaʿnā) | to these (hāulāi) | and their fathers (waābāahum) | until (ḥattā) | grew long (ṭāla) | for them (ʿalayhimu), | the life (l-ʿumuru). | Then do not (afalā) | they see (yarawna) | that We (annā) | We come (natī) | to the land (l-arḍa), | We reduce it (nanquṣuhā) | from (min) | its borders (aṭrāfihā)? | So is it they (afahumu) | who will be overcoming (l-ghālibūna)?

21:45 Say, "Only I warn you by the revelation." But not hear the deaf the call when they are warned.

Say (qul), | "Only (innamā) | I warn you (undhirukum) | by the revelation. (bil-waḥyi)" | But not (walā) | hear (yasmaʿu) | the deaf (l-ṣumu) | the call (l-duʿāa) | when (idhā) | when (mā) | they are warned (yundharūna).

21:46 And if touches them a whiff of the punishment of your Lord, surely they will say, "O woe to us! Indeed, we [we] were wrongdoers."

And if (wala-in) | touches them (massathum) | a whiff (nafḥatun) | of (min) | the punishment (ʿadhābi) | of your Lord (rabbika), | surely they will say (layaqūlunna), | "O woe to us (yāwaylanā)! | Indeed, we (innā) | [we] were (kunnā) | wrongdoers. (ẓālimīna)"

21:47 And We set the scales of the justice for the Day of the Resurrection, so not will be wronged any soul in anything. And if there be weight of a seed of a mustard We will bring [with] it. And sufficient are We as Reckoners.

And We set (wanaḍaʿu) | the scales (l-mawāzīna) | of the justice (l-qis'ṭa) | for the Day (liyawmi) | of the Resurrection (l-qiyāmati), | so not (falā) | will be wronged (tuẓ'lamu) | any soul (nafsun) | in anything (shayan). | And if (wa-in) | there be (kāna) | weight (mith'qāla) | of a seed (ḥabbatin) | of (min) | a mustard (khardalin) | We will bring (ataynā) | [with] it (bihā). | And sufficient (wakafā) | are We (binā) | as Reckoners (ḥāsibīna).

21:48 And verily, We gave Musa and Harun the Criterion and a light and a Reminder for the righteous.

And verily (walaqad), | We gave (ātaynā) | Musa (mūsā) | and Harun (wahārūna) | the Criterion (l-fur'qāna) | and a light (waḍiyāan) | and a Reminder (wadhik'ran) | for the righteous (lil'muttaqīna).

21:49 Those who fear their Lord in the unseen, and they of the Hour are afraid.

Those who (alladhīna) | fear (yakhshawna) | their Lord (rabbahum) | in the unseen (bil-ghaybi), | and they (wahum) | of (mina) | the Hour (l-sāʿati) | are afraid (mush'fiqūna).

21:50 And this is a Reminder blessed, which We have revealed. Then are you of it rejecters?

And this (wahādhā) | is a Reminder (dhik'run) | blessed (mubārakun), | which We have revealed (anzalnāhu). | Then are you (afa-antum) | of it (lahu) | rejecters (munkirūna)?

21:51 And verily, We gave Ibrahim his guidance before, and We were about him Well-Knowing.

And verily (walaqad), | We gave (ātaynā) | Ibrahim (ib'rāhīma) | his guidance (rush'dahu) | before (min), | before (qablu), | and We were (wakunnā) | about him (bihi) | Well-Knowing (ʿālimīna).

21:52 When he said to his father and his people, "What are these [the] statues which you to it are devoted?"

When (idh) | he said (qāla) | to his father (li-abīhi) | and his people (waqawmihi), | "What (mā) | are these (hādhihi) | [the] statues (l-tamāthīlu) | which (allatī) | you (antum) | to it (lahā) | are devoted? (ʿākifūna)"

21:53 They said, "We found our forefathers of them worshippers."

They said (qālū), | "We found (wajadnā) | our forefathers (ābāanā) | of them (lahā) | worshippers. (ʿābidīna)"

21:54 He said, "Verily, you are [you] and your forefathers were in an error manifest."

He said (qāla), | "Verily (laqad), | you are (kuntum) | [you] (antum) | and your forefathers (waābāukum) | were in (fī) | an error (ḍalālin) | manifest. (mubīnin)"

21:55 They said, "Have you come to us with the truth, or you are of those who play?"

They said (qālū), | "Have you come to us (aji'tanā) | with the truth (bil-ḥaqi), | or (am) | you (anta) | are of (mina) | those who play? (l-lāʿibīna)"

21:56 He said, "Nay, your Lord is the Lord of the heavens and the earth, the One Who created them and I am to that of the witnesses.

He said (qāla), | "Nay (bal), | your Lord (rabbukum) | is the Lord (rabbu) | of the heavens (l-samāwāti) | and the earth (wal-arḍi), | the One Who (alladhī) | created them (faṭarahunna) | and I am (wa-anā) | to (ʿalā) | that (dhālikum) | of (mina) | the witnesses (l-shāhidīna).

21:57 And by Allah surely, I will plan against your idols after [that] you go away turning your backs."

And by Allah (watal-lahi) | surely, I will plan (la-akīdanna) | against your idols (aṣnāmakum) | after (baʿda) | [that] (an) | you go away (tuwallū) | turning your backs. (mud'birīna)"

21:58 So he made them into pieces except a large one of them, so that they may to it return.

So he made them (fajaʿalahum) | into pieces (judhādhan) | except (illā) | a large one (kabīran) | of them (lahum), | so that they may (laʿallahum) | to it (ilayhi) | return (yarjiʿūna).

21:59 They said, "Who has done this to our gods? Indeed, he is of the wrongdoers."
They said (qālū), | "Who (man) | has done (faʿala) | this (hādhā) | to our gods (biālihatinā)? | Indeed, he (innahu) | is of (lamina) | the wrongdoers. (l-ẓālimīna)"

21:60 They said, "We heard a youth mention them he is called Ibrahim."
They said (qālū), | "We heard (samiʿ'nā) | a youth (fatan) | mention them (yadhkuruhum) | he is called (yuqālu) | he is called (lahu) | Ibrahim. (ib'rāhīmu)"

21:61 They said, "Then bring him before the eyes of the people so that they may bear witness."
They said (qālū), | "Then bring (fatū) | him (bihi) | before (ʿalā) | the eyes (aʿyuni) | of the people (l-nāsi) | so that they may (laʿallahum) | bear witness. (yashhadūna)"

21:62 They said, "Have you done this to our gods O Ibrahim?"
They said (qālū), | "Have you (a-anta) | done (faʿalta) | this (hādhā) | to our gods (biālihatinā) | O Ibrahim? (yāib'rāhīmu)"

21:63 He said, "Nay, some doer did it. Their chief is this. So ask them if they can speak."
He said (qāla), | "Nay (bal), | some doer did it (faʿalahu). | Their chief (kabīruhum) | is this (hādhā). | So ask them (fasalūhum) | if (in) | they can (kānū) | speak. (yanṭiqūna)"

21:64 So they returned to themselves and said, "Indeed, you [you] are the wrongdoers."
So they returned (farajaʿū) | to (ilā) | themselves (anfusihim) | and said (faqālū), | "Indeed, you (innakum) | [you] (antumu) | are the wrongdoers. (l-ẓālimūna)"

21:65 Then they were turned on their heads, "Verily, you know not these can speak!"
Then (thumma) | they were turned (nukisū) | on (ʿalā) | their heads (ruūsihim), | "Verily (laqad), | you know (ʿalim'ta) | not (mā) | these (hāulāi) | can speak! (yanṭiqūna)"

21:66 He said, "Then do you worship besides Allah what does not benefit you in anything and not harms you?
He said (qāla), | "Then do you worship (afataʿbudūna) | besides (min) | besides (dūni) | Allah (l-lahi) | what (mā) | does not (lā) | benefit you (yanfaʿukum) | in anything (shayan) | and not (walā) | harms you (yaḍurrukum)?

21:67 Uff to you and to what you worship besides Allah. Then will not you use reason?"
Uff (uffin) | to you (lakum) | and to what (walimā) | you worship (taʿbudūna) | besides (min) | besides (dūni) | Allah (l-lahi). | Then will not (afalā) | you use reason? (taʿqilūna)"

21:68 They said, "Burn him and support your gods, if you are doers."
They said (qālū), | "Burn him (ḥarriqūhu) | and support (wa-unṣurū) | your gods (ālihatakum), | if (in) | you are (kuntum) | doers. (fāʿilīna)"

21:69 We said, "O fire! Be cool[ness] and safe[ty] for Ibrahim."
We said (qul'nā), | "O fire (yānāru)! | Be (kūnī) | cool[ness] (bardan) | and safe[ty] (wasalāman) | for (ʿalā) | Ibrahim. (ib'rāhīma)"

21:70 And they intended for him, a plan but We made them the greatest losers.
And they intended (wa-arādū) | for him (bihi), | a plan (kaydan) | but We made them (fajaʿalnāhumu) | the greatest losers (l-akhsarīna).

21:71 And We delivered him and Lut to the land which We had blessed [in it] for the worlds.
And We delivered him (wanajjaynāhu) | and Lut (walūṭan) | to (ilā) | the land (l-arḍi) | which (allatī) | We had blessed (bāraknā) | [in it] (fīhā) | for the worlds (lil'ʿālamīna).

21:72 And We bestowed on him Isaac and Yaqub in addition, and all We made righteous.
And We bestowed (wawahabnā) | on him (lahu) | Isaac (is'ḥāqa) | and Yaqub (wayaʿqūba) | in addition (nāfilatan), | and all (wakullan) | We made (jaʿalnā) | righteous (ṣāliḥīna).

21:73 And We made them leaders, they guide by Our Command. And We inspired to them the doing of good deeds, and establishment of the prayer and giving of zakah; and they were of Us worshippers.
And We made them (wajaʿalnāhum) | leaders (a-immatan), | they guide (yahdūna) | by Our Command (bi-amrinā). | And We inspired (wa-awḥaynā) | to them (ilayhim) | the doing (fiʿ'la) | of good deeds (l-khayrāti), | and establishment (wa-iqāma) | of the prayer (l-ṣalati) | and giving (waītāa) | of zakah (l-zakati); | and they were (wakānū) | of Us (lanā) | worshippers (ʿābidīna).

21:74 And to Lut We gave him judgment and knowledge, and We saved him from the town which was doing wicked deeds. Indeed, they were a people evil, defiantly disobedient.
And to Lut (walūṭan) | We gave him (ātaynāhu) | judgment (ḥuk'man) | and knowledge (waʿil'man), | and We saved him (wanajjaynāhu) | from (mina) | the town (l-qaryati) | which (allatī) | was (kānat) | doing (taʿmalu) | wicked deeds (l-khabāitha). | Indeed, they (innahum) | were (kānū) | a people (qawma) | evil (sawin), | defiantly disobedient (fāsiqīna).

21:75 And We admitted him into Our Mercy. Indeed, he was of the righteous.
And We admitted him (wa-adkhalnāhu) | into (fī) | Our Mercy (raḥmatinā). | Indeed, he (innahu) | was of (mina) | the righteous (l-ṣāliḥīna).

21:76 And Nuh, when he called before, so We responded to him and We saved him and his family from the affliction, [the] great.
And Nuh (wanūḥan), | when (idh) | he called (nādā) | before (min), | before (qablu), | so We responded (fa-is'tajabnā) | to him (lahu) | and We saved him (fanajjaynāhu) | and his family (wa-ahlahu) | from (mina) | the affliction (l-karbi), | [the] great (l-ʿaẓīmi).

21:77 And We helped him from the people who denied Our Signs. Indeed, they were a people evil, so We drowned them all.
And We helped him (wanaṣarnāhu) | from (mina) | the people (l-qawmi) | who (alladhīna) | denied (kadhabū) | Our Signs (biāyātinā). | Indeed, they (innahum) | were (kānū) | a people (qawma) | evil (sawin), | so We drowned them (fa-aghraqnāhum) | all (ajmaʿīna).

21:78 And Dawud and Sulaiman, when they judged concerning the field, when pastured in it sheep of a people, and We were to their judgment witness.
And Dawud (wadāwūda) | and Sulaiman (wasulaymāna), | when (idh) | they judged (yaḥkumāni) | concerning (fī) | the field (l-ḥarthi), | when (idh) | pastured (nafashat) | in it (fīhi) | sheep (ghanamu) | of a people (l-qawmi), | and We were (wakunnā) | to their judgment (liḥuk'mihim) | witness (shāhidīna).

21:79 And We gave understanding of it to Sulaiman, and to each We gave judgment and knowledge. And We subjected with Dawud the mountains to glorify Our praises and the birds. And We were the Doers.
And We gave understanding of it (fafahhamnāhā) | to Sulaiman (sulaymāna), | and to each (wakullan) | We gave (ātaynā) | judgment (ḥuk'man) | and knowledge (waʿil'man). | And We subjected (wasakharnā) | with (maʿa) | Dawud (dāwūda) | the mountains (l-jibāla) | to glorify Our

praises (yusabbiḥ'na) | and the birds (wal-ṭayra). | And We were (wakunnā) | the Doers (fāʿilīna).

21:80 And We taught him the making of coats of armor for you to protect you from your battle. Then will you be grateful?

And We taught him (waʿallamnāhu) | the making (ṣanʿata) | of coats of armor (labūsin) | for you (lakum) | to protect you (lituḥ'ṣinakum) | from (min) | your battle (basikum). | Then will (fahal) | you (antum) | be grateful (shākirūna)?

21:81 And to Sulaiman, the wind forcefully blowing by his command to the land which We blessed [in it]. And We are of every thing Knowers.

And to Sulaiman (walisulaymāna), | the wind (l-rīḥa) | forcefully (ʿāṣifatan) | blowing (tajrī) | by his command (bi-amrihi) | to (ilā) | the land (l-arḍi) | which (allatī) | We blessed (bāraknā) | [in it] (fīhā). | And We are (wakunnā) | of every (bikulli) | thing (shayin) | Knowers (ʿālimīna).

21:82 And of the devils were some who would dive for him and would do work other than that. And We were of them Guardians.

And of (wamina) | the devils (l-shayāṭīni) | were some who (man) | would dive (yaghūṣūna) | for him (lahu) | and would do (wayaʿmalūna) | work (ʿamalan) | other than (dūna) | that (dhālika). | And We were (wakunnā) | of them (lahum) | Guardians (ḥāfiẓīna).

21:83 And Ayub, when he called to his Lord, "Indeed, [I] has touched me the adversity, and You are Most Merciful of the Merciful."

And Ayub (wa-ayyūba), | when (idh) | he called (nādā) | to his Lord (rabbahu), | "Indeed, [I] (annī) | has touched me (massaniya) | the adversity (l-ḍuru), | and You (wa-anta) | are Most Merciful (arḥamu) | of the Merciful. (l-rāḥimīna)"

21:84 So We responded to him and We removed what was on him of the adversity. And We gave him his family and the like thereof with them as Mercy from Ourselves, and a reminder for the worshippers.

So We responded (fa-is'tajabnā) | to him (lahu) | and We removed (fakashafnā) | what (mā) | was on him (bihi) | of (min) | the adversity (ḍurrin). | And We gave him (waātaynāhu) | his family (ahlahu) | and the like thereof (wamith'lahum) | with them (maʿahum) | as Mercy (raḥmatan) | from Ourselves (min), | from Ourselves (ʿindinā), | and a reminder (wadhik'rā) | for the worshippers (lilʿābidīna).

21:85 And Ishmael and Idris and Dhul-Kifl; all were of the patient ones.

And Ishmael (wa-is'māʿīla) | and Idris (wa-id'rīsa) | and Dhul-Kifl (wadhā); | and Dhul-Kifl (l-kif'li); | all (kullun) | were of (mina) | the patient ones (l-ṣābirīna).

21:86 And We admitted them in Our Mercy. Indeed, they were of the righteous.

And We admitted them (wa-adkhalnāhum) | in (fī) | Our Mercy (raḥmatinā). | Indeed, they (innahum) | were of (mina) | the righteous (l-ṣāliḥīna).

21:87 And Dhun-Nun when he went while angry and thought that never We would decree upon him. Then he called in the darknesses that, "There is no god except You, Glory be to You! Indeed, [I] I am of the wrongdoers."

And Dhun-Nun (wadhā) | And Dhun-Nun (l-nūni) | when (idh) | he went (dhahaba) | while angry (mughāḍiban) | and thought (faẓanna) | that (an) | never (lan) | We would decree (naqdira) | upon him (ʿalayhi). | Then he called (fanādā) | in (fī) | the darknesses (l-ẓulumāti) | that (an), | "There is no (lā) | god (ilāha) | except (illā) | You (anta), | Glory be to You (sub'ḥānaka)! | Indeed, [I] (innī) | I am (kuntu) | of (mina) | the wrongdoers. (l-ẓālimīna)"

21:88 So We responded to him, and We saved him from the distress. And thus We save the believers.

So We responded (fa-is'tajabnā) | to him (lahu), | and We saved him (wanajjaynāhu) | from (mina) | the distress (l-ghami). | And thus (wakadhālika) | We save (nunjī) | the believers (l-mu'minīna).

21:89 And Zakariya, when he called to his Lord, "My Lord! Do not leave me alone, while You are [the] Best of the inheritors."

And Zakariya (wazakariyyā), | when (idh) | he called (nādā) | to his Lord (rabbahu), | "My Lord (rabbi)! | Do not (lā) | leave me (tadharnī) | alone (fardan), | while You (wa-anta) | are [the] Best (khayru) | of the inheritors. (l-wārithīna)"

21:90 So We responded to him, and We bestowed on him Yahya, and We cured for him his wife. Indeed, they used to hasten in good deeds, and they supplicate to Us in hope and fear, and they were to Us humbly submissive.

So We responded (fa-is'tajabnā) | to him (lahu), | and We bestowed (wawahabnā) | on him (lahu) | Yahya (yaḥyā), | and We cured (wa-aṣlaḥnā) | for him (lahu) | his wife (zawjahu). | Indeed, they (innahum) | used to (kānū) | hasten (yusāriʿūna) | in (fī) | good deeds (l-khayrāti), | and they supplicate to Us (wayadʿūnanā) | in hope (raghaban) | and fear (warahaban), | and they were (wakānū) | to Us (lanā) | humbly submissive (khāshiʿīna).

21:91 And she who guarded her chastity, so We breathed into her of Our Spirit, and We made her and her son a sign for the worlds.

And she who (wa-allatī) | guarded (aḥṣanat) | her chastity (farjahā), | so We breathed (fanafakhnā) | into her (fīhā) | of (min) | Our Spirit (rūḥinā), | and We made her (wajaʿalnāhā) | and her son (wa-ib'nahā) | a sign (āyatan) | for the worlds (lil'ʿālamīna).

21:92 Indeed, this is your religion - religion one, and I Am your Lord, so worship Me.

Indeed (inna), | this (hādhihi) | is your religion (ummatukum)- | religion (ummatan) | one (wāḥidatan), | and I Am (wa-anā) | your Lord (rabbukum), | so worship Me (fa-u'ʿbudūni).

21:93 But they cut off their affair among themselves, all to Us will return.

But they cut off (wataqaṭṭaʿū) | their affair (amrahum) | among themselves (baynahum), | all (kullun) | to Us (ilaynā) | will return (rājiʿūna).

21:94 Then whoever does [of] [the] righteous deeds while he is a believer then not will be rejected [of] his effort. And indeed, We of it are Recorders.

Then whoever (faman) | does (yaʿmal) | [of] (mina) | [the] righteous deeds (l-ṣāliḥāti) | while he (wahuwa) | is a believer (mu'minun) | then not (falā) | will be rejected (kuf'rāna) | [of] his effort (lisaʿyihi). | And indeed, We (wa-innā) | of it (lahu) | are Recorders (kātibūna).

21:95 And there is prohibition upon a city which We have destroyed, that they not will return.

And there is prohibition (waḥarāmun) | upon (ʿalā) | a city (qaryatin) | which We have destroyed (ahlaknāhā), | that they (annahum) | not (lā) | will return (yarjiʿūna).

21:96 Until when has been opened for the Yajuj and Majuj, and they from every elevation descend.

Until (ḥattā) | when (idhā) | has been opened (futiḥat) | for the Yajuj (yajūju) | and Majuj (wamajūju), | and they (wahum) | from (min) | every (kulli) | elevation (ḥadabin) | descend (yansilūna).

21:97 And has approached the promise [the] true then behold, [it] are staring the eyes of those who disbelieved, "O woe to us! Verily, we had been in heedlessness of this; nay, we were wrongdoers."

And has approached (wa-iq'taraba) | the promise (l-waʿdu) | [the] true (l-ḥaqu) | then behold (fa-idhā), | [it] (hiya) | are staring (shākhiṣatun) | the eyes (abṣāru) | of those who (alladhīna) | disbelieved (kafarū), | "O woe to us (yāwaylanā)! | Verily (qad), | we had been (kunnā) | in (fī) | heedlessness (ghaflatin) | of (min) | this (hādhā); | nay (bal), | we were (kunnā) | wrongdoers. (ẓālimīna)"

21:98 Indeed, you and what you worship besides Allah are firewood of Hell. You to it will come.
Indeed, you (innakum) | and what (wamā) | you worship (taʿbudūna) | besides Allah (min) | besides Allah (dūni) | besides Allah (l-lahi) | are firewood (ḥaṣabu) | of Hell (jahannama). | You (antum) | to it (lahā) | will come (wāridūna).

21:99 If were these gods, not they would have come to it. And all therein will abide forever.
If (law) | were (kāna) | these (hāulāi) | gods (ālihatan), | not (mā) | they would have come to it (waradūhā). | And all (wakullun) | therein (fīhā) | will abide forever (khālidūna).

21:100 For them therein is sighing, and they therein not will hear.
For them (lahum) | therein (fīhā) | is sighing (zafīrun), | and they (wahum) | therein (fīhā) | not (lā) | will hear (yasmaʿūna).

21:101 Indeed, those has gone forth for them from Us the good, those from it will be removed far.
Indeed (inna), | those (alladhīna) | has gone forth (sabaqat) | for them (lahum) | from Us (minnā) | the good (l-ḥus'nā), | those (ulāika) | from it (ʿanhā) | will be removed far (mub'ʿadūna).

21:102 Not they will hear the slightest sound of it and they in what desire their souls will abide forever.
Not (lā) | they will hear (yasmaʿūna) | the slightest sound of it (ḥasīsahā) | and they (wahum) | in (fī) | what (mā) | desire (ish'tahat) | their souls (anfusuhum) | will abide forever (khālidūna).

21:103 Not will grieve them the terror [the] greatest, and will meet them the Angels, "This is your Day which you were promised."
Not (lā) | will grieve them (yaḥzunuhumu) | the terror (l-fazaʿu) | [the] greatest (l-akbaru), | and will meet them (watatalaqqāhumu) | the Angels (l-malāikatu), | "This (hādhā) | is your Day (yawmukumu) | which (alladhı) | you were (kuntum) | promised. (tuʿadūna)"

21:104 The Day We will fold the heaven like the folding of a scroll for records. As We began the first creation We will repeat it, a promise upon Us. Indeed, We - We are the Doers.
The Day (yawma) | We will fold (naṭwī) | the heaven (l-samāa) | like the folding (kaṭayyi) | of a scroll (l-sijili) | for records (lil'kutubi). | As (kamā) | We began (badanā) | the first (awwala) | creation (khalqin) | We will repeat it (nuʿīduhu), | a promise (waʿdan) | upon Us (ʿalaynā). | Indeed, We (innā)- | We are (kunnā) | the Doers (fāʿilīna).

21:105 And verily, We have written in the Scripture after the mention, that the earth - will inherit it My slaves, the righteous.
And verily (walaqad), | We have written (katabnā) | in (fī) | the Scripture (l-zabūri) | after (min) | after (baʿdi) | the mention (l-dhik'ri), | that (anna) | the earth (l-arḍa)- | will inherit it (yarithuhā) | My slaves (ʿibādiya), | the righteous (l-ṣāliḥūna).

21:106 Indeed, in this surely is a Message for a people, worshippers.
Indeed (inna), | in (fī) | this (hādhā) | surely is a Message (labalāghan) | for a people (liqawmin), | worshippers (ʿābidīna).

21:107 And not We have sent you but as a mercy for the worlds.

And not (wamā) | We have sent you (arsalnāka) | but (illā) | as a mercy (raḥmatan) | for the worlds (lil'ʿālamīna).

21:108 Say, "Only it is revealed to me that your god is God One; so will you submit to Him?"

Say (qul), | "Only (innamā) | it is revealed (yūḥā) | to me (ilayya) | that (annamā) | your god (ilāhukum) | is God (ilāhun) | One (wāḥidun); | so will (fahal) | you (antum) | submit to Him? (mus'limūna)"

21:109 But if they turn away then say, "I have announced to you equally And not I know whether is near or far what you are promised.

But if (fa-in) | they turn away (tawallaw) | then say (faqul), | "I have announced to you (ādhantukum) | equally (ʿalā) | equally (sawāin) | And not (wa-in) | I know (adrī) | whether is near (aqarībun) | or (am) | far (baʿīdun) | what (mā) | you are promised (tūʿadūna).

21:110 Indeed, He knows the declared [of] [the] speech and He knows what you conceal.

Indeed, He (innahu) | knows (yaʿlamu) | the declared (l-jahra) | [of] (mina) | [the] speech (l-qawli) | and He knows (wayaʿlamu) | what (mā) | you conceal (taktumūna).

21:111 And not I know, perhaps it may be a trial for you, and an enjoyment for a time."

And not (wa-in) | I know (adrī), | perhaps it may be (laʿallahu) | a trial (fit'natun) | for you (lakum), | and an enjoyment (wamatāʿun) | for (ilā) | a time. (ḥīnin)"

21:112 He said, "My Lord! judge in truth. And our Lord is the Most Gracious, the One Whose help is sought against what you attribute."

He said (qāla), | "My Lord (rabbi)! | judge (uḥ'kum) | in truth (bil-ḥaqi). | And our Lord (warabbunā) | is the Most Gracious (l-raḥmānu), | the One Whose help is sought (l-mus'taʿānu) | against (ʿalā) | what (mā) | you attribute. (taṣifūna)"

Chapter (22) Sūrat l-Ḥaj (The Pilgrimage)

22:1 O mankind! Fear your Lord. Indeed, the convulsion of the Hour is a thing great.

O mankind (yāayyuhā)! | O mankind (l-nāsu)! | Fear (ittaqū) | your Lord (rabbakum). | Indeed (inna), | the convulsion (zalzalata) | of the Hour (l-sāʿati) | is a thing (shayon) | great (ʿaẓīmun).

22:2 The Day you will see it, will forget every nursing mother that which she was nursing, and will deliver every pregnant woman her load, and you will see [the] mankind intoxicated, while not they are intoxicated; but the punishment of Allah will be severe.

The Day (yawma) | you will see it (tarawnahā), | will forget (tadhhalu) | every (kullu) | nursing mother (mur'ḍiʿatin) | that which (ʿammā) | she was nursing (arḍaʿat), | and will deliver (wataḍaʿu) | every (kullu) | pregnant woman (dhāti) | pregnant woman (ḥamlin) | her load (ḥamlahā), | and you will see (watarā) | [the] mankind (l-nāsa) | intoxicated (sukārā), | while not (wamā) | they (hum) | are intoxicated (bisukārā); | but (walākinna) | the punishment (ʿadhāba) | of Allah (l-lahi) | will be severe (shadīdun).

22:3 And among the mankind is he who disputes concerning Allah without knowledge and follows every devil rebellious.

And among (wamina) | the mankind (l-nāsi) | is he who (man) | disputes (yujādilu) | concerning (fī) | Allah (l-lahi) | without (bighayri) | knowledge (ʿil'min) | and follows (wayattabiʿu) | every (kulla) | devil (shayṭānin) | rebellious (marīdin).

22:4 It has been decreed for him that he who befriends him, then indeed, he will misguide him and will guide him to the punishment of the Blaze.

It has been decreed (kutiba) | for him (ʿalayhi) | that he (annahu) | who (man) | befriends him (tawallāhu), | then indeed, he (fa-annahu) | will misguide him (yuḍilluhu) | and will guide him (wayahdīhi) | to (ilā) | the punishment (ʿadhābi) | of the Blaze (l-saʿīri).

22:5 O mankind! If you are in doubt about the Resurrection, then indeed, We We created you from dust, then from a semen-drop then from a clinging substance then from an embryonic lump, formed and unformed, that We may make clear to you. And We cause to remain in the wombs what We will for a term appointed, then We bring you out as a child, [then] that you may reach [your] maturity. And among you is he who dies, and among you is he who is returned to the most abject age, so that not he knows, after having known, anything. And you see the earth barren then when We send down on it water, it gets stirred and it swells and grows of every kind beautiful.

O mankind (yāayyuhā)! | O mankind (l-nāsu)! | If (in) | you are (kuntum) | in (fī) | doubt (raybin) | about (mina) | the Resurrection (l-baʿthi), | then indeed, We (fa-innā) | We created you (khalaqnākum) | from (min) | dust (turābin), | then (thumma) | from (min) | a semen-drop (nuṭ'fatin) | then (thumma) | from (min) | a clinging substance (ʿalaqatin) | then (thumma) | from (min) | an embryonic lump (muḍ'ghatin), | formed (mukhallaqatin) | and unformed (waghayri), | and unformed (mukhallaqatin), | that We may make clear (linubayyina) | to you (lakum). | And We cause to remain (wanuqirru) | in (fī) | the wombs (l-arḥāmi) | what (mā) | We will (nashāu) | for (ilā) | a term (ajalin) | appointed (musamman), | then (thumma) | We bring you out (nukh'rijukum) | as a child (ṭif'lan), | [then] (thumma) | that you may reach (litablughū) | [your] maturity (ashuddakum). | And among you (waminkum) | is he who (man) | dies (yutawaffā), | and among you (waminkum) | is he who (man) | is returned (yuraddu) | to (ilā) | the most abject (ardhali) | age (l-ʿumuri), | so that not (likaylā) | he knows (yaʿlama), | after (min) | after (baʿdi) | having known (ʿil'min), | anything (shayan). | And you see (watarā) | the earth (l-arḍa) | barren (hāmidatan) | then when (fa-idhā) | We send down (anzalnā) | on it (ʿalayhā) | water (l-māa), | it gets stirred (ih'tazzat) | and it swells (warabat) | and grows (wa-anbatat) | of (min) | every (kulli) | kind (zawjin) | beautiful (bahījin).

22:6 That is because, Allah - He is the Truth. And that He [He] gives life to the dead, and that He is over every thing All-Powerful.

That (dhālika) | is because (bi-anna), | Allah (l-laha)- | He (huwa) | is the Truth (l-ḥaqu). | And that He (wa-annahu) | [He] gives life (yuḥ'yī) | to the dead (l-mawtā), | and that He (wa-annahu) | is over (ʿalā) | every (kulli) | thing (shayin) | All-Powerful (qadīrun).

22:7 And that the Hour will come, there is no doubt about it, and that Allah will resurrect those who are in the graves.

And that (wa-anna) | the Hour (l-sāʿata) | will come (ātiyatun), | there is no (lā) | doubt (rayba) | about it (fīhā), | and that (wa-anna) | Allah (l-laha) | will resurrect (yabʿathu) | those who (man) | are in (fī) | the graves (l-qubūri).

22:8 And among mankind is he who disputes concerning Allah without any knowledge and not any guidance and not a Book enlightening,

And among (wamina) | mankind (l-nāsi) | is he who (man) | disputes (yujādilu) | concerning (fī) | Allah (l-lahi) | without (bighayri) | any knowledge (ʿil'min) | and not (walā) | any guidance (hudan) | and not (walā) | a Book (kitābin) | enlightening (munīrin),

22:9 Twisting his neck to mislead from the way of Allah. For him in the world is disgrace, and We will make him taste on the Day of Resurrection the punishment of the Burning Fire.

Twisting (thāniya) | his neck (ʿiṭ'fihi) | to mislead (liyuḍilla) | from (ʿan) | the way (sabīli) | of Allah (l-lahi). | For him (lahu) | in (fī) | the world (l-dun'yā) | is disgrace (khiz'yun), | and We will make him taste (wanudhīquhu) | on the Day (yawma) | of Resurrection (l-qiyāmati) | the punishment (ʿadhāba) | of the Burning Fire (l-ḥarīqi).

22:10 That is for what have sent forth your hands, and that Allah is not unjust to His slaves.

That (dhālika) | is for what (bimā) | have sent forth (qaddamat) | your hands (yadāka), | and that (wa-anna) | Allah (l-laha) | is not (laysa) | unjust (biẓallāmin) | to His slaves (lilʿabīdi).

22:11 And among the mankind is he who worships Allah on an edge. And if befalls him good, he is content with it, and if befalls him a trial he turns on his face. He has lost the world and the Hereafter. That [it] is the loss clear.

And among (wamina) | the mankind (l-nāsi) | is he who (man) | worships (yaʿbudu) | Allah (l-laha) | on (ʿalā) | an edge (ḥarfin). | And if (fa-in) | befalls him (aṣābahu) | good (khayrun), | he is content (iṭ'ma-anna) | with it (bihi), | and if (wa-in) | befalls him (aṣābathu) | a trial (fit'natun) | he turns (inqalaba) | on (ʿalā) | his face (wajhihi). | He has lost (khasira) | the world (l-dun'yā) | and the Hereafter (wal-ākhirata). | That (dhālika) | [it] (huwa) | is the loss (l-khus'rānu) | clear (l-mubīnu).

22:12 He calls besides Allah what not harms him and what not benefits him. That [it] is the straying far away.

He calls (yadʿū) | besides (min) | besides (dūni) | Allah (l-lahi) | what (mā) | not (lā) | harms him (yaḍurruhu) | and what (wamā) | not (lā) | benefits him (yanfaʿuhu). | That (dhālika) | [it] (huwa) | is the straying (l-ḍalālu) | far away (l-baʿīdu).

22:13 He calls one who - his harm is closer than his benefit. Surely, an evil protector and surely an evil friend!

He calls (yadʿū) | one who (laman)- | his harm (ḍarruhu) | is closer (aqrabu) | than (min) | his benefit (nafʿihi). | Surely, an evil (labi'sa) | protector (l-mawlā) | and surely an evil (walabi'sa) | friend (l-ʿashīru)!

22:14 Indeed, Allah will admit those who believe and do the righteous deeds to Gardens flow from underneath it the rivers. Indeed, Allah does what He intends.

Indeed (inna), | Allah (l-laha) | will admit (yud'khilu) | those who (alladhīna) | believe (āmanū) | and do (waʿamilū) | the righteous deeds (l-ṣāliḥāti) | to Gardens (jannātin) | flow (tajrī) | from (min) | underneath it (taḥtihā) | the rivers (l-anhāru). | Indeed (inna), | Allah (l-laha) | does (yafʿalu) | what (mā) | He intends (yurīdu).

22:15 Whoever [is] thinks that not Allah will help him in the world and the Hereafter, then let him extend a rope to the sky, then let him cut off, then let him see whether will remove his plan what enrages.

Whoever (man) | [is] (kāna) | thinks (yaẓunnu) | that (an) | not (lan) | Allah will help him (yanṣurahu) | Allah will help him (l-lahu) | in (fī) | the world (l-dun'yā) | and the Hereafter (wal-ākhirati), | then let him extend (falyamdud) | a rope (bisababin) | to (ilā) | the sky (l-samāi), | then (thumma) | let him cut off (l'yaqṭaʿ), | then let him see (falyanẓur) | whether (hal) | will remove (yudh'hibanna) | his plan (kayduhu) | what (mā) | enrages (yaghīẓu).

22:16 And thus We sent it down as clear Verses, and that Allah guides whom He intends.

And thus (wakadhālika) | We sent it down (anzalnāhu) | as clear Verses (āyātin), | as clear Verses (bayyinātin), | and that (wa-anna) | Allah (l-laha) | guides (yahdī) | whom (man) | He intends (yurīdu).

22:17 Indeed, those who have believed, and those who were Jews and the Sabians and the Christians and the Magians, and those who are polytheists indeed, Allah will judge between them on the Day of the Resurrection. Indeed, Allah over every thing is a Witness.

Indeed (inna), | those who (alladhīna) | have believed (āmanū), | and those who (wa-alladhīna) | were Jews (hādū) | and the Sabians (wal-ṣābiīna) | and the Christians (wal-naṣārā) | and the Magians (wal-majūsa), | and those who (wa-alladhīna) | are polytheists (ashrakū) | indeed (inna), | Allah (l-laha) | will judge (yafṣilu) | between them (baynahum) | on the Day (yawma) | of the Resurrection (l-qiyāmati). | Indeed (inna), | Allah (l-laha) | over (ʿalā) | every (kulli) | thing (shayin) | is a Witness (shahīdun).

22:18 Do not you see that to Allah prostrates to Him whoever is in the heavens and whoever is in the earth, and the sun and the moon and the stars and the mountains, and the trees and the moving creatures and many of the people? But many - is justly due on him the punishment. And whoever Allah humiliates then not for him any bestower of honor. Indeed, Allah does what He wills

Do not (alam) | you see (tara) | that (anna) | to Allah (l-laha) | prostrates (yasjudu) | to Him (lahu) | whoever (man) | is in (fī) | the heavens (l-samāwāti) | and whoever (waman) | is in (fī) | the earth (l-arḍi), | and the sun (wal-shamsu) | and the moon (wal-qamaru) | and the stars (wal-nujūmu) | and the mountains (wal-jibālu), | and the trees (wal-shajaru) | and the moving creatures (wal-dawābu) | and many (wakathīrun) | of (mina) | the people (l-nāsi)? | But many (wakathīrun)- | is justly due (ḥaqqa) | on him (ʿalayhi) | the punishment (l-ʿadhābu). | And whoever (waman) | Allah humiliates (yuhini) | Allah humiliates (l-lahu) | then not (famā) | for him (lahu) | any (min) | bestower of honor (muk'rimin). | Indeed (inna), | Allah (l-laha) | does (yafʿalu) | what (mā) | He wills (yashāu)

22:19 These two opponents dispute concerning their Lord. But those who disbelieved will be cut out for them garments of fire. Will be poured over their heads [the] scalding water.

These two (hādhāni) | opponents (khasmāni) | dispute (ikh'taṣamū) | concerning (fī) | their Lord (rabbihim). | But those who (fa-alladhīna) | disbelieved (kafarū) | will be cut out (quṭṭiʿat) | for them (lahum) | garments (thiyābun) | of (min) | fire (nārin). | Will be poured (yuṣabbu) | over (min) | over (fawqi) | their heads (ruūsihimu) | [the] scalding water (l-ḥamīmu).

22:20 Will be melted with it what is in their bellies and the skins.

Will be melted (yuṣ'haru) | with it (bihi) | what (mā) | is in (fī) | their bellies (buṭūnihim) | and the skins (wal-julūdu).

22:21 And for them are hooked rods of iron.

And for them (walahum) | are hooked rods (maqāmiʿu) | of (min) | iron (ḥadīdin).

22:22 Every time they want to come out from it from anguish, they will be returned therein, "Taste the punishment of the Burning Fire!"

Every time (kullamā) | they want (arādū) | to (an) | come out (yakhrujū) | from it (min'hā) | from (min) | anguish (ghammin), | they will be returned (uʿīdū) | therein (fīhā), | "Taste (wadhūqū) | the punishment (ʿadhāba) | of the Burning Fire! (l-ḥarīqi)"

22:23 Indeed, Allah will admit those who believe and do the righteous deeds, to Gardens flow from underneath it the rivers. They will be adorned therein with bracelets of gold and pearl, and their garments therein will be of silk.

Indeed (inna), | Allah (l-laha) | will admit (yud'khilu) | those who (alladhīna) | believe (āmanū) | and do (waʿamilū) | the righteous deeds (l-ṣāliḥāti), | to Gardens (jannātin) | flow (tajrī) | from (min) | underneath it (taḥtihā) | the rivers (l-anhāru). | They will be adorned (yuḥallawna) | therein (fīhā) | with (min) | bracelets (asāwira) | of (min) | gold (dhahabin) | and pearl (walu'lu-an), | and their garments (walibāsuhum) | therein (fīhā) | will be of silk (ḥarīrun).

22:24 And they were guided to the good of the speech, and they were guided to the path of the Praiseworthy.

And they were guided (wahudū) | to (ilā) | the good (l-ṭayibi) | of (mina) | the speech (l-qawli), | and they were guided (wahudū) | to (ilā) | the path (ṣirāṭi) | of the Praiseworthy (l-ḥamīdi).

22:25 Indeed, those who disbelieved and hinder from the way of Allah and Al-Masjid Al-Haraam, which We made it for the mankind, equal, are the resident therein and the visitor; and whoever intends therein of deviation or wrongdoing, We will make him taste of a punishment painful.

Indeed (inna), | those who (alladhīna) | disbelieved (kafarū) | and hinder (wayaṣuddūna) | from (ʿan) | the way (sabīli) | of Allah (l-lahi) | and Al-Masjid Al-Haraam (wal-masjidi), | and Al-Masjid Al-Haraam (l-ḥarāmi), | which (alladhī) | We made it (jaʿalnāhu) | for the mankind (lilnnāsi), | equal (sawāan), | are the resident (l-ʿākifu) | therein (fīhi) | and the visitor (wal-bādi); | and whoever (waman) | intends (yurid) | therein (fīhi) | of deviation (bi-il'ḥādin) | or wrongdoing (biẓul'min), | We will make him taste (nudhiq'hu) | of (min) | a punishment (ʿadhābin) | painful (alīmin).

22:26 And when We assigned to Ibrahim the site of the House, "That do not associate with Me anything and purify My House for those who circumambulate and those who stand and those who bow, and those who prostrate.

And when (wa-idh) | We assigned (bawwanā) | to Ibrahim (li-ib'rāhīma) | the site (makāna) | of the House (l-bayti), | "That (an) | do not (lā) | associate (tush'rik) | with Me (bī) | anything (shayan) | and purify (waṭahhir) | My House (baytiya) | for those who circumambulate (lilṭṭāifīna) | and those who stand (wal-qāimīna) | and those who bow (wal-rukaʿi), | and those who prostrate (l-sujūdi).

22:27 And proclaim to [the] mankind [of] the Pilgrimage; they will come to you on foot and on every lean camel; they will come from every mountain highway distant.

And proclaim (wa-adhin) | to (fī) | [the] mankind (l-nāsi) | [of] the Pilgrimage (bil-ḥaji); | they will come to you (yatūka) | on foot (rijālan) | and on (waʿalā) | every (kulli) | lean camel (ḍāmirin); | they will come (yatīna) | from (min) | every (kulli) | mountain highway (fajjin) | distant (ʿamīqin).

22:28 That they may witness benefits for them, and mention the name of Allah on days known over what He has provided them of the beast of cattle. So eat of them and feed the miserable, the poor.

That they may witness (liyashhadū) | benefits (manāfiʿa) | for them (lahum), | and mention (wayadhkurū) | the name (is'ma) | of Allah (l-lahi) | on (fī) | days (ayyāmin) | known (maʿlūmātin) | over (ʿalā) | what (mā) | He has provided them (razaqahum) | of (min) | the beast (bahīmati) | of cattle (l-anʿāmi). | So eat (fakulū) | of them (min'hā) | and feed (wa-aṭʿimū) | the miserable (l-bāisa), | the poor (l-faqīra).

22:29 Then let them end their prescribed duties and fulfil their vows, and circumambulate the House [the] Ancient."

Then (thumma) | let them end (l'yaqḍū) | their prescribed duties (tafathahum) | and fulfil (walyūfū) | their vows (nudhūrahum), | and circumambulate (walyaṭṭawwafū) | the House (bil-bayti)

| [the] Ancient. (l-ʿatīqi)"

22:30 That and whoever honors the sacred rites of Allah, then it is best for him near his Lord. And are made lawful to you the cattle except what is recited to you. So avoid the abomination of the idols and avoid the word false.

That (dhālika) | and whoever (waman) | honors (yuʿaẓẓim) | the sacred rites (ḥurumāti) | of Allah (l-lahi), | then it (fahuwa) | is best (khayrun) | for him (lahu) | near (ʿinda) | his Lord (rabbihi). | And are made lawful (wa-uḥillat) | to you (lakumu) | the cattle (l-anʿāmu) | except (illā) | what (mā) | is recited (yut'lā) | to you (ʿalaykum). | So avoid (fa-ij'tanibū) | the abomination (l-rij'sa) | of (mina) | the idols (l-awthāni) | and avoid (wa-ij'tanibū) | the word (qawla) | false (l-zūri).

22:31 Being upright to Allah, not associating partners with Him. And whoever associates partners with Allah then it is as though he had fallen from the sky and had snatched him the birds, or had blown him the wind to a place far off.

Being upright (ḥunafāa) | to Allah (lillahi), | not (ghayra) | associating partners (mush'rikīna) | with Him (bihi). | And whoever (waman) | associates partners (yush'rik) | with Allah (bil-lahi) | then it is as though (faka-annamā) | he had fallen (kharra) | from (mina) | the sky (l-samāi) | and had snatched him (fatakhṭafuhu) | the birds (l-ṭayru), | or (aw) | had blown (tahwī) | him (bihi) | the wind (l-rīḥu) | to (fī) | a place (makānin) | far off (saḥīqin).

22:32 That, and whoever honors the Symbols of Allah then indeed, it is from the piety of the hearts.

That (dhālika), | and whoever (waman) | honors (yuʿaẓẓim) | the Symbols (shaʿāira) | of Allah (l-lahi) | then indeed, it (fa-innahā) | is from (min) | the piety (taqwā) | of the hearts (l-qulūbi).

22:33 For you therein are benefits for a term appointed; then their place of sacrifice is at the House the Ancient.

For you (lakum) | therein (fīhā) | are benefits (manāfiʿu) | for (ilā) | a term (ajalin) | appointed (musamman); | then (thumma) | their place of sacrifice (maḥilluhā) | is at (ilā) | the House (l-bayti) | the Ancient (l-ʿatīqi).

22:34 And for every nation We have appointed a rite, that they may mention the name of Allah over what He has provided them of the beast of cattle. And your God is God One, so to Him submit. And give glad tidings to the humble ones.

And for every (walikulli) | nation (ummatin) | We have appointed (jaʿalnā) | a rite (mansakan), | that they may mention (liyadhkurū) | the name (is'ma) | of Allah (l-lahi) | over (ʿalā) | what (mā) | He has provided them (razaqahum) | of (min) | the beast (bahīmati) | of cattle (l-anʿāmi). | And your God (fa-ilāhukum) | is God (ilāhun) | One (wāḥidun), | so to Him (falahu) | submit (aslimū). | And give glad tidings (wabashiri) | to the humble ones (l-mukh'bitīna).

22:35 Those when is mentioned Allah - fear their hearts, and those who are patient over whatever has afflicted them, and those who establish the prayer, and out of what We have provided them they spend.

Those (alladhīna) | when (idhā) | is mentioned (dhukira) | Allah (l-lahu)- | fear (wajilat) | their hearts (qulūbuhum), | and those who are patient (wal-ṣābirīna) | over (ʿalā) | whatever (mā) | has afflicted them (aṣābahum), | and those who establish (wal-muqīmī) | the prayer (l-ṣalati), | and out of what (wamimmā) | We have provided them (razaqnāhum) | they spend (yunfiqūna).

22:36 And the camels and cattle - We have made them for you among the Symbols of Allah, for you therein is good. So mention the name of Allah over them when lined up; and when are down their sides, then eat from them and feed the needy who do not ask and the needy who ask. Thus We have subjected them to you so that you may be grateful.

And the camels and cattle (wal-bud'na)- | We have made them (jaʿalnāhā) | for you (lakum) | among (min) | the Symbols (shaʿāiri) | of Allah (l-lahi), | for you (lakum) | therein (fīhā) | is good (khayrun). | So mention (fa-udh'kurū) | the name (is'ma) | of Allah (l-lahi) | over them (ʿalayhā) | when lined up (ṣawāffa); | and when (fa-idhā) | are down (wajabat) | their sides (junūbuhā), | then eat (fakulū) | from them (min'hā) | and feed (wa-aṭʿimū) | the needy who do not ask (l-qāniʿa) | and the needy who ask (wal-muʿ'tara). | Thus (kadhālika) | We have subjected them (sakharnāhā) | to you (lakum) | so that you may (laʿallakum) | be grateful (tashkurūna).

22:37 Will not reach Allah their meat and not their blood but reaches Him the piety from you. Thus He subjected them to you so that you may magnify Allah for what He has guided you. And give glad tidings to the good-doers.

Will not (lan) | reach (yanāla) | Allah (l-laha) | their meat (luḥūmuhā) | and not (walā) | their blood (dimāuhā) | but (walākin) | reaches Him (yanāluhu) | the piety (l-taqwā) | from you (minkum). | Thus (kadhālika) | He subjected them (sakharahā) | to you (lakum) | so that you may magnify (litukabbirū) | Allah (l-laha) | for (ʿalā) | what (mā) | He has guided you (hadākum). | And give glad tidings (wabashiri) | to the good-doers (l-muḥ'sinīna).

22:38 Indeed, Allah defends those who believe. Indeed, Allah does not like every treacherous ungrateful.

Indeed (inna), | Allah (l-laha) | defends (yudāfiʿu) | defends (ʿani) | those who (alladhīna) | believe (āmanū). | Indeed (inna), | Allah (l-laha) | does not (lā) | like (yuḥibbu) | every (kulla) | treacherous (khawwānin) | ungrateful (kafūrin).

22:39 Permission is given to those who are being fought because they were wronged. And indeed, Allah for their victory is surely Able.

Permission is given (udhina) | to those who (lilladhīna) | are being fought (yuqātalūna) | because they (bi-annahum) | were wronged (ẓulimū). | And indeed (wa-inna), | Allah (l-laha) | for (ʿalā) | their victory (naṣrihim) | is surely Able (laqadīrun).

22:40 Those who have been evicted from their homes without right except that they said, "Our Lord is Allah." And if not Allah checks the people, some of them by others surely would have been demolished monasteries and churches and synagogues and masajid - is mentioned in it the name of Allah much. And surely Allah will help those who help Him. Indeed, Allah is surely All-Strong, All-Mighty.

Those who (alladhīna) | have been evicted (ukh'rijū) | from (min) | their homes (diyārihim) | without (bighayri) | right (ḥaqqin) | except (illā) | that (an) | they said (yaqūlū), | "Our Lord (rabbunā) | is Allah. (l-lahu)" | And if not (walawlā) | Allah checks (dafʿu) | Allah checks (l-lahi) | the people (l-nāsa), | some of them (baʿḍahum) | by others (bibaʿḍin) | surely would have been demolished (lahuddimat) | monasteries (ṣawāmiʿu) | and churches (wabiyaʿun) | and synagogues (waṣalawātun) | and masajid (wamasājidu)- | is mentioned (yudh'karu) | in it (fīhā) | the name of Allah (us'mu) | the name of Allah (l-lahi) | much (kathīran). | And surely Allah will help (walayanṣuranna) | And surely Allah will help (l-lahu) | those who (man) | help Him (yanṣuruhu). | Indeed (inna), | Allah (l-laha) | is surely All-Strong (laqawiyyun), | All-Mighty (ʿazīzun).

22:41 Those who, if We establish them in the land they establish the prayer and they give zakah and they enjoin the right and forbid from the wrong. And for Allah is the end of the matters.

Those who (alladhīna), | if (in) | We establish them (makkannāhum) | in (fī) | the land (l-arḍi) | they establish (aqāmū) | the prayer (l-ṣalata) | and they give (waātawū) | zakah (l-zakata) | and they enjoin (wa-amarū) | the right (bil-maʿrūfi) | and forbid (wanahaw) | from (ʿani) | the wrong (l-munkari). | And for Allah (walillahi) | is the end (ʿāqibatu) | of the matters (l-umūri).

22:42 And if they deny you, so verily denied before them the people of Nuh and Aad and Thamud,
And if (wa-in) | they deny you (yukadhibūka), | so verily (faqad) | denied (kadhabat) | before them (qablahum) | the people (qawmu) | of Nuh (nūḥin) | and Aad (waʿādun) | and Thamud (wathamūdu),

22:43 And the people of Ibrahim, and the people of Lut
And the people (waqawmu) | of Ibrahim (ib'rāhīma), | and the people (waqawmu) | of Lut (lūṭin)

22:44 And the inhabitants of Madyan. And Musa was denied, so I granted respite to the disbelievers, then I seized them, and how was My punishment.
And the inhabitants (wa-aṣḥābu) | of Madyan (madyana). | And Musa was denied (wakudhiba), | And Musa was denied (mūsā), | so I granted respite (fa-amlaytu) | to the disbelievers (lil'kāfirīna), | then (thumma) | I seized them (akhadhtuhum), | and how (fakayfa) | was (kāna) | My punishment (nakīri).

22:45 And how many of a township We have destroyed it, while it was doing wrong, so it fell on its roofs, and well abandoned, and castle lofty.
And how many (faka-ayyin) | of (min) | a township (qaryatin) | We have destroyed it (ahlaknāhā), | while it (wahiya) | was doing wrong (ẓālimatun), | so it (fahiya) | fell (khāwiyatun) | on (ʿalā) | its roofs (ʿurūshihā), | and well (wabi'rin) | abandoned (muʿaṭṭalatin), | and castle (waqaṣrin) | lofty (mashīdin).

22:46 So have not they traveled in the land and is for them hearts to reason with it or ears to hear with it? For indeed, [it] not are blinded the eyes but are blinded the hearts which are in the breasts.
So have not (afalam) | they traveled (yasīrū) | in (fī) | the land (l-arḍi) | and is (fatakūna) | for them (lahum) | hearts (qulūbun) | to reason (yaʿqilūna) | with it (bihā) | or (aw) | ears (ādhānun) | to hear (yasmaʿūna) | with it (bihā)? | For indeed, [it] (fa-innahā) | not (lā) | are blinded (taʿmā) | the eyes (l-abṣāru) | but (walākin) | are blinded (taʿmā) | the hearts (l-qulūbu) | which (allatī) | are in (fī) | the breasts (l-ṣudūri).

22:47 And they ask you to hasten the punishment. But never will Allah fail in His Promise. And indeed, a day with your Lord is like a thousand years of what you count.
And they ask you to hasten (wayastaʿjilūnaka) | the punishment (bil-ʿadhābi). | But never will (walan) | Allah fail (yukh'lifa) | Allah fail (l-lahu) | in His Promise (waʿdahu). | And indeed (wa-inna), | a day (yawman) | with (ʿinda) | your Lord (rabbika) | is like a thousand (ka-alfi) | years (sanatin) | of what (mimmā) | you count (taʿuddūna).

22:48 And how many of a township I gave respite to it, while it was doing wrong. Then I seized it and to Me is the destination.
And how many (waka-ayyin) | of (min) | a township (qaryatin) | I gave respite (amlaytu) | to it (lahā), | while it (wahiya) | was doing wrong (ẓālimatun). | Then (thumma) | I seized it (akhadhtuhā) | and to Me (wa-ilayya) | is the destination (l-maṣīru).

22:49 Say, "O mankind! Only I am to you a warner clear."
Say (qul), | "O mankind (yāayyuhā)! | "O mankind (l-nāsu)! | Only (innamā) | I am (anā) | to you (lakum) | a warner (nadhīrun) | clear. (mubīnun)"

22:50 So those who believe and do righteous deeds - for them is forgiveness and a provision noble.
So those who (fa-alladhīna) | believe (āmanū) | and do (waʿamilū) | righteous deeds (l-ṣāliḥāti)- | for them (lahum) | is forgiveness (maghfiratun) | and a provision (wariz'qun) | noble (karīmun).

22:51 And those who strove against Our Verses, to cause failure, those are the companions of the Hellfire.

And those who (wa-alladhīna) | strove (saʿaw) | against (fī) | Our Verses (āyātinā), | to cause failure (muʿājizīna), | those (ulāika) | are the companions (aṣḥābu) | of the Hellfire (l-jaḥīmi).

22:52 And not We sent before you any Messenger and not a Prophet but when he recited, threw the Shaitaan in his recitation. But Allah abolishes what throws the Shaitaan, then Allah will establish His Verses. And Allah is All-Knower, All-Wise.

And not (wamā) | We sent (arsalnā) | before you (min) | before you (qablika) | any (min) | Messenger (rasūlin) | and not (walā) | a Prophet (nabiyyin) | but (illā) | when (idhā) | he recited (tamannā), | threw (alqā) | the Shaitaan (l-shayṭānu) | in (fī) | his recitation (um'niyyatihi). | But Allah abolishes (fayansakhu) | But Allah abolishes (l-lahu) | what (mā) | throws (yul'qī) | the Shaitaan (l-shayṭānu), | then (thumma) | Allah will establish (yuḥ'kimu) | Allah will establish (l-lahu) | His Verses (āyātihi). | And Allah (wal-lahu) | is All-Knower (ʿalīmun), | All-Wise (ḥakīmun).

22:53 That He may make what the Shaitaan throws a trial for those in their hearts is a disease, and are hardened their hearts. And indeed, the wrongdoers are surely, in schism far.

That He may make (liyajʿala) | what (mā) | the Shaitaan throws (yul'qī) | the Shaitaan throws (l-shayṭānu) | a trial (fit'natan) | for those (lilladhīna) | in (fī) | their hearts (qulūbihim) | is a disease (maraḍun), | and are hardened (wal-qāsiyati) | their hearts (qulūbuhum). | And indeed (wa-inna), | the wrongdoers (l-ẓālimīna) | are surely, in (lafī) | schism (shiqāqin) | far (baʿīdin).

22:54 And that may know those who have been given the knowledge that it is the truth from your Lord, and they believe in it, and may humbly submit to it their hearts. And indeed, Allah is surely (the) Guide of those who believe, to a Path Straight.

And that may know (waliyaʿlama) | those who (alladhīna) | have been given (ūtū) | the knowledge (l-ʿil'ma) | that it (annahu) | is the truth (l-ḥaqu) | from (min) | your Lord (rabbika), | and they believe (fayu'minū) | in it (bihi), | and may humbly submit (fatukh'bita) | to it (lahu) | their hearts (qulūbuhum). | And indeed (wa-inna), | Allah (l-laha) | is surely (the) Guide (lahādi) | of those who (alladhīna) | believe (āmanū), | to (ilā) | a Path (ṣirāṭin) | Straight (mus'taqīmin).

22:55 And not will cease those who disbelieve to be in doubt of it until comes to them the Hour suddenly or comes to them the punishment of a Day barren.

And not (walā) | will cease (yazālu) | those who (alladhīna) | disbelieve (kafarū) | to be in (fī) | doubt (mir'yatin) | of it (min'hu) | until (ḥattā) | comes to them (tatiyahumu) | the Hour (l-sāʿatu) | suddenly (baghtatan) | or (aw) | comes to them (yatiyahum) | the punishment (ʿadhābu) | of a Day (yawmin) | barren (ʿaqīmin).

22:56 The Sovereignty on that Day will be for Allah, He will judge between them. So those who believe and did righteous deeds will be in Gardens of Delight.

The Sovereignty (al-mul'ku) | on that Day (yawma-idhin) | will be for Allah (lillahi), | He will judge (yaḥkumu) | between them (baynahum). | So those who (fa-alladhīna) | believe (āmanū) | and did (waʿamilū) | righteous deeds (l-ṣāliḥāti) | will be in (fī) | Gardens (jannāti) | of Delight (l-naʿīmi).

22:57 And those who disbelieved and denied Our Verses, then those for them will be a punishment humiliating.

And those who (wa-alladhīna) | disbelieved (kafarū) | and denied (wakadhabū) | Our Verses (biāyātinā), | then those (fa-ulāika) | for them (lahum) | will be a punishment (ʿadhābun) | humiliating (muhīnun).

22:58 And those who emigrated in the way of Allah then were killed or died, surely, Allah will provide them a provision good. And indeed Allah, surely, He is the Best of the Providers.

And those who (wa-alladhīna) | emigrated (hājarū) | in (fī) | the way (sabīli) | of Allah (l-lahi) | then (thumma) | were killed (qutilū) | or (aw) | died (mātū), | surely, Allah will provide them (layarzuqannahumu) | surely, Allah will provide them (l-lahu) | a provision (riz'qan) | good (ḥasanan). | And indeed (wa-inna) | Allah (l-laha), | surely, He (lahuwa) | is the Best (khayru) | of the Providers (l-rāziqīna).

22:59 Surely, He will admit them to an entrance they will be pleased with it. And indeed, Allah surely, is All-Knowing, Most Forbearing.

Surely, He will admit them (layud'khilannahum) | to an entrance (mud'khalan) | they will be pleased with it (yarḍawnahu). | And indeed (wa-inna), | Allah (l-laha) | surely, is All-Knowing (laʿalīmun), | Most Forbearing (ḥalīmun).

22:60 That, and whoever has retaliated, with the like of that he was made to suffer by it, then he was oppressed [on him], Allah will surely help him. Indeed, Allah is surely Oft-Pardoning, Oft-Forgiving.

That (dhālika), | and whoever (waman) | has retaliated (ʿāqaba), | with the like (bimith'li) | of that (mā) | he was made to suffer (ʿūqiba) | by it (bihi), | then (thumma) | he was oppressed (bughiya) | [on him] (ʿalayhi), | Allah will surely help him (layanṣurannahu). | Allah will surely help him (l-lahu). | Indeed (inna), | Allah (l-laha) | is surely Oft-Pardoning (laʿafuwwun), | Oft-Forgiving (ghafūrun).

22:61 That, is because Allah causes to enter the night in to the day, and causes to enter the day in to the night. And indeed, Allah is All-Hearer, All-Seer.

That (dhālika), | is because (bi-anna) | Allah (l-laha) | causes to enter (yūliju) | the night (al-layla) | in to (fī) | the day (l-nahāri), | and causes to enter (wayūliju) | the day (l-nahāra) | in to (fī) | the night (al-layli). | And indeed (wa-anna), | Allah (l-laha) | is All-Hearer (samīʿun), | All-Seer (baṣīrun).

22:62 That is, because Allah, He is the Truth, and that what they invoke besides Him, it is the falsehood. And that Allah, He is the Most High, the Most Great.

That is (dhālika), | because (bi-anna) | Allah (l-laha), | He (huwa) | is the Truth (l-ḥaqu), | and that (wa-anna) | what (mā) | they invoke (yadʿūna) | besides Him (min), | besides Him (dūnihi), | it (huwa) | is the falsehood (l-bāṭilu). | And that (wa-anna) | Allah (l-laha), | He (huwa) | is the Most High (l-ʿaliyu), | the Most Great (l-kabīru).

22:63 Do not you see, that Allah sends down from the sky water then becomes the earth green? Indeed, Allah is surely Subtle, All-Aware.

Do not (alam) | you see (tara), | that (anna) | Allah (l-laha) | sends down (anzala) | from (mina) | the sky (l-samāi) | water (māan) | then becomes (fatuṣ'biḥu) | the earth (l-arḍu) | green (mukh'ḍarratan)? | Indeed (inna), | Allah (l-laha) | is surely Subtle (laṭīfun), | All-Aware (khabīrun).

22:64 For Him is whatever is in the heavens and whatever is in the earth. And indeed, Allah surely, He is Free of need, the Praiseworthy.

For Him (lahu) | is whatever (mā) | is in (fī) | the heavens (l-samāwāti) | and whatever (wamā) | is in (fī) | the earth (l-arḍi). | And indeed (wa-inna), | Allah (l-laha) | surely, He (lahuwa) | is Free of need (l-ghaniyu), | the Praiseworthy (l-ḥamīdu).

22:65 Do not you see that Allah has subjected to you what is in the earth, and the ships that sail through the sea by His Command? And He withholds the sky lest it falls on the earth except by His permission. Indeed, Allah to mankind is Full of Kindness, Most Merciful.

Do not (alam) | you see (tara) | that (anna) | Allah (l-laha) | has subjected (sakhara) | to you (lakum) | what (mā) | is in (fī) | the earth (l-arḍi), | and the ships (wal-ful'ka) | that sail (tajrī) | through (fī) | the sea (l-baḥri) | by His Command (bi-amrihi)? | And He withholds (wayum'siku) | the sky (l-samāa) | lest (an) | it falls (taqaʿa) | on (ʿalā) | the earth (l-arḍi) | except (illā) | by His permission (bi-idh'nihi). | Indeed (inna), | Allah (l-laha) | to mankind (bil-nāsi) | is Full of Kindness (laraūfun), | Most Merciful (raḥīmun).

22:66 And He is the One Who gave you life then He will cause you to die then He will give you life again. Indeed, man is surely ungrateful.

And He (wahuwa) | is the One Who (alladhī) | gave you life (aḥyākum) | then (thumma) | He will cause you to die (yumītukum) | then (thumma) | He will give you life again (yuḥ'yīkum). | Indeed (inna), | man (l-insāna) | is surely ungrateful (lakafūrun).

22:67 For every nation We have made rites, they perform it. So let them not dispute with you in the matter, but invite them to your Lord. Indeed, you are surely on guidance straight.

For every (likulli) | nation (ummatin) | We have made (jaʿalnā) | rites (mansakan), | they (hum) | perform it (nāsikūhu). | So let them not dispute with you (falā) | So let them not dispute with you (yunāziʿunnaka) | in (fī) | the matter (l-amri), | but invite them (wa-ud'ʿu) | to (ilā) | your Lord (rabbika). | Indeed, you (innaka) | are surely on (laʿalā) | guidance (hudan) | straight (mus'taqīmin).

22:68 And if they argue with you then say, "Allah is most knowing of what you do.

And if (wa-in) | they argue with you (jādalūka) | then say (faquli), | "Allah (l-lahu) | is most knowing (aʿlamu) | of what (bimā) | you do (taʿmalūna).

22:69 Allah will judge between you on the Day of the Resurrection, concerning what you used to in it differ."

Allah (al-lahu) | will judge (yaḥkumu) | between you (baynakum) | on the Day (yawma) | of the Resurrection (l-qiyāmati), | concerning what (fīmā) | you used to (kuntum) | in it (fīhi) | differ. (takhtalifūna)"

22:70 Do not you know that Allah knows what is in the heaven and the earth? Indeed, that is in a Record, indeed, that is for Allah easy.

Do not (alam) | you know (taʿlam) | that (anna) | Allah (l-laha) | knows (yaʿlamu) | what (mā) | is in (fī) | the heaven (l-samāi) | and the earth (wal-arḍi)? | Indeed (inna), | that (dhālika) | is in (fī) | a Record (kitābin), | indeed (inna), | that (dhālika) | is for (ʿalā) | Allah (l-lahi) | easy (yasīrun).

22:71 And they worship besides Allah what not He has sent down for it any authority, and what not they have of it any knowledge. And not will be for the wrongdoers any helper.

And they worship (wayaʿbudūna) | besides Allah (min) | besides Allah (dūni) | besides Allah (l-lahi) | what (mā) | not (lam) | He has sent down (yunazzil) | for it (bihi) | any authority (sul'ṭānan), | and what (wamā) | not (laysa) | they have (lahum) | of it (bihi) | any knowledge (ʿil'mun). | And not (wamā) | will be for the wrongdoers (lilẓẓālimīna) | any (min) | helper (naṣīrin).

22:72 And when are recited to them Our Verses clear, you will recognize on the faces of those who disbelieve the denial. They almost attack those who recite to them Our Verses. Say, "Then shall I inform you of worse than that? The Fire, Allah has promised it for those who disbelieve, and wretched is the destination."

And when (wa-idhā) | are recited (tut'lā) | to them (ʿalayhim) | Our Verses (āyātunā) | clear (bayyinātin), | you will recognize (taʿrifu) | on (fī) | the faces (wujūhi) | of those who (alladhīna) | disbelieve (kafarū) | the denial (l-munkara). | They almost (yakādūna) | attack (yasṭūna)

| those who (bi-alladhīna) | recite (yatlūna) | to them (ʿalayhim) | Our Verses (āyātinā). | Say (qul), | "Then shall I inform you (afa-unabbi-ukum) | of worse (bisharrin) | than (min) | that (dhālikumu)? | The Fire (l-nāru), | Allah has promised it (waʿadahā) | Allah has promised it (l-lahu) | for those who (alladhīna) | disbelieve (kafarū), | and wretched (wabi'sa) | is the destination. (l-maṣīru)"

22:73 O mankind! Is set forth an example, so listen to it. Indeed, those whom you invoke besides Allah will never create a fly even if they gathered together for it. And if snatched away from them the fly a thing not they could take it back from it. So weak are the seeker and the one who is sought.

O mankind (yāayyuhā)! | O mankind (l-nāsu)! | Is set forth (ḍuriba) | an example (mathalun), | so listen (fa-is'tamiʿū) | to it (lahu). | Indeed (inna), | those whom (alladhīna) | you invoke (tadʿūna) | besides Allah (min) | besides Allah (dūni) | besides Allah (l-lahi) | will never (lan) | create (yakhluqū) | a fly (dhubāban) | even if (walawi) | they gathered together (ij'tamaʿū) | for it (lahu). | And if (wa-in) | snatched away from them (yaslub'humu) | the fly (l-dhubābu) | a thing (shayan) | not (lā) | they could take it back (yastanqidhūhu) | from it (min'hu). | So weak (ḍaʿufa) | are the seeker (l-ṭālibu) | and the one who is sought (wal-maṭlūbu).

22:74 Not they have estimated Allah with due [His] estimation. Indeed, Allah is surely All-Strong, All-Mighty.

Not (mā) | they have estimated (qadarū) | Allah (l-laha) | with due (ḥaqqa) | [His] estimation (qadrihi). | Indeed (inna), | Allah (l-laha) | is surely All-Strong (laqawiyyun), | All-Mighty (ʿazīzun).

22:75 Allah chooses from the Angels Messengers, and from the mankind. Indeed, Allah is All-Hearer, All-Seer.

Allah (al-lahu) | chooses (yaṣṭafī) | from (mina) | the Angels (l-malāikati) | Messengers (rusulan), | and from (wamina) | the mankind (l-nāsi). | Indeed (inna), | Allah (l-laha) | is All-Hearer (samīʿun), | All-Seer (baṣīrun).

22:76 He knows what is before them and what is after them. And to Allah return all the matters.

He knows (yaʿlamu) | what (mā) | is before them (bayna) | is before them (aydīhim) | and what (wamā) | is after them (khalfahum). | And to (wa-ilā) | Allah (l-lahi) | return (tur'jaʿu) | all the matters (l-umūru).

22:77 O you who believe! Bow and prostrate and worship your Lord and do [the] good so that you may be successful.

O you who believe (yāayyuhā)! | O you who believe (alladhīna)! | O you who believe (āmanū)! | Bow (ir'kaʿū) | and prostrate (wa-us'judū) | and worship (wa-uʿ'budū) | your Lord (rabbakum) | and do (wa-if'ʿalū) | [the] good (l-khayra) | so that you may (laʿallakum) | be successful (tuf'liḥūna).

22:78 And strive for Allah with the striving due (to) Him. He has chosen you and not placed upon you in the religion any difficulty. The religion of your father Ibrahim. He named you Muslims before and in this, that may be the Messenger a witness over you and you may be witnesses on the mankind. So establish the prayer and give zakah and hold fast to Allah. He is your Protector - so an Excellent [the] Protector and an Excellent [the] Helper.

And strive (wajāhidū) | for (fī) | Allah (l-lahi) | with the striving due (to) Him (ḥaqqa). | with the striving due (to) Him (jihādihi). | He (huwa) | has chosen you (ij'tabākum) | and not (wamā) | placed (jaʿala) | upon you (ʿalaykum) | in (fī) | the religion (l-dīni) | any (min) | difficulty (ḥarajin). | The religion (millata) | of your father (abīkum) | Ibrahim (ib'rāhīma). | He (huwa) | named you (sammākumu) | Muslims (l-mus'limīna) | before (min) | before (qablu) | and in (wafī) | this (hādhā), | that may be (liyakūna) | the Messenger (l-rasūlu) | a witness (shahīdan) | over you (ʿalaykum) | and you may be (watakūnū) | witnesses (shuhadāa) | on (ʿalā) | the mankind (l-nāsi). | So establish (fa-aqīmū) | the prayer (l-ṣalata) | and give (waātū) | zakah (l-zakata) | and hold fast (wa-iʿʿtaṣimū) | to Allah (bil-lahi). | He (huwa) | is your Protector (mawlākum)- | so an Excellent (faniʿʿma) | [the] Protector (l-mawlā) | and an Excellent (waniʿʿma) | [the] Helper (l-naṣīru).

Chapter (23) Sūrat l-Mu'minūn (The Believers)

23:1 Indeed, successful are the believers
Indeed (qad), | successful (aflaḥa) | are the believers (l-mu'minūna)

23:2 Those who [they] during their prayers are humbly submissive,
Those who (alladhīna) | [they] (hum) | during (fī) | their prayers (ṣalātihim) | are humbly submissive (khāshiʿūna),

23:3 Those who [they] from the vain talk turn away,
Those who (wa-alladhīna) | [they] (hum) | from (ʿani) | the vain talk (l-laghwi) | turn away (muʿʿriḍūna),

23:4 Those who [they] of purification works are doers,
Those who (wa-alladhīna) | [they] (hum) | of purification works (lilzzakati) | are doers (fāʿilūna),

23:5 And those who [they] of their modesty are guardians
And those who (wa-alladhīna) | [they] (hum) | of their modesty (lifurūjihim) | are guardians (ḥāfiẓūna)

23:6 Except from their spouses or what possess their right hands then indeed, they are not blameworthy.
Except (illā) | from (ʿalā) | their spouses (azwājihim) | or (aw) | what (mā) | possess (malakat) | their right hands (aymānuhum) | then indeed, they (fa-innahum) | are not (ghayru) | blameworthy (malūmīna).

23:7 Then whoever seeks beyond that then those [they] are the transgressors.
Then whoever (famani) | seeks (ib'taghā) | beyond (warāa) | that (dhālika) | then those (fa-ulāika) | [they] (humu) | are the transgressors (l-ʿādūna).

23:8 And those who [they] of their trusts and their promises are observers
And those who (wa-alladhīna) | [they] (hum) | of their trusts (li-amānātihim) | and their promises (waʿahdihim) | are observers (rāʿūna)

23:9 And those who [they] over their prayers they guard
And those who (wa-alladhīna) | [they] (hum) | over (ʿalā) | their prayers (ṣalawātihim) | they guard (yuḥāfiẓūna)

23:10 Those [they] are the inheritors

Those (ulāika) | [they] (humu) | are the inheritors (l-wārithūna)

23:11 Who will inherit the Paradise. They therein will abide forever.
Who (alladhīna) | will inherit (yarithūna) | the Paradise (l-fir'dawsa). | They (hum) | therein (fīhā) | will abide forever (khālidūna).

23:12 And indeed, We created the humankind from an essence of clay.
And indeed (walaqad), | We created (khalaqnā) | the humankind (l-insāna) | from (min) | an essence (sulālatin) | of (min) | clay (ṭīnin).

23:13 Then We placed him as a semen-drop in a resting place firm.
Then (thumma) | We placed him (jaʿalnāhu) | as a semen-drop (nuṭ'fatan) | in (fī) | a resting place (qarārin) | firm (makīnin).

23:14 Then We created the semen-drop into a clinging substance, then We created the clinging substance into an embryonic lump, then We created the embryonic lump, into bones, then We clothed the bones with flesh; then We produce it as a creation another. So blessed is Allah the Best of the Creators.
Then (thumma) | We created (khalaqnā) | the semen-drop (l-nuṭ'fata) | into a clinging substance (ʿalaqatan), | then We created (fakhalaqnā) | the clinging substance (l-ʿalaqata) | into an embryonic lump (muḍ'ghatan), | then We created (fakhalaqnā) | the embryonic lump (l-muḍ'ghata), | into bones (ʿiẓāman), | then We clothed (fakasawnā) | the bones (l-ʿiẓāma) | with flesh (laḥman); | then (thumma) | We produce it (anshanāhu) | as a creation (khalqan) | another (ākhara). | So blessed is (fatabāraka) | Allah (l-lahu) | the Best (aḥsanu) | of the Creators (l-khāliqīna).

23:15 Then indeed, you after that surely will die.
Then (thumma) | indeed, you (innakum) | after (baʿda) | that (dhālika) | surely will die (lamayyitūna).

23:16 Then indeed, you on the Day of the Resurrection, will be resurrected.
Then (thumma) | indeed, you (innakum) | on the Day (yawma) | of the Resurrection (l-qiyāmati), | will be resurrected (tub'ʿathūna).

23:17 And indeed, We have created above you seven paths and not We are of the creation unaware.
And indeed (walaqad), | We have created (khalaqnā) | above you (fawqakum) | seven (sabʿa) | paths (ṭarāiqa) | and not (wamā) | We are (kunnā) | of (ʿani) | the creation (l-khalqi) | unaware (ghāfilīna).

23:18 And We send down from the sky water, in due measure then We cause it to settle in the earth. And indeed, We, on taking it away, surely are Able.
And We send down (wa-anzalnā) | from (mina) | the sky (l-samāi) | water (māan), | in due measure (biqadarin) | then We cause it to settle (fa-askannāhu) | in (fī) | the earth (l-arḍi). | And indeed, We (wa-innā), | on (ʿalā) | taking it away (dhahābin), | taking it away (bihi), | surely are Able (laqādirūna).

23:19 Then We produced for you by it gardens of date-palms and grapevines, for you, in it are fruits abundant and from them you eat.
Then We produced (fa-anshanā) | for you (lakum) | by it (bihi) | gardens (jannātin) | of date-palms (min) | of date-palms (nakhīlin) | and grapevines (wa-aʿnābin), | for you (lakum), | in it (fīhā) | are fruits (fawākihu) | abundant (kathīratun) | and from them (wamin'hā) | you eat (takulūna).

23:20 And a tree that springs forth from Mount Sinai which produces oil and a relish for those who eat.

And a tree (washajaratan) | that springs forth (takhruju) | from (min) | Mount Sinai (ṭūri) | Mount Sinai (saynāa) | which produces (tanbutu) | oil (bil-duh'ni) | and a relish (waṣib'ghin) | for those who eat (lil'ākilīna).

23:21 And indeed, for you in the cattle surely, is a lesson. We give you drink from what is in their bellies, and for you in them are benefits many and of them you eat.

And indeed (wa-inna), | for you (lakum) | in (fī) | the cattle (l-anʿāmi) | surely, is a lesson (laʿib'ratan). | We give you drink (nus'qīkum) | from what (mimmā) | is in (fī) | their bellies (buṭūnihā), | and for you (walakum) | in them (fīhā) | are benefits (manāfiʿu) | many (kathīratun) | and of them (wamin'hā) | you eat (takulūna).

23:22 And on them and on [the] ships you are carried.

And on them (waʿalayhā) | and on (waʿalā) | [the] ships (l-ful'ki) | you are carried (tuḥ'malūna).

23:23 And verily We sent Nuh to his people, and he said, "O my people! Worship Allah; not for you is any god other than Him. Then will not you fear?"

And verily (walaqad) | We sent (arsalnā) | Nuh (nūḥan) | to (ilā) | his people (qawmihi), | and he said (faqāla), | "O my people (yāqawmi)! | Worship (uʿ'budū) | Allah (l-laha); | not (mā) | for you (lakum) | is any (min) | god (ilāhin) | other than Him (ghayruhu). | Then will not (afalā) | you fear? (tattaqūna)"

23:24 But said the chiefs of those who disbelieved among his people, "This is not but a man like you, he wishes to assert his superiority over you, and if Allah had willed surely He would have sent down Angels. Not we heard of this from our forefathers.

But said (faqāla) | the chiefs (l-mala-u) | of those who (alladhīna) | disbelieved (kafarū) | among (min) | his people (qawmihi), | "This is not (mā) | "This is not (hādhā) | but (illā) | a man (basharun) | like you (mith'lukum), | he wishes (yurīdu) | to (an) | assert his superiority (yatafaḍḍala) | over you (ʿalaykum), | and if (walaw) | Allah had willed (shāa) | Allah had willed (l-lahu) | surely He would have sent down (la-anzala) | Angels (malāikatan). | Not (mā) | we heard (samiʿ'nā) | of this (bihādhā) | from (fī) | our forefathers (ābāinā). | our forefathers (l-awalīna).

23:25 Not he is but a man in him is madness, so wait concerning him until a time."

Not (in) | he (huwa) | is but (illā) | a man (rajulun) | in him (bihi) | is madness (jinnatun), | so wait (fatarabbaṣū) | concerning him (bihi) | until (ḥattā) | a time. (ḥīnin)"

23:26 He said, "My Lord! Help me because they deny me."

He said (qāla), | "My Lord (rabbi)! | Help me (unṣur'nī) | because (bimā) | they deny me. (kadhabūni)"

23:27 So We inspired to him, "That construct the ship under Our eyes, and Our inspiration, then when comes Our Command and gushes forth the oven, then put into it of every kind of mates two and your family, except those has preceded against whom the Word thereof. And do not address Me concerning those who wronged, indeed, they are the ones to be drowned.

So We inspired (fa-awḥaynā) | to him (ilayhi), | "That (ani) | construct (iṣ'naʿi) | the ship (l-ful'ka) | under Our eyes (bi-aʿyuninā), | and Our inspiration (wawaḥyinā), | then when (fa-idhā) | comes (jāa) | Our Command (amrunā) | and gushes forth (wafāra) | the oven (l-tanūru), | then put (fa-us'luk) | into it (fīhā) | of (min) | every kind (kullin) | of mates (zawjayni) | two (ith'nayni) | and your family (wa-ahlaka), | except (illā) | those (man) | has preceded (sabaqa) | against whom

(ʿalayhi) | the Word (l-qawlu) | thereof (min'hum). | And do not (walā) | address Me (tukhāṭib'nī) | concerning (fī) | those who (alladhīna) | wronged (ẓalamū), | indeed, they (innahum) | are the ones to be drowned (mugh'raqūna).

23:28 And when you have boarded you, and whoever is with you [on] the ship then say, "Praise be to Allah, Who has saved us from the people - the wrongdoers."

And when (fa-idhā) | you have boarded (is'tawayta) | you (anta), | and whoever (waman) | is with you (maʿaka) | [on] (ʿalā) | the ship (l-ful'ki) | then say (faquli), | "Praise (l-ḥamdu) | be to Allah (lillahi), | Who (alladhī) | has saved us (najjānā) | from (mina) | the people (l-qawmi)- | the wrongdoers. (l-ẓālimīna)"

23:29 And say, "My Lord, cause me to land at a landing place blessed, and You are the Best of those who cause to land.'"

And say (waqul), | "My Lord (rabbi), | cause me to land (anzil'nī) | at a landing place (munzalan) | blessed (mubārakan), | and You (wa-anta) | are the Best (khayru) | of those who cause to land.' (l-munzilīna)"

23:30 Indeed, in that surely are Signs, and indeed, We are surely testing.

Indeed (inna), | in (fī) | that (dhālika) | surely are Signs (laāyātin), | and indeed (wa-in), | We are (kunnā) | surely testing (lamub'talīna).

23:31 Then We produced after them a generation another.

Then (thumma) | We produced (anshanā) | after them (min) | after them (baʿdihim) | a generation (qarnan) | another (ākharīna).

23:32 And We sent among them a Messenger from themselves [that] "Worship Allah; not for you is any god other than Him. Then will not you fear?"

And We sent (fa-arsalna) | among them (fīhim) | a Messenger (rasūlan) | from themselves (min'hum) | [that] (ani) | "Worship (uʿ'budū) | Allah (l-laha); | not (mā) | for you (lakum) | is any (min) | god (ilāhin) | other than Him (ghayruhu). | Then will not (afalā) | you fear? (tattaqūna)"

23:33 And said the chiefs of his people who disbelieved and denied the meeting of the Hereafter, while We had given them luxury in the life of the world, "Not is this but a man like you. He eats of what you eat [from it], and he drinks of what you drink.

And said (waqāla) | the chiefs (l-mala-u) | of (min) | his people (qawmihi) | who (alladhīna) | disbelieved (kafarū) | and denied (wakadhabū) | the meeting (biliqāi) | of the Hereafter (l-ākhirati), | while We had given them luxury (wa-atrafnāhum) | in (fī) | the life (l-ḥayati) | of the world (l-dun'yā), | "Not (mā) | is this (hādhā) | but (illā) | a man (basharun) | like you (mith'lukum). | He eats (yakulu) | of what (mimmā) | you eat (takulūna) | [from it] (min'hu), | and he drinks (wayashrabu) | of what (mimmā) | you drink (tashrabūna).

23:34 And surely if you obey a man like you, indeed, you then surely will be losers.

And surely if (wala-in) | you obey (aṭaʿtum) | a man (basharan) | like you (mith'lakum), | indeed, you (innakum) | then (idhan) | surely will be losers (lakhāsirūna).

23:35 Does he promise you - that you when you are dead and you become dust and bones that you will be brought forth?

Does he promise you (ayaʿidukum)- | that you (annakum) | when (idhā) | you are dead (mittum) | and you become (wakuntum) | dust (turāban) | and bones (waʿiẓāman) | that you (annakum) | will be brought forth (mukh'rajūna)?

23:36 Far-fetched, far-fetched is what you are promised!

Far-fetched (hayhāta), | far-fetched (hayhāta) | is what (limā) | you are promised (tūʿadūna)!

23:37 Not it is but our life of the world, we die and we live, and not we will be resurrected.
Not (in) | it (hiya) | is but (illā) | our life (ḥayātunā) | of the world (l-dun'yā), | we die (namūtu) | and we live (wanaḥyā), | and not (wamā) | we (naḥnu) | will be resurrected (bimabʿūthīna).

23:38 Not is he but a man who has invented about Allah a lie, and not we in him are believers."
Not (in) | is he (huwa) | but (illā) | a man (rajulun) | who has invented (if'tarā) | about (ʿalā) | Allah (l-lahi) | a lie (kadhiban), | and not (wamā) | we (naḥnu) | in him (lahu) | are believers. (bimu'minīna)"

23:39 He said, "My Lord! Help me because they deny me."
He said (qāla), | "My Lord (rabbi)! | Help me (unṣur'nī) | because (bimā) | they deny me. (kadhabūni)"

23:40 He said, "After a little while surely they will become regretful."
He said (qāla), | "After a little while (ʿammā) | "After a little while (qalīlin) | surely they will become (layuṣ'biḥunna) | regretful. (nādimīna)"

23:41 So seized them the awful cry in truth, and We made them as rubbish of dead leaves. So away with the people - the wrongdoers.
So seized them (fa-akhadhathumu) | the awful cry (l-ṣayḥatu) | in truth (bil-ḥaqi), | and We made them (fajaʿalnāhum) | as rubbish of dead leaves (ghuthāan). | So away (fabuʿ'dan) | with the people (lil'qawmi)- | the wrongdoers (l-ẓālimīna).

23:42 Then We produced after them a generation another.
Then (thumma) | We produced (anshanā) | after them (min) | after them (baʿdihim) | a generation (qurūnan) | another (ākharīna).

23:43 Not can precede any nation its term, and not they can delay (it).
Not (mā) | can precede (tasbiqu) | any (min) | nation (ummatin) | its term (ajalahā), | and not (wamā) | they can delay (it) (yastakhirūna).

23:44 Then We sent Our Messengers in succession. Every time came to a nation its Messenger, they denied him, so We made them follow - some of them others, and We made them narrations. So away with a people - not they believe.
Then (thumma) | We sent (arsalnā) | Our Messengers (rusulanā) | in succession (tatrā). | Every time (kulla) | Every time (mā) | came (jāa) | to a nation (ummatan) | its Messenger (rasūluhā), | they denied him (kadhabūhu), | so We made them follow (fa-atbaʿnā)- | some of them (baʿḍahum) | others (baʿḍan), | and We made them (wajaʿalnāhum) | narrations (aḥādītha). | So away (fabuʿ'dan) | with a people (liqawmin)- | not (lā) | they believe (yu'minūna).

23:45 Then We sent Musa and his brother Harun with Our Signs and an authority clear
Then (thumma) | We sent (arsalnā) | Musa (mūsā) | and his brother (wa-akhāhu) | Harun (hārūna) | with Our Signs (biāyātinā) | and an authority (wasul'ṭānin) | clear (mubīnin)

23:46 To Firaun and his chiefs, but they behaved arrogantly and they were a people haughty.
To (ilā) | Firaun (firʿ'awna) | and his chiefs (wamala-ihi), | but they behaved arrogantly (fa-is'takbarū) | and they were (wakānū) | a people (qawman) | haughty (ʿālīna).

23:47 Then they said, "Shall we believe in two men like ourselves while their people for us are slaves."

Then they said (faqālū), | "Shall we believe (anu'minu) | in two men (libasharayni) | like ourselves (mith'linā) | while their people (waqawmuhumā) | for us (lanā) | are slaves. (ʿābidūna)"

23:48 So they denied them and they became of those who were destroyed.

So they denied them (fakadhabūhumā) | and they became (fakānū) | of (mina) | those who were destroyed (l-muh'lakīna).

23:49 And verily, We gave Musa the Scripture so that they may be guided.

And verily (walaqad), | We gave (ātaynā) | Musa (mūsā) | the Scripture (l-kitāba) | so that they may (laʿallahum) | be guided (yahtadūna).

23:50 And We made the son of Maryam and his mother a Sign, and We sheltered them to a high ground, of tranquility and water springs.

And We made (wajaʿalnā) | the son (ib'na) | of Maryam (maryama) | and his mother (wa-ummahu) | a Sign (āyatan), | and We sheltered them (waāwaynāhumā) | to (ilā) | a high ground (rabwatin), | of tranquility (dhāti) | of tranquility (qarārin) | and water springs (wamaʿīnin).

23:51 O Messengers! Eat of the good things and do righteous deeds. Indeed, I Am of what you do All-Knower.

O Messengers (yāayyuhā)! | O Messengers (l-rusulu)! | Eat (kulū) | of (mina) | the good things (l-ṭayibāti) | and do (wa-iʿ'malū) | righteous deeds (ṣāliḥan). | Indeed, I Am (innī) | of what (bimā) | you do (taʿmalūna) | All-Knower (ʿalīmun).

23:52 And indeed this, your religion, is religion one. And I Am your Lord, so fear Me.

And indeed (wa-inna) | this (hādhihi), | your religion (ummatukum), | is religion (ummatan) | one (wāḥidatan). | And I Am (wa-anā) | your Lord (rabbukum), | so fear Me (fa-ittaqūni).

23:53 But they cut off their affair of unity between them into sects, each faction in what they have rejoicing.

But they cut off (fataqaṭṭaʿū) | their affair of unity (amrahum) | between them (baynahum) | into sects (zuburan), | each (kullu) | faction (ḥiz'bin) | in what (bimā) | they have (ladayhim) | rejoicing (fariḥūna).

23:54 So leave them in their confusion until a time.

So leave them (fadharhum) | in (fī) | their confusion (ghamratihim) | until (ḥattā) | a time (ḥīnin).

23:55 Do they think that what We extend to them [with it] of wealth and children

Do they think (ayaḥsabūna) | that what (annamā) | We extend to them (numidduhum) | [with it] (bihi) | of (min) | wealth (mālin) | and children (wabanīna)

23:56 We hasten to them in the good? Nay, not they perceive.

We hasten (nusāriʿu) | to them (lahum) | in (fī) | the good (l-khayrāti)? | Nay (bal), | not (lā) | they perceive (yashʿurūna).

23:57 Indeed, those who [they] from the fear of their Lord are cautious.

Indeed (inna), | those who (alladhīna) | [they] (hum) | from (min) | the fear (khashyati) | of their Lord (rabbihim) | are cautious (mush'fiqūna).

23:58 And those [they] in the Signs of their Lord believe

And those (wa-alladhīna) | [they] (hum) | in the Signs (biāyāti) | of their Lord (rabbihim) | believe (yu'minūna)

23:59 And those [they] with their Lord do not associate partners.
And those (wa-alladhīna) | [they] (hum) | with their Lord (birabbihim) | do not (lā) | associate partners (yush'rikūna).

23:60 And those who give what they give while their hearts are fearful, because they to their Lord will return
And those who (wa-alladhīna) | give (yu'tūna) | what (mā) | they give (ātaw) | while their hearts (waqulūbuhum) | are fearful (wajilatun), | because they (annahum) | to (ilā) | their Lord (rabbihim) | will return (rājiʿūna)

23:61 It is those who hasten in the good deeds and they in them are foremost.
It is those (ulāika) | who hasten (yusāriʿūna) | in (fī) | the good deeds (l-khayrāti) | and they (wahum) | in them (lahā) | are foremost (sābiqūna).

23:62 And not We burden any soul except to its capacity, and with Us is a Record which speaks with the truth; and they will not be wronged.
And not (walā) | We burden (nukallifu) | any soul (nafsan) | except (illā) | to its capacity (wus''ahā), | and with Us (waladaynā) | is a Record (kitābun) | which speaks (yanṭiqu) | with the truth (bil-ḥaqi); | and they (wahum) | will not (lā) | be wronged (yuẓ'lamūna).

23:63 Nay, their hearts are in confusion over this, and for them are deeds besides that, they for it are doers
Nay (bal), | their hearts (qulūbuhum) | are in (fī) | confusion (ghamratin) | over (min) | this (hādhā), | and for them (walahum) | are deeds (aʿmālun) | besides (min) | besides (dūni) | that (dhālika), | they (hum) | for it (lahā) | are doers (ʿāmilūna)

23:64 Until when We seize their affluent ones with the punishment, behold! They cry for help.
Until (ḥattā) | when (idhā) | We seize (akhadhnā) | their affluent ones (mut'rafīhim) | with the punishment (bil-ʿadhābi), | behold (idhā)! | They (hum) | cry for help (yajarūna).

23:65 "Do not cry for help today. Indeed, you from Us not will be helped.
"Do not (lā) | cry for help (tajarū) | today (l-yawma). | Indeed, you (innakum) | from Us (minnā) | not (lā) | will be helped (tunṣarūna).

23:66 Verily, were My Verses recited to you, but you used to on your heels turn back
Verily (qad), | were (kānat) | My Verses (āyātī) | recited (tut'lā) | to you (ʿalaykum), | but you used (fakuntum) | to on (ʿalā) | your heels (aʿqābikum) | turn back (tankiṣūna)

23:67 Being arrogant about it, conversing by night, speaking evil."
Being arrogant (mus'takbirīna) | about it (bihi), | conversing by night (sāmiran), | speaking evil. (tahjurūna)"

23:68 Then, do not they ponder the Word or has come to them what not had come to their forefathers?
Then, do not (afalam) | they ponder (yaddabbarū) | the Word (l-qawla) | or (am) | has come to them (jāahum) | what (mā) | not (lam) | had come (yati) | to their forefathers (ābāahumu)? | to their forefathers (l-awalīna)?

23:69 Or do not they recognize their Messenger, so they are rejecting him?

Or (am) | do not (lam) | they recognize (yaʿrifū) | their Messenger (rasūlahum), | so they (fahum) | are rejecting him (lahu)? | are rejecting him (munkirūna)?

23:70 Or they say, "In him is madness?" Nay, he brought them the truth, but most of them to the truth, are averse.

Or (am) | they say (yaqūlūna), | "In him (bihi) | is madness? (jinnatun)" | Nay (bal), | he brought them (jāahum) | the truth (bil-ḥaqi), | but most of them (wa-aktharuhum) | to the truth (lil'ḥaqqi), | are averse (kārihūna).

23:71 But if had followed the truth their desires, surely would have been corrupted the heavens and the earth and whoever is therein. Nay, We have brought them their reminder, but they, from their reminder, are turning away.

But if (walawi) | had followed (ittabaʿa) | the truth (l-ḥaqu) | their desires (ahwāahum), | surely would have been corrupted (lafasadati) | the heavens (l-samāwātu) | and the earth (wal-arḍu) | and whoever (waman) | is therein (fīhinna). | Nay (bal), | We have brought them (ataynāhum) | their reminder (bidhik'rihim), | but they (fahum), | from (ʿan) | their reminder (dhik'rihim), | are turning away (muʿ'riḍūna).

23:72 Or you ask them for a payment? But the payment of your Lord is best, and He is the Best of the Providers.

Or (am) | you ask them (tasaluhum) | for a payment (kharjan)? | But the payment (fakharāju) | of your Lord (rabbika) | is best (khayrun), | and He (wahuwa) | is the Best (khayru) | of the Providers (l-rāziqīna).

23:73 And indeed, you certainly call them to the Path Straight.

And indeed, you (wa-innaka) | certainly call them (latadʿūhum) | to (ilā) | the Path (ṣirāṭin) | Straight (mus'taqīmin).

23:74 And indeed, those who do not believe in the Hereafter from the path surely are deviating.

And indeed (wa-inna), | those who (alladhīna) | do not (lā) | believe (yu'minūna) | in the Hereafter (bil-ākhirati) | from (ʿani) | the path (l-ṣirāṭi) | surely are deviating (lanākibūna).

23:75 And if We had mercy on them and We removed what was on them of the hardship, surely they would persist in their transgression wandering blindly.

And if (walaw) | We had mercy on them (raḥim'nāhum) | and We removed (wakashafnā) | what (mā) | was on them (bihim) | of (min) | the hardship (ḍurrin), | surely they would persist (lalajjū) | in (fī) | their transgression (ṭugh'yānihim) | wandering blindly (yaʿmahūna).

23:76 And verily We seized them with the punishment but not they submit to their Lord and not they supplicate humbly

And verily (walaqad) | We seized them (akhadhnāhum) | with the punishment (bil-ʿadhābi) | but not (famā) | they submit (is'takānū) | to their Lord (lirabbihim) | and not (wamā) | they supplicate humbly (yataḍarraʿūna)

23:77 Until when We opened for them a gate of a punishment severe, behold! They in it will be in despair.

Until (ḥattā) | when (idhā) | We opened (fataḥnā) | for them (ʿalayhim) | a gate (bāban) | of a punishment (dhā) | of a punishment (ʿadhābin) | severe (shadīdin), | behold (idhā)! | They (hum) | in it (fīhi) | will be in despair (mub'lisūna).

23:78 And He is the One Who produced for you the hearing and the sight and the feeling; little is what you give thanks.

And He (wahuwa) | is the One Who (alladhī) | produced (ansha-a) | for you (lakumu) | the hearing (l-samʿa) | and the sight (wal-abṣāra) | and the feeling (wal-afidata); | little (qalīlan) | is what (mā) | you give thanks (tashkurūna).

23:79 And He is the One Who multiplied you in the earth and to Him you will be gathered.
And He (wahuwa) | is the One Who (alladhī) | multiplied you (dhara-akum) | in (fī) | the earth (l-arḍi) | and to Him (wa-ilayhi) | you will be gathered (tuḥ'sharūna).

23:80 And He is the One Who gives life and causes death and for Him is the alternation of the night and the day. Then will not you reason?
And He (wahuwa) | is the One Who (alladhī) | gives life (yuḥ'yī) | and causes death (wayumītu) | and for Him (walahu) | is the alternation (ikh'tilāfu) | of the night (al-layli) | and the day (wal-nahāri). | Then will not (afalā) | you reason (taʿqilūna)?

23:81 Nay, they say the like of what said the former people.
Nay (bal), | they say (qālū) | the like (mith'la) | of what (mā) | said (qāla) | the former people (l-awalūna).

23:82 They said, "What! When we are dead and become dust and bones, would we surely be resurrected?
They said (qālū), | "What! When (a-idhā) | we are dead (mit'nā) | and become (wakunnā) | dust (turāban) | and bones (waʿiẓāman), | would we (a-innā) | surely be resurrected (lamabʿūthūna)?

23:83 Verily, we have been promised [we] and our forefathers this before; not is this but the tales of the former (people)."
Verily (laqad), | we have been promised (wuʿid'nā) | [we] (naḥnu) | and our forefathers (waābāunā) | this (hādhā) | before (min); | before (qablu); | not (in) | is this (hādhā) | but (illā) | the tales (asāṭīru) | of the former (people). (l-awalīna)"

23:84 Say, "To whom belongs the earth and whoever is in it, if you know?"
Say (qul), | "To whom belongs (limani) | the earth (l-arḍu) | and whoever (waman) | is in it (fīhā), | if (in) | you (kuntum) | know? (taʿlamūna)"

23:85 They will say, "To Allah." Say, "Then will not you remember?"
They will say (sayaqūlūna), | "To Allah. (lillahi)" | Say (qul), | "Then will not (afalā) | you remember? (tadhakkarūna)"

23:86 Say, "Who is the Lord of the seven heavens and the Lord of the Throne the Great?"
Say (qul), | "Who (man) | is the Lord (rabbu) | of the seven heavens (l-samāwāti) | of the seven heavens (l-sabʿi) | and the Lord (warabbu) | of the Throne (l-ʿarshi) | the Great? (l-ʿaẓīmi)"

23:87 They will say, "Allah." Say, "Then will not you fear Him?"
They will say (sayaqūlūna), | "Allah. (lillahi)" | Say (qul), | "Then will not (afalā) | you fear Him? (tattaqūna)"

23:88 Say, Who is it in Whose Hands is the dominion of all things, and He protects and no one can be protected against Him, If you know?"
Say (qul), | Who is it (man) | in Whose Hands (biyadihi) | is the dominion (malakūtu) | of all (kulli) | things (shayin), | and He (wahuwa) | protects (yujīru) | and no one (walā) | can be protected (yujāru) | against Him (ʿalayhi), | If (in) | you (kuntum) | know? (taʿlamūna)"

23:89 They will say, "Allah." Say, "Then how are you deluded?"
They will say (sayaqūlūna), | "Allah. (lillahi)" | Say (qul), | "Then how (fa-annā) | are you deluded? (tus'ḥarūna)"

23:90 Nay, We have brought them the truth, but indeed, they surely, are liars.
Nay (bal), | We have brought them (ataynāhum) | the truth (bil-ḥaqi), | but indeed, they (wa-innahum) | surely, are liars (lakādhibūna).

23:91 Not Allah has taken any son, and not is with Him any god. Then surely would have taken away each god what he created, and surely would have overpowered, some of them [on] others. Glory be to Allah above what they attribute!
Not (mā) | Allah has taken (ittakhadha) | Allah has taken (l-lahu) | any (min) | son (waladin), | and not (wamā) | is (kāna) | with Him (maʿahu) | any (min) | god (ilāhin). | Then (idhan) | surely would have taken away (ladhahaba) | each (kullu) | god (ilāhin) | what (bimā) | he created (khalaqa), | and surely would have overpowered (walaʿalā), | some of them (baʿḍuhum) | [on] (ʿalā) | others (baʿḍin). | Glory be (sub'ḥāna) | to Allah (l-lahi) | above what (ʿammā) | they attribute (yaṣifūna)!

23:92 Knower of the unseen and the witnessed, exalted is He above what they associate.
Knower (ʿālimi) | of the unseen (l-ghaybi) | and the witnessed (wal-shahādati), | exalted is He (fataʿālā) | above what (ʿammā) | they associate (yush'rikūna).

23:93 Say, "My Lord! If You should show me what they are promised
Say (qul), | "My Lord (rabbi)! | If (immā) | You should show me (turiyannī) | what (mā) | they are promised (yūʿadūna)

23:94 My Lord, then do not place me among the people - the wrongdoers."
My Lord (rabbi), | then do not (falā) | place me (tajʿalnī) | among (fī) | the people (l-qawmi)- | the wrongdoers. (l-ẓālimīna)"

23:95 And indeed We on that We show you what We have promised them surely able.
And indeed We (wa-innā) | on (ʿalā) | that (an) | We show you (nuriyaka) | what (mā) | We have promised them (naʿiduhum) | surely able (laqādirūna).

23:96 Repel by that which is best - the evil. We know best of what they attribute.
Repel (id'faʿ) | by that (bi-allatī) | which (hiya) | is best (aḥsanu)- | the evil (l-sayi-ata). | We (naḥnu) | know best (aʿlamu) | of what (bimā) | they attribute (yaṣifūna).

23:97 And say, "My Lord! I seek refuge in You from the suggestions of the evil ones,
And say (waqul), | "My Lord (rabbi)! | I seek refuge (aʿūdhu) | in You (bika) | from (min) | the suggestions (hamazāti) | of the evil ones (l-shayāṭīni),

23:98 And I seek refuge in You, My Lord! Lest they be present with me."
And I seek refuge (wa-aʿūdhu) | in You (bika), | My Lord (rabbi)! | Lest (an) | they be present with me. (yaḥḍurūni)"

23:99 Until when comes to one of them the death he says, "My Lord! Send me back
Until (ḥattā) | when (idhā) | comes (jāa) | to one of them (aḥadahumu) | the death (l-mawtu) | he says (qāla), | "My Lord (rabbi)! | Send me back (ir'jiʿūni)

23:100 That I may do righteous deeds in what I left behind." No! Indeed, it is a word he speaks it, and before them is a barrier till the Day they are resurrected.

That I may (laʿallī) | do (aʿmalu) | righteous deeds (ṣāliḥan) | in what (fīmā) | I left behind. (taraktu)" | No (kallā)! | Indeed, it (innahā) | is a word (kalimatun) | he (huwa) | speaks it (qāiluhā), | and before them (wamin) | and before them (warāihim) | is a barrier (barzakhun) | till (ilā) | the Day (yawmi) | they are resurrected (yubʿathūna).

23:101 So when is blown in the trumpet then not there will be relationship among them that Day, and not will they ask each other.

So when (fa-idhā) | is blown (nufikha) | in (fī) | the trumpet (l-ṣūri) | then not (falā) | there will be relationship (ansāba) | among them (baynahum) | that Day (yawma-idhin), | and not (walā) | will they ask each other (yatasāalūna).

23:102 Then the one whose are heavy his scales, then those - they are the successful.

Then the one whose (faman) | are heavy (thaqulat) | his scales (mawāzīnuhu), | then those (fa-ulāika)- | they (humu) | are the successful (l-muf'liḥūna).

23:103 But the one whose are light his scales, then those they [who] have lost their souls, in Hell they will abide forever.

But the one whose (waman) | are light (khaffat) | his scales (mawāzīnuhu), | then those (fa-ulāika) | they [who] (alladhīna) | have lost (khasirū) | their souls (anfusahum), | in (fī) | Hell (jahannama) | they will abide forever (khālidūna).

23:104 Will burn their faces the Fire, and they in it will grin with displaced lips.

Will burn (talfaḥu) | their faces (wujūhahumu) | the Fire (l-nāru), | and they (wahum) | in it (fīhā) | will grin with displaced lips (kāliḥūna).

23:105 "Were not My Verses recited to you, and you used to deny them?"

"Were not (alam) | "Were not (takun) | My Verses (āyātī) | recited (tut'lā) | to you (ʿalaykum), | and you used to (fakuntum) | deny them? (bihā)" | deny them? (tukadhibūna)"

23:106 They will say, "Our Lord! Overcame [on] us our wretchedness, and we were a people astray.

They will say (qālū), | "Our Lord (rabbanā)! | Overcame (ghalabat) | [on] us (ʿalaynā) | our wretchedness (shiq'watunā), | and we were (wakunnā) | a people (qawman) | astray (ḍāllīna).

23:107 Our Lord! Bring us out from it, then if we return then indeed, we would be wrongdoers."

Our Lord (rabbanā)! | Bring us out (akhrij'nā) | from it (min'hā), | then if (fa-in) | we return (ʿud'nā) | then indeed, we (fa-innā) | would be wrongdoers. (ẓālimūna)"

23:108 He will say, "Remain despised in it and do not speak to Me."

He will say (qāla), | "Remain despised (ikh'saū) | in it (fīhā) | and do not (walā) | speak to Me. (tukallimūni)"

23:109 Indeed, there was a party of My slaves who said, "Our Lord! We believe, so forgive us and have mercy on us, and You are best of those who show mercy."

Indeed (innahu), | there was (kāna) | a party (farīqun) | of (min) | My slaves (ʿibādī) | who said (yaqūlūna), | "Our Lord (rabbanā)! | We believe (āmannā), | so forgive (fa-igh'fir) | us (lanā) | and have mercy on us (wa-ir'ḥamnā), | and You (wa-anta) | are best (khayru) | of those who show mercy. (l-rāḥimīna)"

23:110 But you took them in mockery until they made you forget My remembrance, and you used to at them laugh.

But you took them (fa-ittakhadhtumūhum) | in mockery (sikh'riyyan) | until (ḥattā) | they made you forget (ansawkum) | My remembrance (dhik'rī), | and you used to (wakuntum) | at them (min'hum) | laugh (taḍḥakūna).

23:111 Indeed, I have rewarded them this Day because they were patient, indeed, they [they] are the successful ones.

Indeed, I (innī) | have rewarded them (jazaytuhumu) | this Day (l-yawma) | because (bimā) | they were patient (ṣabarū), | indeed, they (annahum) | [they] (humu) | are the successful ones (l-fāizūna).

23:112 He will say, "How long did you remain in the earth, in number of years?"

He will say (qāla), | "How long (kam) | did you remain (labith'tum) | in (fī) | the earth (l-arḍi), | in number (ʿadada) | of years? (sinīna)"

23:113 They will say, "We remained a day or a part of a day; but ask those who keep count."

They will say (qālū), | "We remained (labith'nā) | a day (yawman) | or (aw) | a part (baʿḍa) | of a day (yawmin); | but ask (fasali) | those who keep count. (l-ʿādīna)"

23:114 He will say, "Not you stayed but a little, if only you [you] knew.

He will say (qāla), | "Not (in) | you stayed (labith'tum) | but (illā) | a little (qalīlan), | if (law) | only you (annakum) | [you] (kuntum) | knew (taʿlamūna).

23:115 Then did you think that We created you uselessly and that you to Us not will be returned?"

Then did you think (afaḥasib'tum) | that (annamā) | We created you (khalaqnākum) | uselessly (ʿabathan) | and that you (wa-annakum) | to Us (ilaynā) | not (lā) | will be returned? (tur'jaʿūna)"

23:116 So exalted is Allah, the King, the Truth. There is no god except Him, the Lord of the Throne Honorable.

So exalted is (fataʿālā) | Allah (l-lahu), | the King (l-maliku), | the Truth (l-ḥaqu). | There is no (lā) | god (ilāha) | except (illā) | Him (huwa), | the Lord (rabbu) | of the Throne (l-ʿarshi) | Honorable (l-karīmi).

23:117 And whoever invokes with Allah god other, no proof for him in it. Then only his account is with his Lord. Indeed, [he] not will succeed the disbelievers.

And whoever (waman) | invokes (yadʿu) | with (maʿa) | Allah (l-lahi) | god (ilāhan) | other (ākhara), | no (lā) | proof (bur'hāna) | for him (lahu) | in it (bihi). | Then only (fa-innamā) | his account (ḥisābuhu) | is with (ʿinda) | his Lord (rabbihi). | Indeed, [he] (innahu) | not (lā) | will succeed (yuf'liḥu) | the disbelievers (l-kāfirūna).

23:118 And say, "My Lord! Forgive and have mercy, and You are the Best of those who show mercy."

And say (waqul), | "My Lord (rabbi)! | Forgive (igh'fir) | and have mercy (wa-ir'ḥam), | and You (wa-anta) | are the Best (khayru) | of those who show mercy. (l-rāḥimīna)"

Chapter (24) Sūrat l-Nūr (The Light)

24:1 A Surah - We have sent it down and We have made it obligatory, and We have revealed therein Verses clear, so that you may take heed.

A Surah (sūratun)- | We have sent it down (anzalnāhā) | and We have made it obligatory (wafaraḍnāhā), | and We have revealed (wa-anzalnā) | therein (fīhā) | Verses (āyātin) | clear (bayyinātin), | so that you may (laʿallakum) | take heed (tadhakkarūna).

24:2 The fornicatress and the fornicator, [then] flog each one of them with hundred lashes. And let not withhold you pity for them concerning the religion of Allah, if you believe in Allah and the Day the Last. And let witness their punishment a group of the believers.

The fornicatress (al-zāniyatu) | and the fornicator (wal-zānī), | [then] flog (fa-ij'lidū) | each (kulla) | one (wāḥidin) | of them (min'humā) | with hundred (mi-ata) | lashes (jaldatin). | And let not (walā) | withhold you (takhudh'kum) | pity for them (bihimā) | pity for them (rafatun) | concerning (fī) | the religion of Allah (dīni), | the religion of Allah (l-lahi), | if (in) | you (kuntum) | believe (tu'minūna) | in Allah (bil-lahi) | and the Day (wal-yawmi) | the Last (l-ākhiri). | And let witness (walyashhad) | their punishment (ʿadhābahumā) | a group (ṭāifatun) | of (mina) | the believers (l-mu'minīna).

24:3 The fornicator will not marry except a fornicatress, or a polytheist woman, and the fornicatress - will not marry her except a fornicator or a polytheist man. And is forbidden that to the believers.

The fornicator (al-zānī) | will not (lā) | marry (yankiḥu) | except (illā) | a fornicatress (zāniyatan), | or (aw) | a polytheist woman (mush'rikatan), | and the fornicatress (wal-zāniyatu)- | will not (lā) | marry her (yankiḥuhā) | except (illā) | a fornicator (zānin) | or (aw) | a polytheist man (mush'rikun). | And is forbidden (waḥurrima) | that (dhālika) | to (ʿalā) | the believers (l-mu'minīna).

24:4 And those who accuse the chaste women, then not they bring four witnesses, then flog them with eighty lashes and do not accept their testimony ever. And those, they are the defiantly disobedient,

And those who (wa-alladhīna) | accuse (yarmūna) | the chaste women (l-muḥ'ṣanāti), | then (thumma) | not (lam) | they bring (yatū) | four (bi-arbaʿati) | witnesses (shuhadāa), | then flog them (fa-ij'lidūhum) | with eighty (thamānīna) | lashes (jaldatan) | and do not (walā) | accept (taqbalū) | their (lahum) | testimony (shahādatan) | ever (abadan). | And those (wa-ulāika), | they (humu) | are the defiantly disobedient (l-fāsiqūna),

24:5 Except those who repent after that and reform. Then indeed, Allah is Oft-Forgiving, Most Merciful.

Except (illā) | those who (alladhīna) | repent (tābū) | after (min) | after (baʿdi) | that (dhālika) | and reform (wa-aṣlaḥū). | Then indeed (fa-inna), | Allah (l-laha) | is Oft-Forgiving (ghafūrun), | Most Merciful (raḥīmun).

24:6 And those who accuse their spouses and not have for them witnesses except themselves, then the testimony of one of them is four testimonies by Allah, that he is surely of the truthful.

And those who (wa-alladhīna) | accuse (yarmūna) | their spouses (azwājahum) | and not (walam) | have (yakun) | for them (lahum) | witnesses (shuhadāu) | except (illā) | themselves (anfusuhum), | then the testimony (fashahādatu) | of one of them (aḥadihim) | is four (arbaʿu) | testimonies (shahādātin) | by Allah (bil-lahi), | that he (innahu) | is surely of (lamina) | the truthful (l-ṣādiqīna).

24:7 And the fifth that the curse of Allah be upon him if he is of the liars.

And the fifth (wal-khāmisatu) | that (anna) | the curse of Allah (laʿnata) | the curse of Allah (l-lahi) | be upon him (ʿalayhi) | if (in) | he is (kāna) | of (mina) | the liars (l-kādhibīna).

24:8 But it would prevent from her the punishment that she bears witness four testimonies by Allah that he is surely of the liars.

But it would prevent (wayadra-u) | from her (ʿanhā) | the punishment (l-ʿadhāba) | that (an) | she bears witness (tashhada) | four (arbaʿa) | testimonies (shahādātin) | by Allah (bil-lahi) | that he (innahu) | is surely of (lamina) | the liars (l-kādhibīna).

24:9 And the fifth, that the wrath of Allah be upon her if he is of the truthful.

And the fifth (wal-khāmisata), | that (anna) | the wrath of Allah (ghaḍaba) | the wrath of Allah (l-lahi) | be upon her (ʿalayhā) | if (in) | he is (kāna) | of (mina) | the truthful (l-ṣādiqīna).

24:10 And if not for the Grace of Allah upon you and His Mercy - and that, Allah is Oft-Returning (to Mercy), All-Wise.

And if not (walawlā) | for the Grace of Allah (faḍlu) | for the Grace of Allah (l-lahi) | upon you (ʿalaykum) | and His Mercy (waraḥmatuhu)- | and that (wa-anna), | Allah (l-laha) | is Oft-Returning (to Mercy) (tawwābun), | All-Wise (ḥakīmun).

24:11 Indeed, those who brought the lie are a group among you. Do not think it bad for you; nay, it is good for you. For every person among them is what he earned of the sin, and the one who took upon himself a greater share of it among them - for him is a punishment great.

Indeed (inna), | those who (alladhīna) | brought (jāū) | the lie (bil-if'ki) | are a group (ʿuṣ'batun) | among you (minkum). | Do not (lā) | think it (taḥsabūhu) | bad (sharran) | for you (lakum); | nay (bal), | it (huwa) | is good (khayrun) | for you (lakum). | For every (likulli) | person (im'ri-in) | among them (min'hum) | is what (mā) | he earned (ik'tasaba) | of (mina) | the sin (l-ith'mi), | and the one who (wa-alladhī) | took upon himself a greater share of it (tawallā) | took upon himself a greater share of it (kib'rahu) | among them (min'hum)- | for him (lahu) | is a punishment (ʿadhābun) | great (ʿaẓīmun).

24:12 Why not, when you heard it, think the believing men and the believing women good of themselves and say, "This is a lie clear?"

Why not (lawlā), | when (idh) | you heard it (samiʿ'tumūhu), | think (ẓanna) | the believing men (l-mu'minūna) | and the believing women (wal-mu'minātu) | good of themselves (bi-anfusihim) | good of themselves (khayran) | and say (waqālū), | "This (hādhā) | is a lie (if'kun) | clear? (mubīnun)"

24:13 Why did not they bring for it four witnesses? Then when not they brought the witnesses, then those near Allah, they are the liars.

Why did not (lawlā) | they bring (jāū) | for it (ʿalayhi) | four (bi-arbaʿati) | witnesses (shuhadāa)? | Then when (fa-idh) | not (lam) | they brought (yatū) | the witnesses (bil-shuhadāi), | then those (fa-ulāika) | near Allah (ʿinda), | near Allah (l-lahi), | they (humu) | are the liars (l-kādhibūna).

24:14 And if not for the Grace of Allah upon you and His Mercy in the world and the Hereafter, surely would have touched you in what you had rushed glibly concerning it a punishment great.

And if not (walawlā) | for the Grace (faḍlu) | of Allah (l-lahi) | upon you (ʿalaykum) | and His Mercy (waraḥmatuhu) | in (fī) | the world (l-dun'yā) | and the Hereafter (wal-ākhirati), | surely would have touched you (lamassakum) | in (fī) | what (mā) | you had rushed glibly (afaḍtum) | concerning it (fīhi) | a punishment (ʿadhābun) | great (ʿaẓīmun).

24:15 When you received it with your tongues and you said with your mouths what not for you of it any knowledge, and you thought it was insignificant, while it was near Allah great.

When (idh) | you received it (talaqqawnahu) | with your tongues (bi-alsinatikum) | and you said (wataqūlūna) | with your mouths (bi-afwāhikum) | what (mā) | not (laysa) | for you (lakum) | of it (bihi) | any knowledge (ʿil'mun), | and you thought it (wataḥsabūnahu) | was insignificant (hayyinan), | while it (wahuwa) | was near Allah (ʿinda) | was near Allah (l-lahi) | great (ʿaẓīmun).

24:16 And why not, when you heard it, you said, "Not it is for us that we speak of this. Glory be to You! This is a slander great?"

And why not (walawlā), | when (idh) | you heard it (samiʿ'tumūhu), | you said (qul'tum), | "Not (mā) | it is (yakūnu) | for us (lanā) | that (an) | we speak (natakallama) | of this (bihādhā). | Glory be to You (sub'ḥānaka)! | This (hādhā) | is a slander (buh'tānun) | great? (ʿaẓīmun)"

24:17 Allah warns you that you return to the like of it ever, if you are believers.

Allah warns you (yaʿiẓukumu) | Allah warns you (l-lahu) | that (an) | you return (taʿūdū) | to the like of it (limith'lihi) | ever (abadan), | if (in) | you are (kuntum) | believers (mu'minīna).

24:18 And Allah makes clear to you the Verses. And Allah is All-Knower, All-Wise.

And Allah makes clear (wayubayyinu) | And Allah makes clear (l-lahu) | to you (lakumu) | the Verses (l-āyāti). | And Allah (wal-lahu) | is All-Knower (ʿalīmun), | All-Wise (ḥakīmun).

24:19 Indeed, those who like that should spread the immorality among those who believe, for them is a punishment painful in the world and the Hereafter. And Allah knows, while you do not know.

Indeed (inna), | those who (alladhīna) | like (yuḥibbūna) | that (an) | should spread (tashīʿa) | the immorality (l-fāḥishatu) | among (fī) | those who (alladhīna) | believe (āmanū), | for them (lahum) | is a punishment (ʿadhābun) | painful (alīmun) | in (fī) | the world (l-dun'yā) | and the Hereafter (wal-ākhirati). | And Allah (wal-lahu) | knows (yaʿlamu), | while you (wa-antum) | do not (lā) | know (taʿlamūna).

24:20 And if not for the Grace of Allah upon you and His Mercy. And that Allah is Full of Kindness, Most Merciful.

And if not (walawlā) | for the Grace of Allah (faḍlu) | for the Grace of Allah (l-lahi) | upon you (ʿalaykum) | and His Mercy (waraḥmatuhu). | And that (wa-anna) | Allah (l-laha) | is Full of Kindness (raūfun), | Most Merciful (raḥīmun).

24:21 O you who believe! Do not follow the footsteps of the Shaitaan, and whoever follows the footsteps of the Shaitaan then indeed, he commands the immorality and the evil. And if not for the Grace of Allah upon you and His Mercy not would have been pure among you anyone ever, but Allah purifies whom He wills. And Allah is All-Hearer, All-Knower.

O you who believe (yāayyuhā)! | O you who believe (alladhīna)! | O you who believe (āmanū)! | Do not (lā) | follow (tattabiʿū) | the footsteps (khuṭuwāti) | of the Shaitaan (l-shayṭāni), | and whoever (waman) | follows (yattabiʿ) | the footsteps (khuṭuwāti) | of the Shaitaan (l-shayṭāni) | then indeed, he (fa-innahu) | commands (yamuru) | the immorality (bil-faḥshāi) | and the evil (wal-munkari). | And if not (walawlā) | for the Grace of Allah (faḍlu) | for the Grace of Allah (l-lahi) | upon you (ʿalaykum) | and His Mercy (waraḥmatuhu) | not (mā) | would have been pure (zakā) | among you (minkum) | anyone (min) | anyone (aḥadin) | ever (abadan), | but (walākinna) | Allah (l-laha) | purifies (yuzakkī) | whom (man) | He wills (yashāu). | And Allah (wal-lahu) | is All-Hearer (samīʿun), | All-Knower (ʿalīmun).

24:22 And not let swear those of virtue among you and the amplitude of means that they give to the near of kin, and the needy and the emigrants in the way of Allah. And let them pardon and let them overlook. Do not you like that Allah should forgive you? And Allah is Oft-Forgiving, Most Merciful.

And not (walā) | let swear (yatali) | those of virtue (ulū) | those of virtue (l-faḍli) | among you (minkum) | and the amplitude of means (wal-saʿati) | that (an) | they give (yu'tū) | to the near of kin (ulī), | to the near of kin (l-qur'bā), | and the needy (wal-masākīna) | and the emigrants (wal-muhājirīna) | in (fī) | the way (sabīli) | of Allah (l-lahi). | And let them pardon (walyaʿfū) | and let them overlook (walyaṣfaḥū). | Do not (alā) | you like (tuḥibbūna) | that (an) | Allah should forgive (yaghfira) | Allah should forgive (l-lahu) | you (lakum)? | And Allah (wal-lahu) | is Oft-Forgiving (ghafūrun), | Most Merciful (raḥīmun).

24:23 Indeed, those who accuse the chaste women, the unaware women and the believing women, are cursed in the world and the Hereafter. And for them is a punishment great.

Indeed (inna), | those who (alladhīna) | accuse (yarmūna) | the chaste women (l-muḥ'ṣanāti), | the unaware women (l-ghāfilāti) | and the believing women (l-mu'mināti), | are cursed (luʿinū) | in (fī) | the world (l-dun'yā) | and the Hereafter (wal-ākhirati). | And for them (walahum) | is a punishment (ʿadhābun) | great (ʿaẓīmun).

24:24 On a Day, will bear witness against them their tongues, and their hands and their feet for what they used to do.

On a Day (yawma), | will bear witness (tashhadu) | against them (ʿalayhim) | their tongues (alsinatuhum), | and their hands (wa-aydīhim) | and their feet (wa-arjuluhum) | for what (bimā) | they used (kānū) | to do (yaʿmalūna).

24:25 That Day, Allah will pay them in full their recompense, the due, and they will know that Allah, He is the Truth the Manifest.

That Day (yawma-idhin), | Allah will pay them in full (yuwaffīhimu) | Allah will pay them in full (l-lahu) | their recompense (dīnahumu), | the due (l-ḥaqa), | and they will know (wayaʿlamūna) | that (anna) | Allah (l-laha), | He (huwa) | is the Truth (l-ḥaqu) | the Manifest (l-mubīnu).

24:26 Evil women are for evil men, and evil men are for evil women. And good women are for good men and good men are for good women. Those are innocent of what they say. For them is forgiveness and a provision noble.

Evil women (al-khabīthātu) | are for evil men (lil'khabīthīna), | and evil men (wal-khabīthūna) | are for evil women (lil'khabīthāti). | And good women (wal-ṭayibātu) | are for good men (lilṭṭayyibīna) | and good men (wal-ṭayibūna) | are for good women (lilṭṭayyibāti). | Those (ulāika) | are innocent (mubarraūna) | of what (mimmā) | they say (yaqūlūna). | For them (lahum) | is forgiveness (maghfiratun) | and a provision (wariz'qun) | noble (karīmun).

24:27 O you who believe! Do not enter houses other than your houses until you have asked permission and you have greeted [on] its inhabitants. That is best for you so that you may pay heed.

O you (yāayyuhā) | who (alladhīna) | believe (āmanū)! | Do not (lā) | enter (tadkhulū) | houses (buyūtan) | other than (ghayra) | your houses (buyūtikum) | until (ḥattā) | you have asked permission (tastanisū) | and you have greeted (watusallimū) | [on] (ʿalā) | its inhabitants (ahlihā). | That (dhālikum) | is best (khayrun) | for you (lakum) | so that you may (laʿallakum) | pay heed (tadhakkarūna).

24:28 But if not you find in it anyone, then do not enter it until permission has been given to you. And if it is said to you "Go back," then go back; it is purer for you. And Allah of what you do is All-Knower.

But if (fa-in) | not (lam) | you find (tajidū) | in it (fīhā) | anyone (aḥadan), | then do not (falā) | enter it (tadkhulūhā) | until (ḥattā) | permission has been given (yu'dhana) | to you (lakum). | And if (wa-in) | it is said (qīla) | to you (lakumu) | "Go back, (ir'jiʿū)" | then go back (fa-ir'jiʿū); | it (huwa) | is purer (azkā) | for you (lakum). | And Allah (wal-lahu) | of what (bimā) | you do (taʿmalūna) | is All-Knower (ʿalīmun).

24:29 Not upon you is any blame that you enter houses not inhabited, in it is a provision for you. And Allah knows what you reveal and what you conceal.

Not (laysa) | upon you (ʿalaykum) | is any blame (junāḥun) | that (an) | you enter (tadkhulū) | houses (buyūtan) | not (ghayra) | inhabited (maskūnatin), | in it (fīhā) | is a provision (matāʿun) | for you (lakum). | And Allah (wal-lahu) | knows (yaʿlamu) | what (mā) | you reveal (tub'dūna) | and what (wamā) | you conceal (taktumūna).

24:30 Say to the believing men they should lower their gaze and they should guard their chastity. That is purer for them. Indeed, Allah is All-Aware of what they do.

Say (qul) | to the believing men (lil'mu'minīna) | they should lower (yaghuḍḍū) | their gaze (min) | their gaze (abṣārihim) | and they should guard (wayaḥfaẓū) | their chastity (furūjahum). | That (dhālika) | is purer (azkā) | for them (lahum). | Indeed (inna), | Allah (l-laha) | is All-Aware (khabīrun) | of what (bimā) | they do (yaṣnaʿūna).

24:31 And say to the believing women that they should lower [of] their gaze and they should guard their chastity, and not to display their adornment except what is apparent of it. And let them draw their head covers over their bosoms, and not to display their adornment except to their husbands, or their fathers or fathers of their husbands or their sons or sons of their husbands or their brothers or sons of their brothers or sons of their sisters, or their women or what possess their right hands or the attendants having no physical desire among [the] men or [the] children who are not aware of private aspects of the women. And not let them stamp their feet to make known what they conceal of their adornment. And turn to Allah altogether O believers! So that you may succeed.

And say (waqul) | to the believing women (lil'mu'mināti) | that they should lower (yaghḍuḍ'na) | [of] (min) | their gaze (abṣārihinna) | and they should guard (wayaḥfaẓna) | their chastity (furūjahunna), | and not (walā) | to display (yub'dīna) | their adornment (zīnatahunna) | except (illā) | what (mā) | is apparent (ẓahara) | of it (min'hā). | And let them draw (walyaḍrib'na) | their head covers (bikhumurihinna) | over (ʿalā) | their bosoms (juyūbihinna), | and not (walā) | to display (yub'dīna) | their adornment (zīnatahunna) | except (illā) | to their husbands (libuʿūlatihinna), | or (aw) | their fathers (ābāihinna) | or (aw) | fathers (ābāi) | of their husbands (buʿūlatihinna) | or (aw) | their sons (abnāihinna) | or (aw) | sons (abnāi) | of their husbands (buʿūlatihinna) | or (aw) | their brothers (ikh'wānihinna) | or (aw) | sons (banī) | of their brothers (ikh'wānihinna) | or (aw) | sons (banī) | of their sisters (akhawātihinna), | or (aw) | their women (nisāihinna) | or (aw) | what (mā) | possess (malakat) | their right hands (aymānuhunna) | or (awi) | the attendants (l-tābiʿīna) | having no physical desire (ghayri) | having no physical desire (ulī) | having no physical desire (l-ir'bati) | among (mina) | [the] men (l-rijāli) | or (awi) | [the] children (l-ṭif'li) | who (alladhīna) | are not (lam) | aware (yaẓharū) | of (ʿalā) | private aspects (ʿawrāti) | of the women (l-nisāi). | And not (walā) | let them stamp (yaḍrib'na) | their feet (bi-arjulihinna) | to make known (liyuʿ'lama) | what (mā) | they conceal (yukh'fīna) | of (min) | their adornment (zīnatihinna). | And turn (watūbū) | to (ilā) | Allah (l-lahi) | altogether (jamīʿan) | O believers (ayyuha)! | O believers (l-mu'minūna)! | So that you may (laʿallakum) | succeed (tuf'liḥūna).

24:32 And marry the single among you and the righteous among your male slaves, and your female slaves. If they are poor, Allah will enrich them from His Bounty. And Allah is All-Encompassing, All-Knowing.

And marry (wa-ankiḥū) | the single (l-ayāmā) | among you (minkum) | and the righteous (wal-ṣāliḥīna) | among (min) | your male slaves (ʿibādikum), | and your female slaves (wa-imāikum). | If (in) | they are (yakūnū) | poor (fuqarāa), | Allah will enrich them (yugh'nihimu) | Allah will enrich them (l-lahu) | from (min) | His Bounty (faḍlihi). | And Allah (wal-lahu) | is All-Encompassing (wāsiʿun), | All-Knowing (ʿalīmun).

24:33 And let be chaste those who do not find means for marriage until Allah enriches them from

His Bounty. And those who seek the writing from those whom possess your right hands, then give them the writing if you know in them any good and give them from the wealth of Allah which He has given you. And do not compel your slave girls to [the] prostitution, if they desire chastity that you may seek temporary gain of the life of the world. And whoever compels them, then indeed, Allah after their compulsion is Oft-Forgiving, Most Merciful.

And let be chaste (walyastaʿfifi) | those who (alladhīna) | do not (lā) | find (yajidūna) | means for marriage (nikāḥan) | until (ḥattā) | Allah enriches them (yugh'niyahumu) | Allah enriches them (l-lahu) | from (min) | His Bounty (faḍlihi). | And those who (wa-alladhīna) | seek (yabtaghūna) | the writing (l-kitāba) | from those whom (mimmā) | possess (malakat) | your right hands (aymānukum), | then give them the writing (fakātibūhum) | if (in) | you know (ʿalim'tum) | in them (fīhim) | any good (khayran) | and give them (waātūhum) | from (min) | the wealth of Allah (māli) | the wealth of Allah (l-lahi) | which (alladhī) | He has given you (ātākum). | And do not (walā) | compel (tuk'rihū) | your slave girls (fatayātikum) | to (ʿalā) | [the] prostitution (l-bighāi), | if (in) | they desire (aradna) | chastity (taḥaṣṣunan) | that you may seek (litabtaghū) | temporary gain (ʿaraḍa) | of the life (l-ḥayati) | of the world (l-dun'yā). | And whoever (waman) | compels them (yuk'rihhunna), | then indeed (fa-inna), | Allah (l-laha) | after (min) | after (baʿdi) | their compulsion (ik'rāhihinna) | is Oft-Forgiving (ghafūrun), | Most Merciful (raḥīmun).

24:34 And verily, We have sent down to you Verses clear, and an example of those who passed away before you, and an admonition for those who fear Allah.

And verily (walaqad), | We have sent down (anzalnā) | to you (ilaykum) | Verses (āyātin) | clear (mubayyinātin), | and an example (wamathalan) | of (mina) | those who (alladhīna) | passed away (khalaw) | before you (min), | before you (qablikum), | and an admonition (wamawʿiẓatan) | for those who fear Allah (lil'muttaqīna).

24:35 Allah is the Light of the heavens and the earth. The example of His Light is like a niche in it is a lamp; the lamp is in a glass, the glass as if it were a star brilliant which is lit from a tree blessed - an olive, not of the east and not of the west, would almost its oil glow, even if not touched it fire. Light upon Light. Allah guides to His Light whom He wills. And Allah sets forth the examples for the mankind. And Allah of every thing is All-Knower.

Allah (al-lahu) | is the Light (nūru) | of the heavens (l-samāwāti) | and the earth (wal-arḍi). | The example (mathalu) | of His Light (nūrihi) | is like a niche (kamish'katin) | in it (fīhā) | is a lamp (miṣ'bāḥun); | the lamp (l-miṣ'bāḥu) | is in (fī) | a glass (zujājatin), | the glass (l-zujājatu) | as if it were (ka-annahā) | a star (kawkabun) | brilliant (durriyyun) | which is lit (yūqadu) | from (min) | a tree (shajaratin) | blessed (mubārakatin)- | an olive (zaytūnatin), | not (lā) | of the east (sharqiyyatin) | and not (walā) | of the west (gharbiyyatin), | would almost (yakādu) | its oil (zaytuhā) | glow (yuḍīu), | even if (walaw) | not (lam) | touched it (tamsashu) | fire (nārun). | Light (nūrun) | upon (ʿalā) | Light (nūrin). | Allah guides (yahdī) | Allah guides (l-lahu) | to His Light (linūrihi) | whom (man) | He wills (yashāu). | And Allah sets forth (wayaḍribu) | And Allah sets forth (l-lahu) | the examples (l-amthāla) | for the mankind (lilnnāsi). | And Allah (wal-lahu) | of every (bikulli) | thing (shayin) | is All-Knower (ʿalīmun).

24:36 In houses which Allah ordered that they be raised and be mentioned in them His name. Glorify [to] Him in them in the mornings and in the evenings.

In (fī) | houses (buyūtin) | which Allah ordered (adhina) | which Allah ordered (l-lahu) | that (an) | they be raised (tur'faʿa) | and be mentioned (wayudh'kara) | in them (fīhā) | His name (us'muhu). | Glorify (yusabbiḥu) | [to] Him (lahu) | in them (fīhā) | in the mornings (bil-ghuduwi) | and in the evenings (wal-āṣāli).

24:37 Men - not distracts them trade and not sale from the remembrance of Allah and from establishing the prayer and giving zakah. They fear a Day will turn about therein the hearts and the eyes.

Men (rijālun)- | not (lā) | distracts them (tul'hīhim) | trade (tijāratun) | and not (walā) | sale (bayʿun) | from (ʿan) | the remembrance of Allah (dhik'ri) | the remembrance of Allah (l-lahi) | and from establishing (wa-iqāmi) | the prayer (l-ṣalati) | and giving (waītāi) | zakah (l-zakati). | They fear (yakhāfūna) | a Day (yawman) | will turn about (tataqallabu) | therein (fīhi) | the hearts (l-qulūbu) | and the eyes (wal-abṣāru).

24:38 That Allah may reward them with the best of what they did, and increase them from His Bounty. And Allah provides whom He wills without measure.

That Allah may reward them (liyajziyahumu) | That Allah may reward them (l-lahu) | with the best (aḥsana) | of what (mā) | they did (ʿamilū), | and increase them (wayazīdahum) | from (min) | His Bounty (faḍlihi). | And Allah (wal-lahu) | provides (yarzuqu) | whom (man) | He wills (yashāu) | without (bighayri) | measure (ḥisābin).

24:39 But those who disbelieve, their deeds are like a mirage in a lowland, thinks it the thirsty one to be water, until when he comes to it, not he finds it to be anything, but he finds Allah before him, He will pay him in full his due. And Allah is swift in the account.

But those who (wa-alladhīna) | disbelieve (kafarū), | their deeds (aʿmāluhum) | are like a mirage (kasarābin) | in a lowland (biqīʿatin), | thinks it (yaḥsabuhu) | the thirsty one (l-ẓamānu) | to be water (māan), | until (ḥattā) | when (idhā) | he comes to it (jāahu), | not (lam) | he finds it (yajid'hu) | to be anything (shayan), | but he finds (wawajada) | Allah (l-laha) | before him (ʿindahu), | He will pay him in full (fawaffāhu) | his due (ḥisābahu). | And Allah (wal-lahu) | is swift (sarīʿu) | in the account (l-ḥisābi).

24:40 Or is like (the) darkness[es] in a sea deep, covers it a wave, on it a wave, on it a cloud, darkness[es] some of it on others. When he puts out his hand hardly he can see it. And for whom not Allah has made for him a light, then not for him is any light.

Or (aw) | is like (the) darkness[es] (kaẓulumātin) | in (fī) | a sea (baḥrin) | deep (lujjiyyin), | covers it (yaghshāhu) | a wave (mawjun), | on it (min) | on it (fawqihi) | a wave (mawjun), | on it (min) | on it (fawqihi) | a cloud (saḥābun), | darkness[es] (ẓulumātun) | some of it (baʿḍuhā) | on (fawqa) | others (baʿḍin). | When (idhā) | he puts out (akhraja) | his hand (yadahu) | hardly (lam) | hardly (yakad) | he can see it (yarāhā). | And for whom (waman) | not (lam) | Allah has made (yajʿali) | Allah has made (l-lahu) | for him (lahu) | a light (nūran), | then not (famā) | for him (lahu) | is any (min) | light (nūrin).

24:41 Do not you see that Allah - glorify Him whoever is in the heavens and the earth and the birds with wings outspread? Each one verily knows its prayer and its glorification. And Allah is All-Knower of what they do.

Do not (alam) | you see (tara) | that (anna) | Allah (l-laha)- | glorify (yusabbiḥu) | Him (lahu) | whoever (man) | is in (fī) | the heavens (l-samāwāti) | and the earth (wal-arḍi) | and the birds (wal-ṭayru) | with wings outspread (ṣāffātin)? | Each one (kullun) | verily (qad) | knows (ʿalima) | its prayer (ṣalātahu) | and its glorification (watasbīḥahu). | And Allah (wal-lahu) | is All-Knower (ʿalīmun) | of what (bimā) | they do (yafʿalūna).

24:42 And to Allah belongs the dominion of the heavens and the earth. And to Allah is the destination.

And to Allah belongs (walillahi) | the dominion (mul'ku) | of the heavens (l-samāwāti) | and the earth (wal-arḍi). | And to (wa-ilā) | Allah (l-lahi) | is the destination (l-maṣīru).

24:43 Do not you see that Allah drives clouds then joins between them then makes them into a mass, then you see the rain come forth from their midst? And He sends down from the sky, [from] mountains within it [of] is hail and He strikes with it whom He wills and averts it from whom He wills. Nearly the flash of its lighting takes away the sight.

Do not (alam) | you see (tara) | that (anna) | Allah (l-laha) | drives (yuz'jī) | clouds (saḥāban) | then (thumma) | joins (yu-allifu) | between them (baynahu) | then (thumma) | makes them (yajʿaluhu) | into a mass (rukāman), | then you see (fatarā) | the rain (l-wadqa) | come forth (yakhruju) | from (min) | their midst (khilālihi)? | And He sends down (wayunazzilu) | from (mina) | the sky (l-samāi), | [from] (min) | mountains (jibālin) | within it (fīhā) | [of] (min) | is hail (baradin) | and He strikes (fayuṣību) | with it (bihi) | whom (man) | He wills (yashāu) | and averts it (wayaṣrifuhu) | from (ʿan) | whom (man) | He wills (yashāu). | Nearly (yakādu) | the flash (sanā) | of its lighting (barqihi) | takes away (yadhhabu) | the sight (bil-abṣāri).

24:44 Allah alternates the night and the day. Indeed, in that surely is a lesson for those who have vision.

Allah alternates (yuqallibu) | Allah alternates (l-lahu) | the night (al-layla) | and the day (wal-nahāra). | Indeed (inna), | in (fī) | that (dhālika) | surely is a lesson (laʿib'ratan) | for those who have vision (li-ulī). | for those who have vision (l-abṣāri).

24:45 And Allah created every moving creature from water. Of them is a kind who walks on its belly, and of them is a kind who walks on two legs, and of them is a kind who walks on four. Allah creates what He wills. Indeed, Allah on every thing is All-Powerful.

And Allah (wal-lahu) | created (khalaqa) | every (kulla) | moving creature (dābbatin) | from (min) | water (māin). | Of them (famin'hum) | is a kind who (man) | walks (yamshī) | on (ʿalā) | its belly (baṭnihi), | and of them (wamin'hum) | is a kind who (man) | walks (yamshī) | on (ʿalā) | two legs (rij'layni), | and of them (wamin'hum) | is a kind who (man) | walks (yamshī) | on (ʿalā) | four (arbaʿin). | Allah creates (yakhluqu) | Allah creates (l-lahu) | what (mā) | He wills (yashāu). | Indeed (inna), | Allah (l-laha) | on (ʿalā) | every (kulli) | thing (shayin) | is All-Powerful (qadīrun).

24:46 Verily, We have sent down Verses clear. And Allah guides whom He wills to a path straight.

Verily (laqad), | We have sent down (anzalnā) | Verses (āyātin) | clear (mubayyinātin). | And Allah (wal-lahu) | guides (yahdī) | whom (man) | He wills (yashāu) | to (ilā) | a path (ṣirāṭin) | straight (mus'taqīmin).

24:47 And they say, "We believe in Allah and in the Messenger and we obey." Then turns away a party of them after that. And not those are believers.

And they say (wayaqūlūna), | "We believe (āmannā) | in Allah (bil-lahi) | and in the Messenger (wabil-rasūli) | and we obey. (wa-aṭaʿnā)" | Then (thumma) | turns away (yatawallā) | a party (farīqun) | of them (min'hum) | after (min) | after (baʿdi) | that (dhālika). | And not (wamā) | those (ulāika) | are believers (bil-mu'minīna).

24:48 And when they are called to Allah and His Messenger, to judge between them, behold, a party of them is averse.

And when (wa-idhā) | they are called (duʿū) | to (ilā) | Allah (l-lahi) | and His Messenger (warasūlihi), | to judge (liyaḥkuma) | between them (baynahum), | behold (idhā), | a party (farīqun) | of them (min'hum) | is averse (muʿ'riḍūna).

24:49 But if is with them the truth, they come to him as promptly obedient.

But if (wa-in) | is (yakun) | with them (lahumu) | the truth (l-ḥaqu), | they come (yatū) | to him (ilayhi) | as promptly obedient (mudh'ʿinīna).

24:50 Is there in their hearts a disease or do they doubt or they fear that Allah will be unjust to them and His Messenger? Nay, those [they] are the wrongdoers.

Is there in (afī) | their hearts (qulūbihim) | a disease (maraḍun) | or (ami) | do they doubt (ir'tābū) | or (am) | they fear (yakhāfūna) | that (an) | Allah will be unjust (yaḥīfa) | Allah will be unjust (l-lahu) | to them (ʿalayhim) | and His Messenger (warasūluhu)? | Nay (bal), | those (ulāika) |

[they] (humu) | are the wrongdoers (l-ẓālimūna).

24:51 Only is the statement of the believers when they are called to Allah and His Messenger to judge between them is that they say, "We hear and we obey." And those [they] are the successful.

Only (innamā) | is (kāna) | the statement (qawla) | of the believers (l-mu'minīna) | when (idhā) | they are called (duʿū) | to (ilā) | Allah (l-lahi) | and His Messenger (warasūlihi) | to judge (liyaḥkuma) | between them (baynahum) | is that (an) | they say (yaqūlū), | "We hear (samiʿnā) | and we obey. (wa-aṭaʿnā)" | And those (wa-ulāika) | [they] (humu) | are the successful (l-muf'liḥūna).

24:52 And whoever obeys Allah and His Messenger and fears Allah and is conscious of Him, then those [they] are the successful ones.

And whoever (waman) | obeys (yuṭiʿi) | Allah (l-laha) | and His Messenger (warasūlahu) | and fears (wayakhsha) | Allah (l-laha) | and is conscious of Him (wayattaqhi), | then those (fa-ulāika) | [they] (humu) | are the successful ones (l-fāizūna).

24:53 And they swear by Allah strong their oaths that if you ordered them, surely they would go forth. Say, "Do not swear. Obedience is known. Indeed, Allah is All-Aware of what you do."

And they swear (wa-aqsamū) | by Allah (bil-lahi) | strong (jahda) | their oaths (aymānihim) | that if (la-in) | you ordered them (amartahum), | surely they would go forth (layakhrujunna). | Say (qul), | "Do not (lā) | swear (tuq'simū). | Obedience (ṭāʿatun) | is known (maʿrūfatun). | Indeed (inna), | Allah (l-laha) | is All-Aware (khabīrun) | of what (bimā) | you do. (taʿmalūna)"

24:54 Say, "Obey Allah and obey the Messenger, but if you turn away then only upon him is what is placed on him, and on you is what is placed on you. And if you obey him, you will be guided. And not is on the Messenger except the conveyance [the] clear."

Say (qul), | "Obey (aṭīʿū) | Allah (l-laha) | and obey (wa-aṭīʿū) | the Messenger (l-rasūla), | but if (fa-in) | you turn away (tawallaw) | then only (fa-innamā) | upon him (ʿalayhi) | is what (mā) | is placed on him (ḥummila), | and on you (waʿalaykum) | is what (mā) | is placed on you (ḥummil'tum). | And if (wa-in) | you obey him (tuṭīʿūhu), | you will be guided (tahtadū). | And not (wamā) | is on (ʿalā) | the Messenger (l-rasūli) | except (illā) | the conveyance (l-balāghu) | [the] clear. (l-mubīnu)"

24:55 Allah has promised those who believe among you and do righteous deeds, surely He will grant them succession in the earth, as He gave succession to those who were before them, and that He will surely establish for them their religion which He has approved for them, and surely He will change for them after their fear, security for they worship Me, not they associate with Me anything. But whoever disbelieved after that, then those [they] are the defiantly disobedient.

Allah has promised (waʿada) | Allah has promised (l-lahu) | those who (alladhīna) | believe (āmanū) | among you (minkum) | and do (waʿamilū) | righteous deeds (l-ṣāliḥāti), | surely He will grant them succession (layastakhlifannahum) | in (fī) | the earth (l-arḍi), | as (kamā) | He gave succession (is'takhlafa) | to those who (alladhīna) | were before them (min), | were before them (qablihim), | and that He will surely establish (walayumakkinanna) | for them (lahum) | their religion (dīnahumu) | which (alladhī) | He has approved (ir'taḍā) | for them (lahum), | and surely He will change for them (walayubaddilannahum) | after (min) | after (baʿdi) | their fear (khawfihim), | security (amnan) | for they worship Me (yaʿbudūnanī), | not (lā) | they associate (yush'rikūna) | with Me (bī) | anything (shayan). | But whoever (waman) | disbelieved (kafara) | after (baʿda) | that (dhālika), | then those (fa-ulāika) | [they] (humu) | are the defiantly disobedient (l-fāsiqūna).

24:56 And establish the prayer and give zakah and obey the Messenger, so that you may receive mercy.

And establish (wa-aqīmū) | the prayer (l-ṣalata) | and give (waātū) | zakah (l-zakata) | and obey (wa-aṭīʿū) | the Messenger (l-rasūla), | so that you may (laʿallakum) | receive mercy (tur'ḥamūna).

24:57 Do not think those who disbelieve can escape in the earth. And their abode will be the Fire and wretched is the destination.

Do not (lā) | think (taḥsabanna) | those who (alladhīna) | disbelieve (kafarū) | can escape (muʿjizīna) | in (fī) | the earth (l-arḍi). | And their abode (wamawāhumu) | will be the Fire (l-nāru) | and wretched is (walabi'sa) | the destination (l-maṣīru).

24:58 O you who believe! Let ask your permission those whom possess your right hands and those who have not reached puberty among you at three times, before the prayer of dawn, and when you put aside your garments at noon and after the prayer of night. These three are times of privacy for you. Not on you and not on them any blame after that as moving about among you, some of you among others. Thus Allah makes clear for you the Verses, and Allah is All-Knower, All-Wise.

O you who believe (yāayyuhā)! | O you who believe (alladhīna)! | O you who believe (āmanū)! | Let ask your permission (liyastadhinkumu) | those whom (alladhīna) | possess (malakat) | your right hands (aymānukum) | and those who (wa-alladhīna) | have not (lam) | reached (yablughū) | puberty (l-ḥuluma) | among you (minkum) | at three (thalātha) | times (marrātin), | before (min) | before (qabli) | the prayer (ṣalati) | of dawn (l-fajri), | and when (waḥīna) | you put aside (taḍaʿūna) | your garments (thiyābakum) | at (mina) | noon (l-ẓahīrati) | and after (wamin) | and after (baʿdi) | the prayer (ṣalati) | of night (l-ʿishāi). | These three (thalāthu) | are times of privacy (ʿawrātin) | for you (lakum). | Not (laysa) | on you (ʿalaykum) | and not (walā) | on them (ʿalayhim) | any blame (junāḥun) | after that (baʿdahunna) | as moving about (ṭawwāfūna) | among you (ʿalaykum), | some of you (baʿḍukum) | among (ʿalā) | others (baʿḍin). | Thus (kadhālika) | Allah makes clear (yubayyinu) | Allah makes clear (l-lahu) | for you (lakumu) | the Verses (l-āyāti), | and Allah (wal-lahu) | is All-Knower (ʿalīmun), | All-Wise (ḥakīmun).

24:59 And when reach the children among you the puberty then let them ask permission as asked permission those who were before them. Thus Allah makes clear for you His Verses. And Allah is All-Knower All-Wise.

And when (wa-idhā) | reach (balagha) | the children (l-aṭfālu) | among you (minkumu) | the puberty (l-ḥuluma) | then let them ask permission (falyastadhinū) | as (kamā) | asked permission (is'tadhana) | those who (alladhīna) | were before them (min). | were before them (qablihim). | Thus (kadhālika) | Allah makes clear (yubayyinu) | Allah makes clear (l-lahu) | for you (lakum) | His Verses (āyātihi). | And Allah (wal-lahu) | is All-Knower (ʿalīmun) | All-Wise (ḥakīmun).

24:60 And postmenopausal among the women who do not have desire for marriage, then not is on them any blame that they put aside their outer garments, not displaying their adornment. And that they modestly refrain is better for them. And Allah is All-Hearer, All-Knower.

And postmenopausal (wal-qawāʿidu) | among (mina) | the women (l-nisāi) | who (allātī) | do not (lā) | have desire (yarjūna) | for marriage (nikāḥan), | then not is (falaysa) | on them (ʿalayhinna) | any blame (junāḥun) | that (an) | they put aside (yaḍaʿna) | their outer garments (thiyābahunna), | not (ghayra) | displaying (mutabarrijātin) | their adornment (bizīnatin). | And that (wa-an) | they modestly refrain (yastaʿfif'na) | is better (khayrun) | for them (lahunna). | And Allah (wal-lahu) | is All-Hearer (samīʿun), | All-Knower (ʿalīmun).

24:61 Not is on the blind any blame and not on the lame any blame and not on the sick any blame and not on yourselves that you eat from your houses or houses of your fathers or houses of your mothers or houses of your brothers or houses of your sisters or houses of your paternal uncles or houses of your paternal aunts or houses of your maternal uncles or houses of your maternal aunts or what you possess its keys or your friend. Not is on you any blame that you eat together or separately. But when you enter houses then greet [on] yourselves a greeting from Allah blessed and good. Thus Allah makes clear for you the Verses so that you may understand.

Not is (laysa) | on (ʿalā) | the blind (l-aʿmā) | any blame (ḥarajun) | and not (walā) | on (ʿalā) | the lame (l-aʿraji) | any blame (ḥarajun) | and not (walā) | on (ʿalā) | the sick (l-marīḍi) | any blame (ḥarajun) | and not (walā) | on (ʿalā) | yourselves (anfusikum) | that (an) | you eat (takulū) | from (min) | your houses (buyūtikum) | or (aw) | houses (buyūti) | of your fathers (ābāikum) | or (aw) | houses (buyūti) | of your mothers (ummahātikum) | or (aw) | houses (buyūti) | of your brothers (ikh'wānikum) | or (aw) | houses (buyūti) | of your sisters (akhawātikum) | or (aw) | houses (buyūti) | of your paternal uncles (aʿmāmikum) | or (aw) | houses (buyūti) | of your paternal aunts (ʿammātikum) | or (aw) | houses (buyūti) | of your maternal uncles (akhwālikum) | or (aw) | houses (buyūti) | of your maternal aunts (khālātikum) | or (aw) | what (mā) | you possess (malaktum) | its keys (mafātiḥahu) | or (aw) | your friend (ṣadīqikum). | Not is (laysa) | on you (ʿalaykum) | any blame (junāḥun) | that (an) | you eat (takulū) | together (jamīʿan) | or (aw) | separately (ashtātan). | But when (fa-idhā) | you enter (dakhaltum) | houses (buyūtan) | then greet (fasallimū) | [on] (ʿalā) | yourselves (anfusikum) | a greeting (taḥiyyatan) | from (min) | from (ʿindi) | Allah (l-lahi) | blessed (mubārakatan) | and good (ṭayyibatan). | Thus (kadhālika) | Allah makes clear (yubayyinu) | Allah makes clear (l-lahu) | for you (lakumu) | the Verses (l-āyāti) | so that you may (laʿallakum) | understand (taʿqilūna).

24:62 Only the believers are those who believe in Allah and His Messenger, and when they are with him for a matter of collective action, not they go until they have asked his permission. Indeed, those who ask your permission, those [those who] believe in Allah and His Messenger. So when they ask your permission for some affair of theirs, then give permission to whom you will among them, and ask forgiveness for them of Allah. Indeed, Allah is Oft-Forgiving, Most Merciful.

Only (innamā) | the believers (l-mu'minūna) | are those who (alladhīna) | believe (āmanū) | in Allah (bil-lahi) | and His Messenger (warasūlihi), | and when (wa-idhā) | they are (kānū) | with him (maʿahu) | for (ʿalā) | a matter (amrin) | of collective action (jāmiʿin), | not (lam) | they go (yadhhabū) | until (ḥattā) | they have asked his permission (yastadhinūhu). | Indeed (inna), | those who (alladhīna) | ask your permission (yastadhinūnaka), | those (ulāika) | [those who] (alladhīna) | believe (yu'minūna) | in Allah (bil-lahi) | and His Messenger (warasūlihi). | So when (fa-idhā) | they ask your permission (is'tadhanūka) | for some (libaʿḍi) | affair of theirs (shanihim), | then give permission (fadhan) | to whom (liman) | you will (shi'ta) | among them (min'hum), | and ask forgiveness (wa-is'taghfir) | for them (lahumu) | of Allah (l-laha). | Indeed (inna), | Allah (l-laha) | is Oft-Forgiving (ghafūrun), | Most Merciful (raḥīmun).

24:63 Do not make the calling of the Messenger among you as the call of some of you to others. Verily, Allah knows those who slip away among you under shelter. So let beware those who oppose [from] his orders lest befalls them a trial or befalls them a punishment painful.

Do not (lā) | make (tajʿalū) | the calling (duʿāa) | of the Messenger (l-rasūli) | among you (baynakum) | as the call (kaduʿāi) | of some of you (baʿḍikum) | to others (baʿḍan). | Verily (qad), | Allah knows (yaʿlamu) | Allah knows (l-lahu) | those who (alladhīna) | slip away (yatasallalūna) | among you (minkum) | under shelter (liwādhan). | So let beware (falyaḥdhari) | those who (alladhīna) | oppose (yukhālifūna) | [from] (ʿan) | his orders (amrihi) | lest (an) | befalls them (tuṣībahum) | a trial (fit'natun) | or (aw) | befalls them (yuṣībahum) | a punishment (ʿadhābun) | painful (alīmun).

24:64 No doubt! Indeed, to Allah belongs whatever is in the heavens and the earth. Verily, He knows what you are on [it], And the Day they will be returned to Him then He will inform them of what they did. And Allah of every thing is All-Knower.

No doubt (alā)! | Indeed (inna), | to Allah belongs (lillahi) | whatever (mā) | is in (fī) | the heavens (l-samāwāti) | and the earth (wal-arḍi). | Verily (qad), | He knows (yaʿlamu) | what (mā) | you (antum) | are on [it] (ʿalayhi), | And the Day (wayawma) | they will be returned (yur'jaʿūna) | to Him (ilayhi) | then He will inform them (fayunabbi-uhum) | of what (bimā) | they did (ʿamilū). | And

Allah (wal-lahu) | of every (bikulli) | thing (shayin) | is All-Knower (ʿalīmun).

Chapter (25) Sūrat l-Fur'qān (The Criterion)

25:1 Blessed is He Who sent down the Criterion upon His slave that he may be to the worlds a warner -

Blessed is He (tabāraka) | Who (alladhī) | sent down (nazzala) | the Criterion (l-fur'qāna) | upon (ʿalā) | His slave (ʿabdihi) | that he may be (liyakūna) | to the worlds (lilʿālamīna) | a warner (nadhīran)-

25:2 The One Who - to Him belongs the dominion of the heavens and the earth, and not He has taken a son, and not He has for Him a partner in the dominion and He has created every thing, and determined it with determination.

The One Who (alladhī)- | to Him belongs (lahu) | the dominion (mul'ku) | of the heavens (l-samāwāti) | and the earth (wal-arḍi), | and not (walam) | He has taken (yattakhidh) | a son (waladan), | and not (walam) | He has (yakun) | for Him (lahu) | a partner (sharīkun) | in (fī) | the dominion (l-mul'ki) | and He has created (wakhalaqa) | every (kulla) | thing (shayin), | and determined it (faqaddarahu) | with determination (taqdīran).

25:3 Yet they have taken besides Him gods not they create anything, while they are created, and not they possess for themselves any harm and not any benefit, and not they control death and not life and not resurrection.

Yet they have taken (wa-ittakhadhū) | besides Him (min) | besides Him (dūnihi) | gods (ālihatan) | not (lā) | they create (yakhluqūna) | anything (shayan), | while they (wahum) | are created (yukh'laqūna), | and not (walā) | they possess (yamlikūna) | for themselves (li-anfusihim) | any harm (ḍarran) | and not (walā) | any benefit (nafʿan), | and not (walā) | they control (yamlikūna) | death (mawtan) | and not (walā) | life (ḥayatan) | and not (walā) | resurrection (nushūran).

25:4 And say those who disbelieve, "Not this is but a lie, he invented it and helped him at it people other." But verily, they have produced an injustice and a lie.

And say (waqāla) | those who (alladhīna) | disbelieve (kafarū), | "Not (in) | this (hādhā) | is but (illā) | a lie (if'kun), | he invented it (if'tarāhu) | and helped him (wa-aʿānahu) | at it (ʿalayhi) | people (qawmun) | other. (ākharūna)" | But verily (faqad), | they have produced (jāū) | an injustice (ẓul'man) | and a lie (wazūran).

25:5 And they say, "Tales of the former people which he has had written and they are dictated to him morning and evening."

And they say (waqālū), | "Tales (asāṭīru) | of the former people (l-awalīna) | which he has had written (ik'tatabahā) | and they (fahiya) | are dictated (tum'lā) | to him (ʿalayhi) | morning (buk'ratan) | and evening. (wa-aṣīlan)"

25:6 Say, "Has sent it down the One Who knows the secret in the heavens and the earth. Indeed, He is Oft-Forgiving, Most Merciful."

Say (qul), | "Has sent it down (anzalahu) | the One Who (alladhī) | knows (yaʿlamu) | the secret (l-sira) | in (fī) | the heavens (l-samāwāti) | and the earth (wal-arḍi). | Indeed, He (innahu) | is (kāna) | Oft-Forgiving (ghafūran), | Most Merciful. (raḥīman)"

25:7 And they say, "Why does this Messenger eat [the] food and walk in the markets? Why not is sent down to him an Angel then he be with him a warner?

And they say (waqālū), | "Why does (māli) | this (hādhā) | Messenger (l-rasūli) | eat (yakulu) | [the] food (l-ṭaʿāma) | and walk (wayamshī) | in (fī) | the markets (l-aswāqi)? | Why not (lawlā) | is sent down (unzila) | to him (ilayhi) | an Angel (malakun) | then he be (fayakūna) | with him (maʿahu) | a warner (nadhīran)?

25:8 Or is delivered to him a treasure or is for him a garden, he may eat from it? And say the wrongdoers, "Not you follow but a man bewitched."

Or (aw) | is delivered (yul'qā) | to him (ilayhi) | a treasure (kanzun) | or (aw) | is (takūnu) | for him (lahu) | a garden (jannatun), | he may eat (yakulu) | from it (min'hā)? | And say (waqāla) | the wrongdoers (l-ẓālimūna), | "Not (in) | you follow (tattabiʿūna) | but (illā) | a man (rajulan) | bewitched. (masḥūran)"

25:9 See how they set forth for you the similitudes, but they have gone astray, so not they are able to find a way.

See (unẓur) | how (kayfa) | they set forth (ḍarabū) | for you (laka) | the similitudes (l-amthāla), | but they have gone astray (faḍallū), | so not (falā) | they are able to find (yastaṭīʿūna) | a way (sabīlan).

25:10 Blessed is He Who if He willed could have made for you better than that - gardens - flow from underneath it the rivers and He could make for you palaces.

Blessed is He (tabāraka) | Who (alladhī) | if (in) | He willed (shāa) | could have made (jaʿala) | for you (laka) | better (khayran) | than (min) | that (dhālika)- | gardens (jannātin)- | flow (tajrī) | from (min) | underneath it (taḥtihā) | the rivers (l-anhāru) | and He could make (wayajʿal) | for you (laka) | palaces (quṣūran).

25:11 Nay, they deny the Hour and We have prepared for those who deny the Hour, a Blazing Fire.

Nay (bal), | they deny (kadhabū) | the Hour (bil-sāʿati) | and We have prepared (wa-aʿtadnā) | for those who (liman) | deny (kadhaba) | the Hour (bil-sāʿati), | a Blazing Fire (saʿīran).

25:12 When it sees them from a place far, they will hear its raging and roaring.

When (idhā) | it sees them (ra-athum) | from (min) | a place (makānin) | far (baʿīdin), | they will hear (samiʿū) | its (lahā) | raging (taghayyuẓan) | and roaring (wazafīran).

25:13 And when they are thrown thereof in a place narrow bound in chains, they will call there for destruction.

And when (wa-idhā) | they are thrown (ul'qū) | thereof (min'hā) | in a place (makānan) | narrow (ḍayyiqan) | bound in chains (muqarranīna), | they will call (daʿaw) | there (hunālika) | for destruction (thubūran).

25:14 "Do not call this day for destruction one, but call for destructions many."

"Do not (lā) | call (tadʿū) | this day (l-yawma) | for destruction (thubūran) | one (wāḥidan), | but call (wa-id''ū) | for destructions (thubūran) | many. (kathīran)"

25:15 Say, "Is that better or Garden of Eternity, which is promised to the righteous? It will be for them a reward and destination.

Say (qul), | "Is that (adhālika) | better (khayrun) | or (am) | Garden (jannatu) | of Eternity (l-khul'di), | which (allatī) | is promised (wuʿida) | to the righteous (l-mutaqūna)? | It will be (kānat) | for them (lahum) | a reward (jazāan) | and destination (wamaṣīran).

25:16 For them therein is whatever they wish, they will abide forever. It is on your Lord a promise requested."

For them (lahum) | therein (fīhā) | is whatever (mā) | they wish (yashāūna), | they will abide forever (khālidīna). | It is (kāna) | on (ʿalā) | your Lord (rabbika) | a promise (waʿdan) | requested. (masūlan)"

25:17 And the Day He will gather them and what they worship besides Allah and He will say, "Did you [you] mislead My slaves these or they went astray from the way?"

And the Day (wayawma) | He will gather them (yaḥshuruhum) | and what (wamā) | they worship (yaʿbudūna) | besides Allah (min) | besides Allah (dūni) | besides Allah (l-lahi) | and He will say (fayaqūlu), | "Did you (a-antum) | [you] mislead (aḍlaltum) | My slaves (ʿibādī) | these (hāulāi) | or (am) | they (hum) | went astray (ḍallū) | from the way? (l-sabīla)"

25:18 They say, "Glory be to You! Not it was proper for us that we take besides You any protectors. But You gave them comforts and their forefathers until they forgot the Message and became a people ruined."

They say (qālū), | "Glory be to You (sub'ḥānaka)! | Not (mā) | it was proper (kāna) | it was proper (yanbaghī) | for us (lanā) | that (an) | we take (nattakhidha) | besides You (min) | besides You (dūnika) | any (min) | protectors (awliyāa). | But (walākin) | You gave them comforts (mattaʿtahum) | and their forefathers (waābāahum) | until (ḥattā) | they forgot (nasū) | the Message (l-dhik'ra) | and became (wakānū) | a people (qawman) | ruined. (būran)"

25:19 "So verily, they deny you in what you say, so not you are able to avert and not to help." And whoever does wrong among you, We will make him taste a punishment great.

"So verily (faqad), | they deny you (kadhabūkum) | in what (bimā) | you say (taqūlūna), | so not (famā) | you are able (tastaṭīʿūna) | to avert (ṣarfan) | and not (walā) | to help. (naṣran)" | And whoever (waman) | does wrong (yaẓlim) | among you (minkum), | We will make him taste (nudhiq'hu) | a punishment (ʿadhāban) | great (kabīran).

25:20 And not We sent before you any Messengers but indeed, they [surely] ate food and walked in the markets. And We have made some of you for others a trial, will you have patience? And is your Lord All-Seer.

And not (wamā) | We sent (arsalnā) | before you (qablaka) | any (mina) | Messengers (l-mur'salīna) | but (illā) | indeed, they (innahum) | [surely] ate (layakulūna) | food (l-ṭaʿāma) | and walked (wayamshūna) | in (fī) | the markets (l-aswāqi). | And We have made (wajaʿalnā) | some of you (baʿḍakum) | for others (libaʿḍin) | a trial (fit'natan), | will you have patience (ataṣbirūna)? | And is (wakāna) | your Lord (rabbuka) | All-Seer (baṣīran).

25:21 And said those who do not expect the meeting with Us, "Why not are sent down to us the Angels or we see our Lord?" Indeed, they have become arrogant within themselves and become insolent with insolence great.

And said (waqāla) | those who (alladhīna) | do not (lā) | expect (yarjūna) | the meeting with Us (liqāanā), | "Why not (lawlā) | are sent down (unzila) | to us (ʿalaynā) | the Angels (l-malāikatu) | or (aw) | we see (narā) | our Lord? (rabbanā)" | Indeed (laqadi), | they have become arrogant (is'takbarū) | within (fī) | themselves (anfusihim) | and become insolent (waʿataw) | with insolence (ʿutuwwan) | great (kabīran).

25:22 The Day they see the Angels, no glad tidings will be that Day for the criminals, and they will say, "A partition forbidden."

The Day (yawma) | they see (yarawna) | the Angels (l-malāikata), | no (lā) | glad tidings (bush'rā) | will be that Day (yawma-idhin) | for the criminals (lil'muj'rimīna), | and they will say (wayaqūlūna), | "A partition (ḥij'ran) | forbidden. (maḥjūran)"

25:23 And We will proceed to whatever they did of the deed(s), and We will make them as dust dispersed.

And We will proceed (waqadim'nā) | to (ilā) | whatever (mā) | they did (ʿamilū) | of (min) | the deed(s) (ʿamalin), | and We will make them (fajaʿalnāhu) | as dust (habāan) | dispersed (manthūran).

25:24 The companions of Paradise, that Day, will be in a better abode, and a better resting-place.

The companions (aṣḥābu) | of Paradise (l-janati), | that Day (yawma-idhin), | will be in a better (khayrun) | abode (mus'taqarran), | and a better (wa-aḥsanu) | resting-place (maqīlan).

25:25 And the Day will split open the heavens with the clouds and will be sent down the Angels, descending.

And the Day (wayawma) | will split open (tashaqqaqu) | the heavens (l-samāu) | with the clouds (bil-ghamāmi) | and will be sent down (wanuzzila) | the Angels (l-malāikatu), | descending (tanzīlan).

25:26 The Sovereignty, that Day will be truly, for the Most Gracious. And it will be a Day for the disbelievers difficult.

The Sovereignty (al-mul'ku), | that Day (yawma-idhin) | will be truly (l-ḥaqu), | for the Most Gracious (lilrraḥmāni). | And it will be (wakāna) | a Day (yawman) | for (ʿalā) | the disbelievers (l-kāfirīna) | difficult (ʿasīran).

25:27 And the Day will bite the wrongdoer [on] his hands, he will say, "O I wish! I had taken with the Messenger a way.

And the Day (wayawma) | will bite (yaʿaḍḍu) | the wrongdoer (l-ẓālimu) | [on] (ʿalā) | his hands (yadayhi), | he will say (yaqūlu), | "O I wish (yālaytanī)! | I had taken (ittakhadhtu) | with (maʿa) | the Messenger (l-rasūli) | a way (sabīlan).

25:28 O woe to me! I wish not I had taken that one as a friend.

O woe to me (yāwaylatā)! | I wish (laytanī) | not (lam) | I had taken (attakhidh) | that one (fulānan) | as a friend (khalīlan).

25:29 Verily, he led me astray from the Reminder after [when] it had come to me. And is the Shaitaan to the man a deserter."

Verily (laqad), | he led me astray (aḍallanī) | from (ʿani) | the Reminder (l-dhik'ri) | after (baʿda) | [when] (idh) | it had come to me (jāanī). | And is (wakāna) | the Shaitaan (l-shayṭānu) | to the man (lil'insāni) | a deserter. (khadhūlan)"

25:30 And said the Messenger, "O my Lord! Indeed, my people took this the Quran as a forsaken thing."

And said (waqāla) | the Messenger (l-rasūlu), | "O my Lord (yārabbi)! | Indeed (inna), | my people (qawmī) | took (ittakhadhū) | this (hādhā) | the Quran (l-qur'āna) | as a forsaken thing. (mahjūran)"

25:31 And thus We have made for every Prophet an enemy, among the criminals. But sufficient is your Lord, as a Guide and a Helper.

And thus (wakadhālika) | We have made (jaʿalnā) | for every (likulli) | Prophet (nabiyyin) | an enemy (ʿaduwwan), | among (mina) | the criminals (l-muj'rimīna). | But sufficient is (wakafā) |

your Lord (birabbika), | as a Guide (hādiyan) | and a Helper (wanaṣīran).

25:32 And said those who disbelieve, "Why not was revealed to him the Quran all at once?" Thus, that We may strengthen thereby your heart, and We have recited it with distinct recitation.

And said (waqāla) | those who (alladhīna) | disbelieve (kafarū), | "Why not (lawlā) | was revealed (nuzzila) | to him (ʿalayhi) | the Quran (l-qur'ānu) | all at once? (jum'latan)" | all at once? (wāḥidatan)" | Thus (kadhālika), | that We may strengthen (linuthabbita) | thereby (bihi) | your heart (fuādaka), | and We have recited it (warattalnāhu) | with distinct recitation (tartīlan).

25:33 And not they come to you with an example but We bring you the truth, and the best explanation.

And not (walā) | they come to you (yatūnaka) | with an example (bimathalin) | but (illā) | We bring you (ji'nāka) | the truth (bil-ḥaqi), | and the best (wa-aḥsana) | explanation (tafsīran).

25:34 Those who will be gathered on their faces to Hell, those are the worst in position and most astray from the way.

Those who (alladhīna) | will be gathered (yuḥ'sharūna) | on (ʿalā) | their faces (wujūhihim) | to (ilā) | Hell (jahannama), | those (ulāika) | are the worst (sharrun) | in position (makānan) | and most astray (wa-aḍallu) | from the way (sabīlan).

25:35 And verily, We gave Musa the Scripture and We appointed with him his brother Harun as an assistant.

And verily (walaqad), | We gave (ātaynā) | Musa (mūsā) | the Scripture (l-kitāba) | and We appointed (wajaʿalnā) | with him (maʿahu) | his brother (akhāhu) | Harun (hārūna) | as an assistant (wazīran).

25:36 Then We said, "Go both of you to the people, those who have denied, Our Signs." Then We destroyed them with destruction.

Then We said (faqul'nā), | "Go both of you (idh'habā) | to (ilā) | the people (l-qawmi), | those who (alladhīna) | have denied (kadhabū), | Our Signs. (biāyātinā)" | Then We destroyed them (fadammarnāhum) | with destruction (tadmīran).

25:37 And the people of Nuh, when they denied the Messengers, We drowned them and We made them for mankind a sign. And We have prepared for the wrongdoers. a punishment painful.

And the people (waqawma) | of Nuh (nūḥin), | when (lammā) | they denied (kadhabū) | the Messengers (l-rusula), | We drowned them (aghraqnāhum) | and We made them (wajaʿalnāhum) | for mankind (lilnnāsi) | a sign (āyatan). | And We have prepared (wa-aʿtadnā) | for the wrongdoers (lilẓẓālimīna). | a punishment (ʿadhāban) | painful (alīman).

25:38 And Ad and Thamud and the dwellers of Ar-rass and generations between that many.

And Ad (waʿādan) | and Thamud (wathamūdā) | and the dwellers (wa-aṣḥāba) | of Ar-rass (l-rasi) | and generations (waqurūnan) | between (bayna) | that (dhālika) | many (kathīran).

25:39 And each We have set forth for him the examples, and each We destroyed with destruction.

And each (wakullan) | We have set forth (ḍarabnā) | for him (lahu) | the examples (l-amthāla), | and each (wakullan) | We destroyed (tabbarnā) | with destruction (tatbīran).

25:40 And verily, they have come upon the town which was showered with a rain of evil. Then do not they [were] see it? Nay, they are not expecting Resurrection.

And verily (walaqad), | they have come (ataw) | upon (ʿalā) | the town (l-qaryati) | which (allatī) | was showered (um'ṭirat) | with a rain (maṭara) | of evil (l-sawi). | Then do not (afalam) | they [were] (yakūnū) | see it (yarawnahā)? | Nay (bal), | they are (kānū) | not (lā) | expecting (yarjūna) | Resurrection (nushūran).

25:41 And when they see you, not they take you except in mockery, "Is this the one whom Allah has sent as a Messenger?

And when (wa-idhā) | they see you (ra-awka), | not (in) | they take you (yattakhidhūnaka) | except (illā) | in mockery (huzuwan), | "Is this (ahādhā) | the one whom (alladhī) | Allah has sent (baʿatha) | Allah has sent (l-lahu) | as a Messenger (rasūlan)?

25:42 He would have almost [surely] misled us from our gods if not that we had been steadfast to them." And soon will know when they will see the punishment, who is more astray from the way.

He would have almost (in) | He would have almost (kāda) | [surely] misled us (layuḍillunā) | from (ʿan) | our gods (ālihatinā) | if not (lawlā) | that (an) | we had been steadfast (ṣabarnā) | to them. (ʿalayhā)" | And soon (wasawfa) | will know (yaʿlamūna) | when (ḥīna) | they will see (yarawna) | the punishment (l-ʿadhāba), | who (man) | is more astray (aḍallu) | from the way (sabīlan).

25:43 Have you seen one who takes as his god his own desire? Then would you be over him a guardian?

Have you seen (ara-ayta) | one who (mani) | takes (ittakhadha) | as his god (ilāhahu) | his own desire (hawāhu)? | Then would you (afa-anta) | be (takūnu) | over him (ʿalayhi) | a guardian (wakīlan)?

25:44 Or do you think that most of them hear or understand? Not they are except like cattle. Nay, they are more astray from the way.

Or (am) | do you think (taḥsabu) | that (anna) | most of them (aktharahum) | hear (yasmaʿūna) | or (aw) | understand (yaʿqilūna)? | Not (in) | they (hum) | are except (illā) | like cattle (kal-anʿāmi). | Nay (bal), | they (hum) | are more astray (aḍallu) | from the way (sabīlan).

25:45 Do you not see [to] your Lord how He extends the shadow? And if He willed, surely He could have made it stationary. Then We made the sun for it an indication.

Do you not (alam) | see (tara) | [to] (ilā) | your Lord (rabbika) | how (kayfa) | He extends (madda) | the shadow (l-ẓila)? | And if (walaw) | He willed (shāa), | surely He could have made it (lajaʿalahu) | stationary (sākinan). | Then (thumma) | We made (jaʿalnā) | the sun (l-shamsa) | for it (ʿalayhi) | an indication (dalīlan).

25:46 Then We withdraw it to Us, a withdrawal gradual.

Then (thumma) | We withdraw it (qabaḍnāhu) | to Us (ilaynā), | a withdrawal (qabḍan) | gradual (yasīran).

25:47 And He is the One Who made for you the night as a covering and the sleep a rest and made the day a resurrection.

And He (wahuwa) | is the One Who (alladhī) | made (jaʿala) | for you (lakumu) | the night (al-layla) | as a covering (libāsan) | and the sleep (wal-nawma) | a rest (subātan) | and made (wajaʿala) | the day (l-nahāra) | a resurrection (nushūran).

25:48 And He is the One Who sends the winds as glad tidings before His Mercy, and We send down from the sky water pure.

And He (wahuwa) | is the One Who (alladhī) | sends (arsala) | the winds (l-riyāḥa) | as glad tidings (bush'ran) | before (bayna) | before (yaday) | His Mercy (raḥmatihi), | and We send down (wa-anzalnā) | from (mina) | the sky (l-samāi) | water (māan) | pure (ṭahūran).

25:49 That We may give life thereby to a land dead and We give drink thereof to those We created, cattle and men many.

That We may give life (linuḥ'yiya) | thereby (bihi) | to a land (baldatan) | dead (maytan) | and We give drink (wanus'qiyahu) | thereof (mimmā) | to those We created (khalaqnā), | cattle (anʿāman) | and men (wa-anāsiyya) | many (kathīran).

25:50 And verily, We have distributed it among them that they may remember, but refuse most of the people except disbelief.

And verily (walaqad), | We have distributed it (ṣarrafnāhu) | among them (baynahum) | that they may remember (liyadhakkarū), | but refuse (fa-abā) | most (aktharu) | of the people (l-nāsi) | except (illā) | disbelief (kufūran).

25:51 And if We willed, surely, We would have raised in every town a warner.

And if (walaw) | We willed (shi'nā), | surely, We would have raised (labaʿathnā) | in (fī) | every (kulli) | town (qaryatin) | a warner (nadhīran).

25:52 So do not obey the disbelievers and strive against them with it, a striving great.

So do not (falā) | obey (tuṭiʿi) | the disbelievers (l-kāfirīna) | and strive against them (wajāhid'hum) | with it (bihi), | a striving (jihādan) | great (kabīran).

25:53 And He is the One Who has released the two seas [this] one palatable and sweet and [this] one salty and bitter, and He has made between them a barrier and a partition forbidden.

And He (wahuwa) | is the One Who (alladhī) | has released (maraja) | the two seas (l-baḥrayni) | [this] one (hādhā) | palatable (ʿadhbun) | and sweet (furātun) | and [this] one (wahādhā) | salty (mil'ḥun) | and bitter (ujājun), | and He has made (wajaʿala) | between them (baynahumā) | a barrier (barzakhan) | and a partition (waḥij'ran) | forbidden (maḥjūran).

25:54 And He is the One Who has created from the water human being and has made for him blood relationship and marriage relationship. And is your Lord All-Powerful.

And He (wahuwa) | is the One Who (alladhī) | has created (khalaqa) | from (mina) | the water (l-māi) | human being (basharan) | and has made for him (fajaʿalahu) | blood relationship (nasaban) | and marriage relationship (waṣih'ran). | And is (wakāna) | your Lord (rabbuka) | All-Powerful (qadīran).

25:55 But they worship besides Allah what not profits them and not harms them, and is the disbeliever against his Lord a helper.

But they worship (wayaʿbudūna) | besides Allah (min) | besides Allah (dūni) | besides Allah (l-lahi) | what (mā) | not profits them (lā) | not profits them (yanfaʿuhum) | and not (walā) | harms them (yaḍurruhum), | and is (wakāna) | the disbeliever (l-kāfiru) | against (ʿalā) | his Lord (rabbihi) | a helper (ẓahīran).

25:56 And not We sent you except as a bearer of glad tidings and a warner.

And not (wamā) | We sent you (arsalnāka) | except (illā) | as a bearer of glad tidings (mubashiran) | and a warner (wanadhīran).

25:57 Say, "Not I ask of you for it any payment, except that whoever wills to take to his Lord a way."

Say (qul), | "Not (mā) | I ask of you (asalukum) | for it (ʿalayhi) | any (min) | payment (ajrin), | except (illā) | that whoever wills (man) | that whoever wills (shāa) | to (an) | take (yattakhidha) | to (ilā) | his Lord (rabbihi) | a way. (sabīlan)"

25:58 And put your trust in the Ever-Living, the One Who does not die, and glorify with His Praise. And sufficient is He regarding the sins of His slaves, All-Aware,

And put your trust (watawakkal) | in (ʿalā) | the Ever-Living (l-ḥayi), | the One Who (alladhī)

| does not die (lā), | does not die (yamūtu), | and glorify (wasabbiḥ) | with His Praise (biḥamdihi). | And sufficient is (wakafā) | He (bihi) | regarding the sins (bidhunūbi) | of His slaves (ʿibādihi), | All-Aware (khabīran),

25:59 The One Who created the heavens and the earth and whatever is between them in six periods, then He established Himself over the Throne - the Most Gracious, so ask Him as He is All-Aware.

The One Who (alladhī) | created (khalaqa) | the heavens (l-samāwāti) | and the earth (wal-arḍa) | and whatever (wamā) | is between them (baynahumā) | in (fī) | six (sittati) | periods (ayyāmin), | then (thumma) | He established Himself (is'tawā) | over (ʿalā) | the Throne (l-ʿarshi)- | the Most Gracious (l-raḥmānu), | so ask (fasal) | Him (bihi) | as He is All-Aware (khabīran).

25:60 And when it is said to them, "Prostrate to the Most Gracious." They say, "And what is the Most Gracious? Should we prostrate to what you order us?" And it increases them in aversion.

And when (wa-idhā) | it is said (qīla) | to them (lahumu), | "Prostrate (us'judū) | to the Most Gracious. (lilrraḥmāni)" | They say (qālū), | "And what (wamā) | is the Most Gracious (l-raḥmānu)? | Should we prostrate (anasjudu) | to what (limā) | you order us? (tamurunā)" | And it increases them (wazādahum) | in aversion (nufūran).

25:61 Blessed is He Who has placed in the skies constellations and has placed therein a lamp and a moon shining.

Blessed is He (tabāraka) | Who (alladhī) | has placed (jaʿala) | in (fī) | the skies (l-samāi) | constellations (burūjan) | and has placed (wajaʿala) | therein (fīhā) | a lamp (sirājan) | and a moon (waqamaran) | shining (munīran).

25:62 And He is the One Who made the night and the day in succession for whoever desires to remember or desires to be thankful.

And He (wahuwa) | is the One Who (alladhī) | made (jaʿala) | the night (al-layla) | and the day (wal-nahāra) | in succession (khil'fatan) | for whoever (liman) | desires (arāda) | to (an) | remember (yadhakkara) | or (aw) | desires (arāda) | to be thankful (shukūran).

25:63 And the slaves of the Most Gracious are those who walk on the earth in humbleness and when address them the ignorant ones, they say, "Peace."

And the slaves (waʿibādu) | of the Most Gracious (l-raḥmāni) | are those who (alladhīna) | walk (yamshūna) | on (ʿalā) | the earth (l-arḍi) | in humbleness (hawnan) | and when (wa-idhā) | address them (khāṭabahumu) | the ignorant ones (l-jāhilūna), | they say (qālū), | "Peace. (salāman)"

25:64 And those who spend the night before their Lord, prostrating and standing.

And those who (wa-alladhīna) | spend the night (yabītūna) | before their Lord (lirabbihim), | prostrating (sujjadan) | and standing (waqiyāman).

25:65 And those who say, "Our Lord! Avert from us the punishment of Hell. Indeed, its punishment is inseparable,

And those who (wa-alladhīna) | say (yaqūlūna), | "Our Lord (rabbanā)! | Avert (iṣ'rif) | from us (ʿannā) | the punishment (ʿadhāba) | of Hell (jahannama). | Indeed (inna), | its punishment (ʿadhābahā) | is (kāna) | inseparable (gharāman),

25:66 Indeed, it is an evil abode and resting place."

Indeed, it (innahā) | is an evil (sāat) | abode (mus'taqarran) | and resting place. (wamuqāman)"

25:67 And those who, when they spend, are not extravagant and are not stingy but are between that - moderate.

And those who (wa-alladhīna), | when (idhā) | they spend (anfaqū), | are not extravagant (lam) | are not extravagant (yus'rifū) | and are not stingy (walam) | and are not stingy (yaqturū) | but are (wakāna) | between (bayna) | that (dhālika)- | moderate (qawāman).

25:68 And those who do not invoke with Allah god another, and do not [they] kill the soul which Allah has forbidden except by right and do not commit unlawful sexual intercourse. And whoever does that will meet a penalty.

And those who (wa-alladhīna) | do not (lā) | invoke (yadʿūna) | with (maʿa) | Allah (l-lahi) | god (ilāhan) | another (ākhara), | and do not (walā) | [they] kill (yaqtulūna) | the soul (l-nafsa) | which (allatī) | Allah has forbidden (ḥarrama) | Allah has forbidden (l-lahu) | except (illā) | by right (bil-ḥaqi) | and do not (walā) | commit unlawful sexual intercourse (yaznūna). | And whoever (waman) | does (yafʿal) | that (dhālika) | will meet (yalqa) | a penalty (athāman).

25:69 Will be doubled for him the punishment on the Day of Resurrection, and he will abide forever therein humiliated

Will be doubled (yuḍāʿaf) | for him (lahu) | the punishment (l-ʿadhābu) | on the Day (yawma) | of Resurrection (l-qiyāmati), | and he will abide forever (wayakhlud) | therein (fīhi) | humiliated (muhānan)

25:70 Except he who repents and believes and does righteous deeds, then for those Allah will replace their evil deeds with good ones. And is Allah Oft-Forgiving, Most Merciful.

Except (illā) | he who (man) | repents (tāba) | and believes (waāmana) | and does (waʿamila) | righteous deeds (ʿamalan), | righteous deeds (ṣāliḥan), | then for those (fa-ulāika) | Allah will replace (yubaddilu) | Allah will replace (l-lahu) | their evil deeds (sayyiātihim) | with good ones (ḥasanātin). | And is (wakāna) | Allah (l-lahu) | Oft-Forgiving (ghafūran), | Most Merciful (raḥīman).

25:71 And whoever repents and does righteous deeds, then indeed, he turns to Allah with repentance.

And whoever (waman) | repents (tāba) | and does (waʿamila) | righteous deeds (ṣāliḥan), | then indeed, he (fa-innahu) | turns (yatūbu) | to (ilā) | Allah (l-lahi) | with repentance (matāban).

25:72 And those who do not bear witness to the falsehood, and when they pass by futility, they pass as dignified ones

And those who (wa-alladhīna) | do not (lā) | bear witness (yashhadūna) | to the falsehood (l-zūra), | and when (wa-idhā) | they pass (marrū) | by futility (bil-laghwi), | they pass (marrū) | as dignified ones (kirāman)

25:73 And those who, when they are reminded of the Verses of their Lord, do not fall upon them deaf and blind.

And those who (wa-alladhīna), | when (idhā) | they are reminded (dhukkirū) | of the Verses (biāyāti) | of their Lord (rabbihim), | do not (lam) | fall (yakhirrū) | upon them (ʿalayhā) | deaf (ṣumman) | and blind (waʿum'yānan).

25:74 And those who say, "Our Lord! Grant to us from our spouses and our offspring comfort to our eyes, and make us for the righteous a leader."

And those who (wa-alladhīna) | say (yaqūlūna), | "Our Lord (rabbanā)! | Grant (hab) | to us (lanā) | from (min) | our spouses (azwājinā) | and our offspring (wadhurriyyātinā) | comfort (qurrata) | to our eyes (aʿyunin), | and make us (wa-ij'ʿalnā) | for the righteous (lil'muttaqīna) | a leader. (imāman)"

25:75 Those will be awarded the Chamber because they were patient and they will be met therein with greetings and peace.

Those (ulāika) | will be awarded (yuj'zawna) | the Chamber (l-ghur'fata) | because (bimā) | they were patient (ṣabarū) | and they will be met (wayulaqqawna) | therein (fīhā) | with greetings (taḥiyyatan) | and peace (wasalāman).

25:76 Will abide forever in it. Good is the settlement and a resting place.

Will abide forever (khālidīna) | in it (fīhā). | Good (ḥasunat) | is the settlement (mus'taqarran) | and a resting place (wamuqāman).

25:77 Say, "Not will care for you my Lord, if not your prayer is to Him. But verily, you have denied, so soon will be the inevitable punishment."

Say (qul), | "Not (mā) | will care (yaʿba-u) | for you (bikum) | my Lord (rabbī), | if not (lawlā) | your prayer is to Him (duʿāukum). | But verily (faqad), | you have denied (kadhabtum), | so soon (fasawfa) | will be (yakūnu) | the inevitable punishment. (lizāman)"

Chapter (26) Sūrat l-Shuʿarā (The Poets)

26:1 Ta Seem Meem.

Ta Seem Meem (tta-seen-meem).

26:2 These are the Verses of the Book clear.

These (til'ka) | are the Verses (āyātu) | of the Book (l-kitābi) | clear (l-mubīni).

26:3 Perhaps you would kill yourself that not they become believers.

Perhaps you (laʿallaka) | would kill (bākhiʿun) | yourself (nafsaka) | that not (allā) | they become (yakūnū) | believers (mu'minīna).

26:4 If We will, We can send down to them from the sky a Sign so would bend their necks to it in humility.

If (in) | We will (nasha), | We can send down (nunazzil) | to them (ʿalayhim) | from (mina) | the sky (l-samāi) | a Sign (āyatan) | so would bend (faẓallat) | their necks (aʿnāquhum) | to it (lahā) | in humility (khāḍiʿīna).

26:5 And does not come to them any reminder from the Most Gracious new, but they from it turn away.

And does not (wamā) | come to them (yatīhim) | any (min) | reminder (dhik'rin) | from (mina) | the Most Gracious (l-raḥmāni) | new (muḥ'dathin), | but (illā) | they (kānū) | from it (ʿanhu) | turn away (muʿ'riḍīna).

26:6 So verily, they have denied, then will come to them the news of what they used at it to mock.

So verily (faqad), | they have denied (kadhabū), | then will come to them (fasayatīhim) | the news (anbāu) | of what (mā) | they used (kānū) | at it (bihi) | to mock (yastahziūna).

26:7 Do not they see at the earth - how many We produced in it of every kind noble.

Do not (awalam) | they see (yaraw) | at (ilā) | the earth (l-arḍi)- | how many (kam) | We produced (anbatnā) | in it (fīhā) | of (min) | every (kulli) | kind (zawjin) | noble (karīmin).

26:8 Indeed, in that surely is a sign, but not are most of them believers.
Indeed (inna), | in (fī) | that (dhālika) | surely is a sign (laāyatan), | but not (wamā) | are (kāna) | most of them (aktharuhum) | believers (mu'minīna).

26:9 And indeed your Lord, surely, He is the All-Mighty, the Most Merciful.
And indeed (wa-inna) | your Lord (rabbaka), | surely, He (lahuwa) | is the All-Mighty (l-ʿazīzu), | the Most Merciful (l-raḥīmu).

26:10 And when your Lord called Musa, [that], "Go to the people who are wrongdoers
And when (wa-idh) | your Lord called (nādā) | your Lord called (rabbuka) | Musa (mūsā), | [that] (ani), | "Go (i'ti) | to the people (l-qawma) | who are wrongdoers (l-ẓālimīna)

26:11 The people of Firaun. Will not they fear?"
The people (qawma) | of Firaun (fir'ʿawna). | Will not (alā) | they fear? (yattaqūna)"

26:12 He said, "My Lord! Indeed, I [I] fear that they will deny me.
He said (qāla), | "My Lord (rabbi)! | Indeed, I (innī) | [I] fear (akhāfu) | that (an) | they will deny me (yukadhibūni).

26:13 And straitens my breast and not expresses well my tongue, so send for Harun.
And straitens (wayaḍīqu) | my breast (ṣadrī) | and not (walā) | expresses well (yanṭaliqu) | my tongue (lisānī), | so send (fa-arsil) | for (ilā) | Harun (hārūna).

26:14 And they have against me a crime, so I fear that they will kill me."
And they have (walahum) | against me (ʿalayya) | a crime (dhanbun), | so I fear (fa-akhāfu) | that (an) | they will kill me. (yaqtulūni)"

26:15 He said, "Nay, go both of you with Our Signs. Indeed, We are with you, listening.
He said (qāla), | "Nay (kallā), | go both of you (fa-idh'habā) | with Our Signs (biāyātinā). | Indeed, We (innā) | are with you (maʿakum), | listening (mus'tamiʿūna).

26:16 So go both of you to Firaun and say, 'Indeed, we are the Messenger of the Lord of the worlds
So go both of you (fatiyā) | to Firaun (fir'ʿawna) | and say (faqūlā), | 'Indeed, we (innā) | are the Messenger (rasūlu) | of the Lord (rabbi) | of the worlds (l-ʿālamīna)

26:17 [That] send with us the Children of Israel.'"
[That] (an) | send (arsil) | with us (maʿanā) | the Children of Israel.' (banī)" | the Children of Israel.' (is'rāīla)"

26:18 He said, "Did not we bring you up among us as a child, and you remained among us of your life years?
He said (qāla), | "Did not (alam) | we bring you up (nurabbika) | among us (fīnā) | as a child (walīdan), | and you remained (walabith'ta) | among us (fīnā) | of (min) | your life (ʿumurika) | years (sinīna)?

26:19 And you did your deed which you did, and you were of the ungrateful."
And you did (wafaʿalta) | your deed (faʿlataka) | which (allatī) | you did (faʿalta), | and you (wa-anta) | were of (mina) | the ungrateful. (l-kāfirīna)"

26:20 He said, "I did it when I was of those who are astray.

He said (qāla), | "I did it (faʿaltuhā) | when (idhan) | I (wa-anā) | was of (mina) | those who are astray (l-ḍālīna).

26:21 So I fled from you when I feared you. But granted to me my Lord, judgment and made me of the Messengers.

So I fled (fafarartu) | from you (minkum) | when (lammā) | I feared you (khif'tukum). | But granted (fawahaba) | to me (lī) | my Lord (rabbī), | judgment (ḥuk'man) | and made me (wajaʿalanī) | of (mina) | the Messengers (l-mur'salīna).

26:22 And this is the favor with which you reproach [on] me, that you have enslaved the Children of Israel."

And this (watil'ka) | is the favor (niʿ'matun) | with which you reproach (tamunnuhā) | [on] me (ʿalayya), | that (an) | you have enslaved (ʿabbadtta) | the Children of Israel. (banī)" | the Children of Israel. (is'rāīla)"

26:23 Firaun said "And what is the Lord of the worlds?"

Firaun said (qāla) | Firaun said (fir'ʿawnu) | "And what (wamā) | is the Lord (rabbu) | of the worlds? (l-ʿālamīna)"

26:24 He said, "Lord of the heavens and the earth and whatever is between them, if you should be convinced."

He said (qāla), | "Lord (rabbu) | of the heavens (l-samāwāti) | and the earth (wal-arḍi) | and whatever (wamā) | is between them (baynahumā), | if (in) | you should be (kuntum) | convinced. (mūqinīna)"

26:25 He said to those around him, "Do not you hear?"

He said (qāla) | to those (liman) | around him (ḥawlahu), | "Do not (alā) | you hear? (tastamiʿūna)"

26:26 He said, "Your Lord and the Lord of your forefathers."

He said (qāla), | "Your Lord (rabbukum) | and the Lord (warabbu) | of your forefathers. (ābāikumu)" | of your forefathers. (l-awalīna)"

26:27 He said, "Indeed, your Messenger who has been sent to you is surely mad."

He said (qāla), | "Indeed (inna), | your Messenger (rasūlakumu) | who (alladhī) | has been sent (ur'sila) | to you (ilaykum) | is surely mad. (lamajnūnun)"

26:28 He said, "Lord of the east and the west and whatever is between them, if you were to reason."

He said (qāla), | "Lord (rabbu) | of the east (l-mashriqi) | and the west (wal-maghribi) | and whatever (wamā) | is between them (baynahumā), | if (in) | you were (kuntum) | to reason. (taʿqilūna)"

26:29 He said, "If you take a god other than me, I will surely make you among those imprisoned."

He said (qāla), | "If (la-ini) | you take (ittakhadhta) | a god (ilāhan) | other than me (ghayrī), | I will surely make you (la-ajʿalannaka) | among (mina) | those imprisoned. (l-masjūnīna)"

26:30 He said, "Even if I bring you something manifest?"

He said (qāla), | "Even if (awalaw) | I bring you (ji'tuka) | something (bishayin) | manifest? (mubīnin)"

26:31 He said, "Then bring it, if you are of the truthful."

He said (qāla), | "Then bring (fati) | it (bihi), | if (in) | you are (kunta) | of (mina) | the truthful. (l-ṣādiqīna)"

26:32 So he threw his staff and behold! It was a serpent, manifest.
So he threw (fa-alqā) | his staff (ʿaṣāhu) | and behold (fa-idhā)! | It (hiya) | was a serpent (thuʿ'bānun), | manifest (mubīnun).

26:33 And he drew out his hand and behold! It was white for the observers.
And he drew out (wanazaʿa) | his hand (yadahu) | and behold (fa-idhā)! | It (hiya) | was white (bayḍāu) | for the observers (lilnnāẓirīna).

26:34 He said to the chiefs around him, "Indeed, this is surely a magician learned.
He said (qāla) | to the chiefs (lil'mala-i) | around him (ḥawlahu), | "Indeed (inna), | this (hādhā) | is surely a magician (lasāḥirun) | learned (ʿalīmun).

26:35 He wants to drive you out from your land by his magic, so what do you advise?"
He wants (yurīdu) | to (an) | drive you out (yukh'rijakum) | from (min) | your land (arḍikum) | by his magic (bisiḥ'rihi), | so what (famādhā) | do you advise? (tamurūna)"

26:36 They said, "Postpone him and his brother, and send in the cities gatherers -
They said (qālū), | "Postpone him (arjih) | and his brother (wa-akhāhu), | and send (wa-ib'ʿath) | in (fī) | the cities (l-madāini) | gatherers (ḥāshirīna)-

26:37 They will bring to you every magician, learned."
They will bring to you (yatūka) | every (bikulli) | magician (saḥḥārin), | learned. (ʿalīmin)"

26:38 So were assembled the magicians for the appointment on a day well-known.
So were assembled (fajumiʿa) | the magicians (l-saḥaratu) | for the appointment (limīqāti) | on a day (yawmin) | well-known (maʿlūmin).

26:39 And it was said to the people, "Will you assemble
And it was said (waqīla) | to the people (lilnnāsi), | "Will (hal) | you (antum) | assemble (muj'tamiʿūna)

26:40 That we may follow the magicians if they are the victorious?"
That we may (laʿallanā) | follow (nattabiʿu) | the magicians (l-saḥarata) | if (in) | they are (kānū) | they are (humu) | the victorious? (l-ghālibīna)"

26:41 So when came the magicians, they said to Firaun, "Is there for us a reward if we are the victorious?"
So when (falammā) | came (jāa) | the magicians (l-saḥaratu), | they said (qālū) | to Firaun (lifir'ʿawna), | "Is there (a-inna) | for us (lanā) | a reward (la-ajran) | if (in) | we are (kunnā) | we are (naḥnu) | the victorious? (l-ghālibīna)"

26:42 He said, "Yes, and indeed you then surely will be of the ones who are brought near."
He said (qāla), | "Yes (naʿam), | and indeed you (wa-innakum) | then (idhan) | surely will be of (lamina) | the ones who are brought near. (l-muqarabīna)"

26:43 Said to them Musa. "Throw what you are going to throw."
Said (qāla) | to them (lahum) | Musa (mūsā). | "Throw (alqū) | what (mā) | you (antum) | are going to throw. (mul'qūna)"

26:44 So they threw their ropes and their staffs and said, "By the might of Firaun, indeed, we surely, we are the victorious."

So they threw (fa-alqaw) | their ropes (ḥibālahum) | and their staffs (waʿiṣiyyahum) | and said (waqālū), | "By the might (biʿizzati) | of Firaun (firʿawna), | indeed, we (innā) | surely, we (lanaḥnu) | are the victorious. (l-ghālibūna)"

26:45 Then threw Musa his staff and behold! It swallowed what they falsified.

Then threw (fa-alqā) | Musa (mūsā) | his staff (ʿaṣāhu) | and behold (fa-idhā)! | It (hiya) | swallowed (talqafu) | what (mā) | they falsified (yafikūna).

26:46 Then fell down the magicians prostrate.

Then fell down (fa-ul'qiya) | the magicians (l-saḥaratu) | prostrate (sājidīna).

26:47 They said, "We believe in the Lord of the worlds,

They said (qālū), | "We believe (āmannā) | in the Lord (birabbi) | of the worlds (l-ʿālamīna),

26:48 Lord of Musa and Harun."

Lord (rabbi) | of Musa (mūsā) | and Harun. (wahārūna)"

26:49 He said, "You believed in him before [that] I gave permission to you. Indeed, he is surely your chief who has taught you the magic, so surely soon you will know. I will surely cut off your hands and your feet of opposite sides, and I will surely crucify you all."

He said (qāla), | "You believed (āmantum) | in him (lahu) | before (qabla) | [that] (an) | I gave permission (ādhana) | to you (lakum). | Indeed, he (innahu) | is surely your chief (lakabīrukumu) | who (alladhī) | has taught you (ʿallamakumu) | the magic (l-siḥ'ra), | so surely soon (falasawfa) | you will know (taʿlamūna). | I will surely cut off (la-uqaṭṭiʿanna) | your hands (aydiyakum) | and your feet (wa-arjulakum) | of (min) | opposite sides (khilāfin), | and I will surely crucify you (wala-uṣallibannakum) | all. (ajmaʿīna)"

26:50 They said, "No harm. Indeed, we to our Lord will return.

They said (qālū), | "No (lā) | harm (ḍayra). | Indeed, we (innā) | to (ilā) | our Lord (rabbinā) | will return (munqalibūna).

26:51 Indeed, we hope that will forgive us our Lord our sins, because we are the first of the believers."

Indeed, we (innā) | hope (naṭmaʿu) | that (an) | will forgive (yaghfira) | us (lanā) | our Lord (rabbunā) | our sins (khaṭāyānā), | because (an) | we are (kunnā) | the first (awwala) | of the believers. (l-mu'minīna)"

26:52 And We inspired to Musa, [that] "Travel by night with My slaves, indeed, you will be followed."

And We inspired (wa-awḥaynā) | to (ilā) | Musa (mūsā), | [that] (an) | "Travel by night (asri) | with My slaves (biʿibādī), | indeed, you (innakum) | will be followed. (muttabaʿūna)"

26:53 Then sent Firaun in the cities gatherers,

Then sent (fa-arsala) | Firaun (firʿawnu) | in (fī) | the cities (l-madāini) | gatherers (ḥāshirīna),

26:54 "Indeed, these are certainly a band small

"Indeed (inna), | these (hāulāi) | are certainly a band (lashir'dhimatun) | small (qalīlūna)

26:55 And indeed, they [to] us are surely enraging,

And indeed, they (wa-innahum) | [to] us (lanā) | are surely enraging (laghāiẓūna),

26:56 And indeed, we are surely a multitude forewarned."
And indeed, we (wa-innā) | are surely a multitude (lajamīʿun) | forewarned. (ḥādhirūna)"

26:57 So We expelled them from gardens and springs,
So We expelled them (fa-akhrajnāhum) | from (min) | gardens (jannātin) | and springs (waʿuyūnin),

26:58 And treasures and a place honorable,
And treasures (wakunūzin) | and a place (wamaqāmin) | honorable (karīmin),

26:59 Thus. And We caused to inherit them the Children of Israel.
Thus (kadhālika). | And We caused to inherit them (wa-awrathnāhā) | the Children of Israel (banī). | the Children of Israel (is'rāīla).

26:60 So they followed them at sunrise.
So they followed them (fa-atbaʿūhum) | at sunrise (mush'riqīna).

26:61 Then when saw each other the two hosts, said the companions of Musa, "Indeed, we are surely to be overtaken."
Then when (falammā) | saw each other (tarāā) | the two hosts (l-jamʿāni), | said (qāla) | the companions (aṣḥābu) | of Musa (mūsā), | "Indeed, we (innā) | are surely to be overtaken. (lamud'rakūna)"

26:62 He said, "Nay, indeed, with me is my Lord, He will guide me."
He said (qāla), | "Nay (kallā), | indeed (inna), | with me (maʿiya) | is my Lord (rabbī), | He will guide me. (sayahdīni)"

26:63 Then We inspired to Musa, [that] "Strike with your staff the sea." So it parted and became each part like the mountain [the] great.
Then We inspired (fa-awḥaynā) | to (ilā) | Musa (mūsā), | [that] (ani) | "Strike (iḍ'rib) | with your staff (biʿaṣāka) | the sea. (l-baḥra)" | So it parted (fa-infalaqa) | and became (fakāna) | each (kullu) | part (fir'qin) | like the mountain (kal-ṭawdi) | [the] great (l-ʿaẓīmi).

26:64 And We brought near there, the others.
And We brought near (wa-azlafnā) | there (thamma), | the others (l-ākharīna).

26:65 And We saved Musa and who were with him all.
And We saved (wa-anjaynā) | Musa (mūsā) | and who (waman) | were with him (maʿahu) | all (ajmaʿīna).

26:66 Then We drowned the others.
Then (thumma) | We drowned (aghraqnā) | the others (l-ākharīna).

26:67 Indeed, in that surely is a Sign, but not are most of them believers.
Indeed (inna), | in (fī) | that (dhālika) | surely is a Sign (laāyatan), | but not (wamā) | are (kāna) | most of them (aktharuhum) | believers (mu'minīna).

26:68 And indeed, your Lord, surely He is the All-Mighty, the Most Merciful.
And indeed (wa-inna), | your Lord (rabbaka), | surely He (lahuwa) | is the All-Mighty (l-ʿazīzu), | the Most Merciful (l-raḥīmu).

26:69 And recite to them the news of Ibrahim,
And recite (wa-ut'lu) | to them (ʿalayhim) | the news (naba-a) | of Ibrahim (ib'rāhīma),

26:70 When he said to his father and his people, "What do you worship?"
When (idh) | he said (qāla) | to his father (li-abīhi) | and his people (waqawmihi), | "What (mā) | do you worship? (taʿbudūna)"

26:71 They said, "We worship idols, so we will remain to them devoted."
They said (qālū), | "We worship (naʿbudu) | idols (aṣnāman), | so we will remain (fanaẓallu) | to them (lahā) | devoted. (ʿākifīna)"

26:72 He said, "Do they hear you when you call?
He said (qāla), | "Do (hal) | they hear you (yasmaʿūnakum) | when (idh) | you call (tadʿūna)?

26:73 Or do they benefit you or they harm you?"
Or (aw) | do they benefit you (yanfaʿūnakum) | or (aw) | they harm you? (yaḍurrūna)"

26:74 They said, "Nay, but we found our forefathers like that - doing."
They said (qālū), | "Nay (bal), | but we found (wajadnā) | our forefathers (ābāanā) | like that (kadhālika)- | doing. (yafʿalūna)"

26:75 He said, "Do you see what you have been worshipping,
He said (qāla), | "Do you see (afara-aytum) | what (mā) | you have been (kuntum) | worshipping (taʿbudūna),

26:76 You and your forefathers.
You (antum) | and your forefathers (waābāukumu). | and your forefathers (l-aqdamūna).

26:77 Indeed, they are enemies to me, except the Lord of the worlds,
Indeed, they (fa-innahum) | are enemies (ʿaduwwun) | to me (lī), | except (illā) | the Lord (rabba) | of the worlds (l-ʿālamīna),

26:78 The One Who created me, and He guides me.
The One Who (alladhī) | created me (khalaqanī), | and He (fahuwa) | guides me (yahdīni).

26:79 And the One Who [He] gives me food and gives me drink.
And the One Who (wa-alladhī) | [He] (huwa) | gives me food (yuṭ'ʿimunī) | and gives me drink (wayasqīni).

26:80 And when I am ill, then He cures me,
And when (wa-idhā) | I am ill (mariḍ'tu), | then He (fahuwa) | cures me (yashfīni),

26:81 And the One Who will cause me to die then he will give me life,
And the One Who (wa-alladhī) | will cause me to die (yumītunī) | then (thumma) | he will give me life (yuḥ'yīni),

26:82 And the One Who - I hope that He will forgive for me my faults on the Day of the Judgment.
And the One Who (wa-alladhī)- | I hope (aṭmaʿu) | that (an) | He will forgive (yaghfira) | for me (lī) | my faults (khaṭīatī) | on the Day (yawma) | of the Judgment (l-dīni).

26:83 My Lord! Grant [for] me wisdom and join me with the righteous.
My Lord (rabbi)! | Grant (hab) | [for] me (lī) | wisdom (ḥuk'man) | and join me (wa-alḥiq'nī) | with the righteous (bil-ṣāliḥīna).

26:84 And grant [for] me a mention of honor among the later generations.
And grant (wa-ij'ʿal) | [for] me (lī) | a mention (lisāna) | of honor (ṣid'qin) | among (fī) | the later generations (l-ākhirīna).

26:85 And make me of the inheritors of Garden(s) of Delight.
And make me (wa-ij'ʿalnī) | of (min) | the inheritors (warathati) | of Garden(s (jannati)) | of Delight (l-naʿīmi).

26:86 And forgive my father. Indeed, he is of those astray.
And forgive (wa-igh'fir) | my father (li-abī). | Indeed, he (innahu) | is (kāna) | of (mina) | those astray (l-ḍālīna).

26:87 And do not disgrace me on the Day they are resurrected,
And do not (walā) | disgrace me (tukh'zinī) | on the Day (yawma) | they are resurrected (yub'ʿathūna),

26:88 The Day not will benefit wealth and not sons,
The Day (yawma) | not (lā) | will benefit (yanfaʿu) | wealth (mālun) | and not (walā) | sons (banūna),

26:89 Except he who comes to Allah with a heart sound."
Except (illā) | he who (man) | comes (atā) | to Allah (l-laha) | with a heart (biqalbin) | sound. (salīmin)"

26:90 And will be brought near the Paradise for the righteous.
And will be brought near (wa-uz'lifati) | the Paradise (l-janatu) | for the righteous (lil'muttaqīna).

26:91 And will be made manifest the Hellfire to the deviators.
And will be made manifest (waburrizati) | the Hellfire (l-jaḥīmu) | to the deviators (lil'ghāwīna).

26:92 And it will be said to them, "Where is that you used to worship
And it will be said (waqīla) | to them (lahum), | "Where (ayna) | is that (mā) | you used (kuntum) | to worship (taʿbudūna)

26:93 Besides Allah? Can they help you or help themselves?"
Besides Allah (min)? | Besides Allah (dūni)? | Besides Allah (l-lahi)? | Can (hal) | they help you (yanṣurūnakum) | or (aw) | help themselves? (yantaṣirūna)"

26:94 Then they will be overturned into it, they and the deviators
Then they will be overturned (fakub'kibū) | into it (fīhā), | they (hum) | and the deviators (wal-ghāwūna)

26:95 And the hosts of Iblis all together.
And the hosts (wajunūdu) | of Iblis (ib'līsa) | all together (ajmaʿūna).

26:96 They will say while they in it are disputing,

They will say (qālū) | while they (wahum) | in it (fīhā) | are disputing (yakhtaṣimūna),

26:97 "By Allah, indeed, we were surely in error clear
"By Allah (tal-lahi), | indeed (in), | we were (kunnā) | surely in (lafī) | error (ḍalālin) | clear (mubīnin)

26:98 When we equated you with the Lord of the worlds.
When (idh) | we equated you (nusawwīkum) | with the Lord (birabbi) | of the worlds (l-ʿālamīna).

26:99 And not misguided us except the criminals.
And not (wamā) | misguided us (aḍallanā) | except (illā) | the criminals (l-muj'rimūna).

26:100 So now not we have any intercessors
So now not (famā) | we have (lanā) | any (min) | intercessors (shāfiʿīna)

26:101 And not a friend close.
And not (walā) | a friend (ṣadīqin) | close (ḥamīmin).

26:102 Then if that we had a return, then we could be of the believers."
Then if (falaw) | that (anna) | we had (lanā) | a return (karratan), | then we could be (fanakūna) | of (mina) | the believers. (l-mu'minīna)"

26:103 Indeed, in that surely is a Sign, but not are most of them believers.
Indeed (inna), | in (fī) | that (dhālika) | surely is a Sign (laāyatan), | but not (wamā) | are (kāna) | most of them (aktharuhum) | believers (mu'minīna).

26:104 And indeed, your Lord, surely He is the All-Mighty, the Most Merciful.
And indeed (wa-inna), | your Lord (rabbaka), | surely He (lahuwa) | is the All-Mighty (l-ʿazīzu), | the Most Merciful (l-raḥīmu).

26:105 Denied the people of Nuh the Messengers
Denied (kadhabat) | the people (qawmu) | of Nuh (nūḥin) | the Messengers (l-mur'salīna)

26:106 When said to them their brother Nuh, "Will not you fear Allah?
When (idh) | said (qāla) | to them (lahum) | their brother (akhūhum) | Nuh (nūḥun), | "Will not (alā) | you fear Allah (tattaqūna)?

26:107 Indeed, I am to you a Messenger trustworthy.
Indeed, I am (innī) | to you (lakum) | a Messenger (rasūlun) | trustworthy (amīnun).

26:108 So fear Allah and obey me.
So fear (fa-ittaqū) | Allah (l-laha) | and obey me (wa-aṭīʿūni).

26:109 And not I ask of you for it any payment. Not is my payment but from the Lord of the worlds.
And not (wamā) | I ask of you (asalukum) | for it (ʿalayhi) | any (min) | payment (ajrin). | Not (in) | is my payment (ajriya) | but (illā) | from (ʿalā) | the Lord (rabbi) | of the worlds (l-ʿālamīna).

26:110 So fear Allah and obey me."
So fear (fa-ittaqū) | Allah (l-laha) | and obey me. (wa-aṭīʿūni)"

26:111 They said, "Should we believe in you while followed you the lowest?"
They said (qālū), | "Should we believe (anu'minu) | in you (laka) | while followed you (wa-ittabaʿaka) | the lowest? (l-ardhalūna)"

26:112 He said, "And what do I know of what they used to do?
He said (qāla), | "And what (wamā) | do I know (ʿil'mī) | of what (bimā) | they used (kānū) | to do (yaʿmalūna)?

26:113 Verily, their account is but upon my Lord, if you perceive.
Verily (in), | their account (ḥisābuhum) | is but (illā) | upon (ʿalā) | my Lord (rabbī), | if (law) | you perceive (tashʿurūna).

26:114 And not I am the one to drive away the believers.
And not (wamā) | I am (anā) | the one to drive away (biṭāridi) | the believers (l-mu'minīna).

26:115 Not I am but a warner clear."
Not (in) | I am (anā) | but (illā) | a warner (nadhīrun) | clear. (mubīnun)"

26:116 They said, "If not you desist, O Nuh! Surely you will be of those who are stoned."
They said (qālū), | "If (la-in) | not (lam) | you desist (tantahi), | O Nuh (yānūḥu)! | Surely you will be (latakūnanna) | of (mina) | those who are stoned. (l-marjūmīna)"

26:117 He said, "My Lord! Indeed, my people have denied me.
He said (qāla), | "My Lord (rabbi)! | Indeed (inna), | my people (qawmī) | have denied me (kadhabūni).

26:118 So judge between me and between them with decisive judgment, and save me and who are with me of the believers."
So judge (fa-if'taḥ) | between me (baynī) | and between them (wabaynahum) | with decisive judgment (fatḥan), | and save me (wanajjinī) | and who (waman) | are with me (maʿiya) | of (mina) | the believers. (l-mu'minīna)"

26:119 So We saved him and who were with him in the ship, laden.
So We saved him (fa-anjaynāhu) | and who (waman) | were with him (maʿahu) | in (fī) | the ship (l-ful'ki), | laden (l-mashḥūni).

26:120 Then We drowned thereafter the remaining ones.
Then (thumma) | We drowned (aghraqnā) | thereafter (baʿdu) | the remaining ones (l-bāqīna).

26:121 Indeed, in that surely, is a sign but not are most of them believers.
Indeed (inna), | in (fī) | that (dhālika) | surely, is a sign (laāyatan) | but not (wamā) | are (kāna) | most of them (aktharuhum) | believers (mu'minīna).

26:122 And indeed, your Lord surely, He is the All-Mighty, the Most Merciful.
And indeed (wa-inna), | your Lord (rabbaka) | surely, He (lahuwa) | is the All-Mighty (l-ʿazīzu), | the Most Merciful (l-raḥīmu).

26:123 Denied the people of Aad the Messengers.
Denied (kadhabat) | the people of Aad (ʿādun) | the Messengers (l-mur'salīna).

26:124 When said to them their brother Hud, "Will not you fear Allah?
When (idh) | said (qāla) | to them (lahum) | their brother (akhūhum) | Hud (hūdun), | "Will not (alā) | you fear Allah (tattaqūna)?

26:125 Indeed, I am to you a Messenger trustworthy.
Indeed, I am (innī) | to you (lakum) | a Messenger (rasūlun) | trustworthy (amīnun).

26:126 So fear Allah and obey me.
So fear (fa-ittaqū) | Allah (l-laha) | and obey me (wa-aṭīʿūni).

26:127 And not I ask you for it any payment. Not is my payment except from the Lord of the worlds.
And not (wamā) | I ask you (asalukum) | for it (ʿalayhi) | any (min) | payment (ajrin). | Not (in) | is my payment (ajriya) | except (illā) | from (ʿalā) | the Lord (rabbi) | of the worlds (l-ʿālamīna).

26:128 Do you construct on every elevation a sign, amusing yourselves,
Do you construct (atabnūna) | on every (bikulli) | elevation (rīʿin) | a sign (āyatan), | amusing yourselves (taʿbathūna),

26:129 And take for yourselves strongholds that you may live forever?
And take for yourselves (watattakhidhūna) | strongholds (maṣāniʿa) | that you may (laʿallakum) | live forever (takhludūna)?

26:130 And when you seize, you seize as tyrants.
And when (wa-idhā) | you seize (baṭashtum), | you seize (baṭashtum) | as tyrants (jabbārīna).

26:131 So fear Allah and obey me.
So fear (fa-ittaqū) | Allah (l-laha) | and obey me (wa-aṭīʿūni).

26:132 And fear the One Who has aided you with what you know,
And fear (wa-ittaqū) | the One Who (alladhī) | has aided you (amaddakum) | with what (bimā) | you know (taʿlamūna),

26:133 He has aided you with cattle and children,
He has aided you (amaddakum) | with cattle (bi-anʿāmin) | and children (wabanīna),

26:134 And gardens and springs.
And gardens (wajannātin) | and springs (waʿuyūnin).

26:135 Indeed, I [I] fear for you the punishment of a Day Great."
Indeed, I (innī) | [I] fear (akhāfu) | for you (ʿalaykum) | the punishment (ʿadhāba) | of a Day (yawmin) | Great. (ʿaẓīmin)"

26:136 They said, "It is same to us whether you advise or not you are of the advisors.
They said (qālū), | "It is same (sawāon) | to us (ʿalaynā) | whether you advise (awaʿaẓta) | or (am) | not (lam) | you are (takun) | of (mina) | the advisors (l-wāʿiẓīna).

26:137 Not is this but the custom of the former (people),
Not (in) | is this (hādhā) | but (illā) | the custom (khuluqu) | of the former (people) (l-awalīna),

26:138 And not we are the ones to be punished."

And not (wamā) | we (naḥnu) | are the ones to be punished. (bimuʿadhabīna)"

26:139 So they denied him, then We destroyed them. Indeed, in that surely, is a sign, but not are most of them believers.

So they denied him (fakadhabūhu), | then We destroyed them (fa-ahlaknāhum). | Indeed (inna), | in (fī) | that (dhālika) | surely, is a sign (laāyatan), | but not (wamā) | are (kāna) | most of them (aktharuhum) | believers (mu'minīna).

26:140 And indeed, your Lord surely, He is the All-Mighty, the Most Merciful.

And indeed (wa-inna), | your Lord (rabbaka) | surely, He (lahuwa) | is the All-Mighty (l-ʿazīzu), | the Most Merciful (l-raḥīmu).

26:141 Denied Thamud, the Messengers

Denied (kadhabat) | Thamud (thamūdu), | the Messengers (l-mur'salīna)

26:142 When, said to them their brother Salih, "Will not you fear Allah?

When (idh), | said (qāla) | to them (lahum) | their brother (akhūhum) | Salih (ṣāliḥun), | "Will not (alā) | you fear Allah (tattaqūna)?

26:143 Indeed, I am to you a Messenger trustworthy.

Indeed, I am (innī) | to you (lakum) | a Messenger (rasūlun) | trustworthy (amīnun).

26:144 So fear Allah and obey me.

So fear (fa-ittaqū) | Allah (l-laha) | and obey me (wa-aṭīʿūni).

26:145 And not I ask you for it any payment. Not is my payment except from the Lord of the worlds.

And not (wamā) | I ask you (asalukum) | for it (ʿalayhi) | any (min) | payment (ajrin). | Not (in) | is my payment (ajriya) | except (illā) | from (ʿalā) | the Lord (rabbi) | of the worlds (l-ʿālamīna).

26:146 Will you be left in what is here secure,

Will you be left (atut'rakūna) | in (fī) | what (mā) | is here (hāhunā) | secure (āminīna),

26:147 In gardens and springs,

In (fī) | gardens (jannātin) | and springs (waʿuyūnin),

26:148 And cornfields and date-palms its spadix soft?

And cornfields (wazurūʿin) | and date-palms (wanakhlin) | its spadix (ṭalʿuhā) | soft (haḍīmun)?

26:149 And you carve of the mountains, houses skillfully.

And you carve (watanḥitūna) | of (mina) | the mountains (l-jibāli), | houses (buyūtan) | skillfully (fārihīna).

26:150 So fear Allah and obey me.

So fear (fa-ittaqū) | Allah (l-laha) | and obey me (wa-aṭīʿūni).

26:151 And do not obey the command of the transgressors,

And do not (walā) | obey (tuṭīʿū) | the command (amra) | of the transgressors (l-mus'rifīna),

26:152 Those who spread corruption in the earth and do not reform."

Those who (alladhīna) | spread corruption (yuf'sidūna) | in (fī) | the earth (l-arḍi) | and do not (walā) | reform. (yuṣ'liḥūna)"

26:153 They said, "Only you are of those bewitched.
They said (qālū), | "Only (innamā) | you (anta) | are of (mina) | those bewitched (l-musaḥarīna).

26:154 Not you are except a man like us, so bring a sign, if you are of the truthful."
Not (mā) | you (anta) | are except (illā) | a man (basharun) | like us (mith'lunā), | so bring (fati) | a sign (biāyatin), | if (in) | you (kunta) | are of (mina) | the truthful. (l-ṣādiqīna)"

26:155 He said, "This is a she-camel. For her is a share of drink, and for you is a share of drink on a day known.
He said (qāla), | "This (hādhihi) | is a she-camel (nāqatun). | For her (lahā) | is a share of drink (shir'bun), | and for you (walakum) | is a share of drink (shir'bu) | on a day (yawmin) | known (maʿlūmin).

26:156 And do not touch her with harm, lest seize you the punishment of a Day Great."
And do not (walā) | touch her (tamassūhā) | with harm (bisūin), | lest seize you (fayakhudhakum) | the punishment (ʿadhābu) | of a Day (yawmin) | Great. (ʿaẓīmin)"

26:157 But they hamstrung her, then they became regretful.
But they hamstrung her (faʿaqarūhā), | then they became (fa-aṣbaḥū) | regretful (nādimīna).

26:158 So seized them the punishment. Indeed, in that surely is a sign, but not are most of them believers.
So seized them (fa-akhadhahumu) | the punishment (l-ʿadhābu). | Indeed (inna), | in (fī) | that (dhālika) | surely is a sign (laāyatan), | but not (wamā) | are (kāna) | most of them (aktharuhum) | believers (mu'minīna).

26:159 And indeed, your Lord, surely He is the All-Mighty, the Most Merciful.
And indeed (wa-inna), | your Lord (rabbaka), | surely He (lahuwa) | is the All-Mighty (l-ʿazīzu), | the Most Merciful (l-raḥīmu).

26:160 Denied, the people of Lut, the Messengers.
Denied (kadhabat), | the people (qawmu) | of Lut (lūṭin), | the Messengers (l-mur'salīna).

26:161 When said to them their brother Lut, "Will not you fear Allah?
When (idh) | said (qāla) | to them (lahum) | their brother (akhūhum) | Lut (lūṭun), | "Will not (alā) | you fear Allah (tattaqūna)?

26:162 Indeed, I am to you a Messenger trustworthy.
Indeed, I am (innī) | to you (lakum) | a Messenger (rasūlun) | trustworthy (amīnun).

26:163 So fear Allah and obey me.
So fear (fa-ittaqū) | Allah (l-laha) | and obey me (wa-aṭīʿūni).

26:164 And not I ask you for it any payment Not is my payment except from the Lord of the worlds.
And not (wamā) | I ask you (asalukum) | for it (ʿalayhi) | any (min) | payment (ajrin) | Not (in) | is my payment (ajriya) | except (illā) | from (ʿalā) | the Lord (rabbi) | of the worlds (l-ʿālamīna).

26:165 Do you approach the males among the worlds

Do you approach (atatūna) | the males (l-dhuk'rāna) | among (mina) | the worlds (l-ʿālamīna)

26:166 And you leave what created for you your Lord, of your mates? Nay, you are a people transgressing."

And you leave (watadharūna) | what (mā) | created (khalaqa) | for you (lakum) | your Lord (rabbukum), | of (min) | your mates (azwājikum)? | Nay (bal), | you (antum) | are a people (qawmun) | transgressing. (ʿādūna)"

26:167 They said, "If not you desist, O Lut! Surely, you will be of the ones driven out."

They said (qālū), | "If (la-in) | not (lam) | you desist (tantahi), | O Lut (yālūṭu)! | Surely, you will be (latakūnanna) | of (mina) | the ones driven out. (l-mukh'rajīna)"

26:168 He said, "Indeed, I am of your deed of those who detest.

He said (qāla), | "Indeed, I am (innī) | of your deed (liʿamalikum) | of (mina) | those who detest (l-qālīna).

26:169 My Lord! Save me and my family from what they do."

My Lord (rabbi)! | Save me (najjinī) | and my family (wa-ahlī) | from what (mimmā) | they do. (yaʿmalūna)"

26:170 So We saved him and his family all,

So We saved him (fanajjaynāhu) | and his family (wa-ahlahu) | all (ajmaʿīna),

26:171 Except an old woman, was among those who remained behind.

Except (illā) | an old woman (ʿajūzan), | was among (fī) | those who remained behind (l-ghābirīna).

26:172 Then We destroyed the others.

Then (thumma) | We destroyed (dammarnā) | the others (l-ākharīna).

26:173 And We rained upon them a rain, and evil was was the rain on those who were warned.

And We rained (wa-amṭarnā) | upon them (ʿalayhim) | a rain (maṭaran), | and evil was (fasāa) | was the rain (maṭaru) | on those who were warned (l-mundharīna).

26:174 Indeed, in that surely is a sign, but not are most of them believers.

Indeed (inna), | in (fī) | that (dhālika) | surely is a sign (laāyatan), | but not (wamā) | are (kāna) | most of them (aktharuhum) | believers (mu'minīna).

26:175 And indeed, your Lord, surely, He is the All-Mighty, the Most Merciful.

And indeed (wa-inna), | your Lord (rabbaka), | surely, He (lahuwa) | is the All-Mighty (l-ʿazīzu), | the Most Merciful (l-raḥīmu).

26:176 Denied the companions of the Wood, the Messengers.

Denied (kadhaba) | the companions (aṣḥābu) | of the Wood (al'aykati), | the Messengers (l-mur'salīna).

26:177 When, said to them Shuaib, "Will not you fear Allah?

When (idh), | said (qāla) | to them (lahum) | Shuaib (shuʿaybun), | "Will not (alā) | you fear Allah (tattaqūna)?

26:178 Indeed, I am to you a Messenger trustworthy.

Indeed, I am (innī) | to you (lakum) | a Messenger (rasūlun) | trustworthy (amīnun).

26:179 So fear Allah and obey me.
So fear (fa-ittaqū) | Allah (l-laha) | and obey me (wa-aṭīʿūni).

26:180 And not I ask of you for it any payment. Not is my payment except from the Lord of the worlds.
And not (wamā) | I ask of you (asalukum) | for it (ʿalayhi) | any (min) | payment (ajrin). | Not (in) | is my payment (ajriya) | except (illā) | from (ʿalā) | the Lord (rabbi) | of the worlds (l-ʿālamīna).

26:181 Give full measure and do not be of those who cause loss.
Give full (awfū) | measure (l-kayla) | and do not (walā) | be (takūnū) | of (mina) | those who cause loss (l-mukh'sirīna).

26:182 And weigh with a balance, [the] even.
And weigh (wazinū) | with a balance (bil-qis'ṭāsi), | [the] even (l-mus'taqīmi).

26:183 And do not deprive people of their things, and do not commit evil in the earth, spreading corruption.
And do not (walā) | deprive (tabkhasū) | people (l-nāsa) | of their things (ashyāahum), | and do not (walā) | commit evil (taʿthaw) | in (fī) | the earth (l-arḍi), | spreading corruption (muf'sidīna).

26:184 And fear the One Who created you and the generations the former."
And fear (wa-ittaqū) | the One Who (alladhī) | created you (khalaqakum) | and the generations (wal-jibilata) | the former. (l-awalīna)"

26:185 They said, "Only you are of those bewitched.
They said (qālū), | "Only (innamā) | you (anta) | are of (mina) | those bewitched (l-musaḥarīna).

26:186 And not you are except a man like us, and indeed, we think you surely are of the liars.
And not (wamā) | you (anta) | are except (illā) | a man (basharun) | like us (mith'lunā), | and indeed (wa-in), | we think you (naẓunnuka) | surely are of (lamina) | the liars (l-kādhibīna).

26:187 Then cause to fall upon us fragments of the sky, if you are of the truthful."
Then cause to fall (fa-asqiṭ) | upon us (ʿalaynā) | fragments (kisafan) | of (mina) | the sky (l-samāi), | if (in) | you are (kunta) | of (mina) | the truthful. (l-ṣādiqīna)"

26:188 He said, "My Lord knows best of what you do."
He said (qāla), | "My Lord (rabbī) | knows best (aʿlamu) | of what (bimā) | you do. (taʿmalūna)"

26:189 But they denied him, so seized them the punishment of the day of the shadow. Indeed, it was the punishment of a Day Great.
But they denied him (fakadhabūhu), | so seized them (fa-akhadhahum) | the punishment (ʿadhābu) | of the day (yawmi) | of the shadow (l-ẓulati). | Indeed, it (innahu) | was (kāna) | the punishment (ʿadhāba) | of a Day (yawmin) | Great (ʿaẓīmin).

26:190 Indeed, in that surely, is a sign but not are most of them believers.
Indeed (inna), | in (fī) | that (dhālika) | surely, is a sign (laāyatan) | but not (wamā) | are

(kāna) | most of them (aktharuhum) | believers (mu'minīna).

26:191 And indeed, your Lord surely, He is the All-Mighty, the Most Merciful.
And indeed (wa-inna), | your Lord (rabbaka) | surely, He (lahuwa) | is the All-Mighty (l-ʿazīzu), | the Most Merciful (l-raḥīmu).

26:192 And indeed, it surely, is a Revelation of the Lord of the worlds.
And indeed, it (wa-innahu) | surely, is a Revelation (latanzīlu) | of the Lord (rabbi) | of the worlds (l-ʿālamīna).

26:193 Has brought it down, the Spirit [the] Trustworthy,
Has brought it down (nazala), | Has brought it down (bihi), | the Spirit (l-rūḥu) | [the] Trustworthy (l-amīnu),

26:194 Upon your heart, that you may be of the warners
Upon (ʿalā) | your heart (qalbika), | that you may be (litakūna) | of (mina) | the warners (l-mundhirīna)

26:195 In language Arabic clear.
In language (bilisānin) | Arabic (ʿarabiyyin) | clear (mubīnin).

26:196 And indeed, it surely, is in the Scriptures of the former (people).
And indeed, it (wa-innahu) | surely, is in (lafī) | the Scriptures (zuburi) | of the former (people) (l-awalīna).

26:197 Is it not to them a sign that know it the scholars of the Children of Israel?
Is it not (awalam) | Is it not (yakun) | to them (lahum) | a sign (āyatan) | that (an) | know it (yaʿlamahu) | the scholars (ʿulamāu) | of the Children (banī) | of Israel (is'rāīla)?

26:198 And if We had revealed it to any of the non-Arabs
And if (walaw) | We had revealed it (nazzalnāhu) | to (ʿalā) | any (baʿḍi) | of the non-Arabs (l-aʿjamīna)

26:199 And he had recited it to them, not they would in it be believers.
And he had recited it (faqara-ahu) | to them (ʿalayhim), | not (mā) | they would (kānū) | in it (bihi) | be believers (mu'minīna).

26:200 Thus We have inserted it into the hearts of the criminals.
Thus (kadhālika) | We have inserted it (salaknāhu) | into (fī) | the hearts (qulūbi) | of the criminals (l-muj'rimīna).

26:201 Not they will believe in it until they see the punishment [the] painful.
Not (lā) | they will believe (yu'minūna) | in it (bihi) | until (ḥattā) | they see (yarawū) | the punishment (l-ʿadhāba) | [the] painful (l-alīma).

26:202 And it will come to them suddenly, while they do not perceive.
And it will come to them (fayatiyahum) | suddenly (baghtatan), | while they (wahum) | do not (lā) | perceive (yashʿurūna).

26:203 Then they will say, "Are we to be reprieved?"
Then they will say (fayaqūlū), | "Are (hal) | we (naḥnu) | to be reprieved? (munẓarūna)"

26:204 So is it for Our punishment they wish to hasten?
So is it for Our punishment (afabiʿadhābinā) | they wish to hasten (yastaʿjilūna)?

26:205 Then have you seen if We let them enjoy for years
Then have you seen (afara-ayta) | if (in) | We let them enjoy (mattaʿnāhum) | for years (sinīna)

26:206 Then comes to them what they were promised
Then (thumma) | comes to them (jāahum) | what (mā) | they were (kānū) | promised (yūʿadūna)

26:207 Not will avail them what enjoyment they were given?
Not (mā) | will avail (aghnā) | them (ʿanhum) | what (mā) | enjoyment they were given (kānū)? | enjoyment they were given (yumattaʿūna)?

26:208 And not We destroyed any town but it had warners
And not (wamā) | We destroyed (ahlaknā) | any (min) | town (qaryatin) | but (illā) | it had (lahā) | warners (mundhirūna)

26:209 To remind, and not We are unjust.
To remind (dhik'rā), | and not (wamā) | We are (kunnā) | unjust (ẓālimīna).

26:210 And not have brought it down the devils.
And not (wamā) | have brought it down (tanazzalat) | have brought it down (bihi) | the devils (l-shayāṭīnu).

26:211 And not it suits [for] them and not they are able.
And not (wamā) | it suits (yanbaghī) | [for] them (lahum) | and not (wamā) | they are able (yastaṭīʿūna).

26:212 Indeed, they from the hearing are surely banished.
Indeed, they (innahum) | from (ʿani) | the hearing (l-samʿi) | are surely banished (lamaʿzūlūna).

26:213 So do not invoke with Allah, god another lest you be of those punished.
So do not (falā) | invoke (tadʿu) | with (maʿa) | Allah (l-lahi), | god (ilāhan) | another (ākhara) | lest you be (fatakūna) | of (mina) | those punished (l-muʿadhabīna).

26:214 And warn your kindred [the] closest.
And warn (wa-andhir) | your kindred (ʿashīrataka) | [the] closest (l-aqrabīna).

26:215 And lower your wing to those who follow you of the believers.
And lower (wa-ikh'fiḍ) | your wing (janāḥaka) | to those who (limani) | follow you (ittabaʿaka) | of (mina) | the believers (l-mu'minīna).

26:216 Then if they disobey you then say, "Indeed, I am innocent of what you do."
Then if (fa-in) | they disobey you (ʿaṣawka) | then say (faqul), | "Indeed, I am (innī) | innocent (barīon) | of what (mimmā) | you do. (taʿmalūna)"

26:217 And put your trust in the All-Mighty, the Most Merciful,
And put your trust (watawakkal) | in (ʿalā) | the All-Mighty (l-ʿazīzi), | the Most Merciful (l-raḥīmi),

26:218 The One Who sees you when you stand up
The One Who (alladhī) | sees you (yarāka) | when (ḥīna) | you stand up (taqūmu)

26:219 And your movements among those who prostrate.
And your movements (wataqallubaka) | among (fī) | those who prostrate (l-sājidīna).

26:220 Indeed, He [He] is the All-Hearer, the All-Knower.
Indeed, He (innahu) | [He] (huwa) | is the All-Hearer (l-samīʿu), | the All-Knower (l-ʿalīmu).

26:221 Shall I inform you upon whom descend the devils?
Shall (hal) | I inform you (unabbi-ukum) | upon (ʿalā) | whom (man) | descend (tanazzalu) | the devils (l-shayāṭīnu)?

26:222 They descend upon every liar sinful.
They descend (tanazzalu) | upon (ʿalā) | every (kulli) | liar (affākin) | sinful (athīmin).

26:223 They pass on what is heard, and most of them are liars.
They pass on (yul'qūna) | what is heard (l-samʿa), | and most of them (wa-aktharuhum) | are liars (kādhibūna).

26:224 And the poets - follow them the deviators.
And the poets (wal-shuʿarāu)- | follow them (yattabiʿuhumu) | the deviators (l-ghāwūna).

26:225 Do not you see that they in every valley [they] roam,
Do not (alam) | you see (tara) | that they (annahum) | in (fī) | every (kulli) | valley (wādin) | [they] roam (yahīmūna),

26:226 And that they say what not they do?
And that they (wa-annahum) | say (yaqūlūna) | what (mā) | not (lā) | they do (yafʿalūna)?

26:227 Except those who believe and do righteous deeds and remember Allah much, and defend themselves after they were wronged. And will come to know those who have wronged to what return they will return.
Except (illā) | those who (alladhīna) | believe (āmanū) | and do (waʿamilū) | righteous deeds (l-ṣāliḥāti) | and remember (wadhakarū) | Allah (l-laha) | much (kathīran), | and defend themselves (wa-intaṣarū) | after (min) | after (baʿdi) | after (mā) | they were wronged (ẓulimū). | And will come to know (wasayaʿlamu) | those who (alladhīna) | have wronged (ẓalamū) | to what (ayya) | return (munqalabin) | they will return (yanqalibūna).

Chapter (27) Sūrat l-Naml (The Ants)

27:1 Ta Seen. These are the Verses of the Quran and a Book clear
Ta Seen (tta-seen). | These (til'ka) | are the Verses (āyātu) | of the Quran (l-qur'āni) | and a Book (wakitābin) | clear (mubīnin)

27:2 A guidance and glad tidings for the believers,
A guidance (hudan) | and glad tidings (wabush'rā) | for the believers (lil'mu'minīna),

27:3 Those who establish the prayer and give zakah and they in the Hereafter [they] believe with certainty.
Those who (alladhīna) | establish (yuqīmūna) | the prayer (l-ṣalata) | and give (wayu'tūna) | zakah (l-zakata) | and they (wahum) | in the Hereafter (bil-ākhirati) | [they] (hum) | believe with certainty (yūqinūna).

27:4 Indeed, those who do not believe in the Hereafter, We have made fair-seeming to them their deeds, so they wander blindly.
Indeed (inna), | those who (alladhīna) | do not (lā) | believe (yu'minūna) | in the Hereafter (bil-ākhirati), | We have made fair-seeming (zayyannā) | to them (lahum) | their deeds (aʿmālahum), | so they (fahum) | wander blindly (yaʿmahūna).

27:5 Those are the ones, for them is an evil [the] punishment and they in the Hereafter [they] will be the greatest losers.
Those (ulāika) | are the ones (alladhīna), | for them (lahum) | is an evil (sūu) | [the] punishment (l-ʿadhābi) | and they (wahum) | in (fī) | the Hereafter (l-ākhirati) | [they] (humu) | will be the greatest losers (l-akhsarūna).

27:6 And indeed, you surely, receive the Quran from [near] the All-Wise, the All-Knower.
And indeed, you (wa-innaka) | surely, receive (latulaqqā) | the Quran (l-qur'āna) | from [near] (min) | from [near] (ladun) | the All-Wise (ḥakīmin), | the All-Knower (ʿalīmin).

27:7 When said Musa to his family, "Indeed, I perceive a fire. I will bring you from it some information or I will bring you a torch burning so that you may warm yourselves."
When (idh) | said (qāla) | Musa (mūsā) | to his family (li-ahlihi), | "Indeed, I (innī) | perceive (ānastu) | a fire (nāran). | I will bring you (saātīkum) | from it (min'hā) | some information (bikhabarin) | or (aw) | I will bring you (ātīkum) | a torch (bishihābin) | burning (qabasin) | so that you may (laʿallakum) | warm yourselves. (taṣṭalūna)"

27:8 But when he came to it, he was called [that] "Blessed is who is at the fire and whoever is around it. And glory be to Allah the Lord of the worlds.
But when (falammā) | he came to it (jāahā), | he was called (nūdiya) | [that] (an) | "Blessed is (būrika) | who (man) | is at (fī) | the fire (l-nāri) | and whoever (waman) | is around it (ḥawlahā). | And glory be (wasub'ḥāna) | to Allah (l-lahi) | the Lord (rabbi) | of the worlds (l-ʿālamīna).

27:9 O Musa! Indeed, I Am Allah, the All-Mighty, the All-Wise."
O Musa (yāmūsā)! | Indeed (innahu), | I Am (anā) | Allah (l-lahu), | the All-Mighty (l-ʿazīzu), | the All-Wise. (l-ḥakīmu)"

27:10 And, "Throw your staff." But when he saw it moving as if it were a snake he turned back in flight and did not look back. "O Musa! Do not fear. Indeed, [I] do not fear in My presence the Messengers.
And, "Throw (wa-alqi) | your staff. (ʿaṣāka)" | But when (falammā) | he saw it (raāhā) | moving (tahtazzu) | as if it (ka-annahā) | were a snake (jānnun) | he turned back (wallā) | in flight (mud'biran) | and did not (walam) | look back (yuʿaqqib). | "O Musa (yāmūsā)! | Do not (lā) | fear (takhaf). | Indeed, [I] (innī) | do not (lā) | fear (yakhāfu) | in My presence (ladayya) | the Messengers (l-mur'salūna).

27:11 Except who wrongs then substitutes good after evil, then indeed, I Am Oft-Forgiving, Most Merciful.

Except (illā) | who (man) | wrongs (ẓalama) | then (thumma) | substitutes (baddala) | good (ḥus'nan) | after (baʿda) | evil (sūin), | then indeed, I Am (fa-innī) | Oft-Forgiving (ghafūrun), | Most Merciful (raḥīmun).

27:12 And enter your hand into your bosom it will come forth white without harm. These are among nine signs to Firaun and his people. Indeed, they are a people defiantly disobedient."

And enter (wa-adkhil) | your hand (yadaka) | into (fī) | your bosom (jaybika) | it will come forth (takhruj) | white (bayḍāa) | without (min) | without (ghayri) | harm (sūin). | These are among (fī) | nine (tisʿi) | signs (āyātin) | to (ilā) | Firaun (firʿawna) | and his people (waqawmihi). | Indeed, they (innahum) | are (kānū) | a people (qawman) | defiantly disobedient. (fāsiqīna)"

27:13 But when came to them Our Signs visible, they said, "This is a magic manifest."

But when (falammā) | came to them (jāathum) | Our Signs (āyātunā) | visible (mub'ṣiratan), | they said (qālū), | "This (hādhā) | is a magic (siḥ'run) | manifest. (mubīnun)"

27:14 And they rejected them, though were convinced with them signs themselves, out of injustice and haughtiness. So see how was the end of the corrupters.

And they rejected (wajaḥadū) | them (bihā), | though were convinced with them signs (wa-is'tayqanathā) | themselves (anfusuhum), | out of injustice (ẓul'man) | and haughtiness (waʿuluwwan). | So see (fa-unẓur) | how (kayfa) | was (kāna) | the end (ʿāqibatu) | of the corrupters (l-muf'sidīna).

27:15 And verily, We gave Dawood and Sulaiman knowledge, and they said, "Praise be to Allah the One Who has favored us over many of His servants the believers."

And verily (walaqad), | We gave (ātaynā) | Dawood (dāwūda) | and Sulaiman (wasulaymāna) | knowledge (ʿil'man), | and they said (waqālā), | "Praise be (l-ḥamdu) | to Allah (lillahi) | the One Who (alladhī) | has favored us (faḍḍalanā) | over (ʿalā) | many (kathīrin) | of (min) | His servants (ʿibādihi) | the believers. (l-mu'minīna)"

27:16 And inherited Sulaiman Dawood. And he said, "O people! We have been taught the language of the birds, and we have been given from every thing. Indeed, this surely, it is the favor evident."

And inherited (wawaritha) | Sulaiman (sulaymānu) | Dawood (dāwūda). | And he said (waqāla), | "O (yāayyuhā) | people (l-nāsu)! | We have been taught (ʿullim'nā) | the language (manṭiqa) | of the birds (l-ṭayri), | and we have been given (waūtīnā) | from (min) | every (kulli) | thing (shayin). | Indeed (inna), | this (hādhā) | surely, it (lahuwa) | is the favor (l-faḍlu) | evident. (l-mubīnu)"

27:17 And were gathered for Sulaiman his hosts of jinn and the men and the birds, and they were set in rows.

And were gathered (waḥushira) | for Sulaiman (lisulaymāna) | his hosts (junūduhu) | of (mina) | jinn (l-jini) | and the men (wal-insi) | and the birds (wal-ṭayri), | and they (fahum) | were set in rows (yūzaʿūna).

27:18 Until, when they came to the valley of the ants, said an ant, "O ants! Enter your dwellings lest not crush you Sulaiman and his hosts while they do not perceive."

Until (ḥattā), | when (idhā) | they came (ataw) | to (ʿalā) | the valley (wādi) | of the ants (l-namli), | said (qālat) | an ant (namlatun), | "O (yāayyuhā) | ants (l-namlu)! | Enter (ud'khulū) | your dwellings (masākinakum) | lest not crush you (lā) | lest not crush you (yaḥṭimannakum) | Sulaiman (sulaymānu) | and his hosts (wajunūduhu) | while they (wahum) | do not perceive. (lā)" | do not perceive. (yashʿurūna)"

27:19 So he smiled - laughing at her speech and said, "My Lord! Grant me the power that I may thank You for Your Favor which You have bestowed on me and on my parents and that I may do righteous deeds, that will please You. And admit me by Your Mercy among Your slaves righteous."

So he smiled (fatabassama)- | laughing (ḍāḥikan) | at (min) | her speech (qawlihā) | and said (waqāla), | "My Lord (rabbi)! | Grant me the power (awzi''nī) | that (an) | I may thank You (ashkura) | for Your Favor (ni''mataka) | which (allatī) | You have bestowed (anʿamta) | on me (ʿalayya) | and on (waʿalā) | my parents (wālidayya) | and that (wa-an) | I may do (aʿmala) | righteous deeds (ṣāliḥan), | that will please You (tarḍāhu). | And admit me (wa-adkhil'nī) | by Your Mercy (biraḥmatika) | among (fī) | Your slaves (ʿibādika) | righteous. (l-ṣāliḥīna)"

27:20 And he inspected the birds and said, "Why not I see the hoopoe or is he from the absent?

And he inspected (watafaqqada) | the birds (l-ṭayra) | and said (faqāla), | "Why (mā) | "Why (liya) | not (lā) | I see (arā) | the hoopoe (l-hud'huda) | or (am) | is he (kāna) | from (mina) | the absent (l-ghāibīna)?

27:21 I will surely punish him with a punishment severe or I will surely slaughter him unless he brings me a reason clear."

I will surely punish him (la-uʿadhibannahu) | with a punishment (ʿadhāban) | severe (shadīdan) | or (aw) | I will surely slaughter him (laādh'baḥannahu) | unless (aw) | he brings me (layatiyannī) | a reason (bisul'ṭānin) | clear. (mubīnin)"

27:22 So he stayed not long, and he said, "I have encompassed that which not you have encompassed it, and I have come to you from Saba with news certain.

So he stayed (famakatha) | not (ghayra) | long (baʿīdin), | and he said (faqāla), | "I have encompassed (aḥaṭtu) | that which (bimā) | not (lam) | you have encompassed (tuḥiṭ) | it (bihi), | and I have come to you (waji'tuka) | from (min) | Saba (saba-in) | with news (binaba-in) | certain (yaqīnin).

27:23 Indeed, I found a woman ruling them and she has been given of every thing and for her is a throne great.

Indeed, I (innī) | found (wajadttu) | a woman (im'ra-atan) | ruling them (tamlikuhum) | and she has been given (waūtiyat) | of (min) | every (kulli) | thing (shayin) | and for her (walahā) | is a throne (ʿarshun) | great (ʿaẓīmun).

27:24 And I found her and her people prostrating to the sun instead of Allah, and has made fair-seeming to them the Shaitaan their deeds, and averted them from the Way, so they are not guided,

And I found her (wajadttuhā) | and her people (waqawmahā) | prostrating (yasjudūna) | to the sun (lilshamsi) | instead of Allah (min), | instead of Allah (dūni), | instead of Allah (l-lahi), | and has made fair-seeming (wazayyana) | to them (lahumu) | the Shaitaan (l-shayṭānu) | their deeds (aʿmālahum), | and averted them (faṣaddahum) | from (ʿani) | the Way (l-sabīli), | so they (fahum) | are not (lā) | guided (yahtadūna),

27:25 That not they prostrate to Allah, the One Who brings forth the hidden in the heavens and the earth and knows what you conceal and what you declare,

That not (allā) | they prostrate (yasjudū) | to Allah (lillahi), | the One Who (alladhī) | brings forth (yukh'riju) | the hidden (l-khaba-a) | in (fī) | the heavens (l-samāwāti) | and the earth (wal-arḍi) | and knows (wayaʿlamu) | what (mā) | you conceal (tukh'fūna) | and what (wamā) | you declare (tu''linūna),

27:26 Allah there is no god but He, the Lord of the Throne the Great."

Allah (al-lahu) | there is no (lā) | god (ilāha) | but (illā) | He (huwa), | the Lord (rabbu) | of the Throne (l-ʿarshi) | the Great. (l-ʿaẓīmi)"

27:27 He said, "We will see whether you speak the truth or you are of the liars.

He said (qāla), | "We will see (sananẓuru) | whether you speak the truth (aṣadaqta) | or (am) | you are (kunta) | of (mina) | the liars (l-kādhibīna).

27:28 Go with my letter, this, and deliver it to them. Then turn away from them and see what they return."

Go (idh'hab) | with my letter (bikitābī), | this (hādhā), | and deliver it (fa-alqih) | to them (ilayhim). | Then (thumma) | turn away (tawalla) | from them (ʿanhum) | and see (fa-unẓur) | what (mādhā) | they return. (yarjiʿūna)"

27:29 She said, "O chiefs! Indeed [I], is delivered to me a letter noble.

She said (qālat), | "O (yāayyuhā) | chiefs (l-mala-u)! | Indeed [I] (innī), | is delivered (ul'qiya) | to me (ilayya) | a letter (kitābun) | noble (karīmun).

27:30 Indeed, it is from Sulaiman and indeed it is, "In the name of Allah, the Most Gracious, the Most Merciful,

Indeed, it (innahu) | is from (min) | Sulaiman (sulaymāna) | and indeed it is (wa-innahu), | "In the name (bis'mi) | of Allah (l-lahi), | the Most Gracious (l-raḥmāni), | the Most Merciful (l-raḥīmi),

27:31 That not exalt yourselves against me, but come to me in submission."

That not (allā) | exalt yourselves (taʿlū) | against me (ʿalayya), | but come to me (watūnī) | in submission. (mus'limīna)"

27:32 She said, "O chiefs! Advise me in my affair. Not I would be the one to decide any matter until you are present with me."

She said (qālat), | "O (yāayyuhā) | chiefs (l-mala-u)! | Advise me (aftūnī) | in (fī) | my affair (amrī). | Not (mā) | I would be (kuntu) | the one to decide (qāṭiʿatan) | any matter (amran) | until (ḥattā) | you are present with me. (tashhadūni)"

27:33 They said, "We are possessors of strength and possessors of might great, and the command is up to you, so look what you will command."

They said (qālū), | "We (naḥnu) | are possessors (ulū) | of strength (quwwatin) | and possessors (wa-ulū) | of might (basin) | great (shadīdin), | and the command (wal-amru) | is up to you (ilayki), | so look (fa-unẓurī) | what (mādhā) | you will command. (tamurīna)"

27:34 She said, "Indeed, the kings, when they enter a town they ruin it and make the most honorable of its people the lowest. And thus they do.

She said (qālat), | "Indeed (inna), | the kings (l-mulūka), | when (idhā) | they enter (dakhalū) | a town (qaryatan) | they ruin it (afsadūhā) | and make (wajaʿalū) | the most honorable (aʿizzata) | of its people (ahlihā) | the lowest (adhillatan). | And thus (wakadhālika) | they do (yafʿalūna).

27:35 But indeed, I am going to send to them a gift and see with what return the messengers."

But indeed, I am (wa-innī) | going to send (mur'silatun) | to them (ilayhim) | a gift (bihadiyyatin) | and see (fanāẓiratun) | with what (bima) | return (yarjiʿu) | the messengers. (l-mur'salūna)"

27:36 So when came to Sulaiman he said, "Will you provide me with wealth? But what Allah has given me is better than what He has given you. Nay, you in your gift rejoice.

So when (falammā) | came (jāa) | to Sulaiman (sulaymāna) | he said (qāla), | "Will you provide me (atumiddūnani) | with wealth (bimālin)? | But what (famā) | Allah has given me (ātāniya) | Allah has given me (l-lahu) | is better (khayrun) | than what (mimmā) | He has given you (ātākum). | Nay (bal), | you (antum) | in your gift (bihadiyyatikum) | rejoice (tafraḥūna).

27:37 Return to them, surely, we will come to them with hosts not is resistance for them of it, and surely, we will drive them out from there in humiliation, and they will be abased."

Return (ir'ji') | to them (ilayhim), | surely, we will come to them (falanatiyannahum) | with hosts (bijunūdin) | not (lā) | is resistance (qibala) | for them (lahum) | of it (bihā), | and surely, we will drive them out (walanukh'rijannahum) | from there (min'hā) | in humiliation (adhillatan), | and they (wahum) | will be abased. (ṣāghirūna)"

27:38 He said, "O chiefs! Which of you will bring me her throne before that they come to me in submission?"

He said (qāla), | "O (yāayyuhā) | chiefs (l-mala-u)! | Which of you (ayyukum) | will bring me (yatīnī) | her throne (bi'arshihā) | before (qabla) | that (an) | they come to me (yatūnī) | in submission? (mus'limīna)"

27:39 Said a strong one of the jinn, "I will bring it to you before [that] you rise from your place. And indeed, I am for it surely, strong, trustworthy."

Said (qāla) | a strong one ('if'rītun) | of (mina) | the jinn (l-jini), | "I (anā) | will bring it to you (ātīka) | will bring it to you (bihi) | before (qabla) | [that] (an) | you rise (taqūma) | from (min) | your place (maqāmika). | And indeed, I am (wa-innī) | for it ('alayhi) | surely, strong (laqawiyyun), | trustworthy. (amīnun)"

27:40 Said one who, with him was knowledge of the Scripture, "I will bring it to you before [that] returns to you your glance." Then when he saw it placed before him, he said, "This is from the Favor of my Lord, to test me whether I am grateful or I am ungrateful. And whoever is grateful then only he is grateful for his own soul. And whoever is ungrateful, then indeed, my Lord is Self-sufficient, Noble."

Said (qāla) | one who (alladhī), | with him ('indahu) | was knowledge ('il'mun) | of (mina) | the Scripture (l-kitābi), | "I (anā) | will bring it to you (ātīka) | will bring it to you (bihi) | before (qabla) | [that] (an) | returns (yartadda) | to you (ilayka) | your glance. (ṭarfuka)" | Then when (falammā) | he saw it (raāhu) | placed (mus'taqirran) | before him ('indahu), | he said (qāla), | "This (hādhā) | is from (min) | the Favor (faḍli) | of my Lord (rabbī), | to test me (liyabluwanī) | whether I am grateful (a-ashkuru) | or (am) | I am ungrateful (akfuru). | And whoever (waman) | is grateful (shakara) | then only (fa-innamā) | he is grateful (yashkuru) | for his own soul (linafsihi). | And whoever (waman) | is ungrateful (kafara), | then indeed (fa-inna), | my Lord (rabbī) | is Self-sufficient (ghaniyyun), | Noble. (karīmun)"

27:41 He said, "Disguise for her her throne; we will see whether she will be guided or will be of those who are not guided."

He said (qāla), | "Disguise (nakkirū) | for her (lahā) | her throne ('arshahā); | we will see (nanẓur) | whether she will be guided (atahtadī) | or (am) | will be (takūnu) | of (mina) | those who (alladhīna) | are not guided. (lā)" | are not guided. (yahtadūna)"

27:42 So when she came, it was said, "Is like this your throne?" She said, "It is like it." "And we were given the knowledge before her and we have been Muslims."

So when (falammā) | she came (jāat), | it was said (qīla), | "Is like this (ahākadhā) | your throne? ('arshuki)" | She said (qālat), | "It is like (ka-annahu) | it. (huwa)" | "And we were given (waūtīnā) | the knowledge (l-'il'ma) | before her (min) | before her (qablihā) | and we have been (wakunnā) | Muslims. (mus'limīna)"

27:43 And has averted her what she used to worship besides Allah. Indeed, she was from a people who disbelieve.

And has averted her (waṣaddahā) | what (mā) | she used to (kānat) | worship (taʿbudu) | besides (min) | besides (dūni) | Allah (l-lahi). | Indeed, she (innahā) | was (kānat) | from (min) | a people (qawmin) | who disbelieve (kāfirīna).

27:44 It was said to her, "Enter the palace." Then when she saw it, she thought it was a pool, and she uncovered [on] her shins. He said, "Indeed, it is a palace made smooth of glass." She said, "My Lord, indeed, I [I] have wronged myself, and I submit with Sulaiman to Allah, the Lord of the worlds."

It was said (qīla) | to her (lahā), | "Enter (ud'khulī) | the palace. (l-ṣarḥa)" | Then when (falammā) | she saw it (ra-athu), | she thought it (ḥasibathu) | was a pool (lujjatan), | and she uncovered (wakashafat) | [on] (ʿan) | her shins (sāqayhā). | He said (qāla), | "Indeed, it (innahu) | is a palace (ṣarḥun) | made smooth (mumarradun) | of (min) | glass. (qawārīra)" | She said (qālat), | "My Lord (rabbi), | indeed, I (innī) | [I] have wronged (ẓalamtu) | myself (nafsī), | and I submit (wa-aslamtu) | with (maʿa) | Sulaiman (sulaymāna) | to Allah (lillahi), | the Lord (rabbi) | of the worlds. (l-ʿālamīna)"

27:45 And certainly, We sent to Thamud their brother Salih that, "Worship Allah." Then behold! They became two parties quarreling.

And certainly (walaqad), | We sent (arsalnā) | to (ilā) | Thamud (thamūda) | their brother (akhāhum) | Salih (ṣāliḥan) | that (ani), | "Worship (uʿ'budū) | Allah. (l-laha)" | Then behold (fa-idhā)! | They (hum) | became two parties (farīqāni) | quarreling (yakhtaṣimūna).

27:46 He said, "O my people! Why do you seek to hasten the evil before the good? Why not you ask forgiveness of Allah so that you may receive mercy?"

He said (qāla), | "O my people (yāqawmi)! | Why (lima) | do you seek to hasten (tastaʿjilūna) | the evil (bil-sayi-ati) | before (qabla) | the good (l-ḥasanati)? | Why not (lawlā) | you ask forgiveness (tastaghfirūna) | of Allah (l-laha) | so that you may (laʿallakum) | receive mercy? (tur'ḥamūna)"

27:47 They said, "We consider you a bad omen and those with you." He said, "Your bad omen is with Allah. Nay, you are a people being tested."

They said (qālū), | "We consider you a bad omen (iṭṭayyarnā) | "We consider you a bad omen (bika) | and those (wabiman) | with you. (maʿaka)" | He said (qāla), | "Your bad omen (ṭāirukum) | is with (ʿinda) | Allah (l-lahi). | Nay (bal), | you (antum) | are a people (qawmun) | being tested. (tuf'tanūna)"

27:48 And were in the city nine family heads, they were spreading corruption in the land and not reforming.

And were (wakāna) | in (fī) | the city (l-madīnati) | nine (tis'ʿatu) | family heads (rahṭin), | they were spreading corruption (yuf'sidūna) | in (fī) | the land (l-arḍi) | and not (walā) | reforming (yuṣ'liḥūna).

27:49 They said, "Swear to each other by Allah surely, we will attack him by night, and his family. Then we will surely say to his heir, "Not we witnessed the destruction of his family, and indeed, we are surely truthful."

They said (qālū), | "Swear to each other (taqāsamū) | by Allah (bil-lahi) | surely, we will attack him by night (lanubayyitannahu), | and his family (wa-ahlahu). | Then (thumma) | we will surely say (lanaqūlanna) | to his heir (liwaliyyihi), | "Not (mā) | we witnessed (shahid'nā) | the destruction (mahlika) | of his family (ahlihi), | and indeed, we (wa-innā) | are surely truthful. (laṣādiqūna)"

27:50 So they plotted a plot and We planned a plan, while they did not perceive.

So they plotted (wamakarū) | a plot (makran) | and We planned (wamakarnā) | a plan (makran), | while they (wahum) | did not (lā) | perceive (yashʿurūna).

27:51 Then see how was the end of their plot, that We destroyed them and their people all.

Then see (fa-unẓur) | how (kayfa) | was (kāna) | the end (ʿāqibatu) | of their plot (makrihim), | that We (annā) | destroyed them (dammarnāhum) | and their people (waqawmahum) | all (ajmaʿīna).

27:52 So, these are their houses, ruined because they wronged. Indeed, in that surely, is a sign for a people who know.

So, these (fatil'ka) | are their houses (buyūtuhum), | ruined (khāwiyatan) | because (bimā) | they wronged (ẓalamū). | Indeed (inna), | in (fī) | that (dhālika) | surely, is a sign (laāyatan) | for a people (liqawmin) | who know (yaʿlamūna).

27:53 And We saved those who believed and used to fear Allah.

And We saved (wa-anjaynā) | those who (alladhīna) | believed (āmanū) | and used to (wakānū) | fear Allah (yattaqūna).

27:54 And Lut, when he said to his people, "Do you commit [the] immorality while you see?

And Lut (walūṭan), | when (idh) | he said (qāla) | to his people (liqawmihi), | "Do you commit (atatūna) | [the] immorality (l-fāḥishata) | while you (wa-antum) | see (tub'ṣirūna)?

27:55 Why do you approach the men with lust instead of the women? Nay, you are a people ignorant."

Why do you (a-innakum) | approach (latatūna) | the men (l-rijāla) | with lust (shahwatan) | instead of (min) | instead of (dūni) | the women (l-nisāi)? | Nay (bal), | you (antum) | are a people (qawmun) | ignorant. (tajhalūna)"

27:56 But not was the answer of his people except that they said, "Drive out the family of Lut from your town. Indeed, they are people who keep clean and pure."

But not (famā) | was (kāna) | the answer (jawāba) | of his people (qawmihi) | except (illā) | that (an) | they said (qālū), | "Drive out (akhrijū) | the family (āla) | of Lut (lūṭin) | from (min) | your town (qaryatikum). | Indeed, they (innahum) | are people (unāsun) | who keep clean and pure. (yataṭahharūna)"

27:57 So We saved him and his family, except his wife; We destined her to be of those who remained behind.

So We saved him (fa-anjaynāhu) | and his family (wa-ahlahu), | except (illā) | his wife (im'ra-atahu); | We destined her (qaddarnāhā) | to be of (mina) | those who remained behind (l-ghābirīna).

27:58 And We rained upon them a rain, and was evil the rain on those who were warned.

And We rained (wa-amṭarnā) | upon them (ʿalayhim) | a rain (maṭaran), | and was evil (fasāa) | the rain (maṭaru) | on those who were warned (l-mundharīna).

27:59 Say, "All praise be to Allah, and peace be upon His slaves those whom He has chosen. Is Allah better or what they associate with Him?"

Say (quli), | "All praise be (l-ḥamdu) | to Allah (lillahi), | and peace be (wasalāmun) | upon

(ʿalā) | His slaves (ʿibādihi) | those whom (alladhīna) | He has chosen (iṣ'ṭafā). | Is Allah (āllahu) | better (khayrun) | or what (ammā) | they associate with Him? (yush'rikūna)"

27:60 Or Who has created the heavens and the earth and sent down for you from the sky water? And We caused to grow thereby gardens of beauty and delight, not it is for you that you cause to grow their trees. Is there any god with Allah? Nay, they are a people who ascribe equals.

Or Who (amman) | has created (khalaqa) | the heavens (l-samāwāti) | and the earth (wal-arḍa) | and sent down (wa-anzala) | for you (lakum) | from (mina) | the sky (l-samāi) | water (māan)? | And We caused to grow (fa-anbatnā) | thereby (bihi) | gardens (ḥadāiqa) | of beauty and delight (dhāta), | of beauty and delight (bahjatin), | not (mā) | it is (kāna) | for you (lakum) | that (an) | you cause to grow (tunbitū) | their trees (shajarahā). | Is there any god (a-ilāhun) | with (maʿa) | Allah (l-lahi)? | Nay (bal), | they (hum) | are a people (qawmun) | who ascribe equals (yaʿdilūna).

27:61 Or Who made the earth a firm abode and made in its midst rivers and made for it firm mountains and made between the two seas a barrier? Is there any god with Allah? Nay, most of them do not know.

Or Who (amman) | made (jaʿala) | the earth (l-arḍa) | a firm abode (qarāran) | and made (wajaʿala) | in its midst (khilālahā) | rivers (anhāran) | and made (wajaʿala) | for it (lahā) | firm mountains (rawāsiya) | and made (wajaʿala) | between (bayna) | the two seas (l-baḥrayni) | a barrier (ḥājizan)? | Is there any god (a-ilāhun) | with (maʿa) | Allah (l-lahi)? | Nay (bal), | most of them (aktharuhum) | do not (lā) | know (yaʿlamūna).

27:62 Or Who responds to the distressed one when he calls Him and He removes the evil and makes you inheritors of the earth? Is there any god with Allah? Little is what you remember.

Or Who (amman) | responds (yujību) | to the distressed one (l-muḍ'ṭara) | when (idhā) | he calls Him (daʿāhu) | and He removes (wayakshifu) | the evil (l-sūa) | and makes you (wayajʿalukum) | inheritors (khulafāa) | of the earth (l-arḍi)? | Is there any god (a-ilāhun) | with (maʿa) | Allah (l-lahi)? | Little (qalīlan) | is what (ma) | you remember (tadhakkarūna).

27:63 Or Who, guides you in the darkness[es] of the land and the sea and Who sends the winds as glad tidings before His Mercy? Is there any god with Allah? High is Allah above what they associate with Him.

Or Who (amman), | guides you (yahdīkum) | in (fī) | the darkness[es] (ẓulumāti) | of the land (l-bari) | and the sea (wal-baḥri) | and Who (waman) | sends (yur'silu) | the winds (l-riyāḥa) | as glad tidings (bush'ran) | before (bayna) | before (yaday) | His Mercy (raḥmatihi)? | Is there any god (a-ilāhun) | with (maʿa) | Allah (l-lahi)? | High is (taʿālā) | Allah (l-lahu) | above what (ʿammā) | they associate with Him (yush'rikūna).

27:64 Or Who originates the creation then repeats it and Who provides you from the heavens and the earth? Is there any god with Allah? Say, "Bring forth your proof if you are truthful."

Or Who (amman) | originates (yabda-u) | the creation (l-khalqa) | then (thumma) | repeats it (yuʿīduhu) | and Who (waman) | provides you (yarzuqukum) | from (mina) | the heavens (l-samāi) | and the earth (wal-arḍi)? | Is there any god (a-ilāhun) | with (maʿa) | Allah (l-lahi)? | Say (qul), | "Bring forth (hātū) | your proof (bur'hānakum) | if (in) | you are (kuntum) | truthful. (ṣādiqīna)"

27:65 Say, "No one knows whoever is in the heavens and the earth of the unseen except Allah, and not they perceive when they will be resurrected."

Say (qul), | "No one (lā) | knows (yaʿlamu) | whoever (man) | is in (fī) | the heavens (l-samāwāti) | and the earth (wal-arḍi) | of the unseen (l-ghayba) | except (illā) | Allah (l-lahu), | and not (wamā) | they perceive (yashʿurūna) | when (ayyāna) | they will be resurrected. (yub'ʿathūna)"

27:66 Nay, is arrested their knowledge of the Hereafter? Nay they are in doubt about it. Nay, they about it are blind.

Nay (bali), | is arrested (iddāraka) | their knowledge (ʿil'muhum) | of (fī) | the Hereafter (l-ākhirati)? | Nay (bal) | they (hum) | are in (fī) | doubt (shakkin) | about it (min'hā). | Nay (bal), | they (hum) | about it (min'hā) | are blind (ʿamūna).

27:67 And say those who disbelieve, "What, when we have become dust and our forefathers, will we surely be brought out?

And say (waqāla) | those who (alladhīna) | disbelieve (kafarū), | "What, when (a-idhā) | we have become (kunnā) | dust (turāban) | and our forefathers (waābāunā), | will we (a-innā) | surely be brought out (lamukh'rajūna)?

27:68 Certainly, we have been promised this, we and our forefathers before. Not is this except tales of the former (people)."

Certainly (laqad), | we have been promised (wuʿid'nā) | this (hādhā), | we (naḥnu) | and our forefathers (waābāunā) | before (min). | before (qablu). | Not (in) | is this (hādhā) | except (illā) | tales (asāṭīru) | of the former (people). (l-awalīna)"

27:69 Say, "Travel in the land, and see how was the end of the criminals."

Say (qul), | "Travel (sīrū) | in (fī) | the land (l-arḍi), | and see (fa-unẓurū) | how (kayfa) | was (kāna) | the end (ʿāqibatu) | of the criminals. (l-muj'rimīna)"

27:70 And do not grieve over them and not be in distress from what they plot.

And do not (walā) | grieve (taḥzan) | over them (ʿalayhim) | and not (walā) | be (takun) | in (fī) | distress (ḍayqin) | from what (mimmā) | they plot (yamkurūna).

27:71 And they say, "When will this promise be fulfilled, if you are truthful."

And they say (wayaqūlūna), | "When (matā) | will this (hādhā) | promise be fulfilled (l-waʿdu), | if (in) | you are (kuntum) | truthful. (ṣādiqīna)"

27:72 Say, "Perhaps that is close behind you, some of that which you seek to hasten."

Say (qul), | "Perhaps (ʿasā) | that (an) | is (yakūna) | close behind (radifa) | you (lakum), | some (baʿḍu) | of that which (alladhī) | you seek to hasten. (tastaʿjilūna)"

27:73 And indeed, your Lord is full of Bounty for the mankind, but most of them are not grateful.

And indeed (wa-inna), | your Lord (rabbaka) | is full of Bounty (ladhū) | is full of Bounty (faḍlin) | for (ʿalā) | the mankind (l-nāsi), | but (walākinna) | most of them (aktharahum) | are not (lā) | grateful (yashkurūna).

27:74 And indeed, your Lord surely knows what conceals their breasts and what they declare.

And indeed (wa-inna), | your Lord (rabbaka) | surely knows (layaʿlamu) | what (mā) | conceals (tukinnu) | their breasts (ṣudūruhum) | and what (wamā) | they declare (yuʿ'linūna).

27:75 And not is any thing hidden in the heavens and the earth but is in a Record clear.

And not is (wamā) | any thing (min) | hidden (ghāibatin) | in (fī) | the heavens (l-samāi) | and the earth (wal-arḍi) | but (illā) | is in (fī) | a Record (kitābin) | clear (mubīnin).

27:76 Indeed, this [the] Quran relates to the Children of Israel, most of that they in it differ.

Indeed (inna), | this (hādhā) | [the] Quran (l-qur'āna) | relates (yaquṣṣu) | to (ʿalā) | the Children (banī) | of Israel (is'rāīla), | most (akthara) | of that (alladhī) | they (hum) | in it (fīhi) | differ (yakhtalifūna).

27:77 And indeed, it is surely a guidance and a mercy for the believers.

And indeed, it (wa-innahu) | is surely a guidance (lahudan) | and a mercy (waraḥmatun) | for the believers (lil'mu'minīna).

27:78 Indeed, your Lord will judge between them by His Judgment, and He is the All-Mighty, the All-Knower.

Indeed (inna), | your Lord (rabbaka) | will judge (yaqḍī) | between them (baynahum) | by His Judgment (biḥuk'mihi), | and He (wahuwa) | is the All-Mighty (l-ʿazīzu), | the All-Knower (l-ʿalīmu).

27:79 So put your trust in Allah, indeed, you are on the truth manifest.

So put your trust (fatawakkal) | in (ʿalā) | Allah (l-lahi), | indeed, you (innaka) | are on (ʿalā) | the truth (l-ḥaqi) | manifest (l-mubīni).

27:80 Indeed, you can not cause to hear the dead and not can you cause to hear the deaf the call when they turn back retreating.

Indeed, you (innaka) | can not (lā) | cause to hear (tus'miʿu) | the dead (l-mawtā) | and not (walā) | can you cause to hear (tus'miʿu) | the deaf (l-ṣuma) | the call (l-duʿāa) | when (idhā) | they turn back (wallaw) | retreating (mud'birīna).

27:81 And not can you guide the blind from their error. Not you can cause to hear except those who believe in Our Signs so they are Muslims.

And not (wamā) | can you (anta) | guide (bihādī) | the blind (l-ʿum'yi) | from (ʿan) | their error (ḍalālatihim). | Not (in) | you can cause to hear (tus'miʿu) | except (illā) | those who (man) | believe (yu'minu) | in Our Signs (biāyātinā) | so they (fahum) | are Muslims (mus'limūna).

27:82 And when is fulfilled the word against them, We will bring forth for them a creature from the earth speaking to them, that the people were, of Our Signs, not certain.

And when (wa-idhā) | is fulfilled (waqaʿa) | the word (l-qawlu) | against them (ʿalayhim), | We will bring forth (akhrajnā) | for them (lahum) | a creature (dābbatan) | from (mina) | the earth (l-arḍi) | speaking to them (tukallimuhum), | that (anna) | the people (l-nāsa) | were (kānū), | of Our Signs (biāyātinā), | not (lā) | certain (yūqinūna).

27:83 And the Day We will gather from every nation a troop of those who deny Our Signs, and they will be set in rows.

And the Day (wayawma) | We will gather (naḥshuru) | from (min) | every (kulli) | nation (ummatin) | a troop (fawjan) | of those who (mimman) | deny (yukadhibu) | Our Signs (biāyātinā), | and they (fahum) | will be set in rows (yūzaʿūna).

27:84 Until, when they come, He will say, "Did you deny My Signs while not you encompassed them in knowledge, or what you used to do?"

Until (ḥattā), | when (idhā) | they come (jāū), | He will say (qāla), | "Did you deny (akadhabtum) | My Signs (biāyātī) | while not (walam) | you encompassed (tuḥīṭū) | them (bihā) | in knowledge (ʿil'man), | or what (ammādhā) | you used to (kuntum) | do? (taʿmalūna)"

27:85 And will be fulfilled the word against them because they wronged, and they will not speak.

And will be fulfilled (wawaqaʿa) | the word (l-qawlu) | against them (ʿalayhim) | because (bimā) | they wronged (ẓalamū), | and they (fahum) | will not (lā) | speak (yanṭiqūna).

27:86 Do not they see that We [We] have made the night that they may rest in it, and the day giving visibility? Indeed, in that surely are Signs for a people who believe.

Do not (alam) | they see (yaraw) | that We (annā) | [We] have made (jaʿalnā) | the night (al-layla) | that they may rest (liyaskunū) | in it (fīhi), | and the day (wal-nahāra) | giving visibility (mub'ṣiran)? | Indeed (inna), | in (fī) | that (dhālika) | surely are Signs (laāyātin) | for a people (liqawmin) | who believe (yu'minūna).

27:87 And the Day will be blown [in] the trumpet and will be terrified whoever is in the heavens and whoever is in the earth except whom Allah wills. And all will come to Him humbled.

And the Day (wayawma) | will be blown (yunfakhu) | [in] (fī) | the trumpet (l-ṣūri) | and will be terrified (fafaziʿa) | whoever (man) | is in (fī) | the heavens (l-samāwāti) | and whoever (waman) | is in (fī) | the earth (l-arḍi) | except (illā) | whom (man) | Allah wills (shāa). | Allah wills (l-lahu). | And all (wakullun) | will come to Him (atawhu) | humbled (dākhirīna).

27:88 And you see the mountains, thinking them firmly fixed, while they will pass as the passing of the clouds. The Work of Allah Who perfected all things. Indeed, He is All-Aware of what you do.

And you see (watarā) | the mountains (l-jibāla), | thinking them (taḥsabuhā) | firmly fixed (jāmidatan), | while they (wahiya) | will pass (tamurru) | as the passing (marra) | of the clouds (l-saḥābi). | The Work (ṣunʿa) | of Allah (l-lahi) | Who (alladhī) | perfected (atqana) | all (kulla) | things (shayin). | Indeed, He (innahu) | is All-Aware (khabīrun) | of what (bimā) | you do (tafʿalūna).

27:89 Whoever comes with the good, then for him will be better than it, and they, from the terror of that Day will be safe.

Whoever (man) | comes (jāa) | with the good (bil-ḥasanati), | then for him (falahu) | will be better (khayrun) | than it (min'hā), | and they (wahum), | from (min) | the terror (fazaʿin) | of that Day (yawma-idhin) | will be safe (āminūna).

27:90 And whoever comes with the evil, will be cast down their faces in the Fire. "Are you recompensed except for what you used to do?"

And whoever (waman) | comes (jāa) | with the evil (bil-sayi-ati), | will be cast down (fakubbat) | their faces (wujūhuhum) | in (fī) | the Fire (l-nāri). | "Are (hal) | you recompensed (tuj'zawna) | except (illā) | for what (mā) | you used to (kuntum) | do? (taʿmalūna)"

27:91 "Only I am commanded that I worship the Lord of this city, the One Who made it sacred and to Him belongs all things. And I am commanded that I be of the Muslims

"Only (innamā) | I am commanded (umir'tu) | that (an) | I worship (aʿbuda) | the Lord (rabba) | of this (hādhihi) | city (l-baldati), | the One Who (alladhī) | made it sacred (ḥarramahā) | and to Him belongs (walahu) | all (kullu) | things (shayin). | And I am commanded (wa-umir'tu) | that (an) | I be (akūna) | of (mina) | the Muslims (l-mus'limīna)

27:92 And that I recite the Quran." And whoever accepts guidance then only he accepts guidance for himself; and whoever goes astray then say, "Only I am of the warners."

And that (wa-an) | I recite (atluwā) | the Quran. (l-qur'āna)" | And whoever (famani) | accepts guidance (ih'tadā) | then only (fa-innamā) | he accepts guidance (yahtadī) | for himself (linafsihi); | and whoever (waman) | goes astray (ḍalla) | then say (faqul), | "Only (innamā) | I am (anā) | of (mina) | the warners. (l-mundhirīna)"

27:93 And say, "All praise be to Allah, He will show you His Signs, and you will recognize them. And your Lord is not unaware of what you do."

And say (waquli), | "All praise be (l-ḥamdu) | to Allah (lillahi), | He will show you (sayurīkum) | His Signs (āyātihi), | and you will recognize them (fataʿrifūnahā). | And your Lord is not (wamā) | And your Lord is not (rabbuka) | unaware (bighāfilin) | of what (ʿammā) | you do. (taʿmalūna)"

Chapter (28) Sūrat l-Qaṣaṣ (The Stories)

28:1 Ta Seem Meem.

Ta Seem Meem (tta-seen-meem).

28:2 These are the Verses of the Book the clear.

These (til'ka) | are the Verses (āyātu) | of the Book (l-kitābi) | the clear (l-mubīni).

28:3 We recite to you from the news of Musa and Firaun in truth for a people who believe.

We recite (natlū) | to you (ʿalayka) | from (min) | the news (naba-i) | of Musa (mūsā) | and Firaun (wafir'ʿawna) | in truth (bil-ḥaqi) | for a people (liqawmin) | who believe (yu'minūna).

28:4 Indeed, Firaun exalted himself in the land and made its people into sects, oppressing a group among them, slaughtering their sons and letting live their women. Indeed, he was of the corrupters.

Indeed (inna), | Firaun (fir'ʿawna) | exalted himself (ʿalā) | in (fī) | the land (l-arḍi) | and made (wajaʿala) | its people (ahlahā) | into sects (shiyaʿan), | oppressing (yastaḍʿifu) | a group (ṭāifatan) | among them (min'hum), | slaughtering (yudhabbiḥu) | their sons (abnāahum) | and letting live (wayastaḥyī) | their women (nisāahum). | Indeed, he (innahu) | was (kāna) | of (mina) | the corrupters (l-muf'sidīna).

28:5 And We wanted to bestow a favor upon those who were oppressed in the land and make them leaders and make them the inheritors,

And We wanted (wanurīdu) | to (an) | bestow a favor (namunna) | upon (ʿalā) | those who (alladhīna) | were oppressed (us'tuḍ'ʿifū) | in (fī) | the land (l-arḍi) | and make them (wanajʿalahum) | leaders (a-immatan) | and make them (wanajʿalahumu) | the inheritors (l-wārithīna),

28:6 And [We] establish them in the land and show Firaun and Haman and their hosts through them what they were fearing.

And [We] establish (wanumakkina) | them (lahum) | in (fī) | the land (l-arḍi) | and show (wanuriya) | Firaun (fir'ʿawna) | and Haman (wahāmāna) | and their hosts (wajunūdahumā) | through them (min'hum) | what (mā) | they were (kānū) | fearing (yaḥdharūna).

28:7 And We inspired [to] the mother of Musa that, "Suckle him, but when you fear for him, then cast him into the river and do not fear and do not grieve. Indeed, We will restore him to you and will make him of the Messengers."

And We inspired (wa-awḥaynā) | [to] (ilā) | the mother (ummi) | of Musa (mūsā) | that (an), | "Suckle him (arḍiʿīhi), | but when (fa-idhā) | you fear (khif'ti) | for him (ʿalayhi), | then cast him (fa-alqīhi) | into (fī) | the river (l-yami) | and do not (walā) | fear (takhāfī) | and do not (walā) | grieve (taḥzanī). | Indeed, We (innā) | will restore him (rāddūhu) | to you (ilayki) | and will make him (wajāʿilūhu) | of (mina) | the Messengers. (l-mur'salīna)"

28:8 Then picked him up the family of Firaun so that he might become to them an enemy and a grief. Indeed, Firaun and Haman and their hosts were sinners.

Then picked him up (fal-taqaṭahu) | the family (ālu) | of Firaun (fir'ʿawna) | so that he might become (liyakūna) | to them (lahum) | an enemy (ʿaduwwan) | and a grief (waḥazanan). | Indeed (inna), | Firaun (fir'ʿawna) | and Haman (wahāmāna) | and their hosts (wajunūdahumā) | were (kānū) | sinners (khāṭiīna).

28:9 And said the wife of Firaun, "A comfort of the eye for me and for you; Do not kill him; perhaps that he may benefit us, or we may take him as a son." And they did not perceive.

And said (waqālati) | the wife (im'ra-atu) | of Firaun (fir'ʿawna), | "A comfort (qurratu) | of the eye (ʿaynin) | for me (lī) | and for you (walaka); | Do not (lā) | kill him (taqtulūhu); | perhaps (ʿasā) | that (an) | he may benefit us (yanfaʿanā), | or (aw) | we may take him (nattakhidhahu) | as a son. (waladan)" | And they (wahum) | did not (lā) | perceive (yashʿurūna).

28:10 And became the heart of the mother of Musa empty. That, she was near to disclosing about him, if not that We strengthened [over] her heart, so that she would be of the believers.

And became (wa-aṣbaḥa) | the heart (fuādu) | of the mother (ummi) | of Musa (mūsā) | empty (fārighan). | That (in), | she was near (kādat) | to disclosing (latub'dī) | about him (bihi), | if not (lawlā) | that (an) | We strengthened (rabaṭnā) | [over] (ʿalā) | her heart (qalbihā), | so that she would be (litakūna) | of (mina) | the believers (l-mu'minīna).

28:11 And she said to his sister, "Follow him." So she watched him from a distance while they did not perceive.

And she said (waqālat) | to his sister (li-ukh'tihi), | "Follow him. (quṣṣīhi)" | So she watched (fabaṣurat) | him (bihi) | from (ʿan) | a distance (junubin) | while they (wahum) | did not (lā) | perceive (yashʿurūna).

28:12 And We had forbidden for him the wet nurses before, so she said, "Shall I direct you to the people of a house who will rear him for you while they to him will be sincere?"

And We had forbidden (waḥarramnā) | for him (ʿalayhi) | the wet nurses (l-marāḍiʿa) | before (min), | before (qablu), | so she said (faqālat), | "Shall I (hal) | direct you (adullukum) | to (ʿalā) | the people (ahli) | of a house (baytin) | who will rear him (yakfulūnahu) | for you (lakum) | while they (wahum) | to him (lahu) | will be sincere? (nāṣiḥūna)"

28:13 So We restored him to his mother that might be comforted her eye, and not she may grieve and that she would know, that the Promise of Allah is true. But most of them do not know.

So We restored him (faradadnāhu) | to (ilā) | his mother (ummihi) | that (kay) | might be comforted (taqarra) | her eye (ʿaynuhā), | and not (walā) | she may grieve (taḥzana) | and that she would know (walitaʿlama), | that (anna) | the Promise of Allah (waʿda) | the Promise of Allah (l-lahi) | is true (ḥaqqun). | But (walākinna) | most of them (aktharahum) | do not (lā) | know (yaʿlamūna).

28:14 And when he reached his full strength and became mature, We bestowed upon him wisdom and knowledge. And thus We reward the good-doers.

And when (walammā) | he reached (balagha) | his full strength (ashuddahu) | and became mature (wa-is'tawā), | We bestowed upon him (ātaynāhu) | wisdom (ḥuk'man) | and knowledge (waʿil'man). | And thus (wakadhālika) | We reward (najzī) | the good-doers (l-muḥ'sinīna).

28:15 And he entered the city at a time of inattention of its people and found therein two men fighting each other; this of his party and this of his enemy. And called him for help the one who was from his party against the one who was from his enemy, so Musa struck him with his fist and killed him. He said, "This is of the deed of Shaitaan. Indeed, he is an enemy - one who misleads clearly."

And he entered (wadakhala) | the city (l-madīnata) | at (ʿalā) | a time (ḥīni) | of inattention (ghaflatin) | of (min) | its people (ahlihā) | and found (fawajada) | therein (fīhā) | two men (rajulayni) | fighting each other (yaqtatilāni); | this (hādhā) | of (min) | his party (shīʿatihi) | and this (wahādhā) | of (min) | his enemy (ʿaduwwihi). | And called him for help (fa-is'taghāthahu) | the one who (alladhī) | was from (min) | his party (shīʿatihi) | against (ʿalā) | the one who (alladhī) | was from (min) | his enemy (ʿaduwwihi), | so Musa struck him with his fist (fawakazahu) | so Musa struck him with his fist (mūsā) | and killed him (faqaḍā). | and killed him (ʿalayhi). | He said (qāla), | "This is (hādhā) | of (min) | the deed (ʿamali) | of Shaitaan (l-shayṭāni). | Indeed, he (innahu) | is an enemy (ʿaduwwun)- | one who misleads (muḍillun) | clearly. (mubīnun)"

28:16 He said, "My Lord! Indeed, I [I] have wronged my soul, so forgive [for] me." Then He forgave

[for] him. Indeed He, He is the Oft-Forgiving, the Most Merciful.

He said (qāla), | "My Lord (rabbi)! | Indeed, I (innī) | [I] have wronged (ẓalamtu) | my soul (nafsī), | so forgive (fa-igh'fir) | [for] me. (lī)" | Then He forgave (faghafara) | [for] him (lahu). | Indeed He (innahu), | He is (huwa) | the Oft-Forgiving (l-ghafūru), | the Most Merciful (l-raḥīmu).

28:17 He said, "My Lord! Because You have favored [on] me, so not I will be a supporter of the criminals."

He said (qāla), | "My Lord (rabbi)! | Because (bimā) | You have favored (anʿamta) | [on] me (ʿalayya), | so not (falan) | I will be (akūna) | a supporter (ẓahīran) | of the criminals. (lil'muj'rimīna)"

28:18 In the morning he was in the city fearful and was vigilant, when behold! The one who sought his help the previous day cried out to him for help. Said to him Musa, "Indeed, you are surely a deviator clear."

In the morning he was (fa-aṣbaḥa) | in (fī) | the city (l-madīnati) | fearful (khāifan) | and was vigilant (yataraqqabu), | when behold (fa-idhā)! | The one who (alladhī) | sought his help (is'tanṣarahu) | the previous day (bil-amsi) | cried out to him for help (yastaṣrikhuhu). | Said (qāla) | to him (lahu) | Musa (mūsā), | "Indeed, you (innaka) | are surely a deviator (laghawiyyun) | clear. (mubīnun)"

28:19 Then when [that] he wanted to strike the one who [he] was an enemy to both of them, he said, "O Musa! Do you intend to kill me as you killed a person yesterday? Not you want but that you become a tyrant in the earth, and not you want that you be of the reformers."

Then when (falammā) | [that] (an) | he wanted (arāda) | to (an) | strike (yabṭisha) | the one who (bi-alladhī) | [he] was (huwa) | an enemy (ʿaduwwun) | to both of them (lahumā), | he said (qāla), | "O Musa (yāmūsā)! | Do you intend (aturīdu) | to (an) | kill me (taqtulanī) | as (kamā) | you killed (qatalta) | a person (nafsan) | yesterday (bil-amsi)? | Not (in) | you want (turīdu) | but (illā) | that (an) | you become (takūna) | a tyrant (jabbāran) | in (fī) | the earth (l-arḍi), | and not (wamā) | you want (turīdu) | that (an) | you be (takūna) | of (mina) | the reformers. (l-muṣ'liḥīna)"

28:20 And came a man from the farthest end of the city running. He said, "O Musa! Indeed, the chiefs are taking counsel about you to kill you, so leave; indeed, I am to you of the sincere advisors."

And came (wajāa) | a man (rajulun) | from (min) | the farthest end (aqṣā) | of the city (l-madīnati) | running (yasʿā). | He said (qāla), | "O Musa (yāmūsā)! | Indeed (inna), | the chiefs (l-mala-a) | are taking counsel (yatamirūna) | about you (bika) | to kill you (liyaqtulūka), | so leave (fa-ukh'ruj); | indeed, I am (innī) | to you (laka) | of (mina) | the sincere advisors. (l-nāṣiḥīna)"

28:21 So he left from it fearing, and vigilant. He said, "My Lord! Save me from the people - the wrongdoers."

So he left (fakharaja) | from it (min'hā) | fearing (khāifan), | and vigilant (yataraqqabu). | He said (qāla), | "My Lord (rabbi)! | Save me (najjinī) | from (mina) | the people (l-qawmi)- | the wrongdoers. (l-ẓālimīna)"

28:22 And when he turned his face towards Madyan, he said, "Perhaps my Lord [that] will guide me to the sound way."

And when (walammā) | he turned his face (tawajjaha) | towards (til'qāa) | Madyan (madyana), | he said (qāla), | "Perhaps (ʿasā) | my Lord (rabbī) | [that] (an) | will guide me (yahdiyanī) | to the sound (sawāa) | way. (l-sabīli)"

28:23 And when he came to the water of Madyan, he found on it a group of men watering, and he found besides them two women keeping back. He said, "What is the matter with both of you?" They said, "We cannot water until take away the shepherds; and our father is a very old man."

And when (walammā) | he came (warada) | to the water (māa) | of Madyan (madyana), | he found (wajada) | on it (ʿalayhi) | a group (ummatan) | of (mina) | men (l-nāsi) | watering (yasqūna), | and he found (wawajada) | besides them (min) | besides them (dūnihimu) | two women (im'ra-atayni) | keeping back (tadhūdāni). | He said (qāla), | "What (mā) | is the matter with both of you? (khaṭbukumā)" | They said (qālatā), | "We cannot water (lā) | "We cannot water (nasqī) | until (ḥattā) | take away (yuṣ'dira) | the shepherds (l-riʿāu); | and our father (wa-abūnā) | is a very old man. (shaykhun)" | is a very old man. (kabīrun)"

28:24 So he watered for them. Then he turned back to the shade and said, "My Lord! Indeed, I am of whatever You send to me of good in need."

So he watered (fasaqā) | for them (lahumā). | Then (thumma) | he turned back (tawallā) | to (ilā) | the shade (l-ẓili) | and said (faqāla), | "My Lord (rabbi)! | Indeed, I am (innī) | of whatever (limā) | You send (anzalta) | to me (ilayya) | of (min) | good (khayrin) | in need. (faqīrun)"

28:25 Then came to him one of the two women walking with shyness. She said, "Indeed, my father calls you, that he may reward you the reward for what you watered for us." So when he came to him and narrated to him the story, he said, "Do not fear. You have escaped from the people - the wrongdoers."

Then came to him (fajāathu) | one of the two women (iḥ'dāhumā) | walking (tamshī) | with (ʿalā) | shyness (is'tiḥ'yāin). | She said (qālat), | "Indeed (inna), | my father (abī) | calls you (yadʿūka), | that he may reward you (liyajziyaka) | the reward (ajra) | for what (mā) | you watered (saqayta) | for us. (lanā)" | So when (falammā) | he came to him (jāahu) | and narrated (waqaṣṣa) | to him (ʿalayhi) | the story (l-qaṣaṣa), | he said (qāla), | "Do not (lā) | fear (takhaf). | You have escaped (najawta) | from (mina) | the people (l-qawmi)- | the wrongdoers. (l-ẓālimīna)"

28:26 Said one of them, "O my father! Hire him. Indeed, the best whom you can hire is the strong, the trustworthy."

Said (qālat) | one of them (iḥ'dāhumā), | "O my father (yāabati)! | Hire him (is'tajir'hu). | Indeed (inna), | the best (khayra) | whom (mani) | you can hire (is'tajarta) | is the strong (l-qawiyu), | the trustworthy. (l-amīnu)"

28:27 He said, "Indeed, I [I] wish to marry you to one of my daughters of these two on that you serve me, for eight years; but if you complete ten, then from you. And not I wish to make it difficult for you. You will find me, if Allah wills, of the righteous."

He said (qāla), | "Indeed, I (innī) | [I] wish (urīdu) | to (an) | marry you to (unkiḥaka) | one (iḥ'dā) | of my daughters (ib'natayya) | of these two (hātayni) | on (ʿalā) | that (an) | you serve me (tajuranī), | for eight (thamāniya) | years (ḥijajin); | but if (fa-in) | you complete (atmamta) | ten (ʿashran), | then from (famin) | you (ʿindika). | And not (wamā) | I wish (urīdu) | to (an) | make it difficult (ashuqqa) | for you (ʿalayka). | You will find me (satajidunī), | if (in) | Allah wills (shāa), | Allah wills (l-lahu), | of (mina) | the righteous. (l-ṣāliḥīna)"

28:28 He said, "That is between me and between you. Whichever of the two terms I complete then no injustice to me, and Allah, over what we say is a Witness."

He said (qāla), | "That (dhālika) | is between me (baynī) | and between you (wabaynaka). | Whichever (ayyamā) | of the two terms (l-ajalayni) | I complete (qaḍaytu) | then no (falā) | injustice (ʿud'wāna) | to me (ʿalayya), | and Allah (wal-lahu), | over (ʿalā) | what (mā) | we say (naqūlu) | is a Witness. (wakīlun)"

28:29 Then when Musa fulfilled the term and was traveling with his family, he saw in the direction of Mount Tur a fire. He said to his family, "Stay here; indeed, I [I] perceive a fire. Perhaps I will bring you from there some information or a burning wood from the fire so that you may warm yourselves."

Then when (falammā) | Musa fulfilled (qaḍā) | Musa fulfilled (mūsā) | the term (l-ajala) | and was traveling (wasāra) | with his family (bi-ahlihi), | he saw (ānasa) | in (min) | the direction (jānibi) | of Mount Tur (l-ṭūri) | a fire (nāran). | He said (qāla) | to his family (li-ahlihi), | "Stay here (um'kuthū); | indeed, I (innī) | [I] perceive (ānastu) | a fire (nāran). | Perhaps (laʿallī) | I will bring you (ātīkum) | from there (min'hā) | some information (bikhabarin) | or (aw) | a burning wood (jadhwatin) | from (mina) | the fire (l-nāri) | so that you may (laʿallakum) | warm yourselves. (taṣṭalūna)"

28:30 But when he came to it, he was called from the side of the valley - the right in the place even, blessed, from the tree that, "O Musa! Indeed, I Am Allah, the Lord of the worlds.

But when (falammā) | he came to it (atāhā), | he was called (nūdiya) | from (min) | the side (shāṭi-i) | of the valley (l-wādi)- | the right (l-aymani) | in (fī) | the place even (l-buqʿati), | blessed (l-mubārakati), | from (mina) | the tree (l-shajarati) | that (an), | "O Musa (yāmūsā)! | Indeed (innī), | I Am (anā) | Allah (l-lahu), | the Lord (rabbu) | of the worlds (l-ʿālamīna).

28:31 And [that] throw your staff." But when he saw it moving as if it were a snake he turned in flight and did not return. "O Musa! Draw near and do not fear. Indeed, you are of the secure.

And [that] (wa-an) | throw (alqi) | your staff. (ʿaṣāka)" | But when (falammā) | he saw it (raāhā) | moving (tahtazzu) | as if it (ka-annahā) | were a snake (jānnun) | he turned (wallā) | in flight (mud'biran) | and did not (walam) | return (yuʿaqqib). | "O Musa (yāmūsā)! | Draw near (aqbil) | and do not (walā) | fear (takhaf). | Indeed, you (innaka) | are of (mina) | the secure (l-āminīna).

28:32 Insert your hand in your bosom it will come forth white without any harm. And draw to yourselves your hand against fear. So these are two evidences from your Lord, to Firaun and his chiefs. Indeed, they are a people defiantly disobedient."

Insert (us'luk) | your hand (yadaka) | in (fī) | your bosom (jaybika) | it will come forth (takhruj) | white (bayḍāa) | without (min) | without (ghayri) | any harm (sūin). | And draw (wa-uḍ'mum) | to yourselves (ilayka) | your hand (janāḥaka) | against (mina) | fear (l-rahbi). | So these (fadhānika) | are two evidences (bur'hānāni) | from (min) | your Lord (rabbika), | to (ilā) | Firaun (fir'ʿawna) | and his chiefs (wamala-ihi). | Indeed, they (innahum) | are (kānū) | a people (qawman) | defiantly disobedient. (fāsiqīna)"

28:33 He said, "My Lord! Indeed, I killed of them a man, and I fear that they will kill me.

He said (qāla), | "My Lord (rabbi)! | Indeed (innī), | I killed (qataltu) | of them (min'hum) | a man (nafsan), | and I fear (fa-akhāfu) | that (an) | they will kill me (yaqtulūni).

28:34 And my brother Harun, he is more eloquent than me in speech, so send him with me as a helper, who will confirm me. Indeed, I fear that they will deny me."

And my brother (wa-akhī) | Harun (hārūnu), | he (huwa) | is more eloquent (afṣaḥu) | than me (minnī) | in speech (lisānan), | so send him (fa-arsil'hu) | with me (maʿiya) | as a helper (rid'an), | who will confirm me (yuṣaddiqunī). | Indeed (innī), | I fear (akhāfu) | that (an) | they will deny me. (yukadhibūni)"

28:35 He said, "We will strengthen your arm through your brother and We will make for both of you an authority, so not they will reach to both of you. Through Our Signs you two and those who follow you, will be the dominant."

He said (qāla), | "We will strengthen (sanashuddu) | your arm (ʿaḍudaka) | through your brother (bi-akhīka) | and We will make (wanajʿalu) | for both of you (lakumā) | an authority (sul'ṭānan), | so not (falā) | they will reach (yaṣilūna) | to both of you (ilaykumā). | Through Our Signs (biāyātinā) | you two (antumā) | and those who (wamani) | follow you (ittabaʿakumā), | will be the dominant. (l-ghālibūna)"

28:36 But when came to them Musa with Our Signs clear, they said, "Not is this except a magic invented, and not we heard of this among our forefathers."

But when (falammā) | came to them (jāahum) | Musa (mūsā) | with Our Signs (biāyātinā) | clear (bayyinātin), | they said (qālū), | "Not (mā) | is this (hādhā) | except (illā) | a magic (siḥ'run) | invented (muf'taran), | and not (wamā) | we heard (sami''nā) | of this (bihādhā) | among (fī) | our forefathers. (ābāinā)" | our forefathers. (l-awalīna)"

28:37 And Musa said, "My Lord knows best of who has come with [the] guidance from Him and who - will be for him the good end in the Hereafter. Indeed, not will be successful the wrongdoers."

And Musa said (waqāla), | And Musa said (mūsā), | "My Lord (rabbī) | knows best (aʿlamu) | of who (biman) | has come (jāa) | with [the] guidance (bil-hudā) | from Him (min) | from Him (ʿindihi) | and who (waman)- | will be (takūnu) | for him (lahu) | the good end in the Hereafter (ʿāqibatu). | the good end in the Hereafter (l-dāri). | Indeed (innahu), | not (lā) | will be successful (yuf'liḥu) | the wrongdoers. (l-ẓālimūna)"

28:38 And Firaun said, "O chiefs! Not I know for you any god other than me. So kindle for me O Haman! Upon the clay and make, for me a lofty tower so that [I] I may look at the God of Musa. And indeed, I [I] think that he is of the liars."

And Firaun said (waqāla), | And Firaun said (fir''awnu), | "O chiefs (yāayyuhā)! | "O chiefs (l-mala-u)! | Not (mā) | I know (ʿalim'tu) | for you (lakum) | any (min) | god (ilāhin) | other than me (ghayrī). | So kindle (fa-awqid) | for me (lī) | O Haman (yāhāmānu)! | Upon (ʿalā) | the clay (l-ṭīni) | and make (fa-ij''al), | for me (lī) | a lofty tower (ṣarḥan) | so that [I] (laʿallī) | I may look (aṭṭaliʿu) | at (ilā) | the God (ilāhi) | of Musa (mūsā). | And indeed, I (wa-innī) | [I] think that he (la-aẓunnuhu) | is of (mina) | the liars. (l-kādhibīna)"

28:39 And he was arrogant, and his hosts in the land without right, and they thought that they to Us not will be returned.

And he was arrogant (wa-is'takbara), | And he was arrogant (huwa), | and his hosts (wajunūduhu) | in (fī) | the land (l-arḍi) | without (bighayri) | right (l-ḥaqi), | and they thought (waẓannū) | that they (annahum) | to Us (ilaynā) | not (lā) | will be returned (yur'jaʿūna).

28:40 So We seized him and his hosts, and We threw them in the sea. So see how was the end of the wrongdoers.

So We seized him (fa-akhadhnāhu) | and his hosts (wajunūdahu), | and We threw them (fanabadhnāhum) | in (fī) | the sea (l-yami). | So see (fa-unẓur) | how (kayfa) | was (kāna) | the end (ʿāqibatu) | of the wrongdoers (l-ẓālimīna).

28:41 And We made them leaders inviting to the Fire, and on the Day of the Resurrection not they will be helped.

And We made them (wajaʿalnāhum) | leaders (a-immatan) | inviting (yadʿūna) | to (ilā) | the Fire (l-nāri), | and on the Day (wayawma) | of the Resurrection (l-qiyāmati) | not (lā) | they will be helped (yunṣarūna).

28:42 And We caused to follow them in this world a curse, and on the Day of the Resurrection they will be of the despised.

And We caused to follow them (wa-atbaʿnāhum) | in (fī) | this (hādhihi) | world (l-dun'yā) | a curse (laʿnatan), | and on the Day (wayawma) | of the Resurrection (l-qiyāmati) | they (hum) | will be of (mina) | the despised (l-maqbūḥīna).

28:43 And verily, We gave Musa the Scripture, after [what] We had destroyed the generations former as an enlightenment for the mankind and a guidance and mercy that they may remember.

And verily (walaqad), | We gave (ātaynā) | Musa (mūsā) | the Scripture (l-kitāba), | after

[what] (min) | after [what] (baʿdi) | after [what] (mā) | We had destroyed (ahlaknā) | the generations (l-qurūna) | former (l-ūlā) | as an enlightenment (baṣāira) | for the mankind (lilnnāsi) | and a guidance (wahudan) | and mercy (waraḥmatan) | that they may (laʿallahum) | remember (yatadhakkarūna).

28:44 And not you were on the side western when We decreed to Musa the Commandment and not you were among the witnesses.

And not (wamā) | you were (kunta) | on the side (bijānibi) | western (l-gharbiyi) | when (idh) | We decreed (qaḍaynā) | to (ilā) | Musa (mūsā) | the Commandment (l-amra) | and not (wamā) | you were (kunta) | among (mina) | the witnesses (l-shāhidīna).

28:45 But We [We] produced generations and prolonged for them the life. And not you were a dweller among the people of Madyan, reciting to them Our Verses, but We [We] were the Senders.

But We (walākinnā) | [We] produced (anshanā) | generations (qurūnan) | and prolonged (fataṭāwala) | for them (ʿalayhimu) | the life (l-ʿumuru). | And not (wamā) | you were (kunta) | a dweller (thāwiyan) | among (fī) | the people (ahli) | of Madyan (madyana), | reciting (tatlū) | to them (ʿalayhim) | Our Verses (āyātinā), | but We (walākinnā) | [We] were (kunnā) | the Senders (mur'silīna).

28:46 And not you were at the side of the Tur when We called. But as a mercy from your Lord so that you warn a people not had come to them any warner before you so that they may remember.

And not (wamā) | you were (kunta) | at the side (bijānibi) | of the Tur (l-ṭūri) | when (idh) | We called (nādaynā). | But (walākin) | as a mercy (raḥmatan) | from (min) | your Lord (rabbika) | so that you warn (litundhira) | a people (qawman) | not (mā) | had come to them (atāhum) | any (min) | warner (nadhīrin) | before you (min) | before you (qablika) | so that they may (laʿallahum) | remember (yatadhakkarūna).

28:47 And if not [that] struck them a disaster for what had sent forth their hands and they would say, "Our Lord! Why not You sent to us a Messenger so we could have followed Your Verses and we would have been of the believers?"

And if not (walawlā) | [that] (an) | struck them (tuṣībahum) | a disaster (muṣībatun) | for what (bimā) | had sent forth (qaddamat) | their hands (aydīhim) | and they would say (fayaqūlū), | "Our Lord (rabbanā)! | Why not (lawlā) | You sent (arsalta) | to us (ilaynā) | a Messenger (rasūlan) | so we could have followed (fanattabiʿa) | Your Verses (āyātika) | and we would have been (wanakūna) | of (mina) | the believers? (l-mu'minīna)"

28:48 But when came to them the truth from Us they said, "Why not he was given the like of what was given to Musa?" Did not they disbelieve in what was given to Musa before? They said, "Two magic works supporting each other." And they said, "Indeed, we in all are disbelievers."

But when (falammā) | came to them (jāahumu) | the truth (l-ḥaqu) | from Us (min) | from Us (ʿindinā) | they said (qālū), | "Why not (lawlā) | he was given (ūtiya) | the like (mith'la) | of what (mā) | was given (ūtiya) | to Musa? (mūsā)" | Did not (awalam) | they disbelieve (yakfurū) | in what (bimā) | was given (ūtiya) | to Musa (mūsā) | before (min)? | before (qablu)? | They said (qālū), | "Two magic works (siḥ'rāni) | supporting each other. (taẓāharā)" | And they said (waqālū), | "Indeed, we (innā) | in all (bikullin) | are disbelievers. (kāfirūna)"

28:49 Say, "Then bring a Book from Allah, which is a better guide than both of them that I may follow it, if you are truthful."

Say (qul), | "Then bring (fatū) | a Book (bikitābin) | from Allah (min), | from Allah (ʿindi), | from Allah (l-lahi), | which (huwa) | is a better guide (ahdā) | than both of them (min'humā) | that I may follow it (attabiʿ'hu), | if (in) | you are (kuntum) | truthful. (ṣādiqīna)"

28:50 But if not they respond to you, then know that only they follow their desires. And who is more astray than one who follows his own desire without guidance from Allah? Indeed, Allah does not guide the people - the wrongdoers.

But if (fa-in) | not (lam) | they respond (yastajībū) | to you (laka), | then know (fa-iʿ'lam) | that only (annamā) | they follow (yattabiʿūna) | their desires (ahwāahum). | And who (waman) | is more astray (aḍallu) | than one who (mimmani) | follows (ittabaʿa) | his own desire (hawāhu) | without (bighayri) | guidance (hudan) | from (mina) | Allah (l-lahi)? | Indeed (inna), | Allah (l-laha) | does not (lā) | guide (yahdī) | the people (l-qawma)- | the wrongdoers (l-ẓālimīna).

28:51 And indeed, We have conveyed to them the Word so that they may remember.

And indeed (walaqad), | We have conveyed (waṣṣalnā) | to them (lahumu) | the Word (l-qawla) | so that they may (laʿallahum) | remember (yatadhakkarūna).

28:52 Those who, We gave them the Scripture before it, they in it believe.

Those who (alladhīna), | We gave them (ātaynāhumu) | the Scripture (l-kitāba) | before it (min), | before it (qablihi), | they (hum) | in it (bihi) | believe (yu'minūna).

28:53 And when it is recited to them they say, "We believe in it. Indeed, it is the truth from our Lord. Indeed, we [we] were before it Muslims."

And when (wa-idhā) | it is recited (yut'lā) | to them (ʿalayhim) | they say (qālū), | "We believe (āmannā) | in it (bihi). | Indeed, it (innahu) | is the truth (l-ḥaqu) | from (min) | our Lord (rabbinā). | Indeed, we (innā) | [we] were (kunnā) | before it (min) | before it (qablihi) | Muslims. (mus'limīna)"

28:54 Those will be given their reward twice because they are patient and they repel with good - the evil and from what We have provided them they spend.

Those (ulāika) | will be given (yu'tawna) | their reward (ajrahum) | twice (marratayni) | because (bimā) | they are patient (ṣabarū) | and they repel (wayadraūna) | with good (bil-ḥasanati)- | the evil (l-sayi-ata) | and from what (wamimmā) | We have provided them (razaqnāhum) | they spend (yunfiqūna).

28:55 And when they hear vain talk, they turn away from it and say, "For us our deeds and for you your deeds. Peace be on you; not we seek the ignorant."

And when (wa-idhā) | they hear (samiʿū) | vain talk (l-laghwa), | they turn away (aʿraḍū) | from it (ʿanhu) | and say (waqālū), | "For us (lanā) | our deeds (aʿmālunā) | and for you (walakum) | your deeds (aʿmālukum). | Peace be (salāmun) | on you (ʿalaykum); | not (lā) | we seek (nabtaghī) | the ignorant. (l-jāhilīna)"

28:56 Indeed, you can not guide whom you love, but Allah guides whom He wills. And He is most knowing of the guided ones.

Indeed, you (innaka) | can not (lā) | guide (tahdī) | whom (man) | you love (aḥbabta), | but (walākinna) | Allah (l-laha) | guides (yahdī) | whom (man) | He wills (yashāu). | And He (wahuwa) | is most knowing (aʿlamu) | of the guided ones (bil-muh'tadīna).

28:57 And they say, "If we follow the guidance with you, we would be swept from our land." Have not We established for them a sanctuary secure, are brought to it fruits of all things, a provision from Us? But most of them do not know.

And they say (waqālū), | "If (in) | we follow (nattabiʿi) | the guidance (l-hudā) | with you (maʿaka), | we would be swept (nutakhaṭṭaf) | from (min) | our land. (arḍinā)" | Have not (awalam) | We established (numakkin) | for them (lahum) | a sanctuary (ḥaraman) | secure (āminan), | are brought (yuj'bā) | to it (ilayhi) | fruits (thamarātu) | of all (kulli) | things (shayin), | a provision (riz'qan) | from (min) | Us (ladunnā)? | But (walākinna) | most of them (aktharahum) | do not (lā) |

know (yaʿlamūna).

28:58 And how many We have destroyed of a town which exulted, in its means of livelihood. And these are their dwellings not have been inhabited after them except a little. And indeed, [We] We are the inheritors.

And how many (wakam) | We have destroyed (ahlaknā) | of (min) | a town (qaryatin) | which exulted (baṭirat), | in its means of livelihood (maʿīshatahā). | And these (fatil'ka) | are their dwellings (masākinuhum) | not (lam) | have been inhabited (tus'kan) | after them (min) | after them (baʿdihim) | except (illā) | a little (qalīlan). | And indeed, [We] (wakunnā) | We (naḥnu) | are the inheritors (l-wārithīna).

28:59 And not was your Lord the one to destroy the towns until He had sent in their mother town a Messenger reciting to them Our Verses. And not We would be the one to destroy the towns except while their people were wrongdoers.

And not (wamā) | was (kāna) | your Lord (rabbuka) | the one to destroy (muh'lika) | the towns (l-qurā) | until (ḥattā) | He had sent (yabʿatha) | in (fī) | their mother town (ummihā) | a Messenger (rasūlan) | reciting (yatlū) | to them (ʿalayhim) | Our Verses (āyātinā). | And not (wamā) | We would be (kunnā) | the one to destroy (muh'likī) | the towns (l-qurā) | except (illā) | while their people (wa-ahluhā) | were wrongdoers (ẓālimūna).

28:60 And whatever you have been given from things, is an enjoyment of the life of the world and its adornment. And what is with Allah, is better and more lasting. So will not you use intellect?

And whatever (wamā) | you have been given (ūtītum) | from (min) | things (shayin), | is an enjoyment (famatāʿu) | of the life (l-ḥayati) | of the world (l-dun'yā) | and its adornment (wazīnatuhā). | And what (wamā) | is with (ʿinda) | Allah (l-lahi), | is better (khayrun) | and more lasting (wa-abqā). | So will not (afalā) | you use intellect (taʿqilūna)?

28:61 Then is he whom We have promised him a promise good, and he will meet it, like the one whom We provided him enjoyment of the life of the world then he on the Day of the Resurrection will be among those presented?

Then is he whom (afaman) | We have promised him (waʿadnāhu) | a promise (waʿdan) | good (ḥasanan), | and he (fahuwa) | will meet it (lāqīhi), | like the one whom (kaman) | We provided him (mattaʿnāhu) | enjoyment (matāʿa) | of the life (l-ḥayati) | of the world (l-dun'yā) | then (thumma) | he (huwa) | on the Day (yawma) | of the Resurrection (l-qiyāmati) | will be among (mina) | those presented (l-muḥ'ḍarīna)?

28:62 And the Day He will call them and say, "Where, are My partners whom you used to claim?"

And the Day (wayawma) | He will call them (yunādīhim) | and say (fayaqūlu), | "Where (ayna), | are My partners (shurakāiya) | whom (alladhīna) | you used to (kuntum) | claim? (tazʿumūna)"

28:63 Will say those - has come true against whom the Word, "Our Lord! These are those whom we led astray. We led them astray as we were astray. We declare our innocence before You. Not they used to worship us."

Will say (qāla) | those (alladhīna)- | has come true (ḥaqqa) | against whom (ʿalayhimu) | the Word (l-qawlu), | "Our Lord (rabbanā)! | These (hāulāi) | are those whom (alladhīna) | we led astray (aghwaynā). | We led them astray (aghwaynāhum) | as (kamā) | we were astray (ghawaynā). | We declare our innocence (tabarranā) | before You (ilayka). | Not (mā) | they used to (kānū) | worship us. (iyyānā)" | worship us. (yaʿbudūna)"

28:64 And it will be said, "Call your partners." And they will call them, but not they will respond to them and they will see the punishment. If only [that] they had been guided!

And it will be said (waqīla), | "Call (id''ū) | your partners. (shurakāakum)" | And they will call them (fadaʿawhum), | but not (falam) | they will respond (yastajībū) | to them (lahum) | and they will see (wara-awū) | the punishment (l-ʿadhāba). | If only (law) | [that] they (annahum) | had been (kānū) | guided (yahtadūna)!

28:65 And the Day He will call them and say, "What did you answer the Messengers?"
And the Day (wayawma) | He will call them (yunādīhim) | and say (fayaqūlu), | "What (mādhā) | did you answer (ajabtumu) | the Messengers? (l-mur'salīna)"

28:66 But will be obscure to them the information that day, so they will not ask one another.
But will be obscure (faʿamiyat) | to them (ʿalayhimu) | the information (l-anbāu) | that day (yawma-idhin), | so they (fahum) | will not ask one another (lā). | will not ask one another (yatasāalūna).

28:67 But as for him who repented and believed, and did righteousness, then perhaps [that] he will be of the successful ones.
But as for (fa-ammā) | him who (man) | repented (tāba) | and believed (waāmana), | and did (waʿamila) | righteousness (ṣāliḥan), | then perhaps (faʿasā) | [that] (an) | he will be (yakūna) | of (mina) | the successful ones (l-muf'liḥīna).

28:68 And your Lord creates what He wills and chooses. Not they have for them the choice. Glory be to Allah and High is He above what they associate with Him.
And your Lord (warabbuka) | creates (yakhluqu) | what (mā) | He wills (yashāu) | and chooses (wayakhtāru). | Not (mā) | they have (kāna) | for them (lahumu) | the choice (l-khiyaratu). | Glory be (sub'ḥāna) | to Allah (l-lahi) | and High is He (wataʿālā) | above what (ʿammā) | they associate with Him (yush'rikūna).

28:69 And your Lord knows what conceals their breasts and what they declare.
And your Lord (warabbuka) | knows (yaʿlamu) | what (mā) | conceals (tukinnu) | their breasts (ṣudūruhum) | and what (wamā) | they declare (yu''linūna).

28:70 And He is Allah; there is no god but He. To Him are due all praises in the first and the last. And for Him is the Decision, and to Him you will be returned.
And He (wahuwa) | is Allah (l-lahu); | there is no (lā) | god (ilāha) | but (illā) | He (huwa). | To Him (lahu) | are due all praises (l-ḥamdu) | in (fī) | the first (l-ūlā) | and the last (wal-ākhirati). | And for Him (walahu) | is the Decision (l-ḥuk'mu), | and to Him (wa-ilayhi) | you will be returned (tur'jaʿūna).

28:71 Say, "Have you seen if Allah made for you the night continuous till the Day of the Resurrection, who is the god besides Allah who could bring you light? Then will not you hear?"
Say (qul), | "Have you seen (ara-aytum) | if (in) | Allah made (jaʿala) | Allah made (l-lahu) | for you (ʿalaykumu) | the night (al-layla) | continuous (sarmadan) | till (ilā) | the Day (yawmi) | of the Resurrection (l-qiyāmati), | who (man) | is the god (ilāhun) | besides (ghayru) | Allah (l-lahi) | who could bring you (yatīkum) | light (biḍiyāin)? | Then will not (afalā) | you hear? (tasmaʿūna)"

28:72 Say, "Have you seen if Allah made for you the day continuous till the Day of the Resurrection, who is the god besides Allah who could bring you night for you (to) rest in it? Then will not you see?"
Say (qul), | "Have you seen (ara-aytum) | if (in) | Allah made (jaʿala) | Allah made (l-lahu) | for you (ʿalaykumu) | the day (l-nahāra) | continuous (sarmadan) | till (ilā) | the Day (yawmi) | of the Resurrection (l-qiyāmati), | who (man) | is the god (ilāhun) | besides (ghayru) | Allah (l-lahi) | who could bring you (yatīkum) | night (bilaylin) | for you (to) rest (taskunūna) | in it (fīhi)? | Then

will not (afalā) | you see? (tub'ṣirūna)"

28:73 And from His Mercy He made for you the night and the day, that you may rest therein and that you may seek from His Bounty, and so that you may be grateful.

And from (wamin) | His Mercy (raḥmatihi) | He made (jaʿala) | for you (lakumu) | the night (al-layla) | and the day (wal-nahāra), | that you may rest (litaskunū) | therein (fīhi) | and that you may seek (walitabtaghū) | from (min) | His Bounty (faḍlihi), | and so that you may (walaʿallakum) | be grateful (tashkurūna).

28:74 And the Day He will call them and say, "Where are My partners whom you used to claim?"

And the Day (wayawma) | He will call them (yunādīhim) | and say (fayaqūlu), | "Where (ayna) | are My partners (shurakāiya) | whom (alladhīna) | you used to (kuntum) | claim? (tazʿumūna)"

28:75 And We will draw forth from every nation a witness and We will say, "Bring your proof?" Then they will know that the truth is for Allah and will be lost from them what they used to invent.

And We will draw forth (wanazaʿnā) | from (min) | every (kulli) | nation (ummatin) | a witness (shahīdan) | and We will say (faqul'nā), | "Bring (hātū) | your proof? (bur'hānakum)" | Then they will know (faʿalimū) | that (anna) | the truth (l-ḥaqa) | is for Allah (lillahi) | and will be lost (waḍalla) | from them (ʿanhum) | what (mā) | they used to (kānū) | invent (yaftarūna).

28:76 Indeed, Qarun, was from the people of Musa, but he oppressed [on] them. And We gave him of the treasures which indeed the keys of it would burden a company of men possessors of great strength. When said to him his people, "Do not exult. Indeed, Allah does not love the exultant.

Indeed (inna), | Qarun (qārūna), | was (kāna) | from (min) | the people (qawmi) | of Musa (mūsā), | but he oppressed (fabaghā) | [on] them (ʿalayhim). | And We gave him (waātaynāhu) | of (mina) | the treasures (l-kunūzi) | which (mā) | indeed (inna) | the keys of it (mafātiḥahu) | would burden (latanūu) | a company of men (bil-ʿuṣ'bati) | possessors of great strength (ulī). | possessors of great strength (l-quwati). | When (idh) | said (qāla) | to him (lahu) | his people (qawmuhu), | "Do not (lā) | exult (tafraḥ). | Indeed (inna), | Allah (l-laha) | does not (lā) | love (yuḥibbu) | the exultant (l-fariḥīna).

28:77 But seek, through what Allah has given you, the home of the Hereafter, and do not forget your share of the world. And do good as Allah has been good to you. And do not seek corruption in the earth. Indeed, Allah does not love the corrupters."

But seek (wa-ib'taghi), | through what (fīmā) | Allah has given you (ātāka), | Allah has given you (l-lahu), | the home (l-dāra) | of the Hereafter (l-ākhirata), | and do not (walā) | forget (tansa) | your share (naṣībaka) | of (mina) | the world (l-dun'yā). | And do good (wa-aḥsin) | as (kamā) | Allah has been good (aḥsana) | Allah has been good (l-lahu) | to you (ilayka). | And do not (walā) | seek (tabghi) | corruption (l-fasāda) | in (fī) | the earth (l-arḍi). | Indeed (inna), | Allah (l-laha) | does not (lā) | love (yuḥibbu) | the corrupters. (l-muf'sidīna)"

28:78 He said, "Only I have been given it on account of knowledge I have." Did not he know that Allah indeed destroyed before him of the generations who [they] were stronger than him in strength and greater in accumulation. And not will be questioned about their sins the criminals.

He said (qāla), | "Only (innamā) | I have been given it (ūtītuhu) | on account (ʿalā) | of knowledge (ʿil'min) | I have. (ʿindī)" | Did not (awalam) | he know (yaʿlam) | that (anna) | Allah (l-laha) | indeed (qad) | destroyed (ahlaka) | before him (min) | before him (qablihi) | of (mina) | the generations (l-qurūni) | who (man) | [they] (huwa) | were stronger (ashaddu) | than him (min'hu) | in strength (quwwatan) | and greater (wa-aktharu) | in accumulation (jamʿan). | And not (walā) | will be questioned (yus'alu) | about (ʿan) | their sins (dhunūbihimu) | the criminals (l-muj'rimūna).

28:79 So he went forth to his people in his adornment. Said those who desire the life of the world, "O! Would that for us the like of what has been given to Qarun. Indeed, he is the owner of fortune great."

So he went forth (fakharaja) | to (ʿalā) | his people (qawmihi) | in (fī) | his adornment (zīnatihi). | Said (qāla) | those who (alladhīna) | desire (yurīdūna) | the life (l-ḥayata) | of the world (l-dun'yā), | "O! Would that (yālayta) | for us (lanā) | the like (mith'la) | of what (mā) | has been given (ūtiya) | to Qarun (qārūnu). | Indeed, he (innahu) | is the owner (ladhū) | of fortune (ḥaẓẓin) | great. (ʿaẓīmin)"

28:80 But said those who were given the knowledge, "Woe to you! The reward of Allah is better for he who believes and does righteous deeds. And not it is granted except to the patient ones."

But said (waqāla) | those who (alladhīna) | were given (ūtū) | the knowledge (l-ʿil'ma), | "Woe to you (waylakum)! | The reward (thawābu) | of Allah (l-lahi) | is better (khayrun) | for he who (liman) | believes (āmana) | and does (waʿamila) | righteous deeds (ṣāliḥan). | And not (walā) | it is granted (yulaqqāhā) | except (illā) | to the patient ones. (l-ṣābirūna)"

28:81 Then We caused to swallow up, him and his home, the earth. Then not was for him any group to help him besides Allah, and not was he of those who could defend themselves.

Then We caused to swallow up (fakhasafnā), | him (bihi) | and his home (wabidārihi), | the earth (l-arḍa). | Then not (famā) | was (kāna) | for him (lahu) | any (min) | group (fi-atin) | to help him (yanṣurūnahu) | besides (min) | besides (dūni) | Allah (l-lahi), | and not (wamā) | was (kāna) | he of (mina) | those who could defend themselves (l-muntaṣirīna).

28:82 And began, those who had wished his position the day before to say, "Ah! That Allah extends the provision for whom He wills of His slaves, and restricts it. If not that Allah had favored [to] us He would have caused it to swallow us. Ah! That not will succeed the disbelievers."

And began (wa-aṣbaḥa), | those who (alladhīna) | had wished (tamannaw) | his position (makānahu) | the day before (bil-amsi) | to say (yaqūlūna), | "Ah! That (wayka-anna) | Allah (l-laha) | extends (yabsuṭu) | the provision (l-riz'qa) | for whom (liman) | He wills (yashāu) | of (min) | His slaves (ʿibādihi), | and restricts it (wayaqdiru). | If not (lawlā) | that (an) | Allah had favored (manna) | Allah had favored (l-lahu) | [to] us (ʿalaynā) | He would have caused it to swallow us (lakhasafa). | He would have caused it to swallow us (binā). | Ah! That (wayka-annahu) | not (lā) | will succeed (yuf'liḥu) | the disbelievers. (l-kāfirūna)"

28:83 That the Home of the Hereafter We assign it to those who do not desire exaltedness in the earth and not corruption. And the good end is for the righteous.

That (til'ka) | the Home (l-dāru) | of the Hereafter (l-ākhiratu) | We assign it (najʿaluhā) | to those who (lilladhīna) | do not (lā) | desire (yurīdūna) | exaltedness (ʿuluwwan) | in (fī) | the earth (l-arḍi) | and not (walā) | corruption (fasādan). | And the good end (wal-ʿāqibatu) | is for the righteous (lil'muttaqīna).

28:84 Whoever comes with a good deed then for him, will be better than it; and whoever comes with an evil deed then not will be recompensed those who do the evil deeds except what they used to do.

Whoever (man) | comes (jāa) | with a good deed (bil-ḥasanati) | then for him (falahu), | will be better (khayrun) | than it (min'hā); | and whoever (waman) | comes (jāa) | with an evil deed (bil-sayi-ati) | then not (falā) | will be recompensed (yuj'zā) | those who (alladhīna) | do (ʿamilū) | the evil deeds (l-sayiāti) | except (illā) | what (mā) | they used to (kānū) | do (yaʿmalūna).

28:85 Indeed, He Who ordained upon you the Quran will surely take you back to a place of return. Say, "My Lord is most knowing of him who comes with the guidance, and who - he is in an error manifest."

Indeed (inna), | He Who (alladhī) | ordained (faraḍa) | upon you (ʿalayka) | the Quran (l-qur'āna) | will surely take you back (larādduka) | to (ilā) | a place of return (maʿādin). | Say (qul), | "My Lord (rabbī) | is most knowing (aʿlamu) | of him who (man) | comes (jāa) | with the guidance (bil-hudā), | and who (waman)- | he (huwa) | is in (fī) | an error (ḍalālin) | manifest. (mubīnin)"

28:86 And not you were expecting that would be sent down to you the Book, except as a mercy from your Lord. So do not be an assistant to the disbelievers.

And not (wamā) | you were (kunta) | expecting (tarjū) | that (an) | would be sent down (yul'qā) | to you (ilayka) | the Book (l-kitābu), | except (illā) | as a mercy (raḥmatan) | from (min) | your Lord (rabbika). | So do not (falā) | be (takūnanna) | an assistant (ẓahīran) | to the disbelievers (lil'kāfirīna).

28:87 And let not avert you from the Verses of Allah after [when] they have been revealed to you. And invite people to your Lord. And do not be of the polytheists.

And let not (walā) | avert you (yaṣuddunnaka) | from (ʿan) | the Verses (āyāti) | of Allah (l-lahi) | after (baʿda) | [when] (idh) | they have been revealed (unzilat) | to you (ilayka). | And invite people (wa-udʿʿu) | to (ilā) | your Lord (rabbika). | And do not (walā) | be (takūnanna) | of (mina) | the polytheists (l-mush'rikīna).

28:88 And do not invoke with Allah god other. There is no god except Him. Every thing will be destroyed except His Face. To Him is the Decision, and to Him you will be returned.

And do not (walā) | invoke (tadʿu) | with (maʿa) | Allah (l-lahi) | god (ilāhan) | other (ākhara). | There is no (lā) | god (ilāha) | except (illā) | Him (huwa). | Every (kullu) | thing (shayin) | will be destroyed (hālikun) | except (illā) | His Face (wajhahu). | To Him (lahu) | is the Decision (l-ḥuk'mu), | and to Him (wa-ilayhi) | you will be returned (tur'jaʿūna).

Chapter (29) Sūrat l-ʿAnkabūt (The Spider)

29:1 Alif Laam Meem.

Alif Laam Meem (alif-lam-meem).

29:2 Do think the people that they will be left because they say, "We believe" and they will not be tested?

Do think (aḥasiba) | the people (l-nāsu) | that (an) | they will be left (yut'rakū) | because (an) | they say (yaqūlū), | "We believe (āmannā)" | and they (wahum) | will not be tested (lā)? | will not be tested (yuf'tanūna)?

29:3 And indeed, We tested those who were before them. And Allah will surely make evident those who are truthful and He will surely make evident the liars.

And indeed (walaqad), | We tested (fatannā) | those who (alladhīna) | were before them (min). | were before them (qablihim). | And Allah will surely make evident (falayaʿlamanna) | And Allah will surely make evident (l-lahu) | those who (alladhīna) | are truthful (ṣadaqū) | and He will surely make evident (walayaʿlamanna) | the liars (l-kādhibīna).

29:4 Or think those who do evil deeds that they can outrun Us. Evil is what they judge.

Or (am) | think (ḥasiba) | those who (alladhīna) | do (yaʿmalūna) | evil deeds (l-sayiāti) | that (an) | they can outrun Us (yasbiqūnā). | Evil is (sāa) | what (mā) | they judge (yaḥkumūna).

29:5 Whoever [is] hopes for the meeting with Allah, then indeed, the Term of Allah is surely coming. And He is the All-Hearer, the All-Knower.

Whoever (man) | [is] (kāna) | hopes (yarjū) | for the meeting (liqāa) | with Allah (l-lahi), | then indeed (fa-inna), | the Term (ajala) | of Allah (l-lahi) | is surely coming (laātin). | And He (wahuwa) | is the All-Hearer (l-samīʿu), | the All-Knower (l-ʿalīmu).

29:6 And whoever strives then only he strives for himself. Indeed, Allah is Free from need of the worlds.

And whoever (waman) | strives (jāhada) | then only (fa-innamā) | he strives (yujāhidu) | for himself (linafsihi). | Indeed (inna), | Allah (l-laha) | is Free from need (laghaniyyun) | of (ʿani) | the worlds (l-ʿālamīna).

29:7 And those who believe and do righteous deeds, surely, We will remove from them their evil deeds, and We will surely reward them the best of what they used to do.

And those who (wa-alladhīna) | believe (āmanū) | and do (waʿamilū) | righteous deeds (l-ṣāliḥāti), | surely, We will remove (lanukaffiranna) | from them (ʿanhum) | their evil deeds (sayyiātihim), | and We will surely reward them (walanajziyannahum) | the best (aḥsana) | of what (alladhī) | they used (kānū) | to do (yaʿmalūna).

29:8 And We have enjoined on man goodness to his parents, but if they both strive against you to make you associate with Me what not you have of it any knowledge, then do not obey both of them. To Me is your return, and I will inform you about what you used to do.

And We have enjoined (wawaṣṣaynā) | on man (l-insāna) | goodness to his parents (biwālidayhi), | goodness to his parents (ḥus'nan), | but if (wa-in) | they both strive against you (jāhadāka) | to make you associate (litush'rika) | with Me (bī) | what (mā) | not (laysa) | you have (laka) | of it (bihi) | any knowledge (ʿil'mun), | then do not (falā) | obey both of them (tuṭiʿ'humā). | To Me (ilayya) | is your return (marjiʿukum), | and I will inform you (fa-unabbi-ukum) | about what (bimā) | you used (kuntum) | to do (taʿmalūna).

29:9 And those who believe and do righteous deeds We will surely admit them among the righteous.

And those who (wa-alladhīna) | believe (āmanū) | and do (waʿamilū) | righteous deeds (l-ṣāliḥāti) | We will surely admit them (lanud'khilannahum) | among (fī) | the righteous (l-ṣāliḥīna).

29:10 And of the people is he who says, "We believe in Allah." But when he is harmed in the Way of Allah he considers the trial of the people as the punishment of Allah. But if comes victory from your Lord, surely they say, "Indeed, we were with you." Is not Allah most knowing of what is in the breasts of the worlds?

And of (wamina) | the people (l-nāsi) | is he who (man) | says (yaqūlu), | "We believe (āmannā) | in Allah. (bil-lahi)" | But when (fa-idhā) | he is harmed (ūdhiya) | in (fī) | the Way of Allah (l-lahi) | he considers (jaʿala) | the trial (fit'nata) | of the people (l-nāsi) | as the punishment (kaʿadhābi) | of Allah (l-lahi). | But if (wala-in) | comes (jāa) | victory (naṣrun) | from (min) | your Lord (rabbika), | surely they say (layaqūlunna), | "Indeed, we (innā) | were (kunnā) | with you. (maʿakum)" | Is not (awalaysa) | Allah (l-lahu) | most knowing (bi-aʿlama) | of what (bimā) | is in (fī) | the breasts (ṣudūri) | of the worlds (l-ʿālamīna)?

29:11 And Allah will surely make evident those who believe, And He will surely make evident the hypocrites.

And Allah will surely make evident (walayaʿlamanna) | And Allah will surely make evident (l-lahu) | those who (alladhīna) | believe (āmanū), | And He will surely make evident (walayaʿlamanna) | the hypocrites (l-munāfiqīna).

29:12 And said, those who disbelieve to those who believe, "Follow our way, and we will carry your sins." But not they are going to carry of their sins any thing. Indeed, they are surely liars.

And said (waqāla), | those who (alladhīna) | disbelieve (kafarū) | to those who (lilladhīna) | believe (āmanū), | "Follow (ittabiʿū) | our way (sabīlanā), | and we will carry (walnaḥmil) | your sins. (khaṭāyākum)" | But not (wamā) | they (hum) | are going to carry (biḥāmilīna) | of (min) | their sins (khaṭāyāhum) | any (min) | thing (shayin). | Indeed, they (innahum) | are surely liars (lakādhibūna).

29:13 But surely they will carry their burdens and burdens with their burdens, and surely they will be questioned on the Day of the Resurrection about what they used to invent.

But surely they will carry (walayaḥmilunna) | their burdens (athqālahum) | and burdens (wa-athqālan) | with (maʿa) | their burdens (athqālihim), | and surely they will be questioned (walayus'alunna) | on the Day (yawma) | of the Resurrection (l-qiyāmati) | about what (ʿammā) | they used (kānū) | to invent (yaftarūna).

29:14 And verily, We sent Nuh to his people, and he remained among them a thousand years, save fifty years, then seized them the flood, while they were wrongdoers.

And verily (walaqad), | We sent (arsalnā) | Nuh (nūḥan) | to (ilā) | his people (qawmihi), | and he remained (falabitha) | among them (fīhim) | a thousand (alfa) | years (sanatin), | save (illā) | fifty (khamsīna) | years (ʿāman), | then seized them (fa-akhadhahumu) | the flood (l-ṭūfānu), | while they (wahum) | were wrongdoers (ẓālimūna).

29:15 But We saved him and the people of the ship, and We made it a Sign for the worlds.

But We saved him (fa-anjaynāhu) | and the people (wa-aṣḥāba) | of the ship (l-safīnati), | and We made it (wajaʿalnāhā) | a Sign (āyatan) | for the worlds (lilʿālamīna).

29:16 And Ibrahim - when he said to his people, "Worship Allah and fear Him. That is better for you if you know.

And Ibrahim (wa-ib'rāhīma)- | when (idh) | he said (qāla) | to his people (liqawmihi), | "Worship (uʿbudū) | Allah (l-laha) | and fear Him (wa-ittaqūhu). | That (dhālikum) | is better (khayrun) | for you (lakum) | if (in) | you (kuntum) | know (taʿlamūna).

29:17 Only you worship besides Allah idols, and you create falsehood. Indeed, those whom you worship besides Allah do not possess for you any provision. So seek from Allah the provision and worship Him and be grateful to Him. To Him you will be returned.

Only (innamā) | you worship (taʿbudūna) | besides (min) | besides (dūni) | Allah (l-lahi) | idols (awthānan), | and you create (watakhluqūna) | falsehood (if'kan). | Indeed (inna), | those whom (alladhīna) | you worship (taʿbudūna) | besides (min) | besides (dūni) | Allah (l-lahi) | do not (lā) | possess (yamlikūna) | for you (lakum) | any provision (riz'qan). | So seek (fa-ib'taghū) | from (ʿinda) | Allah (l-lahi) | the provision (l-riz'qa) | and worship Him (wa-uʿbudūhu) | and be grateful (wa-ush'kurū) | to Him (lahu). | To Him (ilayhi) | you will be returned (tur'jaʿūna).

29:18 And if you deny then verily, denied the nations before you. And not is on the Messenger except the conveyance clear."

And if (wa-in) | you deny (tukadhibū) | then verily (faqad), | denied (kadhaba) | the nations (umamun) | before you (min). | before you (qablikum). | And not (wamā) | is on (ʿalā) | the Messenger (l-rasūli) | except (illā) | the conveyance (l-balāghu) | clear. (l-mubīnu)"

29:19 Do not they see how Allah originates the creation then repeats it? Indeed, that for Allah is easy.

Do not (awalam) | they see (yaraw) | how (kayfa) | Allah originates (yub'di-u) | Allah originates (l-lahu) | the creation (l-khalqa) | then (thumma) | repeats it (yuʿīduhu)? | Indeed (inna), | that (dhālika) | for (ʿalā) | Allah (l-lahi) | is easy (yasīrun).

29:20 Say, "Travel in the earth and see how He originated the creation, Then Allah will produce the creation the last. Indeed, Allah on every thing is All-Powerful."

Say (qul), | "Travel (sīrū) | in (fī) | the earth (l-arḍi) | and see (fa-unẓurū) | how (kayfa) | He originated (bada-a) | the creation (l-khalqa), | Then (thumma) | Allah (l-lahu) | will produce (yunshi-u) | the creation (l-nashata) | the last (l-ākhirata). | Indeed (inna), | Allah (l-laha) | on (ʿalā) | every (kulli) | thing (shayin) | is All-Powerful. (qadīrun)"

29:21 He punishes whom He wills and has mercy on whom He wills, and to Him you will be returned.

He punishes (yuʿadhibu) | whom (man) | He wills (yashāu) | and has mercy (wayarḥamu) | on whom (man) | He wills (yashāu), | and to Him (wa-ilayhi) | you will be returned (tuq'labūna).

29:22 And not you can escape in the earth and not in the heaven. And not for you besides Allah any protector and not a helper.

And not (wamā) | you (antum) | can escape (bimuʿ'jizīna) | in (fī) | the earth (l-arḍi) | and not (walā) | in (fī) | the heaven (l-samāi). | And not (wamā) | for you (lakum) | besides (min) | besides (dūni) | Allah (l-lahi) | any (min) | protector (waliyyin) | and not (walā) | a helper (naṣīrin).

29:23 And those who disbelieve in the Signs of Allah and the meeting (with) Him, those have despaired of My Mercy. And those, for them is a punishment painful.

And those who (wa-alladhīna) | disbelieve (kafarū) | in the Signs (biāyāti) | of Allah (l-lahi) | and the meeting (with) Him (waliqāihi), | those (ulāika) | have despaired (ya-isū) | of (min) | My Mercy (raḥmatī). | And those (wa-ulāika), | for them (lahum) | is a punishment (ʿadhābun) | painful (alīmun).

29:24 And not was the answer of his people except that they said, "Kill him or burn him." But Allah saved him from the fire. Indeed, in that, surely are Signs for a people who believe.

And not (famā) | was (kāna) | the answer (jawāba) | of his people (qawmihi) | except (illā) | that (an) | they said (qālū), | "Kill him (uq'tulūhu) | or (aw) | burn him. (ḥarriqūhu)" | But Allah saved him (fa-anjāhu) | But Allah saved him (l-lahu) | from (mina) | the fire (l-nāri). | Indeed (inna), | in (fī) | that (dhālika), | surely are Signs (laāyātin) | for a people (liqawmin) | who believe (yu'minūna).

29:25 And he said, "Only you have taken besides Allah idols out of love among you in the life of the world. Then on the Day of the Resurrection you will deny one another and curse one another, and your abode will be the Fire and not for you any helpers."

And he said (waqāla), | "Only (innamā) | you have taken (ittakhadhtum) | besides (min) | besides (dūni) | Allah (l-lahi) | idols (awthānan) | out of love (mawaddata) | among you (baynikum) | in (fī) | the life (l-ḥayati) | of the world (l-dun'yā). | Then (thumma) | on the Day (yawma) | of the Resurrection (l-qiyāmati) | you will deny (yakfuru) | one another (baʿḍukum) | one another (bibaʿḍin) | and curse (wayalʿanu) | one another (baʿḍukum), | one another (baʿḍan), | and your abode (wamawākumu) | will be the Fire (l-nāru) | and not (wamā) | for you (lakum) | any (min) | helpers. (nāṣirīna)"

29:26 And believed [in] him Lut, and he said, "Indeed I am emigrating to my Lord. Indeed, He [He] is the All-Mighty, the All-Wise."

And believed (faāmana) | [in] him (lahu) | Lut (lūṭun), | and he said (waqāla), | "Indeed I am (innī) | emigrating (muhājirun) | to (ilā) | my Lord (rabbī). | Indeed, He (innahu) | [He] is (huwa) | the All-Mighty (l-ʿazīzu), | the All-Wise. (l-ḥakīmu)"

29:27 And We granted to him Isaac and Yaqub and We placed in his offsprings the Prophethood and the Book. And We gave him his reward in the world. And indeed, he in the Hereafter is surely, among the righteous.

And We granted (wawahabnā) | to him (lahu) | Isaac (is'ḥāqa) | and Yaqub (wayaʿqūba) | and We placed (wajaʿalnā) | in (fī) | his offsprings (dhurriyyatihi) | the Prophethood (l-nubuwata) | and the Book (wal-kitāba). | And We gave him (waātaynāhu) | his reward (ajrahu) | in (fī) | the world (l-dun'yā). | And indeed, he (wa-innahu) | in (fī) | the Hereafter (l-ākhirati) | is surely, among (lamina) | the righteous (l-ṣāliḥīna).

29:28 And Lut, when he said to his people, "Indeed, you commit the immorality, not has preceded you with it any one from the worlds.

And Lut (walūṭan), | when (idh) | he said (qāla) | to his people (liqawmihi), | "Indeed, you (innakum) | commit (latatūna) | the immorality (l-fāḥishata), | not (mā) | has preceded you (sabaqakum) | with it (bihā) | any (min) | one (aḥadin) | from (mina) | the worlds (l-ʿālamīna).

29:29 Indeed, you approach the men, and you cut off the road and commit in your meetings evil?" And not was the answer of his people except that they said, "Bring upon us the punishment of Allah if you are of the truthful."

Indeed, you (a-innakum) | approach (latatūna) | the men (l-rijāla), | and you cut off (wataqṭaʿūna) | the road (l-sabīla) | and commit (watatūna) | in (fī) | your meetings (nādīkumu) | evil? (l-munkara)" | And not (famā) | was (kāna) | the answer (jawāba) | of his people (qawmihi) | except (illā) | that (an) | they said (qālū), | "Bring upon us (i'tinā) | the punishment (biʿadhābi) | of Allah (l-lahi) | if (in) | you are (kunta) | of (mina) | the truthful. (l-ṣādiqīna)"

29:30 He said, "My Lord! Help me against the people the corrupters."

He said (qāla), | "My Lord (rabbi)! | Help me (unṣur'nī) | against (ʿalā) | the people (l-qawmi) | the corrupters. (l-muf'sidīna)"

29:31 And when came Our messengers to Ibrahim with the glad tidings they said, "Indeed, we are going to destroy the people of this town. Indeed, its people are wrongdoers."

And when (walammā) | came (jāat) | Our messengers (rusulunā) | to Ibrahim (ib'rāhīma) | with the glad tidings (bil-bush'rā) | they said (qālū), | "Indeed, we (innā) | are going to destroy (muh'likū) | the people (ahli) | of this (hādhihi) | town (l-qaryati). | Indeed (inna), | its people (ahlahā) | are (kānū) | wrongdoers. (ẓālimīna)"

29:32 He said, "Indeed, in it is Lut." They said, "We know better who is in it. We will surely save him and his family, except his wife. She is of those who remain behind."

He said (qāla), | "Indeed (inna), | in it (fīhā) | is Lut. (lūṭan)" | They said (qālū), | "We (naḥnu) | know better (aʿlamu) | who (biman) | is in it (fīhā). | We will surely save him (lanunajjiyannahu) | and his family (wa-ahlahu), | except (illā) | his wife (im'ra-atahu). | She (kānat) | is of (mina) | those who remain behind. (l-ghābirīna)"

29:33 And when [that] came Our messengers to Lut he was distressed for them, and felt straitened for them and uneasy. And they said, "Do not fear and do not grieve. Indeed, we will save you and your family, except your wife. She is of those who remain behind.

And when (walammā) | [that] (an) | came (jāat) | Our messengers (rusulunā) | to Lut (lūṭan) | he was distressed (sīa) | for them (bihim), | and felt straitened (waḍāqa) | for them (bihim) | and uneasy (dhar'an). | And they said (waqālū), | "Do not (lā) | fear (takhaf) | and do not (walā) | grieve (taḥzan). | Indeed, we (innā) | will save you (munajjūka) | and your family (wa-ahlaka), |

except (illā) | your wife (im'ra-ataka). | She (kānat) | is of (mina) | those who remain behind (l-ghābirīna).

29:34 Indeed, we will bring down on the people of this town a punishment from the sky, because they have been defiantly disobedient."

Indeed, we (innā) | will bring down (munzilūna) | on (ʿalā) | the people (ahli) | of this (hādhihi) | town (l-qaryati) | a punishment (rij'zan) | from (mina) | the sky (l-samāi), | because (bimā) | they have been (kānū) | defiantly disobedient. (yafsuqūna)"

29:35 And verily, We have left about it a sign, as evidence for a people who use reason.

And verily (walaqad), | We have left (taraknā) | about it (min'hā) | a sign (āyatan), | as evidence (bayyinatan) | for a people (liqawmin) | who use reason (yaʿqilūna).

29:36 And to Madyan their brother Shuaib. And he said, "O my people! Worship Allah and expect the Day the Last, and do not commit evil in the earth as corrupters."

And to (wa-ilā) | Madyan (madyana) | their brother (akhāhum) | Shuaib (shuʿayban). | And he said (faqāla), | "O my people (yāqawmi)! | Worship (uʿ'budū) | Allah (l-laha) | and expect (wa-ir'jū) | the Day (l-yawma) | the Last (l-ākhira), | and do not (walā) | commit evil (taʿthaw) | in (fī) | the earth (l-arḍi) | as corrupters. (muf'sidīna)"

29:37 But they denied him, so seized them the earthquake, and they became in their home fallen prone.

But they denied him (fakadhabūhu), | so seized them (fa-akhadhathumu) | the earthquake (l-rajfatu), | and they became (fa-aṣbaḥū) | in (fī) | their home (dārihim) | fallen prone (jāthimīna).

29:38 And Aad and Thamud, and verily, has become clear to you from their dwellings. And made fair-seeming to them the Shaitaan their deeds and averted them from the Way, though they were endowed with insight.

And Aad (waʿādan) | and Thamud (wathamūdā), | and verily (waqad), | has become clear (tabayyana) | to you (lakum) | from (min) | their dwellings (masākinihim). | And made fair-seeming (wazayyana) | to them (lahumu) | the Shaitaan (l-shayṭānu) | their deeds (aʿmālahum) | and averted them (faṣaddahum) | from (ʿani) | the Way (l-sabīli), | though they were (wakānū) | endowed with insight (mus'tabṣirīna).

29:39 And Qarun, and Firaun and Haman. And certainly came to them Musa with clear evidences, but they were arrogant in the earth, and not they could outstrip Us.

And Qarun (waqārūna), | and Firaun (wafir'ʿawna) | and Haman (wahāmāna). | And certainly (walaqad) | came to them (jāahum) | Musa (mūsā) | with clear evidences (bil-bayināti), | but they were arrogant (fa-is'takbarū) | in (fī) | the earth (l-arḍi), | and not (wamā) | they could (kānū) | outstrip Us (sābiqīna).

29:40 So each We seized for his sin. Then of them was he who, We sent on him a violent storm, and of them was he who, seized him the awful cry and of them was he who, We caused to swallow him, the earth and of them was he who, We drowned. And not was Allah to wrong them but they were themselves doing wrong.

So each (fakullan) | We seized (akhadhnā) | for his sin (bidhanbihi). | Then of them (famin'hum) | was he who (man), | We sent (arsalnā) | on him (ʿalayhi) | a violent storm (ḥāṣiban), | and of them (wamin'hum) | was he who (man), | seized him (akhadhathu) | the awful cry (l-ṣayḥatu) | and of them (wamin'hum) | was he who (man), | We caused to swallow (khasafnā) | him (bihi), | the earth (l-arḍa) | and of them (wamin'hum) | was he who (man), | We drowned (aghraqnā). | And not (wamā) | was (kāna) | Allah (l-lahu) | to wrong them (liyaẓlimahum) | but (walākin) | they were (kānū) | themselves (anfusahum) | doing wrong (yaẓlimūna).

29:41 The example of those who take besides Allah protectors is like the spider who takes a house. And indeed, the weakest of houses is surely (the) house of the spider, if only they know.

The example (mathalu) | of those who (alladhīna) | take (ittakhadhū) | besides (min) | besides (dūni) | Allah (l-lahi) | protectors (awliyāa) | is like (kamathali) | the spider (l-ʿankabūti) | who takes (ittakhadhat) | a house (baytan). | And indeed (wa-inna), | the weakest (awhana) | of houses (l-buyūti) | is surely (the) house (labaytu) | of the spider (l-ʿankabūti), | if only (law) | they (kānū) | know (yaʿlamūna).

29:42 Indeed, Allah knows what they invoke besides Him any thing. And He is the All-Mighty, the All-Wise.

Indeed (inna), | Allah (l-laha) | knows (yaʿlamu) | what (mā) | they invoke (yadʿūna) | besides Him (min) | besides Him (dūnihi) | any (min) | thing (shayin). | And He (wahuwa) | is the All-Mighty (l-ʿazīzu), | the All-Wise (l-ḥakīmu).

29:43 And these examples We set forth to mankind, but not will understand them except those of knowledge.

And these (watil'ka) | examples (l-amthālu) | We set forth (naḍribuhā) | to mankind (lilnnāsi), | but not (wamā) | will understand them (yaʿqiluhā) | except (illā) | those of knowledge (l-ʿālimūna).

29:44 Allah created the heavens and the earth in truth. Indeed, in that is surely a Sign for the believers.

Allah created (khalaqa) | Allah created (l-lahu) | the heavens (l-samāwāti) | and the earth (wal-arḍa) | in truth (bil-ḥaqi). | Indeed (inna), | in (fī) | that (dhālika) | is surely a Sign (laāyatan) | for the believers (lil'mu'minīna).

29:45 Recite what has been revealed to you of the Book, and establish the prayer. Indeed, the prayer prevents from the immorality and evil deeds, and surely the remembrance of Allah is greatest. And Allah knows what you do.

Recite (ut'lu) | what (mā) | has been revealed (ūḥiya) | to you (ilayka) | of (mina) | the Book (l-kitābi), | and establish (wa-aqimi) | the prayer (l-ṣalata). | Indeed (inna), | the prayer (l-ṣalata) | prevents (tanhā) | from (ʿani) | the immorality (l-faḥshāi) | and evil deeds (wal-munkari), | and surely the remembrance (waladhik'ru) | of Allah (l-lahi) | is greatest (akbaru). | And Allah (wal-lahu) | knows (yaʿlamu) | what (mā) | you do (taṣnaʿūna).

29:46 And do not argue with the People of the Book except by which [it] is best, except those who do wrong among them, and say, "We believe in that which has been revealed to us and was revealed to you. And our God and your God is One, and we to Him submit."

And do not (walā) | argue (tujādilū) | with the People of the Book (ahla) | with the People of the Book (l-kitābi) | except (illā) | by which (bi-allatī) | [it] (hiya) | is best (aḥsanu), | except (illā) | those who (alladhīna) | do wrong (ẓalamū) | among them (min'hum), | and say (waqūlū), | "We believe (āmannā) | in that which (bi-alladhī) | has been revealed (unzila) | to us (ilaynā) | and was revealed (wa-unzila) | to you (ilaykum). | And our God (wa-ilāhunā) | and your God (wa-ilāhukum) | is One (wāḥidun), | and we (wanaḥnu) | to Him (lahu) | submit. (mus'limūna)"

29:47 And thus We have revealed to you the Book. So those We gave [them] the Book believe therein. And among these are some who believe therein. And none reject Our Verses except the disbelievers.

And thus (wakadhālika) | We have revealed (anzalnā) | to you (ilayka) | the Book (l-kitāba). | So those (fa-alladhīna) | We gave [them] (ātaynāhumu) | the Book (l-kitāba) | believe (yu'minūna) | therein (bihi). | And among (wamin) | these (hāulāi) | are some who (man) | believe (yu'minu) |

therein (bihi). | And none (wamā) | reject (yajḥadu) | Our Verses (biāyātinā) | except (illā) | the disbelievers (l-kāfirūna).

29:48 And not did you recite before it, any Book, and not did you write it with your right hand, in that case surely would have doubted the falsifiers.

And not (wamā) | did you (kunta) | recite (tatlū) | before it (min), | before it (qablihi), | any (min) | Book (kitābin), | and not (walā) | did you write it (takhuṭṭuhu) | with your right hand (biyamīnika), | in that case (idhan) | surely would have doubted (la-ir'tāba) | the falsifiers (l-mub'ṭilūna).

29:49 Nay, it is Verses clear in the breasts of those who are given the knowledge. And not reject Our Verses except the wrongdoers.

Nay (bal), | it (huwa) | is Verses (āyātun) | clear (bayyinātun) | in (fī) | the breasts (ṣudūri) | of those who (alladhīna) | are given (ūtū) | the knowledge (l-ʿil'ma). | And not (wamā) | reject (yajḥadu) | Our Verses (biāyātinā) | except (illā) | the wrongdoers (l-ẓālimūna).

29:50 And they say, "Why not are sent down to him the Signs from his Lord?" Say, "Only the Signs are with Allah, and only I am a warner clear."

And they say (waqālū), | "Why not (lawlā) | are sent down (unzila) | to him (ʿalayhi) | the Signs (āyātun) | from (min) | his Lord? (rabbihi)" | Say (qul), | "Only (innamā) | the Signs (l-āyātu) | are with (ʿinda) | Allah (l-lahi), | and only (wa-innamā) | I am (anā) | a warner (nadhīrun) | clear. (mubīnun)"

29:51 And is it not sufficient for them that We revealed to you the Book which is recited to them? Indeed, in that, surely is a mercy and a reminder for a people who believe.

And is it not (awalam) | sufficient for them (yakfihim) | that We (annā) | revealed (anzalnā) | to you (ʿalayka) | the Book (l-kitāba) | which is recited (yut'lā) | to them (ʿalayhim)? | Indeed (inna), | in (fī) | that (dhālika), | surely is a mercy (laraḥmatan) | and a reminder (wadhik'rā) | for a people (liqawmin) | who believe (yu'minūna).

29:52 Say, "Sufficient is Allah between me and between you as a Witness. He knows what is in the heavens and the earth. And those who believe in [the] falsehood and disbelieve in Allah, those, they are the losers."

Say (qul), | "Sufficient is (kafā) | Allah (bil-lahi) | between me (baynī) | and between you (wabaynakum) | as a Witness (shahīdan). | He knows (yaʿlamu) | what (mā) | is in (fī) | the heavens (l-samāwāti) | and the earth (wal-arḍi). | And those who (wa-alladhīna) | believe (āmanū) | in [the] falsehood (bil-bāṭili) | and disbelieve (wakafarū) | in Allah (bil-lahi), | those (ulāika), | they (humu) | are the losers. (l-khāsirūna)"

29:53 And they ask you to hasten [with] the punishment. And if not for a term appointed, surely would have come to them the punishment. But it will surely come to them suddenly while they do not perceive.

And they ask you to hasten (wayastaʿjilūnaka) | [with] the punishment (bil-ʿadhābi). | And if not (walawlā) | for a term (ajalun) | appointed (musamman), | surely would have come to them (lajāahumu) | the punishment (l-ʿadhābu). | But it will surely come to them (walayatiyannahum) | suddenly (baghtatan) | while they (wahum) | do not (lā) | perceive (yashʿurūna).

29:54 They ask you to hasten the punishment. And indeed, Hell, will surely, encompass the disbelievers

They ask you to hasten (yastaʿjilūnaka) | the punishment (bil-ʿadhābi). | And indeed (wa-inna), | Hell (jahannama), | will surely, encompass (lamuḥīṭatun) | the disbelievers (bil-kāfirīna)

29:55 On the Day will cover them the punishment from above them and from below their feet, and He will say, "Taste what you used to do."

On the Day (yawma) | will cover them (yaghshāhumu) | the punishment (l-ʿadhābu) | from (min) | above them (fawqihim) | and from (wamin) | below (taḥti) | their feet (arjulihim), | and He will say (wayaqūlu), | "Taste (dhūqū) | what (mā) | you used (kuntum) | to do. (taʿmalūna)"

29:56 O My servants who believe! Indeed, My earth is spacious, so only worship Me.

O My servants (yāʿibādiya) | who (alladhīna) | believe (āmanū)! | Indeed (inna), | My earth (arḍī) | is spacious (wāsiʿatun), | so only (fa-iyyāya) | worship Me (fa-uʿ'budūni).

29:57 Every soul will taste the death. Then to Us you will be returned.

Every (kullu) | soul (nafsin) | will taste (dhāiqatu) | the death (l-mawti). | Then (thumma) | to Us (ilaynā) | you will be returned (tur'jaʿūna).

29:58 And those who believe and do [the] righteous deeds, surely We will give them a place in Paradise lofty dwellings, flow from underneath it the rivers, will abide forever in it. Excellent is the reward of the workers

And those who (wa-alladhīna) | believe (āmanū) | and do (waʿamilū) | [the] righteous deeds (l-ṣāliḥāti), | surely We will give them a place (lanubawwi-annahum) | in (mina) | Paradise (l-janati) | lofty dwellings (ghurafan), | flow (tajrī) | from (min) | underneath it (taḥtihā) | the rivers (l-anhāru), | will abide forever (khālidīna) | in it (fīhā). | Excellent is (niʿ'ma) | the reward (ajru) | of the workers (l-ʿāmilīna)

29:59 Those who are patient and upon their Lord put their trust.

Those who (alladhīna) | are patient (ṣabarū) | and upon (waʿalā) | their Lord (rabbihim) | put their trust (yatawakkalūna).

29:60 And how many of a creature does not carry its provision. Allah provides for it and for you. And He is the All-Hearer, the All-Knower.

And how many (waka-ayyin) | of (min) | a creature (dābbatin) | does not (lā) | carry (taḥmilu) | its provision (riz'qahā). | Allah (l-lahu) | provides for it (yarzuquhā) | and for you (wa-iyyākum). | And He (wahuwa) | is the All-Hearer (l-samīʿu), | the All-Knower (l-ʿalīmu).

29:61 And if you ask them, "Who created the heavens and the earth, and subjected the sun and the moon?" Surely they would say "Allah." Then how are they deluded?

And if (wala-in) | you ask them (sa-altahum), | "Who (man) | created (khalaqa) | the heavens (l-samāwāti) | and the earth (wal-arḍa), | and subjected (wasakhara) | the sun (l-shamsa) | and the moon? (wal-qamara)" | Surely they would say (layaqūlunna) | "Allah. (l-lahu)" | Then how (fa-annā) | are they deluded (yu'fakūna)?

29:62 Allah extends the provision for whom He wills of His slaves and restricts for him. Indeed, Allah of every thing is All-Knower.

Allah (al-lahu) | extends (yabsuṭu) | the provision (l-riz'qa) | for whom (liman) | He wills (yashāu) | of (min) | His slaves (ʿibādihi) | and restricts (wayaqdiru) | for him (lahu). | Indeed (inna), | Allah (l-laha) | of every (bikulli) | thing (shayin) | is All-Knower (ʿalīmun).

29:63 And if you ask them, "Who sends down from the sky water and gives life thereby to the earth after its death?" Surely, they would say, "Allah." Say, "All Praises are for Allah." But most of them do not use reason.

And if (wala-in) | you ask them (sa-altahum), | "Who (man) | sends down (nazzala) | from (mina) | the sky (l-samāi) | water (māan) | and gives life (fa-aḥyā) | thereby (bihi) | to the earth (l-arḍa) | after (min) | after (baʿdi) | its death? (mawtihā)" | Surely, they would say (layaqūlunna), |

"Allah. (l-lahu)" | Say (quli), | "All Praises (l-ḥamdu) | are for Allah. (lillahi)" | But (bal) | most of them (aktharuhum) | do not (lā) | use reason (yaʿqilūna).

29:64 And not is this life of the world but amusement and play. And indeed, the Home of the Hereafter - surely, it is the life, if only they know.

And not (wamā) | is this (hādhihi) | life (l-ḥayatu) | of the world (l-dun'yā) | but (illā) | amusement (lahwun) | and play (walaʿibun). | And indeed (wa-inna), | the Home (l-dāra) | of the Hereafter (l-ākhirata)- | surely, it (lahiya) | is the life (l-ḥayawānu), | if only (law) | they (kānū) | know (yaʿlamūna).

29:65 And when they embark [in] the ship, they call Allah being sincere to Him in the religion. But when He delivers them to the land, behold, they associate partners with Him

And when (fa-idhā) | they embark (rakibū) | [in] (fī) | the ship (l-ful'ki), | they call (daʿawū) | Allah (l-laha) | being sincere (mukh'liṣīna) | to Him (lahu) | in the religion (l-dīna). | But when (falammā) | He delivers them (najjāhum) | to (ilā) | the land (l-bari), | behold (idhā), | they (hum) | associate partners with Him (yush'rikūna)

29:66 So that they may deny [in] what We have given them, and they may enjoy themselves. But soon they will know.

So that they may deny (liyakfurū) | [in] what (bimā) | We have given them (ātaynāhum), | and they may enjoy themselves (waliyatamattaʿū). | But soon (fasawfa) | they will know (yaʿlamūna).

29:67 Do not they see that We have made a Sanctuary secure while are being taken away the people around them? Then do in the falsehood they believe and in the Favor of Allah they disbelieve?

Do not (awalam) | they see (yaraw) | that We (annā) | have made (jaʿalnā) | a Sanctuary (ḥaraman) | secure (āminan) | while are being taken away (wayutakhaṭṭafu) | the people (l-nāsu) | around them (min)? | around them (ḥawlihim)? | Then do in the falsehood (afabil-bāṭili) | they believe (yu'minūna) | and in the Favor (wabiniʿ'mati) | of Allah (l-lahi) | they disbelieve (yakfurūna)?

29:68 And who is more unjust than he who invents against Allah a lie or denies the truth when it has come to him. Is there not in Hell an abode for the disbelievers?

And who (waman) | is more unjust (aẓlamu) | than he who (mimmani) | invents (if'tarā) | against (ʿalā) | Allah (l-lahi) | a lie (kadhiban) | or (aw) | denies (kadhaba) | the truth (bil-ḥaqi) | when (lammā) | it has come to him (jāahu). | Is there not (alaysa) | in (fī) | Hell (jahannama) | an abode (mathwan) | for the disbelievers (lil'kāfirīna)?

29:69 And those who strive for Us, We will surely, guide them to Our ways. And indeed, Allah surely is with the good-doers.

And those who (wa-alladhīna) | strive (jāhadū) | for Us (fīnā), | We will surely, guide them (lanahdiyannahum) | to Our ways (subulanā). | And indeed (wa-inna), | Allah (l-laha) | surely is with (lamaʿa) | the good-doers (l-muḥ'sinīna).

Chapter (30) Sūrat l-Rūm (The Romans)

30:1 Alif Lam Meem.

Alif Lam Meem (alif-lam-meem).

30:2 Have been defeated the Romans

Have been defeated (ghulibati) | the Romans (l-rūmu)

30:3 In the nearest land. But they, after their defeat, will overcome

In (fī) | the nearest (adnā) | land (l-arḍi). | But they (wahum), | after (min) | after (baʿdi) | their defeat (ghalabihim), | will overcome (sayaghlibūna)

30:4 Within a few years. For Allah is the command before and after. And that day will rejoice the believers

Within (fī) | a few (biḍʿi) | years (sinīna). | For Allah (lillahi) | is the command (l-amru) | before (min) | before (qablu) | and after (wamin). | and after (baʿdu). | And that day (wayawma-idhin) | will rejoice (yafraḥu) | the believers (l-mu'minūna)

30:5 With the help of Allah. He helps whom He wills. And He is the All-Mighty, the Most Merciful.

With the help (binaṣri) | of Allah (l-lahi). | He helps (yanṣuru) | whom (man) | He wills (yashāu). | And He (wahuwa) | is the All-Mighty (l-ʿazīzu), | the Most Merciful (l-raḥīmu).

30:6 It is the Promise of Allah. Does not fail Allah in His promise, but most of [the] people do not know.

It is the Promise (waʿda) | of Allah (l-lahi). | Does not (lā) | fail (yukh'lifu) | Allah (l-lahu) | in His promise (waʿdahu), | but (walākinna) | most of (akthara) | [the] people (l-nāsi) | do not (lā) | know (yaʿlamūna).

30:7 They know the apparent of the life of the world, but they, about the Hereafter, [they] are heedless.

They know (yaʿlamūna) | the apparent (ẓāhiran) | of (mina) | the life (l-ḥayati) | of the world (l-dun'yā), | but they (wahum), | about (ʿani) | the Hereafter (l-ākhirati), | [they] (hum) | are heedless (ghāfilūna).

30:8 Do not they ponder within themselves? Not Allah has created the heavens and the earth, and what is between them except in truth and for a term appointed. And indeed, many of the people in the meeting with their Lord surely are disbelievers.

Do not (awalam) | they ponder (yatafakkarū) | within (fī) | themselves (anfusihim)? | Not (mā) | Allah has created (khalaqa) | Allah has created (l-lahu) | the heavens (l-samāwāti) | and the earth (wal-arḍa), | and what (wamā) | is between them (baynahumā) | except (illā) | in truth (bil-ḥaqi) | and for a term (wa-ajalin) | appointed (musamman). | And indeed (wa-inna), | many (kathīran) | of (mina) | the people (l-nāsi) | in the meeting (biliqāi) | with their Lord (rabbihim) | surely are disbelievers (lakāfirūna).

30:9 Have not they traveled in the earth and observed how was the end of those before them? They were mightier than them in strength, and they dug the earth and built on it more than what they have built on it. And came to them their Messengers with clear proofs. So not was Allah to wrong them but they were themselves doing wrong.

Have not (awalam) | they traveled (yasīrū) | in (fī) | the earth (l-arḍi) | and observed (fayanẓurū) | how (kayfa) | was (kāna) | the end (ʿāqibatu) | of those (alladhīna) | before them (min)? | before them (qablihim)? | They were (kānū) | mightier (ashadda) | than them (min'hum) | in strength (quwwatan), | and they dug (wa-athārū) | the earth (l-arḍa) | and built on it (waʿamarūhā) | more (akthara) | than what (mimmā) | they have built on it (ʿamarūhā). | And came to them (wajāathum) | their Messengers (rusuluhum) | with clear proofs (bil-bayināti). | So not (famā) | was (kāna) | Allah (l-lahu) | to wrong them (liyaẓlimahum) | but (walākin) | they were (kānū) | themselves (anfusahum) | doing wrong (yaẓlimūna).

30:10 Then was the end of those who did evil - the evil, because they denied the Signs of Allah and were of them making mockery.

Then (thumma) | was (kāna) | the end (ʿāqibata) | of those who (alladhīna) | did evil (asāū)- | the evil (l-sūā), | because (an) | they denied (kadhabū) | the Signs (biāyāti) | of Allah (l-lahi) | and were (wakānū) | of them (bihā) | making mockery (yastahziūna).

30:11 Allah originates the creation, then He repeats it, then to Him you will be returned.

Allah (al-lahu) | originates (yabda-u) | the creation (l-khalqa), | then (thumma) | He repeats it (yuʿīduhu), | then (thumma) | to Him (ilayhi) | you will be returned (tur'jaʿūna).

30:12 And the Day will be established the Hour, will be in despair the criminals.

And the Day (wayawma) | will be established (taqūmu) | the Hour (l-sāʿatu), | will be in despair (yub'lisu) | the criminals (l-muj'rimūna).

30:13 And not will be for them among theirs partners any intercessors and they will be in their partners disbelievers.

And not (walam) | will be (yakun) | for them (lahum) | among (min) | theirs partners (shurakāihim) | any intercessors (shufaʿāu) | and they will be (wakānū) | in their partners (bishurakāihim) | disbelievers (kāfirīna).

30:14 And the Day will be established the Hour, that Day they will become separated.

And the Day (wayawma) | will be established (taqūmu) | the Hour (l-sāʿatu), | that Day (yawma-idhin) | they will become separated (yatafarraqūna).

30:15 Then as for those who believed and did righteous deeds, so they in a Garden will be delighted.

Then as for (fa-ammā) | those who (alladhīna) | believed (āmanū) | and did (waʿamilū) | righteous deeds (l-ṣāliḥāti), | so they (fahum) | in (fī) | a Garden (rawḍatin) | will be delighted (yuḥ'barūna).

30:16 But as for those who disbelieved and denied Our Signs and the meeting of the Hereafter, then those in the punishment will be brought forth.

But as for (wa-ammā) | those who (alladhīna) | disbelieved (kafarū) | and denied (wakadhabū) | Our Signs (biāyātinā) | and the meeting (waliqāi) | of the Hereafter (l-ākhirati), | then those (fa-ulāika) | in (fī) | the punishment (l-ʿadhābi) | will be brought forth (muḥ'ḍarūna).

30:17 So glory be to Allah when you reach the evening and when you reach the morning.

So glory be to (fasub'ḥāna) | Allah (l-lahi) | when (ḥīna) | you reach the evening (tum'sūna) | and when (waḥīna) | you reach the morning (tuṣ'biḥūna).

30:18 And for Him are all praises in the heavens and the earth and at night and when you are at noon.

And for Him (walahu) | are all praises (l-ḥamdu) | in (fī) | the heavens (l-samāwāti) | and the earth (wal-arḍi) | and at night (waʿashiyyan) | and when (waḥīna) | you are at noon (tuẓ'hirūna).

30:19 He brings forth the living from the dead and He brings forth the dead from the living, and He gives life to the earth after its death, and thus you will be brought forth.

He brings forth (yukh'riju) | the living (l-ḥaya) | from (mina) | the dead (l-mayiti) | and He brings forth (wayukh'riju) | the dead (l-mayita) | from (mina) | the living (l-ḥayi), | and He gives life (wayuḥ'yī) | to the earth (l-arḍa) | after (baʿda) | its death (mawtihā), | and thus (wakadhālika) | you will be brought forth (tukh'rajūna).

30:20 And among His Signs is that He created you from dust then behold! You are human beings dispersing.

And among (wamin) | His Signs (āyātihi) | is that (an) | He created you (khalaqakum) | from (min) | dust (turābin) | then (thumma) | behold (idhā)! | You (antum) | are human beings (basharun) | dispersing (tantashirūna).

30:21 And among His Signs is that He created for you from yourselves mates that you may find tranquility in them; and He placed between you love and mercy. Indeed, in that surely are Signs for a people who reflect.

And among (wamin) | His Signs (āyātihi) | is that (an) | He created (khalaqa) | for you (lakum) | from (min) | yourselves (anfusikum) | mates (azwājan) | that you may find tranquility (litaskunū) | in them (ilayhā); | and He placed (wajaʿala) | between you (baynakum) | love (mawaddatan) | and mercy (waraḥmatan). | Indeed (inna), | in (fī) | that (dhālika) | surely are Signs (laāyātin) | for a people (liqawmin) | who reflect (yatafakkarūna).

30:22 And among His Signs is the creation of the heavens and the earth, and the diversity of your languages and your colors. Indeed, in that surely are Signs for those of knowledge.

And among (wamin) | His Signs (āyātihi) | is the creation (khalqu) | of the heavens (l-samāwāti) | and the earth (wal-arḍi), | and the diversity (wa-ikh'tilāfu) | of your languages (alsinatikum) | and your colors (wa-alwānikum). | Indeed (inna), | in (fī) | that (dhālika) | surely are Signs (laāyātin) | for those of knowledge (lil'ʿālimīna).

30:23 And among His Signs is your sleep by night and the day [and] your seeking of His Bounty. Indeed, in that surely are Signs for a people who listen.

And among (wamin) | His Signs (āyātihi) | is your sleep (manāmukum) | by night (bi-al-layli) | and the day (wal-nahāri) | [and] your seeking (wa-ib'tighāukum) | of (min) | His Bounty (faḍlihi). | Indeed (inna), | in (fī) | that (dhālika) | surely are Signs (laāyātin) | for a people (liqawmin) | who listen (yasmaʿūna).

30:24 And among His Signs He shows you the lightning causing fear and hope, and He sends down from the sky water and gives life therewith to the earth after its death. Indeed, in that surely are Signs for a people who use intellect.

And among (wamin) | His Signs (āyātihi) | He shows you (yurīkumu) | the lightning (l-barqa) | causing fear (khawfan) | and hope (waṭamaʿan), | and He sends down (wayunazzilu) | from (mina) | the sky (l-samāi) | water (māan) | and gives life (fayuḥ'yī) | therewith (bihi) | to the earth (l-arḍa) | after (baʿda) | its death (mawtihā). | Indeed (inna), | in (fī) | that (dhālika) | surely are Signs (laāyātin) | for a people (liqawmin) | who use intellect (yaʿqilūna).

30:25 And among His Signs is that stands the heavens and the earth by His Command. Then when He calls you with a call, from the earth, behold! You will come forth.

And among (wamin) | His Signs (āyātihi) | is that (an) | stands (taqūma) | the heavens (l-samāu) | and the earth (wal-arḍu) | by His Command (bi-amrihi). | Then (thumma) | when (idhā) | He calls you (daʿākum) | with a call (daʿwatan), | from (mina) | the earth (l-arḍi), | behold (idhā)! | You (antum) | will come forth (takhrujūna).

30:26 And to Him belongs whoever is in the heavens and the earth. All to Him are obedient.

And to Him belongs (walahu) | whoever (man) | is in (fī) | the heavens (l-samāwāti) | and the earth (wal-arḍi). | All (kullun) | to Him (lahu) | are obedient (qānitūna).

30:27 And He is the One Who originates the creation then repeats it, and it is easier for Him. And for Him is the description, the highest in the heavens and the earth. And He is the All-Mighty, the All-Wise.

And He (wahuwa) | is the One Who (alladhī) | originates (yabda-u) | the creation (l-khalqa) | then (thumma) | repeats it (yuʿīduhu), | and it (wahuwa) | is easier (ahwanu) | for Him (ʿalayhi). |

And for Him (walahu) | is the description (l-mathalu), | the highest (l-aʿlā) | in (fī) | the heavens (l-samāwāti) | and the earth (wal-arḍi). | And He (wahuwa) | is the All-Mighty (l-ʿazīzu), | the All-Wise (l-ḥakīmu).

30:28 He sets forth to you an example from yourselves. Is for you among what possess your right hands any partners in what We have provided you so you in it are equal, you fear them as you fear yourselves? Thus We explain the Verses for a people who use reason.

He sets forth (ḍaraba) | to you (lakum) | an example (mathalan) | from (min) | yourselves (anfusikum). | Is (hal) | for you (lakum) | among (min) | what (mā) | possess (malakat) | your right hands (aymānukum) | any (min) | partners (shurakāa) | in (fī) | what (mā) | We have provided you (razaqnākum) | so you (fa-antum) | in it (fīhi) | are equal (sawāon), | you fear them (takhāfūnahum) | as you fear (kakhīfatikum) | yourselves (anfusakum)? | Thus (kadhālika) | We explain (nufaṣṣilu) | the Verses (l-āyāti) | for a people (liqawmin) | who use reason (yaʿqilūna).

30:29 Nay, follow those who do wrong, their desires, without knowledge. Then who can guide one whom Allah has let go astray? And not for them any helpers.

Nay (bali), | follow (ittabaʿa) | those who (alladhīna) | do wrong (ẓalamū), | their desires (ahwāahum), | without (bighayri) | knowledge (ʿil'min). | Then who (faman) | can guide (yahdī) | one whom (man) | Allah has let go astray (aḍalla)? | Allah has let go astray (l-lahu)? | And not (wamā) | for them (lahum) | any (min) | helpers (nāṣirīna).

30:30 So set your face to the religion upright. Nature made by Allah upon which He has created mankind [on it]. No change should there be in the creation of Allah. That is the religion the correct, but most men do not know.

So set (fa-aqim) | your face (wajhaka) | to the religion (lilddīni) | upright (ḥanīfan). | Nature (fiṭ'rata) | made by Allah (l-lahi) | upon which (allatī) | He has created (faṭara) | mankind (l-nāsa) | [on it] (ʿalayhā). | No (lā) | change (tabdīla) | should there be in the creation (likhalqi) | of Allah (l-lahi). | That (dhālika) | is the religion (l-dīnu) | the correct (l-qayimu), | but (walākinna) | most (akthara) | men (l-nāsi) | do not (lā) | know (yaʿlamūna).

30:31 Turning to Him, and fear Him and establish the prayer and do not be of the polytheists

Turning (munībīna) | to Him (ilayhi), | and fear Him (wa-ittaqūhu) | and establish (wa-aqīmū) | the prayer (l-ṣalata) | and do not (walā) | be (takūnū) | of (mina) | the polytheists (l-mush'rikīna)

30:32 Of those who divide their religion and become sects, each party in what they have rejoicing.

Of (mina) | those who (alladhīna) | divide (farraqū) | their religion (dīnahum) | and become (wakānū) | sects (shiyaʿan), | each (kullu) | party (ḥiz'bin) | in what (bimā) | they have (ladayhim) | rejoicing (fariḥūna).

30:33 And when touches people hardship, they call their Lord turning to Him. Then when He causes them to taste from Him Mercy behold! A party of them with their Lord associate partners

And when (wa-idhā) | touches (massa) | people (l-nāsa) | hardship (ḍurrun), | they call (daʿaw) | their Lord (rabbahum) | turning (munībīna) | to Him (ilayhi). | Then (thumma) | when (idhā) | He causes them to taste (adhāqahum) | from Him (min'hu) | Mercy (raḥmatan) | behold (idhā)! | A party (farīqun) | of them (min'hum) | with their Lord (birabbihim) | associate partners (yush'rikūna)

30:34 So as to deny [in] what, We have granted them. Then enjoy, but soon you will know.

So as to deny (liyakfurū) | [in] what (bimā), | We have granted them (ātaynāhum). | Then enjoy (fatamattaʿū), | but soon (fasawfa) | you will know (taʿlamūna).

30:35 Or have We sent to them an authority and it speaks of what they were with Him associating?
Or (am) | have We sent (anzalnā) | to them (ʿalayhim) | an authority (sul'ṭānan) | and it (fahuwa) | speaks (yatakallamu) | of what (bimā) | they were (kānū) | with Him (bihi) | associating (yush'rikūna)?

30:36 And when We cause people to taste mercy, they rejoice therein. But if afflicts them an evil for what have sent forth their hands, behold! They despair.
And when (wa-idhā) | We cause people to taste (adhaqnā) | We cause people to taste (l-nāsa) | mercy (raḥmatan), | they rejoice (fariḥū) | therein (bihā). | But if (wa-in) | afflicts them (tuṣib'hum) | an evil (sayyi-atun) | for what (bimā) | have sent forth (qaddamat) | their hands (aydīhim), | behold (idhā)! | They (hum) | despair (yaqnaṭūna).

30:37 Do not they see that Allah extends the provision for whom He wills and straitens it. Indeed, in that surely are Signs for a people who believe.
Do not (awalam) | they see (yaraw) | that (anna) | Allah (l-laha) | extends (yabsuṭu) | the provision (l-riz'qa) | for whom (liman) | He wills (yashāu) | and straitens it (wayaqdiru). | Indeed (inna), | in (fī) | that (dhālika) | surely are Signs (laāyātin) | for a people (liqawmin) | who believe (yu'minūna).

30:38 So give the relative his right and the poor and the wayfarer. That is best for those who desire the Countenance of Allah. And those, they are the successful ones.
So give (faāti) | the relative (dhā) | the relative (l-qur'bā) | his right (ḥaqqahu) | and the poor (wal-mis'kīna) | and the wayfarer (wa-ib'na). | and the wayfarer (l-sabīli). | That (dhālika) | is best (khayrun) | for those who (lilladhīna) | desire (yurīdūna) | the Countenance (wajha) | of Allah (l-lahi). | And those (wa-ulāika), | they (humu) | are the successful ones (l-muf'liḥūna).

30:39 And what you give for usury to increase in the wealth of people, not will increase with Allah. But what you give of zakah desiring the Countenance of Allah, then those [they] will get manifold.
And what (wamā) | you give (ātaytum) | for (min) | usury (riban) | to increase (liyarbuwā) | in (fī) | the wealth (amwāli) | of people (l-nāsi), | not (falā) | will increase (yarbū) | with (ʿinda) | Allah (l-lahi). | But what (wamā) | you give (ātaytum) | of (min) | zakah (zakatin) | desiring (turīdūna) | the Countenance (wajha) | of Allah (l-lahi), | then those (fa-ulāika) | [they] (humu) | will get manifold (l-muḍ'ʿifūna).

30:40 Allah is the One Who created you, then He provided for you, then He will cause you to die then He will give you life. Is there any of your partners who does of that any thing? Glory be to Him and exalted is He above what they associate.
Allah (al-lahu) | is the One Who (alladhī) | created you (khalaqakum), | then (thumma) | He provided for you (razaqakum), | then (thumma) | He will cause you to die (yumītukum) | then (thumma) | He will give you life (yuḥ'yīkum). | Is there (hal) | any (min) | of your partners (shurakāikum) | who (man) | does (yafʿalu) | of (min) | that (dhālikum) | any (min) | thing (shayin)? | Glory be to Him (sub'ḥānahu) | and exalted is He (wataʿālā) | above what (ʿammā) | they associate (yush'rikūna).

30:41 Has appeared the corruption in the land and the sea for what have earned the hands of people, so that He may let them taste a part of that which they have done so that they may return.
Has appeared (ẓahara) | the corruption (l-fasādu) | in (fī) | the land (l-bari) | and the sea (wal-baḥri) | for what (bimā) | have earned (kasabat) | the hands (aydī) | of people (l-nāsi), | so that He may let them taste (liyudhīqahum) | a part (baʿḍa) | of that which (alladhī) | they have done (ʿamilū) | so that they may (laʿallahum) | return (yarjiʿūna).

30:42 Say, "Travel in the earth and see how was the end of those who were before. Most of them were polytheists."

Say (qul), | "Travel (sīrū) | in (fī) | the earth (l-arḍi) | and see (fa-unẓurū) | how (kayfa) | was (kāna) | the end (ʿāqibatu) | of those who (alladhīna) | were before (min). | were before (qablu). | Most of them were (kāna) | Most of them were (aktharuhum) | polytheists. (mush'rikīna)"

30:43 So set your face to the religion right, before [that] comes a Day not can be averted [it] from Allah. That Day, they will be divided.

So set (fa-aqim) | your face (wajhaka) | to the religion (lilddīni) | right (l-qayimi), | before (min) | before (qabli) | [that] (an) | comes (yatiya) | a Day (yawmun) | not (lā) | can be averted (maradda) | [it] (lahu) | from (mina) | Allah (l-lahi). | That Day (yawma-idhin), | they will be divided (yaṣṣaddaʿūna).

30:44 Whoever disbelieves, then against him is his disbelief. And whoever does righteousness, then for themselves they are preparing,

Whoever (man) | disbelieves (kafara), | then against him (faʿalayhi) | is his disbelief (kuf'ruhu). | And whoever (waman) | does (ʿamila) | righteousness (ṣāliḥan), | then for themselves (fali-anfusihim) | they are preparing (yamhadūna),

30:45 That He may reward those who believe and do righteous deeds out of His Bounty. Indeed, He does not like the disbelievers.

That He may reward (liyajziya) | those who (alladhīna) | believe (āmanū) | and do (waʿamilū) | righteous deeds (l-ṣāliḥāti) | out of (min) | His Bounty (faḍlihi). | Indeed, He (innahu) | does not (lā) | like (yuḥibbu) | the disbelievers (l-kāfirīna).

30:46 And among His Signs is that He sends the winds as bearers of glad tidings and to let you taste of His Mercy, and that may sail the ships at His Command, and that you may seek of His Bounty, and that you may be grateful.

And among (wamin) | His Signs (āyātihi) | is that (an) | He sends (yur'sila) | the winds (l-riyāḥa) | as bearers of glad tidings (mubashirātin) | and to let you taste (waliyudhīqakum) | of (min) | His Mercy (raḥmatihi), | and that may sail (walitajriya) | the ships (l-ful'ku) | at His Command (bi-amrihi), | and that you may seek (walitabtaghū) | of (min) | His Bounty (faḍlihi), | and that you may (walaʿallakum) | be grateful (tashkurūna).

30:47 And verily, We sent before you Messengers to their people, and they came to them with clear proofs; then We took retribution from those who committed crimes. And it was incumbent upon Us to help the believers.

And verily (walaqad), | We sent (arsalnā) | before you (min) | before you (qablika) | Messengers (rusulan) | to (ilā) | their people (qawmihim), | and they came to them (fajāūhum) | with clear proofs (bil-bayināti); | then We took retribution (fa-intaqamnā) | from (mina) | those who (alladhīna) | committed crimes (ajramū). | And it was (wakāna) | incumbent (ḥaqqan) | upon Us (ʿalaynā) | to help (naṣru) | the believers (l-mu'minīna).

30:48 Allah is the One Who sends the winds, so they raise the clouds, then He spreads them in the sky, how He wills, and He makes them fragments so you see the rain coming forth from their midst. Then when He causes it to fall on whom He wills of His slaves, behold! They rejoice.

Allah (al-lahu) | is the One Who (alladhī) | sends (yur'silu) | the winds (l-riyāḥa), | so they raise (fatuthīru) | the clouds (saḥāban), | then He spreads them (fayabsuṭuhu) | in (fī) | the sky (l-samāi), | how (kayfa) | He wills (yashāu), | and He makes them (wayajʿaluhu) | fragments (kisafan) | so you see (fatarā) | the rain (l-wadqa) | coming forth (yakhruju) | from (min) | their midst (khilālihi). | Then when (fa-idhā) | He causes it to fall on (aṣāba) | He causes it to fall on (bihi) | whom (man) | He wills (yashāu) | of (min) | His slaves (ʿibādihi), | behold (idhā)! | They (hum) |

rejoice (yastabshirūna).

30:49 And certainly they were, before [that] it was sent down upon them, [before it], surely in despair.

And certainly (wa-in) | they were (kānū), | before (min) | before (qabli) | [that] (an) | it was sent down (yunazzala) | upon them (ʿalayhim), | [before it] (min), | [before it] (qablihi), | surely in despair (lamub'lisīna).

30:50 So look at the effects of the Mercy of Allah, how He gives life to the earth after its death. Indeed, that surely He will give life to the dead. And He is on every thing All-Powerful.

So look (fa-unẓur) | at (ilā) | the effects (āthāri) | of the Mercy (raḥmati) | of Allah (l-lahi), | how (kayfa) | He gives life (yuḥ'yī) | to the earth (l-arḍa) | after (baʿda) | its death (mawtihā). | Indeed (inna), | that (dhālika) | surely He will give life (lamuḥ'yī) | to the dead (l-mawtā). | And He (wahuwa) | is on (ʿalā) | every (kulli) | thing (shayin) | All-Powerful (qadīrun).

30:51 But if We sent a wind and they see it turn yellow, certainly they continue after it in disbelief.

But if (wala-in) | We sent (arsalnā) | a wind (rīḥan) | and they see it (fara-awhu) | turn yellow (muṣ'farran), | certainly they continue (laẓallū) | after it (min) | after it (baʿdihi) | in disbelief (yakfurūna).

30:52 So indeed, you can not make the dead hear and not make the deaf hear the call when they turn, retreating.

So indeed, you (fa-innaka) | can not (lā) | make the dead hear (tus'miʿu) | make the dead hear (l-mawtā) | and not (walā) | make the deaf hear (tus'miʿu) | make the deaf hear (l-ṣuma) | the call (l-duʿāa) | when (idhā) | they turn (wallaw), | retreating (mud'birīna).

30:53 And not you can guide the blind from their error. Not you can make hear except those who believe in Our Verses so they surrender.

And not (wamā) | you (anta) | can guide (bihādi) | the blind (l-ʿum'yi) | from (ʿan) | their error (ḍalālatihim). | Not (in) | you can make hear (tus'miʿu) | except (illā) | those who (man) | believe (yu'minu) | in Our Verses (biāyātinā) | so they (fahum) | surrender (mus'limūna).

30:54 Allah is the One Who created you from weakness, then made after weakness strength, then made after strength weakness and gray hair. He creates what He wills, and He is the All-Knower the All-Powerful.

Allah (al-lahu) | is the One Who (alladhī) | created you (khalaqakum) | from (min) | weakness (ḍaʿfin), | then (thumma) | made (jaʿala) | after (min) | after (baʿdi) | weakness (ḍaʿfin) | strength (quwwatan), | then (thumma) | made (jaʿala) | after (min) | after (baʿdi) | strength (quwwatin) | weakness (ḍaʿfan) | and gray hair (washaybatan). | He creates (yakhluqu) | what (mā) | He wills (yashāu), | and He (wahuwa) | is the All-Knower (l-ʿalīmu) | the All-Powerful (l-qadīru).

30:55 And the Day will be established the Hour will swear the criminals not they remained but an hour. Thus they were deluded.

And the Day (wayawma) | will be established (taqūmu) | the Hour (l-sāʿatu) | will swear (yuq'simu) | the criminals (l-muj'rimūna) | not (mā) | they remained (labithū) | but (ghayra) | an hour (sāʿatin). | Thus (kadhālika) | they were (kānū) | deluded (yu'fakūna).

30:56 But will say those who were given the knowledge and the faith, "Verily you remained by the Decree of Allah until the Day of Resurrection. And this is the Day of the Resurrection but you were not knowing.

But will say (waqāla) | those who (alladhīna) | were given (ūtū) | the knowledge (l-ʿil'ma) | and the faith (wal-īmāna), | "Verily (laqad) | you remained (labith'tum) | by (fī) | the Decree (kitābi)

| of Allah (l-lahi) | until (ilā) | the Day (yawmi) | of Resurrection (l-baʿthi). | And this (fahādhā) | is the Day (yawmu) | of the Resurrection (l-baʿthi) | but you (walākinnakum) | were (kuntum) | not (lā) | knowing (taʿlamūna).

30:57 So that Day, not will profit those who wronged their excuses and not they will be allowed to make amends.

So that Day (fayawma-idhin), | not (lā) | will profit (yanfaʿu) | those who (alladhīna) | wronged (ẓalamū) | their excuses (maʿdhiratuhum) | and not (walā) | they (hum) | will be allowed to make amends (yus'taʿtabūna).

30:58 And verily, We have set forth for mankind in this - [the] Quran of every example. But if you bring them a sign, surely will say those who disbelieve, "Not you are except falsifiers."

And verily (walaqad), | We have set forth (ḍarabnā) | for mankind (lilnnāsi) | in (fī) | this (hādhā)- | [the] Quran (l-qur'āni) | of (min) | every (kulli) | example (mathalin). | But if (wala-in) | you bring them (ji'tahum) | a sign (biāyatin), | surely will say (layaqūlanna) | those who (alladhīna) | disbelieve (kafarū), | "Not (in) | you (antum) | are except (illā) | falsifiers. (mub'ṭilūna)"

30:59 Thus Allah seals [on] the hearts of those who do not know.

Thus (kadhālika) | Allah seals (yaṭbaʿu) | Allah seals (l-lahu) | [on] (ʿalā) | the hearts (qulūbi) | of those who (alladhīna) | do not (lā) | know (yaʿlamūna).

30:60 So be patient. Indeed, the Promise of Allah is true. And let not take you in light estimation those who are not certain in faith.

So be patient (fa-iṣ'bir). | Indeed (inna), | the Promise (waʿda) | of Allah (l-lahi) | is true (ḥaqqun). | And let not (walā) | take you in light estimation (yastakhiffannaka) | those who (alladhīna) | are not (lā) | certain in faith (yūqinūna).

Chapter (31) Sūrat Luq'mān

31:1 Alif Lam Meem.

Alif Lam Meem (alif-lam-meem).

31:2 These are Verses of the Book the Wise,

These (til'ka) | are Verses (āyātu) | of the Book (l-kitābi) | the Wise (l-ḥakīmi),

31:3 A guidance and a mercy for the good-doers,

A guidance (hudan) | and a mercy (waraḥmatan) | for the good-doers (lil'muḥ'sinīna),

31:4 Those who establish the prayer and give zakah and they, in the Hereafter, [they] believe firmly.

Those who (alladhīna) | establish (yuqīmūna) | the prayer (l-ṣalata) | and give (wayu'tūna) | zakah (l-zakata) | and they (wahum), | in the Hereafter (bil-ākhirati), | [they] (hum) | believe firmly (yūqinūna).

31:5 Those are on guidance from their Lord, and those [they] are the successful.

Those (ulāika) | are on (ʿalā) | guidance (hudan) | from (min) | their Lord (rabbihim), | and those (wa-ulāika) | [they] (humu) | are the successful (l-muf'liḥūna).

31:6 And of the mankind is he who purchases, idle tales to mislead from the path of Allah without knowledge, and takes it in ridicule. Those for them is a punishment humiliating.

And of (wamina) | the mankind (l-nāsi) | is he who (man) | purchases (yashtarī), | idle tales (lahwa) | idle tales (l-ḥadīthi) | to mislead (liyuḍilla) | from (ʿan) | the path (sabīli) | of Allah (l-lahi) | without (bighayri) | knowledge (ʿil'min), | and takes it (wayattakhidhahā) | in ridicule (huzuwan). | Those (ulāika) | for them (lahum) | is a punishment (ʿadhābun) | humiliating (muhīnun).

31:7 And when are recited to him Our Verses, he turns away arrogantly as if not he had heard them, as if in his ears is deafness. So give him tidings of a punishment painful.

And when (wa-idhā) | are recited (tut'lā) | to him (ʿalayhi) | Our Verses (āyātunā), | he turns away (wallā) | arrogantly (mus'takbiran) | as if (ka-an) | not (lam) | he had heard them (yasmaʿhā), | as if (ka-anna) | in (fī) | his ears (udhunayhi) | is deafness (waqran). | So give him tidings (fabashir'hu) | of a punishment (biʿadhābin) | painful (alīmin).

31:8 Indeed, those who believe and do righteous deeds, for them are Gardens of Delight,

Indeed (inna), | those who (alladhīna) | believe (āmanū) | and do (waʿamilū) | righteous deeds (l-ṣāliḥāti), | for them (lahum) | are Gardens (jannātu) | of Delight (l-naʿīmi),

31:9 To abide forever in it. The Promise of Allah is true. And He is the All-Mighty, the All-Wise.

To abide forever (khālidīna) | in it (fīhā). | The Promise of Allah (waʿda) | The Promise of Allah (l-lahi) | is true (ḥaqqan). | And He (wahuwa) | is the All-Mighty (l-ʿazīzu), | the All-Wise (l-ḥakīmu).

31:10 He created the heavens without pillars that you see and has cast in the earth firm mountains lest it might shake with you, and He dispersed in it from every creature. And We sent down from the sky water then We caused to grow therein of every kind noble.

He created (khalaqa) | the heavens (l-samāwāti) | without (bighayri) | pillars (ʿamadin) | that you see (tarawnahā) | and has cast (wa-alqā) | in (fī) | the earth (l-arḍi) | firm mountains (rawāsiya) | lest (an) | it might shake (tamīda) | with you (bikum), | and He dispersed (wabatha) | in it (fīhā) | from (min) | every (kulli) | creature (dābbatin). | And We sent down (wa-anzalnā) | from (mina) | the sky (l-samāi) | water (māan) | then We caused to grow (fa-anbatnā) | therein (fīhā) | of (min) | every (kulli) | kind (zawjin) | noble (karīmin).

31:11 This is the creation of Allah. So show Me what have created those besides Him. Nay, the wrongdoers are in error clear.

This (hādhā) | is the creation (khalqu) | of Allah (l-lahi). | So show Me (fa-arūnī) | what (mādhā) | have created (khalaqa) | those (alladhīna) | besides Him (min). | besides Him (dūnihi). | Nay (bali), | the wrongdoers (l-ẓālimūna) | are in (fī) | error (ḍalālin) | clear (mubīnin).

31:12 And verily, We gave Luqman the wisdom that, "Be grateful to Allah." And whoever is grateful then only he is grateful for himself. And whoever is ungrateful, then indeed, Allah is Free of need, Praiseworthy.

And verily (walaqad), | We gave (ātaynā) | Luqman (luq'māna) | the wisdom (l-ḥik'mata) | that (ani), | "Be grateful (ush'kur) | to Allah. (lillahi)" | And whoever (waman) | is grateful (yashkur) | then only (fa-innamā) | he is grateful (yashkuru) | for himself (linafsihi). | And whoever (waman) | is ungrateful (kafara), | then indeed (fa-inna), | Allah (l-laha) | is Free of need (ghaniyyun), | Praiseworthy (ḥamīdun).

31:13 And when said Luqman to his son while he was instructing him, "O my son! Do not associate partners with Allah. Indeed, associating partners is surely an injustice great."

And when (wa-idh) | said (qāla) | Luqman (luq'mānu) | to his son (li-ib'nihi) | while he (wahuwa) | was instructing him (yaʿiẓuhu), | "O my son (yābunayya)! | Do not (lā) | associate partners (tush'rik) | with Allah (bil-lahi). | Indeed (inna), | associating partners (l-shir'ka) | is surely an injustice (laẓul'mun) | great. (ʿaẓīmun)"

31:14 And We have enjoined upon man for his parents - carried him his mother in weakness upon weakness, and his weaning is in two years that "Be grateful to Me and to your parents; towards Me is the destination.

And We have enjoined (wawaṣṣaynā) | upon man (l-insāna) | for his parents (biwālidayhi)- | carried him (ḥamalathu) | his mother (ummuhu) | in weakness (wahnan) | upon (ʿalā) | weakness (wahnin), | and his weaning (wafiṣāluhu) | is in (fī) | two years (ʿāmayni) | that (ani) | "Be grateful (ush'kur) | to Me (lī) | and to your parents (waliwālidayka); | towards Me (ilayya) | is the destination (l-maṣīru).

31:15 But if they strive against you on that you associate partners with Me what not you have of it any knowledge, then do not obey both of them. But accompany them in the world with kindness, and follow the path of him who turns to Me. Then towards Me is your return, then I will inform you of what you used to do."

But if (wa-in) | they strive against you (jāhadāka) | on (ʿalā) | that (an) | you associate partners (tush'rika) | with Me (bī) | what (mā) | not (laysa) | you have (laka) | of it (bihi) | any knowledge (ʿil'mun), | then do not (falā) | obey both of them (tuṭiʿ'humā). | But accompany them (waṣāḥib'humā) | in (fī) | the world (l-dun'yā) | with kindness (maʿrūfan), | and follow (wa-ittabiʿ) | the path (sabīla) | of him who (man) | turns (anāba) | to Me (ilayya). | Then (thumma) | towards Me (ilayya) | is your return (marjiʿukum), | then I will inform you (fa-unabbi-ukum) | of what (bimā) | you used to (kuntum) | do. (taʿmalūna)"

31:16 "O my son! Indeed it, if it be the weight of a grain of a mustard seed, and it be in a rock or in the heavens or in the earth Allah will bring it forth. Indeed, Allah is All-Subtle, All-Aware.

"O my son (yābunayya)! | Indeed it (innahā), | if (in) | it be (taku) | the weight (mith'qāla) | of a grain (ḥabbatin) | of (min) | a mustard seed (khardalin), | and it be (fatakun) | in (fī) | a rock (ṣakhratin) | or (aw) | in (fī) | the heavens (l-samāwāti) | or (aw) | in (fī) | the earth (l-arḍi) | Allah will bring it forth (yati). | Allah will bring it forth (bihā). | Allah will bring it forth (l-lahu). | Indeed (inna), | Allah (l-laha) | is All-Subtle (laṭīfun), | All-Aware (khabīrun).

31:17 O my son! Establish the prayer and enjoin [with] the right and forbid from the wrong, and be patient over what befalls you. Indeed, that is of the matters requiring determination.

O my son (yābunayya)! | Establish (aqimi) | the prayer (l-ṣalata) | and enjoin (wamur) | [with] the right (bil-maʿrūfi) | and forbid (wa-in'ha) | from (ʿani) | the wrong (l-munkari), | and be patient (wa-iṣ'bir) | over (ʿalā) | what (mā) | befalls you (aṣābaka). | Indeed (inna), | that (dhālika) | is of (min) | the matters requiring determination (ʿazmi). | the matters requiring determination (l-umūri).

31:18 And do not turn your cheek from men and do not walk in the earth exultantly. Indeed, Allah does not like every self-conceited boaster.

And do not (walā) | turn (tuṣaʿʿir) | your cheek (khaddaka) | from men (lilnnāsi) | and do not (walā) | walk (tamshi) | in (fī) | the earth (l-arḍi) | exultantly (maraḥan). | Indeed (inna), | Allah (l-laha) | does not (lā) | like (yuḥibbu) | every (kulla) | self-conceited (mukh'tālin) | boaster (fakhūrin).

31:19 And be moderate in your pace and lower [of] your voice. Indeed, the harshest of all sounds is surely (the) voice of the donkeys."

And be moderate (wa-iq'ṣid) | in (fī) | your pace (mashyika) | and lower (wa-ugh'ḍuḍ) | [of] (min) | your voice (ṣawtika). | Indeed (inna), | the harshest (ankara) | of all sounds (l-aṣwāti) | is surely (the) voice (laṣawtu) | of the donkeys. (l-ḥamīri)"

31:20 Do not you see that Allah has subjected to you whatever is in the heavens and whatever is in the earth and amply bestowed upon you His Bounties apparent and hidden? But of the people is he who disputes about Allah without knowledge, and not guidance and not a book enlightening.

Do not (alam) | you see (taraw) | that (anna) | Allah (l-laha) | has subjected (sakhara) | to you (lakum) | whatever (mā) | is in (fī) | the heavens (l-samāwāti) | and whatever (wamā) | is in (fī) | the earth (l-arḍi) | and amply bestowed (wa-asbagha) | upon you (ʿalaykum) | His Bounties (niʿamahu) | apparent (ẓāhiratan) | and hidden (wabāṭinatan)? | But of (wamina) | the people (l-nāsi) | is he who (man) | disputes (yujādilu) | about (fī) | Allah (l-lahi) | without (bighayri) | knowledge (ʿil'min), | and not (walā) | guidance (hudan) | and not (walā) | a book (kitābin) | enlightening (munīrin).

31:21 And when it is said to them, "Follow what Allah has revealed," they say, "Nay, we will follow what we found on it our forefathers." Even if Shaitaan was to call them to the punishment of the Blaze!

And when (wa-idhā) | it is said (qīla) | to them (lahumu), | "Follow (ittabiʿū) | what (mā) | Allah has revealed, (anzala)" | Allah has revealed, (l-lahu)" | they say (qālū), | "Nay (bal), | we will follow (nattabiʿu) | what (mā) | we found (wajadnā) | on it (ʿalayhi) | our forefathers. (ābāanā)" | Even if (awalaw) | Shaitaan was (kāna) | Shaitaan was (l-shayṭānu) | to call them (yadʿūhum) | to (ilā) | the punishment (ʿadhābi) | of the Blaze (l-saʿīri)!

31:22 And whoever submits his face to Allah while he is a good-doer, then indeed, he has grasped the handhold the most trustworthy. And to Allah is the end of the matters.

And whoever (waman) | submits (yus'lim) | his face (wajhahu) | to (ilā) | Allah (l-lahi) | while he (wahuwa) | is a good-doer (muḥ'sinun), | then indeed (faqadi), | he has grasped (is'tamsaka) | the handhold (bil-ʿur'wati) | the most trustworthy (l-wuth'qā). | And to (wa-ilā) | Allah (l-lahi) | is the end (ʿāqibatu) | of the matters (l-umūri).

31:23 And whoever disbelieves, let not grieve you his disbelief. To Us is their return, then We will inform them of what they did. Indeed, Allah is the All-Knower of what is in the breasts.

And whoever (waman) | disbelieves (kafara), | let not (falā) | grieve you (yaḥzunka) | his disbelief (kuf'ruhu). | To Us (ilaynā) | is their return (marjiʿuhum), | then We will inform them (fanunabbi-uhum) | of what (bimā) | they did (ʿamilū). | Indeed (inna), | Allah (l-laha) | is the All-Knower (ʿalīmun) | of what (bidhāti) | is in the breasts (l-ṣudūri).

31:24 We grant them enjoyment for a little, then We will force them to a punishment severe.

We grant them enjoyment (numattiʿuhum) | for a little (qalīlan), | then (thumma) | We will force them (naḍṭarruhum) | to (ilā) | a punishment (ʿadhābin) | severe (ghalīẓin).

31:25 And if you ask them, "Who created the heavens and the earth?" They will surely say, "Allah." Say, "All praises are for Allah." But most of them do not know.

And if (wala-in) | you ask them (sa-altahum), | "Who (man) | created (khalaqa) | the heavens (l-samāwāti) | and the earth? (wal-arḍa)" | They will surely say (layaqūlunna), | "Allah. (l-lahu)" | Say (quli), | "All praises (l-ḥamdu) | are for Allah. (lillahi)" | But (bal) | most of them (aktharuhum) | do not (lā) | know (yaʿlamūna).

31:26 To Allah belongs whatever is in the heavens and the earth. Indeed, Allah, He is Free of need, the Praiseworthy.

To Allah belongs (lillahi) | whatever (mā) | is in (fī) | the heavens (l-samāwāti) | and the earth (wal-arḍi). | Indeed (inna), | Allah (l-laha), | He (huwa) | is Free of need (l-ghaniyu), | the Praiseworthy (l-ḥamīdu).

31:27 And if whatever is in the earth of the trees were pens and the sea, to add to it after it seven seas, not would be exhausted the Words of Allah. Indeed, Allah is All-Mighty, All-Wise.

And if (walaw) | whatever (annamā) | is in (fī) | the earth (l-arḍi) | of (min) | the trees (shajaratin) | were pens (aqlāmun) | and the sea (wal-baḥru), | to add to it (yamudduhu) | after it (min) | after it (baʿdihi) | seven (sabʿatu) | seas (abḥurin), | not (mā) | would be exhausted (nafidat) | the Words (kalimātu) | of Allah (l-lahi). | Indeed (inna), | Allah (l-laha) | is All-Mighty (ʿazīzun), | All-Wise (ḥakīmun).

31:28 Not is your creation and not your resurrection but as a soul single. Indeed, Allah is All-Hearer, All-Seer.

Not (mā) | is your creation (khalqukum) | and not (walā) | your resurrection (baʿthukum) | but (illā) | as a soul (kanafsin) | single (wāḥidatin). | Indeed (inna), | Allah (l-laha) | is All-Hearer (samīʿun), | All-Seer (baṣīrun).

31:29 Do not you see that Allah causes to enter the night into the day, and causes to enter the day into the night and has subjected the sun and the moon, each moving for a term appointed, and that Allah of what you do is All-Aware.

Do not (alam) | you see (tara) | that (anna) | Allah (l-laha) | causes to enter (yūliju) | the night (al-layla) | into (fī) | the day (l-nahāri), | and causes to enter (wayūliju) | the day (l-nahāra) | into (fī) | the night (al-layli) | and has subjected (wasakhara) | the sun (l-shamsa) | and the moon (wal-qamara), | each (kullun) | moving (yajrī) | for (ilā) | a term (ajalin) | appointed (musamman), | and that (wa-anna) | Allah (l-laha) | of what (bimā) | you do (taʿmalūna) | is All-Aware (khabīrun).

31:30 That is because Allah, He is the Truth, and that what they call besides Him is [the] falsehood, and that Allah, He is the Most High, the Most Great.

That (dhālika) | is because (bi-anna) | Allah (l-laha), | He (huwa) | is the Truth (l-ḥaqu), | and that (wa-anna) | what (mā) | they call (yadʿūna) | besides Him (min) | besides Him (dūnihi) | is [the] falsehood (l-bāṭilu), | and that (wa-anna) | Allah (l-laha), | He (huwa) | is the Most High (l-ʿaliyu), | the Most Great (l-kabīru).

31:31 Do not you see that the ships sail through the sea by the Grace of Allah that He may show you of His Signs? Indeed, in that surely are Signs for everyone who is patient, grateful.

Do not (alam) | you see (tara) | that (anna) | the ships (l-ful'ka) | sail (tajrī) | through (fī) | the sea (l-baḥri) | by the Grace (biniʿ'mati) | of Allah (l-lahi) | that He may show you (liyuriyakum) | of (min) | His Signs (āyātihi)? | Indeed (inna), | in (fī) | that (dhālika) | surely are Signs (laāyātin) | for everyone (likulli) | who is patient (ṣabbārin), | grateful (shakūrin).

31:32 And when covers them a wave like canopies, they call Allah, being sincere to Him in religion. But when He delivers them to the land then among them some are moderate. And not deny Our Signs except every traitor ungrateful.

And when (wa-idhā) | covers them (ghashiyahum) | a wave (mawjun) | like canopies (kal-ẓulali), | they call (daʿawū) | Allah (l-laha), | being sincere (mukh'liṣīna) | to Him (lahu) | in religion (l-dīna). | But when (falammā) | He delivers them (najjāhum) | to (ilā) | the land (l-bari) | then among them (famin'hum) | some are moderate (muq'taṣidun). | And not (wamā) | deny (yajḥadu) | Our Signs (biāyātinā) | except (illā) | every (kullu) | traitor (khattārin) | ungrateful (kafūrin).

31:33 O mankind! Fear your Lord and fear a Day not can avail a father [for] his son and not a son, he can avail [for] his father anything. Indeed, the Promise of Allah is True, so let not deceive you the life of the world and let not deceive you about Allah the deceiver.

O (yāayyuhā) | mankind (l-nāsu)! | Fear (ittaqū) | your Lord (rabbakum) | and fear (wa-ikh'shaw) | a Day (yawman) | not (lā) | can avail (yajzī) | a father (wālidun) | [for] (ʿan) | his son (waladihi) | and not (walā) | a son (mawlūdun), | he (huwa) | can avail (jāzin) | [for] (ʿan) | his father (wālidihi) | anything (shayan). | Indeed (inna), | the Promise (waʿda) | of Allah (l-lahi) | is True (ḥaqqun), | so let not deceive you (falā) | so let not deceive you (taghurrannakumu) | the life (l-ḥayatu) | of the world (l-dun'yā) | and let not deceive you (walā) | and let not deceive you (yaghurrannakum) | about Allah (bil-lahi) | the deceiver (l-gharūru).

31:34 Indeed, Allah, with Him is the knowledge of the Hour and He sends down the rain, and knows what is in the wombs. And not knows any soul what it will earn tomorrow, and not knows any soul in what land it will die. Indeed, Allah is All-Knower All-Aware.

Indeed (inna), | Allah (l-laha), | with Him (ʿindahu) | is the knowledge (ʿil'mu) | of the Hour (l-sāʿati) | and He sends down (wayunazzilu) | the rain (l-ghaytha), | and knows (wayaʿlamu) | what (mā) | is in (fī) | the wombs (l-arḥāmi). | And not (wamā) | knows (tadrī) | any soul (nafsun) | what (mādhā) | it will earn (taksibu) | tomorrow (ghadan), | and not (wamā) | knows (tadrī) | any soul (nafsun) | in what (bi-ayyi) | land (arḍin) | it will die (tamūtu). | Indeed (inna), | Allah (l-laha) | is All-Knower (ʿalīmun) | All-Aware (khabīrun).

Chapter (32) Sūrat l-Sajdah (The Prostration)

32:1 Alif Lam Meem.

Alif Lam Meem (alif-lam-meem).

32:2 The revelation of the Book, there is no doubt about it, from the Lord of the worlds.

The revelation (tanzīlu) | of the Book (l-kitābi), | there is no (lā) | doubt (rayba) | about it (fīhi), | from (min) | the Lord (rabbi) | of the worlds (l-ʿālamīna).

32:3 Or do they say, "He invented it?" Nay, it is the truth from your Lord that you may warn a people not has come to them any warner before you so that they may be guided.

Or (am) | do they say (yaqūlūna), | "He invented it? (if'tarāhu)" | Nay (bal), | it (huwa) | is the truth (l-ḥaqu) | from (min) | your Lord (rabbika) | that you may warn (litundhira) | a people (qawman) | not (mā) | has come to them (atāhum) | any (min) | warner (nadhīrin) | before you (min) | before you (qablika) | so that they may (laʿallahum) | be guided (yahtadūna).

32:4 Allah is the One Who created the heavens and the earth and whatever is between them in six periods. Then established Himself on the Throne. Not for you besides Him any protector and not any intercessor. Then will not you take heed?

Allah (al-lahu) | is the One Who (alladhī) | created (khalaqa) | the heavens (l-samāwāti) | and the earth (wal-arḍa) | and whatever (wamā) | is between them (baynahumā) | in (fī) | six (sittati) | periods (ayyāmin). | Then (thumma) | established Himself (is'tawā) | on (ʿalā) | the Throne (l-ʿarshi). | Not (mā) | for you (lakum) | besides Him (min) | besides Him (dūnihi) | any (min) | protector (waliyyin) | and not (walā) | any intercessor (shafīʿin). | Then will not (afalā) | you take heed (tatadhakkarūna)?

32:5 He regulates the affair of the heaven to the earth; then it will ascend to Him in a Day, the measure of which is a thousand years of what you count.

He regulates (yudabbiru) | the affair (l-amra) | of (mina) | the heaven (l-samāi) | to (ilā) | the earth (l-arḍi); | then (thumma) | it will ascend (yaʿruju) | to Him (ilayhi) | in (fī) | a Day (yawmin), | the measure of which is (kāna) | the measure of which is (miq'dāruhu) | a thousand (alfa) | years (sanatin) | of what (mimmā) | you count (taʿuddūna).

32:6 That is the Knower of the hidden and the witnessed, the All-Mighty, the Most Merciful,
That (dhālika) | is the Knower (ʿālimu) | of the hidden (l-ghaybi) | and the witnessed (wal-shahādati), | the All-Mighty (l-ʿazīzu), | the Most Merciful (l-raḥīmu),

32:7 The One Who made good every thing He created, and He began the creation of man from clay.
The One Who (alladhī) | made good (aḥsana) | every (kulla) | thing (shayin) | He created (khalaqahu), | and He began (wabada-a) | the creation (khalqa) | of man (l-insāni) | from (min) | clay (ṭīnin).

32:8 Then He made his progeny from an extract of water despised.
Then (thumma) | He made (jaʿala) | his progeny (naslahu) | from (min) | an extract (sulālatin) | of (min) | water (māin) | despised (mahīnin).

32:9 Then He fashioned him and breathed into him from His spirit and made for you the hearing and the sight and feelings; little [what] thanks you give.
Then (thumma) | He fashioned him (sawwāhu) | and breathed (wanafakha) | into him (fīhi) | from (min) | His spirit (rūḥihi) | and made (wajaʿala) | for you (lakumu) | the hearing (l-samʿa) | and the sight (wal-abṣāra) | and feelings (wal-afidata); | little (qalīlan) | [what] (mā) | thanks you give (tashkurūna).

32:10 And they say, "Is it when we are lost in the earth, will we certainly be in a creation new?" Nay, they in the meeting of their Lord are disbelievers.
And they say (waqālū), | "Is it when (a-idhā) | we are lost (ḍalalnā) | in (fī) | the earth (l-arḍi), | will we (a-innā) | certainly be in (lafī) | a creation (khalqin) | new? (jadīdin)" | Nay (bal), | they (hum) | in the meeting (biliqāi) | of their Lord (rabbihim) | are disbelievers (kāfirūna).

32:11 Say, "Will take your soul the Angel of the death the one who has been put in charge of you. Then to your Lord you will be returned."
Say (qul), | "Will take your soul (yatawaffākum) | the Angel (malaku) | of the death (l-mawti) | the one who (alladhī) | has been put in charge (wukkila) | of you (bikum). | Then (thumma) | to (ilā) | your Lord (rabbikum) | you will be returned. (tur'jaʿūna)"

32:12 And if you could see when the criminals will hang their heads before their Lord, "Our Lord we have seen and we have heard, so return us, we will do righteous deeds. Indeed, we are now certain."
And if (walaw) | you could see (tarā) | when (idhi) | the criminals (l-muj'rimūna) | will hang (nākisū) | their heads (ruūsihim) | before (ʿinda) | their Lord (rabbihim), | "Our Lord (rabbanā) | we have seen (abṣarnā) | and we have heard (wasamiʿ'nā), | so return us (fa-ir'jiʿ'nā), | we will do (naʿmal) | righteous deeds (ṣāliḥan). | Indeed, we (innā) | are now certain. (mūqinūna)"

32:13 And if We had willed, surely We would have given every soul its guidance, but is true the Word from Me that I will surely fill Hell with the jinn and the men together.
And if (walaw) | We had willed (shi'nā), | surely We would have given (laātaynā) | every (kulla) | soul (nafsin) | its guidance (hudāhā), | but (walākin) | is true (ḥaqqa) | the Word (l-qawlu) | from Me (minnī) | that I will surely fill (la-amla-anna) | Hell (jahannama) | with (mina) | the jinn (l-jinati) | and the men (wal-nāsi) | together (ajmaʿīna).

32:14 So taste because you forgot the meeting, of this Day of yours. Indeed, We have forgotten you. And taste the punishment of eternity for what you used to do."

So taste (fadhūqū) | because (bimā) | you forgot (nasītum) | the meeting (liqāa), | of this Day of yours (yawmikum). | of this Day of yours (hādhā). | Indeed, We (innā) | have forgotten you (nasīnākum). | And taste (wadhūqū) | the punishment (ʿadhāba) | of eternity (l-khul'di) | for what (bimā) | you used to (kuntum) | do. (taʿmalūna)"

32:15 Only believe in Our Verses those who when they are reminded of them fall down prostrating and glorify the praises of their Lord, and they are not arrogant.

Only (innamā) | believe (yu'minu) | in Our Verses (biāyātinā) | those who (alladhīna) | when (idhā) | they are reminded (dhukkirū) | of them (bihā) | fall down (kharrū) | prostrating (sujjadan) | and glorify (wasabbaḥū) | the praises (biḥamdi) | of their Lord (rabbihim), | and they (wahum) | are not arrogant (lā). | are not arrogant (yastakbirūna).

32:16 Forsake their sides from their beds; they call their Lord in fear and hope, and out of what We have provided them they spend.

Forsake (tatajāfā) | their sides (junūbuhum) | from (ʿani) | their beds (l-maḍājiʿi); | they call (yadʿūna) | their Lord (rabbahum) | in fear (khawfan) | and hope (waṭamaʿan), | and out of what (wamimmā) | We have provided them (razaqnāhum) | they spend (yunfiqūna).

32:17 And not knows a soul what is hidden for them of the comfort for the eyes as a reward for what they used to do.

And not (falā) | knows (taʿlamu) | a soul (nafsun) | what (mā) | is hidden (ukh'fiya) | for them (lahum) | of (min) | the comfort (qurrati) | for the eyes (aʿyunin) | as a reward (jazāan) | for what (bimā) | they used to (kānū) | do (yaʿmalūna).

32:18 Then is one who is a believer like him who is defiantly disobedient? Not they are equal.

Then is one who (afaman) | is (kāna) | a believer (mu'minan) | like him who (kaman) | is (kāna) | defiantly disobedient (fāsiqan)? | Not (lā) | they are equal (yastawūna).

32:19 As for those who believe and do righteous deeds, then for them are Gardens of Refuge as hospitality for what they used to do.

As for (amma) | those who (alladhīna) | believe (āmanū) | and do (waʿamilū) | righteous deeds (l-ṣāliḥāti), | then for them (falahum) | are Gardens (jannātu) | of Refuge (l-mawā) | as hospitality (nuzulan) | for what (bimā) | they used to (kānū) | do (yaʿmalūna).

32:20 But as for those who are defiantly disobedient then their refuge is the Fire. Every time they wish to come out from it, they will be returned in it, and it will be said to them, "Taste the punishment of the Fire which you used to [in it] deny."

But as for (wa-ammā) | those who (alladhīna) | are defiantly disobedient (fasaqū) | then their refuge (famawāhumu) | is the Fire (l-nāru). | Every time (kullamā) | they wish (arādū) | to (an) | come out (yakhrujū) | from it (min'hā), | they will be returned (uʿīdū) | in it (fīhā), | and it will be said (waqīla) | to them (lahum), | "Taste (dhūqū) | the punishment (ʿadhāba) | of the Fire (l-nāri) | which (alladhī) | you used to (kuntum) | [in it] (bihi) | deny. (tukadhibūna)"

32:21 And surely, We will let them taste of the punishment the nearer before the punishment the greater, so that they may return.

And surely, We will let them taste (walanudhīqannahum) | of (mina) | the punishment (l-ʿadhābi) | the nearer (l-adnā) | before (dūna) | the punishment (l-ʿadhābi) | the greater (l-akbari), | so that they may (laʿallahum) | return (yarjiʿūna).

32:22 And who is more unjust than he who is reminded of the Verses of his Lord, then he turns away from them? Indeed, We from the criminals, will take retribution.

And who (waman) | is more unjust (aẓlamu) | than he who (mimman) | is reminded (dhukkira) | of the Verses (biāyāti) | of his Lord (rabbihi), | then (thumma) | he turns away (aʿraḍa) | from them (ʿanhā)? | Indeed, We (innā) | from (mina) | the criminals (l-muj'rimīna), | will take retribution (muntaqimūna).

32:23 And certainly We gave Musa the Scripture, so do not be in doubt about receiving it. And We made it a guide for the Children of Israel.

And certainly (walaqad) | We gave (ātaynā) | Musa (mūsā) | the Scripture (l-kitāba), | so do not (falā) | be (takun) | in (fī) | doubt (mir'yatin) | about (min) | receiving it (liqāihi). | And We made it (wajaʿalnāhu) | a guide (hudan) | for the Children of Israel (libanī). | for the Children of Israel (is'rāīla).

32:24 And We made from them leaders guiding by Our Command when they were patient and they were of Our Verses certain.

And We made (wajaʿalnā) | from them (min'hum) | leaders (a-immatan) | guiding (yahdūna) | by Our Command (bi-amrinā) | when (lammā) | they were patient (ṣabarū) | and they were (wakānū) | of Our Verses (biāyātinā) | certain (yūqinūna).

32:25 Indeed, your Lord [He] will judge between them on the Day of Resurrection in what they used to [in it] differ.

Indeed (inna), | your Lord (rabbaka) | [He] (huwa) | will judge (yafṣilu) | between them (baynahum) | on the Day (yawma) | of Resurrection (l-qiyāmati) | in what (fīmā) | they used to (kānū) | [in it] (fīhi) | differ (yakhtalifūna).

32:26 Does it not guide [for] them, that how many We have destroyed before them of the generations, they walk about in their dwellings. Indeed, in that surely, are Signs. Then do not they hear?

Does it not (awalam) | guide (yahdi) | [for] them (lahum), | that how many (kam) | We have destroyed (ahlaknā) | before them (min) | before them (qablihim) | of (mina) | the generations (l-qurūni), | they walk about (yamshūna) | in (fī) | their dwellings (masākinihim). | Indeed (inna), | in (fī) | that (dhālika) | surely, are Signs (laāyātin). | Then do not (afalā) | they hear (yasmaʿūna)?

32:27 Do not they see that We drive water to the land [the] barren, then We bring forth thereby crops, eat from it their cattle and they themselves? Then do not they see?

Do not (awalam) | they see (yaraw) | that We (annā) | drive (nasūqu) | water (l-māa) | to (ilā) | the land (l-arḍi) | [the] barren (l-juruzi), | then We bring forth (fanukh'riju) | thereby (bihi) | crops (zarʿan), | eat (takulu) | from it (min'hu) | their cattle (anʿāmuhum) | and they themselves (wa-anfusuhum)? | Then do not (afalā) | they see (yub'ṣirūna)?

32:28 And they say, "When will be this decision, if you are truthful?"

And they say (wayaqūlūna), | "When will be (matā) | this (hādhā) | decision (l-fatḥu), | if (in) | you are (kuntum) | truthful? (ṣādiqīna)"

32:29 Say, "On the Day of the Decision, not will benefit those who disbelieve their belief and not they will be granted respite."

Say (qul), | "On the Day (yawma) | of the Decision (l-fatḥi), | not (lā) | will benefit (yanfaʿu) | those who (alladhīna) | disbelieve (kafarū) | their belief (īmānuhum) | and not (walā) | they (hum) | will be granted respite. (yunẓarūna)"

32:30 So turn away from them and wait. Indeed, they are waiting.

So turn away (fa-aʿriḍ) | from them (ʿanhum) | and wait (wa-intaẓir). | Indeed, they (innahum) | are waiting (muntaẓirūna).

Chapter (33) Sūrat l-Aḥzāb (The Combined Forces)

33:1 O Prophet! Fear Allah and do not obey the disbelievers and the hypocrites. Indeed, Allah is All-Knower, All-Wise.

O Prophet (yāayyuhā)! | O Prophet (l-nabiyu)! | Fear (ittaqi) | Allah (l-laha) | and do not (walā) | obey (tuṭiʿi) | the disbelievers (l-kāfirīna) | and the hypocrites (wal-munāfiqīna). | Indeed (inna), | Allah (l-laha) | is (kāna) | All-Knower (ʿalīman), | All-Wise (ḥakīman).

33:2 And follow what is inspired to you from your Lord. Indeed, Allah is of what you do All-Aware.

And follow (wa-ittabiʿ) | what (mā) | is inspired (yūḥā) | to you (ilayka) | from (min) | your Lord (rabbika). | Indeed (inna), | Allah (l-laha) | is (kāna) | of what (bimā) | you do (taʿmalūna) | All-Aware (khabīran).

33:3 And put your trust in Allah. And Allah is sufficient as Disposer of affairs.

And put your trust (watawakkal) | in (ʿalā) | Allah (l-lahi). | And Allah is sufficient (wakafā) | And Allah is sufficient (bil-lahi) | as Disposer of affairs (wakīlan).

33:4 Not Allah has made for any man [of] two hearts in his interior. And not He has made your wives whom you declare unlawful [of them] as your mothers. And not He has made your adopted sons your sons. That is your saying by your mouths, but Allah says the truth, and He guides to the Way.

Not (mā) | Allah has made (jaʿala) | Allah has made (l-lahu) | for any man (lirajulin) | [of] (min) | two hearts (qalbayni) | in (fī) | his interior (jawfihi). | And not (wamā) | He has made (jaʿala) | your wives (azwājakumu) | whom (allāī) | you declare unlawful (tuẓāhirūna) | [of them] (min'hunna) | as your mothers (ummahātikum). | And not (wamā) | He has made (jaʿala) | your adopted sons (adʿiyāakum) | your sons (abnāakum). | That (dhālikum) | is your saying (qawlukum) | by your mouths (bi-afwāhikum), | but Allah (wal-lahu) | says (yaqūlu) | the truth (l-ḥaqa), | and He (wahuwa) | guides (yahdī) | to the Way (l-sabīla).

33:5 Call them by their fathers; it is more just near Allah. But if not you know their fathers - then they are your brothers in [the] religion and your friends. But not is upon you any blame in what you made a mistake in it, but what intended your hearts. And Allah is Oft-Forgiving, Most Merciful.

Call them (id'ʿūhum) | by their fathers (liābāihim); | it (huwa) | is more just (aqsaṭu) | near (ʿinda) | Allah (l-lahi). | But if (fa-in) | not (lam) | you know (taʿlamū) | their fathers (ābāahum)- | then they are your brothers (fa-ikh'wānukum) | in (fī) | [the] religion (l-dīni) | and your friends (wamawālīkum). | But not is (walaysa) | upon you (ʿalaykum) | any blame (junāḥun) | in what (fīmā) | you made a mistake (akhṭatum) | in it (bihi), | but (walākin) | what (mā) | intended (taʿammadat) | your hearts (qulūbukum). | And Allah (wakāna) | And Allah (l-lahu) | is Oft-Forgiving (ghafūran), | Most Merciful (raḥīman).

33:6 The Prophet is closer to the believers than their own selves, and his wives are their mothers. And possessors of relationships, some of them are closer to another in the Decree of Allah than the believers and the emigrants, except that you do to your friends a kindness. That is in the Book written.

The Prophet (al-nabiyu) | is closer (awlā) | to the believers (bil-mu'minīna) | than (min) | their own selves (anfusihim), | and his wives (wa-azwājuhu) | are their mothers (ummahātuhum). | And possessors (wa-ulū) | of relationships (l-arḥāmi), | some of them (baʿḍuhum) | are closer (awlā) | to another (bibaʿḍin) | in (fī) | the Decree (kitābi) | of Allah (l-lahi) | than (mina) | the believers (l-mu'minīna) | and the emigrants (wal-muhājirīna), | except (illā) | that (an) | you do (tafʿalū) | to (ilā) | your friends (awliyāikum) | a kindness (maʿrūfan). | That is (kāna) | That is (dhālika) | in (fī) | the Book (l-kitābi) | written (masṭūran).

33:7 And when We took from the Prophets their Covenant and from you and from Nuh and Ibrahim and Musa and Isa, son of Maryam. And We took from them a covenant strong

And when (wa-idh) | We took (akhadhnā) | from (mina) | the Prophets (l-nabiyīna) | their Covenant (mīthāqahum) | and from you (waminka) | and from (wamin) | Nuh (nūḥin) | and Ibrahim (wa-ib'rāhīma) | and Musa (wamūsā) | and Isa (waʿīsā), | son (ib'ni) | of Maryam (maryama). | And We took (wa-akhadhnā) | from them (min'hum) | a covenant (mīthāqan) | strong (ghalīẓan)

33:8 That He may ask the truthful about their truth. And He has prepared for the disbelievers a punishment painful.

That He may ask (liyasala) | the truthful (l-ṣādiqīna) | about (ʿan) | their truth (ṣid'qihim). | And He has prepared (wa-aʿadda) | for the disbelievers (lil'kāfirīna) | a punishment (ʿadhāban) | painful (alīman).

33:9 O you who believe! Remember the Favor of Allah upon you when came to you the hosts and We sent upon them a wind and hosts not you could see them. And Allah is of what you do All-Seer.

O you (yāayyuhā) | who (alladhīna) | believe (āmanū)! | Remember (udh'kurū) | the Favor (niʿ'mata) | of Allah (l-lahi) | upon you (ʿalaykum) | when (idh) | came to you (jāatkum) | the hosts (junūdun) | and We sent (fa-arsalnā) | upon them (ʿalayhim) | a wind (rīḥan) | and hosts (wajunūdan) | not (lam) | you could see them (tarawhā). | And Allah is (wakāna) | And Allah is (l-lahu) | of what (bimā) | you do (taʿmalūna) | All-Seer (baṣīran).

33:10 When they came upon you from above you and from below you, and when grew wild the eyes and reached the hearts the throats, and you assumed about Allah the assumptions.

When (idh) | they came upon you (jāūkum) | from (min) | above you (fawqikum) | and from (wamin) | below (asfala) | you (minkum), | and when (wa-idh) | grew wild (zāghati) | the eyes (l-abṣāru) | and reached (wabalaghati) | the hearts (l-qulūbu) | the throats (l-ḥanājira), | and you assumed (wataẓunnūna) | about Allah (bil-lahi) | the assumptions (l-ẓunūnā).

33:11 There - were tried the believers and shaken with a shake severe.

There (hunālika)- | were tried (ub'tuliya) | the believers (l-mu'minūna) | and shaken (wazul'zilū) | with a shake (zil'zālan) | severe (shadīdan).

33:12 And when said the hypocrites and those in their hearts was a disease, "Not Allah promised us and His messenger except delusion."

And when (wa-idh) | said (yaqūlu) | the hypocrites (l-munāfiqūna) | and those (wa-alladhīna) | in (fī) | their hearts (qulūbihim) | was a disease (maraḍun), | "Not (mā) | Allah promised us (waʿadanā) | Allah promised us (l-lahu) | and His messenger (warasūluhu) | except (illā) | delusion. (ghurūran)"

33:13 And when said a party of them, "O People of Yathrib! No stand for you, so return." And asked permission a group of them from the Prophet, saying, "Indeed, our houses are exposed," and not they were exposed. Not they wished but to flee.

And when (wa-idh) | said (qālat) | a party (ṭāifatun) | of them (min'hum), | "O People (yāahla) | of Yathrib (yathriba)! | No (lā) | stand (muqāma) | for you (lakum), | so return. (fa-ir'jiʿū)" | And asked permission (wayastadhinu) | a group (farīqun) | of them (min'humu) | from the Prophet (l-nabiya), | saying (yaqūlūna), | "Indeed (inna), | our houses (buyūtanā) | are exposed, (ʿawratun)" | and not (wamā) | they (hiya) | were exposed (biʿawratin). | Not (in) | they wished (yurīdūna) | but (illā) | to flee (firāran).

33:14 And if had been entered upon them from all its sides then they had been asked the treachery, they would have certainly done it and not they would have hesitated over it except a little.

And if (walaw) | had been entered (dukhilat) | upon them (ʿalayhim) | from (min) | all its sides (aqṭārihā) | then (thumma) | they had been asked (su-ilū) | the treachery (l-fit'nata), | they would have certainly done it (laātawhā) | and not (wamā) | they would have hesitated (talabbathū) | over it (bihā) | except (illā) | a little (yasīran).

33:15 And certainly they had promised Allah before, not they would turn their backs. And is the promise to Allah to be questioned.

And certainly (walaqad) | they had (kānū) | promised (ʿāhadū) | Allah (l-laha) | before (min), | before (qablu), | not (lā) | they would turn (yuwallūna) | their backs (l-adbāra). | And is (wakāna) | the promise (ʿahdu) | to Allah (l-lahi) | to be questioned (masūlan).

33:16 Say, "Never will benefit you the fleeing, if you flee from death or killing, and then not you will be allowed to enjoy except a little."

Say (qul), | "Never (lan) | will benefit you (yanfaʿakumu) | the fleeing (l-firāru), | if (in) | you flee (farartum) | from (mina) | death (l-mawti) | or (awi) | killing (l-qatli), | and then (wa-idhan) | not (lā) | you will be allowed to enjoy (tumattaʿūna) | except (illā) | a little. (qalīlan)"

33:17 Say, "Who is it that can protect you from Allah If He intends for you any harm or He intends for you a mercy?" And not they will find for them besides Allah any protector and not any helper.

Say (qul), | "Who (man) | is it that (dhā) | is it that (alladhī) | can protect you (yaʿṣimukum) | from (mina) | Allah (l-lahi) | If (in) | He intends (arāda) | for you (bikum) | any harm (sūan) | or (aw) | He intends (arāda) | for you (bikum) | a mercy? (raḥmatan)" | And not (walā) | they will find (yajidūna) | for them (lahum) | besides (min) | besides (dūni) | Allah (l-lahi) | any protector (waliyyan) | and not (walā) | any helper (naṣīran).

33:18 Verily, Allah knows those who hinder among you and those who say to their brothers, "Come to us," and not they come to the battle except a few,

Verily (qad), | Allah knows (yaʿlamu) | Allah knows (l-lahu) | those who hinder (l-muʿawiqīna) | among you (minkum) | and those who say (wal-qāilīna) | to their brothers (li-ikh'wānihim), | "Come (halumma) | to us, (ilaynā)" | and not (walā) | they come (yatūna) | to the battle (l-basa) | except (illā) | a few (qalīlan),

33:19 Miserly towards you. But when comes the fear, you see them looking at you, revolving their eyes like one who faints from [the] death. But when departs the fear, they smite you with tongues sharp miserly towards the good. Those - not they have believed, so Allah made worthless their deeds. And is that for Allah easy.

Miserly (ashiḥḥatan) | towards you (ʿalaykum). | But when (fa-idhā) | comes (jāa) | the fear (l-khawfu), | you see them (ra-aytahum) | looking (yanẓurūna) | at you (ilayka), | revolving (tadūru) | their eyes (aʿyunuhum) | like one who (ka-alladhī) | faints (yugh'shā) | faints (ʿalayhi) | from (mina) | [the] death (l-mawti). | But when (fa-idhā) | departs (dhahaba) | the fear (l-khawfu), | they smite you (salaqūkum) | with tongues (bi-alsinatin) | sharp (ḥidādin) | miserly (ashiḥḥatan) | towards (ʿalā) | the good (l-khayri). | Those (ulāika)- | not (lam) | they have believed (yu'minū), | so Allah made worthless (fa-aḥbaṭa) | so Allah made worthless (l-lahu) | their deeds (aʿmālahum). | And is (wakāna) | that (dhālika) | for (ʿalā) | Allah (l-lahi) | easy (yasīran).

33:20 They think the confederates have not withdrawn. And if should come the confederates they would wish if that they were living in the desert among the Bedouins, asking about your news. And if they were among you not they would fight except a little.

They think (yaḥsabūna) | the confederates (l-aḥzāba) | have not (lam) | withdrawn (yadhhabū). | And if (wa-in) | should come (yati) | the confederates (l-aḥzābu) | they would wish (yawaddū) | if (law) | that they were (annahum) | living in the desert (bādūna) | among (fī) | the Bedouins (l-aʿrābi), | asking (yasalūna) | about (ʿan) | your news (anbāikum). | And if (walaw) | they were (kānū) | among you (fīkum) | not (mā) | they would fight (qātalū) | except (illā) | a little (qalīlan).

33:21 Certainly, is for you in the Messenger of Allah an excellent example for one who has hope in Allah and the Day the Last, and remembers Allah much.

Certainly (laqad), | is (kāna) | for you (lakum) | in (fī) | the Messenger (rasūli) | of Allah (l-lahi) | an excellent example (us'watun) | an excellent example (ḥasanatun) | for one who (liman) | has (kāna) | hope (yarjū) | in Allah (l-laha) | and the Day (wal-yawma) | the Last (l-ākhira), | and remembers (wadhakara) | Allah (l-laha) | much (kathīran).

33:22 And when saw the believers the confederates, they said, "This is what Allah promised us and His Messenger, and Allah spoke the truth and His Messenger." And not it increased them except in faith and submission.

And when (walammā) | saw (raā) | the believers (l-mu'minūna) | the confederates (l-aḥzāba), | they said (qālū), | "This (hādhā) | is what (mā) | Allah promised us (waʿadanā) | Allah promised us (l-lahu) | and His Messenger (warasūluhu), | and Allah spoke the truth (waṣadaqa) | and Allah spoke the truth (l-lahu) | and His Messenger. (warasūluhu)" | And not (wamā) | it increased them (zādahum) | except (illā) | in faith (īmānan) | and submission (wataslīman).

33:23 Among the believers are men who have been true to what they promised Allah [on it]. And among them is he who has fulfilled his vow and among them is he who awaits. And not they alter by any alteration -

Among (mina) | the believers (l-mu'minīna) | are men (rijālun) | who have been true (ṣadaqū) | to what (mā) | they promised Allah (ʿāhadū) | they promised Allah (l-laha) | [on it] (ʿalayhi). | And among them (famin'hum) | is he who (man) | has fulfilled (qaḍā) | his vow (naḥbahu) | and among them (wamin'hum) | is he who (man) | awaits (yantaẓiru). | And not (wamā) | they alter (baddalū) | by any alteration (tabdīlan)-

33:24 That Allah may reward the truthful for their truth and punish the hypocrites if He wills or turn in mercy to them. Indeed, Allah is Oft-Forgiving, Most Merciful.

That Allah may reward (liyajziya) | That Allah may reward (l-lahu) | the truthful (l-ṣādiqīna) | for their truth (biṣid'qihim) | and punish (wayuʿadhiba) | the hypocrites (l-munāfiqīna) | if (in) | He wills (shāa) | or (aw) | turn in mercy (yatūba) | to them (ʿalayhim). | Indeed (inna), | Allah (l-laha) | is (kāna) | Oft-Forgiving (ghafūran), | Most Merciful (raḥīman).

33:25 And Allah turned back those who disbelieved, in their rage, not they obtained any good. And sufficient is Allah for the believers in the battle, and Allah is All-Strong, All-Mighty.

And Allah turned back (waradda) | And Allah turned back (l-lahu) | those who (alladhīna) | disbelieved (kafarū), | in their rage (bighayẓihim), | not (lam) | they obtained (yanālū) | any good (khayran). | And sufficient is (wakafā) | Allah (l-lahu) | for the believers (l-mu'minīna) | in the battle (l-qitāla), | and Allah is (wakāna) | and Allah is (l-lahu) | All-Strong (qawiyyan), | All-Mighty (ʿazīzan).

33:26 And He brought down those who backed them among the People of the Scripture from their fortresses and cast into their hearts [the] terror, a group you killed and you took captive a group.

And He brought down (wa-anzala) | those who (alladhīna) | backed them (ẓāharūhum) | among (min) | the People (ahli) | of the Scripture (l-kitābi) | from (min) | their fortresses (ṣayāṣīhim) | and cast (waqadhafa) | into (fī) | their hearts (qulūbihimu) | [the] terror (l-ruʿba), | a group (farīqan) | you killed (taqtulūna) | and you took captive (watasirūna) | a group (farīqan).

33:27 And He caused you to inherit their land, and their houses, and their properties and a land not you had trodden. And Allah is on every thing All-Powerful.

And He caused you to inherit (wa-awrathakum) | their land (arḍahum), | and their houses (wadiyārahum), | and their properties (wa-amwālahum) | and a land (wa-arḍan) | not (lam) | you had trodden (taṭaūhā). | And Allah is (wakāna) | And Allah is (l-lahu) | on (ʿalā) | every (kulli) | thing (shayin) | All-Powerful (qadīran).

33:28 O Prophet! Say to your wives, "If you desire the life of the world and its adornment, then come, I will provide for you and release you with a release good.

O Prophet (yāayyuhā)! | O Prophet (l-nabiyu)! | Say (qul) | to your wives (li-azwājika), | "If (in) | you (kuntunna) | desire (turid'na) | the life (l-ḥayata) | of the world (l-dun'yā) | and its adornment (wazīnatahā), | then come (fataʿālayna), | I will provide for you (umattiʿ'kunna) | and release you (wa-usarriḥ'kunna) | with a release (sarāḥan) | good (jamīlan).

33:29 But if you desire Allah and His Messenger and the Home of the Hereafter, then indeed, Allah has prepared for the good-doers among you a reward great."

But if (wa-in) | you (kuntunna) | desire (turid'na) | Allah (l-laha) | and His Messenger (warasūlahu) | and the Home (wal-dāra) | of the Hereafter (l-ākhirata), | then indeed (fa-inna), | Allah (l-laha) | has prepared (aʿadda) | for the good-doers (lil'muḥ'sināti) | among you (minkunna) | a reward (ajran) | great. (ʿaẓīman)"

33:30 O wives of the Prophet! Whoever commits from you immorality clear, will be doubled for her the punishment two fold. And that is for Allah easy.

O wives (yānisāa) | of the Prophet (l-nabiyi)! | Whoever (man) | commits (yati) | from you (minkunna) | immorality (bifāḥishatin) | clear (mubayyinatin), | will be doubled (yuḍāʿaf) | for her (lahā) | the punishment (l-ʿadhābu) | two fold (ḍiʿ'fayni). | And that is (wakāna) | And that is (dhālika) | for (ʿalā) | Allah (l-lahi) | easy (yasīran).

33:31 And whoever is obedient among you to Allah and His Messenger and does righteousness, We will give her her reward twice; and We have prepared for her a provision noble.

And whoever (waman) | is obedient (yaqnut) | among you (minkunna) | to Allah (lillahi) | and His Messenger (warasūlihi) | and does (wataʿmal) | righteousness (ṣāliḥan), | We will give her (nu'tihā) | her reward (ajrahā) | twice (marratayni); | and We have prepared (wa-aʿtadnā) | for her (lahā) | a provision (riz'qan) | noble (karīman).

33:32 O wives of the Prophet! You are not like anyone among the women. If you fear Allah, then do not be soft in speech, lest should be moved with desire he who, in his heart is a disease, but say a word appropriate.

O wives (yānisāa) | of the Prophet (l-nabiyi)! | You are not (lastunna) | like anyone (ka-aḥadin) | among (mina) | the women (l-nisāi). | If (ini) | you fear Allah (ittaqaytunna), | then do not (falā) | be soft (takhḍaʿna) | in speech (bil-qawli), | lest should be moved with desire (fayaṭmaʿa) | he who (alladhī), | in (fī) | his heart (qalbihi) | is a disease (maraḍun), | but say (waqul'na) | a word (qawlan) | appropriate (maʿrūfan).

33:33 And stay in your houses and do not display yourselves as was the display of the times of ignorance the former. And establish the prayer and give zakah and obey Allah and His Messenger. Only Allah wishes to remove from you the impurity, O People of the House! And to purify you with thorough purification.

And stay (waqarna) | in (fī) | your houses (buyūtikunna) | and do not (walā) | display yourselves (tabarrajna) | as was the display (tabarruja) | of the times of ignorance (l-jāhiliyati) | the former (l-ūlā). | And establish (wa-aqim'na) | the prayer (l-ṣalata) | and give (waātīna) | zakah (l-zakata) | and obey (wa-aṭi''na) | Allah (l-laha) | and His Messenger (warasūlahu). | Only (innamā) | Allah wishes (yurīdu) | Allah wishes (l-lahu) | to remove (liyudh'hiba) | from you (ʿankumu) | the impurity (l-rij'sa), | O People (ahla) | of the House (l-bayti)! | And to purify you (wayuṭahhirakum) | with thorough purification (taṭhīran).

33:34 And remember what is recited in your houses of the Verses of Allah and the wisdom. Indeed, Allah is All-Subtle, All-Aware.

And remember (wa-udh'kur'na) | what (mā) | is recited (yut'lā) | in (fī) | your houses (buyūtikunna) | of (min) | the Verses (āyāti) | of Allah (l-lahi) | and the wisdom (wal-ḥik'mati). | Indeed (inna), | Allah (l-laha) | is (kāna) | All-Subtle (laṭīfan), | All-Aware (khabīran).

33:35 Indeed, the Muslim men and the Muslim women, and the believing men and the believing women, and the obedient men and the obedient women, and the truthful men and the truthful women, and the patient men and the patient women, and the humble men and the humble women, and the men who give charity and the women who give charity and the men who fast and the women who fast, and the men who guard their chastity and the women who guard it, and the men who remember Allah much and the women who remember Allah has prepared for them forgiveness and a reward great.

Indeed (inna), | the Muslim men (l-mus'limīna) | and the Muslim women (wal-mus'limāti), | and the believing men (wal-mu'minīna) | and the believing women (wal-mu'mināti), | and the obedient men (wal-qānitīna) | and the obedient women (wal-qānitāti), | and the truthful men (wal-ṣādiqīna) | and the truthful women (wal-ṣādiqāti), | and the patient men (wal-ṣābirīna) | and the patient women (wal-ṣābirāti), | and the humble men (wal-khāshiʿīna) | and the humble women (wal-khāshiʿāti), | and the men who give charity (wal-mutaṣadiqīna) | and the women who give charity (wal-mutaṣadiqāti) | and the men who fast (wal-ṣāimīna) | and the women who fast (wal-ṣāimāti), | and the men who guard (wal-ḥāfiẓīna) | their chastity (furūjahum) | and the women who guard it (wal-ḥāfiẓāti), | and the men who remember (wal-dhākirīna) | Allah (l-laha) | much (kathīran) | and the women who remember (wal-dhākirāti) | Allah has prepared (aʿadda) | Allah has prepared (l-lahu) | for them (lahum) | forgiveness (maghfiratan) | and a reward (wa-ajran) | great (ʿaẓīman).

33:36 And not it is for a believing man and not for a believing woman, when Allah has decided and His Messenger a matter that there should be for them any choice about their affair. And whoever disobeys Allah and His Messenger certainly, he has strayed into error clear.

And not (wamā) | it is (kāna) | for a believing man (limu'minin) | and not (walā) | for a believing woman (mu'minatin), | when (idhā) | Allah has decided (qaḍā) | Allah has decided (l-lahu) | and His Messenger (warasūluhu) | a matter (amran) | that (an) | there should be (yakūna) | for them (lahumu) | any choice (l-khiyaratu) | about (min) | their affair (amrihim). | And whoever (waman) | disobeys (yaʿṣi) | Allah (l-laha) | and His Messenger (warasūlahu) | certainly (faqad), | he has strayed (ḍalla) | into error (ḍalālan) | clear (mubīnan).

33:37 And when you said to the one, Allah bestowed favor on him and you bestowed favor on him, "Keep to yourself your wife and fear Allah." But you concealed within yourself what Allah was to disclose. And you fear the people, while Allah has more right that you should fear Him. So when ended Zaid from her necessary formalities, We married her to you so that not there be on the believers any discomfort concerning the wives of their adopted sons when they have ended from them necessary formalities. And is the Command of Allah accomplished.

And when (wa-idh) | you said (taqūlu) | to the one (lilladhī), | Allah bestowed favor (anʿama) | Allah bestowed favor (l-lahu) | on him (ʿalayhi) | and you bestowed favor (wa-anʿamta) | on him (ʿalayhi), | "Keep (amsik) | to yourself (ʿalayka) | your wife (zawjaka) | and fear (wa-ittaqi) | Allah. (l-laha)" | But you concealed (watukh'fī) | within (fī) | yourself (nafsika) | what (mā) | Allah (l-lahu) | was to disclose (mub'dīhi). | And you fear (watakhshā) | the people (l-nāsa), | while Allah (wal-lahu) | has more right (aḥaqqu) | that (an) | you should fear Him (takhshāhu). | So when (falammā) | ended (qaḍā) | Zaid (zaydun) | from her (min'hā) | necessary formalities (waṭaran), | We married her to you (zawwajnākahā) | so that (likay) | not (lā) | there be (yakūna) | on (ʿalā) | the believers (l-mu'minīna) | any discomfort (ḥarajun) | concerning (fī) | the wives (azwāji) | of their adopted sons (adʿiyāihim) | when (idhā) | they have ended (qaḍaw) | from them (min'hunna) | necessary formalities (waṭaran). | And is (wakāna) | the Command (amru) | of Allah (l-lahi) | accomplished (mafʿūlan).

33:38 Not there can be upon the Prophet any discomfort in what Allah has imposed on him. That is the Way of Allah concerning those who passed away before. And is the Command of Allah a decree destined.

Not (mā) | there can be (kāna) | upon (ʿalā) | the Prophet (l-nabiyi) | any (min) | discomfort (ḥarajin) | in what (fīmā) | Allah has imposed (faraḍa) | Allah has imposed (l-lahu) | on him (lahu). | That is the Way (sunnata) | of Allah (l-lahi) | concerning (fī) | those who (alladhīna) | passed away (khalaw) | before (min). | before (qablu). | And is (wakāna) | the Command (amru) | of Allah (l-lahi) | a decree (qadaran) | destined (maqdūran).

33:39 Those who convey the Messages of Allah and fear Him and do not fear anyone except Allah. And sufficient is Allah as a Reckoner.

Those who (alladhīna) | convey (yuballighūna) | the Messages (risālāti) | of Allah (l-lahi) | and fear Him (wayakhshawnahu) | and do not (walā) | fear (yakhshawna) | anyone (aḥadan) | except (illā) | Allah (l-laha). | And sufficient is Allah (wakafā) | And sufficient is Allah (bil-lahi) | as a Reckoner (ḥasīban).

33:40 Not is Muhammad the father of anyone of your men but he is the Messenger of Allah and Seal of the Prophets. And Allah is of every thing All-Knower.

Not (mā) | is (kāna) | Muhammad (muḥammadun) | the father (abā) | of anyone (aḥadin) | of (min) | your men (rijālikum) | but (walākin) | he is the Messenger (rasūla) | of Allah (l-lahi) | and Seal (wakhātama) | of the Prophets (l-nabiyīna). | And Allah is (wakāna) | And Allah is (l-lahu) | of every (bikulli) | thing (shayin) | All-Knower (ʿalīman).

33:41 O you who believe! Remember Allah with remembrance much

O you who believe (yāayyuhā)! | O you who believe (alladhīna)! | O you who believe (āmanū)! | Remember (udh'kurū) | Allah (l-laha) | with remembrance (dhik'ran) | much (kathīran)

33:42 And glorify Him morning and evening.

And glorify Him (wasabbiḥūhu) | morning (buk'ratan) | and evening (wa-aṣīlan).

33:43 He is the One Who sends His blessings upon you and His Angels so that He may bring you out from the darkness[es] to the light. And He is to the believers Merciful.

He (huwa) | is the One Who (alladhī) | sends His blessings (yuṣallī) | upon you (ʿalaykum) | and His Angels (wamalāikatuhu) | so that He may bring you out (liyukh'rijakum) | from (mina) | the darkness[es] (l-ẓulumāti) | to (ilā) | the light (l-nūri). | And He is (wakāna) | to the believers (bil-mu'minīna) | Merciful (raḥīman).

33:44 Their greetings on the Day they will meet Him will be, "Peace." and He has prepared for them a reward noble.

Their greetings (taḥiyyatuhum) | on the Day (yawma) | they will meet Him (yalqawnahu) |

will be, "Peace. (salāmun)" | and He has prepared (wa-aʿadda) | for them (lahum) | a reward (ajran) | noble (karīman).

33:45 O Prophet! Indeed, We have sent you as a witness and a bearer of glad tidings and as a warner

O Prophet (yāayyuhā)! | O Prophet (l-nabiyu)! | Indeed, We (innā) | have sent you (arsalnāka) | as a witness (shāhidan) | and a bearer of glad tidings (wamubashiran) | and as a warner (wanadhīran)

33:46 And as one who invites to Allah by His permission, and as a lamp illuminating.

And as one who invites (wadāʿiyan) | to (ilā) | Allah (l-lahi) | by His permission (bi-idh'nihi), | and as a lamp (wasirājan) | illuminating (munīran).

33:47 And give glad tidings to the believers that for them is from Allah a Bounty great.

And give glad tidings (wabashiri) | to the believers (l-mu'minīna) | that (bi-anna) | for them (lahum) | is from (mina) | Allah (l-lahi) | a Bounty (faḍlan) | great (kabīran).

33:48 And do not obey the disbelievers and the hypocrites, and disregard their harm, and put your trust in Allah. And sufficient is Allah as a Trustee.

And do not (walā) | obey (tuṭiʿi) | the disbelievers (l-kāfirīna) | and the hypocrites (wal-munāfiqīna), | and disregard (wadaʿ) | their harm (adhāhum), | and put your trust (watawakkal) | in (ʿalā) | Allah (l-lahi). | And sufficient is Allah (wakafā) | And sufficient is Allah (bil-lahi) | as a Trustee (wakīlan).

33:49 O you who believe! When you marry believing women and then, divorce them before [that] you have touched them, then not for you on them any waiting period to count concerning them. So provide for them and release them with a release good.

O you who believe (yāayyuhā)! | O you who believe (alladhīna)! | O you who believe (āmanū)! | When (idhā) | you marry (nakaḥtumu) | believing women (l-mu'mināti) | and then (thumma), | divorce them (ṭallaqtumūhunna) | before (min) | before (qabli) | [that] (an) | you have touched them (tamassūhunna), | then not (famā) | for you (lakum) | on them (ʿalayhinna) | any (min) | waiting period (ʿiddatin) | to count concerning them (taʿtaddūnahā). | So provide for them (famattiʿūhunna) | and release them (wasarriḥūhunna) | with a release (sarāḥan) | good (jamīlan).

33:50 O Prophet! Indeed, We [We] have made lawful to you your wives to whom you have given their bridal money and whom you rightfully possess from those whom Allah has given to you, and the daughters of your paternal uncles and the daughters of your paternal aunts and the daughters of your maternal uncles and the daughters of your maternal aunts who emigrated with you, and a woman believing if she gives herself to the Prophet if wishes the Prophet to marry her - only for you, excluding the believers. Certainly, We know what We have made obligatory upon them concerning their wives and whom they rightfully possess, that not should be on you any discomfort. And Allah is Oft-Forgiving, Most Merciful

O Prophet (yāayyuhā)! | O Prophet (l-nabiyu)! | Indeed, We (innā) | [We] have made lawful (aḥlalnā) | to you (laka) | your wives (azwājaka) | to whom (allātī) | you have given (ātayta) | their bridal money (ujūrahunna) | and whom (wamā) | you rightfully possess (malakat) | you rightfully possess (yamīnuka) | from those whom (mimmā) | Allah has given (afāa) | Allah has given (l-lahu) | to you (ʿalayka), | and the daughters (wabanāti) | of your paternal uncles (ʿammika) | and the daughters (wabanāti) | of your paternal aunts (ʿammātika) | and the daughters (wabanāti) | of your maternal uncles (khālika) | and the daughters (wabanāti) | of your maternal aunts (khālātika) | who (allātī) | emigrated (hājarna) | with you (maʿaka), | and a woman (wa-im'ra-atan) | believing (mu'minatan) | if (in) | she gives (wahabat) | herself (nafsahā) | to the Prophet (lilnnabiyyi) | if (in) | wishes (arāda) | the Prophet (l-nabiyu) | to (an) | marry her (yastankiḥahā)- | only (khāliṣatan) |

for you (laka), | excluding (min) | excluding (dūni) | the believers (l-mu'minīna). | Certainly (qad), | We know (ʿalim'nā) | what (mā) | We have made obligatory (faraḍnā) | upon them (ʿalayhim) | concerning (fī) | their wives (azwājihim) | and whom (wamā) | they rightfully possess (malakat), | they rightfully possess (aymānuhum), | that not (likaylā) | should be (yakūna) | on you (ʿalayka) | any discomfort (ḥarajun). | And Allah is (wakāna) | And Allah is (l-lahu) | Oft-Forgiving (ghafūran), | Most Merciful (raḥīman)

33:51 You may defer whom you will of them or you may take to yourself whom you will. And whoever you desire of those whom you had set aside - then there is no blame upon you. That is more suitable that may be cooled their eyes and not they grieve and they may be pleased with what you have given them - all of them. And Allah knows what is in your hearts. And Allah is All-Knower, Most Forbearing.

You may defer (tur'jī) | whom (man) | you will (tashāu) | of them (min'hunna) | or you may take (watu'wī) | to yourself (ilayka) | whom (man) | you will (tashāu). | And whoever (wamani) | you desire (ib'taghayta) | of those whom (mimman) | you had set aside (ʿazalta)- | then there is no (falā) | blame (junāḥa) | upon you (ʿalayka). | That (dhālika) | is more suitable (adnā) | that (an) | may be cooled (taqarra) | their eyes (aʿyunuhunna) | and not (walā) | they grieve (yaḥzanna) | and they may be pleased (wayarḍayna) | with what (bimā) | you have given them (ātaytahunna)- | all of them (kulluhunna). | And Allah (wal-lahu) | knows (yaʿlamu) | what (mā) | is in (fī) | your hearts (qulūbikum). | And Allah is (wakāna) | And Allah is (l-lahu) | All-Knower (ʿalīman), | Most Forbearing (ḥalīman).

33:52 It is not lawful for you to marry women after this and not to exchange them for other wives even if pleases you their beauty, except whom you rightfully possess And Allah is over all things an Observer.

It is not (lā) | lawful (yaḥillu) | for you (laka) | to marry women (l-nisāu) | after this (min) | after this (baʿdu) | and not (walā) | to (an) | exchange (tabaddala) | them (bihinna) | for (min) | other wives (azwājin) | even if (walaw) | pleases you (aʿjabaka) | their beauty (ḥus'nuhunna), | except (illā) | whom (mā) | you rightfully possess (malakat) | you rightfully possess (yamīnuka) | And Allah is (wakāna) | And Allah is (l-lahu) | over (ʿalā) | all (kulli) | things (shayin) | an Observer (raqīban).

33:53 O you who believe! Do not enter the houses of the Prophet except when permission is given to you for a meal, without awaiting its preparation. But when you are invited, then enter; and when you have eaten, then disperse and not seeking to remain for a conversation. Indeed, that was troubling the Prophet, and he is shy of dismissing you. But Allah is not shy of the truth. And when you ask them for anything then ask them from behind a screen. That is purer for your hearts and their hearts. And not is for you that you trouble the Messenger of Allah and not that you should marry his wives after him, ever. Indeed, that is near Allah an enormity.

O you who believe (yāayyuhā)! | O you who believe (alladhīna)! | O you who believe (āmanū)! | Do not (lā) | enter (tadkhulū) | the houses (buyūta) | of the Prophet (l-nabiyi) | except (illā) | when (an) | permission is given (yu'dhana) | to you (lakum) | for (ilā) | a meal (ṭaʿāmin), | without (ghayra) | awaiting (nāẓirīna) | its preparation (ināhu). | But (walākin) | when (idhā) | you are invited (duʿītum), | then enter (fa-ud'khulū); | and when (fa-idhā) | you have eaten (ṭaʿim'tum), | then disperse (fa-intashirū) | and not (walā) | seeking to remain (mus'tanisīna) | for a conversation (liḥadīthin). | Indeed (inna), | that (dhālikum) | was (kāna) | troubling (yu'dhī) | the Prophet (l-nabiya), | and he is shy (fayastaḥyī) | of dismissing you (minkum). | But Allah (wal-lahu) | is not shy (lā) | is not shy (yastaḥyī) | of (mina) | the truth (l-ḥaqi). | And when (wa-idhā) | you ask them (sa-altumūhunna) | for anything (matāʿan) | then ask them (fasalūhunna) | from (min) | behind (warāi) | a screen (ḥijābin). | That (dhālikum) | is purer (aṭharu) | for your hearts (liqulūbikum) | and their hearts (waqulūbihinna). | And not (wamā) | is (kāna) | for you (lakum) | that (an) | you trouble (tu'dhū) | the Messenger (rasūla) | of Allah (l-lahi) | and not (walā) | that (an)

| you should marry (tankiḥū) | his wives (azwājahu) | after him (min), | after him (baʿdihi), | ever (abadan). | Indeed (inna), | that (dhālikum) | is (kāna) | near (ʿinda) | Allah (l-lahi) | an enormity (ʿaẓīman).

33:54 Whether you reveal a thing or conceal it, indeed, Allah is of all things All-Knower.

Whether (in) | you reveal (tub'dū) | a thing (shayan) | or (aw) | conceal it (tukh'fūhu), | indeed (fa-inna), | Allah (l-laha) | is (kāna) | of all (bikulli) | things (shayin) | All-Knower (ʿalīman).

33:55 There is no blame upon them concerning their fathers and not their sons and not their brothers and not sons of their brothers and not sons of their sisters and not their women and not what they rightfully possess. And fear Allah. Indeed, Allah is over all things a Witness.

There is no (lā) | blame (junāḥa) | upon them (ʿalayhinna) | concerning (fī) | their fathers (ābāihinna) | and not (walā) | their sons (abnāihinna) | and not (walā) | their brothers (ikh'wānihinna) | and not (walā) | sons (abnāi) | of their brothers (ikh'wānihinna) | and not (walā) | sons (abnāi) | of their sisters (akhawātihinna) | and not (walā) | their women (nisāihinna) | and not (walā) | what (mā) | they rightfully possess (malakat). | they rightfully possess (aymānuhunna). | And fear (wa-ittaqīna) | Allah (l-laha). | Indeed (inna), | Allah (l-laha) | is (kāna) | over (ʿalā) | all (kulli) | things (shayin) | a Witness (shahīdan).

33:56 Indeed, Allah and His Angels send blessings upon the Prophet. O you who believe! Send blessings on him and greet him with greetings.

Indeed (inna), | Allah (l-laha) | and His Angels (wamalāikatahu) | send blessings (yuṣallūna) | upon (ʿalā) | the Prophet (l-nabiyi). | O you who believe (yāayyuhā)! | O you who believe (alladhīna)! | O you who believe (āmanū)! | Send blessings (ṣallū) | on him (ʿalayhi) | and greet him (wasallimū) | with greetings (taslīman).

33:57 Indeed, those who annoy Allah and His Messenger, Allah has cursed them in the world and the Hereafter and prepared for them a punishment humiliating.

Indeed (inna), | those who (alladhīna) | annoy (yu'dhūna) | Allah (l-laha) | and His Messenger (warasūlahu), | Allah has cursed them (laʿanahumu) | Allah has cursed them (l-lahu) | in (fī) | the world (l-dun'yā) | and the Hereafter (wal-ākhirati) | and prepared (wa-aʿadda) | for them (lahum) | a punishment (ʿadhāban) | humiliating (muhīnan).

33:58 And those who harm the believing men and the believing women for other than what they have earned, then certainly, they bear false accusation and sin manifest.

And those who (wa-alladhīna) | harm (yu'dhūna) | the believing men (l-mu'minīna) | and the believing women (wal-mu'mināti) | for other than (bighayri) | what (mā) | they have earned (ik'tasabū), | then certainly (faqadi), | they bear (iḥ'tamalū) | false accusation (buh'tānan) | and sin (wa-ith'man) | manifest (mubīnan).

33:59 O Prophet! Say to your wives and your daughters and the women of the believers to draw over themselves [of] their outer garments. That is more suitable that they should be known and not harmed. And is Allah Oft-Forgiving, Most Merciful.

O Prophet (yāayyuhā)! | O Prophet (l-nabiyu)! | Say (qul) | to your wives (li-azwājika) | and your daughters (wabanātika) | and the women (wanisāi) | of the believers (l-mu'minīna) | to draw (yud'nīna) | over themselves (ʿalayhinna) | [of] (min) | their outer garments (jalābībihinna). | That (dhālika) | is more suitable (adnā) | that (an) | they should be known (yuʿ'rafna) | and not (falā) | harmed (yu'dhayna). | And is (wakāna) | Allah (l-lahu) | Oft-Forgiving (ghafūran), | Most Merciful (raḥīman).

33:60 If do not cease the hypocrites and those who in their hearts is a disease and those who spread rumors in the city, We will let you overpower them, then not they will remain your neighbors therein except for a little,

If (la-in) | do not (lam) | cease (yantahi) | the hypocrites (l-munāfiqūna) | and those who (wa-alladhīna) | in (fī) | their hearts (qulūbihim) | is a disease (maraḍun) | and those who spread rumors (wal-mur'jifūna) | in (fī) | the city (l-madīnati), | We will let you overpower them (lanugh'riyannaka), | We will let you overpower them (bihim), | then (thumma) | not (lā) | they will remain your neighbors (yujāwirūnaka) | therein (fīhā) | except (illā) | for a little (qalīlan),

33:61 Accursed, wherever they are found, they are seized and massacred completely.

Accursed (malʿūnīna), | wherever (aynamā) | they are found (thuqifū), | they are seized (ukhidhū) | and massacred completely (waquttilū). | and massacred completely (taqtīlan).

33:62 Such is the Way of Allah with those who passed away before and never you will find in the Way of Allah any change.

Such is the Way (sunnata) | of Allah (l-lahi) | with (fī) | those who (alladhīna) | passed away (khalaw) | before (min) | before (qablu) | and never (walan) | you will find (tajida) | in the Way (lisunnati) | of Allah (l-lahi) | any change (tabdīlan).

33:63 Ask you the people about the Hour. Say, "Only its knowledge is with Allah. And what will make you know? Perhaps the Hour is near."

Ask you (yasaluka) | the people (l-nāsu) | about (ʿani) | the Hour (l-sāʿati). | Say (qul), | "Only (innamā) | its knowledge (ʿil'muhā) | is with (ʿinda) | Allah (l-lahi). | And what (wamā) | will make you know (yud'rīka)? | Perhaps (laʿalla) | the Hour (l-sāʿata) | is (takūnu) | near. (qarīban)"

33:64 Indeed, Allah has cursed the disbelievers and has prepared for them a Blaze,

Indeed (inna), | Allah (l-laha) | has cursed (laʿana) | the disbelievers (l-kāfirīna) | and has prepared (wa-aʿadda) | for them (lahum) | a Blaze (saʿīran),

33:65 Abiding therein forever, not they will find any protector and not any helper.

Abiding (khālidīna) | therein (fīhā) | forever (abadan), | not (lā) | they will find (yajidūna) | any protector (waliyyan) | and not (walā) | any helper (naṣīran).

33:66 The Day will be turned about their faces in the Fire they will say, "O we wish we had obeyed Allah and obeyed the Messenger!"

The Day (yawma) | will be turned about (tuqallabu) | their faces (wujūhuhum) | in (fī) | the Fire (l-nāri) | they will say (yaqūlūna), | "O we wish (yālaytanā) | we had obeyed (aṭaʿnā) | Allah (l-laha) | and obeyed (wa-aṭaʿnā) | the Messenger! (l-rasūlā)"

33:67 And they will say, "Our Lord! Indeed, we [we] obeyed our chiefs and our great men, and they misled us from the Way.

And they will say (waqālū), | "Our Lord (rabbanā)! | Indeed, we (innā) | [we] obeyed (aṭaʿnā) | our chiefs (sādatanā) | and our great men (wakubarāanā), | and they misled us (fa-aḍallūnā) | from the Way (l-sabīlā).

33:68 Our Lord! Give them double [of] punishment and curse them with a curse great."

Our Lord (rabbanā)! | Give them (ātihim) | double (ḍiʿfayni) | [of] (mina) | punishment (l-ʿadhābi) | and curse them (wal-ʿanhum) | with a curse (laʿnan) | great. (kabīran)"

33:69 O you who believe! Do not be like those who abused Musa then Allah cleared him of what they said. And he was near Allah honorable.

O you who believe (yāayyuhā)! | O you who believe (alladhīna)! | O you who believe (āmanū)! | Do not (lā) | be (takūnū) | like those who (ka-alladhīna) | abused (ādhaw) | Musa (mūsā) | then Allah cleared him (fabarra-ahu) | then Allah cleared him (l-lahu) | of what (mimmā) | they said (qālū). | And he was (wakāna) | near (ʿinda) | Allah (l-lahi) | honorable (wajīhan).

33:70 O you who believe! Fear Allah and speak a word right.

O you who believe (yāayyuhā)! | O you who believe (alladhīna)! | O you who believe (āmanū)! | Fear (ittaqū) | Allah (l-laha) | and speak (waqūlū) | a word (qawlan) | right (sadīdan).

33:71 He will amend for you your deeds and forgive for you your sins. And whoever obeys Allah and His Messenger certainly has attained an attainment great.

He will amend (yuṣ'liḥ) | for you (lakum) | your deeds (aʿmālakum) | and forgive (wayaghfir) | for you (lakum) | your sins (dhunūbakum). | And whoever (waman) | obeys (yuṭiʿi) | Allah (l-laha) | and His Messenger (warasūlahu) | certainly (faqad) | has attained (fāza) | an attainment (fawzan) | great (ʿaẓīman).

33:72 Indeed, We [We] offered the Trust to the heavens and the earth and the mountains, but they refused to bear it and they feared from it; but bore it the man. Indeed, he was unjust ignorant.

Indeed, We (innā) | [We] offered (ʿaraḍnā) | the Trust (l-amānata) | to (ʿalā) | the heavens (l-samāwāti) | and the earth (wal-arḍi) | and the mountains (wal-jibāli), | but they refused (fa-abayna) | to (an) | bear it (yaḥmil'nahā) | and they feared (wa-ashfaqna) | from it (min'hā); | but bore it (waḥamalahā) | the man (l-insānu). | Indeed, he (innahu) | was (kāna) | unjust (ẓalūman) | ignorant (jahūlan).

33:73 So that Allah may punish the hypocrite men and the hypocrite women and the polytheist men and the polytheist women and Allah will turn in Mercy to the believing men and the believing women. And Allah is Oft-Forgiving, Most Merciful.

So that Allah may punish (liyuʿadhiba) | So that Allah may punish (l-lahu) | the hypocrite men (l-munāfiqīna) | and the hypocrite women (wal-munāfiqāti) | and the polytheist men (wal-mush'rikīna) | and the polytheist women (wal-mush'rikāti) | and Allah will turn in Mercy (wayatūba) | and Allah will turn in Mercy (l-lahu) | to (ʿalā) | the believing men (l-mu'minīna) | and the believing women (wal-mu'mināti). | And Allah is (wakāna) | And Allah is (l-lahu) | Oft-Forgiving (ghafūran), | Most Merciful (raḥīman).

Chapter (34) Sūrat Saba (Sheba)

34:1 All praises be to Allah the One to Whom belongs whatever is in the heavens and whatever is in the earth, and for Him are all praises in the Hereafter. And He is the All-Wise, the All-Aware.

All praises (al-ḥamdu) | be to Allah (lillahi) | the One to Whom belongs (alladhī) | the One to Whom belongs (lahu) | whatever (mā) | is in (fī) | the heavens (l-samāwāti) | and whatever (wamā) | is in (fī) | the earth (l-arḍi), | and for Him (walahu) | are all praises (l-ḥamdu) | in (fī) | the Hereafter (l-ākhirati). | And He (wahuwa) | is the All-Wise (l-ḥakīmu), | the All-Aware (l-khabīru).

34:2 He knows what penetrates in the earth and what comes out from it, and what descends from the heaven and what ascends therein. And He is the Most Merciful, the Oft-Forgiving.

He knows (yaʿlamu) | what (mā) | penetrates (yaliju) | in (fī) | the earth (l-arḍi) | and what (wamā) | comes out (yakhruju) | from it (min'hā), | and what (wamā) | descends (yanzilu) | from (mina) | the heaven (l-samāi) | and what (wamā) | ascends (yaʿruju) | therein (fīhā). | And He (wahuwa) | is the Most Merciful (l-raḥīmu), | the Oft-Forgiving (l-ghafūru).

34:3 But say those who disbelieve, "Not will come to us the Hour." Say, "Nay, by my Lord surely it will come to you. He is the Knower of the unseen." Not escapes from Him the weight of an atom in the heavens and not in the earth and not smaller than that and not greater, but is in a Record Clear.

But say (waqāla) | those who (alladhīna) | disbelieve (kafarū), | "Not (lā) | will come to us (tatīnā) | the Hour. (l-sāʿatu)" | Say (qul), | "Nay (balā), | by my Lord (warabbī) | surely it will come to you (latatiyannakum). | He is the Knower (ʿālimi) | of the unseen. (l-ghaybi)" | Not (lā) | escapes (yaʿzubu) | from Him (ʿanhu) | the weight (mith'qālu) | of an atom (dharratin) | in (fī) | the heavens (l-samāwāti) | and not (walā) | in (fī) | the earth (l-arḍi) | and not (walā) | smaller (aṣgharu) | than (min) | that (dhālika) | and not (walā) | greater (akbaru), | but (illā) | is in (fī) | a Record (kitābin) | Clear (mubīnin).

34:4 That He may reward those who believe and do righteous deeds. Those - for them will be forgiveness and a provision noble.

That He may reward (liyajziya) | those who (alladhīna) | believe (āmanū) | and do (waʿamilū) | righteous deeds (l-ṣāliḥāti). | Those (ulāika)- | for them (lahum) | will be forgiveness (maghfiratun) | and a provision (wariz'qun) | noble (karīmun).

34:5 But those who strive against Our Verses to cause failure - those - for them is a punishment of foul nature, painful.

But those who (wa-alladhīna) | strive (saʿaw) | against (fī) | Our Verses (āyātinā) | to cause failure (muʿājizīna)- | those (ulāika)- | for them (lahum) | is a punishment (ʿadhābun) | of (min) | foul nature (rij'zin), | painful (alīmun).

34:6 And see those who have been given the knowledge, that what is revealed to you from your Lord [it] is the Truth, and it guides to the Path of the All-Mighty, the Praiseworthy.

And see (wayarā) | those who (alladhīna) | have been given (ūtū) | the knowledge (l-ʿil'ma), | that what (alladhī) | is revealed (unzila) | to you (ilayka) | from (min) | your Lord (rabbika) | [it] (huwa) | is the Truth (l-ḥaqa), | and it guides (wayahdī) | to (ilā) | the Path (ṣirāṭi) | of the All-Mighty (l-ʿazīzi), | the Praiseworthy (l-ḥamīdi).

34:7 But say those who disbelieve, "Shall we direct you to a man who informs you when you have disintegrated in total disintegration, indeed you surely will be in a creation new?

But say (waqāla) | those who (alladhīna) | disbelieve (kafarū), | "Shall (hal) | we direct you (nadullukum) | to (ʿalā) | a man (rajulin) | who informs you (yunabbi-ukum) | when (idhā) | you have disintegrated (muzziq'tum) | in total (kulla) | disintegration (mumazzaqin), | indeed you (innakum) | surely will be in (lafī) | a creation (khalqin) | new (jadīdin)?

34:8 Has he invented about Allah a lie or in him is madness?" Nay, those who do not believe in the Hereafter will be in the punishment and error far.

Has he invented (aftarā) | about (ʿalā) | Allah (l-lahi) | a lie (kadhiban) | or (am) | in him (bihi) | is madness? (jinnatun)" | Nay (bali), | those who (alladhīna) | do not (lā) | believe (yu'minūna) | in the Hereafter (bil-ākhirati) | will be in (fī) | the punishment (l-ʿadhābi) | and error (wal-ḍalāli) | far (l-baʿīdi).

34:9 Then, do not they see towards what is before them and what is behind them of the heaven and the earth? If We will We could cause to swallow them the earth or cause to fall upon them fragments from the sky. Indeed, in that surely, is a Sign for every slave who turns to Allah.

Then, do not (afalam) | they see (yaraw) | towards (ilā) | what (mā) | is before them (bayna) | is before them (aydīhim) | and what (wamā) | is behind them (khalfahum) | of (mina) | the heaven (l-samāi) | and the earth (wal-arḍi)? | If (in) | We will (nasha) | We could cause to swallow them (nakhsif) | We could cause to swallow them (bihimu) | the earth (l-arḍa) | or (aw) | cause to fall (nus'qiṭ) | upon them (ʿalayhim) | fragments (kisafan) | from (mina) | the sky (l-samāi). | Indeed (inna), | in (fī) | that (dhālika) | surely, is a Sign (laāyatan) | for every (likulli) | slave (ʿabdin) | who turns to Allah (munībin).

34:10 And certainly, We gave Dawood from Us Bounty. "O mountains! Repeat praises with him, and the birds." And We made pliable for him [the] iron,

And certainly (walaqad), | We gave (ātaynā) | Dawood (dāwūda) | from Us (minnā) | Bounty (faḍlan). | "O mountains (yājibālu)! | Repeat praises (awwibī) | with him (maʿahu), | and the birds. (wal-ṭayra)" | And We made pliable (wa-alannā) | for him (lahu) | [the] iron (l-ḥadīda),

34:11 That make full coats of mail and measure precisely [of] the links of armor, and work righteousness. Indeed, I Am of what you do All-Seer.

That (ani) | make (iʿ'mal) | full coats of mail (sābighātin) | and measure precisely (waqaddir) | [of] (fī) | the links of armor (l-sardi), | and work (wa-iʿ'malū) | righteousness (ṣāliḥan). | Indeed, I Am (innī) | of what (bimā) | you do (taʿmalūna) | All-Seer (baṣīrun).

34:12 And to Sulaiman, the wind - its morning course was a month and its afternoon course was a month, and We caused to flow for him a spring of molten copper. And [of] the jinn who worked before him by the permission of his Lord. And whoever deviated among them from Our Command, We will make him taste of the punishment of the Blaze.

And to Sulaiman (walisulaymāna), | the wind (l-rīḥa)- | its morning course (ghuduwwuhā) | was a month (shahrun) | and its afternoon course (warawāḥuhā) | was a month (shahrun), | and We caused to flow (wa-asalnā) | for him (lahu) | a spring (ʿayna) | of molten copper (l-qiṭ'ri). | And [of] (wamina) | the jinn (l-jini) | who (man) | worked (yaʿmalu) | before him (bayna) | before him (yadayhi) | by the permission (bi-idh'ni) | of his Lord (rabbihi). | And whoever (waman) | deviated (yazigh) | among them (min'hum) | from (ʿan) | Our Command (amrinā), | We will make him taste (nudhiq'hu) | of (min) | the punishment (ʿadhābi) | of the Blaze (l-saʿīri).

34:13 They worked for him what he willed of elevated chambers and statues and bowls like reservoirs and cooking-pots fixed. "Work, O family of Dawood! in gratitude." But few of My slaves are grateful.

They worked (yaʿmalūna) | for him (lahu) | what (mā) | he willed (yashāu) | of (min) | elevated chambers (maḥārība) | and statues (watamāthīla) | and bowls (wajifānin) | like reservoirs (kal-jawābi) | and cooking-pots (waqudūrin) | fixed (rāsiyātin). | "Work (iʿ'malū), | O family (āla) | of Dawood (dāwūda)! | in gratitude. (shuk'ran)" | But few (waqalīlun) | of (min) | My slaves (ʿibādiya) | are grateful (l-shakūru).

34:14 Then when We decreed for him the death, not indicated to them [on] his death except a creature of the earth eating his staff. But when he fell down, became clear to the jinn that if they had known the unseen, not they would have remained in the punishment humiliating.

Then when (falammā) | We decreed (qaḍaynā) | for him (ʿalayhi) | the death (l-mawta), | not (mā) | indicated to them (dallahum) | [on] (ʿalā) | his death (mawtihi) | except (illā) | a creature (dābbatu) | of the earth (l-arḍi) | eating (takulu) | his staff (minsa-atahu). | But when (falammā) | he fell down (kharra), | became clear (tabayyanati) | to the jinn (l-jinu) | that (an) | if (law) | they had (kānū) | known (yaʿlamūna) | the unseen (l-ghayba), | not (mā) | they would have remained (labithū) | in (fī) | the punishment (l-ʿadhābi) | humiliating (l-muhīni).

34:15 Certainly, there was for Saba in their dwelling place a sign: Two gardens on the right and on the left. "Eat from the provision of your Lord and be grateful to Him. A land good and a Lord Oft-Forgiving."

Certainly (laqad), | there was (kāna) | for Saba (lisaba-in) | in (fī) | their dwelling place (maskanihim) | a sign (āyatun): | Two gardens (jannatāni) | on (ʿan) | the right (yamīnin) | and on the left (washimālin). | "Eat (kulū) | from (min) | the provision (riz'qi) | of your Lord (rabbikum) | and be grateful (wa-ush'kurū) | to Him (lahu). | A land (baldatun) | good (ṭayyibatun) | and a Lord (warabbun) | Oft-Forgiving. (ghafūrun)"

34:16 But they turned away, so We sent upon them the flood of the dam, and We changed for them their two gardens with two gardens producing fruit bitter, and tamarisks and something of lote trees few.

But they turned away (fa-aʿraḍū), | so We sent (fa-arsalnā) | upon them (ʿalayhim) | the flood (sayla) | of the dam (l-ʿarimi), | and We changed for them (wabaddalnāhum) | their two gardens (bijannatayhim) | with two gardens (jannatayni) | producing fruit (dhawātay) | producing fruit (ukulin) | bitter (khamṭin), | and tamarisks (wa-athlin) | and something (washayin) | of (min) | lote trees (sid'rin) | few (qalīlin).

34:17 That We recompensed them because they disbelieved. And not We recompense except the ungrateful.

That (dhālika) | We recompensed them (jazaynāhum) | because (bimā) | they disbelieved (kafarū). | And not (wahal) | We recompense (nujāzī) | except (illā) | the ungrateful (l-kafūra).

34:18 And We made between them and between the towns which We had blessed in it towns visible. And We determined between them the journey. "Travel between them by night and by day safely."

And We made (wajaʿalnā) | between them (baynahum) | and between (wabayna) | the towns (l-qurā) | which (allatī) | We had blessed (bāraknā) | in it (fīhā) | towns (quran) | visible (ẓāhiratan). | And We determined (waqaddarnā) | between them (fīhā) | the journey (l-sayra). | "Travel (sīrū) | between them (fīhā) | by night (layāliya) | and by day (wa-ayyāman) | safely. (āminīna)"

34:19 But they said, "Our Lord lengthen the distance between our journeys." And they wronged themselves, so We made them narrations and We dispersed them in a total dispersion. Indeed, in that surely are Signs for everyone, patient and grateful.

But they said (faqālū), | "Our Lord (rabbanā) | lengthen the distance (bāʿid) | between (bayna) | our journeys. (asfārinā)" | And they wronged (waẓalamū) | themselves (anfusahum), | so We made them (fajaʿalnāhum) | narrations (aḥādītha) | and We dispersed them (wamazzaqnāhum) | in a total (kulla) | dispersion (mumazzaqin). | Indeed (inna), | in (fī) | that (dhālika) | surely are Signs (laāyātin) | for everyone (likulli), | patient (ṣabbārin) | and grateful (shakūrin).

34:20 And certainly, found true about them Iblis his assumption, so they followed him except a group of the believers.

And certainly (walaqad), | found true (ṣaddaqa) | about them (ʿalayhim) | Iblis (ib'līsu) | his assumption (ẓannahu), | so they followed him (fa-ittabaʿūhu) | except (illā) | a group (farīqan) | of (mina) | the believers (l-mu'minīna).

34:21 And not was for him over them any authority except that We might make evident who believes in the Hereafter from one who [he] about it is in doubt. And your Lord over all things is a Guardian.

And not (wamā) | was (kāna) | for him (lahu) | over them (ʿalayhim) | any (min) | authority (sul'ṭānin) | except (illā) | that We might make evident (linaʿlama) | who (man) | believes (yu'minu) | in the Hereafter (bil-ākhirati) | from one who (mimman) | [he] (huwa) | about it (min'hā) | is in (fī) | doubt (shakkin). | And your Lord (warabbuka) | over (ʿalā) | all (kulli) | things (shayin) | is a Guardian (ḥafīẓun).

34:22 Say, "Call upon those whom you claim besides Allah." Not they possess the weight of an atom in the heavens and not in the earth and not for them in both of them any partnership, and not for Him from them any supporter.

Say (quli), | "Call upon (id'ʿū) | those whom (alladhīna) | you claim (zaʿamtum) | besides (min) | besides (dūni) | Allah. (l-lahi)" | Not (lā) | they possess (yamlikūna) | the weight (mith'qāla) | of an atom (dharratin) | in (fī) | the heavens (l-samāwāti) | and not (walā) | in (fī) | the earth (l-arḍi) | and not (wamā) | for them (lahum) | in both of them (fīhimā) | any (min) | partnership (shir'kin), | and not (wamā) | for Him (lahu) | from them (min'hum) | any (min) | supporter (ẓahīrin).

34:23 And not benefits the intercession with Him except for one whom He permits for him. Until when fear is removed on their hearts, they will say, "What is that - your Lord has said?" They will say, "The truth." And He is the Most High, the Most Great.

And not (walā) | benefits (tanfaʿu) | the intercession (l-shafāʿatu) | with Him (ʿindahu) | except (illā) | for one whom (liman) | He permits (adhina) | for him (lahu). | Until (ḥattā) | when (idhā) | fear is removed (fuzziʿa) | on (ʿan) | their hearts (qulūbihim), | they will say (qālū), | "What is that (mādhā)- | your Lord has said? (qāla)" | your Lord has said? (rabbukum)" | They will say (qālū), | "The truth. (l-ḥaqa)" | And He (wahuwa) | is the Most High (l-ʿaliyu), | the Most Great (l-kabīru).

34:24 Say, "Who provides for you from the heavens and the earth?" Say, "Allah. And indeed, we or you are surely upon guidance or in error clear."

Say (qul), | "Who (man) | provides for you (yarzuqukum) | from (mina) | the heavens (l-samāwāti) | and the earth? (wal-arḍi)" | Say (quli), | "Allah (l-lahu). | And indeed, we (wa-innā) | or (aw) | you (iyyākum) | are surely upon (laʿalā) | guidance (hudan) | or (aw) | in (fī) | error (ḍalālin) | clear. (mubīnin)"

34:25 Say, "Not you will be asked about what sins we committed and not we will be asked about what you do."

Say (qul), | "Not (lā) | you will be asked (tus'alūna) | about what (ʿammā) | sins we committed (ajramnā) | and not (walā) | we will be asked (nus'alu) | about what (ʿammā) | you do. (taʿmalūna)"

34:26 Say, "Will gather us together our Lord, then He will judge between us in truth. And He is the Judge the All-Knowing."

Say (qul), | "Will gather (yajmaʿu) | us together (baynanā) | our Lord (rabbunā), | then (thumma) | He will judge (yaftaḥu) | between us (baynanā) | in truth (bil-ḥaqi). | And He (wahuwa) | is the Judge (l-fatāḥu) | the All-Knowing. (l-ʿalīmu)"

34:27 Say, "Show me those whom you have joined with Him as partners. By no means! Nay, He is Allah the All-Mighty, the All-Wise."

Say (qul), | "Show me (arūniya) | those whom (alladhīna) | you have joined (alḥaqtum) | with Him (bihi) | as partners (shurakāa). | By no means (kallā)! | Nay (bal), | He (huwa) | is Allah (l-lahu) | the All-Mighty (l-ʿazīzu), | the All-Wise. (l-ḥakīmu)"

34:28 And not We have sent you except comprehensively to mankind as a giver of glad tidings and as a warner. But most [the] people do not know.

And not (wamā) | We have sent you (arsalnāka) | except (illā) | comprehensively (kāffatan) | to mankind (lilnnāsi) | as a giver of glad tidings (bashīran) | and as a warner (wanadhīran). | But (walākinna) | most (akthara) | [the] people (l-nāsi) | do not (lā) | know (yaʿlamūna).

34:29 And they say, "When is this promise, if you are truthful?"

And they say (wayaqūlūna), | "When (matā) | is this (hādhā) | promise (l-waʿdu), | if (in) | you are (kuntum) | truthful? (ṣādiqīna)"

34:30 Say, "For you is the appointment of a Day, not you can postpone [of] it for an hour, and not can you precede (it)."

Say (qul), | "For you (lakum) | is the appointment (mīʿādu) | of a Day (yawmin), | not (lā) | you can postpone (tastakhirūna) | [of] it (ʿanhu) | for an hour (sāʿatan), | and not (walā) | can you precede (it). (tastaqdimūna)"

34:31 And say those who disbelieve, "Never will we believe in this Quran and not in that which was before it." But if you could see when the wrongdoers will be made to stand before their Lord, will throw back some of them to others the word. Will say those who were oppressed to those who were arrogant, "If not for you certainly we would have been believers."

And say (waqāla) | those who (alladhīna) | disbelieve (kafarū), | "Never will (lan) | we believe (nu'mina) | in this (bihādhā) | Quran (l-qur'āni) | and not (walā) | in that which (bi-alladhī) | was before it. (bayna)" | was before it. (yadayhi)" | But if (walaw) | you could see (tarā) | when (idhi) | the wrongdoers (l-ẓālimūna) | will be made to stand (mawqūfūna) | before (ʿinda) | their Lord (rabbihim), | will throw back (yarjiʿu) | some of them (baʿḍuhum) | to (ilā) | others (baʿḍin) | the word (l-qawla). | Will say (yaqūlu) | those who (alladhīna) | were oppressed (us'tuḍʿifū) | to those who (lilladhīna) | were arrogant (is'takbarū), | "If not (lawlā) | for you (antum) | certainly we would have been (lakunnā) | believers. (mu'minīna)"

34:32 Will say those who were arrogant to those who were oppressed, "Did we avert you from the guidance after when it had come to you? Nay, you were criminals."

Will say (qāla) | those who (alladhīna) | were arrogant (is'takbarū) | to those (lilladhīna) | who were oppressed (us'tuḍʿifū), | "Did we (anaḥnu) | avert you (ṣadadnākum) | from (ʿani) | the guidance (l-hudā) | after (baʿda) | when (idh) | it had come to you (jāakum)? | Nay (bal), | you were (kuntum) | criminals. (muj'rimīna)"

34:33 And will say those who were oppressed to those who were arrogant, "Nay, it was a plot by night and by day when you were ordering us that we disbelieve in Allah and we set up for Him equals." But they will conceal the regret when they see the punishment. And We will put shackles on the necks of those who disbelieved. Will they be recompensed except for what they used to do?

And will say (waqāla) | those who (alladhīna) | were oppressed (us'tuḍʿifū) | to those who (lilladhīna) | were arrogant (is'takbarū), | "Nay (bal), | it was a plot (makru) | by night (al-layli) | and by day (wal-nahāri) | when (idh) | you were ordering us (tamurūnanā) | that (an) | we disbelieve (nakfura) | in Allah (bil-lahi) | and we set up (wanajʿala) | for Him (lahu) | equals. (andādan)" | But they will conceal (wa-asarrū) | the regret (l-nadāmata) | when (lammā) | they see (ra-awū) | the punishment (l-ʿadhāba). | And We will put (wajaʿalnā) | shackles (l-aghlāla) | on (fī) | the necks (aʿnāqi) | of those who (alladhīna) | disbelieved (kafarū). | Will (hal) | they be recompensed (yuj'zawna) | except (illā) | for what (mā) | they used to (kānū) | do (yaʿmalūna)?

34:34 And not We sent to a town any warner but said its wealthy ones, "Indeed we, in what you have been sent with, are disbelievers."

And not (wamā) | We sent (arsalnā) | to (fī) | a town (qaryatin) | any (min) | warner (nadhīrin) | but (illā) | said (qāla) | its wealthy ones (mut'rafūhā), | "Indeed we (innā), | in what (bimā) | you have been sent (ur'sil'tum) | with (bihi), | are disbelievers. (kāfirūna)"

34:35 And they say, "We have more wealth and children, and not we will be punished."

And they say (waqālū), | "We (naḥnu) | have more (aktharu) | wealth (amwālan) | and children (wa-awlādan), | and not (wamā) | we (naḥnu) | will be punished. (bimuʿadhabīna)"

34:36 Say, "Indeed, my Lord extends the provision for whom He wills and restricts, but most [the] people do not know."

Say (qul), | "Indeed (inna), | my Lord (rabbī) | extends (yabsuṭu) | the provision (l-riz'qa) | for whom (liman) | He wills (yashāu) | and restricts (wayaqdiru), | but (walākinna) | most (akthara) | [the] people (l-nāsi) | do not (lā) | know. (yaʿlamūna)"

34:37 And not your wealth and not your children [that] will bring you close to Us in position, but whoever believes and does righteousness, then those, for them will be reward two-fold for what they did, and they will be in the high dwellings secure.

And not (wamā) | your wealth (amwālukum) | and not (walā) | your children (awlādukum) | [that] (bi-allatī) | will bring you close (tuqarribukum) | to Us (ʿindanā) | in position (zul'fā), | but (illā) | whoever (man) | believes (āmana) | and does (waʿamila) | righteousness (ṣāliḥan), | then those (fa-ulāika), | for them (lahum) | will be reward (jazāu) | two-fold (l-ḍiʿ'fi) | for what (bimā) | they did (ʿamilū), | and they (wahum) | will be in (fī) | the high dwellings (l-ghurufāti) | secure (āminūna).

34:38 And those who strive against Our Verses to cause failure, those into the punishment will be brought.

And those who (wa-alladhīna) | strive (yasʿawna) | against (fī) | Our Verses (āyātinā) | to cause failure (muʿājizīna), | those (ulāika) | into (fī) | the punishment (l-ʿadhābi) | will be brought (muḥ'ḍarūna).

34:39 Say, "Indeed, my Lord extends the provision for whom He wills of His slaves and restricts for him. But what you spend of anything then He will compensate it and He is the Best of the Providers.

Say (qul), | "Indeed (inna), | my Lord (rabbī) | extends (yabsuṭu) | the provision (l-riz'qa) | for whom (liman) | He wills (yashāu) | of (min) | His slaves (ʿibādihi) | and restricts (wayaqdiru) | for him (lahu). | But what (wamā) | you spend (anfaqtum) | of (min) | anything (shayin) | then He (fahuwa) | will compensate it (yukh'lifuhu) | and He (wahuwa) | is the Best (khayru) | of the Providers (l-rāziqīna).

34:40 And the Day He will gather them all, then He will say to the Angels, "Were these you they were worshipping?"

And the Day (wayawma) | He will gather them (yaḥshuruhum) | all (jamīʿan), | then (thumma) | He will say (yaqūlu) | to the Angels (lil'malāikati), | "Were these you (ahāulāi) | "Were these you (iyyākum) | they were (kānū) | worshipping? (yaʿbudūna)"

34:41 They will say, "Glory be to You! You are our Protector, not them. Nay, they used to worship the jinn, most of them in them were believers."

They will say (qālū), | "Glory be to You (sub'ḥānaka)! | You (anta) | are our Protector (waliyyunā), | not them (min). | not them (dūnihim). | Nay (bal), | they used (kānū) | to worship (yaʿbudūna) | the jinn (l-jina), | most of them (aktharuhum) | in them (bihim) | were believers. (mu'minūna)"

34:42 But today not possess power some of you on others to benefit and not to harm, and We will say to those who wronged, "Taste the punishment of the Fire which you used to [it] deny."

But today (fal-yawma) | not (lā) | possess power (yamliku) | some of you (baʿḍukum) | on others (libaʿḍin) | to benefit (nafʿan) | and not (walā) | to harm (ḍarran), | and We will say (wanaqūlu) | to those (lilladhīna) | who wronged (ẓalamū), | "Taste (dhūqū) | the punishment (ʿadhāba) | of the Fire (l-nāri) | which (allatī) | you used (kuntum) | to [it] (bihā) | deny. (tukadhibūna)"

34:43 And when are recited to them Our Verses clear they say, "Not is this but a man who wishes to hinder you from what used to worship your forefathers." And they say, "Not is this except a lie invented." And said those who disbelieved about the truth when it came to them, "Not is this except a magic obvious."

And when (wa-idhā) | are recited (tut'lā) | to them (ʿalayhim) | Our Verses (āyātunā) | clear (bayyinātin) | they say (qālū), | "Not (mā) | is this (hādhā) | but (illā) | a man (rajulun) | who wishes (yurīdu) | to (an) | hinder you (yaṣuddakum) | from what (ʿammā) | used (kāna) | to worship (yaʿbudu) | your forefathers. (ābāukum)" | And they say (waqālū), | "Not (mā) | is this (hādhā) | except (illā) | a lie (if'kun) | invented. (muf'taran)" | And said (waqāla) | those who (alladhīna) | disbelieved (kafarū) | about the truth (lil'ḥaqqi) | when (lammā) | it came to them (jāahum), | "Not (in) | is this (hādhā) | except (illā) | a magic (siḥ'run) | obvious. (mubīnun)"

34:44 And not We had given them any Scriptures which they could study, and not We sent to them before you any warner.

And not (wamā) | We had given them (ātaynāhum) | any (min) | Scriptures (kutubin) | which they could study (yadrusūnahā), | and not (wamā) | We sent (arsalnā) | to them (ilayhim) | before you (qablaka) | any (min) | warner (nadhīrin).

34:45 And denied those who were before them and not they have attained a tenth of what We had given them. But they denied My Messengers, so how was My rejection?

And denied (wakadhaba) | those who (alladhīna) | were before them (min) | were before them (qablihim) | and not (wamā) | they have attained (balaghū) | a tenth (miʿshāra) | of what (mā) | We had given them (ātaynāhum). | But they denied (fakadhabū) | My Messengers (rusulī), | so how (fakayfa) | was (kāna) | My rejection (nakīri)?

34:46 Say, "Only I advise you for one thing, that you stand for Allah in pairs and as individuals, then reflect." Not is in your companion any madness. Not he is except a warner for you before a punishment severe."

Say (qul), | "Only (innamā) | I advise you (aʿiẓukum) | for one thing (biwāḥidatin), | that (an) | you stand (taqūmū) | for Allah (lillahi) | in pairs (mathnā) | and as individuals (wafurādā), | then (thumma) | reflect. (tatafakkarū)" | Not (mā) | is in your companion (biṣāḥibikum) | any (min) | madness (jinnatin). | Not (in) | he (huwa) | is except (illā) | a warner (nadhīrun) | for you (lakum) | before (bayna) | before (yaday) | a punishment (ʿadhābin) | severe. (shadīdin)"

34:47 Say, "Not I ask you for any payment, but it is for you. Not is my payment but from Allah. And He is over all things a Witness."

Say (qul), | "Not (mā) | I ask you (sa-altukum) | for (min) | any payment (ajrin), | but it is (fahuwa) | for you (lakum). | Not (in) | is my payment (ajriya) | but (illā) | from (ʿalā) | Allah (l-lahi). | And He (wahuwa) | is over (ʿalā) | all (kulli) | things (shayin) | a Witness. (shahīdun)"

34:48 Say, "Indeed, my Lord projects the truth, the All-Knower of the unseen."

Say (qul), | "Indeed (inna), | my Lord (rabbī) | projects (yaqdhifu) | the truth (bil-ḥaqi), | the All-Knower (ʿallāmu) | of the unseen. (l-ghuyūbi)"

34:49 Say, "Has come the truth and not can originate the falsehood and not repeat."

Say (qul), | "Has come (jāa) | the truth (l-ḥaqu) | and not (wamā) | can originate (yub'di-u) | the falsehood (l-bāṭilu) | and not (wamā) | repeat. (yuʿīdu)"

34:50 Say, "If I err, then only I will err against myself. But if I am guided, then it is by what reveals to me my Lord. Indeed, He is All-Hearer, Ever-Near."

Say (qul), | "If (in) | I err (ḍalaltu), | then only (fa-innamā) | I will err (aḍillu) | against (ʿalā) | myself (nafsī). | But if (wa-ini) | I am guided (ih'tadaytu), | then it is by what (fabimā) | reveals (yūḥī) | to me (ilayya) | my Lord (rabbī). | Indeed, He (innahu) | is All-Hearer (samīʿun), | Ever-Near.

(qarībun)"

34:51 And if you could see when they will be terrified but there will be no escape, and they will be seized from a place near.

And if (walaw) | you could see (tarā) | when (idh) | they will be terrified (faziʿū) | but there will be no (falā) | escape (fawta), | and they will be seized (wa-ukhidhū) | from (min) | a place (makānin) | near (qarībin).

34:52 And they will say, "We believe in it." But how for them will be the receiving from a place far off?

And they will say (waqālū), | "We believe (āmannā) | in it. (bihi)" | But how (wa-annā) | for them (lahumu) | will be the receiving (l-tanāwushu) | from (min) | a place (makānin) | far off (baʿīdin)?

34:53 And certainly, they disbelieved in it before. And they utter conjectures about the unseen from a place far off.

And certainly (waqad), | they disbelieved (kafarū) | in it (bihi) | before (min). | before (qablu). | And they utter conjectures (wayaqdhifūna) | about the unseen (bil-ghaybi) | from (min) | a place (makānin) | far off (baʿīdin).

34:54 And a barrier will be placed between them and between what they desire, as was done with their kind before. Indeed, they were in doubt disquieting.

And a barrier will be placed (waḥīla) | between them (baynahum) | and between (wabayna) | what (mā) | they desire (yashtahūna), | as (kamā) | was done (fuʿila) | with their kind (bi-ashyāʿihim) | before (min). | before (qablu). | Indeed, they (innahum) | were (kānū) | in (fī) | doubt (shakkin) | disquieting (murībin).

Chapter (35) Sūrat Fāṭir (The Originator)

35:1 All praises be to Allah, Originator of the heavens and the earth, Who makes the Angels messengers having wings two or three or four. He increases in the creation what He wills. Indeed, Allah is on every thing All-Powerful.

All praises (al-ḥamdu) | be to Allah (lillahi), | Originator (fāṭiri) | of the heavens (l-samāwāti) | and the earth (wal-arḍi), | Who makes (jāʿili) | the Angels (l-malāikati) | messengers (rusulan) | having wings (ulī) | having wings (ajniḥatin) | two (mathnā) | or three (wathulātha) | or four (warubāʿa). | He increases (yazīdu) | in (fī) | the creation (l-khalqi) | what (mā) | He wills (yashāu). | Indeed (inna), | Allah (l-laha) | is on (ʿalā) | every (kulli) | thing (shayin) | All-Powerful (qadīrun).

35:2 What Allah grants to mankind of Mercy, then none can withhold it. And what He withholds, then none can release it thereafter. And He is the All-Mighty, the All-Wise.

What (mā) | Allah grants (yaftaḥi) | Allah grants (l-lahu) | to mankind (lilnnāsi) | of (min) | Mercy (raḥmatin), | then none (falā) | can withhold (mum'sika) | it (lahā). | And what (wamā) | He withholds (yum'sik), | then none (falā) | can release (mur'sila) | it (lahu) | thereafter (min). | thereafter (baʿdihi). | And He (wahuwa) | is the All-Mighty (l-ʿazīzu), | the All-Wise (l-ḥakīmu).

35:3 O mankind! Remember the Favor of Allah upon you. Is there any creator other than Allah who provides for you from the sky and the earth? There is no god but He. Then, how are you deluded?

O (yāayyuhā) | mankind (l-nāsu)! | Remember (udh'kurū) | the Favor (niʿʿmata) | of Allah (l-lahi) | upon you (ʿalaykum). | Is (hal) | there any (min) | creator (khāliqin) | other than Allah (ghayru) | other than Allah (l-lahi) | who provides for you (yarzuqukum) | from (mina) | the sky (l-samāi) | and the earth (wal-arḍi)? | There is no (lā) | god (ilāha) | but (illā) | He (huwa). | Then, how (fa-annā) | are you deluded (tu'fakūna)?

35:4 And if they deny you, then certainly were denied Messengers before you. And to Allah return the matters.

And if (wa-in) | they deny you (yukadhibūka), | then certainly (faqad) | were denied (kudhibat) | Messengers (rusulun) | before you (min). | before you (qablika). | And to (wa-ilā) | Allah (l-lahi) | return (tur'jaʿu) | the matters (l-umūru).

35:5 O mankind! Indeed, the promise of Allah is true. So let not deceive you the life of the world, and let not deceive you about Allah the Deceiver.

O (yāayyuhā) | mankind (l-nāsu)! | Indeed (inna), | the promise (waʿda) | of Allah (l-lahi) | is true (ḥaqqun). | So let not (falā) | deceive you (taghurrannakumu) | the life (l-ḥayatu) | of the world (l-dun'yā), | and let not (walā) | deceive you (yaghurrannakum) | about Allah (bil-lahi) | the Deceiver (l-gharūru).

35:6 Indeed, the Shaitaan is to you an enemy, so take him as an enemy. Only he invites his party that they may be among the companions of the Blaze.

Indeed (inna), | the Shaitaan (l-shayṭāna) | is to you (lakum) | an enemy (ʿaduwwun), | so take him (fa-ittakhidhūhu) | as an enemy (ʿaduwwan). | Only (innamā) | he invites (yadʿū) | his party (ḥiz'bahu) | that they may be (liyakūnū) | among (min) | the companions (aṣḥābi) | of the Blaze (l-saʿīri).

35:7 Those who disbelieve, for them will be a punishment severe, and those who believe and do righteous deeds, for them will be forgiveness and a reward great.

Those who (alladhīna) | disbelieve (kafarū), | for them (lahum) | will be a punishment (ʿadhābun) | severe (shadīdun), | and those (wa-alladhīna) | who believe (āmanū) | and do (waʿamilū) | righteous deeds (l-ṣāliḥāti), | for them (lahum) | will be forgiveness (maghfiratun) | and a reward (wa-ajrun) | great (kabīrun).

35:8 Then is he who - is made fair-seeming to him the evil of his deed - so that he sees it as good? For indeed, Allah lets go astray whom He wills and guides whom He wills. So let not go out your soul for them in regrets. Indeed, Allah is All-Knower of what they do.

Then is he who (afaman)- | is made fair-seeming (zuyyina) | to him (lahu) | the evil (sūu) | of his deed (ʿamalihi)- | so that he sees it (faraāhu) | as good (ḥasanan)? | For indeed (fa-inna), | Allah (l-laha) | lets go astray (yuḍillu) | whom (man) | He wills (yashāu) | and guides (wayahdī) | whom (man) | He wills (yashāu). | So let not (falā) | go out (tadhhab) | your soul (nafsuka) | for them (ʿalayhim) | in regrets (ḥasarātin). | Indeed (inna), | Allah (l-laha) | is All-Knower (ʿalīmun) | of what (bimā) | they do (yaṣnaʿūna).

35:9 And Allah is the One Who sends the winds so that they raise the clouds, and We drive them to a land dead and We revive therewith the earth after its death. Thus will be the Resurrection.

And Allah (wal-lahu) | is the One Who (alladhī) | sends (arsala) | the winds (l-riyāḥa) | so that they raise (fatuthīru) | the clouds (saḥāban), | and We drive them (fasuq'nāhu) | to (ilā) | a land (baladin) | dead (mayyitin) | and We revive (fa-aḥyaynā) | therewith (bihi) | the earth (l-arḍa) | after (baʿda) | its death (mawtihā). | Thus (kadhālika) | will be the Resurrection (l-nushūru).

35:10 Whoever [is] desires the honor, then for Allah is the Honor all. To Him ascends the words good, and the deed righteous raises it. But those who plot the evil, for them is a punishment severe, and the plotting of those - it will perish.

Whoever (man) | [is] desires (kāna) | [is] desires (yurīdu) | the honor (l-ʿizata), | then for Allah (falillahi) | is the Honor (l-ʿizatu) | all (jamīʿan). | To Him (ilayhi) | ascends (yaṣʿadu) | the words (l-kalimu) | good (l-ṭayibu), | and the deed (wal-ʿamalu) | righteous (l-ṣāliḥu) | raises it (yarfaʿuhu). | But those who (wa-alladhīna) | plot (yamkurūna) | the evil (l-sayiāti), | for them (lahum) | is a punishment (ʿadhābun) | severe (shadīdun), | and the plotting (wamakru) | of those (ulāika)- | it (huwa) | will perish (yabūru).

35:11 And Allah created you from dust, then from a semen-drop; then He made you pairs. And not conceives any female and not gives birth except with His knowledge. And not is granted life any aged person and not is lessened from his life but is in a Register. Indeed, that for Allah is easy.

And Allah (wal-lahu) | created you (khalaqakum) | from (min) | dust (turābin), | then (thumma) | from (min) | a semen-drop (nuṭ'fatin); | then (thumma) | He made you (jaʿalakum) | pairs (azwājan). | And not (wamā) | conceives (taḥmilu) | any (min) | female (unthā) | and not (walā) | gives birth (taḍaʿu) | except (illā) | with His knowledge (biʿil'mihi). | And not (wamā) | is granted life (yuʿammaru) | any (min) | aged person (muʿammarin) | and not (walā) | is lessened (yunqaṣu) | from (min) | his life (ʿumurihi) | but (illā) | is in (fī) | a Register (kitābin). | Indeed (inna), | that (dhālika) | for (ʿalā) | Allah (l-lahi) | is easy (yasīrun).

35:12 And not are alike the two seas. This is fresh, sweet, pleasant its drink, and this salty and bitter. And from each you eat meat fresh and you extract ornaments you wear them, and you see the ships in it, cleaving, so that you may seek of His Bounty, and that you may be grateful.

And not (wamā) | are alike (yastawī) | the two seas (l-baḥrāni). | This (hādhā) | is fresh (ʿadhbun), | sweet (furātun), | pleasant (sāighun) | its drink (sharābuhu), | and this (wahādhā) | salty (mil'ḥun) | and bitter (ujājun). | And from (wamin) | each (kullin) | you eat (takulūna) | meat (laḥman) | fresh (ṭariyyan) | and you extract (watastakhrijūna) | ornaments (ḥil'yatan) | you wear them (talbasūnahā), | and you see (watarā) | the ships (l-ful'ka) | in it (fīhi), | cleaving (mawākhira), | so that you may seek (litabtaghū) | of (min) | His Bounty (faḍlihi), | and that you may (walaʿallakum) | be grateful (tashkurūna).

35:13 He causes to enter the night in to the day and He causes to enter the day in to the night, and He has subjected the sun and the moon each running for a term appointed. That is Allah, your Lord, for Him is the Dominion. And those whom you invoke besides Him, not they possess even as much as the membrane of a date-seed.

He causes to enter (yūliju) | the night (al-layla) | in to (fī) | the day (l-nahāri) | and He causes to enter (wayūliju) | the day (l-nahāra) | in to (fī) | the night (al-layli), | and He has subjected (wasakhara) | the sun (l-shamsa) | and the moon (wal-qamara) | each (kullun) | running (yajrī) | for a term (li-ajalin) | appointed (musamman). | That is (dhālikumu) | Allah (l-lahu), | your Lord (rabbukum), | for Him (lahu) | is the Dominion (l-mul'ku). | And those whom (wa-alladhīna) | you invoke (tadʿūna) | besides Him (min), | besides Him (dūnihi), | not (mā) | they possess (yamlikūna) | even (min) | as much as the membrane of a date-seed (qiṭ'mīrin).

35:14 If you invoke them not they hear your call; and if they heard, not they would respond to you. And on the Day of the Resurrection they will deny your association. And none can inform you like the All-Aware.

If (in) | you invoke them (tadʿūhum) | not (lā) | they hear (yasmaʿū) | your call (duʿāakum); | and if (walaw) | they heard (samiʿū), | not (mā) | they would respond (is'tajābū) | to you (lakum). | And on the Day (wayawma) | of the Resurrection (l-qiyāmati) | they will deny (yakfurūna) | your association (bishir'kikum). | And none (walā) | can inform you (yunabbi-uka) | like (mith'lu) | the

All-Aware (khabīrin).

35:15 O mankind! You are those in need of Allah, while Allah, He is Free of need the Praiseworthy.
O (yāayyuhā) | mankind (l-nāsu)! | You (antumu) | are those in need (l-fuqarāu) | of (ilā) | Allah (l-lahi), | while Allah (wal-lahu), | He (huwa) | is Free of need (l-ghaniyu) | the Praiseworthy (l-ḥamīdu).

35:16 If He wills, He can do away with you and bring in a creation new.
If (in) | He wills (yasha), | He can do away with you (yudh'hib'kum) | and bring (wayati) | in a creation (bikhalqin) | new (jadīdin).

35:17 And not that is on Allah difficult.
And not (wamā) | that (dhālika) | is on (ʿalā) | Allah (l-lahi) | difficult (biʿazīzin).

35:18 And not will bear bearer of burdens burden of another. And if calls a heavily laden to carry its load, not will be carried of it anything even if he be near of kin. Only you can warn those who fear their Lord - unseen and establish the prayer. And whoever purifies himself, then only he purifies for his own self. And to Allah is the destination.
And not (walā) | will bear (taziru) | bearer of burdens (wāziratun) | burden (wiz'ra) | of another (ukh'rā). | And if (wa-in) | calls (tadʿu) | a heavily laden (muth'qalatun) | to (ilā) | carry its load (ḥim'lihā), | not (lā) | will be carried (yuḥ'mal) | of it (min'hu) | anything (shayon) | even if (walaw) | he be (kāna) | near of kin (dhā). | near of kin (qur'bā). | Only (innamā) | you can warn (tundhiru) | those who (alladhīna) | fear (yakhshawna) | their Lord (rabbahum)- | unseen (bil-ghaybi) | and establish (wa-aqāmū) | the prayer (l-ṣalata). | And whoever (waman) | purifies himself (tazakkā), | then only (fa-innamā) | he purifies (yatazakkā) | for his own self (linafsihi). | And to (wa-ilā) | Allah (l-lahi) | is the destination (l-maṣīru).

35:19 And not equal are the blind and the seeing,
And not (wamā) | equal (yastawī) | are the blind (l-aʿmā) | and the seeing (wal-baṣīru),

35:20 And not the darkness[es] and not [the] light,
And not (walā) | the darkness[es] (l-ẓulumātu) | and not (walā) | [the] light (l-nūru),

35:21 And not the shade and not the heat,
And not (walā) | the shade (l-ẓilu) | and not (walā) | the heat (l-ḥarūru),

35:22 And not equal are the living and not the dead. Indeed, Allah causes to hear whom He wills, and not you can make hear those who are in the graves.
And not (wamā) | equal (yastawī) | are the living (l-aḥyāu) | and not (walā) | the dead (l-amwātu). | Indeed (inna), | Allah (l-laha) | causes to hear (yus'miʿu) | whom (man) | He wills (yashāu), | and not (wamā) | you (anta) | can make hear (bimus'miʿin) | those who (man) | are in (fī) | the graves (l-qubūri).

35:23 Not you are but a warner.
Not (in) | you are (anta) | but (illā) | a warner (nadhīrun).

35:24 Indeed, We [We] have sent you with the truth, as a bearer of glad tidings and as a warner. And not was any nation but had passed within it a warner.
Indeed, We (innā) | [We] have sent you (arsalnāka) | with the truth (bil-ḥaqi), | as a bearer of glad tidings (bashīran) | and as a warner (wanadhīran). | And not (wa-in) | was any (min) | nation (ummatin) | but (illā) | had passed (khalā) | within it (fīhā) | a warner (nadhīrun).

35:25 And if they deny you, then certainly, denied those who were before them. Came to them their Messengers with clear signs and with Scriptures and with the Book [the] enlightening.

And if (wa-in) | they deny you (yukadhibūka), | then certainly (faqad), | denied (kadhaba) | those who (alladhīna) | were before them (min). | were before them (qablihim). | Came to them (jāathum) | their Messengers (rusuluhum) | with clear signs (bil-bayināti) | and with Scriptures (wabil-zuburi) | and with the Book (wabil-kitābi) | [the] enlightening (l-munīri).

35:26 Then I seized those who disbelieved, and how was My rejection!

Then (thumma) | I seized (akhadhtu) | those who (alladhīna) | disbelieved (kafarū), | and how (fakayfa) | was (kāna) | My rejection (nakīri)!

35:27 Do not you see that Allah sends down from the sky water, then We bring forth therewith fruits of various [their] colors? And in the mountains are tracts, white and red of various [their] colors, and intensely black.

Do not (alam) | you see (tara) | that (anna) | Allah (l-laha) | sends down (anzala) | from (mina) | the sky (l-samāi) | water (māan), | then We bring forth (fa-akhrajnā) | therewith (bihi) | fruits (thamarātin) | of various (mukh'talifan) | [their] colors (alwānuhā)? | And in (wamina) | the mountains (l-jibāli) | are tracts (judadun), | white (bīḍun) | and red (waḥum'run) | of various (mukh'talifun) | [their] colors (alwānuhā), | and intensely black (wagharābību). | and intensely black (sūdun).

35:28 And among men and moving creatures and the cattle are various [their] colors likewise. Only fear Allah among His slaves those who have knowledge. Indeed, Allah is All-Mighty, Oft-Forgiving.

And among (wamina) | men (l-nāsi) | and moving creatures (wal-dawābi) | and the cattle (wal-anʿāmi) | are various (mukh'talifun) | [their] colors (alwānuhu) | likewise (kadhālika). | Only (innamā) | fear (yakhshā) | Allah (l-laha) | among (min) | His slaves (ʿibādihi) | those who have knowledge (l-ʿulamāu). | Indeed (inna), | Allah (l-laha) | is All-Mighty (ʿazīzun), | Oft-Forgiving (ghafūrun).

35:29 Indeed, those who recite the Book of Allah, and establish the prayer and spend out of what We have provided them, secretly and openly, hope for a commerce - never it will perish.

Indeed (inna), | those who (alladhīna) | recite (yatlūna) | the Book (kitāba) | of Allah (l-lahi), | and establish (wa-aqāmū) | the prayer (l-ṣalata) | and spend (wa-anfaqū) | out of what (mimmā) | We have provided them (razaqnāhum), | secretly (sirran) | and openly (waʿalāniyatan), | hope (yarjūna) | for a commerce (tijāratan)- | never (lan) | it will perish (tabūra).

35:30 That He may give them in full their rewards and increase for them of His Bounty. Indeed, He is Oft-Forgiving, Most Appreciative.

That He may give them in full (liyuwaffiyahum) | their rewards (ujūrahum) | and increase for them (wayazīdahum) | of (min) | His Bounty (faḍlihi). | Indeed, He (innahu) | is Oft-Forgiving (ghafūrun), | Most Appreciative (shakūrun).

35:31 And that which We have revealed to you of the Book, it is the truth confirming what was before it. Indeed, Allah of His slaves surely, is All-Aware, All-Seer.

And that which (wa-alladhī) | We have revealed (awḥaynā) | to you (ilayka) | of (mina) | the Book (l-kitābi), | it (huwa) | is the truth (l-ḥaqu) | confirming (muṣaddiqan) | what was (limā) | before it (bayna). | before it (yadayhi). | Indeed (inna), | Allah (l-laha) | of His slaves (biʿibādihi) | surely, is All-Aware (lakhabīrun), | All-Seer (baṣīrun).

35:32 Then We caused to inherit the Book those whom We have chosen of Our slaves; and among them is he who wrongs himself, and among them is he who is moderate, and among them is he who is foremost in good deeds by permission of Allah. That is the Bounty the great.

Then (thumma) | We caused to inherit (awrathnā) | the Book (l-kitāba) | those whom (alladhīna) | We have chosen (iṣ'ṭafaynā) | of (min) | Our slaves (ʿibādinā); | and among them (famin'hum) | is he who wrongs (ẓālimun) | himself (linafsihi), | and among them (wamin'hum) | is he who is moderate (muq'taṣidun), | and among them (wamin'hum) | is he who is foremost (sābiqun) | in good deeds (bil-khayrāti) | by permission (bi-idh'ni) | of Allah (l-lahi). | That (dhālika) | is (huwa) | the Bounty (l-faḍlu) | the great (l-kabīru).

35:33 Gardens of Eternity, they will enter them. They will be adorned therein with bracelets of gold and pearls, and their garments therein will be of silk.

Gardens (jannātu) | of Eternity (ʿadnin), | they will enter them (yadkhulūnahā). | They will be adorned (yuḥallawna) | therein (fīhā) | with (min) | bracelets (asāwira) | of (min) | gold (dhahabin) | and pearls (walu'lu-an), | and their garments (walibāsuhum) | therein (fīhā) | will be of silk (ḥarīrun).

35:34 And they will say, "All praises be to Allah the One Who has removed from us the sorrow. Indeed, our Lord is surely Oft-Forgiving, Most Appreciative,

And they will say (waqālū), | "All praises (l-ḥamdu) | be to Allah (lillahi) | the One Who (alladhī) | has removed (adhhaba) | from us (ʿannā) | the sorrow (l-ḥazana). | Indeed (inna), | our Lord (rabbanā) | is surely Oft-Forgiving (laghafūrun), | Most Appreciative (shakūrun),

35:35 The One Who has settled us in a Home of Eternity out of His Bounty. Not touches us therein any fatigue and not touches therein weariness."

The One Who (alladhī) | has settled us (aḥallanā) | in a Home (dāra) | of Eternity (l-muqāmati) | out of (min) | His Bounty (faḍlihi). | Not (lā) | touches us (yamassunā) | therein (fīhā) | any fatigue (naṣabun) | and not (walā) | touches (yamassunā) | therein (fīhā) | weariness. (lughūbun)"

35:36 And those who disbelieve, for them will be the Fire of Hell. Not is decreed for them that they die, and not will be lightened for them of its torment. Thus We recompense every ungrateful one.

And those who (wa-alladhīna) | disbelieve (kafarū), | for them (lahum) | will be the Fire (nāru) | of Hell (jahannama). | Not (lā) | is decreed (yuq'ḍā) | for them (ʿalayhim) | that they die (fayamūtū), | and not (walā) | will be lightened (yukhaffafu) | for them (ʿanhum) | of (min) | its torment (ʿadhābihā). | Thus (kadhālika) | We recompense (najzī) | every (kulla) | ungrateful one (kafūrin).

35:37 And they will cry therein, "Our Lord! Bring us out; we will do righteous deeds other than that which we used to do." Did not We give you life long enough that would receive admonition therein whoever receives admonition? And came to you the warner. So taste, then not is for the wrongdoers any helper.

And they (wahum) | will cry (yaṣṭarikhūna) | therein (fīhā), | "Our Lord (rabbanā)! | Bring us out (akhrij'nā); | we will do (naʿmal) | righteous deeds (ṣāliḥan) | other than (ghayra) | that which (alladhī) | we used (kunnā) | to do. (naʿmalu)" | Did not (awalam) | We give you life long enough (nuʿammir'kum) | that (mā) | would receive admonition (yatadhakkaru) | therein (fīhi) | whoever (man) | receives admonition (tadhakkara)? | And came to you (wajāakumu) | the warner (l-nadhīru). | So taste (fadhūqū), | then not (famā) | is for the wrongdoers (lilẓẓālimīna) | any (min) | helper (naṣīrin).

35:38 Indeed, Allah is the Knower of the unseen of the heavens and the earth. Indeed, He is the All-Knower of what is in the breasts.

Indeed (inna), | Allah (l-laha) | is the Knower (ʿālimu) | of the unseen (ghaybi) | of the heavens (l-samāwāti) | and the earth (wal-arḍi). | Indeed, He (innahu) | is the All-Knower (ʿalīmun) | of what is in the breasts (bidhāti). | of what is in the breasts (l-ṣudūri).

35:39 He is the One Who made you successors in the earth. And whoever disbelieves, then upon him is his disbelief. And not increase the disbelievers their disbelief near their Lord, except in hatred; and not increase the disbelievers their disbelief except in loss.

He (huwa) | is the One Who (alladhī) | made you (jaʿalakum) | successors (khalāifa) | in (fī) | the earth (l-arḍi). | And whoever (faman) | disbelieves (kafara), | then upon him (faʿalayhi) | is his disbelief (kuf'ruhu). | And not (walā) | increase (yazīdu) | the disbelievers (l-kāfirīna) | their disbelief (kuf'ruhum) | near (ʿinda) | their Lord (rabbihim), | except (illā) | in hatred (maqtan); | and not (walā) | increase (yazīdu) | the disbelievers (l-kāfirīna) | their disbelief (kuf'ruhum) | except (illā) | in loss (khasāran).

35:40 Say, "Have you seen your partners those whom you call besides Allah?" Show Me what they have created from the earth, or for them is a share in the heavens. Or have We given them a Book so they are on a clear proof therefrom? Nay, not promise the wrongdoers some of them to others except delusion.

Say (qul), | "Have you seen (ara-aytum) | your partners (shurakāakumu) | those whom (alladhīna) | you call (tadʿūna) | besides (min) | besides (dūni) | Allah? (l-lahi)" | Show Me (arūnī) | what (mādhā) | they have created (khalaqū) | from (mina) | the earth (l-arḍi), | or (am) | for them (lahum) | is a share (shir'kun) | in (fī) | the heavens (l-samāwāti). | Or (am) | have We given them (ātaynāhum) | a Book (kitāban) | so they (fahum) | are on (ʿalā) | a clear proof (bayyinatin) | therefrom (min'hu)? | Nay (bal), | not (in) | promise (yaʿidu) | the wrongdoers (l-ẓālimūna) | some of them (baʿḍuhum) | to others (baʿḍan) | except (illā) | delusion (ghurūran).

35:41 Indeed, Allah upholds the heavens and the earth, lest they cease. And if they should cease, not can uphold them any one after Him. Indeed, He is Most Forbearing, Oft-Forgiving.

Indeed (inna), | Allah (l-laha) | upholds (yum'siku) | the heavens (l-samāwāti) | and the earth (wal-arḍa), | lest (an) | they cease (tazūlā). | And if (wala-in) | they should cease (zālatā), | not (in) | can uphold them (amsakahumā) | any (min) | one (aḥadin) | after Him (min). | after Him (baʿdihi). | Indeed, He (innahu) | is (kāna) | Most Forbearing (ḥalīman), | Oft-Forgiving (ghafūran).

35:42 And they swore by Allah the strongest of their oaths that if came to them a warner, surely, they would be more guided than any of the nations. But when came to them a warner, not it increased them but in aversion,

And they swore (wa-aqsamū) | by Allah (bil-lahi) | the strongest (jahda) | of their oaths (aymānihim) | that if (la-in) | came to them (jāahum) | a warner (nadhīrun), | surely, they would be (layakūnunna) | more guided (ahdā) | than (min) | any (iḥ'dā) | of the nations (l-umami). | But when (falammā) | came to them (jāahum) | a warner (nadhīrun), | not (mā) | it increased them (zādahum) | but (illā) | in aversion (nufūran),

35:43 Due to arrogance in the land and plotting of the evil; but not encompasses the plot of the evil except its own people. Then do they wait except the way of the former (people)? But never you will find in the way of Allah any change, and never you will find in the way of Allah any alteration.

Due to arrogance (is'tik'bāran) | in (fī) | the land (l-arḍi) | and plotting (wamakra) | of the evil (l-sayi-i); | but not (walā) | encompasses (yaḥīqu) | the plot (l-makru) | of the evil (l-sayi-u) | except (illā) | its own people (bi-ahlihi). | Then do (fahal) | they wait (yanẓurūna) | except (illā) | the way (sunnata) | of the former (people) (l-awalīna)? | But never (falan) | you will find (tajida) | in the way (lisunnati) | of Allah (l-lahi) | any change (tabdīlan), | and never (walan) | you will find (tajida) | in the way (lisunnati) | of Allah (l-lahi) | any alteration (taḥwīlan).

35:44 Have they not traveled in the land and seen how was the end of those who were before them? And they were stronger than them in power. But not is Allah that can escape from Him any thing in the heavens and not in the earth. Indeed, He is All-Knower, All-Powerful.

Have they not (awalam) | traveled (yasīrū) | in (fī) | the land (l-arḍi) | and seen (fayanẓurū) | how (kayfa) | was (kāna) | the end (ʿāqibatu) | of those who (alladhīna) | were before them (min)? | were before them (qablihim)? | And they were (wakānū) | stronger (ashadda) | than them (min'hum) | in power (quwwatan). | But not (wamā) | is (kāna) | Allah (l-lahu) | that can escape from Him (liyuʿʾjizahu) | any (min) | thing (shayin) | in (fī) | the heavens (l-samāwāti) | and not (walā) | in (fī) | the earth (l-arḍi). | Indeed, He (innahu) | is (kāna) | All-Knower (ʿalīman), | All-Powerful (qadīran).

35:45 And if Allah were to punish the people for what they have earned, not He would leave on its back any creature. But He gives them respite till a term appointed. And when comes their term, then indeed, Allah is of His slaves All-Seer.

And if (walaw) | Allah were to punish (yuākhidhu) | Allah were to punish (l-lahu) | the people (l-nāsa) | for what (bimā) | they have earned (kasabū), | not (mā) | He would leave (taraka) | on (ʿalā) | its back (ẓahrihā) | any (min) | creature (dābbatin). | But (walākin) | He gives them respite (yu-akhiruhum) | till (ilā) | a term (ajalin) | appointed (musamman). | And when (fa-idhā) | comes (jāa) | their term (ajaluhum), | then indeed (fa-inna), | Allah (l-laha) | is (kāna) | of His slaves (biʿibādihi) | All-Seer (baṣīran).

Chapter (36) Sūrat Yā Sīn

36:1 Ya Seen.

Ya Seen (ya-seen).

36:2 By the Quran the Wise.

By the Quran (wal-qur'āni) | the Wise (l-ḥakīmi).

36:3 Indeed, you are among the Messengers,

Indeed, you (innaka) | are among (lamina) | the Messengers (l-mur'salīna),

36:4 On a Path Straight.

On (ʿalā) | a Path (ṣirāṭin) | Straight (mus'taqīmin).

36:5 A revelation of the All-Mighty, the Most Merciful,

A revelation (tanzīla) | of the All-Mighty (l-ʿazīzi), | the Most Merciful (l-raḥīmi),

36:6 That you may warn a people not were warned their forefathers, so they are heedless.

That you may warn (litundhira) | a people (qawman) | not (mā) | were warned (undhira) | their forefathers (ābāuhum), | so they (fahum) | are heedless (ghāfilūna).

36:7 Certainly, has proved true the word upon most of them so they do not believe.

Certainly (laqad), | has proved true (ḥaqqa) | the word (l-qawlu) | upon (ʿalā) | most of them (aktharihim) | so they (fahum) | do not (lā) | believe (yu'minūna).

36:8 Indeed, We [We] have placed on their necks iron collars, and they are up to the chins, so they are with heads raised up.

Indeed, We (innā) | [We] have placed (jaʿalnā) | on (fī) | their necks (aʿnāqihim) | iron collars (aghlālan), | and they (fahiya) | are up to (ilā) | the chins (l-adhqāni), | so they (fahum) | are with heads raised up (muq'maḥūna).

36:9 And We have made before them a barrier and behind them a barrier. and We covered them, so they do not see.

And We have made (wajaʿalnā) | before them (min) | before them (bayni) | before them (aydīhim) | a barrier (saddan) | and behind them (wamin) | and behind them (khalfihim) | a barrier (saddan). | and We covered them (fa-aghshaynāhum), | so they (fahum) | do not (lā) | see (yub'ṣirūna).

36:10 And it is same to them whether you warn them or do not warn them, not they will believe.

And it is same (wasawāon) | to them (ʿalayhim) | whether you warn them (a-andhartahum) | or (am) | do not (lam) | warn them (tundhir'hum), | not (lā) | they will believe (yu'minūna).

36:11 Only you can warn him who follows the Reminder and fears the Most Gracious in the unseen. So give him glad tidings of forgiveness and a reward noble.

Only (innamā) | you can warn (tundhiru) | him who (mani) | follows (ittabaʿa) | the Reminder (l-dhik'ra) | and fears (wakhashiya) | the Most Gracious (l-raḥmāna) | in the unseen (bil-ghaybi). | So give him glad tidings (fabashir'hu) | of forgiveness (bimaghfiratin) | and a reward (wa-ajrin) | noble (karīmin).

36:12 Indeed, We [We] [We] give life to the dead and We record what they have sent before and their footprints, and every thing We have enumerated it in a Register clear.

Indeed, We (innā) | [We] (naḥnu) | [We] give life (nuḥ'yī) | to the dead (l-mawtā) | and We record (wanaktubu) | what (mā) | they have sent before (qaddamū) | and their footprints (waāthārahum), | and every (wakulla) | thing (shayin) | We have enumerated it (aḥṣaynāhu) | in (fī) | a Register (imāmin) | clear (mubīnin).

36:13 And set forth to them an example of the companions of the city, when came to it the Messengers,

And set forth (wa-iḍ'rib) | to them (lahum) | an example (mathalan) | of the companions (aṣḥāba) | of the city (l-qaryati), | when (idh) | came to it (jāahā) | the Messengers (l-mur'salūna),

36:14 When We sent to them two Messengers but they denied both of them, so We strengthened them with a third, and they said, "Indeed, We to you are Messengers."

When (idh) | We sent (arsalnā) | to them (ilayhimu) | two Messengers (ith'nayni) | but they denied both of them (fakadhabūhumā), | so We strengthened them (faʿazzaznā) | with a third (bithālithin), | and they said (faqālū), | "Indeed, We (innā) | to you (ilaykum) | are Messengers. (mur'salūna)"

36:15 They said, "Not you are but human beings like us, and not has revealed the Most Gracious any thing. Not you are but lying."

They said (qālū), | "Not (mā) | you (antum) | are but (illā) | human beings (basharun) | like us (mith'lunā), | and not (wamā) | has revealed (anzala) | the Most Gracious (l-raḥmānu) | any (min) | thing (shayin). | Not (in) | you (antum) | are but (illā) | lying. (takdhibūna)"

36:16 They said, "Our Lord, knows that we to you are surely Messengers,

They said (qālū), | "Our Lord (rabbunā), | knows (yaʿlamu) | that we (innā) | to you (ilaykum) | are surely Messengers (lamur'salūna),

36:17 And not is on us except the conveyance clear."

And not (wamā) | is on us (ʿalaynā) | except (illā) | the conveyance (l-balāghu) | clear. (l-mubīnu)"

36:18 They said, "Indeed, we [we] see an evil omen from you. If not you desist, surely, we will stone you, and surely will touch you from us a punishment painful."

They said (qālū), | "Indeed, we (innā) | [we] see an evil omen (taṭayyarnā) | from you (bikum). | If (la-in) | not (lam) | you desist (tantahū), | surely, we will stone you (lanarjumannakum), | and surely will touch you (walayamassannakum) | from us (minnā) | a punishment (ʿadhābun) | painful. (alīmun)"

36:19 They said, "Your evil omen be with you! Is it because you are admonished? Nay, you are a people transgressing."

They said (qālū), | "Your evil omen (ṭāirukum) | be with you (maʿakum)! | Is it because (a-in) | you are admonished (dhukkir'tum)? | Nay (bal), | you (antum) | are a people (qawmun) | transgressing. (mus'rifūna)"

36:20 And came from the farthest end of the city a man running. He said, "O my People! Follow the Messengers.

And came (wajāa) | from (min) | the farthest end (aqṣā) | of the city (l-madīnati) | a man (rajulun) | running (yasʿā). | He said (qāla), | "O my People (yāqawmi)! | Follow (ittabiʿū) | the Messengers (l-mur'salīna).

36:21 Follow those who do not ask of you any payment, and they are rightly guided.

Follow (ittabiʿū) | those who (man) | do not (lā) | ask of you (yasalukum) | any payment (ajran), | and they (wahum) | are rightly guided (muh'tadūna).

36:22 And what is for me that not I worship the One Who created me and to Whom you will be returned?

And what (wamā) | is for me (liya) | that not (lā) | I worship (aʿbudu) | the One Who (alladhī) | created me (faṭaranī) | and to Whom (wa-ilayhi) | you will be returned (tur'jaʿūna)?

36:23 Should I take besides Him gods? If intends for me the Most Gracious any harm not will avail [from] me their intercession in anything, and not they can save me.

Should I take (a-attakhidhu) | besides Him (min) | besides Him (dūnihi) | gods (ālihatan)? | If (in) | intends for me (yurid'ni) | the Most Gracious (l-raḥmānu) | any harm (biḍurrin) | not (lā) | will avail (tugh'ni) | [from] me (ʿannī) | their intercession (shafāʿatuhum) | in anything (shayan), | and not (walā) | they can save me (yunqidhūni).

36:24 Indeed, I then surely would be in an error clear.

Indeed, I (innī) | then (idhan) | surely would be in (lafī) | an error (ḍalālin) | clear (mubīnin).

36:25 Indeed, I [I] have believed in your Lord, so listen to me."

Indeed, I (innī) | [I] have believed (āmantu) | in your Lord (birabbikum), | so listen to me. (fa-is'maʿūni)"

36:26 It was said, "Enter Paradise." He said, "I wish my people knew

It was said (qīla), | "Enter (ud'khuli) | Paradise. (l-janata)" | He said (qāla), | "I wish (yālayta) | my people (qawmī) | knew (yaʿlamūna)

36:27 Of how has forgiven me my Lord and placed me among the honored ones."

Of how (bimā) | has forgiven (ghafara) | me (lī) | my Lord (rabbī) | and placed me (wajaʿalanī) | among (mina) | the honored ones. (l-muk'ramīna)"

36:28 And not We sent down upon his people after him any host from the heaven, and not were We to send down.

And not (wamā) | We sent down (anzalnā) | upon (ʿalā) | his people (qawmihi) | after him (min) | after him (baʿdihi) | any (min) | host (jundin) | from (mina) | the heaven (l-samāi), | and not (wamā) | were We (kunnā) | to send down (munzilīna).

36:29 Not it was but a shout one then behold! They were extinguished.

Not (in) | it was (kānat) | but (illā) | a shout (ṣayḥatan) | one (wāḥidatan) | then behold (fa-idhā)! | They (hum) | were extinguished (khāmidūna).

36:30 Alas for the servants! Not came to them any Messenger but they did mock at him.

Alas (yāḥasratan) | for (ʿalā) | the servants (l-ʿibādi)! | Not (mā) | came to them (yatīhim) | any (min) | Messenger (rasūlin) | but (illā) | they did (kānū) | mock at him (bihi). | mock at him (yastahziūna).

36:31 Do not they see how many We destroyed before them of the generations? That they to them will not return.

Do not (alam) | they see (yaraw) | how many (kam) | We destroyed (ahlaknā) | before them (qablahum) | of (mina) | the generations (l-qurūni)? | That they (annahum) | to them (ilayhim) | will not return (lā). | will not return (yarjiʿūna).

36:32 And surely all then together, before Us will be brought.

And surely (wa-in) | all (kullun) | then (lammā) | together (jamīʿun), | before Us (ladaynā) | will be brought (muḥ'ḍarūna).

36:33 And a Sign for them is the earth dead. We give it life and We bring forth from it grain, and from it they eat.

And a Sign (waāyatun) | for them (lahumu) | is the earth (l-arḍu) | dead (l-maytatu). | We give it life (aḥyaynāhā) | and We bring forth (wa-akhrajnā) | from it (min'hā) | grain (ḥabban), | and from it (famin'hu) | they eat (yakulūna).

36:34 And We placed therein gardens of date-palms and grapevines, and We caused to gush forth in it of the springs,

And We placed (wajaʿalnā) | therein (fīhā) | gardens (jannātin) | of (min) | date-palms (nakhīlin) | and grapevines (wa-aʿnābin), | and We caused to gush forth (wafajjarnā) | in it (fīhā) | of (mina) | the springs (l-ʿuyūni),

36:35 That they may eat of its fruit. And not made it their hands. So will not they be grateful?

That they may eat (liyakulū) | of (min) | its fruit (thamarihi). | And not (wamā) | made it (ʿamilathu) | their hands (aydīhim). | So will not (afalā) | they be grateful (yashkurūna)?

36:36 Glory be to the One Who created in pairs all of what grows the earth and of themselves, and of what not they know.

Glory be (sub'ḥāna) | to the One Who (alladhī) | created (khalaqa) | in pairs (l-azwāja) | all (kullahā) | of what (mimmā) | grows (tunbitu) | the earth (l-arḍu) | and of (wamin) | themselves (anfusihim), | and of what (wamimmā) | not (lā) | they know (yaʿlamūna).

36:37 And a Sign for them is the night. We withdraw from it the day. Then behold! They are those in darkness.

And a Sign (waāyatun) | for them (lahumu) | is the night (al-laylu). | We withdraw (naslakhu) | from it (min'hu) | the day (l-nahāra). | Then behold (fa-idhā)! | They (hum) | are those in darkness (muẓ'limūna).

36:38 And the sun runs to a term appointed for it. That is the Decree of the All-Mighty, the All-Knowing.

And the sun (wal-shamsu) | runs (tajrī) | to a term appointed (limus'taqarrin) | for it (lahā). | That (dhālika) | is the Decree (taqdīru) | of the All-Mighty (l-ʿazīzi), | the All-Knowing (l-ʿalīmi).

36:39 And the moon - We have ordained for it phases until, it returns like the date stalk, the old.

And the moon (wal-qamara)- | We have ordained for it (qaddarnāhu) | phases (manāzila) | until (ḥattā), | it returns (ʿāda) | like the date stalk (kal-ʿur'jūni), | the old (l-qadīmi).

36:40 Not the sun is permitted for it - that it overtakes the moon, and not the night can outstrip the day, but all in an orbit they are floating.

Not (lā) | the sun (l-shamsu) | is permitted (yanbaghī) | for it (lahā)- | that (an) | it overtakes (tud'rika) | the moon (l-qamara), | and not (walā) | the night (al-laylu) | can outstrip (sābiqu) | the day (l-nahāri), | but all (wakullun) | in (fī) | an orbit (falakin) | they are floating (yasbaḥūna).

36:41 And a Sign for them is that We carried their offspring in the ship laden.

And a Sign (waāyatun) | for them (lahum) | is that (annā) | We carried (ḥamalnā) | their offspring (dhurriyyatahum) | in (fī) | the ship (l-ful'ki) | laden (l-mashḥūni).

36:42 And We created for them from the likes of it what they ride.

And We created (wakhalaqnā) | for them (lahum) | from (min) | the likes of it (mith'lihi) | what (mā) | they ride (yarkabūna).

36:43 And if We will, We could drown them; then not would be a responder to a cry for them, and not they would be saved,

And if (wa-in) | We will (nasha), | We could drown them (nugh'riq'hum); | then not (falā) | would be a responder to a cry (ṣarīkha) | for them (lahum), | and not (walā) | they (hum) | would be saved (yunqadhūna),

36:44 Except by Mercy from Us and provision for a time.

Except (illā) | by Mercy (raḥmatan) | from Us (minnā) | and provision (wamatāʿan) | for (ilā) | a time (ḥīnin).

36:45 And when it is said to them, "Fear what is before you and what is behind you so that you may receive mercy."

And when (wa-idhā) | it is said (qīla) | to them (lahumu), | "Fear (ittaqū) | what (mā) | is before you (bayna) | is before you (aydīkum) | and what (wamā) | is behind you (khalfakum) | so that you may (laʿallakum) | receive mercy. (tur'ḥamūna)"

36:46 And not comes to them of a Sign from the Signs of their Lord, but they from it turn away.

And not (wamā) | comes to them (tatīhim) | of (min) | a Sign (āyatin) | from (min) | the Signs (āyāti) | of their Lord (rabbihim), | but (illā) | they (kānū) | from it (ʿanhā) | turn away (muʿ'riḍīna).

36:47 And when it is said to them, "Spend from what has provided you Allah." Said those who disbelieved to those who believed, "Should we feed whom if Allah willed - He would have fed him?" Not are you except in an error clear.

And when (wa-idhā) | it is said (qīla) | to them (lahum), | "Spend (anfiqū) | from what (mimmā) | has provided you (razaqakumu) | Allah. (l-lahu)" | Said (qāla) | those who (alladhīna) | disbelieved (kafarū) | to those who (lilladhīna) | believed (āmanū), | "Should we feed (anuṭ'ʿimu) |

whom (man) | if (law) | Allah willed (yashāu)- | Allah willed (l-lahu)- | He would have fed him? (aṭʿamahu)" | Not (in) | are you (antum) | except (illā) | in (fī) | an error (ḍalālin) | clear (mubīnin).

36:48 And they say, "When is this promise, if you are truthful?"
And they say (wayaqūlūna), | "When is (matā) | this (hādhā) | promise (l-waʿdu), | if (in) | you are (kuntum) | truthful? (ṣādiqīna)"

36:49 Not they await except a shout one, it will seize them while they are disputing.
Not (mā) | they await (yanẓurūna) | except (illā) | a shout (ṣayḥatan) | one (wāḥidatan), | it will seize them (takhudhuhum) | while they (wahum) | are disputing (yakhiṣṣimūna).

36:50 Then not they will be able to make a will, and not to their people they can return.
Then not (falā) | they will be able (yastaṭīʿūna) | to make a will (tawṣiyatan), | and not (walā) | to (ilā) | their people (ahlihim) | they can return (yarjiʿūna).

36:51 And will be blown [in] the trumpet, and behold! They from the graves to their Lord [they] will hasten.
And will be blown (wanufikha) | [in] (fī) | the trumpet (l-ṣūri), | and behold (fa-idhā)! | They (hum) | from (mina) | the graves (l-ajdāthi) | to (ilā) | their Lord (rabbihim) | [they] will hasten (yansilūna).

36:52 They [will] say, "O woe to us! Who has raised us from our sleeping place?" "This is what had promised the Most Gracious, and told the truth the Messengers."
They [will] say (qālū), | "O woe to us (yāwaylanā)! | Who (man) | has raised us (baʿathanā) | from (min) | our sleeping place? (marqadinā)" | "This is (hādhā) | what (mā) | had promised (waʿada) | the Most Gracious (l-raḥmānu), | and told the truth (waṣadaqa) | the Messengers. (l-mur'salūna)"

36:53 Not it will be but a shout single, so behold! They all before Us will be brought.
Not (in) | it will be (kānat) | but (illā) | a shout (ṣayḥatan) | single (wāḥidatan), | so behold (fa-idhā)! | They (hum) | all (jamīʿun) | before Us (ladaynā) | will be brought (muḥ'ḍarūna).

36:54 So this Day not will be wronged a soul in anything and not you will be recompensed except for what you used to do.
So this Day (fal-yawma) | not (lā) | will be wronged (tuẓ'lamu) | a soul (nafsun) | in anything (shayan) | and not (walā) | you will be recompensed (tuj'zawna) | except (illā) | for what (mā) | you used to (kuntum) | do (taʿmalūna).

36:55 Indeed, the companions of Paradise this Day [in] will be occupied in amusement,
Indeed (inna), | the companions (aṣḥāba) | of Paradise (l-janati) | this Day (l-yawma) | [in] (fī) | will be occupied (shughulin) | in amusement (fākihūna),

36:56 They and their spouses in shades, on [the] couches reclining.
They (hum) | and their spouses (wa-azwājuhum) | in (fī) | shades (ẓilālin), | on (ʿalā) | [the] couches (l-arāiki) | reclining (muttakiūna).

36:57 For them therein are fruits, and for them is whatever they call for.
For them (lahum) | therein (fīhā) | are fruits (fākihatun), | and for them (walahum) | is whatever (mā) | they call for (yaddaʿūna).

36:58 "Peace." A word from a Lord Most Merciful.
"Peace. (salāmun)" | A word (qawlan) | from (min) | a Lord (rabbin) | Most Merciful

(raḥīmin).

36:59 "But stand apart today O criminals!
"But stand apart (wa-im'tāzū) | today (l-yawma) | O criminals (ayyuhā)! | O criminals (l-muj'rimūna)!

36:60 Did not I enjoin upon you O Children of Adam! That do not worship the Shaitaan, indeed, he is for you an enemy clear,
Did not (alam) | I enjoin (aʿhad) | upon you (ilaykum) | O Children of Adam (yābanī)! | O Children of Adam (ādama)! | That (an) | do not (lā) | worship (taʿbudū) | the Shaitaan (l-shayṭāna), | indeed, he (innahu) | is for you (lakum) | an enemy (ʿaduwwun) | clear (mubīnun),

36:61 And that you worship Me? This is a Path Straight.
And that (wa-ani) | you worship Me (uʿ'budūnī)? | This (hādhā) | is a Path (ṣirāṭun) | Straight (mus'taqīmun).

36:62 And indeed, he led astray from you a multitude great. Then did not you use reason?
And indeed (walaqad), | he led astray (aḍalla) | from you (minkum) | a multitude (jibillan) | great (kathīran). | Then did not (afalam) | you (takūnū) | use reason (taʿqilūna)?

36:63 This is the Hell which you were promised.
This is (hādhihi) | the Hell (jahannamu) | which (allatī) | you were (kuntum) | promised (tūʿadūna).

36:64 Burn therein today because you used to disbelieve."
Burn therein (iṣ'lawhā) | today (l-yawma) | because (bimā) | you used to (kuntum) | disbelieve. (takfurūna)"

36:65 This Day We will seal [on] their mouths, and will speak to Us their hands, and will bear witness their feet about what they used to earn.
This Day (al-yawma) | We will seal (nakhtimu) | [on] (ʿalā) | their mouths (afwāhihim), | and will speak to Us (watukallimunā) | their hands (aydīhim), | and will bear witness (watashhadu) | their feet (arjuluhum) | about what (bimā) | they used to (kānū) | earn (yaksibūna).

36:66 And if We willed, We would have surely obliterated [over] their eyes, then they would race to find the path, then how could they see?
And if (walaw) | We willed (nashāu), | We would have surely obliterated (laṭamasnā) | [over] (ʿalā) | their eyes (aʿyunihim), | then they would race (fa-is'tabaqū) | to find the path (l-ṣirāṭa), | then how (fa-annā) | could they see (yub'ṣirūna)?

36:67 And if We willed surely, We would have transformed them in their places then not they would have been able to proceed and not return.
And if (walaw) | We willed (nashāu) | surely, We would have transformed them (lamasakhnāhum) | in (ʿalā) | their places (makānatihim) | then not (famā) | they would have been able (is'taṭāʿū) | to proceed (muḍiyyan) | and not (walā) | return (yarjiʿūna).

36:68 And he whom We grant him long life, We reverse him in the creation. Then will not they use intellect?
And he whom (waman) | We grant him long life (nuʿammir'hu), | We reverse him (nunakkis'hu) | in (fī) | the creation (l-khalqi). | Then will not (afalā) | they use intellect (yaʿqilūna)?

36:69 And not We taught him [the] poetry, and not it is befitting for him. Not it is except a Reminder and a Quran clear,

And not (wamā) | We taught him (ʿallamnāhu) | [the] poetry (l-shiʿra), | and not (wamā) | it is befitting (yanbaghī) | for him (lahu). | Not (in) | it (huwa) | is except (illā) | a Reminder (dhik'run) | and a Quran (waqur'ānun) | clear (mubīnun),

36:70 To warn him who is alive and may be proved true the Word against the disbelievers.

To warn (liyundhira) | him who (man) | is (kāna) | alive (ḥayyan) | and may be proved true (wayaḥiqqa) | the Word (l-qawlu) | against (ʿalā) | the disbelievers (l-kāfirīna).

36:71 Do not they see that We [We] created for them from what have made Our hands, cattle, then they [for them] are the owners?

Do not (awalam) | they see (yaraw) | that We (annā) | [We] created (khalaqnā) | for them (lahum) | from what (mimmā) | have made (ʿamilat) | Our hands (aydīnā), | cattle (anʿāman), | then they (fahum) | [for them] (lahā) | are the owners (mālikūna)?

36:72 And We have tamed them for them, so some of them - they ride them, and some of them they eat.

And We have tamed them (wadhallalnāhā) | for them (lahum), | so some of them (famin'hā)- | they ride them (rakūbuhum), | and some of them (wamin'hā) | they eat (yakulūna).

36:73 And for them therein are benefits and drinks, so will not they give thanks?

And for them (walahum) | therein (fīhā) | are benefits (manāfiʿu) | and drinks (wamashāribu), | so will not (afalā) | they give thanks (yashkurūna)?

36:74 But they have taken besides Allah gods, that they may be helped.

But they have taken (wa-ittakhadhū) | besides (min) | besides (dūni) | Allah (l-lahi) | gods (ālihatan), | that they may (laʿallahum) | be helped (yunṣarūna).

36:75 Not they are able to help them, but they - for them are hosts who will be brought.

Not (lā) | they are able (yastaṭīʿūna) | to help them (naṣrahum), | but they (wahum)- | for them (lahum) | are hosts (jundun) | who will be brought (muḥ'ḍarūna).

36:76 So let not grieve you their speech. Indeed, We [We] know what they conceal and what they declare.

So let not (falā) | grieve you (yaḥzunka) | their speech (qawluhum). | Indeed, We (innā) | [We] know (naʿlamu) | what (mā) | they conceal (yusirrūna) | and what (wamā) | they declare (yuʿ'linūna).

36:77 Does not see [the] man that We [We] created him from a semen-drop Then behold! He is an opponent clear.

Does not (awalam) | see (yara) | [the] man (l-insānu) | that We (annā) | [We] created him (khalaqnāhu) | from (min) | a semen-drop (nuṭ'fatin) | Then behold (fa-idhā)! | He (huwa) | is an opponent (khaṣīmun) | clear (mubīnun).

36:78 And he sets forth for Us an example and forgets his own creation. He says, "Who will give life to the bones while they are decomposed?"

And he sets forth (waḍaraba) | for Us (lanā) | an example (mathalan) | and forgets (wanasiya) | his own creation (khalqahu). | He says (qāla), | "Who (man) | will give life (yuḥ'yī) | to the bones (l-ʿiẓāma) | while they (wahiya) | are decomposed? (ramīmun)"

36:79 Say, "He will give them life Who produced them the first time; and He is of every creation All-Knower."

Say (qul), | "He will give them life (yuḥ'yīhā) | Who (alladhī) | produced them (ansha-ahā) | the first (awwala) | time (marratin); | and He (wahuwa) | is of every (bikulli) | creation (khalqin) | All-Knower. (ʿalīmun)"

36:80 The One Who made for you from the tree [the] green - fire, and behold! You from it ignite.

The One Who (alladhī) | made (jaʿala) | for you (lakum) | from (mina) | the tree (l-shajari) | [the] green (l-akhḍari)- | fire (nāran), | and behold (fa-idhā)! | You (antum) | from it (min'hu) | ignite (tūqidūna).

36:81 Is it not He Who created the heavens and the earth Able to [that] create the like of them. Yes, indeed! and He is the Supreme Creator, the All-Knower.

Is it not (awalaysa) | He Who (alladhī) | created (khalaqa) | the heavens (l-samāwāti) | and the earth (wal-arḍa) | Able (biqādirin) | to (ʿalā) | [that] (an) | create (yakhluqa) | the like of them (mith'lahum). | Yes, indeed (balā)! | and He (wahuwa) | is the Supreme Creator (l-khalāqu), | the All-Knower (l-ʿalīmu).

36:82 Only His Command when He intends a thing that He says to it, "Be," and it is.

Only (innamā) | His Command (amruhu) | when (idhā) | He intends (arāda) | a thing (shayan) | that (an) | He says (yaqūla) | to it (lahu), | "Be, (kun)" | and it is (fayakūnu).

36:83 So glory be to the One who in Whose hand is the dominion of all things, and to Him you will be returned.

So glory be (fasub'ḥāna) | to the One who (alladhī) | in Whose hand (biyadihi) | is the dominion (malakūtu) | of all (kulli) | things (shayin), | and to Him (wa-ilayhi) | you will be returned (tur'jaʿūna).

Chapter (37) Sūrat l-Ṣāfāt (Those Ranges in Ranks)

37:1 By those lined in rows,

By those lined (wal-ṣāfāti) | in rows (ṣaffan),

37:2 And those who drive strongly,

And those who drive (fal-zājirāti) | strongly (zajran),

37:3 And those who recite the Message,

And those who recite (fal-tāliyāti) | the Message (dhik'ran),

37:4 Indeed, your Lord is surely One,

Indeed (inna), | your Lord (ilāhakum) | is surely One (lawāḥidun),

37:5 Lord of the heavens and the earth, and what is between both of them and Lord of each point of sunrise.

Lord (rabbu) | of the heavens (l-samāwāti) | and the earth (wal-arḍi), | and what (wamā) | is between both of them (baynahumā) | and Lord (warabbu) | of each point of sunrise (l-mashāriqi).

37:6 Indeed, We [We] adorned the sky [the world] with an adornment of the stars.

Indeed, We (innā) | [We] adorned (zayyannā) | the sky (l-samāa) | [the world] (l-dun'yā) | with an adornment (bizīnatin) | of the stars (l-kawākibi).

37:7 And to guard against every devil rebellious,

And to guard (waḥif'ẓan) | against (min) | every (kulli) | devil (shayṭānin) | rebellious (māridin),

37:8 Not they may listen to the assembly [the] exalted, are pelted from every side,

Not (lā) | they may listen (yassammaʿūna) | to (ilā) | the assembly (l-mala-i) | [the] exalted (l-aʿlā), | are pelted (wayuq'dhafūna) | from (min) | every (kulli) | side (jānibin),

37:9 Repelled; and for them is a punishment perpetual,

Repelled (duḥūran); | and for them (walahum) | is a punishment (ʿadhābun) | perpetual (wāṣibun),

37:10 Except him who snatches by theft but follows him a burning flame, piercing.

Except (illā) | him who (man) | snatches (khaṭifa) | by theft (l-khaṭfata) | but follows him (fa-atbaʿahu) | a burning flame (shihābun), | piercing (thāqibun).

37:11 Then ask them, "Are they a stronger creation or those whom We have created?" Indeed, We created them from a clay sticky.

Then ask them (fa-is'taftihim), | "Are they (ahum) | a stronger (ashaddu) | creation (khalqan) | or (am) | those whom (man) | We have created? (khalaqnā)" | Indeed, We (innā) | created them (khalaqnāhum) | from (min) | a clay (ṭīnin) | sticky (lāzibin).

37:12 Nay, you wonder, while they mock.

Nay (bal), | you wonder (ʿajib'ta), | while they mock (wayaskharūna).

37:13 And when they are reminded, not they receive admonition.

And when (wa-idhā) | they are reminded (dhukkirū), | not (lā) | they receive admonition (yadhkurūna).

37:14 And when they see a Sign, they mock,

And when (wa-idhā) | they see (ra-aw) | a Sign (āyatan), | they mock (yastaskhirūna),

37:15 And they say, "Not is this except a magic clear.

And they say (waqālū), | "Not (in) | is this (hādhā) | except (illā) | a magic (siḥ'run) | clear (mubīnun).

37:16 Is it when we are dead and have become dust and bones, shall we then be certainly resurrected,

Is it when (a-idhā) | we are dead (mit'nā) | and have become (wakunnā) | dust (turāban) | and bones (waʿiẓāman), | shall we then (a-innā) | be certainly resurrected (lamabʿūthūna),

37:17 Or our fathers former?"

Or our fathers (awaābāunā) | former? (l-awalūna)"

37:18 Say, "Yes, and you will be humiliated."

Say (qul), | "Yes (naʿam), | and you (wa-antum) | will be humiliated. (dākhirūna)"

37:19 Then only it will be a cry single, then, behold! They will see.
Then only (fa-innamā) | it (hiya) | will be a cry (zajratun) | single (wāḥidatun), | then, behold (fa-idhā)! | They (hum) | will see (yanẓurūna).

37:20 And they will say, "O woe to us! This is the Day of the Recompense."
And they will say (waqālū), | "O woe to us (yāwaylanā)! | This (hādhā) | is the Day (yawmu) | of the Recompense. (l-dīni)"

37:21 "This is the Day of Judgment which you used to [of it] deny."
"This (hādhā) | is the Day (yawmu) | of Judgment (l-faṣli) | which (alladhī) | you used to (kuntum) | [of it] (bihi) | deny. (tukadhibūna)"

37:22 Gather those who wronged, and their kinds and what they used to worship
Gather (uḥ'shurū) | those who (alladhīna) | wronged (ẓalamū), | and their kinds (wa-azwājahum) | and what (wamā) | they used to (kānū) | worship (yaʿbudūna)

37:23 Besides Allah, then lead them to the Path of the Hellfire.
Besides (min) | Besides (dūni) | Allah (l-lahi), | then lead them (fa-ih'dūhum) | to (ilā) | the Path (ṣirāṭi) | of the Hellfire (l-jaḥīmi).

37:24 And stop them; indeed, they are to be questioned."
And stop them (waqifūhum); | indeed, they (innahum) | are to be questioned. (masūlūna)"

37:25 "What is for you? Why not you help one another?"
"What (mā) | is for you (lakum)? | Why not (lā) | you help one another? (tanāṣarūna)"

37:26 Nay, they on that Day will surrender.
Nay (bal), | they (humu) | on that Day (l-yawma) | will surrender (mus'taslimūna).

37:27 And will approach some of them to others questioning one another.
And will approach (wa-aqbala) | some of them (baʿḍuhum) | to (ʿalā) | others (baʿḍin) | questioning one another (yatasāalūna).

37:28 They will say, "Indeed, you [you] used to come to us from the right."
They will say (qālū), | "Indeed, you (innakum) | [you] used to (kuntum) | come to us (tatūnanā) | from (ʿani) | the right. (l-yamīni)"

37:29 They will say, "Nay, not you were believers,
They will say (qālū), | "Nay (bal), | not (lam) | you were (takūnū) | believers (mu'minīna),

37:30 And not was for us over you any authority. Nay, you were a people transgressing.
And not (wamā) | was (kāna) | for us (lanā) | over you (ʿalaykum) | any (min) | authority (sul'ṭānin). | Nay (bal), | you were (kuntum) | a people (qawman) | transgressing (ṭāghīna).

37:31 So has been proved true against us the Word of our Lord; indeed, we will certainly taste.
So has been proved true (faḥaqqa) | against us (ʿalaynā) | the Word (qawlu) | of our Lord (rabbinā); | indeed, we (innā) | will certainly taste (ladhāiqūna).

37:32 So we led you astray; indeed, we were astray."
So we led you astray (fa-aghwaynākum); | indeed, we (innā) | were (kunnā) | astray.

(ghāwīna)"

37:33 Then indeed, they that Day in the punishment will be sharers.
Then indeed, they (fa-innahum) | that Day (yawma-idhin) | in (fī) | the punishment (l-ʿadhābi) | will be sharers (mush'tarikūna).

37:34 Indeed, We thus, We deal with the criminals.
Indeed, We (innā) | thus (kadhālika), | We deal (nafʿalu) | with the criminals (bil-muj'rimīna).

37:35 Indeed, they were, when it was said to them, "There is no god except Allah," were arrogant
Indeed, they (innahum) | were (kānū), | when (idhā) | it was said (qīla) | to them (lahum), | "There is no (lā) | god (ilāha) | except (illā) | Allah, (l-lahu)" | were arrogant (yastakbirūna)

37:36 And they say, "Are we to leave our gods for a poet mad?"
And they say (wayaqūlūna), | "Are we (a-innā) | to leave (latārikū) | our gods (ālihatinā) | for a poet (lishāʿirin) | mad? (majnūnin)"

37:37 Nay, he has brought the truth and confirmed the Messengers.
Nay (bal), | he has brought (jāa) | the truth (bil-ḥaqi) | and confirmed (waṣaddaqa) | the Messengers (l-mur'salīna).

37:38 Indeed, you will surely taste the punishment painful,
Indeed, you (innakum) | will surely taste (ladhāiqū) | the punishment (l-ʿadhābi) | painful (l-alīmi),

37:39 And not you will be recompensed except what you used to do,
And not (wamā) | you will be recompensed (tuj'zawna) | except (illā) | what (mā) | you used to (kuntum) | do (taʿmalūna),

37:40 Except the slaves of Allah the chosen ones.
Except (illā) | the slaves (ʿibāda) | of Allah (l-lahi) | the chosen ones (l-mukh'laṣīna).

37:41 Those for them will be a provision determined,
Those (ulāika) | for them (lahum) | will be a provision (riz'qun) | determined (maʿlūmun),

37:42 Fruits and they will be honored
Fruits (fawākihu) | and they (wahum) | will be honored (muk'ramūna)

37:43 In Gardens of Delight
In (fī) | Gardens (jannāti) | of Delight (l-naʿīmi)

37:44 On thrones facing each other.
On (ʿalā) | thrones (sururin) | facing each other (mutaqābilīna).

37:45 Will be circulated among them a cup from a flowing spring,
Will be circulated (yuṭāfu) | among them (ʿalayhim) | a cup (bikasin) | from (min) | a flowing spring (maʿīnin),

37:46 White, delicious for the drinkers;
White (bayḍāa), | delicious (ladhatin) | for the drinkers (lilshāribīna);

37:47 Not in it is bad effect and not they from it will be intoxicated.
Not (lā) | in it (fīhā) | is bad effect (ghawlun) | and not (walā) | they (hum) | from it (ʿanhā) | will be intoxicated (yunzafūna).

37:48 And with them will be companions of modest gaze having beautiful eyes,
And with them (waʿindahum) | will be companions of modest gaze (qāṣirātu) | will be companions of modest gaze (l-ṭarfi) | having beautiful eyes (ʿīnun),

37:49 As if they were eggs, well protected.
As if they were (ka-annahunna) | eggs (bayḍun), | well protected (maknūnun).

37:50 And will approach some of them to others questioning one another.
And will approach (fa-aqbala) | some of them (baʿḍuhum) | to (ʿalā) | others (baʿḍin) | questioning one another (yatasāalūna).

37:51 Will say a speaker among them, "Indeed, I had for me a companion,
Will say (qāla) | a speaker (qāilun) | among them (min'hum), | "Indeed, I (innī) | had (kāna) | for me (lī) | a companion (qarīnun),

37:52 Who would say, "Are you indeed surely of those who believe?
Who would say (yaqūlu), | "Are you indeed (a-innaka) | surely of (lamina) | those who believe (l-muṣadiqīna)?

37:53 Is it when we have died and become dust and bones, will we surely be brought to Judgment?"
Is it when (a-idhā) | we have died (mit'nā) | and become (wakunnā) | dust (turāban) | and bones (waʿiẓāman), | will we (a-innā) | surely be brought to Judgment? (lamadīnūna)"

37:54 He will say, "Will you be looking?"
He will say (qāla), | "Will (hal) | you (antum) | be looking? (muṭṭaliʿūna)"

37:55 Then he will look and see him in the midst of the Hellfire.
Then he will look (fa-iṭṭalaʿa) | and see him (faraāhu) | in (fī) | the midst (sawāi) | of the Hellfire (l-jaḥīmi).

37:56 He will say, "By Allah, verily, you almost ruined me.
He will say (qāla), | "By Allah (tal-lahi), | verily (in), | you almost (kidtta) | ruined me (latur'dīni).

37:57 And if not for the Grace of my Lord, certainly, I would have been among those brought."
And if not (walawlā) | for the Grace (niʿ'matu) | of my Lord (rabbī), | certainly, I would have been (lakuntu) | among (mina) | those brought. (l-muḥ'ḍarīna)"

37:58 Then are not we to die,
Then are not (afamā) | we (naḥnu) | to die (bimayyitīna),

37:59 Except our death the first, and not we will be punished?"
Except (illā) | our death (mawtatanā) | the first (l-ūlā), | and not (wamā) | we (naḥnu) | will be punished? (bimuʿadhabīna)"

37:60 Indeed, this surely is the attainment great.
Indeed (inna), | this (hādhā) | surely (lahuwa) | is the attainment (l-fawzu) | great (l-ʿaẓīmu).

37:61 For the like of this, let work the workers.
For the like (limith'li) | of this (hādhā), | let work (falyaʿmali) | the workers (l-ʿāmilūna).

37:62 Is that better as hospitality or the tree of Zaqqum?
Is that (adhālika) | better (khayrun) | as hospitality (nuzulan) | or (am) | the tree (shajaratu) | of Zaqqum (l-zaqūmi)?

37:63 Indeed, We [We] have made it a trial for the wrongdoers.
Indeed, We (innā) | [We] have made it (jaʿalnāhā) | a trial (fit'natan) | for the wrongdoers (lilẓẓālimīna).

37:64 Indeed, it is a tree that grows in the bottom of the Hellfire,
Indeed, it (innahā) | is a tree (shajaratun) | that grows (takhruju) | in (fī) | the bottom (aṣli) | of the Hellfire (l-jaḥīmi),

37:65 Its emerging fruit is as if it was heads of the devils.
Its emerging fruit (ṭalʿuhā) | is as if it (ka-annahu) | was heads (ruūsu) | of the devils (l-shayāṭīni).

37:66 And indeed, they will surely eat from it and fill with it their bellies.
And indeed, they (fa-innahum) | will surely eat (laākilūna) | from it (min'hā) | and fill (famāliūna) | with it (min'hā) | their bellies (l-buṭūna).

37:67 Then indeed, for them in it is a mixture of boiling water.
Then (thumma) | indeed (inna), | for them (lahum) | in it (ʿalayhā) | is a mixture (lashawban) | of (min) | boiling water (ḥamīmin).

37:68 Then indeed, their return will surely be to the Hellfire.
Then (thumma) | indeed (inna), | their return (marjiʿahum) | will surely be to (la-ilā) | the Hellfire (l-jaḥīmi).

37:69 Indeed, they found their fathers astray.
Indeed, they (innahum) | found (alfaw) | their fathers (ābāahum) | astray (ḍāllīna).

37:70 So they on their footsteps they hastened.
So they (fahum) | on (ʿalā) | their footsteps (āthārihim) | they hastened (yuh'raʿūna).

37:71 And verily, went astray before them most of the former (people),
And verily (walaqad), | went astray (ḍalla) | before them (qablahum) | most (aktharu) | of the former (people) (l-awalīna),

37:72 And verily, We sent among them warners.
And verily (walaqad), | We sent (arsalnā) | among them (fīhim) | warners (mundhirīna).

37:73 Then see how was the end of those who were warned,
Then see (fa-unẓur) | how (kayfa) | was (kāna) | the end (ʿāqibatu) | of those who were warned (l-mundharīna),

37:74 Except the slaves of Allah the chosen ones.
Except (illā) | the slaves (ʿibāda) | of Allah (l-lahi) | the chosen ones (l-mukh'laṣīna).

37:75 And verily, called Us Nuh; and Best are We as Responders!
And verily (walaqad), | called Us (nādānā) | Nuh (nūḥun); | and Best (falaniʿma) | are We as Responders (l-mujībūna)!

37:76 And We saved him and his family from the distress, the great.
And We saved him (wanajjaynāhu) | and his family (wa-ahlahu) | from (mina) | the distress (l-karbi), | the great (l-ʿaẓīmi).

37:77 And We made his offspring [they] the survivors.
And We made (wajaʿalnā) | his offspring (dhurriyyatahu) | [they] (humu) | the survivors (l-bāqīna).

37:78 And We left for him among the later generations.
And We left (wataraknā) | for him (ʿalayhi) | among (fī) | the later generations (l-ākhirīna).

37:79 "Peace be upon Nuh among the worlds."
"Peace be (salāmun) | upon (ʿalā) | Nuh (nūḥin) | among (fī) | the worlds. (l-ʿālamīna)"

37:80 Indeed, We thus [We] reward the good-doers.
Indeed, We (innā) | thus (kadhālika) | [We] reward (najzī) | the good-doers (l-muḥ'sinīna).

37:81 Indeed, he was of Our slaves believing.
Indeed, he (innahu) | was of (min) | Our slaves (ʿibādinā) | believing (l-mu'minīna).

37:82 Then We drowned the others.
Then (thumma) | We drowned (aghraqnā) | the others (l-ākharīna).

37:83 And indeed, among his kind was surely Ibrahim,
And indeed (wa-inna), | among (min) | his kind (shīʿatihi) | was surely Ibrahim (la-ib'rāhīma),

37:84 When he came to his Lord with a heart sound,
When (idh) | he came (jāa) | to his Lord (rabbahu) | with a heart (biqalbin) | sound (salīmin),

37:85 When he said to his father and his people, "What is it you worship?
When (idh) | he said (qāla) | to his father (li-abīhi) | and his people (waqawmihi), | "What is it (mādhā) | you worship (taʿbudūna)?

37:86 Is it falsehood - gods other than Allah - that you desire?
Is it falsehood (a-if'kan)- | gods (ālihatan) | other than (dūna) | Allah (l-lahi)- | that you desire (turīdūna)?

37:87 Then what do you think about the Lord of the worlds?"
Then what (famā) | do you think (ẓannukum) | about the Lord (birabbi) | of the worlds? (l-ʿālamīna)"

37:88 Then he glanced a glance at the stars,
Then he glanced (fanaẓara) | a glance (naẓratan) | at (fī) | the stars (l-nujūmi),

37:89 And he said, "Indeed, I am sick."
And he said (faqāla), | "Indeed, I am (innī) | sick. (saqīmun)"

37:90 So they turned away from him departing.
So they turned away (fatawallaw) | from him (ʿanhu) | departing (mud'birīna).

37:91 Then he turned to their gods and said, "Do not you eat?
Then he turned (farāgha) | to (ilā) | their gods (ālihatihim) | and said (faqāla), | "Do not (alā) | you eat (takulūna)?

37:92 What is for you not you speak?"
What is (mā) | for you (lakum) | not (lā) | you speak? (tanṭiqūna)"

37:93 Then he turned upon them striking with the right hand.
Then he turned (farāgha) | upon them (ʿalayhim) | striking (ḍarban) | with the right hand (bil-yamīni).

37:94 Then they advanced towards him, hastening.
Then they advanced (fa-aqbalū) | towards him (ilayhi), | hastening (yaziffūna).

37:95 He said, "Do you worship what you carve
He said (qāla), | "Do you worship (ataʿbudūna) | what (mā) | you carve (tanḥitūna)

37:96 While Allah created you and what you make?"
While Allah (wal-lahu) | created you (khalaqakum) | and what (wamā) | you make? (taʿmalūna)"

37:97 They said, "Build for him a structure and throw him into the blazing Fire."
They said (qālū), | "Build (ib'nū) | for him (lahu) | a structure (bun'yānan) | and throw him (fa-alqūhu) | into (fī) | the blazing Fire. (l-jaḥīmi)"

37:98 And they intended for him a plot, but We made them the lowest.
And they intended (fa-arādū) | for him (bihi) | a plot (kaydan), | but We made them (fajaʿalnāhumu) | the lowest (l-asfalīna).

37:99 And he said, "Indeed, I am going to my Lord, He will guide me.
And he said (waqāla), | "Indeed, I am (innī) | going (dhāhibun) | to (ilā) | my Lord (rabbī), | He will guide me (sayahdīni).

37:100 My Lord grant me of the righteous."
My Lord (rabbi) | grant (hab) | me (lī) | of (mina) | the righteous. (l-ṣāliḥīna)"

37:101 So We gave him the glad tidings of a boy forbearing.
So We gave him the glad tidings (fabasharnāhu) | of a boy (bighulāmin) | forbearing (ḥalīmin).

37:102 Then when he reached the age of working with him he said, "O my son! Indeed, I have seen in the dream that I am sacrificing you, so look what you see." He said, "O my father! Do what you are commanded. You will find me, if Allah wills, of the patient ones."
Then when (falammā) | he reached (balagha) | the age of working with him (maʿahu) | the age of working with him (l-saʿya) | he said (qāla), | "O my son (yābunayya)! | Indeed, I (innī) | have seen (arā) | in (fī) | the dream (l-manāmi) | that I am (annī) | sacrificing you (adhbaḥuka), | so look (fa-unẓur) | what (mādhā) | you see. (tarā)" | He said (qāla), | "O my father (yāabati)! | Do (if'ʿal) | what (mā) | you are commanded (tu'maru). | You will find me (satajidunī), | if (in) | Allah wills

(shāa), | Allah wills (l-lahu), | of (mina) | the patient ones. (l-ṣābirīna)"

37:103 Then when both of them had submitted and he put him down upon his forehead,
Then when (falammā) | both of them had submitted (aslamā) | and he put him down (watallahu) | upon his forehead (lil'jabīni),

37:104 And We called out to him that "O Ibrahim!
And We called out to him (wanādaynāhu) | that (an) | "O Ibrahim (yāib'rāhīmu)!

37:105 Verily, you have fulfilled the vision." Indeed, We thus [We] reward the good-doers.
Verily (qad), | you have fulfilled (ṣaddaqta) | the vision. (l-ru'yā)" | Indeed, We (innā) | thus (kadhālika) | [We] reward (najzī) | the good-doers (l-muḥ'sinīna).

37:106 Indeed, this was surely [it] the trial clear.
Indeed (inna), | this (hādhā) | was surely [it] (lahuwa) | the trial (l-balāu) | clear (l-mubīnu).

37:107 And We ransomed him with a sacrifice great,
And We ransomed him (wafadaynāhu) | with a sacrifice (bidhib'ḥin) | great (ʿaẓīmin),

37:108 And We left for him among the later generations.
And We left (wataraknā) | for him (ʿalayhi) | among (fī) | the later generations (l-ākhirīna).

37:109 "Peace be on Ibrahim."
"Peace be (salāmun) | on (ʿalā) | Ibrahim. (ib'rāhīma)"

37:110 Thus We reward the good-doers.
Thus (kadhālika) | We reward (najzī) | the good-doers (l-muḥ'sinīna).

37:111 Indeed, he was of Our slaves believing.
Indeed, he was (innahu) | of (min) | Our slaves (ʿibādinā) | believing (l-mu'minīna).

37:112 And We gave him glad tidings of Isaac, a Prophet among the righteous.
And We gave him glad tidings (wabasharnāhu) | of Isaac (bi-is'ḥāqa), | a Prophet (nabiyyan) | among (mina) | the righteous (l-ṣāliḥīna).

37:113 And We blessed him and [on] Isaac. And of their offspring are good-doers and unjust to himself clear.
And We blessed (wabāraknā) | him (ʿalayhi) | and [on] (waʿalā) | Isaac (is'ḥāqa). | And of (wamin) | their offspring (dhurriyyatihimā) | are good-doers (muḥ'sinun) | and unjust (waẓālimun) | to himself (linafsihi) | clear (mubīnun).

37:114 And verily, We conferred Favor upon Musa and Harun.
And verily (walaqad), | We conferred Favor (manannā) | upon (ʿalā) | Musa (mūsā) | and Harun (wahārūna).

37:115 And We saved both of them and their people from the distress the great,
And We saved both of them (wanajjaynāhumā) | and their people (waqawmahumā) | from (mina) | the distress (l-karbi) | the great (l-ʿaẓīmi),

37:116 And We helped them, so they became the victors.
And We helped them (wanaṣarnāhum), | so they became (fakānū) | so they became

(humu) | the victors (l-ghālibīna).

37:117 And We gave both of them the Book the clear.
And We gave both of them (waātaynāhumā) | the Book (l-kitāba) | the clear (l-mus'tabīna).

37:118 And We guided both of them to the Path the Straight.
And We guided both of them (wahadaynāhumā) | to the Path (l-ṣirāṭa) | the Straight (l-mus'taqīma).

37:119 And We left for both of them, among the later generations.
And We left (wataraknā) | for both of them (ʿalayhimā), | among (fī) | the later generations (l-ākhirīna).

37:120 "Peace be upon Musa and Harun."
"Peace be (salāmun) | upon (ʿalā) | Musa (mūsā) | and Harun. (wahārūna)"

37:121 Indeed, We thus reward the good-doers.
Indeed, We (innā) | thus (kadhālika) | reward (najzī) | the good-doers (l-muḥ'sinīna).

37:122 Indeed, both of them were of Our slaves believing.
Indeed, both of them (innahumā) | were of (min) | Our slaves (ʿibādinā) | believing (l-mu'minīna).

37:123 And indeed, Elijah was surely of the Messengers.
And indeed (wa-inna), | Elijah (il'yāsa) | was surely of (lamina) | the Messengers (l-mur'salīna).

37:124 When he said to his people, "Will not you fear?
When (idh) | he said (qāla) | to his people (liqawmihi), | "Will not (alā) | you fear (tattaqūna)?

37:125 Do you call Baal and you forsake the Best of Creators -
Do you call (atadʿūna) | Baal (baʿlan) | and you forsake (watadharūna) | the Best (aḥsana) | of Creators (l-khāliqīna)-

37:126 Allah, your Lord and the Lord of your forefathers?"
Allah (al-laha), | your Lord (rabbakum) | and the Lord (warabba) | of your forefathers? (ābāikumu)" | of your forefathers? (l-awalīna)"

37:127 But they denied him, so indeed, they will surely be brought,
But they denied him (fakadhabūhu), | so indeed, they (fa-innahum) | will surely be brought (lamuḥ'ḍarūna),

37:128 Except the slaves of Allah the chosen ones.
Except (illā) | the slaves (ʿibāda) | of Allah (l-lahi) | the chosen ones (l-mukh'laṣīna).

37:129 And We left for him among the later generations.
And We left (wataraknā) | for him (ʿalayhi) | among (fī) | the later generations (l-ākhirīna).

37:130 "Peace be upon Elijah."
"Peace be (salāmun) | upon (ʿalā) | Elijah. (il yāsīna)"

37:131 Indeed, We thus reward the good-doers.
Indeed, We (innā) | thus (kadhālika) | reward (najzī) | the good-doers (l-muḥ'sinīna).

37:132 Indeed, he was of Our slaves believing.
Indeed, he was (innahu) | of (min) | Our slaves (ʿibādinā) | believing (l-mu'minīna).

37:133 And indeed, Lut was of the Messengers.
And indeed (wa-inna), | Lut (lūṭan) | was of (lamina) | the Messengers (l-mur'salīna).

37:134 When We saved him and his family all,
When (idh) | We saved him (najjaynāhu) | and his family (wa-ahlahu) | all (ajmaʿīna),

37:135 Except an old woman was among those who remained behind.
Except (illā) | an old woman (ʿajūzan) | was among (fī) | those who remained behind (l-ghābirīna).

37:136 Then We destroyed the others.
Then (thumma) | We destroyed (dammarnā) | the others (l-ākharīna).

37:137 And indeed, you surely pass by them in the morning,
And indeed, you (wa-innakum) | surely pass (latamurrūna) | by them (ʿalayhim) | in the morning (muṣ'biḥīna),

37:138 And at night. Then will not you use reason?
And at night (wabi-al-layli). | Then will not (afalā) | you use reason (taʿqilūna)?

37:139 And indeed, Yunus was surely of the Messengers.
And indeed (wa-inna), | Yunus (yūnusa) | was surely of (lamina) | the Messengers (l-mur'salīna).

37:140 When he ran away to the ship laden.
When (idh) | he ran away (abaqa) | to (ilā) | the ship (l-ful'ki) | laden (l-mashḥūni).

37:141 Then he drew lots and was of the losers.
Then he drew lots (fasāhama) | and was (fakāna) | of (mina) | the losers (l-mud'ḥaḍīna).

37:142 Then swallowed him the fish, while he was blameworthy.
Then swallowed him (fal-taqamahu) | the fish (l-ḥūtu), | while he (wahuwa) | was blameworthy (mulīmun).

37:143 And if not that he was of those who glorify
And if not (falawlā) | that he (annahu) | was (kāna) | of (mina) | those who glorify (l-musabiḥīna)

37:144 Certainly, he would have remained in its belly until the Day they are resurrected.
Certainly, he would have remained (lalabitha) | in (fī) | its belly (baṭnihi) | until (ilā) | the Day (yawmi) | they are resurrected (yub'ʿathūna).

37:145 But We cast him onto the open shore while he was ill.
But We cast him (fanabadhnāhu) | onto the open shore (bil-ʿarāi) | while he (wahuwa) | was ill (saqīmun).

37:146 And We caused to grow over him a plant of gourd.
And We caused to grow (wa-anbatnā) | over him (ʿalayhi) | a plant (shajaratan) | of (min) | gourd (yaqṭīnin).

37:147 And We sent him to a hundred thousand or more.
And We sent him (wa-arsalnāhu) | to (ilā) | a hundred (mi-ati) | thousand (alfin) | or (aw) | more (yazīdūna).

37:148 And they believed, so We gave them enjoyment for a while.
And they believed (faāmanū), | so We gave them enjoyment (famattaʿnāhum) | for (ilā) | a while (ḥīnin).

37:149 Then ask them, "Does your Lord have daughters while for them are sons?"
Then ask them (fa-is'taftihim), | "Does your Lord (alirabbika) | have daughters (l-banātu) | while for them (walahumu) | are sons? (l-banūna)"

37:150 Or did We create the Angels females while they were witnesses?
Or (am) | did We create (khalaqnā) | the Angels (l-malāikata) | females (ināthan) | while they (wahum) | were witnesses (shāhidūna)?

37:151 No doubt, indeed, they of their falsehood [they] say,
No doubt (alā), | indeed, they (innahum) | of (min) | their falsehood (if'kihim) | [they] say (layaqūlūna),

37:152 "Allah has begotten," and indeed, they surely are liars.
"Allah has begotten, (walada)" | "Allah has begotten, (l-lahu)" | and indeed, they (wa-innahum) | surely are liars (lakādhibūna).

37:153 Has He chosen [the] daughters over sons?
Has He chosen (aṣṭafā) | [the] daughters (l-banāti) | over (ʿalā) | sons (l-banīna)?

37:154 What is with you? How you judge?
What is with you (mā)? | What is with you (lakum)? | How (kayfa) | you judge (taḥkumūna)?

37:155 Then will not you pay heed?
Then will not (afalā) | you pay heed (tadhakkarūna)?

37:156 Or is for you an authority clear?
Or (am) | is for you (lakum) | an authority (sul'ṭānun) | clear (mubīnun)?

37:157 Then bring your book, if you are truthful.
Then bring (fatū) | your book (bikitābikum), | if (in) | you are (kuntum) | truthful (ṣādiqīna).

37:158 And they have made between Him and between the jinn a relationship, but certainly, know the jinn that they will surely be brought.
And they have made (wajaʿalū) | between Him (baynahu) | and between (wabayna) | the jinn (l-jinati) | a relationship (nasaban), | but certainly (walaqad), | know (ʿalimati) | the jinn (l-jinatu) | that they (innahum) | will surely be brought (lamuḥ'ḍarūna).

37:159 Glory be to Allah above what they attribute,

Glory be (sub'ḥāna) | to Allah (l-lahi) | above what (ʿammā) | they attribute (yaṣifūna),

37:160 Except the slaves of Allah the chosen.
Except (illā) | the slaves (ʿibāda) | of Allah (l-lahi) | the chosen (l-mukh'laṣīna).

37:161 So indeed, you and what you worship,
So indeed, you (fa-innakum) | and what (wamā) | you worship (taʿbudūna),

37:162 Not you from Him can tempt away anyone.
Not (mā) | you (antum) | from Him (ʿalayhi) | can tempt away anyone (bifātinīna).

37:163 Except who he is to burn in the Hellfire.
Except (illā) | who (man) | he (huwa) | is to burn (ṣāli) | in the Hellfire (l-jaḥīmi).

37:164 "And not among us except for him is a position known.
"And not (wamā) | among us (minnā) | except (illā) | for him (lahu) | is a position (maqāmun) | known (maʿlūmun).

37:165 And indeed, we surely, [we] stand in rows.
And indeed, we (wa-innā) | surely, [we] (lanaḥnu) | stand in rows (l-ṣāfūna).

37:166 And indeed, we surely, [we] glorify Allah."
And indeed, we (wa-innā) | surely, [we] (lanaḥnu) | glorify Allah. (l-musabiḥūna)"

37:167 And indeed, they used to say,
And indeed (wa-in), | they used to (kānū) | say (layaqūlūna),

37:168 "If that we had a reminder from the former people,
"If (law) | that (anna) | we had (ʿindanā) | a reminder (dhik'ran) | from (mina) | the former people (l-awalīna),

37:169 Certainly, we would have been slaves of Allah the chosen."
Certainly, we would have been (lakunnā) | slaves (ʿibāda) | of Allah (l-lahi) | the chosen. (l-mukh'laṣīna)"

37:170 But they disbelieved in it, so soon they will know.
But they disbelieved (fakafarū) | in it (bihi), | so soon (fasawfa) | they will know (yaʿlamūna).

37:171 And verily, has preceded Our Word for Our slaves, the Messengers,
And verily (walaqad), | has preceded (sabaqat) | Our Word (kalimatunā) | for Our slaves (liʿibādinā), | the Messengers (l-mur'salīna),

37:172 Indeed they, surely they would be the victorious.
Indeed they (innahum), | surely they (lahumu) | would be the victorious (l-manṣūrūna).

37:173 And indeed, Our host surely, they will be those who overcome.
And indeed (wa-inna), | Our host (jundanā) | surely, they (lahumu) | will be those who overcome (l-ghālibūna).

37:174 So turn away from them until a time.
So turn away (fatawalla) | from them (ʿanhum) | until (ḥattā) | a time (ḥīnin).

37:175 And see them, so soon they will see.
And see them (wa-abṣir'hum), | so soon (fasawfa) | they will see (yub'ṣirūna).

37:176 Then is it for Our punishment they hasten?
Then is it for Our punishment (afabiʿadhābinā) | they hasten (yastaʿjilūna)?

37:177 But when it descends in their territory, then evil will be the morning for those who were warned.
But when (fa-idhā) | it descends (nazala) | in their territory (bisāḥatihim), | then evil will be (fasāa) | the morning (ṣabāḥu) | for those who were warned (l-mundharīna).

37:178 So turn away from them for a time.
So turn away (watawalla) | from them (ʿanhum) | for (ḥattā) | a time (ḥīnin).

37:179 And see, so soon they will see.
And see (wa-abṣir), | so soon (fasawfa) | they will see (yub'ṣirūna).

37:180 Glory be to your Lord, the Lord of Honor, above what they attribute.
Glory (sub'ḥāna) | be to your Lord (rabbika), | the Lord (rabbi) | of Honor (l-ʿizati), | above what (ʿammā) | they attribute (yaṣifūna).

37:181 And peace be upon the Messengers.
And peace be (wasalāmun) | upon (ʿalā) | the Messengers (l-mur'salīna).

37:182 And all praise be to Allah, the Lord of the worlds.
And all praise (wal-ḥamdu) | be to Allah (lillahi), | the Lord (rabbi) | of the worlds (l-ʿālamīna).

Chapter (38) Sūrat Ṣād

38:1 Saad. By the Quran full of reminder.
Saad (sad). | By the Quran (wal-qur'āni) | full of reminder (dhī). | full of reminder (l-dhik'ri).

38:2 Nay, those who disbelieve are in self-glory and opposition.
Nay (bali), | those who (alladhīna) | disbelieve (kafarū) | are in (fī) | self-glory (ʿizzatin) | and opposition (washiqāqin).

38:3 How many We destroyed before them of a generation, then they called out when there was no longer time for escape.
How many (kam) | We destroyed (ahlaknā) | before them (min) | before them (qablihim) | of (min) | a generation (qarnin), | then they called out (fanādaw) | when there was no longer (walāta) | time (ḥīna) | for escape (manāṣin).

38:4 And they wonder that has come to them a warner from themselves. And said the disbelievers, "This is a magician, a liar.

And they wonder (wa'ajibū) | that (an) | has come to them (jāahum) | a warner (mundhirun) | from themselves (min'hum). | And said (waqāla) | the disbelievers (l-kāfirūna), | "This (hādhā) | is a magician (sāḥirun), | a liar (kadhābun).

38:5 Has he made the gods into one god? Indeed this is certainly a thing curious."

Has he made (aja'ala) | the gods (l-ālihata) | into one god (ilāhan)? | into one god (wāḥidan)? | Indeed (inna) | this (hādhā) | is certainly a thing (lashayon) | curious. ('ujābun)"

38:6 And went forth the chiefs among them that, "Continue, and be patient over your gods. Indeed, this is certainly a thing intended.

And went forth (wa-inṭalaqa) | the chiefs (l-mala-u) | among them (min'hum) | that (ani), | "Continue (im'shū), | and be patient (wa-iṣ'birū) | over ('alā) | your gods (ālihatikum). | Indeed (inna), | this (hādhā) | is certainly a thing (lashayon) | intended (yurādu).

38:7 Not we heard of this in the religion the last. Not is this but a fabrication.

Not (mā) | we heard (sami''nā) | of this (bihādhā) | in (fī) | the religion (l-milati) | the last (l-ākhirati). | Not (in) | is this (hādhā) | but (illā) | a fabrication (ikh'tilāqun).

38:8 Has been revealed to him the Message from among us?" Nay, They are in doubt about My Message. Nay, not yet they have tasted My punishment.

Has been revealed (a-unzila) | to him ('alayhi) | the Message (l-dhik'ru) | from (min) | among us? (bayninā)" | Nay (bal), | They (hum) | are in (fī) | doubt (shakkin) | about (min) | My Message (dhik'rī). | Nay (bal), | not yet (lammā) | they have tasted (yadhūqū) | My punishment ('adhābi).

38:9 Or have they the treasures of the Mercy of your Lord the All-Mighty, the Bestower?

Or (am) | have they ('indahum) | the treasures (khazāinu) | of the Mercy (raḥmati) | of your Lord (rabbika) | the All-Mighty (l-'azīzi), | the Bestower (l-wahābi)?

38:10 Or for them is the dominion of the heavens and the earth and whatever is between them? Then let them ascend by the means.

Or (am) | for them (lahum) | is the dominion (mul'ku) | of the heavens (l-samāwāti) | and the earth (wal-arḍi) | and whatever (wamā) | is between them (baynahumā)? | Then let them ascend (falyartaqū) | by (fī) | the means (l-asbābi).

38:11 Soldiers - there they will be defeated among the companies.

Soldiers (jundun)- | there (mā) | there (hunālika) | they will be defeated (mahzūmun) | among (mina) | the companies (l-aḥzābi).

38:12 Denied before them the people of Nuh and Aad and Firaun, the owner of the stakes.

Denied (kadhabat) | before them (qablahum) | the people (qawmu) | of Nuh (nūḥin) | and Aad (wa'ādun) | and Firaun (wafir''awnu), | the owner (dhū) | of the stakes (l-awtādi).

38:13 And Thamud and the people of Lut and the companions of the wood. Those were the companies.

And Thamud (wathamūdu) | and the people (waqawmu) | of Lut (lūṭin) | and the companions (wa-aṣḥābu) | of the wood (al'aykati). | Those (ulāika) | were the companies (l-aḥzābu).

38:14 Not all of them but denied the Messengers, so was just My penalty.
Not (in) | all of them (kullun) | but (illā) | denied (kadhaba) | the Messengers (l-rusula), | so was just (faḥaqqa) | My penalty (ʿiqābi).

38:15 And not await these but a shout one; not for it any delay.
And not (wamā) | await (yanẓuru) | these (hāulāi) | but (illā) | a shout (ṣayḥatan) | one (wāḥidatan); | not (mā) | for it (lahā) | any (min) | delay (fawāqin).

38:16 And they say, "Our Lord! Hasten for us our share before the Day of the Account."
And they say (waqālū), | "Our Lord (rabbanā)! | Hasten (ʿajjil) | for us (lanā) | our share (qiṭṭanā) | before (qabla) | the Day (yawmi) | of the Account. (l-ḥisābi)"

38:17 Be patient over what they say, and remember Our slave, Dawood, the possessor of strength. Indeed, he was repeatedly turning.
Be patient (iṣ'bir) | over (ʿalā) | what (mā) | they say (yaqūlūna), | and remember (wa-udh'kur) | Our slave (ʿabdanā), | Dawood (dāwūda), | the possessor of strength (dhā). | the possessor of strength (l-aydi). | Indeed, he was (innahu) | repeatedly turning (awwābun).

38:18 Indeed, We subjected the mountains with him glorifying in the evening and [the] sunrise.
Indeed, We (innā) | subjected (sakharnā) | the mountains (l-jibāla) | with him (maʿahu) | glorifying (yusabbiḥ'na) | in the evening (bil-ʿashiyi) | and [the] sunrise (wal-ish'rāqi).

38:19 And the birds assembled, all with him repeatedly turning.
And the birds (wal-ṭayra) | assembled (maḥshūratan), | all (kullun) | with him (lahu) | repeatedly turning (awwābun).

38:20 And We strengthened his kingdom and We gave him [the] wisdom and decisive speech.
And We strengthened (washadadnā) | his kingdom (mul'kahu) | and We gave him (waātaynāhu) | [the] wisdom (l-ḥik'mata) | and decisive (wafaṣla) | speech (l-khiṭābi).

38:21 And has there come to you the news of the litigants, when they climbed over the wall of the chamber?
And has there (wahal) | come to you (atāka) | the news (naba-u) | of the litigants (l-khaṣmi), | when (idh) | they climbed over the wall (tasawwarū) | of the chamber (l-miḥ'rāba)?

38:22 When they entered upon Dawood and he was afraid of them, they said, "Do not fear. We are two litigants, has wronged one of us to another, so judge between us in truth and do not be unjust and guide us to an even [the] path.
When (idh) | they entered (dakhalū) | upon (ʿalā) | Dawood (dāwūda) | and he was afraid (fafaziʿa) | of them (min'hum), | they said (qālū), | "Do not (lā) | fear (takhaf). | We are two litigants (khaṣmāni), | has wronged (baghā) | one of us (baʿḍunā) | to (ʿalā) | another (baʿḍin), | so judge (fa-uḥ'kum) | between us (baynanā) | in truth (bil-ḥaqi) | and do not (walā) | be unjust (tush'ṭiṭ) | and guide us (wa-ih'dinā) | to (ilā) | an even (sawāi) | [the] path (l-ṣirāṭi).

38:23 Indeed, this is my brother, he has ninety-nine ewes while I have ewe one; so he said, "Entrust her to me," and he overpowered me in [the] speech."
Indeed (inna), | this (hādhā) | is my brother (akhī), | he has (lahu) | ninety-nine (tis'ʿun) | ninety-nine (watis'ʿūna) | ewes (naʿjatan) | while I have (waliya) | ewe (naʿjatun) | one (wāḥidatun); | so he said (faqāla), | "Entrust her to me, (akfil'nīhā)" | and he overpowered me (waʿazzanī) | in (fī) | [the] speech. (l-khiṭābi)"

38:24 He said, "Certainly, he has wronged you by demanding your ewe to his ewes. And indeed, many of the partners certainly oppress some of them [on] another except those who believe and do righteous deeds and few are they." And became certain Dawood that We had tried him, and he asked forgiveness of his Lord and fell down bowing and turned in repentance.

He said (qāla), | "Certainly (laqad), | he has wronged you (ẓalamaka) | by demanding (bisuāli) | your ewe (naʿjatika) | to (ilā) | his ewes (niʿājihi). | And indeed (wa-inna), | many (kathīran) | of (mina) | the partners (l-khulaṭāi) | certainly oppress (layabghī) | some of them (baʿḍuhum) | [on] (ʿalā) | another (baʿḍin) | except (illā) | those who (alladhīna) | believe (āmanū) | and do (waʿamilū) | righteous deeds (l-ṣāliḥāti) | and few (waqalīlun) | are they. (mā)" | are they. (hum)" | And became certain (waẓanna) | Dawood (dāwūdu) | that (annamā) | We had tried him (fatannāhu), | and he asked forgiveness (fa-is'taghfara) | of his Lord (rabbahu) | and fell down (wakharra) | bowing (rākiʿan) | and turned in repentance (wa-anāba).

38:25 So We forgave for him that. And indeed, for him with Us surely is a near access and a good place of return.

So We forgave (faghafarnā) | for him (lahu) | that (dhālika). | And indeed (wa-inna), | for him (lahu) | with Us (ʿindanā) | surely is a near access (lazul'fā) | and a good (waḥus'na) | place of return (maābin).

38:26 "O Dawood! Indeed, We [We] have made you a vicegerent in the earth, so judge between [the] men in truth and do not follow the desire, for it will lead you astray from the way of Allah. Indeed, those who go astray from the way of Allah, for them is a punishment severe because they forgot the Day of Account."

"O Dawood (yādāwūdu)! | Indeed, We (innā) | [We] have made you (jaʿalnāka) | a vicegerent (khalīfatan) | in (fī) | the earth (l-arḍi), | so judge (fa-uḥ'kum) | between (bayna) | [the] men (l-nāsi) | in truth (bil-ḥaqi) | and do not (walā) | follow (tattabiʿi) | the desire (l-hawā), | for it will lead you astray (fayuḍillaka) | from (ʿan) | the way (sabīli) | of Allah (l-lahi). | Indeed (inna), | those who (alladhīna) | go astray (yaḍillūna) | from (ʿan) | the way (sabīli) | of Allah (l-lahi), | for them (lahum) | is a punishment (ʿadhābun) | severe (shadīdun) | because (bimā) | they forgot (nasū) | the Day (yawma) | of Account. (l-ḥisābi)"

38:27 And not We created the heaven and the earth and whatever is between them without purpose. That is the assumption of those who disbelieve. So woe to those who disbelieve, from the Fire.

And not (wamā) | We created (khalaqnā) | the heaven (l-samāa) | and the earth (wal-arḍa) | and whatever (wamā) | is between them (baynahumā) | without purpose (bāṭilan). | That (dhālika) | is the assumption (ẓannu) | of those who (alladhīna) | disbelieve (kafarū). | So woe (fawaylun) | to those (lilladhīna) | who disbelieve (kafarū), | from (mina) | the Fire (l-nāri).

38:28 Or should We treat those who believe and do righteous deeds like those who spread corruption in the earth? Or should We treat the pious like the wicked?

Or (am) | should We treat (najʿalu) | those who (alladhīna) | believe (āmanū) | and do (waʿamilū) | righteous deeds (l-ṣāliḥāti) | like those who spread corruption (kal-muf'sidīna) | in (fī) | the earth (l-arḍi)? | Or (am) | should We treat (najʿalu) | the pious (l-mutaqīna) | like the wicked (kal-fujāri)?

38:29 This is a Book We have revealed it to you, blessed, that they may ponder over its Verses and may be reminded those of understanding.

This is a Book (kitābun) | We have revealed it (anzalnāhu) | to you (ilayka), | blessed (mubārakun), | that they may ponder (liyaddabbarū) | over its Verses (āyātihi) | and may be reminded (waliyatadhakkara) | those of understanding (ulū). | those of understanding (l-albābi).

38:30 And We gave to Dawood Sulaiman, an excellent slave. Indeed, he was one who repeatedly turned.

And We gave (wawahabnā) | to Dawood (lidāwūda) | Sulaiman (sulaymāna), | an excellent (ni‘'ma) | slave (l-‘abdu). | Indeed, he (innahu) | was one who repeatedly turned (awwābun).

38:31 When were displayed to him in the afternoon excellent bred steeds.

When (idh) | were displayed (‘uriḍa) | to him (‘alayhi) | in the afternoon (bil-‘ashiyi) | excellent bred steeds (l-ṣāfinātu). | excellent bred steeds (l-jiyādu).

38:32 And he said, "Indeed, I [I] preferred the love of the good over the remembrance of my Lord." Until they were hidden in the veil;

And he said (faqāla), | "Indeed, I (innī) | [I] preferred (aḥbabtu) | the love (ḥubba) | of the good (l-khayri) | over (‘an) | the remembrance (dhik'ri) | of my Lord. (rabbī)" | Until (ḥattā) | they were hidden (tawārat) | in the veil (bil-ḥijābi);

38:33 "Return them to me." Then he began to pass (his hand) over the legs and the necks.

"Return them (ruddūhā) | to me. (‘alayya)" | Then he began (faṭafiqa) | to pass (his hand (masḥan)) | over the legs (bil-sūqi) | and the necks (wal-a‘nāqi).

38:34 And certainly We tried Sulaiman, and We placed on his throne a body; then he turned.

And certainly (walaqad) | We tried (fatannā) | Sulaiman (sulaymāna), | and We placed (wa-alqaynā) | on (‘alā) | his throne (kur'siyyihi) | a body (jasadan); | then (thumma) | he turned (anāba).

38:35 He said, "O my Lord! Forgive me and grant me a kingdom, not will belong to anyone after me. Indeed, You [You] are the Bestower."

He said (qāla), | "O my Lord (rabbi)! | Forgive (igh'fir) | me (lī) | and grant (wahab) | me (lī) | a kingdom (mul'kan), | not (lā) | will belong (yanbaghī) | to anyone (li-aḥadin) | after me (min). | after me (ba‘dī). | Indeed, You (innaka) | [You] (anta) | are the Bestower. (l-wahābu)"

38:36 Then We subjected to him the wind to flow by his command, gently, wherever he directed,

Then We subjected (fasakharnā) | to him (lahu) | the wind (l-rīḥa) | to flow (tajrī) | by his command (bi-amrihi), | gently (rukhāan), | wherever (ḥaythu) | he directed (aṣāba),

38:37 And the devils, every builder and diver,

And the devils (wal-shayāṭīna), | every (kulla) | builder (bannāin) | and diver (waghawwāṣin),

38:38 And others bound in chains.

And others (waākharīna) | bound (muqarranīna) | in (fī) | chains (l-aṣfādi).

38:39 "This is Our gift, so grant or withhold without account."

"This (hādhā) | is Our gift (‘aṭāunā), | so grant (fa-um'nun) | or (aw) | withhold (amsik) | without (bighayri) | account. (ḥisābin)"

38:40 And indeed, for him with Us surely is a near access and a good place of return.

And indeed (wa-inna), | for him (lahu) | with Us (‘indanā) | surely is a near access (lazul'fā) | and a good (waḥus'na) | place of return (maābin).

38:41 And remember Our slave Ayyub, when he called his Lord, "That [I], has touched me Shaitaan with distress and suffering."

And remember (wa-udh'kur) | Our slave (‘abdanā) | Ayyub (ayyūba), | when (idh) | he called (nādā) | his Lord (rabbahu), | "That [I] (annī), | has touched me (massaniya) | Shaitaan (l-shayṭānu) | with distress (binuṣ'bin) | and suffering. (wa'adhābin)"

38:42 "Strike with your foot. This is a spring of water to bathe, cool and a drink."

"Strike (ur'kuḍ) | with your foot (birij'lika). | This (hādhā) | is a spring of water to bathe (mugh'tasalun), | cool (bāridun) | and a drink. (washarābun)"

38:43 And We granted [to] him his family and a like of them with them, a Mercy from Us and a Reminder for those of understanding.

And We granted (wawahabnā) | [to] him (lahu) | his family (ahlahu) | and a like of them (wamith'lahum) | with them (ma'ahum), | a Mercy (raḥmatan) | from Us (minnā) | and a Reminder (wadhik'rā) | for those of understanding (li-ulī). | for those of understanding (l-albābi).

38:44 "And take in your hand a bunch and strike with it and do not break your oath." Indeed, We [We] found him patient, an excellent slave. Indeed, he repeatedly turned.

"And take (wakhudh) | in your hand (biyadika) | a bunch (ḍigh'than) | and strike (fa-iḍ'rib) | with it (bihi) | and do not (walā) | break your oath. (taḥnath)" | Indeed, We (innā) | [We] found him (wajadnāhu) | patient (ṣābiran), | an excellent (ni''ma) | slave (l-'abdu). | Indeed, he (innahu) | repeatedly turned (awwābun).

38:45 And remember Our slaves Ibrahim and Isaac and Ayyub, possessors of strength and vision.

And remember (wa-udh'kur) | Our slaves ('ibādanā) | Ibrahim (ib'rāhīma) | and Isaac (wa-is'ḥāqa) | and Ayyub (waya'qūba), | possessors (ulī) | of strength (l-aydī) | and vision (wal-abṣāri).

38:46 Indeed, We [We] chose them for an exclusive quality; remembrance of the Home.

Indeed, We (innā) | [We] chose them (akhlaṣnāhum) | for an exclusive quality (bikhāliṣatin); | remembrance (dhik'rā) | of the Home (l-dāri).

38:47 And indeed, they to Us are from the chosen ones, the best.

And indeed, they (wa-innahum) | to Us ('indanā) | are from (lamina) | the chosen ones (l-muṣ'ṭafayna), | the best (l-akhyāri).

38:48 And remember Ishmael and Elisha and Dhul-kifl, and all are from the best.

And remember (wa-udh'kur) | Ishmael (is'mā'īla) | and Elisha (wal-yasa'a) | and Dhul-kifl (wadhā), | and Dhul-kifl (l-kif'li), | and all (wakullun) | are from (mina) | the best (l-akhyāri).

38:49 This is a Reminder. And indeed, for the righteous surely, is a good place of return,

This (hādhā) | is a Reminder (dhik'run). | And indeed (wa-inna), | for the righteous (lil'muttaqīna) | surely, is a good (laḥus'na) | place of return (maābin),

38:50 Gardens of Eternity, will be opened for them the gates.

Gardens (jannāti) | of Eternity ('adnin), | will be opened (mufattaḥatan) | for them (lahumu) | the gates (l-abwābu).

38:51 Reclining therein, they will call therein for fruit many and drink.

Reclining (muttakiīna) | therein (fīhā), | they will call (yad'ūna) | therein (fīhā) | for fruit (bifākihatin) | many (kathīratin) | and drink (washarābin).

38:52 And with them will be companions of modest gaze well-matched.

And with them (wa'indahum) | will be companions of modest gaze (qāṣirātu) | will be companions of modest gaze (l-ṭarfi) | well-matched (atrābun).

38:53 This is what you are promised for the Day of Account.
This (hādhā) | is what (mā) | you are promised (tūʿadūna) | for the Day (liyawmi) | of Account (l-ḥisābi).

38:54 Indeed, this is surely Our provision; not for it any depletion.
Indeed (inna), | this (hādhā) | is surely Our provision (lariz'qunā); | not (mā) | for it (lahu) | any (min) | depletion (nafādin).

38:55 This is so! And indeed, for the transgressors surely is an evil place of return.
This is so (hādhā)! | And indeed (wa-inna), | for the transgressors (lilṭṭāghīna) | surely is an evil (lasharra) | place of return (maābin).

38:56 Hell; they will burn therein and wretched is the resting place.
Hell (jahannama); | they will burn therein (yaṣlawnahā) | and wretched is (fabi'sa) | the resting place (l-mihādu).

38:57 This is so! Then let them taste it, boiling fluid and purulence.
This is so (hādhā)! | Then let them taste it (falyadhūqūhu), | boiling fluid (ḥamīmun) | and purulence (waghassāqun).

38:58 And other of its type of various kinds.
And other (waākharu) | of (min) | its type (shaklihi) | of various kinds (azwājun).

38:59 This is a company bursting in with you. No welcome for them. Indeed, they will burn in the Fire.
This (hādhā) | is a company (fawjun) | bursting (muq'taḥimun) | in with you (maʿakum). | No (lā) | welcome (marḥaban) | for them (bihim). | Indeed, they (innahum) | will burn (ṣālū) | in the Fire (l-nāri).

38:60 They say, "Nay! You - no welcome for you. You brought this upon us. So wretched is the settlement."
They say (qālū), | "Nay (bal)! | You (antum)- | no (lā) | welcome (marḥaban) | for you (bikum). | You (antum) | brought this (qaddamtumūhu) | upon us (lanā). | So wretched is (fabi'sa) | the settlement. (l-qarāru)"

38:61 They will say, "Our Lord, whoever brought upon us this; increase for him a punishment double in the Fire."
They will say (qālū), | "Our Lord (rabbanā), | whoever (man) | brought (qaddama) | upon us (lanā) | this (hādhā); | increase for him (fazid'hu) | a punishment (ʿadhāban) | double (ḍiʿ'fan) | in (fī) | the Fire. (l-nāri)"

38:62 And they will say, "What is for us not we see men we used to count them among the bad ones?
And they will say (waqālū), | "What is (mā) | for us (lanā) | not (lā) | we see (narā) | men (rijālan) | we used to (kunnā) | count them (naʿudduhum) | among (mina) | the bad ones (l-ashrāri)?

38:63 Did we take them in ridicule or has turned away from them the vision?"
Did we take them (attakhadhnāhum) | in ridicule (sikh'riyyan) | or (am) | has turned away (zāghat) | from them (ʿanhumu) | the vision? (l-abṣāru)"

38:64 Indeed, that is surely (the) truth - the quarreling of the people of the Fire.

Indeed (inna), | that (dhālika) | is surely (the) truth (laḥaqqun)- | the quarreling (takhāṣumu) | of the people (ahli) | of the Fire (l-nāri).

38:65 Say, "Only I am a warner, and not is there any god except Allah, the One the Irresistible,
Say (qul), | "Only (innamā) | I am (anā) | a warner (mundhirun), | and not (wamā) | is there any (min) | god (ilāhin) | except (illā) | Allah (l-lahu), | the One (l-wāḥidu) | the Irresistible (l-qahāru),

38:66 Lord of the heavens and the earth and whatever is between them, the All-Mighty, the Oft-Forgiving."
Lord (rabbu) | of the heavens (l-samāwāti) | and the earth (wal-arḍi) | and whatever (wamā) | is between them (baynahumā), | the All-Mighty (l-ʿazīzu), | the Oft-Forgiving. (l-ghafāru)"

38:67 Say, "It is a news great,
Say (qul), | "It is (huwa) | a news (naba-on) | great (ʿaẓīmun),

38:68 You from it turn away
You (antum) | from it (ʿanhu) | turn away (muʿriḍūna)

38:69 Not is for me any knowledge of the chiefs, the exalted when they were disputing.
Not (mā) | is (kāna) | for me (liya) | any (min) | knowledge (ʿil'min) | of the chiefs (bil-mala-i), | the exalted (l-aʿlā) | when (idh) | they were disputing (yakhtaṣimūna).

38:70 Not has been revealed to me except that only I am a warner clear."
Not (in) | has been revealed (yūḥā) | to me (ilayya) | except (illā) | that only (annamā) | I am (anā) | a warner (nadhīrun) | clear. (mubīnun)"

38:71 When said your Lord to the Angels, "Indeed, I Am going to create a human being from clay.
When (idh) | said (qāla) | your Lord (rabbuka) | to the Angels (lil'malāikati), | "Indeed, I Am (innī) | going to create (khāliqun) | a human being (basharan) | from (min) | clay (ṭīnin).

38:72 So when I have proportioned him and breathed into him of My spirit, then fall down to him prostrating."
So when (fa-idhā) | I have proportioned him (sawwaytuhu) | and breathed (wanafakhtu) | into him (fīhi) | of (min) | My spirit (rūḥī), | then fall down (faqaʿū) | to him (lahu) | prostrating. (sājidīna)"

38:73 So prostrated the Angels all of them together.
So prostrated (fasajada) | the Angels (l-malāikatu) | all of them (kulluhum) | together (ajmaʿūna).

38:74 Except Iblis; he was arrogant and became of the disbelievers.
Except (illā) | Iblis (ib'līsa); | he was arrogant (is'takbara) | and became (wakāna) | of (mina) | the disbelievers (l-kāfirīna).

38:75 He said, "O Iblis! What prevented you that you should prostrate to one whom I created with My Hands? Are you arrogant or are you of the exalted ones."
He said (qāla), | "O Iblis (yāib'līsu)! | What (mā) | prevented you (manaʿaka) | that (an) | you should prostrate (tasjuda) | to one whom (limā) | I created (khalaqtu) | with My Hands (biyadayya)? | Are you arrogant (astakbarta) | or (am) | are you (kunta) | of (mina) | the exalted ones. (l-ʿālīna)"

38:76 He said, "I am better than him. You created me from fire and You created him from clay."
He said (qāla), | "I am (anā) | better (khayrun) | than him (min'hu). | You created me (khalaqtanī) | from (min) | fire (nārin) | and You created him (wakhalaqtahu) | from (min) | clay. (ṭīnin)"

38:77 He said, "Then get out of it, for indeed, you are accursed.
He said (qāla), | "Then get out (fa-ukh'ruj) | of it (min'hā), | for indeed, you (fa-innaka) | are accursed (rajīmun).

38:78 And indeed, upon you is My curse until the Day of Judgment."
And indeed (wa-inna), | upon you (ʿalayka) | is My curse (laʿnatī) | until (ilā) | the Day (yawmi) | of Judgment. (l-dīni)"

38:79 He said, "My Lord! Then give me respite until the Day they are resurrected."
He said (qāla), | "My Lord (rabbi)! | Then give me respite (fa-anẓir'nī) | until (ilā) | the Day (yawmi) | they are resurrected. (yub'ʿathūna)"

38:80 He said, "Then indeed, you are of those given respite,
He said (qāla), | "Then indeed, you (fa-innaka) | are of (mina) | those given respite (l-munẓarīna),

38:81 Until the Day of the time well-known."
Until (ilā) | the Day (yawmi) | of the time (l-waqti) | well-known. (l-maʿlūmi)"

38:82 He said, "Then by Your might I will surely mislead them all.
He said (qāla), | "Then by Your might (fabiʿizzatika) | I will surely mislead them (la-ugh'wiyannahum) | all (ajmaʿīna).

38:83 Except Your slaves among them the chosen ones."
Except (illā) | Your slaves (ʿibādaka) | among them (min'humu) | the chosen ones. (l-mukh'laṣīna)"

38:84 He said, "Then it is the truth and the truth I say,
He said (qāla), | "Then it is the truth (fal-ḥaqu) | and the truth (wal-ḥaqa) | I say (aqūlu),

38:85 Surely I will fill Hell with you and those who follow you among them all."
Surely I will fill (la-amla-anna) | Hell (jahannama) | with you (minka) | and those who (wamimman) | follow you (tabiʿaka) | among them (min'hum) | all. (ajmaʿīna)"

38:86 Say, "Not I ask of you for it any payment, and not I am of the ones who pretend.
Say (qul), | "Not (mā) | I ask of you (asalukum) | for it (ʿalayhi) | any (min) | payment (ajrin), | and not (wamā) | I am (anā) | of (mina) | the ones who pretend (l-mutakalifīna).

38:87 Not it is except a Reminder to the worlds.
Not (in) | it is (huwa) | except (illā) | a Reminder (dhik'run) | to the worlds (lil'ʿālamīna).

38:88 And surely you will know its information after a time."
And surely you will know (walataʿlamunna) | its information (naba-ahu) | after (baʿda) | a time. (ḥīnin)"

Chapter (39) Sūrat l-Zumar (The Groups)

39:1 The revelation of the Book is from Allah the All-Mighty, the All-Wise.

The revelation (tanzīlu) | of the Book (l-kitābi) | is from (mina) | Allah (l-lahi) | the All-Mighty (l-ʿazīzi), | the All-Wise (l-ḥakīmi).

39:2 Indeed, We [We] have revealed to you the Book in truth; so worship Allah being sincere to Him in the religion.

Indeed, We (innā) | [We] have revealed (anzalnā) | to you (ilayka) | the Book (l-kitāba) | in truth (bil-ḥaqi); | so worship (fa-uʿ'budi) | Allah (l-laha) | being sincere (mukh'liṣan) | to Him (lahu) | in the religion (l-dīna).

39:3 Unquestionably, for Allah is the religion the pure. And those who take besides Him protectors, "Not we worship them except that they may bring us near to Allah in nearness." Indeed, Allah will judge between them in what they [in it] differ. Indeed, Allah does not guide one who [he] is a liar and a disbeliever.

Unquestionably (alā), | for Allah (lillahi) | is the religion (l-dīnu) | the pure (l-khāliṣu). | And those who (wa-alladhīna) | take (ittakhadhū) | besides Him (min) | besides Him (dūnihi) | protectors (awliyāa), | "Not (mā) | we worship them (naʿbuduhum) | except (illā) | that they may bring us near (liyuqarribūnā) | to (ilā) | Allah (l-lahi) | in nearness. (zul'fā)" | Indeed (inna), | Allah (l-laha) | will judge (yaḥkumu) | between them (baynahum) | in (fī) | what (mā) | they (hum) | [in it] (fīhi) | differ (yakhtalifūna). | Indeed (inna), | Allah (l-laha) | does not (lā) | guide (yahdī) | one who (man) | [he] (huwa) | is a liar (kādhibun) | and a disbeliever (kaffārun).

39:4 If Allah had intended to take a son, surely, He could have chosen from what He creates whatever He willed. Glory be to Him! He is Allah the One, the Irresistible.

If (law) | Allah had intended (arāda) | Allah had intended (l-lahu) | to (an) | take (yattakhidha) | a son (waladan), | surely, He could have chosen (la-iṣ'ṭafā) | from what (mimmā) | He creates (yakhluqu) | whatever (mā) | He willed (yashāu). | Glory be to Him (sub'ḥānahu)! | He (huwa) | is Allah (l-lahu) | the One (l-wāḥidu), | the Irresistible (l-qahāru).

39:5 He created the heavens and the earth in [the] truth. He wraps the night over the day and wraps the day over the night. And He subjected the sun and the moon, each running for a term specified. Unquestionably, He is the All-Mighty, the Oft-Forgiving.

He created (khalaqa) | the heavens (l-samāwāti) | and the earth (wal-arḍa) | in [the] truth (bil-ḥaqi). | He wraps (yukawwiru) | the night (al-layla) | over (ʿalā) | the day (l-nahāri) | and wraps (wayukawwiru) | the day (l-nahāra) | over (ʿalā) | the night (al-layli). | And He subjected (wasakhara) | the sun (l-shamsa) | and the moon (wal-qamara), | each (kullun) | running (yajrī) | for a term (li-ajalin) | specified (musamman). | Unquestionably (alā), | He (huwa) | is the All-Mighty (l-ʿazīzu), | the Oft-Forgiving (l-ghafāru).

39:6 He created you from a soul single. Then He made from it its mate. And He sent down for you of the cattle eight kinds. He creates you in the wombs of your mothers, creation after creation, in darkness[es] three. That is Allah your Lord; for Him is the dominion. There is no god except He. Then how are you turning away?

He created you (khalaqakum) | from (min) | a soul (nafsin) | single (wāḥidatin). | Then (thumma) | He made (jaʿala) | from it (min'hā) | its mate (zawjahā). | And He sent down (wa-anzala) | for you (lakum) | of (mina) | the cattle (l-anʿāmi) | eight (thamāniyata) | kinds (azwājin). | He creates you (yakhluqukum) | in (fī) | the wombs (buṭūni) | of your mothers (ummahātikum), | creation (khalqan) | after (min) | after (baʿdi) | creation (khalqin), | in (fī) | darkness[es] (ẓulumātin) | three (thalāthin). | That (dhālikumu) | is Allah (l-lahu) | your Lord (rabbukum); | for Him (lahu) | is the dominion (l-mul'ku). | There is no (lā) | god (ilāha) | except (illā) | He (huwa). | Then how (fa-annā) | are you turning away (tuṣ'rafūna)?

39:7 If you disbelieve then indeed, Allah is free from need of you. And not He likes in His slaves ungratefulness. And if you are grateful He likes it in you. And not will bear bearer of burdens the burden of another. Then to your Lord is your return, then He will inform you about what you used to do. Indeed, He is the All-Knower of what is in the breasts.

If (in) | you disbelieve (takfurū) | then indeed (fa-inna), | Allah (l-laha) | is free from need (ghaniyyun) | of you (ʿankum). | And not (walā) | He likes (yarḍā) | in His slaves (liʿibādihi) | ungratefulness (l-kuf'ra). | And if (wa-in) | you are grateful (tashkurū) | He likes it (yarḍahu) | in you (lakum). | And not (walā) | will bear (taziru) | bearer of burdens (wāziratun) | the burden (wiz'ra) | of another (ukh'rā). | Then (thumma) | to (ilā) | your Lord (rabbikum) | is your return (marjiʿukum), | then He will inform you (fayunabbi-ukum) | about what (bimā) | you used to (kuntum) | do (taʿmalūna). | Indeed, He (innahu) | is the All-Knower (ʿalīmun) | of what is in the breasts (bidhāti). | of what is in the breasts (l-ṣudūri).

39:8 And when touches [the] man adversity, he calls his Lord turning to Him; then when He bestows on him a favor from Himself, he forgets for what he used to call [to] Him before, and he sets up to Allah rivals to mislead from His Path. Say, "Enjoy in your disbelief for a little. Indeed, you are of the companions of the Fire."

And when (wa-idhā) | touches (massa) | [the] man (l-insāna) | adversity (ḍurrun), | he calls (daʿā) | his Lord (rabbahu) | turning (munīban) | to Him (ilayhi); | then (thumma) | when (idhā) | He bestows on him (khawwalahu) | a favor (niʿ'matan) | from Himself (min'hu), | he forgets (nasiya) | for what (mā) | he used to call (kāna) | he used to call (yadʿū) | [to] Him (ilayhi) | before (min), | before (qablu), | and he sets up (wajaʿala) | to Allah (lillahi) | rivals (andādan) | to mislead (liyuḍilla) | from (ʿan) | His Path (sabīlihi). | Say (qul), | "Enjoy (tamattaʿ) | in your disbelief (bikuf'rika) | for a little (qalīlan). | Indeed, you (innaka) | are of (min) | the companions (aṣḥābi) | of the Fire. (l-nāri)"

39:9 Is one who [he] is devoutly obedient - during hours of the night, prostrating and standing, fearing the Hereafter and hoping for the Mercy of his Lord? Say, "Are equal those who know and those who do not know?" Only will take heed those of understanding.

Is one who (amman) | [he] (huwa) | is devoutly obedient (qānitun)- | during hours (ānāa) | of the night (al-layli), | prostrating (sājidan) | and standing (waqāiman), | fearing (yaḥdharu) | the Hereafter (l-ākhirata) | and hoping (wayarjū) | for the Mercy (raḥmata) | of his Lord (rabbihi)? | Say (qul), | "Are (hal) | equal (yastawī) | those who (alladhīna) | know (yaʿlamūna) | and those who (wa-alladhīna) | do not (lā) | know? (yaʿlamūna)" | Only (innamā) | will take heed (yatadhakkaru) | those of understanding (ulū). | those of understanding (l-albābi).

39:10 Say, "O My slaves [those] who believe! Fear your Lord. For those who do good in this world is good, and the earth of Allah is spacious. Only will be paid back in full the patient ones their reward without account."

Say (qul), | "O My slaves (yāʿibādi) | [those] who (alladhīna) | believe (āmanū)! | Fear (ittaqū) | your Lord (rabbakum). | For those who (lilladhīna) | do good (aḥsanū) | in (fī) | this (hādhihi) | world (l-dun'yā) | is good (ḥasanatun), | and the earth (wa-arḍu) | of Allah (l-lahi) | is spacious (wāsiʿatun). | Only (innamā) | will be paid back in full (yuwaffā) | the patient ones (l-ṣābirūna) | their reward (ajrahum) | without (bighayri) | account. (ḥisābin)"

39:11 Say, "Indeed, I [I] am commanded that I worship Allah, being sincere to Him in the religion.

Say (qul), | "Indeed, I (innī) | [I] am commanded (umir'tu) | that (an) | I worship (aʿbuda) | Allah (l-laha), | being sincere (mukh'liṣan) | to Him (lahu) | in the religion (l-dīna).

39:12 And I am commanded that I be the first of those who submit."

And I am commanded (wa-umir'tu) | that (li-an) | I be (akūna) | the first (awwala) | of those who submit. (l-mus'limīna)"

39:13 Say, "Indeed, I [I] fear, if I disobey my Lord, the punishment of a Day great."

Say (qul), | "Indeed, I (innī) | [I] fear (akhāfu), | if (in) | I disobey (ʿaṣaytu) | my Lord (rabbī), | the punishment (ʿadhāba) | of a Day (yawmin) | great. (ʿaẓīmin)"

39:14 Say, "I worship Allah being sincere to Him in my religion.

Say (quli), | "I worship Allah (l-laha) | "I worship Allah (aʿbudu) | being sincere (mukh'liṣan) | to Him (lahu) | in my religion (dīnī).

39:15 So worship what you will besides Him." Say, "Indeed, the losers are those who will lose themselves and their families on the Day of the Resurrection. Unquestionably, that - it is the loss the clear."

So worship (fa-uʿ'budū) | what (mā) | you will (shi'tum) | besides Him. (min)" | besides Him. (dūnihi)" | Say (qul), | "Indeed (inna), | the losers (l-khāsirīna) | are those who (alladhīna) | will lose (khasirū) | themselves (anfusahum) | and their families (wa-ahlīhim) | on the Day (yawma) | of the Resurrection (l-qiyāmati). | Unquestionably (alā), | that (dhālika)- | it (huwa) | is the loss (l-khus'rānu) | the clear. (l-mubīnu)"

39:16 For them from above them coverings of the Fire and from below them coverings. With that threatens Allah [with it] His slaves, "O My slaves! So fear Me."

For them (lahum) | from (min) | above them (fawqihim) | coverings (ẓulalun) | of (mina) | the Fire (l-nāri) | and from (wamin) | below them (taḥtihim) | coverings (ẓulalun). | With that (dhālika) | threatens (yukhawwifu) | Allah (l-lahu) | [with it] (bihi) | His slaves (ʿibādahu), | "O My slaves (yāʿibādi)! | So fear Me. (fa-ittaqūni)"

39:17 And those who avoid the false gods lest they worship them and turn to Allah, for them are glad tidings. So give glad tidings to My slaves

And those who (wa-alladhīna) | avoid (ij'tanabū) | the false gods (l-ṭāghūta) | lest (an) | they worship them (yaʿbudūhā) | and turn (wa-anābū) | to (ilā) | Allah (l-lahi), | for them (lahumu) | are glad tidings (l-bush'rā). | So give glad tidings (fabashir) | to My slaves (ʿibādi)

39:18 Those who they listen to the Word, then follow the best thereof, those are they whom Allah has guided them, and those are [they] the men of understanding.

Those who (alladhīna) | they listen to (yastamiʿūna) | the Word (l-qawla), | then follow (fayattabiʿūna) | the best thereof (aḥsanahu), | those (ulāika) | are they whom (alladhīna) | Allah has guided them (hadāhumu), | Allah has guided them (l-lahu), | and those (wa-ulāika) | are [they] (hum) | the men of understanding (ulū). | the men of understanding (l-albābi).

39:19 Then, is one who, became due on him the word of the punishment? Then can you save one who is in the Fire?

Then, is one who (afaman), | became due (ḥaqqa) | on him (ʿalayhi) | the word (kalimatu) | of the punishment (l-ʿadhābi)? | Then can you (afa-anta) | save (tunqidhu) | one who (man) | is in (fī) | the Fire (l-nāri)?

39:20 But those who fear their Lord, for them are lofty mansions, above them lofty mansions built high, flow from beneath it the rivers. The Promise of Allah. Not Allah fails in His promise.

But (lākini) | those who (alladhīna) | fear (ittaqaw) | their Lord (rabbahum), | for them (lahum) | are lofty mansions (ghurafun), | above them (min) | above them (fawqihā) | lofty mansions (ghurafun) | built high (mabniyyatun), | flow (tajrī) | from (min) | beneath it (taḥtihā) | the rivers (l-anhāru). | The Promise (waʿda) | of Allah (l-lahi). | Not (lā) | Allah fails (yukh'lifu) | Allah fails (l-lahu) | in His promise (l-mīʿāda).

39:21 Do not you see that Allah sends down from the sky water and He makes it flow as springs in the earth; then He produces with it crops of different colors; then they wither and you see it turn yellow; then He makes them debris? Indeed, in that surely, is a reminder for those of understanding.

Do not (alam) | you see (tara) | that (anna) | Allah (l-laha) | sends down (anzala) | from (mina) | the sky (l-samāi) | water (māan) | and He makes it flow (fasalakahu) | as springs (yanābīʿa) | in (fī) | the earth (l-arḍi); | then (thumma) | He produces (yukh'riju) | with it (bihi) | crops (zarʿan) | of different (mukh'talifan) | colors (alwānuhu); | then (thumma) | they wither (yahīju) | and you see it (fatarāhu) | turn yellow (muṣ'farran); | then (thumma) | He makes them (yajʿaluhu) | debris (ḥuṭāman)? | Indeed (inna), | in (fī) | that (dhālika) | surely, is a reminder (ladhik'rā) | for those of understanding (li-ulī). | for those of understanding (l-albābi).

39:22 So is one for whom Allah has expanded his breast for Islam so he is upon a light from his Lord. So woe to those are hardened their hearts from the remembrance of Allah. Those are in error clear.

So is one for whom (afaman) | Allah has expanded (sharaḥa) | Allah has expanded (l-lahu) | his breast (ṣadrahu) | for Islam (lil'is'lāmi) | so he (fahuwa) | is upon (ʿalā) | a light (nūrin) | from (min) | his Lord (rabbihi). | So woe (fawaylun) | to those are hardened (lil'qāsiyati) | their hearts (qulūbuhum) | from (min) | the remembrance of Allah (dhik'ri). | the remembrance of Allah (l-lahi). | Those (ulāika) | are in (fī) | error (ḍalālin) | clear (mubīnin).

39:23 Allah has revealed the best of [the] statement - a Book its parts resembling each other oft-repeated. Shiver from it the skins of those who fear their Lord, then relax their skins and their hearts at the remembrance of Allah. That is the guidance of Allah, He guides with it whom He wills. And whoever Allah lets go astray then not for him any guide.

Allah (al-lahu) | has revealed (nazzala) | the best (aḥsana) | of [the] statement (l-ḥadīthi)- | a Book (kitāban) | its parts resembling each other (mutashābihan) | oft-repeated (mathāniya). | Shiver (taqshaʿirru) | from it (min'hu) | the skins (julūdu) | of those who (alladhīna) | fear (yakhshawna) | their Lord (rabbahum), | then (thumma) | relax (talīnu) | their skins (julūduhum) | and their hearts (waqulūbuhum) | at (ilā) | the remembrance (dhik'ri) | of Allah (l-lahi). | That (dhālika) | is the guidance (hudā) | of Allah (l-lahi), | He guides (yahdī) | with it (bihi) | whom (man) | He wills (yashāu). | And whoever (waman) | Allah lets go astray (yuḍ'lili) | Allah lets go astray (l-lahu) | then not (famā) | for him (lahu) | any (min) | guide (hādin).

39:24 Then is he who will shield with his face the worst punishment on the Day of the Resurrection? And it will be said to the wrongdoers, "Taste what you used to earn."

Then is he who (afaman) | will shield (yattaqī) | with his face (biwajhihi) | the worst (sūa) | punishment (l-ʿadhābi) | on the Day (yawma) | of the Resurrection (l-qiyāmati)? | And it will be said (waqīla) | to the wrongdoers (lilẓẓālimīna), | "Taste (dhūqū) | what (mā) | you used to (kuntum) | earn. (taksibūna)"

39:25 Denied those who were before them, so came upon them the punishment from where not they perceive.

Denied (kadhaba) | those who (alladhīna) | were before them (min), | were before them (qablihim), | so came upon them (fa-atāhumu) | the punishment (l-ʿadhābu) | from (min) | where (ḥaythu) | not (lā) | they perceive (yashʿurūna).

39:26 So Allah made them the disgrace in the life of the world, and certainly the punishment of the Hereafter is greater, if they knew.

So Allah made them (fa-adhāqahumu) | So Allah made them (l-lahu) | the disgrace (l-khiz'ya) | in (fī) | the life (l-ḥayati) | of the world (l-dun'yā), | and certainly the punishment (walaʿadhābu) | of the Hereafter (l-ākhirati) | is greater (akbaru), | if (law) | they (kānū) | knew (yaʿlamūna).

39:27 And indeed, We have set forth for people in this Quran of every example so that they may take heed.
And indeed (walaqad), | We have set forth (ḍarabnā) | for people (lilnnāsi) | in (fī) | this (hādhā) | Quran (l-qur'āni) | of (min) | every (kulli) | example (mathalin) | so that they may (laʿallahum) | take heed (yatadhakkarūna).

39:28 A Quran in Arabic without any crookedness so that they may become righteous.
A Quran (qur'ānan) | in Arabic (ʿarabiyyan) | without (ghayra) | any (dhī) | crookedness (ʿiwajin) | so that they may (laʿallahum) | become righteous (yattaqūna).

39:29 Allah sets forth an example - a man about him partners quarreling and a man belonging exclusively to one man - are they both equal in comparison? All praise be to Allah! Nay, most of them do not know.
Allah sets forth (ḍaraba) | Allah sets forth (l-lahu) | an example (mathalan)- | a man (rajulan) | about him (fīhi) | partners (shurakāu) | quarreling (mutashākisūna) | and a man (warajulan) | belonging exclusively (salaman) | to one man (lirajulin)- | are (hal) | they both equal (yastawiyāni) | in comparison (mathalan)? | All praise (l-ḥamdu) | be to Allah (lillahi)! | Nay (bal), | most of them (aktharuhum) | do not (lā) | know (yaʿlamūna).

39:30 Indeed, you will die and indeed, they will also die.
Indeed, you (innaka) | will die (mayyitun) | and indeed, they (wa-innahum) | will also die (mayyitūna).

39:31 Then indeed you, on the Day of the Resurrection, before your Lord, will dispute.
Then (thumma) | indeed you (innakum), | on the Day (yawma) | of the Resurrection (l-qiyāmati), | before (ʿinda) | your Lord (rabbikum), | will dispute (takhtaṣimūna).

39:32 Then who is more unjust than one who lies against Allah and denies the truth when it comes to him? Is there not in Hell an abode for the disbelievers?
Then who (faman) | is more unjust (aẓlamu) | than one who (mimman) | lies (kadhaba) | against (ʿalā) | Allah (l-lahi) | and denies (wakadhaba) | the truth (bil-ṣid'qi) | when (idh) | it comes to him (jāahu)? | Is there not (alaysa) | in (fī) | Hell (jahannama) | an abode (mathwan) | for the disbelievers (lil'kāfirīna)?

39:33 And the one who brought the truth and believed in it, those [they] are the righteous.
And the one who (wa-alladhī) | brought (jāa) | the truth (bil-ṣid'qi) | and believed (waṣaddaqa) | in it (bihi), | those (ulāika) | [they] (humu) | are the righteous (l-mutaqūna).

39:34 For them is what they wish with their Lord. That is the reward of the good-doers
For them (lahum) | is what (mā) | they wish (yashāūna) | with (ʿinda) | their Lord (rabbihim). | That (dhālika) | is the reward (jazāu) | of the good-doers (l-muḥ'sinīna)

39:35 That Allah will remove from them the worst of what they did and reward them their due for the best of what they used to do.
That Allah will remove (liyukaffira) | That Allah will remove (l-lahu) | from them (ʿanhum) | the worst (aswa-a) | of what (alladhī) | they did (ʿamilū) | and reward them (wayajziyahum) | their due (ajrahum) | for the best (bi-aḥsani) | of what (alladhī) | they used to (kānū) | do (yaʿmalūna).

39:36 Is not Allah sufficient for His slave? And they threaten you with those besides Him. And whoever Allah lets go astray - then not for him any guide.

Is not (alaysa) | Allah (l-lahu) | sufficient (bikāfin) | for His slave (ʿabdahu)? | And they threaten you (wayukhawwifūnaka) | with those (bi-alladhīna) | besides Him (min). | besides Him (dūnihi). | And whoever (waman) | Allah lets go astray (yuḍ'lili)- | Allah lets go astray (l-lahu)- | then not (famā) | for him (lahu) | any (min) | guide (hādin).

39:37 And whoever Allah guides, then not for him any misleader. Is not Allah All-Mighty, All-Able of retribution?

And whoever (waman) | Allah guides (yahdi), | Allah guides (l-lahu), | then not (famā) | for him (lahu) | any (min) | misleader (muḍillin). | Is not (alaysa) | Allah (l-lahu) | All-Mighty (biʿazīzin), | All-Able of retribution (dhī)? | All-Able of retribution (intiqāmin)?

39:38 And if you ask them who created the heavens and the earth? Surely, they will say, "Allah." Say, "Then do you see what you invoke besides Allah? if Allah intended for me harm, are they removers of harm (from) Him; or if He intended for me mercy, are they withholders of His mercy?" Say, "Sufficient is Allah for me; upon Him put trust those who trust."

And if (wala-in) | you ask them (sa-altahum) | who (man) | created (khalaqa) | the heavens (l-samāwāti) | and the earth (wal-arḍa)? | Surely, they will say (layaqūlunna), | "Allah. (l-lahu)" | Say (qul), | "Then do you see (afara-aytum) | what (mā) | you invoke (tadʿūna) | besides (min) | besides (dūni) | Allah (l-lahi)? | if (in) | Allah intended for me (arādaniya) | Allah intended for me (l-lahu) | harm (biḍurrin), | are (hal) | they (hunna) | removers (kāshifātu) | of harm (from) Him (ḍurrihi); | or (aw) | if He intended for me (arādanī) | mercy (biraḥmatin), | are (hal) | they (hunna) | withholders (mum'sikātu) | of His mercy? (raḥmatihi)" | Say (qul), | "Sufficient is Allah for me (ḥasbiya); | "Sufficient is Allah for me (l-lahu); | upon Him (ʿalayhi) | put trust (yatawakkalu) | those who trust. (l-mutawakilūna)"

39:39 Say, "O my people! Work according to your position, indeed, I am working; then soon you will know

Say (qul), | "O my people (yāqawmi)! | Work (iʿ'malū) | according to (ʿalā) | your position (makānatikum), | indeed, I am (innī) | working (ʿāmilun); | then soon (fasawfa) | you will know (taʿlamūna)

39:40 Upon whom will come a punishment disgracing him and descends on him a punishment everlasting."

Upon whom (man) | will come (yatīhi) | a punishment (ʿadhābun) | disgracing him (yukh'zīhi) | and descends (wayaḥillu) | on him (ʿalayhi) | a punishment (ʿadhābun) | everlasting. (muqīmun)"

39:41 Indeed We, We revealed to you the Book for [the] mankind in truth. So whoever accepts guidance, then it is for his soul; and whoever goes astray then only he strays against his soul. And not you are over them a manager.

Indeed We (innā), | We revealed (anzalnā) | to you (ʿalayka) | the Book (l-kitāba) | for [the] mankind (lilnnāsi) | in truth (bil-ḥaqi). | So whoever (famani) | accepts guidance (ih'tadā), | then it is for his soul (falinafsihi); | and whoever (waman) | goes astray (ḍalla) | then only (fa-innamā) | he strays (yaḍillu) | against his soul (ʿalayhā). | And not (wamā) | you (anta) | are over them (ʿalayhim) | a manager (biwakīlin).

39:42 Allah takes the souls at the time of their death, and the one who does not die in their sleep. Then He keeps the one whom, He has decreed for them the death, and sends the others for a term specified. Indeed, in that surely are signs for a people who ponder.

Allah (al-lahu) | takes (yatawaffā) | the souls (l-anfusa) | at the time (ḥīna) | of their death (mawtihā), | and the one who (wa-allatī) | does not (lam) | die (tamut) | in (fī) | their sleep (manāmihā). | Then He keeps (fayum'siku) | the one whom (allatī), | He has decreed (qaḍā) | for them (ʿalayhā) | the death (l-mawta), | and sends (wayur'silu) | the others (l-ukh'rā) | for (ilā) | a term (ajalin) | specified (musamman). | Indeed (inna), | in (fī) | that (dhālika) | surely are signs (laāyātin) | for a people (liqawmin) | who ponder (yatafakkarūna).

39:43 Or have they taken besides Allah intercessors? Say, "Even though they were not possessing anything, and not they understand?"

Or (ami) | have they taken (ittakhadhū) | besides (min) | besides (dūni) | Allah (l-lahi) | intercessors (shufaʿāa)? | Say (qul), | "Even though (awalaw) | they were (kānū) | not (lā) | possessing (yamlikūna) | anything (shayan), | and not (walā) | they understand? (yaʿqilūna)"

39:44 Say, "To Allah belongs the intercession all. For Him is the dominion of the heavens and the earth. Then to Him you will be returned."

Say (qul), | "To Allah belongs (lillahi) | the intercession (l-shafāʿatu) | all (jamīʿan). | For Him (lahu) | is the dominion (mul'ku) | of the heavens (l-samāwāti) | and the earth (wal-arḍi). | Then (thumma) | to Him (ilayhi) | you will be returned. (tur'jaʿūna)"

39:45 And when Allah is mentioned Alone, shrink with aversion the hearts of those who do not believe in the Hereafter, and when are mentioned those besides Him, behold! They rejoice.

And when (wa-idhā) | Allah is mentioned (dhukira) | Allah is mentioned (l-lahu) | Alone (waḥdahu), | shrink with aversion (ish'ma-azzat) | the hearts (qulūbu) | of those who (alladhīna) | do not (lā) | believe (yu'minūna) | in the Hereafter (bil-ākhirati), | and when (wa-idhā) | are mentioned (dhukira) | those (alladhīna) | besides Him (min), | besides Him (dūnihi), | behold (idhā)! | They (hum) | rejoice (yastabshirūna).

39:46 Say, "O Allah! Creator of the heavens and the earth, Knower of the unseen and the witnessed, You will judge between Your slaves in what they used to therein differ."

Say (quli), | "O Allah (l-lahuma)! | Creator (fāṭira) | of the heavens (l samāwāti) | and the earth (wal-arḍi), | Knower (ʿālima) | of the unseen (l-ghaybi) | and the witnessed (wal-shahādati), | You (anta) | will judge (taḥkumu) | between (bayna) | Your slaves (ʿibādika) | in (fī) | what (mā) | they used to (kānū) | therein (fīhi) | differ. (yakhtalifūna)"

39:47 And if those who did wrong had whatever is in the earth all and the like of it with it, they would ransom with it from the evil of the punishment on the Day of the Resurrection. And will appear to them from Allah what not they had taken into account.

And if (walaw) | And if (anna) | those who (lilladhīna) | did wrong (ẓalamū) | had whatever (mā) | is in (fī) | the earth (l-arḍi) | all (jamīʿan) | and the like of it (wamith'lahu) | with it (maʿahu), | they would ransom (la-if'tadaw) | with it (bihi) | from (min) | the evil (sūi) | of the punishment (l-ʿadhābi) | on the Day (yawma) | of the Resurrection (l-qiyāmati). | And will appear (wabadā) | to them (lahum) | from (mina) | Allah (l-lahi) | what (mā) | not (lam) | they had (yakūnū) | taken into account (yaḥtasibūna).

39:48 And will become apparent to them the evils of what they earned, and will surround them what they used to [in it] mock.

And will become apparent (wabadā) | to them (lahum) | the evils (sayyiātu) | of what (mā) | they earned (kasabū), | and will surround (waḥāqa) | them (bihim) | what (mā) | they used to (kānū) | [in it] (bihi) | mock (yastahziūna).

39:49 So when touches [the] man adversity, he calls upon Us; then when We bestow on him a favor from Us, he says, "Only, I have been given it for knowledge." Nay, it is a trial, but most of them do not know.

So when (fa-idhā) | touches (massa) | [the] man (l-insāna) | adversity (ḍurrun), | he calls upon Us (daʿānā); | then (thumma) | when (idhā) | We bestow on him (khawwalnāhu) | a favor (niʿ'matan) | from Us (minnā), | he says (qāla), | "Only (innamā), | I have been given it (ūtītuhu) | for (ʿalā) | knowledge. (ʿil'min)" | Nay (bal), | it (hiya) | is a trial (fit'natun), | but (walākinna) | most of them (aktharahum) | do not (lā) | know (yaʿlamūna).

39:50 Indeed, said it those before them, but did not avail them what they used to earn.

Indeed (qad), | said it (qālahā) | those (alladhīna) | before them (min), | before them (qablihim), | but did not (famā) | avail (aghnā) | them (ʿanhum) | what (mā) | they used to (kānū) | earn (yaksibūna).

39:51 Then struck them the evils of what they earned. And those who have wronged of these, will strike them the evils of what they earned; and not they will be able to escape.

Then struck them (fa-aṣābahum) | the evils (sayyiātu) | of what (mā) | they earned (kasabū). | And those who (wa-alladhīna) | have wronged (ẓalamū) | of (min) | these (hāulāi), | will strike them (sayuṣībuhum) | the evils (sayyiātu) | of what (mā) | they earned (kasabū); | and not (wamā) | they (hum) | will be able to escape (bimuʿ'jizīna).

39:52 Do not they know that Allah extends the provision for whom He wills and restricts. Indeed, in that surely are signs for a people who believe.

Do not (awalam) | they know (yaʿlamū) | that (anna) | Allah (l-laha) | extends (yabsuṭu) | the provision (l-riz'qa) | for whom (liman) | He wills (yashāu) | and restricts (wayaqdiru). | Indeed (inna), | in (fī) | that (dhālika) | surely are signs (laāyātin) | for a people (liqawmin) | who believe (yu'minūna).

39:53 Say, "O My slaves! Those who have transgressed against themselves, do not despair of the Mercy of Allah. Indeed, Allah forgives the sins all. Indeed He, He is the Oft-Forgiving, the Most Merciful.

Say (qul), | "O My slaves (yāʿibādiya)! | Those who (alladhīna) | have transgressed (asrafū) | against (ʿalā) | themselves (anfusihim), | do not (lā) | despair (taqnaṭū) | of (min) | the Mercy (raḥmati) | of Allah (l-lahi). | Indeed (inna), | Allah (l-laha) | forgives (yaghfiru) | the sins (l-dhunūba) | all (jamīʿan). | Indeed He (innahu), | He (huwa) | is the Oft-Forgiving (l-ghafūru), | the Most Merciful (l-raḥīmu).

39:54 And turn to your Lord and submit to Him before [that] comes to you the punishment; then not you will be helped.

And turn (wa-anībū) | to (ilā) | your Lord (rabbikum) | and submit (wa-aslimū) | to Him (lahu) | before (min) | before (qabli) | [that] (an) | comes to you (yatiyakumu) | the punishment (l-ʿadhābu); | then (thumma) | not (lā) | you will be helped (tunṣarūna).

39:55 And follow the best of what is revealed to you from your Lord before [that] comes to you the punishment suddenly, while you do not perceive,

And follow (wa-ittabiʿū) | the best (aḥsana) | of what (mā) | is revealed (unzila) | to you (ilaykum) | from (min) | your Lord (rabbikum) | before (min) | before (qabli) | [that] (an) | comes to you (yatiyakumu) | the punishment (l-ʿadhābu) | suddenly (baghtatan), | while you (wa-antum) | do not (lā) | perceive (tashʿurūna),

39:56 Lest should say a soul, "Oh! My regret over what I neglected in regard to Allah and that I was surely, among the mockers."

Lest (an) | should say (taqūla) | a soul (nafsun), | "Oh! My regret (yāḥasratā) | over (ʿalā) | what (mā) | I neglected (farraṭtu) | in (fī) | regard to (janbi) | Allah (l-lahi) | and that (wa-in) | I was (kuntu) | surely, among (lamina) | the mockers. (l-sākhirīna)"

39:57 Or it should say, "If that Allah had guided me, surely, I would have been among the righteous."

Or (aw) | it should say (taqūla), | "If that (law) | "If that (anna) | Allah (l-laha) | had guided me (hadānī), | surely, I would have been (lakuntu) | among (mina) | the righteous. (l-mutaqīna)"

39:58 Or it should say when it sees the punishment, "If only for me another chance then I could be among the good-doers."

Or (aw) | it should say (taqūla) | when (ḥīna) | it sees (tarā) | the punishment (l-ʿadhāba), | "If (law) | only (anna) | for me (lī) | another chance (karratan) | then I could be (fa-akūna) | among (mina) | the good-doers. (l-muḥ'sinīna)"

39:59 "Yes, verily came to you My Verses, but you denied them and were arrogant, and you were among the disbelievers.

"Yes (balā), | verily (qad) | came to you (jāatka) | My Verses (āyātī), | but you denied (fakadhabta) | them (bihā) | and were arrogant (wa-is'takbarta), | and you were (wakunta) | among (mina) | the disbelievers (l-kāfirīna).

39:60 And on the Day of the Resurrection you will see those who lied about Allah, their faces will be blackened. Is there not in Hell an abode for the arrogant?

And on the Day (wayawma) | of the Resurrection (l-qiyāmati) | you will see (tarā) | those who (alladhīna) | lied (kadhabū) | about (ʿalā) | Allah (l-lahi), | their faces (wujūhuhum) | will be blackened (mus'waddatun). | Is there not (alaysa) | in (fī) | Hell (jahannama) | an abode (mathwan) | for the arrogant (lil'mutakabbirīna)?

39:61 And Allah will deliver those who feared Him to their place of salvation; not will touch them the evil, and not they will grieve.

And Allah will deliver (wayunajjī) | And Allah will deliver (l-lahu) | those who (alladhīna) | feared Him (ittaqaw) | to their place of salvation (bimafāzatihim); | not (lā) | will touch them (yamassuhumu) | the evil (l-sūu), | and not (walā) | they (hum) | will grieve (yaḥzanūna).

39:62 Allah is the Creator of all things, and He is over all things a Guardian.

Allah (al-lahu) | is the Creator (khāliqu) | of all (kulli) | things (shayin), | and He (wahuwa) | is over (ʿalā) | all (kulli) | things (shayin) | a Guardian (wakīlun).

39:63 For Him are the keys of the heavens and the earth. And those who disbelieve in the Verses of Allah, those - they are the losers.

For Him (lahu) | are the keys (maqālīdu) | of the heavens (l-samāwāti) | and the earth (wal-arḍi). | And those who (wa-alladhīna) | disbelieve (kafarū) | in the Verses (biāyāti) | of Allah (l-lahi), | those (ulāika)- | they (humu) | are the losers (l-khāsirūna).

39:64 Say, "Is it other than Allah you order me to worship, O ignorant ones?"

Say (qul), | "Is it other than (afaghayra) | Allah (l-lahi) | you order me (tamurūnnī) | to worship (aʿbudu), | O (ayyuhā) | ignorant ones? (l-jāhilūna)"

39:65 And verily, it has been revealed to you and to those who were before you, if you associate with Allah surely, will become worthless your deeds and you will surely be among the losers.

And verily (walaqad), | it has been revealed (ūḥiya) | to you (ilayka) | and to (wa-ilā) | those who (alladhīna) | were before you (min), | were before you (qablika), | if (la-in) | you associate with Allah (ashrakta) | surely, will become worthless (layaḥbaṭanna) | your deeds (ʿamaluka) | and you will surely be (walatakūnanna) | among (mina) | the losers (l-khāsirīna).

39:66 Nay! But worship Allah and be among the thankful ones.

Nay (bali)! | But worship Allah (l-laha) | But worship Allah (fa-uʿ'bud) | and be (wakun) | among (mina) | the thankful ones (l-shākirīna).

39:67 And not they appraised Allah with true appraisal, while the earth entirely will be in His Grip on the Day of the Resurrection, and the heavens will be folded in His Right Hand. Glory be to Him! And High is He above what they associate with Him.

And not (wamā) | they appraised (qadarū) | Allah (l-laha) | with true (ḥaqqa) | appraisal (qadrihi), | while the earth (wal-arḍu) | entirely (jamīʿan) | will be in His Grip (qabḍatuhu) | on the Day (yawma) | of the Resurrection (l-qiyāmati), | and the heavens (wal-samāwātu) | will be folded (maṭwiyyātun) | in His Right Hand (biyamīnihi). | Glory be to Him (sub'ḥānahu)! | And High is He (wataʿālā) | above what (ʿammā) | they associate with Him (yush'rikūna).

39:68 And will be blown [in] the trumpet, then will fall dead whoever is in the heavens and whoever is on the earth except whom Allah wills. Then it will be blown [in it] a second time, and behold! They will be standing waiting.

And will be blown (wanufikha) | [in] (fī) | the trumpet (l-ṣūri), | then will fall dead (faṣaʿiqa) | whoever (man) | is in (fī) | the heavens (l-samāwāti) | and whoever (waman) | is on (fī) | the earth (l-arḍi) | except (illā) | whom (man) | Allah wills (shāa). | Allah wills (l-lahu). | Then (thumma) | it will be blown (nufikha) | [in it] (fīhi) | a second time (ukh'rā), | and behold (fa-idhā)! | They (hum) | will be standing (qiyāmun) | waiting (yanẓurūna).

39:69 And will shine the earth with the light of its Lord and will be placed the Record and will be brought the Prophets and the witnesses, and it will be judged between them in truth, and they will not be wronged.

And will shine (wa-ashraqati) | the earth (l-arḍu) | with the light (binūri) | of its Lord (rabbihā) | and will be placed (wawuḍiʿa) | the Record (l-kitābu) | and will be brought (wajīa) | the Prophets (bil-nabiyīna) | and the witnesses (wal-shuhadāi), | and it will be judged (waquḍiya) | between them (baynahum) | in truth (bil-ḥaqi), | and they (wahum) | will not be wronged (lā). | will not be wronged (yuẓ'lamūna).

39:70 And will be paid in full every soul what it did; and He is the Best-Knower of what they do.

And will be paid in full (wawuffiyat) | every (kullu) | soul (nafsin) | what (mā) | it did (ʿamilat); | and He (wahuwa) | is the Best-Knower (aʿlamu) | of what (bimā) | they do (yafʿalūna).

39:71 And will be driven those who disbelieve to Hell in groups until when they reach it, will be opened its gates and will say to them its keepers, "Did not come to you Messengers from you reciting to you the Verses of your Lord and warning you of the meeting of your Day this?" They will say, "Yes!" But has been justified the word of punishment against the disbelievers.

And will be driven (wasīqa) | those who (alladhīna) | disbelieve (kafarū) | to (ilā) | Hell (jahannama) | in groups (zumaran) | until (ḥattā) | when (idhā) | they reach it (jāūhā), | will be opened (futiḥat) | its gates (abwābuhā) | and will say (waqāla) | to them (lahum) | its keepers (khazanatuhā), | "Did not (alam) | come to you (yatikum) | Messengers (rusulun) | from you (minkum) | reciting (yatlūna) | to you (ʿalaykum) | the Verses (āyāti) | of your Lord (rabbikum) | and warning you (wayundhirūnakum) | of the meeting (liqāa) | of your Day (yawmikum) | this? (hādhā)" | They will say (qālū), | "Yes! (balā)" | But (walākin) | has been justified (ḥaqqat) | the word (kalimatu) | of punishment (l-ʿadhābi) | against (ʿalā) | the disbelievers (l-kāfirīna).

39:72 It will be said, "Enter the gates of Hell to abide eternally therein, and wretched is the abode of the arrogant."

It will be said (qīla), | "Enter (ud'khulū) | the gates (abwāba) | of Hell (jahannama) | to abide eternally (khālidīna) | therein (fīhā), | and wretched is (fabi'sa) | the abode (mathwā) | of the arrogant. (l-mutakabirīna)"

39:73 And will be driven those who feared their Lord, to Paradise in groups until when they reach it and will be opened its gates and will say to them its keepers, "Peace be upon you, you have done well, so enter it to abide eternally."

And will be driven (wasīqa) | those who (alladhīna) | feared (ittaqaw) | their Lord (rabbahum), | to (ilā) | Paradise (l-janati) | in groups (zumaran) | until (ḥattā) | when (idhā) | they reach it (jāūhā) | and will be opened (wafutiḥat) | its gates (abwābuhā) | and will say (waqāla) | to them (lahum) | its keepers (khazanatuhā), | "Peace be (salāmun) | upon you (ʿalaykum), | you have done well (ṭib'tum), | so enter it (fa-ud'khulūhā) | to abide eternally. (khālidīna)"

39:74 And they will say, "All praise be to Allah, Who has fulfilled for us His promise and has made us inherit the earth, we may settle [from] in Paradise wherever we wish. So excellent is the reward of the workers."

And they will say (waqālū), | "All praise (l-ḥamdu) | be to Allah (lillahi), | Who (alladhī) | has fulfilled for us (ṣadaqanā) | His promise (waʿdahu) | and has made us inherit (wa-awrathanā) | the earth (l-arḍa), | we may settle (natabawwa-u) | [from] (mina) | in Paradise (l-janati) | wherever (ḥaythu) | we wish (nashāu). | So excellent (faniʿ'ma) | is the reward (ajru) | of the workers. (l-ʿāmilīna)"

39:75 And you will see the Angels surrounding [from] around the Throne glorifying the praise of their Lord. And will be judged between them in truth, and it will be said, "All praise be to Allah, the Lord of the worlds."

And you will see (watarā) | the Angels (l-malāikata) | surrounding (ḥāffīna) | [from] (min) | around (ḥawli) | the Throne (l-ʿarshi) | glorifying (yusabbiḥūna) | the praise (biḥamdi) | of their Lord (rabbihim). | And will be judged (waquḍiya) | between them (baynahum) | in truth (bil-ḥaqi), | and it will be said (waqīla), | "All praise be (l-ḥamdu) | to Allah (lillahi), | the Lord (rabbi) | of the worlds. (l ʿālamīna)"

Chapter (40) Sūrat Ghāfir (The Forgiver God)

40:1 Ha Meem.

Ha Meem (hha-meem).

40:2 The revelation of the Book is from Allah the All-Mighty, the All-Knower.

The revelation (tanzīlu) | of the Book (l-kitābi) | is from (mina) | Allah (l-lahi) | the All-Mighty (l-ʿazīzi), | the All-Knower (l-ʿalīmi).

40:3 The Forgiver of the sin, and the Acceptor of [the] repentance, severe in the punishment, Owner of the abundance. There is no god except Him; to Him, is the final return.

The Forgiver (ghāfiri) | of the sin (l-dhanbi), | and the Acceptor (waqābili) | of [the] repentance (l-tawbi), | severe (shadīdi) | in the punishment (l-ʿiqābi), | Owner of the abundance (dhī). | Owner of the abundance (l-ṭawli). | There is no (lā) | god (ilāha) | except (illā) | Him (huwa); | to Him (ilayhi), | is the final return (l-maṣīru).

40:4 Not dispute concerning the Verses of Allah except those who disbelieve, so let not deceive you their movement in the cities.

Not (mā) | dispute (yujādilu) | concerning (fī) | the Verses (āyāti) | of Allah (l-lahi) | except (illā) | those who (alladhīna) | disbelieve (kafarū), | so let not (falā) | deceive you (yaghrur'ka) | their movement (taqallubuhum) | in (fī) | the cities (l-bilādi).

40:5 Denied before them the people of Nuh and the factions after them, and plotted every nation against their Messenger, to seize him, and they disputed by falsehood to refute thereby the truth. So I seized them. Then how was My penalty?

Denied (kadhabat) | before them (qablahum) | the people (qawmu) | of Nuh (nūḥin) | and the factions (wal-aḥzābu) | after them (min), | after them (baʿdihim), | and plotted (wahammat) | every (kullu) | nation (ummatin) | against their Messenger (birasūlihim), | to seize him (liyakhudhūhu), | and they disputed (wajādalū) | by falsehood (bil-bāṭili) | to refute (liyud'ḥiḍū) | thereby (bihi) | the truth (l-ḥaqa). | So I seized them (fa-akhadhtuhum). | Then how (fakayfa) | was (kāna) | My penalty (ʿiqābi)?

40:6 And thus has been justified the Word of your Lord against those who disbelieved that they are companions of the Fire.

And thus (wakadhālika) | has been justified (ḥaqqat) | the Word (kalimatu) | of your Lord (rabbika) | against (ʿalā) | those who (alladhīna) | disbelieved (kafarū) | that they (annahum) | are companions (aṣḥābu) | of the Fire (l-nāri).

40:7 Those who bear the Throne and who are around it glorify the praises of their Lord and believe in Him and ask forgiveness for those who believe, "Our Lord! You encompass all things by Your Mercy and knowledge, so forgive those who repent and follow Your Way and save them from the punishment of the Hellfire.

Those who (alladhīna) | bear (yaḥmilūna) | the Throne (l-ʿarsha) | and who (waman) | are around it (ḥawlahu) | glorify (yusabbiḥūna) | the praises (biḥamdi) | of their Lord (rabbihim) | and believe (wayu'minūna) | in Him (bihi) | and ask forgiveness (wayastaghfirūna) | for those who (lilladhīna) | believe (āmanū), | "Our Lord (rabbanā)! | You encompass (wasiʿ'ta) | all (kulla) | things (shayin) | by Your Mercy (raḥmatan) | and knowledge (waʿil'man), | so forgive (fa-igh'fir) | those who (lilladhīna) | repent (tābū) | and follow (wa-ittabaʿū) | Your Way (sabīlaka) | and save them from (waqihim) | the punishment (ʿadhāba) | of the Hellfire (l-jaḥīmi).

40:8 Our Lord! And admit them to Gardens of Eden which You have promised them and whoever was righteous among their fathers and their spouses and their offspring. Indeed You, You are the All-Mighty, the All-Wise.

Our Lord (rabbanā)! | And admit them (wa-adkhil'hum) | to Gardens (jannāti) | of Eden (ʿadnin) | which (allatī) | You have promised them (waʿadttahum) | and whoever (waman) | was righteous (ṣalaḥa) | among (min) | their fathers (ābāihim) | and their spouses (wa-azwājihim) | and their offspring (wadhurriyyātihim). | Indeed You (innaka), | You (anta) | are the All-Mighty (l-ʿazīzu), | the All-Wise (l-ḥakīmu).

40:9 And protect them from the evils. And whoever you protect from the evils that Day, then verily You have bestowed mercy on him. And that [it] is the success, the great."

And protect them (waqihimu) | from the evils (l-sayiāti). | And whoever (waman) | you protect (taqi) | from the evils (l-sayiāti) | that Day (yawma-idhin), | then verily (faqad) | You have bestowed mercy on him (raḥim'tahu). | And that (wadhālika) | [it] (huwa) | is the success (l-fawzu), | the great. (l-ʿaẓīmu)"

40:10 Indeed, those who disbelieved will be cried out to them, "Certainly Allah's hatred was greater than your hatred of yourselves when you were called to the faith, and you disbelieved.

Indeed (inna), | those who (alladhīna) | disbelieved (kafarū) | will be cried out to them (yunādawna), | "Certainly Allah's hatred (lamaqtu) | "Certainly Allah's hatred (l-lahi) | was greater (akbaru) | than (min) | your hatred (maqtikum) | of yourselves (anfusakum) | when (idh) | you were called (tudʿawna) | to (ilā) | the faith (l-īmāni), | and you disbelieved (fatakfurūna).

40:11 They will say, "Our Lord! You gave us death twice and You gave us life twice, and we confess our sins. So is there to get out any way?"

They will say (qālū), | "Our Lord (rabbanā)! | You gave us death (amattanā) | twice (ith'natayni) | and You gave us life (wa-aḥyaytanā) | twice (ith'natayni), | and we confess (fa-iʿtarafnā) | our sins (bidhunūbinā). | So is there (fahal) | to (ilā) | get out (khurūjin) | any (min) | way? (sabīlin)"

40:12 "That is because, when Allah was invoked Alone you disbelieved; but if others were associated with Him, you believed. So the judgment is with Allah, the Most High, the Most Great."

"That (dhālikum) | is because (bi-annahu), | when (idhā) | Allah was invoked (duʿiya) | Allah was invoked (l-lahu) | Alone (waḥdahu) | you disbelieved (kafartum); | but if (wa-in) | others were associated (yush'rak) | with Him (bihi), | you believed (tu'minū). | So the judgment (fal-ḥuk'mu) | is with Allah (lillahi), | the Most High (l-ʿaliyi), | the Most Great. (l-kabīri)"

40:13 He is the One Who shows you His Signs and sends down for you from the sky provision. But does not take heed except one who turns.

He (huwa) | is the One Who (alladhī) | shows you (yurīkum) | His Signs (āyātihi) | and sends down (wayunazzilu) | for you (lakum) | from (mina) | the sky (l-samāi) | provision (riz'qan). | But does not (wamā) | take heed (yatadhakkaru) | except (illā) | one who (man) | turns (yunību).

40:14 So invoke Allah, being sincere to Him in the religion, even though dislike it the disbelievers.

So invoke (fa-idʿū) | Allah (l-laha), | being sincere (mukh'liṣīna) | to Him (lahu) | in the religion (l-dīna), | even though (walaw) | dislike it (kariha) | the disbelievers (l-kāfirūna).

40:15 Possessor of the Highest Ranks, Owner of the Throne; He places the inspiration of His Command upon whom He wills of His slaves, to warn of the Day of the Meeting.

Possessor of the Highest Ranks (rafīʿu), | Possessor of the Highest Ranks (l-darajāti), | Owner of the Throne (dhū); | Owner of the Throne (l-ʿarshi); | He places (yul'qī) | the inspiration (l-rūḥa) | of (min) | His Command (amrihi) | upon (ʿalā) | whom (man) | He wills (yashāu) | of (min) | His slaves (ʿibādihi), | to warn (liyundhira) | of the Day (yawma) | of the Meeting (l-talāqi).

40:16 The Day they come forth, not is hidden from Allah about them anything. For whom is the Dominion this Day? For Allah the One, the Irresistible.

The Day (yawma) | they (hum) | come forth (bārizūna), | not (lā) | is hidden (yakhfā) | from (ʿalā) | Allah (l-lahi) | about them (min'hum) | anything (shayon). | For whom (limani) | is the Dominion (l-mul'ku) | this Day (l-yawma)? | For Allah (lillahi) | the One (l-wāḥidi), | the Irresistible (l-qahāri).

40:17 This Day will be recompensed every soul for what it earned. No injustice today! Indeed, Allah is Swift in Account.

This Day (al-yawma) | will be recompensed (tuj'zā) | every (kullu) | soul (nafsin) | for what (bimā) | it earned (kasabat). | No (lā) | injustice (ẓul'ma) | today (l-yawma)! | Indeed (inna), | Allah (l-laha) | is Swift (sarīʿu) | in Account (l-ḥisābi).

40:18 And warn them of the Day the Approaching, when the hearts are at the throats, choked. Not for the wrongdoers any intimate friend and no intercessor who is obeyed.

And warn them (wa-andhir'hum) | of the Day (yawma) | the Approaching (l-āzifati), | when (idhi) | the hearts (l-qulūbu) | are at (ladā) | the throats (l-ḥanājiri), | choked (kāẓimīna). | Not (mā) | for the wrongdoers (lilẓẓālimīna) | any (min) | intimate friend (ḥamīmin) | and no (walā)

| intercessor (shafīʿin) | who is obeyed (yuṭāʿu).

40:19 He knows the stealthy glance and what conceal the breasts.
He knows (yaʿlamu) | the stealthy glance (khāinata) | the stealthy glance (l-aʿyuni) | and what (wamā) | conceal (tukh'fī) | the breasts (l-ṣudūru).

40:20 And Allah judges in truth, while those whom they invoke besides Him not they judge with anything. Indeed, Allah - He is the All-Hearer, the All-Seer.
And Allah (wal-lahu) | judges (yaqḍī) | in truth (bil-ḥaqi), | while those whom (wa-alladhīna) | they invoke (yadʿūna) | besides Him (min) | besides Him (dūnihi) | not (lā) | they judge (yaqḍūna) | with anything (bishayin). | Indeed (inna), | Allah (l-laha)- | He (huwa) | is the All-Hearer (l-samīʿu), | the All-Seer (l-baṣīru).

40:21 Do not they travel in the earth and see how was the end of those who were before them? They were [they] superior to them in strength and in impressions in the land, but Allah seized them for their sins, and not was for them against Allah any protector.
Do not (awalam) | they travel (yasīrū) | in (fī) | the earth (l-arḍi) | and see (fayanẓurū) | how (kayfa) | was (kāna) | the end (ʿāqibatu) | of those who (alladhīna) | were (kānū) | before them (min)? | before them (qablihim)? | They were (kānū) | [they] (hum) | superior (ashadda) | to them (min'hum) | in strength (quwwatan) | and in impressions (waāthāran) | in (fī) | the land (l-arḍi), | but Allah seized them (fa-akhadhahumu) | but Allah seized them (l-lahu) | for their sins (bidhunūbihim), | and not (wamā) | was (kāna) | for them (lahum) | against (mina) | Allah (l-lahi) | any (min) | protector (wāqin).

40:22 That was because [they] used to come to them their Messengers with clear proofs but they disbelieved, So Allah seized them. Indeed, He is All-Strong, severe in punishment.
That (dhālika) | was because [they] (bi-annahum) | used to come to them (kānat) | used to come to them (tatīhim) | their Messengers (rusuluhum) | with clear proofs (bil-bayināti) | but they disbelieved (fakafarū), | So Allah seized them (fa-akhadhahumu). | So Allah seized them (l-lahu). | Indeed, He (innahu) | is All-Strong (qawiyyun), | severe (shadīdu) | in punishment (l-ʿiqābi).

40:23 And certainly, We sent Musa with Our Signs and an authority clear,
And certainly (walaqad), | We sent (arsalnā) | Musa (mūsā) | with Our Signs (biāyātinā) | and an authority (wasul'ṭānin) | clear (mubīnin),

40:24 To Firaun, Haman and Qarun, but they said, "A magician, a liar."
To (ilā) | Firaun (fir'ʿawna), | Haman (wahāmāna) | and Qarun (waqārūna), | but they said (faqālū), | "A magician (sāḥirun), | a liar. (kadhābun)"

40:25 Then when he brought to them the truth from Us they said, "Kill the sons of those who believe with him, and let live their women." And not is the plot of the disbelievers but in error.
Then when (falammā) | he brought to them (jāahum) | the truth (bil-ḥaqi) | from (min) | Us (ʿindinā) | they said (qālū), | "Kill (uq'tulū) | the sons (abnāa) | of those who (alladhīna) | believe (āmanū) | with him (maʿahu), | and let live (wa-is'taḥyū) | their women. (nisāahum)" | And not (wamā) | is the plot (kaydu) | of the disbelievers (l-kāfirīna) | but (illā) | in (fī) | error (ḍalālin).

40:26 And said Firaun, "Leave me so that I kill Musa and let him call his Lord. Indeed, I [I] fear that he will change your religion or that he may cause to appear in the land the corruption."
And said (waqāla) | Firaun (fir'ʿawnu), | "Leave me (dharūnī) | so that I kill (aqtul) | Musa (mūsā) | and let him call (walyadʿu) | his Lord (rabbahu). | Indeed, I (innī) | [I] fear (akhāfu) | that (an) | he will change (yubaddila) | your religion (dīnakum) | or (aw) | that (an) | he may cause to appear (yuẓ'hira) | in (fī) | the land (l-arḍi) | the corruption. (l-fasāda)"

40:27 And said Musa, "Indeed, I [I] seek refuge in my Lord and your Lord from every arrogant one not who believes in the Day of the Account."

And said (waqāla) | Musa (mūsā), | "Indeed, I (innī) | [I] seek refuge (ʿudh'tu) | in my Lord (birabbī) | and your Lord (warabbikum) | from (min) | every (kulli) | arrogant one (mutakabbirin) | not (lā) | who believes (yu'minu) | in the Day (biyawmi) | of the Account. (l-ḥisābi)"

40:28 And said a man, believing, from the family of Firaun who concealed his faith, "Will you kill a man because he says, "My Lord is Allah," and indeed he has brought you clear proofs from your Lord? And if he is a liar, then upon him is his lie; and if he is truthful, there will strike you some of that which he threatens you. Indeed, Allah does not guide one who [he] is a transgressor, a liar.

And said (waqāla) | a man (rajulun), | believing (mu'minun), | from (min) | the family (āli) | of Firaun (fir'ʿawna) | who concealed (yaktumu) | his faith (īmānahu), | "Will you kill (ataqtulūna) | a man (rajulan) | because (an) | he says (yaqūla), | "My Lord (rabbiya) | is Allah, (l-lahu)" | and indeed (waqad) | he has brought you (jāakum) | clear proofs (bil-bayināti) | from (min) | your Lord (rabbikum)? | And if (wa-in) | he is (yaku) | a liar (kādhiban), | then upon him (faʿalayhi) | is his lie (kadhibuhu); | and if (wa-in) | he is (yaku) | truthful (ṣādiqan), | there will strike you (yuṣib'kum) | some of (baʿḍu) | that which (alladhī) | he threatens you (yaʿidukum). | Indeed (inna), | Allah (l-laha) | does not (lā) | guide (yahdī) | one who (man) | [he] (huwa) | is a transgressor (mus'rifun), | a liar (kadhābun).

40:29 O my people! For you is the kingdom today, dominant in the land, but who will help us from the punishment of Allah, if it came to us." Said Firaun, "Not I show you except what I see and not I guide you except to the path the right."

O my people (yāqawmi)! | For you (lakumu) | is the kingdom (l-mul'ku) | today (l-yawma), | dominant (ẓāhirīna) | in (fī) | the land (l-arḍi), | but who (faman) | will help us (yanṣurunā) | from (min) | the punishment (basi) | of Allah (l-lahi), | if (in) | it came to us. (jāanā)" | Said (qāla) | Firaun (fir'ʿawnu), | "Not (mā) | I show you (urīkum) | except (illā) | what (mā) | I see (arā) | and not (wamā) | I guide you (ahdīkum) | except (illā) | to the path (sabīla) | the right. (l-rashādi)"

40:30 And said he who believed, "O my people! Indeed I, [I] fear for you like the day of the companies,

And said (waqāla) | he who (alladhī) | believed (āmana), | "O my people (yāqawmi)! | Indeed I (innī), | [I] fear (akhāfu) | for you (ʿalaykum) | like (mith'la) | the day (yawmi) | of the companies (l-aḥzābi),

40:31 Like the plight of the people of Nuh and Aad and Thamud and those after them. And Allah does not want injustice for His slaves.

Like (mith'la) | the plight (dabi) | of the people (qawmi) | of Nuh (nūḥin) | and Aad (waʿādin) | and Thamud (wathamūda) | and those (wa-alladhīna) | after them (min). | after them (baʿdihim). | And Allah does not (wamā) | And Allah does not (l-lahu) | want (yurīdu) | injustice (ẓul'man) | for His slaves (lil'ʿibādi).

40:32 And O my people! Indeed, I [I] fear for you the Day of Calling,

And O my people (wayāqawmi)! | Indeed, I (innī) | [I] fear (akhāfu) | for you (ʿalaykum) | the Day (yawma) | of Calling (l-tanādi),

40:33 A Day you will turn back fleeing; not for you from Allah any protector. And whoever Allah lets go astray, then not for him any guide.

A Day (yawma) | you will turn back (tuwallūna) | fleeing (mud'birīna); | not (mā) | for you (lakum) | from (mina) | Allah (l-lahi) | any (min) | protector (ʿāṣimin). | And whoever (waman) | Allah lets go astray (yuḍ'lili), | Allah lets go astray (l-lahu), | then not (famā) | for him (lahu) | any (min) | guide (hādin).

40:34 And indeed, came to you Yusuf before with clear proofs, but not you ceased in doubt about what he brought to you [with it], until when he died, you said, "Never will Allah raise after him a Messenger." Thus, Allah lets go astray who [he] is a transgressor, a doubter."

And indeed (walaqad), | came to you (jāakum) | Yusuf (yūsufu) | before (min) | before (qablu) | with clear proofs (bil-bayināti), | but not (famā) | you ceased (zil'tum) | in (fī) | doubt (shakkin) | about what (mimmā) | he brought to you (jāakum) | [with it] (bihi), | until (ḥattā) | when (idhā) | he died (halaka), | you said (qul'tum), | "Never (lan) | will Allah raise (yabʿatha) | will Allah raise (l-lahu) | after him (min) | after him (baʿdihi) | a Messenger. (rasūlan)" | Thus (kadhālika), | Allah lets go astray (yuḍillu) | Allah lets go astray (l-lahu) | who (man) | [he] (huwa) | is a transgressor (mus'rifun), | a doubter. (mur'tābun)"

40:35 Those who dispute concerning the Signs of Allah without any authority having come to them, it is greatly hateful near Allah and near those who believe. Thus Allah sets a seal over every heart of an arrogant tyrant."

Those who (alladhīna) | dispute (yujādilūna) | concerning (fī) | the Signs (āyāti) | of Allah (l-lahi) | without (bighayri) | any authority (sul'ṭānin) | having come to them (atāhum), | it is greatly (kabura) | hateful (maqtan) | near Allah (ʿinda) | near Allah (l-lahi) | and near (waʿinda) | those (alladhīna) | who believe (āmanū). | Thus (kadhālika) | Allah sets a seal (yaṭbaʿu) | Allah sets a seal (l-lahu) | over (ʿalā) | every (kulli) | heart (qalbi) | of an arrogant (mutakabbirin) | tyrant. (jabbārin)"

40:36 And said Firaun, "O Haman! Construct for me a tower that I may reach the ways

And said (waqāla) | Firaun (fir'ʿawnu), | "O Haman (yāhāmānu)! | Construct (ib'ni) | for me (lī) | a tower (ṣarḥan) | that I may (laʿallī) | reach (ablughu) | the ways (l-asbāba)

40:37 The ways to the heavens so I may look at the God of Musa; and indeed, I [I] surely think him to be a liar." And thus was made fair-seeming to Firaun the evil of his deed, and he was averted from the way. And not was the plot of Firaun except in ruin.

The ways (asbāba) | to the heavens (l-samāwāti) | so I may look (fa-aṭṭaliʿa) | at (ilā) | the God (ilāhi) | of Musa (mūsā); | and indeed, I (wa-innī) | [I] surely think him (la-aẓunnuhu) | to be a liar. (kādhiban)" | And thus (wakadhālika) | was made fair-seeming (zuyyina) | to Firaun (lifir'ʿawna) | the evil (sūu) | of his deed (ʿamalihi), | and he was averted (waṣudda) | from (ʿani) | the way (l-sabīli). | And not (wamā) | was the plot (kaydu) | of Firaun (fir'ʿawna) | except (illā) | in (fī) | ruin (tabābin).

40:38 And said the one who believed, "O my people! Follow me; I will guide you to the way, the right.

And said (waqāla) | the one who (alladhī) | believed (āmana), | "O my people (yāqawmi)! | Follow me (ittabiʿūni); | I will guide you (ahdikum) | to the way (sabīla), | the right (l-rashādi).

40:39 O my people! Only this, the life of the world, is enjoyment, and indeed, the Hereafter - it is the home, of settlement.

O my people (yāqawmi)! | Only (innamā) | this (hādhihi), | the life (l-ḥayatu) | of the world (l-dun'yā), | is enjoyment (matāʿun), | and indeed (wa-inna), | the Hereafter (l-ākhirata)- | it (hiya) | is the home (dāru), | of settlement (l-qarāri).

40:40 Whoever does an evil then not he will be recompensed but the like thereof; and whoever does righteous deeds, of male or female, while he is a believer, then those will enter Paradise, they will be given provision in it without account.

Whoever (man) | does (ʿamila) | an evil (sayyi-atan) | then not (falā) | he will be recompensed (yuj'zā) | but (illā) | the like thereof (mith'lahā); | and whoever (waman) | does

(ʿamila) | righteous deeds (ṣāliḥan), | of (min) | male (dhakarin) | or (aw) | female (unthā), | while he (wahuwa) | is a believer (mu'minun), | then those (fa-ulāika) | will enter (yadkhulūna) | Paradise (l-janata), | they will be given provision (yur'zaqūna) | in it (fīhā) | without (bighayri) | account (ḥisābin).

40:41 And O my people! What is for me that I call you to the salvation while you call me to the Fire!
And O my people (wayāqawmi)! | What is (mā) | for me (lī) | that I call you (adʿūkum) | to (ilā) | the salvation (l-najati) | while you call me (watadʿūnanī) | to (ilā) | the Fire (l-nāri)!

40:42 You call me that I disbelieve in Allah and to associate with Him what not for me of it any knowledge, and I call you to the All-Mighty, the Oft-Forgiving.
You call me (tadʿūnanī) | that I disbelieve (li-akfura) | in Allah (bil-lahi) | and to associate (wa-ush'rika) | with Him (bihi) | what (mā) | not (laysa) | for me (lī) | of it (bihi) | any knowledge (ʿil'mun), | and I (wa-anā) | call you (adʿūkum) | to (ilā) | the All-Mighty (l-ʿazīzi), | the Oft-Forgiving (l-ghafāri).

40:43 No doubt that what you call me to it not for it a claim in the world and not in the Hereafter; and that our return is to Allah, and that the transgressors - they will be the companions of the Fire.
No (lā) | doubt (jarama) | that what (annamā) | you call me (tadʿūnanī) | to it (ilayhi) | not (laysa) | for it (lahu) | a claim (daʿwatun) | in (fī) | the world (l-dun'yā) | and not (walā) | in (fī) | the Hereafter (l-ākhirati); | and that (wa-anna) | our return (maraddanā) | is to (ilā) | Allah (l-lahi), | and that (wa-anna) | the transgressors (l-mus'rifīna)- | they (hum) | will be the companions (aṣḥābu) | of the Fire (l-nāri).

40:44 And you will remember what I say to you, and I entrust my affair to Allah. Indeed, Allah is All-Seer of His slaves."
And you will remember (fasatadhkurūna) | what (mā) | I say (aqūlu) | to you (lakum), | and I entrust (wa-ufawwiḍu) | my affair (amrī) | to (ilā) | Allah (l-lahi). | Indeed (inna), | Allah (l-laha) | is All-Seer (baṣīrun) | of His slaves. (bil-ʿibādi)"

40:45 So Allah protected him from the evils that they plotted, and enveloped the people of Firaun the worst punishment,
So Allah protected him (fawaqāhu) | So Allah protected him (l-lahu) | from the evils (sayyiāti) | that (mā) | they plotted (makarū), | and enveloped (waḥāqa) | the people (biāli) | of Firaun (fir'ʿawna) | the worst (sūu) | punishment (l-ʿadhābi),

40:46 The Fire; they are exposed to it morning and evening. And the Day will be established the Hour, "Cause to enter the people of Firaun in the severest punishment."
The Fire (al-nāru); | they are exposed (yu'ʿraḍūna) | to it (ʿalayhā) | morning (ghuduwwan) | and evening (waʿashiyyan). | And the Day (wayawma) | will be established (taqūmu) | the Hour (l-sāʿatu), | "Cause to enter (adkhilū) | the people (āla) | of Firaun (fir'ʿawna) | in the severest (ashadda) | punishment. (l-ʿadhābi)"

40:47 And when they will dispute in the Fire, then will say the weak to those who were arrogant, "Indeed, we [we] were for you followers, so can you avert from us a portion of the Fire?"
And when (wa-idh) | they will dispute (yataḥājjūna) | in (fī) | the Fire (l-nāri), | then will say (fayaqūlu) | the weak (l-ḍuʿafāu) | to those who (lilladhīna) | were arrogant (is'takbarū), | "Indeed, we (innā) | [we] were (kunnā) | for you (lakum) | followers (tabaʿan), | so can (fahal) | you (antum) | avert (mugh'nūna) | from us (ʿannā) | a portion (naṣīban) | of (mina) | the Fire? (l-nāri)"

40:48 Will say those who were arrogant, "Indeed, we all are in it. Indeed, Allah certainly has judged between His slaves"

Will say (qāla) | those who (alladhīna) | were arrogant (is'takbarū), | "Indeed, we (innā) | all (kullun) | are in it (fīhā). | Indeed (inna), | Allah (l-laha) | certainly (qad) | has judged (ḥakama) | between (bayna) | His slaves (l-ʿibādi)"

40:49 And will say those in the Fire to the keepers of Hell, "Call your Lord to lighten for us a day of the punishment."

And will say (waqāla) | those (alladhīna) | in (fī) | the Fire (l-nāri) | to the keepers (likhazanati) | of Hell (jahannama), | "Call (idʿū) | your Lord (rabbakum) | to lighten (yukhaffif) | for us (ʿannā) | a day (yawman) | of (mina) | the punishment. (l-ʿadhābi)"

40:50 They will say, "Did there not come to you your Messengers with clear proofs?" They will say, "Yes." They will say, "Then call, but not is the call of the disbelievers except in error."

They will say (qālū), | "Did there not (awalam) | "Did there not (taku) | come to you (tatīkum) | your Messengers (rusulukum) | with clear proofs? (bil-bayināti)" | They will say (qālū), | "Yes. (balā)" | They will say (qālū), | "Then call (fa-idʿū), | but not (wamā) | is the call (duʿāu) | of the disbelievers (l-kāfirīna) | except (illā) | in (fī) | error. (ḍalālin)"

40:51 Indeed We, We will surely help Our Messengers and those who believe in the life of the world and on the Day when will stand the witnesses,

Indeed We (innā), | We will surely help (lananṣuru) | Our Messengers (rusulanā) | and those who (wa-alladhīna) | believe (āmanū) | in (fī) | the life (l-ḥayati) | of the world (l-dun'yā) | and on the Day (wayawma) | when will stand (yaqūmu) | the witnesses (l-ashhādu),

40:52 The Day not will benefit the wrongdoers their excuse, and for them is the curse and for them is the worst home.

The Day (yawma) | not (lā) | will benefit (yanfaʿu) | the wrongdoers (l-ẓālimīna) | their excuse (maʿdhiratuhum), | and for them (walahumu) | is the curse (l-laʿnatu) | and for them (walahum) | is the worst (sūu) | home (l-dāri).

40:53 And certainly, We gave Musa the guidance and We caused to inherit the Children of Israel the Book,

And certainly (walaqad), | We gave (ātaynā) | Musa (mūsā) | the guidance (l-hudā) | and We caused to inherit (wa-awrathnā) | the Children of Israel (banī) | the Children of Israel (is'rāīla) | the Book (l-kitāba),

40:54 A guide and a reminder for those of understanding.

A guide (hudan) | and a reminder (wadhik'rā) | for those (li-ulī) | of understanding (l-albābi).

40:55 So be patient; indeed, the Promise of Allah is true. And ask forgiveness for your sin and glorify the praise of your Lord in the evening and the morning.

So be patient (fa-iṣ'bir); | indeed (inna), | the Promise of Allah (waʿda) | the Promise of Allah (l-lahi) | is true (ḥaqqun). | And ask forgiveness (wa-is'taghfir) | for your sin (lidhanbika) | and glorify (wasabbiḥ) | the praise (biḥamdi) | of your Lord (rabbika) | in the evening (bil-ʿashiyi) | and the morning (wal-ib'kāri).

40:56 Indeed, those who dispute concerning the Signs of Allah without any authority which came to them, not is in their breasts but greatness, not they can reach it. So seek refuge in Allah. Indeed He, He is the All-Hearer the All-Seer.

Indeed (inna), | those who (alladhīna) | dispute (yujādilūna) | concerning (fī) | the Signs (āyāti) | of Allah (l-lahi) | without (bighayri) | any authority (sul'ṭānin) | which came to them (atāhum), | not (in) | is in (fī) | their breasts (ṣudūrihim) | but (illā) | greatness (kib'run), | not (mā)

| they (hum) | can reach it (bibālighīhi). | So seek refuge (fa-is'taʿidh) | in Allah (bil-lahi). | Indeed He (innahu), | He (huwa) | is the All-Hearer (l-samīʿu) | the All-Seer (l-baṣīru).

40:57 Surely, the creation of the heavens and the earth is greater than the creation of the mankind, but most of the people do not know.

Surely, the creation (lakhalqu) | of the heavens (l-samāwāti) | and the earth (wal-arḍi) | is greater (akbaru) | than (min) | the creation (khalqi) | of the mankind (l-nāsi), | but (walākinna) | most (akthara) | of the people (l-nāsi) | do not (lā) | know (yaʿlamūna).

40:58 And not are equal the blind and the seeing and those who believe and do righteous deeds and not the evildoer. Little is what you take heed.

And not (wamā) | are equal (yastawī) | the blind (l-aʿmā) | and the seeing (wal-baṣīru) | and those who (wa-alladhīna) | believe (āmanū) | and do (waʿamilū) | righteous deeds (l-ṣāliḥāti) | and not (walā) | the evildoer (l-musīu). | Little (qalīlan) | is what (mā) | you take heed (tatadhakkarūna).

40:59 Indeed, the Hour is surely coming, no doubt in it, but most of the people do not believe.

Indeed (inna), | the Hour (l-sāʿata) | is surely coming (laātiyatun), | no (lā) | doubt (rayba) | in it (fīhā), | but (walākinna) | most (akthara) | of the people (l-nāsi) | do not (lā) | believe (yu'minūna).

40:60 And said your Lord, "Call upon Me; I will respond to you. Indeed, those who are proud to worship Me will enter Hell in humiliation."

And said (waqāla) | your Lord (rabbukumu), | "Call upon Me (id'ʿūnī); | I will respond (astajib) | to you (lakum). | Indeed (inna), | those who (alladhīna) | are proud (yastakbirūna) | to (ʿan) | worship Me (ʿibādatī) | will enter (sayadkhulūna) | Hell (jahannama) | in humiliation. (dākhirīna)"

40:61 Allah is the One Who made for you the night that you may rest in it, and the day giving visibility. Indeed, Allah is Full (of) Bounty to the people, but most of the people do not give thanks.

Allah (al-lahu) | is the One Who (alladhī) | made (jaʿala) | for you (lakumu) | the night (al-layla) | that you may rest ( ) | in it (fīhi), | and the day (wal-nahāra) | giving visibility (mub'ṣiran). | Indeed (inna), | Allah (l-laha) | is Full (of) Bounty (ladhū) | is Full (of) Bounty (faḍlin) | to (ʿalā) | the people (l-nāsi), | but (walākinna) | most (akthara) | of the people (l-nāsi) | do not (lā) | give thanks (yashkurūna).

40:62 That is Allah your Lord, the Creator of all things, there is no god except Him. So how are you deluded?

That (dhālikumu) | is Allah (l-lahu) | your Lord (rabbukum), | the Creator (khāliqu) | of all (kulli) | things (shayin), | there is no (lā) | god (ilāha) | except (illā) | Him (huwa). | So how (fa-annā) | are you deluded (tu'fakūna)?

40:63 Thus were deluded those who were - the Signs of Allah, rejecting.

Thus (kadhālika) | were deluded (yu'faku) | those who (alladhīna) | were (kānū)- | the Signs (biāyāti) | of Allah (l-lahi), | rejecting (yajḥadūna).

40:64 Allah is the One Who made for you the earth a place of settlement and the sky a canopy and He formed you and perfected your forms, and provided you of the good things. That is Allah, your Lord. Then blessed is Allah, the Lord of the worlds.

Allah (al-lahu) | is the One Who (alladhī) | made (jaʿala) | for you (lakumu) | the earth (l-arḍa) | a place of settlement (qarāran) | and the sky (wal-samāa) | a canopy (bināan) | and He formed you (waṣawwarakum) | and perfected (fa-aḥsana) | your forms (ṣuwarakum), | and provided you (warazaqakum) | of (mina) | the good things (l-ṭayibāti). | That (dhālikumu) | is Allah (l-lahu), | your Lord (rabbukum). | Then blessed is (fatabāraka) | Allah (l-lahu), | the Lord (rabbu) | of the worlds (l-ʿālamīna).

40:65 He is the Ever-Living; there is no god but He, so call Him, being sincere to Him in the religion. All praise be to Allah, the Lord of the worlds.

He (huwa) | is the Ever-Living (l-ḥayu); | there is no (lā) | god (ilāha) | but (illā) | He (huwa), | so call Him (fa-id'ʿūhu), | being sincere (mukh'liṣīna) | to Him (lahu) | in the religion (l-dīna). | All praise be (l-ḥamdu) | to Allah (lillahi), | the Lord (rabbi) | of the worlds (l-ʿālamīna).

40:66 Say, "Indeed, I [I] have been forbidden to worship those whom you call besides Allah when have come to me the clear proofs from my Lord, and I am commanded to submit to the Lord of the worlds.

Say (qul), | "Indeed, I (innī) | [I] have been forbidden (nuhītu) | to (an) | worship (aʿbuda) | those whom (alladhīna) | you call (tadʿūna) | besides (min) | besides (dūni) | Allah (l-lahi) | when (lammā) | have come to me (jāaniya) | the clear proofs (l-bayinātu) | from (min) | my Lord (rabbī), | and I am commanded (wa-umir'tu) | to (an) | submit (us'lima) | to the Lord (lirabbi) | of the worlds (l-ʿālamīna).

40:67 He is the One Who created you from dust, then from a semen-drop, then from a clinging substance, then He brings you out as a child; then lets you reach your maturity, then lets you become old - and among you is he who dies before - and lets you reach a term specified, and that you may use reason.

He (huwa) | is the One Who (alladhī) | created you (khalaqakum) | from (min) | dust (turābin), | then (thumma) | from (min) | a semen-drop (nuṭ'fatin), | then (thumma) | from (min) | a clinging substance (ʿalaqatin), | then (thumma) | He brings you out (yukh'rijukum) | as a child (ṭif'lan); | then (thumma) | lets you reach (litablughū) | your maturity (ashuddakum), | then (thumma) | lets you become (litakūnū) | old (shuyūkhan)- | and among you (waminkum) | is he who (man) | dies (yutawaffā) | before (min)- | before (qablu)- | and lets you reach (walitablughū) | a term (ajalan) | specified (musamman), | and that you may (walaʿallakum) | use reason (taʿqilūna).

40:68 He is the One Who gives life and causes death. And when He decrees a matter, then only He says to it, "Be," and it is.

He (huwa) | is the One Who (alladhī) | gives life (yuḥ'yī) | and causes death (wayumītu). | And when (fa-idhā) | He decrees (qaḍā) | a matter (amran), | then only (fa-innamā) | He says (yaqūlu) | to it (lahu), | "Be, (kun)" | and it is (fayakūnu).

40:69 Do not you see [to] those who dispute concerning the Signs of Allah? How they are turned away?

Do not (alam) | you see (tara) | [to] (ilā) | those who (alladhīna) | dispute (yujādilūna) | concerning (fī) | the Signs (āyāti) | of Allah (l-lahi)? | How (annā) | they are turned away (yuṣ'rafūna)?

40:70 Those who deny the Book and with what We sent with it Our Messengers; but soon they will know.

Those who (alladhīna) | deny (kadhabū) | the Book (bil-kitābi) | and with what (wabimā) | We sent (arsalnā) | with it (bihi) | Our Messengers (rusulanā); | but soon (fasawfa) | they will know (yaʿlamūna).

40:71 When the iron collars will be around their necks and the chains, they will be dragged,

When (idhi) | the iron collars (l-aghlālu) | will be around (fī) | their necks (aʿnāqihim) | and the chains (wal-salāsilu), | they will be dragged (yus'ḥabūna),

40:72 In the boiling water; then in the Fire they will be burned.

In (fī) | the boiling water (l-ḥamīmi); | then (thumma) | in (fī) | the Fire (l-nāri) | they will be burned (yus'jarūna).

40:73 Then it will be said to them, "Where is that which you used to associate

Then (thumma) | it will be said (qīla) | to them (lahum), | "Where (ayna) | is that which (mā) | you used to (kuntum) | associate (tush'rikūna)

40:74 Other than Allah?" They will say, "They have departed from us. Nay! Not we used to [we] call before anything." Thus Allah lets go astray the disbelievers.

Other than (min) | Other than (dūni) | Allah? (l-lahi)" | They will say (qālū), | "They have departed (ḍallū) | from us (ʿannā). | Nay (bal)! | Not (lam) | we used to (nakun) | [we] call (nadʿū) | before (min) | before (qablu) | anything. (shayan)" | Thus (kadhālika) | Allah lets go astray (yuḍillu) | Allah lets go astray (l-lahu) | the disbelievers (l-kāfirīna).

40:75 "That was because you used to rejoice in the earth without right and because you used to be insolent.

"That was (dhālikum) | because (bimā) | you used to (kuntum) | rejoice (tafraḥūna) | in (fī) | the earth (l-arḍi) | without (bighayri) | right (l-ḥaqi) | and because (wabimā) | you used to (kuntum) | be insolent (tamraḥūna).

40:76 Enter the gates of Hell to abide forever in it, and wretched is the abode of the arrogant."

Enter (ud'khulū) | the gates (abwāba) | of Hell (jahannama) | to abide forever (khālidīna) | in it (fīhā), | and wretched is (fabi'sa) | the abode (mathwā) | of the arrogant. (l-mutakabirīna)"

40:77 So be patient; indeed, the Promise of Allah is true. And whether We show you some of what We have promised them or We cause you to die, then to Us they will be returned.

So be patient (fa-iṣ'bir); | indeed (inna), | the Promise (waʿda) | of Allah (l-lahi) | is true (ḥaqqun). | And whether (fa-immā) | We show you (nuriyannaka) | some (baʿḍa) | of what (alladhī) | We have promised them (naʿiduhum) | or (aw) | We cause you to die (natawaffayannaka), | then to Us (fa-ilaynā) | they will be returned (yur'jaʿūna).

40:78 And certainly We have sent Messengers before you. Among them are who - We have related to you, and among them are who - not We have related to you. And not is for any Messenger that he brings a Sign except by the permission of Allah. So when comes the Command of Allah, it will be decided in truth, and will lose there the falsifiers.

And certainly (walaqad) | We have sent (arsalnā) | Messengers (rusulan) | before you (min). | before you (qablika). | Among them (min'hum) | are who (man)- | We have related (qaṣaṣnā) | to you (ʿalayka), | and among them (wamin'hum) | are who (man)- | not (lam) | We have related (naqṣuṣ) | to you (ʿalayka). | And not (wamā) | is (kāna) | for any Messenger (lirasūlin) | that (an) | he brings (yatiya) | a Sign (biāyatin) | except (illā) | by the permission (bi-idh'ni) | of Allah (l-lahi). | So when (fa-idhā) | comes (jāa) | the Command (amru) | of Allah (l-lahi), | it will be decided (quḍiya) | in truth (bil-ḥaqi), | and will lose (wakhasira) | there (hunālika) | the falsifiers (l-mub'ṭilūna).

40:79 Allah is the One Who made for you the cattle, that you may ride some of them and some of them you eat.

Allah (al-lahu) | is the One Who (alladhī) | made (jaʿala) | for you (lakumu) | the cattle (l-anʿāma), | that you may ride (litarkabū) | some of them (min'hā) | and some of them (wamin'hā) | you eat (takulūna).

40:80 And for you in them are benefits and that you may reach through them a need that is in your breasts; and upon them and upon the ships you are carried.

And for you (walakum) | in them (fīhā) | are benefits (manāfiʿu) | and that you may reach (walitablughū) | through them (ʿalayhā) | a need (ḥājatan) | that is in (fī) | your breasts (ṣudūrikum); | and upon them (waʿalayhā) | and upon (waʿalā) | the ships (l-ful'ki) | you are carried (tuḥ'malūna).

40:81 And He shows you His Signs. Then which of the Signs of Allah will you deny?

And He shows you (wayurīkum) | His Signs (āyātihi). | Then which (fa-ayya) | of the Signs (āyāti) | of Allah (l-lahi) | will you deny (tunkirūna)?

40:82 Do they not travel through the land and see how was the end of those who were before them? They were more numerous than them and mightier in strength and impressions in the land, but not availed them what they used to earn.

Do they not (afalam) | travel (yasīrū) | through (fī) | the land (l-arḍi) | and see (fayanẓurū) | how (kayfa) | was (kāna) | the end (ʿāqibatu) | of those who (alladhīna) | were before them (min)? | were before them (qablihim)? | They were (kānū) | more numerous (akthara) | than them (min'hum) | and mightier (wa-ashadda) | in strength (quwwatan) | and impressions (waāthāran) | in (fī) | the land (l-arḍi), | but not (famā) | availed (aghnā) | them (ʿanhum) | what (mā) | they used to (kānū) | earn (yaksibūna).

40:83 Then when came to them their Messengers with clear proofs they rejoiced in what they had of the knowledge, and enveloped them what they used to [at it] mock.

Then when (falammā) | came to them (jāathum) | their Messengers (rusuluhum) | with clear proofs (bil-bayināti) | they rejoiced (fariḥū) | in what (bimā) | they had (ʿindahum) | of (mina) | the knowledge (l-ʿil'mi), | and enveloped (waḥāqa) | them (bihim) | what (mā) | they used to (kānū) | [at it] (bihi) | mock (yastahziūna).

40:84 So when they saw Our punishment they said, "We believe in Allah Alone and we disbelieve in what we used to with Him associate."

So when (falammā) | they saw (ra-aw) | Our punishment (basanā) | they said (qālū), | "We believe (āmannā) | in Allah (bil-lahi) | Alone (waḥdahu) | and we disbelieve (wakafarnā) | in what (bimā) | we used to (kunnā) | with Him (bihi) | associate. (mush'rikīna)"

40:85 But did not benefit them their faith when they saw Our punishment. Such is the Way of Allah which has indeed preceded among His slaves. And are lost there the disbelievers.

But did not (falam) | But did not (yaku) | benefit them (yanfaʿuhum) | their faith (īmānuhum) | when (lammā) | they saw (ra-aw) | Our punishment (basanā). | Such is the Way (sunnata) | of Allah (l-lahi) | which (allatī) | has indeed (qad) | preceded (khalat) | among (fī) | His slaves (ʿibādihi). | And are lost (wakhasira) | there (hunālika) | the disbelievers (l-kāfirūna).

Chapter (41) Sūrat Fuṣṣilat (Explained in Detail)

41:1 Ha Meem.

Ha Meem (hha-meem).

41:2 A revelation from the Most Gracious, the Most Merciful,

A revelation (tanzīlun) | from (mina) | the Most Gracious (l-raḥmāni), | the Most Merciful (l-raḥīmi),

41:3 A Book, are detailed its Verses, a Quran in Arabic for a people who know,

A Book (kitābun), | are detailed (fuṣṣilat) | its Verses (āyātuhu), | a Quran (qur'ānan) | in Arabic (ʿarabiyyan) | for a people (liqawmin) | who know (yaʿlamūna),

41:4 A giver of glad tidings and a warner; but turn away most of them, so they do not hear.
A giver of glad tidings (bashīran) | and a warner (wanadhīran); | but turn away (fa-aʿraḍa) | most of them (aktharuhum), | so they (fahum) | do not (lā) | hear (yasmaʿūna).

41:5 And they say, "Our hearts are in coverings from what you call us to it, and in our ears is deafness, and between us and between you is a screen. So work, indeed, we are working."
And they say (waqālū), | "Our hearts (qulūbunā) | are in (fī) | coverings (akinnatin) | from what (mimmā) | you call us (tadʿūnā) | to it (ilayhi), | and in (wafī) | our ears (ādhāninā) | is deafness (waqrun), | and between us (wamin) | and between us (bayninā) | and between you (wabaynika) | is a screen (ḥijābun). | So work (fa-iʿ'mal), | indeed, we (innanā) | are working. (ʿāmilūna)"

41:6 Say, "Only I am a man like you, it is revealed to me that your god is God One; so take a Straight Path to Him and ask His forgiveness." And woe to the polytheists,
Say (qul), | "Only (innamā) | I am (anā) | a man (basharun) | like you (mith'lukum), | it is revealed (yūḥā) | to me (ilayya) | that (annamā) | your god (ilāhukum) | is God (ilāhun) | One (wāḥidun); | so take a Straight Path (fa-is'taqīmū) | to Him (ilayhi) | and ask His forgiveness. (wa-is'taghfirūhu)" | And woe (wawaylun) | to the polytheists (lil'mush'rikīna),

41:7 Those who do not give the zakah, and they in the Hereafter they are disbelievers.
Those who (alladhīna) | do not (lā) | give (yu'tūna) | the zakah (l-zakata), | and they (wahum) | in the Hereafter (bil-ākhirati) | they (hum) | are disbelievers (kāfirūna).

41:8 Indeed, those who believe and do righteous deeds, for them is a reward never ending.
Indeed (inna), | those who (alladhīna) | believe (āmanū) | and do (waʿamilū) | righteous deeds (l-ṣāliḥāti), | for them (lahum) | is a reward (ajrun) | never ending (ghayru). | never ending (mamnūnin).

41:9 Say, "Do you indeed [surely] disbelieve in the One Who created the earth in two periods and you set up with Him rivals? That is the Lord of the worlds."
Say (qul), | "Do you indeed (a-innakum) | [surely] disbelieve (latakfurūna) | in the One Who (bi-alladhī) | created (khalaqa) | the earth (l-arḍa) | in (fī) | two periods (yawmayni) | and you set up (watajʿalūna) | with Him (lahu) | rivals (andādan)? | That (dhālika) | is the Lord (rabbu) | of the worlds. (l-ʿālamīna)"

41:10 And He placed therein firmly-set mountains above it and He blessed therein, and determined therein its sustenance in four periods equal, for those who ask.
And He placed (wajaʿala) | therein (fīhā) | firmly-set mountains (rawāsiya) | above it (min) | above it (fawqihā) | and He blessed (wabāraka) | therein (fīhā), | and determined (waqaddara) | therein (fīhā) | its sustenance (aqwātahā) | in (fī) | four (arbaʿati) | periods (ayyāmin) | equal (sawāan), | for those who ask (lilssāilīna).

41:11 Then He directed Himself towards the heaven while it was smoke, and He said to it and to the earth, "Come both of you willingly or unwillingly." They both said, "We come willingly."
Then (thumma) | He directed Himself (is'tawā) | towards (ilā) | the heaven (l-samāi) | while it was (wahiya) | smoke (dukhānun), | and He said (faqāla) | to it (lahā) | and to the earth (walil'arḍi), | "Come both of you (i'tiyā) | willingly (ṭawʿan) | or (aw) | unwillingly. (karhan)" | They both said (qālatā), | "We come (ataynā) | willingly. (ṭāiʿīna)"

41:12 Then He completed them as seven heavens in two periods and He revealed in each heaven its affair. And We adorned the heaven, [the world] with lamps and to guard. That is the Decree of the All-Mighty, the All-Knower.

Then He completed them (faqaḍāhunna) | as seven (sabʿa) | heavens (samāwātin) | in (fī) | two periods (yawmayni) | and He revealed (wa-awḥā) | in (fī) | each (kulli) | heaven (samāin) | its affair (amrahā). | And We adorned (wazayyannā) | the heaven (l-samāa), | [the world] (l-dun'yā) | with lamps (bimaṣābīḥa) | and to guard (waḥif'ẓan). | That (dhālika) | is the Decree (taqdīru) | of the All-Mighty (l-ʿazīzi), | the All-Knower (l-ʿalīmi).

41:13 But if they turn away, then say, "I have warned you of a thunderbolt like the thunderbolt of Aad and Thamud."

But if (fa-in) | they turn away (aʿraḍū), | then say (faqul), | "I have warned you (andhartukum) | of a thunderbolt (ṣāʿiqatan) | like (mith'la) | the thunderbolt (ṣāʿiqati) | of Aad (ʿādin) | and Thamud. (wathamūda)"

41:14 When came to them the Messengers from before them and from behind them, saying "Do not worship except Allah." They said, "If had willed our Lord, surely, He would have sent down Angels. So indeed, we in what you have been sent with are disbelievers."

When (idh) | came to them (jāathumu) | the Messengers (l-rusulu) | from before them (min) | from before them (bayni) | from before them (aydīhim) | and from (wamin) | behind them (khalfihim), | saying "Do not (allā) | worship (taʿbudū) | except (illā) | Allah. (l-laha)" | They said (qālū), | "If (law) | had willed (shāa) | our Lord (rabbunā), | surely, He would have sent down (la-anzala) | Angels (malāikatan). | So indeed, we (fa-innā) | in what (bimā) | you have been sent (ur'sil'tum) | with (bihi) | are disbelievers. (kāfirūna)"

41:15 Then as for Aad, they were arrogant in the land without [the] right and they said, "Who is mightier than us in strength?" Do not they see that Allah, the One Who created them, He is Mightier than them in strength? But they used to, in Our Signs, deny.

Then as for (fa-ammā) | Aad (ʿādun), | they were arrogant (fa-is'takbarū) | in (fī) | the land (l-arḍi) | without (bighayri) | [the] right (l-ḥaqi) | and they said (waqālū), | "Who (man) | is mightier (ashaddu) | than us (minnā) | in strength? (quwwatan)" | Do not (awalam) | they see (yaraw) | that (anna) | Allah (l-laha), | the One Who (alladhī) | created them (khalaqahum), | He (huwa) | is Mightier (ashaddu) | than them (min'hum) | in strength (quwwatan)? | But they used to (wakānū), | in Our Signs (biāyātinā), | deny (yajḥadūna).

41:16 So We sent upon them a wind furious in the days of misfortune, that We may make them taste the punishment of disgrace in the life of the world. And surely, the punishment of the Hereafter is more disgracing, and they will not be helped.

So We sent (fa-arsalnā) | upon them (ʿalayhim) | a wind (rīḥan) | furious (ṣarṣaran) | in (fī) | the days (ayyāmin) | of misfortune (naḥisātin), | that We may make them taste (linudhīqahum) | the punishment (ʿadhāba) | of disgrace (l-khiz'yi) | in (fī) | the life (l-ḥayati) | of the world (l-dun'yā). | And surely, the punishment (walaʿadhābu) | of the Hereafter (l-ākhirati) | is more disgracing (akhzā), | and they (wahum) | will not be helped (lā). | will not be helped (yunṣarūna).

41:17 And as for Thamud, We guided them, but they preferred [the] blindness over the guidance, so seized them a thunderbolt of the punishment humiliating, for what they used to earn.

And as for (wa-ammā) | Thamud (thamūdu), | We guided them (fahadaynāhum), | but they preferred (fa-is'taḥabbū) | [the] blindness (l-ʿamā) | over (ʿalā) | the guidance (l-hudā), | so seized them (fa-akhadhathum) | a thunderbolt (ṣāʿiqatu) | of the punishment (l-ʿadhābi) | humiliating (l-hūni), | for what (bimā) | they used to (kānū) | earn (yaksibūna).

41:18 And We saved those who believed and used to fear Allah.

And We saved (wanajjaynā) | those who (alladhīna) | believed (āmanū) | and used to (wakānū) | fear Allah (yattaqūna).

41:19 And the Day will be gathered the enemies of Allah to the Fire, then they will be assembled in rows,

And the Day (wayawma) | will be gathered (yuḥ'sharu) | the enemies (aʿdāu) | of Allah (l-lahi) | to (ilā) | the Fire (l-nāri), | then they (fahum) | will be assembled in rows (yūzaʿūna),

41:20 Until, when they come to it will testify against them their hearing, and their sight, and their skins, as to what they used to do.

Until (ḥattā), | when (idhā) | when (mā) | they come to it (jāūhā) | will testify (shahida) | against them (ʿalayhim) | their hearing (samʿuhum), | and their sight (wa-abṣāruhum), | and their skins (wajulūduhum), | as to what (bimā) | they used to (kānū) | do (yaʿmalūna).

41:21 And they will say to their skins, "Why do you testify against us?" They will say, "Allah made us speak, the One Who makes speak every thing; and He created you the first time, and to Him you will be returned."

And they will say (waqālū) | to their skins (lijulūdihim), | "Why do (lima) | you testify (shahidttum) | against us? (ʿalaynā)" | They will say (qālū), | "Allah made us speak (anṭaqanā), | "Allah made us speak (l-lahu), | the One Who (alladhī) | makes speak (anṭaqa) | every (kulla) | thing (shayin); | and He (wahuwa) | created you (khalaqakum) | the first (awwala) | time (marratin), | and to Him (wa-ilayhi) | you will be returned. (tur'jaʿūna)"

41:22 And not you were covering yourselves lest testify against you your hearing and not your sight and not your skins, but you assumed that Allah does not know much of what you do.

And not (wamā) | you were (kuntum) | covering yourselves (tastatirūna) | lest (an) | testify (yashhada) | against you (ʿalaykum) | your hearing (samʿukum) | and not (walā) | your sight (abṣārukum) | and not (walā) | your skins (julūdukum), | but (walākin) | you assumed (ẓanantum) | that (anna) | Allah (l-laha) | does not (lā) | know (yaʿlamu) | much (kathīran) | of what (mimmā) | you do (taʿmalūna).

41:23 And that was your assumption which you assumed about your Lord. It has ruined you, and you have become of the losers.

And that (wadhālikum) | was your assumption (ẓannukumu) | which (alladhī) | you assumed (ẓanantum) | about your Lord (birabbikum). | It has ruined you (ardākum), | and you have become (fa-aṣbaḥtum) | of (mina) | the losers (l-khāsirīna).

41:24 Then if they endure, the Fire is an abode for them; and if they ask for favor, then not they will be of those who receive favor.

Then if (fa-in) | they endure (yaṣbirū), | the Fire (fal-nāru) | is an abode (mathwan) | for them (lahum); | and if (wa-in) | they ask for favor (yastaʿtibū), | then not (famā) | they (hum) | will be of (mina) | those who receive favor (l-muʿ'tabīna).

41:25 And We have destined for them companions who made fair-seeming to them, what was before them and what was behind them, and is justified against them the Word among nations that have passed away before them of the jinn and the men. Indeed, they were losers.

And We have destined (waqayyaḍnā) | for them (lahum) | companions (quranāa) | who made fair-seeming (fazayyanū) | to them (lahum), | what (mā) | was before them (bayna) | was before them (aydīhim) | and what (wamā) | was behind them (khalfahum), | and is justified (waḥaqqa) | against them (ʿalayhimu) | the Word (l-qawlu) | among (fī) | nations (umamin) | that have passed away (qad) | that have passed away (khalat) | before them (min) | before them (qablihim) | of (mina) | the jinn (l-jini) | and the men (wal-insi). | Indeed, they (innahum) | were (kānū) | losers (khāsirīna).

41:26 And said those who disbelieve, "Do not listen to this Quran, and make noise therein, so that you may overcome."

And said (waqāla) | those who (alladhīna) | disbelieve (kafarū), | "Do not (lā) | listen (tasmaʿū) | to this (lihādhā) | Quran (l-qur'āni), | and make noise (wal-ghaw) | therein (fīhi), | so that you may (laʿallakum) | overcome. (taghlibūna)"

41:27 But surely We will cause to taste those who disbelieve a punishment severe, and surely We will recompense them the worst of what they used to do.

But surely We will cause to taste (falanudhīqanna) | those who (alladhīna) | disbelieve (kafarū) | a punishment (ʿadhāban) | severe (shadīdan), | and surely We will recompense them (walanajziyannahum) | the worst (aswa-a) | of what (alladhī) | they used to (kānū) | do (yaʿmalūna).

41:28 That is the recompense of the enemies of Allah - the Fire; for them therein is the home of the eternity as recompense for what they used to, of Our Verses, reject.

That (dhālika) | is the recompense (jazāu) | of the enemies (aʿdāi) | of Allah (l-lahi)- | the Fire (l-nāru); | for them (lahum) | therein (fīhā) | is the home (dāru) | of the eternity (l-khul'di) | as recompense (jazāan) | for what (bimā) | they used to (kānū), | of Our Verses (biāyātinā), | reject (yajḥadūna).

41:29 And will say those who disbelieve, "Our Lord! Show us those who misled us of the jinn and the men, so we may put them under our feet, that they be of the lowest."

And will say (waqāla) | those who (alladhīna) | disbelieve (kafarū), | "Our Lord (rabbanā)! | Show us (arinā) | those who (alladhayni) | misled us (aḍallānā) | of (mina) | the jinn (l-jini) | and the men (wal-insi), | so we may put them (najʿalhumā) | under (taḥta) | our feet (aqdāminā), | that they be (liyakūnā) | of (mina) | the lowest. (l-asfalīna)"

41:30 Indeed, those who say, "Our Lord, is Allah," then stand firm - will descend on them the Angels, "Do not fear, and do not grieve but receive the glad tidings of Paradise which you were promised.

Indeed (inna), | those who (alladhīna) | say (qālū), | "Our Lord (rabbunā), | is Allah, (l-lahu)" | then (thumma) | stand firm (is'taqāmū)- | will descend (tatanazzalu) | on them (ʿalayhimu) | the Angels (l-malāikatu), | "Do not (allā) | fear (takhāfū), | and do not (walā) | grieve (taḥzanū) | but receive the glad tidings (wa-abshirū) | of Paradise (bil-janati) | which (allatī) | you were (kuntum) | promised (tūʿadūna).

41:31 We are your protectors in the life of the world and in the Hereafter. And for you therein whatever desire your souls, and for you therein what you ask,

We (naḥnu) | are your protectors (awliyāukum) | in (fī) | the life (l-ḥayati) | of the world (l-dun'yā) | and in (wafī) | the Hereafter (l-ākhirati). | And for you (walakum) | therein (fīhā) | whatever (mā) | desire (tashtahī) | your souls (anfusukum), | and for you (walakum) | therein (fīhā) | what (mā) | you ask (taddaʿūna),

41:32 A hospitable gift from the Oft-Forgiving, the Most Merciful."

A hospitable gift (nuzulan) | from (min) | the Oft-Forgiving (ghafūrin), | the Most Merciful. (raḥīmin)"

41:33 And who is better in speech than one who invites to Allah and does righteous deeds and says, "Indeed, I am of those who submit?"

And who (waman) | is better (aḥsanu) | in speech (qawlan) | than one who (mimman) | invites (daʿā) | to (ilā) | Allah (l-lahi) | and does (waʿamila) | righteous deeds (ṣāliḥan) | and says (waqāla), | "Indeed, I am (innanī) | of (mina) | those who submit? (l-mus'limīna)"

41:34 And not are equal the good deed and the evil deed. Repel by that which [it] is better; then behold! One who, between you and between him, was enmity, will become as if he was a friend intimate.

And not (walā) | are equal (tastawī) | the good deed (l-ḥasanatu) | and (walā) | the evil deed (l-sayi-atu). | Repel (id'faʿ) | by that which (bi-allatī) | [it] (hiya) | is better (aḥsanu); | then behold (fa-idhā)! | One who (alladhī), | between you (baynaka) | and between him (wabaynahu), | was enmity (ʿadāwatun), | will become as if he (ka-annahu) | was a friend (waliyyun) | intimate (ḥamīmun).

41:35 And not it is granted except to those who are patient and not it is granted except to the owner of fortune great.

And not (wamā) | it is granted (yulaqqāhā) | except (illā) | to those who (alladhīna) | are patient (ṣabarū) | and not (wamā) | it is granted (yulaqqāhā) | except (illā) | to the owner (dhū) | of fortune (ḥaẓẓin) | great (ʿaẓīmin).

41:36 And if whisper comes to you from the Shaitaan, an evil suggestion, then seek refuge in Allah. Indeed, He [He] is the All-Hearer, the All-Knower.

And if (wa-immā) | whisper comes to you (yanzaghannaka) | from (mina) | the Shaitaan (l-shayṭāni), | an evil suggestion (nazghun), | then seek refuge (fa-is'taʿidh) | in Allah (bil-lahi). | Indeed, He (innahu) | [He] (huwa) | is the All-Hearer (l-samīʿu), | the All-Knower (l-ʿalīmu).

41:37 And of His Signs are the night and the day and the sun and the moon. Do not prostrate to the sun and not to the moon, but prostrate to Allah the One Who created them, if you, Him alone, worship.

And of (wamin) | His Signs (āyātihi) | are the night (al-laylu) | and the day (wal-nahāru) | and the sun (wal-shamsu) | and the moon (wal-qamaru). | Do not (lā) | prostrate (tasjudū) | to the sun (lilshamsi) | and not (walā) | to the moon (lil'qamari), | but prostrate (wa-us'judū) | to Allah (lillahi) | the One Who (alladhī) | created them (khalaqahunna), | if (in) | you (kuntum), | Him alone (iyyāhu), | worship (taʿbudūna).

41:38 But if they are arrogant, then those who are near your Lord, glorify Him by night and day. And they do not tire.

But if (fa-ini) | they are arrogant (is'takbarū), | then those who (fa-alladhīna) | are near (ʿinda) | your Lord (rabbika), | glorify (yusabbiḥūna) | Him (lahu) | by night (bi-al-layli) | and day (wal-nahāri). | And they (wahum) | do not (lā) | tire (yasamūna).

41:39 And among His Signs is that you see the earth barren, but when We send down upon it water it is stirred to life and grows. Indeed, the One Who gives it life, is surely the Giver of life to the dead. Indeed, He is on every thing All-Powerful.

And among (wamin) | His Signs (āyātihi) | is that you (annaka) | see (tarā) | the earth (l-arḍa) | barren (khāshiʿatan), | but when (fa-idhā) | We send down (anzalnā) | upon it (ʿalayhā) | water (l-māa) | it is stirred to life (ih'tazzat) | and grows (warabat). | Indeed (inna), | the One Who (alladhī) | gives it life (aḥyāhā), | is surely the Giver of life (lamuḥ'yī) | to the dead (l-mawtā). | Indeed, He (innahu) | is on (ʿalā) | every (kulli) | thing (shayin) | All-Powerful (qadīrun).

41:40 Indeed, those who distort [in] Our Verses are not hidden from Us. So, is he who is cast in the Fire better or he who comes secure on the Day of Resurrection? Do what you will. Indeed, He of what you do is All-Seer.

Indeed (inna), | those who (alladhīna) | distort (yul'ḥidūna) | [in] (fī) | Our Verses (āyātinā) | are not (lā) | hidden (yakhfawna) | from Us (ʿalaynā). | So, is he who (afaman) | is cast (yul'qā) | in (fī) | the Fire (l-nāri) | better (khayrun) | or (am) | he who (man) | comes (yatī) | secure (āminan) | on the Day (yawma) | of Resurrection (l-qiyāmati)? | Do (i''malū) | what (mā) | you will (shi'tum). | Indeed, He (innahu) | of what (bimā) | you do (taʿmalūna) | is All-Seer (baṣīrun).

41:41 Indeed, those who disbelieve in the Reminder when it comes to them. And indeed, it is surely a Book mighty.

Indeed (inna), | those who (alladhīna) | disbelieve (kafarū) | in the Reminder (bil-dhik'ri) | when (lammā) | it comes to them (jāahum). | And indeed, it (wa-innahu) | is surely a Book (lakitābun) | mighty (ʿazīzun).

41:42 Not comes to it the falsehood from before it and not from behind it. A Revelation from the All-Wise, the Praiseworthy.

Not (lā) | comes to it (yatīhi) | the falsehood (l-bāṭilu) | from (min) | before it (bayni) | before it (yadayhi) | and not (walā) | from (min) | behind it (khalfihi). | A Revelation (tanzīlun) | from (min) | the All-Wise (ḥakīmin), | the Praiseworthy (ḥamīdin).

41:43 Not is said to you except what was said to the Messengers before you. Indeed, your Lord is Possessor of forgiveness, and Possessor of penalty painful.

Not (mā) | is said (yuqālu) | to you (laka) | except (illā) | what (mā) | was said (qad) | was said (qīla) | to the Messengers (lilrrusuli) | before you (min). | before you (qablika). | Indeed (inna), | your Lord (rabbaka) | is Possessor (ladhū) | of forgiveness (maghfiratin), | and Possessor (wadhū) | of penalty (ʿiqābin) | painful (alīmin).

41:44 And if We had made it a Quran in a foreign (language), they would have said, "Why not are explained in detail its verses? Is it a foreign (language) and an Arab?" Say, "It is for those who believe, a guidance and a healing." And those who do not believe, in their ears is deafness, and it is for them blindness. Those are being called from a place far."

And if (walaw) | We had made it (jaʿalnāhu) | a Quran (qur'ānan) | in a foreign (language) (aʿjamiyyan), | they would have said (laqālū), | "Why not (lawlā) | are explained in detail (fuṣṣilat) | its verses (āyātuhu)? | Is it a foreign (language (ā''jamiyyun)) | and an Arab? (waʿarabiyyun)" | Say (qul), | "It is (huwa) | for those who (lilladhīna) | believe (āmanū), | a guidance (hudan) | and a healing. (washifāon)" | And those who (wa-alladhīna) | do not (lā) | believe (yu'minūna), | in (fī) | their ears (ādhānihim) | is deafness (waqrun), | and it (wahuwa) | is for them (ʿalayhim) | blindness (ʿaman). | Those (ulāika) | are being called (yunādawna) | from (min) | a place (makānin) | far. (baʿīdin)"

41:45 And certainly, We gave Musa the Book, but disputes arose therein. And had it not been for a word that preceded from your Lord, surely, would have been settled between them. But indeed, they surely are in doubt about it disquieting.

And certainly (walaqad), | We gave (ātaynā) | Musa (mūsā) | the Book (l-kitāba), | but disputes arose (fa-ukh'tulifa) | therein (fīhi). | And had it not been (walawlā) | for a word (kalimatun) | that preceded (sabaqat) | from (min) | your Lord (rabbika), | surely, would have been settled (laquḍiya) | between them (baynahum). | But indeed, they (wa-innahum) | surely are in (lafī) | doubt (shakkin) | about it (min'hu) | disquieting (murībin).

41:46 Whoever does righteous deeds then it is for his soul; and whoever does evil, then it is against it. And not is your Lord unjust to His slaves.

Whoever (man) | does (ʿamila) | righteous deeds (ṣāliḥan) | then it is for his soul (falinafsihi); | and whoever (waman) | does evil (asāa), | then it is against it (faʿalayhā). | And not (wamā) | is your Lord (rabbuka) | unjust (biẓallāmin) | to His slaves (lil''abīdi).

41:47 To Him is referred the knowledge of the Hour. And not comes out any fruits from their coverings, and not bears any female and not gives birth except with His knowledge. And the Day He will call them, "Where are My partners?" They will say, "We announce to You, not among us any witness."

To Him (ilayhi) | is referred (yuraddu) | the knowledge (ʿil'mu) | of the Hour (l-sāʿati). | And not (wamā) | comes out (takhruju) | any (min) | fruits (thamarātin) | from (min) | their coverings (akmāmihā), | and not (wamā) | bears (taḥmilu) | any (min) | female (unthā) | and not (walā) | gives birth (taḍaʿu) | except (illā) | with His knowledge (biʿil'mihi). | And the Day (wayawma) | He will call them (yunādīhim), | "Where are (ayna) | My partners? (shurakāī)" | They will say (qālū), | "We announce to You (ādhannāka), | not (mā) | among us (minnā) | any (min) | witness. (shahīdin)"

41:48 And lost from them what they were invoking before, and they will be certain that not for them any place of escape.

And lost (waḍalla) | from them (ʿanhum) | what (mā) | they were (kānū) | invoking (yadʿūna) | before (min), | before (qablu), | and they will be certain (waẓannū) | that not (mā) | for them (lahum) | any (min) | place of escape (maḥīṣin).

41:49 Does not get tired man of praying for the good, but if touches him the evil then he gives up hope and despairs.

Does not (lā) | get tired (yasamu) | man (l-insānu) | of (min) | praying (duʿāi) | for the good (l-khayri), | but if (wa-in) | touches him (massahu) | the evil (l-sharu) | then he gives up hope (fayaūsun) | and despairs (qanūṭun).

41:50 And verily, if We let him taste mercy from Us after an adversity has touched him, he will surely say, "This is due to me and not I think the Hour will be established, and if I am returned to my Lord, indeed, for me with Him will be the best." But We will surely inform those who disbelieved about what they did, and We will surely make them taste of a punishment severe.

And verily, if (wala-in) | We let him taste (adhaqnāhu) | mercy (raḥmatan) | from Us (minnā) | after (min) | after (baʿdi) | an adversity (ḍarrāa) | has touched him (massathu), | he will surely say (layaqūlanna), | "This is (hādhā) | due to me (lī) | and not (wamā) | I think (aẓunnu) | the Hour (l-sāʿata) | will be established (qāimatan), | and if (wala-in) | I am returned (rujiʿtu) | to (ilā) | my Lord (rabbī), | indeed (inna), | for me (lī) | with Him (ʿindahu) | will be the best. (lalḥus'nā)" | But We will surely inform (falanunabbi-anna) | those who (alladhīna) | disbelieved (kafarū) | about what (bimā) | they did (ʿamilū), | and We will surely make them taste (walanudhīqannahum) | of (min) | a punishment (ʿadhābin) | severe (ghalīẓin).

41:51 And when We bestow favor upon man, he turns away - and distances himself; but when touches him the evil, then he is full of supplication lengthy.

And when (wa-idhā) | We bestow favor (anʿamnā) | upon (ʿalā) | man (l-insāni), | he turns away (aʿraḍa)- | and distances himself (wanaā); | and distances himself (bijānibihi); | but when (wa-idhā) | touches him (massahu) | the evil (l-sharu), | then he is full (fadhū) | of supplication (duʿāin) | lengthy (ʿarīḍin).

41:52 Say, "You see - if it is from Allah then you disbelieve in it, who is more astray than one who - he is in opposition far?"

Say (qul), | "You see (ara-aytum)- | if (in) | it is (kāna) | from (min) | from (ʿindi) | Allah (l-lahi) | then (thumma) | you disbelieve (kafartum) | in it (bihi), | who (man) | is more astray (aḍallu) | than one who (mimman)- | he (huwa) | is in (fī) | opposition (shiqāqin) | far? (baʿīdin)"

41:53 Soon We will show them Our Signs in the horizons and in themselves until becomes clear to them, that it is the truth. Is it not sufficient concerning your Lord, that He is over all things a Witness?

Soon We will show them (sanurīhim) | Our Signs (āyātinā) | in (fī) | the horizons (l-āfāqi) | and in (wafī) | themselves (anfusihim) | until (ḥattā) | becomes clear (yatabayyana) | to them (lahum), | that it (annahu) | is the truth (l-ḥaqu). | Is it not (awalam) | sufficient (yakfi) | concerning your Lord (birabbika), | that He (annahu) | is over (ʿalā) | all (kulli) | things (shayin) | a Witness (shahīdun)?

41:54 Unquestionably, they are in doubt about the meeting with their Lord? Unquestionably, indeed, He is of all things encompassing.

Unquestionably (alā), | they (innahum) | are in (fī) | doubt (mir'yatin) | about (min) | the meeting (liqāi) | with their Lord (rabbihim)? | Unquestionably (alā), | indeed, He (innahu) | is of all (bikulli) | things (shayin) | encompassing (muḥīṭun).

Chapter (42) Sūrat l-Shūrā (Consultation)

42:1 Ha Meem.

Ha Meem (hha-meem).

42:2 Ayn Seen Qaaf.

Ayn Seen Qaaf (ain-seen-qaf).

42:3 Thus reveals to you, and to those before you - Allah the All-Mighty, the All-Wise.

Thus (kadhālika) | reveals (yūḥī) | to you (ilayka), | and to (wa-ilā) | those (alladhīna) | before you (min)- | before you (qablika)- | Allah (l-lahu) | the All-Mighty (l-ʿazīzu), | the All-Wise (l-ḥakīmu).

42:4 To Him belong whatever is in the heavens and whatever is in the earth, and He is the Most High, the Most Great.

To Him (lahu) | belong whatever (mā) | is in (fī) | the heavens (l-samāwāti) | and whatever (wamā) | is in (fī) | the earth (l-arḍi), | and He (wahuwa) | is the Most High (l-ʿaliyu), | the Most Great (l-ʿaẓīmu).

42:5 Almost the heavens break up from above them, and the Angels glorify the praise of their Lord and ask for forgiveness for those on the earth. Unquestionably, indeed, Allah, He is the Oft-Forgiving, the Most Merciful.

Almost (takādu) | the heavens (l-samāwātu) | break up (yatafaṭṭarna) | from (min) | above them (fawqihinna), | and the Angels (wal-malāikatu) | glorify (yusabbiḥūna) | the praise (biḥamdi) | of their Lord (rabbihim) | and ask for forgiveness (wayastaghfirūna) | for those (liman) | on (fī) | the earth (l-arḍi). | Unquestionably (alā), | indeed (inna), | Allah (l-laha), | He (huwa) | is the Oft-Forgiving (l-ghafūru), | the Most Merciful (l-raḥīmu).

42:6 And those who take besides protectors, Allah is a Guardian over them, and not you are over them a manager.

And those who (wa-alladhīna) | take (ittakhadhū) | besides (min) | besides (dūnihi) | protectors (awliyāa), | Allah (l-lahu) | is a Guardian (ḥafīẓun) | over them (ʿalayhim), | and not (wamā) | you (anta) | are over them (ʿalayhim) | a manager (biwakīlin).

42:7 And thus We have revealed to you a Quran in Arabic, that you may warn the mother of the towns, and whoever is around it, and warn of the Day of Assembly, there is no doubt in it. A party will be in Paradise and a party in the Blazing Fire.

And thus (wakadhālika) | We have revealed (awḥaynā) | to you (ilayka) | a Quran (qur'ānan) | in Arabic (ʿarabiyyan), | that you may warn (litundhira) | the mother (umma) | of the towns (l-qurā), | and whoever (waman) | is around it (ḥawlahā), | and warn (watundhira) | of the Day (yawma) | of Assembly (l-jamʿi), | there is no (lā) | doubt (rayba) | in it (fīhi). | A party (farīqun) | will be in (fī) | Paradise (l-janati) | and a party (wafarīqun) | in (fī) | the Blazing Fire (l-saʿīri).

42:8 And if Allah willed, He could have made them a community one, but He admits whom He wills in to His Mercy. And the wrongdoers, not for them any protector and not any helper.

And if (walaw) | Allah willed (shāa), | Allah willed (l-lahu), | He could have made them (lajaʿalahum) | a community (ummatan) | one (wāḥidatan), | but (walākin) | He admits (yud'khilu) | whom (man) | He wills (yashāu) | in to (fī) | His Mercy (raḥmatihi). | And the wrongdoers (wal-ẓālimūna), | not (mā) | for them (lahum) | any (min) | protector (waliyyin) | and not (walā) | any helper (naṣīrin).

42:9 Or have they taken besides Him protectors? But Allah - He is the Protector, and He gives life to the dead. And He is on every thing All-Powerful.

Or (ami) | have they taken (ittakhadhū) | besides Him (min) | besides Him (dūnihi) | protectors (awliyāa)? | But Allah (fal-lahu)- | He (huwa) | is the Protector (l-waliyu), | and He (wahuwa) | gives life (yuḥ'yī) | to the dead (l-mawtā). | And He (wahuwa) | is on (ʿalā) | every (kulli) | thing (shayin) | All-Powerful (qadīrun).

42:10 And whatever you differ in it of a thing, then its ruling is to Allah. That is Allah, my Lord, upon Him I put my trust and to Him I turn.

And whatever (wamā) | you differ (ikh'talaftum) | in it (fīhi) | of (min) | a thing (shayin), | then its ruling (faḥuk'muhu) | is to (ilā) | Allah (l-lahi). | That (dhālikumu) | is Allah (l-lahu), | my Lord (rabbī), | upon Him (ʿalayhi) | I put my trust (tawakkaltu) | and to Him (wa-ilayhi) | I turn (unību).

42:11 The Creator of the heavens and the earth. He made for you from yourselves, mates, and among the cattle mates; He multiplies you thereby. There is not like Him anything, and He is the All-Hearer, the All-Seer.

The Creator (fāṭiru) | of the heavens (l-samāwāti) | and the earth (wal-arḍi). | He made (jaʿala) | for you (lakum) | from (min) | yourselves (anfusikum), | mates (azwājan), | and among (wamina) | the cattle (l-anʿāmi) | mates (azwājan); | He multiplies you (yadhra-ukum) | thereby (fīhi). | There is not (laysa) | like Him (kamith'lihi) | anything (shayon), | and He (wahuwa) | is the All-Hearer (l-samīʿu), | the All-Seer (l-baṣīru).

42:12 To Him belongs the keys of the heavens and the earth. He extends the provision for whom He wills and restricts. Indeed, He of every thing is All-Knower.

To Him belongs (lahu) | the keys (maqālīdu) | of the heavens (l-samāwāti) | and the earth (wal-arḍi). | He extends (yabsuṭu) | the provision (l-riz'qa) | for whom (liman) | He wills (yashāu) | and restricts (wayaqdiru). | Indeed, He (innahu) | of every (bikulli) | thing (shayin) | is All-Knower (ʿalīmun).

42:13 He has ordained for you of the religion what He enjoined upon Nuh, and that which We have revealed to you, and what We enjoined upon Ibrahim and Musa and Isa. To establish the religion and not be divided therein. Is difficult on the polytheists what you call them to it. Allah chooses for Himself whom He wills, and guides to Himself whoever turns.

He has ordained (sharaʿa) | for you (lakum) | of (mina) | the religion (l-dīni) | what (mā) | He enjoined (waṣṣā) | upon (bihi) | Nuh (nūḥan), | and that which (wa-alladhī) | We have revealed (awḥaynā) | to you (ilayka), | and what (wamā) | We enjoined (waṣṣaynā) | upon (bihi) | Ibrahim (ib'rāhīma) | and Musa (wamūsā) | and Isa (waʿīsā). | To (an) | establish (aqīmū) | the religion (l-dīna) | and not (walā) | be divided (tatafarraqū) | therein (fīhi). | Is difficult (kabura) | on (ʿalā) | the polytheists (l-mush'rikīna) | what (mā) | you call them (tadʿūhum) | to it (ilayhi). | Allah (l-lahu)

| chooses (yajtabī) | for Himself (ilayhi) | whom (man) | He wills (yashāu), | and guides (wayahdī) | to Himself (ilayhi) | whoever (man) | turns (yunību).

42:14 And not they became divided until after [what] came to them the knowledge out of rivalry, among them. And if not for a word that preceded from your Lord for a term specified, surely, it would have been settled between them. And indeed, those who were made to inherit the Book after them are surely in doubt concerning it - disquieting.

And not (wamā) | they became divided (tafarraqū) | until (illā) | after (min) | after (baʿdi) | [what] (mā) | came to them (jāahumu) | the knowledge (l-ʿil'mu) | out of rivalry (baghyan), | among them (baynahum). | And if not (walawlā) | for a word (kalimatun) | that preceded (sabaqat) | from (min) | your Lord (rabbika) | for (ilā) | a term (ajalin) | specified (musamman), | surely, it would have been settled (laquḍiya) | between them (baynahum). | And indeed (wa-inna), | those who (alladhīna) | were made to inherit (ūrithū) | the Book (l-kitāba) | after them (min) | after them (baʿdihim) | are surely in (lafī) | doubt (shakkin) | concerning it (min'hu)- | disquieting (murībin).

42:15 So to that then invite, and stand firm as you are commanded and do not follow their desires, but say, "I believe in what Allah has sent down of the Book, and I am commanded that I do justice between you. Allah is our Lord and your Lord. For us our deeds and for you your deeds. There is no argument between us and between you. Allah will assemble [between] us, and to Him is the final return."

So to that (falidhālika) | then invite (fa-udʿʿu), | and stand firm (wa-is'taqim) | as (kamā) | you are commanded (umir'ta) | and do not (walā) | follow (tattabiʿ) | their desires (ahwāahum), | but say (waqul), | "I believe (āmantu) | in what (bimā) | Allah has sent down (anzala) | Allah has sent down (l-lahu) | of (min) | the Book (kitābin), | and I am commanded (wa-umir'tu) | that I do justice (li-aʿdila) | between you (baynakumu). | Allah (l-lahu) | is our Lord (rabbunā) | and your Lord (warabbukum). | For us (lanā) | our deeds (aʿmālunā) | and for you (walakum) | your deeds (aʿmālukum). | There is no (lā) | argument (ḥujjata) | between us (baynanā) | and between you (wabaynakumu). | Allah (l-lahu) | will assemble (yajmaʿu) | [between] us (baynanā), | and to Him (wa-ilayhi) | is the final return. (l-maṣīru)"

42:16 And those who argue concerning Allah after [what] response has been made to Him, their argument is invalid with their Lord, and upon them is wrath, and for them is a punishment severe.

And those who (wa-alladhīna) | argue (yuḥājjūna) | concerning (fī) | Allah (l-lahi) | after (min) | after (baʿdi) | [what] (mā) | response has been made to Him (us'tujība), | response has been made to Him (lahu), | their argument (ḥujjatuhum) | is invalid (dāḥiḍatun) | with (ʿinda) | their Lord (rabbihim), | and upon them (waʿalayhim) | is wrath (ghaḍabun), | and for them (walahum) | is a punishment (ʿadhābun) | severe (shadīdun).

42:17 Allah is the One Who has sent down the Book in truth, and the Balance. And what will make you know? Perhaps the Hour is near.

Allah (al-lahu) | is the One Who (alladhī) | has sent down (anzala) | the Book (l-kitāba) | in truth (bil-ḥaqi), | and the Balance (wal-mīzāna). | And what (wamā) | will make you know (yud'rīka)? | Perhaps (laʿalla) | the Hour (l-sāʿata) | is near (qarībun).

42:18 Seek to hasten [of] it those who do not believe in it, and those who believe are fearful of it and know that it is the truth. Unquestionably, indeed, those who dispute concerning the Hour are certainly in error far.

Seek to hasten (yastaʿjilu) | [of] it (bihā) | those who (alladhīna) | do not (lā) | believe (yu'minūna) | in it (bihā), | and those who (wa-alladhīna) | believe (āmanū) | are fearful (mush'fiqūna) | of it (min'hā) | and know (wayaʿlamūna) | that it (annahā) | is the truth (l-ḥaqu). | Unquestionably (alā), | indeed (inna), | those who (alladhīna) | dispute (yumārūna) | concerning (fī) | the Hour (l-sāʿati) | are certainly in (lafī) | error (ḍalālin) | far (baʿīdin).

42:19 Allah is Subtle with His slaves; He gives provision to whom He wills. And He is the All-Strong, the All-Mighty.

Allah (al-lahu) | is Subtle (laṭīfun) | with His slaves (biʿibādihi); | He gives provision (yarzuqu) | to whom (man) | He wills (yashāu). | And He (wahuwa) | is the All-Strong (l-qawiyu), | the All-Mighty (l-ʿazīzu).

42:20 Whoever is desiring the harvest of the Hereafter - We increase for him in his harvest. And whoever is desiring the harvest of the world, We give him of it, but not for him in the Hereafter any share.

Whoever (man) | is (kāna) | desiring (yurīdu) | the harvest (ḥartha) | of the Hereafter (l-ākhirati)- | We increase (nazid) | for him (lahu) | in (fī) | his harvest (ḥarthihi). | And whoever (waman) | is (kāna) | desiring (yurīdu) | the harvest (ḥartha) | of the world (l-dun'yā), | We give him (nu'tihi) | of it (min'hā), | but not (wamā) | for him (lahu) | in (fī) | the Hereafter (l-ākhirati) | any (min) | share (naṣībin).

42:21 Or for them are partners who have ordained for them of the religion what not Allah has given permission of it And if not for a word decisive, surely, it would have been judged between them. And indeed, the wrongdoers, for them is a punishment painful.

Or (am) | for them (lahum) | are partners (shurakāu) | who have ordained (sharaʿū) | for them (lahum) | of (mina) | the religion (l-dīni) | what (mā) | not (lam) | Allah has given permission of it (yadhan) | Allah has given permission of it (bihi) | Allah has given permission of it (l-lahu) | And if not (walawlā) | for a word (kalimatu) | decisive (l-faṣli), | surely, it would have been judged (laquḍiya) | between them (baynahum). | And indeed (wa-inna), | the wrongdoers (l-ẓālimīna), | for them (lahum) | is a punishment (ʿadhābun) | painful (alīmun).

42:22 You will see the wrongdoers fearful of what they earned, and it will befall [on] them. And those who believe and do righteous deeds will be in flowering meadows of the Gardens, for them is whatever they wish with their Lord. That - it is the Bounty the Great.

You will see (tarā) | the wrongdoers (l-ẓālimīna) | fearful (mush'fiqīna) | of what (mimmā) | they earned (kasabū), | and it (wahuwa) | will befall (wāqiʿun) | [on] them (bihim). | And those who (wa-alladhīna) | believe (āmanū) | and do (waʿamilū) | righteous deeds (l-ṣāliḥāti) | will be in (fī) | flowering meadows (rawḍāti) | of the Gardens (l-janāti), | for them (lahum) | is whatever (mā) | they wish (yashāūna) | with (ʿinda) | their Lord (rabbihim). | That (dhālika)- | it (huwa) | is the Bounty (l-faḍlu) | the Great (l-kabīru).

42:23 That is of which Allah gives glad tidings to His slaves - those who believe and do righteous deeds. Say, "Not I ask you for it any payment except the love among the relatives." And whoever earns any good, We increase for him therein good. Indeed, Allah is Oft-Forgiving, All-Appreciative.

That (dhālika) | is of which (alladhī) | Allah gives glad tidings (yubashiru) | Allah gives glad tidings (l-lahu) | to His slaves (ʿibādahu)- | those who (alladhīna) | believe (āmanū) | and do (waʿamilū) | righteous deeds (l-ṣāliḥāti). | Say (qul), | "Not (lā) | I ask you (asalukum) | for it (ʿalayhi) | any payment (ajran) | except (illā) | the love (l-mawadata) | among (fī) | the relatives. (l-qur'bā)" | And whoever (waman) | earns (yaqtarif) | any good (ḥasanatan), | We increase (nazid) | for him (lahu) | therein (fīhā) | good (ḥus'nan). | Indeed (inna), | Allah (l-laha) | is Oft-Forgiving (ghafūrun), | All-Appreciative (shakūrun).

42:24 Or do they say, "He has invented about Allah a lie?" But if Allah willed He would seal [over] your heart. And Allah eliminates the falsehood and establishes the truth by His Words. Indeed, He is All-Knowing of what is in the breasts.

Or (am) | do they say (yaqūlūna), | "He has invented (if'tarā) | about (ʿalā) | Allah (l-lahi) | a lie? (kadhiban)" | But if (fa-in) | Allah willed (yasha-i) | Allah willed (l-lahu) | He would seal (yakhtim) | [over] (ʿalā) | your heart (qalbika). | And Allah eliminates (wayamḥu) | And Allah eliminates (l-lahu) | the falsehood (l-bāṭila) | and establishes (wayuḥiqqu) | the truth (l-ḥaqa) | by His Words (bikalimātihi). | Indeed, He (innahu) | is All-Knowing (ʿalīmun) | of what (bidhāti) | is in the breasts (l-ṣudūri).

42:25 And He is the One Who accepts the repentance of His slaves and pardons [of] the evil, and He knows what you do.

And He (wahuwa) | is the One Who (alladhī) | accepts (yaqbalu) | the repentance (l-tawbata) | of (ʿan) | His slaves (ʿibādihi) | and pardons (wayaʿfū) | [of] (ʿani) | the evil (l-sayiāti), | and He knows (wayaʿlamu) | what (mā) | you do (tafʿalūna).

42:26 And He answers those who believe and do righteous deeds and increases for them from His Bounty. And the disbelievers - for them will be a punishment severe.

And He answers (wayastajību) | those who (alladhīna) | believe (āmanū) | and do (waʿamilū) | righteous deeds (l-ṣāliḥāti) | and increases for them (wayazīduhum) | from (min) | His Bounty (faḍlihi). | And the disbelievers (wal-kāfirūna)- | for them (lahum) | will be a punishment (ʿadhābun) | severe (shadīdun).

42:27 And if Allah extends the provision for His slaves, surely they would rebel in the earth; but He sends down in due measure what He wills. Indeed, He of His slaves is All-Aware, All-Seer.

And if (walaw) | Allah extends (basaṭa) | Allah extends (l-lahu) | the provision (l-riz'qa) | for His slaves (liʿibādihi), | surely they would rebel (labaghaw) | in (fī) | the earth (l-arḍi); | but (walākin) | He sends down (yunazzilu) | in due measure (biqadarin) | what (mā) | He wills (yashāu). | Indeed, He (innahu) | of His slaves (biʿibādihi) | is All-Aware (khabīrun), | All-Seer (baṣīrun).

42:28 And He is the One Who sends down the rain after [what] they have despaired, and spreads His mercy. And He is the Protector, the Praiseworthy.

And He (wahuwa) | is the One Who (alladhī) | sends down (yunazzilu) | the rain (l-ghaytha) | after (min) | after (baʿdi) | [what] (mā) | they have despaired (qanaṭū), | and spreads (wayanshuru) | His mercy (raḥmatahu). | And He (wahuwa) | is the Protector (l-waliyu), | the Praiseworthy (l-ḥamīdu).

42:29 And among His Signs is the creation of the heavens and the earth and whatever He has dispersed in both of them of the creatures. And He is over their gathering, when He wills, All-Powerful.

And among (wamin) | His Signs (āyātihi) | is the creation (khalqu) | of the heavens (l-samāwāti) | and the earth (wal-arḍi) | and whatever (wamā) | He has dispersed (batha) | in both of them (fīhimā) | of (min) | the creatures (dābbatin). | And He (wahuwa) | is over (ʿalā) | their gathering (jamʿihim), | when (idhā) | He wills (yashāu), | All-Powerful (qadīrun).

42:30 And whatever befalls you of the misfortune, is because of what have earned your hands. But He pardons [from] much.

And whatever (wamā) | befalls you (aṣābakum) | of (min) | the misfortune (muṣībatin), | is because of what (fabimā) | have earned (kasabat) | your hands (aydīkum). | But He pardons (wayaʿfū) | [from] (ʿan) | much (kathīrin).

42:31 And not you can escape in the earth, and not for you besides Allah any protector and not any helper.

And not (wamā) | you (antum) | can escape (bimuʿjizīna) | in (fī) | the earth (l-arḍi), | and not (wamā) | for you (lakum) | besides (min) | besides (dūni) | Allah (l-lahi) | any (min) | protector (waliyyin) | and not (walā) | any helper (naṣīrin).

42:32 And among His Signs are the ships in the sea, like [the] mountains.
And among (wamin) | His Signs (āyātihi) | are the ships (l-jawāri) | in (fī) | the sea (l-baḥri), | like [the] mountains (kal-aʿlāmi).

42:33 If He wills, He can cause the wind to become still then they would remain motionless on its back. Indeed, in that surely are Signs for everyone patient and grateful.
If (in) | He wills (yasha), | He can cause the wind to become still (yus'kini) | He can cause the wind to become still (l-rīḥa) | then they would remain (fayaẓlalna) | motionless (rawākida) | on (ʿalā) | its back (ẓahrihi). | Indeed (inna), | in (fī) | that (dhālika) | surely are Signs (laāyātin) | for everyone (likulli) | patient (ṣabbārin) | and grateful (shakūrin).

42:34 Or He could destroy them for what they have earned; but He pardons [from] much.
Or (aw) | He could destroy them (yūbiq'hunna) | for what (bimā) | they have earned (kasabū); | but He pardons (wayaʿfu) | [from] (ʿan) | much (kathīrin).

42:35 And may know those who dispute concerning Our Signs that not for them any place of refuge.
And may know (wayaʿlama) | those who (alladhīna) | dispute (yujādilūna) | concerning (fī) | Our Signs (āyātinā) | that not (mā) | for them (lahum) | any (min) | place of refuge (maḥīṣin).

42:36 So whatever you are given of a thing, is but a passing enjoyment for the life of the world. But what is with Allah is better and more lasting for those who believe and upon their Lord put their trust.
So whatever (famā) | you are given (ūtītum) | of (min) | a thing (shayin), | is but a passing enjoyment (famatāʿu) | for the life (l-ḥayati) | of the world (l-dun'yā). | But what (wamā) | is with (ʿinda) | Allah (l-lahi) | is better (khayrun) | and more lasting (wa-abqā) | for those who (lilladhīna) | believe (āmanū) | and upon (waʿalā) | their Lord (rabbihim) | put their trust (yatawakkalūna).

42:37 And those who avoid the greater sins and the immoralities, and when they are angry, they forgive,
And those who (wa-alladhīna) | avoid (yajtanibūna) | the greater (kabāira) | sins (l-ith'mi) | and the immoralities (wal-fawāḥisha), | and when (wa-idhā) | and when (mā) | they are angry (ghaḍibū), | they (hum) | forgive (yaghfirūna),

42:38 And those who respond to their Lord and establish prayer and their affairs are conducted by consultation among them, and from what We have provided them they spend,
And those who (wa-alladhīna) | respond (is'tajābū) | to their Lord (lirabbihim) | and establish (wa-aqāmū) | prayer (l-ṣalata) | and their affairs (wa-amruhum) | are conducted by consultation (shūrā) | among them (baynahum), | and from what (wamimmā) | We have provided them (razaqnāhum) | they spend (yunfiqūna),

42:39 And those who, when strikes them tyranny, they defend themselves.
And those who (wa-alladhīna), | when (idhā) | strikes them (aṣābahumu) | tyranny (l-baghyu), | they (hum) | defend themselves (yantaṣirūna).

42:40 The recompense of an evil is an evil like it. But whoever pardons and makes reconciliation, then his reward is on Allah. Indeed, He does not like the wrongdoers.
The recompense (wajazāu) | of an evil (sayyi-atin) | is an evil (sayyi-atun) | like it (mith'luhā). | But whoever (faman) | pardons (ʿafā) | and makes reconciliation (wa-aṣlaḥa), | then his reward (fa-ajruhu) | is on (ʿalā) | Allah (l-lahi). | Indeed, He (innahu) | does not (lā) | like (yuḥibbu) | the wrongdoers (l-ẓālimīna).

42:41 And surely whosoever defends himself after he has been wronged, then those not is against them any way.

And surely whosoever (walamani) | defends himself (intaṣara) | after (baʿda) | he has been wronged (ẓul'mihi), | then those (fa-ulāika) | not (mā) | is against them (ʿalayhim) | any (min) | way (sabīlin).

42:42 Only the way against those who oppress the people and rebel in the earth without right. Those for them is a punishment painful.

Only (innamā) | the way (l-sabīlu) | against (ʿalā) | those who (alladhīna) | oppress (yaẓlimūna) | the people (l-nāsa) | and rebel (wayabghūna) | in (fī) | the earth (l-arḍi) | without (bighayri) | right (l-ḥaqi). | Those (ulāika) | for them (lahum) | is a punishment (ʿadhābun) | painful (alīmun).

42:43 And whoever is patient and forgives, indeed, that is surely of matters of determination.

And whoever (walaman) | is patient (ṣabara) | and forgives (waghafara), | indeed (inna), | that (dhālika) | is surely of (lamin) | matters of determination (ʿazmi). | matters of determination (l-umūri).

42:44 And whoever Allah lets go astray then not for him any protector after Him. And you will see the wrongdoers, when they see the punishment saying, "Is there for return any way?"

And whoever (waman) | Allah lets go astray (yuḍ'lili) | Allah lets go astray (l-lahu) | then not (famā) | for him (lahu) | any (min) | protector (waliyyin) | after Him (min). | after Him (baʿdihi). | And you will see (watarā) | the wrongdoers (l-ẓālimīna), | when (lammā) | they see (ra-awū) | the punishment (l-ʿadhāba) | saying (yaqūlūna), | "Is (hal) | there for (ilā) | return (maraddin) | any (min) | way? (sabīlin)"

42:45 And you will see them being exposed to it, humbled by disgrace, looking with a glance stealthy. And will say those who believed, "Indeed, the losers are those who lost themselves and their families on the Day of the Resurrection. Unquestionably! Indeed, the wrongdoers are in a punishment lasting.

And you will see them (watarāhum) | being exposed (yuʿ'raḍūna) | to it (ʿalayhā), | humbled (khāshiʿīna) | by (mina) | disgrace (l-dhuli), | looking (yanẓurūna) | with (min) | a glance (ṭarfin) | stealthy (khafiyyin). | And will say (waqāla) | those who (alladhīna) | believed (āmanū), | "Indeed (inna), | the losers (l-khāsirīna) | are those who (alladhīna) | lost (khasirū) | themselves (anfusahum) | and their families (wa-ahlīhim) | on the Day (yawma) | of the Resurrection (l-qiyāmati). | Unquestionably (alā)! | Indeed (inna), | the wrongdoers (l-ẓālimīna) | are in (fī) | a punishment (ʿadhābin) | lasting (muqīmin).

42:46 And not will be for them any protector who will help them besides Allah. And whom Allah lets go astray then not for him any way.

And not (wamā) | will be (kāna) | for them (lahum) | any (min) | protector (awliyāa) | who will help them (yanṣurūnahum) | besides (min) | besides (dūni) | Allah (l-lahi). | And whom (waman) | Allah lets go astray (yuḍ'lili) | Allah lets go astray (l-lahu) | then not (famā) | for him (lahu) | any (min) | way (sabīlin).

42:47 Respond to your Lord before [that] comes a Day there is no averting for it from Allah. Not is for you any refuge on that Day and not for you any denial.

Respond (is'tajībū) | to your Lord (lirabbikum) | before (min) | before (qabli) | [that] (an) | comes (yatiya) | a Day (yawmun) | there is no (lā) | averting (maradda) | for it (lahu) | from (mina) | Allah (l-lahi). | Not (mā) | is for you (lakum) | any (min) | refuge (malja-in) | on that Day (yawma-idhin) | and not (wamā) | for you (lakum) | any (min) | denial (nakīrin).

42:48 Then if they turn away, then not We have sent you over them as a guardian. Not is on you except the conveyance. And indeed, when We cause to taste [the] man from Us Mercy, he rejoices in it. But if befalls them evil, for what have sent forth their hands then indeed, [the] man is ungrateful.

Then if (fa-in) | they turn away (aʿraḍū), | then not (famā) | We have sent you (arsalnāka) | over them (ʿalayhim) | as a guardian (ḥafīẓan). | Not (in) | is on you (ʿalayka) | except (illā) | the conveyance (l-balāghu). | And indeed (wa-innā), | when (idhā) | We cause to taste (adhaqnā) | [the] man (l-insāna) | from Us (minnā) | Mercy (raḥmatan), | he rejoices (fariḥa) | in it (bihā). | But if (wa-in) | befalls them (tuṣib'hum) | evil (sayyi-atun), | for what (bimā) | have sent forth (qaddamat) | their hands (aydīhim) | then indeed (fa-inna), | [the] man (l-insāna) | is ungrateful (kafūrun).

42:49 To Allah belongs the dominion of the heavens and the earth. He creates what He wills. He grants to whom He wills females, and He grants to whom He wills [the] males.

To Allah (lillahi) | belongs the dominion (mul'ku) | of the heavens (l-samāwāti) | and the earth (wal-arḍi). | He creates (yakhluqu) | what (mā) | He wills (yashāu). | He grants (yahabu) | to whom (liman) | He wills (yashāu) | females (ināthan), | and He grants (wayahabu) | to whom (liman) | He wills (yashāu) | [the] males (l-dhukūra).

42:50 Or He grants them males and females; and He makes whom He wills barren. Indeed, He is All-Knower, All-Powerful.

Or (aw) | He grants them (yuzawwijuhum) | males (dhuk'rānan) | and females (wa-ināthan); | and He makes (wayajʿalu) | whom (man) | He wills (yashāu) | barren (ʿaqīman). | Indeed, He (innahu) | is All-Knower (ʿalīmun), | All-Powerful (qadīrun).

42:51 And not is for any human that Allah should speak to him except by revelation or from behind a veil or by sending a messenger then he reveals by His permission what He wills. Indeed, He is Most High, Most Wise.

And not (wamā) | is (kāna) | for any human (libasharin) | that (an) | Allah should speak to him (yukallimahu) | Allah should speak to him (l-lahu) | except (illā) | by revelation (waḥyan) | or (aw) | from (min) | behind (warāi) | a veil (ḥijābin) | or (aw) | by sending (yur'sila) | a messenger (rasūlan) | then he reveals (fayūḥiya) | by His permission (bi-idh'nihi) | what (mā) | He wills (yashāu). | Indeed, He (innahu) | is Most High (ʿaliyyun), | Most Wise (ḥakīmun).

42:52 And thus We have revealed to you an inspiration by Our Command. Not did you know what the Book is and not the faith. But We have made it a light, We guide with it whom We will of Our slaves. And indeed, you surely guide to the Path Straight,

And thus (wakadhālika) | We have revealed (awḥaynā) | to you (ilayka) | an inspiration (rūḥan) | by (min) | Our Command (amrinā). | Not (mā) | did you (kunta) | know (tadrī) | what (mā) | the Book is (l-kitābu) | and not (walā) | the faith (l-īmānu). | But (walākin) | We have made it (jaʿalnāhu) | a light (nūran), | We guide (nahdī) | with it (bihi) | whom (man) | We will (nashāu) | of (min) | Our slaves (ʿibādinā). | And indeed, you (wa-innaka) | surely guide (latahdī) | to (ilā) | the Path (ṣirāṭin) | Straight (mus'taqīmin),

42:53 The path of Allah, the One to Whom belongs whatever is in the heavens and whatever is in the earth. Unquestionably! To Allah reach all affairs.

The path (ṣirāṭi) | of Allah (l-lahi), | the One (alladhī) | to Whom (lahu) | belongs whatever (mā) | is in (fī) | the heavens (l-samāwāti) | and whatever (wamā) | is in (fī) | the earth (l-arḍi). | Unquestionably (alā)! | To (ilā) | Allah (l-lahi) | reach (taṣīru) | all affairs (l-umūru).

Chapter (43) Sūrat l-Zukh'ruf (The Gold Adornment)

43:1 Ha Meem.

Ha Meem (hha-meem).

43:2 By the Book the clear,

By the Book (wal-kitābi) | the clear (l-mubīni),

43:3 Indeed, We have made it a Quran in Arabic so that you may understand.

Indeed, We (innā) | have made it (jaʿalnāhu) | a Quran (qur'ānan) | in Arabic (ʿarabiyyan) | so that you may (laʿallakum) | understand (taʿqilūna).

43:4 And indeed, it is in the Mother of the Book with Us, surely exalted, full of wisdom.

And indeed, it (wa-innahu) | is in (fī) | the Mother (ummi) | of the Book (l-kitābi) | with Us (ladaynā), | surely exalted (laʿaliyyun), | full of wisdom (ḥakīmun).

43:5 Then should We take away from you the Reminder, disregarding you, because you are a people transgressing?

Then should We take away (afanaḍribu) | from you (ʿankumu) | the Reminder (l-dhik'ra), | disregarding you (ṣafḥan), | because (an) | you are (kuntum) | a people (qawman) | transgressing (mus'rifīna)?

43:6 And how many We sent of a Prophet among the former people,

And how many (wakam) | We sent (arsalnā) | of (min) | a Prophet (nabiyyin) | among (fī) | the former people (l-awalīna),

43:7 And not came to them any Prophet but they used to mock at him.

And not (wamā) | came to them (yatīhim) | any Prophet (min) | any Prophet (nabiyyin) | but (illā) | they used to (kānū) | mock at him (bihi). | mock at him (yastahziūna).

43:8 Then We destroyed stronger than them in power and has passed the example of the former (people).

Then We destroyed (fa-ahlaknā) | stronger (ashadda) | than them (min'hum) | in power (baṭshan) | and has passed (wamaḍā) | the example (mathalu) | of the former (people) (l-awalīna).

43:9 And if you ask them, "Who created the heavens and the earth?" They will surely say, "Created them the All-Mighty, the All-Knower,"

And if (wala-in) | you ask them (sa-altahum), | "Who (man) | created (khalaqa) | the heavens (l-samāwāti) | and the earth? (wal-arḍa)" | They will surely say (layaqūlunna), | "Created them (khalaqahunna) | the All-Mighty (l-ʿazīzu), | the All-Knower, (l-ʿalīmu)"

43:10 The One Who made for you the earth a bed, and made for you therein roads so that you may be guided,

The One Who (alladhī) | made (jaʿala) | for you (lakumu) | the earth (l-arḍa) | a bed (mahdan), | and made (wajaʿala) | for you (lakum) | therein (fīhā) | roads (subulan) | so that you may (laʿallakum) | be guided (tahtadūna),

43:11 And the One Who sends down from the sky water in due measure, then We revive with it a land dead, thus you will be brought forth,

And the One Who (wa-alladhī) | sends down (nazzala) | from (mina) | the sky (l-samāi) | water (māan) | in due measure (biqadarin), | then We revive (fa-ansharnā) | with it (bihi) | a land (baldatan) | dead (maytan), | thus (kadhālika) | you will be brought forth (tukh'rajūna),

43:12 And the One Who created the pairs all of them and made for you [of] the ships and the cattle what you ride,

And the One Who (wa-alladhī) | created (khalaqa) | the pairs (l-azwāja) | all of them (kullahā) | and made (wajaʿala) | for you (lakum) | [of] (mina) | the ships (l-ful'ki) | and the cattle (wal-anʿāmi) | what (mā) | you ride (tarkabūna),

43:13 That you may sit firmly, on their backs, then remember the favor of your Lord when you sit firmly on them and say, "Glory be to the One Who has subjected to us this, and not we were of it capable.

That you may sit firmly (litastawū), | on (ʿalā) | their backs (ẓuhūrihi), | then (thumma) | remember (tadhkurū) | the favor (niʿmata) | of your Lord (rabbikum) | when (idhā) | you sit firmly (is'tawaytum) | on them (ʿalayhi) | and say (wataqūlū), | "Glory be to (sub'ḥāna) | the One Who (alladhī) | has subjected (sakhara) | to us (lanā) | this (hādhā), | and not (wamā) | we were (kunnā) | of it (lahu) | capable (muq'rinīna).

43:14 And indeed, we to our Lord, will surely return."

And indeed, we (wa-innā) | to (ilā) | our Lord (rabbinā), | will surely return. (lamunqalibūna)"

43:15 But they attribute to Him from His slaves a portion. Indeed, man surely is clearly ungrateful.

But they attribute (wajaʿalū) | to Him (lahu) | from (min) | His slaves (ʿibādihi) | a portion (juz'an). | Indeed (inna), | man (l-insāna) | surely is clearly ungrateful (lakafūrun). | surely is clearly ungrateful (mubīnun).

43:16 Or has He taken of what, He has created, daughters and He has chosen for you sons.

Or (ami) | has He taken (ittakhadha) | of what (mimmā), | He has created (yakhluqu), | daughters (banātin) | and He has chosen for you (wa-aṣfākum) | sons (bil-banīna).

43:17 And when is given good news, to one of them, of what he sets up for the Most Gracious as a likeness, becomes his face dark and he is filled with grief.

And when (wa-idhā) | is given good news (bushira), | to one of them (aḥaduhum), | of what (bimā) | he sets up (ḍaraba) | for the Most Gracious (lilrraḥmāni) | as a likeness (mathalan), | becomes (ẓalla) | his face (wajhuhu) | dark (mus'waddan) | and he (wahuwa) | is filled with grief (kaẓīmun).

43:18 Then is one who is brought up in ornaments and he in the dispute is not clear.

Then is one who (awaman) | is brought up (yunasha-u) | in (fī) | ornaments (l-ḥil'yati) | and he (wahuwa) | in (fī) | the dispute (l-khiṣāmi) | is not (ghayru) | clear (mubīnin).

43:19 And they made, the Angels, those who themselves are slaves of the Most Gracious, females. Did they witness their creation? Will be recorded their testimony, and they will be questioned.

And they made (wajaʿalū), | the Angels (l-malāikata), | those who (alladhīna) | themselves (hum) | are slaves (ʿibādu) | of the Most Gracious (l-raḥmāni), | females (ināthan). | Did they witness (ashahidū) | their creation (khalqahum)? | Will be recorded (satuk'tabu) | their testimony (shahādatuhum), | and they will be questioned (wayus'alūna).

43:20 And they say, "If had willed the Most Gracious, we would not have worshipped them." Not they have about that any knowledge. Nothing they do but lie.

And they say (waqālū), | "If (law) | had willed (shāa) | the Most Gracious (l-raḥmānu), | we would not have worshipped them. (mā)" | we would not have worshipped them. (ʿabadnāhum)" |

Not (mā) | they have (lahum) | about that (bidhālika) | any (min) | knowledge (ʿil'min). | Nothing (in) | they do (hum) | but (illā) | lie (yakhruṣūna).

43:21 Or have We given them a book before it, so they to it are holding fast?

Or (am) | have We given them (ātaynāhum) | a book (kitāban) | before it (min), | before it (qablihi), | so they (fahum) | to it (bihi) | are holding fast (mus'tamsikūna)?

43:22 Nay, they say, "Indeed, we [we] found our forefathers upon a religion and indeed, we on their footsteps are guided."

Nay (bal), | they say (qālū), | "Indeed, we (innā) | [we] found (wajadnā) | our forefathers (ābāanā) | upon (ʿalā) | a religion (ummatin) | and indeed, we (wa-innā) | on (ʿalā) | their footsteps (āthārihim) | are guided. (muh'tadūna)"

43:23 And thus not We sent before you in a town any warner except said the wealthy ones of it, "Indeed, we [we] found our forefathers on a religion, and indeed, we [on] their footsteps are following."

And thus (wakadhālika) | not (mā) | We sent (arsalnā) | before you (min) | before you (qablika) | in (fī) | a town (qaryatin) | any (min) | warner (nadhīrin) | except (illā) | said (qāla) | the wealthy ones of it (mut'rafūhā), | "Indeed, we (innā) | [we] found (wajadnā) | our forefathers (ābāanā) | on (ʿalā) | a religion (ummatin), | and indeed, we (wa-innā) | [on] (ʿalā) | their footsteps (āthārihim) | are following. (muq'tadūna)"

43:24 He said, "Even if I brought you better guidance than what you found on it your forefathers?" They said, "Indeed, we with what you are sent with [it] are disbelievers."

He said (qāla), | "Even if (awalaw) | I brought you (ji'tukum) | better guidance (bi-ahdā) | than what (mimmā) | you found (wajadttum) | on it (ʿalayhi) | your forefathers? (ābāakum)" | They said (qālū), | "Indeed, we (innā) | with what (bimā) | you are sent (ur'sil'tum) | with [it] (bihi) | are disbelievers. (kāfirūna)"

43:25 So We took retribution from them. Then see how was the end of the deniers.

So We took retribution (fa-intaqamnā) | from them (min'hum). | Then see (fa-unẓur) | how (kayfa) | was (kāna) | the end (ʿāqibatu) | of the deniers (l-mukadhibīna).

43:26 And when Ibrahim Said to his father and his people, "Indeed, I am disassociated from what you worship

And when (wa-idh) | Ibrahim Said (qāla) | Ibrahim Said (ib'rāhīmu) | to his father (li-abīhi) | and his people (waqawmihi), | "Indeed, I am (innanī) | disassociated (barāon) | from what (mimmā) | you worship (taʿbudūna)

43:27 Except the One Who created me; and indeed, He will guide me."

Except (illā) | the One Who (alladhī) | created me (faṭaranī); | and indeed, He (fa-innahu) | will guide me. (sayahdīni)"

43:28 And he made it a word lasting among his descendents, so that they may return.

And he made it (wajaʿalahā) | a word (kalimatan) | lasting (bāqiyatan) | among (fī) | his descendents (ʿaqibihi), | so that they may (laʿallahum) | return (yarjiʿūna).

43:29 Nay, I gave enjoyment to these and their forefathers until came to them the truth and a Messenger clear.

Nay (bal), | I gave enjoyment (mattaʿtu) | to these (hāulāi) | and their forefathers (waābāahum) | until (ḥattā) | came to them (jāahumu) | the truth (l-ḥaqu) | and a Messenger (warasūlun) | clear (mubīnun).

43:30 And when came to them the truth, they said, "This is magic, and indeed, we of it are disbelievers."

And when (walammā) | came to them (jāahumu) | the truth (l-ḥaqu), | they said (qālū), | "This (hādhā) | is magic (siḥ'run), | and indeed, we (wa-innā) | of it (bihi) | are disbelievers. (kāfirūna)"

43:31 And they say, "Why not was sent down this the Quran to a man, from the two towns, great?"

And they say (waqālū), | "Why not (lawlā) | was sent down (nuzzila) | this (hādhā) | the Quran (l-qur'ānu) | to (ʿalā) | a man (rajulin), | from (mina) | the two towns (l-qaryatayni), | great? (ʿaẓīmin)"

43:32 Do they distribute the Mercy of your Lord? We [We] distribute among them their livelihood in the life of the world, and We raise some of them above others in degrees so that may take, some of them, others, for service. But the Mercy of your Lord is better than what they accumulate.

Do they (ahum) | distribute (yaqsimūna) | the Mercy (raḥmata) | of your Lord (rabbika)? | We (naḥnu) | [We] distribute (qasamnā) | among them (baynahum) | their livelihood (maʿīshatahum) | in (fī) | the life (l-ḥayati) | of the world (l-dun'yā), | and We raise (warafaʿnā) | some of them (baʿḍahum) | above (fawqa) | others (baʿḍin) | in degrees (darajātin) | so that may take (liyattakhidha), | some of them (baʿḍuhum), | others (baʿḍan), | for service (sukh'riyyan). | But the Mercy (waraḥmatu) | of your Lord (rabbika) | is better (khayrun) | than what (mimmā) | they accumulate (yajmaʿūna).

43:33 And if not that would become [the] mankind a community one, We would have made for one who disbelieves in the Most Gracious for their houses roofs of silver and stairways upon which they mount

And if not (walawlā) | that (an) | would become (yakūna) | [the] mankind (l-nāsu) | a community (ummatan) | one (wāḥidatan), | We would have made (lajaʿalnā) | for one who (liman) | disbelieves (yakfuru) | in the Most Gracious (bil-raḥmāni) | for their houses (libuyūtihim) | roofs (suqufan) | of (min) | silver (fiḍḍatin) | and stairways (wamaʿārija) | upon which (ʿalayhā) | they mount (yaẓharūna)

43:34 And for their houses doors and couches upon which they recline

And for their houses (walibuyūtihim) | doors (abwāban) | and couches (wasururan) | upon which (ʿalayhā) | they recline (yattakiūna)

43:35 And ornaments of gold. And not is all that but an enjoyment of the life of the world. And the Hereafter with your Lord is for the righteous.

And ornaments of gold (wazukh'rufan). | And not is (wa-in) | all (kullu) | that (dhālika) | but (lammā) | an enjoyment (matāʿu) | of the life (l-ḥayati) | of the world (l-dun'yā). | And the Hereafter (wal-ākhiratu) | with (ʿinda) | your Lord (rabbika) | is for the righteous (lil'muttaqīna).

43:36 And whoever turns away from the remembrance of the Most Gracious, We appoint for him a devil, then he is to him a companion.

And whoever (waman) | turns away (yaʿshu) | from (ʿan) | the remembrance (dhik'ri) | of the Most Gracious (l-raḥmāni), | We appoint (nuqayyiḍ) | for him (lahu) | a devil (shayṭānan), | then he (fahuwa) | is to him (lahu) | a companion (qarīnun).

43:37 And indeed, they surely, turn them from the Path and they think that they are guided.

And indeed, they (wa-innahum) | surely, turn them (layaṣuddūnahum) | from (ʿani) | the Path (l-sabīli) | and they think (wayaḥsabūna) | that they (annahum) | are guided (muh'tadūna).

43:38 Until when he comes to Us he says, "O would that between me and between you were the distance of the East and the West." How wretched is the companion!

Until (ḥattā) | when (idhā) | he comes to Us (jāanā) | he says (qāla), | "O would that (yālayta) | between me (baynī) | and between you (wabaynaka) | were the distance (buʿ'da) | of the East and the West. (l-mashriqayni)" | How wretched is (fabi'sa) | the companion (l-qarīnu)!

43:39 And never will benefit you the Day, when you have wronged, that you will be in the punishment sharing.

And never (walan) | will benefit you (yanfaʿakumu) | the Day (l-yawma), | when (idh) | you have wronged (ẓalamtum), | that you (annakum) | will be in (fī) | the punishment (l-ʿadhābi) | sharing (mush'tarikūna).

43:40 Then can you cause to hear the deaf or guide the blind and one who is in an error clear?

Then can you (afa-anta) | cause to hear (tus'miʿu) | the deaf (l-ṣuma) | or (aw) | guide (tahdī) | the blind (l-ʿum'ya) | and one who (waman) | is (kāna) | in (fī) | an error (ḍalālin) | clear (mubīnin)?

43:41 And whether We take you away, then indeed, We, from them will take retribution.

And whether (fa-immā) | We take you away (nadhhabanna), | We take you away (bika), | then indeed, We (fa-innā), | from them (min'hum) | will take retribution (muntaqimūna).

43:42 Or We show you that which We have promised them, then indeed, We over them have full power.

Or (aw) | We show you (nuriyannaka) | that which (alladhī) | We have promised them (waʿadnāhum), | then indeed, We (fa-innā) | over them (ʿalayhim) | have full power (muq'tadirūna).

43:43 So hold fast to that which is revealed to you. Indeed, you are on a Path Straight.

So hold fast (fa-is'tamsik) | to that which (bi-alladhī) | is revealed (ūḥiya) | to you (ilayka). | Indeed, you (innaka) | are on (ʿalā) | a Path (ṣirāṭin) | Straight (mus'taqīmin).

43:44 And indeed, it is surely, a Reminder for you and your people, and soon you will be questioned.

And indeed, it (wa-innahu) | is surely, a Reminder (ladhik'run) | for you (laka) | and your people (waliqawmika), | and soon (wasawfa) | you will be questioned (tus'alūna).

43:45 And ask those whom We sent before you of Our Messengers; did We make besides the Most Gracious gods to be worshipped?

And ask (wasal) | those whom (man) | We sent (arsalnā) | before you (min) | before you (qablika) | of (min) | Our Messengers (rusulinā); | did We make (ajaʿalnā) | besides (min) | besides (dūni) | the Most Gracious (l-raḥmāni) | gods (ālihatan) | to be worshipped (yuʿ'badūna)?

43:46 And certainly We sent Musa with Our Signs to Firaun and his chiefs, and he said, "Indeed, I am a Messenger of the Lord of the worlds."

And certainly (walaqad) | We sent (arsalnā) | Musa (mūsā) | with Our Signs (biāyātinā) | to (ilā) | Firaun (firʿ'awna) | and his chiefs (wamala-ihi), | and he said (faqāla), | "Indeed, I am (innī) | a Messenger (rasūlu) | of the Lord (rabbi) | of the worlds. (l-ʿālamīna)"

43:47 But when he came to them with Our Signs, behold! They at them laughed.

But when (falammā) | he came to them (jāahum) | with Our Signs (biāyātinā), | behold (idhā)! | They (hum) | at them (min'hā) | laughed (yaḍḥakūna).

43:48 And not We showed them of a Sign but it was greater than its sister, and We seized them with the punishment so that they may return.

And not (wamā) | We showed them (nurīhim) | of (min) | a Sign (āyatin) | but (illā) | it (hiya) | was greater (akbaru) | than (min) | its sister (ukh'tihā), | and We seized them (wa-akhadhnāhum) | with the punishment (bil-ʿadhābi) | so that they may (laʿallahum) | return (yarjiʿūna).

43:49 And they said, "O [the] magician! Invoke for us your Lord by what He has made covenant with you. Indeed, we will surely be guided."

And they said (waqālū), | "O (yāayyuha) | [the] magician (l-sāḥiru)! | Invoke (ud'ʿu) | for us (lanā) | your Lord (rabbaka) | by what (bimā) | He has made covenant (ʿahida) | with you (ʿindaka). | Indeed, we (innanā) | will surely be guided. (lamuh'tadūna)"

43:50 But when We removed from them the punishment behold! They broke their word.

But when (falammā) | We removed (kashafnā) | from them (ʿanhumu) | the punishment (l-ʿadhāba) | behold (idhā)! | They (hum) | broke their word (yankuthūna).

43:51 And called out Firaun among his people; he said, "O my people! Is not for me the kingdom of Egypt and these [the] rivers flowing underneath me? Then do not you see?

And called out (wanādā) | Firaun (fir'ʿawnu) | among (fī) | his people (qawmihi); | he said (qāla), | "O my people (yāqawmi)! | Is not (alaysa) | for me (lī) | the kingdom (mul'ku) | of Egypt (miṣ'ra) | and these (wahādhihi) | [the] rivers (l-anhāru) | flowing (tajrī) | underneath me (min)? | underneath me (taḥtī)? | Then do not (afalā) | you see (tub'ṣirūna)?

43:52 Or am I better than this, one who - he is insignificant and hardly clear?

Or (am) | am I (anā) | better (khayrun) | than (min) | this (hādhā), | one who (alladhī)- | he (huwa) | is insignificant (mahīnun) | and hardly (walā) | and hardly (yakādu) | clear (yubīnu)?

43:53 Then why not are placed on him bracelets of gold or come with him the Angels accompanying him?"

Then why not (falawlā) | are placed (ul'qiya) | on him (ʿalayhi) | bracelets (aswiratun) | of (min) | gold (dhahabin) | or (aw) | come (jāa) | with him (maʿahu) | the Angels (l-malāikatu) | accompanying him? (muq'tarinīna)"

43:54 So he bluffed his people, and they obeyed him. Indeed, they were a people defiantly disobedient.

So he bluffed (fa-is'takhaffa) | his people (qawmahu), | and they obeyed him (fa-aṭāʿūhu). | Indeed, they (innahum) | were (kānū) | a people (qawman) | defiantly disobedient (fāsiqīna).

43:55 So when they angered Us, We took retribution from them, and We drowned them all.

So when (falammā) | they angered Us (āsafūnā), | We took retribution (intaqamnā) | from them (min'hum), | and We drowned them (fa-aghraqnāhum) | all (ajmaʿīna).

43:56 And We made them a precedent and an example for the later generations.

And We made them (fajaʿalnāhum) | a precedent (salafan) | and an example (wamathalan) | for the later generations (lil'ākhirīna).

43:57 And when is presented, the son of Maryam, as an example behold! Your people about it laughed aloud.

And when (walammā) | is presented (ḍuriba), | the son (ub'nu) | of Maryam (maryama), | as an example (mathalan) | behold (idhā)! | Your people (qawmuka) | about it (min'hu) | laughed aloud (yaṣiddūna).

43:58 And they said, "Are our gods better or he?" Not they present it to you except for argument. Nay, they are a people argumentative.

And they said (waqālū), | "Are our gods (aālihatunā) | better (khayrun) | or (am) | he? (huwa)" | Not (mā) | they present it (ḍarabūhu) | to you (laka) | except (illā) | for argument (jadalan). | Nay (bal), | they (hum) | are a people (qawmun) | argumentative (khaṣimūna).

43:59 Not he was except a slave, We bestowed Our favor on him and We made him an example for the Children of Israel.

Not (in) | he (huwa) | was except (illā) | a slave (ʿabdun), | We bestowed Our favor (anʿamnā) | on him (ʿalayhi) | and We made him (wajaʿalnāhu) | an example (mathalan) | for the Children of Israel (libanī). | for the Children of Israel (is'rāīla).

43:60 And if We willed, surely We could have made among you Angels in the earth succeeding.

And if (walaw) | We willed (nashāu), | surely We could have made (lajaʿalnā) | among you (minkum) | Angels (malāikatan) | in (fī) | the earth (l-arḍi) | succeeding (yakhlufūna).

43:61 And indeed, it surely is a knowledge of the Hour. So do not be doubtful about it, and follow Me. This is the Path Straight.

And indeed, it (wa-innahu) | surely is a knowledge (laʿil'mun) | of the Hour (lilssāʿati). | So do not (falā) | be doubtful (tamtarunna) | about it (bihā), | and follow Me (wa-ittabiʿūni). | This (hādhā) | is the Path (ṣirāṭun) | Straight (mus'taqīmun).

43:62 And let not avert you the Shaitaan. Indeed, he is for you an enemy clear.

And let not (walā) | avert you (yaṣuddannakumu) | the Shaitaan (l-shayṭānu). | Indeed, he (innahu) | is for you (lakum) | an enemy (ʿaduwwun) | clear (mubīnun).

43:63 And when came Isa with clear proofs, he said, "Verily, I have come to you with wisdom and that I make clear to you some of that which you differ in it. So fear Allah and obey me.

And when (walammā) | came (jāa) | Isa (ʿīsā) | with clear proofs (bil-bayināti), | he said (qāla), | "Verily (qad), | I have come to you (ji'tukum) | with wisdom (bil-ḥik'mati) | and that I make clear (wali-ubayyina) | to you (lakum) | some (baʿḍa) | of that which (alladhī) | you differ (takhtalifūna) | in it (fīhi). | So fear (fa-ittaqū) | Allah (l-laha) | and obey me (wa-aṭīʿūni).

43:64 Indeed, Allah, He is my Lord and your Lord, so worship Him. This is a Path Straight."

Indeed (inna), | Allah (l-laha), | He (huwa) | is my Lord (rabbī) | and your Lord (warabbukum), | so worship Him (fa-uʿ'budūhu). | This (hādhā) | is a Path (ṣirāṭun) | Straight. (mus'taqīmun)"

43:65 But differed the factions from among them, so woe to those who wronged from the punishment of the Day painful.

But differed (fa-ikh'talafa) | the factions (l-aḥzābu) | from (min) | among them (baynihim), | so woe (fawaylun) | to those who (lilladhīna) | wronged (ẓalamū) | from (min) | the punishment (ʿadhābi) | of the Day (yawmin) | painful (alīmin).

43:66 Are they waiting except for the Hour that it should come on them suddenly while they do not perceive?

Are (hal) | they waiting (yanẓurūna) | except (illā) | for the Hour (l-sāʿata) | that (an) | it should come on them (tatiyahum) | suddenly (baghtatan) | while they (wahum) | do not (lā) | perceive (yashʿurūna)?

43:67 Friends that Day, some of them to others will be enemies except the righteous,

Friends (al-akhilāu) | that Day (yawma-idhin), | some of them (baʿḍuhum) | to others (libaʿḍin) | will be enemies (ʿaduwwun) | except (illā) | the righteous (l-mutaqīna),

43:68 "O My slaves! No fear on you this Day and not you will grieve,
"O My slaves (yāʿibādi)! | No (lā) | fear (khawfun) | on you (ʿalaykumu) | this Day (l-yawma) | and not (walā) | you (antum) | will grieve (taḥzanūna),

43:69 Those who believed in Our Verses and were submissive.
Those who (alladhīna) | believed (āmanū) | in Our Verses (biāyātinā) | and were (wakānū) | submissive (mus'limīna).

43:70 Enter Paradise, you and your spouses delighted."
Enter (ud'khulū) | Paradise (l-janata), | you (antum) | and your spouses (wa-azwājukum) | delighted. (tuḥ'barūna)"

43:71 Will be circulated for them plates of gold and cups. And therein is what desires the souls and delights the eyes, and you therein will abide forever.
Will be circulated (yuṭāfu) | for them (ʿalayhim) | plates (biṣiḥāfin) | of (min) | gold (dhahabin) | and cups (wa-akwābin). | And therein (wafīhā) | is what (mā) | desires (tashtahīhi) | the souls (l-anfusu) | and delights (wataladhu) | the eyes (l-aʿyunu), | and you (wa-antum) | therein (fīhā) | will abide forever (khālidūna).

43:72 And this is the Paradise which you are made to inherit for what you used to do.
And this (watil'ka) | is the Paradise (l-janatu) | which (allatī) | you are made to inherit (ūrith'tumūhā) | for what (bimā) | you used to (kuntum) | do (taʿmalūna).

43:73 For you therein are fruits abundant, from it you will eat.
For you (lakum) | therein (fīhā) | are fruits (fākihatun) | abundant (kathīratun), | from it (min'hā) | you will eat (takulūna).

43:74 Indeed, the criminals will be in the punishment of Hell abiding forever.
Indeed (inna), | the criminals (l-muj'rimīna) | will be in (fī) | the punishment (ʿadhābi) | of Hell (jahannama) | abiding forever (khālidūna).

43:75 Not will it subside for them, and they in it will despair.
Not (lā) | will it subside (yufattaru) | for them (ʿanhum), | and they (wahum) | in it (fīhi) | will despair (mub'lisūna).

43:76 And not We wronged them but they were themselves wrongdoers.
And not (wamā) | We wronged them (ẓalamnāhum) | but (walākin) | they were (kānū) | themselves (humu) | wrongdoers (l-ẓālimīna).

43:77 And they will call, "O Malik! Let put an end to us your Lord." He will say, "Indeed, you will remain."
And they will call (wanādaw), | "O Malik (yāmāliku)! | Let put an end (liyaqḍi) | to us (ʿalaynā) | your Lord. (rabbuka)" | He will say (qāla), | "Indeed, you (innakum) | will remain. (mākithūna)"

43:78 Certainly, We have brought you the truth, but most of you, to the truth are averse.
Certainly (laqad), | We have brought you (ji'nākum) | the truth (bil-ḥaqi), | but (walākinna) | most of you (aktharakum), | to the truth (lil'ḥaqqi) | are averse (kārihūna).

43:79 Or have they determined an affair? Then indeed, We are determined.

Or (am) | have they determined (abramū) | an affair (amran)? | Then indeed, We (fa-innā) | are determined (mub'rimūna).

43:80 Or do they think that We can not hear their secrets and their private counsels? Nay, and Our Messengers with them, are recording.

Or (am) | do they think (yaḥsabūna) | that We (annā) | can not (lā) | hear (nasmaʿu) | their secrets (sirrahum) | and their private counsels (wanajwāhum)? | Nay (balā), | and Our Messengers (warusulunā) | with them (ladayhim), | are recording (yaktubūna).

43:81 Say, "If had the Most Gracious a son. Then, I would be the first of the worshippers."

Say (qul), | "If (in) | had (kāna) | the Most Gracious (lilrraḥmāni) | a son (waladun). | Then, I (fa-anā) | would be the first (awwalu) | of the worshippers. (l-ʿābidīna)"

43:82 Glory be to the Lord, of the heavens and the earth, the Lord of the Throne, above what they ascribe.

Glory be (sub'ḥāna) | to the Lord (rabbi), | of the heavens (l-samāwāti) | and the earth (wal-arḍi), | the Lord (rabbi) | of the Throne (l-ʿarshi), | above what (ʿammā) | they ascribe (yaṣifūna).

43:83 So leave them to converse vainly and play until they meet their Day which they are promised

So leave them (fadharhum) | to converse vainly (yakhūḍū) | and play (wayalʿabū) | until (ḥattā) | they meet (yulāqū) | their Day (yawmahumu) | which (alladhī) | they are promised (yūʿadūna)

43:84 And He is the One Who is in the heaven - God, and in the earth - God. And He is the All-Wise, the All-Knower.

And He (wahuwa) | is the One Who (alladhī) | is in (fī) | the heaven (l-samāi)- | God (ilāhun), | and in (wafī) | the earth (l-arḍi)- | God (ilāhun). | And He (wahuwa) | is the All-Wise (l-ḥakīmu), | the All-Knower (l-ʿalīmu).

43:85 And blessed is the One Who - to Whom belongs the dominion of the heavens and the earth and whatever is between both of them and with Him is the knowledge of the Hour, and to Him you will be returned.

And blessed is (watabāraka) | the One Who (alladhī)- | to Whom (lahu) | belongs the dominion (mul'ku) | of the heavens (l-samāwāti) | and the earth (wal-arḍi) | and whatever (wamā) | is between both of them (baynahumā) | and with Him (waʿindahu) | is the knowledge (ʿil'mu) | of the Hour (l-sāʿati), | and to Him (wa-ilayhi) | you will be returned (tur'jaʿūna).

43:86 And not have power those whom they invoke besides Him for the intercession; except who testifies to the truth, and they know.

And not (walā) | have power (yamliku) | those whom (alladhīna) | they invoke (yadʿūna) | besides Him (min) | besides Him (dūnihi) | for the intercession (l-shafāʿata); | except (illā) | who (man) | testifies (shahida) | to the truth (bil-ḥaqi), | and they (wahum) | know (yaʿlamūna).

43:87 And if you ask them who created them, they will certainly say, "Allah." Then how are they deluded?

And if (wala-in) | you ask them (sa-altahum) | who (man) | created them (khalaqahum), | they will certainly say (layaqūlunna), | "Allah. (l-lahu)" | Then how (fa-annā) | are they deluded (yu'fakūna)?

43:88 And his saying, "O my Lord! Indeed, these are a people who do not believe."

And his saying (waqīlihi), | "O my Lord (yārabbi)! | Indeed (inna), | these (hāulāi) | are a people (qawmun) | who do not (lā) | believe. (yu'minūna)"

43:89 So turn away from them and say, "Peace." But soon they will know.
So turn away (fa-iṣ'faḥ) | from them (ʿanhum) | and say (waqul), | "Peace. (salāmun)" | But soon (fasawfa) | they will know (yaʿlamūna).

Chapter (44) Sūrat l-Dukhān (The Smoke)

44:1 Ha Meem.
Ha Meem (hha-meem).

44:2 By the Book the clear,
By the Book (wal-kitābi) | the clear (l-mubīni),

44:3 Indeed, We revealed it in a Night Blessed. Indeed, We [We] are ever warning.
Indeed, We (innā) | revealed it (anzalnāhu) | in (fī) | a Night (laylatin) | Blessed (mubārakatin). | Indeed, We (innā) | [We] are (kunnā) | ever warning (mundhirīna).

44:4 Therein is made distinct every affair, wise,
Therein (fīhā) | is made distinct (yuf'raqu) | every (kullu) | affair (amrin), | wise (ḥakīmin),

44:5 A command from Us. Indeed, We [We] are ever sending,
A command (amran) | from (min) | Us (ʿindinā). | Indeed, We (innā) | [We] are (kunnā) | ever sending (mur'silīna),

44:6 As Mercy from your Lord. Indeed, He [He] is the All-Hearer, the All-Knower.
As Mercy (raḥmatan) | from (min) | your Lord (rabbika). | Indeed, He (innahu) | [He] (huwa) | is the All-Hearer (l-samīʿu), | the All-Knower (l-ʿalīmu).

44:7 Lord of the heavens and the earth and whatever is between both of them, if you are certain.
Lord (rabbi) | of the heavens (l-samāwāti) | and the earth (wal-arḍi) | and whatever (wamā) | is between both of them (baynahumā), | if (in) | you are (kuntum) | certain (mūqinīna).

44:8 There is no god except Him; He gives life and causes death, your Lord and the Lord of your fathers the former.
There is no (lā) | god (ilāha) | except (illā) | Him (huwa); | He gives life (yuḥ'yī) | and causes death (wayumītu), | your Lord (rabbukum) | and the Lord (warabbu) | of your fathers (ābāikumu) | the former (l-awalīna).

44:9 Nay, they are in doubt - playing.
Nay (bal), | they (hum) | are in (fī) | doubt (shakkin)- | playing (yalʿabūna).

44:10 Then watch for the Day when will bring the sky smoke visible,
Then watch (fa-ir'taqib) | for the Day (yawma) | when will bring (tatī) | the sky (l-samāu) | smoke (bidukhānin) | visible (mubīnin),

44:11 Enveloping the people. This will be a punishment painful.
Enveloping (yaghshā) | the people (l-nāsa). | This (hādhā) | will be a punishment (ʿadhābun) | painful (alīmun).

44:12 "Our Lord! Remove from us the punishment; indeed, we are believers."
"Our Lord (rabbanā)! | Remove (ik'shif) | from us (ʿannā) | the punishment (l-ʿadhāba); | indeed, we (innā) | are believers. (mu'minūna)"

44:13 How can there be for them the reminder, when verily, had come to them a Messenger clear.
How can (annā) | there be for them (lahumu) | the reminder (l-dhik'rā), | when verily (waqad), | had come to them (jāahum) | a Messenger (rasūlun) | clear (mubīnun).

44:14 Then they turned away from him and said, "One taught, a mad man."
Then (thumma) | they turned away (tawallaw) | from him (ʿanhu) | and said (waqālū), | "One taught (muʿallamun), | a mad man. (majnūnun)"

44:15 Indeed, We will remove the punishment a little, indeed, you will return.
Indeed, We (innā) | will remove (kāshifū) | the punishment (l-ʿadhābi) | a little (qalīlan), | indeed, you (innakum) | will return (ʿāidūna).

44:16 The Day We will seize with the seizure the greatest, indeed, We will take retribution.
The Day (yawma) | We will seize (nabṭishu) | with the seizure (l-baṭshata) | the greatest (l-kub'rā), | indeed, We (innā) | will take retribution (muntaqimūna).

44:17 And certainly, We tried before them the people of Firaun, and came to them a Messenger noble.
And certainly (walaqad), | We tried (fatannā) | before them (qablahum) | the people (qawma) | of Firaun (fir'ʿawna), | and came to them (wajāahum) | a Messenger (rasūlun) | noble (karīmun).

44:18 That, "Deliver to me the servants of Allah. Indeed, I am to you a Messenger trustworthy.
That (an), | "Deliver (addū) | to me (ilayya) | the servants (ʿibāda) | of Allah (l-lahi). | Indeed, I am (innī) | to you (lakum) | a Messenger (rasūlun) | trustworthy (amīnun).

44:19 And that do not exalt yourselves against Allah. Indeed, I [I] have come to you with an authority clear.
And that (wa-an) | do not (lā) | exalt yourselves (taʿlū) | against (ʿalā) | Allah (l-lahi). | Indeed, I (innī) | [I] have come to you (ātīkum) | with an authority (bisul'ṭānin) | clear (mubīnin).

44:20 And indeed, I [I] seek refuge with my Lord and your Lord lest you stone me.
And indeed, I (wa-innī) | [I] seek refuge (ʿudh'tu) | with my Lord (birabbī) | and your Lord (warabbikum) | lest (an) | you stone me (tarjumūni).

44:21 And if not you believe me, then leave me alone."
And if (wa-in) | not (lam) | you believe (tu'minū) | me (lī), | then leave me alone. (fa-i'ʿtazilūni)"

44:22 So he called his Lord, "That these are a people criminals."
So he called (fadaʿā) | his Lord (rabbahu), | "That (anna) | these (hāulāi) | are a people (qawmun) | criminals. (muj'rimūna)"

44:23 Then "Set out with My slaves by night. Indeed, you will be followed.

Then "Set out (fa-asri) | with My slaves (biʿibādī) | by night (laylan). | Indeed, you (innakum) | will be followed (muttabaʿūna).

44:24 And leave the sea at rest. Indeed, they are an army to be drowned."
And leave (wa-ut'ruki) | the sea (l-baḥra) | at rest (rahwan). | Indeed, they (innahum) | are an army (jundun) | to be drowned. (mugh'raqūna)"

44:25 How many did they leave of gardens and springs,
How many (kam) | did they leave (tarakū) | of (min) | gardens (jannātin) | and springs (waʿuyūnin),

44:26 And cornfields and places noble,
And cornfields (wazurūʿin) | and places (wamaqāmin) | noble (karīmin),

44:27 And pleasant things they used to therein take delight!
And pleasant things (wanaʿmatin) | they used to (kānū) | therein (fīhā) | take delight (fākihīna)!

44:28 Thus. And We made it an inherit(ance) for a people another.
Thus (kadhālika). | And We made it an inherit(ance (wa-awrathnāhā)) | for a people (qawman) | another (ākharīna).

44:29 And not wept for them the heaven and the earth and not they were given respite.
And not (famā) | wept (bakat) | for them (ʿalayhimu) | the heaven (l-samāu) | and the earth (wal-arḍu) | and not (wamā) | they were (kānū) | given respite (munẓarīna).

44:30 And certainly, We saved the Children of Israel from the punishment the humiliating,
And certainly (walaqad), | We saved (najjaynā) | the Children of Israel (banī) | the Children of Israel (is'rāīla) | from (mina) | the punishment (l-ʿadhābi) | the humiliating (l-muhīni),

44:31 From Firaun. Indeed, he was arrogant among the transgressors.
From (min) | Firaun (fir'ʿawna). | Indeed, he (innahu) | was (kāna) | arrogant (ʿāliyan) | among (mina) | the transgressors (l-mus'rifīna).

44:32 And certainly We chose them by knowledge over the worlds.
And certainly (walaqadi) | We chose them (ikh'tarnāhum) | by (ʿalā) | knowledge (ʿil'min) | over (ʿalā) | the worlds (l-ʿālamīna).

44:33 And We gave them of the Signs that in it was a trial clear.
And We gave them (waātaynāhum) | of (mina) | the Signs (l-āyāti) | that (mā) | in it (fīhi) | was a trial (balāon) | clear (mubīnun).

44:34 Indeed, these surely, they say,
Indeed (inna), | these (hāulāi) | surely, they say (layaqūlūna),

44:35 "Not it is but our death the first and not we will be raised again.
"Not (in) | it (hiya) | is but (illā) | our death (mawtatunā) | the first (l-ūlā) | and not (wamā) | we (naḥnu) | will be raised again (bimunsharīna).

44:36 Then bring our forefathers, if you are truthful."
Then bring (fatū) | our forefathers (biābāinā), | if (in) | you are (kuntum) | truthful. (ṣādiqīna)"

44:37 Are they better or the people of Tubba and those before them? We destroyed them, indeed, they were criminals.

Are they (ahum) | better (khayrun) | or (am) | the people (qawmu) | of Tubba (tubbaʿin) | and those (wa-alladhīna) | before them (min)? | before them (qablihim)? | We destroyed them (ahlaknāhum), | indeed, they (innahum) | were (kānū) | criminals (muj'rimīna).

44:38 And not We created the heavens and the earth and whatever is between them in play.

And not (wamā) | We created (khalaqnā) | the heavens (l-samāwāti) | and the earth (wal-arḍa) | and whatever (wamā) | is between them (baynahumā) | in play (lāʿibīna).

44:39 Not We created both of them but in [the] truth, but most of them do not know.

Not (mā) | We created both of them (khalaqnāhumā) | but (illā) | in [the] truth (bil-ḥaqi), | but (walākinna) | most of them (aktharahum) | do not (lā) | know (yaʿlamūna).

44:40 Indeed, the Day of Judgment is an appointed term for them all.

Indeed (inna), | the Day of Judgment (yawma) | the Day of Judgment (l-faṣli) | is an appointed term for them (mīqātuhum) | all (ajmaʿīna).

44:41 The Day not will avail a relation for a relation anything and not they will be helped.

The Day (yawma) | not (lā) | will avail (yugh'nī) | a relation (mawlan) | for (ʿan) | a relation (mawlan) | anything (shayan) | and not (walā) | they (hum) | will be helped (yunṣarūna).

44:42 Except, on whom Allah has mercy. Indeed, He [He] is the All-Mighty, the Most Merciful.

Except (illā), | on whom (man) | Allah has mercy (raḥima). | Allah has mercy (l-lahu). | Indeed, He (innahu) | [He] (huwa) | is the All-Mighty (l-ʿazīzu), | the Most Merciful (l-raḥīmu).

44:43 Indeed, the tree of Zaqqum

Indeed (inna), | the tree (shajarata) | of Zaqqum (l-zaqūmi)

44:44 Will be food of the sinner(s).

Will be food (ṭaʿāmu) | of the sinner(s) (l-athīmi).

44:45 Like the murky oil, it will boil in the bellies,

Like the murky oil (kal-muh'li), | it will boil (yaghlī) | in (fī) | the bellies (l-buṭūni),

44:46 Like boiling of scalding water.

Like boiling (kaghalyi) | of scalding water (l-ḥamīmi).

44:47 "Seize him and drag him into the midst of the Hellfire,

"Seize him (khudhūhu) | and drag him (fa-iʿ'tilūhu) | into (ilā) | the midst (sawāi) | of the Hellfire (l-jaḥīmi),

44:48 Then pour over his head of the punishment of the scalding water.

Then (thumma) | pour (ṣubbū) | over (fawqa) | his head (rasihi) | of (min) | the punishment (ʿadhābi) | of the scalding water (l-ḥamīmi).

44:49 Taste! Indeed, you [you] were the mighty, the noble.

Taste (dhuq)! | Indeed, you (innaka) | [you] were (anta) | the mighty (l-ʿazīzu), | the noble (l-karīmu).

44:50 Indeed, this is what you used to [about it] doubt."

Indeed (inna), | this (hādhā) | is what (mā) | you used to (kuntum) | [about it] (bihi) | doubt. (tamtarūna)"

44:51 Indeed, the righteous will be in a place secure,
Indeed (inna), | the righteous (l-mutaqīna) | will be in (fī) | a place (maqāmin) | secure (amīnin),

44:52 In gardens and springs,
In (fī) | gardens (jannātin) | and springs (waʿuyūnin),

44:53 Wearing garments of fine silk and heavy silk, facing each other.
Wearing garments (yalbasūna) | of (min) | fine silk (sundusin) | and heavy silk (wa-is'tabraqin), | facing each other (mutaqābilīna).

44:54 Thus. And We will marry them to companions with beautiful eyes.
Thus (kadhālika). | And We will marry them (wazawwajnāhum) | to companions with beautiful eyes (biḥūrin). | to companions with beautiful eyes (ʿīnin).

44:55 They will call therein for every kind of fruit, secure.
They will call (yadʿūna) | therein (fīhā) | for every kind (bikulli) | of fruit (fākihatin), | secure (āminīna).

44:56 Not they will taste therein the death except the death the first. And He will protect them from the punishment of the Hellfire,
Not (lā) | they will taste (yadhūqūna) | therein (fīhā) | the death (l-mawta) | except (illā) | the death (l-mawtata) | the first (l-ūlā). | And He will protect them (wawaqāhum) | from the punishment (ʿadhāba) | of the Hellfire (l-jaḥımi),

44:57 A Bounty from your Lord. That - it will be the success the great.
A Bounty (faḍlan) | from (min) | your Lord (rabbika). | That (dhālika)- | it (huwa) | will be the success (l-fawzu) | the great (l-ʿaẓīmu).

44:58 Indeed, We have made it easy in your tongue so that they may take heed.
Indeed (fa-innamā), | We have made it easy (yassarnāhu) | in your tongue (bilisānika) | so that they may (laʿallahum) | take heed (yatadhakkarūna).

44:59 So watch; indeed, they too are watching.
So watch (fa-ir'taqib); | indeed, they (innahum) | too are watching (mur'taqibūna).

Chapter (45) Sūrat l-Jāthiyah (Crouching)

45:1 Ha Meem.
Ha Meem (hha-meem).

45:2 The revelation of the Book is from Allah the All-Mighty, the All-Wise.
The revelation (tanzīlu) | of the Book (l-kitābi) | is from (mina) | Allah (l-lahi) | the

All-Mighty (l-ʿazīzi), | the All-Wise (l-ḥakīmi).

45:3 Indeed, in the heavens and the earth surely are Signs for the believers.
Indeed (inna), | in (fī) | the heavens (l-samāwāti) | and the earth (wal-arḍi) | surely are Signs (laāyātin) | for the believers (lil'mu'minīna).

45:4 And in your creation and what He disperses of the moving creatures are Signs for a people who are certain.
And in (wafī) | your creation (khalqikum) | and what (wamā) | He disperses (yabuthu) | of (min) | the moving creatures (dābbatin) | are Signs (āyātun) | for a people (liqawmin) | who are certain (yūqinūna).

45:5 And in the alternation of the night and the day and what Allah sends down from the sky of the provision and gives life thereby to the earth after its death, and in directing the winds are Signs for a people who reason.
And in the alternation (wa-ikh'tilāfi) | of the night (al-layli) | and the day (wal-nahāri) | and what (wamā) | Allah sends down (anzala) | Allah sends down (l-lahu) | from (mina) | the sky (l-samāi) | of (min) | the provision (riz'qin) | and gives life (fa-aḥyā) | thereby (bihi) | to the earth (l-arḍa) | after (baʿda) | its death (mawtihā), | and in directing (wataṣrīfi) | the winds (l-riyāḥi) | are Signs (āyātun) | for a people (liqawmin) | who reason (yaʿqilūna).

45:6 These are the Verses, of Allah We recite them to you in truth. Then in what statement after Allah and His Verses will they believe?
These (til'ka) | are the Verses (āyātu), | of Allah (l-lahi) | We recite them (natlūhā) | to you (ʿalayka) | in truth (bil-ḥaqi). | Then in what (fabi-ayyi) | statement (ḥadīthin) | after (baʿda) | Allah (l-lahi) | and His Verses (waāyātihi) | will they believe (yu'minūna)?

45:7 Woe to every liar sinful
Woe (waylun) | to every (likulli) | liar (affākin) | sinful (athīmin)

45:8 Who hears the Verses of Allah recited to him, then persists arrogantly as if not he heard them. So give him tidings of a punishment painful.
Who hears (yasmaʿu) | the Verses (āyāti) | of Allah (l-lahi) | recited (tut'lā) | to him (ʿalayhi), | then (thumma) | persists (yuṣirru) | arrogantly (mus'takbiran) | as if (ka-an) | not (lam) | he heard them (yasmaʿhā). | So give him tidings (fabashir'hu) | of a punishment (biʿadhābin) | painful (alīmin).

45:9 And when he knows of Our Verses, anything, he takes them in ridicule. Those - for them is a punishment humiliating.
And when (wa-idhā) | he knows (ʿalima) | of (min) | Our Verses (āyātinā), | anything (shayan), | he takes them (ittakhadhahā) | in ridicule (huzuwan). | Those (ulāika)- | for them (lahum) | is a punishment (ʿadhābun) | humiliating (muhīnun).

45:10 Before them is Hell and not will avail them what they had earned anything, and not what they had taken besides Allah as protectors. And for them is a punishment great.
Before them (min) | Before them (warāihim) | is Hell (jahannamu) | and not (walā) | will avail (yugh'nī) | them (ʿanhum) | what (mā) | they had earned (kasabū) | anything (shayan), | and not (walā) | what (mā) | they had taken (ittakhadhū) | besides (min) | besides (dūni) | Allah (l-lahi) | as protectors (awliyāa). | And for them (walahum) | is a punishment (ʿadhābun) | great (ʿaẓīmun).

45:11 This is guidance. And those who disbelieve in the Verses of their Lord, for them is a punishment of filth, painful.

This (hādhā) | is guidance (hudan). | And those who (wa-alladhīna) | disbelieve (kafarū) | in the Verses (biāyāti) | of their Lord (rabbihim), | for them (lahum) | is a punishment (ʿadhābun) | of (min) | filth (rij'zin), | painful (alīmun).

45:12 Allah is the One Who subjected to you the sea that may sail the ships therein by His Command, and that you may seek of His Bounty and that you may give thanks.

Allah (al-lahu) | is the One Who (alladhī) | subjected (sakhara) | to you (lakumu) | the sea (l-baḥra) | that may sail (litajriya) | the ships (l-ful'ku) | therein (fīhi) | by His Command (bi-amrihi), | and that you may seek (walitabtaghū) | of (min) | His Bounty (faḍlihi) | and that you may (walaʿallakum) | give thanks (tashkurūna).

45:13 And He has subjected to you whatever is in the heavens and whatever is in the earth - all from Him. Indeed, in that surely are Signs for a people who give thought.

And He has subjected (wasakhara) | to you (lakum) | whatever (mā) | is in (fī) | the heavens (l-samāwāti) | and whatever (wamā) | is in (fī) | the earth (l-arḍi)- | all (jamīʿan) | from Him (min'hu). | Indeed (inna), | in (fī) | that (dhālika) | surely are Signs (laāyātin) | for a people (liqawmin) | who give thought (yatafakkarūna).

45:14 Say to those who believe to forgive those who do not hope for the days of Allah; that He may recompense a people for what they used to earn.

Say (qul) | to those who (lilladhīna) | believe (āmanū) | to forgive (yaghfirū) | those who (lilladhīna) | do not (lā) | hope (yarjūna) | for the days (ayyāma) | of Allah (l-lahi); | that He may recompense (liyajziya) | a people (qawman) | for what (bimā) | they used to (kānū) | earn (yaksibūna).

45:15 Whoever does a righteous deed, then it is for his soul, and whoever does evil, then it is against it. Then to your Lord you will be returned.

Whoever (man) | does (ʿamila) | a righteous deed (ṣāliḥan), | then it is for his soul (falinafsihi), | and whoever (waman) | does evil (asāa), | then it is against it (faʿalayhā). | Then (thumma) | to (ilā) | your Lord (rabbikum) | you will be returned (tur'jaʿūna).

45:16 And certainly, We gave the Children of Israel the Book and the wisdom and the Prophethood, and We provided them of the good things and We preferred them over the worlds.

And certainly (walaqad), | We gave (ātaynā) | the Children of Israel (banī) | the Children of Israel (is'rāīla) | the Book (l-kitāba) | and the wisdom (wal-ḥuk'ma) | and the Prophethood (wal-nubuwata), | and We provided them (warazaqnāhum) | of (mina) | the good things (l-ṭayibāti) | and We preferred them (wafaḍḍalnāhum) | over (ʿalā) | the worlds (l-ʿālamīna).

45:17 And We gave them clear proofs of the matter. And not they differed except after [what] came to them the knowledge, out of envy between themselves. Indeed, your Lord will judge between them on the Day of the Resurrection about what they used to therein differ.

And We gave them (waātaynāhum) | clear proofs (bayyinātin) | of (mina) | the matter (l-amri). | And not (famā) | they differed (ikh'talafū) | except (illā) | after (min) | after (baʿdi) | [what] (mā) | came to them (jāahumu) | the knowledge (l-ʿil'mu), | out of envy (baghyan) | between themselves (baynahum). | Indeed (inna), | your Lord (rabbaka) | will judge (yaqḍī) | between them (baynahum) | on the Day (yawma) | of the Resurrection (l-qiyāmati) | about what (fīmā) | they used to (kānū) | therein (fīhi) | differ (yakhtalifūna).

45:18 Then We put you on an ordained way of the matter; so follow it and do not follow the desires of those who do not know.

Then (thumma) | We put you (jaʿalnāka) | on (ʿalā) | an ordained way (sharīʿatin) | of (mina) | the matter (l-amri); | so follow it (fa-ittabiʿ'hā) | and do not (walā) | follow (tattabiʿ) | the desires (ahwāa) | of those who (alladhīna) | do not (lā) | know (yaʿlamūna).

45:19 Indeed, they never will avail you against Allah in anything. And indeed, the wrongdoers some of them are allies of others, and Allah is the Protector of the righteous.

Indeed, they (innahum) | never (lan) | will avail (yugh'nū) | you (ʿanka) | against (mina) | Allah (l-lahi) | in anything (shayan). | And indeed (wa-inna), | the wrongdoers (l-ẓālimīna) | some of them (baʿḍuhum) | are allies (awliyāu) | of others (baʿḍin), | and Allah (wal-lahu) | is the Protector (waliyyu) | of the righteous (l-mutaqīna).

45:20 This is enlightenment for mankind and guidance and mercy for a people who are certain.

This (hādhā) | is enlightenment (baṣāiru) | for mankind (lilnnāsi) | and guidance (wahudan) | and mercy (waraḥmatun) | for a people (liqawmin) | who are certain (yūqinūna).

45:21 Do think those who commit evil deeds that We will make them like those who believed and did righteous deeds equal in their life and their death? Evil is what they judge!

Do (am) | think (ḥasiba) | those who (alladhīna) | commit (ij'taraḥū) | evil deeds (l-sayiāti) | that (an) | We will make them (najʿalahum) | like those who (ka-alladhīna) | believed (āmanū) | and did (waʿamilū) | righteous deeds (l-ṣāliḥāti) | equal (sawāan) | in their life (maḥyāhum) | and their death (wamamātuhum)? | Evil is (sāa) | what (mā) | they judge (yaḥkumūna)!

45:22 And Allah created the heavens and the earth in truth and that may be recompensed every soul for what it has earned, and they will not be wronged.

And Allah created (wakhalaqa) | And Allah created (l-lahu) | the heavens (l-samāwāti) | and the earth (wal-arḍa) | in truth (bil-ḥaqi) | and that may be recompensed (walituj'zā) | every (kullu) | soul (nafsin) | for what (bimā) | it has earned (kasabat), | and they (wahum) | will not be wronged (lā). | will not be wronged (yuẓ'lamūna).

45:23 Have you seen he who takes as his god his desire and Allah lets him go astray knowingly, and He sets a seal upon his hearing and his heart and puts over his vision a veil? Then who will guide him after Allah? Then will not you receive admonition?

Have you seen (afara-ayta) | he who (mani) | takes (ittakhadha) | as his god (ilāhahu) | his desire (hawāhu) | and Allah lets him go astray (wa-aḍallahu) | and Allah lets him go astray (l-lahu) | knowingly (ʿalā), | knowingly (ʿil'min), | and He sets a seal (wakhatama) | upon (ʿalā) | his hearing (samʿihi) | and his heart (waqalbihi) | and puts (wajaʿala) | over (ʿalā) | his vision (baṣarihi) | a veil (ghishāwatan)? | Then who (faman) | will guide him (yahdīhi) | after (min) | after (baʿdi) | Allah (l-lahi)? | Then will not (afalā) | you receive admonition (tadhakkarūna)?

45:24 And they say, "Not it is but our life of the world, we die and we live, and not destroys us except the time." And not for them of that any knowledge; not, they do but guess.

And they say (waqālū), | "Not (mā) | it (hiya) | is but (illā) | our life (ḥayātunā) | of the world (l-dun'yā), | we die (namūtu) | and we live (wanaḥyā), | and not (wamā) | destroys us (yuh'likunā) | except (illā) | the time. (l-dahru)" | And not (wamā) | for them (lahum) | of that (bidhālika) | any (min) | knowledge (ʿil'min); | not (in), | they (hum) | do but (illā) | guess (yaẓunnūna).

45:25 And when are recited to them Our Verses clear, not is their argument except that they say, "Bring our forefathers if you are truthful."

And when (wa-idhā) | are recited (tut'lā) | to them (ʿalayhim) | Our Verses (āyātunā) | clear (bayyinātin), | not (mā) | is (kāna) | their argument (ḥujjatahum) | except (illā) | that (an) | they say (qālū), | "Bring (i'tū) | our forefathers (biābāinā) | if (in) | you are (kuntum) | truthful. (ṣādiqīna)"

45:26 Say, "Allah gives you life, then causes you to die; then He will gather you to the Day of the Resurrection, no doubt about it." But most of the people do not know.

Say (quli), | "Allah (l-lahu) | gives you life (yuḥ'yīkum), | then (thumma) | causes you to die (yumītukum); | then (thumma) | He will gather you (yajmaʿukum) | to (ilā) | the Day (yawmi) | of the Resurrection (l-qiyāmati), | no (lā) | doubt (rayba) | about it. (fīhi)" | But (walākinna) | most (akthara) | of the people (l-nāsi) | do not (lā) | know (yaʿlamūna).

45:27 And for Allah is the dominion of the heavens and the earth; and the Day is established the Hour, that Day will lose the falsifiers.

And for Allah (walillahi) | is the dominion (mul'ku) | of the heavens (l-samāwāti) | and the earth (wal-arḍi); | and the Day (wayawma) | is established (taqūmu) | the Hour (l-sāʿatu), | that Day (yawma-idhin) | will lose (yakhsaru) | the falsifiers (l-mub'ṭilūna).

45:28 And you will see every nation kneeling. Every nation will be called to its record, "Today you will be recompensed for what you used to do.

And you will see (watarā) | every (kulla) | nation (ummatin) | kneeling (jāthiyatan). | Every (kullu) | nation (ummatin) | will be called (tud'ʿā) | to (ilā) | its record (kitābihā), | "Today (l-yawma) | you will be recompensed (tuj'zawna) | for what (mā) | you used to (kuntum) | do (taʿmalūna).

45:29 This, Our Record, speaks about you in truth. Indeed, We [We] used to transcribe what you used to do."

This (hādhā), | Our Record (kitābunā), | speaks (yanṭiqu) | about you (ʿalaykum) | in truth (bil-ḥaqi). | Indeed, We (innā) | [We] used to (kunnā) | transcribe (nastansikhu) | what (mā) | you used to (kuntum) | do. (taʿmalūna)"

45:30 Then as for those who believed and did [the] righteous deeds, will admit them their Lord into His mercy. That [it] is the success clear.

Then as for (fa-ammā) | those who (alladhīna) | believed (āmanū) | and did (waʿamilū) | [the] righteous deeds (l-ṣāliḥāti), | will admit them (fayud'khiluhum) | their Lord (rabbuhum) | into (fī) | His mercy (raḥmatihi). | That (dhālika) | [it] (huwa) | is the success (l-fawzu) | clear (l-mubīnu).

45:31 But as for those who disbelieved, "Then were not My Verses recited to you but you were proud and you became a people criminals?"

But as for (wa-ammā) | those who (alladhīna) | disbelieved (kafarū), | "Then were not (afalam) | "Then were not (takun) | My Verses (āyātī) | recited (tut'lā) | to you (ʿalaykum) | but you were proud (fa-is'takbartum) | and you became (wakuntum) | a people (qawman) | criminals? (muj'rimīna)"

45:32 And when it was said, "Indeed the Promise of Allah is true and the Hour - there is no doubt about it, you said, "Not we know what the Hour is. Not we think except an assumption, and not we are convinced."

And when (wa-idhā) | it was said (qīla), | "Indeed (inna) | the Promise (waʿda) | of Allah (l-lahi) | is true (ḥaqqun) | and the Hour (wal-sāʿatu)- | there is no (lā) | doubt (rayba) | about it (fīhā), | you said (qul'tum), | "Not (mā) | we know (nadrī) | what (mā) | the Hour is (l-sāʿatu). | Not (in) | we think (naẓunnu) | except (illā) | an assumption (ẓannan), | and not (wamā) | we (naḥnu) | are convinced. (bimus'tayqinīna)"

45:33 And will appear to them the evil of what they did and will envelop them what they used [at it] to mock.

And will appear (wabadā) | to them (lahum) | the evil (sayyiātu) | of what (mā) | they did (ʿamilū) | and will envelop (waḥāqa) | them (bihim) | what (mā) | they used (kānū) | [at it] (bihi) | to mock (yastahziūna).

45:34 And it will be said, "Today We forget you as you forgot the meeting of this Day of yours, and your abode is the Fire, and not for you any helpers.

And it will be said (waqīla), | "Today (l-yawma) | We forget you (nansākum) | as (kamā) | you forgot (nasītum) | the meeting (liqāa) | of this Day of yours (yawmikum), | of this Day of yours (hādhā), | and your abode (wamawākumu) | is the Fire (l-nāru), | and not (wamā) | for you (lakum) | any (min) | helpers (nāṣirīna).

45:35 That is because you took the Verses of Allah in ridicule and deceived you the life of the world." So this Day not they will be brought forth from it and not they will be asked to appease.

That (dhālikum) | is because you (bi-annakumu) | took (ittakhadhtum) | the Verses (āyāti) | of Allah (l-lahi) | in ridicule (huzuwan) | and deceived you (wagharratkumu) | the life (l-ḥayatu) | of the world. (l-dun'yā)" | So this Day (fal-yawma) | not (lā) | they will be brought forth (yukh'rajūna) | from it (min'hā) | and not (walā) | they (hum) | will be asked to appease (yus'taʿtabūna).

45:36 Then for Allah is all the praise, the Lord of the heavens and the Lord of the earth, the lord of the worlds.

Then for Allah (falillahi) | is all the praise (l-ḥamdu), | the Lord (rabbi) | of the heavens (l-samāwāti) | and the Lord (warabbi) | of the earth (l-arḍi), | the lord (rabbi) | of the worlds (l-ʿālamīna).

45:37 And for Him is the greatness in the heavens and the earth, and He is the All-Mighty, the All-Wise.

And for Him (walahu) | is the greatness (l-kib'riyāu) | in (fī) | the heavens (l-samāwāti) | and the earth (wal-arḍi), | and He (wahuwa) | is the All-Mighty (l-ʿazīzu), | the All-Wise (l-ḥakīmu).

Chapter (46) Sūrat l-Aḥqāf (The Curved Sand-hills)

46:1 Ha Meem.

Ha Meem (hha-meem).

46:2 The revelation of the Book is from Allah the All-Mighty, the All-Wise

The revelation (tanzīlu) | of the Book (l-kitābi) | is from (mina) | Allah (l-lahi) | the All-Mighty (l-ʿazīzi), | the All-Wise (l-ḥakīmi)

46:3 Not We created the heavens and the earth and what is between both of them except in truth and for a term appointed. But those who disbelieve, from what they are warned, are turning away.

Not (mā) | We created (khalaqnā) | the heavens (l-samāwāti) | and the earth (wal-arḍa) | and what (wamā) | is between both of them (baynahumā) | except (illā) | in truth (bil-ḥaqi) | and for a term (wa-ajalin) | appointed (musamman). | But those who (wa-alladhīna) | disbelieve (kafarū), | from what (ʿammā) | they are warned (undhirū), | are turning away (muʿriḍūna).

46:4 Say, "Do you see what you call besides Allah? Show me what they have created of the earth or for them is any share in the heavens? Bring me a book from before this or a trace of knowledge, if you are truthful."

Say (qul), | "Do you see (ara-aytum) | what (mā) | you call (tadʿūna) | besides (min) | besides (dūni) | Allah (l-lahi)? | Show me (arūnī) | what (mādhā) | they have created (khalaqū) | of (mina) | the earth (l-arḍi) | or (am) | for them (lahum) | is any share (shir'kun) | in (fī) | the heavens (l-samāwāti)? | Bring me (i'tūnī) | a book (bikitābin) | from (min) | before (qabli) | this (hādhā) | or (aw) | a trace (athāratin) | of (min) | knowledge (ʿil'min), | if (in) | you are (kuntum) | truthful. (ṣādiqīna)"

46:5 And who is more astray than he who calls besides Allah, who will not respond to him until the Day of Resurrection, and they of their calls are unaware.

And who (waman) | is more astray (aḍallu) | than he who (mimman) | calls (yadʿū) | besides (min) | besides (dūni) | Allah (l-lahi), | who (man) | will not respond (lā) | will not respond (yastajību) | to him (lahu) | until (ilā) | the Day (yawmi) | of Resurrection (l-qiyāmati), | and they (wahum) | of (ʿan) | their calls (duʿāihim) | are unaware (ghāfilūna).

46:6 And when are gathered the people, they will be for them enemies and they will be of their worship deniers.

And when (wa-idhā) | are gathered (ḥushira) | the people (l-nāsu), | they will be (kānū) | for them (lahum) | enemies (aʿdāan) | and they will be (wakānū) | of their worship (biʿibādatihim) | deniers (kāfirīna).

46:7 And when are recited to them Our Verses clear, say those who disbelieve of the truth when it comes to them, "This is a magic clear."

And when (wa-idhā) | are recited (tut'lā) | to them (ʿalayhim) | Our Verses (āyātunā) | clear (bayyinātin), | say (qāla) | those who (alladhīna) | disbelieve (kafarū) | of the truth (lil'ḥaqqi) | when (lammā) | it comes to them (jāahum), | "This (hādhā) | is a magic (siḥ'run) | clear. (mubīnun)"

46:8 Or they say, "He has invented it." Say, "If I have invented it then not you have power for me against Allah anything. He knows best of what you utter concerning it. Sufficient is He as a Witness between me and between you, and He is the Oft-Forgiving, the Most Merciful.

Or (am) | they say (yaqūlūna), | "He has invented it. (if'tarāhu)" | Say (qul), | "If (ini) | I have invented it (if'taraytuhu) | then not (falā) | you have power (tamlikūna) | for me (lī) | against (mina) | Allah (l-lahi) | anything (shayan). | He (huwa) | knows best (aʿlamu) | of what (bimā) | you utter (tufīḍūna) | concerning it (fīhi). | Sufficient is He (kafā) | Sufficient is He (bihi) | as a Witness (shahīdan) | between me (baynī) | and between you (wabaynakum), | and He (wahuwa) | is the Oft-Forgiving (l-ghafūru), | the Most Merciful (l-raḥīmu).

46:9 Say, "Not I am a new one among the Messengers and not I know what will be done with me and not with you. Not I follow but what is revealed to me and not I am but a warner clear."

Say (qul), | "Not (mā) | I am (kuntu) | a new one (bidʿ'an) | among (mina) | the Messengers (l-rusuli) | and not (wamā) | I know (adrī) | what (mā) | will be done (yufʿ'alu) | with me (bī) | and not (walā) | with you (bikum). | Not (in) | I follow (attabiʿu) | but (illā) | what (mā) | is revealed (yūḥā) | to me (ilayya) | and not (wamā) | I am (anā) | but (illā) | a warner (nadhīrun) | clear. (mubīnun)"

46:10 Say, "Do you see if it is from Allah and you disbelieve in it, and testifies a witness from the Children of Israel to the like thereof, then he believed while you are arrogant?" Indeed, Allah does not guide the people the wrongdoers.

Say (qul), | "Do you see (ara-aytum) | if (in) | it is (kāna) | from Allah (min) | from Allah (ʿindi) | from Allah (l-lahi) | and you disbelieve (wakafartum) | in it (bihi), | and testifies (washahida) | a witness (shāhidun) | from (min) | the Children of Israel (banī) | the Children of Israel (is'rāīla) | to (ʿalā) | the like thereof (mith'lihi), | then he believed (faāmana) | while you are arrogant? (wa-is'takbartum)" | Indeed (inna), | Allah (l-laha) | does not (lā) | guide (yahdī) | the people (l-qawma) | the wrongdoers (l-ẓālimīna).

46:11 And say those who disbelieve of those who believe, "If it had been good, not they would have preceded us to it." And when not they are guided by it, they say, "This is a lie ancient."

And say (waqāla) | those who (alladhīna) | disbelieve (kafarū) | of those who (lilladhīna) | believe (āmanū), | "If (law) | it had been (kāna) | good (khayran), | not (mā) | they would have preceded us (sabaqūnā) | to it. (ilayhi)" | And when (wa-idh) | not (lam) | they are guided (yahtadū) | by it (bihi), | they say (fasayaqūlūna), | "This (hādhā) | is a lie (if'kun) | ancient. (qadīmun)"

46:12 And before it was the Scripture of Musa as a guide and a mercy. And this is a Book confirming, in language Arabic to warn those who do wrong and as glad tidings for the good-doers.

And before it (wamin) | And before it (qablihi) | was the Scripture (kitābu) | of Musa (mūsā) | as a guide (imāman) | and a mercy (waraḥmatan). | And this (wahādhā) | is a Book (kitābun) | confirming (muṣaddiqun), | in language (lisānan) | Arabic (ʿarabiyyan) | to warn (liyundhira) | those who (alladhīna) | do wrong (ẓalamū) | and as glad tidings (wabush'rā) | for the good-doers (lil'muḥ'sinīna).

46:13 Indeed, those who say, "Our Lord is Allah," then remain firm, then no fear on them and not they will grieve.

Indeed (inna), | those who (alladhīna) | say (qālū), | "Our Lord (rabbunā) | is Allah, (l-lahu)" | then (thumma) | remain firm (is'taqāmū), | then no (falā) | fear (khawfun) | on them (ʿalayhim) | and not (walā) | they (hum) | will grieve (yaḥzanūna).

46:14 Those are the companions of Paradise abiding forever therein, a reward for what they used to do.

Those (ulāika) | are the companions (aṣḥābu) | of Paradise (l-janati) | abiding forever (khālidīna) | therein (fīhā), | a reward (jazāan) | for what (bimā) | they used to (kānū) | do (yaʿmalūna).

46:15 And We have enjoined on man to his parents kindness. Carried him his mother with hardship and gave birth to him with hardship. And the bearing of him and the weaning of him is thirty months until, when he reaches his maturity and reaches forty years, he says, "My Lord, grant me the power that I may be grateful for Your favor which You have bestowed upon me and upon my parents and that I do righteous deeds which please You, and make righteous for me among my offspring, indeed, I turn to You and indeed, I am of those who submit."

And We have enjoined (wawaṣṣaynā) | on man (l-insāna) | to his parents (biwālidayhi) | kindness (iḥ'sānan). | Carried him (ḥamalathu) | his mother (ummuhu) | with hardship (kur'han) | and gave birth to him (wawaḍaʿathu) | with hardship (kur'han). | And the bearing of him (waḥamluhu) | and the weaning of him (wafiṣāluhu) | is thirty (thalāthūna) | months (shahran) | until (ḥattā), | when (idhā) | he reaches (balagha) | his maturity (ashuddahu) | and reaches (wabalagha) | forty (arbaʿīna) | years (sanatan), | he says (qāla), | "My Lord (rabbi), | grant me the power (awziʿ'nī) | that (an) | I may be grateful (ashkura) | for Your favor (niʿ'mataka) | which (allatī) | You have bestowed (anʿamta) | upon me (ʿalayya) | and upon (waʿalā) | my parents (wālidayya) | and that (wa-an) | I do (aʿmala) | righteous deeds (ṣāliḥan) | which please You (tarḍāhu), | and make righteous (wa-aṣliḥ) | for me (lī) | among (fī) | my offspring (dhurriyyatī), | indeed (innī), | I turn (tub'tu) | to You (ilayka) | and indeed, I am (wa-innī) | of (mina) | those who submit. (l-mus'limīna)"

46:16 Those are the ones We will accept from them the best of what they did and We will overlook [from] their evil deeds, among the companions of Paradise. A promise true which they were promised.

Those (ulāika) | are the ones (alladhīna) | We will accept (nataqabbalu) | from them

(ʿanhum) | the best (aḥsana) | of what (mā) | they did (ʿamilū) | and We will overlook (wanatajāwazu) | [from] (ʿan) | their evil deeds (sayyiātihim), | among (fī) | the companions (aṣḥābi) | of Paradise (l-janati). | A promise (waʿda) | true (l-ṣid'qi) | which (alladhī) | they were (kānū) | promised (yūʿadūna).

46:17 But the one who says to his parents, "Uff to both of you! Do you promise me that I will be brought forth, and have already passed away the generations before me?" And they both seek help of Allah. "Woe to you! Believe! Indeed, the Promise of Allah is true." But he says, "Not is this but the stories of the former (people)."

But the one who (wa-alladhī) | says (qāla) | to his parents (liwālidayhi), | "Uff (uffin) | to both of you (lakumā)! | Do you promise me (ataʿidāninī) | that (an) | I will be brought forth (ukh'raja), | and have already passed away (waqad) | and have already passed away (khalati) | the generations (l-qurūnu) | before me? (min)" | before me? (qablī)" | And they both (wahumā) | seek help (yastaghīthāni) | of Allah (l-laha). | "Woe to you (waylaka)! | Believe (āmin)! | Indeed (inna), | the Promise (waʿda) | of Allah (l-lahi) | is true. (ḥaqqun)" | But he says (fayaqūlu), | "Not (mā) | is this (hādhā) | but (illā) | the stories (asāṭīru) | of the former (people). (l-awalīna)"

46:18 Those - are the ones has proved true against them the word among nations that already passed away before them of the jinn and the men. Indeed, they are the losers.

Those (ulāika)- | are the ones (alladhīna) | has proved true (ḥaqqa) | against them (ʿalayhimu) | the word (l-qawlu) | among (fī) | nations (umamin) | that already passed away (qad) | that already passed away (khalat) | before them (min) | before them (qablihim) | of (mina) | the jinn (l-jini) | and the men (wal-insi). | Indeed, they (innahum) | are (kānū) | the losers (khāsirīna).

46:19 And for all are degrees for what they did, and that He may fully compensate them for their deeds, and they will not be wronged.

And for all (walikullin) | are degrees (darajātun) | for what (mimmā) | they did (ʿamilū), | and that He may fully compensate them (waliyuwaffiyahum) | for their deeds (aʿmālahum), | and they (wahum) | will not be wronged (lā). | will not be wronged (yuẓ'lamūna).

46:20 And the Day will be exposed those who disbelieved to the Fire. "You exhausted your good things in your life of the world, and you took your pleasures therein. So today you will be recompensed with a punishment humiliating because you were arrogant in the earth without [the] right and because you were defiantly disobedient."

And the Day (wayawma) | will be exposed (yuʿ'raḍu) | those who (alladhīna) | disbelieved (kafarū) | to (ʿalā) | the Fire (l-nāri). | "You exhausted (adhhabtum) | your good things (ṭayyibātikum) | in (fī) | your life (ḥayātikumu) | of the world (l-dun'yā), | and you took your pleasures (wa-is'tamtaʿtum) | therein (bihā). | So today (fal-yawma) | you will be recompensed (tuj'zawna) | with a punishment (ʿadhāba) | humiliating (l-hūni) | because (bimā) | you were (kuntum) | arrogant (tastakbirūna) | in (fī) | the earth (l-arḍi) | without (bighayri) | [the] right (l-ḥaqi) | and because (wabimā) | you were (kuntum) | defiantly disobedient. (tafsuqūna)"

46:21 And mention the brother of Aad, when he warned his people in the Al-Ahqaf - and had already passed away [the] warners before him and after him, "That not you worship except Allah. Indeed, I [I] fear for you a punishment of a Day Great."

And mention (wa-udh'kur) | the brother (akhā) | of Aad (ʿādin), | when (idh) | he warned (andhara) | his people (qawmahu) | in the Al-Ahqaf (bil-aḥqāfi)- | and had already passed away (waqad) | and had already passed away (khalati) | [the] warners (l-nudhuru) | before him (min) | before him (bayni) | before him (yadayhi) | and after him (wamin), | and after him (khalfihi), | "That not (allā) | you worship (taʿbudū) | except (illā) | Allah (l-laha). | Indeed, I (innī) | [I] fear (akhāfu) | for you (ʿalaykum) | a punishment (ʿadhāba) | of a Day (yawmin) | Great. (ʿaẓīmin)"

46:22 They said, "Have you come to us to turn us away from our gods? Then bring us what you threaten us, if you are of the truthful."

They said (qālū), | "Have you come to us (aji'tanā) | to turn us away (litafikanā) | from (ʿan) | our gods (ālihatinā)? | Then bring us (fatinā) | what (bimā) | you threaten us (taʿidunā), | if (in) | you are (kunta) | of (mina) | the truthful. (l-ṣādiqīna)"

46:23 He said, "Only the knowledge is with Allah and I convey to you what I am sent with it, but I see you a people ignorant."

He said (qāla), | "Only (innamā) | the knowledge (l-ʿil'mu) | is with Allah (ʿinda) | is with Allah (l-lahi) | and I convey to you (wa-uballighukum) | what (mā) | I am sent (ur'sil'tu) | with it (bihi), | but (walākinnī) | I see you (arākum) | a people (qawman) | ignorant. (tajhalūna)"

46:24 Then when they saw it as a cloud approaching their valleys, they said, "This is a cloud bringing us rain." Nay, it is what you were asking it to be hastened, a wind in it is a punishment painful,

Then when (falammā) | they saw it (ra-awhu) | as a cloud (ʿāriḍan) | approaching (mus'taqbila) | their valleys (awdiyatihim), | they said (qālū), | "This (hādhā) | is a cloud (ʿāriḍun) | bringing us rain. (mum'ṭirunā)" | Nay (bal), | it (huwa) | is what (mā) | you were asking it to be hastened (is'taʿjaltum), | you were asking it to be hastened (bihi), | a wind (rīḥun) | in it (fīhā) | is a punishment (ʿadhābun) | painful (alīmun),

46:25 Destroying every thing by the command of its Lord. Then they became such, not is seen except their dwellings. Thus We recompense the people [the] criminals.

Destroying (tudammiru) | every (kulla) | thing (shayin) | by the command (bi-amri) | of its Lord (rabbihā). | Then they became such (fa-aṣbaḥū), | not (lā) | is seen (yurā) | except (illā) | their dwellings (masākinuhum). | Thus (kadhālika) | We recompense (najzī) | the people (l-qawma) | [the] criminals (l-muj'rimīna).

46:26 And certainly, We had established them in what not We have established you in it, and We made for them hearing and vision and hearts. But not availed them their hearing and not their vision and not their hearts any thing, when they were rejecting the Signs of Allah and enveloped them what they used to [at it] ridicule.

And certainly (walaqad), | We had established them (makkannāhum) | in what (fīmā) | not (in) | We have established you (makkannākum) | in it (fīhi), | and We made (wajaʿalnā) | for them (lahum) | hearing (samʿan) | and vision (wa-abṣāran) | and hearts (wa-afidatan). | But not (famā) | availed (aghnā) | them (ʿanhum) | their hearing (samʿuhum) | and not (walā) | their vision (abṣāruhum) | and not (walā) | their hearts (afidatuhum) | any (min) | thing (shayin), | when (idh) | they were (kānū) | rejecting (yajḥadūna) | the Signs (biāyāti) | of Allah (l-lahi) | and enveloped (waḥāqa) | them (bihim) | what (mā) | they used to (kānū) | [at it] (bihi) | ridicule (yastahziūna).

46:27 And certainly We destroyed what surrounds you of the towns, and We have diversified the Signs, that they may return.

And certainly (walaqad) | We destroyed (ahlaknā) | what (mā) | surrounds you (ḥawlakum) | of (mina) | the towns (l-qurā), | and We have diversified (waṣarrafnā) | the Signs (l-āyāti), | that they may (laʿallahum) | return (yarjiʿūna).

46:28 Then why did not help them those whom they had taken besides Allah gods as a way of approach? Nay, they were lost from them. And that was their falsehood and what they were inventing.

Then why did not (falawlā) | help them (naṣarahumu) | those whom (alladhīna) | they had taken (ittakhadhū) | besides (min) | besides (dūni) | Allah (l-lahi) | gods as a way of approach (qur'bānan)? | gods as a way of approach (ālihatan)? | Nay (bal), | they were lost (ḍallū) | from them (ʿanhum). | And that (wadhālika) | was their falsehood (if'kuhum) | and what (wamā) | they were (kānū) | inventing (yaftarūna).

46:29 And when We directed to you a party of the jinn, listening to the Quran. And when they attended it, they said, "Listen quietly." And when it was concluded, they turned back to their people as warners.

And when (wa-idh) | We directed (ṣarafnā) | to you (ilayka) | a party (nafaran) | of (mina) | the jinn (l-jini), | listening (yastamiʿūna) | to the Quran (l-qur'āna). | And when (falammā) | they attended it (ḥaḍarūhu), | they said (qālū), | "Listen quietly. (anṣitū)" | And when (falammā) | it was concluded (quḍiya), | they turned back (wallaw) | to (ilā) | their people (qawmihim) | as warners (mundhirīna).

46:30 They said, "O our people! Indeed, we [we] have heard a Book revealed after Musa confirming what was before it, guiding to the truth and to a Path Straight.

They said (qālū), | "O our people (yāqawmanā)! | Indeed, we (innā) | [we] have heard (samiʿ'nā) | a Book (kitāban) | revealed (unzila) | after (min) | after (baʿdi) | Musa (mūsā) | confirming (muṣaddiqan) | what (limā) | was before it (bayna), | was before it (yadayhi), | guiding (yahdī) | to (ilā) | the truth (l-ḥaqi) | and to (wa-ilā) | a Path (ṭarīqin) | Straight (mus'taqīmin).

46:31 O our people! Respond to the caller of Allah and believe in him. He will forgive for you of your sins and will protect you from a punishment painful.

O our people (yāqawmanā)! | Respond (ajībū) | to the caller (dāʿiya) | of Allah (l-lahi) | and believe (waāminū) | in him (bihi). | He will forgive (yaghfir) | for you (lakum) | of (min) | your sins (dhunūbikum) | and will protect you (wayujir'kum) | from (min) | a punishment (ʿadhābin) | painful (alīmin).

46:32 And whoever does not respond to the caller of Allah, then not he can escape in the earth, and not for him besides Him protectors. Those are in error clear."

And whoever (waman) | does not (lā) | respond (yujib) | to the caller (dāʿiya) | of Allah (l-lahi), | then not (falaysa) | he can escape (bimuʿ'jizin) | in (fī) | the earth (l-arḍi), | and not (walaysa) | for him (lahu) | besides Him (min) | besides Him (dūnihi) | protectors (awliyāu). | Those (ulāika) | are in (fī) | error (ḍalālin) | clear. (mubīnin)"

46:33 Do not they see that Allah, is the One Who created the heavens and the earth and was not tired by their creation, is able to give life to the dead? Yes, indeed He is on every thing All-Powerful.

Do not (awalam) | they see (yaraw) | that (anna) | Allah (l-laha), | is the One Who (alladhī) | created (khalaqa) | the heavens (l-samāwāti) | and the earth (wal-arḍa) | and was not (walam) | tired (yaʿya) | by their creation (bikhalqihinna), | is able (biqādirin) | to give life (ʿalā) | to give life (an) | to give life (yuḥ'yiya) | to the dead (l-mawtā)? | Yes (balā), | indeed He (innahu) | is on (ʿalā) | every (kulli) | thing (shayin) | All-Powerful (qadīrun).

46:34 And the Day, are exposed those who disbelieved to the Fire, "Is not this the truth?" They will say, "Yes by our Lord." He will say, "Then taste the punishment because you used to disbelieve."

And the Day (wayawma), | are exposed (yuʿ'raḍu) | those who (alladhīna) | disbelieved (kafarū) | to (ʿalā) | the Fire (l-nāri), | "Is not (alaysa) | this (hādhā) | the truth? (bil-ḥaqi)" | They will say (qālū), | "Yes (balā) | by our Lord. (warabbinā)" | He will say (qāla), | "Then taste (fadhūqū) | the punishment (l-ʿadhāba) | because (bimā) | you used to (kuntum) | disbelieve. (takfurūna)"

46:35 So be patient, as had patience those of determination of the Messengers, and do not seek to hasten for them. As if they had, the Day they see what they were promised, not remained except an hour of a day. A notification. But will any be destroyed except the people - the defiantly disobedient?

So be patient (fa-iṣ'bir), | as (kamā) | had patience (ṣabara) | those of determination (ulū)

| those of determination (l-ʿazmi) | of (mina) | the Messengers (l-rusuli), | and do not (walā) | seek to hasten (tastaʿjil) | for them (lahum). | As if they had (ka-annahum), | the Day (yawma) | they see (yarawna) | what (mā) | they were promised (yūʿadūna), | not (lam) | remained (yalbathū) | except (illā) | an hour (sāʿatan) | of (min) | a day (nahārin). | A notification (balāghun). | But will (fahal) | any be destroyed (yuh'laku) | except (illā) | the people (l-qawmu)- | the defiantly disobedient (l-fāsiqūna)?

Chapter (47) Sūrat Muḥammad

47:1 Those who disbelieve and turn away from the way of Allah, He will cause to be lost their deeds.

Those who (alladhīna) | disbelieve (kafarū) | and turn away (waṣaddū) | from (ʿan) | the way of Allah (sabīli), | the way of Allah (l-lahi), | He will cause to be lost (aḍalla) | their deeds (aʿmālahum).

47:2 And those who believe and do righteous deeds, and believe in what is revealed to Muhammad, and it is the truth from their Lord, He will remove from them their misdeeds, and improve their condition.

And those who (wa-alladhīna) | believe (āmanū) | and do (waʿamilū) | righteous deeds (l-ṣāliḥāti), | and believe (waāmanū) | in what (bimā) | is revealed (nuzzila) | to (ʿalā) | Muhammad (muḥammadin), | and it (wahuwa) | is the truth (l-ḥaqu) | from (min) | their Lord (rabbihim), | He will remove (kaffara) | from them (ʿanhum) | their misdeeds (sayyiātihim), | and improve (wa-aṣlaḥa) | their condition (bālahum).

47:3 That is because those who disbelieve follow falsehood and that those who believe follow the truth from their Lord. Thus Allah presents to the people their similitudes.

That (dhālika) | is because (bi-anna) | those who (alladhīna) | disbelieve (kafarū) | follow (ittabaʿū) | falsehood (l-bāṭila) | and that (wa-anna) | those who (alladhīna) | believe (āmanū) | follow (ittabaʿū) | the truth (l-ḥaqa) | from (min) | their Lord (rabbihim). | Thus (kadhālika) | Allah presents (yaḍribu) | Allah presents (l-lahu) | to the people (lilnnāsi) | their similitudes (amthālahum).

47:4 So when you meet those who disbelieve, then strike the necks until when you have subdued them, then bind firmly the bond, then either a favor afterwards or ransom until lays down the war its burdens. That. And if Allah had willed surely, He could have taken retribution from them, but to test some of you with others. And those who are killed in the way of Allah, then never He will cause to be lost their deeds.

So when (fa-idhā) | you meet (laqītumu) | those who (alladhīna) | disbelieve (kafarū), | then strike (faḍarba) | the necks (l-riqābi) | until (ḥattā) | when (idhā) | you have subdued them (athkhantumūhum), | then bind firmly (fashuddū) | the bond (l-wathāqa), | then either (fa-immā) | a favor (mannan) | afterwards (baʿdu) | or (wa-immā) | ransom (fidāan) | until (ḥattā) | lays down (taḍaʿa) | the war (l-ḥarbu) | its burdens (awzārahā). | That (dhālika). | And if (walaw) | Allah had willed (yashāu) | Allah had willed (l-lahu) | surely, He could have taken retribution (la-intaṣara) |

from them (min'hum), | but (walākin) | to test (liyabluwā) | some of you (baʿḍakum) | with others (bibaʿḍin). | And those who (wa-alladhīna) | are killed (qutilū) | in (fī) | the way of Allah (sabīli), | the way of Allah (l-lahi), | then never (falan) | He will cause to be lost (yuḍilla) | their deeds (aʿmālahum).

47:5 He will guide them and improve their condition,

He will guide them (sayahdīhim) | and improve (wayuṣ'liḥu) | their condition (bālahum),

47:6 And admit them to Paradise, He has made it known to them.

And admit them (wayud'khiluhumu) | to Paradise (l-janata), | He has made it known (ʿarrafahā) | to them (lahum).

47:7 O you who believe! If you help Allah, He will help you and make firm your feet.

O you who believe (yāayyuhā)! | O you who believe (alladhīna)! | O you who believe (āmanū)! | If (in) | you help (tanṣurū) | Allah (l-laha), | He will help you (yanṣur'kum) | and make firm (wayuthabbit) | your feet (aqdāmakum).

47:8 But those who disbelieve, destruction is for them, and He will cause to be lost their deeds.

But those who (wa-alladhīna) | disbelieve (kafarū), | destruction is (fataʿsan) | for them (lahum), | and He will cause to be lost (wa-aḍalla) | their deeds (aʿmālahum).

47:9 That is because they hate what Allah has revealed, so He has made worthless their deeds.

That (dhālika) | is because they (bi-annahum) | hate (karihū) | what (mā) | Allah has revealed (anzala), | Allah has revealed (l-lahu), | so He has made worthless (fa-aḥbaṭa) | their deeds (aʿmālahum).

47:10 Do not they travel in the earth and see how was the end of those before them? Allah destroyed [over] them, and for the disbelievers its likeness.

Do not (afalam) | they travel (yasīrū) | in (fī) | the earth (l-arḍi) | and see (fayanẓurū) | how (kayfa) | was (kāna) | the end (ʿāqibatu) | of those (alladhīna) | before them (min)? | before them (qablihim)? | Allah destroyed (dammara) | Allah destroyed (l-lahu) | [over] them (ʿalayhim), | and for the disbelievers (walil'kāfirīna) | its likeness (amthāluhā).

47:11 That is because Allah is the Protector of those who believe, and that the disbelievers - there is no protector for them.

That (dhālika) | is because (bi-anna) | Allah (l-laha) | is the Protector (mawlā) | of those who (alladhīna) | believe (āmanū), | and that (wa-anna) | the disbelievers (l-kāfirīna)- | there is no (lā) | protector (mawlā) | for them (lahum).

47:12 Indeed, Allah will admit those who believe and do righteous deeds to Gardens, flow from underneath it the rivers, but those who disbelieve they enjoy and eat as eat the cattle, and the Fire will be an abode for them.

Indeed (inna), | Allah (l-laha) | will admit (yud'khilu) | those who (alladhīna) | believe (āmanū) | and do (waʿamilū) | righteous deeds (l-ṣāliḥāti) | to Gardens (jannātin), | flow (tajrī) | from (min) | underneath it (taḥtihā) | the rivers (l-anhāru), | but those who (wa-alladhīna) | disbelieve (kafarū) | they enjoy (yatamattaʿūna) | and eat (wayakulūna) | as (kamā) | eat (takulu) | the cattle (l-anʿāmu), | and the Fire (wal-nāru) | will be an abode (mathwan) | for them (lahum).

47:13 And how many of a town, which was stronger in strength than your town which has driven you out? We destroyed them, so no helper for them.

And how many (waka-ayyin) | of (min) | a town (qaryatin), | which (hiya) | was stronger (ashaddu) | in strength (quwwatan) | than (min) | your town (qaryatika) | which (allatī) | has driven you out (akhrajatka)? | We destroyed them (ahlaknāhum), | so no (falā) | helper (nāṣira) | for them (lahum).

47:14 Then is he who is on a clear proof from his Lord like he who, is made attractive to him the evil of his deeds while they follow their desires.

Then is he who (afaman) | is (kāna) | on (ʿalā) | a clear proof (bayyinatin) | from (min) | his Lord (rabbihi) | like he who (kaman), | is made attractive (zuyyina) | to him (lahu) | the evil (sūu) | of his deeds (ʿamalihi) | while they follow (wa-ittabaʿū) | their desires (ahwāahum).

47:15 A parable of Paradise which is promised to the righteous. Therein are rivers of water not polluted, and rivers of milk not changes its taste, and rivers of wine delicious for the drinkers, and rivers of honey purified, and for them therein of all fruits and forgiveness from their Lord like he who will abide forever in the Fire and they will be given to drink water boiling so it cuts into pieces their intestines.

A parable (mathalu) | of Paradise (l-janati) | which (allatī) | is promised (wuʿida) | to the righteous (l-mutaqūna). | Therein (fīhā) | are rivers (anhārun) | of (min) | water (māin) | not (ghayri) | polluted (āsinin), | and rivers (wa-anhārun) | of (min) | milk (labanin) | not (lam) | changes (yataghayyar) | its taste (ṭaʿmuhu), | and rivers (wa-anhārun) | of (min) | wine (khamrin) | delicious (ladhatin) | for the drinkers (lilshāribīna), | and rivers (wa-anhārun) | of (min) | honey (ʿasalin) | purified (muṣaffan), | and for them (walahum) | therein (fīhā) | of (min) | all (kulli) | fruits (l-thamarāti) | and forgiveness (wamaghfiratun) | from (min) | their Lord (rabbihim) | like he who (kaman) | like he who (huwa) | will abide forever (khālidun) | in (fī) | the Fire (l-nāri) | and they will be given to drink (wasuqū) | water (māan) | boiling (ḥamīman) | so it cuts into pieces (faqaṭṭaʿa) | their intestines (amʿāahum).

47:16 And among them are some who listen to you, until when they depart from you, they say to those who were given the knowledge, "What has he said just now?" Those - are the ones Allah has set a seal upon their hearts and they follow their desires.

And among them (wamin'hum) | are some who (man) | listen (yastamiʿu) | to you (ilayka), | until (ḥattā) | when (idhā) | they depart (kharajū) | from (min) | you (ʿindika), | they say (qālū) | to those who (lilladhīna) | were given (ūtū) | the knowledge (l-ʿil'ma), | "What (mādhā) | has he said (qāla) | just now? (ānifan)" | Those (ulāika)- | are the ones (alladhīna) | Allah has set a seal (ṭabaʿa) | Allah has set a seal (l-lahu) | upon (ʿalā) | their hearts (qulūbihim) | and they follow (wa-ittabaʿū) | their desires (ahwāahum).

47:17 And those who accept guidance, He increases them in guidance and gives them their righteousness.

And those who (wa-alladhīna) | accept guidance (ih'tadaw), | He increases them (zādahum) | in guidance (hudan) | and gives them (waātāhum) | their righteousness (taqwāhum).

47:18 Then do they wait but for the Hour that it should come to them suddenly? But indeed, have come its indications. Then how to them when has come to them their reminder.

Then do (fahal) | they wait (yanẓurūna) | but (illā) | for the Hour (l-sāʿata) | that (an) | it should come to them (tatiyahum) | suddenly (baghtatan)? | But indeed (faqad), | have come (jāa) | its indications (ashrāṭuhā). | Then how (fa-annā) | to them (lahum) | when (idhā) | has come to them (jāathum) | their reminder (dhik'rāhum).

47:19 So know that [He] - there is no god but Allah and ask forgiveness for your sin and for the believing men and the believing women. And Allah knows your movement and your resting places.

So know (fa-iʿ'lam) | that [He] (annahu)- | there is no (lā) | god (ilāha) | but (illā) | Allah (l-lahu) | and ask forgiveness (wa-is'taghfir) | for your sin (lidhanbika) | and for the believing men (walil'mu'minīna) | and the believing women (wal-mu'mināti). | And Allah (wal-lahu) | knows (ya'lamu) | your movement (mutaqallabakum) | and your resting places (wamathwākum).

47:20 And say those who believe, "Why not has been revealed a Surah?" But when is revealed a Surah precise and is mentioned in it the fighting, you see those who, in their hearts, is a disease looking at you - a look of one fainting from the death. But more appropriate for them

And say (wayaqūlu) | those who (alladhīna) | believe (āmanū), | "Why not (lawlā) | has been revealed (nuzzilat) | a Surah? (sūratun)" | But when (fa-idhā) | is revealed (unzilat) | a Surah (sūratun) | precise (muḥ'kamatun) | and is mentioned (wadhukira) | in it (fīhā) | the fighting (l-qitālu), | you see (ra-ayta) | those who (alladhīna), | in (fī) | their hearts (qulūbihim), | is a disease (maraḍun) | looking (yanẓurūna) | at you (ilayka)- | a look (naẓara) | of one fainting (l-maghshiyi) | of one fainting ('alayhi) | from (mina) | the death (l-mawti). | But more appropriate (fa-awlā) | for them (lahum)

47:21 Is obedience and a word kind. And when is determined the matter, then if they had been true to Allah, surely, it would have been better for them.

Is obedience (ṭā'atun) | and a word (waqawlun) | kind (ma'rūfun). | And when (fa-idhā) | is determined ('azama) | the matter (l-amru), | then if (falaw) | they had been true (ṣadaqū) | to Allah (l-laha), | surely, it would have been (lakāna) | better (khayran) | for them (lahum).

47:22 Then would you perhaps, if you are given authority that you cause corruption in the earth and cut off your ties of kinship.

Then would (fahal) | you perhaps ('asaytum), | if (in) | you are given authority (tawallaytum) | that (an) | you cause corruption (tuf'sidū) | in (fī) | the earth (l-arḍi) | and cut off (watuqaṭṭi'ū) | your ties of kinship (arḥāmakum).

47:23 Those, are the ones Allah has cursed them, so He made them deaf and blinded their vision.

Those (ulāika), | are the ones (alladhīna) | Allah has cursed them (la'anahumu), | Allah has cursed them (l-lahu), | so He made them deaf (fa-aṣammahum) | and blinded (wa-a'mā) | their vision (abṣārahum).

47:24 Then do not they ponder over the Quran or upon their hearts are locks?

Then do not (afalā) | they ponder (yatadabbarūna) | over the Quran (l-qur'āna) | or (am) | upon ('alā) | their hearts (qulūbin) | are locks (aqfāluhā)?

47:25 Indeed, those who return on their backs after what has become clear to them of the guidance, Shaitaan enticed [for] them and prolonged hope for them.

Indeed (inna), | those who (alladhīna) | return (ir'taddū) | on ('alā) | their backs (adbārihim) | after (min) | after (ba'di) | what (mā) | has become clear (tabayyana) | to them (lahumu) | of the guidance (l-hudā), | Shaitaan (l-shayṭānu) | enticed (sawwala) | [for] them (lahum) | and prolonged hope (wa-amlā) | for them (lahum).

47:26 That is because they [they] said to those who hate what Allah has revealed, "We will obey you in part of the matter." But Allah knows their secrets.

That (dhālika) | is because they (bi-annahum) | [they] said (qālū) | to those who (lilladhīna) | hate (karihū) | what (mā) | Allah has revealed (nazzala), | Allah has revealed (l-lahu), | "We will obey you (sanuṭī'ukum) | in (fī) | part (ba'ḍi) | of the matter. (l-amri)" | But Allah (wal-lahu) | knows (ya'lamu) | their secrets (is'rārahum).

47:27 Then how, when take them in death the Angels, striking their faces and their backs?

Then how (fakayfa), | when (idhā) | take them in death (tawaffathumu) | the Angels (l-malāikatu), | striking (yaḍribūna) | their faces (wujūhahum) | and their backs (wa-adbārahum)?

47:28 That is because they followed what angered Allah and hated His pleasure, so He made worthless their deeds.

That (dhālika) | is because they (bi-annahumu) | followed (ittabaʿū) | what (mā) | angered (askhaṭa) | Allah (l-laha) | and hated (wakarihū) | His pleasure (riḍ'wānahu), | so He made worthless (fa-aḥbaṭa) | their deeds (aʿmālahum).

47:29 Or do think those who in their hearts is a disease that never will Allah bring forth their hatred?

Or do (am) | think (ḥasiba) | those who (alladhīna) | in (fī) | their hearts (qulūbihim) | is a disease (maraḍun) | that (an) | never (lan) | will Allah bring forth (yukh'rija) | will Allah bring forth (l-lahu) | their hatred (aḍghānahum)?

47:30 And if We willed surely, We could show them to you and you would know them by their marks; but surely, you will know them by the tone of their speech. And Allah knows your deeds.

And if (walaw) | We willed (nashāu) | surely, We could show them to you (la-araynākahum) | and you would know them (falaʿaraftahum) | by their marks (bisīmāhum); | but surely, you will know them (walataʿrifannahum) | by (fī) | the tone (laḥni) | of their speech (l-qawli). | And Allah (wal-lahu) | knows (yaʿlamu) | your deeds (aʿmālakum).

47:31 And surely We will test you until We make evident those who strive among you and the patient ones, and We will test your affairs.

And surely We will test you (walanabluwannakum) | until (ḥattā) | We make evident (naʿlama) | those who strive (l-mujāhidīna) | among you (minkum) | and the patient ones (wal-ṣābirīna), | and We will test (wanabluwā) | your affairs (akhbārakum).

47:32 Indeed, those who disbelieve and turn away from the way of Allah and oppose the Messenger after [what] has been made clear to them the guidance, never will they harm Allah in anything, and He will make worthless their deeds.

Indeed (inna), | those who (alladhīna) | disbelieve (kafarū) | and turn away (waṣaddū) | from (ʿan) | the way of Allah (sabīli) | the way of Allah (l-lahi) | and oppose (washāqqū) | the Messenger (l-rasūla) | after (min) | after (baʿdi) | [what] (mā) | has been made clear (tabayyana) | to them (lahumu) | the guidance (l-hudā), | never (lan) | will they harm (yaḍurrū) | Allah (l-laha) | in anything (shayan), | and He will make worthless (wasayuḥ'biṭu) | their deeds (aʿmālahum).

47:33 O you who believe! Obey Allah and obey the Messenger, and do not make vain your deeds.

O you who believe (yāayyuhā)! | O you who believe (alladhīna)! | O you who believe (āmanū)! | Obey (aṭīʿū) | Allah (l-laha) | and obey (wa-aṭīʿū) | the Messenger (l-rasūla), | and do not (walā) | make vain (tub'ṭilū) | your deeds (aʿmālakum).

47:34 Indeed, those who disbelieve and turn away from the way of Allah, then died while they were disbelievers, never will Allah forgive them.

Indeed (inna), | those who (alladhīna) | disbelieve (kafarū) | and turn away (waṣaddū) | from (ʿan) | the way (sabīli) | of Allah (l-lahi), | then (thumma) | died (mātū) | while they (wahum) | were disbelievers (kuffārun), | never (falan) | will Allah forgive (yaghfira) | will Allah forgive (l-lahu) | them (lahum).

47:35 So do not weaken and call for peace while you are superior, and Allah is with you and never will deprive you of your deeds.

So do not (falā) | weaken (tahinū) | and call (watadʿū) | for (ilā) | peace (l-salmi) | while you (wa-antumu) | are superior (l-aʿlawna), | and Allah (wal-lahu) | is with you (maʿakum) | and never (walan) | will deprive you (yatirakum) | of your deeds (aʿmālakum).

47:36 Only the life of the world is play and amusement. And if you believe and fear Allah He will give you your rewards and not will ask you for your wealth.

Only (innamā) | the life (l-ḥayatu) | of the world (l-dun'yā) | is play (laʿibun) | and amusement (walahwun). | And if (wa-in) | you believe (tu'minū) | and fear Allah (watattaqū) | He will give you (yu'tikum) | your rewards (ujūrakum) | and not (walā) | will ask you (yasalkum) | for your wealth (amwālakum).

47:37 If He were to ask you for it and press you, you will withhold and He will bring forth your hatred.

If (in) | He were to ask you for it (yasalkumūhā) | and press you (fayuḥ'fikum), | you will withhold (tabkhalū) | and He will bring forth (wayukh'rij) | your hatred (aḍghānakum).

47:38 Here you are - these, called to spend in the way of Allah - but among you are some who withhold, and whoever withholds, then only he withholds from himself. But Allah is Free of need, while you are the needy. And if you turn away He will replace you with a people other than you, then not they will be the likes of you.

Here you are (hāantum)- | these (hāulāi), | called (tud'ʿawna) | to spend (litunfiqū) | in (fī) | the way (sabīli) | of Allah (l-lahi)- | but among you (faminkum) | are some who (man) | withhold (yabkhalu), | and whoever (waman) | withholds (yabkhal), | then only (fa-innamā) | he withholds (yabkhalu) | from (ʿan) | himself (nafsihi). | But Allah (wal-lahu) | is Free of need (l-ghaniyu), | while you (wa-antumu) | are the needy (l-fuqarāu). | And if (wa-in) | you turn away (tatawallaw) | He will replace you (yastabdil) | with a people (qawman) | other than you (ghayrakum), | then (thumma) | not (lā) | they will be (yakūnū) | the likes of you (amthālakum).

Chapter (48) Sūrat l-Fatḥ (The Victory)

48:1 Indeed, We have given victory, to you a victory clear.

Indeed (innā), | We have given victory (fataḥnā), | to you (laka) | a victory (fatḥan) | clear (mubīnan).

48:2 That may forgive for you Allah what preceded of your sins and what will follow and complete His favor upon you and guide you to a Path Straight,

That may forgive (liyaghfira) | for you (laka) | Allah (l-lahu) | what (mā) | preceded (taqaddama) | of (min) | your sins (dhanbika) | and what (wamā) | will follow (ta-akhara) | and complete (wayutimma) | His favor (niʿ'matahu) | upon you (ʿalayka) | and guide you (wayahdiyaka) | to a Path (ṣirāṭan) | Straight (mus'taqīman),

48:3 And Allah may help you with a help mighty.

And Allah may help you (wayanṣuraka) | And Allah may help you (l-lahu) | with a help (naṣran) | mighty (ʿazīzan).

48:4 He is the One Who sent down [the] tranquility into the hearts of the believers that they may increase in faith with their faith. And for Allah are the hosts of the heavens and the earth, and Allah is All-Knower, All-Wise.

He (huwa) | is the One Who (alladhī) | sent down (anzala) | [the] tranquility (l-sakīnata) | into (fī) | the hearts (qulūbi) | of the believers (l-mu'minīna) | that they may increase (liyazdādū) |

in faith (īmānan) | with (maʿa) | their faith (īmānihim). | And for Allah (walillahi) | are the hosts (junūdu) | of the heavens (l-samāwāti) | and the earth (wal-arḍi), | and Allah (wakāna) | and Allah (l-lahu) | is All-Knower (ʿalīman), | All-Wise (ḥakīman).

48:5 That He may admit the believing men and the believing women to Gardens flow from underneath them the rivers to abide forever therein, and to remove from them their misdeeds, and is that with Allah a success great.

That He may admit (liyud'khila) | the believing men (l-mu'minīna) | and the believing women (wal-mu'mināti) | to Gardens (jannātin) | flow (tajrī) | from (min) | underneath them (taḥtihā) | the rivers (l-anhāru) | to abide forever (khālidīna) | therein (fīhā), | and to remove (wayukaffira) | from them (ʿanhum) | their misdeeds (sayyiātihim), | and is (wakāna) | that (dhālika) | with (ʿinda) | Allah (l-lahi) | a success (fawzan) | great (ʿaẓīman).

48:6 And He may punish the hypocrite men and the hypocrite women and the polytheist men and the polytheist women, who assume about Allah an assumption evil. Upon them is a turn of evil, and Allah's wrath is upon them and He has cursed them and prepared for them Hell, and evil is the destination.

And He may punish (wayuʿadhiba) | the hypocrite men (l-munāfiqīna) | and the hypocrite women (wal-munāfiqāti) | and the polytheist men (wal-mush'rikīna) | and the polytheist women (wal-mush'rikāti), | who assume (l-ẓānīna) | about Allah (bil-lahi) | an assumption (ẓanna) | evil (l-sawi). | Upon them (ʿalayhim) | is a turn (dāiratu) | of evil (l-sawi), | and Allah's wrath is (waghaḍiba) | and Allah's wrath is (l-lahu) | upon them (ʿalayhim) | and He has cursed them (walaʿanahum) | and prepared (wa-aʿadda) | for them (lahum) | Hell (jahannama), | and evil (wasāat) | is the destination (maṣīran).

48:7 And for Allah are the hosts of the heavens and the earth. and Allah is All-Mighty, All-Wise.

And for Allah (walillahi) | are the hosts (junūdu) | of the heavens (l-samāwāti) | and the earth (wal-arḍi). | and Allah (wakāna) | and Allah (l-lahu) | is All-Mighty (ʿazīzan), | All-Wise (ḥakīman).

48:8 Indeed, We [We] have sent you as a witness and as a bearer of glad tidings and as a warner,

Indeed, We (innā) | [We] have sent you (arsalnāka) | as a witness (shāhidan) | and as a bearer of glad tidings (wamubashiran) | and as a warner (wanadhīran),

48:9 That you may believe in Allah and His Messenger and may honor him and respect him and glorify Him morning and evening.

That you may believe (litu'minū) | in Allah (bil-lahi) | and His Messenger (warasūlihi) | and may honor him (watuʿazzirūhu) | and respect him (watuwaqqirūhu) | and glorify Him (watusabbiḥūhu) | morning (buk'ratan) | and evening (wa-aṣīlan).

48:10 Indeed, those who pledge allegiance to you only they pledge allegiance to Allah. The Hand of Allah is over their hands. Then whoever breaks his oath then only he breaks against himself, and whoever fulfils what he has covenanted with Allah, soon He will give him a reward great.

Indeed (inna), | those who (alladhīna) | pledge allegiance to you (yubāyiʿūnaka) | only (innamā) | they pledge allegiance (yubāyiʿūna) | to Allah (l-laha). | The Hand (yadu) | of Allah (l-lahi) | is over (fawqa) | their hands (aydīhim). | Then whoever (faman) | breaks his oath (nakatha) | then only (fa-innamā) | he breaks (yankuthu) | against (ʿalā) | himself (nafsihi), | and whoever (waman) | fulfils (awfā) | what (bimā) | he has covenanted (ʿāhada) | with (ʿalayhu) | Allah (l-laha), | soon He will give him (fasayu'tīhi) | a reward (ajran) | great (ʿaẓīman).

48:11 Will say to you those who remained behind of the Bedouins, "Kept us busy our properties and our families, so ask forgiveness for us." They say with their tongues what is not in their hearts. Say,

"Then who has power for you against Allah in anything, if He intends for you harm or He intends for you a benefit? Nay, is Allah of what you do All-Aware.

Will say (sayaqūlu) | to you (laka) | those who remained behind (l-mukhalafūna) | of (mina) | the Bedouins (l-aʿrābi), | "Kept us busy (shaghalatnā) | our properties (amwālunā) | and our families (wa-ahlūnā), | so ask forgiveness (fa-is'taghfir) | for us. (lanā)" | They say (yaqūlūna) | with their tongues (bi-alsinatihim) | what (mā) | is not (laysa) | in (fī) | their hearts (qulūbihim). | Say (qul), | "Then who (faman) | has power (yamliku) | for you (lakum) | against (mina) | Allah (l-lahi) | in anything (shayan), | if (in) | He intends (arāda) | for you (bikum) | harm (ḍarran) | or (aw) | He intends (arāda) | for you (bikum) | a benefit (nafʿan)? | Nay (bal), | is (kāna) | Allah (l-lahu) | of what (bimā) | you do (taʿmalūna) | All-Aware (khabīran).

48:12 Nay, you thought that would never return the Messenger and the believers to their families ever, that was made fair-seeming in your hearts. And you assumed an assumption evil, and you became a people ruined."

Nay (bal), | you thought (ẓanantum) | that (an) | would never (lan) | return (yanqaliba) | the Messenger (l-rasūlu) | and the believers (wal-mu'minūna) | to (ilā) | their families (ahlīhim) | ever (abadan), | that was made fair-seeming (wazuyyina) | that was made fair-seeming (dhālika) | in (fī) | your hearts (qulūbikum). | And you assumed (waẓanantum) | an assumption (ẓanna) | evil (l-sawi), | and you became (wakuntum) | a people (qawman) | ruined. (būran)"

48:13 And whoever has not believed in Allah and His Messenger then indeed, We [We] have prepared for the disbelievers a Blazing Fire.

And whoever (waman) | has not believed (lam) | has not believed (yu'min) | in Allah (bil-lahi) | and His Messenger (warasūlihi) | then indeed, We (fa-innā) | [We] have prepared (aʿtadnā) | for the disbelievers (lil'kāfirīna) | a Blazing Fire (saʿīran).

48:14 And for Allah is the kingdom of the heavens and the earth. He forgives whom He wills and punishes whom He wills. And is Allah Oft-Forgiving, Most Merciful.

And for Allah (walillahi) | is the kingdom (mul'ku) | of the heavens (l-samāwāti) | and the earth (wal-arḍi). | He forgives (yaghfiru) | whom (liman) | He wills (yashāu) | and punishes (wayuʿadhibu) | whom (man) | He wills (yashāu). | And is (wakāna) | Allah (l-lahu) | Oft-Forgiving (ghafūran), | Most Merciful (raḥīman).

48:15 Will say those who remained behind when you set forth towards the spoils of war to take it, "Allow us to follow you." They wish to change the Words of Allah. Say, "Never will you follow us. Thus Allah said before." Then they will say, "Nay, you envy us." Nay, they were not understanding except a little.

Will say (sayaqūlu) | those who remained behind (l-mukhalafūna) | when (idhā) | you set forth (inṭalaqtum) | towards (ilā) | the spoils of war (maghānima) | to take it (litakhudhūhā), | "Allow us (dharūnā) | to follow you. (nattabiʿkum)" | They wish (yurīdūna) | to (an) | change (yubaddilū) | the Words (kalāma) | of Allah (l-lahi). | Say (qul), | "Never (lan) | will you follow us (tattabiʿūnā). | Thus (kadhālikum) | Allah said (qāla) | Allah said (l-lahu) | before. (min)" | before. (qablu)" | Then they will say (fasayaqūlūna), | "Nay (bal), | you envy us. (taḥsudūnanā)" | Nay (bal), | they were (kānū) | not (lā) | understanding (yafqahūna) | except (illā) | a little (qalīlan).

48:16 Say to those who remained behind of the Bedouins, "You will be called to a people, possessors of military might great; you will fight them, or they will submit. Then if you obey, Allah will give you a reward good; but if you turn away as you turned away before, He will punish you with a punishment painful."

Say (qul) | to those who remained behind (lil'mukhallafīna) | of (mina) | the Bedouins (l-aʿrābi), | "You will be called (satudʿawna) | to (ilā) | a people (qawmin), | possessors of military might (ulī) | possessors of military might (basin) | great (shadīdin); | you will fight them (tuqātilūnahum), | or (aw) | they will submit (yus'limūna). | Then if (fa-in) | you obey (tuṭīʿū), | Allah will give you (yu'tikumu) | Allah will give you (l-lahu) | a reward (ajran) | good (ḥasanan); | but if (wa-in) | you turn away (tatawallaw) | as (kamā) | you turned away (tawallaytum) | before (min), | before (qablu), | He will punish you (yuʿadhib'kum) | with a punishment (ʿadhāban) | painful. (alīman)"

48:17 Not is upon the blind any blame and not on the lame any blame and not on the sick any blame. And whoever obeys Allah and His Messenger, He will admit him to Gardens flow from underneath them the rivers, but whoever turns away, He will punish him with a punishment painful.

Not is (laysa) | upon (ʿalā) | the blind (l-aʿmā) | any blame (ḥarajun) | and not (walā) | on (ʿalā) | the lame (l-aʿraji) | any blame (ḥarajun) | and not (walā) | on (ʿalā) | the sick (l-marīḍi) | any blame (ḥarajun). | And whoever (waman) | obeys (yuṭiʿi) | Allah (l-laha) | and His Messenger (warasūlahu), | He will admit him (yud'khil'hu) | to Gardens (jannātin) | flow (tajrī) | from (min) | underneath them (taḥtihā) | the rivers (l-anhāru), | but whoever (waman) | turns away (yatawalla), | He will punish him (yuʿadhib'hu) | with a punishment (ʿadhāban) | painful (alīman).

48:18 Certainly Allah was pleased with the believers when they pledged allegiance to you under the tree, and He knew what was in their hearts, so He sent down the tranquility upon them and rewarded them with a victory near,

Certainly (laqad) | Allah was pleased (raḍiya) | Allah was pleased (l-lahu) | with (ʿani) | the believers (l-mu'minīna) | when (idh) | they pledged allegiance to you (yubāyiʿūnaka) | under (taḥta) | the tree (l-shajarati), | and He knew (faʿalima) | what (mā) | was in (fī) | their hearts (qulūbihim), | so He sent down (fa-anzala) | the tranquility (l-sakīnata) | upon them (ʿalayhim) | and rewarded them (wa-athābahum) | with a victory (fatḥan) | near (qarīban),

48:19 And spoils of war much that they will take; and is Allah All-Mighty, All-Wise.

And spoils of war (wamaghānima) | much (kathīratan) | that they will take (yakhudhūnahā); | and is (wakāna) | Allah (l-lahu) | All-Mighty (ʿazīzan), | All-Wise (ḥakīman).

48:20 Allah has promised you spoils of war much that you will take it, and He has hastened for you this and has withheld the hands of the people from you - that it may be a sign for the believers and He may guide you to the Path Straight.

Allah has promised you (waʿadakumu) | Allah has promised you (l-lahu) | spoils of war (maghānima) | much (kathīratan) | that you will take it (takhudhūnahā), | and He has hastened (faʿajjala) | for you (lakum) | this (hādhihi) | and has withheld (wakaffa) | the hands (aydiya) | of the people (l-nāsi) | from you (ʿankum)- | that it may be (walitakūna) | a sign (āyatan) | for the believers (lil'mu'minīna) | and He may guide you (wayahdiyakum) | to the Path (ṣirāṭan) | Straight (mus'taqīman).

48:21 And others, not you had power over them surely Allah encompassed them, and is Allah over all things All-Powerful.

And others (wa-ukh'rā), | not (lam) | you had power (taqdirū) | over them (ʿalayhā) | surely (qad) | Allah encompassed (aḥāṭa) | Allah encompassed (l-lahu) | them (bihā), | and is (wakāna) | Allah (l-lahu) | over (ʿalā) | all (kulli) | things (shayin) | All-Powerful (qadīran).

48:22 And if, fight you, those who disbelieve, surely they would turn the backs. Then not they would find any protector and not any helper.

And if (walaw), | fight you (qātalakumu), | those who (alladhīna) | disbelieve (kafarū), | surely they would turn (lawallawū) | the backs (l-adbāra). | Then (thumma) | not (lā) | they would find (yajidūna) | any protector (waliyyan) | and not (walā) | any helper (naṣīran).

48:23 The established way of Allah which passed away before, and never you will find in the way of

Allah any change.

The established way (sunnata) | of Allah (l-lahi) | which (allatī) | passed away (qad) | passed away (khalat) | before (min), | before (qablu), | and never (walan) | you will find (tajida) | in the way of Allah (lisunnati) | in the way of Allah (l-lahi) | any change (tabdīlan).

48:24 And He is the One Who withheld their hands from you and your hands from them within Makkah, after that He gave you victory over them. And is Allah of what you do All-Seer.

And He (wahuwa) | is the One Who (alladhī) | withheld (kaffa) | their hands (aydiyahum) | from you (ʿankum) | and your hands (wa-aydiyakum) | from them (ʿanhum) | within (bibaṭni) | Makkah (makkata), | after (min) | after (baʿdi) | that (an) | He gave you victory (aẓfarakum) | over them (ʿalayhim). | And is (wakāna) | Allah (l-lahu) | of what (bimā) | you do (taʿmalūna) | All-Seer (baṣīran).

48:25 They are those who disbelieved and hindered you from Al-Masjid Al-Haraam while the offering was prevented from reaching its place of sacrifice. And if not for men believing and women believing not you knew them that you may trample them and would befall you from them any harm without knowledge. That Allah may admit to His Mercy whom He wills. If they had been apart surely, We would have punished those who disbelieved among them with a punishment painful.

They (humu) | are those who (alladhīna) | disbelieved (kafarū) | and hindered you (waṣaddūkum) | from (ʿani) | Al-Masjid Al-Haraam (l-masjidi) | Al-Masjid Al-Haraam (l-ḥarāmi) | while the offering (wal-hadya) | was prevented (maʿkūfan) | from (an) | reaching (yablugha) | its place of sacrifice (maḥillahu). | And if not (walawlā) | for men (rijālun) | believing (mu'minūna) | and women (wanisāon) | believing (mu'minātun) | not (lam) | you knew them (taʿlamūhum) | that (an) | you may trample them (taṭaūhum) | and would befall you (fatuṣībakum) | from them (min'hum) | any harm (maʿarratun) | without (bighayri) | knowledge (ʿil'min). | That Allah may admit (liyud'khila) | That Allah may admit (l-lahu) | to (fī) | His Mercy (raḥmatihi) | whom (man) | He wills (yashāu). | If (law) | they had been apart (tazayyalū) | surely, We would have punished (laʿadhabnā) | those who (alladhīna) | disbelieved (kafarū) | among them (min'hum) | with a punishment (ʿadhāban) | painful (alīman).

48:26 When had put those who disbelieved in their hearts disdain - the disdain of the time of ignorance. Then Allah sent down His tranquility upon His Messenger and upon the believers and made them adhere to the word of righteousness, and they were more deserving of it and worthy of it. And is Allah of every thing All-Knower.

When (idh) | had put (jaʿala) | those who (alladhīna) | disbelieved (kafarū) | in (fī) | their hearts (qulūbihimu) | disdain (l-ḥamiyata)- | the disdain (ḥamiyyata) | of the time of ignorance (l-jāhiliyati). | Then Allah sent down (fa-anzala) | Then Allah sent down (l-lahu) | His tranquility (sakīnatahu) | upon (ʿalā) | His Messenger (rasūlihi) | and upon (waʿalā) | the believers (l-mu'minīna) | and made them adhere (wa-alzamahum) | to the word (kalimata) | of righteousness (l-taqwā), | and they were (wakānū) | more deserving (aḥaqqa) | of it (bihā) | and worthy of it (wa-ahlahā). | And is (wakāna) | Allah (l-lahu) | of every (bikulli) | thing (shayin) | All-Knower (ʿalīman).

48:27 Certainly, Allah has fulfilled His Messenger's vision in truth. Surely, you will enter Al-Masjid Al-Haraam if Allah wills, secure, having shaved your heads and shortened, not fearing. But He knew what not you knew, and He made besides that a victory near.

Certainly (laqad), | Allah has fulfilled (ṣadaqa) | Allah has fulfilled (l-lahu) | His Messenger's (rasūlahu) | vision (l-ru'yā) | in truth (bil-ḥaqi). | Surely, you will enter (latadkhulunna) | Al-Masjid Al-Haraam (l-masjida) | Al-Masjid Al-Haraam (l-ḥarāma) | if (in) | Allah wills (shāa), | Allah wills (l-lahu), | secure (āminīna), | having shaved (muḥalliqīna) | your heads (ruūsakum) | and shortened (wamuqaṣṣirīna), | not (lā) | fearing (takhāfūna). | But He knew (faʿalima) | what (mā) | not (lam) | you knew (taʿlamū), | and He made (fajaʿala) | besides (min) | besides (dūni) | that (dhālika) | a victory (fatḥan) | near (qarīban).

48:28 He is the One Who has sent His Messenger with guidance and the religion, the true that He may make it prevail over the religions all. And sufficient is Allah as a Witness.

He (huwa) | is the One Who (alladhī) | has sent (arsala) | His Messenger (rasūlahu) | with guidance (bil-hudā) | and the religion (wadīni), | the true (l-ḥaqi) | that He may make it prevail (liyuẓ'hirahu) | over (ʿalā) | the religions (l-dīni) | all (kullihi). | And sufficient is (wakafā) | Allah (bil-lahi) | as a Witness (shahīdan).

48:29 Muhammad is the Messenger of Allah, and those who are with him are firm against the disbelievers and merciful among themselves. You see them bowing and prostrating, seeking Bounty from Allah and pleasure. Their mark is on their faces from the trace of the prostration. That is their similitude in the Taurah. And their similitude in the Injeel, is like a seed which sends forth its shoot then strengthens it, then it becomes thick and it stands upon its stem delighting the sowers that He may enrage by them the disbelievers. Allah has promised those who believe and do righteous deeds among them, forgiveness and a reward great.

Muhammad (muḥammadun) | is the Messenger of Allah (rasūlu), | is the Messenger of Allah (l-lahi), | and those who (wa-alladhīna) | are with him (maʿahu) | are firm (ashiddāu) | against (ʿalā) | the disbelievers (l-kufāri) | and merciful (ruḥamāu) | among themselves (baynahum). | You see them (tarāhum) | bowing (rukkaʿan) | and prostrating (sujjadan), | seeking (yabtaghūna) | Bounty (faḍlan) | from Allah (mina) | from Allah (l-lahi) | and pleasure (wariḍ'wānan). | Their mark (sīmāhum) | is on (fī) | their faces (wujūhihim) | from (min) | the trace (athari) | of the prostration (l-sujūdi). | That (dhālika) | is their similitude (mathaluhum) | in (fī) | the Taurah (l-tawrāti). | And their similitude (wamathaluhum) | in (fī) | the Injeel (l-injīli), | is like a seed (kazarʿin) | which sends forth (akhraja) | its shoot (shaṭahu) | then strengthens it (faāzarahu), | then it becomes thick (fa-is'taghlaẓa) | and it stands (fa-is'tawā) | upon (ʿalā) | its stem (sūqihi) | delighting (yuʿʾjibu) | the sowers (l-zurāʿa) | that He may enrage (liyaghīẓa) | by them (bihimu) | the disbelievers (l-kufāra). | Allah has promised (waʿada) | Allah has promised (l-lahu) | those who (alladhīna) | believe (āmanū) | and do (waʿamilū) | righteous deeds (l-ṣāliḥāti) | among them (min'hum), | forgiveness (maghfiratan) | and a reward (wa-ajran) | great (ʿaẓīman).

Chapter (49) Sūrat l-Ḥujurāt (The Dwellings)

49:1 O you who believe! Do not put yourselves forward - before Allah and His Messenger and fear Allah. Indeed, Allah is All-Hearer, All-Knower.

O you who believe (yāayyuhā)! | O you who believe (alladhīna)! | O you who believe (āmanū)! | Do not (lā) | put yourselves forward (tuqaddimū)- | before Allah (bayna) | before Allah (yadayi) | before Allah (l-lahi) | and His Messenger (warasūlihi) | and fear Allah (wa-ittaqū). | and fear Allah (l-laha). | Indeed (inna), | Allah (l-laha) | is All-Hearer (samīʿun), | All-Knower (ʿalīmun).

49:2 O you who believe! Do not raise your voices above the voice of the Prophet, and do not be loud to him in speech like the loudness of some of you to others, lest become worthless your deeds while you do not perceive.

O you who believe (yāayyuhā)! | O you who believe (alladhīna)! | O you who believe (āmanū)! | Do not (lā) | raise (tarfaʿū) | your voices (aṣwātakum) | above (fawqa) | the voice (ṣawti) | of the Prophet (l-nabiyi), | and do not (walā) | be loud (tajharū) | to him (lahu) | in speech (bil-qawli) | like the loudness (kajahri) | of some of you (baʿḍikum) | to others (libaʿḍin), | lest (an) |

become worthless (taḥbaṭa) | your deeds (aʿmālukum) | while you (wa-antum) | do not (lā) | perceive (tashʿurūna).

49:3 Indeed, those who lower their voices in presence of the Messenger of Allah - those, are the ones Allah has tested their hearts for righteousness. For them is forgiveness and a reward great.

Indeed (inna), | those who (alladhīna) | lower (yaghuḍḍūna) | their voices (aṣwātahum) | in presence (ʿinda) | of the Messenger of Allah (rasūli)- | of the Messenger of Allah (l-lahi)- | those (ulāika), | are the ones (alladhīna) | Allah has tested (im'taḥana) | Allah has tested (l-lahu) | their hearts (qulūbahum) | for righteousness (lilttaqwā). | For them (lahum) | is forgiveness (maghfiratun) | and a reward (wa-ajrun) | great (ʿaẓīmun).

49:4 Indeed, those who call you from behind the private chambers, most of them do not understand.

Indeed (inna), | those who (alladhīna) | call you (yunādūnaka) | from (min) | behind (warāi) | the private chambers (l-ḥujurāti), | most of them (aktharuhum) | do not (lā) | understand (yaʿqilūna).

49:5 And if they had been patient until you came out to them certainly it would be better for them. And Allah is Oft-Forgiving, Most Merciful.

And if (walaw) | they (annahum) | had been patient (ṣabarū) | until (ḥattā) | you came out (takhruja) | to them (ilayhim) | certainly it would be (lakāna) | better (khayran) | for them (lahum). | And Allah (wal-lahu) | is Oft-Forgiving (ghafūrun), | Most Merciful (raḥīmun).

49:6 O you who believe! If comes to you a wicked person with information, investigate, lest you harm a people in ignorance, then you become, over what you have done, regretful.

O you who believe (yāayyuhā)! | O you who believe (alladhīna)! | O you who believe (āmanū)! | If (in) | comes to you (jāakum) | a wicked person (fāsiqun) | with information (binaba-in), | investigate (fatabayyanū), | lest (an) | you harm (tuṣībū) | a people (qawman) | in ignorance (bijahālatin), | then you become (fatuṣ'biḥū), | over (ʿalā) | what (mā) | you have done (faʿaltum), | regretful (nādimīna).

49:7 And know that among you is the Messenger of Allah. If he were to obey you in much of the matter, surely you would be in difficulty, but Allah has endeared to you the Faith and has made it pleasing in your hearts and has made hateful to you disbelief and defiance and disobedience. Those are they - the guided ones.

And know (wa-iʿ'lamū) | that (anna) | among you (fīkum) | is the Messenger of Allah (rasūla). | is the Messenger of Allah (l-lahi). | If (law) | he were to obey you (yuṭīʿukum) | in (fī) | much (kathīrin) | of (mina) | the matter (l-amri), | surely you would be in difficulty (laʿanittum), | but (walākinna) | Allah (l-laha) | has endeared (ḥabbaba) | to you (ilaykumu) | the Faith (l-īmāna) | and has made it pleasing (wazayyanahu) | in (fī) | your hearts (qulūbikum) | and has made hateful (wakarraha) | to you (ilaykumu) | disbelief (l-kuf'ra) | and defiance (wal-fusūqa) | and disobedience (wal-ʿiṣ'yāna). | Those (ulāika) | are they (humu)- | the guided ones (l-rāshidūna).

49:8 A Bounty from Allah and favor. And Allah is All-Knower, All-Wise.

A Bounty (faḍlan) | from Allah (mina) | from Allah (l-lahi) | and favor (waniʿ'matan). | And Allah (wal-lahu) | is All-Knower (ʿalīmun), | All-Wise (ḥakīmun).

49:9 And if two parties among the believers fight, then make peace between both of them. But if oppresses one of them on the other, then fight one which oppresses until it returns to the command of Allah. Then if it returns, then make peace between them with justice, and act justly. Indeed, Allah loves those who act justly.

And if (wa-in) | two parties (ṭāifatāni) | among (mina) | the believers (l-mu'minīna) | fight (iq'tatalū), | then make peace (fa-aṣliḥū) | between both of them (baynahumā). | But if (fa-in) | oppresses (baghat) | one of them (iḥ'dāhumā) | on (ʿalā) | the other (l-ukh'rā), | then fight (faqātilū) | one which (allatī) | oppresses (tabghī) | until (ḥattā) | it returns (tafīa) | to (ilā) | the command (amri) | of Allah (l-lahi). | Then if (fa-in) | it returns (fāat), | then make peace (fa-aṣliḥū) | between them (baynahumā) | with justice (bil-ʿadli), | and act justly (wa-aqsiṭū). | Indeed (inna), | Allah (l-laha) | loves (yuḥibbu) | those who act justly (l-muq'siṭīna).

49:10 Only the believers are brothers, so make peace between your brothers, and fear Allah so that you may receive mercy.

Only (innamā) | the believers (l-mu'minūna) | are brothers (ikh'watun), | so make peace (fa-aṣliḥū) | between (bayna) | your brothers (akhawaykum), | and fear Allah (wa-ittaqū) | and fear Allah (l-laha) | so that you may (laʿallakum) | receive mercy (tur'ḥamūna).

49:11 O you who believe! Let not ridicule a people [of] another people, perhaps that they may be better than them; and let not women [of] other women perhaps that they may be better than them. And do not insult yourselves and do not call each other by nicknames. Wretched is the name of disobedience after the faith. And whoever does not repent, then those - they are the wrongdoers.

O you who believe (yāayyuhā)! | O you who believe (alladhīna)! | O you who believe (āmanū)! | Let not (lā) | ridicule (yaskhar) | a people (qawmun) | [of] (min) | another people (qawmin), | perhaps (ʿasā) | that (an) | they may be (yakūnū) | better (khayran) | than them (min'hum); | and let not (walā) | women (nisāon) | [of] (min) | other women (nisāin) | perhaps (ʿasā) | that (an) | they may be (yakunna) | better (khayran) | than them (min'hunna). | And do not (walā) | insult (talmizū) | yourselves (anfusakum) | and do not (walā) | call each other (tanābazū) | by nicknames (bil-alqābi). | Wretched is (bi'sa) | the name (l-s'mu) | of disobedience (l-fusūqu) | after (baʿda) | the faith (l-īmāni). | And whoever (waman) | does not (lam) | repent (yatub), | then those (fa-ulāika)- | they (humu) | are the wrongdoers (l-ẓālimūna).

49:12 O you who believe! Avoid much of the assumption. Indeed, some assumption is sin. And do not spy and do not backbite some of you to others. Would like one of you to eat the flesh of his brother, dead? Nay, you would hate it. And fear Allah; indeed, Allah is Oft-Returning, Most Merciful.

O you who believe (yāayyuhā)! | O you who believe (alladhīna)! | O you who believe (āmanū)! | Avoid (ij'tanibū) | much (kathīran) | of (mina) | the assumption (l-ẓani). | Indeed (inna), | some (baʿḍa) | assumption (l-ẓani) | is sin (ith'mun). | And do not (walā) | spy (tajassasū) | and do not (walā) | backbite (yaghtab) | some of you (baʿḍukum) | to others (baʿḍan). | Would like (ayuḥibbu) | one of you (aḥadukum) | to (an) | eat (yakula) | the flesh (laḥma) | of his brother (akhīhi), | dead (maytan)? | Nay, you would hate it (fakarih'tumūhu). | And fear Allah (wa-ittaqū); | And fear Allah (l-laha); | indeed (inna), | Allah (l-laha) | is Oft-Returning (tawwābun), | Most Merciful (raḥīmun).

49:13 O mankind! Indeed, We created you from a male and a female and We made you nations and tribes that you may know one another. Indeed, the most noble of you near Allah is the most righteous of you. Indeed, Allah is All-Knower, All-Aware.

O mankind (yāayyuhā)! | O mankind (l-nāsu)! | Indeed, We (innā) | created you (khalaqnākum) | from (min) | a male (dhakarin) | and a female (wa-unthā) | and We made you (wajaʿalnākum) | nations (shuʿūban) | and tribes (waqabāila) | that you may know one another (litaʿārafū). | Indeed (inna), | the most noble of you (akramakum) | near (ʿinda) | Allah (l-lahi) | is the most righteous of you (atqākum). | Indeed (inna), | Allah (l-laha) | is All-Knower (ʿalīmun), | All-Aware (khabīrun).

49:14 Say the Bedouins, "We believe." Say, "Not you believe; but say, "We have submitted," and has not yet entered the faith in your hearts. But if you obey Allah and His Messenger, not He will deprive you of your deeds anything. Indeed, Allah is Oft-Forgiving, Most Merciful.

Say (qālati) | the Bedouins (l-aʿrābu), | "We believe. (āmannā)" | Say (qul), | "Not (lam) | you believe (tu'minū); | but (walākin) | say (qūlū), | "We have submitted, (aslamnā)" | and has not yet (walammā) | entered (yadkhuli) | the faith (l-īmānu) | in (fī) | your hearts (qulūbikum). | But if (wa-in) | you obey (tuṭīʿū) | Allah (l-laha) | and His Messenger (warasūlahu), | not (lā) | He will deprive you (yalit'kum) | of (min) | your deeds (aʿmālikum) | anything (shayan). | Indeed (inna), | Allah (l-laha) | is Oft-Forgiving (ghafūrun), | Most Merciful (raḥīmun).

49:15 Only the believers are those who believe in Allah and His Messenger, then do not doubt but strive with their wealth and their lives in the way of Allah. Those [they] are the truthful."

Only (innamā) | the believers (l-mu'minūna) | are those who (alladhīna) | believe (āmanū) | in Allah (bil-lahi) | and His Messenger (warasūlihi), | then (thumma) | do not (lam) | doubt (yartābū) | but strive (wajāhadū) | with their wealth (bi-amwālihim) | and their lives (wa-anfusihim) | in (fī) | the way (sabīli) | of Allah (l-lahi). | Those (ulāika) | [they] (humu) | are the truthful. (l-ṣādiqūna)"

49:16 Say, "Will you acquaint Allah with your religion while Allah knows what is in the heavens and what is in the earth. And Allah of every thing is All-Knower."

Say (qul), | "Will you acquaint (atuʿallimūna) | Allah (l-laha) | with your religion (bidīnikum) | while Allah (wal-lahu) | knows (yaʿlamu) | what (mā) | is in (fī) | the heavens (l-samāwāti) | and what (wamā) | is in (fī) | the earth (l-arḍi). | And Allah (wal-lahu) | of every (bikulli) | thing (shayin) | is All-Knower. (ʿalīmun)"

49:17 They consider it a favor to you that they have accepted Islam. Say, "Do not consider a favor on me - your Islam. Nay, Allah has conferred a favor upon you that He has guided you to the faith, if you are truthful.

They consider it a favor (yamunnūna) | to you (ʿalayka) | that (an) | they have accepted Islam (aslamū). | Say (qul), | "Do not (lā) | consider a favor (tamunnū) | on me (ʿalayya)- | your Islam (is'lāmakum). | Nay (bali), | Allah (l-lahu) | has conferred a favor (yamunnu) | upon you (ʿalaykum) | that (an) | He has guided you (hadākum) | to the faith (lil'īmāni), | if (in) | you are (kuntum) | truthful (ṣādiqīna).

49:18 Indeed, Allah knows the unseen of the heavens and the earth. And Allah is All-Seer of what you do."

Indeed (inna), | Allah (l-laha) | knows (yaʿlamu) | the unseen (ghayba) | of the heavens (l-samāwāti) | and the earth (wal-arḍi). | And Allah (wal-lahu) | is All-Seer (baṣīrun) | of what (bimā) | you do. (taʿmalūna)"

Chapter (50) Sūrat Qāf

50:1 Qaf. By the Quran, the Glorious.

Qaf (qaf). | By the Quran (wal-qur'āni), | the Glorious (l-majīdi).

50:2 Nay, they wonder that has come to them a warner from them. So say the disbelievers, "This is a thing amazing.

Nay (bal), | they wonder (ʿajibū) | that (an) | has come to them (jāahum) | a warner (mundhirun) | from them (min'hum). | So say (faqāla) | the disbelievers (l-kāfirūna), | "This (hādhā) | is a thing (shayon) | amazing (ʿajībun).

50:3 What! When we die and have become dust. That is a return far."
What! When (a-idhā) | we die (mit'nā) | and have become (wakunnā) | dust (turāban). | That (dhālika) | is a return (rajʿun) | far. (baʿīdun)"

50:4 Certainly, We know what diminishes the earth of them, and with Us is a Book guarded.
Certainly (qad), | We know (ʿalim'nā) | what (mā) | diminishes (tanquṣu) | the earth (l-arḍu) | of them (min'hum), | and with Us (waʿindanā) | is a Book (kitābun) | guarded (ḥafīẓun).

50:5 Nay, they denied the truth when it came to them, so they are in a state confused.
Nay (bal), | they denied (kadhabū) | the truth (bil-ḥaqi) | when (lammā) | it came to them (jāahum), | so they (fahum) | are in (fī) | a state (amrin) | confused (marījin).

50:6 Then do not they look at the sky above them - how We structured it and adorned it and not for it any rifts?
Then do not (afalam) | they look (yanẓurū) | at (ilā) | the sky (l-samāi) | above them (fawqahum)- | how (kayfa) | We structured it (banaynāhā) | and adorned it (wazayyannāhā) | and not (wamā) | for it (lahā) | any (min) | rifts (furūjin)?

50:7 And the earth, We have spread it out and cast therein firmly set mountains and We made to grow therein of every kind beautiful,
And the earth (wal-arḍa), | We have spread it out (madadnāhā) | and cast (wa-alqaynā) | therein (fīhā) | firmly set mountains (rawāsiya) | and We made to grow (wa-anbatnā) | therein (fīhā) | of (min) | every (kulli) | kind (zawjin) | beautiful (bahījin),

50:8 Giving insight and a reminder for every slave who turns.
Giving insight (tabṣiratan) | and a reminder (wadhik'rā) | for every (likulli) | slave (ʿabdin) | who turns (munībin).

50:9 And We have sent down from the sky water blessed, then We made to grow thereby gardens and grain for the harvest,
And We have sent down (wanazzalnā) | from (mina) | the sky (l-samāi) | water (māan) | blessed (mubārakan), | then We made to grow (fa-anbatnā) | thereby (bihi) | gardens (jannātin) | and grain (waḥabba) | for the harvest (l-ḥaṣīdi),

50:10 And the palms trees tall - for it are layers arranged.
And the palms trees (wal-nakhla) | tall (bāsiqātin)- | for it (lahā) | are layers (ṭalʿun) | arranged (naḍīdun).

50:11 A provision for the slaves, and We give life therewith to a land dead. Thus will be the coming forth.
A provision (riz'qan) | for the slaves (lilʿibādi), | and We give life (wa-aḥyaynā) | therewith (bihi) | to a land (baldatan) | dead (maytan). | Thus (kadhālika) | will be the coming forth (l-khurūju).

50:12 Denied before them the people of Nuh and the companions of Ar-Raas and Thamud,
Denied (kadhabat) | before them (qablahum) | the people (qawmu) | of Nuh (nūḥin) | and the companions (wa-aṣḥābu) | of Ar-Raas (l-rasi) | and Thamud (wathamūdu),

50:13 And Aad and Firaun and the brothers of Lut,

And Aad (waʿādun) | and Firaun (wafir'ʿawnu) | and the brothers (wa-ikh'wānu) | of Lut (lūṭin),

50:14 And the companions of the wood and the people of Tubba. All denied the Messengers, so was fulfilled My Threat.

And the companions (wa-aṣḥābu) | of the wood (l-aykati) | and the people (waqawmu) | of Tubba (tubbaʿin). | All (kullun) | denied (kadhaba) | the Messengers (l-rusula), | so was fulfilled (faḥaqqa) | My Threat (waʿīdi).

50:15 Were We then tired with the creation the first? Nay, they are in doubt about a creation new.

Were We then tired (afaʿayīnā) | with the creation (bil-khalqi) | the first (l-awali)? | Nay (bal), | they (hum) | are in (fī) | doubt (labsin) | about (min) | a creation (khalqin) | new (jadīdin).

50:16 And certainly We created man and We know what whispers to him his soul, and We are nearer to him than his jugular vein.

And certainly (walaqad) | We created (khalaqnā) | man (l-insāna) | and We know (wanaʿlamu) | what (mā) | whispers (tuwaswisu) | to him (bihi) | his soul (nafsuhu), | and We (wanaḥnu) | are nearer (aqrabu) | to him (ilayhi) | than (min) | his jugular vein (ḥabli). | his jugular vein (l-warīdi).

50:17 When receive the two receivers on the right and on the left seated.

When (idh) | receive (yatalaqqā) | the two receivers (l-mutalaqiyāni) | on (ʿani) | the right (l-yamīni) | and on (waʿani) | the left (l-shimāli) | seated (qaʿīdun).

50:18 Not he utters any word but with him is an observer ready.

Not (mā) | he utters (yalfiẓu) | any (min) | word (qawlin) | but (illā) | with him (ladayhi) | is an observer (raqībun) | ready (ʿatīdun).

50:19 And will come the stupor of death in truth, "That is what you were [from it] avoiding."

And will come (wajāat) | the stupor (sakratu) | of death (l-mawti) | in truth (bil-ḥaqi), | "That (dhālika) | is what (mā) | you were (kunta) | [from it] (min'hu) | avoiding. (taḥīdu)"

50:20 And will be blown [in] the trumpet. That is the Day of the Warning.

And will be blown (wanufikha) | [in] (fī) | the trumpet (l-ṣūri). | That (dhālika) | is the Day (yawmu) | of the Warning (l-waʿīdi).

50:21 And will come every soul, with it a driver and a witness.

And will come (wajāat) | every (kullu) | soul (nafsin), | with it (maʿahā) | a driver (sāiqun) | and a witness (washahīdun).

50:22 "Certainly you were in heedlessness of this. So We have removed from you your cover, so your sight today is sharp."

"Certainly (laqad) | you were (kunta) | in (fī) | heedlessness (ghaflatin) | of (min) | this (hādhā). | So We have removed (fakashafnā) | from you (ʿanka) | your cover (ghiṭāaka), | so your sight (fabaṣaruka) | today (l-yawma) | is sharp. (ḥadīdun)"

50:23 And will say his companion, "This is what is with me ready."

And will say (waqāla) | his companion (qarīnuhu), | "This (hādhā) | is what (mā) | is with me (ladayya) | ready. (ʿatīdun)"

50:24 "Throw in to Hell every disbeliever stubborn,

"Throw (alqiyā) | in to (fī) | Hell (jahannama) | every (kulla) | disbeliever (kaffārin) |

stubborn (ʿanīdin),

50:25 Forbidder of good, transgressor doubter,
Forbidder (mannāʿin) | of good (lil'khayri), | transgressor (muʿ'tadin) | doubter (murībin),

50:26 Who made with Allah a god another; so throw him into the punishment the severe."
Who (alladhī) | made (jaʿala) | with (maʿa) | Allah (l-lahi) | a god (ilāhan) | another (ākhara); | so throw him (fa-alqiyāhu) | into (fī) | the punishment (l-ʿadhābi) | the severe. (l-shadīdi)"

50:27 Will say his companion, "Our Lord, not I made him transgress, but he was in error far."
Will say (qāla) | his companion (qarīnuhu), | "Our Lord (rabbanā), | not (mā) | I made him transgress (aṭghaytuhu), | but (walākin) | he was (kāna) | in (fī) | error (ḍalālin) | far. (baʿīdin)"

50:28 He will say, "Do not dispute in My presence and indeed, I sent forth to you the Warning.
He will say (qāla), | "Do not (lā) | dispute (takhtaṣimū) | in My presence (ladayya) | and indeed (waqad), | I sent forth (qaddamtu) | to you (ilaykum) | the Warning (bil-waʿīdi).

50:29 Not will be changed the word with Me, and not I Am unjust to My slaves."
Not (mā) | will be changed (yubaddalu) | the word (l-qawlu) | with Me (ladayya), | and not (wamā) | I Am (anā) | unjust (biẓallāmin) | to My slaves. (lil'ʿabīdi)"

50:30 The Day We will say to Hell, "Are you filled?" And it will say, "Are there any more?"
The Day (yawma) | We will say (naqūlu) | to Hell (lijahannama), | "Are (hali) | you filled? (im'talati)" | And it will say (wataqūlu), | "Are (hal) | there any (min) | more? (mazīdin)"

50:31 And will be brought near the Paradise to the righteous, not far.
And will be brought near (wa-uz'lifati) | the Paradise (l-janatu) | to the righteous (lil'muttaqīna), | not (ghayra) | far (baʿīdin).

50:32 "This is what you were promised, for everyone who turns and who keeps,
"This (hādhā) | is what (mā) | you were promised (tūʿadūna), | for everyone (likulli) | who turns (awwābin) | and who keeps (ḥafīẓin),

50:33 Who feared the Most Gracious in the unseen, and came with a heart returning.
Who (man) | feared (khashiya) | the Most Gracious (l-raḥmāna) | in the unseen (bil-ghaybi), | and came (wajāa) | with a heart (biqalbin) | returning (munībin).

50:34 Enter it in peace. That is a Day of Eternity."
Enter it (ud'khulūhā) | in peace (bisalāmin). | That (dhālika) | is a Day (yawmu) | of Eternity. (l-khulūdi)"

50:35 For them whatever they wish therein and with Us is more.
For them (lahum) | whatever (mā) | they wish (yashāūna) | therein (fīhā) | and with Us (waladaynā) | is more (mazīdun).

50:36 And how many We destroyed before them of a generation, they were stronger than them in power. so they explored throughout the lands. Is there any place of escape?
And how many (wakam) | We destroyed (ahlaknā) | before them (qablahum) | of (min) | a generation (qarnin), | they (hum) | were stronger (ashaddu) | than them (min'hum) | in power (baṭshan). | so they explored (fanaqqabū) | throughout (fī) | the lands (l-bilādi). | Is there (hal) | any (min) | place of escape (maḥīṣin)?

50:37 Indeed, in that surely, is a reminder for one who, is - for him a heart or who gives ear while he is a witness.

Indeed (inna), | in (fī) | that (dhālika) | surely, is a reminder (ladhik'rā) | for one who (liman), | is (kāna)- | for him (lahu) | a heart (qalbun) | or (aw) | who gives ear (alqā) | who gives ear (l-samʿa) | while he (wahuwa) | is a witness (shahīdun).

50:38 And certainly, We created the heavens and the earth and whatever is between both of them in six periods, and did not touch Us any fatigue.

And certainly (walaqad), | We created (khalaqnā) | the heavens (l-samāwāti) | and the earth (wal-arḍa) | and whatever (wamā) | is between both of them (baynahumā) | in (fī) | six (sittati) | periods (ayyāmin), | and did not (wamā) | touch Us (massanā) | any (min) | fatigue (lughūbin).

50:39 So be patient over what they say and glorify the praise of your Lord, before the rising of the sun and before the setting,

So be patient (fa-iṣ'bir) | over (ʿalā) | what (mā) | they say (yaqūlūna) | and glorify (wasabbiḥ) | the praise (biḥamdi) | of your Lord (rabbika), | before (qabla) | the rising (ṭulūʿi) | of the sun (l-shamsi) | and before (waqabla) | the setting (l-ghurūbi),

50:40 And of the night glorify Him and after the prostration.

And of (wamina) | the night (al-layli) | glorify Him (fasabbiḥ'hu) | and after (wa-adbāra) | the prostration (l-sujūdi).

50:41 And listen! The Day will call the caller from a place near,

And listen (wa-is'tamiʿ)! | The Day (yawma) | will call (yunādi) | the caller (l-munādi) | from (min) | a place (makānin) | near (qarībin),

50:42 The Day they will hear the Blast in truth. That is the Day of coming forth.

The Day (yawma) | they will hear (yasmaʿūna) | the Blast (l-ṣayḥata) | in truth (bil-ḥaqi). | That (dhālika) | is the Day (yawmu) | of coming forth (l-khurūji).

50:43 Indeed, We [We] [We] give life and [We] cause death, and to Us is the final return.

Indeed, We (innā) | [We] (naḥnu) | [We] give life (nuḥ'yī) | and [We] cause death (wanumītu), | and to Us (wa-ilaynā) | is the final return (l-maṣīru).

50:44 The Day will split the earth from them, hurrying. That is a gathering for Us easy.

The Day (yawma) | will split (tashaqqaqu) | the earth (l-arḍu) | from them (ʿanhum), | hurrying (sirāʿan). | That (dhālika) | is a gathering (ḥashrun) | for Us (ʿalaynā) | easy (yasīrun).

50:45 We know best [of] what they say, and not are you over them the one to compel. But remind with the Quran whoever fears My threat.

We (naḥnu) | know best (aʿlamu) | [of] what (bimā) | they say (yaqūlūna), | and not (wamā) | are you (anta) | over them (ʿalayhim) | the one to compel (bijabbārin). | But remind (fadhakkir) | with the Quran (bil-qur'āni) | whoever (man) | fears (yakhāfu) | My threat (waʿīdi).

Chapter (51) Sūrat l-Dhāriyāt (The Wind that Scatter)

51:1 By those scattering, dispersing,
By those scattering (wal-dhāriyāti), | dispersing (dharwan),

51:2 And those carrying a load,
And those carrying (fal-ḥāmilāti) | a load (wiq'ran),

51:3 And those sailing with ease,
And those sailing (fal-jāriyāti) | with ease (yus'ran),

51:4 And those distributing Command,
And those distributing (fal-muqasimāti) | Command (amran),

51:5 Indeed, what you are promised is surely true,
Indeed, what (innamā) | you are promised (tūʿadūna) | is surely true (laṣādiqun),

51:6 And indeed, the Judgment is surely to occur.
And indeed (wa-inna), | the Judgment (l-dīna) | is surely to occur (lawāqiʿun).

51:7 By the heaven full of pathways.
By the heaven (wal-samāi) | full of (dhāti) | pathways (l-ḥubuki).

51:8 Indeed, you are surely in a speech differing.
Indeed, you (innakum) | are surely in (lafī) | a speech (qawlin) | differing (mukh'talifin).

51:9 Deluded away from it is he who is deluded.
Deluded away (yu'faku) | from it (ʿanhu) | is he who (man) | is deluded (ufika).

51:10 Cursed be the liars,
Cursed be (qutila) | the liars (l-kharāṣūna),

51:11 Those who [they] are in flood of heedlessness.
Those who (alladhīna) | [they] (hum) | are in (fī) | flood (ghamratin) | of heedlessness (sāhūna).

51:12 They ask, "When is the Day of Judgment?"
They ask (yasalūna), | "When (ayyāna) | is the Day (yawmu) | of Judgment? (l-dīni)"

51:13 A Day, they over the Fire will be tried,
A Day (yawma), | they (hum) | over (ʿalā) | the Fire (l-nāri) | will be tried (yuf'tanūna),

51:14 "Taste your trial. This is what you were for it seeking to hasten."
"Taste (dhūqū) | your trial (fit'natakum). | This (hādhā) | is what (alladhī) | you were (kuntum) | for it (bihi) | seeking to hasten. (tastaʿjilūna)"

51:15 Indeed, the righteous will be in Gardens and springs,
Indeed (inna), | the righteous (l-mutaqīna) | will be in (fī) | Gardens (jannātin) | and springs (waʿuyūnin),

51:16 Taking what their Lord has given them. Indeed, they were before that good-doers.

Taking (ākhidhīna) | what (mā) | their Lord has given them (ātāhum). | their Lord has given them (rabbuhum). | Indeed, they (innahum) | were (kānū) | before (qabla) | that (dhālika) | good-doers (muḥ'sinīna).

51:17 They used to little of the night [what] sleep.
They used to (kānū) | little (qalīlan) | of (mina) | the night (al-layli) | [what] (mā) | sleep (yahjaʿūna).

51:18 And in the hours before dawn they would ask forgiveness,
And in the hours before dawn (wabil-asḥāri) | they (hum) | would ask forgiveness (yastaghfirūna),

51:19 And in their wealth was the right of those who asked and the deprived.
And in (wafī) | their wealth (amwālihim) | was the right (ḥaqqun) | of those who asked (lilssāili) | and the deprived (wal-maḥrūmi).

51:20 And in the earth are signs for those who are certain,
And in (wafī) | the earth (l-arḍi) | are signs (āyātun) | for those who are certain (lil'mūqinīna),

51:21 And in yourselves. Then will not you see?
And in (wafī) | yourselves (anfusikum). | Then will not (afalā) | you see (tub'ṣirūna)?

51:22 And in the heaven is your provision and what you are promised.
And in (wafī) | the heaven (l-samāi) | is your provision (riz'qukum) | and what (wamā) | you are promised (tūʿadūna).

51:23 Then by the Lord of the heaven and the earth, indeed, it is surely (the) truth just as [what] you speak.
Then by the Lord (fawarabbi) | of the heaven (l-samāi) | and the earth (wal-arḍi), | indeed, it (innahu) | is surely (the) truth (laḥaqqun) | just as (mith'la) | [what] (mā) | you (annakum) | speak (tanṭiqūna).

51:24 Has reached you the narration of the guests of Ibrahim the honored?
Has (hal) | reached you (atāka) | the narration (ḥadīthu) | of the guests (ḍayfi) | of Ibrahim (ib'rāhīma) | the honored (l-muk'ramīna)?

51:25 When they entered upon him and said, "Peace." He said, "Peace, a people unknown."
When (idh) | they entered (dakhalū) | upon him (ʿalayhi) | and said (faqālū), | "Peace. (salāman)" | He said (qāla), | "Peace (salāmun), | a people (qawmun) | unknown. (munkarūna)"

51:26 Then he went to his household and came with a calf fat,
Then he went (farāgha) | to (ilā) | his household (ahlihi) | and came (fajāa) | with a calf (biʿij'lin) | fat (samīnin),

51:27 And he placed it near [to] them, he said, "Will not you eat?"
And he placed it near (faqarrabahu) | [to] them (ilayhim), | he said (qāla), | "Will not (alā) | you eat? (takulūna)"

51:28 Then he felt from them a fear. They said, "Do not fear," and they gave him glad tidings of a son learned.
Then he felt (fa-awjasa) | from them (min'hum) | a fear (khīfatan). | They said (qālū), | "Do

not (lā) | fear, (takhaf)" | and they gave him glad tidings (wabasharūhu) | of a son (bighulāmin) | learned (ʿalīmin).

51:29 Then came forward his wife with a loud voice, and struck her face and she said, "An old woman barren!"

Then came forward (fa-aqbalati) | his wife (im'ra-atuhu) | with (fī) | a loud voice (ṣarratin), | and struck (faṣakkat) | her face (wajhahā) | and she said (waqālat), | "An old woman (ʿajūzun) | barren! (ʿaqīmun)"

51:30 They said, "Thus said your Lord. Indeed, He [He] is the All-Wise, the All-Knower."

They said (qālū), | "Thus (kadhāliki) | said (qāla) | your Lord (rabbuki). | Indeed, He (innahu) | [He] (huwa) | is the All-Wise (l-ḥakīmu), | the All-Knower. (l-ʿalīmu)"

51:31 He said, "Then what is your mission, O messengers?"

He said (qāla), | "Then what (famā) | is your mission (khaṭbukum), | O messengers? (ayyuhā)" | O messengers? (l-mur'salūna)"

51:32 They said, "Indeed, we [we] have been sent to a people criminal,

They said (qālū), | "Indeed, we (innā) | [we] have been sent (ur'sil'nā) | to (ilā) | a people (qawmin) | criminal (muj'rimīna),

51:33 That we may send down upon them stones of clay,

That we may send down (linur'sila) | upon them (ʿalayhim) | stones (ḥijāratan) | of (min) | clay (ṭīnin),

51:34 Marked by your Lord for the transgressors."

Marked (musawwamatan) | by your Lord (ʿinda) | by your Lord (rabbika) | for the transgressors. (lil'mus'rifīna)"

51:35 Then We brought out those who were therein of the believers.

Then We brought out (fa-akhrajnā) | those who (man) | were (kāna) | therein (fīhā) | of (mina) | the believers (l-mu'minīna).

51:36 But not We found therein other than a house of the Muslims.

But not (famā) | We found (wajadnā) | therein (fīhā) | other than (ghayra) | a house (baytin) | of (mina) | the Muslims (l-mus'limīna).

51:37 And We left therein a Sign for those who fear the punishment the painful.

And We left (wataraknā) | therein (fīhā) | a Sign (āyatan) | for those who (lilladhīna) | fear (yakhāfūna) | the punishment (l-ʿadhāba) | the painful (l-alīma).

51:38 And in Musa, when We sent him to Firaun with an authority clear.

And in (wafī) | Musa (mūsā), | when (idh) | We sent him (arsalnāhu) | to (ilā) | Firaun (fir'ʿawna) | with an authority (bisul'ṭānin) | clear (mubīnin).

51:39 But he turned away with his supporters and said, "A magician or a madman."

But he turned away (fatawallā) | with his supporters (biruk'nihi) | and said (waqāla), | "A magician (sāḥirun) | or (aw) | a madman. (majnūnun)"

51:40 So We took him and his hosts and threw them into the sea, while he was blameworthy.

So We took him (fa-akhadhnāhu) | and his hosts (wajunūdahu) | and threw them (fanabadhnāhum) | into (fī) | the sea (l-yami), | while he (wahuwa) | was blameworthy (mulīmun).

51:41 And in Aad, when We sent against them the wind the barren.
And in (wafī) | Aad (ʿādin), | when (idh) | We sent (arsalnā) | against them (ʿalayhimu) | the wind (l-rīḥa) | the barren (l-ʿaqīma).

51:42 Not it left any thing it came upon it, but it made it like disintegrated ruins.
Not (mā) | it left (tadharu) | any (min) | thing (shayin) | it came (atat) | upon it (ʿalayhi), | but (illā) | it made it (jaʿalathu) | like disintegrated ruins (kal-ramīmi).

51:43 And in Thamud, when was said to them, "Enjoy yourselves for a time."
And in (wafī) | Thamud (thamūda), | when (idh) | was said (qīla) | to them (lahum), | "Enjoy yourselves (tamattaʿū) | for (ḥattā) | a time. (ḥīnin)"

51:44 But they rebelled against the Command of their Lord, so seized them the thunderbolt while they were looking.
But they rebelled (faʿataw) | against (ʿan) | the Command (amri) | of their Lord (rabbihim), | so seized them (fa-akhadhathumu) | the thunderbolt (l-ṣāʿiqatu) | while they (wahum) | were looking (yanẓurūna).

51:45 Then not they were able to [of] stand and not they could help themselves.
Then not (famā) | they were able to (is'taṭāʿū) | [of] (min) | stand (qiyāmin) | and not (wamā) | they could (kānū) | help themselves (muntaṣirīna).

51:46 And the people of Nuh before; indeed, they were a people defiantly disobedient.
And the people (waqawma) | of Nuh (nūḥin) | before (min); | before (qablu); | indeed, they (innahum) | were (kānū) | a people (qawman) | defiantly disobedient (fāsiqīna).

51:47 And the heaven We constructed it with strength, and indeed, We are surely (its) Expanders.
And the heaven (wal-samāa) | We constructed it (banaynāhā) | with strength (bi-aydin), | and indeed, We (wa-innā) | are surely (its) Expanders (lamūsiʿūna).

51:48 And the earth, We have spread it; how excellent are the Spreaders!
And the earth (wal-arḍa), | We have spread it (farashnāhā); | how excellent (faniʿ'ma) | are the Spreaders (l-māhidūna)!

51:49 And of every thing We have created pairs, so that you may remember.
And of (wamin) | every (kulli) | thing (shayin) | We have created (khalaqnā) | pairs (zawjayni), | so that you may (laʿallakum) | remember (tadhakkarūna).

51:50 So flee to Allah, indeed, I am to you from Him a warner clear.
So flee (fafirrū) | to (ilā) | Allah (l-lahi), | indeed, I am (innī) | to you (lakum) | from Him (min'hu) | a warner (nadhīrun) | clear (mubīnun).

51:51 And do not make with Allah god another. Indeed, I am to you from Him a warner clear.
And do not (walā) | make (tajʿalū) | with (maʿa) | Allah (l-lahi) | god (ilāhan) | another (ākhara). | Indeed, I am (innī) | to you (lakum) | from Him (min'hu) | a warner (nadhīrun) | clear (mubīnun).

51:52 Likewise not came to those before them any Messenger but they said, "A magician or a madman."
Likewise (kadhālika) | not (mā) | came (atā) | to those (alladhīna) | before them (min) | before them (qablihim) | any (min) | Messenger (rasūlin) | but (illā) | they said (qālū), | "A magician

(sāḥirun) | or (aw) | a madman. (majnūnun)"

51:53 Have they transmitted it to them? Nay, they are a people transgressing.
Have they transmitted it to them (atawāṣaw)? | Have they transmitted it to them (bihi)? | Nay (bal), | they (hum) | are a people (qawmun) | transgressing (ṭāghūna).

51:54 So turn away from them, for not you are to be blamed.
So turn away (fatawalla) | from them (ʿanhum), | for not (famā) | you (anta) | are to be blamed (bimalūmin).

51:55 And remind, for indeed, the reminder benefits the believers.
And remind (wadhakkir), | for indeed (fa-inna), | the reminder (l-dhik'rā) | benefits (tanfaʿu) | the believers (l-mu'minīna).

51:56 And not I have created the jinn and the mankind except that they worship Me.
And not (wamā) | I have created (khalaqtu) | the jinn (l-jina) | and the mankind (wal-insa) | except (illā) | that they worship Me (liyaʿbudūni).

51:57 Not I want from them any provision and not I want that they should feed Me.
Not (mā) | I want (urīdu) | from them (min'hum) | any (min) | provision (riz'qin) | and not (wamā) | I want (urīdu) | that (an) | they should feed Me (yuṭ'ʿimūni).

51:58 Indeed, Allah, He is the All-Provider, Possessor of Power the Strong.
Indeed (inna), | Allah (l-laha), | He (huwa) | is the All-Provider (l-razāqu), | Possessor (dhū) | of Power (l-quwati) | the Strong (l-matīnu).

51:59 So indeed, for those who do wrong, is a portion like the portion of their companions, so let them not ask Me to hasten.
So indeed (fa-inna), | for those who (lilladhīna) | do wrong (ẓalamū), | is a portion (dhanūban) | like (mith'la) | the portion (dhanūbi) | of their companions (aṣḥābihim), | so let them not ask Me to hasten (falā). | so let them not ask Me to hasten (yastaʿjilūni).

51:60 Then woe to those who disbelieve from their Day which they are promised.
Then woe (fawaylun) | to those who (lilladhīna) | disbelieve (kafarū) | from (min) | their Day (yawmihimu) | which (alladhī) | they are promised (yūʿadūna).

Chapter (52) Sūrat l-Ṭūr (The Mount)

52:1 By the Mount,
By the Mount (wal-ṭūri),

52:2 And by the Book written
And by the Book (wakitābin) | written (masṭūrin)

52:3 In parchment unrolled,
In (fī) | parchment (raqqin) | unrolled (manshūrin),

52:4 By the House frequented
By the House (wal-bayti) | frequented (l-maʿmūri)

52:5 By the roof raised high
By the roof (wal-saqfi) | raised high (l-marfūʿi)

52:6 By the sea filled
By the sea (wal-baḥri) | filled (l-masjūri)

52:7 Indeed, the punishment of your Lord will surely occur.
Indeed (inna), | the punishment (ʿadhāba) | of your Lord (rabbika) | will surely occur (lawāqiʿun).

52:8 Not for it any preventer.
Not (mā) | for it (lahu) | any (min) | preventer (dāfiʿin).

52:9 On the Day will shake the heaven with violent shake
On the Day (yawma) | will shake (tamūru) | the heaven (l-samāu) | with violent shake (mawran)

52:10 And will move away, the mountains with an awful movement
And will move away (watasīru), | the mountains (l-jibālu) | with an awful movement (sayran)

52:11 Then woe, that Day, to the deniers,
Then woe (fawaylun), | that Day (yawma-idhin), | to the deniers (lil'mukadhibīna),

52:12 Who [they] in vain discourse are playing.
Who (alladhīna) | [they] (hum) | in (fī) | vain discourse (khawḍin) | are playing (yalʿabūna).

52:13 The Day they will be thrust into the Fire of Hell with a thrust.
The Day (yawma) | they will be thrust (yudaʿʿūna) | into (ilā) | the Fire (nāri) | of Hell (jahannama) | with a thrust (daʿʿan).

52:14 "This is the Fire which you used to [of it] deny.
"This (hādhihi) | is the Fire (l-nāru) | which (allatī) | you used to (kuntum) | [of it] (bihā) | deny (tukadhibūna).

52:15 Then is this magic, or you do not see?
Then is this magic (afasiḥ'run), | Then is this magic (hādhā), | or (am) | you (antum) | do not (lā) | see (tub'ṣirūna)?

52:16 Burn in it then be patient or do not be patient, it is same for you. Only you are being recompensed for what you used to do."
Burn in it (iṣ'lawhā) | then be patient (fa-iṣ'birū) | or (aw) | do not (lā) | be patient (taṣbirū), | it is same (sawāon) | for you (ʿalaykum). | Only (innamā) | you are being recompensed (tuj'zawna) | for what (mā) | you used to (kuntum) | do. (taʿmalūna)"

52:17 Indeed, the righteous will be in Gardens and pleasure,
Indeed (inna), | the righteous (l-mutaqīna) | will be in (fī) | Gardens (jannātin) | and pleasure (wanaʿīmin),

52:18 Enjoying in what has given them their Lord, and protected them their Lord from the punishment of Hellfire.

Enjoying (fākihīna) | in what (bimā) | has given them (ātāhum) | their Lord (rabbuhum), | and protected them (wawaqāhum) | their Lord (rabbuhum) | from the punishment (ʿadhāba) | of Hellfire (l-jaḥīmi).

52:19 "Eat and drink in satisfaction for what you used to do."

"Eat (kulū) | and drink (wa-ish'rabū) | in satisfaction (hanīan) | for what (bimā) | you used to (kuntum) | do. (taʿmalūna)"

52:20 Reclining on thrones lined up, and We will marry them to fair ones with large eyes.

Reclining (muttakiīna) | on (ʿalā) | thrones (sururin) | lined up (maṣfūfatin), | and We will marry them (wazawwajnāhum) | to fair ones (biḥūrin) | with large eyes (ʿīnin).

52:21 And those who believed and followed them their offspring in faith, We will join with them their offspring and not We will deprive them of their deeds in any thing. Every person for what he earned is pledged.

And those who (wa-alladhīna) | believed (āmanū) | and followed them (wa-ittabaʿathum) | their offspring (dhurriyyatuhum) | in faith (biīmānin), | We will join (alḥaqnā) | with them (bihim) | their offspring (dhurriyyatahum) | and not (wamā) | We will deprive them (alatnāhum) | of (min) | their deeds (ʿamalihim) | in any (min) | thing (shayin). | Every (kullu) | person (im'ri-in) | for what (bimā) | he earned (kasaba) | is pledged (rahīnun).

52:22 And We will provide them with fruit and meat from what they desire.

And We will provide them (wa-amdadnāhum) | with fruit (bifākihatin) | and meat (walaḥmin) | from what (mimmā) | they desire (yashtahūna).

52:23 They will pass to one another therein a cup, no ill speech therein and no sin.

They will pass to one another (yatanāzaʿūna) | therein (fīhā) | a cup (kasan), | no (lā) | ill speech (laghwun) | therein (fīhā) | and no (walā) | sin (tathīmun).

52:24 And will circulate among them boys for them, as if they were pearls well-protected.

And will circulate (wayaṭūfu) | among them (ʿalayhim) | boys (ghil'mānun) | for them (lahum), | as if they were (ka-annahum) | pearls (lu'lu-on) | well-protected (maknūnun).

52:25 And will approach some of them to others inquiring.

And will approach (wa-aqbala) | some of them (baʿḍuhum) | to (ʿalā) | others (baʿḍin) | inquiring (yatasāalūna).

52:26 They will say, "Indeed, we [we] were before among our families fearful,

They will say (qālū), | "Indeed, we (innā) | [we] were (kunnā) | before (qablu) | among (fī) | our families (ahlinā) | fearful (mush'fiqīna),

52:27 But Allah conferred favor upon us, and protected us from the punishment of the Scorching Fire.

But Allah conferred favor (famanna) | But Allah conferred favor (l-lahu) | upon us (ʿalaynā), | and protected us (wawaqānā) | from the punishment (ʿadhāba) | of the Scorching Fire (l-samūmi).

52:28 Indeed, we [we] used to before call Him. Indeed, He [He] is the Most Kind, the Most Merciful."

Indeed, we (innā) | [we] used to (kunnā) | before (min) | before (qablu) | call Him (nadʿūhu). | Indeed, He (innahu) | [He] (huwa) | is the Most Kind (l-baru), | the Most Merciful.

(l-raḥīmu)"

52:29 Therefore remind, for not you are by (the) grace of your Lord a soothsayer, and not a madman.
Therefore remind (fadhakkir), | for not (famā) | you (anta) | are by (the) grace (biniʿmati) | of your Lord (rabbika) | a soothsayer (bikāhinin), | and not (walā) | a madman (majnūnin).

52:30 Or do they say, "A poet, we wait for him a misfortune of time."
Or (am) | do they say (yaqūlūna), | "A poet (shāʿirun), | we wait (natarabbaṣu) | for him (bihi) | a misfortune of time. (rayba)" | a misfortune of time. (l-manūni)"

52:31 Say, "Wait, for indeed I am, with you, among those who wait."
Say (qul), | "Wait (tarabbaṣū), | for indeed I am (fa-innī), | with you (maʿakum), | among (mina) | those who wait. (l-mutarabiṣīna)"

52:32 Or command them their minds this, or they are a people transgressing?
Or (am) | command them (tamuruhum) | their minds (aḥlāmuhum) | this (bihādhā), | or (am) | they (hum) | are a people (qawmun) | transgressing (ṭāghūna)?

52:33 Or do they say, "He has made it up" Nay, not they believe.
Or (am) | do they say (yaqūlūna), | "He has made it up (taqawwalahu)" | Nay (bal), | not (lā) | they believe (yu'minūna).

52:34 Then let them bring a statement like it, if they are truthful.
Then let them bring (falyatū) | a statement (biḥadīthin) | like it (mith'lihi), | if (in) | they are (kānū) | truthful (ṣādiqīna).

52:35 Or they were created of nothing, or are they the creators?
Or (am) | they were created (khuliqū) | of (min) | nothing (ghayri), | nothing (shayin), | or (am) | are they (humu) | the creators (l-khāliqūna)?

52:36 Or did they create the heavens and the earth? Nay, not they are certain.
Or (am) | did they create (khalaqū) | the heavens (l-samāwāti) | and the earth (wal-arḍa)? | Nay (bal), | not (lā) | they are certain (yūqinūna).

52:37 Or with them are the treasures of your Lord or are they the controllers?
Or (am) | with them (ʿindahum) | are the treasures (khazāinu) | of your Lord (rabbika) | or (am) | are they (humu) | the controllers (l-muṣayṭirūna)?

52:38 Or for them is a stairway, they listen therewith? Then let bring, their listener, an authority clear.
Or (am) | for them (lahum) | is a stairway (sullamun), | they listen (yastamiʿūna) | therewith (fīhi)? | Then let bring (falyati), | their listener (mus'tamiʿuhum), | an authority (bisul'ṭānin) | clear (mubīnin).

52:39 Or for Him are daughters while for you are sons?
Or (am) | for Him (lahu) | are daughters (l-banātu) | while for you (walakumu) | are sons (l-banūna)?

52:40 Or do you ask from them a payment, so they from a debt are overburdened.
Or (am) | do you ask from them (tasaluhum) | a payment (ajran), | so they (fahum) | from (min) | a debt (maghramin) | are overburdened (muth'qalūna).

52:41 Or with them is the unseen, so they write it down?
Or (am) | with them (ʿindahumu) | is the unseen (l-ghaybu), | so they (fahum) | write it down (yaktubūna)?

52:42 Or do they intend a plot? But those who disbelieve, themselves are in the plot.
Or (am) | do they intend (yurīdūna) | a plot (kaydan)? | But those who (fa-alladhīna) | disbelieve (kafarū), | themselves (humu) | are in the plot (l-makīdūna).

52:43 Or for them a god other than Allah? Glory be to Allah from what they associate with Him.
Or (am) | for them (lahum) | a god (ilāhun) | other than (ghayru) | Allah (l-lahi)? | Glory be (sub'ḥāna) | to Allah (l-lahi) | from what (ʿammā) | they associate with Him (yush'rikūna).

52:44 And if they were to see a portion from the sky falling, they will say, "Clouds heaped up."
And if (wa-in) | they were to see (yaraw) | a portion (kis'fan) | from (mina) | the sky (l-samāi) | falling (sāqiṭan), | they will say (yaqūlū), | "Clouds (saḥābun) | heaped up. (markūmun)"

52:45 So leave them until they meet their Day which in it they will faint.
So leave them (fadharhum) | until (ḥattā) | they meet (yulāqū) | their Day (yawmahumu) | which (alladhī) | in it (fīhi) | they will faint (yuṣ'ʿaqūna).

52:46 The Day not will avail to them their plotting in anything, and not they will be helped.
The Day (yawma) | not (lā) | will avail (yugh'nī) | to them (ʿanhum) | their plotting (kayduhum) | in anything (shayan), | and not (walā) | they (hum) | will be helped (yunṣarūna).

52:47 And indeed, for those who do wrong, is a punishment before that, but most of them do not know.
And indeed (wa-inna), | for those who (lilladhīna) | do wrong (ẓalamū), | is a punishment (ʿadhāban) | before (dūna) | that (dhālika), | but (walākinna) | most of them (aktharahum) | do not (lā) | know (yaʿlamūna).

52:48 So be patient, for the Command of your Lord, for indeed, you are in Our Eyes. And glorify the praise of your Lord when you arise,
So be patient (wa-iṣ'bir), | for the Command (liḥuk'mi) | of your Lord (rabbika), | for indeed, you (fa-innaka) | are in Our Eyes (bi-aʿyuninā). | And glorify (wasabbiḥ) | the praise (biḥamdi) | of your Lord (rabbika) | when (ḥīna) | you arise (taqūmu),

52:49 And of the night, glorify Him, and after the stars.
And of (wamina) | the night (al-layli), | glorify Him (fasabbiḥ'hu), | and after (wa-id'bāra) | the stars (l-nujūmi).

Chapter (53) Sūrat l-Najm (The Star)

53:1 By the star when it goes down,
By the star (wal-najmi) | when (idhā) | it goes down (hawā),

53:2 Not has strayed your companion and not has he erred,
Not (mā) | has strayed (ḍalla) | your companion (ṣāḥibukum) | and not (wamā) | has he erred (ghawā),

53:3 And not he speaks from the desire.
And not (wamā) | he speaks (yanṭiqu) | from (ʿani) | the desire (l-hawā).

53:4 Not it is except a revelation revealed,
Not (in) | it (huwa) | is except (illā) | a revelation (waḥyun) | revealed (yūḥā),

53:5 Has taught him the one mighty in power,
Has taught him (ʿallamahu) | the one mighty (shadīdu) | in power (l-quwā),

53:6 Possessor of soundness. And he rose,
Possessor of soundness (dhū). | Possessor of soundness (mirratin). | And he rose (fa-is'tawā),

53:7 While he was in the horizon - the highest.
While he (wahuwa) | was in the horizon (bil-ufuqi)- | the highest (l-aʿlā).

53:8 Then he approached and came down,
Then (thumma) | he approached (danā) | and came down (fatadallā),

53:9 And was at a distance of two bow-(lengths) or nearer.
And was (fakāna) | at a distance (qāba) | of two bow-(lengths (qawsayni)) | or (aw) | nearer (adnā).

53:10 So he revealed to His slave what he revealed.
So he revealed (fa-awḥā) | to (ilā) | His slave (ʿabdihi) | what (mā) | he revealed (awḥā).

53:11 Not lied the heart what it saw.
Not (mā) | lied (kadhaba) | the heart (l-fuādu) | what (mā) | it saw (raā).

53:12 Then will you dispute with him about what he saw?
Then will you dispute with him (afatumārūnahu) | about (ʿalā) | what (mā) | he saw (yarā)?

53:13 And certainly he saw him in descent another,
And certainly (walaqad) | he saw him (raāhu) | in descent (nazlatan) | another (ukh'rā),

53:14 Near the Lote Tree of the utmost boundary,
Near (ʿinda) | the Lote Tree (sid'rati) | of the utmost boundary (l-muntahā),

53:15 Near it is the Garden of Abode.
Near it (ʿindahā) | is the Garden (jannatu) | of Abode (l-mawā).

53:16 When covered the Lote Tree what covers,
When (idh) | covered (yaghshā) | the Lote Tree (l-sid'rata) | what (mā) | covers (yaghshā),

53:17 Not swerved the sight and not it transgressed.
Not (mā) | swerved (zāgha) | the sight (l-baṣaru) | and not (wamā) | it transgressed (ṭaghā).

53:18 Certainly he saw of the Signs of his Lord the Greatest.
Certainly (laqad) | he saw (raā) | of (min) | the Signs (āyāti) | of his Lord (rabbihi) | the Greatest (l-kub'rā).

53:19 So have you seen the Lat and the Uzza,
So have you seen (afara-aytumu) | the Lat (l-lāta) | and the Uzza (wal-ʿuzā),

53:20 And Manat the third, the other?
And Manat (wamanata) | the third (l-thālithata), | the other (l-ukh'rā)?

53:21 Is for you the male and for Him the female?
Is for you (alakumu) | the male (l-dhakaru) | and for Him (walahu) | the female (l-unthā)?

53:22 This, then, is a division unfair.
This (til'ka), | then (idhan), | is a division (qis'matun) | unfair (ḍīzā).

53:23 Not they are except names you have named them, you and your forefathers, not has Allah sent down for it any authority. Not they follow except assumption and what desire their souls. And certainly has come to them from their Lord the guidance.
Not (in) | they (hiya) | are except (illā) | names (asmāon) | you have named them (sammaytumūhā), | you (antum) | and your forefathers (waābāukum), | not (mā) | has Allah sent down (anzala) | has Allah sent down (l-lahu) | for it (bihā) | any (min) | authority (sul'ṭānin). | Not (in) | they follow (yattabiʿūna) | except (illā) | assumption (l-ẓana) | and what (wamā) | desire (tahwā) | their souls (l-anfusu). | And certainly (walaqad) | has come to them (jāahum) | from (min) | their Lord (rabbihimu) | the guidance (l-hudā).

53:24 Or is for man what he wishes?
Or (am) | is for man (lil'insāni) | what (mā) | he wishes (tamannā)?

53:25 But for Allah is the last and the first.
But for Allah (falillahi) | is the last (l-ākhiratu) | and the first (wal-ūlā).

53:26 And how many of the Angels in the heavens not will avail their intercession anything except after [that] Allah has given permission for whom He wills and approves.
And how many (wakam) | of (min) | the Angels (malakin) | in (fī) | the heavens (l-samāwāti) | not (lā) | will avail (tugh'nī) | their intercession (shafāʿatuhum) | anything (shayan) | except (illā) | after (min) | after (baʿdi) | [that] (an) | Allah has given permission (yadhana) | Allah has given permission (l-lahu) | for whom (liman) | He wills (yashāu) | and approves (wayarḍā).

53:27 Indeed, those who do not believe in the Hereafter, surely they name the Angels names of female,
Indeed (inna), | those who (alladhīna) | do not (lā) | believe (yu'minūna) | in the Hereafter (bil-ākhirati), | surely they name (layusammūna) | the Angels (l-malāikata) | names (tasmiyata) | of female (l-unthā),

53:28 And not for them about it any knowledge. Not they follow but assumption. And indeed, the assumption does not avail against the truth anything.
And not (wamā) | for them (lahum) | about it (bihi) | any (min) | knowledge (ʿil'min). | Not (in) | they follow (yattabiʿūna) | but (illā) | assumption (l-ẓana). | And indeed (wa-inna), | the assumption (l-ẓana) | does not (lā) | avail (yugh'nī) | against (mina) | the truth (l-ḥaqi) | anything (shayan).

53:29 So turn away from him who turns away from Our Reminder and not he desires except the life of the world.

So turn away (fa-aʿriḍ) | from (ʿan) | him who (man) | turns away (tawallā) | from (ʿan) | Our Reminder (dhik'rinā) | and not (walam) | he desires (yurid) | except (illā) | the life (l-ḥayata) | of the world (l-dun'yā).

53:30 That is their sum of knowledge. Indeed, your Lord is He (Who) knows best he who strays from His Path, and He knows best he who is guided.

That (dhālika) | is their sum (mablaghuhum) | of (mina) | knowledge (l-ʿil'mi). | Indeed (inna), | your Lord (rabbaka) | is He (Who (huwa)) | knows best (aʿlamu) | he who (biman) | strays (ḍalla) | from (ʿan) | His Path (sabīlihi), | and He (wahuwa) | knows best (aʿlamu) | he who (bimani) | is guided (ih'tadā).

53:31 And for Allah is whatever is in the heavens and whatever is in the earth that He may recompense those who do evil with what they have done and recompense those who do good with the best.

And for Allah (walillahi) | is whatever (mā) | is in (fī) | the heavens (l-samāwāti) | and whatever (wamā) | is in (fī) | the earth (l-arḍi) | that He may recompense (liyajziya) | those who (alladhīna) | do evil (asāū) | with what (bimā) | they have done (ʿamilū) | and recompense (wayajziya) | those who (alladhīna) | do good (aḥsanū) | with the best (bil-ḥus'nā).

53:32 Those who avoid great sins and the immoralities except the small faults; indeed, your Lord is vast in forgiveness. He is most knowing about you when He produced you from the earth and when you were fetuses in the wombs of your mothers. So do not ascribe purity to yourselves. He knows best he who fears.

Those who (alladhīna) | avoid (yajtanibūna) | great (kabāira) | sins (l-ith'mi) | and the immoralities (wal-fawāḥisha) | except (illā) | the small faults (l-lamama); | indeed (inna), | your Lord (rabbaka) | is vast (wāsiʿu) | in forgiveness (l-maghfirati). | He (huwa) | is most knowing about you (aʿlamu) | is most knowing about you (bikum) | when (idh) | He produced you (ansha-akum) | from (mina) | the earth (l-arḍi) | and when (wa-idh) | you were (antum) | fetuses (ajinnatun) | in (fī) | the wombs (buṭūni) | of your mothers (ummahātikum). | So do not (falā) | ascribe purity (tuzakkū) | to yourselves (anfusakum). | He (huwa) | knows best (aʿlamu) | he who (bimani) | fears (ittaqā).

53:33 Did you see the one who turned away

Did you see (afara-ayta) | the one who (alladhī) | turned away (tawallā)

53:34 And gave a little, and withheld?

And gave (wa-aʿṭā) | a little (qalīlan), | and withheld (wa-akdā)?

53:35 Is with him the knowledge of the unseen, so he sees?

Is with him (aʿindahu) | the knowledge (ʿil'mu) | of the unseen (l-ghaybi), | so he (fahuwa) | sees (yarā)?

53:36 Or not he was informed with what was in the Scriptures of Musa,

Or (am) | not (lam) | he was informed (yunabba) | with what (bimā) | was in (fī) | the Scriptures (ṣuḥufi) | of Musa (mūsā),

53:37 And Ibrahim, who fulfilled?

And Ibrahim (wa-ib'rāhīma), | who (alladhī) | fulfilled (waffā)?

53:38 That not will bear a bearer of burdens the burden of another,

That not (allā) | will bear (taziru) | a bearer of burdens (wāziratun) | the burden (wiz'ra) |

of another (ukh'rā),

53:39 And that is not for man except what he strives for,
And that (wa-an) | is not (laysa) | for man (lil'insāni) | except (illā) | what (mā) | he strives for (saʿā),

53:40 And that his striving will soon be seen.
And that (wa-anna) | his striving (saʿyahu) | will soon (sawfa) | be seen (yurā).

53:41 Then he will be recompensed for it the recompense the fullest.
Then (thumma) | he will be recompensed for it (yuj'zāhu) | the recompense (l-jazāa) | the fullest (l-awfā).

53:42 And that to your Lord is the final goal.
And that (wa-anna) | to (ilā) | your Lord (rabbika) | is the final goal (l-muntahā).

53:43 And that He [He] makes one laugh and makes one weep.
And that He (wa-annahu) | [He] (huwa) | makes one laugh (aḍḥaka) | and makes one weep (wa-abkā).

53:44 And that He [He] causes death and gives life.
And that He (wa-annahu) | [He] (huwa) | causes death (amāta) | and gives life (wa-aḥyā).

53:45 And that He created the pairs, the male and the female
And that He (wa-annahu) | created (khalaqa) | the pairs (l-zawjayni), | the male (l-dhakara) | and the female (wal-unthā)

53:46 From a semen-drop when it is emitted.
From (min) | a semen-drop (nuṭ'fatin) | when (idhā) | it is emitted (tum'nā).

53:47 And that upon Him is the bringing forth another.
And that (wa-anna) | upon Him (ʿalayhi) | is the bringing forth (l-nashata) | another (l-ukh'rā).

53:48 And that He [He] enriches and suffices.
And that He (wa-annahu) | [He] (huwa) | enriches (aghnā) | and suffices (wa-aqnā).

53:49 And that He [He] is the Lord of Sirius
And that He (wa-annahu) | [He] (huwa) | is the Lord (rabbu) | of Sirius (l-shiʿ'rā)

53:50 And that He destroyed Aad the first,
And that He (wa-annahu) | destroyed (ahlaka) | Aad (ʿādan) | the first (l-ūlā),

53:51 And Thamud, so not He spared,
And Thamud (wathamūdā), | so not (famā) | He spared (abqā),

53:52 And the people of Nuh before. Indeed, they they were more unjust and more rebellious.
And the people (waqawma) | of Nuh (nūḥin) | before (min). | before (qablu). | Indeed, they (innahum) | they were (kānū) | they were (hum) | more unjust (aẓlama) | and more rebellious (wa-aṭghā).

53:53 And the overturned cities He overthrew

And the overturned cities (wal-mu'tafikata) | He overthrew (ahwā)

53:54 So covered them what covered.
So covered them (faghashāhā) | what (mā) | covered (ghashā).

53:55 Then which of the Favors of your Lord, will you doubt?
Then which of (fabi-ayyi) | the Favors (ālāi) | of your Lord (rabbika), | will you doubt (tatamārā)?

53:56 This is a warner, from the warners the former.
This (hādhā) | is a warner (nadhīrun), | from (mina) | the warners (l-nudhuri) | the former (l-ūlā).

53:57 Has approached the Approaching Day.
Has approached (azifati) | the Approaching Day (l-āzifatu).

53:58 Not is for it besides Allah any remover.
Not is (laysa) | for it (lahā) | besides (min) | besides (dūni) | Allah (l-lahi) | any remover (kāshifatun).

53:59 Then of this statement you wonder?
Then of (afamin) | this (hādhā) | statement (l-ḥadīthi) | you wonder (taʿjabūna)?

53:60 And you laugh and do not weep,
And you laugh (wataḍḥakūna) | and do not (walā) | weep (tabkūna),

53:61 While you amuse yourselves?
While you (wa-antum) | amuse yourselves (sāmidūna)?

53:62 So prostrate to Allah and worship Him.
So prostrate (fa-us'judū) | to Allah (lillahi) | and worship Him (wa-uʿbudū).

Chapter (54) Sūrat l-Qamar (The Moon)

54:1 Has come near the Hour and has split the moon.
Has come near (iq'tarabati) | the Hour (l-sāʿatu) | and has split (wa-inshaqqa) | the moon (l-qamaru).

54:2 And if they see a Sign, they turn away and say, "Magic continuing."
And if (wa-in) | they see (yaraw) | a Sign (āyatan), | they turn away (yuʿriḍū) | and say (wayaqūlū), | "Magic (siḥ'run) | continuing. (mus'tamirrun)"

54:3 And they denied and followed their desires, but for every matter will be a settlement.
And they denied (wakadhabū) | and followed (wa-ittabaʿū) | their desires (ahwāahum), |

but for every (wakullu) | matter (amrin) | will be a settlement (mus'taqirrun).

54:4 And certainly has come to them of the information wherein is deterrence,
And certainly (walaqad) | has come to them (jāahum) | of (mina) | the information (l-anbāi) | wherein (mā) | wherein (fīhi) | is deterrence (muz'dajarun),

54:5 Wisdom perfect, but not will avail the warnings.
Wisdom (ḥik'matun) | perfect (bālighatun), | but not (famā) | will avail (tugh'ni) | the warnings (l-nudhuru).

54:6 So turn away from them. The Day, will call the caller to a thing terrible,
So turn away (fatawalla) | from them (ʿanhum). | The Day (yawma), | will call (yadʿu) | the caller (l-dāʿi) | to (ilā) | a thing (shayin) | terrible (nukurin),

54:7 Will be humbled their eyes they will come forth from the graves as if they were locusts spreading,
Will be humbled (khushaʿan) | their eyes (abṣāruhum) | they will come forth (yakhrujūna) | from (mina) | the graves (l-ajdāthi) | as if they were (ka-annahum) | locusts (jarādun) | spreading (muntashirun),

54:8 Racing ahead towards the caller. Will say the disbelievers, "This is a Day difficult."
Racing ahead (muh'ṭiʿīna) | towards (ilā) | the caller (l-dāʿi). | Will say (yaqūlu) | the disbelievers (l-kāfirūna), | "This (hādhā) | is a Day (yawmun) | difficult. (ʿasirun)"

54:9 Denied before them the people of Nuh, and they denied Our slave and said, "A madman," and he was repelled.
Denied (kadhabat) | before them (qablahum) | the people (qawmu) | of Nuh (nūḥin), | and they denied (fakadhabū) | Our slave (ʿabdanā) | and said (waqālū), | "A madman, (majnūnun)" | and he was repelled (wa-uz'dujira).

54:10 So he called his Lord, "I am one overpowered, so help."
So he called (fadaʿā) | his Lord (rabbahu), | "I am (annī) | one overpowered (maghlūbun), | so help. (fa-intaṣir)"

54:11 So We opened the gates of heaven with water pouring down
So We opened (fafataḥnā) | the gates (abwāba) | of heaven (l-samāi) | with water (bimāin) | pouring down (mun'hamirin)

54:12 And We caused to burst the earth with springs, so met the waters for a matter already predestined.
And We caused to burst (wafajjarnā) | the earth (l-arḍa) | with springs (ʿuyūnan), | so met (fal-taqā) | the waters (l-māu) | for (ʿalā) | a matter (amrin) | already (qad) | predestined (qudira).

54:13 And We carried him on ark made of planks and nails,
And We carried him (waḥamalnāhu) | on (ʿalā) | ark made of planks (dhāti) | ark made of planks (alwāḥin) | and nails (wadusurin),

54:14 Sailing before Our eyes, a reward for he who was denied.
Sailing (tajrī) | before Our eyes (bi-aʿyuninā), | a reward (jazāan) | for he who (liman) | was (kāna) | denied (kufira).

54:15 And certainly We left it as a Sign, so is there any who will receive admonition?

And certainly (walaqad) | We left it (taraknāhā) | as a Sign (āyatan), | so is there (fahal) | any (min) | who will receive admonition (muddakirin)?

54:16 So how was My punishment and My warnings?
So how (fakayfa) | was (kāna) | My punishment (ʿadhābī) | and My warnings (wanudhuri)?

54:17 And certainly We have made easy the Quran for remembrance, so is there any who will receive admonition?
And certainly (walaqad) | We have made easy (yassarnā) | the Quran (l-qur'āna) | for remembrance (lildhik'ri), | so is there (fahal) | any (min) | who will receive admonition (muddakirin)?

54:18 Denied Aad; so how was My punishment and My warnings?
Denied (kadhabat) | Aad (ʿādun); | so how (fakayfa) | was (kāna) | My punishment (ʿadhābī) | and My warnings (wanudhuri)?

54:19 Indeed, We [We] sent upon them a wind furious on a day of misfortune continuous,
Indeed, We (innā) | [We] sent (arsalnā) | upon them (ʿalayhim) | a wind (rīḥan) | furious (ṣarṣaran) | on (fī) | a day (yawmi) | of misfortune (naḥsin) | continuous (mus'tamirrin),

54:20 Plucking out men as if they were trunks of date-palms uprooted.
Plucking out (tanziʿu) | men (l-nāsa) | as if they were (ka-annahum) | trunks (aʿjāzu) | of date-palms (nakhlin) | uprooted (munqaʿirin).

54:21 So how was My punishment and My warnings?
So how (fakayfa) | was (kāna) | My punishment (ʿadhābī) | and My warnings (wanudhuri)?

54:22 And certainly, We have made easy the Quran for remembrance, so is there any who will receive admonition?
And certainly (walaqad), | We have made easy (yassarnā) | the Quran (l-qur'āna) | for remembrance (lildhik'ri), | so is there (fahal) | any (min) | who will receive admonition (muddakirin)?

54:23 Denied Thamud the warnings,
Denied (kadhabat) | Thamud (thamūdu) | the warnings (bil-nudhuri),

54:24 And said, "Is it a human being among us one, that we should follow him? Indeed, we then will be surely in error and madness.
And said (faqālū), | "Is it a human being (abasharan) | among us (minnā) | one (wāḥidan), | that we should follow him (nattabiʿuhu)? | Indeed, we (innā) | then (idhan) | will be surely in (lafī) | error (ḍalālin) | and madness (wasuʿurin).

54:25 Has been sent the Reminder to him from among us? Nay, he is a liar insolent."
Has been sent (a-ul'qiya) | the Reminder (l-dhik'ru) | to him (ʿalayhi) | from (min) | among us (bayninā)? | Nay (bal), | he (huwa) | is a liar (kadhābun) | insolent. (ashirun)"

54:26 They will know tomorrow who is the liar, the insolent one.
They will know (sayaʿlamūna) | tomorrow (ghadan) | who (mani) | is the liar (l-kadhābu), | the insolent one (l-ashiru).

54:27 Indeed, We are sending the she-camel as a trial for them, so watch them and be patient.
Indeed, We (innā) | are sending (mur'silū) | the she-camel (l-nāqati) | as a trial (fit'natan) |

for them (lahum), | so watch them (fa-ir'taqib'hum) | and be patient (wa-iṣ'ṭabir).

54:28 And inform them that the water is to be shared between them, each drink attended.
And inform them (wanabbi'hum) | that (anna) | the water (l-māa) | is to be shared (qis'matun) | between them (baynahum), | each (kullu) | drink (shir'bin) | attended (muḥ'taḍarun).

54:29 But they called their companion and he took and hamstrung.
But they called (fanādaw) | their companion (ṣāḥibahum) | and he took (fataʿāṭā) | and hamstrung (faʿaqara).

54:30 So how was My punishment and My warnings.
So how (fakayfa) | was (kāna) | My punishment (ʿadhābī) | and My warnings (wanudhuri).

54:31 Indeed, We [We] sent upon them thunderous blast single, and they became like dry twig fragments used by a fence builder.
Indeed, We (innā) | [We] sent (arsalnā) | upon them (ʿalayhim) | thunderous blast (ṣayḥatan) | single (wāḥidatan), | and they became (fakānū) | like dry twig fragments (kahashīmi) | used by a fence builder (l-muḥ'taẓiri).

54:32 And certainly We have made easy the Quran for remembrance, so is there any who will receive admonition?
And certainly (walaqad) | We have made easy (yassarnā) | the Quran (l-qur'āna) | for remembrance (lildhik'ri), | so is there (fahal) | any (min) | who will receive admonition (muddakirin)?

54:33 Denied the people of Lut, the warnings.
Denied (kadhabat) | the people (qawmu) | of Lut (lūṭin), | the warnings (bil-nudhuri).

54:34 Indeed, We [We] sent upon them a storm of stones, except the family of Lut, We saved them by dawn
Indeed, We (innā) | [We] sent (arsalnā) | upon them (ʿalayhim) | a storm of stones (ḥāṣiban), | except (illā) | the family (āla) | of Lut (lūṭin), | We saved them (najjaynāhum) | by dawn (bisaḥarin)

54:35 As a favor from Us. Thus We reward one who is grateful.
As a favor (niʿ'matan) | from (min) | Us (ʿindinā). | Thus (kadhālika) | We reward (najzī) | one who (man) | is grateful (shakara).

54:36 And certainly he warned them of Our seizure, but they disputed the warnings.
And certainly (walaqad) | he warned them (andharahum) | of Our seizure (baṭshatanā), | but they disputed (fatamāraw) | the warnings (bil-nudhuri).

54:37 And certainly they demanded from him his guests, so We blinded their eyes. "So taste My punishment and My warnings."
And certainly (walaqad) | they demanded from him (rāwadūhu) | they demanded from him (ʿan) | his guests (ḍayfihi), | so We blinded (faṭamasnā) | their eyes (aʿyunahum). | "So taste (fadhūqū) | My punishment (ʿadhābī) | and My warnings. (wanudhuri)"

54:38 And certainly seized them in the morning early a punishment abiding.
And certainly (walaqad) | seized them in the morning (ṣabbaḥahum) | early (buk'ratan) | a punishment (ʿadhābun) | abiding (mus'taqirrun).

54:39 So taste My punishment and My warnings.
So taste (fadhūqū) | My punishment (ʿadhābī) | and My warnings (wanudhuri).

54:40 And certainly We have made easy the Quran for remembrance, so is there any who will receive admonition?
And certainly (walaqad) | We have made easy (yassarnā) | the Quran (l-qur'āna) | for remembrance (lildhik'ri), | so is there (fahal) | any (min) | who will receive admonition (muddakirin)?

54:41 And certainly came to the people of Firaun warnings.
And certainly (walaqad) | came (jāa) | to the people (āla) | of Firaun (fir'ʿawna) | warnings (l-nudhuru).

54:42 They denied Our Signs, all of them, so We seized them with a seizure of All-Mighty, the Powerful One.
They denied (kadhabū) | Our Signs (biāyātinā), | all of them (kullihā), | so We seized them (fa-akhadhnāhum) | with a seizure (akhdha) | of All-Mighty (ʿazīzin), | the Powerful One (muq'tadirin).

54:43 Are your disbelievers, better than those, or for you is an exemption in the Scriptures?
Are your disbelievers (akuffārukum), | better (khayrun) | than (min) | those (ulāikum), | or (am) | for you (lakum) | is an exemption (barāatun) | in (fī) | the Scriptures (l-zuburi)?

54:44 Or do they say, "We are an assembly helping each other?"
Or (am) | do they say (yaqūlūna), | "We (naḥnu) | are an assembly (jamīʿun) | helping each other? (muntaṣirun)"

54:45 Soon will be defeated their assembly, and they will turn their backs.
Soon will be defeated (sayuh'zamu) | their assembly (l-jamʿu), | and they will turn (wayuwallūna) | their backs (l-dubura).

54:46 Nay, the Hour is their promised time, and the Hour will be more grievous and more bitter.
Nay (bali), | the Hour (l-sāʿatu) | is their promised time (mawʿiduhum), | and the Hour (wal-sāʿatu) | will be more grievous (adhā) | and more bitter (wa-amarru).

54:47 Indeed, the criminals are in an error and madness.
Indeed (inna), | the criminals (l-muj'rimīna) | are in (fī) | an error (ḍalālin) | and madness (wasuʿurin).

54:48 The Day they will be dragged into the Fire on their faces, "Taste the touch of Hell."
The Day (yawma) | they will be dragged (yus'ḥabūna) | into (fī) | the Fire (l-nāri) | on (ʿalā) | their faces (wujūhihim), | "Taste (dhūqū) | the touch (massa) | of Hell. (saqara)"

54:49 Indeed, [We] every thing We created it by a measure.
Indeed, [We] (innā) | every (kulla) | thing (shayin) | We created it (khalaqnāhu) | by a measure (biqadarin).

54:50 And not is Our Command but one, like the twinkling of the eye.
And not (wamā) | is Our Command (amrunā) | but (illā) | one (wāḥidatun), | like the twinkling (kalamḥin) | of the eye (bil-baṣari).

54:51 And certainly We destroyed your kinds, so is there any who will receive admonition?

And certainly (walaqad) | We destroyed (ahlaknā) | your kinds (ashyāʿakum), | so is there (fahal) | any (min) | who will receive admonition (muddakirin)?

54:52 And every thing they did is in the written records.
And every (wakullu) | thing (shayin) | they did (faʿalūhu) | is in (fī) | the written records (l-zuburi).

54:53 And every small and big is written down.
And every (wakullu) | small (ṣaghīrin) | and big (wakabīrin) | is written down (mus'taṭarun).

54:54 Indeed, the righteous will be in gardens and river,
Indeed (inna), | the righteous (l-mutaqīna) | will be in (fī) | gardens (jannātin) | and river (wanaharin),

54:55 In a seat of honor near a King Most Powerful.
In (fī) | a seat (maqʿadi) | of honor (ṣid'qin) | near (ʿinda) | a King (malīkin) | Most Powerful (muq'tadirin).

Chapter (55) Sūrat l-Raḥmān (The Most Gracious)

55:1 The Most Gracious
The Most Gracious (al-raḥmānu)

55:2 He taught the Quran.
He taught (ʿallama) | the Quran (l-qur'āna).

55:3 He created [the] man.
He created (khalaqa) | [the] man (l-insāna).

55:4 He taught him [the] speech.
He taught him (ʿallamahu) | [the] speech (l-bayāna).

55:5 The sun and the moon by precise calculation,
The sun (al-shamsu) | and the moon (wal-qamaru) | by precise calculation (biḥus'bānin),

55:6 And the stars and the trees both prostrate.
And the stars (wal-najmu) | and the trees (wal-shajaru) | both prostrate (yasjudāni).

55:7 And the heaven, He raised it and He has set up the balance,
And the heaven (wal-samāa), | He raised it (rafaʿahā) | and He has set up (wawaḍaʿa) | the balance (l-mīzāna),

55:8 That not you may transgress in the balance.
That not (allā) | you may transgress (taṭghaw) | in (fī) | the balance (l-mīzāni).

55:9 And establish the weight in justice and do not make deficient the balance.
And establish (wa-aqīmū) | the weight (l-wazna) | in justice (bil-qis'ṭi) | and do not (walā) | make deficient (tukh'sirū) | the balance (l-mīzāna).

55:10 And the earth, He laid it for the creatures,
And the earth (wal-arḍa), | He laid it (waḍaʿahā) | for the creatures (lil'anāmi),

55:11 Therein is fruit and date-palms having sheaths,
Therein (fīhā) | is fruit (fākihatun) | and date-palms (wal-nakhlu) | having (dhātu) | sheaths (l-akmāmi),

55:12 And the grain having husk and scented plants.
And the grain (wal-ḥabu) | having (dhū) | husk (l-ʿaṣfi) | and scented plants (wal-rayḥānu).

55:13 So which of the favors of your Lord will you both deny?
So which (fabi-ayyi) | of the favors (ālāi) | of your Lord (rabbikumā) | will you both deny (tukadhibāni)?

55:14 He created the man from clay like the pottery.
He created (khalaqa) | the man (l-insāna) | from (min) | clay (ṣalṣālin) | like the pottery (kal-fakhāri).

55:15 And He created the jinn from a smokeless flame of fire.
And He created (wakhalaqa) | the jinn (l-jāna) | from (min) | a smokeless flame (mārijin) | of (min) | fire (nārin).

55:16 So which of the favors of your Lord will you both deny?
So which (fabi-ayyi) | of the favors (ālāi) | of your Lord (rabbikumā) | will you both deny (tukadhibāni)?

55:17 Lord of the two Easts and Lord of the two Wests.
Lord (rabbu) | of the two Easts (l-mashriqayni) | and Lord (warabbu) | of the two Wests (l-maghribayni).

55:18 So which of the favors of your Lord will you both deny?
So which (fabi-ayyi) | of the favors (ālāi) | of your Lord (rabbikumā) | will you both deny (tukadhibāni)?

55:19 He released the two seas, meeting.
He released (maraja) | the two seas (l-baḥrayni), | meeting (yaltaqiyāni).

55:20 Between both of them is a barrier, not they transgress.
Between both of them (baynahumā) | is a barrier (barzakhun), | not (lā) | they transgress (yabghiyāni).

55:21 So which of the favors of your Lord will you both deny?
So which (fabi-ayyi) | of the favors (ālāi) | of your Lord (rabbikumā) | will you both deny (tukadhibāni)?

55:22 Come forth from both of them the pearl and the coral.
Come forth (yakhruju) | from both of them (min'humā) | the pearl (l-lu'lu-u) | and the coral (wal-marjānu).

55:23 So which of the favors of your Lord will you both deny?
So which (fabi-ayyi) | of the favors (ālāi) | of your Lord (rabbikumā) | will you both deny (tukadhibāni)?

55:24 And for Him are the ships elevated in the sea like mountains.
And for Him (walahu) | are the ships (l-jawāri) | elevated (l-munshaātu) | in (fī) | the sea (l-baḥri) | like mountains (kal-aʿlāmi).

55:25 So which of the favors of your Lord will you both deny?
So which (fabi-ayyi) | of the favors (ālāi) | of your Lord (rabbikumā) | will you both deny (tukadhibāni)?

55:26 Everyone who is on it will perish.
Everyone (kullu) | who (man) | is on it (ʿalayhā) | will perish (fānin).

55:27 But will remain the Face of your Lord, the Owner of Majesty and Honor.
But will remain (wayabqā) | the Face (wajhu) | of your Lord (rabbika), | the Owner (dhū) | of Majesty (l-jalāli) | and Honor (wal-ik'rāmi).

55:28 So which of the favors of your Lord will you both deny?
So which (fabi-ayyi) | of the favors (ālāi) | of your Lord (rabbikumā) | will you both deny (tukadhibāni)?

55:29 Asks Him whoever is in the heavens and the earth. Every day He is in a matter.
Asks Him (yasaluhu) | whoever (man) | is in (fī) | the heavens (l-samāwāti) | and the earth (wal-arḍi). | Every (kulla) | day (yawmin) | He (huwa) | is in (fī) | a matter (shanin).

55:30 So which of the favors of your Lord will you both deny?
So which (fabi-ayyi) | of the favors (ālāi) | of your Lord (rabbikumā) | will you both deny (tukadhibāni)?

55:31 Soon We will attend to you, O you two classes!
Soon We will attend (sanafrughu) | to you (lakum), | O you (ayyuha) | two classes (l-thaqalāni)!

55:32 So which of the favors of your Lord will you both deny?
So which (fabi-ayyi) | of the favors (ālāi) | of your Lord (rabbikumā) | will you both deny (tukadhibāni)?

55:33 O assembly of the jinn and the men! If you are able to pass beyond [of] the regions of the heavens and the earth, then pass. Not you can pass except by authority.
O assembly (yāmaʿshara) | of the jinn (l-jini) | and the men (wal-insi)! | If (ini) | you are able (is'taṭaʿtum) | to (an) | pass beyond (tanfudhū) | [of] (min) | the regions (aqṭāri) | of the heavens (l-samāwāti) | and the earth (wal-arḍi), | then pass (fa-unfudhū). | Not (lā) | you can pass (tanfudhūna) | except (illā) | by authority (bisul'ṭānin).

55:34 So which of the favors of your Lord will you both deny?
So which (fabi-ayyi) | of the favors (ālāi) | of your Lord (rabbikumā) | will you both deny (tukadhibāni)?

55:35 Will be sent against both of you a flame of fire and smoke, and not you will be able to defend

yourselves.
Will be sent (yur'salu) | against both of you ('alaykumā) | a flame (shuwāẓun) | of (min) | fire (nārin) | and smoke (wanuḥāsun), | and not (falā) | you will be able to defend yourselves (tantaṣirāni).

55:36 So which of the favors of your Lord will you both deny?
So which (fabi-ayyi) | of the favors (ālāi) | of your Lord (rabbikumā) | will you both deny (tukadhibāni)?

55:37 Then when is split the heaven, and it becomes rose-colored like murky oil.
Then when (fa-idhā) | is split (inshaqqati) | the heaven (l-samāu), | and it becomes (fakānat) | rose-colored (wardatan) | like murky oil (kal-dihāni).

55:38 So which of the favors of your Lord will you both deny?
So which (fabi-ayyi) | of the favors (ālāi) | of your Lord (rabbikumā) | will you both deny (tukadhibāni)?

55:39 Then on that Day not will be asked about his sin any man and not any jinn.
Then on that Day (fayawma-idhin) | not (lā) | will be asked (yus'alu) | about ('an) | his sin (dhanbihi) | any man (insun) | and not (walā) | any jinn (jānnun).

55:40 So which of the favors of your Lord will you both deny?
So which (fabi-ayyi) | of the favors (ālāi) | of your Lord (rabbikumā) | will you both deny (tukadhibāni)?

55:41 Will be known the criminals by their marks and will be seized by the forelocks and the feet.
Will be known (yu''rafu) | the criminals (l-muj'rimūna) | by their marks (bisīmāhum) | and will be seized (fayu'khadhu) | by the forelocks (bil-nawāṣī) | and the feet (wal-aqdāmi).

55:42 So which of the favors of your Lord will you both deny?
So which (fabi-ayyi) | of the favors (ālāi) | of your Lord (rabbikumā) | will you both deny (tukadhibāni)?

55:43 This is Hell which deny [of it] the criminals.
This (hādhihi) | is Hell (jahannamu) | which (allatī) | deny (yukadhibu) | [of it] (bihā) | the criminals (l-muj'rimūna).

55:44 They will go around between it and between scalding water, heated.
They will go around (yaṭūfūna) | between it (baynahā) | and between (wabayna) | scalding water (ḥamīmin), | heated (ānin).

55:45 So which of the favors of your Lord will you both deny?
So which (fabi-ayyi) | of the favors (ālāi) | of your Lord (rabbikumā) | will you both deny (tukadhibāni)?

55:46 But for him who fears the standing before his Lord are two gardens.
But for him who (waliman) | fears (khāfa) | the standing (maqāma) | before his Lord (rabbihi) | are two gardens (jannatāni).

55:47 So which of the favors of your Lord will you both deny?
So which (fabi-ayyi) | of the favors (ālāi) | of your Lord (rabbikumā) | will you both deny (tukadhibāni)?

55:48 Having branches.
Having (dhawātā) | branches (afnānin).

55:49 So which of the favors of your Lord will you both deny?
So which (fabi-ayyi) | of the favors (ālāi) | of your Lord (rabbikumā) | will you both deny (tukadhibāni)?

55:50 In both of them are two springs, flowing.
In both of them (fīhimā) | are two springs (ʿaynāni), | flowing (tajriyāni).

55:51 So which of the favors of your Lord will you both deny?
So which (fabi-ayyi) | of the favors (ālāi) | of your Lord (rabbikumā) | will you both deny (tukadhibāni)?

55:52 In both of them [of] are every fruits in pairs.
In both of them (fīhimā) | [of] (min) | are every (kulli) | fruits (fākihatin) | in pairs (zawjāni).

55:53 So which of the favors of your Lord will you both deny?
So which (fabi-ayyi) | of the favors (ālāi) | of your Lord (rabbikumā) | will you both deny (tukadhibāni)?

55:54 Reclining on couches, whose inner linings are of brocade, and the fruit of both the gardens is near.
Reclining (muttakiīna) | on (ʿalā) | couches (furushin), | whose inner linings (baṭāinuhā) | are of (min) | brocade (is'tabraqin), | and the fruit (wajanā) | of both the gardens (l-janatayni) | is near (dānin).

55:55 So which of the favors of your Lord will you both deny?
So which (fabi-ayyi) | of the favors (ālāi) | of your Lord (rabbikumā) | will you both deny (tukadhibāni)?

55:56 In them will be companions of modest gaze not has touched them any man before them and not any jinn.
In them (fīhinna) | will be companions of modest gaze (qāṣirātu) | will be companions of modest gaze (l-ṭarfi) | not (lam) | has touched them (yaṭmith'hunna) | any man (insun) | before them (qablahum) | and not (walā) | any jinn (jānnun).

55:57 So which of the favors of your Lord will you both deny?
So which (fabi-ayyi) | of the favors (ālāi) | of your Lord (rabbikumā) | will you both deny (tukadhibāni)?

55:58 As if they were rubies and coral.
As if they were (ka-annahunna) | rubies (l-yāqūtu) | and coral (wal-marjānu).

55:59 So which of the favors of your Lord will you both deny?
So which (fabi-ayyi) | of the favors (ālāi) | of your Lord (rabbikumā) | will you both deny (tukadhibāni)?

55:60 Is the reward for the good but good?
Is (hal) | the reward (jazāu) | for the good (l-iḥ'sāni) | but (illā) | good (l-iḥ'sānu)?

55:61 So which of the favors of your Lord will you both deny?
So which (fabi-ayyi) | of the favors (ālāi) | of your Lord (rabbikumā) | will you both deny (tukadhibāni)?

55:62 Besides these two are two gardens.
Besides these two (wamin) | Besides these two (dūnihimā) | are two gardens (jannatāni).

55:63 So which of the favors of your Lord will you both deny?
So which (fabi-ayyi) | of the favors (ālāi) | of your Lord (rabbikumā) | will you both deny (tukadhibāni)?

55:64 Dark green.
Dark green (mud'hāmmatāni).

55:65 So which of the favors of your Lord will you both deny?
So which (fabi-ayyi) | of the favors (ālāi) | of your Lord (rabbikumā) | will you both deny (tukadhibāni)?

55:66 In both of them are two springs, gushing forth.
In both of them (fīhimā) | are two springs (ʿaynāni), | gushing forth (naḍḍākhatāni).

55:67 So which of the favors of your Lord will you both deny?
So which (fabi-ayyi) | of the favors (ālāi) | of your Lord (rabbikumā) | will you both deny (tukadhibāni)?

55:68 In both of them are fruits and date-palms and pomegranates.
In both of them (fīhimā) | are fruits (fākihatun) | and date-palms (wanakhlun) | and pomegranates (warummānun).

55:69 So which of the favors of your Lord will you both deny?
So which (fabi-ayyi) | of the favors (ālāi) | of your Lord (rabbikumā) | will you both deny (tukadhibāni)?

55:70 In them are good and beautiful ones.
In them (fīhinna) | are good (khayrātun) | and beautiful ones (ḥisānun).

55:71 So which of the favors of your Lord will you both deny?
So which (fabi-ayyi) | of the favors (ālāi) | of your Lord (rabbikumā) | will you both deny (tukadhibāni)?

55:72 Fair ones restrained in the pavilions.
Fair ones (ḥūrun) | restrained (maqṣūrātun) | in (fī) | the pavilions (l-khiyāmi).

55:73 So which of the favors of your Lord will you both deny?
So which (fabi-ayyi) | of the favors (ālāi) | of your Lord (rabbikumā) | will you both deny (tukadhibāni)?

55:74 Not has touched them any man before them and not any jinn.
Not (lam) | has touched them (yaṭmith'hunna) | any man (insun) | before them (qablahum) | and not (walā) | any jinn (jānnun).

55:75 So which of the favors of your Lord will you both deny?
So which (fabi-ayyi) | of the favors (ālāi) | of your Lord (rabbikumā) | will you both deny (tukadhibāni)?

55:76 Reclining on cushions green, and carpets beautiful.
Reclining (muttakiīna) | on (ʿalā) | cushions (rafrafin) | green (khuḍ'rin), | and carpets (waʿabqariyyin) | beautiful (ḥisānin).

55:77 So which of the favors of your Lord will you both deny?
So which (fabi-ayyi) | of the favors (ālāi) | of your Lord (rabbikumā) | will you both deny (tukadhibāni)?

55:78 Blessed is the name of your Lord, Owner of Majesty and Honor.
Blessed is (tabāraka) | the name (us'mu) | of your Lord (rabbika), | Owner (dhī) | of Majesty (l-jalāli) | and Honor (wal-ik'rāmi).

Chapter (56) Sūrat l-Wāqiʿah (The Event)

56:1 When occurs the Event,
When (idhā) | occurs (waqaʿati) | the Event (l-wāqiʿatu),

56:2 Not at its occurrence a denial
Not (laysa) | at its occurrence (liwaqʿatihā) | a denial (kādhibatun)

56:3 Bringing down, raising up,
Bringing down (khāfiḍatun), | raising up (rāfiʿatun),

56:4 When will be shaken the earth with a shaking,
When (idhā) | will be shaken (rujjati) | the earth (l-arḍu) | with a shaking (rajjan),

56:5 And will be crumbled the mountains with awful crumbling.
And will be crumbled (wabussati) | the mountains (l-jibālu) | with awful crumbling (bassan).

56:6 So they become dust particles dispersing.
So they become (fakānat) | dust particles (habāan) | dispersing (munbathan).

56:7 And you will become kinds three.
And you will become (wakuntum) | kinds (azwājan) | three (thalāthatan).

56:8 Then the companions of the right, what are the companions of the right?
Then the companions (fa-aṣḥābu) | of the right (l-maymanati), | what (mā) | are the companions (aṣḥābu) | of the right (l-maymanati)?

56:9 And the companions of the left, what are the companions of the left?
And the companions (wa-aṣḥābu) | of the left (l-mashamati), | what (mā) | are the

companions (aṣḥābu) | of the left (l-mashamati)?

56:10 And the foremost are the foremost,
And the foremost (wal-sābiqūna) | are the foremost (l-sābiqūna),

56:11 Those are the nearest ones.
Those (ulāika) | are the nearest ones (l-muqarabūna).

56:12 In Gardens of Pleasure,
In (fī) | Gardens (jannāti) | of Pleasure (l-naʿīmi),

56:13 A company of the former people,
A company (thullatun) | of (mina) | the former people (l-awalīna),

56:14 And a few of the later people,
And a few (waqalīlun) | of (mina) | the later people (l-ākhirīna),

56:15 On thrones decorated,
On (ʿalā) | thrones (sururin) | decorated (mawḍūnatin),

56:16 Reclining, on them facing each other.
Reclining (muttakiīna), | on them (ʿalayhā) | facing each other (mutaqābilīna).

56:17 Will circulate among them boys immortal,
Will circulate (yaṭūfu) | among them (ʿalayhim) | boys (wil'dānun) | immortal (mukhalladūna),

56:18 With vessels and jugs and a cup from a flowing stream,
With vessels (bi-akwābin) | and jugs (wa-abārīqa) | and a cup (wakasin) | from (min) | a flowing stream (maʿīnin),

56:19 Not they will get headache therefrom and not they will get intoxicated
Not (lā) | they will get headache (yuṣaddaʿūna) | therefrom (ʿanhā) | and not (walā) | they will get intoxicated (yunzifūna)

56:20 And fruits of what they select,
And fruits (wafākihatin) | of what (mimmā) | they select (yatakhayyarūna),

56:21 And the flesh of fowls of what they desire.
And the flesh (walaḥmi) | of fowls (ṭayrin) | of what (mimmā) | they desire (yashtahūna).

56:22 And fair ones with large eyes,
And fair ones (waḥūrun) | with large eyes (ʿīnun),

56:23 Like pearls well-protected,
Like (ka-amthāli) | pearls (l-lu'lu-i) | well-protected (l-maknūni),

56:24 A reward for what they used to do.
A reward (jazāan) | for what (bimā) | they used to (kānū) | do (yaʿmalūna).

56:25 Not they will hear therein vain talk and not sinful speech,
Not (lā) | they will hear (yasmaʿūna) | therein (fīhā) | vain talk (laghwan) | and not (walā) |

sinful speech (tathīman),

56:26 Except a saying, "Peace, Peace."
Except (illā) | a saying (qīlan), | "Peace (salāman), | Peace. (salāman)"

56:27 And the companions of the right, what are the companions of the right?
And the companions (wa-aṣḥābu) | of the right (l-yamīni), | what (mā) | are the companions (aṣḥābu) | of the right (l-yamīni)?

56:28 Among lote trees thornless,
Among (fī) | lote trees (sid'rin) | thornless (makhḍūdin),

56:29 And banana trees layered,
And banana trees (waṭalḥin) | layered (manḍūdin),

56:30 And shade extended,
And shade (waẓillin) | extended (mamdūdin),

56:31 And water poured forth,
And water (wamāin) | poured forth (maskūbin),

56:32 And fruit abundant,
And fruit (wafākihatin) | abundant (kathīratin),

56:33 Not limited and not forbidden,
Not (lā) | limited (maqṭūʿatin) | and not (walā) | forbidden (mamnūʿatin),

56:34 And on couches raised.
And on couches (wafurushin) | raised (marfūʿatin).

56:35 Indeed, We [We] have produced them into a creation,
Indeed, We (innā) | [We] have produced them (anshanāhunna) | into a creation (inshāan),

56:36 And We have made them virgins,
And We have made them (fajaʿalnāhunna) | virgins (abkāran),

56:37 Devoted, equals in age.
Devoted (ʿuruban), | equals in age (atrāban).

56:38 For the companions of the right,
For the companions (li-aṣḥābi) | of the right (l-yamīni),

56:39 A company of the former people,
A company (thullatun) | of (mina) | the former people (l-awalīna),

56:40 And a company of the later people.
And a company (wathullatun) | of (mina) | the later people (l-ākhirīna).

56:41 And the companions of the left, what are the companions of the left?
And the companions (wa-aṣḥābu) | of the left (l-shimāli), | what (mā) | are the companions (aṣḥābu) | of the left (l-shimāli)?

56:42 In scorching fire and scalding water,
In (fī) | scorching fire (samūmin) | and scalding water (waḥamīmin),

56:43 And a shade of black smoke,
And a shade (waẓillin) | of (min) | black smoke (yaḥmūmin),

56:44 Not cool and not pleasant.
Not (lā) | cool (bāridin) | and not (walā) | pleasant (karīmin).

56:45 Indeed, they were before that indulging in affluence.
Indeed, they (innahum) | were (kānū) | before (qabla) | that (dhālika) | indulging in affluence (mut'rafīna).

56:46 And were persisting in the sin the great,
And were (wakānū) | persisting (yuṣirrūna) | in (ʿalā) | the sin (l-ḥinthi) | the great (l-ʿaẓīmi),

56:47 And they used to say, "When we die and become dust and bones, will we surely be resurrected?
And they used to (wakānū) | say (yaqūlūna), | "When (a-idhā) | we die (mit'nā) | and become (wakunnā) | dust (turāban) | and bones (waʿiẓāman), | will we (a-innā) | surely be resurrected (lamabʿūthūna)?

56:48 And also our fathers former?
And also our fathers (awaābāunā) | former (l-awalūna)?

56:49 Say, "Indeed, the former and the later people
Say (qul), | "Indeed (inna), | the former (l-awalīna) | and the later people (wal-ākhirīna)

56:50 Surely, will be gathered for the appointment of a Day well-known."
Surely, will be gathered (lamajmūʿūna) | for (ilā) | the appointment (mīqāti) | of a Day (yawmin) | well-known. (maʿlūmin)"

56:51 "Then indeed you, O those astray! the deniers,
"Then (thumma) | indeed you (innakum), | O those astray (ayyuhā)! | O those astray (l-ḍālūna)! | the deniers (l-mukadhibūna),

56:52 Will surely eat from the tree of Zaqqum.
Will surely eat (laākilūna) | from (min) | the tree (shajarin) | of (min) | Zaqqum (zaqqūmin).

56:53 Then will fill with it the bellies,
Then will fill (famāliūna) | with it (min'hā) | the bellies (l-buṭūna),

56:54 And drink over it [from] the scalding water,
And drink (fashāribūna) | over it (ʿalayhi) | [from] (mina) | the scalding water (l-ḥamīmi),

56:55 And will drink as drinking of the thirsty camels."
And will drink (fashāribūna) | as drinking (shur'ba) | of the thirsty camels. (l-hīmi)"

56:56 This is their hospitality on the Day of Judgment.
This (hādhā) | is their hospitality (nuzuluhum) | on the Day (yawma) | of Judgment (l-dīni).

56:57 We [We] created you, so why do not you admit the truth?
We (naḥnu) | [We] created you (khalaqnākum), | so why do not (falawlā) | you admit the truth (tuṣaddiqūna)?

56:58 Do you see what you emit?
Do you see (afara-aytum) | what (mā) | you emit (tum'nūna)?

56:59 Is it you who create it or are We the Creators?
Is it you (a-antum) | who create it (takhluqūnahu) | or (am) | are We (naḥnu) | the Creators (l-khāliqūna)?

56:60 We [We] have decreed among you the death and not We are outrun,
We (naḥnu) | [We] have decreed (qaddarnā) | among you (baynakumu) | the death (l-mawta) | and not (wamā) | We (naḥnu) | are outrun (bimasbūqīna),

56:61 In that We will change your likeness[es] and produce you in what not you know.
In (ʿalā) | that (an) | We will change (nubaddila) | your likeness[es] (amthālakum) | and produce you (wanunshi-akum) | in (fī) | what (mā) | not (lā) | you know (taʿlamūna).

56:62 And certainly you know the creation the first, so why not you take heed?
And certainly (walaqad) | you know (ʿalim'tumu) | the creation (l-nashata) | the first (l-ūlā), | so why not (falawlā) | you take heed (tadhakkarūna)?

56:63 And do you see what you sow?
And do you see (afara-aytum) | what (mā) | you sow (taḥruthūna)?

56:64 Is it you who cause it to grow or are We the Ones Who grow?
Is it you who (a-antum) | cause it to grow (tazraʿūnahu) | or (am) | are We (naḥnu) | the Ones Who grow (l-zāriʿūna)?

56:65 If We willed We would surely, make it debris, then you would remain wondering,
If (law) | We willed (nashāu) | We would surely, make it (lajaʿalnāhu) | debris (ḥuṭāman), | then you would remain (faẓaltum) | wondering (tafakkahūna),

56:66 "Indeed, we surely are laden with debt,
"Indeed, we (innā) | surely are laden with debt (lamugh'ramūna),

56:67 Nay, we are deprived."
Nay (bal), | we (naḥnu) | are deprived. (maḥrūmūna)"

56:68 Do you see the water, which you drink?
Do you see (afara-aytumu) | the water (l-māa), | which (alladhī) | you drink (tashrabūna)?

56:69 Is it you who send it down from the rain clouds, or We are the Ones to send?
Is it you (a-antum) | who send it down (anzaltumūhu) | from (mina) | the rain clouds (l-muz'ni), | or (am) | We (naḥnu) | are the Ones to send (l-munzilūna)?

56:70 If We willed, We could make it salty, then why are you not grateful?
If (law) | We willed (nashāu), | We could make it (jaʿalnāhu) | salty (ujājan), | then why are you not grateful (falawlā)? | then why are you not grateful (tashkurūna)?

56:71 Do you see the Fire, which you ignite?
Do you see (afara-aytumu) | the Fire (l-nāra), | which (allatī) | you ignite (tūrūna)?

56:72 Is it you who produced its tree or We are the Producers?
Is it you (a-antum) | who produced (anshatum) | its tree (shajaratahā) | or (am) | We (naḥnu) | are the Producers (l-munshiūna)?

56:73 We have made it a reminder and a provision for the wayfarers in the desert.
We (naḥnu) | have made it (jaʿalnāhā) | a reminder (tadhkiratan) | and a provision (wamatāʿan) | for the wayfarers in the desert (lil'muq'wīna).

56:74 So glorify the name of your Lord, the Most Great.
So glorify (fasabbiḥ) | the name (bi-is'mi) | of your Lord (rabbika), | the Most Great (l-ʿaẓīmi).

56:75 But nay, I swear by setting of the stars,
But nay (falā), | I swear (uq'simu) | by setting (bimawāqiʿi) | of the stars (l-nujūmi),

56:76 And indeed, it is surely an oath, if you know - great,
And indeed, it (wa-innahu) | is surely an oath (laqasamun), | if (law) | you know (taʿlamūna)- | great (ʿaẓīmun),

56:77 Indeed, it is surely, a Quran noble,
Indeed, it (innahu) | is surely, a Quran (laqur'ānun) | noble (karīmun),

56:78 In a Book well-guarded,
In (fī) | a Book (kitābin) | well-guarded (maknūnin),

56:79 None touch it except the purified.
None (lā) | touch it (yamassuhu) | except (illā) | the purified (l-muṭaharūna).

56:80 A Revelation from the Lord of the worlds.
A Revelation (tanzīlun) | from (min) | the Lord (rabbi) | of the worlds (l-ʿālamīna).

56:81 Then is it to this statement that you are indifferent?
Then is it to this (afabihādhā) | statement (l-ḥadīthi) | that you (antum) | are indifferent (mud'hinūna)?

56:82 And you make your provision that you deny.
And you make (watajʿalūna) | your provision (riz'qakum) | that you (annakum) | deny (tukadhibūna).

56:83 Then why not when it reaches the throat,
Then why not (falawlā) | when (idhā) | it reaches (balaghati) | the throat (l-ḥul'qūma),

56:84 And you at that time look on,
And you (wa-antum) | at that time (ḥīna-idhin) | look on (tanẓurūna),

56:85 And We are nearer to him than you but you do not see,
And We (wanaḥnu) | are nearer (aqrabu) | to him (ilayhi) | than you (minkum) | but (walākin) | you do not see (lā), | you do not see (tub'ṣirūna),

56:86 Then why not, if you are not to be recompensed,
Then why not (falawlā), | if (in) | you are (kuntum) | not (ghayra) | to be recompensed (madīnīna),

56:87 Bring it back, if you are truthful.
Bring it back (tarjiʿūnahā), | if (in) | you are (kuntum) | truthful (ṣādiqīna).

56:88 Then if he was of those brought near,
Then (fa-ammā) | if (in) | he was (kāna) | of (mina) | those brought near (l-muqarabīna),

56:89 Then rest and bounty and a Garden of Pleasure.
Then rest (farawḥun) | and bounty (warayḥānun) | and a Garden (wajannatu) | of Pleasure (naʿīmin).

56:90 And if he was of the companions of the right,
And (wa-ammā) | if (in) | he was (kāna) | of (min) | the companions (aṣḥābi) | of the right (l-yamīni),

56:91 Then, peace for you; [from] the companions of the right.
Then, peace (fasalāmun) | for you (laka); | [from] (min) | the companions (aṣḥābi) | of the right (l-yamīni).

56:92 But if he was of the deniers, the astray,
But (wa-ammā) | if (in) | he was (kāna) | of (mina) | the deniers (l-mukadhibīna), | the astray (l-ḍālīna),

56:93 Then, hospitality of the scalding water,
Then, hospitality (fanuzulun) | of (min) | the scalding water (ḥamīmin),

56:94 And burning in Hellfire.
And burning (wataṣliyatu) | in Hellfire (jaḥīmin).

56:95 Indeed, this surely, it is the truth certain.
Indeed (inna), | this (hādhā) | surely, it (lahuwa) | is the truth (ḥaqqu) | certain (l-yaqīni).

56:96 So glorify the name of your Lord, the Most Great.
So glorify (fasabbiḥ) | the name (bi-is'mi) | of your Lord (rabbika), | the Most Great (l-ʿaẓīmi).

Chapter (57) Sūrat l-Ḥadīd (The Iron)

57:1 Glorifies [to] Allah whatever is in the heavens and the earth, and He is the All-Mighty, the All-Wise.
Glorifies (sabbaḥa) | [to] Allah (lillahi) | whatever (mā) | is in (fī) | the heavens (l-samāwāti) | and the earth (wal-arḍi), | and He (wahuwa) | is the All-Mighty (l-ʿazīzu), | the All-Wise (l-ḥakīmu).

57:2 For Him is the dominion of the heavens and the earth, He gives life and causes death, and He is over all things All-Powerful.

For Him (lahu) | is the dominion (mul'ku) | of the heavens (l-samāwāti) | and the earth (wal-arḍi), | He gives life (yuḥ'yī) | and causes death (wayumītu), | and He (wahuwa) | is over (ʿalā) | all (kulli) | things (shayin) | All-Powerful (qadīrun).

57:3 He is the First and the Last, and the Apparent and the Unapparent, and He is of every thing All-Knower.

He (huwa) | is the First (l-awalu) | and the Last (wal-ākhiru), | and the Apparent (wal-ẓāhiru) | and the Unapparent (wal-bāṭinu), | and He (wahuwa) | is of every (bikulli) | thing (shayin) | All-Knower (ʿalīmun).

57:4 He is the One Who created the heavens and the earth in six periods, then He rose over the Throne. He knows what penetrates into the earth and what comes forth from it, and what descends from the heaven and what ascends therein; and He is with you wherever you are. And Allah of what you do is All-seer.

He (huwa) | is the One Who (alladhī) | created (khalaqa) | the heavens (l-samāwāti) | and the earth (wal-arḍa) | in (fī) | six (sittati) | periods (ayyāmin), | then (thumma) | He rose (is'tawā) | over (ʿalā) | the Throne (l-ʿarshi). | He knows (yaʿlamu) | what (mā) | penetrates (yaliju) | into (fī) | the earth (l-arḍi) | and what (wamā) | comes forth (yakhruju) | from it (min'hā), | and what (wamā) | descends (yanzilu) | from (mina) | the heaven (l-samāi) | and what (wamā) | ascends (yaʿruju) | therein (fīhā); | and He (wahuwa) | is with you (maʿakum) | wherever (ayna) | wherever (mā) | you are (kuntum). | And Allah (wal-lahu) | of what (bimā) | you do (taʿmalūna) | is All-seer (baṣīrun).

57:5 For Him is the dominion of the heavens and the earth, and to Allah will be returned the matters.

For Him (lahu) | is the dominion (mul'ku) | of the heavens (l-samāwāti) | and the earth (wal-arḍi), | and to (wa-ilā) | Allah (l-lahi) | will be returned (tur'jaʿu) | the matters (l-umūru).

57:6 He merges the night into the day and He merges the day into the night, and He is All-Knower of what is in the breasts.

He merges (yūliju) | the night (al-layla) | into (fī) | the day (l-nahāri) | and He merges (wayūliju) | the day (l-nahāra) | into (fī) | the night (al-layli), | and He (wahuwa) | is All-Knower (ʿalīmun) | of what is in the breasts (bidhāti). | of what is in the breasts (l-ṣudūri).

57:7 Believe in Allah and His Messenger and spend of what He has made you trustees therein. And those who believe among you and spend, for them is a reward great.

Believe (āminū) | in Allah (bil-lahi) | and His Messenger (warasūlihi) | and spend (wa-anfiqū) | of what (mimmā) | He has made you (jaʿalakum) | trustees (mus'takhlafīna) | therein (fīhi). | And those (fa-alladhīna) | who believe (āmanū) | among you (minkum) | and spend (wa-anfaqū), | for them (lahum) | is a reward (ajrun) | great (kabīrun).

57:8 And what is for you that not you believe in Allah while the Messenger calls you that you believe in your Lord, and indeed, He has taken your covenant if you are believers.

And what (wamā) | is for you (lakum) | that not (lā) | you believe (tu'minūna) | in Allah (bil-lahi) | while the Messenger (wal-rasūlu) | calls you (yadʿūkum) | that you believe (litu'minū) | in your Lord (birabbikum), | and indeed (waqad), | He has taken (akhadha) | your covenant (mīthāqakum) | if (in) | you are (kuntum) | believers (mu'minīna).

57:9 He is the One Who sends down upon His slave Verses clear that He may bring you out from the darkness[es] into the light. And indeed, Allah to you is the Most Kind, the Most Merciful.

He (huwa) | is the One Who (alladhī) | sends down (yunazzilu) | upon (ʿalā) | His slave (ʿabdihi) | Verses (āyātin) | clear (bayyinātin) | that He may bring you out (liyukh'rijakum) | from (mina) | the darkness[es] (l-ẓulumāti) | into (ilā) | the light (l-nūri). | And indeed (wa-inna), | Allah (l-laha) | to you (bikum) | is the Most Kind (laraūfun), | the Most Merciful (raḥīmun).

57:10 And what is for you that not you spend in the way of Allah? while for Allah is the heritage of the heavens and the earth? Not are equal among you those who spent before the victory and fought. Those are greater in degree than those who spent afterwards and fought. But to all, Allah has promised the best. And Allah of what you do is All-Aware.

And what (wamā) | is for you (lakum) | that not (allā) | you spend (tunfiqū) | in (fī) | the way (sabīli) | of Allah (l-lahi)? | while for Allah (walillahi) | is the heritage (mīrāthu) | of the heavens (l-samāwāti) | and the earth (wal-arḍi)? | Not (lā) | are equal (yastawī) | among you (minkum) | those who (man) | spent (anfaqa) | before (min) | before (qabli) | the victory (l-fatḥi) | and fought (waqātala). | Those (ulāika) | are greater (aʿẓamu) | in degree (darajatan) | than (mina) | those who (alladhīna) | spent (anfaqū) | afterwards (min) | afterwards (baʿdu) | and fought (waqātalū). | But to all (wakullan), | Allah has promised (waʿada) | Allah has promised (l-lahu) | the best (l-ḥus'nā). | And Allah (wal-lahu) | of what (bimā) | you do (taʿmalūna) | is All-Aware (khabīrun).

57:11 Who is the one who will loan to Allah a loan goodly, so He will multiply it for him and for him is a reward noble?

Who is (man) | the one who (dhā) | the one who (alladhī) | will loan (yuq'riḍu) | to Allah (l-laha) | a loan (qarḍan) | goodly (ḥasanan), | so He will multiply it (fayuḍāʿifahu) | for him (lahu) | and for him (walahu) | is a reward (ajrun) | noble (karīmun)?

57:12 On the Day you will see the believing men and the believing women, running, their light before them and on their right, "Glad tidings for you this Day - gardens flowing from underneath it the rivers, abiding forever therein. That [it] is the success the great."

On the Day (yawma) | you will see (tarā) | the believing men (l-mu'minīna) | and the believing women (wal-mu'mināti), | running (yasʿā), | their light (nūruhum) | before them (bayna) | before them (aydīhim) | and on their right (wabi-aymānihim), | "Glad tidings for you (bush'rākumu) | this Day (l-yawma)- | gardens (jannātun) | flowing (tajrī) | from (min) | underneath it (taḥtihā) | the rivers (l-anhāru), | abiding forever (khālidīna) | therein (fīhā). | That (dhālika) | [it] is (huwa) | the success (l-fawzu) | the great. (l-ʿaẓīmu)"

57:13 On the Day will say the hypocrite men and the hypocrite women to those who believed, "Wait for us, we may acquire of your light." It will be said, "Go back behind you and seek light." Then will be put up between them a wall, for it a gate its interior, in it is mercy but its exterior, facing towards [it] the punishment.

On the Day (yawma) | will say (yaqūlu) | the hypocrite men (l-munāfiqūna) | and the hypocrite women (wal-munāfiqātu) | to those who (lilladhīna) | believed (āmanū), | "Wait for us (unẓurūnā), | we may acquire (naqtabis) | of (min) | your light. (nūrikum)" | It will be said (qīla), | "Go back (ir'jiʿū) | behind you (warāakum) | and seek (fal-tamisū) | light. (nūran)" | Then will be put up (faḍuriba) | between them (baynahum) | a wall (bisūrin), | for it (lahu) | a gate (bābun) | its interior (bāṭinuhu), | in it (fīhi) | is mercy (l-raḥmatu) | but its exterior (waẓāhiruhu), | facing towards [it] (min) | facing towards [it] (qibalihi) | the punishment (l-ʿadhābu).

57:14 They will call them, "Were not we with you?" They will say, "Yes, but you led to temptation yourselves and you awaited and you doubted and deceived you the wishful thinking until came the Command of Allah. And deceived you about Allah the deceiver.

They will call them (yunādūnahum), | "Were not (alam) | we (nakun) | with you? (maʿakum)" | They will say (qālū), | "Yes (balā), | but you (walākinnakum) | led to temptation (fatantum) | yourselves (anfusakum) | and you awaited (watarabbaṣtum) | and you doubted (wa-ir'tabtum) | and deceived you (wagharratkumu) | the wishful thinking (l-amāniyu) | until (ḥattā) | came (jāa) | the Command (amru) | of Allah (l-lahi). | And deceived you (wagharrakum) | about Allah (bil-lahi) | the deceiver (l-gharūru).

57:15 So today not will be accepted from you any ransom and not from those who disbelieved. Your abode is the Fire; it is your protector and wretched is the destination.

So today (fal-yawma) | not (lā) | will be accepted (yu'khadhu) | from you (minkum) | any ransom (fid'yatun) | and not (walā) | from (mina) | those who (alladhīna) | disbelieved (kafarū). | Your abode (mawākumu) | is the Fire (l-nāru); | it is (hiya) | your protector (mawlākum) | and wretched is (wabi'sa) | the destination (l-maṣīru).

57:16 Has not come the time for those who believed that become humble their hearts at the remembrance (of) Allah and what has come down of the truth? And not they become like those who were given the Book before, and was prolonged for them the term, so hardened their hearts; and many of them are defiantly disobedient.

Has not (alam) | come the time (yani) | for those who (lilladhīna) | believed (āmanū) | that (an) | become humble (takhshaʿa) | their hearts (qulūbuhum) | at the remembrance (of) Allah (lidhik'ri) | at the remembrance (of) Allah (l-lahi) | and what (wamā) | has come down (nazala) | of (mina) | the truth (l-ḥaqi)? | And not (walā) | they become (yakūnū) | like those who (ka-alladhīna) | were given (ūtū) | the Book (l-kitāba) | before (min), | before (qablu), | and was prolonged (faṭāla) | for them (ʿalayhimu) | the term (l-amadu), | so hardened (faqasat) | their hearts (qulūbuhum); | and many (wakathīrun) | of them (min'hum) | are defiantly disobedient (fāsiqūna).

57:17 Know that Allah gives life to the earth after its death. Indeed, We have made clear to you the Signs so that you may understand.

Know (iʿlamū) | that (anna) | Allah (l-laha) | gives life (yuḥ'yī) | to the earth (l-arḍa) | after (baʿda) | its death (mawtihā). | Indeed (qad), | We have made clear (bayyannā) | to you (lakumu) | the Signs (l-āyāti) | so that you may (laʿallakum) | understand (taʿqilūna).

57:18 Indeed, the men who give charity and the women who give charity, and who lend to Allah a loan goodly, it will be multiplied for them, and for them is a reward noble.

Indeed (inna), | the men who give charity (l-muṣadiqīna) | and the women who give charity (wal-muṣadiqāti), | and who lend (wa-aqraḍū) | to Allah (l-laha) | a loan (qarḍan) | goodly (ḥasanan), | it will be multiplied (yuḍāʿafu) | for them (lahum), | and for them (walahum) | is a reward (ajrun) | noble (karīmun).

57:19 And those who believe in Allah and His Messengers, [those] they are the truthful and the martyrs, are with their Lord. For them is their reward and their light. But those who disbelieve and deny Our Verses, those are the companions of the Hellfire.

And those who (wa-alladhīna) | believe (āmanū) | in Allah (bil-lahi) | and His Messengers (warusulihi), | [those] (ulāika) | they (humu) | are the truthful (l-ṣidīqūna) | and the martyrs (wal-shuhadāu), | are with (ʿinda) | their Lord (rabbihim). | For them (lahum) | is their reward (ajruhum) | and their light (wanūruhum). | But those who (wa-alladhīna) | disbelieve (kafarū) | and deny (wakadhabū) | Our Verses (biāyātinā), | those (ulāika) | are the companions (aṣḥābu) | of the Hellfire (l-jaḥīmi).

57:20 Know that the life of the world is play and amusement and adornment and boasting among you and competition in increase of the wealth and the children, like the example of a rain, pleases the tillers its growth; then it dries and you see it turning yellow; then becomes debris. And in the Hereafter is a punishment severe and forgiveness from Allah and Pleasure. But not is the life of the world except the enjoyment of delusion.

Know (iʿlamū) | that (annamā) | the life (l-ḥayatu) | of the world (l-dun'yā) | is play (laʿibun) | and amusement (walahwun) | and adornment (wazīnatun) | and boasting (watafākhurun) | among you (baynakum) | and competition in increase (watakāthurun) | of (fī) | the wealth (l-amwāli) | and the children (wal-awlādi), | like the example (kamathali) | of a rain (ghaythin), | pleases (aʿjaba) | the tillers (l-kufāra) | its growth (nabātuhu); | then (thumma) | it dries (yahīju) | and you see it (fatarāhu) | turning yellow (muṣ'farran); | then (thumma) | becomes (yakūnu) | debris (ḥuṭāman). | And in (wafī) | the Hereafter (l-ākhirati) | is a punishment (ʿadhābun) | severe (shadīdun) | and forgiveness (wamaghfiratun) | from (mina) | Allah (l-lahi) | and Pleasure (wariḍ'wānun). | But not (wamā) | is the life (l-ḥayatu) | of the world (l-dun'yā) | except (illā) | the enjoyment (matāʿu) | of delusion (l-ghurūri).

57:21 Race to the forgiveness from your Lord and a Garden its width is like (the) width of the heaven and the earth, prepared for those who believe in Allah and His Messengers. That is the Bounty of Allah, He gives to whom He wills. And Allah is the Possessor of Bounty, the Great.

Race (sābiqū) | to (ilā) | the forgiveness (maghfiratin) | from (min) | your Lord (rabbikum) | and a Garden (wajannatin) | its width (ʿarḍuhā) | is like (the) width (kaʿarḍi) | of the heaven (l-samāi) | and the earth (wal-arḍi), | prepared (uʿiddat) | for those who (lilladhīna) | believe (āmanū) | in Allah (bil-lahi) | and His Messengers (warusulihi). | That (dhālika) | is the Bounty (faḍlu) | of Allah (l-lahi), | He gives (yu'tīhi) | to whom (man) | He wills (yashāu). | And Allah (wal-lahu) | is the Possessor of Bounty (dhū), | is the Possessor of Bounty (l-faḍli), | the Great (l-ʿaẓīmi).

57:22 Not strikes any disaster in the earth and not in yourselves, but in a Register before that We bring it into existence. Indeed, that for Allah is easy.

Not (mā) | strikes (aṣāba) | any (min) | disaster (muṣībatin) | in (fī) | the earth (l-arḍi) | and not (walā) | in (fī) | yourselves (anfusikum), | but (illā) | in (fī) | a Register (kitābin) | before (min) | before (qabli) | that (an) | We bring it into existence (nabra-ahā). | Indeed (inna), | that (dhālika) | for (ʿalā) | Allah (l-lahi) | is easy (yasīrun).

57:23 So that you may not grieve over what has escaped you, and do not exult at what He has given you. And Allah does not love every self-deluded boaster,

So that you may not (likaylā) | grieve (tasaw) | over (ʿalā) | what (mā) | has escaped you (fātakum), | and do not (walā) | exult (tafraḥū) | at what (bimā) | He has given you (ātākum). | And Allah (wal-lahu) | does not (lā) | love (yuḥibbu) | every (kulla) | self-deluded (mukh'tālin) | boaster (fakhūrin),

57:24 Those who are stingy and enjoin on the people stinginess. And whoever turns away, then indeed, Allah, He is Free of need, the Praiseworthy.

Those who (alladhīna) | are stingy (yabkhalūna) | and enjoin (wayamurūna) | on the people (l-nāsa) | stinginess (bil-bukh'li). | And whoever (waman) | turns away (yatawalla), | then indeed (fa-inna), | Allah (l-laha), | He (huwa) | is Free of need (l-ghaniyu), | the Praiseworthy (l-ḥamīdu).

57:25 Certainly We sent Our Messengers with clear proofs and We sent down with them the Scripture and the Balance that may establish the people justice. And We sent down [the] iron, wherein is power mighty and benefits for the people, and so that Allah may make evident he who helps Him and His Messengers, unseen. Indeed, Allah is All-Strong All-Mighty.

Certainly (laqad) | We sent (arsalnā) | Our Messengers (rusulanā) | with clear proofs (bil-bayināti) | and We sent down (wa-anzalnā) | with them (maʿahumu) | the Scripture (l-kitāba) | and the Balance (wal-mīzāna) | that may establish (liyaqūma) | the people (l-nāsu) | justice (bil-qis'ṭi). | And We sent down (wa-anzalnā) | [the] iron (l-ḥadīda), | wherein (fīhi) | is power (basun) | mighty (shadīdun) | and benefits (wamanāfiʿu) | for the people (lilnnāsi), | and so that Allah may make evident (waliyaʿlama) | and so that Allah may make evident (l-lahu) | he who (man) | helps Him (yanṣuruhu) | and His Messengers (warusulahu), | unseen (bil-ghaybi). | Indeed (inna),

| Allah (l-laha) | is All-Strong (qawiyyun) | All-Mighty (ʿazīzun).

57:26 And certainly We sent Nuh and Ibrahim, and We placed in their offspring Prophethood and the Scripture; and among them is a guided one, but most of them are defiantly disobediently.

And certainly (walaqad) | We sent (arsalnā) | Nuh (nūḥan) | and Ibrahim (wa-ib'rāhīma), | and We placed (wajaʿalnā) | in (fī) | their offspring (dhurriyyatihimā) | Prophethood (l-nubuwata) | and the Scripture (wal-kitāba); | and among them (famin'hum) | is a guided one (muh'tadin), | but most (wakathīrun) | of them (min'hum) | are defiantly disobediently (fāsiqūna).

57:27 Then We sent on their footsteps Our Messengers and We followed with Isa, son of Maryam, and We gave him the Injeel. And We placed in the hearts of those who followed him compassion and mercy. But monasticism they innovated - not We prescribed it for them - only seeking the pleasure of Allah, but not they observed it with right observance. So We gave those who believed among them their reward, but most of them are defiantly disobediently.

Then (thumma) | We sent (qaffaynā) | on (ʿalā) | their footsteps (āthārihim) | Our Messengers (birusulinā) | and We followed (waqaffaynā) | with Isa (biʿīsā), | son (ib'ni) | of Maryam (maryama), | and We gave him (waātaynāhu) | the Injeel (l-injīla). | And We placed (wajaʿalnā) | in (fī) | the hearts (qulūbi) | of those who (alladhīna) | followed him (ittabaʿūhu) | compassion (rafatan) | and mercy (waraḥmatan). | But monasticism (warahbāniyyatan) | they innovated (ib'tadaʿūhā)- | not (mā) | We prescribed it (katabnāhā) | for them (ʿalayhim)- | only (illā) | seeking (ib'tighāa) | the pleasure (riḍ'wāni) | of Allah (l-lahi), | but not (famā) | they observed it (raʿawhā) | with right (ḥaqqa) | observance (riʿāyatihā). | So We gave (faātaynā) | those who (alladhīna) | believed (āmanū) | among them (min'hum) | their reward (ajrahum), | but most (wakathīrun) | of them (min'hum) | are defiantly disobediently (fāsiqūna).

57:28 O you who believe! Fear Allah and believe in His Messenger; He will give you double portion of His Mercy and He will make for you a light, you will walk with it, and He will forgive you. And Allah is Oft-Forgiving, Most Merciful.

O you who believe (yāayyuhā)! | O you who believe (alladhīna)! | O you who believe (āmanū)! | Fear (ittaqū) | Allah (l-laha) | and believe (waāminū) | in His Messenger (birasūlihi); | He will give you (yu'tikum) | double portion (kif'layni) | of (min) | His Mercy (raḥmatihi) | and He will make (wayajʿal) | for you (lakum) | a light (nūran), | you will walk (tamshūna) | with it (bihi), | and He will forgive (wayaghfir) | you (lakum). | And Allah (wal-lahu) | is Oft-Forgiving (ghafūrun), | Most Merciful (raḥīmun).

57:29 So that may know the People of the Book that not they have power over anything from the Bounty of Allah, and that the Bounty is in Allah's Hand; He gives it whom He wills. And Allah is the Possessor of Bounty the Great.

So that (li-allā) | may know (yaʿlama) | the People (ahlu) | of the Book (l-kitābi) | that not (allā) | they have power (yaqdirūna) | over (ʿalā) | anything (shayin) | from (min) | the Bounty (faḍli) | of Allah (l-lahi), | and that (wa-anna) | the Bounty (l-faḍla) | is in Allah's Hand (biyadi); | is in Allah's Hand (l-lahi); | He gives it (yu'tīhi) | whom (man) | He wills (yashāu). | And Allah (wal-lahu) | is the Possessor of Bounty (dhū) | is the Possessor of Bounty (l-faḍli) | the Great (l-ʿaẓīmi).

Chapter (58) Sūrat l-Mujādilah (She That Disputeth)

58:1 Indeed, Allah has heard the speech of one who disputes with you concerning her husband and she directs her complaint to Allah. And Allah hears the dialogue of both of you. Indeed, Allah is All-Hearer, All-Seer.

Indeed (qad), | Allah has heard (samiʿa) | Allah has heard (l-lahu) | the speech (qawla) | of one who (allatī) | disputes with you (tujādiluka) | concerning (fī) | her husband (zawjihā) | and she directs her complaint (watashtakī) | to (ilā) | Allah (l-lahi). | And Allah (wal-lahu) | hears (yasmaʿu) | the dialogue of both of you (taḥāwurakumā). | Indeed (inna), | Allah (l-laha) | is All-Hearer (samīʿun), | All-Seer (baṣīrun).

58:2 Those who pronounce zihar among you [from] to their wives, not they are their mothers. Not are their mothers except those who gave them birth. And indeed, they surely say an evil [of] [the] word and a lie. But indeed, Allah is surely, Oft-Pardoning, Oft-Forgiving.

Those who (alladhīna) | pronounce zihar (yuẓāhirūna) | among you (minkum) | [from] (min) | to their wives (nisāihim), | not (mā) | they (hunna) | are their mothers (ummahātihim). | Not (in) | are their mothers (ummahātuhum) | except (illā) | those who (allāī) | gave them birth (waladnahum). | And indeed, they (wa-innahum) | surely say (layaqūlūna) | an evil (munkaran) | [of] (mina) | [the] word (l-qawli) | and a lie (wazūran). | But indeed (wa-inna), | Allah (l-laha) | is surely, Oft-Pardoning (laʿafuwwun), | Oft-Forgiving (ghafūrun).

58:3 And those who pronounce zihar [from] to their wives then go back on what they said, then freeing of a slave before [that] they touch each other. That you are admonished to it. And Allah of what you do is All-Aware.

And those who (wa-alladhīna) | pronounce zihar (yuẓāhirūna) | [from] (min) | to their wives (nisāihim) | then (thumma) | go back (yaʿūdūna) | on what (limā) | they said (qālū), | then freeing (fataḥrīru) | of a slave (raqabatin) | before (min) | before (qabli) | [that] (an) | they touch each other (yatamāssā). | That (dhālikum) | you are admonished (tūʿaẓūna) | to it (bihi). | And Allah (wal-lahu) | of what (bimā) | you do (taʿmalūna) | is All-Aware (khabīrun).

58:4 Then whoever does not find, then fasting for two months consecutively before [that] they both touch each other. But he who not is able then the feeding of sixty needy ones. That - so that you may believe in Allah and His Messenger, and these are the limits of Allah, and for the disbelievers is a punishment painful.

Then whoever (faman) | does not (lam) | find (yajid), | then fasting (faṣiyāmu) | for two months (shahrayni) | consecutively (mutatābiʿayni) | before (min) | before (qabli) | [that] (an) | they both touch each other (yatamāssā). | But he who (faman) | not (lam) | is able (yastaṭiʿ) | then the feeding (fa-iṭʿāmu) | of sixty (sittīna) | needy ones (mis'kīnan). | That (dhālika)- | so that you may believe (litu'minū) | in Allah (bil-lahi) | and His Messenger (warasūlihi), | and these (watil'ka) | are the limits (ḥudūdu) | of Allah (l-lahi), | and for the disbelievers (walil'kāfirīna) | is a punishment (ʿadhābun) | painful (alīmun).

58:5 Indeed, those who oppose Allah and His Messenger will be disgraced as were disgraced those before them. And certainly We have sent down Verses clear. And for the disbelievers is a punishment humiliating.

Indeed (inna), | those who (alladhīna) | oppose (yuḥāddūna) | Allah (l-laha) | and His Messenger (warasūlahu) | will be disgraced (kubitū) | as (kamā) | were disgraced (kubita) | those (alladhīna) | before them (min). | before them (qablihim). | And certainly (waqad) | We have sent down (anzalnā) | Verses (āyātin) | clear (bayyinātin). | And for the disbelievers (walil'kāfirīna) | is a punishment (ʿadhābun) | humiliating (muhīnun).

58:6 On the Day when Allah will raise them all and inform them of what they did. Allah has recorded it while they forgot it. And Allah is over all things a Witness.

On the Day (yawma) | when Allah will raise them (yabʿathuhumu) | when Allah will raise them (l-lahu) | all (jamīʿan) | and inform them (fayunabbi-uhum) | of what (bimā) | they did (ʿamilū). | Allah has recorded it (aḥṣāhu) | Allah has recorded it (l-lahu) | while they forgot it (wanasūhu). | And Allah (wal-lahu) | is over (ʿalā) | all (kulli) | things (shayin) | a Witness (shahīdun).

58:7 Do not you see that Allah knows whatever is in the heavens and whatever is in the earth? Not there is any secret counsel of three but He is the fourth of them, and not five but He is the sixth of them, and not less than that and not more but He is with them wherever they are. Then He will inform them of what they did on the Day of the Resurrection. Indeed, Allah of every thing is All-Knower.

Do not (alam) | you see (tara) | that (anna) | Allah (l-laha) | knows (yaʿlamu) | whatever (mā) | is in (fī) | the heavens (l-samāwāti) | and whatever (wamā) | is in (fī) | the earth (l-arḍi)? | Not (mā) | there is (yakūnu) | any (min) | secret counsel (najwā) | of three (thalāthatin) | but (illā) | He is (huwa) | the fourth of them (rābiʿuhum), | and not (walā) | five (khamsatin) | but (illā) | He is (huwa) | the sixth of them (sādisuhum), | and not (walā) | less (adnā) | than (min) | that (dhālika) | and not (walā) | more (akthara) | but (illā) | He (huwa) | is with them (maʿahum) | wherever (ayna) | wherever (mā) | they are (kānū). | Then (thumma) | He will inform them (yunabbi-uhum) | of what (bimā) | they did (ʿamilū) | on the Day (yawma) | of the Resurrection (l-qiyāmati). | Indeed (inna), | Allah (l-laha) | of every (bikulli) | thing (shayin) | is All-Knower (ʿalīmun).

58:8 Do not you see [to] those who were forbidden from secret counsels, then they return to what they were forbidden from [it], and they hold secret counsels for sin and aggression and disobedience to the Messenger? And when they come to you, they greet you with what not greets you therewith Allah, and they say among themselves, "Why does not Allah punish us for what we say?" Sufficient for them is Hell, they will burn in it and worst is the destination.

Do not (alam) | you see (tara) | [to] (ilā) | those who (alladhīna) | were forbidden (nuhū) | from (ʿani) | secret counsels (l-najwā), | then (thumma) | they return (yaʿūdūna) | to what (limā) | they were forbidden (nuhū) | from [it] (ʿanhu), | and they hold secret counsels (wayatanājawna) | for sin (bil-ith'mi) | and aggression (wal-ʿud'wāni) | and disobedience (wamaʿṣiyati) | to the Messenger (l-rasūli)? | And when (wa-idhā) | they come to you (jāūka), | they greet you (ḥayyawka) | with what (bimā) | not (lam) | greets you (yuḥayyika) | therewith (bihi) | Allah (l-lahu), | and they say (wayaqūlūna) | among (fī) | themselves (anfusihim), | "Why does not (lawlā) | Allah punish us (yuʿadhibunā) | Allah punish us (l-lahu) | for what (bimā) | we say? (naqūlu)" | Sufficient for them (ḥasbuhum) | is Hell (jahannamu), | they will burn in it (yaṣlawnahā) | and worst is (fabi'sa) | the destination (l-maṣīru).

58:9 O you who believe! When you hold secret counsel then do not hold secret counsel for sin and aggression and disobedience to the Messenger, but hold secret counsel for righteousness and piety. And fear Allah, the One Who, to Him you will be gathered.

O you who believe (yāayyuhā)! | O you who believe (alladhīna)! | O you who believe (āmanū)! | When (idhā) | you hold secret counsel (tanājaytum) | then do not (falā) | hold secret counsel (tatanājaw) | for sin (bil-ith'mi) | and aggression (wal-ʿud'wāni) | and disobedience (wamaʿṣiyati) | to the Messenger (l-rasūli), | but hold secret counsel (watanājaw) | for righteousness (bil-biri) | and piety (wal-taqwā). | And fear (wa-ittaqū) | Allah (l-laha), | the One Who (alladhī), | to Him (ilayhi) | you will be gathered (tuḥ'sharūna).

58:10 Only the secret counsels are from the Shaitaan that he may grieve those who believe, but not he can harm them in anything except by Allah's permission. And upon Allah let put their trust the believers.

Only (innamā) | the secret counsels (l-najwā) | are from (mina) | the Shaitaan (l-shayṭāni) |

that he may grieve (liyaḥzuna) | those who (alladhīna) | believe (āmanū), | but not (walaysa) | he can harm them (biḍārrihim) | in anything (shayan) | except (illā) | by Allah's permission (bi-idh'ni). | by Allah's permission (l-lahi). | And upon (waʿalā) | Allah (l-lahi) | let put their trust (falyatawakkali) | the believers (l-mu'minūna).

58:11 O you who believe! When it is said to you "Make room," in the assemblies then make room, Allah will make room for you. And when it is said "Rise up," then rise up; Allah will raise those who believe among you and those who were given the knowledge, in degrees. And Allah of what you do is All-Aware.

O you who believe (yāayyuhā)! | O you who believe (alladhīna)! | O you who believe (āmanū)! | When (idhā) | it is said (qīla) | to you (lakum) | "Make room, (tafassaḥū)" | in (fī) | the assemblies (l-majālisi) | then make room (fa-if'saḥū), | Allah will make room (yafsaḥi) | Allah will make room (l-lahu) | for you (lakum). | And when (wa-idhā) | it is said (qīla) | "Rise up, (unshuzū)" | then rise up (fa-unshuzū); | Allah will raise (yarfaʿi) | Allah will raise (l-lahu) | those who (alladhīna) | believe (āmanū) | among you (minkum) | and those who (wa-alladhīna) | were given (ūtū) | the knowledge (l-ʿil'ma), | in degrees (darajātin). | And Allah (wal-lahu) | of what (bimā) | you do (taʿmalūna) | is All-Aware (khabīrun).

58:12 O you who believe! When you privately consult the Messenger, then offer before your private consultation, charity. That is better for you and purer. But if not you find, then indeed, Allah is Oft-Forgiving, Most Merciful.

O you who believe (yāayyuhā)! | O you who believe (alladhīna)! | O you who believe (āmanū)! | When (idhā) | you privately consult (nājaytumu) | the Messenger (l-rasūla), | then offer (faqaddimū) | before (bayna) | before (yaday) | your private consultation (najwākum), | charity (ṣadaqatan). | That (dhālika) | is better (khayrun) | for you (lakum) | and purer (wa-aṭharu). | But if (fa-in) | not (lam) | you find (tajidū), | then indeed (fa-inna), | Allah (l-laha) | is Oft-Forgiving (ghafūrun), | Most Merciful (raḥīmun).

58:13 Are you afraid to offer before your private consultation charities? Then when you do not and Allah has forgiven you, then establish the prayer and give the zakah, and obey Allah and His Messenger. And Allah is All-Aware of what you do.

Are you afraid (a-ashfaqtum) | to (an) | offer (tuqaddimū) | before (bayna) | before (yaday) | your private consultation (najwākum) | charities (ṣadaqātin)? | Then when (fa-idh) | you do not (lam) | you do not (tafʿalū) | and Allah has forgiven (watāba) | and Allah has forgiven (l-lahu) | you (ʿalaykum), | then establish (fa-aqīmū) | the prayer (l-ṣalata) | and give (waātū) | the zakah (l-zakata), | and obey (wa-aṭīʿū) | Allah (l-laha) | and His Messenger (warasūlahu). | And Allah (wal-lahu) | is All-Aware (khabīrun) | of what (bimā) | you do (taʿmalūna).

58:14 Do not you see [to] those who take as allies a people, wrath of Allah is upon them? They are not of you and not of them, and they swear to the lie while they know.

Do not (alam) | you see (tara) | [to] (ilā) | those who (alladhīna) | take as allies (tawallaw) | a people (qawman), | wrath (ghaḍiba) | of Allah (l-lahu) | is upon them (ʿalayhim)? | They are not (mā) | They are not (hum) | of you (minkum) | and not (walā) | of them (min'hum), | and they swear (wayaḥlifūna) | to (ʿalā) | the lie (l-kadhibi) | while they (wahum) | know (yaʿlamūna).

58:15 Allah has prepared for them a punishment severe. Indeed, [they] evil is what they used to do.

Allah has prepared (aʿadda) | Allah has prepared (l-lahu) | for them (lahum) | a punishment (ʿadhāban) | severe (shadīdan). | Indeed, [they] (innahum) | evil is (sāa) | what (mā) | they used to (kānū) | do (yaʿmalūna).

58:16 They have taken their oaths as a cover, so they hinder from the way of Allah, so for them is a punishment humiliating.

They have taken (ittakhadhū) | their oaths (aymānahum) | as a cover (junnatan), | so they hinder (faṣaddū) | from (ʿan) | the way of Allah (sabīli), | the way of Allah (l-lahi), | so for them (falahum) | is a punishment (ʿadhābun) | humiliating (muhīnun).

58:17 Never will avail them their wealth and not their children against Allah in anything. Those will be companions of the Fire, they, in it, will abide forever.

Never (lan) | will avail (tugh'niya) | them (ʿanhum) | their wealth (amwāluhum) | and not (walā) | their children (awlāduhum) | against (mina) | Allah (l-lahi) | in anything (shayan). | Those (ulāika) | will be companions (aṣḥābu) | of the Fire (l-nāri), | they (hum), | in it (fīhā), | will abide forever (khālidūna).

58:18 On the Day Allah will raise them all, then they will swear to Him as they swear to you. And they think that they are on something. No doubt! Indeed, they [they] are the liars.

On the Day (yawma) | Allah will raise them (yabʿathuhumu) | Allah will raise them (l-lahu) | all (jamīʿan), | then they will swear (fayaḥlifūna) | to Him (lahu) | as (kamā) | they swear (yaḥlifūna) | to you (lakum). | And they think (wayaḥsabūna) | that they (annahum) | are on (ʿalā) | something (shayin). | No doubt (alā)! | Indeed, they (innahum) | [they] (humu) | are the liars (l-kādhibūna).

58:19 Has overcome them the Shaitaan, so he made them forget the remembrance of Allah. Those are the party of the Shaitaan. No doubt! Indeed, the party of the Shaitaan, they will be the losers.

Has overcome (is'taḥwadha) | them (ʿalayhimu) | the Shaitaan (l-shayṭānu), | so he made them forget (fa-ansāhum) | the remembrance (dhik'ra) | of Allah (l-lahi). | Those (ulāika) | are the party (ḥiz'bu) | of the Shaitaan (l-shayṭāni). | No doubt (alā)! | Indeed (inna), | the party (ḥiz'ba) | of the Shaitaan (l-shayṭāni), | they (humu) | will be the losers (l-khāsirūna).

58:20 Indeed, those who oppose Allah and His Messenger, those will be among the most humiliated.

Indeed (inna), | those who (alladhīna) | oppose (yuḥāddūna) | Allah (l-laha) | and His Messenger (warasūlahu), | those (ulāika) | will be among (fī) | the most humiliated (l-adhalīna).

58:21 Allah has decreed, "Surely, I will overcome, I and My Messengers." Indeed, Allah is All-Strong, All-Mighty.

Allah has decreed (kataba), | Allah has decreed (l-lahu), | "Surely, I will overcome (la-aghlibanna), | I (anā) | and My Messengers. (warusulī)" | Indeed (inna), | Allah (l-laha) | is All-Strong (qawiyyun), | All-Mighty (ʿazīzun).

58:22 You will not find a people who believe in Allah and the Day the Last loving those who oppose Allah and His Messenger even if they were their fathers or their sons or their brothers or their kindred. Those - He has decreed within their hearts faith and supported them with a spirit from Him. And He will admit them to Gardens, flow from underneath it the rivers, will abide forever in it. Allah is pleased with them, and they are pleased with Him. Those are the party of Allah. No doubt! Indeed, the party of Allah, they are the successful ones.

You will not find (lā) | You will not find (tajidu) | a people (qawman) | who believe (yu'minūna) | in Allah (bil-lahi) | and the Day (wal-yawmi) | the Last (l-ākhiri) | loving (yuwāddūna) | those who (man) | oppose (ḥādda) | Allah (l-laha) | and His Messenger (warasūlahu) | even if (walaw) | they were (kānū) | their fathers (ābāahum) | or (aw) | their sons (abnāahum) | or (aw) | their brothers (ikh'wānahum) | or (aw) | their kindred (ʿashīratahum). | Those (ulāika)- | He has decreed (kataba) | within (fī) | their hearts (qulūbihimu) | faith (l-īmāna) | and supported them (wa-ayyadahum) | with a spirit (birūḥin) | from Him (min'hu). | And He will admit them (wayud'khiluhum) | to Gardens (jannātin), | flow (tajrī) | from (min) | underneath it (taḥtihā) | the rivers (l-anhāru), | will abide forever (khālidīna) | in it (fīhā). | Allah is pleased (raḍiya) | Allah is pleased (l-lahu) | with them (ʿanhum), | and they are pleased (waraḍū) | with Him (ʿanhu). | Those (ulāika) | are the party (ḥiz'bu) | of Allah (l-lahi). | No doubt (alā)! | Indeed (inna), | the party (ḥiz'ba) | of Allah (l-lahi), | they (humu) | are the successful ones (l-muf'liḥūna).

Chapter (59) Sūrat l-Ḥashr (The Gathering)

59:1 Glorifies [to] Allah whatever is in the heavens and whatever is in the earth. And He is the All-Mighty, the All-Wise.

Glorifies (sabbaḥa) | [to] Allah (lillahi) | whatever (mā) | is in (fī) | the heavens (l-samāwāti) | and whatever (wamā) | is in (fī) | the earth (l-arḍi). | And He (wahuwa) | is the All-Mighty (l-ʿazīzu), | the All-Wise (l-ḥakīmu).

59:2 He is the One Who expelled those who disbelieved from the People of the Scripture from their homes at the first gathering. Not you think that they would leave, and they thought that [they] would defend them their fortresses against Allah. But came to them Allah from where not they expected, and He cast into their hearts [the] terror, they destroyed their houses with their hands and the hands of the believers. So take a lesson, O those endowed with insight!

He (huwa) | is the One Who (alladhī) | expelled (akhraja) | those who (alladhīna) | disbelieved (kafarū) | from (min) | the People (ahli) | of the Scripture (l-kitābi) | from (min) | their homes (diyārihim) | at the first (li-awwali) | gathering (l-ḥashri). | Not (mā) | you think (ẓanantum) | that (an) | they would leave (yakhrujū), | and they thought (waẓannū) | that [they] (annahum) | would defend them (māniʿatuhum) | their fortresses (ḥuṣūnuhum) | against (mina) | Allah (l-lahi). | But came to them (fa-atāhumu) | Allah (l-lahu) | from (min) | where (ḥaythu) | not (lam) | they expected (yaḥtasibū), | and He cast (waqadhafa) | into (fī) | their hearts (qulūbihimu) | [the] terror (l-ruʿ'ba), | they destroyed (yukh'ribūna) | their houses (buyūtahum) | with their hands (bi-aydīhim) | and the hands (wa-aydī) | of the believers (l-mu'minīna). | So take a lesson (fa-iʿ'tabirū), | O those endowed (yāulī) | with insight (l-abṣāri)!

59:3 And if not [that] had decreed Allah for them the exile, certainly He would have punished them in the world, and for them in the Hereafter is a punishment of the Fire.

And if not (walawlā) | [that] (an) | had decreed (kataba) | Allah (l-lahu) | for them (ʿalayhimu) | the exile (l-jalāa), | certainly He would have punished them (laʿadhabahum) | in (fī) | the world (l-dun'yā), | and for them (walahum) | in (fī) | the Hereafter (l-ākhirati) | is a punishment (ʿadhābu) | of the Fire (l-nāri).

59:4 That is because [they] they opposed Allah and His Messenger. And whoever opposes Allah then indeed, Allah is severe in penalty.

That (dhālika) | is because [they] (bi-annahum) | they opposed (shāqqū) | Allah (l-laha) | and His Messenger (warasūlahu). | And whoever (waman) | opposes (yushāqqi) | Allah (l-laha) | then indeed (fa-inna), | Allah (l-laha) | is severe (shadīdu) | in penalty (l-ʿiqābi).

59:5 Whatever you cut down of the palm-trees or you left them standing on their roots, it was by the permission of Allah, and that He may disgrace the defiantly disobedient.

Whatever (mā) | you cut down (qaṭaʿtum) | of (min) | the palm-trees (līnatin) | or (aw) | you left them (taraktumūhā) | standing (qāimatan) | on (ʿalā) | their roots (uṣūlihā), | it was by the permission (fabi-idh'ni) | of Allah (l-lahi), | and that He may disgrace (waliyukh'ziya) | the defiantly disobedient (l-fāsiqīna).

59:6 And what was restored by Allah to His Messenger from them, then not you made expedition for it of horses and not camels, but Allah gives power to His Messengers over whom He wills. And Allah is on every thing All-Powerful.

And what (wamā) | was restored (afāa) | by Allah (l-lahu) | to (ʿalā) | His Messenger (rasūlihi) | from them (min'hum), | then not (famā) | you made expedition (awjaftum) | for it (ʿalayhi) | of (min) | horses (khaylin) | and not (walā) | camels (rikābin), | but (walākinna) | Allah (l-laha) | gives power (yusalliṭu) | to His Messengers (rusulahu) | over (ʿalā) | whom (man) | He wills (yashāu). | And Allah (wal-lahu) | is on (ʿalā) | every (kulli) | thing (shayin) | All-Powerful (qadīrun).

59:7 What was restored by Allah to His Messenger from the people of the towns, it is for Allah and His Messenger and for those of the kindred and the orphans and the needy and the wayfarer, that not it becomes a perpetual circulation between the rich among you. And whatever gives you the Messenger, take it and whatever he forbids you from it, refrain. And fear Allah. Indeed, Allah is severe in penalty.

What (mā) | was restored (afāa) | by Allah (l-lahu) | to (ʿalā) | His Messenger (rasūlihi) | from (min) | the people (ahli) | of the towns (l-qurā), | it is for Allah (falillahi) | and His Messenger (walilrrasūli) | and for those (walidhī) | of the kindred (l-qur'bā) | and the orphans (wal-yatāmā) | and the needy (wal-masākīni) | and (wa-ib'ni) | the wayfarer (l-sabīli), | that (kay) | not (lā) | it becomes (yakūna) | a perpetual circulation (dūlatan) | between (bayna) | the rich (l-aghniyāi) | among you (minkum). | And whatever (wamā) | gives you (ātākumu) | the Messenger (l-rasūlu), | take it (fakhudhūhu) | and whatever (wamā) | he forbids you (nahākum) | from it (ʿanhu), | refrain (fa-intahū). | And fear (wa-ittaqū) | Allah (l-laha). | Indeed (inna), | Allah (l-laha) | is severe (shadīdu) | in penalty (l-ʿiqābi).

59:8 For the poor emigrants, those who were expelled from their homes and their properties, seeking bounty from Allah and pleasure and helping Allah and His Messenger. Those, they are the truthful.

For the poor (lil'fuqarāi) | emigrants (l-muhājirīna), | those who (alladhīna) | were expelled (ukh'rijū) | from (min) | their homes (diyārihim) | and their properties (wa-amwālihim), | seeking (yabtaghūna) | bounty (faḍlan) | from (mina) | Allah (l-lahi) | and pleasure (wariḍ'wānan) | and helping (wayanṣurūna) | Allah (l-laha) | and His Messenger (warasūlahu). | Those (ulāika), | they (humu) | are the truthful (l-ṣādiqūna).

59:9 And those who settled in the home and accepted faith from before them love those who emigrated to them, and not they find in their breasts any want of what they were given but prefer over themselves, even though was with them poverty. And whoever is saved from stinginess of his soul, then those [they] are the successful ones.

And those who (wa-alladhīna) | settled (tabawwaū) | in the home (l-dāra) | and accepted faith (wal-īmāna) | from (min) | before them (qablihim) | love (yuḥibbūna) | those who (man) | emigrated (hājara) | to them (ilayhim), | and not (walā) | they find (yajidūna) | in (fī) | their breasts (ṣudūrihim) | any want (ḥājatan) | of what (mimmā) | they were given (ūtū) | but prefer (wayu'thirūna) | over (ʿalā) | themselves (anfusihim), | even though (walaw) | was (kāna) | with them (bihim) | poverty (khaṣāṣatun). | And whoever (waman) | is saved (yūqa) | from stinginess (shuḥḥa) | of his soul (nafsihi), | then those (fa-ulāika) | [they] (humu) | are the successful ones (l-muf'liḥūna).

59:10 And those who came from after them they say, "Our Lord, forgive us and our brothers who preceded us in faith, and do not put in our hearts any rancor towards those who believed. Our Lord, indeed You are Full of Kindness, Most Merciful."

And those who (wa-alladhīna) | came (jāū) | from (min) | after them (baʿdihim) | they say (yaqūlūna), | "Our Lord (rabbanā), | forgive (igh'fir) | us (lanā) | and our brothers (wali-ikh'wāninā) | who (alladhīna) | preceded us (sabaqūnā) | in faith (bil-īmāni), | and do not (walā) | put (taj'al) | in (fī) | our hearts (qulūbinā) | any rancor (ghillan) | towards those who (lilladhīna) | believed (āmanū). | Our Lord (rabbanā), | indeed You (innaka) | are Full of Kindness (raūfun), | Most Merciful. (raḥīmun)"

59:11 Do not you see [to] those who were hypocrites, saying to their brothers, those who disbelieved, among the People of the Scripture, "If you are expelled, surely we will leave with you, and not we will obey concerning you anyone, ever; and if you are fought, certainly we will help you." And Allah bears witness that they are surely liars.

Do not (alam) | you see (tara) | [to] (ilā) | those who (alladhīna) | were hypocrites (nāfaqū), | saying (yaqūlūna) | to their brothers (li-ikh'wānihimu), | those who (alladhīna) | disbelieved (kafarū), | among (min) | the People (ahli) | of the Scripture (l-kitābi), | "If (la-in) | you are expelled (ukh'rij'tum), | surely we will leave (lanakhrujanna) | with you (ma'akum), | and not (walā) | we will obey (nuṭī'u) | concerning you (fīkum) | anyone (aḥadan), | ever (abadan); | and if (wa-in) | you are fought (qūtil'tum), | certainly we will help you. (lananṣurannakum)" | And Allah (wal-lahu) | bears witness (yashhadu) | that they (innahum) | are surely liars (lakādhibūna).

59:12 If they are expelled, not they will leave with them, and if they are fought not they will help them. And if they help them, certainly they will turn their backs; then not they will be helped.

If (la-in) | they are expelled (ukh'rijū), | not (lā) | they will leave (yakhrujūna) | with them (ma'ahum), | and if (wala-in) | they are fought (qūtilū) | not (lā) | they will help them (yanṣurūnahum). | And if (wala-in) | they help them (naṣarūhum), | certainly they will turn (layuwallunna) | their backs (l-adbāra); | then (thumma) | not (lā) | they will be helped (yunṣarūna).

59:13 Certainly you are more intense in fear in their breasts than Allah. That is because they are a people who do not understand.

Certainly you (la-antum) | are more intense (ashaddu) | in fear (rahbatan) | in (fī) | their breasts (ṣudūrihim) | than (mina) | Allah (l-lahi). | That (dhālika) | is because they (bi-annahum) | are a people (qawmun) | who do not (lā) | understand (yafqahūna).

59:14 Not will they fight you all except in towns fortified or from behind walls. Their violence among themselves is severe. You think they are united, but their hearts are divided. That is because they are a people, not they reason.

Not (lā) | will they fight you (yuqātilūnakum) | all (jamī'an) | except (illā) | in (fī) | towns (quran) | fortified (muḥaṣṣanatin) | or (aw) | from (min) | behind (warāi) | walls (judurin). | Their violence (basuhum) | among themselves (baynahum) | is severe (shadīdun). | You think they (taḥsabuhum) | are united (jamī'an), | but their hearts (waqulūbuhum) | are divided (shattā). | That (dhālika) | is because they (bi-annahum) | are a people (qawmun), | not (lā) | they reason (ya'qilūna).

59:15 Like the example of those from before them shortly, they tasted the evil result of their affair, and for them is a punishment painful.

Like the example (kamathali) | of those (alladhīna) | from (min) | before them (qablihim) | shortly (qarīban), | they tasted (dhāqū) | the evil result (wabāla) | of their affair (amrihim), | and for them (walahum) | is a punishment ('adhābun) | painful (alīmun).

59:16 Like the example of the Shaitaan, when he says to man, "Disbelieve." But when he disbelieves, he says, "Indeed, I am disassociated from you. Indeed, [I] I fear Allah, the Lord of the worlds."

Like the example (kamathali) | of the Shaitaan (l-shayṭāni), | when (idh) | he says (qāla) | to man (lil'insāni), | "Disbelieve. (uk'fur)" | But when (falammā) | he disbelieves (kafara), | he says (qāla), | "Indeed, I am (innī) | disassociated (barīon) | from you (minka). | Indeed, [I] (innī) | I fear (akhāfu) | Allah (l-laha), | the Lord (rabba) | of the worlds. (l-ʿālamīna)"

59:17 So will be the end of both of them, that they will be in the Fire abiding forever therein. And that is the recompense of the wrongdoers.

So will be (fakāna) | the end of both of them (ʿāqibatahumā), | that they (annahumā) | will be in (fī) | the Fire (l-nāri) | abiding forever (khālidayni) | therein (fīhā). | And that (wadhālika) | is the recompense (jazāu) | of the wrongdoers (l-ẓālimīna).

59:18 O you who believe! Fear Allah and let look every soul what it has sent forth for tomorrow, and fear Allah. Indeed, Allah is All-Aware of what you do.

O (yāayyuhā) | you who (alladhīna) | believe (āmanū)! | Fear (ittaqū) | Allah (l-laha) | and let look (waltanẓur) | every soul (nafsun) | what (mā) | it has sent forth (qaddamat) | for tomorrow (lighadin), | and fear (wa-ittaqū) | Allah (l-laha). | Indeed (inna), | Allah (l-laha) | is All-Aware (khabīrun) | of what (bimā) | you do (taʿmalūna).

59:19 And do not be like those who forgot Allah, so He made them forget themselves. Those [they] are the defiantly disobedient.

And do not (walā) | be (takūnū) | like those who (ka-alladhīna) | forgot (nasū) | Allah (l-laha), | so He made them forget (fa-ansāhum) | themselves (anfusahum). | Those (ulāika) | [they] (humu) | are the defiantly disobedient (l-fāsiqūna).

59:20 Not equal are the companions of the Fire and the companions of Paradise. The companions of Paradise they are the achievers.

Not (lā) | equal (yastawī) | are the companions (aṣḥābu) | of the Fire (l-nāri) | and the companions (wa-aṣḥābu) | of Paradise (l-janati). | The companions (aṣḥābu) | of Paradise (l-janati) | they (humu) | are the achievers (l-fāizūna).

59:21 If We had sent down this Quran on a mountain, surely you would have seen it humbled, breaking asunder from the fear of Allah. And these examples, We present them to the people so that they may give thought.

If (law) | We had sent down (anzalnā) | this (hādhā) | Quran (l-qur'āna) | on (ʿalā) | a mountain (jabalin), | surely you would have seen it (lara-aytahu) | humbled (khāshiʿan), | breaking asunder (mutaṣaddiʿan) | from (min) | the fear (khashyati) | of Allah (l-lahi). | And these (watil'ka) | examples (l-amthālu), | We present them (naḍribuhā) | to the people (lilnnāsi) | so that they may (laʿallahum) | give thought (yatafakkarūna).

59:22 He is Allah, the One Who, there is no god but He, the All-Knower of the unseen and the witnessed. He is the Most Gracious, the Most Merciful.

He (huwa) | is Allah (l-lahu), | the One Who (alladhī), | there is no (lā) | god (ilāha) | but (illā) | He (huwa), | the All-Knower (ʿālimu) | of the unseen (l-ghaybi) | and the witnessed (wal-shahādati). | He (huwa) | is the Most Gracious (l-raḥmānu), | the Most Merciful (l-raḥīmu).

59:23 He is Allah, the One Who, there is no god but He, the Sovereign, the Holy One, the Giver of Peace, the Giver of Security, the Guardian, the All-Mighty, the Irresistible, the Supreme. Glory be to Allah from what they associate with Him.

He (huwa) | is Allah (l-lahu), | the One Who (alladhī), | there is no (lā) | god (ilāha) | but (illā) | He (huwa), | the Sovereign (l-maliku), | the Holy One (l-qudūsu), | the Giver of Peace (l-salāmu), | the Giver of Security (l-mu'minu), | the Guardian (l-muhayminu), | the All-Mighty (l-ʿazīzu), | the Irresistible (l-jabāru), | the Supreme (l-mutakabiru). | Glory be to (sub'ḥāna) | Allah (l-lahi) | from what (ʿammā) | they associate with Him (yush'rikūna).

59:24 He is Allah, the Creator, the Inventor, the Fashioner. For Him are the names the beautiful.

Glorifies Him whatever is in the heavens and the earth. And He is the All-Mighty, the All-Wise.

He (huwa) | is Allah (l-lahu), | the Creator (l-khāliqu), | the Inventor (l-bāri-u), | the Fashioner (l-muṣawiru). | For Him (lahu) | are the names (l-asmāu) | the beautiful (l-ḥus'nā). | Glorifies (yusabbiḥu) | Him (lahu) | whatever (mā) | is in (fī) | the heavens (l-samāwāti) | and the earth (wal-arḍi). | And He (wahuwa) | is the All-Mighty (l-ʿazīzu), | the All-Wise (l-ḥakīmu).

Chapter (60) Sūrat l-Mum'taḥanah (The Woman to be examined)

60:1 O you who believe! Do not take My enemies and your enemies as allies offering them love while they have disbelieved in what came to you of the truth, driving out the Messenger and yourselves because you believe in Allah, your Lord. If you come forth to strive in My way and to seek My Pleasure. You confide to them love, but I Am most knowing of what you conceal and what you declare. And whoever does it among you then certainly he has strayed from the straight path.

O you (yāayyuhā) | who (alladhīna) | believe (āmanū)! | Do not (lā) | take (tattakhidhū) | My enemies (ʿaduwwī) | and your enemies (waʿaduwwakum) | as allies (awliyāa) | offering (tul'qūna) | them (ilayhim) | love (bil-mawadati) | while (waqad) | they have disbelieved (kafarū) | in what (bimā) | came to you (jāakum) | of (mina) | the truth (l-ḥaqi), | driving out (yukh'rijūna) | the Messenger (l-rasūla) | and yourselves (wa-iyyākum) | because (an) | you believe (tu'minū) | in Allah (bil-lahi), | your Lord (rabbikum). | If (in) | you (kuntum) | come forth (kharajtum) | to strive (jihādan) | in (fī) | My way (sabīlī) | and to seek (wa-ib'tighāa) | My Pleasure (marḍātī). | You confide (tusirrūna) | to them (ilayhim) | love (bil-mawadati), | but I Am (wa-anā) | most knowing (aʿlamu) | of what (bimā) | you conceal (akhfaytum) | and what (wamā) | you declare (aʿlantum). | And whoever (waman) | does it (yafʿalhu) | among you (minkum) | then certainly (faqad) | he has strayed (ḍalla) | from the straight (sawāa) | path (l-sabīli).

60:2 If they gain dominance over you, they would be to you enemies and extend against you their hands and their tongues with evil, and they desire that you would disbelieve.

If (in) | they gain dominance over you (yathqafūkum), | they would be (yakūnū) | to you (lakum) | enemies (aʿdāan) | and extend (wayabsuṭū) | against you (ilaykum) | their hands (aydiyahum) | and their tongues (wa-alsinatahum) | with evil (bil-sūi), | and they desire (wawaddū) | that (law) | you would disbelieve (takfurūna).

60:3 Never will benefit you your relatives and not your children on the Day of the Resurrection. He will judge between you. And Allah of what you do is All-Seer.

Never (lan) | will benefit you (tanfaʿakum) | your relatives (arḥāmukum) | and not (walā) | your children (awlādukum) | on the Day (yawma) | of the Resurrection (l-qiyāmati). | He will judge (yafṣilu) | between you (baynakum). | And Allah (wal-lahu) | of what (bimā) | you do (taʿmalūna) | is All-Seer (baṣīrun).

60:4 Indeed, there is for you an example good in Ibrahim and those with him, when they said to their people, "Indeed, we are disassociated from you and from what you worship from besides Allah. We have denied you, and has appeared between us and between you enmity and hatred forever until you believe in Allah Alone." Except the saying of Ibrahim to his father, "Surely I ask forgiveness for you, but not I have power for you from Allah of anything. Our Lord, upon You we put our trust, and to You we turn, and to You is the final return.

Indeed (qad), | there is (kānat) | for you (lakum) | an example (us'watun) | good (ḥasanatun) | in (fī) | Ibrahim (ib'rāhīma) | and those (wa-alladhīna) | with him (maʿahu), | when (idh) | they said (qālū) | to their people (liqawmihim), | "Indeed, we (innā) | are disassociated (buraāu) | from you (minkum) | and from what (wamimmā) | you worship (taʿbudūna) | from (min) | besides (dūni) | Allah (l-lahi). | We have denied (kafarnā) | you (bikum), | and has appeared (wabadā) | between us (baynanā) | and between you (wabaynakumu) | enmity (l-ʿadāwatu) | and hatred (wal-baghḍāu) | forever (abadan) | until (ḥattā) | you believe (tu'minū) | in Allah (bil-lahi) | Alone. (waḥdahu)" | Except (illā) | the saying (qawla) | of Ibrahim (ib'rāhīma) | to his father (li-abīhi), | "Surely I ask forgiveness (la-astaghfiranna) | for you (laka), | but not (wamā) | I have power (amliku) | for you (laka) | from (mina) | Allah (l-lahi) | of (min) | anything (shayin). | Our Lord (rabbanā), | upon You (ʿalayka) | we put our trust (tawakkalnā), | and to You (wa-ilayka) | we turn (anabnā), | and to You (wa-ilayka) | is the final return (l-maṣīru).

60:5 Our Lord, do not make us a trial for those who disbelieve, and forgive us, our Lord. Indeed You [You] are the All-Mighty, the All-Wise."

Our Lord (rabbanā), | do not (lā) | make us (tajʿalnā) | a trial (fit'natan) | for those who (lilladhīna) | disbelieve (kafarū), | and forgive (wa-igh'fir) | us (lanā), | our Lord (rabbanā). | Indeed You (innaka) | [You] (anta) | are the All-Mighty (l-ʿazīzu), | the All-Wise. (l-ḥakīmu)"

60:6 Certainly, there is for you in them an example good for he who is hopeful in Allah and the Day the Last. And whoever turns away, then indeed, Allah, He, is Free of need, the Praiseworthy.

Certainly (laqad), | there is (kāna) | for you (lakum) | in them (fīhim) | an example (us'watun) | good (ḥasanatun) | for he who (liman) | is (kāna) | hopeful (yarjū) | in Allah (l-laha) | and the Day (wal-yawma) | the Last (l-ākhira). | And whoever (waman) | turns away (yatawalla), | then indeed (fa-inna), | Allah (l-laha), | He (huwa), | is Free of need (l-ghaniyu), | the Praiseworthy (l-ḥamīdu).

60:7 Perhaps Allah [that] will put between you and between those to whom you have been enemies, among them love. And Allah is All-Powerful. And Allah is Oft-Forgiving, Most Merciful.

Perhaps (ʿasā) | Allah (l-lahu) | [that] (an) | will put (yajʿala) | between you (baynakum) | and between (wabayna) | those to whom (alladhīna) | you have been enemies (ʿādaytum), | among them (min'hum) | love (mawaddatan). | And Allah (wal-lahu) | is All-Powerful (qadīrun). | And Allah (wal-lahu) | is Oft-Forgiving (ghafūrun), | Most Merciful (raḥīmun).

60:8 Not does forbid you Allah from those who do not fight you in the religion and do not drive you out of your homes that you deal kindly and deal justly with them. Indeed, Allah loves those who act justly.

Not (lā) | does forbid you (yanhākumu) | Allah (l-lahu) | from (ʿani) | those who (alladhīna) | do not (lam) | fight you (yuqātilūkum) | in (fī) | the religion (l-dīni) | and do not (walam) | drive you out (yukh'rijūkum) | of (min) | your homes (diyārikum) | that (an) | you deal kindly (tabarrūhum) | and deal justly (watuq'siṭū) | with them (ilayhim). | Indeed (inna), | Allah (l-laha) | loves (yuḥibbu) | those who act justly (l-muq'siṭīna).

60:9 Only forbids you Allah from those who fight you in the religion and drive you out of your homes and support in your expulsion, that you make them allies. And whoever makes them allies, then those [they] are the wrongdoers.

Only (innamā) | forbids you (yanhākumu) | Allah (l-lahu) | from (ʿani) | those who (alladhīna) | fight you (qātalūkum) | in (fī) | the religion (l-dīni) | and drive you out (wa-akhrajūkum) | of (min) | your homes (diyārikum) | and support (waẓāharū) | in (ʿalā) | your expulsion (ikh'rājikum), | that (an) | you make them allies (tawallawhum). | And whoever (waman) | makes them allies (yatawallahum), | then those (fa-ulāika) | [they] (humu) | are the wrongdoers (l-ẓālimūna).

60:10 O you who believe! When come to you the believing women as emigrants, then examine them. Allah is most knowing of their faith. And if you know them to be believers, then do not return them to the disbelievers. Not they are lawful for them and not they are lawful for them. But give them what they have spent. And not any blame upon you if you marry them when you have given them their bridal dues. And do not hold to marriage bonds with disbelieving women, but ask for what you have spent, and let them ask what they have spent. That is the Judgment of Allah. He judges between you. And Allah is All-Knowing, All-Wise.

O you (yāayyuhā) | who (alladhīna) | believe (āmanū)! | When (idhā) | come to you (jāakumu) | the believing women (l-mu'minātu) | as emigrants (muhājirātin), | then examine them (fa-im'taḥinūhunna). | Allah (l-lahu) | is most knowing (aʿlamu) | of their faith (biīmānihinna). | And if (fa-in) | you know them (ʿalim'tumūhunna) | to be believers (mu'minātin), | then do not (falā) | return them (tarjiʿūhunna) | to (ilā) | the disbelievers (l-kufāri). | Not (lā) | they (hunna) | are lawful (ḥillun) | for them (lahum) | and not (walā) | they (hum) | are lawful (yaḥillūna) | for them (lahunna). | But give them (waātūhum) | what (mā) | they have spent (anfaqū). | And not (walā) | any blame (junāḥa) | upon you (ʿalaykum) | if (an) | you marry them (tankiḥūhunna) | when (idhā) | you have given them (ātaytumūhunna) | their bridal dues (ujūrahunna). | And do not (walā) | hold (tum'sikū) | to marriage bonds (biʿiṣami) | with disbelieving women (l-kawāfiri), | but ask for (wasalū) | what (mā) | you have spent (anfaqtum), | and let them ask (walyasalū) | what (mā) | they have spent (anfaqū). | That (dhālikum) | is the Judgment (ḥuk'mu) | of Allah (l-lahi). | He judges (yaḥkumu) | between you (baynakum). | And Allah (wal-lahu) | is All-Knowing (ʿalīmun), | All-Wise (ḥakīmun).

60:11 And if have gone from you any of your wives to the disbelievers then your turn comes, then give to those who have gone, their wives, the like of what they had spent. And fear Allah in Whom, you, [in Him] are believers.

And if (wa-in) | have gone from you (fātakum) | any (shayon) | of (min) | your wives (azwājikum) | to (ilā) | the disbelievers (l-kufāri) | then your turn comes (faʿāqabtum), | then give (faātū) | to those who (alladhīna) | have gone (dhahabat), | their wives (azwājuhum), | the like (mith'la) | of what (mā) | they had spent (anfaqū). | And fear (wa-ittaqū) | Allah (l-laha) | in Whom (alladhī), | you (antum), | [in Him] (bihi) | are believers (mu'minūna).

60:12 O Prophet! When come to you the believing women pledging to you [on] that not they will associate with Allah anything, and not they will steal, and not they will commit adultery, and not they will kill their children, and not they bring slander, they invent it between their hands and their feet, and not they will disobey you in the right, then accept their pledge and ask forgiveness for them from Allah. Indeed, Allah is Oft-Forgiving, Most Merciful.

O (yāayyuhā) | Prophet (l-nabiyu)! | When (idhā) | come to you (jāaka) | the believing women (l-mu'minātu) | pledging to you (yubāyiʿ'naka) | [on] (ʿalā) | that (an) | not (lā) | they will associate (yush'rik'na) | with Allah (bil-lahi) | anything (shayan), | and not (walā) | they will steal (yasriq'na), | and not (walā) | they will commit adultery (yaznīna), | and not (walā) | they will kill (yaqtul'na) | their children (awlādahunna), | and not (walā) | they bring (yatīna) | slander (bibuh'tānin), | they invent it (yaftarīnahu) | between (bayna) | their hands (aydīhinna) | and their feet (wa-arjulihinna), | and not (walā) | they will disobey you (yaʿṣīnaka) | in (fī) | the right (maʿrūfin), | then accept their pledge (fabāyiʿ'hunna) | and ask forgiveness (wa-is'taghfir) | for them (lahunna) | from Allah (l-laha). | Indeed (inna), | Allah (l-laha) | is Oft-Forgiving (ghafūrun), | Most Merciful (raḥīmun).

60:13 O you who believe! Do not make allies of a people, The wrath of Allah is upon them. Indeed, they despair of the Hereafter as despair the disbelievers of the companions of the graves.

O you (yāayyuhā) | who (alladhīna) | believe (āmanū)! | Do not (lā) | make allies (tatawallaw) | of a people (qawman), | The wrath (ghaḍiba) | of Allah (l-lahu) | is upon them (ʿalayhim). | Indeed (qad), | they despair (ya-isū) | of (mina) | the Hereafter (l-ākhirati) | as (kamā) | despair (ya-isa) | the disbelievers (l-kufāru) | of (min) | the companions (aṣḥābi) | of the graves (l-qubūri).

Chapter (61) Sūrat l-Ṣaf (The Row)

61:1 Glorifies Allah whatever is in the heavens and whatever is in the earth. And He is the All-Mighty, the All-Wise.

Glorifies (sabbaḥa) | Allah (lillahi) | whatever (mā) | is in (fī) | the heavens (l-samāwāti) | and whatever (wamā) | is in (fī) | the earth (l-arḍi). | And He (wahuwa) | is the All-Mighty (l-ʿazīzu), | the All-Wise (l-ḥakīmu).

61:2 O you who believe! Why do you say what not you do?

O (yāayyuhā) | you who (alladhīna) | believe (āmanū)! | Why (lima) | do you say (taqūlūna) | what (mā) | not (lā) | you do (tafʿalūna)?

61:3 Great is hatred with Allah that you say what not you do?

Great is (kabura) | hatred (maqtan) | with (ʿinda) | Allah (l-lahi) | that (an) | you say (taqūlū) | what (mā) | not (lā) | you do (tafʿalūna)?

61:4 Indeed, Allah loves those who fight in His Way in a row as if they were a structure joined firmly.

Indeed (inna), | Allah (l-laha) | loves (yuḥibbu) | those who (alladhīna) | fight (yuqātilūna) | in (fī) | His Way (sabīlihi) | in a row (ṣaffan) | as if they (ka-annahum) | were a structure (bun'yānun) | joined firmly (marṣūṣun).

61:5 And when said Musa to his people, "O my people! Why do you hurt me while certainly you know that I am the Messenger of Allah to you?" Then when they deviated, was caused to deviate by Allah their hearts. And Allah does not guide the people, the defiantly disobedient.

And when (wa-idh) | said (qāla) | Musa (mūsā) | to his people (liqawmihi), | "O my people (yāqawmi)! | Why (lima) | do you hurt me (tu'dhūnanī) | while certainly (waqad) | you know (taʿlamūna) | that I am (annī) | the Messenger (rasūlu) | of Allah (l-lahi) | to you? (ilaykum)" | Then when (falammā) | they deviated (zāghū), | was caused to deviate (azāgha) | by Allah (l-lahu) | their hearts (qulūbahum). | And Allah (wal-lahu) | does not (lā) | guide (yahdī) | the people (l-qawma), | the defiantly disobedient (l-fāsiqīna).

61:6 And when said Isa, son of Maryam, "O Children of Israel! Indeed, I am the Messenger of Allah to you, confirming that which was between my hands of the Taurat and bringing glad tidings of a Messenger to come from after me, whose name will be Ahmad." But when he came to them with clear proofs, they said, "This is a magic clear."

And when (wa-idh) | said (qāla) | Isa (ʿīsā), | son (ub'nu) | of Maryam (maryama), | "O Children (yābanī) | of Israel (is'rāīla)! | Indeed, I am (innī) | the Messenger (rasūlu) | of Allah (l-lahi) | to you (ilaykum), | confirming (muṣaddiqan) | that which (limā) | was between (bayna) | my hands (yadayya) | of (mina) | the Taurat (l-tawrāti) | and bringing glad tidings (wamubashiran) | of a Messenger (birasūlin) | to come (yatī) | from (min) | after me (baʿdī), | whose name will be (us'muhu) | Ahmad. (aḥmadu)" | But when (falammā) | he came to them (jāahum) | with clear proofs (bil-bayināti), | they said (qālū), | "This (hādhā) | is a magic (siḥ'run) | clear. (mubīnun)"

61:7 And who is more wrong than one who invents upon Allah the lie while he is invited to Islam? And Allah does not guide the people [the] wrongdoers.

And who (waman) | is more wrong (aẓlamu) | than one who (mimmani) | invents (if'tarā) | upon (ʿalā) | Allah (l-lahi) | the lie (l-kadhiba) | while he (wahuwa) | is invited (yud''ā) | to (ilā) | Islam (l-is'lāmi)? | And Allah (wal-lahu) | does not (lā) | guide (yahdī) | the people (l-qawma) | [the] wrongdoers (l-ẓālimīna).

61:8 They intend to put out the light of Allah with their mouths, but Allah will perfect His Light although dislike the disbelievers.

They intend (yurīdūna) | to put out (liyuṭ'fiū) | the light (nūra) | of Allah (l-lahi) | with their mouths (bi-afwāhihim), | but Allah (wal-lahu) | will perfect (mutimmu) | His Light (nūrihi) | although (walaw) | dislike (kariha) | the disbelievers (l-kāfirūna).

61:9 He is the One Who sent His Messenger with guidance and the religion of the truth, to make it prevail over the religion all of them, although dislike it the polytheists.

He (huwa) | is the One Who (alladhī) | sent (arsala) | His Messenger (rasūlahu) | with guidance (bil-hudā) | and the religion (wadīni) | of the truth (l-ḥaqi), | to make it prevail (liyuẓ'hirahu) | over (ʿalā) | the religion (l-dīni) | all of them (kullihi), | although (walaw) | dislike it (kariha) | the polytheists (l-mush'rikūna).

61:10 O you who believe! Shall I guide you to a transaction that will save you from a punishment painful?

O (yāayyuhā) | you who (alladhīna) | believe (āmanū)! | Shall (hal) | I guide you (adullukum) | to (ʿalā) | a transaction (tijāratin) | that will save you (tunjīkum) | from (min) | a punishment (ʿadhābin) | painful (alīmin)?

61:11 Believe in Allah and His Messenger and strive in the way of Allah with your wealth and your lives. That is better for you if you know.

Believe (tu'minūna) | in Allah (bil-lahi) | and His Messenger (warasūlihi) | and strive (watujāhidūna) | in (fī) | the way (sabīli) | of Allah (l-lahi) | with your wealth (bi-amwālikum) | and your lives (wa-anfusikum). | That (dhālikum) | is better (khayrun) | for you (lakum) | if (in) | you (kuntum) | know (taʿlamūna).

61:12 He will forgive for you your sins and admit you in Gardens flow from underneath it the rivers and dwellings pleasant in Gardens of Eternity. That is the success the great.

He will forgive (yaghfir) | for you (lakum) | your sins (dhunūbakum) | and admit you (wayud'khil'kum) | in Gardens (jannātin) | flow (tajrī) | from (min) | underneath it (taḥtihā) | the rivers (l-anhāru) | and dwellings (wamasākina) | pleasant (ṭayyibatan) | in (fī) | Gardens (jannāti) | of Eternity (ʿadnin). | That (dhālika) | is the success (l-fawzu) | the great (l-ʿaẓīmu).

61:13 And another that you love - a help from Allah and a victory near; and give glad tidings to the believers.

And another (wa-ukh'rā) | that you love (tuḥibbūnahā)- | a help (naṣrun) | from (mina) | Allah (l-lahi) | and a victory (wafatḥun) | near (qarībun); | and give glad tidings (wabashiri) | to the believers (l-mu'minīna).

61:14 O you who believe! Be helpers of Allah as said Isa, son of Maryam, to the disciples, "Who are my helpers for Allah?" Said the disciples, "We are the helpers of Allah." Then believed a group of Children of Israel and disbelieved a group. So We supported those who believed against their enemy and they became dominant.

O you (yāayyuhā) | who (alladhīna) | believe (āmanū)! | Be (kūnū) | helpers (anṣāra) | of Allah (l-lahi) | as (kamā) | said (qāla) | Isa (ʿīsā), | son (ub'nu) | of Maryam (maryama), | to the disciples (lil'ḥawāriyyīna), | "Who (man) | are my helpers (anṣārī) | for (ilā) | Allah? (l-lahi)" | Said (qāla) | the disciples (l-ḥawāriyūna), | "We (naḥnu) | are the helpers (anṣāru) | of Allah. (l-lahi)" | Then believed (faāmanat) | a group (ṭāifatun) | of (min) | Children (banī) | of Israel (is'rāīla) | and disbelieved (wakafarat) | a group (ṭāifatun). | So We supported (fa-ayyadnā) | those who (alladhīna) | believed (āmanū) | against (ʿalā) | their enemy (ʿaduwwihim) | and they became (fa-aṣbaḥū) | dominant (ẓāhirīna).

Chapter (62) Sūrat l-Jumuʿah (Friday)

62:1 Glorifies Allah whatever is in the heavens and whatever is in the earth, the Sovereign, the Holy, the All-Mighty, the All-Wise.

Glorifies (yusabbiḥu) | Allah (lillahi) | whatever (mā) | is in (fī) | the heavens (l-samāwāti) | and whatever (wamā) | is in (fī) | the earth (l-arḍi), | the Sovereign (l-maliki), | the Holy (l-qudūsi), | the All-Mighty (l-ʿazīzi), | the All-Wise (l-ḥakīmi).

62:2 He is the One Who sent among the unlettered a Messenger from themselves reciting to them His Verses, and purifying them and teaching them the Book and the wisdom although they were from before surely in an error clear.

He (huwa) | is the One Who (alladhī) | sent (baʿatha) | among (fī) | the unlettered (l-umiyīna) | a Messenger (rasūlan) | from themselves (min'hum) | reciting (yatlū) | to them (ʿalayhim) | His Verses (āyātihi), | and purifying them (wayuzakkīhim) | and teaching them (wayuʿallimuhumu) | the Book (l-kitāba) | and the wisdom (wal-ḥik'mata) | although (wa-in) | they were (kānū) | from (min) | before (qablu) | surely in (lafī) | an error (ḍalālin) | clear (mubīnin).

62:3 And others among them who have not yet joined them; and He is the All-Mighty, the All-Wise.

And others (waākharīna) | among them (min'hum) | who have not yet (lammā) | joined (yalḥaqū) | them (bihim); | and He (wahuwa) | is the All-Mighty (l-ʿazīzu), | the All-Wise (l-ḥakīmu).

62:4 That is the Bounty of Allah, He gives it to whom He wills. And Allah is the Possessor of Bounty the Great.

That (dhālika) | is the Bounty (faḍlu) | of Allah (l-lahi), | He gives it (yu'tīhi) | to whom (man) | He wills (yashāu). | And Allah (wal-lahu) | is the Possessor (dhū) | of Bounty (l-faḍli) | the Great (l-ʿaẓīmi).

62:5 The likeness of those who were entrusted with the Taurat then not they bore it, is like the donkey who carries books. Wretched is the example of the people who deny the Signs of Allah. And Allah does not guide the people, the wrongdoers.

The likeness (mathalu) | of those who (alladhīna) | were entrusted (ḥummilū) | with the Taurat (l-tawrāta) | then (thumma) | not (lam) | they bore it (yaḥmilūhā), | is like (kamathali) | the donkey (l-ḥimāri) | who carries (yaḥmilu) | books (asfāran). | Wretched is (bi'sa) | the example (mathalu) | of the people (l-qawmi) | who (alladhīna) | deny (kadhabū) | the Signs (biāyāti) | of Allah (l-lahi). | And Allah (wal-lahu) | does not (lā) | guide (yahdī) | the people (l-qawma), | the wrongdoers (l-ẓālimīna).

62:6 Say, "O you who are Jews! If you claim that you are allies of Allah. from excluding the people, then wish for the death, if you are truthful."

Say (qul), | "O (yāayyuhā) | you who (alladhīna) | are Jews (hādū)! | If (in) | you claim (zaʿamtum) | that you (annakum) | are allies (awliyāu) | of Allah (lillahi). | from (min) | excluding (dūni) | the people (l-nāsi), | then wish (fatamannawū) | for the death (l-mawta), | if (in) | you are (kuntum) | truthful. (ṣādiqīna)"

62:7 But not they will wish for it, ever, for what have sent forth their hands. And Allah is All-Knowing of the wrongdoers.

But not (walā) | they will wish for it (yatamannawnahu), | ever (abadan), | for what (bimā) | have sent forth (qaddamat) | their hands (aydīhim). | And Allah (wal-lahu) | is All-Knowing (ʿalīmun) | of the wrongdoers (bil-ẓālimīna).

62:8 Say, "Indeed, the death which you flee from it, then surely it will meet you. Then you will be sent back to the All-Knower of the unseen and the witnessed, and He will inform you [of] what you used to do."

Say (qul), | "Indeed (inna), | the death (l-mawta) | which (alladhī) | you flee (tafirrūna) | from it (min'hu), | then surely it (fa-innahu) | will meet you (mulāqīkum). | Then (thumma) | you will be sent back (turaddūna) | to (ilā) | the All-Knower (ʿālimi) | of the unseen (l-ghaybi) | and the witnessed (wal-shahādati), | and He will inform you (fayunabbi-ukum) | [of] what (bimā) | you used to (kuntum) | do. (taʿmalūna)"

62:9 O you who believe! When the call is made for the prayer on the day of Friday, then hasten to the remembrance of Allah and leave the business. That is better for you, if you know.

O (yāayyuhā) | you who (alladhīna) | believe (āmanū)! | When (idhā) | the call is made (nūdiya) | for the prayer (lilṣṣalati) | on (min) | the day (yawmi) | of Friday (l-jumuʿati), | then hasten (fa-is'ʿaw) | to (ilā) | the remembrance (dhik'ri) | of Allah (l-lahi) | and leave (wadharū) | the business (l-bayʿa). | That (dhālikum) | is better (khayrun) | for you (lakum), | if (in) | you (kuntum) | know (taʿlamūna).

62:10 Then when is concluded the prayer, then disperse in the land and seek from the Bounty of Allah, and remember Allah much so that you may succeed.

Then when (fa-idhā) | is concluded (quḍiyati) | the prayer (l-ṣalatu), | then disperse (fa-intashirū) | in (fī) | the land (l-arḍi) | and seek (wa-ib'taghū) | from (min) | the Bounty (faḍli) | of Allah (l-lahi), | and remember (wa-udh'kurū) | Allah (l-laha) | much (kathīran) | so that you may (laʿallakum) | succeed (tuf'liḥūna).

62:11 And when they saw a transaction or a sport, they rushed to it and left you standing. Say, "What is with Allah is better than the sport and from any transaction. And Allah is the Best of the Providers."

And when (wa-idhā) | they saw (ra-aw) | a transaction (tijāratan) | or (aw) | a sport (lahwan), | they rushed (infaḍḍū) | to it (ilayhā) | and left you (watarakūka) | standing (qāiman). | Say (qul), | "What (mā) | is with (ʿinda) | Allah (l-lahi) | is better (khayrun) | than (mina) | the sport (l-lahwi) | and from (wamina) | any transaction (l-tijārati). | And Allah (wal-lahu) | is the Best (khayru) | of the Providers. (l-rāziqīna)"

Chapter (63) Sūrat l-Munāfiqūn (The Hypocrites)

63:1 When come to you the hypocrites, they say, "We testify that you are surely (the) Messenger of Allah." And Allah knows that you are surely His Messenger, and Allah testifies that the hypocrites are surely liars.

When (idhā) | come to you (jāaka) | the hypocrites (l-munāfiqūna), | they say (qālū), | "We testify (nashhadu) | that you (innaka) | are surely (the) Messenger (larasūlu) | of Allah. (l-lahi)" | And Allah (wal-lahu) | knows (yaʿlamu) | that you (innaka) | are surely His Messenger (larasūluhu), | and Allah (wal-lahu) | testifies (yashhadu) | that (inna) | the hypocrites (l-munāfiqīna) | are surely liars (lakādhibūna).

63:2 They take their oaths as a cover, so they turn away from the Way of Allah. Indeed, [they] evil is what they used to do.

They take (ittakhadhū) | their oaths (aymānahum) | as a cover (junnatan), | so they turn away (faṣaddū) | from (ʿan) | the Way (sabīli) | of Allah (l-lahi). | Indeed, [they] (innahum) | evil is (sāa) | what (mā) | they used to (kānū) | do (yaʿmalūna).

63:3 That is because they believed, then they disbelieved; so were sealed [upon] their hearts, so they do not understand.

That (dhālika) | is because (bi-annahum) | they believed (āmanū), | then (thumma) | they disbelieved (kafarū); | so were sealed (faṭubiʿa) | [upon] (ʿalā) | their hearts (qulūbihim), | so they (fahum) | do not (lā) | understand (yafqahūna).

63:4 And when you see them pleases you their bodies, and if they speak, you listen to their speech, as if they were pieces of wood propped up. They think every shout is against them. They are the enemy, so beware of them. May destroy them Allah! How are they deluded?

And when (wa-idhā) | you see them (ra-aytahum) | pleases you (tuʿʾjibuka) | their bodies (ajsāmuhum), | and if (wa-in) | they speak (yaqūlū), | you listen (tasmaʿ) | to their speech (liqawlihim), | as if they were (ka-annahum) | pieces of wood (khushubun) | propped up (musannadatun). | They think (yaḥsabūna) | every (kulla) | shout (ṣayḥatin) | is against them (ʿalayhim). | They (humu) | are the enemy (l-ʿaduwu), | so beware of them (fa-iḥ'dharhum). | May destroy them (qātalahumu) | Allah (l-lahu)! | How (annā) | are they deluded (yu'fakūna)?

63:5 And when it is said to them, "Come, will ask forgiveness for you the Messenger of Allah." They turn aside their heads and you see them turning away while they are arrogant.

And when (wa-idhā) | it is said (qīla) | to them (lahum), | "Come (taʿālaw), | will ask forgiveness (yastaghfir) | for you (lakum) | the Messenger (rasūlu) | of Allah. (l-lahi)" | They turn aside (lawwaw) | their heads (ruūsahum) | and you see them (wara-aytahum) | turning away (yaṣuddūna) | while they (wahum) | are arrogant (mus'takbirūna).

63:6 It is same for them whether you ask forgiveness for them or do not ask forgiveness for them. Never will forgive Allah [to] them. Indeed, Allah does not guide the people, the defiantly disobedient.

It is same (sawāon) | for them (ʿalayhim) | whether you ask forgiveness (astaghfarta) | for them (lahum) | or (am) | do not (lam) | ask forgiveness (tastaghfir) | for them (lahum). | Never (lan) | will forgive (yaghfira) | Allah (l-lahu) | [to] them (lahum). | Indeed (inna), | Allah (l-laha) | does not (lā) | guide (yahdī) | the people (l-qawma), | the defiantly disobedient (l-fāsiqīna).

63:7 They are those who say, "Do not spend on those who are with the Messenger of Allah until they disband." And for Allah are the treasures of the heavens and the earth, but the hypocrites do not understand.

They (humu) | are those who (alladhīna) | say (yaqūlūna), | "Do not (lā) | spend (tunfiqū) | on (ʿalā) | those who (man) | are with (ʿinda) | the Messenger (rasūli) | of Allah (l-lahi) | until (ḥattā) | they disband. (yanfaḍḍū)" | And for Allah (walillahi) | are the treasures (khazāinu) | of the heavens (l-samāwāti) | and the earth (wal-arḍi), | but (walākinna) | the hypocrites (l-munāfiqīna) | do not (lā) | understand (yafqahūna).

63:8 They say, "If we return to Al-Madinah, surely, will expel the more honorable from it the more humble." But for Allah is the honor and for His Messenger and for the believers, but the hypocrites do not know.

They say (yaqūlūna), | "If (la-in) | we return (rajaʿnā) | to (ilā) | Al-Madinah (l-madīnati), | surely, will expel (layukh'rijanna) | the more honorable (l-aʿazu) | from it (min'hā) | the more humble. (l-adhala)" | But for Allah (walillahi) | is the honor (l-ʿizatu) | and for His Messenger (walirasūlihi) | and for the believers (walil'mu'minīna), | but (walākinna) | the hypocrites (l-munāfiqīna) | do not (lā) | know (yaʿlamūna).

63:9 O you who believe! Let not divert you your wealth and not your children from the remembrance of Allah. And whoever does that, then those [they] are the losers.

O (yāayyuhā) | you who (alladhīna) | believe (āmanū)! | Let not (lā) | divert you (tul'hikum) | your wealth (amwālukum) | and not (walā) | your children (awlādukum) | from (ʿan) | the remembrance (dhik'ri) | of Allah (l-lahi). | And whoever (waman) | does (yafʿal) | that (dhālika), | then those (fa-ulāika) | [they] (humu) | are the losers (l-khāsirūna).

63:10 And spend from what We have provided you from before [that] comes to one of you the death and he says, "My Lord! Why not You delay me for a term near so I would give charity and be among the righteous."

And spend (wa-anfiqū) | from (min) | what (mā) | We have provided you (razaqnākum) | from (min) | before (qabli) | [that] (an) | comes (yatiya) | to one of you (aḥadakumu) | the death (l-mawtu) | and he says (fayaqūla), | "My Lord (rabbi)! | Why not (lawlā) | You delay me (akhartanī) | for (ilā) | a term (ajalin) | near (qarībin) | so I would give charity (fa-aṣṣaddaqa) | and be (wa-akun) | among (mina) | the righteous. (l-ṣāliḥīna)"

63:11 But never will be delayed by Allah a soul when has come its term. And Allah is All-Aware of what you do.

But never (walan) | will be delayed (yu-akhira) | by Allah (l-lahu) | a soul (nafsan) | when (idhā) | has come (jāa) | its term (ajaluhā). | And Allah (wal-lahu) | is All-Aware (khabīrun) | of what (bimā) | you do (taʿmalūna).

Chapter (64) Sūrat l-Taghābun (Mutual Loss & Gain)

64:1 Glorifies [to] Allah whatever is in the heavens and whatever is in the earth. For Him is the dominion and for Him is the praise. And He is on every thing All-Powerful.

Glorifies (yusabbiḥu) | [to] Allah (lillahi) | whatever (mā) | is in (fī) | the heavens (l-samāwāti) | and whatever (wamā) | is in (fī) | the earth (l-arḍi). | For Him (lahu) | is the dominion (l-mul'ku) | and for Him (walahu) | is the praise (l-ḥamdu). | And He (wahuwa) | is on (ʿalā) | every (kulli) | thing (shayin) | All-Powerful (qadīrun).

64:2 He is the One Who created you and among you is a disbeliever and among you is a believer. And Allah of what you do is All-Seer.

He (huwa) | is the One Who (alladhī) | created you (khalaqakum) | and among you (faminkum) | is a disbeliever (kāfirun) | and among you (waminkum) | is a believer (mu'minun). | And Allah (wal-lahu) | of what (bimā) | you do (taʿmalūna) | is All-Seer (baṣīrun).

64:3 He created the heavens and the earth with truth, and He formed you and made good your forms, and to Him is the final return.

He created (khalaqa) | the heavens (l-samāwāti) | and the earth (wal-arḍa) | with truth (bil-ḥaqi), | and He formed you (waṣawwarakum) | and made good (fa-aḥsana) | your forms (ṣuwarakum), | and to Him (wa-ilayhi) | is the final return (l-maṣīru).

64:4 He knows what is in the heavens and the earth, and He knows what you conceal and what you declare. And Allah is All-Knowing of what is in the breasts.

He knows (yaʿlamu) | what (mā) | is in (fī) | the heavens (l-samāwāti) | and the earth (wal-arḍi), | and He knows (wayaʿlamu) | what (mā) | you conceal (tusirrūna) | and what (wamā) | you declare (tuʿʾlinūna). | And Allah (wal-lahu) | is All-Knowing (ʿalīmun) | of what (bidhāti) | is in the breasts (l-ṣudūri).

64:5 Has not come to you the news of those who disbelieved from before? So they tasted the bad consequence of their affair, and for them is a punishment painful.

Has not (alam) | come to you (yatikum) | the news (naba-u) | of those who (alladhīna) | disbelieved (kafarū) | from (min) | before (qablu)? | So they tasted (fadhāqū) | the bad consequence (wabāla) | of their affair (amrihim), | and for them (walahum) | is a punishment (ʿadhābun) | painful (alīmun).

64:6 That is because had come to them their Messengers with clear proofs, but they said, "Shall human beings guide us?" So they disbelieved and turned away. And can do without them Allah. And Allah is Self-sufficient, Praiseworthy.

That (dhālika) | is because (bi-annahu) | had (kānat) | come to them (tatīhim) | their Messengers (rusuluhum) | with clear proofs (bil-bayināti), | but they said (faqālū), | "Shall human beings (abasharun) | guide us? (yahdūnanā)" | So they disbelieved (fakafarū) | and turned away (watawallaw). | And can do without them (wa-is'taghnā) | Allah (l-lahu). | And Allah (wal-lahu) | is Self-sufficient (ghaniyyun), | Praiseworthy (ḥamīdun).

64:7 Claim those who disbelieve that never will they be raised. Say, "Yes, by my Lord, surely you will be raised; then surely you will be informed of what you did. And that for Allah is easy."

Claim (zaʿama) | those who (alladhīna) | disbelieve (kafarū) | that (an) | never (lan) | will they be raised (yub'ʿathū). | Say (qul), | "Yes (balā), | by my Lord (warabbī), | surely you will be raised (latub'ʿathunna); | then (thumma) | surely you will be informed (latunabba-unna) | of what (bimā) | you did (ʿamil'tum). | And that (wadhālika) | for (ʿalā) | Allah (l-lahi) | is easy. (yasīrun)"

64:8 So believe in Allah and His Messenger and the Light which We have sent down. And Allah, of what you do, is All-Aware.

So believe (faāminū) | in Allah (bil-lahi) | and His Messenger (warasūlihi) | and the Light (wal-nūri) | which (alladhī) | We have sent down (anzalnā). | And Allah (wal-lahu), | of what (bimā) | you do (taʿmalūna), | is All-Aware (khabīrun).

64:9 The Day He will assemble you for the Day of the Assembly, that will be the Day of mutual loss and gain. And whoever believes in Allah and does righteous deeds He will remove from him his evil deeds and He will admit him to Gardens flow from underneath it the rivers, abiding therein forever. That is the success the great.

The Day (yawma) | He will assemble you (yajmaʿukum) | for the Day (liyawmi) | of the Assembly (l-jamʿi), | that (dhālika) | will be the Day (yawmu) | of mutual loss and gain (l-taghābuni). | And whoever (waman) | believes (yu'min) | in Allah (bil-lahi) | and does (wayaʿmal) | righteous deeds (ṣāliḥan) | He will remove (yukaffir) | from him (ʿanhu) | his evil deeds (sayyiātihi) | and He will admit him (wayud'khil'hu) | to Gardens (jannātin) | flow (tajrī) | from (min) | underneath it (taḥtihā) | the rivers (l-anhāru), | abiding (khālidīna) | therein (fīhā) | forever (abadan). | That (dhālika) | is the success (l-fawzu) | the great (l-ʿaẓīmu).

64:10 But those who disbelieved and denied [in] Our Verses, those are the companions of the Fire, abiding forever therein. And wretched is the destination.

But those who (wa-alladhīna) | disbelieved (kafarū) | and denied (wakadhabū) | [in] Our Verses (biāyātinā), | those (ulāika) | are the companions (aṣḥābu) | of the Fire (l-nāri), | abiding forever (khālidīna) | therein (fīhā). | And wretched is (wabi'sa) | the destination (l-maṣīru).

64:11 Not strikes any disaster except by the permission of Allah. And whoever believes in Allah, He guides his heart. And Allah of every thing is All-Knowing.

Not (mā) | strikes (aṣāba) | any (min) | disaster (muṣībatin) | except (illā) | by the permission (bi-idh'ni) | of Allah (l-lahi). | And whoever (waman) | believes (yu'min) | in Allah (bil-lahi), | He guides (yahdi) | his heart (qalbahu). | And Allah (wal-lahu) | of every (bikulli) | thing (shayin) | is All-Knowing (ʿalīmun).

64:12 So obey Allah and obey the Messenger; but if you turn away, then only upon Our Messenger is the conveyance clear.

So obey (wa-aṭīʿū) | Allah (l-laha) | and obey (wa-aṭīʿū) | the Messenger (l-rasūla); | but if (fa-in) | you turn away (tawallaytum), | then only (fa-innamā) | upon (ʿalā) | Our Messenger (rasūlinā) | is the conveyance (l-balāghu) | clear (l-mubīnu).

64:13 Allah, there is no god except Him. And upon Allah let put their trust the believers.

Allah (al-lahu), | there is no (lā) | god (ilāha) | except (illā) | Him (huwa). | And upon (waʿalā) | Allah (l-lahi) | let put their trust (falyatawakkali) | the believers (l-mu'minūna).

64:14 O you who believe! Indeed, from your spouses and your children are enemies to you, so beware of them. But if you pardon and overlook and forgive, then indeed, Allah is Oft-Forgiving, Most Merciful.

O (yāayyuhā) | you who (alladhīna) | believe (āmanū)! | Indeed (inna), | from (min) | your spouses (azwājikum) | and your children (wa-awlādikum) | are enemies (ʿaduwwan) | to you (lakum), | so beware of them (fa-iḥ'dharūhum). | But if (wa-in) | you pardon (taʿfū) | and overlook (wataṣfaḥū) | and forgive (wataghfirū), | then indeed (fa-inna), | Allah (l-laha) | is Oft-Forgiving (ghafūrun), | Most Merciful (raḥīmun).

64:15 Only your wealth and your children are a trial, and Allah - with Him is a reward great.

Only (innamā) | your wealth (amwālukum) | and your children (wa-awlādukum) | are a trial (fit'natun), | and Allah (wal-lahu)- | with Him (ʿindahu) | is a reward (ajrun) | great (ʿaẓīmun).

64:16 So fear Allah what you are able and listen and obey and spend; it is better for yourselves. And whoever is saved from the greediness of his soul, then those [they] are the successful ones.

So fear (fa-ittaqū) | Allah (l-laha) | what (mā) | you are able (is'taṭaʿtum) | and listen (wa-is'maʿū) | and obey (wa-aṭīʿū) | and spend (wa-anfiqū); | it is better (khayran) | for yourselves (li-anfusikum). | And whoever (waman) | is saved (yūqa) | from the greediness (shuḥḥa) | of his soul (nafsihi), | then those (fa-ulāika) | [they] (humu) | are the successful ones (l-muf'liḥūna).

64:17 If you loan to Allah a loan goodly, He will multiply it for you and will forgive you. And Allah is Most Appreciative, Most Forbearing,

If (in) | you loan (tuq'riḍū) | to Allah (l-laha) | a loan (qarḍan) | goodly (ḥasanan), | He will multiply it (yuḍāʿif'hu) | for you (lakum) | and will forgive (wayaghfir) | you (lakum). | And Allah (wal-lahu) | is Most Appreciative (shakūrun), | Most Forbearing (ḥalīmun),

64:18 The Knower of the unseen and the witnessed, the All-Mighty, the All-Wise.

The Knower (ʿālimu) | of the unseen (l-ghaybi) | and the witnessed (wal-shahādati), | the All-Mighty (l-ʿazīzu), | the All-Wise (l-ḥakīmu).

Chapter (65) Sūrat l-Ṭalāq (The Divorce)

65:1 O Prophet! When you divorce [the] women, then divorce them for their waiting period, and keep count of the waiting period, and fear Allah, your Lord. Do not expel them from their houses, and not they should leave except that they commit an immorality clear. And these are the limits of Allah. And whoever transgresses the limits of Allah then certainly he has wronged himself. Not you know; Perhaps Allah will bring about, after that, a matter.

O (yāayyuhā) | Prophet (l-nabiyu)! | When (idhā) | you divorce (ṭallaqtumu) | [the] women (l-nisāa), | then divorce them (faṭalliqūhunna) | for their waiting period (liʿiddatihinna), | and keep count (wa-aḥṣū) | of the waiting period (l-ʿidata), | and fear (wa-ittaqū) | Allah (l-laha), | your Lord (rabbakum). | Do not (lā) | expel them (tukh'rijūhunna) | from (min) | their houses (buyūtihinna), | and not (walā) | they should leave (yakhruj'na) | except (illā) | that (an) | they commit (yatīna) | an immorality (bifāḥishatin) | clear (mubayyinatin). | And these (watil'ka) | are the limits (ḥudūdu) | of Allah (l-lahi). | And whoever (waman) | transgresses (yataʿadda) | the limits (ḥudūda) | of Allah (l-lahi) | then certainly (faqad) | he has wronged (ẓalama) | himself (nafsahu). | Not (lā) | you know (tadrī); | Perhaps (laʿalla) | Allah (l-laha) | will bring about (yuḥ'dithu), | after (baʿda) | that (dhālika), | a matter (amran).

65:2 Then when they have reached their term, then retain them with kindness or part with them with kindness. And take witness two men just among you and establish the testimony for Allah. That is instructed, with it, whoever [is] believes in Allah and the Day the Last. And whoever fears Allah, He will make for him a way out,

Then when (fa-idhā) | they have reached (balaghna) | their term (ajalahunna), | then retain them (fa-amsikūhunna) | with kindness (bimaʿrūfin) | or (aw) | part with them (fāriqūhunna) | with kindness (bimaʿrūfin). | And take witness (wa-ashhidū) | two men (dhaway) | just (ʿadlin) | among you (minkum) | and establish (wa-aqīmū) | the testimony (l-shahādata) | for Allah (lillahi). | That (dhālikum) | is instructed (yūʿaẓu), | with it (bihi), | whoever (man) | [is] (kāna) | believes (yu'minu) | in Allah (bil-lahi) | and the Day (wal-yawmi) | the Last (l-ākhiri). | And whoever (waman) | fears (yattaqi) | Allah (l-laha), | He will make (yajʿal) | for him (lahu) | a way out (makhrajan),

65:3 And He will provide for him from where not he thinks. And whoever puts his trust upon Allah, then He is sufficient for him. Indeed, Allah will accomplish His purpose. Indeed, has set Allah for every thing a measure.

And He will provide for him (wayarzuq'hu) | from (min) | where (ḥaythu) | not (lā) | he thinks (yaḥtasibu). | And whoever (waman) | puts his trust (yatawakkal) | upon (ʿalā) | Allah (l-lahi), | then He (fahuwa) | is sufficient for him (ḥasbuhu). | Indeed (inna), | Allah (l-laha) | will accomplish (bālighu) | His purpose (amrihi). | Indeed (qad), | has set (jaʿala) | Allah (l-lahu) | for every (likulli) | thing (shayin) | a measure (qadran).

65:4 And those who have despaired of the menstruation among your women, if you doubt, then their waiting period is three months, and the ones who not [they] menstruated. And those who are pregnant, their term until they deliver their burdens. And whoever fears Allah, He will make for him of his affair ease.

And those who (wa-allāī) | have despaired (ya-is'na) | of (mina) | the menstruation (l-maḥīḍi) | among (min) | your women (nisāikum), | if (ini) | you doubt (ir'tabtum), | then their waiting period (faʿiddatuhunna) | is three (thalāthatu) | months (ashhurin), | and the ones who (wa-allāī) | not (lam) | [they] menstruated (yaḥiḍ'na). | And those who are (wa-ulātu) | pregnant (l-aḥmāli), | their term (ajaluhunna) | until (an) | they deliver (yaḍaʿna) | their burdens (ḥamlahunna). | And whoever (waman) | fears (yattaqi) | Allah (l-laha), | He will make (yajʿal) | for him (lahu) | of (min) | his affair (amrihi) | ease (yus'ran).

65:5 That is the Command of Allah, which He has sent down to you; and whoever fears Allah, He will remove from him his evil deeds and make great for him his reward.

That (dhālika) | is the Command (amru) | of Allah (l-lahi), | which He has sent down (anzalahu) | to you (ilaykum); | and whoever (waman) | fears (yattaqi) | Allah (l-laha), | He will remove (yukaffir) | from him (ʿanhu) | his evil deeds (sayyiātihi) | and make great (wayuʿ'ẓim) | for him (lahu) | his reward (ajran).

65:6 Lodge them from where you dwell, out of your means and do not harm them to distress [on] them. And if they are those who are pregnant, then spend on them until they deliver their burden.

Then if they suckle for you, then give them their payment, and consult among yourselves with kindness, but if you disagree, then may suckle for him another women.

Lodge them (askinūhunna) | from (min) | where (ḥaythu) | you dwell (sakantum), | out of (min) | your means (wuj'dikum) | and do not (walā) | harm them (tuḍārrūhunna) | to distress (lituḍayyiqū) | [on] them (ʿalayhinna). | And if (wa-in) | they are (kunna) | those who are (ulāti) | pregnant (ḥamlin), | then spend (fa-anfiqū) | on them (ʿalayhinna) | until (ḥattā) | they deliver (yaḍaʿna) | their burden (ḥamlahunna). | Then if (fa-in) | they suckle (arḍaʿna) | for you (lakum), | then give them (faātūhunna) | their payment (ujūrahunna), | and consult (watamirū) | among yourselves (baynakum) | with kindness (bimaʿrūfin), | but if (wa-in) | you disagree (taʿāsartum), | then may suckle (fasatur'ḍiʿu) | for him (lahu) | another women (ukh'rā).

65:7 Let spend owner of ample means from his ample means, and he who, is restricted on him his provision, let him spend from what he has been given by Allah. Does not burden Allah any soul except with what He has given it. Will bring about Allah after hardship ease.

Let spend (liyunfiq) | owner (dhū) | of ample means (saʿatin) | from (min) | his ample means (saʿatihi), | and he who (waman), | is restricted (qudira) | on him (ʿalayhi) | his provision (riz'quhu), | let him spend (falyunfiq) | from what (mimmā) | he has been given (ātāhu) | by Allah (l-lahu). | Does not (lā) | burden (yukallifu) | Allah (l-lahu) | any soul (nafsan) | except (illā) | with what (mā) | He has given it (ātāhā). | Will bring about (sayajʿalu) | Allah (l-lahu) | after (baʿda) | hardship (ʿus'rin) | ease (yus'ran).

65:8 And how many of a town rebelled against the Command of its Lord and His Messengers, so We took it to account, an account severe; and We punished it, a punishment terrible.

And how many (waka-ayyin) | of (min) | a town (qaryatin) | rebelled (ʿatat) | against (ʿan) | the Command (amri) | of its Lord (rabbihā) | and His Messengers (warusulihi), | so We took it to account (faḥāsabnāhā), | an account (ḥisāban) | severe (shadīdan); | and We punished it (waʿadhabnāhā), | a punishment (ʿadhāban) | terrible (nuk'ran).

65:9 So it tasted the bad consequence of its affair, and was the end of its affair loss.

So it tasted (fadhāqat) | the bad consequence (wabāla) | of its affair (amrihā), | and was (wakāna) | the end (ʿāqibatu) | of its affair (amrihā) | loss (khus'ran).

65:10 Has prepared Allah for them a punishment severe. So fear Allah, O men of understanding, those who have believed! Indeed, Has sent down Allah to you a Message.

Has prepared (aʿadda) | Allah (l-lahu) | for them (lahum) | a punishment (ʿadhāban) | severe (shadīdan). | So fear (fa-ittaqū) | Allah (l-laha), | O men (yāulī) | of understanding (l-albābi), | those who (alladhīna) | have believed (āmanū)! | Indeed (qad), | Has sent down (anzala) | Allah (l-lahu) | to you (ilaykum) | a Message (dhik'ran).

65:11 A Messenger reciting to you the Verses of Allah clear, that he may bring out those who believe and do righteous deeds from the darkness[es] towards the light. And whoever believes in Allah and does righteous deeds, He will admit him into Gardens flow from underneath it the rivers, abiding therein forever. Indeed, Has been granted good by Allah for him provision.

A Messenger (rasūlan) | reciting (yatlū) | to you (ʿalaykum) | the Verses (āyāti) | of Allah (l-lahi) | clear (mubayyinātin), | that he may bring out (liyukh'rija) | those who (alladhīna) | believe (āmanū) | and do (waʿamilū) | righteous deeds (l-ṣāliḥāti) | from (mina) | the darkness[es] (l-ẓulumāti) | towards (ilā) | the light (l-nūri). | And whoever (waman) | believes (yu'min) | in Allah (bil-lahi) | and does (wayaʿmal) | righteous deeds (ṣāliḥan), | He will admit him (yud'khil'hu) | into Gardens (jannātin) | flow (tajrī) | from (min) | underneath it (taḥtihā) | the rivers (l-anhāru), | abiding (khālidīna) | therein (fīhā) | forever (abadan). | Indeed (qad), | Has been granted good (aḥsana) | by Allah (l-lahu) | for him (lahu) | provision (riz'qan).

65:12 Allah is He Who created seven heavens and of the earth, the like of them. Descends the command between them that you may know that Allah is on every thing All-Powerful. And that, Allah indeed, encompasses all things in knowledge.

Allah (al-lahu) | is He Who (alladhī) | created (khalaqa) | seven (sabʿa) | heavens (samāwātin) | and of (wamina) | the earth (l-arḍi), | the like of them (mith'lahunna). | Descends (yatanazzalu) | the command (l-amru) | between them (baynahunna) | that you may know (litaʿlamū) | that (anna) | Allah (l-laha) | is on (ʿalā) | every (kulli) | thing (shayin) | All-Powerful (qadīrun). | And that (wa-anna), | Allah (l-laha) | indeed (qad), | encompasses (aḥāṭa) | all (bikulli) | things (shayin) | in knowledge (ʿil'man).

Chapter (66) Sūrat l-Taḥrīm (The Prohibition)

66:1 O Prophet! Why do you prohibit what has made lawful Allah for you, seeking to please your wives? And Allah is Oft-Forgiving, Most Merciful.

O (yāayyuhā) | Prophet (l-nabiyu)! | Why do (lima) | you prohibit (tuḥarrimu) | what (mā) | has made lawful (aḥalla) | Allah (l-lahu) | for you (laka), | seeking (tabtaghī) | to please (marḍāta) | your wives (azwājika)? | And Allah (wal-lahu) | is Oft-Forgiving (ghafūrun), | Most Merciful (raḥīmun).

66:2 Indeed, has ordained Allah for you the dissolution of your oaths. And Allah is your Protector and He is the All-Knower, the All-Wise.

Indeed (qad), | has ordained (faraḍa) | Allah (l-lahu) | for you (lakum) | the dissolution (taḥillata) | of your oaths (aymānikum). | And Allah (wal-lahu) | is your Protector (mawlākum) | and He (wahuwa) | is the All-Knower (l-ʿalīmu), | the All-Wise (l-ḥakīmu).

66:3 And when confided the Prophet to one of his wives a statement, and when she informed about it and made it apparent Allah to him, he made known a part of it and avoided [of] a part. Then when he informed her about it, she said, "Who informed you this?" He said, "Has informed me the All-Knower, the All-Aware."

And when (wa-idh) | confided (asarra) | the Prophet (l-nabiyu) | to (ilā) | one (baʿḍi) | of his wives (azwājihi) | a statement (ḥadīthan), | and when (falammā) | she informed (nabba-at) | about it (bihi) | and made it apparent (wa-aẓharahu) | Allah (l-lahu) | to him (ʿalayhi), | he made known (ʿarrafa) | a part of it (baʿḍahu) | and avoided (wa-aʿraḍa) | [of] (ʿan) | a part (baʿḍin). | Then when (falammā) | he informed her (nabba-ahā) | about it (bihi), | she said (qālat), | "Who (man) | informed you (anba-aka) | this? (hādhā)" | He said (qāla), | "Has informed me (nabba-aniya) | the All-Knower (l-ʿalīmu), | the All-Aware. (l-khabīru)"

66:4 If you both turn to Allah, so indeed, are inclined your hearts; but if you backup each other against him, then indeed, Allah, He is his Protector, and Jibreel, and the righteous believers, and the Angels, after that are his assistants.

If (in) | you both turn (tatūbā) | to (ilā) | Allah (l-lahi), | so indeed (faqad), | are inclined (ṣaghat) | your hearts (qulūbukumā); | but if (wa-in) | you backup each other (taẓāharā) | against him (ʿalayhi), | then indeed (fa-inna), | Allah (l-laha), | He (huwa) | is his Protector (mawlāhu), | and Jibreel (wajib'rīlu), | and the righteous (waṣāliḥu) | believers (l-mu'minīna), | and the Angels (wal-malāikatu), | after (baʿda) | that (dhālika) | are his assistants (ẓahīrun).

66:5 Perhaps his Lord, if he divorced you, [that] He will substitute for him wives better than you submissive, faithful, obedient, repentant, who worship, who fast, previously married and virgins.

Perhaps (ʿasā) | his Lord (rabbuhu), | if (in) | he divorced you (ṭallaqakunna), | [that] (an) | He will substitute for him (yub'dilahu) | wives (azwājan) | better (khayran) | than you (minkunna) | submissive (mus'limātin), | faithful (mu'minātin), | obedient (qānitātin), | repentant (tāibātin), | who worship (ʿābidātin), | who fast (sāiḥātin), | previously married (thayyibātin) | and virgins (wa-abkāran).

66:6 O you who believe! Protect yourselves and your families from a Fire whose fuel is people and stones, over it are Angels stern, severe; not they disobey Allah in what He Commands them but they do what they are commanded.

O (yāayyuhā) | you who (alladhīna) | believe (āmanū)! | Protect (qū) | yourselves (anfusakum) | and your families (wa-ahlīkum) | from a Fire (nāran) | whose fuel (waqūduhā) | is people (l-nāsu) | and stones (wal-ḥijāratu), | over it (ʿalayhā) | are Angels (malāikatun) | stern (ghilāẓun), | severe (shidādun); | not (lā) | they disobey (yaʿṣūna) | Allah (l-laha) | in what (mā) | He Commands them (amarahum) | but they do (wayafʿalūna) | what (mā) | they are commanded (yu'marūna).

66:7 "O you who disbelieve! Do not make excuses today. Only you will be recompensed for what you used to do."

"O (yāayyuhā) | you who (alladhīna) | disbelieve (kafarū)! | Do not (lā) | make excuses (taʿtadhirū) | today (l-yawma). | Only (innamā) | you will be recompensed (tuj'zawna) | for what (mā) | you used to (kuntum) | do. (taʿmalūna)"

66:8 O you who believe believe! Turn to Allah in repentance sincere! Perhaps your Lord will remove from you your evil deeds and admit you into Gardens flow from underneath it the rivers, on the Day not will be disgraced by Allah the Prophet and those who believed with him. Their light will run before their hands and on their right; they will say, "Our Lord Perfect for us our light and grant forgiveness to us. Indeed, You are over every thing All-Powerful."

O (yāayyuhā) | you who believe (alladhīna) | believe (āmanū)! | Turn (tūbū) | to (ilā) | Allah (l-lahi) | in repentance (tawbatan) | sincere (naṣūḥan)! | Perhaps (ʿasā) | your Lord (rabbukum) | will (an) | remove (yukaffira) | from you (ʿankum) | your evil deeds (sayyiātikum) | and admit you (wayud'khilakum) | into Gardens (jannātin) | flow (tajrī) | from (min) | underneath it (taḥtihā) | the rivers (l-anhāru), | on the Day (yawma) | not (lā) | will be disgraced (yukh'zī) | by Allah (l-lahu) | the Prophet (l-nabiya) | and those who (wa-alladhīna) | believed (āmanū) | with him (maʿahu). | Their light (nūruhum) | will run (yasʿā) | before (bayna) | their hands (aydīhim) | and on their right (wabi-aymānihim); | they will say (yaqūlūna), | "Our Lord (rabbanā) | Perfect (atmim) | for us (lanā) | our light (nūranā) | and grant forgiveness (wa-igh'fir) | to us (lanā). | Indeed, You (innaka) | are over (ʿalā) | every (kulli) | thing (shayin) | All-Powerful. (qadīrun)"

66:9 O Prophet! Strive against the disbelievers and the hypocrites, and be stern with them. And their abode is Hell, and wretched is the destination.

O (yāayyuhā) | Prophet (l-nabiyu)! | Strive (jāhidi) | against the disbelievers (l-kufāra) | and the hypocrites (wal-munāfiqīna), | and be stern (wa-ugh'luẓ) | with them (ʿalayhim). | And their abode (wamawāhum) | is Hell (jahannamu), | and wretched is (wabi'sa) | the destination (l-maṣīru).

66:10 Presents Allah an example for those who disbelieved - the wife of Nuh and the wife of Lut. They were under two [slaves] of Our slaves righteous, but they both betrayed them, so not they availed, both of them, from Allah in anything, and it was said, "Enter the Fire with those who enter."

Presents (ḍaraba) | Allah (l-lahu) | an example (mathalan) | for those who (lilladhīna) | disbelieved (kafarū)- | the wife (im'ra-ata) | of Nuh (nūḥin) | and the wife (wa-im'ra-ata) | of Lut (lūṭin). | They were (kānatā) | under (taḥta) | two [slaves] (ʿabdayni) | of (min) | Our slaves (ʿibādinā) | righteous (ṣāliḥayni), | but they both betrayed them (fakhānatāhumā), | so not (falam) | they availed (yugh'niyā), | both of them (ʿanhumā), | from (mina) | Allah (l-lahi) | in anything (shayan), | and it was said (waqīla), | "Enter (ud'khulā) | the Fire (l-nāra) | with (maʿa) | those who enter. (l-dākhilīna)"

66:11 And presents Allah an example for those who believed - the wife of Firaun, when she said, "My Lord! Build for me near You a house in Paradise, and save me from Firaun and his deeds and save me from the people the wrongdoers."

And presents (waḍaraba) | Allah (l-lahu) | an example (mathalan) | for those who (lilladhīna) | believed (āmanū)- | the wife (im'ra-ata) | of Firaun (fir'ʿawna), | when (idh) | she said (qālat), | "My Lord (rabbi)! | Build (ib'ni) | for me (lī) | near You (ʿindaka) | a house (baytan) | in (fī) | Paradise (l-janati), | and save me (wanajjinī) | from (min) | Firaun (fir'ʿawna) | and his deeds (waʿamalihi) | and save me (wanajjinī) | from (mina) | the people (l-qawmi) | the wrongdoers. (l-ẓālimīna)"

66:12 And Maryam, the daughter of Imran who guarded her chastity, so We breathed into it of Our Spirit. And she believed in the Words of her Lord and His Books, and she was of the devoutly obedient.

And Maryam (wamaryama), | the daughter (ib'nata) | of Imran (ʿim'rāna) | who (allatī) | guarded (aḥṣanat) | her chastity (farjahā), | so We breathed (fanafakhnā) | into it (fīhi) | of (min) | Our Spirit (rūḥinā). | And she believed (waṣaddaqat) | in the Words (bikalimāti) | of her Lord (rabbihā) | and His Books (wakutubihi), | and she was (wakānat) | of (mina) | the devoutly obedient (l-qānitīna).

Chapter (67) Sūrat l-Mulk (Dominion)

67:1 Blessed is He in Whose Hand is the Dominion, and He is over every thing All-Powerful.

Blessed is (tabāraka) | He (alladhī) | in Whose Hand (biyadihi) | is the Dominion (l-mul'ku), | and He (wahuwa) | is over (ʿalā) | every (kulli) | thing (shayin) | All-Powerful (qadīrun).

67:2 The One Who created death and life that He may test you, which of you is best in deed. And He is the All-Mighty, the Oft-Forgiving.

The One Who (alladhī) | created (khalaqa) | death (l-mawta) | and life (wal-ḥayata) | that He may test you (liyabluwakum), | which of you (ayyukum) | is best (aḥsanu) | in deed (ʿamalan). | And He (wahuwa) | is the All-Mighty (l-ʿazīzu), | the Oft-Forgiving (l-ghafūru).

67:3 The One Who created seven heavens one above another. Not you see in the creation of the Most Gracious any fault. So return the vision, can you see any flaw?

The One Who (alladhī) | created (khalaqa) | seven (sabʿa) | heavens (samāwātin) | one above another (ṭibāqan). | Not (mā) | you see (tarā) | in (fī) | the creation (khalqi) | of the Most Gracious (l-raḥmāni) | any (min) | fault (tafāwutin). | So return (fa-ir'jiʿi) | the vision (l-baṣara), | can (hal) | you see (tarā) | any (min) | flaw (fuṭūrin)?

67:4 Then return the vision twice again. Will return to you the vision humbled while it is fatigued.

Then (thumma) | return (ir'jiʿi) | the vision (l-baṣara) | twice again (karratayni). | Will return (yanqalib) | to you (ilayka) | the vision (l-baṣaru) | humbled (khāsi-an) | while it (wahuwa) | is fatigued (ḥasīrun).

67:5 And certainly We have beautified the heaven nearest with lamps, and We have made them as missiles for the devils, and We have prepared for them punishment of the Blaze.

And certainly (walaqad) | We have beautified (zayyannā) | the heaven (l-samāa) | nearest (l-dun'yā) | with lamps (bimaṣābīḥa), | and We have made them (wajaʿalnāhā) | as missiles (rujūman) | for the devils (lilshayāṭīni), | and We have prepared (wa-aʿtadnā) | for them (lahum) | punishment (ʿadhāba) | of the Blaze (l-saʿīri).

67:6 And for those who disbelieved in their Lord is the punishment of Hell, and wretched is the destination.

And for those who (walilladhīna) | disbelieved (kafarū) | in their Lord (birabbihim) | is the punishment (ʿadhābu) | of Hell (jahannama), | and wretched is (wabi'sa) | the destination (l-maṣīru).

67:7 When they are thrown therein, they will hear from it an inhaling while it boils up.

When (idhā) | they are thrown (ul'qū) | therein (fīhā), | they will hear (samiʿū) | from it (lahā) | an inhaling (shahīqan) | while it (wahiya) | boils up (tafūru).

67:8 It almost bursts from rage. Every time is thrown therein a group, will ask them its keepers, "Did not come to you a warner?"

It almost (takādu) | bursts (tamayyazu) | from (mina) | rage (l-ghayẓi). | Every time (kullamā) | is thrown (ul'qiya) | therein (fīhā) | a group (fawjun), | will ask them (sa-alahum) | its keepers (khazanatuhā), | "Did not (alam) | come to you (yatikum) | a warner? (nadhīrun)"

67:9 They will say "Yes, indeed came to us a warner, but we denied and we said, "Not has sent down Allah any thing. Not you are but in error great."

They will say (qālū) | "Yes (balā), | indeed (qad) | came to us (jāanā) | a warner (nadhīrun), | but we denied (fakadhabnā) | and we said (waqul'nā), | "Not (mā) | has sent down (nazzala) | Allah (l-lahu) | any (min) | thing (shayin). | Not (in) | you are (antum) | but (illā) | in (fī) | error (ḍalālin) | great. (kabīrin)"

67:10 And they will say, "If we had listened or reasoned, not we would have been among the companions of the Blaze."

And they will say (waqālū), | "If (law) | we had (kunnā) | listened (nasmaʿu) | or (aw) | reasoned (naʿqilu), | not (mā) | we would have been (kunnā) | among (fī) | the companions (aṣḥābi) | of the Blaze. (l-saʿīri)"

67:11 Then they will confess their sins, so away with the companions of the Blaze.

Then they will confess (fa-iʿ'tarafū) | their sins (bidhanbihim), | so away with (fasuḥ'qan) | the companions (li-aṣḥābi) | of the Blaze (l-saʿīri).

67:12 Indeed, those who fear their Lord unseen, for them is forgiveness and a reward great.

Indeed (inna), | those who (alladhīna) | fear (yakhshawna) | their Lord (rabbahum) | unseen (bil-ghaybi), | for them (lahum) | is forgiveness (maghfiratun) | and a reward (wa-ajrun) | great (kabīrun).

67:13 And conceal your speech or proclaim it. Indeed, He is the All-Knower of what is in the breasts.

And conceal (wa-asirrū) | your speech (qawlakum) | or (awi) | proclaim (ij'harū) | it (bihi). | Indeed, He (innahu) | is the All-Knower (ʿalīmun) | of what is in (bidhāti) | the breasts (l-ṣudūri).

67:14 Does not know the One Who created? And He is the Subtle, the All-Aware.
Does not (alā) | know (yaʿlamu) | the One Who (man) | created (khalaqa)? | And He (wahuwa) | is the Subtle (l-laṭīfu), | the All-Aware (l-khabīru).

67:15 He is the One Who made for you the earth subservient, so walk in the paths thereof and eat of His provision, and to Him is the Resurrection.
He (huwa) | is the One Who (alladhī) | made (jaʿala) | for you (lakumu) | the earth (l-arḍa) | subservient (dhalūlan), | so walk (fa-im'shū) | in (fī) | the paths thereof (manākibihā) | and eat (wakulū) | of (min) | His provision (riz'qihi), | and to Him (wa-ilayhi) | is the Resurrection (l-nushūru).

67:16 Do you feel secure from Him Who is in the heaven not He will cause to swallow you the earth when it sways?
Do you feel secure (a-amintum) | from Him Who (man) | is in (fī) | the heaven (l-samāi) | not (an) | He will cause to swallow (yakhsifa) | you (bikumu) | the earth (l-arḍa) | when (fa-idhā) | it (hiya) | sways (tamūru)?

67:17 Or do you feel secure from Him Who is in the heaven, that He will send against you a storm of stones? Then you would know how was My warning?
Or (am) | do you feel secure (amintum) | from Him Who (man) | is in (fī) | the heaven (l-samāi), | that (an) | He will send (yur'sila) | against you (ʿalaykum) | a storm of stones (ḥāṣiban)? | Then you would know (fasataʿlamūna) | how (kayfa) | was My warning (nadhīri)?

67:18 And indeed, denied those from before them, and how was My rejection.
And indeed (walaqad), | denied (kadhaba) | those (alladhīna) | from (min) | before them (qablihim), | and how (fakayfa) | was (kāna) | My rejection (nakīri).

67:19 Do not they see [to] the birds above them spreading their wings and folding? Not holds them except the Most Gracious. Indeed, He is of every thing All-Seer.
Do not (awalam) | they see (yaraw) | [to] (ilā) | the birds (l-ṭayri) | above them (fawqahum) | spreading their wings (ṣāffātin) | and folding (wayaqbiḍ'na)? | Not (mā) | holds them (yum'sikuhunna) | except (illā) | the Most Gracious (l-raḥmānu). | Indeed, He (innahu) | is of every (bikulli) | thing (shayin) | All-Seer (baṣīrun).

67:20 Who is this, the one, he is an army for you to help you from besides the Most Gracious? Not are the disbelievers but in delusion.
Who is (amman) | this (hādhā), | the one (alladhī), | he (huwa) | is an army (jundun) | for you (lakum) | to help you (yanṣurukum) | from (min) | besides (dūni) | the Most Gracious (l-raḥmāni)? | Not (ini) | are the disbelievers (l-kāfirūna) | but (illā) | in (fī) | delusion (ghurūrin).

67:21 Who is this, the one, to provide you if He withheld His provision. Nay, they persist in pride and aversion.
Who is (amman) | this (hādhā), | the one (alladhī), | to provide you (yarzuqukum) | if (in) | He withheld (amsaka) | His provision (riz'qahu). | Nay (bal), | they persist (lajjū) | in (fī) | pride (ʿutuwwin) | and aversion (wanufūrin).

67:22 Then is he who walks fallen on his face better guided, or he who walks upright on the Path Straight?
Then is he who (afaman) | walks (yamshī) | fallen (mukibban) | on (ʿalā) | his face (wajhihi) | better guided (ahdā), | or he who (amman) | walks (yamshī) | upright (sawiyyan) | on (ʿalā) | the Path (ṣirāṭin) | Straight (mus'taqīmin)?

67:23 Say, "He is the One Who produced you and made for you the hearing, and the vision and the feelings. Little is what you give thanks."

Say (qul), | "He (huwa) | is the One Who (alladhī) | produced you (ansha-akum) | and made (wajaʿala) | for you (lakumu) | the hearing (l-samʿa), | and the vision (wal-abṣāra) | and the feelings (wal-afidata). | Little (qalīlan) | is what (mā) | you give thanks. (tashkurūna)"

67:24 Say, "He is the One Who multiplied you in the earth and to Him you will be gathered."

Say (qul), | "He (huwa) | is the One Who (alladhī) | multiplied you (dhara-akum) | in (fī) | the earth (l-arḍi) | and to Him (wa-ilayhi) | you will be gathered. (tuḥ'sharūna)"

67:25 And they say, "When is this promise, if you are truthful?"

And they say (wayaqūlūna), | "When (matā) | is this (hādhā) | promise (l-waʿdu), | if (in) | you are (kuntum) | truthful? (ṣādiqīna)"

67:26 Say, "Only the knowledge is with Allah, and only I am a warner clear."

Say (qul), | "Only (innamā) | the knowledge (l-ʿil'mu) | is with (ʿinda) | Allah (l-lahi), | and only (wa-innamā) | I am (anā) | a warner (nadhīrun) | clear. (mubīnun)"

67:27 But when they will see it approaching, will be distressed the faces of those who disbelieved, and it will be said, "This is that which you used to for it call."

But when (falammā) | they will see it (ra-awhu) | approaching (zul'fatan), | will be distressed (sīat) | the faces (wujūhu) | of those who (alladhīna) | disbelieved (kafarū), | and it will be said (waqīla), | "This (hādhā) | is that which (alladhī) | you used to (kuntum) | for it (bihi) | call. (taddaʿūna)"

67:28 Say, "Have you seen, if destroys me Allah and whoever is with me or has mercy upon us, then who can protect the disbelievers from a punishment painful."

Say (qul), | "Have you seen (ara-aytum), | if (in) | destroys me (ahlakaniya) | Allah (l-lahu) | and whoever (waman) | is with me (maʿiya) | or (aw) | has mercy upon us (raḥimanā), | then who (faman) | can protect (yujīru) | the disbelievers (l-kāfirīna) | from (min) | a punishment (ʿadhābin) | painful. (alīmin)"

67:29 Say, "He is the Most Gracious; we believe in Him, and upon Him we put our trust. So you will know who is it that is in error clear."

Say (qul), | "He (huwa) | is the Most Gracious (l-raḥmānu); | we believe (āmannā) | in Him (bihi), | and upon Him (waʿalayhi) | we put our trust (tawakkalnā). | So you will know (fasataʿlamūna) | who (man) | is it (huwa) | that is in (fī) | error (ḍalālin) | clear. (mubīnin)"

67:30 Say, "Have you seen, if becomes your water sunken, then who could bring you water flowing?"

Say (qul), | "Have you seen (ara-aytum), | if (in) | becomes (aṣbaḥa) | your water (māukum) | sunken (ghawran), | then who (faman) | could bring you (yatīkum) | water (bimāin) | flowing? (maʿīnin)"

Chapter (68) Sūrat l-Qalam (The Pen)

68:1 Nun. By the pen and what they write,
Nun (noon). | By the pen (wal-qalami) | and what (wamā) | they write (yasṭurūna),

68:2 Not you are, by the Grace of your Lord, a madman.
Not (mā) | you are (anta), | by the Grace (bini''mati) | of your Lord (rabbika), | a madman (bimajnūnin).

68:3 And indeed, for you surely is a reward without end.
And indeed (wa-inna), | for you (laka) | surely is a reward (la-ajran) | without (ghayra) | end (mamnūnin).

68:4 And indeed, you surely are of a moral character great.
And indeed, you (wa-innaka) | surely are (laʿalā) | of a moral character (khuluqin) | great (ʿaẓīmin).

68:5 So you will see and they will see,
So you will see (fasatub'ṣiru) | and they will see (wayub'ṣirūna),

68:6 Which of you is the afflicted one.
Which of you (bi-ayyikumu) | is the afflicted one (l-maftūnu).

68:7 Indeed, your Lord, He is most knowing of he who has strayed from His way, and He is most knowing of the guided ones.
Indeed (inna), | your Lord (rabbaka), | He (huwa) | is most knowing (aʿlamu) | of he who (biman) | has strayed (ḍalla) | from (ʿan) | His way (sabīlihi), | and He (wahuwa) | is most knowing (aʿlamu) | of the guided ones (bil-muh'tadīna).

68:8 So do not obey the deniers.
So do not (falā) | obey (tuṭiʿi) | the deniers (l-mukadhibīna).

68:9 They wish that you should compromise, so they would compromise.
They wish (waddū) | that (law) | you should compromise (tud'hinu), | so they would compromise (fayud'hinūna).

68:10 And do not obey every habitual swearer worthless,
And do not (walā) | obey (tuṭiʿ) | every (kulla) | habitual swearer (ḥallāfin) | worthless (mahīnin),

68:11 Defamer going about with malicious gossip,
Defamer (hammāzin) | going about (mashāin) | with malicious gossip (binamīmin),

68:12 A preventer, of the good, transgressor, sinful,
A preventer (mannāʿin), | of the good (lil'khayri), | transgressor (mu''tadin), | sinful (athīmin),

68:13 Cruel, after all that utterly useless.
Cruel (ʿutullin), | after (baʿda) | all that (dhālika) | utterly useless (zanīmin).

68:14 Because he is a possessor of wealth and children,

Because (an) | he is (kāna) | a possessor (dhā) | of wealth (mālin) | and children (wabanīna),

68:15 When are recited to him Our Verses, he says, "Stories of the former (people)."
When (idhā) | are recited (tut'lā) | to him (ʿalayhi) | Our Verses (āyātunā), | he says (qāla), | "Stories (asāṭīru) | of the former (people). (l-awalīna)"

68:16 We will brand him on the snout.
We will brand him (sanasimuhu) | on (ʿalā) | the snout (l-khur'ṭūmi).

68:17 Indeed, We have tried them as We tried the companions of the garden, when they swore to pluck its fruit in the morning,
Indeed, We (innā) | have tried them (balawnāhum) | as (kamā) | We tried (balawnā) | the companions (aṣḥāba) | of the garden (l-janati), | when (idh) | they swore (aqsamū) | to pluck its fruit (layaṣrimunnahā) | in the morning (muṣ'biḥīna),

68:18 And not making exception.
And not (walā) | making exception (yastathnūna).

68:19 So there came upon it a visitation from your Lord, while they were asleep.
So there came (faṭāfa) | upon it (ʿalayhā) | a visitation (ṭāifun) | from (min) | your Lord (rabbika), | while they (wahum) | were asleep (nāimūna).

68:20 So it became as if reaped.
So it became (fa-aṣbaḥat) | as if reaped (kal-ṣarīmi).

68:21 And they called one another at morning,
And they called one another (fatanādaw) | at morning (muṣ'biḥīna),

68:22 That "Go early to your crop if you would pluck the fruit."
That (ani) | "Go early (igh'dū) | to (ʿalā) | your crop (ḥarthikum) | if (in) | you would (kuntum) | pluck the fruit. (ṣārimīna)"

68:23 So they went, while they lowered their voices,
So they went (fa-inṭalaqū), | while they (wahum) | lowered their voices (yatakhāfatūna),

68:24 That "Not will enter it today upon you any poor person."
That (an) | "Not (lā) | will enter it (yadkhulannahā) | today (l-yawma) | upon you (ʿalaykum) | any poor person. (mis'kīnun)"

68:25 And they went early with determination able.
And they went early (waghadaw) | with (ʿalā) | determination (ḥardin) | able (qādirīna).

68:26 But when they saw it, they said, "Indeed, we are surely lost.
But when (falammā) | they saw it (ra-awhā), | they said (qālū), | "Indeed, we (innā) | are surely lost (laḍāllūna).

68:27 Nay! We are deprived."
Nay (bal)! | We (naḥnu) | are deprived. (maḥrūmūna)"

68:28 Said the most moderate of them, "Did not I tell you, 'Why not you glorify Allah?'"
Said (qāla) | the most moderate of them (awsaṭuhum), | "Did not (alam) | I tell (aqul) |

you (lakum), | 'Why not (lawlā) | you glorify Allah?' (tusabbiḥūna)"

68:29 They said, "Glory be to our Lord! Indeed, we [we] were wrongdoers."
They said (qālū), | "Glory be (sub'ḥāna) | to our Lord (rabbinā)! | Indeed, we (innā) | [we] were (kunnā) | wrongdoers. (ẓālimīna)"

68:30 Then approached, some of them to others blaming each other.
Then approached (fa-aqbala), | some of them (baʿḍuhum) | to (ʿalā) | others (baʿḍin) | blaming each other (yatalāwamūna).

68:31 They said, "O woe to us! Indeed, we [we] were transgressors.
They said (qālū), | "O woe to us (yāwaylanā)! | Indeed, we (innā) | [we] were (kunnā) | transgressors (ṭāghīna).

68:32 Perhaps, our Lord, [that] will substitute for us a better than it. Indeed, we to our Lord turn devoutly."
Perhaps (ʿasā), | our Lord (rabbunā), | [that] (an) | will substitute for us (yub'dilanā) | a better (khayran) | than it (min'hā). | Indeed, we (innā) | to (ilā) | our Lord (rabbinā) | turn devoutly. (rāghibūna)"

68:33 Such is the punishment. And surely the punishment of the Hereafter is greater, if they know.
Such (kadhālika) | is the punishment (l-ʿadhābu). | And surely the punishment (walaʿadhābu) | of the Hereafter (l-ākhirati) | is greater (akbaru), | if (law) | they (kānū) | know (yaʿlamūna).

68:34 Indeed, for the righteous with their Lord are Gardens of Delight.
Indeed (inna), | for the righteous (lil'muttaqīna) | with (ʿinda) | their Lord (rabbihim) | are Gardens (jannāti) | of Delight (l-naʿīmi).

68:35 Then will We treat the Muslims like the criminals?
Then will We treat (afanajʿalu) | the Muslims (l-mus'limīna) | like the criminals (kal-muj'rimīna)?

68:36 What is for you? How do you judge?
What (mā) | is for you (lakum)? | How (kayfa) | do you judge (taḥkumūna)?

68:37 Or is for you a book wherein you learn,
Or (am) | is for you (lakum) | a book (kitābun) | wherein (fīhi) | you learn (tadrusūna),

68:38 Indeed for you in it what you choose?
Indeed (inna) | for you (lakum) | in it (fīhi) | what (lamā) | you choose (takhayyarūna)?

68:39 Or for you oaths from us, reaching to the Day of the Resurrection, indeed, for you is what you judge?
Or (am) | for you (lakum) | oaths (aymānun) | from us (ʿalaynā), | reaching (bālighatun) | to (ilā) | the Day (yawmi) | of the Resurrection (l-qiyāmati), | indeed (inna), | for you (lakum) | is what (lamā) | you judge (taḥkumūna)?

68:40 Ask them, which of them for that is responsible.
Ask them (salhum), | which of them (ayyuhum) | for that (bidhālika) | is responsible (zaʿīmun).

68:41 Or are for them partners? Then let them bring their partners, if they are truthful.
Or (am) | are for them (lahum) | partners (shurakāu)? | Then let them bring (falyatū) | their partners (bishurakāihim), | if (in) | they are (kānū) | truthful (ṣādiqīna).

68:42 The Day will be uncovered from the shin and they will be called to prostrate, but not they will be able,
The Day (yawma) | will be uncovered (yuk'shafu) | from (ʿan) | the shin (sāqin) | and they will be called (wayud''awna) | to (ilā) | prostrate (l-sujūdi), | but not (falā) | they will be able (yastaṭīʿūna),

68:43 Humbled, their eyes, will cover them humiliation. And indeed, they were called to prostrate while they were sound.
Humbled (khāshiʿatan), | their eyes (abṣāruhum), | will cover them (tarhaquhum) | humiliation (dhillatun). | And indeed (waqad), | they were (kānū) | called (yud''awna) | to (ilā) | prostrate (l-sujūdi) | while they (wahum) | were sound (sālimūna).

68:44 So leave Me and whoever denies this Statement, We will progressively lead them from where not they know.
So leave Me (fadharnī) | and whoever (waman) | denies (yukadhibu) | this (bihādhā) | Statement (l-ḥadīthi), | We will progressively lead them (sanastadrijuhum) | from (min) | where (ḥaythu) | not (lā) | they know (yaʿlamūna).

68:45 And I will give respite to them. Indeed, My plan is firm.
And I will give respite (wa-um'lī) | to them (lahum). | Indeed (inna), | My plan (kaydī) | is firm (matīnun).

68:46 Or you ask them a payment, so they from the debt are burdened?
Or (am) | you ask them (tasaluhum) | a payment (ajran), | so they (fahum) | from (min) | the debt (maghramin) | are burdened (muth'qalūna)?

68:47 Or is with them the unseen, so they write it?
Or (am) | is with them (ʿindahumu) | the unseen (l-ghaybu), | so they (fahum) | write it (yaktubūna)?

68:48 So be patient for the decision of your Lord, and do not be like the companion of the fish, when he called out, while he was distressed.
So be patient (fa-iṣ'bir) | for the decision (liḥuk'mi) | of your Lord (rabbika), | and do not (walā) | be (takun) | like the companion (kaṣāḥibi) | of the fish (l-ḥūti), | when (idh) | he called out (nādā), | while he (wahuwa) | was distressed (makẓūmun).

68:49 If not that overtook him a Favor from his Lord, surely he would have been thrown onto the naked shore while he was blamed.
If not (lawlā) | that (an) | overtook him (tadārakahu) | a Favor (ni''matun) | from (min) | his Lord (rabbihi), | surely he would have been thrown (lanubidha) | onto the naked shore (bil-ʿarāi) | while he (wahuwa) | was blamed (madhmūmun).

68:50 But chose him, his Lord, and made him of the righteous.
But chose him (fa-ij'tabāhu), | his Lord (rabbuhu), | and made him (fajaʿalahu) | of (mina) | the righteous (l-ṣāliḥīna).

68:51 And indeed, would almost those who disbelieve, surely make you slip with their look when they hear the Message, and they say, "Indeed, he is surely mad."

And indeed (wa-in), | would almost (yakādu) | those who (alladhīna) | disbelieve (kafarū), | surely make you slip (layuz'liqūnaka) | with their look (bi-abṣārihim) | when (lammā) | they hear (samiʿū) | the Message (l-dhik'ra), | and they say (wayaqūlūna), | "Indeed, he (innahu) | is surely mad. (lamajnūnun)"

68:52 And not it is but a Reminder to the worlds.
And not (wamā) | it is (huwa) | but (illā) | a Reminder (dhik'run) | to the worlds (lil'ʿālamīna).

Chapter (69) Sūrat l-Ḥāqah (The Inevitable)

69:1 The Inevitable Reality!
The Inevitable Reality (al-ḥāqatu)!

69:2 What is the Inevitable Reality?
What (mā) | is the Inevitable Reality (l-ḥāqatu)?

69:3 And what will make you know what is the Inevitable Reality?
And what (wamā) | will make you know (adrāka) | what (mā) | is the Inevitable Reality (l-ḥāqatu)?

69:4 Denied Thamud and Aad the Striking Calamity.
Denied (kadhabat) | Thamud (thamūdu) | and Aad (waʿādun) | the Striking Calamity (bil-qāriʿati).

69:5 So as for Thamud, they were destroyed by the overpowering blast.
So as for (fa-ammā) | Thamud (thamūdu), | they were destroyed (fa-uh'likū) | by the overpowering blast (bil-ṭāghiyati).

69:6 And as for Aad, they were destroyed by a wind screaming violent,
And as for (wa-ammā) | Aad (ʿādun), | they were destroyed (fa-uh'likū) | by a wind (birīḥin) | screaming (ṣarṣarin) | violent (ʿātiyatin),

69:7 Which He imposed upon them for seven nights and eight days in succession, so you would see the people therein fallen as if they were trunks of date-palms hollow.
Which He imposed (sakharahā) | upon them (ʿalayhim) | for seven (sabʿa) | nights (layālin) | and eight (wathamāniyata) | days (ayyāmin) | in succession (ḥusūman), | so you would see (fatarā) | the people (l-qawma) | therein (fīhā) | fallen (ṣarʿā) | as if they were (ka-annahum) | trunks (aʿjāzu) | of date-palms (nakhlin) | hollow (khāwiyatin).

69:8 Then do you see of them any remains?
Then do (fahal) | you see (tarā) | of them (lahum) | any (min) | remains (bāqiyatin)?

69:9 And came Firaun, and those before him, and the overturned cities with sin.
And came (wajāa) | Firaun (fir'ʿawnu), | and those (waman) | before him (qablahu), | and the overturned cities (wal-mu'tafikātu) | with sin (bil-khāṭi-ati).

69:10 And they disobeyed the Messenger of their Lord, so He seized them with a seizure exceeding.
And they disobeyed (faʿaṣaw) | the Messenger (rasūla) | of their Lord (rabbihim), | so He seized them (fa-akhadhahum) | with a seizure (akhdhatan) | exceeding (rābiyatan).

69:11 Indeed, We when overflowed the water, We carried you in the sailing ship.
Indeed, We (innā) | when (lammā) | overflowed (ṭaghā) | the water (l-māu), | We carried you (ḥamalnākum) | in (fī) | the sailing ship (l-jāriyati).

69:12 That We might make it for you a reminder and would be conscious of it an ear conscious.
That We might make it (linajʿalahā) | for you (lakum) | a reminder (tadhkiratan) | and would be conscious of it (wataʿiyahā) | an ear (udhunun) | conscious (wāʿiyatun).

69:13 Then when is blown in the trumpet - a blast single,
Then when (fa-idhā) | is blown (nufikha) | in (fī) | the trumpet (l-ṣūri)- | a blast (nafkhatun) | single (wāḥidatun),

69:14 And are lifted the earth and the mountains and crushed with a crushing single.
And are lifted (waḥumilati) | the earth (l-arḍu) | and the mountains (wal-jibālu) | and crushed (fadukkatā) | with a crushing (dakkatan) | single (wāḥidatan).

69:15 Then on that Day will occur the Occurrence,
Then on that Day (fayawma-idhin) | will occur (waqaʿati) | the Occurrence (l-wāqiʿatu),

69:16 And will split the heaven, so it is on that Day frail.
And will split (wa-inshaqqati) | the heaven (l-samāu), | so it (fahiya) | is on that Day (yawma-idhin) | frail (wāhiyatun).

69:17 And the Angels will be on its edges, and will bear the Throne of your Lord above them, that Day, eight.
And the Angels (wal-malaku) | will be on (ʿalā) | its edges (arjāihā), | and will bear (wayaḥmilu) | the Throne (ʿarsha) | of your Lord (rabbika) | above them (fawqahum), | that Day (yawma-idhin), | eight (thamāniyatun).

69:18 That Day, you will be exhibited, not will be hidden among you any secret.
That Day (yawma-idhin), | you will be exhibited (tuʿraḍūna), | not (lā) | will be hidden (takhfā) | among you (minkum) | any secret (khāfiyatun).

69:19 Then as for him who is given his record in his right hand will say, "Here, read my record!
Then as for (fa-ammā) | him who (man) | is given (ūtiya) | his record (kitābahu) | in his right hand (biyamīnihi) | will say (fayaqūlu), | "Here (hāumu), | read (iq'raū) | my record (kitābiyah)!

69:20 Indeed, I was certain that I will meet my account."
Indeed, I (innī) | was certain (ẓanantu) | that I (annī) | will meet (mulāqin) | my account. (ḥisābiyah)"

69:21 So he will be in a life pleasant,
So he (fahuwa) | will be in (fī) | a life (ʿīshatin) | pleasant (rāḍiyatin),

69:22 In a Garden elevated,
In (fī) | a Garden (jannatin) | elevated (ʿāliyatin),

69:23 Its clusters of fruits hanging near.
Its clusters of fruits (quṭūfuhā) | hanging near (dāniyatun).

69:24 "Eat and drink in satisfaction for what you sent before you in the days past."
"Eat (kulū) | and drink (wa-ish'rabū) | in satisfaction (hanīan) | for what (bimā) | you sent before you (aslaftum) | in (fī) | the days (l-ayāmi) | past. (l-khāliyati)"

69:25 But as for him who is given his record in his left hand will say, "O! I wish not I had been given my record
But as for (wa-ammā) | him who (man) | is given (ūtiya) | his record (kitābahu) | in his left hand (bishimālihi) | will say (fayaqūlu), | "O! I wish (yālaytanī) | not (lam) | I had been given (ūta) | my record (kitābiyah)

69:26 And not I had known what is my account.
And not (walam) | I had known (adri) | what (mā) | is my account (ḥisābiyah).

69:27 O! I wish it had been the end
O! I wish it (yālaytahā) | had been (kānati) | the end (l-qāḍiyata)

69:28 Not has availed me my wealth,
Not (mā) | has availed (aghnā) | me (ʿannī) | my wealth (māliyah),

69:29 Is gone from me my authority."
Is gone (halaka) | from me (ʿannī) | my authority. (sul'ṭāniyah)"

69:30 "Seize him and shackle him,
"Seize him (khudhūhu) | and shackle him (faghullūhu),

69:31 Then into the Hellfire burn him.
Then (thumma) | into the Hellfire (l-jaḥīma) | burn him (ṣallūhu).

69:32 Then into a chain, its length is seventy cubits, insert him."
Then (thumma) | into (fī) | a chain (sil'silatin), | its length (dharʿuhā) | is seventy (sabʿūna) | cubits (dhirāʿan), | insert him. (fa-us'lukūhu)"

69:33 Indeed, he was not believing in Allah the Most Great,
Indeed, he (innahu) | was (kāna) | not (lā) | believing (yu'minu) | in Allah (bil-lahi) | the Most Great (l-ʿaẓīmi),

69:34 And did not feel the urge on the feeding of the poor.
And did not (walā) | feel the urge (yaḥuḍḍu) | on (ʿalā) | the feeding (ṭaʿāmi) | of the poor (l-mis'kīni).

69:35 So not for him today here any devoted friend,
So not (falaysa) | for him (lahu) | today (l-yawma) | here (hāhunā) | any devoted friend (ḥamīmun),

69:36 And not any food except from the discharge of wounds,
And not (walā) | any food (ṭaʿāmun) | except (illā) | from (min) | the discharge of wounds (ghis'līnin),

69:37 Not will eat it except the sinners.

Not (lā) | will eat it (yakuluhu) | except (illā) | the sinners (l-khāṭiūna).

69:38 But nay! I swear by what you see,
But nay (falā)! | I swear (uq'simu) | by what (bimā) | you see (tub'ṣirūna),

69:39 And what not you see,
And what (wamā) | not (lā) | you see (tub'ṣirūna),

69:40 Indeed, it is surely the Word of a Messenger noble.
Indeed, it is (innahu) | surely the Word (laqawlu) | of a Messenger (rasūlin) | noble (karīmin).

69:41 And not it is the word of a poet; little is what you believe!
And not (wamā) | it (huwa) | is the word (biqawli) | of a poet (shāʿirin); | little (qalīlan) | is what (mā) | you believe (tu'minūna)!

69:42 And not it is the word of a soothsayer; little is what you take heed.
And not (walā) | it is the word (biqawli) | of a soothsayer (kāhinin); | little (qalīlan) | is what (mā) | you take heed (tadhakkarūna).

69:43 It is a revelation from the Lord of the worlds.
It is a revelation (tanzīlun) | from (min) | the Lord (rabbi) | of the worlds (l-ʿālamīna).

69:44 And if he had fabricated against Us some sayings,
And if (walaw) | he had fabricated (taqawwala) | against Us (ʿalaynā) | some (baʿḍa) | sayings (l-aqāwīli),

69:45 Certainly We would have seized him by the right hand;
Certainly We would have seized (la-akhadhnā) | him (min'hu) | by the right hand (bil-yamīni);

69:46 Then certainly We would have cut off from him the aorta.
Then (thumma) | certainly We would have cut off (laqaṭaʿnā) | from him (min'hu) | the aorta (l-watīna).

69:47 And not from you any one [from him] who could prevent (it).
And not (famā) | from you (minkum) | any (min) | one (aḥadin) | [from him] (ʿanhu) | who could prevent (it) (ḥājizīna).

69:48 And indeed, it is surely a reminder for the Allah-fearing.
And indeed, it (wa-innahu) | is surely a reminder (latadhkiratun) | for the Allah-fearing (lil'muttaqīna).

69:49 And indeed, We surely know that among you are deniers.
And indeed, We (wa-innā) | surely know (lanaʿlamu) | that (anna) | among you (minkum) | are deniers (mukadhibīna).

69:50 And indeed, it is surely a regret upon the disbelievers.
And indeed, it (wa-innahu) | is surely a regret (laḥasratun) | upon (ʿalā) | the disbelievers (l-kāfirīna).

69:51 And indeed, it is surely the truth of certainty.

And indeed, it is (wa-innahu) | surely the truth (laḥaqqu) | of certainty (l-yaqīni).

69:52 So glorify the name of your Lord, the Most Great.
So glorify (fasabbiḥ) | the name (bi-is'mi) | of your Lord (rabbika), | the Most Great (l-ʿaẓīmi).

Chapter (70) Sūrat l-Maʿārij (The Ways of Ascent)

70:1 Asked a questioner about a punishment bound to happen
Asked (sa-ala) | a questioner (sāilun) | about a punishment (biʿadhābin) | bound to happen (wāqiʿin)

70:2 To the disbelievers, not of it any preventer.
To the disbelievers (lil'kāfirīna), | not (laysa) | of it (lahu) | any preventer (dāfiʿun).

70:3 From Allah, Owner of the ways of ascent.
From (mina) | Allah (l-lahi), | Owner (dhī) | of the ways of ascent (l-maʿāriji).

70:4 Ascend the Angels and the Spirit to Him in a Day, [is] its measure is fifty thousand years.
Ascend (taʿruju) | the Angels (l-malāikatu) | and the Spirit (wal-rūḥu) | to Him (ilayhi) | in (fī) | a Day (yawmin), | [is] (kāna) | its measure (miq'dāruhu) | is fifty (khamsīna) | thousand (alfa) | years (sanatin).

70:5 So be patient, a patience good.
So be patient (fa-iṣ'bir), | a patience (ṣabran) | good (jamīlan).

70:6 Indeed, they see it as far off.
Indeed, they (innahum) | see it (yarawnahu) | as far off (baʿīdan).

70:7 But We see it near.
But We see it (wanarāhu) | near (qarīban).

70:8 The Day - will be the sky like molten copper,
The Day (yawma)- | will be (takūnu) | the sky (l-samāu) | like molten copper (kal-muh'li),

70:9 And will be the mountains like wool,
And will be (watakūnu) | the mountains (l-jibālu) | like wool (kal-ʿih'ni),

70:10 And not will ask a friend about a friend.
And not (walā) | will ask (yasalu) | a friend (ḥamīmun) | about a friend (ḥamīman).

70:11 They will be made to see each other. Would wish the criminal if he could be ransomed from the punishment of that Day by his children,
They will be made to see each other (yubaṣṣarūnahum). | Would wish (yawaddu) | the criminal (l-muj'rimu) | if (law) | he could be ransomed (yaftadī) | from (min) | the punishment (ʿadhābi) | of that Day (yawmi-idhin) | by his children (bibanīhi),

70:12 And his spouse and his brother,
And his spouse (waṣāḥibatihi) | and his brother (wa-akhīhi),

70:13 And his nearest kindred who sheltered him,
And his nearest kindred (wafaṣīlatihi) | who (allatī) | sheltered him (tu'wīhi),

70:14 And whoever is on the earth all, then it could save him.
And whoever (waman) | is on (fī) | the earth (l-arḍi) | all (jamīʿan), | then (thumma) | it could save him (yunjīhi).

70:15 By no means! Indeed, it is surely a Flame of Hell,
By no means (kallā)! | Indeed, it is (innahā) | surely a Flame of Hell (laẓā),

70:16 A remover of the skin of the head,
A remover (nazzāʿatan) | of the skin of the head (lilshawā),

70:17 Inviting him who turned his back and went away
Inviting (tadʿū) | him who (man) | turned his back (adbara) | and went away (watawallā)

70:18 And collected and hoarded.
And collected (wajamaʿa) | and hoarded (fa-awʿā).

70:19 Indeed, the man was created anxious -
Indeed (inna), | the man (l-insāna) | was created (khuliqa) | anxious (halūʿan)-

70:20 When touches him the evil, distressed.
When (idhā) | touches him (massahu) | the evil (l-sharu), | distressed (jazūʿan).

70:21 And when touches him the good, withholding,
And when (wa-idhā) | touches him (massahu) | the good (l-khayru), | withholding (manūʿan),

70:22 Except those who pray -
Except (illā) | those who pray (l-muṣalīna)-

70:23 Those who [they] at their prayer are constant,
Those who (alladhīna) | [they] (hum) | at (ʿalā) | their prayer (ṣalātihim) | are constant (dāimūna),

70:24 And those who in their wealth is a right known,
And those who (wa-alladhīna) | in (fī) | their wealth (amwālihim) | is a right (ḥaqqun) | known (maʿlūmun),

70:25 For the one who asks and the deprived,
For the one who asks (lilssāili) | and the deprived (wal-maḥrūmi),

70:26 And those who accept the truth of the Day of the Judgment,
And those who (wa-alladhīna) | accept the truth (yuṣaddiqūna) | of the Day (biyawmi) | of the Judgment (l-dīni),

70:27 And those who [they] of the punishment of their Lord are fearful -
And those who (wa-alladhīna) | [they] (hum) | of (min) | the punishment (ʿadhābi) | of

their Lord (rabbihim) | are fearful (mush'fiqūna)-

70:28 Indeed, the punishment of your Lord is not to be felt secure of -
Indeed (inna), | the punishment (ʿadhāba) | of your Lord (rabbihim) | is not (ghayru) | to be felt secure of (mamūnin)-

70:29 And those who [they] their modesty are guardians,
And those who (wa-alladhīna) | [they] (hum) | their modesty (lifurūjihim) | are guardians (ḥāfiẓūna),

70:30 Except from their spouses or what they possess rightfully then indeed, they are not blameworthy,
Except (illā) | from (ʿalā) | their spouses (azwājihim) | or (aw) | what (mā) | they possess (malakat) | rightfully (aymānuhum) | then indeed, they (fa-innahum) | are not (ghayru) | blameworthy (malūmīna),

70:31 But whoever seeks beyond that, then those [they] are the transgressors -
But whoever (famani) | seeks (ib'taghā) | beyond (warāa) | that (dhālika), | then those (fa-ulāika) | [they] (humu) | are the transgressors (l-ʿādūna)-

70:32 And those who [they] of their trusts and their promise are observers,
And those who (wa-alladhīna) | [they] (hum) | of their trusts (li-amānātihim) | and their promise (waʿahdihim) | are observers (rāʿūna),

70:33 And those who [they] in their testimonies stand firm,
And those who (wa-alladhīna) | [they] (hum) | in their testimonies (bishahādātihim) | stand firm (qāimūna),

70:34 And those who, [they] on their prayer keep a guard -
And those who (wa-alladhīna), | [they] (hum) | on (ʿalā) | their prayer (ṣalātihim) | keep a guard (yuḥāfiẓūna)-

70:35 Those will be in Gardens, honored.
Those (ulāika) | will be in (fī) | Gardens (jannātin), | honored (muk'ramūna).

70:36 So what is with those who disbelieve, before you they hasten,
So what is with (famāli) | those who (alladhīna) | disbelieve (kafarū), | before you (qibalaka) | they hasten (muh'ṭiʿīna),

70:37 On the right and on the left, in separate groups?
On (ʿani) | the right (l-yamīni) | and on (waʿani) | the left (l-shimāli), | in separate groups (ʿizīna)?

70:38 Does long every person, among them that he enters a Garden of Delight?
Does long (ayaṭmaʿu) | every (kullu) | person (im'ri-in), | among them (min'hum) | that (an) | he enters (yud'khala) | a Garden (jannata) | of Delight (naʿīmin)?

70:39 By no means! Indeed, We [We] have created them from what they know.
By no means (kallā)! | Indeed, We (innā) | [We] have created them (khalaqnāhum) | from what (mimmā) | they know (yaʿlamūna).

70:40 But nay! I swear by the Lord of the risings and the settings, that We are surely Able

But nay (falā)! | I swear (uq'simu) | by the Lord (birabbi) | of the risings (l-mashāriqi) | and the settings (wal-maghāribi), | that We (innā) | are surely Able (laqādirūna)

70:41 [On] to [We] replace with better than them; and not We are to be outrun.
[On] (ʿalā) | to (an) | [We] replace (nubaddila) | with better (khayran) | than them (min'hum); | and not (wamā) | We (naḥnu) | are to be outrun (bimasbūqīna).

70:42 So leave them to converse vainly and amuse themselves until they meet their Day, which they are promised,
So leave them (fadharhum) | to converse vainly (yakhūḍū) | and amuse themselves (wayalʿabū) | until (ḥattā) | they meet (yulāqū) | their Day (yawmahumu), | which (alladhī) | they are promised (yūʿadūna),

70:43 The Day they will come out from the graves rapidly as if they were to a goal hastening,
The Day (yawma) | they will come out (yakhrujūna) | from (mina) | the graves (l-ajdāthi) | rapidly (sirāʿan) | as if they were (ka-annahum) | to (ilā) | a goal (nuṣubin) | hastening (yūfiḍūna),

70:44 Humbled their eyesights, will cover them humiliation. That is the Day which they were promised.
Humbled (khāshiʿatan) | their eyesights (abṣāruhum), | will cover them (tarhaquhum) | humiliation (dhillatun). | That (dhālika) | is the Day (l-yawmu) | which (alladhī) | they were (kānū) | promised (yūʿadūna).

Chapter (71) Sūrat Nūḥ (Noah)

71:1 Indeed, We [We] sent Nuh to his people, that "Warn your people from before [that] comes to them a punishment painful."
Indeed, We (innā) | [We] sent (arsalnā) | Nuh (nūḥan) | to (ilā) | his people (qawmihi), | that (an) | "Warn (andhir) | your people (qawmaka) | from (min) | before (qabli) | [that] (an) | comes to them (yatiyahum) | a punishment (ʿadhābun) | painful. (alīmun)"

71:2 He said, "O my people! Indeed, I am to you a warner clear.
He said (qāla), | "O my people (yāqawmi)! | Indeed, I am (innī) | to you (lakum) | a warner (nadhīrun) | clear (mubīnun).

71:3 That Worship Allah, and fear Him and obey me.
That (ani) | Worship (uʿʿbudū) | Allah (l-laha), | and fear Him (wa-ittaqūhu) | and obey me (wa-aṭīʿūni).

71:4 He will forgive for you [of] your sins and give you respite for a term specified. Indeed, the term, of Allah, when it comes not is delayed, if you know."
He will forgive (yaghfir) | for you (lakum) | [of] (min) | your sins (dhunūbikum) | and give you respite (wayu-akhir'kum) | for (ilā) | a term (ajalin) | specified (musamman). | Indeed (inna), | the term (ajala), | of Allah (l-lahi), | when (idhā) | it comes (jāa) | not (lā) | is delayed (yu-akharu), | if (law) | you (kuntum) | know. (taʿlamūna)"

71:5 He said, "My Lord! Indeed, I invited my people night and day.

He said (qāla), | "My Lord (rabbi)! | Indeed, I (innī) | invited (daʿawtu) | my people (qawmī) | night (laylan) | and day (wanahāran).

71:6 But not increased them my invitation except in flight.

But not (falam) | increased them (yazid'hum) | my invitation (duʿāī) | except (illā) | in flight (firāran).

71:7 And indeed, I every time, I invited them that You may forgive them, they put their fingers in their ears and covered themselves with their garments and persisted and were arrogant with pride.

And indeed, I (wa-innī) | every time (kullamā), | I invited them (daʿawtuhum) | that You may forgive (litaghfira) | them (lahum), | they put (jaʿalū) | their fingers (aṣābiʿahum) | in (fī) | their ears (ādhānihim) | and covered themselves (wa-is'taghshaw) | with their garments (thiyābahum) | and persisted (wa-aṣarrū) | and were arrogant (wa-is'takbarū) | with pride (is'tik'bāran).

71:8 Then indeed, I invited them publicly.

Then (thumma) | indeed, I (innī) | invited them (daʿawtuhum) | publicly (jihāran).

71:9 Then indeed, I announced to them and I confided to them secretly,

Then (thumma) | indeed, I (innī) | announced (aʿlantu) | to them (lahum) | and I confided (wa-asrartu) | to them (lahum) | secretly (is'rāran),

71:10 Then I said, "Ask forgiveness from your Lord. Indeed, He is Oft-Forgiving.

Then I said (faqul'tu), | "Ask forgiveness (is'taghfirū) | from your Lord (rabbakum). | Indeed, He (innahu) | is (kāna) | Oft-Forgiving (ghaffāran).

71:11 He will send down rain from the sky upon you in abundance,

He will send down (yur'sili) | rain from the sky (l-samāa) | upon you (ʿalaykum) | in abundance (mid'rāran),

71:12 And provide you with wealth and children, and make for you gardens and make for you rivers.

And provide you (wayum'did'kum) | with wealth (bi-amwālin) | and children (wabanīna), | and make (wayajʿal) | for you (lakum) | gardens (jannātin) | and make (wayajʿal) | for you (lakum) | rivers (anhāran).

71:13 What is for you, not you attribute to Allah grandeur?

What (mā) | is for you (lakum), | not (lā) | you attribute (tarjūna) | to Allah (lillahi) | grandeur (waqāran)?

71:14 And indeed, He created you in stages.

And indeed (waqad), | He created you (khalaqakum) | in stages (aṭwāran).

71:15 Do not you see how did create Allah the seven heavens in layers,

Do not (alam) | you see (taraw) | how (kayfa) | did create (khalaqa) | Allah (l-lahu) | the seven (sabʿa) | heavens (samāwātin) | in layers (ṭibāqan),

71:16 And made the moon therein a light and made the sun a lamp?

And made (wajaʿala) | the moon (l-qamara) | therein (fīhinna) | a light (nūran) | and made (wajaʿala) | the sun (l-shamsa) | a lamp (sirājan)?

71:17 And Allah has caused you to grow from the earth as a growth.

And Allah (wal-lahu) | has caused you to grow (anbatakum) | from (mina) | the earth (l-arḍi) | as a growth (nabātan).

71:18 Then He will return you into it and bring you forth, a new bringing forth.

Then (thumma) | He will return you (yuʿīdukum) | into it (fīhā) | and bring you forth (wayukh'rijukum), | a new bringing forth (ikh'rājan).

71:19 And Allah made for you the earth an expanse,

And Allah (wal-lahu) | made (jaʿala) | for you (lakumu) | the earth (l-arḍa) | an expanse (bisāṭan),

71:20 That you may go along therein in paths wide."

That you may go along (litaslukū) | therein (min'hā) | in paths (subulan) | wide. (fijājan)"

71:21 Said Nuh, "My Lord! Indeed, they disobeyed me and followed the one who, did not increase him his wealth, and his children except in loss.

Said (qāla) | Nuh (nūḥun), | "My Lord (rabbi)! | Indeed, they (innahum) | disobeyed me (ʿaṣawnī) | and followed (wa-ittabaʿū) | the one who (man), | did not (lam) | increase him (yazid'hu) | his wealth (māluhu), | and his children (wawaladuhu) | except (illā) | in loss (khasāran).

71:22 And they have planned, a plan great.

And they have planned (wamakarū), | a plan (makran) | great (kubbāran).

71:23 And they said, "Do not leave your gods, and do not leave Wadd and not Suwa and not Yaguth and Yauq and Nasr."

And they said (waqālū), | "Do not (lā) | leave (tadharunna) | your gods (ālihatakum), | and do not (walā) | leave (tadharunna) | Wadd (waddan) | and not (walā) | Suwa (suwāʿan) | and not (walā) | Yaguth (yaghūtha) | and Yauq (wayaʿūqa) | and Nasr. (wanasran)"

71:24 And indeed, they have led astray many. And not increase the wrongdoers except in error."

And indeed (waqad), | they have led astray (aḍallū) | many (kathīran). | And not (walā) | increase (tazidi) | the wrongdoers (l-ẓālimīna) | except (illā) | in error. (ḍalālan)"

71:25 Because of their sins they were drowned, then made to enter the Fire, and not they found for themselves from besides Allah any helpers.

Because of (mimmā) | their sins (khaṭīātihim) | they were drowned (ugh'riqū), | then made to enter (fa-ud'khilū) | the Fire (nāran), | and not (falam) | they found (yajidū) | for themselves (lahum) | from (min) | besides (dūni) | Allah (l-lahi) | any helpers (anṣāran).

71:26 And said Nuh, "My Lord! Do not leave on the earth any of the disbelievers as an inhabitant.

And said (waqāla) | Nuh (nūḥun), | "My Lord (rabbi)! | Do not (lā) | leave (tadhar) | on (ʿalā) | the earth (l-arḍi) | any (mina) | of the disbelievers (l-kāfirīna) | as an inhabitant (dayyāran).

71:27 Indeed, You, if You leave them they will mislead Your slaves and not they will beget except a wicked, a disbeliever.

Indeed, You (innaka), | if (in) | You leave them (tadharhum) | they will mislead (yuḍillū) | Your slaves (ʿibādaka) | and not (walā) | they will beget (yalidū) | except (illā) | a wicked (fājiran), | a disbeliever (kaffāran).

71:28 My Lord! Forgive me and my parents, and whoever enters my house - a believer and the believing men and the believing women. And do not increase the wrongdoers except in destruction."

My Lord (rabbi)! | Forgive (igh'fir) | me (lī) | and my parents (waliwālidayya), | and whoever (waliman) | enters (dakhala) | my house (baytiya)- | a believer (mu'minan) | and the believing men (walil'mu'minīna) | and the believing women (wal-mu'mināti). | And do not (walā) | increase (tazidi) | the wrongdoers (l-ẓālimīna) | except (illā) | in destruction. (tabāran)"

Chapter (72) Sūrat l-Jin (The Jinn)

72:1 Say, "It has been revealed to me that listened a group of the jinn, and they said, "Indeed, we heard a Quran amazing,

Say (qul), | "It has been revealed (ūḥiya) | to me (ilayya) | that (annahu) | listened (is'tamaʿa) | a group (nafarun) | of (mina) | the jinn (l-jini), | and they said (faqālū), | "Indeed, we (innā) | heard (samiʿ'nā) | a Quran (qur'ānan) | amazing (ʿajaban),

72:2 It guides to the right way, so we believe in it, and never we will associate with our Lord anyone.

It guides (yahdī) | to (ilā) | the right way (l-rush'di), | so we believe (faāmannā) | in it (bihi), | and never (walan) | we will associate (nush'rika) | with our Lord (birabbinā) | anyone (aḥadan).

72:3 And that He - Exalted is the Majesty of our Lord - not He has taken a wife and not a son,

And that He (wa-annahu)- | Exalted is (taʿālā) | the Majesty (jaddu) | of our Lord (rabbinā)- | not (mā) | He has taken (ittakhadha) | a wife (ṣāḥibatan) | and not (walā) | a son (waladan),

72:4 And that he used to speak - the foolish among us against Allah an excessive transgression.

And that he (wa-annahu) | used to (kāna) | speak (yaqūlu)- | the foolish among us (safīhunā) | against (ʿalā) | Allah (l-lahi) | an excessive transgression (shaṭaṭan).

72:5 And that we thought that never will say the men and the jinn, against Allah any lie.

And that we (wa-annā) | thought (ẓanannā) | that (an) | never (lan) | will say (taqūla) | the men (l-insu) | and the jinn (wal-jinu), | against (ʿalā) | Allah (l-lahi) | any lie (kadhiban).

72:6 And that there were men among mankind who sought refuge in the men from the jinn, so they increased them in burden.

And that (wa-annahu) | there were (kāna) | men (rijālun) | among (mina) | mankind (l-insi) | who sought refuge (yaʿūdhūna) | in the men (birijālin) | from (mina) | the jinn (l-jini), | so they increased them (fazādūhum) | in burden (rahaqan).

72:7 And that they thought as you thought that never will raise Allah anyone.

And that they (wa-annahum) | thought (ẓannū) | as (kamā) | you thought (ẓanantum) | that (an) | never (lan) | will raise (yabʿatha) | Allah (l-lahu) | anyone (aḥadan).

72:8 And that we sought to touch the heaven but we found it filled with guards severe, and flaming fires.

And that we (wa-annā) | sought to touch (lamasnā) | the heaven (l-samāa) | but we found it (fawajadnāhā) | filled with (muli-at) | guards (ḥarasan) | severe (shadīdan), | and flaming fires (washuhuban).

72:9 And that we used to sit there in positions for hearing, but he who listens now will find for him a flaming fire waiting.

And that we (wa-annā) | used to (kunnā) | sit (naqʿudu) | there in (min'hā) | positions (maqāʿida) | for hearing (lilssamʿi), | but he who (faman) | listens (yastamiʿi) | now (l-āna) | will find (yajid) | for him (lahu) | a flaming fire (shihāban) | waiting (raṣadan).

72:10 And that we - not we know whether evil is intended for those who are in the earth or intends for them their Lord a right path.

And that we (wa-annā)- | not (lā) | we know (nadrī) | whether evil (asharrun) | is intended (urīda) | for those who (biman) | are in (fī) | the earth (l-arḍi) | or (am) | intends (arāda) | for them (bihim) | their Lord (rabbuhum) | a right path (rashadan).

72:11 And that [we] among us are the righteous and among us are other than that. We are on ways different.

And that [we] (wa-annā) | among us (minnā) | are the righteous (l-ṣāliḥūna) | and among us (waminnā) | are other than (dūna) | that (dhālika). | We (kunnā) | are on ways (ṭarāiqa) | different (qidadan).

72:12 And that we [we] have become certain that never we will cause failure to Allah in the earth and never we can escape Him by flight.

And that we (wa-annā) | [we] have become certain (ẓanannā) | that (an) | never (lan) | we will cause failure (nuʿʿjiza) | to Allah (l-laha) | in (fī) | the earth (l-arḍi) | and never (walan) | we can escape Him (nuʿʿjizahu) | by flight (haraban).

72:13 And that [we] when we heard the Guidance we believed in it. And whoever believes in his Lord, then not he will fear any loss and not any burden.

And that [we] (wa-annā) | when (lammā) | we heard (samiʿʿnā) | the Guidance (l-hudā) | we believed (āmannā) | in it (bihi). | And whoever (faman) | believes (yu'min) | in his Lord (birabbihi), | then not (falā) | he will fear (yakhāfu) | any loss (bakhsan) | and not (walā) | any burden (rahaqan).

72:14 And that we, among us are Muslims and among us are unjust. And whoever submits, then those have sought the right path.

And that we (wa-annā), | among us (minnā) | are Muslims (l-mus'limūna) | and among us (waminnā) | are unjust (l-qāsiṭūna). | And whoever (faman) | submits (aslama), | then those (fa-ulāika) | have sought (taḥarraw) | the right path (rashadan).

72:15 And as for the unjust, they will be, for Hell, firewood."

And as for (wa-ammā) | the unjust (l-qāsiṭūna), | they will be (fakānū), | for Hell (lijahannama), | firewood. (ḥaṭaban)"

72:16 And that if they had remained on the Way, surely We would have given them to drink water in abundance,

And that if (wa-allawi) | they had remained (is'taqāmū) | on (ʿalā) | the Way (l-ṭarīqati), | surely We would have given them to drink (la-asqaynāhum) | water (māan) | in abundance (ghadaqan),

72:17 That We might test them therein. And whoever turns away from the Remembrance of his Lord, He will make him enter a punishment severe.

That We might test them (linaftinahum) | therein (fīhi). | And whoever (waman) | turns away (yuʿʿriḍ) | from (ʿan) | the Remembrance (dhik'ri) | of his Lord (rabbihi), | He will make him enter (yasluk'hu) | a punishment (ʿadhāban) | severe (ṣaʿadan).

72:18 And that the masjids are for Allah, so do not call with Allah anyone.
And that (wa-anna) | the masjids (l-masājida) | are for Allah (lillahi), | so do not (falā) | call (tadʿū) | with (maʿa) | Allah (l-lahi) | anyone (aḥadan).

72:19 And that when stood up the slave of Allah calling upon Him, they almost became around him a compacted mass.
And that (wa-annahu) | when (lammā) | stood up (qāma) | the slave (ʿabdu) | of Allah (l-lahi) | calling upon Him (yadʿūhu), | they almost (kādū) | became (yakūnūna) | around him (ʿalayhi) | a compacted mass (libadan).

72:20 Say, "Only I call upon my Lord, and not I associate with Him anyone."
Say (qul), | "Only (innamā) | I call upon (adʿū) | my Lord (rabbī), | and not (walā) | I associate (ush'riku) | with Him (bihi) | anyone. (aḥadan)"

72:21 Say, "Indeed, I do not possess for you any harm and not right path."
Say (qul), | "Indeed, I (innī) | do not (lā) | possess (amliku) | for you (lakum) | any harm (ḍarran) | and not (walā) | right path. (rashadan)"

72:22 Say, "Indeed I, never can protect me from Allah anyone, and never can I find from besides Him any refuge.
Say (qul), | "Indeed I (innī), | never (lan) | can protect me (yujīranī) | from (mina) | Allah (l-lahi) | anyone (aḥadun), | and never (walan) | can I find (ajida) | from (min) | besides Him (dūnihi) | any refuge (mul'taḥadan).

72:23 But the notification from Allah and His Messages." And whoever disobeys Allah and His Messenger, then indeed, for him is the Fire of Hell, they will abide therein forever.
But (illā) | the notification (balāghan) | from (mina) | Allah (l-lahi) | and His Messages. (warisālātihi)" | And whoever (waman) | disobeys (yaʿṣi) | Allah (l-laha) | and His Messenger (warasūlahu), | then indeed (fa-inna), | for him (lahu) | is the Fire (nāra) | of Hell (jahannama), | they will abide (khālidīna) | therein (fīhā) | forever (abadan).

72:24 Until, when they see what they are promised, then they will know who is weaker in helpers and fewer in number.
Until (ḥattā), | when (idhā) | they see (ra-aw) | what (mā) | they are promised (yūʿadūna), | then they will know (fasayaʿlamūna) | who (man) | is weaker (aḍʿafu) | in helpers (nāṣiran) | and fewer (wa-aqallu) | in number (ʿadadan).

72:25 Say, "Not I know whether is near what you are promised or whether will appoint for it my Lord a distant term.
Say (qul), | "Not (in) | I know (adrī) | whether is near (aqarībun) | what (mā) | you are promised (tūʿadūna) | or whether (am) | will appoint (yajʿalu) | for it (lahu) | my Lord (rabbī) | a distant term (amadan).

72:26 The All-Knower of the unseen, so not He reveals from His unseen to anyone,
The All-Knower (ʿālimu) | of the unseen (l-ghaybi), | so not (falā) | He reveals (yuẓ'hiru) | from (ʿalā) | His unseen (ghaybihi) | to anyone (aḥadan),

72:27 Except whom He has approved of a Messenger, and indeed, He makes to march from before him and from behind him a guard,
Except (illā) | whom (mani) | He has approved (ir'taḍā) | of (min) | a Messenger (rasūlin), | and indeed, He (fa-innahu) | makes to march (yasluku) | from (min) | before (bayni) | him (yadayhi)

| and from (wamin) | behind him (khalfihi) | a guard (raṣadan),

72:28 That He may make evident that indeed, they have conveyed the Messages of their Lord; and He has encompassed what is with them and He takes account of all things in number."

That He may make evident (liyaʿlama) | that (an) | indeed (qad), | they have conveyed (ablaghū) | the Messages (risālāti) | of their Lord (rabbihim); | and He has encompassed (wa-aḥāṭa) | what (bimā) | is with them (ladayhim) | and He takes account (wa-aḥṣā) | of all (kulla) | things (shayin) | in number. (ʿadadan)"

Chapter (73) Sūrat l-Muzamil (The One wrapped in Garments)

73:1 O you who wraps himself!

O you (yāayyuhā) | who wraps himself (l-muzamilu)!

73:2 Stand in the night, except a little,

Stand (qumi) | in the night (al-layla), | except (illā) | a little (qalīlan),

73:3 Half of it, or lessen from it a little,

Half of it (niṣ'fahu), | or (awi) | lessen (unquṣ) | from it (min'hu) | a little (qalīlan),

73:4 Or add to it, and recite the Quran with measured rhythmic recitation.

Or (aw) | add (zid) | to it (ʿalayhi), | and recite (warattili) | the Quran (l-qur'āna) | with measured rhythmic recitation (tartīlan).

73:5 Indeed, We will cast upon you a Word heavy.

Indeed, We (innā) | will cast (sanul'qī) | upon you (ʿalayka) | a Word (qawlan) | heavy (thaqīlan).

73:6 Indeed, the rising at the night, it is very hard and most potent and more suitable for Word.

Indeed (inna), | the rising (nāshi-ata) | at the night (al-layli), | it (hiya) | is very hard (ashaddu) | and most potent (waṭan) | and more suitable (wa-aqwamu) | for Word (qīlan).

73:7 Indeed, for you in the day is occupation prolonged.

Indeed (inna), | for you (laka) | in (fī) | the day (l-nahāri) | is occupation (sabḥan) | prolonged (ṭawīlan).

73:8 And remember the name of your Lord and devote yourself to Him with devotion.

And remember (wa-udh'kuri) | the name (is'ma) | of your Lord (rabbika) | and devote yourself (watabattal) | to Him (ilayhi) | with devotion (tabtīlan).

73:9 The Lord of the east and the west; there is no god except Him, so take Him as Disposer of Affairs.

The Lord (rabbu) | of the east (l-mashriqi) | and the west (wal-maghribi); | there is no (lā) |

god (ilāha) | except (illā) | Him (huwa), | so take Him (fa-ittakhidh'hu) | as Disposer of Affairs (wakīlan).

73:10 And be patient over what they say, and avoid them, an avoidance gracious.
And be patient (wa-iṣ'bir) | over (ʿalā) | what (mā) | they say (yaqūlūna), | and avoid them (wa-uh'jur'hum), | an avoidance (hajran) | gracious (jamīlan).

73:11 And leave Me and the deniers, possessors of the ease, and allow them respite - a little.
And leave Me (wadharnī) | and the deniers (wal-mukadhibīna), | possessors (ulī) | of the ease (l-naʿmati), | and allow them respite (wamahhil'hum)- | a little (qalīlan).

73:12 Indeed, with Us are shackles and burning fire,
Indeed (inna), | with Us (ladaynā) | are shackles (ankālan) | and burning fire (wajaḥīman),

73:13 And food that chokes and a punishment painful.
And food (waṭaʿāman) | that (dhā) | chokes (ghuṣṣatin) | and a punishment (waʿadhāban) | painful (alīman).

73:14 On the Day will quake the earth and the mountains, and will become the mountains a heap of sand pouring down.
On the Day (yawma) | will quake (tarjufu) | the earth (l-arḍu) | and the mountains (wal-jibālu), | and will become (wakānati) | the mountains (l-jibālu) | a heap of sand (kathīban) | pouring down (mahīlan).

73:15 Indeed, We [We] have sent to you a Messenger as a witness upon you, as We sent to Firaun a Messenger.
Indeed, We (innā) | [We] have sent (arsalnā) | to you (ilaykum) | a Messenger (rasūlan) | as a witness (shāhidan) | upon you (ʿalaykum), | as (kamā) | We sent (arsalnā) | to (ilā) | Firaun (fir'ʿawna) | a Messenger (rasūlan).

73:16 But disobeyed Firaun the Messenger, so We seized him with a seizure ruinous.
But disobeyed (faʿaṣā) | Firaun (fir'ʿawnu) | the Messenger (l-rasūla), | so We seized him (fa-akhadhnāhu) | with a seizure (akhdhan) | ruinous (wabīlan).

73:17 Then how will you guard yourselves, if you disbelieve, a Day that will make the children gray-haired?
Then how (fakayfa) | will you guard yourselves (tattaqūna), | if (in) | you disbelieve (kafartum), | a Day (yawman) | that will make (yajʿalu) | the children (l-wil'dāna) | gray-haired (shīban)?

73:18 The heaven will break apart therefrom, is His Promise to be fulfilled.
The heaven (al-samāu) | will break apart (munfaṭirun) | therefrom (bihi), | is (kāna) | His Promise (waʿduhu) | to be fulfilled (mafʿūlan).

73:19 Indeed, this is a Reminder, then whoever wills let him take to his Lord a way.
Indeed (inna), | this (hādhihi) | is a Reminder (tadhkiratun), | then whoever (faman) | wills (shāa) | let him take (ittakhadha) | to (ilā) | his Lord (rabbihi) | a way (sabīlan).

73:20 Indeed, your Lord knows that you stand a little less than two-thirds of the night, and half of it and a third of it and so do a group of those who are with you. And Allah determines the night and the day. He knows that not you count it, so He has turned to you, so recite what is easy of the Quran. He knows that there will be among you sick and others traveling in the land seeking of the

Bounty of Allah, and others fighting in the way of Allah. So recite what is easy of it, and establish the prayer and give the zakah and loan Allah a loan goodly. And whatever you send forth for yourselves of good, you will find it with Allah. It will be better and greater in reward. And seek forgiveness of Allah. Indeed, Allah is Oft-Forgiving, Most Merciful.

Indeed (inna), | your Lord (rabbaka) | knows (yaʿlamu) | that you (annaka) | stand (taqūmu) | a little less (adnā) | than (min) | two-thirds (thuluthayi) | of the night (al-layli), | and half of it (waniṣ'fahu) | and a third of it (wathuluthahu) | and so do a group (waṭāifatun) | of (mina) | those who (alladhīna) | are with you (maʿaka). | And Allah (wal-lahu) | determines (yuqaddiru) | the night (al-layla) | and the day (wal-nahāra). | He knows (ʿalima) | that (an) | not (lan) | you count it (tuḥ'ṣūhu), | so He has turned (fatāba) | to you (ʿalaykum), | so recite (fa-iq'raū) | what (mā) | is easy (tayassara) | of (mina) | the Quran (l-qur'āni). | He knows (ʿalima) | that (an) | there will be (sayakūnu) | among you (minkum) | sick (marḍā) | and others (waākharūna) | traveling (yaḍribūna) | in (fī) | the land (l-arḍi) | seeking (yabtaghūna) | of (min) | the Bounty (faḍli) | of Allah (l-lahi), | and others (waākharūna) | fighting (yuqātilūna) | in (fī) | the way (sabīli) | of Allah (l-lahi). | So recite (fa-iq'raū) | what (mā) | is easy (tayassara) | of it (min'hu), | and establish (wa-aqīmū) | the prayer (l-ṣalata) | and give (waātū) | the zakah (l-zakata) | and loan (wa-aqriḍū) | Allah (l-laha) | a loan (qarḍan) | goodly (ḥasanan). | And whatever (wamā) | you send forth (tuqaddimū) | for yourselves (li-anfusikum) | of (min) | good (khayrin), | you will find it (tajidūhu) | with (ʿinda) | Allah (l-lahi). | It (huwa) | will be better (khayran) | and greater (wa-aʿẓama) | in reward (ajran). | And seek forgiveness (wa-is'taghfirū) | of Allah (l-laha). | Indeed (inna), | Allah (l-laha) | is Oft-Forgiving (ghafūrun), | Most Merciful (raḥīmun).

Chapter (74) Sūrat l-Mudathir (The One Enveloped)

74:1 O you who covers himself!
O you (yāayyuhā) | who covers himself (l-mudathiru)!

74:2 Stand up and warn,
Stand up (qum) | and warn (fa-andhir),

74:3 And your Lord magnify,
And your Lord (warabbaka) | magnify (fakabbir),

74:4 And your clothing purify,
And your clothing (wathiyābaka) | purify (faṭahhir),

74:5 And uncleanliness avoid,
And uncleanliness (wal-ruj'za) | avoid (fa-uh'jur),

74:6 And do not confer favor to acquire more,
And do not (walā) | confer favor (tamnun) | to acquire more (tastakthiru),

74:7 And for your Lord be patient.
And for your Lord (walirabbika) | be patient (fa-iṣ'bir).

74:8 Then when is blown in the trumpet,

Then when (fa-idhā) | is blown (nuqira) | in (fī) | the trumpet (l-nāqūri),

74:9 That Day, will be a Day difficult,
That (fadhālika) | Day (yawma-idhin), | will be a Day (yawmun) | difficult (ʿasīrun),

74:10 For the disbelievers - not easy.
For (ʿalā) | the disbelievers (l-kāfirīna)- | not (ghayru) | easy (yasīrin).

74:11 Leave Me and whom I created alone,
Leave Me (dharnī) | and whom (waman) | I created (khalaqtu) | alone (waḥīdan),

74:12 And I granted to him wealth extensive,
And I granted (wajaʿaltu) | to him (lahu) | wealth (mālan) | extensive (mamdūdan),

74:13 And children present,
And children (wabanīna) | present (shuhūdan),

74:14 And I spread for him, ease.
And I spread (wamahhadttu) | for him (lahu), | ease (tamhīdan).

74:15 Then he desires that I should add more.
Then (thumma) | he desires (yaṭmaʿu) | that (an) | I should add more (azīda).

74:16 By no means! Indeed, he has been to Our Verses stubborn.
By no means (kallā)! | Indeed, he (innahu) | has been (kāna) | to Our Verses (liāyātinā) | stubborn (ʿanīdan).

74:17 Soon I will cover Him with a laborious punishment.
Soon I will cover Him (sa-ur'hiquhu) | with a laborious punishment (ṣaʿūdan).

74:18 Indeed, he thought and plotted.
Indeed, he (innahu) | thought (fakkara) | and plotted (waqaddara).

74:19 So may he be destroyed, how he plotted!
So may he be destroyed (faqutila), | how (kayfa) | he plotted (qaddara)!

74:20 Then may he be destroyed, how he plotted!
Then (thumma) | may he be destroyed (qutila), | how (kayfa) | he plotted (qaddara)!

74:21 Then he looked;
Then (thumma) | he looked (naẓara);

74:22 Then he frowned and scowled;
Then (thumma) | he frowned (ʿabasa) | and scowled (wabasara);

74:23 Then he turned back and was proud,
Then (thumma) | he turned back (adbara) | and was proud (wa-is'takbara),

74:24 Then he said, "Not is this but magic imitated.
Then he said (faqāla), | "Not (in) | is this (hādhā) | but (illā) | magic (siḥ'run) | imitated (yu'tharu).

74:25 Not is this but the word of a human being."
Not (in) | is this (hādhā) | but (illā) | the word (qawlu) | of a human being. (l-bashari)"

74:26 Soon I will drive him into Hell.
Soon I will drive him (sa-uṣ'līhi) | into Hell (saqara).

74:27 And what can make you know what is Hell?
And what (wamā) | can make you know (adrāka) | what (mā) | is Hell (saqaru)?

74:28 Not it lets remain and not it leaves,
Not (lā) | it lets remain (tub'qī) | and not (walā) | it leaves (tadharu),

74:29 Scorching the human skin.
Scorching (lawwāḥatun) | the human skin (lil'bashari).

74:30 Over it are nine- -teen.
Over it (ʿalayhā) | are nine (tis'ʿata)- | -teen (ʿashara).

74:31 And not We have made keepers of the Fire except Angels. And not We have made their number except as a trial for those who disbelieve - that may be certain those who were given the Scripture and may increase those who believe in faith, and not may doubt those who were given the Scripture and the believers, and that may say those in their hearts is a disease and the disbelievers "What does intend Allah by this example?" Thus does let go astray Allah whom He wills and guides whom He wills. And none knows the hosts of your Lord except Him. And not it is but a reminder to the human beings.

And not (wamā) | We have made (jaʿalnā) | keepers (aṣḥāba) | of the Fire (l-nāri) | except (illā) | Angels (malāikatan). | And not (wamā) | We have made (jaʿalnā) | their number (ʿiddatahum) | except (illā) | as a trial (fit'natan) | for those who (lilladhīna) | disbelieve (kafarū)- | that may be certain (liyastayqina) | those who (alladhīna) | were given (ūtū) | the Scripture (l-kitāba) | and may increase (wayazdāda) | those who (alladhīna) | believe (āmanū) | in faith (īmānan), | and not (walā) | may doubt (yartāba) | those who (alladhīna) | were given (ūtū) | the Scripture (l-kitāba) | and the believers (wal-mu'minūna), | and that may say (waliyaqūla) | those (alladhīna) | in (fī) | their hearts (qulūbihim) | is a disease (maraḍun) | and the disbelievers (wal-kāfirūna) | "What (mādhā) | does intend (arāda) | Allah (l-lahu) | by this (bihādhā) | example? (mathalan)" | Thus (kadhālika) | does let go astray (yuḍillu) | Allah (l-lahu) | whom (man) | He wills (yashāu) | and guides (wayahdī) | whom (man) | He wills (yashāu). | And none (wamā) | knows (yaʿlamu) | the hosts (junūda) | of your Lord (rabbika) | except (illā) | Him (huwa). | And not (wamā) | it (hiya) | is but (illā) | a reminder (dhik'rā) | to the human beings (lil'bashari).

74:32 Nay! By the moon,
Nay (kallā)! | By the moon (wal-qamari),

74:33 And the night when it departs,
And the night (wa-al-layli) | when (idh) | it departs (adbara),

74:34 And the morning when it brightens,
And the morning (wal-ṣub'ḥi) | when (idhā) | it brightens (asfara),

74:35 Indeed, it is surely one of the greatest,
Indeed, it (innahā) | is surely one (la-iḥ'dā) | of the greatest (l-kubari),

74:36 A warning to the human being,

A warning (nadhīran) | to the human being (lil'bashari),

74:37 To whoever wills among you to proceed or stay behind.
To whoever (liman) | wills (shāa) | among you (minkum) | to (an) | proceed (yataqaddama) | or (aw) | stay behind (yata-akhara).

74:38 Every soul, for what it has earned, is pledged,
Every (kullu) | soul (nafsin), | for what (bimā) | it has earned (kasabat), | is pledged (rahīnatun),

74:39 Except the companions of the right,
Except (illā) | the companions (aṣḥāba) | of the right (l-yamīni),

74:40 In Gardens, asking each other,
In (fī) | Gardens (jannātin), | asking each other (yatasāalūna),

74:41 About the criminals,
About (ʿani) | the criminals (l-muj'rimīna),

74:42 "What led you into Hell?"
"What (mā) | led you (salakakum) | into (fī) | Hell? (saqara)"

74:43 They will say, "Not we were of those who prayed,
They will say (qālū), | "Not (lam) | we were (naku) | of (mina) | those who prayed (l-muṣalīna),

74:44 And not we used to feed the poor,
And not (walam) | we used to (naku) | feed (nuṭ''imu) | the poor (l-mis'kīna),

74:45 And we used to indulge in vain talk with the vain talkers,
And we used to (wakunnā) | indulge in vain talk (nakhūḍu) | with (maʿa) | the vain talkers (l-khāiḍīna),

74:46 And we used to deny the Day of the Judgment,
And we used to (wakunnā) | deny (nukadhibu) | the Day (biyawmi) | of the Judgment (l-dīni),

74:47 Until, came to us the certainty."
Until (ḥattā), | came to us (atānā) | the certainty. (l-yaqīnu)"

74:48 Then not will benefit them intercession of the intercessors.
Then not (famā) | will benefit them (tanfaʿuhum) | intercession (shafāʿatu) | of the intercessors (l-shāfiʿīna).

74:49 Then what is for them, that from the Reminder they are turning away
Then what (famā) | is for them (lahum), | that from (ʿani) | the Reminder (l-tadhkirati) | they are turning away (muʿ'riḍīna)

74:50 As if they were donkeys frightened,
As if they were (ka-annahum) | donkeys (ḥumurun) | frightened (mus'tanfiratun),

74:51 Fleeing from a lion?

Fleeing (farrat) | from (min) | a lion (qaswaratin)?

74:52 Nay! Desires every person of them that he may be given pages spread out.
Nay (bal)! | Desires (yurīdu) | every (kullu) | person (im'ri-in) | of them (min'hum) | that (an) | he may be given (yu'tā) | pages (ṣuḥufan) | spread out (munasharatan).

74:53 Nay! But not they fear the Hereafter.
Nay (kallā)! | But (bal) | not (lā) | they fear (yakhāfūna) | the Hereafter (l-ākhirata).

74:54 Nay! Indeed, it is a Reminder.
Nay (kallā)! | Indeed, it (innahu) | is a Reminder (tadhkiratun).

74:55 So whoever wills, may pay heed to it.
So whoever (faman) | wills (shāa), | may pay heed to it (dhakarahu).

74:56 And not will pay heed except that wills Allah. He is worthy to be feared, and worthy to forgive.
And not (wamā) | will pay heed (yadhkurūna) | except (illā) | that (an) | wills (yashāa) | Allah (l-lahu). | He (huwa) | is worthy (ahlu) | to be feared (l-taqwā), | and worthy (wa-ahlu) | to forgive (l-maghfirati).

Chapter (75) Sūrat l-Qiyāmah (The Resurrection)

75:1 Nay! I swear by the Day of the Resurrection.
Nay (lā)! | I swear (uq'simu) | by the Day (biyawmi) | of the Resurrection (l-qiyāmati).

75:2 And nay! I swear by the soul self-accusing.
And nay (walā)! | I swear (uq'simu) | by the soul (bil-nafsi) | self-accusing (l-lawāmati).

75:3 Does think [the] man that not We will assemble his bones?
Does think (ayaḥsabu) | [the] man (l-insānu) | that not (allan) | We will assemble (najmaʿa) | his bones (ʿiẓāmahu)?

75:4 Nay! We are Able on that We can restore his fingertips.
Nay (balā)! | We are Able (qādirīna) | on (ʿalā) | that (an) | We can restore (nusawwiya) | his fingertips (banānahu).

75:5 Nay! Desires [the] man to give the lie to what is before him.
Nay (bal)! | Desires (yurīdu) | [the] man (l-insānu) | to give the lie (liyafjura) | to what is before him (amāmahu).

75:6 He asks, "When is the Day of the Resurrection?"
He asks (yasalu), | "When (ayyāna) | is the Day (yawmu) | of the Resurrection? (l-qiyāmati)"

75:7 So when is dazzled the vision,

So when (fa-idhā) | is dazzled (bariqa) | the vision (l-baṣaru),

75:8 And becomes dark the moon,
And becomes dark (wakhasafa) | the moon (l-qamaru),

75:9 And are joined the sun and the moon,
And are joined (wajumiʿa) | the sun (l-shamsu) | and the moon (wal-qamaru),

75:10 Will say [the] man that Day, "Where is the escape?"
Will say (yaqūlu) | [the] man (l-insānu) | that Day (yawma-idhin), | "Where (ayna) | is the escape? (l-mafaru)"

75:11 By no means! There is no refuge.
By no means (kallā)! | There is no (lā) | refuge (wazara).

75:12 To your Lord, that Day, is the place of rest.
To (ilā) | your Lord (rabbika), | that Day (yawma-idhin), | is the place of rest (l-mus'taqaru).

75:13 Will be informed [the] man that Day of what he sent forth and kept back.
Will be informed (yunabba-u) | [the] man (l-insānu) | that Day (yawma-idhin) | of what (bimā) | he sent forth (qaddama) | and kept back (wa-akhara).

75:14 Nay! [The] man against himself will be a witness.
Nay (bali)! | [The] man (l-insānu) | against (ʿalā) | himself (nafsihi) | will be a witness (baṣīratun).

75:15 Even if he presents his excuses.
Even if (walaw) | he presents (alqā) | his excuses (maʿādhīrahu).

75:16 Not move with it your tongue to hasten with it.
Not (lā) | move (tuḥarrik) | with it (bihi) | your tongue (lisānaka) | to hasten (litaʿjala) | with it (bihi).

75:17 Indeed, upon Us is its collection and its recitation.
Indeed (inna), | upon Us (ʿalaynā) | is its collection (jamʿahu) | and its recitation (waqur'ānahu).

75:18 And when We have recited it, then follow its recitation.
And when (fa-idhā) | We have recited it (qaranāhu), | then follow (fa-ittabiʿ) | its recitation (qur'ānahu).

75:19 Then indeed, upon Us is its explanation.
Then (thumma) | indeed (inna), | upon Us (ʿalaynā) | is its explanation (bayānahu).

75:20 No! But you love the immediate,
No (kallā)! | But (bal) | you love (tuḥibbūna) | the immediate (l-ʿājilata),

75:21 And leave the Hereafter.
And leave (watadharūna) | the Hereafter (l-ākhirata).

75:22 Faces that Day will be radiant,
Faces (wujūhun) | that Day (yawma-idhin) | will be radiant (nāḍiratun),

75:23 Towards their Lord looking,
Towards (ilā) | their Lord (rabbihā) | looking (nāẓiratun),

75:24 And faces that Day will be distorted,
And faces (wawujūhun) | that Day (yawma-idhin) | will be distorted (bāsiratun),

75:25 Thinking that will be done to them backbreaking.
Thinking (taẓunnu) | that (an) | will be done (yuf''ala) | to them (bihā) | backbreaking (fāqiratun).

75:26 No! When it reaches the collar bones
No (kallā)! | When (idhā) | it reaches (balaghati) | the collar bones (l-tarāqiya)

75:27 And it is said, "Who will cure?"
And it is said (waqīla), | "Who (man) | will cure? (rāqin)"

75:28 And he is certain that it is the parting.
And he is certain (waẓanna) | that it (annahu) | is the parting (l-firāqu).

75:29 And is wound, the leg about the leg,
And is wound (wal-tafati), | the leg (l-sāqu) | about the leg (bil-sāqi),

75:30 To your Lord that Day will be the driving.
To (ilā) | your Lord (rabbika) | that Day (yawma-idhin) | will be the driving (l-masāqu).

75:31 And not he accepted the truth and not he prayed.
And not (falā) | he accepted the truth (ṣaddaqa) | and not (walā) | he prayed (ṣallā).

75:32 But he denied and turned away.
But (walākin) | he denied (kadhaba) | and turned away (watawallā).

75:33 Then he went to his family, swaggering.
Then (thumma) | he went (dhahaba) | to (ilā) | his family (ahlihi), | swaggering (yatamaṭṭā).

75:34 Woe to you, and woe!
Woe (awlā) | to you (laka), | and woe (fa-awlā)!

75:35 Then woe to you, and woe!
Then (thumma) | woe (awlā) | to you (laka), | and woe (fa-awlā)!

75:36 Does think man that he will be left neglected?
Does think (ayaḥsabu) | man (l-insānu) | that (an) | he will be left (yut'raka) | neglected (sudan)?

75:37 Was not he a semen-drop of semen emitted?
Was not (alam) | he (yaku) | a semen-drop (nuṭ'fatan) | of (min) | semen (maniyyin) | emitted (yum'nā)?

75:38 Then he was a clinging substance, then He created and proportioned.
Then (thumma) | he was (kāna) | a clinging substance (ʿalaqatan), | then He created

(fakhalaqa) | and proportioned (fasawwā).

75:39 Then made of him two kinds, the male and the female.
Then made (faja'ala) | of him (min'hu) | two kinds (l-zawjayni), | the male (l-dhakara) | and the female (wal-unthā).

75:40 Is not [that] He Able [over] to give life to the dead?
Is not (alaysa) | [that] (dhālika) | He Able (biqādirin) | [over] ('alā) | to (an) | give life (yuḥ'yiya) | to the dead (l-mawtā)?

Chapter (76) Sūrat l-Insān (Man)

76:1 Has there come upon man a period of time not he was a thing mentioned?
Has (hal) | there come (atā) | upon ('alā) | man (l-insāni) | a period (ḥīnun) | of (mina) | time (l-dahri) | not (lam) | he was (yakun) | a thing (shayan) | mentioned (madhkūran)?

76:2 Indeed, We [We] created man from a semen-drop, a mixture, that We test him; so We made for him hearing and sight.
Indeed, We (innā) | [We] created (khalaqnā) | man (l-insāna) | from (min) | a semen-drop (nuṭ'fatin), | a mixture (amshājin), | that We test him (nabtalīhi); | so We made for him (faja'alnāhu) | hearing (samī'an) | and sight (baṣīran).

76:3 Indeed, We guided him to the way whether he be grateful and whether he be ungrateful.
Indeed, We (innā) | guided him (hadaynāhu) | to the way (l-sabīla) | whether (immā) | he be grateful (shākiran) | and whether (wa-immā) | he be ungrateful (kafūran).

76:4 Indeed, We [We] have prepared for the disbelievers chains and shackles and a Blazing Fire.
Indeed, We (innā) | [We] have prepared (a'tadnā) | for the disbelievers (lil'kāfirīna) | chains (salāsilā) | and shackles (wa-aghlālan) | and a Blazing Fire (wasa'īran).

76:5 Indeed, the righteous will drink from a cup, is its mixture of Kafur,
Indeed (inna), | the righteous (l-abrāra) | will drink (yashrabūna) | from (min) | a cup (kasin), | is (kāna) | its mixture (mizājuhā) | of Kafur (kāfūran),

76:6 A spring - will drink from it the slaves of Allah; causing it to gush forth abundantly.
A spring ('aynan)- | will drink (yashrabu) | from it (bihā) | the slaves ('ibādu) | of Allah (l-lahi); | causing it to gush forth (yufajjirūnahā) | abundantly (tafjīran).

76:7 They fulfill the vows and fear a Day - which is its evil widespread.
They fulfill (yūfūna) | the vows (bil-nadhri) | and fear (wayakhāfūna) | a Day (yawman)- | which is (kāna) | its evil (sharruhu) | widespread (mus'taṭīran).

76:8 And they feed the food in spite of love for it, to the needy, and the orphan and the captive,
And they feed (wayuṭ''imūna) | the food (l-ṭa'āma) | in spite of ('alā) | love for it (ḥubbihi), | to the needy (mis'kīnan), | and the orphan (wayatīman) | and the captive (wa-asīran),

76:9 "Only we feed you for the Countenance of Allah. Not we desire from you any reward and not thanks.

"Only (innamā) | we feed you (nuṭ''imukum) | for the Countenance (liwajhi) | of Allah (l-lahi). | Not (lā) | we desire (nurīdu) | from you (minkum) | any reward (jazāan) | and not (walā) | thanks (shukūran).

76:10 Indeed, we fear from our Lord a Day - harsh and distressful."

Indeed, we (innā) | fear (nakhāfu) | from (min) | our Lord (rabbinā) | a Day (yawman)- | harsh (ʿabūsan) | and distressful. (qamṭarīran)"

76:11 But will protect them Allah from the evil of that Day and will cause them to meet radiance and happiness.

But will protect them (fawaqāhumu) | Allah (l-lahu) | from the evil (sharra) | of that (dhālika) | Day (l-yawmi) | and will cause them to meet (walaqqāhum) | radiance (naḍratan) | and happiness (wasurūran).

76:12 And will reward them because they were patient, with a Garden and silk.

And will reward them (wajazāhum) | because (bimā) | they were patient (ṣabarū), | with a Garden (jannatan) | and silk (waḥarīran).

76:13 Reclining therein on couches. Not they will see therein sun and not freezing cold.

Reclining (muttakiīna) | therein (fīhā) | on (ʿalā) | couches (l-arāiki). | Not (lā) | they will see (yarawna) | therein (fīhā) | sun (shamsan) | and not (walā) | freezing cold (zamharīran).

76:14 And near above them are its shades and will hang low its cluster of fruits dangling low.

And near (wadāniyatan) | above them (ʿalayhim) | are its shades (ẓilāluhā) | and will hang low (wadhullilat) | its cluster of fruits (quṭūfuhā) | dangling low (tadhlīlan).

76:15 And will be circulated among them vessels of silver and cups that are of crystal.

And will be circulated (wayuṭāfu) | among them (ʿalayhim) | vessels (biāniyatin) | of (min) | silver (fiḍḍatin) | and cups (wa-akwābin) | that are (kānat) | of crystal (qawārīrā).

76:16 Crystal-clear of silver. They will determine its measure.

Crystal-clear (qawārīrā) | of (min) | silver (fiḍḍatin). | They will determine its (qaddarūhā) | measure (taqdīran).

76:17 And they will be given to drink therein a cup - is its mixture of Zanjabil,

And they will be given to drink (wayus'qawna) | therein (fīhā) | a cup (kasan)- | is (kāna) | its mixture (mizājuhā) | of Zanjabil (zanjabīlan),

76:18 A spring therein, named Salsabil.

A spring (ʿaynan) | therein (fīhā), | named (tusammā) | Salsabil (salsabīlan).

76:19 And will circulate among them young boys made eternal. When you see them, you would think them to be pearls scattered.

And will circulate (wayaṭūfu) | among them (ʿalayhim) | young boys (wil'dānun) | made eternal (mukhalladūna). | When (idhā) | you see them (ra-aytahum), | you would think them (ḥasib'tahum) | to be pearls (lu'lu-an) | scattered (manthūran).

76:20 And when you look, then you will see blessings and a kingdom great.

And when (wa-idhā) | you look (ra-ayta), | then (thamma) | you will see (ra-ayta) | blessings (naʿīman) | and a kingdom (wamul'kan) | great (kabīran).

76:21 Upon them will be garments of fine silk green and heavy brocade. And they will be adorned with bracelets of silver, and will give them to drink their Lord, a drink pure.

Upon them (ʿāliyahum) | will be garments (thiyābu) | of fine silk (sundusin) | green (khuḍ'run) | and heavy brocade (wa-is'tabraqun). | And they will be adorned (waḥullū) | with bracelets (asāwira) | of (min) | silver (fiḍḍatin), | and will give them to drink (wasaqāhum) | their Lord (rabbuhum), | a drink (sharāban) | pure (ṭahūran).

76:22 "Indeed, this is for you a reward, and has been your effort appreciated."

"Indeed (inna), | this (hādhā) | is (kāna) | for you (lakum) | a reward (jazāan), | and has been (wakāna) | your effort (saʿyukum) | appreciated. (mashkūran)"

76:23 Indeed, We [We] [We] revealed to you the Quran progressively.

Indeed, We (innā) | [We] (naḥnu) | [We] revealed (nazzalnā) | to you (ʿalayka) | the Quran (l-qur'āna) | progressively (tanzīlan).

76:24 So be patient for the Command of your Lord and do not obey from them any sinner or disbeliever.

So be patient (fa-iṣ'bir) | for the Command (liḥuk'mi) | of your Lord (rabbika) | and do not (walā) | obey (tuṭiʿ) | from them (min'hum) | any sinner (āthiman) | or (aw) | disbeliever (kafūran).

76:25 And remember the name of your Lord morning and evening.

And remember (wa-udh'kuri) | the name (is'ma) | of your Lord (rabbika) | morning (buk'ratan) | and evening (wa-aṣīlan).

76:26 And of the night prostrate to Him, and glorify Him a night long.

And of (wamina) | the night (al-layli) | prostrate (fa-us'jud) | to Him (lahu), | and glorify Him (wasabbiḥ'hu) | a night (laylan) | long (ṭawīlan).

76:27 Indeed, these love the immediate, and leave behind them a Day grave.

Indeed (inna), | these (hāulāi) | love (yuḥibbūna) | the immediate (l-ʿājilata), | and leave (wayadharūna) | behind them (warāahum) | a Day (yawman) | grave (thaqīlan).

76:28 We, created them and We strengthened their forms, and when We will, We can change their likeness[es] with a change.

We (naḥnu), | created them (khalaqnāhum) | and We strengthened (washadadnā) | their forms (asrahum), | and when (wa-idhā) | We will (shi'nā), | We can change (baddalnā) | their likeness[es] (amthālahum) | with a change (tabdīlan).

76:29 Indeed, this is a reminder, so whoever wills, let him take to his Lord a way.

Indeed (inna), | this (hādhihi) | is a reminder (tadhkiratun), | so whoever (faman) | wills (shāa), | let him take (ittakhadha) | to (ilā) | his Lord (rabbihi) | a way (sabīlan).

76:30 And not you will except that wills Allah. Indeed, Allah is All-Knower, All-Wise.

And not (wamā) | you will (tashāūna) | except (illā) | that (an) | wills (yashāa) | Allah (l-lahu). | Indeed (inna), | Allah (l-laha) | is (kāna) | All-Knower (ʿalīman), | All-Wise (ḥakīman).

76:31 He admits whom He wills into His mercy, but for the wrongdoers, He has prepared for them a punishment painful.

He admits (yud'khilu) | whom (man) | He wills (yashāu) | into (fī) | His mercy (raḥmatihi), | but for the wrongdoers (wal-ẓālimīna), | He has prepared (aʿadda) | for them (lahum) | a punishment (ʿadhāban) | painful (alīman).

Chapter (77) Sūrat l-Mur'salāt (Those sent forth)

77:1 By the ones sent forth, one after another,
By the ones sent forth (wal-mur'salāti), | one after another (ʿur'fan),

77:2 And the winds that blow violently,
And the winds that blow (fal-ʿāṣifāti) | violently (ʿaṣfan),

77:3 And the ones that scatter far and wide,
And the ones that scatter (wal-nāshirāti) | far and wide (nashran),

77:4 And those who separate by the Criterion,
And those who separate (fal-fāriqāti) | by the Criterion (farqan),

77:5 And those who bring down the Reminder,
And those who bring down (fal-mul'qiyāti) | the Reminder (dhik'ran),

77:6 As justification or warning,
As justification (ʿudh'ran) | or (aw) | warning (nudh'ran),

77:7 Indeed, what you are promised will surely occur.
Indeed, what (innamā) | you are promised (tūʿadūna) | will surely occur (lawāqiʿun).

77:8 So when the stars are obliterated,
So when (fa-idhā) | the stars (l-nujūmu) | are obliterated (ṭumisat),

77:9 And when the heaven is cleft asunder,
And when (wa-idhā) | the heaven (l-samāu) | is cleft asunder (furijat),

77:10 And when the mountains are blown away,
And when (wa-idhā) | the mountains (l-jibālu) | are blown away (nusifat),

77:11 And when the Messengers are gathered to their appointed time.
And when (wa-idhā) | the Messengers (l-rusulu) | are gathered to their appointed time (uqqitat).

77:12 For what Day are these postponed?
For what (li-ayyi) | Day (yawmin) | are these postponed (ujjilat)?

77:13 For the Day of Judgment.
For the Day (liyawmi) | of Judgment (l-faṣli).

77:14 And what will make you know what is the Day of the Judgment?
And what (wamā) | will make you know (adrāka) | what (mā) | is the Day (yawmu) | of the Judgment (l-faṣli)?

77:15 Woe that Day to the deniers
Woe (waylun) | that Day (yawma-idhin) | to the deniers (lil'mukadhibīna)

77:16 Did not We destroy the former people?
Did not (alam) | We destroy (nuh'liki) | the former people (l-awalīna)?

77:17 Then We follow them up with the later ones.
Then (thumma) | We follow them up (nut'bi'uhumu) | with the later ones (l-ākhirīna).

77:18 Thus We deal with the criminals.
Thus (kadhālika) | We deal (naf'alu) | with the criminals (bil-muj'rimīna).

77:19 Woe that Day to the deniers.
Woe (waylun) | that Day (yawma-idhin) | to the deniers (lil'mukadhibīna).

77:20 Did not We create you from a water despicable?
Did not (alam) | We create you (nakhluqkkum) | from (min) | a water (māin) | despicable (mahīnin)?

77:21 Then We placed it in an abode safe
Then We placed it (faja'alnāhu) | in (fī) | an abode (qarārin) | safe (makīnin)

77:22 For a period known.
For (ilā) | a period (qadarin) | known (ma'lūmin).

77:23 So We measured, and Best are We to measure!
So We measured (faqadarnā), | and Best (fani''ma) | are We to measure (l-qādirūna)!

77:24 Woe that Day to the deniers.
Woe (waylun) | that Day (yawma-idhin) | to the deniers (lil'mukadhibīna).

77:25 Have not We made the earth a receptacle
Have not (alam) | We made (naj'ali) | the earth (l-arḍa) | a receptacle (kifātan)

77:26 For the living and the dead,
For the living (aḥyāan) | and the dead (wa-amwātan),

77:27 And We made therein firmly set mountains lofty, and We gave you to drink water - sweet?
And We made (waja'alnā) | therein (fīhā) | firmly set mountains (rawāsiya) | lofty (shāmikhātin), | and We gave you to drink (wa-asqaynākum) | water (māan)- | sweet (furātan)?

77:28 Woe that Day to the deniers.
Woe (waylun) | that Day (yawma-idhin) | to the deniers (lil'mukadhibīna).

77:29 "Proceed to what you used to in it deny,
"Proceed (inṭaliqū) | to (ilā) | what (mā) | you used to (kuntum) | in it (bihi) | deny (tukadhibūna),

77:30 Proceed to a shadow having three columns
Proceed (inṭaliqū) | to (ilā) | a shadow (ẓillin) | having (dhī) | three (thalāthi) | columns (shu'abin)

77:31 No cool shade and not availing against the flame.
No (lā) | cool shade (ẓalīlin) | and not (walā) | availing (yugh'nī) | against (mina) | the flame (l-lahabi).

77:32 Indeed, it throws up sparks as the fortress,

Indeed, it (innahā) | throws up (tarmī) | sparks (bishararin) | as the fortress (kal-qaṣri),

77:33 As if they were camels yellow.
As if they were (ka-annahu) | camels (jimālatun) | yellow (ṣuf'run).

77:34 Woe that Day to the deniers.
Woe (waylun) | that Day (yawma-idhin) | to the deniers (lil'mukadhibīna).

77:35 This is a Day not they will speak,
This (hādhā) | is a Day (yawmu) | not (lā) | they will speak (yanṭiqūna),

77:36 And not will it be permitted for them to make excuses.
And not (walā) | will it be permitted (yu'dhanu) | for them (lahum) | to make excuses (fayaʿtadhirūna).

77:37 Woe that Day to the deniers.
Woe (waylun) | that Day (yawma-idhin) | to the deniers (lil'mukadhibīna).

77:38 This is the Day of Judgment; We have gathered you and the former people.
This (hādhā) | is the Day (yawmu) | of Judgment (l-faṣli); | We have gathered you (jamaʿnākum) | and the former people (wal-awalīna).

77:39 So if is for you a plan, then plan against Me.
So if (fa-in) | is (kāna) | for you (lakum) | a plan (kaydun), | then plan against Me (fakīdūni).

77:40 Woe that Day to the deniers.
Woe (waylun) | that Day (yawma-idhin) | to the deniers (lil'mukadhibīna).

77:41 Indeed, the righteous will be in shades and springs,
Indeed (inna), | the righteous (l-mutaqīna) | will be in (fī) | shades (ẓilālin) | and springs (waʿuyūnin),

77:42 And fruits from what they desire.
And fruits (wafawākiha) | from what (mimmā) | they desire (yashtahūna).

77:43 "Eat and drink in satisfaction for what you used to do."
"Eat (kulū) | and drink (wa-ish'rabū) | in satisfaction (hanīan) | for what (bimā) | you used to (kuntum) | do. (taʿmalūna)"

77:44 Indeed, We thus reward the good-doers.
Indeed, We (innā) | thus (kadhālika) | reward (najzī) | the good-doers (l-muḥ'sinīna).

77:45 Woe that Day to the deniers.
Woe (waylun) | that Day (yawma-idhin) | to the deniers (lil'mukadhibīna).

77:46 Eat and enjoy yourselves a little; indeed, you are criminals."
Eat (kulū) | and enjoy yourselves (watamattaʿū) | a little (qalīlan); | indeed, you (innakum) | are criminals. (muj'rimūna)"

77:47 Woe that Day to the deniers.
Woe (waylun) | that Day (yawma-idhin) | to the deniers (lil'mukadhibīna).

77:48 And when it is said to them, "Bow," not they bow.
And when (wa-idhā) | it is said (qīla) | to them (lahumu), | "Bow, (ir'kaʿū)" | not (lā) | they bow (yarkaʿūna).

77:49 Woe that Day to the deniers.
Woe (waylun) | that Day (yawma-idhin) | to the deniers (lil'mukadhibīna).

77:50 Then in what statement after it will they believe?
Then in what (fabi-ayyi) | statement (ḥadīthin) | after it (baʿdahu) | will they believe (yu'minūna)?

Chapter (78) Sūrat l-Naba (The Great News)

78:1 About what are they asking one another?
About what (ʿamma) | are they asking one another (yatasāalūna)?

78:2 About the News the Great,
About (ʿani) | the News (l-naba-i) | the Great (l-ʿaẓīmi),

78:3 About which they are concerning it in disagreement.
About which (alladhī) | they (hum) | are concerning it (fīhi) | in disagreement (mukh'talifūna).

78:4 Nay! soon they will know.
Nay (kallā)! | soon they will know (sayaʿlamūna).

78:5 Then Nay! soon they will know.
Then (thumma) | Nay (kallā)! | soon they will know (sayaʿlamūna).

78:6 Have not We made the earth a resting place?
Have not (alam) | We made (najʿali) | the earth (l-arḍa) | a resting place (mihādan)?

78:7 And the mountains as pegs,
And the mountains (wal-jibāla) | as pegs (awtādan),

78:8 And We created you in pairs,
And We created you (wakhalaqnākum) | in pairs (azwājan),

78:9 And We made your sleep for rest,
And We made (wajaʿalnā) | your sleep (nawmakum) | for rest (subātan),

78:10 And We made the night as covering,
And We made (wajaʿalnā) | the night (al-layla) | as covering (libāsan),

78:11 And We made the day for livelihood,
And We made (wajaʿalnā) | the day (l-nahāra) | for livelihood (maʿāshan),

78:12 And We constructed over you seven strong,
And We constructed (wabanaynā) | over you (fawqakum) | seven (sabʿan) | strong (shidādan),

78:13 And We placed a lamp burning,
And We placed (wajaʿalnā) | a lamp (sirājan) | burning (wahhājan),

78:14 And We sent down from the rain clouds water pouring abundantly,
And We sent down (wa-anzalnā) | from (mina) | the rain clouds (l-muʿṣirāti) | water (māan) | pouring abundantly (thajjājan),

78:15 That We may bring forth thereby grain and vegetation,
That We may bring forth (linukh'rija) | thereby (bihi) | grain (ḥabban) | and vegetation (wanabātan),

78:16 And gardens of thick foliage.
And gardens (wajannātin) | of thick foliage (alfāfan).

78:17 Indeed, the Day of the Judgment is an appointed time,
Indeed (inna), | the Day (yawma) | of the Judgment (l-faṣli) | is (kāna) | an appointed time (mīqātan),

78:18 The Day in which shall be blown in the trumpet and you will come forth in crowds,
The Day (yawma) | in which shall be blown (yunfakhu) | in (fī) | the trumpet (l-ṣūri) | and you will come forth (fatatūna) | in crowds (afwājan),

78:19 And is opened the heaven and becomes gateways,
And is opened (wafutiḥati) | the heaven (l-samāu) | and becomes (fakānat) | gateways (abwāban),

78:20 And are moved the mountains and become a mirage.
And are moved (wasuyyirati) | the mountains (l-jibālu) | and become (fakānat) | a mirage (sarāban).

78:21 Indeed, Hell is lying in wait,
Indeed (inna), | Hell (jahannama) | is (kānat) | lying in wait (mir'ṣādan),

78:22 For the transgressors a place of return,
For the transgressors (lilṭṭāghīna) | a place of return (maāban),

78:23 They will be remaining therein for ages.
They will be remaining (lābithīna) | therein (fīhā) | for ages (aḥqāban).

78:24 Not they will taste therein coolness and not any drink,
Not (lā) | they will taste (yadhūqūna) | therein (fīhā) | coolness (bardan) | and not (walā) | any drink (sharāban),

78:25 Except scalding water and purulence,
Except (illā) | scalding water (ḥamīman) | and purulence (waghassāqan),

78:26 A recompense appropriate.

A recompense (jazāan) | appropriate (wifāqan).

78:27 Indeed, they were not expecting an account,
Indeed, they (innahum) | were (kānū) | not (lā) | expecting (yarjūna) | an account (ḥisāban),

78:28 And they denied Our Signs with denial.
And they denied (wakadhabū) | Our Signs (biāyātinā) | with denial (kidhāban).

78:29 And every thing We have enumerated it in a Book.
And every (wakulla) | thing (shayin) | We have enumerated it (aḥṣaynāhu) | in a Book (kitāban).

78:30 So taste, and never We will increase you except in punishment.
So taste (fadhūqū), | and never (falan) | We will increase you (nazīdakum) | except (illā) | in punishment (ʿadhāban).

78:31 Indeed, for the righteous is success,
Indeed (inna), | for the righteous (lil'muttaqīna) | is success (mafāzan),

78:32 Gardens and grapevines,
Gardens (ḥadāiqa) | and grapevines (wa-aʿnāban),

78:33 And splendid companions well-matched,
And splendid companions (wakawāʿiba) | well-matched (atrāban),

78:34 And a cup full.
And a cup (wakasan) | full (dihāqan).

78:35 Not they will hear therein any vain talk and not any falsehood,
Not (lā) | they will hear (yasmaʿūna) | therein (fīhā) | any vain talk (laghwan) | and not (walā) | any falsehood (kidhāban),

78:36 As a reward from your Lord, a gift according to account,
As a reward (jazāan) | from (min) | your Lord (rabbika), | a gift (ʿaṭāan) | according to account (ḥisāban),

78:37 Lord of the heavens and the earth and whatever is between both of them the Most Gracious, not they have power from Him to address.
Lord (rabbi) | of the heavens (l-samāwāti) | and the earth (wal-arḍi) | and whatever (wamā) | is between both of them (baynahumā) | the Most Gracious (l-raḥmāni), | not (lā) | they have power (yamlikūna) | from Him (min'hu) | to address (khiṭāban).

78:38 The Day will stand the Spirit and the Angels in rows, not they will speak except one who - permits [for] him the Most Gracious, and he will say what is correct.
The Day (yawma) | will stand (yaqūmu) | the Spirit (l-rūḥu) | and the Angels (wal-malāikatu) | in rows (ṣaffan), | not (lā) | they will speak (yatakallamūna) | except (illā) | one who (man)- | permits (adhina) | [for] him (lahu) | the Most Gracious (l-raḥmānu), | and he will say (waqāla) | what is correct (ṣawāban).

78:39 That is the Day the True. So whoever wills let him take towards his Lord a return.
That (dhālika) | is the Day (l-yawmu) | the True (l-ḥaqu). | So whoever (faman) | wills (shāa)

| let him take (ittakhadha) | towards (ilā) | his Lord (rabbihi) | a return (maāban).

78:40 Indeed We [We] have warned you of a punishment near the Day will see the man what have sent forth his hands and will say the disbeliever, "O I wish! I were dust!"

Indeed We (innā) | [We] have warned you (andharnākum) | of a punishment (ʿadhāban) | near (qarīban) | the Day (yawma) | will see (yanẓuru) | the man (l-maru) | what (mā) | have sent forth (qaddamat) | his hands (yadāhu) | and will say (wayaqūlu) | the disbeliever (l-kāfiru), | "O I wish (yālaytanī)! | I were (kuntu) | dust! (turāban)"

Chapter (79) Sūrat l-Nāziʿāt (Those who Pull Out)

79:1 By those who extract violently,

By those who extract (wal-nāziʿāti) | violently (gharqan),

79:2 And those who draw out gently,

And those who draw out (wal-nāshiṭāti) | gently (nashṭan),

79:3 And those who glide swimming,

And those who glide (wal-sābiḥāti) | swimming (sabḥan),

79:4 And those who race each other in a race,

And those who race each other (fal-sābiqāti) | in a race (sabqan),

79:5 And those who arrange the matter.

And those who arrange (fal-mudabirāti) | the matter (amran).

79:6 The Day will quake the quaking one,

The Day (yawma) | will quake (tarjufu) | the quaking one (l-rājifatu),

79:7 Follows it the subsequent,

Follows it (tatbaʿuhā) | the subsequent (l-rādifatu),

79:8 Hearts, that Day, will palpitate,

Hearts (qulūbun), | that Day (yawma-idhin), | will palpitate (wājifatun),

79:9 Their eyes humbled.

Their eyes (abṣāruhā) | humbled (khāshiʿatun).

79:10 They say, "Will we indeed be returned to the former state?

They say (yaqūlūna), | "Will we (a-innā) | indeed be returned (lamardūdūna) | to (fī) | the former state (l-ḥāfirati)?

79:11 What! When we are bones decayed?"

What! When (a-idhā) | we are (kunnā) | bones (ʿiẓāman) | decayed? (nakhiratan)"

79:12 They say, "This then would be a return losing."

They say (qālū), | "This (til'ka) | then (idhan) | would be a return (karratun) | losing. (khāsiratun)"

79:13 Then only it will be a shout single,
Then only (fa-innamā) | it (hiya) | will be a shout (zajratun) | single (wāḥidatun),

79:14 And behold! They will be awakened.
And behold (fa-idhā)! | They (hum) | will be awakened (bil-sāhirati).

79:15 Has there come to you the story of Musa?
Has (hal) | there come to you (atāka) | the story (ḥadīthu) | of Musa (mūsā)?

79:16 When called him his Lord in the valley the sacred of Tuwa,
When (idh) | called him (nādāhu) | his Lord (rabbuhu) | in the valley (bil-wādi) | the sacred (l-muqadasi) | of Tuwa (ṭuwan),

79:17 "Go to Firaun. Indeed, he has transgressed.
"Go (idh'hab) | to (ilā) | Firaun (fir''awna). | Indeed, he (innahu) | has transgressed (ṭaghā).

79:18 And say, "Would [for] you [to] [that] purify yourself?
And say (faqul), | "Would (hal) | [for] you (laka) | [to] (ilā) | [that] (an) | purify yourself (tazakkā)?

79:19 And I will guide you to your Lord so you would fear."
And I will guide you (wa-ahdiyaka) | to (ilā) | your Lord (rabbika) | so you would fear. (fatakhshā)"

79:20 Then he showed him the sign the great.
Then he showed him (fa-arāhu) | the sign (l-āyata) | the great (l-kub'rā).

79:21 But he denied and disobeyed.
But he denied (fakadhaba) | and disobeyed (waʿaṣā).

79:22 Then he turned his back, striving,
Then (thumma) | he turned his back (adbara), | striving (yasʿā),

79:23 And he gathered and called out,
And he gathered (faḥashara) | and called out (fanādā),

79:24 Then he said, "I am your Lord, the Most High."
Then he said (faqāla), | "I am (anā) | your Lord (rabbukumu), | the Most High. (l-aʿlā)"

79:25 So seized him Allah with an exemplary punishment for the last and the first.
So seized him (fa-akhadhahu) | Allah (l-lahu) | with an exemplary punishment (nakāla) | for the last (l-ākhirati) | and the first (wal-ūlā).

79:26 Indeed, in that surely is a lesson for whoever fears.
Indeed (inna), | in (fī) | that (dhālika) | surely is a lesson (laʿib'ratan) | for whoever (liman) | fears (yakhshā).

79:27 Are you a more difficult creation or the heaven. He constructed it?
Are you (a-antum) | a more difficult (ashaddu) | creation (khalqan) | or (ami) | the heaven

(l-samāu). | He constructed it (banāhā)?

79:28 He raised its ceiling and proportioned it.
He raised (rafaʿa) | its ceiling (samkahā) | and proportioned it (fasawwāhā).

79:29 And He darkened its night and brought out its brightness.
And He darkened (wa-aghṭasha) | its night (laylahā) | and brought out (wa-akhraja) | its brightness (ḍuḥāhā).

79:30 And the earth after that He spread it.
And the earth (wal-arḍa) | after (baʿda) | that (dhālika) | He spread it (daḥāhā).

79:31 He brought forth from it, its water and its pasture,
He brought forth (akhraja) | from it (min'hā), | its water (māahā) | and its pasture (wamarʿāhā),

79:32 And the mountains, He made them firm,
And the mountains (wal-jibāla), | He made them firm (arsāhā),

79:33 As a provision for you and for your cattle.
As a provision (matāʿan) | for you (lakum) | and for your cattle (wali-anʿāmikum).

79:34 But when comes the Overwhelming Calamity the great,
But when (fa-idhā) | comes (jāati) | the Overwhelming Calamity (l-ṭāmatu) | the great (l-kub'rā),

79:35 The Day will remember man what he strove for,
The Day (yawma) | will remember (yatadhakkaru) | man (l-insānu) | what (mā) | he strove for (saʿā),

79:36 And will be made manifest the Hellfire to him who sees,
And will be made manifest (waburrizati) | the Hellfire (l-jaḥīmu) | to him who (liman) | sees (yarā),

79:37 Then as for him who transgressed,
Then as for (fa-ammā) | him who (man) | transgressed (ṭaghā),

79:38 And preferred the life of the world,
And preferred (waāthara) | the life (l-ḥayata) | of the world (l-dun'yā),

79:39 Then indeed, the Hellfire, it is the refuge.
Then indeed (fa-inna), | the Hellfire (l-jaḥīma), | it (hiya) | is the refuge (l-mawā).

79:40 But as for him who feared standing before his Lord, and restrained his soul from the vain desires,
But as for (wa-ammā) | him who (man) | feared (khāfa) | standing (maqāma) | before his Lord (rabbihi), | and restrained (wanahā) | his soul (l-nafsa) | from (ʿani) | the vain desires (l-hawā),

79:41 Then indeed, Paradise - it is the refuge.
Then indeed (fa-inna), | Paradise (l-janata)- | it is (hiya) | the refuge (l-mawā).

79:42 They ask you about the Hour, when is its arrival?

They ask you (yasalūnaka) | about (ʿani) | the Hour (l-sāʿati), | when (ayyāna) | is its arrival (mur'sāhā)?

79:43 In what are you [of] to mention it?
In what (fīma) | are you (anta) | [of] (min) | to mention it (dhik'rāhā)?

79:44 To your Lord is its finality.
To (ilā) | your Lord (rabbika) | is its finality (muntahāhā).

79:45 Only you are a warner for him who fears it.
Only (innamā) | you (anta) | are a warner (mundhiru) | for him who (man) | fears it (yakhshāhā).

79:46 As though they, the Day they see it, not they had remained except an evening or a morning thereof.
As though they (ka-annahum), | the Day (yawma) | they see it (yarawnahā), | not (lam) | they had remained (yalbathū) | except (illā) | an evening (ʿashiyyatan) | or (aw) | a morning thereof (ḍuḥāhā).

Chapter (80) Sūrat ʿAbasa (He frowned)

80:1 He frowned and turned away,
He frowned (ʿabasa) | and turned away (watawallā),

80:2 Because came to him the blind man.
Because (an) | came to him (jāahu) | the blind man (l-aʿmā).

80:3 But what would make you know that he might purify himself,
But what (wamā) | would make you know (yud'rīka) | that he might (laʿallahu) | purify himself (yazzakkā),

80:4 Or be reminded so would benefit him the reminder?
Or (aw) | be reminded (yadhakkaru) | so would benefit him (fatanfaʿahu) | the reminder (l-dhik'rā)?

80:5 As for him who considers himself free from need,
As for (ammā) | him who (mani) | considers himself free from need (is'taghnā),

80:6 So you to him give attention.
So you (fa-anta) | to him (lahu) | give attention (taṣaddā).

80:7 And not upon you that not he purifies himself.
And not (wamā) | upon you (ʿalayka) | that not (allā) | he purifies himself (yazzakkā).

80:8 But as for he who came to you striving,

But as for (wa-ammā) | he who (man) | came to you (jāaka) | striving (yasʿā),

80:9 While he fears,
While he (wahuwa) | fears (yakhshā),

80:10 But you from him are distracted.
But you (fa-anta) | from him (ʿanhu) | are distracted (talahhā).

80:11 Nay! Indeed, it is a reminder,
Nay (kallā)! | Indeed, it (innahā) | is a reminder (tadhkiratun),

80:12 So whosoever wills may remember it.
So whosoever (faman) | wills (shāa) | may remember it (dhakarahu).

80:13 In sheets honored,
In (fī) | sheets (ṣuḥufin) | honored (mukarramatin),

80:14 Exalted, purified,
Exalted (marfūʿatin), | purified (muṭahharatin),

80:15 In the hands of scribes.
In the hands (bi-aydī) | of scribes (safaratin).

80:16 Noble, dutiful.
Noble (kirāmin), | dutiful (bararatin).

80:17 Is destroyed [the] man, how ungrateful is he!
Is destroyed (qutila) | [the] man (l-insānu), | how (mā) | ungrateful is he (akfarahu)!

80:18 From what thing He created him?
From (min) | what (ayyi) | thing (shayin) | He created him (khalaqahu)?

80:19 From a semen-drop He created him, then He proportioned him,
From (min) | a semen-drop (nuṭ'fatin) | He created him (khalaqahu), | then He proportioned him (faqaddarahu),

80:20 Then the way, He made easy for him,
Then (thumma) | the way (l-sabīla), | He made easy for him (yassarahu),

80:21 Then He causes him to die and provides a grave for him,
Then (thumma) | He causes him to die (amātahu) | and provides a grave for him (fa-aqbarahu),

80:22 Then when He wills, He will resurrect him.
Then (thumma) | when (idhā) | He wills (shāa), | He will resurrect him (ansharahu).

80:23 Nay! Not he has accomplished what He commanded him.
Nay (kallā)! | Not (lammā) | he has accomplished (yaqḍi) | what (mā) | He commanded him (amarahu).

80:24 Then let look the man at his food,
Then let look (falyanẓuri) | the man (l-insānu) | at (ilā) | his food (ṭaʿāmihi),

80:25 That [We] [We] poured the water in abundance,
That [We] (annā) | [We] poured (ṣababnā) | the water (l-māa) | in abundance (ṣabban),

80:26 Then We cleaved the earth splitting,
Then (thumma) | We cleaved (shaqaqnā) | the earth (l-arḍa) | splitting (shaqqan),

80:27 Then We caused to grow therein grain,
Then We caused to grow (fa-anbatnā) | therein (fīhā) | grain (ḥabban),

80:28 And grapes and green fodder,
And grapes (waʿinaban) | and green fodder (waqaḍban),

80:29 And olive and date-palms,
And olive (wazaytūnan) | and date-palms (wanakhlan),

80:30 And gardens of thick foliage,
And gardens (waḥadāiqa) | of thick foliage (ghul'ban),

80:31 And fruits and grass,
And fruits (wafākihatan) | and grass (wa-abban),

80:32 As a provision for you and for your cattle.
As a provision (matāʿan) | for you (lakum) | and for your cattle (wali-anʿāmikum).

80:33 But when comes the Deafening Blast,
But when (fa-idhā) | comes (jāati) | the Deafening Blast (l-ṣākhatu),

80:34 The Day will flee a man from his brother,
The Day (yawma) | will flee (yafirru) | a man (l-maru) | from (min) | his brother (akhīhi),

80:35 And his mother and his father,
And his mother (wa ummihi) | and his father (wa-abīhi),

80:36 And his wife and his children,
And his wife (waṣāḥibatihi) | and his children (wabanīhi),

80:37 For every man among them that Day will be a matter occupying him.
For every (likulli) | man (im'ri-in) | among them (min'hum) | that Day (yawma-idhin) | will be a matter (shanun) | occupying him (yugh'nīhi).

80:38 Faces, that Day will be bright,
Faces (wujūhun), | that Day (yawma-idhin) | will be bright (mus'firatun),

80:39 Laughing, rejoicing at good news.
Laughing (ḍāḥikatun), | rejoicing at good news (mus'tabshiratun).

80:40 And faces, that Day, upon them will be dust,
And faces (wawujūhun), | that Day (yawma-idhin), | upon them (ʿalayhā) | will be dust (ghabaratun),

80:41 Will cover them darkness.

Will cover them (tarhaquhā) | darkness (qataratun).

80:42 Those [they] are the disbelievers, the wicked ones.
Those (ulāika) | [they] (humu) | are the disbelievers (l-kafaratu), | the wicked ones (l-fajaratu).

Chapter (81) Sūrat l-Takwīr (The Overthrowing)

81:1 When the sun is wrapped up,
When (idhā) | the sun (l-shamsu) | is wrapped up (kuwwirat),

81:2 And when the stars fall, losing their luster
And when (wa-idhā) | the stars (l-nujūmu) | fall, losing their luster (inkadarat)

81:3 And when the mountains are moved away,
And when (wa-idhā) | the mountains (l-jibālu) | are moved away (suyyirat),

81:4 And when the full-term she-camels are left untended;
And when (wa-idhā) | the full-term she-camels (l-ʿishāru) | are left untended (ʿuṭṭilat);

81:5 And when the wild beasts are gathered,
And when (wa-idhā) | the wild beasts (l-wuḥūshu) | are gathered (ḥushirat),

81:6 And when the seas are made to overflow,
And when (wa-idhā) | the seas (l-biḥāru) | are made to overflow (sujjirat),

81:7 And when the souls are paired,
And when (wa-idhā) | the souls (l-nufūsu) | are paired (zuwwijat),

81:8 And when the female infant buried alive is asked
And when (wa-idhā) | the female infant buried alive (l-mawūdatu) | is asked (su-ilat)

81:9 For what sin she was killed.
For what (bi-ayyi) | sin (dhanbin) | she was killed (qutilat).

81:10 And when the pages are laid open,
And when (wa-idhā) | the pages (l-ṣuḥufu) | are laid open (nushirat),

81:11 And when the sky is stripped away,
And when (wa-idhā) | the sky (l-samāu) | is stripped away (kushiṭat),

81:12 And when the Hellfire is set ablaze,
And when (wa-idhā) | the Hellfire (l-jaḥīmu) | is set ablaze (suʿʿirat),

81:13 And when Paradise is brought near,
And when (wa-idhā) | Paradise (l-janatu) | is brought near (uz'lifat),

81:14 Will know a soul what it has brought.
Will know (ʿalimat) | a soul (nafsun) | what (mā) | it has brought (aḥḍarat).

81:15 But nay! I swear by the retreating planets,
But nay (falā)! | I swear (uq'simu) | by the retreating planets (bil-khunasi),

81:16 Those that run and disappear,
Those that run (al-jawāri) | and disappear (l-kunasi),

81:17 And the night when it departs,
And the night (wa-al-layli) | when (idhā) | it departs (ʿasʿasa),

81:18 And the dawn when it breathes
And the dawn (wal-ṣub'ḥi) | when (idhā) | it breathes (tanaffasa)

81:19 Indeed, it is surely a word of a Messenger noble,
Indeed, it (innahu) | is surely a word (laqawlu) | of a Messenger (rasūlin) | noble (karīmin),

81:20 Possessor of power, with the Owner of the Throne secure,
Possessor of (dhī) | power (quwwatin), | with (ʿinda) | the Owner of (dhī) | the Throne (l-ʿarshi) | secure (makīnin),

81:21 One to be obeyed and trustworthy,
One to be obeyed (muṭāʿin) | and (thamma) | trustworthy (amīnin),

81:22 And not is your companion mad.
And not (wamā) | is your companion (ṣāḥibukum) | mad (bimajnūnin).

81:23 And certainly he saw him in the horizon the clear.
And certainly (walaqad) | he saw him (raāhu) | in the horizon (bil-ufuqi) | the clear (l-mubīni).

81:24 And not he is on the unseen a withholder.
And not (wamā) | he is (huwa) | on (ʿalā) | the unseen (l-ghaybi) | a withholder (biḍanīnin).

81:25 And not it is the word of Shaitaan accursed.
And not (wamā) | it (huwa) | is the word (biqawli) | of Shaitaan (shayṭānin) | accursed (rajīmin).

81:26 So where are you going?
So where (fa-ayna) | are you going (tadhhabūna)?

81:27 Not it is except a reminder to the worlds,
Not (in) | it (huwa) | is except (illā) | a reminder (dhik'run) | to the worlds (lil'ʿālamīna),

81:28 For whoever wills among you to take a straight way.
For whoever (liman) | wills (shāa) | among you (minkum) | to (an) | take a straight way (yastaqīma).

81:29 And not you will except that wills Allah, Lord of the worlds.

And not (wamā) | you will (tashāūna) | except (illā) | that (an) | wills (yashāa) | Allah (l-lahu), | Lord (rabbu) | of the worlds (l-ʿālamīna).

Chapter (82) Sūrat l-Infiṭār (The Cleaving)

82:1 When the sky is cleft asunder,
When (idhā) | the sky (l-samāu) | is cleft asunder (infaṭarat),

82:2 And when the stars scatter,
And when (wa-idhā) | the stars (l-kawākibu) | scatter (intatharat),

82:3 And when the seas are made to gush forth,
And when (wa-idhā) | the seas (l-biḥāru) | are made to gush forth (fujjirat),

82:4 And when the graves are overturned,
And when (wa-idhā) | the graves (l-qubūru) | are overturned (buʿthirat),

82:5 Will know a soul what it has sent forth and left behind.
Will know (ʿalimat) | a soul (nafsun) | what (mā) | it has sent forth (qaddamat) | and left behind (wa-akharat).

82:6 O man! What has deceived you concerning your Lord the Most Noble,
O (yāayyuhā) | man (l-insānu)! | What (mā) | has deceived you (gharraka) | concerning your Lord (birabbika) | the Most Noble (l-karīmi),

82:7 Who created you, then fashioned you then balanced you?
Who (alladhī) | created you (khalaqaka), | then fashioned you (fasawwāka) | then balanced you (faʿadalaka)?

82:8 In whatever form what He willed, He assembled you.
In (fī) | whatever (ayyi) | form (ṣūratin) | what (mā) | He willed (shāa), | He assembled you (rakkabaka).

82:9 Nay! But you deny the Judgment.
Nay (kallā)! | But (bal) | you deny (tukadhibūna) | the Judgment (bil-dīni).

82:10 And indeed, over you are surely guardians,
And indeed (wa-inna), | over you (ʿalaykum) | are surely guardians (laḥāfiẓīna),

82:11 Noble recording,
Noble (kirāman) | recording (kātibīna),

82:12 They know whatever you do.
They know (yaʿlamūna) | whatever (mā) | you do (tafʿalūna).

82:13 Indeed, the righteous will be surely in bliss,

Indeed (inna), | the righteous (l-abrāra) | will be surely in (lafī) | bliss (naʿīmin),

82:14 And indeed, the wicked will be surely in Hellfire.
And indeed (wa-inna), | the wicked (l-fujāra) | will be surely in (lafī) | Hellfire (jaḥīmin).

82:15 They will burn in it on the Day of the Judgment,
They will burn in it (yaṣlawnahā) | on the Day (yawma) | of the Judgment (l-dīni),

82:16 And not they from it will be absent.
And not (wamā) | they (hum) | from it (ʿanhā) | will be absent (bighāibīna).

82:17 And what can make you know what is the Day of the Judgment?
And what (wamā) | can make you know (adrāka) | what (mā) | is the Day (yawmu) | of the Judgment (l-dīni)?

82:18 Then, what can make you know what is the Day of the Judgment?
Then (thumma), | what (mā) | can make you know (adrāka) | what (mā) | is the Day (yawmu) | of the Judgment (l-dīni)?

82:19 The Day not will have power a soul for a soul anything, and the Command that Day will be with Allah.
The Day (yawma) | not (lā) | will have power (tamliku) | a soul (nafsun) | for a soul (linafsin) | anything (shayan), | and the Command (wal-amru) | that Day (yawma-idhin) | will be with Allah (lillahi).

Chapter (83) Sūrat l-Muṭafifīn (Those Who Deal in Fraud)

83:1 Woe to those who give less,
Woe (waylun) | to those who give less (lil'muṭaffifīna),

83:2 Those who when they take a measure from the people, they take in full,
Those who (alladhīna) | when (idhā) | they take a measure (ik'tālū) | from (ʿalā) | the people (l-nāsi), | they take in full (yastawfūna),

83:3 But when they give by measure to them or they weigh for them they give less.
But when (wa-idhā) | they give by measure to them (kālūhum) | or (aw) | they weigh for them (wazanūhum) | they give less (yukh'sirūna).

83:4 Do not think those that they will be resurrected,
Do not (alā) | think (yaẓunnu) | those (ulāika) | that they (annahum) | will be resurrected (mabʿūthūna),

83:5 For a Day Great,

For a Day (liyawmin) | Great (ʿaẓīmin),

83:6 The Day will stand mankind before the Lord of the worlds?
The Day (yawma) | will stand (yaqūmu) | mankind (l-nāsu) | before the Lord (lirabbi) | of the worlds (l-ʿālamīna)?

83:7 Nay! Indeed, the record of the wicked is surely in Sijjin.
Nay (kallā)! | Indeed (inna), | the record (kitāba) | of the wicked (l-fujāri) | is surely in (lafī) | Sijjin (sijjīnin).

83:8 And what can make you know what is Sijjin?
And what (wamā) | can make you know (adrāka) | what (mā) | is Sijjin (sijjīnun)?

83:9 A book written.
A book (kitābun) | written (marqūmun).

83:10 Woe that Day to the deniers,
Woe (waylun) | that Day (yawma-idhin) | to the deniers (lil'mukadhibīna),

83:11 Those who deny the Day of the Judgment.
Those who (alladhīna) | deny (yukadhibūna) | the Day (biyawmi) | of the Judgment (l-dīni).

83:12 And not can deny [of] it except every transgressor sinful.
And not (wamā) | can deny (yukadhibu) | [of] it (bihi) | except (illā) | every (kullu) | transgressor (muʿʿtadin) | sinful (athīmin).

83:13 When are recited to him Our Verses, he says, "Stories of the former (people)."
When (idhā) | are recited (tut'lā) | to him (ʿalayhi) | Our Verses (āyātunā), | he says (qāla), | "Stories (asāṭīru) | of the former (people). (l-awalīna)"

83:14 Nay! But, the stain has covered [over] their hearts for what they used to earn.
Nay (kallā)! | But (bal), | the stain has covered (rāna) | [over] (ʿalā) | their hearts (qulūbihim) | for what (mā) | they used to (kānū) | earn (yaksibūna).

83:15 Nay! Indeed, they from their Lord that Day surely will be partitioned.
Nay (kallā)! | Indeed, they (innahum) | from (ʿan) | their Lord (rabbihim) | that Day (yawma-idhin) | surely will be partitioned (lamaḥjūbūna).

83:16 Then indeed, they surely will burn in the Hellfire.
Then (thumma) | indeed, they (innahum) | surely will burn (laṣālū) | in the Hellfire (l-jaḥīmi).

83:17 Then it will be said, "This is what you used to [of it] deny."
Then (thumma) | it will be said (yuqālu), | "This (hādhā) | is what (alladhī) | you used to (kuntum) | [of it] (bihi) | deny. (tukadhibūna)"

83:18 Nay! Indeed, the record of the righteous will be surely in Illiyin.
Nay (kallā)! | Indeed (inna), | the record (kitāba) | of the righteous (l-abrāri) | will be surely in (lafī) | Illiyin (ʿilliyyīna).

83:19 And what can make you know what is Illiyun?
And what (wamā) | can make you know (adrāka) | what (mā) | is Illiyun (ʿilliyyūna)?

83:20 A book written,
A book (kitābun) | written (marqūmun),

83:21 Witness it those brought near.
Witness it (yashhaduhu) | those brought near (l-muqarabūna).

83:22 Indeed, the righteous will be surely in bliss,
Indeed (inna), | the righteous (l-abrāra) | will be surely in (lafī) | bliss (na'īmin),

83:23 On thrones observing.
On ('alā) | thrones (l-arāiki) | observing (yanẓurūna).

83:24 You will recognize in their faces the radiance of bliss.
You will recognize (ta'rifu) | in (fī) | their faces (wujūhihim) | the radiance (naḍrata) | of bliss (l-na'īmi).

83:25 They will be given to drink of a pure wine sealed,
They will be given to drink (yus'qawna) | of (min) | a pure wine (raḥīqin) | sealed (makhtūmin),

83:26 Its seal will be of musk. And for that let aspire the aspirers.
Its seal (khitāmuhu) | will be of musk (mis'kun). | And for (wafī) | that (dhālika) | let aspire (falyatanāfasi) | the aspirers (l-mutanāfisūna).

83:27 And its mixture is of Tasneem,
And its mixture (wamizājuhu) | is of (min) | Tasneem (tasnīmin),

83:28 A spring, will drink from it, those brought near.
A spring ('aynan), | will drink (yashrabu) | from it (bihā), | those brought near (l-muqarabūna).

83:29 Indeed, those who committed crimes used to at those who believed laugh.
Indeed (inna), | those who (alladhīna) | committed crimes (ajramū) | used to (kānū) | at (mina) | those who (alladhīna) | believed (āmanū) | laugh (yaḍḥakūna).

83:30 And when they passed by them, they winked at one another.
And when (wa-idhā) | they passed (marrū) | by them (bihim), | they winked at one another (yataghāmazūna).

83:31 And when they returned to their people, they would return jesting.
And when (wa-idhā) | they returned (inqalabū) | to (ilā) | their people (ahlihimu), | they would return (inqalabū) | jesting (fakihīna).

83:32 And when they saw them, they said, "Indeed, these surely have gone astray."
And when (wa-idhā) | they saw them (ra-awhum), | they said (qālū), | "Indeed (inna), | these (hāulāi) | surely have gone astray. (laḍāllūna)"

83:33 But not they had been sent over them as guardians.
But not (wamā) | they had been sent (ur'silū) | over them ('alayhim) | as guardians (ḥāfiẓīna).

83:34 So today those who believed - at the disbelievers they will laugh,
So today (fal-yawma) | those who (alladhīna) | believed (āmanū)- | at (mina) | the disbelievers (l-kufāri) | they will laugh (yaḍḥakūna),

83:35 On the thrones observing.
On (ʿalā) | the thrones (l-arāiki) | observing (yanẓurūna).

83:36 Have not been rewarded the disbelievers for what they used to do?
Have not (hal) | been rewarded (thuwwiba) | the disbelievers (l-kufāru) | for what (mā) | they used to (kānū) | do (yafʿalūna)?

Chapter (84) Sūrat l-Inshiqāq (The Splitting Asunder)

84:1 When the sky is split asunder,
When (idhā) | the sky (l-samāu) | is split asunder (inshaqqat),

84:2 And has listened to its Lord and was obligated,
And has listened (wa-adhinat) | to its Lord (lirabbihā) | and was obligated (waḥuqqat),

84:3 And when the earth is spread,
And when (wa-idhā) | the earth (l-arḍu) | is spread (muddat),

84:4 And has cast out what is in it and becomes empty,
And has cast out (wa-alqat) | what (mā) | is in it (fīhā) | and becomes empty (watakhallat),

84:5 And has listened to its Lord and was obligated.
And has listened (wa-adhinat) | to its Lord (lirabbihā) | and was obligated (waḥuqqat).

84:6 O mankind! Indeed, you are laboring to your Lord with exertion and you will meet Him.
O (yāayyuhā) | mankind (l-insānu)! | Indeed, you (innaka) | are laboring (kādiḥun) | to (ilā) | your Lord (rabbika) | with exertion (kadḥan) | and you will meet Him (famulāqīhi).

84:7 Then as for him who is given his record in his right hand,
Then as for (fa-ammā) | him who (man) | is given (ūtiya) | his record (kitābahu) | in his right hand (biyamīnihi),

84:8 Then soon his account will be taken an account, easy,
Then soon (fasawfa) | his account will be taken (yuḥāsabu) | an account (ḥisāban), | easy (yasīran),

84:9 And he will return to his people happily.
And he will return (wayanqalibu) | to (ilā) | his people (ahlihi) | happily (masrūran).

84:10 But as for him who is given his record behind his back,
But as for (wa-ammā) | him who (man) | is given (ūtiya) | his record (kitābahu) | behind (warāa) | his back (ẓahrihi),

84:11 Then soon he will call for destruction,
Then soon (fasawfa) | he will call (yadʿū) | for destruction (thubūran),

84:12 And he will burn in a Blaze.
And he will burn (wayaṣlā) | in a Blaze (saʿīran).

84:13 Indeed, he had been among his people happy,
Indeed, he (innahu) | had been (kāna) | among (fī) | his people (ahlihi) | happy (masrūran),

84:14 Indeed, he had thought that never he would return.
Indeed, he (innahu) | had thought (ẓanna) | that (an) | never (lan) | he would return (yaḥūra).

84:15 Yes! Indeed, his Lord was of him All-Seer.
Yes (balā)! | Indeed (inna), | his Lord (rabbahu) | was (kāna) | of him (bihi) | All-Seer (baṣīran).

84:16 But nay! I swear by the twilight glow,
But nay (falā)! | I swear (uq'simu) | by the twilight glow (bil-shafaqi),

84:17 And the night and what it envelops,
And the night (wa-al-layli) | and what (wamā) | it envelops (wasaqa),

84:18 And the moon when it becomes full,
And the moon (wal-qamari) | when (idhā) | it becomes full (ittasaqa),

84:19 You will surely embark to stage from stage.
You will surely embark (latarkabunna) | to stage (ṭabaqan) | from (ʿan) | stage (ṭabaqin).

84:20 So what is for them not they believe,
So what (famā) | is for them (lahum) | not (lā) | they believe (yu'minūna),

84:21 And when is recited to them the Quran, not they prostrate?
And when (wa-idhā) | is recited (quri-a) | to them (ʿalayhimu) | the Quran (l-qur'ānu), | not (lā) | they prostrate (yasjudūna)?

84:22 Nay! Those who disbelieved deny,
Nay (bali)! | Those who (alladhīna) | disbelieved (kafarū) | deny (yukadhibūna),

84:23 And Allah is most knowing of what they keep within themselves
And Allah (wal-lahu) | is most knowing (aʿlamu) | of what (bimā) | they keep within themselves (yūʿūna)

84:24 so give them tidings of a punishment painful,
so give them tidings (fabashir'hum) | of a punishment (biʿadhābin) | painful (alīmin),

84:25 Except those who believe and do righteous deeds. For them is a reward never ending.
Except (illā) | those who (alladhīna) | believe (āmanū) | and do (waʿamilū) | righteous deeds (l-ṣāliḥāti). | For them (lahum) | is a reward (ajrun) | never (ghayru) | ending (mamnūnin).

Chapter (85) Sūrat l-Burūj (The Big Stars)

85:1 By the sky, containing the constellations,

By the sky (wal-samāi), | containing (dhāti) | the constellations (l-burūji),

85:2 And the Day Promised,

And the Day (wal-yawmi) | Promised (l-mawʿūdi),

85:3 And the witness and what is witnessed,

And the witness (washāhidin) | and what is witnessed (wamashhūdin),

85:4 Destroyed were the companions of the pit,

Destroyed were (qutila) | the companions (aṣḥābu) | of the pit (l-ukh'dūdi),

85:5 Of the fire full of the fuel,

Of the fire (al-nāri) | full (dhāti) | of the fuel (l-waqūdi),

85:6 When they by it were sitting,

When (idh) | they (hum) | by it (ʿalayhā) | were sitting (quʿūdun),

85:7 And they over what they were doing to the believers witnesses.

And they (wahum) | over (ʿalā) | what (mā) | they were doing (yafʿalūna) | to the believers (bil-mu'minīna) | witnesses (shuhūdun).

85:8 And not they resented [of] them except that they believed in Allah the All-Mighty, the Praiseworthy,

And not (wamā) | they resented (naqamū) | [of] them (min'hum) | except (illā) | that (an) | they believed (yu'minū) | in Allah (bil-lahi) | the All-Mighty (l-ʿazīzi), | the Praiseworthy (l-ḥamīdi),

85:9 The One Who, for Him is the dominion of the heavens and the earth; and Allah on every thing is a Witness.

The One Who (alladhī), | for Him (lahu) | is the dominion (mul'ku) | of the heavens (l-samāwāti) | and the earth (wal-arḍi); | and Allah (wal-lahu) | on (ʿalā) | every (kulli) | thing (shayin) | is a Witness (shahīdun).

85:10 Indeed, those who persecuted the believing men and the believing women, then not they repented, then for them is the punishment of Hell and for them is the punishment of the Burning Fire.

Indeed (inna), | those who (alladhīna) | persecuted (fatanū) | the believing men (l-mu'minīna) | and the believing women (wal-mu'mināti), | then (thumma) | not (lam) | they repented (yatūbū), | then for them (falahum) | is the punishment (ʿadhābu) | of Hell (jahannama) | and for them (walahum) | is the punishment (ʿadhābu) | of the Burning Fire (l-ḥarīqi).

85:11 Indeed, those who believe and do the righteous deeds, for them will be Gardens flow from underneath it the rivers. That is the success the great.

Indeed (inna), | those who (alladhīna) | believe (āmanū) | and do (waʿamilū) | the righteous deeds (l-ṣāliḥāti), | for them (lahum) | will be Gardens (jannātun) | flow (tajrī) | from (min) | underneath it (taḥtihā) | the rivers (l-anhāru). | That (dhālika) | is the success (l-fawzu) | the great (l-kabīru).

85:12 Indeed, the Grip of your Lord is surely strong.

Indeed (inna), | the Grip (baṭsha) | of your Lord (rabbika) | is surely strong (lashadīdun).

85:13 Indeed He, He originates and repeats,
Indeed He (innahu), | He (huwa) | originates (yub'di-u) | and repeats (wayuʿīdu),

85:14 And He is the Oft-Forgiving, the Most Loving,
And He (wahuwa) | is the Oft-Forgiving (l-ghafūru), | the Most Loving (l-wadūdu),

85:15 Owner of the Throne the Glorious,
Owner of (dhū) | the Throne (l-ʿarshi) | the Glorious (l-majīdu),

85:16 Doer of what He intends.
Doer (faʿʿālun) | of what (limā) | He intends (yurīdu).

85:17 Has come to you the story of the hosts,
Has (hal) | come to you (atāka) | the story (ḥadīthu) | of the hosts (l-junūdi),

85:18 Firaun and Thamud?
Firaun (firʿawna) | and Thamud (wathamūda)?

85:19 Nay! Those who disbelieve are in denial.
Nay (bali)! | Those who (alladhīna) | disbelieve (kafarū) | are in (fī) | denial (takdhībin).

85:20 But Allah from behind them, encompasses.
But Allah (wal-lahu) | from (min) | behind them (warāihim), | encompasses (muḥīṭun).

85:21 Nay! It is a Quran Glorious,
Nay (bal)! | It (huwa) | is a Quran (qur'ānun) | Glorious (majīdun),

85:22 In a Tablet, Guarded.
In (fī) | a Tablet (lawḥin), | Guarded (maḥfūẓin).

Chapter (86) Sūrat l-Ṭāriq (The Night-Comer)

86:1 By the sky and the night comer,
By the sky (wal-samāi) | and the night comer (wal-ṭāriqi),

86:2 And what can make you know what the night comer is?
And what (wamā) | can make you know (adrāka) | what (mā) | the night comer is (l-ṭāriqu)?

86:3 It is the star, the piercing!
It is the star (al-najmu), | the piercing (l-thāqibu)!

86:4 Not is every soul but over it is a protector.
Not (in) | is every (kullu) | soul (nafsin) | but (lammā) | over it (ʿalayhā) | is a protector (ḥāfiẓun).

86:5 So let see man from what he is created.
So let see (falyanẓuri) | man (l-insānu) | from what (mimma) | he is created (khuliqa).

86:6 He is created from a water, ejected,
He is created (khuliqa) | from (min) | a water (māin), | ejected (dāfiqin),

86:7 Coming forth from between the backbone and the ribs.
Coming forth (yakhruju) | from (min) | between (bayni) | the backbone (l-ṣul'bi) | and the ribs (wal-tarāibi).

86:8 Indeed, He to return him is Able.
Indeed, He (innahu) | to (ʿalā) | return him (rajʿihi) | is Able (laqādirun).

86:9 The Day will be tested the secrets,
The Day (yawma) | will be tested (tub'lā) | the secrets (l-sarāiru),

86:10 Then not is for him any power and not any helper.
Then not (famā) | is for him (lahu) | any (min) | power (quwwatin) | and not (walā) | any helper (nāṣirin).

86:11 By the sky which returns,
By the sky (wal-samāi) | which (dhāti) | returns (l-rajʿi),

86:12 And the earth which cracks open,
And the earth (wal-arḍi) | which (dhāti) | cracks open (l-ṣadʿi),

86:13 Indeed, it is surely a Word decisive,
Indeed, it (innahu) | is surely a Word (laqawlun) | decisive (faṣlun),

86:14 And not it is for amusement.
And not (wamā) | it (huwa) | is for amusement (bil-hazli).

86:15 Indeed, they are plotting a plot,
Indeed, they (innahum) | are plotting (yakīdūna) | a plot (kaydan),

86:16 But I am planning a plan.
But I am planning (wa-akīdu) | a plan (kaydan).

86:17 So give respite to the disbelievers. Give respite to them - little.
So give respite (famahhili) | to the disbelievers (l-kāfirīna). | Give respite to them (amhil'hum)- | little (ruwaydan).

Chapter (87) Sūrat l-Aʿlā (The Most High)

87:1 Glorify the name of your Lord, the Most High,
Glorify (sabbiḥi) | the name (is'ma) | of your Lord (rabbika), | the Most High (l-aʿlā),

87:2 The One Who created, then proportioned,
The One Who (alladhī) | created (khalaqa), | then proportioned (fasawwā),

87:3 And the One Who measured then guided,
And the One Who (wa-alladhī) | measured (qaddara) | then guided (fahadā),

87:4 And the One Who brings forth the pasture,
And the One Who (wa-alladhī) | brings forth (akhraja) | the pasture (l-marʿā),

87:5 And then makes it stubble, dark.
And then makes it (fajaʿalahu) | stubble (ghuthāan), | dark (aḥwā).

87:6 We will make you recite so not you will forget,
We will make you recite (sanuq'ri-uka) | so not (falā) | you will forget (tansā),

87:7 Except what wills Allah Indeed, He knows the manifest and what is hidden.
Except (illā) | what (mā) | wills (shāa) | Allah (l-lahu) | Indeed, He (innahu) | knows (yaʿlamu) | the manifest (l-jahra) | and what (wamā) | is hidden (yakhfā).

87:8 And We will ease you to the ease.
And We will ease you (wanuyassiruka) | to the ease (lil'yus'rā).

87:9 So remind, if benefits the reminder.
So remind (fadhakkir), | if (in) | benefits (nafaʿati) | the reminder (l-dhik'rā).

87:10 He will pay heed - one who fears Allah.
He will pay heed (sayadhakkaru)- | one who (man) | fears Allah (yakhshā).

87:11 And will avoid it the wretched one.
And will avoid it (wayatajannabuhā) | the wretched one (l-ashqā).

87:12 The one who will burn in the Fire [the] great.
The one who (alladhī) | will burn (yaṣlā) | in the Fire (l-nāra) | [the] great (l-kub'rā).

87:13 Then not he will die therein and not will live.
Then (thumma) | not (lā) | he will die (yamūtu) | therein (fīhā) | and not (walā) | will live (yaḥyā).

87:14 Certainly, has succeeded one who purifies himself,
Certainly (qad), | has succeeded (aflaḥa) | one who (man) | purifies himself (tazakkā),

87:15 And remembers the name of his Lord and prays.
And remembers (wadhakara) | the name (is'ma) | of his Lord (rabbihi) | and prays (faṣallā).

87:16 Nay! You prefer the life of the world,
Nay (bal)! | You prefer (tu'thirūna) | the life (l-ḥayata) | of the world (l-dun'yā),

87:17 While the Hereafter is better and everlasting.
While the Hereafter (wal-ākhiratu) | is better (khayrun) | and everlasting (wa-abqā).

87:18 Indeed, this surely is in the Scriptures [the] former,

Indeed (inna), | this (hādhā) | surely is in (lafī) | the Scriptures (l-ṣuḥufi) | [the] former (l-ūlā),

87:19 The Scriptures of Ibrahim and Musa.
The Scriptures (ṣuḥufi) | of Ibrahim (ib'rāhīma) | and Musa (wamūsā).

Chapter (88) Sūrat l-Ghāshiyah (The Overwhelming)

88:1 Has there come to you the news of the Overwhelming?
Has (hal) | there come to you (atāka) | the news (ḥadīthu) | of the Overwhelming (l-ghāshiyati)?

88:2 Faces that Day will be humbled,
Faces (wujūhun) | that Day (yawma-idhin) | will be humbled (khāshiʿatun),

88:3 Laboring, exhausted.
Laboring (ʿāmilatun), | exhausted (nāṣibatun).

88:4 They will burn in a Fire intensely hot.
They will burn (taṣlā) | in a Fire (nāran) | intensely hot (ḥāmiyatan).

88:5 They will be given to drink from a spring, boiling.
They will be given to drink (tus'qā) | from (min) | a spring (ʿaynin), | boiling (āniyatin).

88:6 Not is for them food except from a bitter thorny plant,
Not is (laysa) | for them (lahum) | food (ṭaʿāmun) | except (illā) | from (min) | a bitter thorny plant (ḍarīʿin),

88:7 Not it nourishes and not it avails from hunger.
Not (lā) | it nourishes (yus'minu) | and not (walā) | it avails (yugh'nī) | from (min) | hunger (jūʿin).

88:8 Faces that Day will be joyful.
Faces (wujūhun) | that Day (yawma-idhin) | will be joyful (nāʿimatun).

88:9 With their effort satisfied,
With their effort (lisaʿyihā) | satisfied (rāḍiyatun),

88:10 In a garden elevated.
In (fī) | a garden (jannatin) | elevated (ʿāliyatin).

88:11 Not they will hear therein vain talk.
Not (lā) | they will hear (tasmaʿu) | therein (fīhā) | vain talk (lāghiyatan).

88:12 Therein will be a spring flowing,
Therein (fīhā) | will be a spring (ʿaynun) | flowing (jāriyatun),

88:13 Therein will be thrones raised high,
Therein (fīhā) | will be thrones (sururun) | raised high (marfūʿatun),

88:14 And cups put in place,
And cups (wa-akwābun) | put in place (mawḍūʿatun),

88:15 And cushions lined up,
And cushions (wanamāriqu) | lined up (maṣfūfatun),

88:16 And carpets spread out.
And carpets (wazarābiyyu) | spread out (mabthūthatun).

88:17 Then do not they look towards the camels, how they are created?
Then do not (afalā) | they look (yanẓurūna) | towards (ilā) | the camels (l-ibili), | how (kayfa) | they are created (khuliqat)?

88:18 And towards the sky, how it is raised?
And towards (wa-ilā) | the sky (l-samāi), | how (kayfa) | it is raised (rufiʿat)?

88:19 And towards the mountains, how they are fixed?
And towards (wa-ilā) | the mountains (l-jibāli), | how (kayfa) | they are fixed (nuṣibat)?

88:20 And towards the earth, how it is spread out?
And towards (wa-ilā) | the earth (l-arḍi), | how (kayfa) | it is spread out (suṭiḥat)?

88:21 So remind, only you are a reminder.
So remind (fadhakkir), | only (innamā) | you (anta) | are a reminder (mudhakkirun).

88:22 You are not over them a controller,
You are not (lasta) | over them (ʿalayhim) | a controller (bimuṣayṭirin),

88:23 But whoever turns away and disbelieves,
But (illā) | whoever (man) | turns away (tawallā) | and disbelieves (wakafara),

88:24 Then will punish him Allah with the punishment greatest.
Then will punish him (fayuʿadhibuhu) | Allah (l-lahu) | with the punishment (l-ʿadhāba) | greatest (l-akbara).

88:25 Indeed, to Us will be their return,
Indeed (inna), | to Us (ilaynā) | will be their return (iyābahum),

88:26 Then indeed, upon Us is their account.
Then (thumma) | indeed (inna), | upon Us (ʿalaynā) | is their account (ḥisābahum).

Chapter (89) Sūrat l-Fajr (The Dawn)

89:1 By the dawn,
By the dawn (wal-fajri),

89:2 And the nights ten.
And the nights (walayālin) | ten (ʿashrin).

89:3 And the even and the odd,
And the even (wal-shafʿi) | and the odd (wal-watri),

89:4 And the night when it passes.
And the night (wa-al-layli) | when (idhā) | it passes (yasri).

89:5 Is in that not an oath for those who understand?
Is (hal) | in (fī) | that (dhālika) | not an oath (qasamun) | for those (lidhī) | who understand (ḥij'rin)?

89:6 Did not you see how dealt your Lord with Aad,
Did not (alam) | you see (tara) | how (kayfa) | dealt (faʿala) | your Lord (rabbuka) | with Aad (biʿādin),

89:7 Iram, possessors of, lofty pillars,
Iram (irama), | possessors of (dhāti), | lofty pillars (l-ʿimādi),

89:8 Which not had been created like them in the cities,
Which (allatī) | not (lam) | had been created (yukh'laq) | like them (mith'luhā) | in (fī) | the cities (l-bilādi),

89:9 And Thamud, who carved out the rocks in the valley,
And Thamud (wathamūda), | who (alladhīna) | carved out (jābū) | the rocks (l-ṣakhra) | in the valley (bil-wādi),

89:10 And Firaun, owner of stakes?
And Firaun (wafir'ʿawna), | owner of (dhī) | stakes (l-awtādi)?

89:11 Who transgressed in the lands,
Who (alladhīna) | transgressed (ṭaghaw) | in (fī) | the lands (l-bilādi),

89:12 And made much therein corruption.
And made much (fa-aktharū) | therein (fīhā) | corruption (l-fasāda).

89:13 So poured on them your Lord scourge of punishment.
So poured (faṣabba) | on them (ʿalayhim) | your Lord (rabbuka) | scourge (sawṭa) | of punishment (ʿadhābin).

89:14 Indeed, your Lord is surely Ever Watchful.
Indeed (inna), | your Lord (rabbaka) | is surely Ever Watchful (labil-mir'ṣādi).

89:15 And as for man, when does try him his Lord and is generous to him and favors him, he says, "My Lord has honored me."

And as for (fa-ammā) | man (l-insānu), | when (idhā) | does (mā) | try him (ib'talāhu) | his Lord (rabbuhu) | and is generous to him (fa-akramahu) | and favors him (wanaʿʿamahu), | he says (fayaqūlu), | "My Lord (rabbī) | has honored me. (akramani)"

89:16 But when does He try him and restricts for him his provision, then he says "My Lord has humiliated me."

But (wa-ammā) | when (idhā) | does (mā) | He try him (ib'talāhu) | and restricts (faqadara) | for him (ʿalayhi) | his provision (riz'qahu), | then he says (fayaqūlu) | "My Lord (rabbī) | has humiliated me. (ahānani)"

89:17 Nay! But not you honor the orphan,

Nay (kallā)! | But (bal) | not (lā) | you honor (tuk'rimūna) | the orphan (l-yatīma),

89:18 And not you feel the urge to feed the poor.

And not (walā) | you feel the urge (taḥāḍḍūna) | to (ʿalā) | feed (ṭaʿāmi) | the poor (l-mis'kīni).

89:19 And you consume the inheritance devouring altogether,

And you consume (watakulūna) | the inheritance (l-turātha) | devouring (aklan) | altogether (lamman),

89:20 And you love wealth with love immense.

And you love (watuḥibbūna) | wealth (l-māla) | with love (ḥubban) | immense (jamman).

89:21 Nay! When is leveled the earth, pounded, and crushed,

Nay (kallā)! | When (idhā) | is leveled (dukkati) | the earth (l-arḍu), | pounded (dakkan), | and crushed (dakkan),

89:22 And comes your Lord and the Angels, rank, upon rank,

And comes (wajāa) | your Lord (rabbuka) | and the Angels (wal-malaku), | rank (ṣaffan), | upon rank (ṣaffan),

89:23 And is brought, that Day, Hell. That Day will remember man, but how will be for him the remembrance?

And is brought (wajīa), | that Day (yawma-idhin), | Hell (bijahannama). | That Day (yawma-idhin) | will remember (yatadhakkaru) | man (l-insānu), | but how (wa-annā) | will be for him (lahu) | the remembrance (l-dhik'rā)?

89:24 He will say, "O I wish! I had sent forth for my life."

He will say (yaqūlu), | "O I wish (yālaytanī)! | I had sent forth (qaddamtu) | for my life. (liḥayātī)"

89:25 So that Day not will punish, as His punishment anyone.

So that Day (fayawma-idhin) | not (lā) | will punish (yuʿadhibu), | as His punishment (ʿadhābahu) | anyone (aḥadun).

89:26 And not will bind as His binding anyone.

And not (walā) | will bind (yūthiqu) | as His binding (wathāqahu) | anyone (aḥadun).

89:27 "O soul! who is satisfied,

"O (yāayyatuhā) | soul (l-nafsu)! | who is satisfied (l-muṭ'ma-inatu),

89:28 Return to your Lord well pleased, and pleasing.
Return (ir'jiʿī) | to (ilā) | your Lord (rabbiki) | well pleased (rāḍiyatan), | and pleasing (marḍiyyatan).

89:29 So enter among My slaves,
So enter (fa-ud'khulī) | among (fī) | My slaves (ʿibādī),

89:30 And enter My Paradise."
And enter (wa-ud'khulī) | My Paradise. (jannatī)"

Chapter (90) Sūrat l-Balad (The City)

90:1 Nay! I swear by this city,
Nay (lā)! | I swear (uq'simu) | by this (bihādhā) | city (l-baladi),

90:2 And you are free (to dwell) in this city.
And you (wa-anta) | are free (to dwell (ḥillun)) | in this (bihādhā) | city (l-baladi).

90:3 And the begetter and what he begot.
And the begetter (wawālidin) | and what (wamā) | he begot (walada).

90:4 Certainly, We have created man to be in hardship.
Certainly (laqad), | We have created (khalaqnā) | man (l-insāna) | to be in (fī) | hardship (kabadin).

90:5 Does he think that not has power over him anyone?
Does he think (ayaḥsabu) | that (an) | not (lan) | has power (yaqdira) | over him (ʿalayhi) | anyone (aḥadun)?

90:6 He will say, "I have squandered wealth abundant."
He will say (yaqūlu), | "I have squandered (ahlaktu) | wealth (mālan) | abundant. (lubadan)"

90:7 Does he think that not sees him anyone?
Does he think (ayaḥsabu) | that (an) | not (lam) | sees him (yarahu) | anyone (aḥadun)?

90:8 Have not We made for him two eyes?
Have not (alam) | We made (najʿal) | for him (lahu) | two eyes (ʿaynayni)?

90:9 And a tongue, and two lips?
And a tongue (walisānan), | and two lips (washafatayni)?

90:10 And shown him the two ways?
And shown him (wahadaynāhu) | the two ways (l-najdayni)?

90:11 But not he has attempted the steep path.
But not (falā) | he has attempted (iq'taḥama) | the steep path (l-ʿaqabata).

90:12 And what can make you know what the steep path is?
And what (wamā) | can make you know (adrāka) | what (mā) | the steep path is (l-ʿaqabatu)?

90:13 It is freeing a neck,
It is freeing (fakku) | a neck (raqabatin),

90:14 Or feeding in a day of severe hunger.
Or (aw) | feeding (iṭ'ʿāmun) | in (fī) | a day (yawmin) | of (dhī) | severe hunger (masghabatin).

90:15 An orphan of near relationship,
An orphan (yatīman) | of (dhā) | near relationship (maqrabatin),

90:16 Or a needy person in misery,
Or (aw) | a needy person (mis'kīnan) | in (dhā) | misery (matrabatin),

90:17 Then he is of those who believe and enjoin each other to patience, and enjoin each other to compassion.
Then (thumma) | he is (kāna) | of (mina) | those who (alladhīna) | believe (āmanū) | and enjoin each other (watawāṣaw) | to patience (bil-ṣabri), | and enjoin each other (watawāṣaw) | to compassion (bil-marḥamati).

90:18 Those are the companions of the right (hand)
Those (ulāika) | are the companions (aṣḥābu) | of the right (hand (l-maymanati))

90:19 But those who disbelieve in Our Verses, they are the companions of the left (hand).
But those who (wa-alladhīna) | disbelieve (kafarū) | in Our Verses (biāyātinā), | they (hum) | are the companions (aṣḥābu) | of the left (hand) (l-mashamati).

90:20 Over them, will be the Fire closed in.
Over them (ʿalayhim), | will be the Fire (nārun) | closed in (mu'ṣadatun).

Chapter (91) Sūrat l-Shams (The Sun)

91:1 By the sun and its brightness,
By the sun (wal-shamsi) | and its brightness (waḍuḥāhā),

91:2 And the moon when it follows it,
And the moon (wal-qamari) | when (idhā) | it follows it (talāhā),

91:3 And the day when it displays it,
And the day (wal-nahāri) | when (idhā) | it displays it (jallāhā),

91:4 And the night when it covers it,

And the night (wa-al-layli) | when (idhā) | it covers it (yaghshāhā),

91:5 And the heaven and He Who constructed it,
And the heaven (wal-samāi) | and He Who (wamā) | constructed it (banāhā),

91:6 And the earth and by He Who spread it,
And the earth (wal-arḍi) | and by He Who (wamā) | spread it (ṭaḥāhā),

91:7 And the soul and He Who proportioned it,
And the soul (wanafsin) | and He Who (wamā) | proportioned it (sawwāhā),

91:8 And He inspired it to distinguish its wickedness and its righteousness
And He inspired it (fa-alhamahā) | to distinguish its wickedness (fujūrahā) | and its righteousness (wataqwāhā)

91:9 Indeed, he succeeds who purifies it,
Indeed (qad), | he succeeds (aflaḥa) | who (man) | purifies it (zakkāhā),

91:10 And indeed, he fails who buries it.
And indeed (waqad), | he fails (khāba) | who (man) | buries it (dassāhā).

91:11 Denied Thamud by their transgression,
Denied (kadhabat) | Thamud (thamūdu) | by their transgression (biṭaghwāhā),

91:12 When was sent forth the most wicked of them.
When (idhi) | was sent forth (inbaʿatha) | the most wicked of them (ashqāhā).

91:13 But said to them the Messenger of Allah, "It is the she-camel of Allah and her drink."
But said (faqāla) | to them (lahum) | the Messenger (rasūlu) | of Allah (l-lahi), | "It is the she-camel (nāqata) | of Allah (l-lahi) | and her drink. (wasuq'yāhā)"

91:14 But they denied him, and they hamstrung her. So destroyed them their Lord for their sin and leveled them.
But they denied him (fakadhabūhu), | and they hamstrung her (faʿaqarūhā). | So destroyed (fadamdama) | them (ʿalayhim) | their Lord (rabbuhum) | for their sin (bidhanbihim) | and leveled them (fasawwāhā).

91:15 And not He fears its consequences.
And not (walā) | He fears (yakhāfu) | its consequences (ʿuq'bāhā).

Chapter (92) Sūrat l-Layl (The Night)

92:1 By the night when it covers,
By the night (wa-al-layli) | when (idhā) | it covers (yaghshā),

92:2 And the day when it shines in brightness,

And the day (wal-nahāri) | when (idhā) | it shines in brightness (tajallā),

92:3 And He Who created the male and the female,
And He Who (wamā) | created (khalaqa) | the male (l-dhakara) | and the female (wal-unthā),

92:4 Indeed, your efforts are surely diverse.
Indeed (inna), | your efforts (saʿyakum) | are surely diverse (lashattā).

92:5 Then as for him who gives and fears,
Then as for (fa-ammā) | him who (man) | gives (aʿṭā) | and fears (wa-ittaqā),

92:6 And believes in the best,
And believes (waṣaddaqa) | in the best (bil-ḥus'nā),

92:7 Then We will ease him towards [the] ease.
Then We will ease him (fasanuyassiruhu) | towards [the] ease (lil'yus'rā).

92:8 But as for him who withholds and considers himself free from need,
But as for (wa-ammā) | him who (man) | withholds (bakhila) | and considers himself free from need (wa-is'taghnā),

92:9 And denies the best,
And denies (wakadhaba) | the best (bil-ḥus'nā),

92:10 Then We will ease him towards [the] difficulty.
Then We will ease him (fasanuyassiruhu) | towards [the] difficulty (lil'ʿus'rā).

92:11 And not will avail him his wealth when he falls.
And not (wamā) | will avail (yugh'nī) | him (ʿanhu) | his wealth (māluhu) | when (idhā) | he falls (taraddā).

92:12 Indeed, upon Us is the guidance.
Indeed (inna), | upon Us (ʿalaynā) | is the guidance (lalhudā).

92:13 And indeed, for Us is the Hereafter and the first life.
And indeed (wa-inna), | for Us (lanā) | is the Hereafter (lalākhirata) | and the first life (wal-ūlā).

92:14 So I warn you of a Fire blazing,
So I warn you (fa-andhartukum) | of a Fire (nāran) | blazing (talaẓẓā),

92:15 Not will burn in it except the most wretched,
Not (lā) | will burn in it (yaṣlāhā) | except (illā) | the most wretched (l-ashqā),

92:16 The one who denied and turned away.
The one who (alladhī) | denied (kadhaba) | and turned away (watawallā).

92:17 But will be removed from it the righteous,
But will be removed from it (wasayujannabuhā) | the righteous (l-atqā),

92:18 The one who gives his wealth to purify himself,

The one who (alladhī) | gives (yu'tī) | his wealth (mālahu) | to purify himself (yatazakkā),

92:19 And not for anyone with him any favor to be recompensed
And not (wamā) | for anyone (li-aḥadin) | with him (ʿindahu) | any (min) | favor (niʿʿmatin) | to be recompensed (tuj'zā)

92:20 Except seeking the Countenance of his Lord, the Most High.
Except (illā) | seeking (ib'tighāa) | the Countenance (wajhi) | of his Lord (rabbihi), | the Most High (l-aʿlā).

92:21 And soon, surely he will be pleased.
And soon, surely (walasawfa) | he will be pleased (yarḍā).

Chapter (93) Sūrat l-Ḍuḥā (The Forenoon)

93:1 By the morning brightness,
By the morning brightness (wal-ḍuḥā),

93:2 And the night when it covers with darkness,
And the night (wa-al-layli) | when (idhā) | it covers with darkness (sajā),

93:3 Not has forsaken you your Lord and not He is displeased,
Not (mā) | has forsaken you (waddaʿaka) | your Lord (rabbuka) | and not (wamā) | He is displeased (qalā),

93:4 And surely the Hereafter is better for you than the first.
And surely the Hereafter (walalākhiratu) | is better (khayrun) | for you (laka) | than (mina) | the first (l-ūlā).

93:5 And soon will give you your Lord then you will be satisfied.
And soon (walasawfa) | will give you (yuʿʿṭīka) | your Lord (rabbuka) | then you will be satisfied (fatarḍā).

93:6 Did not He find you an orphan and give shelter?
Did not (alam) | He find you (yajid'ka) | an orphan (yatīman) | and give shelter (faāwā)?

93:7 And He found you lost, so He guided,
And He found you (wawajadaka) | lost (ḍāllan), | so He guided (fahadā),

93:8 And He found you in need, so He made self-sufficient.
And He found you (wawajadaka) | in need (ʿāilan), | so He made self-sufficient (fa-aghnā).

93:9 So as for the orphan, then do not oppress,
So as for (fa-ammā) | the orphan (l-yatīma), | then do not (falā) | oppress (taqhar),

93:10 And as for one who asks, then do not repel,

And as for (wa-ammā) | one who asks (l-sāila), | then do not (falā) | repel (tanhar),

93:11 But as for the Favor of your Lord narrate.
But as for (wa-ammā) | the Favor (biniʿmati) | of your Lord (rabbika) | narrate (faḥaddith).

Chapter (94) Sūrat l-Sharḥ (The Opening Forth)

94:1 Have not We expanded for you your breast?
Have not (alam) | We expanded (nashraḥ) | for you (laka) | your breast (ṣadraka)?

94:2 And We removed from you your burden
And We removed (wawaḍaʿnā) | from you (ʿanka) | your burden (wiz'raka)

94:3 Which weighed upon your back,
Which (alladhī) | weighed upon (anqaḍa) | your back (ẓahraka),

94:4 And We raised high for you your reputation
And We raised high (warafaʿnā) | for you (laka) | your reputation (dhik'raka)

94:5 So indeed, with the hardship is ease.
So indeed (fa-inna), | with (maʿa) | the hardship (l-ʿus'ri) | is ease (yus'ran).

94:6 Indeed, with the hardship is ease.
Indeed (inna), | with (maʿa) | the hardship (l-ʿus'ri) | is ease (yus'ran).

94:7 So when you have finished then labor hard.
So when (fa-idhā) | you have finished (faraghta) | then labor hard (fa-inṣab).

94:8 And to your Lord turn your attention.
And to (wa-ilā) | your Lord (rabbika) | turn your attention (fa-ir'ghab).

Chapter (95) Sūrat l-Tīn (The Fig)

95:1 By the fig, and the olive,
By the fig (wal-tīni), | and the olive (wal-zaytūni),

95:2 And the Mount Sinai,
And the Mount (waṭūri) | Sinai (sīnīna),

95:3 And this [the] city, [the] secure,
And this (wahādhā) | [the] city (l-baladi), | [the] secure (l-amīni),

95:4 Indeed, We created man in the best mould.
Indeed (laqad), | We created (khalaqnā) | man (l-insāna) | in (fī) | the best (aḥsani) | mould (taqwīmin).

95:5 Then We returned him to the lowest of the low,
Then (thumma) | We returned him (radadnāhu) | to the lowest (asfala) | of the low (sāfilīna),

95:6 Except those who believe and do righteous deeds, then for them is a reward never ending.
Except (illā) | those who (alladhīna) | believe (āmanū) | and do (waʿamilū) | righteous deeds (l-ṣāliḥāti), | then for them (falahum) | is a reward (ajrun) | never (ghayru) | ending (mamnūnin).

95:7 Then what causes you to deny after this the judgment?
Then what (famā) | causes you to deny (yukadhibuka) | after this (baʿdu) | the judgment (bil-dīni)?

95:8 Is not Allah the Most Just of the Judges?
Is not (alaysa) | Allah (l-lahu) | the Most Just (bi-aḥkami) | of the Judges (l-ḥākimīna)?

Chapter (96) Sūrat l-ʿAlaq (The Clot)

96:1 Read in the name of your Lord the One Who created -
Read (iq'ra) | in the name (bi-is'mi) | of your Lord (rabbika) | the One Who (alladhī) | created (khalaqa)-

96:2 He created man from a clinging substance.
He created (khalaqa) | man (l-insāna) | from (min) | a clinging substance (ʿalaqin).

96:3 Read, and your Lord is the Most Generous,
Read (iq'ra), | and your Lord (warabbuka) | is the Most Generous (l-akramu),

96:4 The One Who taught by the pen,
The One Who (alladhī) | taught (ʿallama) | by the pen (bil-qalami),

96:5 Taught man what not he knew.
Taught (ʿallama) | man (l-insāna) | what (mā) | not (lam) | he knew (yaʿlam).

96:6 Nay! Indeed, man surely transgresses,
Nay (kallā)! | Indeed (inna), | man (l-insāna) | surely transgresses (layaṭghā),

96:7 That he sees himself self-sufficient.
That (an) | he sees himself (raāhu) | self-sufficient (is'taghnā).

96:8 Indeed, to your Lord is the return.
Indeed (inna), | to (ilā) | your Lord (rabbika) | is the return (l-ruj'ʿā).

96:9 Have you seen the one who forbids
Have you seen (ara-ayta) | the one who (alladhī) | forbids (yanhā)

96:10 A slave when he prays?
A slave (ʿabdan) | when (idhā) | he prays (ṣallā)?

96:11 Have you seen if he is upon [the] guidance,
Have you seen (ara-ayta) | if (in) | he is (kāna) | upon (ʿalā) | [the] guidance (l-hudā),

96:12 Or he enjoins [of the] righteousness?
Or (aw) | he enjoins (amara) | [of the] righteousness (bil-taqwā)?

96:13 Have you seen if he denies and turns away?
Have you seen (ara-ayta) | if (in) | he denies (kadhaba) | and turns away (watawallā)?

96:14 Does not he know that Allah sees?
Does not (alam) | he know (yaʿlam) | that (bi-anna) | Allah (l-laha) | sees (yarā)?

96:15 Nay! If not he desists, surely We will drag him by the forelock,
Nay (kallā)! | If (la-in) | not (lam) | he desists (yantahi), | surely We will drag him (lanasfaʿan) | by the forelock (bil-nāṣiyati),

96:16 A forelock lying, sinful.
A forelock (nāṣiyatin) | lying (kādhibatin), | sinful (khāṭi-atin).

96:17 Then let him call his associates,
Then let him call (falyadʿu) | his associates (nādiyahu),

96:18 We will call the Angels of Hell.
We will call (sanadʿu) | the Angels of Hell (l-zabāniyata).

96:19 Nay! Do not obey him. But prostrate and draw near to Allah.
Nay (kallā)! | Do not (lā) | obey him (tuṭi'ʿhu). | But prostrate (wa-us'jud) | and draw near to Allah (wa-iq'tarib).

Chapter (97) Sūrat l-Qadr (The Night of Decree)

97:1 Indeed, We revealed it in the Night of Power.
Indeed, We (innā) | revealed it (anzalnāhu) | in (fī) | the Night (laylati) | of Power (l-qadri).

97:2 And what can make you know what the Night of Power (is)?
And what (wamā) | can make you know (adrāka) | what (mā) | the Night (laylatu) | of

Power (is) (l-qadri)?

97:3 The Night of Power is better than a thousand months.
The Night (laylatu) | of Power (l-qadri) | is better (khayrun) | than (min) | a thousand (alfi) | months (shahrin).

97:4 Descend the Angels and the Spirit therein, by the permission of their Lord, for every affair,
Descend (tanazzalu) | the Angels (l-malāikatu) | and the Spirit (wal-rūḥu) | therein (fīhā), | by the permission (bi-idh'ni) | of their Lord (rabbihim), | for (min) | every (kulli) | affair (amrin),

97:5 Peace it is until the emergence of the dawn.
Peace (salāmun) | it is (hiya) | until (ḥattā) | the emergence (maṭlaʿi) | of the dawn (l-fajri).

Chapter (98) Sūrat l-Bayinah (The Clear Evidence)

98:1 Not were those who disbelieved from the People of the Book and the polytheists, to be abandoned until there comes to them the clear evidence,
Not (lam) | were (yakuni) | those who (alladhīna) | disbelieved (kafarū) | from (min) | the People (ahli) | of the Book (l-kitābi) | and the polytheists (wal-mush'rikīna), | to be abandoned (munfakkīna) | until (ḥattā) | there comes to them (tatiyahumu) | the clear evidence (l-bayinatu),

98:2 A Messenger from Allah, reciting pages purified,
A Messenger (rasūlun) | from (mina) | Allah (l-lahi), | reciting (yatlū) | pages (ṣuḥufan) | purified (muṭahharatan),

98:3 Wherein are writings correct.
Wherein (fīhā) | are writings (kutubun) | correct (qayyimatun).

98:4 And not became divided those who were given the Book, until from after what came to them of the clear evidence.
And not (wamā) | became divided (tafarraqa) | those who (alladhīna) | were given (ūtū) | the Book (l-kitāba), | until (illā) | from (min) | after (baʿdi) | what (mā) | came to them (jāathumu) | of the clear evidence (l-bayinatu).

98:5 And not they were commanded except to worship Allah being sincere to Him in the religion, upright, and to establish the prayer, and to give the zakah And that is the religion the correct.
And not (wamā) | they were commanded (umirū) | except (illā) | to worship (liyaʿbudū) | Allah (l-laha) | being sincere (mukh'liṣīna) | to Him (lahu) | in the religion (l-dīna), | upright (ḥunafāa), | and to establish (wayuqīmū) | the prayer (l-ṣalata), | and to give (wayu'tū) | the zakah (l-zakata) | And that (wadhālika) | is the religion (dīnu) | the correct (l-qayimati).

98:6 Indeed, those who disbelieve from the People of the Book and the polytheists will be in the Fire of Hell abiding eternally therein. Those - they are the worst of the creatures.
Indeed (inna), | those who (alladhīna) | disbelieve (kafarū) | from (min) | the People (ahli) | of the Book (l-kitābi) | and the polytheists (wal-mush'rikīna) | will be in (fī) | the Fire (nāri) | of Hell (jahannama) | abiding eternally (khālidīna) | therein (fīhā). | Those (ulāika)- | they (hum) |

are the worst (sharru) | of the creatures (l-bariyati).

98:7 Indeed, those who believe and do righteous deeds, those - they are the best of the creatures.
Indeed (inna), | those who (alladhīna) | believe (āmanū) | and do (waʿamilū) | righteous deeds (l-ṣāliḥāti), | those (ulāika)- | they (hum) | are the best (khayru) | of the creatures (l-bariyati).

98:8 Their reward is with their Lord - Gardens of Eternity, flow from underneath them the rivers, will abide therein forever. will be pleased Allah with them and they will be pleased with Him. That is for whoever feared his Lord.
Their reward (jazāuhum) | is with (ʿinda) | their Lord (rabbihim)- | Gardens (jannātu) | of Eternity (ʿadnin), | flow (tajrī) | from (min) | underneath them (taḥtihā) | the rivers (l-anhāru), | will abide (khālidīna) | therein (fīhā) | forever (abadan). | will be pleased (raḍiya) | Allah (l-lahu) | with them (ʿanhum) | and they will be pleased (waraḍū) | with Him (ʿanhu). | That (dhālika) | is for whoever (liman) | feared (khashiya) | his Lord (rabbahu).

Chapter (99) Sūrat l-Zalzalah (The Earthquake)

99:1 When is shaken the earth with its earthquake,
When (idhā) | is shaken (zul'zilati) | the earth (l-arḍu) | with its earthquake (zil'zālahā),

99:2 And brings forth the earth its burdens,
And brings forth (wa-akhrajati) | the earth (l-arḍu) | its burdens (athqālahā),

99:3 And says man, "What is with it?"
And says (waqāla) | man (l-insānu), | "What (mā) | is with it? (lahā)"

99:4 That Day, it will report its news,
That Day (yawma-idhin), | it will report (tuḥaddithu) | its news (akhbārahā),

99:5 Because your Lord inspired [to] it.
Because (bi-anna) | your Lord (rabbaka) | inspired (awḥā) | [to] it (lahā).

99:6 That Day will proceed the mankind in scattered groups to be shown their deeds.
That Day (yawma-idhin) | will proceed (yaṣduru) | the mankind (l-nāsu) | in scattered groups (ashtātan) | to be shown (liyuraw) | their deeds (aʿmālahum).

99:7 So whoever does equal to the weight of an atom good, will see it,
So whoever (faman) | does (yaʿmal) | equal to the weight (mith'qāla) | of an atom (dharratin) | good (khayran), | will see it (yarahu),

99:8 And whoever does equal to the weight of an atom evil, will see it.
And whoever (waman) | does (yaʿmal) | equal to the weight (mith'qāla) | of an atom (dharratin) | evil (sharran), | will see it (yarahu).

Chapter (100) Sūrat l-ʿĀdiyāt (Those That Run)

100:1 By the racers panting,
By the racers (wal-ʿādiyāti) | panting (ḍabḥan),

100:2 And the producers of sparks, striking
And the producers of sparks (fal-mūriyāti), | striking (qadḥan)

100:3 And the chargers at dawn,
And the chargers (fal-mughīrāti) | at dawn (ṣub'ḥan),

100:4 Then raise thereby dust,
Then raise (fa-atharna) | thereby (bihi) | dust (naqʿan),

100:5 Then penetrate in the center thereby collectively
Then penetrate in the center (fawasaṭna) | thereby (bihi) | collectively (jamʿan)

100:6 Indeed, mankind, to his Lord, is surely ungrateful.
Indeed (inna), | mankind (l-insāna), | to his Lord (lirabbihi), | is surely ungrateful (lakanūdun).

100:7 And indeed, he on that surely is a witness,
And indeed, he (wa-innahu) | on (ʿalā) | that (dhālika) | surely is a witness (lashahīdun),

100:8 And indeed he in the love of wealth is surely intense.
And indeed he (wa-innahu) | in the love (liḥubbi) | of wealth (l-khayri) | is surely intense (lashadīdun).

100:9 But does not he know when will be scattered what is in the graves,
But does not (afalā) | he know (yaʿlamu) | when (idhā) | will be scattered (buʿthira) | what (mā) | is in (fī) | the graves (l-qubūri),

100:10 And is made apparent what is in the breasts?
And is made apparent (waḥuṣṣila) | what (mā) | is in (fī) | the breasts (l-ṣudūri)?

100:11 Indeed, their Lord about them, that Day, is surely All-Aware.
Indeed (inna), | their Lord (rabbahum) | about them (bihim), | that Day (yawma-idhin), | is surely All-Aware (lakhabīrun).

Chapter (101) Sūrat l-Qāriʿah (The Striking Hour)

101:1 The Striking Calamity!
The Striking Calamity (al-qāriʿatu)!

101:2 What is the Striking Calamity?

What (mā) | is the Striking Calamity (l-qāriʿatu)?

101:3 And what will make you know what is the Striking Calamity?
And what (wamā) | will make you know (adrāka) | what (mā) | is the Striking Calamity (l-qāriʿatu)?

101:4 The Day will be the mankind like moths, scattered,
The Day (yawma) | will be (yakūnu) | the mankind (l-nāsu) | like moths (kal-farāshi), | scattered (l-mabthūthi),

101:5 And will be the mountains like wool, fluffed up.
And will be (watakūnu) | the mountains (l-jibālu) | like wool (kal-ʿih'ni), | fluffed up (l-manfūshi).

101:6 Then as for him whose are heavy his scales,
Then as for (fa-ammā) | him whose (man) | are heavy (thaqulat) | his scales (mawāzīnuhu),

101:7 Then he will be in a life, pleasant.
Then he (fahuwa) | will be in (fī) | a life (ʿīshatin), | pleasant (rāḍiyatin).

101:8 But as for him whose are light his scales,
But as for (wa-ammā) | him whose (man) | are light (khaffat) | his scales (mawāzīnuhu),

101:9 His abode will be the Pit.
His abode (fa-ummuhu) | will be the Pit (hāwiyatun).

101:10 And what will make you know what it is?
And what (wamā) | will make you know (adrāka) | what (mā) | it is (hiyah)?

101:11 A Fire, intensely hot.
A Fire (nārun), | intensely hot (ḥāmiyatun).

Chapter (102) Sūrat l-Takāthur (The piling Up)

102:1 Diverts you the competition to increase
Diverts you (alhākumu) | the competition to increase (l-takāthuru)

102:2 Until you visit the graves.
Until (ḥattā) | you visit (zur'tumu) | the graves (l-maqābira).

102:3 Nay! Soon you will know.
Nay (kallā)! | Soon (sawfa) | you will know (taʿlamūna).

102:4 Then, nay! Soon you will know.
Then (thumma), | nay (kallā)! | Soon (sawfa) | you will know (taʿlamūna).

102:5 Nay! If you know with a knowledge of certainty.
Nay (kallā)! | If (law) | you know (taʿlamūna) | with a knowledge (ʿil'ma) | of certainty (l-yaqīni).

102:6 Surely you will see the Hellfire.
Surely you will see (latarawunna) | the Hellfire (l-jaḥīma).

102:7 Then surely you will see it with the eye of certainty.
Then (thumma) | surely you will see it (latarawunnahā) | with the eye (ʿayna) | of certainty (l-yaqīni).

102:8 Then, surely you will be asked that Day about the pleasures.
Then (thumma), | surely you will be asked (latus'alunna) | that Day (yawma-idhin) | about (ʿani) | the pleasures (l-naʿīmi).

Chapter (103) Sūrat l-ʿAṣr (Time)

103:1 By the time,
By the time (wal-ʿaṣri),

103:2 Indeed, mankind is surely, in loss,
Indeed (inna), | mankind (l-insāna) | is surely, in (lafī) | loss (khus'rin),

103:3 Except those who believe and do righteous deeds and enjoin each other to the truth and enjoin each other to [the] patience.
Except (illā) | those who (alladhīna) | believe (āmanū) | and do (waʿamilū) | righteous deeds (l-ṣāliḥāti) | and enjoin each other (watawāṣaw) | to the truth (bil-ḥaqi) | and enjoin each other (watawāṣaw) | to [the] patience (bil-ṣabri).

Chapter (104) Sūrat l-Humazah (The Slanderer)

104:1 Woe to every slanderer backbiter!
Woe (waylun) | to every (likulli) | slanderer (humazatin) | backbiter (lumazatin)!

104:2 The one who collects wealth and counts it.
The one who (alladhī) | collects (jamaʿa) | wealth (mālan) | and counts it (waʿaddadahu).

104:3 Thinking that his wealth will make him immortal

Thinking (yaḥsabu) | that (anna) | his wealth (mālahu) | will make him immortal (akhladahu)

104:4 Nay! Surely he will be thrown in the Crusher.
Nay (kallā)! | Surely he will be thrown (layunbadhanna) | in (fī) | the Crusher (l-ḥuṭamati).

104:5 And what will make you know what the Crusher is?
And what (wamā) | will make you know (adrāka) | what (mā) | the Crusher is (l-ḥuṭamatu)?

104:6 A Fire Allah kindled,
A Fire (nāru) | Allah (l-lahi) | kindled (l-mūqadatu),

104:7 Which mounts up to the hearts.
Which (allatī) | mounts up (taṭṭaliʿu) | to (ʿalā) | the hearts (l-afidati).

104:8 Indeed, it will be upon them closed over,
Indeed, it (innahā) | will be upon them (ʿalayhim) | closed over (mu'ṣadatun),

104:9 In columns extended.
In (fī) | columns (ʿamadin) | extended (mumaddadatin).

Chapter (105) Sūrat l-Fīl (The Elephant)

105:1 Have not you seen how dealt your Lord with the Companions of the Elephant?
Have not (alam) | you seen (tara) | how (kayfa) | dealt (faʿala) | your Lord (rabbuka) | with the Companions (bi-aṣḥābi) | of the Elephant (l-fīli)?

105:2 Did not He make their plan go astray?
Did not (alam) | He make (yajʿal) | their plan (kaydahum) | go (fī) | astray (taḍlīlin)?

105:3 And He sent against them birds in flocks.
And He sent (wa-arsala) | against them (ʿalayhim) | birds (ṭayran) | in flocks (abābīla).

105:4 Striking them with stones of baked clay.
Striking them (tarmīhim) | with stones (biḥijāratin) | of (min) | baked clay (sijjīlin).

105:5 Then He made them like straw eaten up.
Then He made them (fajaʿalahum) | like straw (kaʿaṣfin) | eaten up (makūlin).

Chapter (106) Sūrat Quraysh

106:1 For the familiarity of the Quraish,
For the familiarity (liīlāfi) | of the Quraish (qurayshin),

106:2 Their familiarity with the journey of winter and summer,
Their familiarity (īlāfihim) | with the journey (riḥ'lata) | of winter (l-shitāi) | and summer (wal-ṣayfi),

106:3 So let them worship the Lord of this House,
So let them worship (falyaʿbudū) | the Lord (rabba) | of this (hādhā) | House (l-bayti),

106:4 The One Who feeds them [from] against hunger and gives them security from fear.
The One Who (alladhī) | feeds them (aṭʿamahum) | [from] (min) | against hunger (jūʿin) | and gives them security (waāmanahum) | from (min) | fear (khawfin).

Chapter (107) Sūrat l-Māʿūn (Small Kindnesses)

107:1 Have you seen the one who denies the Judgment?
Have you seen (ara-ayta) | the one who (alladhī) | denies (yukadhibu) | the Judgment (bil-dīni)?

107:2 Then that is the one who repulses the orphan,
Then that (fadhālika) | is the one who (alladhī) | repulses (yaduʿʿu) | the orphan (l-yatīma),

107:3 And does not feel the urge to feed the poor.
And does not (walā) | feel the urge (yaḥuḍḍu) | to (ʿalā) | feed (ṭaʿāmi) | the poor (l-mis'kīni).

107:4 So woe to those who pray,
So woe (fawaylun) | to those who pray (lil'muṣallīna),

107:5 Those who [they] about their prayers are neglectful,
Those who (alladhīna) | [they] (hum) | about (ʿan) | their prayers (ṣalātihim) | are neglectful (sāhūna),

107:6 Those who [they] make show.
Those who (alladhīna) | [they] (hum) | make show (yurāūna).

107:7 And they deny [the] small kindnesses.
And they deny (wayamnaʿūna) | [the] small kindnesses (l-māʿūna).

Chapter (108) Sūrat l-Kawthar (A River in Paradise)

108:1 Indeed, We, We have given you Al-Kauthar,
Indeed, We (innā), | We have given you (aʿṭaynāka) | Al-Kauthar (l-kawthara),

108:2 So pray to your Lord and sacrifice.
So pray (faṣalli) | to your Lord (lirabbika) | and sacrifice (wa-in'ḥar).

108:3 Indeed, your enemy - he is the one cut off.
Indeed (inna), | your enemy (shāni-aka)- | he is (huwa) | the one cut off (l-abtaru).

Chapter (109) Sūrat l-Kāfirūn (The Disbelievers)

109:1 Say, "O disbelievers!
Say (qul), | "O (yāayyuhā) | disbelievers (l-kāfirūna)!

109:2 Not I worship what you worship.
Not (lā) | I worship (aʿbudu) | what (mā) | you worship (taʿbudūna).

109:3 And not you are worshippers of what I worship
And not (walā) | you (antum) | are worshippers (ʿābidūna) | of what (mā) | I worship (aʿbudu)

109:4 And not I am a worshipper of what you worship.
And not (walā) | I am (anā) | a worshipper (ʿābidun) | of what (mā) | you worship (ʿabadttum).

109:5 And not you are worshippers of what I worship.
And not (walā) | you (antum) | are worshippers (ʿābidūna) | of what (mā) | I worship (aʿbudu).

109:6 For you is your religion, and for me is my religion."
For you (lakum) | is your religion (dīnukum), | and for me (waliya) | is my religion. (dīni)"

Chapter (110) Sūrat l-Naṣr (The Help)

110:1 When comes the Help of Allah and the Victory,
When (idhā) | comes (jāa) | the Help (naṣru) | of Allah (l-lahi) | and the Victory (wal-fatḥu),

110:2 And you see the people entering into the religion of Allah in multitudes.
And you see (wara-ayta) | the people (l-nāsa) | entering (yadkhulūna) | into (fī) | the religion (dīni) | of Allah (l-lahi) | in multitudes (afwājan).

110:3 Then glorify with the praises of your Lord and ask His forgiveness. Indeed, He is Oft-Returning.
Then glorify (fasabbiḥ) | with the praises (biḥamdi) | of your Lord (rabbika) | and ask His forgiveness (wa-is'taghfir'hu). | Indeed, He (innahu) | is (kāna) | Oft-Returning (tawwāban).

Chapter (111) Sūrat l-Masad (The Palm Fibre)

111:1 Perish the hands of Abu Lahab and perish he.
Perish (tabbat) | the hands (yadā) | of Abu (abī) | Lahab (lahabin) | and perish he (watabba).

111:2 Not will avail him his wealth and what he earned.
Not (mā) | will avail (aghnā) | him (ʿanhu) | his wealth (māluhu) | and what (wamā) | he earned (kasaba).

111:3 He will be burnt in a Fire of Blazing Flames,
He will be burnt (sayaṣlā) | in a Fire (nāran) | of (dhāta) | Blazing Flames (lahabin),

111:4 And his wife, the carrier of firewood,
And his wife (wa-im'ra-atuhu), | the carrier (ḥammālata) | of firewood (l-ḥaṭabi),

111:5 In her neck will be a rope of palm-fiber.
In (fī) | her neck (jīdihā) | will be a rope (ḥablun) | of (min) | palm-fiber (masadin).

Chapter (112) Sūrat l-Ikhlāṣ (Sincerity)

112:1 Say, "He is Allah, the One.
Say (qul), | "He (huwa) | is Allah (l-lahu), | the One (aḥadun).

112:2 Allah, the Eternal, the Absolute.
Allah (al-lahu), | the Eternal, the Absolute (l-ṣamadu).

112:3 Not He begets and not He is begotten.
Not (lam) | He begets (yalid) | and not (walam) | He is begotten (yūlad).

112:4 And not is for Him equivalent any [one]."
And not (walam) | is (yakun) | for Him (lahu) | equivalent (kufuwan) | any [one]. (aḥadun)"

Chapter (113) Sūrat l-Falaq (The Daybreak)

113:1 Say, "I seek refuge in the Lord of the dawn,
Say (qul), | "I seek refuge (aʿūdhu) | in the Lord (birabbi) | of the dawn (l-falaqi),

113:2 From the evil of what He created,
From (min) | the evil (sharri) | of what (mā) | He created (khalaqa),

113:3 And from the evil of darkness when it spreads
And from (wamin) | the evil (sharri) | of darkness (ghāsiqin) | when (idhā) | it spreads (waqaba)

113:4 And from the evil of the blowers in the knots,
And from (wamin) | the evil (sharri) | of the blowers (l-nafāthāti) | in (fī) | the knots (l-ʿuqadi),

113:5 And from the evil of an envier when he envies."
And from (wamin) | the evil (sharri) | of an envier (ḥāsidin) | when (idhā) | he envies. (ḥasada)"

Chapter (114) Sūrat l-Nās (Mankind)

114:1 Say, "I seek refuge in the Lord of mankind,
Say (qul), | "I seek refuge (aʿūdhu) | in the Lord (birabbi) | of mankind (l-nāsi),

114:2 The King of mankind,
The King (maliki) | of mankind (l-nāsi),

114:3 The God of mankind,
The God (ilāhi) | of mankind (l-nāsi),

114:4 From the evil of the whisperer, the one who withdraws,
From (min) | the evil (sharri) | of the whisperer (l-waswāsi), | the one who withdraws (l-khanāsi),

114:5 The one who whispers in the breasts of mankind,

The one who (alladhī) | whispers (yuwaswisu) | in (fī) | the breasts (ṣudūri) | of mankind (l-nāsi),

114:6 From the jinn and men.
From (mina) | the jinn (l-jinati) | and men (wal-nāsi).